T
HANDBOOK

Purchased in Nepal 1995

Author Victor Chan was born in Hong Kong and graduated as a particle physicist in Canada and the U.S. Chan's interest in Tibet began when he met the Dalai Lama in Dharamsala in 1969 and Chögyam Trungpa Rinpoche a year later in Colorado. Since his first visit to Tibet in 1984, he has covered 42,000 kilometers on foot, by horse and yak, coracle, truck and bus. Chan is the first person to have reached Lhasa from Kathmandu by mountain bike and the only non-Tibetan to have made all three of the most sacred pilgrimages in Tibet: Kailash, Tsari and Lapchi.

TIBET
HANDBOOK

VICTOR CHAN

MOON
PUBLICATIONS INC.

TIBET HANDBOOK

Published in 1994 by Moon Publications, Inc.
P.O. Box 3040
Chico, California 95927, USA

© Victor Chan 1994
Maps © Victor Chan 1994

Please send all comments
corrections, additions,
amendments and critiques to:

TIBET HANDBOOK
c/o Moon Publications
P.O. Box 3040
Chico, California 95927
USA

PRINTING HISTORY
1st Edition
February 1994

Library of Congress Cataloging in Publication Data

    Chan, Victor, 1945–
    Tibet Handbook: A Pilgrimage Guide / Victor Chan.
        p.   cm.
    Includes bibliographical references and index.
    ISBN 0-918373-90-5 : $30.00
    1. Buddhist pilgrims and pilgrimages — China — Tibet — Guidebooks.
    2. Tibet (China) — Guidebooks.   I. Title.
    BQ7910. C43   1994
    915.15'04 — dc20
                                 – 93-25186
                                        CIP

Editorial: The Guidebook Company Ltd / Odyssey Guides, Hong Kong
Design: De•Style Studio
Printed in China by Twin Age Ltd

To Daphne,

and to Susanne

CONTENTS

Acknowledgements   12

Preface   14

PART ONE: INTRODUCTION

A Short History of Tibet   26
Tibetan Buddhism and its Sects   32
Tibetan Concepts of Pilgrimage   36
A Short History of Tibetan Art   47

PART TWO: LHASA–THE HOLY CITY

Early Years to Gelugpa Dominance   60
Yarlung-Dynasty Lhasa
  Jokhang: Tibet's Most Sacred Temple   62
  Potala: Monumental Palace of Kings and Dalai Lamas   97
  Ramoche: The Monastery of Princess Wencheng   116
  Meru Nyingba: Where Thönmi Sambhota Created the Tibetan
    Alphabet   119
  Dragla Lugug: A Cave Temple with Early Rock Carvings   121
  Rigsum Gönpo: Chapels of the Gods of the Gate   128
  Pabonka: King Songtsen Gampo's Tower of the Turtle Rock   129
  Tsamkhung: The Principal Nunnery of Lhasa   136
  Chakpo Ri: Rock Carvings on Lhasa's Holy Mountain   138
Gelugpa Monasteries and Monuments
  Ganden: The Main Seat of the Gelugpa   140
  Drepung: Tibet's Largest Monastery   145
  Sera: One of Gelugpa's Great Six Institutions   157
  Nechung: Seat of the State Oracle   165
  The Four Royal Monasteries   168
  The Tratsangs: Monastic Colleges   171
  Lukhang: The Water-dragon Temple   175
  Gesar Lhakhang: King Gesar's Chinese Temple   178

Norbu Lingka: Summer Palace of the Dalai Lamas 180
The Dode Valley: Monasteries and Cliff-top Retreats near Sera 193
Dorings: Historical Stelae 195
The Tshalpa–Kagyüpa Monasteries 197
Other Sites 200

PART THREE:
PRINCIPAL PILGRIMAGE AND HISTORICAL SITES

Tibet's Three Paramount Pilgrimages
  Tsari: Southeast Tibet's Most Celebrated Pilgrimage 208
  Lapchi: Milarepa's Magical Hermitages 248
  Kailash: The Most Sacred of Mountains 273
The Samye Mandala
  Samye: Tibet's First Monastery 295
  Ganden to Samye: A Traverse of the Kyi Chu–Tsangpo Divide 314
Guru Rinpoche's Incredible Cave Complexes
  Drakyul: Two Labyrinthine Hermitages 317
  Jinka: The Six-Tunneled Mandala Cave 327
Ritrö: Mountain Hermitages and Mystics' Haunts
  Drak Yerpa: A Retreat Founded by King Songsten Gampo 338
  Terdrom: An 8th-Century Nunnery and its Medicinal Hotspring 344
  Rechung Phuk: The Yarlung Cave Temple of Milarepa's Disciple 347
  Nyangtö Kyi Phuk: Where Monks were Trained in the Arts of
    Long-Distance Running and Levitation 349
  Daglha Gampo: Principal Retreat of the Kagyü Sect 352
Necropolises of the 7th and 8th centuries
  Chongye: Colossal Tombs of the Yarlung Kings 355
  Yala Shampo: Four Yarlung-Valley Tombs 362
  Drachi: The Tombs of Khongcha, Changra and Dhoku Ri 365
  Dranang: The Serkhung Tombs and the Stone Coffins
    of Dhelekling 367
  Yön: The Largest Yarlung Burial Site in Central Tibet 371
  Lishan: Ancient Tombs in Southeast Tibet 373
  Chögong: Neolithic Relics in Lhasa 375

PART FOUR:
TIBET'S PRE-EMINENT MONUMENTS OF ART

The Early Monasteries
    Kachu: Tibet's Sole-Surviving Yarlung Temple   378
    Yemar: Central Asian-Pala Statues in a Derelict Roadside
        Temple   390
    Dranang: Xixia-Pala Murals Long Thought Lost to the World   393
    Shalu: A 14th-Century Art Gallery   400
    Gyantse: An Introduction to its Art and Architecture   412
    Gyantse Castle: Rare Newari-Style Paintings   417
    Palkhor Chöde: The Great Temple of Gyantse   419
    Tholing: A Royal Temple with Guge-Style Paintings   425
    Tsaparang: Lost City of the Guge Kingdom   430
Great Multi-Chapel Chörtens
    Gyantse Kumbum: A Monumental Showcase for
        15th-century Painters   447
    Chung Riwoche: A Tangton Gyalpo Chörten   451
    The Jonang, Gyang Bumoche and Jampaling Kumbums:
        Three Ruined Architectural Wonders   463

PART FIVE:
PILGRIMAGE AND TREKKING ROUTES

Historic Valleys East of the Kyi Chu-Tsangpo Junction
    Holy Places Along the Lhasa–Tsethang Highway   470
    Lower Kyi Chu: A Pilgrimage to Shugseb Nunnery   487
    Drachi: The Valley of Mindroling Monastery, a Principal
        Shrine of the Nyingmapas   495
    Dranang: Valley of the 13 Buddha-Lamas   501
    Yön: The Temple of Kachu, Tsong Khapa's Hermitage, and
        Princess Karchen's Retreat   510
The Yarlung Valley: Fountainhead of Tibetan Civilization
    Yarlung: Three Sanctuaries, Three Chörtens, and
        Other Sacred Sites   515

Trandruk: Yarlung's Valley's Most Ancient Monastery 533
Yumbu Lagang: First Palace of the Yarlung Kings 539
Upper Reaches of the Kyi Chu River
The Drigung, Jang and Phanyul Districts 544
Gyalam: The Old Tibet–China Caravan Route
A Trek from Kongpo to the Bön Enclave of Khyungpo
Tengcheng through the Salween–Tsangpo Divide 570
Sacred Lakes
Yamdrok: A One-week Circuit of the Scorpion Lake 587
Lhasa to the Yarlung Valley via Lake Yamdrok 595
Lake Phurma: Yamdrok to Lhodrak and Ralung Monastery 606
Manasarovar: Ritual Circumambulation of Mt Kailash's
Holy Lake 614
Lhamo Latso: A Journey to Tibet's Premier Oracle Lake via
Samye Monastery 623
An Alternate Route to Lhamo Latso via Rutok and Dzinchi
Monasteries 642
Draksum Latso: Around the Soul-Lake of King Gesar 647
Namtso: A Pilgrimage to Sky Lake and the Bird Sanctuary
of Tashi Dorje Hermitage 657
Tölung Valley: Stronghold of the Karma Kagyü
Tsurphu: Principal Temple of the Black Hat Lamas 671
Lhodrak: The Pilgrim Sites of South Tibet
From Yarlung to Milarepa's Nine-story Tower, a Guru Rinpoche
Cave, and a Walk around Lake Pemaling 681
Mt Namche Barwa and the Tsangpo Gorges: A Botanist's Paradise
The Ningchi Road: Linking Lhasa with Kongpo 707
Mt Namche Barwa: The Great Bend of the Tsangpo 712
Nyima La: From the Tsangpo to the Flower Gardens of
the Rong Valley 729
Left Bank of the Tsangpo: From Mt Namche Barwa to Gyatsa 735
The Holy Places of Pre-Buddhist Bön
Bönri: A Circumambulation of Bon's Most Sacred Mountain 741
Yungdrungling and Menri: The Major Bön Monasteries 763
Lake Dangra and Mt Targo: A One-month Expedition to
the Sacred Lake and Mountain of Bön 767
The Tibet–Sikkim Himalayas
Chumbi Valley: The Tibet–Sikkim Caravan Route 787

Chörten Nyima: A Guru Rinpoche "Hidden Valley"   801
Shigatse: Capital of Tsang
Lhasa to Shigatse: The Friendship Highway North Route   815
Tashilhunpo: Monastic City of the Panchen Lamas   822
The Rhe and Ku Valleys: Nomad Territory between Shigatse
and the Tibet–Sikkim Border   831
Rinpung Dzong: From Shigatse to Lake Yamdrok via the
Rong Chu Valley   841
**Trans-Nyenchen Tanglha Valleys: Longitudinal Corridors of the
Tsangpo–Changtang Divide**
North Bank of the Tsangpo from Shigatse to Lhatse   847
Shang Valley: Treks to the Zabso Pilgrimage   869
The Sakya Principality
Sakya Monastery: The Massive Citadel of the Sakyapas   880
Lhatse to Sakya: From the Friendship Highway past the
Valley of the Thirteen Caves   890
Mt Everest: The Kangshung Face and Rongphuk
The Kangshung Face: Extensive Treks in the Eastern Regions
of Mt Everest   895
Rongphuk: A Trek to the Everest North Face Base Camp   913
Dingri: Monasteries of the Dingri–Everest Region   918
Tzipri: The Holy Mountain of Dingri   921
Kyirong: Milarepa Country in the Tibet–Nepal Himalayas
Valley of Happiness: A Songsten Gampo Demon-Subjugating
Temple, Guru Rinpoche Caves and the Birthplace of
Milarepa   924
The Shishapangma Massif: Treks near Tibet's Highest
Mountain   940
West Tibet: The Ancient Kingdoms of Guge, Purang, and Rutok
West Tibet Routes: From Central Tibet, Nepal and Xinjiang to
Guge and Mt Kailash   943
Tirthapuri: The Third Major Pilgrimage Site in West Tibet   961
Upper Satlej River: Canyon Country from Lake Manasarovar to
Tholing Monastery   964
Rutok: Recently Discovered Prehistoric Rock Carvings   979
Source of the Indus: Mt Kailash to the Lion-mouthed River   983
The Friendship Highway
Lhasa to the Tibet–Nepal Border via Gyantse   987

PART SIX : PRACTICAL INFORMATION

Traveling in Tibet   994
Health and Medicine   1007
Spoken Tibetan   1018

PART SEVEN: APPENDICES

Glossary   1044
Tibetan Festivals   1053
Iconography   1055
Bibliography   1062
Map Index   1065
General Index   1068

ACKNOWLEDGEMENTS

Near the end of this large project, it is gratifying to compose an acknowledgement. Yet writing this last segment seems so ill-suited and inadequate an effort to express what I owe to so many. Nonetheless, here is some small fraction of my thanks.

Above all, two people I cannot thank enough are the dynamic and inseparable duo of Robi and Cicci. They provided the single most important influence on the project, especially on those sections of Tibet's art history and early relics. Since 1985, the Vitalis and I have traveled, lived, and worked together on projects Tibetan. They provided careful advice and showed unswerving faith in me throughout. Their warmth and friendship are especially treasured.

Many other friends deserve special thanks for their invaluable help. I am indebted to all those who walked with me. Together we negotiated the heartbreaking passes and managed to reach destinations of uncommon sanctity. We were comrades rejoicing together in various far-flung parts of Tibet—Hanneke Swart, Bradley Rowe, Regina Klene, Charles Ramble, Christine and Jean-Paul Shupisser, Brian Stanley, Anders Blomquist, Michel and Missy Peissel, Abe Genack, Mark Baxter, Dinnie Goldring and Nick Lyttle.

I am deeply grateful to Mac McCoy of Washington, DC who, against all odds, came through with a vital set of topographical maps. These provided a firm grounding for all the trekking and pilgrimage routes in the Handbook. Francis Herbert of the Royal Geographic Society was also most helpful.

Many people contributed trekking and pilgrimage information. Others gave moral support and encouragement. In particularly I would like to thank Kesang Namgyal for translation of Tibetan texts, Sylvie Grand-Clement for unstinting help throughout the project, and for her section on spoken Tibetan, and Dr Robin Houston for the section on high-altitude medicine. Lisa Chogyal and Caroline Blunden were staunch supporters of the book in its earliest stages and they have been indefatigable in their advice and generous assistance. Steve Graf, over the years, helped ferret out obscure maps and other research material, and acted as my translator for half a dozen European languages. I am indebted to Evelyn Zeidler, Michele Gareau, Alex and Boojum von Freisen, Guy Dehn, Ian Baker, Michelle Bongiorno, John Bellezza, Kate Roddick, Linda Thomas, David Reed, Ulrich Wiswesser, Chris Drysdale, Annabel Huxley, Chris Barker, Martin Brauen, Martin Parenchio, John Dryden, Peter Garson, Paul Murray-John, Peter Kessler, Keith Dowman, Jane Blunden, Heather Stoddard, Anthony and Marie-Laure Aris, Michael Aris, Eugen Wehrli, Fernand Meyer, Mark Salmon, Bob Gibbons, Trevor McCurdie, E.P. Bass, Sian Pritchard-Jones, Leonard van der Kuijp, Eric Valle, Diane Summers, Stanley Wong, Tsultrim Tersey, Kesang Tsetan, Elliot Sperling, Hugh Swift, H E Richardson, Steve Marshall, Marc Moniez, Dan Meyrowitsch, Althea and Richard, Craig Moffet, Tom Laird, John Hammond, Cyrus Stearn, David Jackson, Charlie and Jill Hadfield, Gerd Mevissen, Steve Shapiro, Eric Rougeot, Jo Hunter, Lobsang Ghelek, Rheinhold Messner, Gabriella Galati, Peter Gold, David Fishley, Ed Bernbaum, Barbara Adams, Dawa Sherpa, Eric Andersen, Katia Buffetrille, Aileen Burns, Deborah Hammond, Robin and Wendy Marsten, Chris Giannotis, Michael Frank, Marilyn Silverstone, and Matthieu Ricard.

I am also deeply grateful to Dr and Mrs F Vitali of Pino Torinese, Vicki Harris of Bristol, Janet and Geoff Rockwell of Kathmandu, Christine and Jean-Paul Shupisser of Lausanne,

Maya Hitz and Esther Krebs of Zürich, Elisabeth Booz of Yvoire, Michael Frank of Kathmandu, Bill and Maureen Newlin of Hong Kong, and Werner and Jutta Martin of Dresden for providing the comforts of home away from home.

Chino Roncoroni and David Salmon were my early patron saints. They kindly provided financial assistance when it was most needed. Magnus Bartlett of Moon Publications (Chico, California) and Odyssey (Hong Kong) has been long-suffering and gentlemanly in his efforts to nurse the author and the project through three difficult years. Paddy Booz had the monumental task of organizing, editing, and condensing 2,800 manuscript pages. I owe a large debt to him for incisive criticism, judgement and hard work. Claire Banham, Anna Claridge, Tom Le Bas and David Clive Price smoothed and groomed; finally Bill Newlin, wielding a big stick, got the horse into the gate.

Lastly, I wish to thank my father, a modern-day *bodhisattva*, for steadfast support and endless patience for his itinerant son.

PREFACE

The structure of this book has been influenced strongly by the uniquely spiritual character of Tibet and the result is a work somewhat different from most regional guidebooks. On the one hand it is a pilgrimage guide. It follows an age-old genre in Tibetan literature which chronicles the religious geography of the land. To provide relevant information to travelers with more than a passing interest in the country's culture, it was necessary to research and translate original Tibetan texts dealing with descriptions of monasteries (*karchag*) and pilgrimate routes (*neyig* or *lamyig*). This process was augmented by interviews with lamas and professional pilgrims who spend a good deal of their lives wandering from one sacred site to another. But the *Tibet Handbook* is also a trekking guide, a practical *aide-memoire* designed for use on foot-trails. Over the course of five years, I have traversed a large part of the country and made numerous hikes along a network of ancient trails, most of which are accessible only on foot. The detailed field information thus obtained has been incorporated into the guide.

Written from the perspective of a would-be pilgrim walking from one shrine to the next, the book describes the monasteries, their contents, and the natural pilgrimage environment along the way. The latter is particularly meaningful: the countryside of Tibet is richly endowed with rocks, rivers and trees imbued with powerful spiritual properties. Many of these, however, are easy to miss. A stone next to the path, smeared with butter, has definite religious connotations for Tibetans, but its importance may be lost on a foreign visitor out on a trek simply to savour the exhilarating wide open spaces. What I have done is to underline the background of this seemingly innocuous object: to give an account of some fundamental but obscure aspects of pilgrimage culture. Important chapels and their collections of sanctified relics are sketched in some detail. In certain cases, I recount the legends of eminent personalities associated with the routes. In the description of the acclaimed Lapchi pilgrimage on the border of Tibet and Nepal, a good deal of emphasis is given to the poet-saint, Milarepa, who meditated in many of the secluded hermitages of the region. His exploits and teachings form an integral part of the chapter.

A primary objective of the *Tibet Handbook* is to give people wishing to go on a pilgrimage or an extended trek sufficient information to do so entirely on their own. With a little help now and then from a friendly villager or nomad, there should be no serious problems in completing any journey. I also try to achieve a certain degree of comprehensiveness, including as many secondary trails, pilgrimages and treks in as many different parts of the country as possible. Over 200 itineraries are included—the chapter on the sacred enclave of Tsari alone has reports on 19. Besides the pilgrimages, there are treks to the base camps of selected mountains, such as Everest, and to areas noted for their nomadic culture or natural history. Most of the routes are of one to three weeks in duration. By linking them together, however, it is entirely possible to backpack for an extended period, staying well away from urban centers. Short jaunts on the outskirts of major towns like Lhasa are also described.

Many of the excursions are arranged for ease of access, with a minimum of logistical complications. Unnecessary expenses and hassles, such as vehicle rental or taking a bus to the trail-head, are avoided as much as is practicable. It is not easy to hitchhike in Tibet so some effort has been made to design journeys that circumvent this problem. There is nothing more satisfying than just putting on a pack and walking out of a city into the countryside.

With this book you can begin directly from a number of convenient staging points. Lhasa, of course, is an important one. Others include major stops on the Tibet–Nepal highway: you can easily reach Dingri by bus, walk around the holy mountain of Tzipri, trek to the Valley of the Roses, and then continue your journey along the Friendship Highway. If you feel like spending a month or two in the Shigatse area, there are enough treks starting from the regional capital to keep you well occupied.

It is difficult to write about Tibet's pilgrimage culture without also referring to the visual arts. Inside the chapels of most monasteries are seemingly inexhaustible quantities of wall paintings, *thangkas* and statues. Unfortunately, because of the ravages of the Cultural Revolution, many are of quite recent vintage and generally possess little artistic or historical value. But in a handful of places, art works of critical significance have miraculously survived. To this day, they retain the power to astound and captivate. To do justice to these exquisite works, a substantial part of the book is devoted to their appreciation and assessment. A good example is the 11th C. Pala-style wall paintings of the Dranang Monastery. These works are unique to Tibet, and also to the Indian subcontinent, the region where the genre first developed. Wherever relevant, the genesis of a particular art style and its subsequent development are traced. On rare occasions, some ancient and hitherto unknown monuments, with their original artwork mercifully intact, were discovered on one of my 11 field trips to the country. These are chronicled for the first time. Kachu Monastery, with its evocative statues, is a good case in point. Another is the imposing monument of Chung Riwoche which, together with the well-known Gyantse Kumbum, comprise the only two surviving multi-chapel chörtens of Tibet.

I have grouped together a variety of related destinations of singular spiritual and geographical importance. Kailash, Tsari, and Lapchi are, by common consensus among Tibetan pilgrims, the three most powerful pilgrimages in Tibet. They are all located in regions of exceptional spirituality. Extended foot-travels to these veritable Shangri-La's are described from the standpoint of a pious pilgrim performing a ritual circumambulation. Seldom-traveled South Tibet forms a substantial part of the book. Lhodrak, a district bordering on Bhutan, and many of its myriad hermitages, are detailed. Travels along the headwaters of the Siyom and Subansiri rivers, within Lhoka, are combined with treks to the delightful valleys and passes of the Pachakshiri (Assam Himalayas), prime plant-hunting territories all. A separate chapter describes the holy places of the Chörten Nyima range. Here, hard by the glaciers of the Tibet–Sikkim Divide, are a number of retreats consecrated to Guru Rinpoche, the Indian tantric master who introduced Buddhism to Tibet in the 8th century.

For many intrepid explorers and eccentrics of the past and present century, the Great Bend of the Tsangpo, where Tibet's principal river drops 3000 m in an excruciatingly short distance, has always been an enigma. One chapter is devoted to the exploration of this part of southeast Tibet, documenting excursions to the environs of Mt Namche Barwa. Near Nepal, the Kangshung Face of Mt Everest is very much off the beaten track; most travelers concentrate instead on reaching the standard base camp of the North Face. In its vicinity are some of the most fabled hideaways of the Himalayas (the first British Everest expedition in the early 1920s waxed eloquent about the enchanting valleys of Kharta, Kama and the Valley of the Lakes). A little further to the west, also amid the Tibet–Nepal Himalayas, is Kyirong, the Valley of Happiness. Heinrich Harrer, of *Seven Years in Tibet* fame, wrote that this was where he would like to spend his last years. Milarepa, the ascetic patriarch of the Kagyü sect, spent much time in splendid isolation among the cave-shrines here.

The renowned 'Tombs of the Kings' in Chongye have always been recognized by scholars as among Tibet's most significant archeological finds. Since the 1980s, however, other burial sites—found within a number of easily accessible Central Tibet valleys—have been unearthed. Preliminary analysis concluded that these reliquaries date back to the Yarlung Dynasty (7th–9th centuries). Going further back in time, look out for a number of particularly hallowed Bönpo (Tibet's pre-Buddhist religion) pilgrimages. There are visits to the major Bönpo shrines of the Wuyuk and Tobgyal valleys and to Kongpo Bönri, the most sacred mountain of Bön, whose *khora* is carefully recorded. The enclave of Lake Dangra and Mount Targo on the inhospitable Changtang (Northern Plateau) is a month's walk from Shigatse. The famous Swedish explorer, Sven Hedin, pulled out all stops to try to reach this very sacred and beautiful place much worshipped by the Bönpos. But he was frustrated ultimately by the intractable Tibetan bureaucracy.

Some of the routes I managed to walk in the course of my pilgrimage research are not entirely unknown to the Western world. A few were first pioneered by clandestine Indian pandits serving the British Raj. Others were ferreted out by assorted European adventurers and scholar-explorers during the last hundred years. Over time, the details of their journeys have become increasingly buried. The British botanists, Sherriff and Ludlow, for example, went to some fascinating places in southeast Tibet in the 1930s. Before retracing their footsteps, it was necessary to first hunt down their original expedition diaries. I have tried to contribute to the knowledge base of these early travelers: to up-date and to incorporate a focused cultural dimension. My own field notes, additional research from primary (usually Tibetan) and secondary literary sources, the travels of friends, etc, are used to this end.

It is my hope that the different elements of this book—pilgrimage, geography, trek routes, art history, and archaeology—will provide a broad introduction to Tibet. But no guide, no matter how thorough, can anticipate the uncharted territory into which travelers will stumble. In any case, it is the little accidents—the chance encounter with an itinerant monk, the surprise discovery of a nameless hermitage, the good will of a villager—that are the finest rewards of travel. So, although this book packs an abundance of detail, its aim is to encourage you to explore the alien but magical universe of Tibet for yourself. And to blaze new trails.

NOTES ON USING THE BOOK AND TRAVELING IN TIBET

In the pilgrimage and trekking portions of the book, route descriptions give information on trekking time from point to point. In general, both days and hours are given. 'Day 4 Pemba–Shekar 4 3/4 hr' means that it was convenient, for various reasons, to budget one day, walking a total of 4 3/4 hr, to go from Pemba to Shekar on the fourth day of the excursion. This is hardly a fixed guideline. If you feel like it, walk 7 hr instead and go beyond Shekar. The 4 3/4 hr 'flag' is the actual time spent walking and does not include time for meals, rests or diversions. Expect to average a 7- to 10-hr day. Perhaps two-thirds is spent actually walking. In a few cases, the itinerary only gives days or distances; there is no breakdown on the walking time between each landmark or village.

The given trekking times are imprecise and largely subjective. Many factors can and do affect the speed of a walk. It is my experience that it fluctuates with weather, temperature, altitude, weight of the pack and how good one feels. Take it as nothing but a rough guide. The same applies to the daily stages. They are a convenient device to confer readability and to give a sense of trip duration. Add or delete days according to your whims and physical conditioning.

The reliability of trail information varies in the trekking portion of the book. This is partly due to the diversity of sources used to compile the data: my own field work, treks made by friends, expedition diaries of bygone travelers, information gleaned from Tibetan pilgrims. The trail details, however, are sufficiently close to reality to allow anyone, with a healthy dose of patience and resourcefulness, to complete a particular itinerary. At any rate, the ultimate guide that can provide idiot-proof trekking notes has yet to be written. It simply is not possible, nor practical, to chronicle exhaustively every landmark, every trail junction. A 'complete' description of any given route would need far more space than any publisher is willing to give. In my years of trekking in the Himalayas, I have learned that I will get to where I want to go once I know a few village names along the way. Most of the treks described in the Handbook follow age-old pilgrimage or pasturage trails; there is always the odd villager (or nomad) willing to point you to the next settlement. Complications can occur during an approach to a pass. Once you have left the last nomad camps, usually the only signs of life on higher ground, you are on your own. Chances are there won't be anyone around to give directions. This is when small stone cairns—a few stones piled one upon another—are invaluable. Try not to lose sight of these all-important trail markers. In the event that there are none, look for yak droppings. A compass can be most helpful. A word about directional information in the Trail Notes: the right or left bank of a river is always defined with you facing downstream.

Seasons and regional climatic conditions are major factors influencing the success of a trip. Even in the middle of summer, snow storms in the higher reaches may be severe enough to completely close a pass for a few days. Some rivers may become unfordable after the increased snow melt of hot summer weather. In these cases, seek out alternative routes or wait it out. I cannot stress enough the importance of respecting the country's tremendously rugged nature. Travelers through the centuries have suffered and died needlessly because they have not taken seriously the severity of Tibet's weather and altitude. Be conservative during your journeys, be well-equipped for contingencies, and take no unnecessary risks. The most common danger is inadequate gear; bring the best that money can buy. If the situation deteriorates—turn back! You can always try again another day. The most common folly is trekking with inadequate gear; bring the best that money can buy (or you can afford) and test it out before you start.

Routes are divided into two categories: standard and exploratory. The former, by far the majority, includes all those with fairly accurate trail information. They should cause no undue difficulties to the average, rather inexperienced trekker. The latter, clearly marked as 'Exploratory treks', are located in uncommonly isolated regions of the country where the availability of food and shelter is uncertain. They often have sketchier trail details and may have unusually difficult sections. These itineraries should only be attempted by those who have extensive wilderness experience and who have brought the right gear to cope with inclement conditions.

In Tibet, virtually nothing stays the same from one season to the next. This is especially true of official policies concerning visitors. The main reasons are the infant state of the tourist industry and the highly volatile political situation. From 1988 to 1992, because of serious conflicts between Tibetans and Chinese, only the more enterprising individual travellers were able to enter the country (organised groups with well-defined itineraries are the exceptions).

This restriction was only lifted in the winter of 1992. By and large, you are likely to encounter conflicting rules as well as plenty of surprises. Expect the unexpected and be prepared for the worst. If you plan to hitchike to reach a trailhead, be flexible and budget extra days. Hitchhiking, almost always time-consuming and frustrating, is definitely not easy. On the plus side, an increasing number of Chinese and Tibetan drivers are now thoroughly market-orientated. They will pick you up for a flat fee—usually about Rmb 10 per 100 km.

Tibetan monasteries are also undergoing rapid changes these days. Several thousand existed before the arrival of the Chinese. During the Cultural Revolution of the 1960s and 1970s practically all were severely damaged. In the 1980s, many were rebuilt; 500–1,000 monasteries are now fully functioning monastic institutions conducting occasional or regular services. Because of ongoing efforts to rebuild chapels and reconsecrate statues do not be surprised to find significant variations from those described in the book. They are inevitable. Even as I write, the second floor of the Jokhang, the holiest temple in the land, was abruptly closed for 'renovations'

Happily, some good things in the country are surprisingly resilient to change. Outside the main urban areas there exists a Tibet that has remained largely true to its traditional roots. Even just a few kilometers beyond Lhasa it is entirely possible to stumble across a village whose architecture and way of life have remained constant over the past couple of centuries. In the wide open spaces, you will find an intricate network of time-worn trails that few foreigners have ever set foot upon. Frequently, paths have been widened for vehicular traffic, usually for the benefit of the few tractors and trucks of the more prosperous communes. However, there is very little traffic; these 'upgraded trails' actually make for quite pleasant and relaxed walking. Expect permanent settlements along any route to be just that; villages do not usually disappear over time. Nomad camps do move from place to place, depending on the season and pasturage.

The topographical maps in this work are based on relatively up-to-date, large scale maps (1:250,000) published by the US Department of Defense. Known as Joint Operations

---

Legend for topographic maps

▲	Mountain	• *5000*	Altitude in metres
●	County town	)(	Pass
•	Village		River
———	Road class I		Lake
———	Road class II		Glacier
———	Road class III	▬•▬	National boundary
– – – – –	Track	▬•▬	Boundary in dispute
～～～	Ridgeline	•	Gompa (monastery, temple) (abbr. to 'G')

Graphic (JOG) Series 1501, they are quasi-classified and difficult to obtain. Short of high-security military maps, they are probably the best available at this time. However, although physical features are adequately portrayed, details on settlements, religious centers and secondary footpaths are extremely sketchy, so I have added my own field research, as well as information collated from other map and literary sources. These include original manuscript maps drawn by early explorers, Survey of India maps (L500 series, 1:250,000), Tactical Pilot Charts (Series TPC, 1:500,000) Tibetan pilgrimage guides, historical works, and others. In certain cases, scarce 1:50,000 scale Chinese maps contribute cultural and geographical information. On the majority of the maps the actual course of rivers has been omitted to avoid confusion resulting from seasonal changes. The names of the valleys, and the paths themselves, indicate the rough river course.

All practical matters—logistics of travel, food and lodging, trekking equipment checklists—are in Part Six. Additionally, Health and Medicine emphasizes emergency procedures in high-altitude areas and includes information on standard health problems encountered during travelling, acute mountain sickness, exposure and hypothermia. A Tibetan language primer, based on a situational approach, covers a wide variety of language needs. You'll learn rudimentary conversation that will allow you to ask for trail directions and to converse with monks on aspects of monastic culture. This is an important section for those who plan a longish stay. The grammar, over time, should give a reasonable grounding for the fundamentals of spoken Tibetan. Nothing enhances your experience of the country and its people than your ability to communicate, albeit at a pidgin-Tibetan level.

Victor Chan, Bowen Island, October 1st 1993

*Publisher's Note: The maps in this book have been compiled from the best sources available. However, as the area has yet to be definitively mapped on a large scale, caution is advised.

*Due to the unavailability of certain source maps, nos. NH45-15B, NH45-15D, NH46-11A and NH46-11C are regrettably omitted from this guide.

Map Location Index

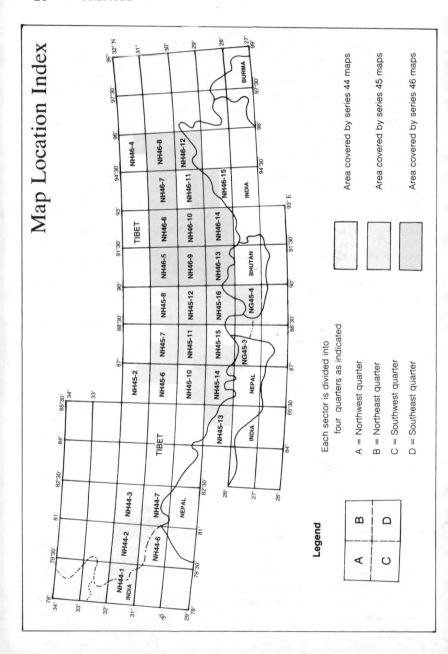

Legend

A	B
C	D

Each sector is divided into four quarters as indicated

A = Northwest quarter

B = Northeast quarter

C = Southwest quarter

D = Southeast quarter

Area covered by series 44 maps

Area covered by series 45 maps

Area covered by series 46 maps

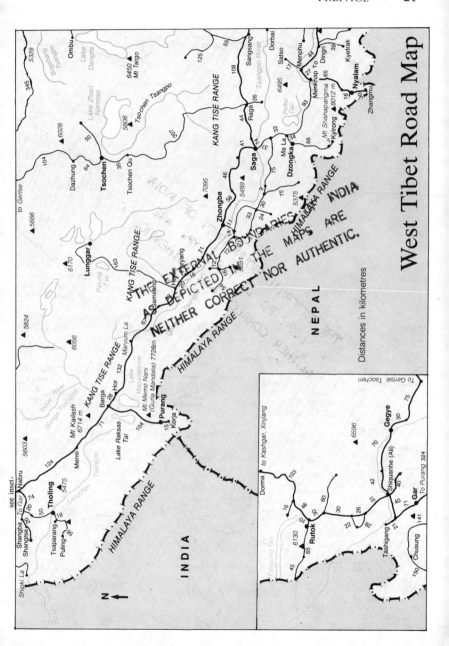

West Tibet Road Map

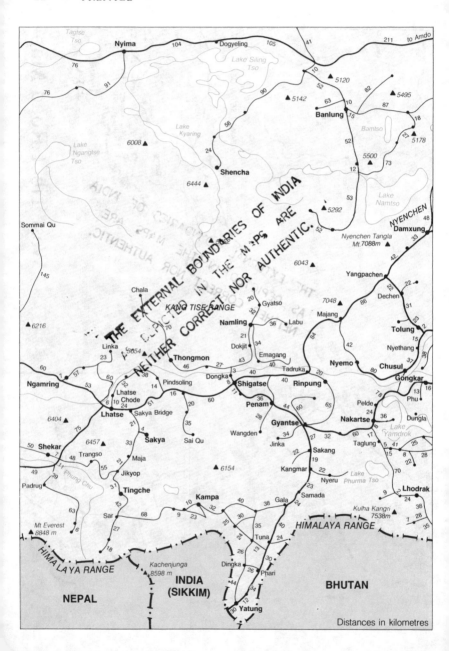

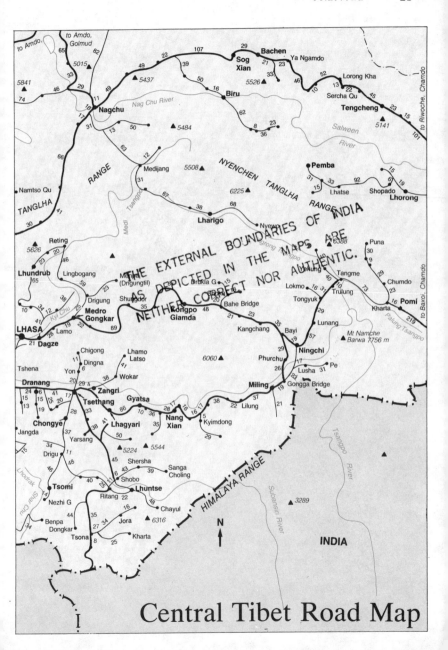

Central Tibet Road Map

Introduction

A SHORT HISTORY
OF TIBET

THE YARLUNG EMPIRE

According to legend, the Tibetan people originated from the union of a monkey and an ogress. This mythical event took place within a cave on Mt Gönpo Ri, a ridge overlooking the historic Yarlung Valley. A firmer historical perspective is given by the authoritative *Tang Annals*, a 10th-C. Chinese text, which recorded that the Tibetans were derived from the Qiang (Ch'iang) tribes, a nomadic and pastoral people that lived on the steppes northwest of China. Prior mention of these tribes has surfaced as early as 200 BC.

Credible Tibetan history begins in the late 6th century AD. Namri Songtsen (ca 570–619) of the Yarlung Valley was a chieftain who ruled part of the divided country. After joining forces with rival factions, he began to exert control over much of Central Tibet and became a significant military force in Inner Asia. He subjugated several Qiang tribes on the Chinese border and was known to the Sui Dynasty (581–617) as 'Commander of 100,000 Warriors'. Tibetan tradition considers him the 32nd king in a line that started with Nyatri Tsenpo, the mythical ruler who miraculously descended from the sky to Mt Yala Shampo at the head of the Yarlung Valley (during the reign of Lhatotori, the 28th king, Buddhist scriptures fell from the sky, heralding the transmission of Buddhism throughout the country).

Namri Songtsen's son, Songtsen Gampo (ca 617–50), was crowned king in 629. He continued to expand the fledgling empire and threatened China's western border during the third decade of the 7th century. To appease him, in 641, Emperor Taizong (r 626–49) of the Tang Dynasty gave him one of his daughters, Princess Wencheng, in marriage. Even before that, however, Songtsen Gampo had subjugated Nepal and annexed the Bönpo kingdom of Shangshung in West Tibet, marrying in 632 the Nepalese Princess Tritsun (Brikuti). She was the daughter of Anshuvarman, minister of King Shivadeva and until 621 *de facto* ruler of Nepal. By 648, Songtsen has also invaded northern India.

Songtsen Gampo was known as the First Religious King (Chögyal). Through marriage he was naturally influenced by Buddhism and it was he who founded Jokhang and Ramoche, the foremost temples of the land. Tibetan religious culture was given a further boost when his minister, Thönmi Sambhota, devised the Tibetan alphabet, based on an Indian script. This enabled Buddhist scriptures from India to be freely translated. The Tibet of the first half of the 7th C. looked west as well as east for its cultural, religious, and political inspiration. In addition to India, both Nepal and China contributed vital influences: vestiges of Nepalese art, particularly Newari woodwork, can still be seen today in the magnificent door frames and columns of the Jokhang.

Two decades after the death of Songtsen Gampo, border hostilities between Tibet and China resumed in the present-day Chinese provinces of Qinghai and Xinjiang. This state of conflict lasted for the next two centuries and the Tibetans, sometimes with the help of the Western Turks, fought the Chinese for control of the lucrative Central Asian Silk Routes.

Trisong Detsen (742–97) was the Second Religious King. A century after Songtsen Gampo, he ascended the Yarlung throne (755), and over the following half-century, he further extended Tibetan military power. In 763, his army actually occupied Chang'an (modern Xi'an), the Chinese capital, and for a short time supported a puppet emperor. However, his most important contribution to Tibetan history was not territorial. He was immortalized for nurturing Buddhism. At the age of 21, Trisong Detsen invited some of the greatest Buddhists of India and China to come to Tibet. He founded Samye (ca 779), Tibet's first monastery, with the expert help of the Indian masters, Guru Rinpoche (Padmasambhava) and Santarakshita. There, for the first time, Tibetans were trained and ordained as monks.

The Third Religious King was Ralpachen (806–38). One of his most important legacies was the establishment of peaceful relations with China, a fact commemorated by a stone pillar in front of the Jokhang. Ralpachen was responsible for the long period of harmony between the two countries. His reign also saw the translation of many different Buddhist texts, from both India and China. The diverse renderings, however, made study of the doctrine difficult; Ralpachen ordered a fresh translation direct from the Sanskrit originals. He built or renovated eight temples in Central Tibet, including the nine-story monastery (now destroyed) at Onchangdo, on the left bank of the Kyi Chu River below Lhasa, and the still intact Yarlung temple of Kachu.

Ralpachen was assassinated in 838 and his elder brother, Langdarma, became the empire's 42nd and last king. Bitterly opposed to Buddhism, he dismantled the religious institutions painstakingly built up by his predecessors. Within a few years, Buddhism was completely suppressed and the Yarlung empire was fragmented into a number of independent principalities.

THE SECOND DIFFUSION OF BUDDHISM

During these dark days, three monks escaped from Central Tibet into the northeast territories of Amdo. Rabsel of Tsang, Yo Gejung of Pötong, and Mar Sakyamuni of Tölung, all from Chuwori Monastery, managed to spirit away crucial Vinaya and Abhidharma texts. They first traveled west, then north into the oasis states of Central Asia, which had been under Buddhist influence for centuries. Some, like Khotan and Dunhuang, were actually controlled by the Yarlung kings. Later, the monks continued east, perhaps through Minyag (Xixia), another region with close ties to Buddhist Tibet, and finally reached the shores of the Koko Nor in Amdo.

Their most important act was to ordain Gongpo Rabsal (832–915, or 855–939), the celebrated monk who, together with Atisha, spearheaded the Second Diffusion of Buddhism in Tibet. After furthering his studies in Minyag at Kanchou and southern Kham, Gongpo Rabsal established Dantig Monastery near present-day Xining and Lanzhou. His renown as a Vinaya master spread and he was soon addressed solely by the epithet, Lachen ('Great Lama'). Many young men of Tibet went to Dantig to learn from him and his disciples.

A group of ten monks, having studied with the masters of Amdo, returned to Central Tibet and Lhasa in 978, 64 years before the arrival of Atisha in Guge (in 1042). Their leader was Lumé Tsultrim, a gifted young man possibly ordained by Yeshe Gyaltsen, who in turn was ordained by Lachen. They refurbished important monastic institutions—such as the Jokhang,

Katsal, and Drak Yerpa—in the Lhasa area. Later, in the late 10th and early 11th C., they founded vigorous new monasteries of their own, including Neten Lhakhang of Drak Yerpa, Lamo (1009) in the Kyi Chu Valley, Dranang (1081) in the Dranang Valley, Tsongdu Tsokpa in Drachi, and Sonak Tangboche (1017) near Chongye.

A parallel development of revitalized religious activity occurred in Tibet's far west. Descendants of Wösung, one of Langdarma's sons, founded new kingdoms in Guge, Rutok, and Purang. One of them, Khorde, became a monk and took the religious name of Yeshe Ö. From Tsaparang, the capital of Guge, he invited masters from Kashmir and India. His protégé, Rinchen Zangpo, who studied in Kashmir, built many *chörtens* and monasteries along the banks of the Satlej River. The most famous was Tholing, the principal monastic institution of Guge. In neighboring Ladakh and Spiti, the important centers of Alchi and Tapho were also built.

During that fecund time, Yeshe Ö invited Atisha (982–1054) from Vikramasila University, Bengal, to West Tibet. The master accepted and taught extensively in West and Central Tibet; his chief disciple, Dromtönpa (1004–64), helped to establish the Kadampa sect. In the 11th C., many principal Kadampa monasteries were founded, including Reting in Central Tibet (1056), Drölma Lhakhang at Netang (between 1045 and 1054), Sangphu Neutok (1073), Langtang (1093), and Yerpa Drubde (ca 1047).

Contemporary to Atisha and Dromtönpa was Marpa (1012–97), teacher of the celebrated poet-saint, Milarepa. Born of a wealthy family in Lhodrak (South Tibet), he visited India three times to collect sacred texts and to study with Naropa, the renowned former abbot of Nalanda Monastery. Milarepa's disciples, in particular Gampopa, founded the Kagyü lineage, which subsequented split into the sub-sects of Karma, Tshalpa, Phagmo Dru, Taklung, Drigung, and others. Major Kagyü monasteries founded in the 12th C. include Daglha Gampo (1121) founded by Dromtönpa, Densatil (1158) founded by Dorje Gyalpo, Tshal Gungthang (1175), Drigungtil (1179), Ralung (1180), Tsurphu (1185), and Taklung (1185). The last five were built within a ten-year period by five remarkable Kagyü masters: Shang Lama, Drigung Kyapgön, Tsangpa Gyare, Düsum Khyenpa, and Taklung Tangpa.

THE SAKYAPA AND THE MONGOLS

In 1073, Kon Chögyal Pho (1034–1102) founded the first chapels of Sakya Monastery, seat of the Sakyapa sect. This was a time of great religious activity and various chieftains of petty kingdoms as well as renowned lamas occupied themselves with temple building. Translation of the doctrine was renewed.

At the beginning of the 13th C., Genghis Khan, leader of the Mongols, was endangering the western borders of Central Asia and China. In 1239, his second son, Godan Khan, invaded Tibet and came within 80 km of Lhasa. Five years later, Godan summoned Sakya's abbot, Sakya Pandita, to his court at Lanzhou. When the two finally met in 1247, the Mongol was so impressed by the spiritual presence of the Sakya lama that he symbolically invested him with temporal authority over all Tibet. This established a *yöncho* (patron–priest) relationship between the Mongols and the Sakyapa, an arrangement further advanced by the next generation. Godan's son, Kublai Khan, ardently supported Phagpa, Sakya Pandita's nephew. And the title Tishih (Imperial Preceptor)—*de facto* ruler of Tibet—was bestowed on Phagpa. In return, Kublai Khan himself converted to Buddhism and underwent the Hevajra initiation. Under the Mongols, the vast country was organized into 13 myriarchies—administrative districts each containing 10,000 families.

For nearly 75 years after the death of Phagpa (1280), the Sakyapa lamas continued to serve as viceroys of Tibet on behalf of the Mongol emperors. Later, Sakyapa authority was contested by the rival schools of the Drigungpa and Phagmo Drupa, both Kagyü sub-sects.

THE PHAGMO DRUPA DYNASTY AND THE KINGS OF TSANG

Two principal factors contributed to the demise of Sakyapa supremacy. The first was the subjugation of the Mongol Yuan Dynasty (1271–1368) by the indigenous Chinese Ming Dynasty. In one stroke, the Sakyapa lamas lost their powerful patron and protector. The second was the ascendancy of the Phagmo Drupa. Under Jangchub Gyaltsen (1302–73), they defeated the Sakyapa in outright battle in 1354. Although they were derived from the Kagyüpa, the new rulers had substantial connections with the Kadampa and Sakyapa. Their power center was Densatil Monastery, founded by Phagmo Drupa (1110–70) in 1158.

The fall of the Sakyapa and the end of the yöncho relationship freed Tibet from foreign jurisdiction. Jangchub Gyaltsen and his eleven successors governed the country from 1354 to 1435 and, like the Sakyapa before them, exercised both spiritual and secular authority. This auspicious period also saw the rediscovery of many sacred texts, known as terma, concealed by Guru Rinpoche in the 8th century.

The end of the dynasty occurred when the Rinpung princes of Tsang displaced the Phagmo Drupa, signalling a return to secular monarchy. The princes ruled the country through four generations, from 1435 to 1565, and were followed by the three kings of Tsang, who held court at Shigatse from 1566 to 1642. These leaders were actively supported by the powerful Karmapa order, whose main seat was at Tsurphu Monastery near Lhasa.

THE GELUGPA AND THE DALAI LAMAS

The prodigious lama, Tsong Khapa (1357–1419), grew up during the heyday of the Phagmo Drupa Dynasty. After studying with leading teachers, he expounded his own doctrine which emphasized the moral and philosophical rigors of Atisha rather than the mysticism of the Sakyapa. In 1409, he founded the great monastery of Ganden, dedicated to the renaissance of strict monastic discipline. His disciples established the pivotal monasteries of Sera, Drepung, and Tashilhunpo, which rapidly grew in size and influence. A distinctive new order of Tibetan Buddhism began to emerge, known initially as the Gandenpa (after Tsong Khapa's monastery), but later renamed the Gelugpa ('Virtuous Ones').

Foreign intervention again occurred during the tenure of the third Gelugpa leader, Sonam Gyatso (1543–88). Like the Sakyapa, he established a patron–priest relationship with the powerful Tümed Mongol leader, Altan Khan, a descendant of Genghis. The chieftain genuinely believed in Tibet's religion and a majority of the Mongols actually became Gelugpa followers. During this time, the title of Dalai ('Ocean-wide') Lama was conferred on Sonam Gyatso and then retrospectively applied to his two predecessors. This lineage is maintained by the discovery of a young child born soon after the death of a previous Dalai Lama. It is believed that the life-spirit of the deceased transfers to the new-found child, who takes on the pre-ordained mantle of the 'Dalai Lama'. This cosy relationship between the Gelugpa and the Mongols greatly concerned the Tsang king and his Karmapa allies. Tension rose between the two factions and in 1640, the Mongol chieftain, Gushri Khan, invaded Tibet, convincingly defeating the Tsang king and his supporters. Two years later, the Fifth Dalai Lama was enthroned as the undisputed ruler of the country, with Lhasa as his capital. At the same time, the Ming Dynasty (1368–1644) in China was succeeded by the Qing Dynasty of the Manchus (1644–1911).

The Gelugpa consolidated their power base by greatly enlarging the monasteries of Ganden, Sera, and Drepung; the Fifth Dalai Lama began construction of the monumental Potala Palace. Ngawang Lobsang Gyatso (1617–82) was perhaps the greatest Dalai Lama Tibet has ever seen. A forceful and effective administrator, he brought genuine peace and unity. He was a prolific scholar who wrote many seminal treatises and was responsible for the renovation of decayed temples and the building of numerous new ones. In 1655, Gushri Khan died and, from then on, the Dalai Lamas became both spiritual and temporal heads of the land.

The death of the Fifth Dalai Lama was concealed from the public and, most importantly, from the Chinese for a total of 12 years. During this time, Regent Sangye Gyatso effectively governed the country and continued the immense project of finishing the Potala. Afterwards, Tibet entered a period of instability, exacerbated by the weak leadership of the Sixth Dalai Lama, who much preferred poetry to politics. The Qing Emperor Kangxi was quick to exploit this. He did so by encouraging the ambitions of the Mongolian prince, Lhabzang Khan, who invaded Tibet in 1706 and killed Sangye Gyatso. This usurper was himself murdered when the Mongol Dzungars, formerly allies of Sangye Gyatso, overran the country in 1717. Kangxi immediately intervened and forced the Dzungars to withdraw. He installed the Seventh Dalai Lama and proclaimed Tibet a protectorate of China. Ambans, representatives of the emperor, were stationed in Lhasa to look after Manchu interests. For the next 200 years no hostilities existed between the Chinese and the Tibetans; the latter were generally allowed to manage their own affairs in what was a nominal protectorate.

THE 20TH CENTURY AND THE CHINESE OCCUPATION

No Dalai Lama, until the 13th (1876–1933), approached the personal authority of the Great Fifth. The Ninth through 12th all died before their majority, and lacklustre regents governed the country in their stead. During the reign of the 13th, the British invaded Lhasa and Chinese overlordship of Tibet came to an end. The invasion occurred in 1904, when Colonel Younghusband led an expedition designed to open Tibet to trade and to exclude both Russian and Chinese interests from the country. British influence was continued by a series of competent and sympathetic residents. Towards the end of the Qing Dynasty, after the Chinese Republican Revolution (1911–12), the Tibetans expelled all Chinese from the country and declared their independence.

Tibet's government functioned independently until 1951. In 1947, the British withdrew from India and Tibet lost its only ally; in 1949, Mao Tsetung announced the creation of the People's Republic of China and immediately made threatening noises towards Lhasa. Finally, in October 1950, the Chinese invaded and overran East Tibet. A Tibetan delegation was summoned to Beijing in 1951 and, under duress, signed a treaty that allowed Chinese forces to be garrisoned in Lhasa. Tensions between the two peoples finally culiminated in a popular uprising in the capital in 1959. The 14th Dalai Lama and his followers escaped across the Himalayas to India. After a short but bloody battle, Tibetan resistance succumbed to the vastly superior forces of the occupier. From this time on, the Chinese set out to formally incorporate Tibet into the People's Republic and, in 1965, Tibet was renamed the Xizang Autonomous Region.

During the next decade, the disastrous Cultural Revolution of China boiled over into Tibet. Virtually the entire inventory of its cultural and religious institutions was systematically destroyed by dynamite, bare hands, or taken as loot by young fanatics. Monks and dissenters were tortured, executed, or simply subjected to never-ending sessions of brainwashing. Thousands were jailed for their refusal to denounce the Dalai Lama. The holocaust abated after Mao's death in 1976, when the Chinese officially acknowledged the havoc wrought by the excesses of the Cultural Revolution. In the late 1970s and early 1980s, Deng Xiaoping's new policy of tolerance led to the rebuilding of many monasteries and the revival of religious practices. In 1979, the Jokhang, the most sacred shrine in Tibet, re-opened for worship. By 1984, further economic and religious freedom was restored and tourism began in earnest for the first time in the country's history. Tibet enjoyed a period of relative prosperity and peace until 1988–89, when a series of monk-led demonstrations in Lhasa led to bloody riots around the Jokhang. The brutal military suppression that followed was swift and widespread. In March 1989, martial law was declared in the capital and the country was closed to foreigners. This was rescinded in May 1990 and, in October 1991, China once again permitted individual travelers to enter Tibet, albeit under a tight leash. There have been further riots and demonstrations in 1993, again highlighting the disatisfaction of the Tibetans towards the ongoing Chinese occupation of the country.

TIBETAN BUDDHISM
AND ITS SECTS

Tibetan Buddhism is a synthesis of two major Buddhist systems: Mahayana and Tantrism. Both concern themselves with the attainment of Buddhahood or enlightenment. Mahayana Buddhism, the so-called Great Vehicle, evolved from Theravada, the early form of Buddhism, around the 1st C. AD. Centering on the intellectual problem of being, it focuses on a gradual but ultimately complete understanding of a well-established body of spiritual knowledge. The Mahayana ideal is the *bodhisattva*, a person who seeks enlightenment not for his own sake but for the salvation of all living things. He delays entry into *nirvana*, the final escape from the vicious cycle of existence, in order to save others from suffering.

The development of Tantrism (Vajrayana, the 'Diamond Vehicle') began in the 2nd or 4th C. in India and Ceylon. It focuses on existential problems. Philosophically, it follows Mahayana precepts, but in practice, the student of tantra is able to achieve enlightenment through a calibrated process of meditation under the guidance of an initiated teacher. It can be said that Mahayana looks at Being, whereas Tantrism acts through Being. Mahayana documents theoretical aspects of Buddhism; tantric literature depicts Buddhism as individually lived.

Tantrism is generally non-doctrinal. It employs yogic and meditative methods to effect an abrupt and complete transformation of the practitioner. A central precept is the identification of emptiness (*sunyata*) with compassion (*karuna*). The realization of this basic truth, which leads to ultimate enlightenment, must be by experiential rather than cognitive means. To achieve this profound change, it is necessary for the student to harness his physical and mental processes instead of being enslaved by them.

The arduous journey begins with the student being accepted by a recognized teacher, who first initiates him into the practice. A direct understanding of compassion is attained through meditation. This allows insight into the transitory nature of life and the suffering of mankind. The second stage involves yogic or contemplative exercises, which includes specific spiritual experiences. These include the use of meditative gestures and postures (*mudras*), sacred syllables, phrases (*mantras*) and icons. Through them the student is trained to visualize, and then subsequently identify himself with, various divinities, each of which represents a particular cosmic force. He comes to realize an essential truth—that each divinity is finally equated with emptiness. This is when he acquires an extraordinary consciousness, a state beyond all duality, which embodies eternal bliss.

Despite great differences, Mahayana and Tantrism invigorated and interacted with each other. During the 7th–11th C., they were brought to Tibet from northern India, primarily through the efforts of the Three Religious Kings of the Yarlung Dynasty (see above, page 26). The Second Diffusion of Buddhism occurred during the 10th–11th C., a period when King Yeshe Ö and the great translator Rinchen Zangpo led the revival in West Tibet. Atisha and other renowned Indian masters were invited to Tibet, where they encouraged a vigorous program of translation of sacred Sanskrit texts and the building of many temples (see above, page 27). In the 14th C., having access to all relevant Buddhist texts, the Tibetans proceeded to produce their own canonical literature: the Kangyur (Translation of the Word of the Buddha) and the Tengyur (Translation of Teachings). The former contains works that supposedly represent the Buddha's sermons. Included in the latter are hymns of praise, commentaries on the tantras, and commentaries on the sutras.

At this time, with students congregating around various charismatic masters, rival sects developed. As a result, a number of distinctive schools developed, each with its own style and emphasis. In the contest for spiritual and political dominance, monasteries squared off against each other, forging alliances with local lords. This internecine strife came to a head when the Gelugpa sect appealed to the Mongol chieftain, Gushri Khan, for help against the Kadampa, who were allied with the princes of Tsang Province (a central Tibetan territory centered on Shigatse). The Mongols won decisively, and from the middle of the 17th C. up to the Chinese invasion of Tibet in the 1950s, the Dalai Lamas, supreme heads of the Gelugpa, became effective rulers of the country.

MAIN SECTS OF TIBETAN BUDDHISM
NYINGMA
The Nyingma is the Old School sect, founded during the First Diffusion of Buddhism in Tibet in the 8th century. Its first and most important proponent was the Indian tantric master, Guru Rinpoche (Padmasambhava), a teacher revered as the Second Buddha. The Nyingmapa's outstanding characteristic is its emphasis on 'rediscovered' texts, known as terma. This sacred literature (teachings), attributed to Guru Rinpoche, was hidden in special sites during the dark age of Buddhism in the 9th century. Hundreds of years elapsed before these works resurfaced again, unearthed by illustrious Nyingmapa lamas called tertons (text discoverers). Among the most important were Orgyan Lingpa, Longchenpa, Jigme Lingpa, and Minling Terchen.

The Nyingma hold that there are nine paths to enlightenment, the first three based on the sutras and the other six on the tantras. Dzokchen ('Great Perfection') is a tantric discipline transmitted within the sect. Imbued with a Zen-like quality, it is based on a program of accelerated meditation, which enables the student to achieve enlightenment within a relatively short time.

Nyingmapa monks often marry and work individually in small village chapels and remote cave retreats. The sect's most visible practitioner is the wandering ngakpa, a long-haired adept who supports himself by dispensing occult services (rainmaking, exorcism, divination). Among the most important Nyingma monasteries are Mindroling and Dorje Drak, both sited on the banks of the Tsangpo near the Yarlung–Kyi Chu River confluence. The last supreme head was Dudjom Rinpoche, an incarnation of Dudjom Lingpa (1835–1904).

SAKYA
This school was named after its principal monastery, founded during the Second Diffusion of Buddhism by Kon Chögyal Pho (1034–1102). Its systematically organized teachings derive from the Indian tantric sage, Birupa, and were brought to Tibet by Drokmi Lötsawa, translator of the Hevajra Tantra, a basic text of the Sakyapa. The Lamdre ('The Way and Its Fruit'), introduced by the 9th-C. Indian master, Virupa, is another widely practiced teaching. It

integrates the precepts of *sutra* and *tantra* into a discipline designed to bring about Buddhahood in a single lifetime.

Sakya's rise to prominence in the 13th–14th C. was largely due to the heroic efforts of five masters, the so-called Five Patriarchs. The greatest were Sakya Pandita and Phagpa. They allied themselves with the Mongol empire in China, and effectively governed the country under a patron–priest (*yöncho*) relationship with their Mongol overlords. The Sakyapa influence faded with the decline of Mongol power; the sect later divided into the Ngor and Tsar branches. One notable feature of the sect is that its abbotship (Sakya Trisin) is hereditary, passing from uncle to nephew, rather than through a continuous line of incarnations.

KAGYÜ

Kagyü means 'orally transmitted precepts'. It places fundamental emphasis on the direct transmission of esoteric teachings from master to pupil. The lineage, characterized by asceticism, started with the Indian master, Tilopa. It was subsequently passed to Naropa, Marpa, and Milarepa, Tibet's greatest poet. Milarepa was in turn the teacher of two highly respected masters, Rechungpa and Gampopa. The latter authored the *Jewel Ornament of Liberation* and his mantle passed to two gifted students, Drogön Phagmo Drupa and Karmapa Düsum Khyenpa. These two later founded the influential Kagyüpa sub-schools of Densatil and Tsurphu (center of the Black Hat Karma-Kagyus). Phagmo Drupa taught Drigung Kyapgön, Taklung Tangpa Tashi Pel, and Tsangpa Gyare, who respectively founded the monasteries of Drigungtil, Taklung, and Ralung. All five centers survive to this day.

The Kagyü system focuses strongly on aspects of practical mysticism. A basic discipline is Hatha Yoga, which specializes in breathing techniques and postures. Its supreme goal is the Great Seal (*mahamudra*), the overcoming of dichotomous thought in the very being of Buddhahood. To achieve enlightenment within a lifetime, or at the moment of death, the practitioner relies on the Six Yogas of Naropa (self-produced heat, illusory body, dreams, the experience of light, the intermediate state between death and rebirth, the passing from one existence into another). Following the tradition of Marpa, the school does not demand celibacy or association with a religious institution.

KADAM

The patriarch of the Kadam ('Bound by Precept') school was Atisha, whose teachings stressed the need for austere monastic discipline and devotion to a teacher prior to the start of tantric practice. The Mahayana *sutras* were given a prominent role and the *tantras* were relegated to a secondary position. Dromtönpa was Atisha's main student; he founded Reting Monastery, and codified the Kadampa system. Other renowned masters of the sect included Sharapa, Potowa, and Puchungwa; all founded important monasteries in the Phanyul and Kyi Chu valleys.

Students observed four fundamental rules: celibacy, abstinence from intoxicants, prohibition of travel and of money-handling. The central practice was purification of the mind, the purging of all intellectual and moral shortcomings, a process that led to a clear perception of emptiness. The sect's primary text was the Perfection of Wisdom Discourses (*Prajnaparamita*) and its major centers were Reting, Langtang, and Sangphu. The Gelugpas absorbed the Kadampas in the 15th century.

GELUG

The Gelug ('Virtuous Ones') is Tibet's reformed sect. Tsong Khapa (1357–1419), its founder, immersed himself in Sakya, Kadam, and Kagyü teachings before enunciating his new formulation of Tibetan Buddhism. The essential teachings of this so-called Yellow Hat sect are a continuation of the Kadampa system. This new doctrine was in part a reaction against the moral laxity of the era and the religion's deviations in the interpretation of the *tantras*. Tsong Khapa imposed rigorous devotion to the traditional rules of the Vinaya (monastic rules of conduct), and students had to master dogmatics and logic as a means to Buddhahood. Monasticism was emphasized and intensive study of texts and methodical practice according to the *Lamrim Chenmo* ('Great Gradual Path') were mandatory.

The *Lamrim Chenmo*, Tsong Khapa's great work, is based on the *Bodhipathapradipa* by Atisha. Codifying the way to enlightenment, it details the process of mental purification through ten spiritual levels that lead ultimately to salvation. Another important text, the *Ngagrim Chenmo* ('Great Graduated Tantric Path'), is a highly technical treatise of ritual and mystical practice that provided guidance on the tantra. However, this course was only open to students already fluent in theoretical learning. Like Atisha before him, Tsong Khapa stressed the thorough learning of the *sutras* before graduating to the *tantras*. Additionally, he instigated a system of examinations, of which the highest degree granted was *geshe*. In 1409, he founded Ganden, his first and greatest monastery.

From Tsong Khapa's chief disciples came the line of the Dalai Lamas, considered the incarnations of Chenresi (Avalokiteshvara), the Bodhisattva of Compassion. This title of the sect's paramount leader was first conferred posthumously upon Gedundrub (1391–1474), disciple and nephew of Tsong Khapa. Another reincarnating lineage within the Gelugpa system is that of the Panchen Lamas, the abbots of Tashilhunpo Monastery in Shigatse.

In the 17th C., the Fifth Dalai Lama, under the patronage of the Mongols, became Tibet's ruler. The Gelugpa became the pre-eminent sect and all rival schools were restructured and curtailed. Over the ensuing century, the Dalai Lamas came to be regarded as the spiritual and temporal leaders of the country (see above, page 29).

TIBETAN CONCEPTS
OF PILGRIMAGE

All mountains, all rivers, holy lakes, tirthas (places of pilgrimage), the abodes of seers, cow-pens, and temples of gods are sin-destroying localities.

Sakyamuni

MYTHIC ORIGINS OF PILGRIMAGE SITES

Just before Buddha died, he designated four places that should inspire his followers: Lumbini, his place of birth; Bodh Gaya, where he attained enlightenment; Sarnath, where he gave his first sermon; and Kushinagara, where he died. These places, all in India except for Lumbini, became the four greatest pilgrimage sites of Buddhism. The most important is Bodh Gaya, regarded as the 'diamond seat' of enlightenment for all Buddhas, and thus the spiritual center of the universe.

In Hindu mythology, pilgrimage sites represent places, known as *pitha*, where parts of the body of the mother goddess (Sati) fell to earth. In Tibetan Tantric Buddhism, the soil of India is venerated as the spiritual body of the Buddha, divided into 24 parts corresponding to 24 famous holy places in northeast India. Tibetans have duplicated them by taking their relics to specific places within Tibet and shrines to house them. For example, Pabonka Monastery on the outskirts of Lhasa (see page 129) is said to be a replica of Devikota, a temple in Gauhati (Assam), which in turn was based on Kushinagara, the place of Buddha's death. There are at least three copies of Devikota in Tibet; each was consecrated with a piece of rock from Devikota itself. These 24 geographical pilgrimage places constitute an outer (*chi*), visible series of sacred sites. The inner (*nang*) series is located within one's own body, providing specific centers for the process of meditation. Lastly, there are the 24 symbolic spheres of the mandala, which constitute the secret (*sang*) division.

HOW A SITE CAME TO BE SANCTIFIED
GEOMANTIC ATTRIBUTES

Geomancy, or the art of divination by means of geographical features, plays a vital role in determining Tibet's pilgrimage places. The sanctity of a site is largely derived from its special natural and physical attributes, rather than from the shrine erected there. The image consecrated in a monastery is of course important and pilgrims have a natural wish to pay homage to it. However, for the most significant sites, it is the geomantic and metaphysical character of the place that makes it worthy of worship.

Certain naturally-occurring pilgrimage sites (caves, rivers, mountains, lakes, river sources) are endowed with subtle and ineffable powers that can trigger unusual responses from pilgrims. There is a widespread Tibetan belief that they are the abodes of local deities capable of helping or harming pilgrims, who propitiate these deities by making regular offerings. Mountains are particularly important. In ancient myths, heavenly beings used them as vehicles to enter this world. Seven of Tibet's early kings descended to earth via sacred mountains, including Yala Shampo and Lhabab Ri. These personify the 'soul' (la) of the communities that worship them as ancestral deities. This 'soul' could be physically represented not only by a mountain (lari) but by a lake (latso); the former takes on a male aspect, the latter female. The 'soul' or 'life-spirit' of Tibet is associated with Lhamo Latso (see page 623 for further details)—'Soul-lake of the Goddess' (the goddess in this case is Palden Lhamo, Protectress of Tibet). The 'soul' of an individual, on the other hand, may reside in a tree (lashing) or in a turquoise (layü) worn around the neck. Tibetans take particular care to maintain the well-being of the collective or individual 'souls' by means of offerings. In the event of calamities brought on by the 'loss of soul', the ritual of lakhug—the retrieval of the 'soul'—is performed.

ASSOCIATION WITH PAST MASTERS AND HISTORICAL FIGURES

Important pilgrim sites are often closely connected with the lives of saints, ascetics, and important historical figures. In many cases, these shrines began as simple retreat caves or hermitages inhabited by renowned yogins. The most important are places frequented by the Buddha in his travels and the caves used for meditation by Guru Rinpoche (Padmasambhava), the Indian tantric master who first introduced Buddhism into Tibet in the 8th century. Most of the latter are located in hard-to-reach places, at the top of isolated valleys or near the summit of a mountain. Examples are the Sheldrak hermitage (see page 522) high above the town of Tsethang and Drak Yong Dzong (see page 321), a grotto complex far up the Drak Valley. Many of Guru Rinpoche's caves are at the center of a geographic mandala that has powerful geomantic attributes. Like many of Tibet's earliest temples, they often face eastwards. Milarepa, the beloved poet-saint of the 11th C., is another celebrated master who consecrated many cave retreats in his lifetime. The most famous of these can be found in the Lapchi area (see page 248) and the Kyirong Valley (see page 924). Temples built by the first Buddhist king, Songtsen Gampo, and his consorts, are also highly sanctified places of pilgrimage.

THE CONSECRATION OF A SITE BY SACRED OBJECTS

Pilgrimage sites were often consecrated when they became repositories for sacred objects. These fall broadly into three categories:

1) Kuten—images of the Buddha and other divinities, symbolizing the sacred body (ku);
2) Sungten—sacred books, representing the sacred speech (sung);
3) Thugten—chörtens, symbolizing sacred thought (thug).

Thus a pilgrimage can be made to a monastery housing a statue of the Jowo (Sakyamuni) or to a chörten that contains the relics of a saint. Tibet's most famous shrine, the Jokhang of Lhasa, used to contain an abundance of these three classes of sacred relics. During the Cultural Revolution, most were plundered or destroyed by the Red Guards. Its principal image, Jowo, which confers immense spiritual power on the temple, somehow survived. In recent years, many new statues have been erected and consecrated; the Jokhang is slowly taking on new life. It should be noted that a statue, *chörten*, or any religious object made by man has no liturgical properties unless it has been subsequently sanctified in the proper manner: a consecration ceremony known as *rabne* must be held. When this occurs, life-force is imbued into the object, usually by means of the *sogshing* (life-tree). In statues, this takes the form of a blessed wooden stick, inscribed with prayers or *mantras*, placed inside the body.

Chörtens may be built to commemorate some noteworthy activity of a holy person. This may be the place where he experienced a profound insight or where he was ordained. Sometimes certain highly blessed *chörtens* can be classified as *thongdröl*—'Liberation on Sight'. Before its near-total destruction in the 1960s, the Jampaling *chörten* in the Dranang Valley (see page 465) was considered such a monument. It was thought to have the power to enlighten any true believer who had the good fortune to set eyes on it.

Chörtens are monuments where the relics of important religious personages are deposited—a tradition passed down the ages since the time of the Buddha himself. His relics were kept in various specific places, which became major sites of pilgrimage for all Buddhists. The practice of keeping and perhaps displaying the relics of a holy person is quintessentially Buddhist and does not derive from any known Hindu precedents.

SOME SPECIAL CHARACTERISTICS OF SACRED OBJECTS

Quite often, Tibetans attach a miraculous quality to a particular image or object. For example, a Drölma statue might be known as Drölma Sungjönma—the 'Talking Tara'—if legends tell of it having spoken aloud at some early time; to give admonishments or predictions. Another class of well-known miraculous objects are the stones whose surfaces are ostensibly imprinted with the hand or footprints of a master. These relics are highly venerated in monasteries, sometimes transcending other conventional religious objects. In Bodh Gaya, the Buddha's footprint is over 60 cm long. A third attribute is *rangjung* ('self-manifestation'). Tibetans believe that an object can be formed supernaturally by itself, with no apparent intervention by man. Certain revered statues are considered *rangjung*, having come into being miraculously—crystallizations of a mystic process. Pilgrims believe that these objects are endowed with special power; they make a special point of viewing and touching them with their foreheads. Sometimes, they are said to dispense holy liquid or ambrosia (*dutsi*) to the worthy, usually through their finger tips.

MOTIVATIONS OF PILGRIMAGE

The overriding purpose of pilgrimage is generally the desire to benefit mankind. Most authentic pilgrims make offerings and prayers so that their fellow beings may share the merits gained from the pilgrimage. However, personal gains, both spiritual and material, are also motives for the trip. It is hoped that by undertaking an arduous journey, for example, the sins accrued in the past might be wiped out, religious consciousness expanded. This would promote a better rebirth during the next lifetime, so that the privations of the present life may be exchanged for a better future. The attainment of physical well-being is another common desire. Some women go on pilgrimage with the hope of begetting an offspring. Perhaps the most common wish is simply to have personal contact with the icon or divine object at the end of the journey. This may be a face-to-face encounter with the Jowo of the Jokhang in Lhasa, or a successful circumambulation of sacred Mt Kailash (see page 273).

The pilgrimage experience is highly subjective. Pilgrims through the ages have reported their own personal vision of events experienced. Quite a few tell of how they heard the strains of divine music in the depths of lakes, and some recount sighting mythical creatures coming out of the water. These supernatural encounters are likely to be triggered by the heightened spirituality of the pilgrimage experience. The varieties of religious experience, described by different persons performing the same journey, can be rather surprising.

Casual pilgrims only travel for a limited time. They tend to imitate the behaviour of a *sannyasi* (one who has taken the vows of abandonment and who formally renounces all earthly ties, embracing the pilgrimage discipline full-time in order to seek enlightenment) in regard to dress, food restrictions, and behavior. This allows them a taste of spirituality, but they may also make invaluable contact with dedicated pilgrims. Through this they gain true insight and deepen their understanding of the pilgrimage process. At the end of the day, they may sense that they have achieved something meaningful. Indeed, for some, the result may be so rewarding that they become full-time pilgrims.

THE BUDDHIST IDEA OF PARADISE

Inherent in naturally sanctified sites are the various ideals of paradise. The entry into a Buddhist paradise is the same as attaining *nirvana*—the final liberation from the never-ending cycle of rebirth and of suffering. The most popular is Sukhavati, the mythical 'Western Paradise' of the Buddha Amitabha (Wöpame). According to a Tibetan text, this fabulous retreat is full of wish-fulfilling trees, where no wish is denied. There is no suffering or sorrow; the finest silk, food, and precious stones are there for the taking. Caves have springs where milk flows perpetually, lakes bestow clarity of mind, and certain caves promote full enlightenment. While here, the *bodhicitta* ('Buddha mind') of a pilgrim increases and ignorance is wiped out. The admission into Sukhavati has one proviso: once entered, it can never be left, for the return route is impossible to find.

According to Tibetan pilgrimage literature, there are a number of paradisiacal sites already in existence in Tibet. Some have long been 'opened' by appropriate masters but others still await discovery. Dremojong and Chörten Nyima on the Tibet–Sikkim border, Khembalung in Nepal, Lapchi and Rongshar on the Nepal–Tibet border, and the Pemakö Valley in southeast Tibet, are probably the best-known 'hidden valleys' (bey*uls*). It is widely believed that when wars and other calamities threaten the very survival of mankind, these special places will serve as refuges for the followers of Buddhism.

To gain entry to an 'opened' *beyul*, the pilgrim must first possess profound faith that the *beyul* actually exists. Secondly, he must have accumulated much merit in his lifetime and be completely detached from worldly goods and desires. Finally, the pilgrim must have access to the proper guidebook and the timing has to be right. Usually this knowledge of a specified date of entry is passed from *guru* to disciple by secret oral transmission. The approach on foot has to be from one of the pre-ordained cardinal points, depending on the time of the year. In order to reach Dremojong in the autumn, for example, it is necessary to use the east gate.

One of the best-known mythical earthly paradises is Shambala. Although much has been written about it in Tibetan sacred literature, no one has been able to pinpoint exactly the whereabouts of this hidden kingdom. Texts that describe the routes to the site underline the fact that only accomplished *yogins*, steeped in the practice of meditation and spiritual transformation, can possibly overcome the supernatural obstacles along the way. Shambala is one of five major Buddhist sites of pilgrimage situated at the cardinal points of the compass. Bodh Gaya is at the center, Wutai Shan is to the east, Potala (not to be confused with Lhasa's Potala) in the south, Uddiyana in the west, and Shambala in the north.

DEVOTIONAL ACTS OF PILGRIMS

In order to gain access to a paradisiacal inner sanctum—the final goal of many pilgrimages—pilgrims first must purify themselves, make appropriate offerings, and pass a series of tests that may have both physical and mental components. Dangerous situations, such as negotiating a precipitous catwalk to reach the inner recesses of a cave, test the concentration of the pilgrim's mind. These procedures ensure a level of spirituality sufficient to identify and worship the mythical objects that a non-believer cannot see. A simple cave near the top of a ridge may possess extraordinarily potent power, fully charged with the vibrations of great *yogis*. An indistinct outline on a rock face may manifest a clear image of Chenresi, the Bodhisattva of Compassion, to the pious. The ability to discern the supernatural is considered a vital sign of a pilgrim's progress. It is a measure of transcendental awareness; a significant increase in merit. Those who have it may follow in the footsteps of past masters, who were usually depicted as humble persons, succeeding against all odds in reaching the promised land.

The most important religious observances of a pilgrim visiting sacred sites are as follows:

CIRCUMAMBULATION

'Pilgrimage' in Tibetan is *nekhor*, which literally means 'the circumambulation of a sacred place'. The practice was derived from Buddhist India, where it began as a means of paying homage to a sacred person or object. The holy site can be a monastery, lake, mountain (in particular Mt Kailash), *chörten*, or tree. The act of walking clockwise around it, usually many times and accompanied by prayers, is a show of devotion and a means of acquiring merit. It also helps one to be spiritually centered. In India (especially in the south) as well as in Tibet, temples still have corridors (*khorlam*) designed specifically for this purpose. Some good examples are at the Jokhang in Lhasa and at Shalu Monastery.

PROSTRATION

Prostration (*chaktshal*) is a predominantly Tibetan tradition. To show his faith, the pilgrim stretches himself fully on the ground and his progress around the circuit is measured in repetitions of this arduous performance. Usually, every time a pilgrim enters a monastery, he prostrates three times as a matter of course. In each instance, his folded hands touch his forehead, the mouth-throat area, and his heart. This three-pointed contact symbolizes mind, speech, and body.

MANTRAS

Mantras are not to be equated with the prayers that often accompany the act of offering. They are formulae used by pilgrims to achieve a meditative state and are usually recited during a journey from sacred site to sacred site. *Mantras* are considered to be imbued with magic and their incantation supposedly produces supernatural results. For example, the recitation of a certain *mantra* in a certain site can help cure blindness. The Shara Bumpa *chörten*, in the Phanyul Valley north of Lhasa, is just such a monument.

In Tibet, the most ubiquitous *mantra* is 'Om Mani Padme Hum'. The verbal symbol of Chenresi, the Bodhisattva of Compassion and the protector of Tibet, it is often seen carved on stones and large rocks. Guru Rinpoche's mantra is 'Om Ah Hum Vajra Guru Padme Siddhi Hum'. Pilgrims believe the blessing of this supreme master will be conferred on those who recite it. Printed on prayer flags (*lungta*) are printed thousands of powerful *mantras*. Likewise, the interior of properly consecrated images contains numerous mantras.

Very often a Tibetan performs three prostrations in front of an image, or recites a *mantra* three times. The first performance prevents the practitioner from falling into the lower realms of existence (*nyensong*); the second helps the person to attain a higher level of rebirth; and the third helps to sublimate negative feelings like anger and hatred.

Offerings

Tibetans on pilgrimage regularly make offerings (*chöpa*), to express thanks and obeisance to the divinities within monasteries or natural places. This gesture, one of the most important for the pilgrim, allows him to propitiate the deities and in so doing ask that particular wishes be granted. By making offerings regularly, the pilgrim knows that he is also accumulating merit for the future.

The object most frequently used in offering is the ceremonial scarf (*khata*), which is usually draped around the neck of a statue or a lama. Others include the five grains, butter lamps (*marme*), and barley beer (*chang*). The last is traditionally offered to shrines associated with Guru Rinpoche and Palden Lhamo, the female divinity. One type of tribute derived from pre-Buddhist practices is incense (*sang*); fragrant juniper is burned at sacred sites and on top of passes or mountains. The way in which the smoke rises indicates good or bad omens.

Fundamentally, the concept of offerings implies giving (*jinpa*); it becomes a path to knowledge, fulfilment, peace, and other desired qualities. The most extreme form is to give one's life. One necessary condition for the art of giving, however, is that the pilgrim must do so of his own volition with no thought of rewards. The other is compassion. An interesting practice of the Tibetans is the purchase from the butcher of condemned animals. After the transaction, the animal, usually a goat or a sheep, is then set free and allowed to live out its days.

Another simple practice of giving can be seen on mountain tops or passes. The pilgrim who finally reaches the summit puts one stone on top of a cairn (*lhatse*), which in turn is formed of the efforts of many bygone pilgrims. This is known as the 'eye-viewed' offering (*chezing*). The stone cairns allow travelers to see the tops of passes, even from afar, and they provide necessary landmarks for a journey. The offering of a prayer flag on a pass is for the same motive.

Ritual Water Splashing

Tibetans, unlike Hindus, have no tradition of purifying themselves by immersion in sanctified water such as the Ganges. For the Hindus, this is one of the most notable ways of expressing devotion. Water is an important element of purification in Tibetan Buddhism, but it is abstracted to such an extent that there is no custom of ritual bathing in sacred rivers or lakes. This fact is well illustrated at the glacial lake called Thukje Dzingbu ('Lake of Compassion'), or

Gourikund, on the Mt Kailash circumambulation circuit. While Hindus plunge themselves into the icy water, Tibetans merely splash a few drops in all directions and on their heads. There is a notable Tibetan saying: 'Hindus clean outside, Tibetans clean inside'.

Lakes and rivers are important centers of pilgrimage. A good example is the Oracle Lake of Tibet, known as Lhamo Latso. In order to divine their past and future, the Dalai Lamas were obliged to visit it at least once in their lives. Some sacred lakes are associated with the birth of important saints: Guru Rinpoche is said to have been born from a lotus in a lake called Pema Tso. The source of the Indus, a short distance north of Mt Kailash, is a place of veneration for Tibetan pilgrims.

AUDIENCE

One primary aspect of pilgrimage is to obtain an audience (*darsan*) with the lama or guru of a sanctuary. Quite often, the spirituality of a place is derived from the person who stays there. Lapchi is one of the most important pilgrimages in Tibet because Milarepa lived and died there. Dharamsala, which three decades ago had no religious significance whatsoever, is now one of the major centers for pilgrims simply by virtue of the Dalai Lama's presence.

Affiliated with the concept of *darsan* is the practice of blessing (*jinlab*). This is usually a touch on the head by the lama, a gift of an offering cake (*torma*); or the bestowing of a blessed knotted string or cloth (*sungdud*), usually red or yellow, to be worn around the neck. It is believed that a sacred person has the power to consecrate by touch. He can transfer this blessing onto an object by blowing on it and reciting a *mantra*. Perfected medicine (*mandrub*) is another highly prized substance. These small granules are usually dispensed by the lama with a tiny silver spoon and are received with immense care and appreciation. They are believed to possess supernatural curative powers and may often save lives during an emergency.

TANTRIC PILGRIMAGE

Pilgrimage for the believer is a conscious choice rather than an onerous duty. It need not necessarily conform to a fixed, rigidly prescribed itinerary. There are also no specific ceremonies to be performed in any one place. Taking this idea of the unstructured journey further, it is feasible for a pilgrimage to be internalized. The entire journey is visualized in the mind's eye, thus eliminating the need for an actual voyage.

The basis of a Tantric Pilgrimage is to correlate the outer, geographical sites with the inner regions or organs in the body of the practitioner. For example, the spinal column is imagined to be Mt Meru, the four limbs to be the four mystic subcontinents around it. Actual physical pilgrimage is thus not an absolute requirement in the search for enlightenment. It is eminently possible to realize ultimate emancipation without ever setting foot in any shrines or walking any pilgrimage routes.

THE PRINCIPAL HOLY PLACES OF TIBET
LHASA

Lhasa is Tibet's sacred city. It first became a site of worship when King Songtsen Gampo built his principal temple, the Tsuglag Khang (commonly known as the Jokhang) in the 7th century. The Jokhang, without doubt the holiest shrine in Tibet, is the repository of

Tibet's paramount statue, the magnificently embellished image of Jowo Sakyamuni.

Throughout the Yarlung Dynasty and subsequent epochs, the fledgling city evolved as the spiritual and temporal center of the Buddhist kingdom. Foundations of other ancient edifices, attributed to Songtsen Gampo, the First Religious King, include the original Potala (traces remain in the Phakpa Lhakhang and the Chögyal Drubphuk), Pabonka, Dragla Lugug, Ramoche, and others. These are potent pilgrim sites fervently venerated to this day.

Three of the Gelugpa 'Great Six' monasteries—Sera, Drepung, and Ganden—are located near Lhasa. In the vicinity of these monastic cities are caves and retreats associated with their illustrious founders, including the originator of the order, Tsong Khapa.

Three pilgrimage circuits exist in Lhasa: the long Lingkhor, which completely encloses the city's old district; the Barkhor circling the Jokhang; and the Nangkhor, which provides a ritual corridor around the inner chapels of the Jokhang. Numerous pilgrims can often be found walking or prostrating themselves along these and visiting the shrines en route.

KING SONGTSEN GAMPO'S DEMON-SUPPRESSING TEMPLES

King Songtsen Gampo's greatest accomplishment was his introduction of Buddhism into Tibet. According to the *Mani Kabum*, a 13th-C. text chronicling his exploits, the Yarlung-dynasty monarch founded 12 so-called Runo, Tandul, and Yangdul temples in the 7th century. The chain of events leading up to their construction began with the Buddhist Princess Wencheng's arrival from China (in 641) to marry the king. She divined the presence of a demoness who was exerting powerful negative forces over the land, preventing the full development of the Buddhist faith. It was thought imperative that this demoness be supressed before Tibet's all-important central temple, the Jokhang (Tsuglag Khang), was constructed. Lying with her head to the east and feet to the west across the expanse of Tibet, her extremities had to be pinned down. To do this, Songtsen Gampo founded four Runo temples in Central Tibet—'the Four Great Horn-suppressors'—which formed an invisible, protective square enclosing Lhasa (supposedly the heart that pumped the blood of the demoness). To pacify the border regions, he constructed four Tandul or 'Taming the Borders' temples. Finally, he built four Yangdul temples for 'Taming the Areas beyond the Borders.' These twelve monastic institutions were perceived as so many potent stakes driven through the limbs of the demoness, subduing her forever. (For their exact configuration, which resembles a mandala, see the diagram on page 44.)

Central Tibet's four Runo temples—Trandruk, Katsal (Katse), Tsang Dram, and Drampa Gyang—form a rough square, with Lhasa and the Jokhang at the center (some sources claim Tsi Nesar near Gyantse and Tangkya near Drigung Qu are two of the four). *Ru* (horn, ring) was a Tibetan term for a basic administrative and geographic unit. The four 'horns' of Tibet's central zone represented the shoulders and hips of the demoness, and each of the four shrines were supposedly built by architects (*lagpön*) from different regions: Minyag (Xixia), Thökhar (Tokharistan), Balpo (Nepal), and Hor (Turkestan). Trandruk (page 533), situated in the Yarlung district of the Left Horn (Yuru, Yarlung, and Dakpo), is the largest and most important of the surviving royal monasteries in the area. It controlled the demoness's left shoulder. Katsal (page 550), near Medro Gongkar, is within the Central Horn (Uru, Kyi Chu Valley) and was designed to hold down the right shoulder. Tsang Dram (unlocated), suppressing the right hip, is at the Right Horn (Yeru, eastern Tsang), on the banks of the Phari Tsangchu River, Tobgyal district. Finally, Drampa Gyang (page 867), in the Supplementary Horn (Rulag, western Tsang) is in southwestern Tsang, near Lhatse Dzong; it pinioned the left hip.

The four Tandul temples are: Phurchu, Khothing, Mön Bumthang, and Pradün Tse. They respectively pin down the right elbow, left elbow, left knee, and right knee of the demoness. Each shrine was said to be linked to a branch temple and a hermitage, although this is not confirmed. Phurchu (page 746), on the right bank of the Nyang Chu, is in the Kongpo district near Bayi and Ningchi. Khothing (page 692) in Lhodrak is just north of Mön Bumthang (Jampa Lhakhang) in Bhutan's Chökhor Valley. Pradun Tse is west of Saga Dzong, a major staging post on the Central Tibet–West Tibet road.

The Yangdul temples, pacifiers of regions beyond the borders, are Dokham Longtang Drönma(in Dankhog), Mangyul Jamtrin (Chamding), Jang Tsangpa Lungnön and Paro Kyerchu. They were built to hold firm the demon's right hand, right foot, left hand, and left foot. Each monastery is associated with a celestial animal of the Chinese geomantic tradition (black tortoise in the north; azure dragon in the east; red bird in the south; white tiger in the west). Dokham Longtang Drönma in Kham is far to the east, 258 km northwest of Ganze and 114

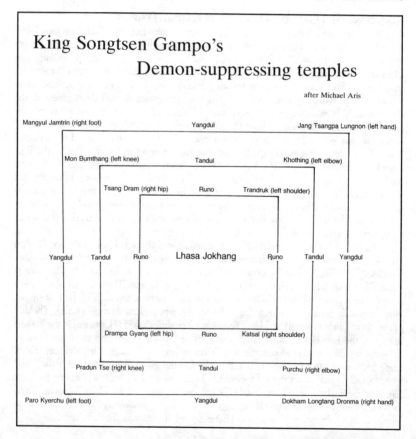

King Songtsen Gampo's Demon-suppressing temples

after Michael Aris

km southeast of Dzogchen Monastery. Jang Tshangpa Lungnön ('Wind Suppressor') Monastery (unlocated) is supposed to be in Tshangpa district in the north (Jang). Other sources, however, claim it is near Nyethang Monastery on the Kyi Chu's right bank, only a short distance from Lhasa—if this were the case, the geographical symmetry of the Yangdul group of temples would be impaired. Mangyul Jamtrin (page 935) in the celebrated Kyirong Valley, is only a short distance north of the town of Kyirong near the Tibet–Nepal border. Paro Kyerchu, the second temple in Bhutan, is sited in the Paro Valley.

GURU RINPOCHE'S EIGHT SECLUDED PLACES OF PRACTICE:

Drak Yong Dzong, Samye Chimpu, Lhodrak Karchu, Yarlung Sheldrak, Nering Senge Dzong, Drakmar Yamalung, Monka Nering Senge Dzong, Monka Sridzong, Paro Taktsang Phuk

During the reign of Trisong Detsen (755–97), Santarakshita, the famous head of Vikramasila University in India advised the king to invite Guru Rinpoche (Padmasambhava) to Tibet. it was hoped that the lotus-born tantric master from Uddiyana, an ancient region of the Swat Valley, would be able to overcome the negative forces existing in the country. (The Chinese pilgrim, Xuan Zang, visited there in the 7th C. and saw over a 1,000 temples, attestation of the valley's uncommon spirituality.) Trisong Detson sent five emissaries with his invitation. Guru Rinpoche accepted and, on arrival, managed to subdue the entire pantheon of local demons. He and Santarakshita founded Samye, Tibet's first monastery. The edifice provided a firm foundation for Buddhist practice in the centuries to come.

Guru Rinpoche also bequeathed to the country the very special tradition of *terma*. Before his departure, he dictated his entire teachings to his consort Yeshe Tsogyal who then transcribed them into Tibetan, Sanskrit, and Uddiyana. These valuable texts, together with ritual objects like *dorjes* and *phurpas*, were carefully hidden in special places imbued with remarkable geomantic qualities. In later periods, *tertons*—reincarnations of Guru Rinpoche's disciples— would use prophecies and visions to rediscover these relics. *Terma* were designed to preserve intact the teachings of the guru for future generations of Buddhist practitioners. Guru Rinpoche predicted three grand, eight great, 21 powerful, 108 intermediate, and 1,000 lesser *tertons*. The three grand ones were Nyima Wöser (12th C.), Chökyi Wangchuk (13th C.), and Rigdzin Godem Truchen (14th C.). The eight great *tertons* were Ratna Lingpa, Padma Lingpa, Orgyan Lingpa, Sangye Lingpa, Dorje Lingpa, Karma Lingpa, Orgyan Dorje Lingpa, and Orgyan Padma Lingpa. They all lived in the 14th and 15th centuries.

Guru Rinpoche's eight most important cave retreats were also supremely sacred repositories of *terma*. Later, other illustrious masters came to these eight sites and hid religiously significant treasures there as well. For example, at Samye Chimpu, a retreat representing Guru Rinpoche's 'speech' (*sung*), the renowned Nyingmapa lama, Nyang Tingedzin, buried texts that one day would be rediscovered by a spiritually qualified person.

Legends recount how Guru Rinpoche used his magical powers to exorcize Bön spirits and local demons, staying in retreat for long periods at each locale. These remote, mountain-top sanctuaries are all located in absolutely extraordinary settings. Lhodrak Karchu, the embodiment of Guru Rinpoche's mind (*thug*), for example, is a lush Shangri-la in the Tibet–Bhutan Himalayas. It stands in stark contrast to Yarlung Sheldrak, a retreat cave at the top of the Sheldrak range in the heart of the Yarlung Valley. Although endowed with equally superb vistas, this locale lies in a barren, moon-like landscape.

The eight places, conceived as the focus of spiritually potent environments, are the symbolic centers of sacred mandalas. Over time, other enlightened teachers contributed their power presence to the caves. The labyrinthine cave system of Drak Yong Dzong, identified as Guru Rinpoche's Buddha-body (*ku*), is famous for being the place where 55 ascetics reached enlightenment in the 8th century. Guru Rinpoche also concealed all the major Dorje Phurpa texts here. Samye and Yarlung held the most significance for Indian master. Of the five indigenous Tibetan sanctuaries, four are located within these two areas. The last is in Lhodrak, South Tibet. Three cave retreats in Bhutan (Senge Dzong, Sridzong, Taktsang Phuk) complete the total of eight.

The list of Guru Rinpoche's most powerful hermitages is extracted from his biographies, the most important of which is the *Padma Thangyig Sheldrakma*, a text discovered by Orgyan Lingpa within Yarlung. It is said that Guru Rinpoche performed 10,900 heroic deeds to expound his teachings. These were faithfully recorded in writing by his five wives and then concealed as *terma* for the benefit of future generations. Other important texts that detailed sacred places frequented by the master are the *Zanglingma* by Nyangral Nyima Wösel (1124–92 or 1136–1204), the *Kathang Denga* discovered by Orgyan Lingpa (1329–67), and the *Soldeb Lewu Dünma* by Zangpo Drakpa.

KAILASH, TSARI, AND LAPCHI

By common consensus, Tibetan pilgrims recognize three pilgrimages as the most sacred in the country: Kailash, Tsari, and Lapchi. These far-flung havens are once-in-a-lifetime destinations, the imagined mystical paradises of most devotees. All three are consecrated to Demchok, the wrathful emanation of Buddha Sakyamuni. Kailash, known by Tibetans as Kang Rinpoche ('Precious Mountain'), is the center of the universe for both Hindus and Buddhists. For the former, it is the abode of Shiva; the latter revere it as the dwelling of Demchok, a tantric transformation of Shiva, and the haunt of Milarepa, the 11th-C. ascetic. Throughout the ages, Kailash has been the foremost place of pilgrimage for Indians, Tibetans, and Nepalis.

The sacred Lapchi Kang range and its Shangri-La retreats are also intimately associated with Milarepa. Considered the Paradise of Demchok, it was first pacified by Guru Rinpoche, who went there to subdue local demons. Located within the heart of the Tibet-Nepal Himalayas, its many cave-shrines are secluded in an astonishingly un-Tibetan environment reminiscent of the lush, alpine regions of Nepal. Beneath the snows of the Lapchi Kang is the Rongshar Valley. Lined with countless wild rose bushes, it is the renowned 'Valley of Roses'.

Tsari is perhaps the most hauntingly beautiful of pilgrimages in Tibet. The very etymology of its name implies the quintessence of nature. Its center is sacred Mt Takpa Shelri, a spectacular snow peak within the Tsari Valley. Seen by Guru Rinpoche in a vision, Tsari represents the three foremost aspects of the Buddha: body, mind, and speech. It is perceived as 'Dewachen', the living paradise of Wöpame (Buddha of Infinite Light), where the lotus energy transmutes passion into spiritual purity. Once in every 12 years, pilgrims from all over Tibet perform the difficult but spectacular Rongkhor pilgrimage. This circumambulates the headwaters of the Subansiri, a principal branch of the Brahmaputra, which flows through the Tibet Himalayas to Assam.

A SHORT HISTORY
OF TIBETAN ART

Beginning with the country's unification in the 7th C., various foreign influences played decisive roles in shaping Tibet's art styles. Monastery murals often reveal artistic elements that originated in India, Nepal, Kashmir, Central Asia, and China. The strongest contributions to Tibetan art probably came from the Indic tradition, encompassing the cultural sensibilities of ancient Magadha (modern Bihar), Kashmir, and Nepal.

The following is an introduction to the main forces that shaped Tibetan art from its tentative beginnings in the Yarlung period to the development of an authentic Tibetan form of expression in the 15th C. onwards. The emphasis falls on those surviving monasteries that still have important early collections of murals and monumental statues. Such large, immovable works provide a generally reliable chronology of Tibetan art.

The Yarlung Period (7th–9th Century)

The Yarlung period coincided with the introduction of Buddhism into Tibet by King Songtsen Gampo and its flowering under Tride Tsugtsen, Trisong Detsen, Ralpachen, and others. A number of key temples were built at this time.

The most significant Tibetan building was the Jokhang, a temple in Lhasa founded by Songtsen Gampo and Princess Tritsun of Nepal. Its earliest structures were conceived and decorated in the Indo–Nepalese style and remnants, in the form of columns, capitals, and entrance door frames, still survive. Their wood carvings and basic design go back to the Indian Gupta art of the 5th C., the stylistic elements of which were absorbed by Nepal—among others—in the 6th and 7th centuries. Superb examples of the genre in the Jokhang are the elaborately carved door frames, made up of a number of concentric borders. Nepalese paintings, possibly of that very early era, survived on the walls of the Jokhang's second floor until the early 1980s. They have since disappeared.

Another Yarlung temple of great importance is the recently discovered Kachu Lhakhang. Begun in the early 8th C., during the rule of King Tride Tsugtsen and his Chinese wife, Princess Jincheng, its foundation was fully half a century earlier than Samye, the acknowledged First Monastery of Tibet. Within this temple are original statues that date back to the 8th and 9th century. These, probably the most ancient images of Central Tibet, are the only ones extant that can be properly attributed to the Yarlung period. The historically significant monumental Buddha, whose style is derived from the Central Asian oasis of Khotan, was crafted in the 8th century. It is an unique synthesis of Gupta (4th-7th C.) spirituality and Tang Dynasty (7th-10th C.) solemnity. Surrounding this image are splendid 9th-C. *bodhisattvas* created during the reign of Ralpachen (806–838). These life-size statues are products of local artists who were obviously conversant with an art style that had its antecedents in Dunhuang (the Yarlung kings controlled this Silk Road oasis at that time). Its roots probably came from the Newar art of the Kathmandu Valley, which managed— by way of itinerant Tibetan traders and pilgrims—to penetrate Central Asia. Stylistic elements from the two civilizations of Nepal and Central Asia became integrated, forming a new mode of artistic expression. Within the small, apparently insignificant chapel of Kachu are outstanding works of art from the reigns of both Tride Tsugtsen and Ralpachen.

The famous Samye Monastery was built in the late 8th C. by King Trisong Detsen. This mandala-like architectural complex owed its inspiration to the great monasteries of India, the *mahaviharas*. Few early remains have survived; notable exceptions are the stone pillar (*doring*) bearing Trisong Detsen's edict, two stone lions (placed within wood enclosures), and the bronze bell with ancient inscriptions at the entrance.

Although the monumental Potala was essentially attributed to the Fifth Dalai Lama (1617–82), parts of the vast complex perhaps date back to the time of Songtsen Gampo, who built a palace on the top of Marpo Ri. These consist of the Chögyal Drubphuk—the king's meditation cave—and the Phakpa Lhakhang. Within the former are statues of the king and his two foreign wives, Wencheng and Tritsun, which can feasibly be dated to the early 9th C. Among the many statues of this triad found in Central Tibetan monasteries, those in the Chögyal Drubphuk are the most unusual in style.

The Dragla Lugug cave temple, a stone's throw from the Potala, has bas-relief rock sculptures that might have been crafted by Nepalese artists working in Lhasa during the Yarlung period. This cave monastery, and its gallery of 71 rock-carved images, is probably the only one in Central Tibet to echo, albeit in a remote manner, the great cave temples and fabulous rock sculptures of the Silk Road. Immediately behind Dragla Lugug, on the rock surfaces of the Chakpo Ri's cliffs, are thousands of rock-carved images. Literary sources mention that King Songtsen Gampo personally ordered their execution; some may be relics from his 7th-C. reign.

NEPALESE INFLUENCE

Nepalese art began to exert its influence in Tibet from an early time. According to both the new and old Tang Annals, Nepal was for a short time a dependency of Tibet prior to the 8th century. The presence of the Nepalese Princess Tritsun (Bhrikuti), who married King Songtsen Gampo (ca 641), had a palpable influence on the Jokhang. 7th-C. Nepalese (Newari) traits can clearly be discerned, for example, in the original door frames.

During Tibet's early history, however, Nepal left only a limited cultural imprint. The great Licchavi Dynasty of Nepal (300–879) had minimal impact. It was not until the late 13th C., when the Sakyapa became dominant, that Nepalese art began to make itself profoundly felt. Of all the foreign artists who have influenced Tibet, the Newars of Nepal have consistently maintained the most prolonged and creative relationship.

CENTRAL ASIAN INFLUENCE

At the time of China's Tang Dynasty, Tibet was a major political power as well as a notable participant in the history and development of Central Asian art. In the 8th and 9th C., many Silk Road oases belonged to Tibet—before their destruction by war and encroaching sand.

Central Asian culture, emanating principally from the states of Dunhuang and Khotan, helped shape the arts of Tibet during the Yarlung period. Tibet also absorbed influences from

India, China, and, to a lesser extent, from Persia. All these disparate sources diffused into the country by way of the great crossroads of Central Asia. Tibetan artists worked in the Tarim Basin area as early as the 8th C. and, exposed to the rich artistic milieu, returned to Tibet to paint in the newly adopted style. Chinese art from this region, strongly shaped by Gupta India, also had considerable impact on the Yarlung Dynasty. However, with the exception of Kachu, Dranang, and Yemar (Iwang), it is difficult to precisely determine the Central Asian stylistic traits of surviving Tibetan temples. Such traits had been largely absorbed by the 11th century.

GUPTA INFLUENCE ON CENTRAL ASIA

From the second half of the 4th C., the Gupta kings united much of northern India. Like the Maurya and the Kushan empires before it, the Gupta Dynasty was so politically and culturally dominant that its influence went far beyond its actual boundaries. This was the Golden, or Classical, period of India; it would not see another empire like it until the Mughal in the 16th century. The country enjoyed unprecedented prosperity, especially in its main centers and prominent Buddhist monasteries. Works of incomparable beauty and elegance were created. Indian arts, architecture, and philosophy flowered, setting standards unmatched in the rest of Indian history.

Gupta art combined spirituality and sensuality. With rare ability, the artists projected an ineffable quality of inner peace into their images of Buddha and other divinities. A major characteristic of Gupta statues was the diaphanous robe, with string-like ridges as folds, worn by the Buddha. The body, perfectly proportioned, gained a sense of almost tangible reality from this veil. The easy and fluid solemnity was further amplified by a dignified calm, the trademark of Gupta sculpture. This artistic tradition strongly influenced the neighboring regions of Central Asia, Nepal, China, Ceylon, and Southeast Asia. It had an important effect on Kashmir, one of Buddhism's strongholds in the Indian subcontinent. Most Kashmiri sculpture of the 5th to the 7th C. was indebted to both Gupta and late Gandharan (northwest Indian) art.

As early as the 7th C., Tibetans must have learned much about Buddhist religion and culture from Kashmir. It is well known that Thönmi Sambhota, Songtsen Gampo's minister, went there for sacred texts and teachings. Kashmir at that time was also one of the centers of trade on the subcontinent. Central Asian and Tibetan merchants arrived frequently, while Kashmiri Buddhist missionaries regularly undertook long trips, via the Silk Road, to China and beyond. In the early 8th C., when Buddhist monks in Khotan suffered persecution, they fled the southern Tarim Basin city-state to seek asylum in Central Tibet, bringing with them Gupta artistic traditions from Central Asia. Although the Gupta empire collapsed by the end of the 6th C., its impact on the arts lingered for a further 50 years throughout most of the Indian subcontinent and surrounding regions.

THE KHOTAN FACTOR

Early Khotanese civilization was chronicled by the famed Chinese pilgrims, Fa Xian (399) and Xuan Zang (644), as they passed through the city-state en route to India. According to them, Khotan was a thriving Buddhist center. Xuan Zang reported 5,000 practicing monks and 100 monasteries, an indication—supported by Buddhist texts—that this was the center of Buddhism for the entire Tarim Basin area and beyond. Artistic influences from the oasis shaped such early Tibetan relics as the monumental Buddha at Kachu Lhakhang. In the 11th C., when Buddhism in the region finally succumbed to Islam, the monks carried their art works and scriptures south to Tibet, where Buddhism was undergoing a rejuvenation.

THE SECOND DIFFUSION OF BUDDHISM (11TH–12TH CENTURY)

The Second Diffusion of Buddhism in Tibet is characterized by two phases. The first centered around the early activities of Gongpo Rabsal (832–915) and his disciples, Lume (ca 950–1025) and Sumpa. Spearheaded by Atisha, the Indian master, the second phase was largely confined to West Tibet.

Some of the major temples in Ü (Central Tibet), founded in that period by Lume et al were: Moragyel by Lume; Gyal Lhakhang by Nanam Dorje Wangchuk (1012); Solnag Tangboche by Tsultrim Jungne (1017). In the neighboring province of Tsang, a flurry of activity predated the arrival of Atisha. Important temples established here were: Gyangong by Löton Dorje Wangchuk (997); Tsi Nesar (1037); Yemar (early 11th C.); Shalu by Sherab Jungne (1027). After his West Tibet sojourn, Atisha's arrival in Central Tibet in 1045 sparked the further building of numerous monasteries. Later, his disciple, Dromtönpa, founded the Kadampa sect, fostering the rapid spread of Buddhism. The most significant monasteries founded at this time were Reting (1056), Sakya (1073), Nethang (mid-11th C.), and Dranang (1081). Few temples from the early years of the Second Diffusion have survived with their cultural relics intact. Exceptions are Dranang, Nethang, and Yemar.

After the fall of the Yarlung empire, part of the royal family was exiled to West Tibet. Under the patronage of King Yeshe Ö and the spiritual guidance of the translator Rinchen Zangpo and Atisha, Buddhism and Buddhist art revived in the 10th century. A number of artistically important monasteries, influenced by Kashmiri styles, were built at this time. These included Tapho (in Spiti, Himachal Pradesh), Alchi (Ladakh), and Tholing (West Tibet). The first two still preserve extraordinary sculptures and murals belonging to the period (10th–11th C.).

Four centuries later, in the late 15th-C., murals and statues of the temples of Tsaparang, West Tibet, were executed in the indigeneous Guge style, whose origins can be traced to Kashmir and Nepal. Most of Tsaparang's murals (within the Red and White Lhakhang) and some damaged statues have survived.

Yemar (see page 390) is a small, abandoned chapel next to the Tibet–Sikkim highway. Within are remarkable life-size statues very different in style from virtually all Central Tibet monasteries. Yemar and Dranang are the only surviving temples founded at the start of the Second Diffusion. The former's magnificent statues were created during the first decades of the 11th C. and represent an unparalleled synthesis of East Indian Pala style and the Buddhist Xixia style from Central Asia. In all likelihood, these works were crafted by Tibetan masters familiar with the Pala idiom and who, through long-standing cultural contact with Central Asia, also embraced the idioms of Xixia. A striking feature of the statues is the uncommon use of medallions in the design of the robes. This motif can perhaps be traced to the Persian Sassanid empire, whose culture penetrated most of the Silk Road territories. Unfortunately, Yemar's Pala-style murals have not survived.

Dranang Monastery (see page 393), founded near the Yarlung Valley in the early phase of the Second Diffusion, still retains 11th-C. murals strongly influenced by the Pala style. This school of art (9th–11th C.), originating in northeast India, is characterized by its strong emphasis on the human figure and its graceful depiction. The Pala roots of these unique works in Dranang are unusual in not being moderated by a Nepalese interpretation, so often the case with late Pala-style paintings in Tibet. Instead, distinctive stylistic elements from Central Asia (Xixia) can be discerned. Dranang's stunning murals are perhaps the earliest and only example of this kind of art in Tibet today. Almost no Pala *thangkas* or murals survive in India, the only extant works being early manuscript covers, with which the Dranang paintings compare favorably.

A recently discovered room (see page 88) in Lhasa's Jokhang contains 12th-C. murals drawn in the original Pala style (albeit moderated by local aesthetics). In one panel, however, the Nepalese–Pala style is more evident. The artist, consummate in both idioms, painted a third panel as a synthesis of the two related, if dissimilar styles.

Some 17 km (10 miles) south of Lhasa is the well-preserved Nethang Drölma Lhakhang (see page 472), a small temple next to the airport road. Atisha, who helped resurrect Buddhism in Tibet, died here in 1054. Remarkably, much of Nethang's original artwork is intact. The most artistical-ly important of its three small chapels is the Tsepame Lhakhang, the very site where Atisha taught his disciples. Here, elaborately costumed, monumental clay statues may date back to the late 12th century. Stylistically, they retain Indian elements of the 12th–13th C. and can be regarded as an evolution of the Yemar–Dranang style.

PALA: INFLUENCES FROM EAST INDIA

The Pala school (8th–12th C.) was the next major phase of Indian art after the Gupta (4th–7th century). It flourished in northeastern India and was sponsored by the Buddhist Pala kings, who ruled the ancient states of Magadha and Bengal. They built many of the great monasteries of the day, including Nalanda and Vikramasila—from which Atisha embarked for Tibet at the beginning of the 11th century. As a descendant of the Gupta idiom, which immeasurably enriched the cultures of Asia, the strongly figural Pala style was one of the most influential art forms ever developed in India. Much of the acclaimed art of Nepal, Tibet, and Central Asia was inspired by it. From the 9th–12th C., Nepal was virtually its second center. But examples have also been found in other parts of Central Asia: an ancient site at Karakhoto, in the Xixia kingdom, has revealed an important group of *thangkas* related to the style; some of the Dunhuang cave murals, probably completed in the late 13th C., show kinship to typical Pala works.

However, although stones and bronzes abound, very few examples of Pala paintings have survived. Among the most important paintings is a small group of Pala manuscripts and manuscript covers dating from the 11th to 13th century. These early works are characterized by a certain figural uniformity. The form of the body is distinguished by broad rounded shoulders, a tapered waist, slender tapering limbs, a three-quarter view of the head, and a high angular nose. After the Moslem conquests, all original works of art—from southern Nepal to Orissa—were systematically destroyed. To see authentic vestiges of this splendid phase of Indian creativity, it is necessary to go to the early Kadampa monasteries (11th–12th C.) in Central Tibet (see above, page 50). Direct Indian influence on Tibet came to an end with the Moslem dominance of the 12th–13th C., which also contributed to the demise of Buddhism in India.

After the 13th C., the subcontinent no longer gave cultural guidance to Tibet, with the possible exception of its western regions.

Generally speaking, the works of Pala art focus on the human figure (see, for example, the Dranang murals) and consist of a main Buddha surrounded by *bodhisattvas*, which are liberally ornamented with jewels and diadems. More *bodhisattvas* and Buddhas, seated in a uniform manner, are usually placed on either side of the central figure's head. (In most cases, 12 figures surround the Buddha.) Finally, a horizontal row of deities is placed below the Buddha's lotus throne, along the painting's bottom register. Unlike Nepalese works, the figures are not confined within signature motifs of elaborate arches or other architectural elements. Other favorite subjects of Pala-style works are Drölma (Tara), cycles of Demchok (Chakrasamvara), Dorje Phagmo (Vajravarahi), Nagpo Chenpo (Mahakala), and portraits of important lamas. The figural type in these early paintings of the Second Diffusion are easily recognized. The *bodhisattvas* are characterized by lithe, graceful bodies; the faces are long and the chins pointed. Their posture is unmistakable. Rendered in the *tribhanga* fashion, they have an exaggerated, out-thrusting of hips which imparts a distinctive, lethargic sway. A prominent feature are the garments worn by standing figures: tight fitting undershorts, which become diaphanous from the top of the thighs down to the ankles; the striped cloth worn by the central figure around the waist (the torso is naked). This type of Pala-inspired work is also renowned for its remarkably rich palette: the colors are even but vibrant and, although red predominates, it is complemented by luminous yellows, greens, and blues.

THE XIXIA FACTOR

For more than 200 years (ca 632–848), Tibet dominated vast tracts of Chinese Turkestan, and was a constant thorn in the side of her powerful neighbor to the east—the Tang empire. Later, the Xixia kingdom (1032–1226), part of northwest China, became a strongly Tibetanized state with a mixed population of Tibetans, Turko-Mongols, Chinese, Qiang, and Sumpas. This area included Kokonor and parts of Gansu. Xixia assimilated considerable elements of Tibet's artistic culture; its predominant religious sects were the Karmapa, Drigungpa and the Tshalpa. The result was that both Dunhuang and Karakhoto displayed unmistakable Tibetan currents in their paintings. Xixia came to an abrupt end when the Mongols, under Genghis Khan (1162–1227), invaded. The murals of Dranang and the statues of Yemar contain stylistic elements from this region.

KASHMIRI ART

The full flowering of Kashmiri Buddhist art occurred during the 7th–8th C. By the late 10th and early 11th C., this art form was mostly found only in neighboring Ladakh, West Tibet, and the western Himalayas. (Although many Buddhist monasteries were built in Kashmir, they were subsequently destroyed.) The bronzes and paintings of Kashmir were highly regarded by its neighboring countries. The royal family of Guge brought Kashmiri statues and artists to West Tibet during the founding of the Tholing Monastery at the turn of the millennium. Mangnang, a West Tibet monastery founded in the 11th c. by the banks of the Satlej River, had murals painted in the Kashmiri style. This artistically important monastery was destroyed during China's Cultural Revolution and all its paintings lost.

Much of the Kashmiri idiom, characterized by sumptuous colors and designs, evolved from composite artistic influences whose main sources were Gupta and late Gandhara formulations that flourished in the 5th and 6th C. The figural style of this genre is renowned for its subtle suggestion of nudity, which gently exerts itself through sensuous, diaphanous garments. The bodies are softly modeled; the limbs taper gently, there is a pronounced elongation of the torso; and the body has a rhythmic bend. Gupta inspiration is apparent in the anatomy: the distinctive pectoral muscles and their breast-like undulations beneath the clothing, the tapered and elongated torso, and especially the abdominal cleavage visible through the garments. The lush colors, largely limited to primary hues, have a radiant, luminous quality. Their range and brilliance are peerless.

A particular characteristic of this genre is its ability to depict richly detailed and luxuriant garments and textiles. Another hallmark is its emphasis on narrative forms. Each episode is self-contained and enclosed in a frame. Consecutive painted panels resemble a long scroll.

Kashmiri influence on Tibet was most strongly felt in the kingdom of Guge, especially with the inception of the Guge style of West Tibet in the 15th century. Superb examples can still be seen today in Tsaparang.

RISE OF THE SAKYAPA

The ascendancy of the Sakyapa sect began with the Mongol conquest of China and Central Asia at the beginning of the 13th century. In Tibet, the military might of Godan Khan, the second son of Genghis Khan, penetrated as far south as Reting and Drigungtil monasteries. But in 1244, aware of the tremendous influence wielded by the great lamas, Godan initiated a patron–priest relationship with Sakya Pandita (1182–1251). This alliance of convenience lasted until the fall of the Yuan Dynasty in 1361. Phagpa (nephew of Sakya Pandita), a great personality of the Sakya lineage, strongly encouraged political and religious cooperation between the Mongols and the Tibetans. He was named Preceptor by Kublai Khan and had jurisdiction over all religious matters within the Yuan (Mongol) empire. Although Sakyapa political dominance lasted less than a century, its cultural impact on 14th–16th C. Tibet was substantial. Tibetan paintings of this period are generally considered Sakyapa in style, a form inspired by Nepal and moderated by Chinese trends. The second half of the 15th C. saw the Sakyapa style move west to influence the arts of Guge.

THE SAKYAPA STYLE (14TH–16TH CENTURY)

As a consequence of the Mongol–Sakyapa link, the Sakyapa received substantial donations which it put to good use by building and lavishly decorating monasteries. Major Sakyapa monuments, such as Sakya and Shalu, were embellished during the 13th–14th century. Because of Mongol generosity, the powerful Sakyapa lamas were able to invite renowned Nepalese artists to work on newly built or recently renovated chapels. Sakya and Shalu, with its superb 13th–14th C. murals executed principally by Newari artists, are considered the developmental centers of the Sakyapa style. Indeed, the Sakyapa genre closely resembles that of the Newari, which in turn owes much to the Pala idiom. The Newars of Nepal, already sharing a close cultural affinity with the Tibetans, deepened this relationship after the 13th century. They often traveled north for trade and work, and thousands of Nepalese Buddhist pilgrims visited the great monasteries of Central Tibet. For Tibetans, India was no longer a source of religious inspiration, and so they turned instead to Nepal, where the Buddhist tradition thrived and original Sanskrit scriptures were widely available. Famed Newari artists, most notably Arniko (1243–1306), made immeasurable contributions to the arts of Tibet and China.

Today, few original Sakyapa artworks survive (most of Sakya Monastery's murals were repainted in the 16th C.). The most important monument of the Sakyapa style is the Shalu Monastery. Here, a treasure trove of breathtaking 14th-C. murals remains virtually intact. The Shalu murals, which inspired generations of Tibetan painters, are distinguished by their quintessentially Newari figurative motifs, of both mortals and divinities. Relegated to the background are the Chinese themes of landscape and nature. Currents of the Tibetan extension of the Pala style can also be detected.

The Shalu figures were executed in typically languorous poses; human and divine forms depicted against a flat, unvarying background of subdued red and blue. They are usually drawn with no attempt at shading, thus creating flat, two-dimensional bodies. Light is uniformly distributed and shadows almost non-existent. Outlines, carefully delineated, are elegant and meticulous; contours are soft, and facial features subtle and gentle. Usually clothed in luxuriant, delicately patterned clothing, the figures are sometimes embellished with exquisite crowns and jewels.

One well-defined characteristic of the Sakyapa-style paintings, as seen on the walls of Shalu, are the elaborate shrines enclosing various figures. Here, the Newari love of detail and extremely fine motifs comes through dramatically. Among the shrines and arches is minute vegetal scrollwork. The rich detailing and design of the thrones are typical. Often lurking within these architectural elements are mythical creatures such as garudas, makaras, and nagas. Along the top and bottom of the paintings are rows of small figures completely separated from each other by elegant and intricate miniature shrines made up of arches, columns, and swirling floral patterns. This geometric arrangement of figures is common among Sakyapa paintings, as is the subtle background behind the principal figures. Dense, whorled scrollwork is sometimes accompanied by a stylized fringe of flames both delicate and lacy. The way in which rocks are painted is derived directly from the 5th-C. Ajanta murals of southwest India. These conventionalized, multi-hued rocks are uniformly geometric and cubic. In the Shalu paintings, the color red prevails, another typical feature of the Sakyapa style. Infused with exuberance, it is considered more animated than its Pala counterpart.

BIRTH OF LOCAL SCHOOLS (15TH–16TH CENTURY)

During the 15th C., a number of regional art schools, each distinct, began to emerge in different parts of Tibet. The Latö and Gyantse schools were based fundamentally on the Sakyapa–Newar style, while the Guge school was more a product of indigenous West Tibetan sensibilities, influenced strongly by Kashmiri traditions.

THE LATÖ SCHOOL

Chung Riwoche (see page 451), a recently discovered nine-story chörten located at a bend of the Tsangpo River due north of Dingri, is, together with the Gyantse Kumbum, the only surviving large, multi-chapel chörten in Tibet. Unlike other famous chörtens—Tröphu, Narthang, Gyang, Jampaling—this monument still contains original and reasonably preserved mid-15th-C. murals. These works mark the early beginning of a fledgling Tibetan art school. Local artists, having fully absorbed the artistic influences of neighboring Nepal (inspired by the Pala) and Yuan China, now added their own interpretation to form a school of art centering on Latö, the westernmost territory of Tsang Province. From the mid-14th to mid-15th C., this uniquely Tibetan painting style co-existed with the Gyantse school (see below).

The artists of Chung Riwoche pioneered a Tibetan art style that was inspired by the paintings of Shalu and Sakya, created during the first decade of the 14th century. The Latö school first came into being at the Jonang Kumbum, before the Gyantse Kumbum (erected 1417–27) was finished. Although the Latö paintings are less accomplished than those of cosmopolitan Gyantse, they cannot be regarded as the precursors. The Latö school is an autonomous and fully separate expression.

THE GYANTSE SCHOOL

Gyantse, a quintessentially Tibetan town, was the main seat of the Shakhapa princes. Its fort was established in the late 14th C. on top of a craggy ridge in the center of the settlement. Palkhor Chöde Monastery and the Kumbum, the great multi-chapel chörten, were completed during the first half of the 15th century. The sheer quantity and quality of artwork preserved in these monuments is remarkable.

Art historians consider the murals of Gyantse to be among the finest examples of Tibetan art extant in the world today. Surviving works of the badly damaged Gyantse fort, however, must be regarded as the beginning of the Gyantse style, essentially an offspring of the Shalu style. At the same time as these were painted, a precursor of the Palkhor Chöde was built. This was later expanded during the years of the Kumbum's completion. In these two monuments the Gyantse style achieved its finest flowering. Alhough the roots of the style are undoubtedly Nepalese, its expression was moderated by Tibetan trends. The result are murals distinguished by a surprisingly varied palette; pale tones are judiciously combined with rich colors.

Another dominant element of the Gyantse school is its highly expressive figurative tradition. Good examples are the mahasiddha figures found in the Gyantse Kumbum, distinctive for their slim elegance and grace. Unusually strong emphasis was placed on well-modeled physiognomy: rounded heads, long curvilinear eyes, extended thin noses, small smiling mouths, sloping shoulders, articulated torsos and limbs. There was also a tendency for lavish displays of decoration, such as complex jewelry, intricate and ornate robes or thrones.

Gyantse is the first clear example in Tibet's art history of a local school that severed its connections with prior foreign influences. Although stylistic contributions from Nepal, and subtler hints from China, are still present, they were assimilated in a fresh and innovative manner. The result is a small but relevant number of sub-styles, which constitute an outstanding achievement of Tibetan creativity.

In China, the Gyantse style had a brief but strong impact on the arts of the Ming Dynasty court. During the Yongle (1402–25) and Xuande (1426–36) reigns, the production of Chinese portable bronzes precisely followed the details laid down by the Gyantse canons. In no other period, with the exception of the Qianlong era (1711–99), did Tibetan stylistic trends make such a strong impact on China.

THE GUGE SCHOOL

A separate artistic movement established itself in the late 15th and early 16th C. in West Tibet, during the time of the Guge Dynasty. This kingdom, geographically and politically isolated from Central Tibet and Lhasa, looked to Kashmir, India, and Nepal for its artistic and religious inspiration. The Red and White chapels of Tsaparang, the capital, have surviving murals and statues from that period.

In general, the Guge style remained confined to the monasteries of Tsaparang and Tapho (Himachal Pradesh, India) and was short-lived. Kashmir exerted a strong influence. The diffusion of the Kashmiri genre began in the 11th C., when Rinchen Zangpo, under the patronage of King Yeshe Ö, built major temples such as Tholing (see page 425) with the help of Kashmiri artists. Kashmir's inroad at Tsaparang was probably inspired by the surviving echoes of the Kashmiri-Tibetan arts of the 11th century. Also critical was the fact that, during the late period of Sakyapa dominance in Tibet, many major monasteries, particularly those in Tsang, were decorated by Newari artists or Tibetans well versed in Newari art. This Newari-Sakyapa tradition helped to shape Guge's art works. The Tsaparang murals, easily differentiated from those of Central Tibetan monuments, are strongly figural and are characterized by their resplendent colors which are unmatched elsewhere.

Considerable stylistic similarities exist between the Tsaparang paintings and the Newari-inspired murals of the 15th-C. Gyantse Kumbum. These include the treatment of clouds, mountains, and garments. The bejeweled trees and floral designs of Tsaparang murals follow closely the decorative tradition of Nepalese works. Although numerous figures and decorative details densely pack the Guge murals, they lack the rigid compartmentalization of the Nepalese. The Guge figures are freer; they do not sit stiffly in symmetrical arrangement, but rather in a variety of postures. This Guge style reached its creative zenith in the chapels of Tsaparang during the second half of the 15th century. Unlike the local art schools of Latö and Gyantse, the paintings of West Tibet of that period were virtually devoid of Chinese influence. In the 16th C., the style was significantly modified by the arrival of Central Tibetan/Gelugpa sensibilities. Good examples of this trend are the murals of the Chapel of the Prefect (ca 16th century). Rendered somewhat later than the Red and White chapels' murals, they seem uninspired in comparison.

THE RULE OF THE DALAI LAMAS (17TH–19TH CENTURY)

In the 17th C., with the support of Gushri Khan, leader of the powerful Qosot Mongols, Tibet once again became a unified country under the Fifth Dalai Lama. By 1656, when Gushri Khan died, most of Tibet, from Guge and Ladakh in the west to Kham in the east, was under the control of the Gelugpa. This was the first time in Tibet's history that a single power, combining spiritual and secular authority, truly dominated the vast territory. From this time on, the major Gelugpa monasteries, such as Tashilhunpo and Drepung, became centers of pilgrimage and patrons of art. Lhasa outstripped other ancient centers of commerce (Shigatse, Gyantse) to become the political and religious capital of the country.

An art style called Üri emanated from Lhasa, a consolidation of past influences. Beginning in the 16th C., the murals of monasteries all across the country were painted in a much more uniform manner. This standardization was applied with equal zeal from Ngari Khorsum in West Tibet to the Chinese borders in the east. Vestiges of the Newari–Sakyapa style, however, can be seen clearly on the walls of some of Central Tibet's monuments. The same can be said of the modified Pala style, often called the Kadampa style. Generally, the Newari–Sakyapa and Pala genres did not survive into the 17th century.

In the age of the Dalai Lamas, the landscape tradition, imported from China as early as the 14th C., grew in importance. This was China's fundamental contribution to Tibetan painting. Landscapes now became an integral part of the painters' repertoire and displaced the strongly figural styles that marked the Indo-Nepalese works. Natural forms appeared in all subjects. For example, the background of many murals, essentially depicting lamas and deities, now featured elements like skies, clouds, and snowy mountains. In time, these landscapes became static and ossified when compared to the superb, creative murals of Shalu and Gyantse. Many more architectural subjects, such as monasteries and hermitages, were painted during the 17th and 18th centuries.

However, there are some magnificent examples of the Central Tibetan landscape genre, and one of these covers the impressive ground-floor cloister walls surrounding the Ütse Temple of Samye. These ca 18th-C. works were executed with great care and precision. The colors are generally green or dark blue, and many of the figures are outlined in gold. A prominent feature of the murals are the blue-green mountains which are distinctive elements in works of this period. Secondary figures, robed in Chinese costumes, are surrounded by imaginatively inflated flowers and leaves. The background *toranas* (halos), unlike Nepalese models—which tend to have more animals lurking within—are depicted here with far more floral and vegetal motifs. Temples with pagoda roofs in the Chinese style are prominent.

In general, Tibetan painters have little use for the pragmatic representation of the real world. They use landscape and the shapes and forms of nature. But these are employed to portray imaginary and transcendental concepts, and to augment religious symbols and stories. Within these panels at Samye Ütse, landscape and architecture are presented with an extraordinarily skilful combination of fantasy and naturalism.

Lhasa: The Holy City

EARLY YEARS TO
GELUGPA DOMINANCE

In November 1984, the Neolithic site of Chögong was discovered near Lhasa's Sera Monastery, Tibet's third such site (the others are Karu and Ningchi, both in the eastern part of the country). Subsequent small-scale excavations turned up stone and bone implements as well as pottery shards. Chögong has thus provided important clues to Lhasa's early history; the area was inhabited some thousands of years ago, well before the advent of the Yarlung Dynasty (7th–9th C.).

In the latter half of the 6th C., Tagri Nyanzig, grandfather of Songtsen Gampo, commanded a substantial political force in the Yarlung Valley region and had his base at the castle of Chingwa Tagtse (present-day Chongye). Tibet at that time consisted of 12 petty kingdoms, about half under Tagri's control. Competing against him for domination of the country were prominent nobles. Among these were Takyawo, a lord of Nyenkar in the region of Medro Gongkar and Drigung, and Tripang Sum, who controlled the Penpo region immediately north of Lhasa. Takyawo was an inept ruler and he lost the confidence of a key aide named Nyan, who formed an alliance with Tripang Sum. Together they defeated Takyawo and took over the entire Kyi Chu Valley. The inhabitants of the area, however, disliked their rulers and four clans—the Wa, Nyang, Non, and Tshepong—were so disenchanted that they sought the assistance of Tagri Nyanzig. Despite being Tripang Sum's brother-in-law, he was willing to plot his downfall. Tagri died before the rebellion could be carried out, but his son Songtsen, father of Songtsen Gampo, succeeded in raising an army of 10,000 men and defeated Tripang Sum. In the process, all the territory around Lhasa was subjugated and Songtsen took the new name of Namri (Sky Mountain). Despite being wise and just, he was poisoned by his discontented ministers. Songtsen Gampo succeeded his father and moved the capital from Chingwa Tagtse to Lhasa.

Under him, Lhasa developed rapidly. With the help of his foreign wives, he built the great edifices of the Jokhang, Ramoche, and the original Potala Palace. According to a well-known myth, before the Jokhang could be constructed, the king needed to immobilize a mighty, mythic demoness who lied supine over the land; to do so, Songtsen Gampo erected 12 special demon-suppressing temples, located in ever-expanding concentric rings outside Lhasa (see page 43). During this period of heightened Buddhist activities in the capital, the king built the nine-story tower of Pabonka as his meditation retreat. One of his wives, Mongza Tricham, founded a temple at Drak Yerpa, a holy mountain just east of Lhasa. Others created hermitages and retreat centers, namely Meru Nyingba, Tshamkhung, one of four Rigsum Gönpo lhakhangs, and the rock-carved grotto of Dragla Lugug.

The Yarlung Dynasty eventually collapsed in the 9th C. as a consequence of King Langdarma's persecution of Buddhism, and the country entered a period of civil war. Power reverted to local feudal lords and Tibet was once again fragmented. Lhasa's religious centers—Ramoche and the Jokhang—were closed and desecrated, and the young city went into a long spiritual and material decline. Although Lhasa remained a place of commerce and trade, it could only nominally be considered the capital.

The city's next period of development occurred in the early 15th C., when Tsong Khapa, founder of the Gelugpa sect, established the great Monlam Chenmo festival in Lhasa. It was attended by over 10,000 people and signaled Lhasa's revival as a religious center. In the same year (1409) he founded Ganden, the Yellow Sect's most important monastery, on the outskirts of the city. In following years, his disciples built the monastic cities of Sera and Drepung which, with Ganden, consolidated Lhasa as Tibet's premier pilgrimage site.

In 1642, Gushri Khan, leader of the Qosot Mongols, entered Tibet at the request of the Gelugpa to crush the country's ruler, the King of Tsang, and his Karmapa allies. The Tsang king was deposed and the Fifth Dalai Lama (1617–82) installed as regent over the land. With Mongolian support, he united the country under the Gelugpa, the first time a single indigenous regime, vested with both temporal and spiritual authority, truly dominated Tibet. Lhasa became the formal capital and many monasteries, including the Jokhang, underwent substantial renovations. The most ambitious building program ever undertaken in Tibet began during the reign of the Fifth Dalai Lama; he oversaw construction of the monumental Potala Palace.

Lhasa's historic and religious monuments are classified below into two sections. The first deals only with structures founded during the Yarlung era (7th–9th C.). The second describes institutions and relics established in later periods, particularly during the time of the Gelugpa (15th–20th C.).

YARLUNG-DYNASTY LHASA

JOKHANG:
TIBET'S MOST SACRED TEMPLE

OVERVIEW

Pilgrims come from all over the country to pay homage to the Jokhang, Tibet's most sacred temple. Located in the very heart of Lhasa's colorful Tibetan quarter, Jokhang is the focus of devotion day and night. Multitudes of Tibetans circle it while going round and round the Barkhor, gaining spiritual merit and generally having a wonderful time. This, the spiritual center of Tibet, is also the heart of Lhasa.

The temple was built by King Songtsen Gampo in the 7th century. It predates Samye, the acknowledged first monastery, by over a century and is in all likelihood Tibet's first significant religious institution. Formally known as the 'Tsuglag Khang', the vast majority of its extant statues date from 1980 onwards, whereas most of its murals are from the 18th and 19th centuries. The Jokhang's *sanctum sanctorum* is the Jowo Lhakhang, the best-preserved room in the large complex. It somehow escaped irrevocable damage during the Cultural Revolution. In the pilgrimage season, long queues of pilgrims wait patiently for hours just to touch their foreheads to the sacred image of Jowo Sakyamuni. Two ancient elements of the temple can safely be attributed to the 7th century. These are the short columns in front of the Jowo chapel and the door frames of the inner chapels (*tsangkhangs*) on the ground floor and second floors. These spectacular works of art, the earliest in Tibet, attest to the sophisticated cosmo-politan nature of the Yarlung Dynasty (7th–9th C.). Accomplished Newari artists from Nepal, versed in the fabled art of Gupta India (4th–7th C.), created them. (The lion sculptures above the magnificent atrium of the Khyamra Chenmo also contain Gupta stylistic elements and may date back to the 7th century.)

The four ground-floor inner chapels with original door frames are: Thuje Chenpo, Wöpame, Jowo Sakyamuni, and Jampa Gönpo. Of the second-floor inner chapels with rare door frames, one stands at the center of the destroyed north wing; the other two are on either side of the Zhelre Lhakhang, itself a recently discovered repository of 12th-C. murals inspired by the Pala tradition (9th–11th century). As late as 1985, 7th-C. murals adorned the north gallery. These unique relics have now disappeared, brutally detached from the walls. Songtsen Gampo's principal chapel is also a highlight of this floor. On the top floor, one of the chapels that draws the most pilgrims is that consecrated to Palden Lhamo, the divine protectress of Tibet.

THE FOUNDING OF THE TSUGLAG KHANG

During the first half of the 7th C., the fledgling Yarlung empire looked beyond its borders for cultural, religious, and political inspiration. Nepal and China greatly influenced Tibet at this stage of its development. Songtsen Gampo (born ca 617) was crowned in 629 and married the Nepalese princess, Tritsun (Brikuti), in 632 (or 634). She was the daughter of Anshuvarman, minister of King Shivadeva, *de facto* ruler of Nepal until 621. A few years later, during the reign of the usurper Jisnugupta, Tritsun's brother, Prince Narendradeva, and his retinue fled to Tibet in exile and stayed until 641. The prince then returned to Nepal and became king. Nepalese influence on Tibet was most pronounced during this period. Newari artists accompanying Narendradeva created the sculpted images and paintings of the Jokhang, and vestiges of their artistry, particularly the wood carvings, can be seen today in the temple's magnificent door frames and columns (see page 78).

The Jokhang's exact date of construction is not known. Chinese scientists conducted carbon-dating analyses on the ancient columns in front of the Jowo chapel and confirmed them to be from the 7th century. Contemporary Chinese and Tibetan sources claim the Jokhang was built in 647, although traditional Tibetan works propose 639. In either case, the building would have coincided with the Chinese phase of Songtsen Gampo's reign, which lasted from 641 until his death in 649. China became a dominant influence when the king took as his second wife Princess Wencheng, who arrived in Lhasa in 641 from Chang'an, the Chinese capital. Princess Tritsun's dowry had included a statue of the Buddha as an eight-year-old boy; it was known as Jowo Mikyo Dorje (Akshobhya). Princess Wencheng's dowry also included a Buddha statue, known as the Jowo Sakyamuni, and also called Mikyo Dorje. The statue originally belonged to the King of Magadha (Bengal), who presented it to Wencheng's father, Tang Taizong (r 627–49), as a reward for his aid against the invading Yavanas. It still resides in the Jokhang, and is generally recognized as Tibet's most sacred object.

However, it was not the only gift the Chinese princess brought with her. She also brought treatises on astrology, medicine, and the techniques of silk culture from China. In order to house such remarkable gifts, Songtsen Gampo decided to build a special temple for them. After consulting the astrological charts, Wencheng determined that the temple's site should be Lake Wothang, a body of water covering part of today's Lhasa. This suprising choice was confirmed when the king, meditating on his tutelary deity, Chenresi, had a vision that convinced him of the site's auspiciousness.

For the foundation, long beams were placed across the lake—a technique that soon failed. Finally, goats were used to carry earth to fill the lake, and in time construction began. All went well until it was discovered that work accomplished during the day was being mysteriously undone at night. Faced with this obstacle, the king and his two queens went to nearby Pabonka to pray for guidance to the important deity, Thuje Chenpo. They received a startling vision; Tibet lay on top of a massive, sleeping demoness that could be pacified only by building monasteries and erecting statues at appropriate geomantic points in the environs of Lhasa. The king immediately embarked on an ambitious program to establish 12 monastic institutions to securely pin down the troublesome demoness (see page 43). Only when Songtsen Gampo had completed these works could he turn his energies back to the building of the Jokhang.

After the ground floor was completed, Queen Tritsun invited Newari architects and craftsmen to collaborate with Tibetan artists on the second floor. The resulting temple design replicated the Vikramasila University at Bodh Gaya, India. To honor the earth-carrying goats that established the Jokhang's physical foundation, the temple was christened 'Rasa Trulnang Tsuglag Khang': *ra* ('goat'), *sa* ('earth'), *trulnang* ('miraculous imagination'), *tsuglag khang*

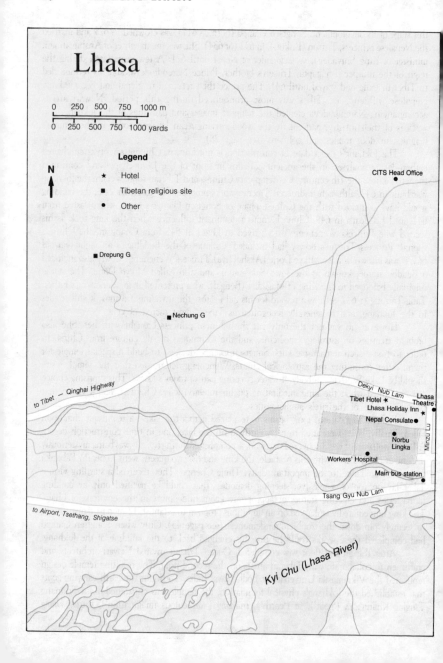

Lhasa

0   250   500   750   1000 m

0   250   500   750   1000 yards

Legend

★ Hotel

■ Tibetan religious site

● Other

N

CITS Head Office ●

■ Drepung G

■ Nechung G

to Tibet – Qinghai Highway

Dekyi Nub Lam

Lhasa Theatre

Tibet Hotel ★

Lhasa Holiday Inn ★

Nepal Consulate ●

● Norbu Lingka

Workers' Hospital ●

Main bus station

Minzu Lu

Tsang Gyu Nub Lam

to Airport, Tsethang, Shigatse

Kyi Chu (Lhasa River)

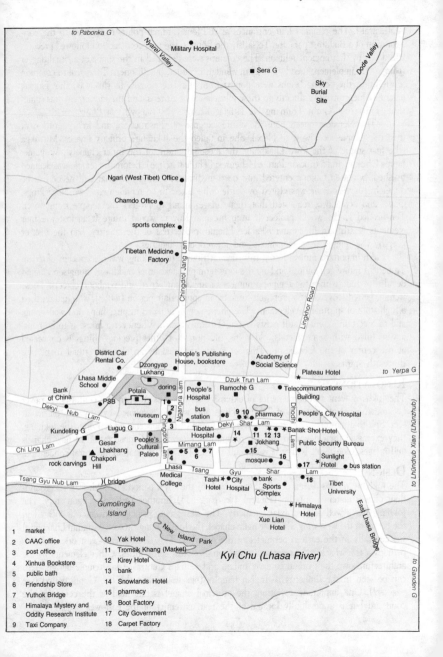

to Pabonka G

Nyarel Valley

Military Hospital

■ Sera G

Sky Burial Site

Dode Valley

Chingdrol Jang Lam

Lingkhor Road

Ngari (West Tibet) Office ●

Chamdo Office ●

sports complex ●

Tibetan Medicine Factory ●

District Car Rental Co. ●

People's Publishing House, bookstore ●

Academy of Social Science ●

Plateau Hotel ★

to Yerpa G

Dzongyap Lukhang ■

Lhasa Middle School ●

Bank of China ■

Potala

PSB ■

Dekyi   Nub   Lam

doring

museum ●

Chingdrol Lam

Ngangra Lam

1

2

3

Dzuk Trun Lam

People's Hospital ●

Ramoche G ●

Telecommunications Building ●

bus station

8 ● 9 10 ★

pharmacy

People's City Hospital ●

Tibetan Hospital ●

Dekyi   Shar   Lam

14 ★

11 ● 12 13 ★

Banak Shol Hotel ●

Dhodhi Lam

Kundeling G ■

Gesar Lhakhang ■

People's Cultural Palace ●

Mimang Lam

4

5 ● 6 ● 7 ●

Jokhang ■

Public Security Bureau ●

Chi Ling Lam

rock carvings

▲ Chakpori Hill

15 ●

mosque ●

16 ●

Sunlight Hotel ★

17 ★

bus station ●

Tsang Gyu Nub Lam   )(bridge

Lhasa Medical College

Tsang

Gyu   Shar   Lam

bank

18 ●

Tashi Hotel ★

City Hospital ●

Sports Complex

Tibet University

Gumolingka Island

New Island Park

Himalaya Hotel ★

Xue Lian Hotel ●

Kyi Chu (Lhasa River)

East Lhasa Bridge

to Lhündrub Xian (Lhünzhub)

to Ganden G

1   market
2   CAAC office
3   post office
4   Xinhua Bookstore
5   public bath
6   Friendship Store
7   Yuthok Bridge
8   Himalaya Mystery and Oddity Research Institute
9   Taxi Company
10 Yak Hotel
11 Tromsik Khang (Market)
12 Kirey Hotel
13 bank
14 Snowlands Hotel
15 pharmacy
16 Boot Factory
17 City Government
18 Carpet Factory

('cathedral'). The temple's four entrances at the four cardinal points conformed to the configuration of a Buddhist paradise. To satisfy the Bönpos, the wall construction followed precepts laid down by that ancient religion. The columns were designed in the shape of a ritual dagger (*phurpa*), an implement used by Ngakpas, wandering tantric practitioners. To appeal to common sensibilities, the ceiling beams were copied from standard houses. In this way, the Tsuglag Khang's blueprint spoke directly to these four classes of citizens, and the monument was sometimes known as 'Gazhi Trulnang Gi Tsuglag Khang': *ga* ('happy'), *zhi* ('four').

The Nepalese queen bore the entire expense of construction, and in recognition of this, the temple faces west to Nepal. She installed the Jokhang's primary images: Mitrukpa (the first statue of the Jowo Lhakhang, the most important of the inner chapels), Wöpame, Jampa Chökor, and a thousand-armed Chenresi (Thuje Chenpo). Before the temple was deemed finished, Songtsen Gampo entered into deep meditation to find out what still needed to be done. In his visions he was visited by deities who asked to be represented. Two Naga kings, Gowa and Nyergawo, requested that their images stand to protect the temple from water. Ten-headed Lanka would protect it from fire and Kuvera would insure it against the four elements (earth, air, fire, water). Palden Lhamo, protectress of the country, had the task of keeping the temple from man-made and mysterious calamities.

An important innovation at this time, attributed to the king, was the concept of *terma*. To benefit future generations and aid the long-term propagation of Buddhism, Songtsen Gampo decided to hide within the temple a number of important actual and symbolic objects. These were to be rediscovered at a propitious time by an appropriate person (*terton*), who had reached a high state of spiritual development. The phenomenon of *terma* inspires hope and well-being, and to a certain extent it still exists among Tibetans today. Whenever a house is to be built, a vase filled with gems, metals, old coins, old notes, or other precious things is concealed at the center of the foundation. This act is accompanied by an elaborate ritual to placate the earth spirits.

Renovations

The Jokhang went through a series of extensive renovations through the centuries. It never became the private domain of Tibetan kings and was never owned by any one particular sect. Spiritual masters of diverse sects were sheltered in its cloisters and to honor the Jokhang, they expressed their devotion through restoration, renewal, and consecration of new chapels and images. One result is that it is difficult to establish the original architectural conception.

Design

The Jokhang retains design details that go back to the royal period (7th–9th C.). Its ground-floor plan is matched only by Trandruk (see page 533), another Yarlung-era monastery. The Jokhang has a well-defined axial symmetry. The west-facing principal entrance is located in the center of the west wing while the main chapel, the Jowo Khang (Jowo Sakyamuni Lhakhang) sits centrally in the eastern perimeter of the complex. This obvious east–west orientation is perhaps a throwback to ancient, animistic, pre-Buddhist sensibilities. Other elements in the architecture owe their origin to early Indian and perhaps Central Asian temple design. This can be seen in the similarity to Indian temples (*mahaviharas*) of the late Gupta period (see page 49). One important deviation: the principal chapel is not sited at the center of the courtyard but is anomalously located at the rear extremity of the east–west axis.

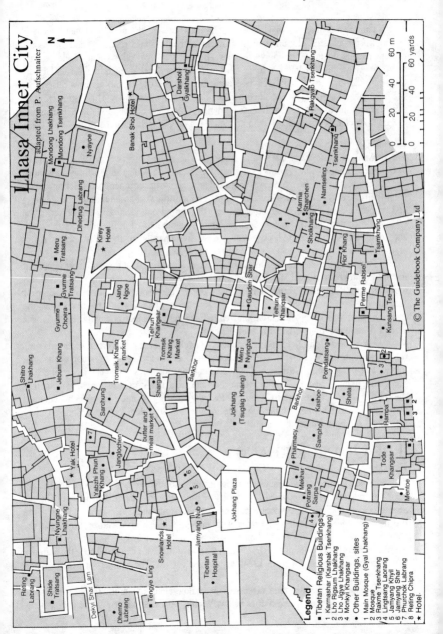

Lhasa Inner City
adapted from P. Aufschnaiter

© The Guidebook Company Ltd

Legend

■ Tibetan Religious Buildings
1 Karmashar (Karshak Tsenkhang)
2 Lho Rigsum Lhakhang
3 Lho Jigye Lhakhang
4 Monkyi Khangsar

• Other Buildings, sites
1 Main Mosque (Gyal Lhakhang)
2 Mosque
3 Lakme Tsenkhang
4 Lingang Laorang
5 Jamyang Khyil
6 Jamyang Shar
7 Phurchok Labrang
8 Reting Chipra
★ Hotel

Reting Labrang
Shide Tratsang
Dhemo Labrang
Tengye Ling
Dekyi Shar Lam
Shitro Lhakhang
Jebum Khang
Gyurme Choera
Gyurme Tratsang
Meru Tratsang
Dhedrug Labrang
Mondong Lhakhang
Mondong Tsenkhang
Nyayoe
Darshol Gyalkhang
Banak Shol Hotel
Kirey Hotel
Jang Ngoe
Telhun Khangsar
Tromsik Khang market
Nyunghe Lhakhang
Yak Hotel
Yabzhi Phun Khang
Sarchung
Janglochen
butter and meat market
Shargab
Tromsik Khang Market
Meru Nyingba
Gauden Shar
Telhun Khangsar
Karma Sharchen
Namseling
Sholkhang
Tsenkhang
Rakgyab Tsenkhang
Hor Khang
Tsamkhung
Perme Rabsel
Kunsang Tse
Pomdatsang
Barkhor
Jokhang (Tsuglag Khang)
Kashoe
Sheta
Rampa
Barkhor
Samphol
Tode Khangsar
Mentoe
Pharmacy
Mekhar
Potrang Sarpa
Jamyang Nub
Jokhang Plaza
Snowlands Hotel
Tibetan Hospital

0   20   40   60 m
0   20   40   60 yards

The ground floor is a quadrangle. Along each side are the primary chapels, enclosed by a multi-story cloister. This unusual outer envelope, chiefly monks' residences and storerooms, perhaps had its origin in the Gupta temples (4th–6th C.). A good example would be cave no. 11 at Ajanta, in Maharashtra, India. This prototype was later adopted by the Pala Dynasty (8th–12th C.) of Bengal and Bihar (see page 51). At one end of the main east–west axis is a monumental entranceway; at the other, the large *sanctum sanctorum*. This distinctive floor plan supports the hypothesis that Lhasa's Jokhang is older than Samye Monastery. The latter's ground floor plan is designed as a cosmic mandala, a development inspired by the early Palas.

LAYOUT

The original structure was conceived as a square. The ground floor was popularly attributed to Songtsen Gampo while Tritsun took credit for the second floor; the third was built much later. In the beginning, the temple was organized around five major inner chapels (*tsangkhangs*). Later, cells next to these were converted into minor shrines to accommodate more images and statues of deities. The five *tsangkhangs* are: the central one located in the center of the east wing, two flanking this central chamber, and two more located in the center of the north and south wings. Thus, in today's Jokhang, these five chapels are the most ancient rooms of the complex.

The Tsuglag Khang today consists of two basic structures. The first and most important is the Inner Jokhang (Chökhang, Offering Hall), identified with the Jokhang proper, and surrounded by the Nangkhor circumambulatory corridor. It resembles a square mandala, measuring 82.5 m, 246 feet, (north–south) by 97 m, 290 feet, (east–west). It has three floors (plus the roof), the first two being the oldest, and each floor has a number of small chapels ranged around a central atrium called Khyamra Chenmo.

The ancient Inner Jokhang is completely enveloped by a massive perimeter structure, the Outer Jokhang. Within this outer complex are secondary chapels, storerooms, kitchens, toilets, and other rooms. Although it has openings on all four sides, the main entrance of the Outer Jokhang and the whole temple complex is a two-story structure that comprises the central portion of the western wing. The Jokhang's north, east, and south sides are enclosed by large Tibetan buildings, former residences of the nobility. Meru Nyingba Monastery (see page 119) is appended to the east wing.

THE OUTER JOKHANG

ENTRANCE

The entrance portico (Khyamra Gochor) is distinguished by six large, fluted columns. For centuries, pilgrims have prostrated themselves in the courtyard (*dhochal*) in front of the big double doors, wearing deep, smooth grooves into the stone slabs. A narrow cloister flanks the main double doors and is decorated with murals of the Four Guardian Kings and the Four Friendly Brothers (Thumpa Punzhi)—elephant, hare, monkey, and parrot. A large painting depicts the famous monkey and ogress, parents of the first Tibetans. Above the entrance is a balcony screened off by a thick, black, yak-hair curtain. The cabinet sat here to watch ceremonies.

Overlooking the Khyamra Gochor is a window along the north facade from where the Dalai Lama watched the festivities below. Within this wing, known as the Labrangteng,

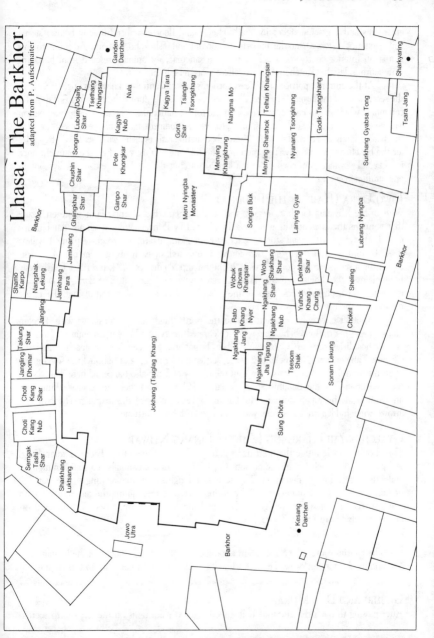

Lhasa: The Barkhor

adapted from P. Aufschnaiter

Ganden Darchen

Tsethang Khangsar

Lubum Dojang

Nula

Songra Shar

Kagya Nub

Chushin Shar

Pole Khongkar

Ghangkhar Shar

Ganpo Shar

Kagya Tara

Tsangle Tsongkhang

Gora Shar

Nangma Mo

Menying Khangkhung

Menying Sharshok

Telhun Khangsar

Nyanang Tsongkhang

Godik Tsongkhang

Surkhang Gyabsa Tong

Tsara Jang

Sharkyaring

Barkhor

Meru Nyingba Monastery

Songra Buk

Lanying Gyar

Labrang Nyingba

Shamo Karpo

Nangshak Lekung

Jamkhang

Jamkhang Para

Wobuk Ghowa Khangsar

Woto Shukhang Shar

Denkhang Shar

Sheling

Barkhor

Jangling

Rato Khang Nyer

Ngakhang Shar

Ngakhang Nub

Yuthok Khang Chung

Takung Shar

Ngakhang Jang

Chokril

Jangling Dhomar

Choti Kang Shar

Ngakhang Jha Tigang

Tsesom Shak

Sonam Lekung

Choti Kang Nub

Serngak Tashi Shar

Sharkhang Luktsang

Jokhang (Tsuglag Khang)

Sung Chöra

Jowo Utra

Kesang Darchen

Barkhor

are rooms and a gracious reception hall. The ground floor chamber (directly below) stored edible offering's (*torma*) for the important Monlam and Tshokchö festivals. Adjacent to this is a small interior courtyard, which serves as a sanctuary for animals rescued from butchers. The south side, the Panchen Lama's offices, was rebuilt in 1986.

At the entrance portico's southeast corner is a special entrance known as Lugong Sanggo, the secret door of the *lugong* ('scapegoat'). It was used primarily during the New Year's Tshokchö ceremony, when an ordinary citizen took on the role of national scapegoat. This hapless person was given a fortune in gold, horses, and property to compensate for his permanent exile to the border lands of South Tibet. As the embodiment of all evil, he was sacrificed (by exile) for the benefit of the country. You can enter the Jokhang by this way when the main entrance is locked. Two huge prayer wheels (*mani khorlo*) stand at the northeast and reputedly contain one million *mantras*.

JOWO UTRA (HAIR OF THE BUDDHA)
West of the Khyamra Gochor, towards the open-air plaza, is a recently built stone enclosure that contains the ancient willow supposedly planted by Princess Wencheng; all that remains is a short stump, with *mani* stones at its base. Flanking it are two recently planted willow trees. In front of the stump are two *dorings* (stone steles), each about 3 m tall. The first, topped by a semi-circular stone carving, is the Smallpox Edict of 1794, inscribed in Chinese. It proclaimed the disease a plague and suggested ways to combat it. The *doring's* lower part is pock-marked; pilgrims took parts of the pillar as protection against the disease. There are no inscriptions on the second *doring*.

Another enclosure, adjacent and to the north, holds a 6 m-tall *doring* with Tibetan and Chinese inscriptions. The text is the celebrated treaty of 822, which commemorates the end of hostilities between China and Tibet. Negotiated between King Ralpachen and the Chinese Tang emperor, it proclaimed peace, settled border issues, and honored the sovereignty of each country. Another notable event in the history of Tibet also happened here. Langdarma was assassinated by the Buddhist monk, Lhalung Paldhor, who shot the renegade king with an arrow while he was performing the Cham dances in front of the Jokhang. The bow and arrows were hidden in his specially designed long-sleeved costume.

GYALCHEN ZHI LHAKHANG (ZIMGO CHINANG NYIWAR)
This short vestibule inside the front doors contains seated statues of the Four Guardian Kings and paintings of angels (*driza*) and demons (*nag*). Above these are murals of a guardian monkey and other protectors of Buddhism. To the left and right are works relating to the Paradise of Kuntu Zangpo (Samantabhadra). All paintings were executed during the reigns of the Fifth and 13th Dalai Lamas. Refined gold, silver, and mineral colors were used. The inner doors of the vestibule are called Zimgo Nangma.

> **The pilgrim route** The classic pilgrim route circles the inner perimeter of the Jokhang and its chapels clockwise. The following description generally conforms to this circuit.

GUSHRI AND DESI MURAL
After passing through the entrance hall, this renowned painting is on the left (north section

of the west wall). An embroidered canopy protects it. The mural shows the bearded Qosot Mongolian prince, Gushri Tenzin Chogyal (Gushri Khan), offering tribute to Tibet's Regent (Desi), Sangye Gyatso, in the 17th century. Gushri (d 1655) was instrumental in consolidating the power of the Fifth Dalai Lama, and he is said to have instructed the artist to paint him standing up so he would not have to rise to greet the Dalai Lama. Other major figures in the panel are the Fifth Dalai Lama and the First Panchen Lama. The remainder of the wall depicts the 1,000 Buddhas who will appear during the current eon. These paintings were commissioned during the time of the 13th Dalai Lama.

The wall south of the entrance has murals of Sera, Drepung, and Ganden monasteries, and scenes from the Buddha's life. Above the entrance are paintings of the Nine Amitayus, Kalachakra, Sangdhe Jigsum, and Rigsum Gönpo. Charming flying lions adorn the beams.

KHYAMRA CHENMO (MAIN ASSEMBLY HALL)
This 32 m-by-39 m columned hall (also known as the Dukhang) lies immediately after the entrance hall. It is open to the sky and receives additional lighting through windows at ceiling level. The Khyamra Chenmo, built primarily for the Mönlam (Great Prayer) Festival, was started by Tsong Khapa in 1409; during important festivals and ceremonies, thousands of butter lamps are lighted. The large murals along the cloister walls were painted in 1648.

A terrace runs above and around the Khyamra. On the north side is the charming facade of a two-story building with a gilded pagoda roof that contains rooms for the Dalai Lama. A large window opens from the pretty, yellow-trimmed balcony and overlooks the courtyard. The roof of the Dukhang affords a fine view of the Jokhang's dazzling architecture. Particularly impressive is the western facade of the central building. Over 300 figurines of deities, people, and mythical animals, each 0.5 m tall, decorate a gilded parapet just above the roof line. A white wall along the lower portion has fine bas-relief stucco images. At each corner is a human-headed bird (shangshang); and in the center of each side is a Dharma wheel (khorlo) flanked by deers. Crowning the central structure are the golden pagoda roofs (gyaphip), one on each of the four sides.

NAMTHER GOSUM LHAKHANG
One of two that front the Khyamra, this is the Chapel of the Three Doors to Enlightenment. Sited along the north wing, its entrance (notice the ornate doors) is just west of the Dalai Lama's Throne. Inside the chamber are images of the Past, Present, and Future Buddhas, the Eight Bodhisattvas, and the guardians Tamdrin (Hayagriva) and Chana Dorje (Vajrapani). A set of stairs allowed the Dalai Lama to descend from his private quarters to the Khyamra.

SHUGTRI CHENMO (DALAI LAMA'S GREAT THRONE)
On the south side of the Main Hall is the throne, a simple masonry seat with cushions. Directly behind it is a painting of Sakyamuni, flanked by Chenresi on the left and Jampelyang on the right. One thousand Buddha images surround these.

During important gatherings, the Shartse Chöje and Jangtse Chöje, head lamas from Ganden, flanked the Dalai Lama. The leader of prayers from Drepung's Tshokchen Chapel sat in front of the throne on a seat called Tshokchen Uze. Monks from Sera sat along the hall's north side, those from Drepung in the center, and Ganden monks sat the south. The Supreme Abbot (Tri Rinpoche) of Ganden presided over the ceremonies.

Drölma Lhakhang

This important chapel, east of the Namther Gosum, has an east-facing entrance at the northeastern end of the Main Hall; it stands at the beginning of the Nangkhor inner circuit. Paintings to the left of the entrance show the Dalai Lamas (First to Seventh) next to Mahakala, Palden Lhamo, and Dorje Drakden. Another painting depicts the Eighth Dalai Lama, Jampel Gyatso (1758–1804), and his attendants, with Palden Lhamo and Zimara. A carved stone on the floor in front of the doors is supposedly a 'self-manifesting' (rangjung) image of Tsong Khapa's pointed hat. The chapel is dominated in the center by an elaborate brass-and-glass shrine that holds in its front row three statues of Drölma. The central Drölma Tsidharmani (Heart Drolma) is a new image. (The original, crafted from clay by the Mahasiddha Nyaknyön Sewa Rinchen, was a principal statue of the Jokhang.) It is flanked by a White Tara and Green Tara. Behind them on the left is Nyaknyön's image; Atisha is on the right. A door on the north side enters the shrine. Behind the door is Nyaknyon's bag for collecting the special clay used to sculpt the Drölma.

Left of the chapel's entrance in the southeast corner is an alcove 2 m above the floor. Within it are the images of, from left to right, Tsong Khapa's father, Tsong Khapa, Tsong Khapa's son and the 13th Dalai Lama. At the far left (southeast) corner is a shrine containing the statue of Trulnyi. The rear (west) wall has two tiers of the 21 Drölmas, commissioned by the Seventh Dalai Lama (now replaced by 21 new ones in ornate cabinets). Along the north wall are six more statues. The three closest to the Drölmas are Santarakshita, Guru Rinpoche, and Trisong Detsen. Next to these are the Yabse Sum (Tsong Khapa and his two principal disciples). Below these six are storage cabinets painted in the Chinese style. A ritual corridor encircles the large central shrine and sooty murals cover the walls flanking the entrance.

Just outside the chapel, immediately left of the entrance frame at shoulder height, are two exposed stones one on top of the other. The top one has on its surface the rangjung Six Syllables. The lower has the distinct handprint of Longdhöl Lama. As an apprentice, he was once beaten for serving tea sloppily. Falling to the floor, he put his hand on the stone and cried out ama ('mother'). The Drölma statue responded and said, yes, she was there.

Tsang Nyön Gi Phang Pedho

Look out for a group of four columns (arrayed in a square) to the left of the inner Jokhang entrance, near the start of the Nangkhor corridor. Embedded within the one at the northwest corner of the square is a rock supposedly thrown by Heruka Sangye Gyaltsen (Tsang Nyon), a Sakyapa master. A similar stone was thrown by another Sakyapa adept, Ueyon Kung Sangpo. This is also embedded within the same column; one is partially retained in place by a steel plate. The two lamas also left their mark at another place within the temple. In front of the Lhogo (south exit, at the end of a corridor leading south from the Khyamra's southeast corner; the door exiting to the south side of the Barkhor is here), a section of the floor is made up of marble and stones that, according to legend, the two miraculously created.

Nangkhor

This circumambulatory corridor surrounds the inner Jokhang complex and is partially open to the sky. After passing through the Khyamra, pilgrims at the northeast corner of the large hall head east past the Drölma Lhakhang to enter the Nangkhor. The corridor is lined with prayer wheels and murals in gold outline on a red background. Along portions of the wall are *chörtens* and diverse bas-relief images. Behind the north wall are four chapels, usually reached through the westernmost Tamdrin Sangdrub chapel. These 4-m-wide chambers are connected by interior openings and each has windows that look out onto the Nangkhor. The recently renovated rooms (all original statues destroyed) are from west to east:

Tamdrin Sangdrub Lhakhang Consecrated to Tamdrin and Rigje Lhamo.

Thuje Chenpo Lhakhang The principal image here is a thousand-armed Chenresi.

Kunrik Lhakhang This chapel contained statues of Kunrik and Vairocana.

Desheg Gye Lhakhang This held silver statues of the Eight Medicine Buddhas.

At the end of the Nangkhor's first leg (west to east) is the entrance to the Nechu Lhakhang, a chapel dedicated to the 16 Arhats. Next (to the south) is the Gurubum Lhakhang, chapel of the 100,000 Gurus. At this point on the Nangkhor, the highly unusual enlargement of the Jowo Sakyamuni chapel within the Jokhang can be seen. The rear wall (easternmost portion) of this room juts 2.5 m into the corridor.

NECHU LHAKHANG

This chapel is distinguished by three ornate west-facing entrances (always locked). The Regent Sangye Gyatso (1653–1705) sponsored the images of the 16 Arhats. Within was a secret room with a hidden statue; pilgrims were never allowed to see it. On the outside wall (south portion) is a painting of forests and eight Taras. These expertly rendered goddesses are minute.

GURUBUM LHAKHANG

Like its neighbour, this chapel south of the Nechu Lhakhang has two impressive entrances. Within were different images of Guru Rinpoche, sponsored by the 13th Dalai Lama. Three lion-faced statues (Senge Dhongma) were surrounded by 100,000 small statues of Guru Rinpoche (Gurubum). (This chapel is always locked.)

SERA DHAGGO

Directly across the corridor from the Jowo Lhakhang's rear wall is an open-air entranceway, the Sera Dhaggo. This ancient passage leads to a courtyard and connects Meru Nyingba Monastery with the Jokhang. In the past, monks from Sera's Thekchenling Chapel gathered here during the Monlam Festival. The passageway door, opened just once a year, led into the huge kitchen of Dhaggo Rungkhang, where the monks brewed huge quantities of butter tea in 3 m-wide iron cauldrons.

SUNG CHÖRA

This south-oriented debate courtyard, attached to the Jokhang's outer perimeter walls, was renovated in 1986. A large stone platform, enclosed by a yak-wool awning, contained thrones for Tsong Khapa (stone), the Dalai Lama, and the Ganden Tripa. Behind it is a recent mural of Tsong Khapa.

Norbu Khungshak

On the full moon of the seventh month in 1988, a mushroom was found growing in the cracks along the front of the Sung Chöra stone platform. All Lhasa took this as an auspicious omen—when the 13th Dalai Lama was born (1876), a similar mushroom had appeared (now preserved inside the Potala). The city celebrated for four days and thousands of people viewed the plant, taking it as a sign for the 14th Dalai Lama's return. However, the situation soon turned ugly as police appeared to control the crowds. For safekeeping, the mushroom (Norbu Khungshak), now growing out of a yellow bag filled with soil, was transferred to a small shrine and placed on top of the Dalai Lama's throne. The stone crack is marked with a painted floral design. Left of the platform is a side door that leads into the Jokhang. Immediately behind the door, on the floor, is a stone slab painted in gold and white that resembles an eye. Apparently, the center of this stone began to bulge up at the same time as the mushroom was discovered. The paint marks the supernatural protuberance.

There are four chapels (all closed) attached to the outside wall of the third (south) leg: Menlha Desheg Lhakhang, Nechu Lhakhang, Lamrin Lhakhang, Desheg Gye Lhakhang.

THE NANGKHOR PAINTINGS

Murals on the walls of the Nangkhor depict the 108 episodes of the Buddha's final and previous lives. This cycle was conceived in the early 11th C. by the popular Kashmiri poet, Ksemendra, and expressed in his epic *Avadanakalpalata*. The Thousand Buddhas of the Bhadrakalpa also decorate the walls. During the last century, the 13th Dalai Lama commissioned these paintings; they probably cover previous faded ones, created at the time of the Fifth and Eighth Dalai Lamas. Along the northern section are renditions of the various paradises and stages of Prajnaparamita, Sukhavati, and the ten most significant events of the Jampa Buddha. The east walls depict the Buddha surrounded by his spiritual sons, Jampelyang and Chenresi, the Arhats, divinities (*devas*) and well-known lamas. Along the south wall, Sakyamuni and six heretics compete in performing miracles. Another mural shows kings Segyal and Vimvisara of Magadha inviting the Buddha and his disciples to teach. Tiny images of Guru Rinpoche are on the side.

The Nangkhor paintings along the external walls of the inner Jokhang complex (after the Jowo Lhakhang) show scenes of the Buddha's 15 incarnations, one for each of the first 15 days of the first lunar month. These are quite remarkable images.

After completing the Nangkhor circuit, enter the ground floor of the Jokhang proper.

THE INNER JOKHANG: GROUND FLOOR
ZHUNGO (ALSO TSENDEN GO, 'SANDALWOOD DOOR')

This principal entrance to the Jokhang proper leads from the east wing of the Khyamra via a short passage. The door has finely carved frames and lintel; the style is early Tibetan with perhaps Nepalese influence. It is ornamented with distinctive Dege metalwork: intricate patterns engraved on iron strips, inlaid with gold. Above the door are the 'Om Mani Padme Hum' *mantra*, seven snow lion sculptures, and the Yabse Sum. Left of the door is a painting of Mipham Gönpo (Future Buddha), and on the right is Sangye Marma Ze (Past Buddha).Embedded in front of the entrance is an unusual fossil, known as Amolongkha. Pilgrims believe it to be 'self-manifesting' (*rangjung*). Next to it is the 13th Dalai Lama's footprint enshrined in a small cabinet.

ENTRANCE HALL

The entrance foyer is divided into east and west sections, separated by a set of large double doors. The west walls (closest to the Zhungo) are whitewashed and two locked, empty rooms, known as Driza Zurphu Ngapa, open onto the corridor. Notice the ceiling, which is brass-plated with patterned floral carvings. A small, insignificant bell hangs above the double doors, a sad reminder of the Yeshu Gong Chenpo (Great Bell of Jesus), a relic of the Capuchin chapel (destroyed 1745). The original disappeared during the Cultural Revolution. An uneven stone slab inset into the floor just beyond the doors is known as Dorpita (bellows-shaped). Pilgrims stand reverently on it to assure that the prayers they recited inside the Jokhang will be answered. Two small chapels that flank the entrance hall's eastern section house the earth (*nojin*) and water (*lu*) divinities.

Nojin Khang

This north chapel is dedicated to the Nojins (Disa), wrathful earth divinities, male and female. Their statues (each with four red faces) are at the northwest corner. Palden Lhamo is at the northwest and Gönpo, wearing Chinese armor, is at the southeast. The new murals show soldiers dressed in Chinese garb.

Lukhang

Within this south chapel are the benign images of the three subterranean dragon kings (Lu Gyalpo); the last holds a snake. Paintings on the back wall show the Wheel of Life and more soldiers in Chinese armor. Next to the Lu Gyalpo altar is a flagstone, the mythical seal that shuts in Lake Wöthang, precursor of Lhasa and the Tsuglag Khang. This stone is removed every year during the second lunar month, and offerings are given to the water divinities below. If not propitiated, it is said they would cause the lake to rise and destroy the city.

KYILKHOR THIL

Straight ahead after the entrance hall is the magnificent two-story inner courtyard and atrium. The Jokhang's largest statues and most important chapels are in and around the Kyilkhor Thil. On the left (west wall) of the courtyard is a painting of Dorje Sempa (Vajrasattva). Two long rows of short pillars, running north–south, are just beyond the entrance passage. Impressive old *thangkas* of the 16 Arhats, painted in the strongly Chinese-influenced Karma Gadri style of East Tibet, hang from the southern pillars.

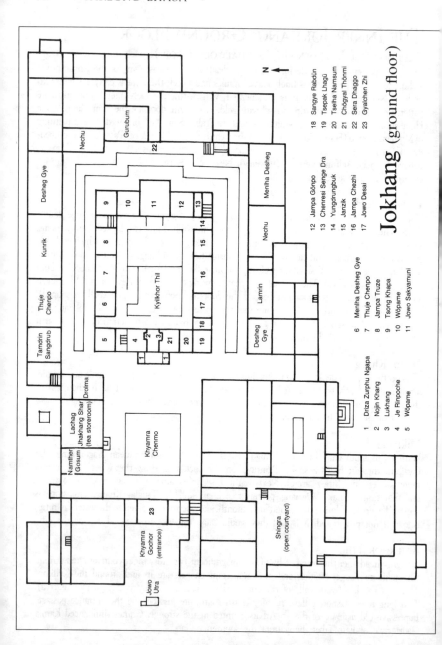

Jokhang (ground floor)

N

1 Driza Zurphu Ngapa
2 Nojin Khang
3 Lukhang
4 Je Rinpoche
5 Wöpame
6 Menlha Desheg Gye
7 Thuje Chenpo
8 Jampa Truze
9 Tsong Khapa
10 Wöpame
11 Jowo Sakyamuni
12 Jampa Gönpo
13 Chenresi Senge Dra
14 Yungdrungbuk
15 Janzik
16 Jampa Chezhi
17 Jowo Desai
18 Sangye Rabdün
19 Tsepak Lhagü
20 Tselha Namsum
21 Chögyal Thönmi
22 Sera Dhaggo
23 Gyalchen Zhi

There are six major statues in the Kyilkhor Thil. To the northwest is a 6 m-tall image of Guru Rinpoche, facing west, erected in 1955 following to a prediction by Khentse Rinpoche and consecrated by Minling Chung Rinpoche. A 4m- (13 feet)-high Jampa (Barzhi Jampa), facing north, is to the southwest. Immediately northeast of it is a larger Jampa, half-seated, facing west. This statue, also known as Thuwang Zangthama, is 10m- (33 feet)-high. Another Jampa (Jamchen, Miwang Jampa) faces north and is at the southeast corner. It was commissioned by the nobleman, Miwang Polha, in 1736. A gold-and-copper, 11-faced Chenresi, 4m- (13 feet)-tall, stands on a dais at the center of the hall. Behind it (east) is a small Guru Rinpoche within a cabinet.

Lion sculptures

The cornice encircling the courtyard has two rows of wooden lion-faced figures. Only one of the 144 carvings is a sphinx (human face and lion's body). These marvelous, archaic works, unknown in other monasteries, date from an early period (7th–8th C.). The short, rounded muzzle and the distinctive mane are stylistic elements reminiscent of Gupta art of the 5th–6th centuries. Tradition ascribes them to a 7th-C. Nepalese sculptor.

Along the hall's east end in front of the Jowo Sakyamuni Chapel is a row of unpainted wooden columns. Considered some of the Jokhang's most important relics, they may well be over 1,300 years old (see page 80).

Before the Cultural Revolution, a stone slab lay next to a column near the center of the north wing, outside the Thuje Chenpo Lhakhang (see page 78). The sacred *mantra* 'Om Mani Padme Hum' was carved on it; the stone supposedly dated from the 7th century. Now destroyed, it has been replaced by a wooden replica inside the chapel. This was one of Jokhang's three sacred 'receptacles' (*ten*) and represented the holy speech. The Tagpa Chörten (mind) stood outside the Wöpame Lhakhang, and a mural (body) of the Gyalwa Rigna (Five Dhyani Buddhas) completed the trinity. Below are the chapels surrounding the Kyilkhor Thil. Starting from the entrance hall, progress clockwise:

JE RINPOCHE (DAKPA NAMGYE) LHAKHANG

This chapel, on the left after the entrance hall, contains statues of Tsong Khapa and his eight disciples (Khor Dakpa Namgye). The two principal ones are Kedrub Je (right) and Gyaltsab Je (left). Outside the room, above and astride the entrance, are paintings of the Five Dhyani Buddhas. A door next to this chapel leads to a hall with stairs to the second floor. In front of this chapel sits a monk whose job is to inscribe with gold ink on red paper names of the deceased or the petitioner. These are then purchased by pilgrims and burned in offering before the Jowo.

WÖPAME LHAKHANG

This northernmost chapel of the west wing is consecrated to Wöpame (Bodhisattva of Infinite Light), one of the Five Dhyani Buddhas. The Panchen Lama is considered its incarnation. Outside the entrance is the Tagpa Chörten ('Chörten of Permanence'), a replica of an original made by Sakya Pandita in the 13th century. It was said to contain relics of Songtsen Gampo. The gold image on the *chörten* is the female deity, Vijaya. Nearby, on the north wall, is a painting of Jampa.

MENLHA DESHEG GYE LHAKHANG

The first chapel of the north wing is dedicated to the Eight Medicine Buddhas; the original sculptures were destroyed and the present ones recently consecrated. Dark murals consist of red line drawings on a yellow background. To the left of the entrance is a painting of Chenresi, to the right (east) an earthen platform that once displayed a seated statue of Milarepa. On the wall behind is a painting of the four-armed Chenresi.

THUJE CHENPO LHAKHANG (CHAPEL OF CHENRESI)

This chapel's door frame is an authentic example of the best woodcarving in ancient Tibet. The 7th-C. frame was a product of expert Nepalese craftsmen, and the unpainted patina of the wood, aged through centuries, is exquisite. The splendid carvings of figural and vegetal motifs show late Gupta and early Pala influence (see pages 49, 51). Its bottom sections are protected by a brass cover and the painted parts belong to a later period. Notice the finely crafted, chain metal curtain that hangs at the door.

Door frames

The Jokhang's ground floor has four magnificent door frames dating back to the 7th century. Their carvings resemble Nepalese Licchavi work (ascribed to the 7th C.) and their execution is attributed to the Newars of Nepal, whose workmanship can be traced back to Indian prototypes, such as the elaborate 5th-C. doorways at Deogarh (Bodh Gaya).

One such door-frame belongs to the Jampa Lhakhang, located immediately south of the Jowo Lhakhang. This elaborate relic has a number of concentric borders each intricately decorated with floral and animal motifs. Individual panels on the top display high-relief figures of humans and animals. Flanking the door are two pilasters. At the top corners of the frame are two lions protruding laterally. Similar designs are found on a stone portal from Bodh Gaya, attributed to the late-Gupta/early-Pala period (7th–9th century). By the 11th C, Tibetan door frames had lost the pilasters, lions at the top corners, and high-relief carvings. They had become formal and rigid. The door frame of the Jowo Sakyamuni chapel, most important of the five inner chapels, is stylistically more restrained and its carvings less elaborate than others. It is smaller and a thick coat of paint rather than naked wood covers the frame. It is certain, however, that it also belongs to the Jokhang's earliest stage. The only ancient door frames on the second floor are the two flanking the empty east central chapel and one in the center of the north wing. Their workmanship and design are identical to those on the ground floor.

Inside, the principal image is an original 11-headed Chenresi image, which was damaged and then restored. After the Jowo Sakyamuni, it is the Jokhang's most important statue. Parts of it were smuggled to Dharamsala, India. Its full name is Thuje Chenpo Rangjung Ngaden: 'self-manifesting' (rangjung) and imbued with the spirits of the Five Entities (ngaden). These five are King Songtsen Gampo, who commissioned the sculpture; his two wives; and the wrathful, protective deities, Amritakundala and Hayagriva. According to legend, Lodro Jungne, an emanation of the king, brought from India religious relics to place inside the statue. These included remains of Tathagatas from Bodh Gaya, holy water from the Ganga and Nerazana rivers, leaves from the bodhi tree, and earth and rocks (prasads) from India's holy places.

Left of the Thuje Chenpo (enclosed in a glass cabinet) are images of Chenresi Kharsapani, Drölma, Wöser Chenma (a form of Drölma), and Tamdrin. On the right are Jikten Wongchuk (a form of Chenresi), Trönyer Chenma (a form of Drölma), Yangchenma, and Dutsi Khilwa. Wöser Chenma and Trönyer Chenma are Drölma's manifestations created miraculously from the tears of Thuje Chenpo. Jampelyang and Chana Dorje are at the end of the left and right side walls. All these images around the Thuje Chenpo are replicas.

Notice three small and two large brass mandala panels on the ceiling, intricately inset with statues. A painting left of the entrance on an outside wall depicts the Rigsum Gönpo. Underneath is a charming painting of Sakyamuni bathing in a pool. The mural right of the entrance shows various episodes of the Buddha's life. Also of interest is the old, dirty wood floor (pungjal) in front of the entrance, which is one of only two wooden floors in the Jokhang. The other, in front of the Jowo Lhakhang, is new and polished.

JAMPA TRUZE LHAKHANG

Within the chapel is the seated image of Jampa Truze, which has an impressive, stucco aureole (torana). A sandalwood figure of Jampelyang is on its knees. The Jampa is new but the Jampelyang is perhaps a restored original. Wöpame flanks Jampa on the left. On the left side wall are four statues (starting from Wöpame): Drölma Karpo, Chana Dorje, Chenresi, and Jampelyang. The right side wall features a statue of Tsong Khapa flanked by two chörten-tombs. One belongs to Ngaripa Tsondru Nyingpo, sculptor of this chapel's original statues., and the other to the historian Lekpe Sherab.

In the center of the room is a square stone stand supporting an antique stone butter bowl. This remarkable relic, supposedly made by Tsong Khapa, is one of the Jokhang's few original objects. Notice the fine lotus carvings. Over the door is a new wood plaque carved with the sacred 'Om Mani Padme Hum' mantra. A stone original was one of three sacred receptacles (ten) of the Jokhang (see page 77).

Outside the chapel is a stone platform (with lotus flower carvings) called Padma Pungpa, the seat used by Songtsen Gampo and his wives when bathing. The original Jampa statue inside the chapel was made with earth mixed with the used bath water (truze means 'made by washing').

Northeast corner East of the Jampa Truze Lhakhang is a low door that purportedly leads into the Wöthang Gyamtso Lhakhang (see below). Walk to the right around this room to some stone stairs that lead up to the Tsong Khapa Lhakhang.

TSONG KHAPA LHAKHANG

This chapel, opening like a gallery to the outside, is built half a story above the ground floor and has a low, 2m ceiling. Tsong Khapa is the central statue, at the northwest corner. The original, known as Nangnyen Ngadrama, was made by Tsong Khapa and resembled him precisely. To its left are two Black-hat lamas, Sakya Chöje Kungpa Tashi (royal priest of Emperor Daming) and Buton, sculpted by Lochen Jangchub Tsemo. On Tsong Khapa's right, along the wall running east–west, are four statues, two with black hats and two with white hair. These represent Arya Sanga, Sonam Gyaltsen, Dorje Gyaltsen, and Karma Rangjung Dorje. The chapel still has original murals.

WÖTHANG GYAMTSO LHAKHANG

This chapel (location uncertain) was consecrated to Lake Wöthang, the original site of Lhasa and the Jokhang. A stone slab within was said to give access to the lake, and offerings were thrown into the water once a year by government officials.

Ancient columns

Short columns These original, unpainted columns have square bases and round shafts. They are known as *kawa thung-thung* and date to the 7th century. Ancient influences from India and Nepal can be seen in the bases, capitals, and shafts; the carving technique resembles that used on stone. Good examples are the capitals at the central hall's northwest corner. They compare favorably to the columns in cave no. 11 at Ajanta (4th–7th century). The distinctive elements are the curvature of the brackets (capital supports), the lotus petal decoration at the top, and the human figures carved on the surfaces of the brackets. After the 11th C., the relief carving on capitals lost its lively plasticity and became rigid and dull. There are 12 columns ranging alongside this north–south wing, six to the left of the Jowo Sakyamuni chapel, and six to the right. No two are exactly the same. The four closest to the central chapel form two double-pillars. (Such early pillars are also found along the east wing of the second floor.)

Plaster columns The three columns at the north end and two at the south end have an intriguing, 3 cm-thick outer covering of plaster. This is molded ingeniously with the column to create a result similar to real wood. The plaster extends to the carved figures on the capitals as well. In some places, chunks have fallen off to expose geometric, floral wood carvings beneath. This design is only seen elsewhere on the two double-columns closest to the Jowo Chapel. These do not have plaster coats. The thick plaster was probably added during the 14th C., to reinforce the columns or to protect against fire. This addition was undertaken by Gadhe Zangpo, abbot of Tshal Gungthang Monastery, and his son, Mönlam Dorje.

Tall columns West of the short columns are four groups of tall columns (*kawa ringpo*) that support the Kyilkhor Thil skylight. These have been repainted with gold floral patterns on a red background. The group just south of the Jowo Sakyamuni Lhakhang's foyer has an engaging, archaic carved figure holding up the columns. These 14th-C. tall columns are attributed to the Tshalpa Tripon Gadhe Zangpo.

WÖPAME LHAKHANG

The first chapel along the north-south wing, it is smaller than the other chapels because the inordinately large Jowo Lhakhang has appropriated part of its space. Flanking the entrance's left side is a big blue statue of Chana Dorje. The anti-Buddhist King Langdarma ordered it to be thrown in a river, but when his minions tried to remove it with a rope they were seized with paranoia and gave up. Guarding the entrance's right side is a wrathful statue of Trowo Mewa Tsegpa (one form of Hayagriva). Legend has it that after Songtsen Gampo's death, an invincible army materialized from within the red protector's stomach to repel Chinese invaders. The statue's entrails are still exposed.

The beautiful unpainted door frame has a gorgeous patina and is one of the Jokhang's best (notice the Nepalese-styled cubic rocks surrounding the figures and crowns on their heads). The unusual, sloping sides of the door frame were purposely designed to reflect a cave opening. In the center of the room are two slender columns covered with plaster (see below). The central image of Wöpame is enclosed within a wood and chicken-wire frame. On its left is a wrathful image of Chana Dorje. To the right is Tamdrin, with a broken arm and also wrathful. Four statues along the left wall and the four along the right represent the Eight Spiritual Sons of Buddha (Nyewe Sechengye). The originals were made by Newari artists according to a vision of Songtsen Gampo.

This is the last chapel pilgrims visit before going into Tibet's most important shrine. The pious often offer a prayer here in the hope of clearing away obstacles that might prevent the long sought-for communion with the Jowo Sakyamuni. Outside the room, immediately south of the Trowo Mewa Tsegpa statue, is a stone platform. On it are statues of Songtsen Gampo, his two queens, and Guru Zahor Rinpoche. Traditionally, this platform held the Four Great Kings (Gyalchen Zhi), created by Tripon Mönlam Dorje from an offering of earth taken from Samye Monastery's original foundation. The unusual Guru Rinpoche image (under an umbrella) was commissioned by the 13th Dalai Lama.

ENTRANCE FOYER OF THE JOWO SAKYAMUNI LHAKHANG

The foyer's many unique artistic and architectural elements are examples of some of the best of 11th-C. Tibetan art (1088 is the likely construction date). Myriads of fascinating details are crammed into this small space and the workmanship is extraordinary. The impressive high ceiling displays human figures, lions, birds, and mythical creatures with human faces. The interface between columns and beams has many delightful sphinxes. Adjacent to these, around a corner, is a row of unusual, polychrome carved human faces within small niches. The physiognomy, the headdresses and clothing (short pants above the knees) diverge from traditional Tibetan design and show marked influences from the subcontinent. Artists from Magadha or Nepal were perhaps responsible. Four rows of shelves immediately below the ceiling hold many small Buddha figures. The wood floor (pungjal) before the chapel entrance is meticulously polished every day (one of two in the Jokhang, see page 79).

Two Guardian Kings stand guard outside the entrance on the right; these are stern-faced Migmi Zang and Namse (God of Wealth). The smiling Guardian Kings on the left are Yulkhor Sung and Phak Kyebu. As pilgrims progress through the foyer to enter the sacred chapel, the first images they see are the unsmiling ones, but after they make their offerings, they leave the room beneath much friendlier looks. According to tradition, the original statues came with Wencheng from China. More plausibly they date from the 8th C., perhaps created by Trisong Detsen. (In any case, all were rebuilt after the Cultural Revolution.)

Round, ornate columns stand east of the Guardian Kings and the sensational ancient door frame is partially covered with brass. Beyond the foyer, just west of the tall pillars, is a statue of Guru Rinpoche enclosed in a glass-and-wood cabinet near the eastern perimeter of the Kyilkhor Thil. The figure directly faces the Jowo Sakyamuni and embodies an admonishment: keep away from the water divinities (*lu*) that dwell beneath the world. This image was made by Ugyen Dudul Lingpa in the mid-18th century. To the right (north) of this, within a glass cabinet, is the female divinity Namgyalma in her peaceful form.

JOWO SAKYAMUNI LHAKHANG (TSANGKHANG)

This is the principal shrine of Tibet and the largest, loftiest chamber in the Jokhang. The room is lit by countless butter lamps and is at all times the temple's brightest place. A beautiful, heavy, iron-mesh curtain drapes across the entrance. Beyond is the 1.5m (5 feet)–tall gilded statue of Jowo Rinpoche, Tibet's most sacred image. It represents the Buddha at the age of 12, at his home in Kapilavastu, and was brought to Tibet by Songtsen Gampo's Chinese wife, Princess Wencheng. According to one tradition, the statue was made in Magadha during the Buddha's life by the celestial artist, Visvakarman, under the guidance of Indra. It was cast from an alloy of gold, silver, zinc, iron, and copper mixed with five heavenly substances— probably diamonds, rubies, lapis-lazuli, emeralds, and indranila. It went from India to Chang'an, capital of Tang China, and finally to Lhasa. The famous scholar of things Tibetan, G. Tucci, noted that one source claimed the sculpture was destroyed in 1717 by the Dzungars. If so, the present image is not the original.

The Jowo's first home was the Ramoche Monastery (see page 116), a short distance north of the Jokhang. After Songtsen Gampo's death, Wencheng, fearing a Chinese invasion, concealed the statue within a south chapel of the Jokhang, behind a painting of Jampelyang. It was later recovered by Jincheng, the wife of King Me Agtshom, and installed in its present place. Later still, Bönpo enemies of Trisong Detsen, being opponents of Buddhism, wanted to send the statue back to China. Unable to move it, they buried it instead. However, the Buddhist faction eventually held sway—the Jowo was unearthed and sent to the Kyirong Valley (see page 924) for safekeeping. During King Langdarma's persecution of Buddhism in the 9th C., the Jowo was buried once more. Eventually, it went back to the Jokhang. Significantly, the statue and chapel did not sustain any damage during the Cultural Revolution.

The Jowo sits on top of a majestic, massive three-tiered stone platform. Two silver-plated dragons (*druk*) presented by a Chinese emperor entwine the ornate pillars that support an intricate double canopy over the Jowo. Small images of Jampa and Jampelyang flank the Jowo beneath the canopy. A celebrated silver sphere hangs from the center (a gift from a descendant of Genghis Khan). Steps from the north and south sides enable pilgrims to touch the knees of the statue with their heads and drape offering scarves around its neck. Four tall, ancient (7th C.) columns stand near the corners of the Jowo statue.

An ornate crown of coral, turquoise, diamonds, rubies, and other precious gems, sits on the Jowo's head. Tsong Khapa offered this crown and the equally elaborate shoulder-cover (*nagyen*). Pearl-studded robes, largely hidden by the shoulder-cover, were contributed by the Chinese Daming Emperor. Above the crown is a *garuda* (*jakhyung*) with wonderfully crafted wings. Notice the large diamond that adorns the statue's forehead. Directly behind the Jowo is a copper plaque decorated with figures and an inscription. It commemorates Yöntan Gyatso's restoration of the back of the Jowo's throne. According to some scholars, this plaque was a work of the Nepalese artist, Arniko, probably executed during the latter half of the 13th century. This artist also created the elaborate repoussé aureole behind the Jowo.

In front (east) of the plaque is a statue of Marma Ze Buddha (Atisha was an incarnation), popularly called Mitrukpa—'I won't go.' Legend says this was the main temple's image before the Jowo's arrival. It refused to make way during the Jowo's installation, not out of jealousy but out of devotion; it wanted to protect the new image. Mitrukpa faces east (Jowo faces west) and only its head and shoulders are visible. It is probably a replica, although Jokhang monks claim otherwise.

Farther to the east towards the back of the chapel, separated from Mitrukpa by a narrow corridor (nangkhor), is the 6m- (20 feet)-tall statue of the deity, Thupa Gangchen (Thuwang), made by the Zangkar Lotsawa during the second half of the 11th century. It sits on a massive, old stone platform. Ranged along the north and south walls are larger-than-life statues of the Sema Jungne, Thupa's disciples, six on each side. Here also are images of wrathful Chana Dorje and Tamdrin (all made by the Zangkar Lotsawa). Other statues include the Seventh and 13th Dalai Lamas and Tsong Khapa. The ceiling above the Jowo is dark but the rich colors and patterns of ancient satin coverings are visible.

Outside and south of the Jowo Sakyamuni Lhakhang is a recessed, L-shaped alcove. Atisha is the central image on a raised platform, flanked on the left by the Nagtsho Lotsawa and on the right by Dromtönpa, Atisha's chief disciples. Behind Dromtönpa is a painting of Drölma, supposedly sungjönma ('spoken').

JETSUN JAMPA GÖNPO LHAKHANG

The original naked door-frame, as beautifully preserved as the Wöpame Lhakhang's, is also the work of 7th-C. Nepalese artists. The main statue here is Jampa Chökor (a replica), part of Princess Tritsun's dowry. People believe it stood up and walked during difficult, trans-Himalayan passages. Above the statue is a finely carved torana, perhaps the original, certainly more interesting than the statue itself. A repoussé ceiling covers this section.

Flanking the main image along the two side walls are eight Taras (Drölma Jikgyema), guardian against the Eight Fears. A statue of Chenresi (Samnyi Ngalso—'have a rest') stands in front (right) of the stone platform. At the chapel's northwest corner is a small stove molded into the wall, a poor replica of the ancient stove used by Princess Wencheng. Lhasa's housewives believe they will become excellent cooks after rubbing their hands on this stove. Over the lintel of the door is a sacred tiger skin (hidden), believed to be an emanation of Songtsen Gampo. Outside, left of the entrance, is Changpa, the protector with four faces and blue hair. He holds a wheel in his left hand. To the right is a statue of Lho Gyalchen; his right hand holds a conch. To his right, on a beautifully crafted stone platform, are images of Tsepame, Jonangpa (Jonang Kunkhyen Dolpa), and four-armed Chenresi. Jonangpa founded the monumental Jonang Chörten (see page 463) and Pindsoling Monastery near Lhatse (see page 863).

CHENRESI SENGE DRA LHAKHANG

Along the north and south walls of this small chapel are six statues, the manifestations of Chenresi. The central image (east wall) is Amitabha, protected by glass. The chapel's name derives from one of Chenresi's manifestations: Chenresi Senge Dra (first on the left), the deity riding a lion. Outside the chapel, south of the door and cemented to the wall, is a 1.5 m (5 feet)-high stone column with a hole at the top. Pilgrims stop here and put their ears to it to hear the *angba* bird that dwells at the bottom of Lake Wöthang. Traces of paintings covered in soot are on the wall. Next to this chapel are stairs to the second floor.

YUNGDRUNG PHUK (SOUTHEAST CORNER)

After the stairs are two statues of Guru Rinpoche and one of King Trisong Detsen. Next to these, attached to the west side wall, is a wood and chicken-wire box at eye level. Inside is a painting of Menlha, the Medicine Buddha. Supposedly, eight rays of light emanated from Chenresi's heart and one of them created this painting, known as Menlha Chengye. Below it is an old stone platform with a basin that holds a large, beautifully crafted butter lamp.

JANZIK LHAKHANG (CLOSED)

Outside this chapel, west of the entrance, are new murals of Songtsen Gampo and his two wives. Next to them are his ministers Thönmi Sambhota (carrying a book, standing over a portrait of a wife of Songtsen Gampo) and Gar Tongtsen. The originals were commissioned by Möinlam Dorje, abbot of Tshal Gungthang Monastery (see page 198).

JAMPA CHEZHI LHAKHANG

This important Jampa (Future Buddha) chapel is one of four in the Jokhang that merits a gilded roof (the others are: Jowo Sakyamuni, east; Thuje Chenpo, north; Songtsen Gampo, west). The original Jampa statue, made of an ancient silver alloy that supposedly came from the belly of Zangbala (God of Wealth), was taken around the Barkhor in procession during the Mönlam Festival each 25th day of the first lunar month. This ceremony, known as Jampa Dandren, hastens the arrival on earth of the Future Buddha. The present Jampa is a replacement from Drepung Monastery.

Other statues in the chapel are Jampelyang (left of Jampa), Khasapani (right of Jampa), 11-faced Chenresi, Dorje Sempa, Tongchen Rabjam, Sosor Drangma, Shinje Tharje, Pema Tharje, Gek Tharje, and Zambala Nakpo. Next to a butter lamp is Lharje Gewabum, an image with yellow hair made by the lama himself. It was commissioned after he stopped the Kyi Chu River from flooding by building a dyke. Behind Gek Tharje, at the northeast corner (left of the entrance) is a 0.5-m, gold-painted sculpture of the legendary Queen of Goats, Ramo Gyalpo, bearer of earth to fill Lake Wöthang. The original clay bust of the mystical goat is said to be 'self-originating' (the head is new). A Guru Rinpoche statue is next to the goat. Right of the entrance is a Guardian King; pilgrims have left money and scarves in front of it.

JOWO DESAI LHAKHANG (MENLHA DESHEG GYE LHAKHANG)

Princess Wencheng hid the Jowo in this chapel during a threatened Chinese invasion. A secret doorway called Lhogo Melongchen, behind the Tathagata statue in the center of the east wall, was walled up to conceal the statue. The cavity remains. This chapel contains images of Wöpame and the Eight Medicine Buddhas. Its walls are newly decorated with line paintings on a gold background. The outside walls have paintings of Jampelyang and Sakyamuni. Another popular legend recounts how the Jowo Sakyamuni's statue was concealed by the Jampelyang painting. When Princess Jincheng, wife of Tride Tsugten and patron of the amazing Kachu Monastery, discovered this hiding place, she wanted to remove the statue but was prevented from doing so. Jampelyang then spoke to her, saying he would move aside. Hence the painting became known as Jampelyang Kho Yölma. It is behind a canopied statue of Kunga Tendzin. West of the entrance are new statues of the Sakyapa patriarchs. The five Red-Hat lamas (left to right) are Sonam Tsemo, Drakpa Gyaltsen, Kunga Tendzin, Kunga Gyaltsen (Sakya Pandita), and Chögyal Phagpa.

SANGYE RABDÜN LHAKHANG

The Chapel of Buddha's Seven Successors had six original statues made of precious metals. One empty space represents a statue that supposedly flew to India. The walls are orange with red line paintings.

TSEPAK LHAGU LHAKHANG

The Chapel of the Nine Statues of Tsepame is at the Jokhang's southwest corner. Within are paintings of the Potala, Chakpo Ri, and various festivals. The nine are the Nine Buddhas of Longevity.

TSELHA NAMSUM LHAKHANG

The Chapel of the Gods of Longevity has the three Gods of Longevity: Tsepame (Amitayus), Namgyalma (a goddess), and Drölma Karpo (White Drölma).

CHÖGYAL THÖNMI LHAKHANG

The Chapel of Songtsen Gampo and Thönmi Sambhota is the last chapel on the ground floor *khora*, next to the entrance hall. It contains the principal image of Songtsen Gampo (center), flanked by Ralpachen and Trisong Detsen. East of Trisong Detsen is Nyatri Tsenpo, legendary First King of Tibet. Statues of Songtsen Gampo's queens are also here. Images of Thönmi Sambhota (holding a book) and Gar (another minister) are next to the entrance. The chapel once held statues of Mongza Tricham, Gungru Gungtsen, and Zhang Lonnyi. Original offering bowls and butter lamps are still here, and the repaired walls have red line drawings on a yellow background.

Walls outside the chapel have murals depicting Mentsi Khang, the former medical college on top of Chakpo Ri Hill, the Jokhang, and the Potala at the time of Songtsen Gampo. The scenes of the founding and construction of the Jokhang are full of charming and instructive details.

THE INNER JOKHANG: SECOND FLOOR

A set of stairs at the southeast corner of the ground floor lead to the second-floor chapels. They open onto a rectangular gallery that encircles the central, open-air atrium.

The Zhelre Lhakhang, directly above the Jowo Lhakhang and behind a thick wall, has been remodeled into a small, hidden room.

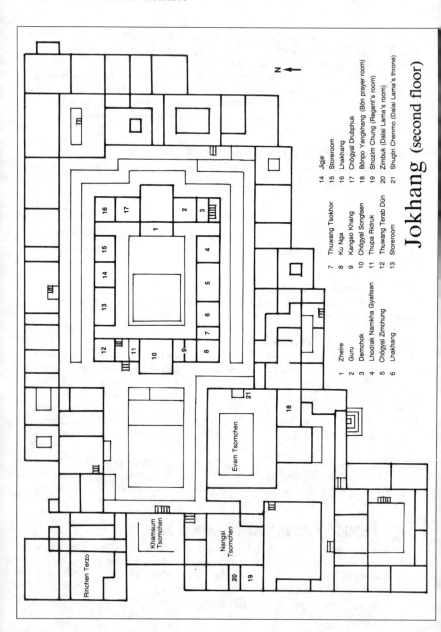

Jokhang (second floor)

1 Zhelre
2 Guru
3 Demchok
4 Lhodrak Namkha Gyaltsan
5 Chögyal Zimchung
6 Lhakhang

7 Thuwang Tsokhor
8 Ku Nga
9 Kangso Khang
10 Chögyal Songtsen
11 Thupa Ridruk
12 Thuwang Terab Dün
13 Storeroom

14 Jigje
15 Storeroom
16 Lhakhang
17 Chögyal Drubphuk
18 Bönpo Yangkhang (Bön prayer room)
19 Shozim Chung (Regent's room)
20 Zimbuk (Dalai Lama's room)
21 Shugtri Chenmo (Dalai Lama's throne)

Rinchen Terzo

Khamsum Tsomchen

Nangsi Tsomchen

Evam Tsomchen

Zhelre Lhakhang (Chapel of the Buddha's Face)

(The following section is a summary from Roberto Vitali's *The Early Temples of Central Tibet*.)`

The southeast corner of the second floor has stairs connecting the ground floor with the upper ones. Immediately north of the stairwell are the Demchok and Guru Rinpoche chapels. Just beyond the latter to its north is a thick wall that prevents access beyond the Guru Rinpoche chapel. Its purpose is to stop pilgrims from entering the Zhelre Lhakhang and thus walking over the head of the Jowo statue located one floor down. A bare room (3 m by 3 m) opens from the end of a narrow catwalk that by-passes the thick wall. (The end of the catwalk looks down on the sculpture shelves above the Jowo Lhakhang entrance.) This room is part of the Zhelre Lhakhang (now defunct) and contains rare murals, some of the earliest and best-preserved of the Jokhang.

Renovations to the Zhelre Lhakhang

Zangkar Lotsawa of West Tibet instigated the first major renovation of the Jokhang in the 11th century. He remodeled the Jowo Lhakhang, the paramount chapel at the center of the east wing, by extending its rear wall. This irregular extension is best seen today in the Nangkhor. To accommodate the giant images of the 12 *bodhisattvas*, he also raised the ceiling to create a two-story chamber. The Zhelre Lhakhang was created immediately west of the newly appropriated space on the second floor, directly above the entrance foyer. Columns are embedded within a new wall that served as the Zhelre Lhakhang's southern limit. Formerly freestanding, these columns confirm an 11th-C. renovation. The outside surface of this wall depicts a large lotus throne with animals; its style is similar to the wall mural (recently renovated) a few meters away—on the exterior wall separating the Guru Lhakhang from Demchok Lhakhang (see page 90). These paintings show a well-defined Pala style; it is therefore possible to date them to the 11th century.

The small chapel

This small part of the original Zhelre Lhakhang is made of two recent and two ancient walls. The new walls, to the north and west, were created to define the space after the floor's center portion was demolished to allow for the heightening of the Jowo Lhakhang. The south wall, built by Zangkar Lotsawa, has the painted lotus throne on its outer surface. On the east wall are original paintings that adorned the rear wall of the former Zhelre Lhakhang.

Four pilasters, two at the rear wall, and one at each of the room's northwest and southwest corners, date back to the 7th century. Before Zangkar Lotsawa's renovations they were freestanding columns. The northwest column has valuable carvings on its capital, while the two at the rear wall are small and have unusual diagonally striped patterns on their surfaces, similar to the two columns of the north wall. (A Newar-style mural, Tibet's earliest-known painting, was on this wall. It was removed in the

➠

late-1980s by Chinese art historians and has since disappeared.)

The rear wall, divided into three sections by the two pillars, is framed by an intricate floral border that gives it an integrated wholeness. Depicted in the center panel are two lamas in flowing robes, one above the other. The face of the upper lama is repainted. Both have long hair and are probably ascetics (*siddhas*). Around them are other *siddhas* and *bodhisattvas*. The right (south) panel's main image is a naked ascetic with long hair; above him are rows of *bodhisattvas*. Along the lower portion is a charming menagerie (bird, elephant, wild ass) and a row of *bodhisattvas*. The north section depicts the worship of a Buddha by *siddhas* and *bodhisattvas*. This strong presence of ascetics suggests a Kagyupa connection.

Murals of the Zhelre Lhakhang

The style of each panel is different though only one artist was involved. These paintings in three panels on the rear wall differ from those of the north and south walls. The 7th-C. mural of the north wall (now removed) showed a definitive Newar hand, and the 11th-C. south wall, with lotus throne fragment, shows strong Pala traits. These rear wall paintings of the small chapel are later.

After Zangkar Lotsawa and another lama, Dagpo Gompa Tsultrim Nyingpo (1116–69), began refurbishing the Jokhang in 1160, they built the Nangkhor and supervised the painting of its murals. It is most probable that the Zhelre Lhakhang's three-panel mural was executed at this time. The south panel was painted in a local idiom with strong overtones from Pala India. Its absorption of the foreign influence is less clear than the mural on the south wall's outer surface. Here, local traits are

➡

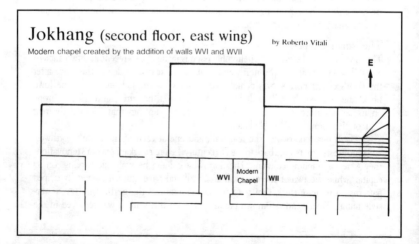

Jokhang (second floor, east wing) by Roberto Vitali

Modern chapel created by the addition of walls WVI and WVII

E
↑

Modern Chapel

WVI   WVII

more apparent. This painting makes no attempt at shading; the figures appear more two-dimensional than typically Indian works. Distinctive protruding eyes, a Pala characteristic, are rendered carefully. The tall hair buns (*ushnishas*) and ovoid Haloes conform to the Pala prototype, as do the trees, used to fill empty spaces. These trees, however, are elongated, thus imparting a peculiarly Tibetan element. The flowers are also Tibetan in execution.

The central panel's greater exuberance is expressed by copious jewelry and elaborate decorations. In the background are trees and giant flowers. All are traits derived from the Nepalese Pala style, a near parallel development with East Indian Pala. There are two different types of eyes. The bulging, almond-shaped ones of the main images indicate spiritual attainment, a device indicative of Nepalese interpretation; the others—protruding eyes—follow the south panel. The mural's deep reds, greens, and blues are another characteristic of Nepalese works. It is interesting that the north panel is a synthesis, a forum for the versatile artist to show off his expertise in both the Pala and Nepalese styles.

Thus, within the contracted Zhelre Lhakhang, are two art styles co-existing together: Tibeto-Indian Pala and Tibeto-Nepalese Pala. The north panel merges the two while retaining signatures from both idioms. It is now known that the Nepalese Pala and Indian Pala styles flourished in Tibet during the 12th century. A totally integrated Tibeto-Newar form of expression did not appear until the 15th century (see page 55).

In the absence of the missing murals that once adorned the north gallery walls of the first floor, it can be claimed that these paintings are among the best preserved

➠

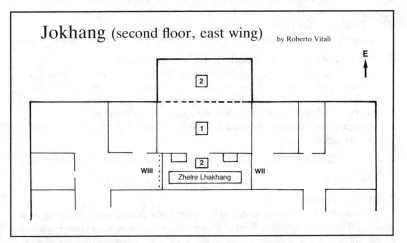

Jokhang (second floor, east wing) by Roberto Vitali

1 Original 7th-century structure
2 11th-century expansion by Zangkar Lotsawa (extension of the Jowo Lhakhang at the rear and creation of the Zhelre Lhakhang by the addition of wall WII and grille WIII)

> early paintings in Lhasa. (Those outside the Demchok and Guru Lhakhangs are older but have been recently restored.) The three panels represent the first paintings executed by Tibetans with separate and overt influences from the Indian Pala and Nepalese Pala styles exhibited side by side.

Chapels of the second floor are described below, clockwise from the southeast corner:

GURU LHAKHANG (BARKHANG LOPON)

This principal chapel of Guru Rinpoche has a beautiful, unpainted, 7th-C. door-frame and the entrance is closed by a metal lattice door. The outside walls adjacent to the entrance were darkened with smoke and the ancient Pala-style paintings were barely legible until they were restored in 1991. The entranceway, like the Wöpame Lhakhang downstairs, is shaped to resemble a cave opening; wider at the bottom than the top. The chapel's interior walls are covered with patterned cloth. Guru Rinpoche, surrounded by his two consorts, is the central statue. Notice the bone rosary around his neck, supposedly a powerful magic talisman. Along the side walls are his eight manifestations (Guru Tsengye), four on each side. The central manifestation is called Guru Namsi, most common of the eight. A figure of the Medicine Buddha is above the entrance. On leaving, visitors are sometimes offered barley beer (chang), known as 'nectar' (dutsi), in skull cups rather than the usual holy water—a special practice peculiar to Guru Rinpoche and other tantric figures.

DEMCHOK LHAKHANG (CHAPEL OF CHAKRASAMVARA)

Demchok and his red-faced consort, Dorje Phagmo, symbolize the union of emptiness and bliss. Their huge clay statue (replaced), in yabyum, is the only one here. Pilgrims rub their backs on the wall between the Demchok Lhakhang and the Guru Lhakhang, in order to extract sin from their body and to cure backaches. Next to the Demchok Lhakhang (south) are stairs to the ground floor and second floor. Known as Pelchok Dolam, they lead up to the chapel of the Goddess Palden Lhamo.

Murals outside the Demchok and Guru Lhakhangs

These murals probably owe their inspiration to the Indian Pala era (9th–11th C.) and were part of Zangkar Lotsawa's 11th-C. additions. On the thick north wall adjacent to the Guru Rinpoche chapel are parts of a deity on a lotus throne. The interesting Haloes of the images are discontinuous, being made up of numerous discreet rectangles. The paintings, darkened by centuries of soot and pilgrims, were until recently almost illegible.

Go west along the south wing past three empty chapels to reach the Thuwang Tsokhor.

THUWANG TSOKHOR

This Chapel of Sakyamuni, surrounded by his Eight Great Bodhisattvas (Nyewe Segye) has an ornate door frame (repainted). West of the entrance is a painting of Sakyamuni, and Tsong Khapa. Along the west wall are statues of the Jowo and his two principal disciples.

Ku Nga Gönkhang (Gönkhangphuk)

The Chapel of the Five Protectors is the fifth chapel along the pilgrim route from the southeast corner stairs. Its five principal statues within this tantric room are known collectively as Gyalpo Ku Nga, guardians of the center and the four directions. Nine 1.5 m-tall statues enclosed in red wood and glass cabinets fill the room. The central image is Tamdrin (Hayagriva), flanked on the left by Palden Lhamo, Tibet's most admired female protector, and on the right by the oracle Nechung (see page 165). Just inside the entrance are the guardians Dütsen, a spirit being (left), and Lutsen, a water spirit (right). A door at the south wall leads to the Ku Nga Gönkhang's inner room.

Kangso Khang (Tachok Lhakhang)

This locked chapel had paintings of the eight sacred symbols of Buddhism: *dharma* wheel, goldfish, conch shell, vase, endless knot, umbrella, banner of victory, and lotus flower. It was an offering prayer room.

Chögyal Songtsen Lhakhang

The principal chapel of Songtsen Gampo in the Jokhang, topped with a gilded roof, is at the center of the west wing. It has two impressive, ornate entrances. The 7th-C. door frames have recently been repainted. Next to the east wall (between the two entrances, on a wood stand in a cabinet) is the Chögyal Trungben, the king's beer container, a round, potbellied silver vessel with a long spout. A horse's head with protruding ears is the terminal decoration. Notice the exaggerated, drunken figures at the bottom of the pot. The workmanship is clearly not Tibetan. The repoussé decorations (garments, boots, hair styles) show a possible Indo-Iranian influence and are often seen in Kushan artwork (late 1st–3rd century). One source suggests a Scythian origin for this vessel. Tradition asserts that this *chang* bowl was concealed in a gorge of the Kyere Valley in west-central Tibet. Tsong Khapa later discovered it and brought it to the Jokhang.

At the back wall, the king sits on a gold throne flanked by his two foreign wives. Tradition states these statues were commissioned by Tritsun and made by Nepalese craftsmen after the Jokhang's construction. The king is a 'true-likeness' (*ngadrama*) statue. Pilgrims believe its middle finger is Songtsen Gampo's actual finger. Behind the king along the west wall are replicas of blue-haired statues of the Seven Past Buddhas (Sangye Rabdün), originally made by Songtsen Gampo himself. Murals behind them consist of many mandalas. Tsong Khapa and his two disciples are along the north wall. The south has another statue of Songtsen Gampo, flanked on his left by Wencheng and on his right by a Tibetan wife.

Thupa Ridruk Lhakhang

The last chapel near the northwest corner is consecrated to Chenresi. The *Bodhisattva* of Compassion as a four-armed Chenresi is the central figure. Along the side walls are the six blue-haired images of Thupa Ridruk, the six manifestations of Sakyamuni, which appeared during the Buddha's emancipation of the six different classes of existence (animal, human, ghost, demigod, celestial, hell); Indra, holding a stringed instrument, is the first manifestation. The chapels of the north wing and those north of the Zhelre Lhakhang along the east gallery have been destroyed. They were Thuwang Terab Dün, Jigje Lhakhang, Chögyal Drubphuk, and Zhelre Lhakhang (Chapel of the Buddha's Face, see page 87).

THE INNER JOKHANG: THIRD FLOOR

Stairs to the third floor are at the temple's southeast corner (a second set is at the northwest corner), reached after the Demchok and the Guru Lhakhangs. The third floor is dedicated to Palden Lhamo, principal protectress of Tibet and the Gelugpa. An open-air cloister runs around the exterior of the chapels, of which only three are open: Pelhachok Dukhang, Palden Lhamo Lhakhang, and Pelha Bedhongma Lhakhang. They are described below, clockwise from the southeast corner.

PELHACHOK DUKHANG (MERU TSHOKHANG)

This assembly room, dedicated to Palden Lhamo, was cared for by the monks of Meru Tratsang. New murals outlined in white, gold, and red on a black background depict Palden Lhamo, Nagpo Chenpo, and Jigje, the main protectors of the Gelugpa. Notice the *thangkas* on the west wall, especially one of Gönpo with small, fantastical figures. There are two doorways; one at the southeast corner leads to the other open chapels, and one at the northeast leads to the terrace. The terrace murals are recent.

Pelha Gönkhang Zimgo This gilt-copper door (destroyed) of Nepalese design had embossed images of precious gems and animals.

PALDEN LHAMO LHAKHANG

The first chapel after the Zimgo is partitoned from the Pelha Bedhongma by a partial wall. The peaceful image (new) of Palden Lhamo resides along the east wall. Next to it is a metal *chakra-dharma* wheel. This chapel is well-known for being infested by tame mice, considered children of the deity.

PELHA BEDHONGMA LHAKHANG

The wrathful image of Palden Lhamo stands next to her peaceful form, the two separated by the partial wall. This fierce figure holds a sword and is always veiled; under the veil she has the face of a frog. The original frog mask was discovered on Mt Khardrak near Tshal Gungthang Monastery by the *terton*, Tsondu Drak. It was made of stone and laden with heavy ornaments and jewelry. Every year on the 13th day of the 10th lunar month, the image was displayed for three days on an open balcony. On the day of the full moon, it was carried out of the Jokhang around the Barkhor for the festival of the Pelhe Ridra. Next to the image on the north wall is the sculpture of a horned deer with the snout of a pig. Steps lead from the west down to the second floor.

During the autumn and winter pilgrimage seasons, crowds wait for hours to enter these chapels. Other chapels on this floor (all closed) are Lama Lhakhang, Tsepak Lhakhang, Sangdhe Jigsum Kyilkhor, Nechu Lhakhang, Menlha Desheg Gye Lhakhang, Menlha Tsokhor Lhakhang, Tönpa Tsokhor Lhakhang, Drelzam, Desheg Gye Lhakhang, Thuwang Tsokhor, and Jowo Uthoe Lhakhang.

MURALS

South wall (outside the Pelhachok Dukhang)

A six-armed Mahakala is surrounded by female deities and four Nojins. To the left are the Fifth Dalai Lama, Regent Sangye Gyatso, and Go Shri Tenzin Chögyal. Next to these are the female divinities Magzorma, Palden Lhamo, and the 12 Tenmas.

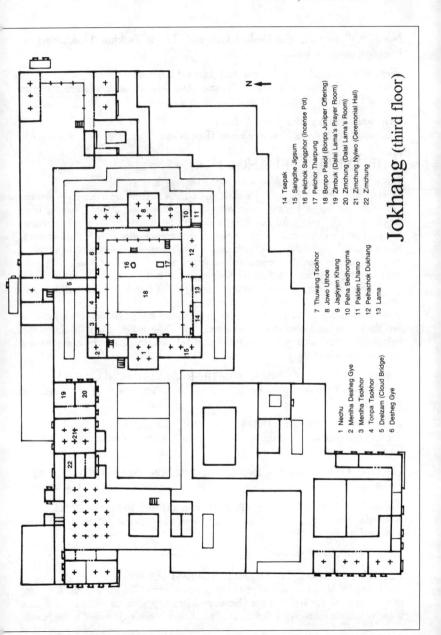

Jokhang (third floor)

7 Thuwang Tsokhor
8 Jowo Uthoe
9 Jagkyen Khang
10 Pelha Bedhongma
11 Palden Lhamo
12 Pelhachok Dukhang
13 Lama

14 Tsepak
15 Sangdhe Jigsum
16 Pelchok Sangphor (Incense Pot)
17 Pelchor Tharpung
18 Bonpo Pasol (Bonpo Juniper Offering)
19 Zimbuk (Dalai Lama's Prayer Room)
20 Zimchung (Dalai Lama's Room)
21 Zimchung Nyiwo (Ceremonial Hall)
22 Zimchung

1 Nechu
2 Menlha Desheg Gye
3 Menlha Tsokhor
4 Tonpa Tsokhor
5 Drelzam (Cloud Bridge)
6 Desheg Gye

North wall (outside the Desheg Gye and Tönpa Tsokhor Lhakhangs)
Numerous images of Buddha.

West wall (outside the Nechu and Lama Lhakhangs)
Dewachen (Sukhavati)— the Pure Land (Paradise) of the West—has a central image of Tsepame and the Paradise of Drölma, surrounded by green Taras.

East wall (outside the Jowo Uthoe)
The Paradise of Wöpame is surrounded by Dorje Sempa.

THE INNER JOKHANG: ROOF

This is one of the most delightful areas of the Jokhang. It is refreshing to come here after spending considerable time inside the dark, greasy chapels. There are a number of different roof levels, the highest being a narrow ledge, protected by a gilded railing, running round the perimeter. The main gilded roof, dating to the early 14th C., rises with impressive intricacy over the Jowo Lhakhang. Its distinct Chinese form and ornamentation embody Buddhist motifs. Notice under the eaves the myriad bells engraved with *mantras* and decorated with mystical animals. Inscriptions on the tongues of the bells and also on the gilded roofs call for peace and prosperity. Metalwork covering the walls under the roofs has richly decorated carvings of divinities and icons: four-faced Indra (Tshangpa) riding a duck, wrathful Mahakala on a *garuda*, a figure with an elephant's trunk riding a rat.

Walk under the northeast corner of Jowo Sakyamuni's gilded roof. On a ledge just over the parapet are a stone phallus and a stone lion. These and other mystical objects were erected to repel evil forces from the earth. Four gilded roofs (*serthok gyaphip*) crown the most important chapels of the Jokhang.

JOWO GYAPHIP (EAST-CENTER, OVER THE JOWO SAKYAMUNI CHAPEL)
This gilded roof was donated in the 14th-C. by Tew Mul, ruler of the Yartse Kingdom of West Tibet.

JAMPA GYAPHIP (SOUTH-CENTER, OVER THE JAMPA CHAPEL)
The roof was once owned by the Nepalese King Amshuvarma, a contemporary of Songtsen Gampo.

CHÖGYAL GYAPHIP (WEST-CENTER, OVER THE SONGTSEN GAMPO CHAPEL)
This was commissioned by the government during the reign of the Fifth Dalai Lama.

THUJE GYAPHIP (NORTH-CENTER, OVER THE THUJE CHENPO CHAPEL)
A donation of King Puni Mul of Yartse and his minister. His son was Prati Mul (Prati Malla), who ruled in the late-14th century.

The following chapels are built at the roof's four corners:

PELHA YUM DRAKMO LHAKHANG (SOUTHEAST CORNER)
The Chapel of Magsorma, mother of the three Pelha sisters. The image of the first sister, in wrathful form, was kept at Tshal Gungthang Monastery, while the second, and fiercest, is the veiled one in the Pelha Bedhongma Chapel directly below. The third is the peaceful

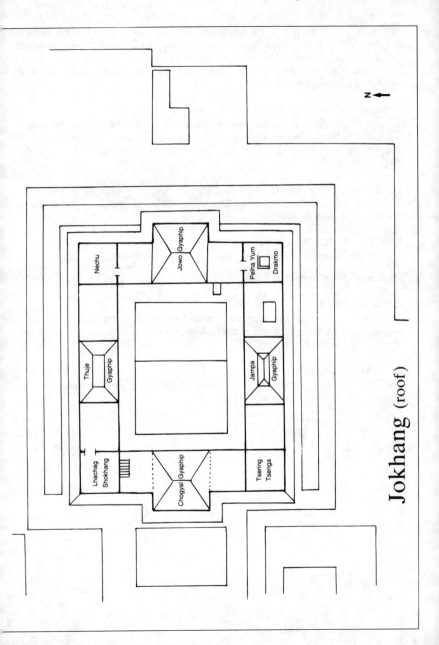

Jokhang (roof)

form of Palden Lhamo, next to the latter. The chapel has many victory banners (*gyaltsen*) and prayer flags are between them. Within the chamber was once displayed the original wrathful Palden Lhamo mask (Palden Lhamo Drakmo), made by the Fifth Dalai Lama. According to one source, at a certain point along the east wall, one can at all times enjoy a jet of air smelling of rotten corpses. This chapel is closed.

TSERING TSENGA LHAKHANG (SOUTHWEST CORNER)
The chapel of the five female goddesses whose responsibilities are to look after Palden Lhamo. It was dedicated to the peace and prosperity of Tibet, and the goddesses made a vow to Wopame that they will protect and serve Buddhism. Monks from Tsurphu Monastery cared for this chapel (closed).

NECHU LHAKHANG (NORTHEAST CORNER)
The chapel of the 16 Arhats was usually occupied by monks and government officials during the Mönlam Festival (closed).

LHACHAG SHOKHANG (NORTHWEST CORNER)
This was the government stationer; it supplied only the best-quality paper (closed).

Other sites on the roof are:

LHABUM LUBUM
This small enclosure contained many vases wrapped with sacred scarves (*kata*). Inside were earth and jewels, elements to protect against misfortune and illness. Lamas held periodic rituals to renew the elements' powers.

TAMNYEN DARCHEN
The 'Flagpole of Sweet News' was erected by Regent Sonam Chöphel after vanquishing the King of Beri in Upper Kham.

POTALA: MONUMENTAL PALACE OF KINGS AND DALAI LAMAS

OVERVIEW

The Potala, the most monumental of structures in Tibet, is best admired from the outside. Slowly circumambulate the palace by following the pilgrim's path around it, noting different aspects and moods of the sophisticated design from varying view points. At some point simply sit with a good vantage (for example, from the island in the middle of the Lhasa River or from the top of Chakpo Ri) and gradually let the Potala's myriad details sink in. This massive edifice embodies the best of 17th-C. Tibetan architecture; no buildings, before or after, compare with it.

Once inside, the most poignant areas are the roof terraces housing the Dalai Lama's residences and the large courtyard known as Deyang Shar. Both places, distinguished by their superb sense of space, reveal the enormity of the Potala and its special relationship with Lhasa. The view of the holy city from the roofs is unforgettable.

From the historical and religious point of view, two tiny chapels, the Phakpa Lhakhang and the Chögyal Drubphuk, both within the White Palace, are the most important. These are probably the only surviving structures from the 7th C., when King Songtsen Gampo first conceived of building a great palace. Images of the king and his retinue within the Chögyal Drubphuk are among the earliest (8th–9th C.) in Tibet. Their style is significant for being neither overtly Chinese nor Indian-inspired; the statues are probably the works of an artist familiar with the idioms of Central Asia. The Potala's most sacred statue, the Arya Lokeshvara, is inside the Phakpa Lhakhang, the holiest shrine for pilgrims.

Eight Dalai Lamas are entombed within the Potala. The most spectacular are the elaborate, ornate burial *chörtens* of the Fifth and the Thirteenth. As a counterpoint to these massive relics spend some time in the Dukhor Lhakhang, which houses an intricate three-dimensional mandala. The two great halls of the Red and White Palaces, Tshomchen Shar and Tshomchen Nub, give some respite from the dark chapels. Both have spectacular multi-storied interior atriums that extend upwards all the way to the roof terraces. Ranged around the inside of these wondrously illuminated spaces are chapels and galleries noted for their murals. The Potala has never been severely damaged. Unlike most Tibetan monasteries, it was not sacked by Red Guards during the 1960s and 1970s. As a result, all the chapels and their artefacts are remarkably well preserved.

FUNCTION

The Potala, the most complex monument ever built in Tibet, was designed to serve numerous diverse functions. First and foremost, it was the palace where the Dalai Lama and his large entourage resided and where all ceremonies of state were held. It was also the seat of Tibet's government, and prior to the mid-18th C. it served as a fortress in tumultuous times. All political and administrative decisions concerning the country emanated from here. In addition, since the Dalai Lamas were considered to be incarnations of Chenresi, Bodhisattva of Compassion, the Potala was a major destination for pilgrims. Riches, sacred images, the spectacular tombs of the Dalai Lamas themselves—all contributed to the Potala's extraordinary status. Finally, within the staggering interior space of 130,000 sq m were sited the Dalai Lama's personal monastery (Namgyal Tratsang), a school for religious officials (Tse Lobdra), numerous chapels, large halls, storage chambers, cells, larders, and treasuries.

NAMING THE POTALA

Nothing in the historical records tells us who named the Potala or how the name originated. We do know that Thönmi Sambhota, a minister of King Songtsen Gampo in the 8th C., was the first Tibetan to be sent to India for advanced Buddhist studies. He was also the country's first translator, having rendered a number of Sanskrit texts into Tibetan. In one of these he mentioned that Riwo Potala, the mystical abode of Chenresi in South India, was identified with the Paradise of Chenresi. Since Songtsen Gampo was widely regarded as the incarnation of Chenresi, and given that he founded the Potala, it seems plausible that Sambhota coined the name for the palace.

The site

The early Dalai Lamas lived within the monastic compound of Drepung Monastery, inside the palace known as Ganden Potrang. When Tibet was unified in the 17th C. under the authority of the Fifth Dalai Lama, this residence became the seat of government as well. Henceforth, the Tibetan Government was known by the name Ganden Potrang, the original site where the Dalai Lamas' power began to exert itself.

In the beginning, however, severe limitations existed for the nascent administration of the Great Fifth. It was difficult to rule all of Tibet from the strict confines of a monastery; the Dalai Lama's prestige was initially shaky and subject to challenge by the large, entrenched monastic powers such as Sera and Drepung. As the government grew in size, the Ganden Potrang was simply too small for its needs. The Fifth and his ministers decided it was time to build a bigger structure to serve as both palace and seat of government.

The Fifth was an admirer a former ruler of Tibet, Jangchub Gyaltsen (1302–73), the abbot-prince of Phagmodru who pioneered the system of dividing vast territorial holdings into districts, each administered from a fortress (*dzongs*). Therefore, abandoning the example of Ganden Potrang, the Fifth decreed that his new palace would be built like a castle, sited in a strategically commanding position. The choice of locations finally narrowed down to two—Lhasa and Gongkar Dzong (close to present-day Lhasa Airport). This latter, near the junction of the Kyi Chu and Tsangpo rivers, was a strong contender; it was a principal power center of the Phagmo Drupas, avid supporters of the Gelugpas, and its large, imposing fortifications made it a logical choice. However, it had a major drawback—its distance from the three chief monasteries of Sera, Drepung and Ganden. This was one of the reasons why Lhasa was finally chosen as the palace site, but there were others: a palace tradition already existed there, for during the times of the Yarlung kings (7th–9th C.), it was the capital of Songtsen Gampo and his successors; Tsong Khapa, the founder of the Gelugpas, had established the Mönlam (Great Prayer) Festival at the Jokhang in Lhasa—the biggest, most prestigious public event in the entire year, drawing vast numbers of monks, laymen and pilgrims from all over the country at the beginning of each Tibetan New Year. In other words, Lhasa was fast becoming the most important pilgrimage site in the country.

Eventually, Marpo Ri (Red Mountain) was designated as the location for the new palace.

It was a good choice. Rising 130 m above the Lhasa Valley and situated near the monastic cities of Drepung and Sera, the top of the mount was centrally located with a commanding position over the entire valley. It was also ideal in a geomantic sense. Sandwiched between a range of impregnable 5200 m-high mountains and the Kyi Chu River with its tracts of grassy marshland, Marpo Ri, resembling a huge heap of grain, could not be more auspicious. This was also the site where Songtsen Gampo located his palace; Marpo Ri was considered the sacred dwelling place of Chenresi, and in fact the most sacred object in the present-day Potala, an ancient statue of Arya Lokeshvara—the 'chosen' divinity of Songtsen Gampo—was found in a cave on Marpo Ri long before the Potala's foundation was laid.

FOUNDATION OF POTRANG KARPO (WHITE PALACE)

In ancient times, the original Potrang Karpo, one of two major components of the Potala, was situated in Chusul near the confluence of the Tsangpo and Kyi Chu rivers. The Fifth Dalai Lama began to draw up plans for a new Potrang Karpo on Marpo Ri in 1645. This mammoth project was entrusted to his personal secretary and treasurer, who supervised the entire construction. It took three years to complete the nine-story structure. In 1648, the murals of the palace's eastern section were completed, as was the Kangyur Lhakhang. After this, artists began to decorate the Namgyal Tratsang, and the Great Fifth moved from the Ganden Potrang to the Potala in 1649.

It is possible to get a visual idea of the original Potala, Songtsen Gampo's 7th-C. palace, by viewing a painting on the outer wall of Lamrin Lhakhang. Judging from this, the Fifth Dalai Lama did not make any major changes to the earlier structure. He simply added new buildings to the west and east of the old ones. The painting shows the main assembly hall of the palace surrounded by four principal buildings: Gyalpo Chok, Tenma Chok, Yugyal Chok, and Sharchen Chok. There was a second assembly hall located in an upper floor, to the north.

FOUNDATION OF POTRANG MARPO (RED PALACE)

Some 45 years after the completion of Potrang Karpo, Sangye Gyatso came to power as Regent of Tibet and ruled the country from 1679 to 1703. After the death of the Great Fifth in 1682, Sangye Gyatso became Tibet's unchallenged ruler. (The Fifth's death was scrupulously concealed until 1694, fully 12 years after the fact.) In 1690, Sangye Gyatso laid the foundation for Potrang Marpo and produced a set of plans designed to increase the size of the palace around Songtsen Gampo's earlier structures by expanding existing facilities. Apparently, the southwestern part of Potrang Karpo was dismantled to make way for new additions. Bokgong Mönpa Lodro Gyaltsen was appointed as the chief civil engineer. Work began in earnest in 1691 and finished in 1693, although it took four more years to complete the interior. The dedicatory stele known as Doring Nangma was erected at that time and this can still be seen in the center of Zhöl Village, below the stairway ramp leading to the Potala.

According to a well-known oral tradition, this particular chronology of Potrang Marpo is subject to dispute. Apparently in 1682, when the Fifth died, two storys of the palace were already completed. It seems that the Fifth had decided to build a monumental palace to house his *chörten*-tomb, much as King Songtsen Gampo had done a millennium earlier. A Jesuit priest visited Lhasa in 1661 and made a drawing that proves that the Potala, as it exists today, was already advanced in its planning. The encircling walls of the entire complex were in place and the entire east–west span (360 m) of the palace were envisaged. If the construction was well underway in 1682, it seems odd that Potrang Marpo was not completed until 1694, especially when we knew that Potrang Karpo took only three years to complete. One plausible explanation holds that both the announcement of the Great Fifth's death and the completion of the Potrang Marpo were purposely delayed to prevent China from meddling in Tibet's affairs.

Work on the funerary chapel of the Fifth Dalai Lama started in 1692. The elaborate chamber was completed by 1694, at which point Sangye Gyatso finally chose to tell the Tibetan people that their beloved Great Fifth was dead. Potrang Marpo was the biggest construction project undertaken in the history of Tibet. Seven thousand workers were conscripted along with more than 1500 artists and craftsmen. Emperor Kangxi of China (r 1662–1722) sent seven Chinese and ten Manchu master craftsmen. From the south, Nepal provided 182 Nepali artists.

20TH-CENTURY RENOVATIONS

In 1922, the 13th Dalai Lama renovated all the chapels and assembly halls near the Phakpa Lhakhang; many of the beams and ceiling panels of these rooms were replaced. The eastern section of Potrang Karpo was demolished and the size of the chapels and halls expanded; the Dukhor Lhakhang was extensively repaired. Additionally, the printing press at the back of Potrang Karpo was enlarged significantly.

In 1959, when the Chinese invaded, the south facade was shelled. Miraculously, only the Potrang Marpo porch and Tse Lobtra were damaged. Under the orders of Beijing's Cultural Relics Bureau, the Potala was left untouched during the Cultural Revolution.

Layout

At the southern foot of Marpo Ri is Zhöl Village, Lhasa's traditional red light district. Located here are auxiliary buildings associated with the Potala. These include the Barkhang (printing press), some government offices, a tribunal and prison, and extensive residential quarters. The Kashag, a building where Tibet's cabinet held meetings, is in the center of the village, near the notorious jail. Zhöl, essentially a quadrangle, is closed off on three sides by long perimeter walls, each nearly 300 m in length. The fourth side, the north, is Marpo Ri crowned with the Potala.

Entrances in the form of fortified gateways stand on the east, south, and west sides. At the southeast and southwest corners of the quadrangle are two watch towers. This configuration is reminiscent of the 13th-C. Sakya Monastery, which was heavily influenced by Yuan Dynasty (1279–1368) military architecture. From the main south entrance, next to the People's Museum on Dekyi Nub Lam, a series of crooked streets bordered by low buildings provide an irregular route towards the wide, impressive south access ramps. These eventually lead up to the Potala.

Potrang Marpo (the Red Palace) is the central, dark red structure that rises majestically from the surrounding whiteness of Potrang Karpo (the White Palace). All religious functions took place within Potrang Marpo. This complicated structure is centered around a spacious inner atrium situated directly above the vast Tshomchen Nub (Great Western Assembly Hall). Abutting on the four sides of the hall are four large, two-story chapels. The western one houses the famed burial *chörten* of the Fifth Dalai Lama. Immediately to the east of Potrang Marpo is Potrang Karpo, site of all activities related to the Dalai Lamas' household and government. This is the oldest part of the Potala. A huge open-air courtyard, the Deyang Shar, adjoins this palace on its eastern side. The two entities together comprise a complete architectural

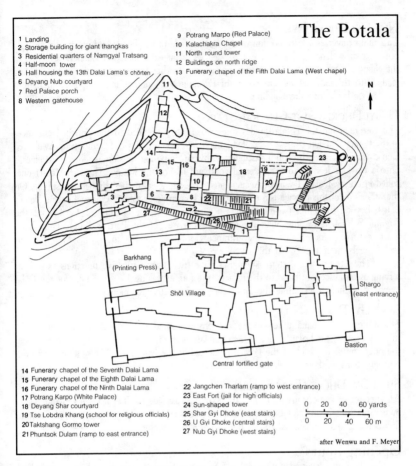

The Potala

1 Landing
2 Storage building for giant thangkas
3 Residential quarters of Namgyal Tratsang
4 Half-moon tower
5 Hall housing the 13th Dalai Lama's chörten
6 Deyang Nub courtyard
7 Red Palace porch
8 Western gatehouse
9 Potrang Marpo (Red Palace)
10 Kalachakra Chapel
11 North round tower
12 Buildings on north ridge
13 Funerary chapel of the Fifth Dalai Lama (West chapel)

14 Funerary chapel of the Seventh Dalai Lama
15 Funerary chapel of the Eighth Dalai Lama
16 Funerary chapel of the Ninth Dalai Lama
17 Potrang Karpo (White Palace)
18 Deyang Shar courtyard
19 Tse Lobdra Khang (school for religious officials)
20 Taktshang Gormo tower
21 Phuntsok Dulam (ramp to east entrance)

22 Jangchen Tharlam (ramp to west entrance)
23 East Fort (jail for high officials)
24 Sun-shaped tower
25 Shar Gyi Dhoke (east stairs)
26 U Gyi Dhoke (central stairs)
27 Nub Gyi Dhoke (west stairs)

0 20 40 60 yards
0 20 40 60 m

after Wenwu and F. Meyer

unit independent of the surrounding structures. From the courtyard, a distinctive and steep triple-staircase leads up into Potrang Karpo, which is also arranged around a huge inner atrium. This three-story enclosed space extends upwards from the Tsomchen Shar (Great Eastern Assembly Hall) all the way to the roof terrace of the palace. Here, at the very top, are the personal quarters of the Dalai Lamas.

Access

Two access ramps from Zhöl zigzag up Marpo Ri from its southern base, ascending to the Potala. Another entrance ramp climbs the northern face of the hill to enter Potrang Marpo by way of an adjacent building. This route enters the palace at a higher level than the southern ones.

NUB GYI DHOKE (WEST STAIRS)

This ramp traverses a large portion of the front facade of the Potala and eventually emerges onto a narrow landing. From here a passage leads into the monks' residences attached to the Namgyal Tratsang, the Potala's own monastery. Another entryway from the narrow landing leads onto the external western courtyard (Deyang Nub) of Potrang Marpo. From here, a small door leads into the building.

Ü GYI DHOKE (EAST-CENTRAL STAIRS)

The east ramp up the Potala divides into two. Both paths lead to the principal entrances of the Potala. The left (west) one, called Jangchen Tharlam ('Way of Liberation by Awakened Consciousness'), goes through a vestibule, within an imposing six-story gatehouse, to emerge onto a corridor leading to the external courtyard of Potrang Marpo. The right (east) one, called Phuntsok Dulam ('Way of Accumulated Perfection'), also goes through a vestibule. On the other side of this passage is a rounded tower known as Tagtshang Gormo ('Round Tiger's Lair'). Beyond this, after passing through a corridor under the building of Tse Lobdra, the Summit School, is Deyang Shar, the external courtyard of the Potrang Karpo. From here, a set of triple-stairs leads up to the entrance cloister of the Potrang Karpo. Most pilgrims and officials enter the Potala this way.

The eastern and western gatehouses have their own distinctive functions as well as serving as entrance vestibules to the palaces: the former was used as residences for the Dalai Lamas' household staff, while the latter contained quarters for monks.

JANG GYI DHOKE (NORTH STAIRS)

This route avoids the many steps of the southern ramps and enters the Potala from the north. In the past, only the Dalai Lama and high officials used this entry. The north palace entrance, the only one at the back of the Potala, is located at the base of a building attached to the northern flank of Potrang Marpo.

SHAR GYI DHOKE (EAST STAIRS)

Another set of stone stairs located at the extreme east side of Zhöl leads up to the Potala by first reaching Sharchen Chok (the Potala's Eastern Fort), used to jail high officials. Beyond this building is a sun-shaped tower, the easternmost structure.

Opening hours

The Potala is open every day from 0900–1600, except Sunday, when it is closed. Expect long queues on Wednesdays and Saturdays, traditional days for pilgrims, when it is open all day. Some parts of the Potala may be locked during lunch from 1230–1430. Admission is Rmb 3. The best day of the year to visit the Potala is the fourth day of the sixth lunar month, the Feast of the Buddha's first sermon. All chapels are open to the public. Tour groups enter the Potala from the back (north) side. Individuals walk up to the East Gate of the Potrang Karpo via the Zhöl Village (the East Gate is reached by a long series of wide stone steps). Inside, a ticket office on the left precedes the Deyang Shar, which is straight ahead. A small shop sells postcards. Be sure to bring a flashlight for viewing murals and dark chambers.

POTRANG KARPO ('THE WHITE PALACE')

This section assumes that you have reached the Potala via the east access, have passed through Tagtshang Gormo and Tse Lobdra, and are now at the Deyang Shar, about to enter Potrang Karpo.

TSE LOBDRA KHANG

Tse Lobdra, the Summit School, founded by the Seventh Dalai Lama (1708–57), trained religious officials. Its teachers came from Mindroling as well as the major monasteries of Lhasa. There were only 40–70 students at any one time.

DEYANG SHAR

This large (1500 sq m) courtyard, about 70 m above Marpo Ri's slopes, flanks the eastern limits of the Potrang Karpo. Along the sides of this courtyard are two-story monks' residences and storage facilities. The eastern facade of the Potrang Karpo overlooks the Deyang Shar, whose four levels of centrally placed galleries provided viewing areas for officials and dignitaries during various performances. The Dalai Lama held court in the top gallery. The north side has a souvenir shop and tour office. Tse Lobdra is to the east. Beneath the flagstoned courtyard are several floors of rooms that are used for storage, especially tea. At the northeast corner, stone steps lead up to Sumke Go, the set of stairs that lead into Potrang Karpo.

SUMKE GO

This prestigious set of steep wooden stairs, the main entryway into the Potrang Karpo, is humble and archaic in design. The Sumke Go is nothing but three sets of ladders, bound side by side, and tilted upwards at an uncomfortable angle. The central ladder is reserved for the exclusive use of the Dalai Lamas.

SUMKE GOCHOR WOK

At the top of the triple-stairs is Sumke Gochor Wok, an entrance foyer that leads to the Potrang Karpo Zimgo (Door of the White Palace). It is worthwhile to spend time here to admire the intricately carved supporting structures of pillars and beams, especially the elaborate entablature. These are among the most richly decorated in the Potala. On the south wall are the liquid gold handprints (*chakje*) of the 13th Dalai Lama, and the Fifth Dalai Lama's edict, written in cursive Tibetan, proclaiming Sangye Gyatso as regent. Murals show the Four Guardian Kings and the construction of the Medical College on Chakpo Ri. On the north side is a painting of Princess Wencheng entering Tibet in the 7th century. Above the door are eight sculptures depicting mythical animals. Another mural in the foyer shows the construction of the Jokhang. The red entrance doors are decorated with Dege metalwork, famed for its elaborate gilt-copper inlay. Go through this set of doors and ascend several flights of stairs to reach the roof. The Dalai Lama's residential quarters are here. Heinrich Harrer recounts how, in the 1940s, the young 14th Dalai Lama set up a brass telescope to watch Lhasa's street life, to gain a glimpse of the world as it existed outside the rarefied atmosphere of the palace. Views of the mountains, the Kyi Chu Valley and Lhasa are superb.

Dalai Lama's Quarters The residences of the 13th and the 14th Dalai Lamas are on the east side of the roof.

NYIWÖ SHAR GADHEN NANGSEL
('EASTERN SUNLIGHT HALL': QUARTERS OF THE 14TH DALAI LAMA)

Reception Hall

A large throne on top of a raised platform dominates this sumptuously decorated room, located around the corner as you ascend the stairs. Flanking the throne are portraits of the two most recent Dalai Lamas; the 14th is to the left. Two small ante-chambers, one on each side of the throne, lead to the private quarters. This hall was once a chapel used exclusively by the god-kings. Its balcony overlooks the Deyang Shar, where Cham dances were performed. Note the elaborate carvings of the Six Long-living Beings (Tshering Drukhor)—man, tree, water, bird, mountain, deer—and of the Four Friendly Brothers (Thumpa Punzhi)—elephant, monkey, bird, and rabbit. The cabinet-shrines (chösam), used for housing statues, are remarkable for their intricacy.

Zurchung Rabsel

The first room behind the Reception Hall is a small audience chamber used for receiving foreign visitors. Dalai Lamas sealed their official documents here and from time to time held personal debates on philosophical subjects. Along the right wall are three large chösams containing some fine bronzes, including three animal-headed deities and a Vijaya (Namgyalma).

Gönpo Khang

Beyond Zurchung Rabsel is Gönpo Khang, a small square chapel. This is the personal chapel of the Dalai Lama and contains statues of the protector Mahakala in its multiple forms. The principal deities are the six-armed Mahakala, Palden Lhamo, and Dorje Drakden.

Zimchung Chime Namgyal ('Bedroom of Immortal Happiness')

The innermost chamber of the Nyiwö Shar suite is the small ornate bedroom of the 14th Dalai Lama. His yellow iron bed and personal belongings (clock, calendar) remain in the exact condition they were in when the clock stopped in 1959. The principal statues on the large altar form the longevity triad of Tsepame, Tara, and Vijaya. Above the bed is a mural of Tsong Khapa.

NYIWÖ NUB SONAM LEKHYIL (QUARTERS OF THE 13TH DALAI LAMA; WEST)

These are the original chambers used by the Great Fifth and all successive Dalai Lamas except the 14th, who took the Nyiwö Shar (or eastern) suite. The Sonam Lekhyil, like its counterpart the Gadhen Kunsel, is ornate. Used primarily as the personal chapel of the Dalai Lama, this was where minor official ceremonies took place. A special ritual was enacted here every year when the Dalai Lama changed into his summer dress. Cabinet ministers met with him in this room and the Chinese Ambans were granted audiences here.

Zimchung Phuntsok Dhokhyil (Bedroom)

The murals in this bedroom are purported to be by the hand of the 13th Dalai Lama.

Zimchung Ganden Yangtse

This chamber was the resting room of the Dalai Lama, where he sometimes discussed official matters with his secretary and cabinet ministers. Thubwang Tazurma, a tutelary divinity of the Dalai Lamas, is the main image. Other statues in the room include Je Tashi Dhokharma, Drölma Lingma, Lopön Rinpoche, and the Fifth Dalai Lama.

Tshomchen Shar (Great Eastern Assembly Hall)

The centerpiece and largest room of the Potrang Karpo is the Tshomchen Shar, site of all the most important state ceremonies. Above this hall is a vast interior atrium, fully three storys high, which extends from the roof terrace down to the Tshomchen. The entire palace is configured around this magnificent hall and its airy open spaces. With a south-facing entrance, it measures 25.8 m by 27.8 m. All the Dalai Lamas were crowned here. Indeed, numerous ceremonies and rituals took place in the Tschomchen Shar, including the acceptance of credentials and gifts from Chinese envoys, and the formal offering of New Year wishes to the Dalai Lama by high clergy and officials. Above the throne of the Dalai Lama is a plaque with Chinese and Tibetan inscriptions given by the Qing Emperor Tongzhi. It reads: 'May the emancipating service of Dharma be spread over all the Universe.' Most of the murals were commissioned by the Fifth Dalai Lama. These depict the origin and evolution of the Tibetan people, and the subsequent development of the country's culture, religion, and history. Other paintings tell the history and legends associated with the various Dalai Lamas. These were painted by Sonam Rabten, personal treasurer of the Fifth.

POTRANG MARPO ('THE RED PALACE')

Potrang Marpo's primary function was religious. It contained, first and foremost, the golden tombs of eight Dalai Lamas. The rest of the edifice is made up of the main assembly hall, numerous chapels and shrines, and libraries for the Buddhist canon, the *Tengyur* and the *Kangyur*. The yellow building between the Red and White Palaces housed giant *thangkas*, which hung across the south face of the Potala during New Year's festivals. On the four sides of the main assembly hall (Tshomchen Nub) are the large two-story chapels, the most important in the palace after those associated with Songtsen Gampo. Above the great hall, three floors

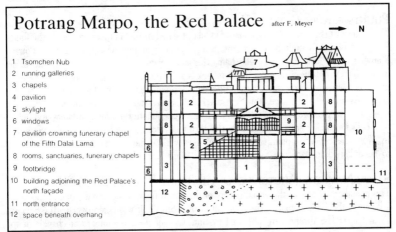

Potrang Marpo, the Red Palace after F. Meyer → N

1 Tsomchen Nub
2 running galleries
3 chapels
4 pavilion
5 skylight
6 windows
7 pavilion crowning funerary chapel of the Fifth Dalai Lama
8 rooms, sanctuaries, funerary chapels
9 footbridge
10 building adjoining the Red Palace's north façade
11 north entrance
12 space beneath overhang

of running galleries extend along the sides of the atrium. To the rear of these are more chapels. Access between each gallery level is by means of ladders through trap doors. Note that the galleries to the west open to the building that houses the tomb of the 13th Dalai Lama.

The south facade of the Potrang Marpo actually extends four more floors below Tshomchen Nub (the Great Western Hall). Behind this lower facade of the palace is a narrow internal space whose northern limits are defined by the slopes of Marpo Ri. This anomalous extension below the hall serves no real function. It was constructed for aesthetic reasons, to harmoniously integrate the south facade of the Potrang Marpo with the Potrang Karpo. The back, or northern, part of the Great Hall rests on solid rock; its front projects out from the slopes and is supported independently.

Access

The Potrang Marpo is reached via a doorway on the west side of the Potrang Karpo's roof. From here travel in a clockwise fashion, slowly descending four floors through the chapels and halls of the Potrang Marpo. The first chapel is the Jamkhang.

Fourth Floor
JAMKHANG; GANDEN PHUNTSOK KHYIL (MAITREYA CHAPEL)

The Jamkhang, on the east side of the fourth floor, was damaged by fire in June, 1984 and later restored. Sadly, many fine *thangkas* were destroyed. The giant seated Jampa (Maitreya) is a finely crafted gilt-copper statue commissioned by the Eighth Dalai Lama. It was erected to honor the deceased mother of the Sixth Panchen Lama, Pelden Yeshe, who was a cousin of the Eighth. According to some sources, the brain of Atisha resides inside the head of the image. On the altar, to the far left, is a statue of the Fifth Dalai Lama, and apparently it contains some of his hair clippings. Other statues in the room include silver images of the Tselha Namsum, Miyowa, Dondrupa Drölma, Misum Gompo, Dukhor, and Guru Rinpoche. The libraries contain the complete sets of the *Kangyur* and *Tengyur*, and to the right of the entrance are shelves of the collected works of the Fifth Dalai Lama.

PHUNTSOK KÖPA (LOLANG KHANG)

The Chapel of the Three Dimensional Mandalas, located in the southeast corner of the fourth floor, was originally built by the regent, Sangye Gyatso, during the construction of Potrang Marpo. In 1749, the Seventh Dalai Lama, Kelsang Gyatso, added to the chapel the three-dimensional mandalas of Jikje (west), Demchok (east), and Sangwa Düpa (center). These mandalas represent the three principal tantric deities propitiated by the Gelugpa.

As an act of homage, the Seventh Dalai Lama's statue rests at the far end of the room, next to his throne. A few hundred small statues denote the principal lamas and deities of Tibet's four major sects. Murals from the 18th C. depict the life history of Kelsang Gyatso. In 1756, the Seventh commissioned several new works. One depicts the first seven monks to be ordained in Tibet by Santarakshita and Guru Rinpoche.

SASUM NAMGYAL (VICTORY OVER THE THREE WORLDS CHAPEL)

This chamber, off the south-central gallery of the fourth floor, was originally one of the living quarters of the Dalai Lama. In the first half of the 18th C., it was taken over by the Seventh Dalai Lama. The throne here was used by him. One of the most important chapels in the

Potrang Marpo, this room witnessed a number of momentous ceremonies and rituals. Among these was the lottery test to determine the legitimacy of a new Dalai Lama.

The most remarkable statue here is the thousand-armed Chenresi at the west side of the chapel. It was commissioned by the 13th Dalai Lama and required over 285 kilos of silver. North of this is the Seventh Dalai Lama's throne. A painting of the Chinese Emperor Qianlong (1735–97), the great Manchu ruler who helped drive the Gurkhas out of Tibet, hangs on the north wall. Beneath this is an ornate plaque framed by four dragons, inscribed in four languages: Tibetan, Chinese, Manchu, and Mongolian. It proclaims, 'May Emperor Kangxi live for thousands and thousands of years.' This plaque was commissioned in 1722 and presented to the Seventh Dalai Lama, then only 14 years old, to celebrate the 61st anniversary of Kangxi's coronation. The painting served as a gift for the occasion of the Eighth Dalai Lama's coronation in 1762. Around the plaque are statues of Yabse Sum, Atisha, the Seventh Dalai Lama, the Fourth and Sixth Panchen Lamas, and others.

On the wall to the left of the glass-covered altar are the 120 volumes of the Manchu edition of the *Kangyur*, the most valuable set of texts in the Potala. Display cases show off these finely crafted works. The colorful manuscript covers are especially sumptuous. Inscriptions, on a black background, are in the three languages of Manchu, Chinese, and Tibetan, bordered by elaborate jewel-encrusted images of *bodhisattvas* and the Buddha.

ZIMCHUNG KADAM KHYIL; CHIME DHEDHEN ('CHAPEL OF IMMORTAL HAPPINESS')

Located in the southwest corner of the fourth floor, this chapel is sometimes called Tsepak Lhakhang. Designed as a residence, this elaborate room, which is the largest on the floor, was taken over by the Sixth Dalai Lama for his private quarters. He lived here between 1697 and 1706. The throne in the chamber was used by him. In 1797, the Eighth turned this into a chapel and erected new statues to commemorate the Sixth. Centered on the altar is the statue of Amitayus.

An important object here is the unusual, probably early, image of Lokeshvara, which stylistically resembles the famous one inside the Phakpa Lhakhang. A thousand small statues of the Longevity deity (Tsepame) sit in small niches around the walls. Also in the chapel are statues of the Lamrin lineage, all in gilt, the 16 Arhats, the Four Guardians and many others. A statue of Tsong Khapa on the west wall came from China, and an unusual image in gilt-copper of Ekajati, the red, wrathful guardian of the Dzokchen practice, is encircled by a ring of flames. The wall paintings depict all major Kadampa lamas as well as important Indian kings.

SERDHUNG GELEK DHOJO (TOMB OF 13TH DALAI LAMA)

Outside the Chime Dhedhen is a long corridor that leads west to a large chapel housing the celebrated tomb of the 13th Dalai Lama. At the end of this passage is a small chamber. From here you can either walk down to enter the chapel at ground level or go in directly to arrive at a high, encircling gallery. The tomb itself is an ornate structure built between 1934 and 1936. Within it, the body of the 13th Dalai Lama, like those of his predecessors, is entombed in salt. Unlike other Dalai Lama tombs, this one is well lit by sunlight streaming in from the chapel windows. The tomb is the second highest in the Potala at 13 m. In front of the *chörten* is a silver statue of the 13th Dalai Lama. Inside the *chörten* window is a gilt-copper statue of the 11-faced Chenresi. On the altar is the celebrated three-dimensional mandala called Mutik Mandal, made of more than 20,000 pearls. Notice the intricate pagoda, studded with turquoise on top, and the small pearl-crafted figures of horses and human figures at the base. Ceiling hangings (*drachi rawa*) are suspended from the galleries. The myriad pieces of fine brocade and embroidery, creating images of lamas, *bodhisattvas*, and *garudas*, are meticulously joined together to form the decoration. Wall murals trace the principal events in the Dalai Lama's prolific life. On either side of the entrance is a modern painting showing him surrounded by ministers, teachers, and other 20th-C. personages. One of the most interesting scenes shows the 13th on a pilgrimage to India, his visit to the British India Office, and his meeting with India's foreign minister.

PHAKPA LHAKHANG

Near the northwest corner of the fourth floor is a small cramped room. Tradition claims this is the all-important chapel built by King Songtsen Gampo in the 7th century. This and its counterpart, the Chögyal Drubphuk, located one floor below, together constitute the most ancient part of the Potala. The two chambers were integrated into the Potrang Marpo 1,100 years later.

The Phakpa Lhakhang, filled to the brim with priceless statues, is considered by Tibetan pilgrims to be the most sacred shrine in the Potala. The primary object of veneration is a statue of Arya Lokeshvara, a deified object that appeared on earth through self-manifestation (*rangjung*). Access to the chapel is via a set of steep triple-stairs. The central stairs, for exclusive use by the Dalai Lama, are barricaded. Above the entrance is a large plaque in Chinese, Tibetan, and Manchu characters. Presented by the 19th-C. Manchu Emperor Tongzhi, the inscription proclaims Buddhism a 'Blessed Field of Amazing Fruits'. The small central statue of Arya Lokeshvara, a standing Padmapani representing the chosen tutelary divinity of Songtsen Gampo, is ancient and jewel-encrusted. Flanking it are two attendants: the right one a blue Drölma, the left a Chenresi; both are made of white sandalwood. After the original palace's construction on Marpo Ri, Songtsen Gampo's monk attendant, known for his magical powers, brought back from the forests of southern Tibet four sandalwood statues. These 'self-manifested' when the trunk of a sandalwood tree split open. One of the four is here in this chapel.

Left of these three central figures are the statues of the Tenth Dalai Lama and Tsong Khapa. To the right are the Eighth and Ninth Dalai Lamas. Along the walls are numerous other statues: a Chenresi Karsapani brought from Tsang Tanak, the Eight Spiritual Sons made of red sandalwood and commissioned by the Fifth Dalai Lama, an 11-faced Chenresi, a Sakyamuni and the attendant 16 Arhats, brought from China, and three silver statues of the Rigsum Gönpo.

On the left wall, within a cabinet, are three sacred stones impressed with footprints. Tradition states that the left one belongs to Guru Rinpoche. It was brought from the Gungthang La near Dzongka, north of the Mangyul Kyirong Valley (see page 924), when the Indian teacher finally left Tibet for Zangdhok Pelri, his mythical paradise. The center footprint is Tsong Khapa's while the right belongs to Nagarjuna, the renowned Indian master. Opposite this cabinet is a large, wrathful Vajrapani. To the right of the door, inside a shrine, sits an old image of Atisha. One of the most striking works of art within this sacred chapel is a jade (*yangtri*) statue of Drogön Phagpa Lodrö Gyaltsen seated on a jade throne.

TASHI WÖBAR SERDHUNG (TOMB OF THE SEVENTH DALAI LAMA)

To the right of the Phakpa Lhakhang, this chapel with an elaborate multi-doored entrance is usually closed to the public. The Jangchub ('Enlightenment') *chörten*-tomb (9 m), containing much gold and nearly 100,000 precious stones, is surrounded by four large statues. In front of the reliquary is a three-dimensional Paradise of Jampa. Along the south wall is a seated Jampa flanked by *chösam* and library shelves.

GELEK ZIBAR SERDHUNG (TOMB OF THE EIGHTH DALAI LAMA)

Left of the Phakpa Lhakhang. Built in 1805, the *chörten* is placed close to the north wall. A statue of the Eighth sits in the southwest. In the tomb's window is a solid gold statue of 11-faced Chenresi. An embroidered *thangka* of Nyatri Tsenpo, the mythical first king of Tibet, hangs in front of the *chörten*. There is also a valuable Sakyamuni statue called Thuwang Dhudhul, erected by the Ninth Dalai Lama. This tomb is to the left of Phakpa Lhakhang, on the fourth floor.

SASUM NGONGA SERDHUNG (TOMB OF THE NINTH DALAI LAMA)

This tomb, on the west side of the fourth floor, holds the opulent, gold *chörten* of the Ninth. Flanking the *chörten* are library shelves and a silver image of the Ninth rests in the room's southwest corner. Across the room is a silver Tsong Khapa, next to 114 volumes of a gold-written *Kangyur*, gift of Sangye Gyatso. Statues of the 16 Arhats were commissioned by the Eighth Dalai Lama; to their right are clay images of various tutelary deities. The wall paintings depict the 1,000 Tsepames. On either side of the tomb are auxiliary chapels, the Gönkhang to the west, and the Neten Lhakhang to the east.

Third Floor

DÜKHOR LHAKHANG (THE KALACHAKRA CHAPEL)

The Kalachakra Chapel stands on the east side extension of the third floor. Its most striking object is a large, gilt-copper three-dimensional mandala on a round dais. Known as Langzak Chengyi Dükhor, it represents the mystical paradise-palace of the principal deity of Dukhor (Kalachakra). This superbly crafted artefact, with its numerous levels filled with figures and shrines, was erected by Sangye Gyatso and remains in excellent condition. The meticulously detailed mandala measures 6.2 m in diameter. Notice also the beautiful Chinese brocades covering the ceiling above the model.

A life-size image of the Dükhor with its consort stands by the window, while small statues of the 172 lamas who held the lineage of the Kalachakra practice line the wall to the left. On the right are shelves containing the seven religious kings of mythical Shambala and the 25 spiritual leaders (*kalki*) who ruled the kingdom after the royal dynasties. Other objects of note: one gilt Jangchub *chörten*, eight silver Dheshek *chörtens*, one gilt Jangchub *chörten* containing an 11-faced Chenresi, and 38 statues of the divinities belonging to the Kalachakra *tantra*. At the far end of the room, opposite the chapel entrance, is an image of Jampelyang (Manjusri) riding a lion. Pelden Lhamo, within a small shrine, is by the window at the right hand corner. Next to the door is a seated figure of Guru Rinpoche.

The murals duplicate the statues and show the lineages of Shambala, and the Kalachakra lamas. An interesting panel shows the king of Shambala and his troops waging a war against the human world. According to Buddhist cosmology, this is the battle that destroys the universe.

THÜWANG KHANG (THE SAKYAMUNI CHAPEL)

The main images in this chapel are along the west wall; flanking the central Sakyamuni are the Eight Spiritual Sons. The throne was once used by the Seventh Dalai Lama, although it was the Eighth who decorated most of this chapel. Across from the throne is a set of hand-written Kangyur, and above this are thangkas of the Eight Medicine Buddhas.

TSEPAK LHAKHANG (CHAPEL OF THE AMITAYUS)

The Nine Buddhas of Longevity are the principal images of this chapel. Next to these are the Drölkar (White Tara) and Dröljang (Green Tara). In the center of the room is a U-shaped altar. Partitions to the east, west and north sides allow for circumambulation. A mural shows the Potala during the reign of the Eighth Dalai Lama. Another mural, by the left window, depicts the master builder, Tangton Gyalpo, and his monastery of Chuwori Chaksam at Chusul.

CHÖGYAL DRUBPHUK

(Near the northwest corner; directly below the Phakpa Lhakhang on the fourth floor.) The Chögyal Drubphuk and the Phakpa Lhakhang are the Potala's most ancient chambers. Tradition holds that this was the cave where King Songtsen Gampo meditated, and it is positioned on the same level as the Marpo Ri. On its east side, a small room contains a white chörten that corresponds to the sacred stone cairn (lhatse) usually found on mountain tops or passes.

The small, dim chapel, with a total of 28 statues, has only one principal column. This, the most massive and most ancient, is located off center, towards the northeast corner. The secondary, less substantial square columns, (seven; one near the west wall and six in a cluster near the east wall) seem to be later additions. They are poorly integrated into the overall design. The principal column, unlike the others, has no capital or entablature at the top to provide the usual interface between column and ceiling. Perhaps this is because it actually extends upwards into the floor above to the Phakpa Lhakhang. The south face of the column's upper portion holds a small statue of the Fifth Dalai Lama, and at the base is a stove supposedly used by King Songtsen Gampo. Along the side walls are benches used to display the 28 statues. Most of the images are made of clay and richly robed. The freshness of the paint around the hairdos and the new clothing suggest that they have been restored recently.

Chögyal Drubphuk contains a total of seven representations of deities; the rest of the images depict temporal figures. Chenresi appears twice, once behind and to the left of the main Songtsen Gampo (north wall) statue and once in the southeast corner. A small Sakyamuni sits in front of the Seventh Dalai Lama (west). The Buddha Bhagavat, also along the west wall, is behind Thönmi Sambhota. Namthose, sitting on a white lion, is to the right of the entrance. The largest (1.5 m) of these seven statues is Jampa, second image from the left of the entrance. Its striking wood halo, similar in color and design to the main column, has beneath it a five-pointed diadem studded with precious stones—this crowns Jampa's head. To the left of this is a Drölkar statue.

The Great Fifth is at the center of the north wall, to the right of Songtsen Gampo. His facial features are unusually fine. On the chapel's main pillar is the second image of the Fifth. Along the west wall, to the right of the single pillar, are statues of two Dalai Lamas. Gungru Gungtsen, Songtsen Gampo's son, is at the northwest corner, while Tsong Khapa is at the northeast. The Gungtang Lama is right of the entrance, to the left of Chenresi. The most important group of images depicts King Songtsen Gampo and his retinue. There are three statues of the king. The main one (see below), at the north wall, corresponds stylistically to the two queens to his left. It has a high turban from the center of which emerges the head of Wöpame. The other two kings are smaller and have white turbans. The southernmost of these is flanked by his Chinese and Nepalese queens. The other has Tsong Khapa and Thönmi Sambhota at his sides; the Tibetan queen, Mongza Tricham, is behind, to his right.

There are two statues of the Nepalese Queen Tritsun, incarnation of the Green Tara. One is near the center of the north wall, the other near the center of the east wall. The Chinese Princess Wencheng can be seen at the northeast and the southeast corners; she personifies the White Tara. A notable statue is Queen Mongza. Resting on an elevated dais, by her left knee is a baby clothed in gold and green—the future king of Tibet, Gungru Gungtsen.

Statues of Thönmi Sambhota, the king's minister, stand near the northwest corner, next to Sakyamuni, and at the center of the east wall. The former wears an orange turban; its counterpart has a white turban and holds a book. The larger of two Gar images is placed immediately east of the main pillar, curiously out of alignment with the rest of the statues along the east wall. Stylistically, it is one of the most exceptional in the chapel. The visage is markedly aquiline: sharp nose, elongated eyes, and well-defined eyebrows. Under the outer brocade robes, an inner one with straight pleats can be glimpsed. In general, the facial expression of this image is livelier and more refined than that of the principal statue of the king (north wall), which is perhaps blunted by the repeated applications of thick gold paint. There is no doubt that Gar's visage is distinctly more European than Asian.

The statues of Songtsen Gampo and his wives are unique among the many representing the triad in Tibet. Their features are neither overtly Chinese nor Indian. A touch of Greco–Buddhist influence, reminiscent of the Gupta Gandhara era (4th–7th C.), is a probable element in these exceptional works of art. The archaic, well-preserved statues (north wall) of King Songtsen Gampo and his two wives also differ significantly from the Tibetan style found in later monastic institutions (the early 15th-C. statues of the three kings in Gyantse, for example, are quite different). Songtsen Gampo wears a loose, belted dress under a shawl. Because of its flowing nature, the dress hints at a Chinese inspiration. Its design, however, with some similarities to a fitted tunic, reminds one of a Central Asian origin, perhaps Persian. The shawl, loosely draped over the shoulders, looks like the shoulder scarves typically worn by bodhisattvas in mid- and late-Tang paintings at Dunhuang. Its use, unique to this depiction of the king, is not part of the vocabulary of Chinese or Persian design. Like traditional Chinese costume, the wide borders of the dress overlap diagonally on the chest regions; the right side crosses over to the left. The wide, prominent belt is made of square plaques, each decorated with a floral design. Its craftsmanship resembles a Kushan-period (1st–2nd C.) statue of King Kanishka, first Buddhist king of the Kushans. Such plaques occur with regularity on various bodhisattva statues attributed to the mid-Tang era (8th C.) at Dunhuang. Although this design probably had its genesis in the Persian–Kushan period, it was later adopted in Central Asian Buddhist art, especially at the Silk Road oases. The belt seems also to indicate rank or royalty; it is wider than ones worn by his ministers.

In general, Songtsen Gampo's attire owes its stylistic origins to the Persians. These characteristics, however, have been modified over time by religious conventions and Chinese influences. The king's body and his smooth, relaxed face are distinguished by a sense of realism untouched by exaggeration. These characteristics set it apart from most Tibetan statues. The refined structure of the face recalls aspects of Gandharan and Central Asian sculpture that first surfaced in the Kushan era and then survived in Central Asia and northwest India into the 7th century. It reminds the onlooker that Tibet imported a good deal of Buddhism and its attendant artistic culture from Kashmir in the 7th century.

A striking attribute of the statue is the steadfastness of its features; the king is at ease and at peace with the world. There is none of the powerful, penetrating projection of personality usually associated with a major figure. His authority is understated, and yet subtly apparent. This trait of gentleness is in common with other sculptural works of the mid-8th to mid-9th century. Works of the 10th C. and later generally show more tension in the body and face, thus imbuing a sense of drama and forcefulness. The sophisticated and diverse renderings of the clothing draped over the body are similar to forms crafted in the mid- and late-Tang Dynasty (750–850). The folds over the lap, the arms, and the pedestal of the king are characteristic of that period. Perhaps the most unusual textural features are the strongly creased triangular patterns around the waist-belt. One possible source for this seldom-seen technique is Central Asia of the mid-8th century.

From a purely stylistic point of view, it is likely that the statue was created between 750–850. During the reigns of the great Buddhist kings, Trisong Detsen (r 755–97) and Ralpachen (r 815–38), literary sources confirm that foreign artists from China, Nepal, and Khotan came to Tibet to help decorate the temples of Samye and Ushangdo. The sculptor who worked on this terracotta image showed no overwhelmingly Chinese, Nepalese, or Indic stylistic signatures. Thus the case may be made that a Tibetan or Central Asian was responsible for this masterpiece. The body's strong and sturdy form, imbued with a well-defined gentleness, points to a distinct Tibetan sensibility.

Images of the two queens flanking Songtsen Gampo are stylistically similar to the king and are probably derived from the same period. The tall alert figure of Wencheng, with prominent rounded breasts, recalls female sculptures of Persia, and of Gandhara. Her face is typically Central Asian. Tritsun, the Nepalese queen, resembles closely the Pala tradition. Wencheng is in a meditative pose, connoting wisdom; Tritsun is in the adorative pose, radiating faith. The two are in perfect harmony with Songtsen Gampo's compassion. This trio of 8th–9th C. statues is unquestionably among the earliest and most magnificent in all Tibet. In artistic terms, it is the equal of Buddha and his cycle of eight bodhisattvas at the 8th-C. monastery of Kachu (see page 378).

KUNZANG JEDRO KHANG

This chapel, east of the Chögyal Drubphuk, is comprised of an outer and inner room (Lima Lhakhang). Both contain numerous statues made of solid li, a special Tibetan alloy. At the center is the throne of Nyiwö Sonam Lekhyil, the lama who introduced the Samantabhadra practice. Statues include Tsong Khapa, Tsepame, the six-armed Gönpo, and Palden Lhamo.

Second Floor

All the chapels on this floor are closed to the public. The galleries running along the interior atrium are well known for their extensive murals, created at the time of the the Potrang Marpo's construction but repainted at a later date. The building of the Potala and important monasteries are the most interesting subjects. Other scenes depict the Mönlam ('Great Prayer') Festival and the funeral procession of the Great Fifth. A most charming panel shows various events, such as archery, horse racing, and wrestling, enacted during the festival for the completion of the Potrang Marpo.

Ground Floor

The large Tshomchen Nub, the geographic center of the Potrang Marpo, is reached by climbing down a number of steep, dark stairwells from the second floor.

TSHOMCHEN NUB; SIZHI PHUNTSOK
(THE GREAT WESTERN ASSEMBLY HALL)

The Tshomchen Nub, the largest hall in the Potala (725 sq m), is dedicated to the Fifth Dalai Lama. It has eight tall and 36 short pillars, all wrapped in thick woven woollens; this strong, white material is typically Bhutanese in style and pattern. A striking pair of huge embroidered curtains hangs along the west wall. A gift from the Kangxi Emperor, these magnificent textiles are among the most revered and priceless works of art in the Potala. The curtains took skilled workmen a year to complete and depict the Three Yarlung Kings, Songtsen Gampo, Trisong Detsen, and Ralpachen, the Dalai Lamas, and other famous historical figures.

Large embroidered *thangkas* hang at the cardinal points of the hall. To the north is a hanging called 'Bozo Yölma Tshedrubma'. Its right half displays Wöpame and flanking this are the figures of the Indian Emperor Ashoka (Nya Ngenme) and Serzang Drime. The principal image on the left is Chödrak Gyatso Yang; Ngön Khyen Gyalpo and Gyalwa Jampa are to the right and left. These are surrounded by the 35 Tathagatas. Along the east wall a similar *thangka* depicts the four principal divinities of the Kadampa sect. These are flanked by the Eight Great Bodhisattvas and the Eight Manifestations of Drölma. Sakyamuni is the main figure of the large southern *thangka*. He is flanked by Wösung and Jampa. The 16 Arhats surround them. To the left are the Medicine Buddha, Yongdrak Palgyi Gyalpo and Drayang Gyalpo, encircled by seven Buddhas, Rigsum Gönpo and the Eight Medicine Buddhas.

A large throne used exclusively by the Sixth Dalai Lama dominates the assembly hall in the west. Above it is a plaque in Chinese from the Qianlong Emperor. Over 280 sq m of original murals date from the end of the 17th century. Many small scenes illustrating the life of the Fifth Dalai Lama surround large images of the Tibetan Buddhist pantheon. Paintings also show the mythical Paradise of Potala and the various historical Kings of Tibet.

The elaborately carved capitals and entablatures of the pillars are some of the finest and most intricate work in the Potala. Notice the small shrines at the top of each pillar, all housing tiny deities.

Four of the largest and most important chapels in the Potala abut the Tshomchen Nub, creating a floor plan deliberately designed as part of a giant mandala. The western one houses the Fifth Dalai Lama's incredible tomb. These four side chapels (see below) contain primarily funerary *chörtens* and large gilt-silver statues commissioned by the Regent Sangye Gyatso. The statues were most likely cast from similar molds.

LAMRIN ('STAGES ON THE PATH TO ENLIGHTENMENT') LHAKHANG

This chapel, attached to the Tshomchen Nub's east side, is smaller than the other three. Tsong Khapa, founder of the Gelugpa sect, wrote a definitive study on the Lamrin—a detailed step-by-step practice that ultimately leads to enlightenment. The Lamrin Lhakhang is dedicated to this tradition of instruction and the two primary teachers of its lineage, Gyachen Chögyue and Zabmo Tagyue. Statues of the chapel represent Kadampa and Gelugpa personages associated with Lamrin. In the center is Tsong Khapa, a statue made of solid silver, painted in gold. To the right is Thokme, a teacher in the Gyachen Chögyue tradition. Next to him are lamas of the same lineage. Left of Tsong Khapa is Gönpo Ludrub, better known as Nagarjuna, founder of the Madyamika. Along the right wall are two Jangchub *chörtens*. Notice the charming, finely worked wood carvings of horses, mythical creatures (*shang shang*), and elephants below the statue cabinets.

RIGDZIN LHAKHANG (THE PRECEPTOR CHAPEL)

This chapel, to the south, has 20 columns. The preceptors are Guru Rinpoche and seven other Indian masters who lived during or just before the 8th century. Masters of the Mahayoga tradition, these eight—known as Rigdzin Chenpo Gye—each received a particular tantric practice (*sadhana*) from the hallowed burial ground of Bodh Gaya, India, site of Buddha's enlightenment. Guru Rinpoche took the teachings to Tibet and taught them to 25 disciples at Samye Chimpu (see page 631).

The central image of this two-story room is Guru Rinpoche, backed by an elaborate halo and topped with a finely worked *garuda*. This silver statue weighs nearly 40 kilos. Flanking it are small gilt-copper statues of the Guru's consorts, Yeshe Tsogyal and Mandarawa. Next to Yeshe Tsogyal are the eight statues of Rigdzin Chenpo Gye. On the right wall, next to Mandarawa, are the Eight Manifestations of Guru Rinpoche, known collectively as Guru Tsengye. All statues are of silver and painted gold. Along the east, south, and west walls are tomes of a superb *Kangyur* written in gold and black ink.

SERDHUNG DZAMLING GYENCHIK ('SOLE ORNAMENT OF THE UNIVERSE')

The tomb of the Fifth Dalai Lama is housed in the west chapel. This monumental funerary *chörten*, built of sandalwood and measuring over 14 m in height, nearly reaches the roof-terrace of the Potrang Marpo. It is the highest *chörten* in the Potala. A gilt-copper pagoda roof above the chapel underscores the significance of the site. A staggering 3,700 kilos of gold 'thick as a cow's hide' embellish the tomb's outer walls. In addition, its large upper window has a solid gold 11-faced Chenresi statue.

The Tenth and 12th Dalai Lamas did not live long enough to rule and thus were not accorded personal funerary chapels. Their *chörten* tombs instead are placed in the western part of the Dzamling Gyenchik chapel.

The Sixth Dalai Lama, Tsangyang Gyatso, was well known for his unorthodox views and behavior. He was the only Dalai Lama, out of 14, who can be truly considered a maverick. His love songs are well known among Tibetans, a reflection of his love of women and wine. He was deposed by Lhajang Khan, the Qosot Mongol, who invaded Tibet and conquered Lhasa in 1705. Tsangyang Gyatso was exiled to China and died en route. His tomb is reputed to be in the Tsho Ngön Serkhok Monastery near Kokonor.

The small tomb, Serdhung Khamsum Gyenchok, of the Tenth Dalai Lama stands to the right. Gold-written sets of the *Kangyur* and *Tengyur* as well as the complete works of Tsong Khapa and his disciples rest near this tomb. The murals depict Palden Lhamo, Mahakala, and other divinities. On the left is the tomb, Serdhung Tshejin Wöbar, of the 12th Dalai Lama. Its butter lamps are made of solid gold. Flanking the Fifth Dalai Lama's tomb are eight lesser *chörtens* called Tathagata Chörtens, receptacles for supposed relics of the Buddha. A mural of the Great Fifth is on the east wall, and three fine large *thangkas* hang in the hall.

TRUNGRAB LHAKHANG (THE LINEAGE CHAPEL)

This north chapel derives its name from the array of statues of the first five Dalai Lamas. A surprising feature here is the equal status given the Great Fifth and Sakyamuni Buddha. Similarly sized images share a joint throne; Sakyamuni is solid gold, and the Fifth is solid silver. In front are expertly carved birds and animals, all in wood. Notice the fine *toranas* behind the statues, carved with *garuda* and *lumo* (female subterranean deity) statues.

To the right of the Fifth are Chenresi, Songtsen Gampo, and Dromtönpa. By the entrance (north) is the tomb containing the relics of the 17-year-old 11th Dalai Lama. Built as a Jangchub *chörten*, this monument is known as Serdhung Phendhe Wöbar. Within its window is a solid silver statue of Songtsen Gampo. Between this and the center altar are statues of the Eight Medicine Buddhas and the Buddhas of the Three Ages. At the far right of the hall is a statue of Tsarchen Lösel Gyatso, the Sakyapa founder of the Tsar sub-sect. A complete set of *Tengyur*, on library shelves ranged along the east and north walls and behind the principal images, was offered to the Seventh Dalai Lama by the Emperor Yongle in 1725. The set of gold *Kangyur* was a gift from Sangye Gyatso. A plaque over the entrance proclaims in Chinese and Tibetan: 'The most precious and excellent Yellow Hat tradition'.

DEYANG NUB

The external western courtyard fronting the entrance porch of the Potrang Marpo serves to center and create a point of unity for the various components of Namgyal Tratsang, the Potala's own monastery. Below the courtyard's flagstone floor are several levels of storerooms. The southern perimeter of the Deyang Nub is a row of monks' residences perched on top of a high wall, which displays the giant cloth appliqué *thangkas* (*gheku*) during festivals.

NAMGYAL TRATSANG

The Potala's own monastery was founded by the Third Dalai Lama, Sonam Gyatso, before he left for Mongolia. Its original premises were within Drepung Monastery, but the Fifth Dalai Lama later moved the monastery here. The murals are noteworthy; they mainly depict the various protectors and the principal lamas of Tibet's four main sects. The Four Guardians, The Five Protectors, and other divinities adorn the outer walls. To the right and left of the Deyang Nub stairs are paintings of the Four Guardians, Tenma, Chamsing, and Dorje Drakden.

RAMOCHE: THE MONASTERY OF PRINCESS WENCHENG

OVERVIEW

Ramoche's historical importance is only exceeded by the Jokhang. In 641, the Chinese Princess Wencheng came to Tibet to marry King Songtsen Gampo. Part of her dowry was the sacred Jowo statue, a representation of Sakyamuni as a 12-year-old boy. After a long and arduous journey, it finally arrived in Lhasa on a wooden cart, which then became thoroughly mired in the sand at Ramoche's present site. Wencheng divined that beneath the earth was the Paradise of the Water Divinities. As an appropriate offering to the subterranean King of the Nagas, she built a monastery to house the Jowo. Local and Chinese artists and craftsmen took one year to construct Ramoche; it was completed at the same time as the Jokhang (mid-7th C.).

During the reign of Mangsong Mangtsen (649–76), there were rumors that armies of the Tang empire were about to invade Tibet. The Jowo statue was therefore hidden inside a secret chamber (Menlha Desheg Gye chapel) in the Jokhang. The expected invasion never materialized. In 710, another Chinese princess, Jincheng, arrived from China to marry King Tride Tsugten (see page 386). She took the statue out of hiding and placed it within the Jowo chapel, its present location in the Jokhang. Ramoche needed a substitute statue as a centerpiece, so one brought by the Nepalese Princess Tritsun (Brikuti) was installed.

The original temple of Ramoche was entirely a Chinese-style structure. After a number of fires, it was rebuilt in the Tibetan manner. In 1474, Kunga Döndrup, a disciple of Tsong Khapa, presided over Ramoche. It then became the assembly hall of the Gyürtö Tratsang, Lhasa's Upper Tantric College (now destroyed). Ramoche presently has about 60 monks.

The site

Ramoche is located 1/2 km north of the junction of Dekyi Shar Lam and the Barkhor market (Tsomsikhang). Having undergone intensive restoration since 1985, it is now in good shape and has a thriving monastic community. The site, facing east, consists of a gatehouse, a *khorlam*, and the main three-story temple; a large courtyard precedes all these. The foyer, part of the three-story gatehouse, has ten 16-sided columns. Flanking the entrance are two rows of eight *mani* wheels. Along the foyer's back walls are damaged murals (Four Guardians, various paradises). The second and third floors have makeshift chapels and rooms for monks; this part of Ramoche is a late addition. Beyond the entrance is the *khorlam* corridor that completely encloses the main monastery. Its south, west, and north sections have long rows of new *mani* wheels similar to those of the Jokhang Nangkhor. The walls have newly painted images of Tsepame, Drölkar, Namgyalma, and other deities.

THE MAIN BUILDING

After entering the main building, reach a wide entrance corridor. The entire left side opens onto a chapel called the *drubkhang*. Behind a glass window along the chapel's west wall is an unusual Gönpo statue constructed of tree branches. One of four interesting pillars once supported a stone slab with Princess Wencheng's handprint. On the surfaces of the capitals, near the ceiling, are wood carvings depicting lions, humans, cloud-and-vase designs, and Atlantis-type figures upholding the ceiling. The beams have inscriptions in Sanskrit of the holy Six Syllables. All the bas-reliefs are archaic and might date from Ramoche's inception. The corridor's right wall has a painting of Dorje Yudruma, the protectress of the Gyürtö College. At the far end of the corridor is the *dukhang's* entrance. Right of this is a statue of Chana Dorje.

DUKHANG

This assembly hall, renovated in 1985, has 27 lion sculptures below the central skylight. All original murals have been destroyed. A long row of images, enclosed in wood-and-glass shrines, sits at the back of the hall (these obscure the inner Jowo Khang and its entrance). The Dalai Lama's throne is at the *dukhang's* center. Left of it is Kunga Thöndrup, first abbot of the Gyürtö Tratsang, enclosed in a shrine. A cabinet contains the three statues of Jowo, Chenresi, and Drölma. Farther to the left is an image of Sangwa Düpa (Guhyasamaja) in a glass case. Along the left wall are the protective deities, Jigje, Demchok, and Sangwa Düpa. Right of the throne are Tsong Khapa, the Fifth Dalai Lama and Sakyamuni. Behind these, inside a glass-and-wood shrine, are the three images of Yabse Sum. All statues are new. Go behind this row of shrines to enter the inner *tsangkhang*.

TSANGKHANG

Facing the west entrance is the all-important Jowo statue, Ramoche's most sacred object. Sitting on a massive stone platform in the center of the room, it is also known as Akshobhya Vajra, a representation of Sakyamuni at the age of eight. The statue is adorned with amazing quantity of precious ornaments and brocade. In spite of its venerable appearance, this Jowo is almost certainly not the 7th-C. original. Flanking the entrance doorway are statues of the Four Guardians; above it are seven small Buddhas.

The *tsangkhang* measures only 5.4 m by 4.4 m and has only two pillars, encased in 3 cm of plaster. Beneath the plaster is a layer of rope; both materials acted to prevent fire and rot. The pillars' upper parts are carved with simple lotus thrones and their capitals have no carvings, a typical feature of early architecture. Nearly all the remaining murals are covered by a thick black coat of soot and smoke. Near the entrance are a few barely legible line paintings. Left and right of the Jowo are clay statues of the Eight Bodhisattvas. Along the rear wall are images of Tsong Khapa and Jampa. Flanking the door are the wrathful figures of Chana Dorje and Tamdrin. Above it is a picture of the Dalai Lama's senior tutor.

Nangkhor The enclosed inner corridor surrounding the *tsangkhang* is narrow but high. This design implies it was built before the 14th C. though the construction material seems to be later.

SECOND FLOOR

The second floor is used primarily as residences. To the rear of the central skylight is a six-column chapel with images of Sangye Lu Gyalpo and the 16 Arhats. An inner chapel has statues of the Eight Medicine Buddhas and a set of the *Kangyur*.

THIRD FLOOR

This floor has six large and small chambers. Its front suite of rooms is reserved for the Dalai Lama. At the back, beyond the open roof (marvelous views), is a chapel crowned with the original gilt, Chinese-style, pagoda roof. It retains mythical decorative ornaments. This east-facing room, enclosed by a narrow *khorlam* (wood balustrade), is Tibetan in design.

TSEPAK LHAKHANG

After visiting Ramoche, walk through the entrance gate onto the street. Make an immediate right turn southward to enter the newly refurbished Tsepak Lhakhang. Pass prayer wheels to the chapel of Tsepame, dominated by three large, new sculptures. Tsepame is flanked on the left by Sakya Thupa and on the right by Jampa. On the walls are the 35 Buddhas and the major lamas of Tibet's four sects; these are outlined in gold on a red background. A *khorlam* surrounds the chamber. Its walls are painted with 1,127 images of Tsepame.

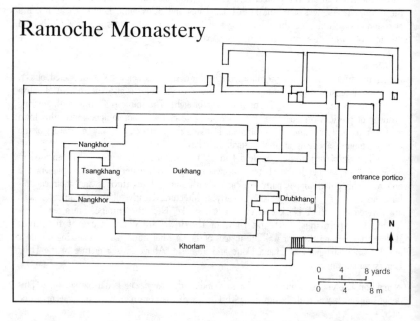

MERU NYINGBA: WHERE THÖNMI SAMBHOTA CREATED THE TIBETAN ALPHABET

The foundation of Meru Nyingba dates back to the 7th C.; King Songtsen Gampo's minister, Thönmi Sambhota, finalized his creation of the Tibetan script at this site. Later, Meru was one of six temples that Ralpachen ordered to be built around the Jokhang. After Langdarma's persecution of Buddhism and Atisha's arrival in Tibet (1042), the community at Meru re-established itself. It converted to the Gelugpa at the time of the Third Dalai Lama (1543–89). The oldest existing structure today is the Zangbala Lhakhang; the main building was constructed in the early 20th C., but the basic configuration of the complex reflects an earlier design. Meru Nyingba is consecrated to the Chökyongs, Guardians of the Buddhist Law. These oracles interpret and communicate the visions and desires of the divinities. Meru Nyingba's prime protector is Dorje Drakden, animator of the Nechung Oracle (see page 165). The safety of all Tibet was entrusted to the Chökyongs. For this reason, the monastery was administered by the Nyingmapa, Gelugpa, and Sakyapa.

Location

The out-of-the-way monastery abuts the Jokhang's southeast corner and is entered via the market along the north section of the Barkhor. From here, a lane goes due south towards the Jokhang complex (right of the lane is Nangtseshag, Lhasa's jail). Follow it past a stone archway to a flight of stairs on the right that leads to a chapel, a branch of Gongkar Chöde, on the second floor. Beyond the set of stairs is a courtyard with an incense burner. The entrance to Meru Nyingba is at the courtyard's north side. Sera Dhaggo is an old wooden entrance on the west side of the complex. By means of this, Sera's monks were able to enter directly into the Jokhang.

GONGKAR CHÖDE BRANCH CHAPEL

The chamber has as its principal image Gönpo Palgön Dramse, a manifestation of Mahakala. This statue resides within an ornate wood shrine flanked by two dragons. Clay statues of Gönpo Gur, Palden Lhamo, and Gönpo with six arms once stood by the west wall; their destroyed bases remains. Attached to a column before the shrine is a long trident and the horns of a deer, ritual implements used by the deity, Gönpo Palgön Dramse. Tibetans know this chapel as part of Meru Nyingba. It is a busy place and an obligatory stop for pilgrims.

ZANGBALA LHAKHANG

This chapel, directly below the Gongkar Chöde branch chapel, constitutes the most ancient section of Meru Nyingba. Ralpachen supposedly constructed this original building, which faces to the east and is only 7.5 m by 7.2 m. Immediately after the entrance is a dim, narrow, circumambulatory corridor. It encircles a tiny shrine, which formerly contained the statue of Zangbala, God of Wealth. The chapel's unusually low ceiling is constructed of thick, heavy beams; the architecture, typical of the Yarlung Dynasty, can be compared to the 8th-C. Kachu

Lhakhang (see page 378). This chapel is said to be the very place where Thönmi Sambhota finished his Tibetan alphabet. Zangbala Lhakhang is considered to be a branch of Nechung Monastery; the State Oracle resided here when in Lhasa. During the Mönlam festival, Nechung's monks congregate at this chapel.

MERU NYINGBA

The principal building of the complex is a three-story structure whose front entrance faces south. Surrounding it on three sides are two-story monks' residences fronted by galleries. This typical cloister design indicates an early construction. During the reign of the 13th Dalai Lama (1895–1933), the Nechung abbot, Sakya Ngape, built the main building along the north wing. The original entrance to the complex, sited at the south wing, was relocated to the northwest corner. Meru Sarpa Monastery was also built at this time (see page 173). The assembly hall was renovated in 1986 and now fairly hums with continuous religious activities.

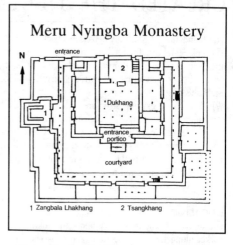

Meru Nyingba Monastery

1 Zangbala Lhakhang 2 Tsangkhang

Two *mani* wheels stand left and right of the main entrance. Murals on the left wall depict Dorje Drakden, the protector who speaks through the Nechung Oracle. Paintings around the skylight show Tsong Khapa and his two disciples, Atisha and retinue, Guru Rinpoche and Trisong Detsen.

The central statue of the *dukhang*, placed on a shrine near the back of the room, is a new Chenresi. To its right is a large, new copper statue of Guru Rinpoche. To the left of Chenresi, under a pagoda shrine, is a mandala constructed of colored sands. Behind the central altar, steps lead to an inner chapel. Flanking this open entranceway are two small ornate shrines enclosing images of the protectors, Dorje Drakden (left) and Palden Lhamo (right). Butter sculptures next to the former depict the episodes of Rigdzin Dungdruk. The main image of this inner chapel is Guru Rinpoche manifested as Guru Nangse Silnyon (one foot sticks out to suppress demons). Above him are: Tsong Khapa, Kuntu Sangpo, and the 13th Dalai Lama. To the left of Guru Rinpoche, from right to left, are: Tamdrin, Sungi Gyalpo, Nyima Zhonnu, and Yönten Gyalpo. Right of him, from left to right, are: Thinle Gyalpo, Thuki Gyalpo, Kuyi Gyalpo, and Thoktsen. Beyond Thoktsen is the miniature palace (*potrang*) of the protective deities, including all-important Pehar Gyalpo. Next to this is the palace for the goddesses (*lhamo*). These rare intricate models, painstakingly constructed of colored strings, are known as *tendho*. Upstairs (first room to the left) is the Tsepame Lhakhang. The central image of Tsepame is surrounded by 1,000 small Tsepame statues.

DRAGLA LUGUG:
A CAVE TEMPLE WITH
EARLY ROCK CARVINGS

OVERVIEW

Dragla Lugug, also known as the Sleeping Cave of the King (Chögyal Zimphuk), is one of the most fascinating religious monuments in Lhasa. This remarkable grotto-hermitage has ancient rock carvings, some similar to Indian prototypes, which date back over a thousand years. The cave temple was founded in the 7th C. by a Tibetan wife of King Songtsen Gampo. Important Buddhist masters, such as Guru Rinpoche and Nyang Tingedzin (Samye's first abbot) stayed and meditated at Dragla Lugug. Tradition considers this the site where subterranean water deities (lu) were imprisoned after they tried to prevent the draining of Lhasa's lake—part of the preparation for the foundation of the Jokhang (see page 63).

The Dragla Lugug (also Palha Lupuk) grotto has an amazing gallery of 71 sculptures, of which all but two are carved directly on sheer granite. According to literary sources, the most ancient carvings were the work of Nepalese artists, perhaps created during the Yarlung era (7th–9th centuries). This is tentatively confirmed by stylistic considerations—it is fortunate that most of these works are comparatively well-preserved. Early Buddhist civilizations (Afghanistan, China, India) commonly have monastic grottoes decorated with spectacular rock carvings. The Bamian, Dunhuang, and Ajanta complexes are well known. Not so in Tibet; Dragla Lugug is the rare exception. In conception, although certainly not in scope, it resembles the celebrated rock carvings of Dunhuang and Ajanta.

The existence of this type of grotto in Central Tibet raises intriguing questions about the diffusion of Buddhism. It has always been held that Buddhist culture came to Tibet from northwest Indian via the Silk Road. The discovery in Lhasa of a cave temple with rock carvings similar to Central Asian cave complexes might feasibly suggest direct transmission from India and Nepal to Tibet over the high Himalayan passes.

Next to Dragla Lugug is a recently rebuilt Neten Lhakhang, consecrated to the 16 Arhats. The meditation cave of Princess Wencheng, Songtsen Gampo's Chinese queen, is here. Nearby is the nunnery of the Drubthob Lhakhang, once the retreat of Tangton Gyalpo (1385–1464), master builder of iron bridges and multi-chapel chörtens (see page 451). The legendary founder of Tibetan medicine, Yutok Yönten Gönpo, was also associated with the nunnery.

History

Pawo Tsuklak Trengwa (16th C.), a Tibetan historian, recorded that Dragla Lugug and its magnificent carvings were begun during Songtsen Gampo's reign (627–50). The shrine was supposedly founded by the Tibetan, Ruyong Gyalmo Tsün, one of the five queens of the king. Along with the Jokhang, Ramoche, the Tsamkhung nunnery, Pabonka, Trandruk, Kachu, and Samye, the monastery is therefore one of the oldest surviving monuments in Central Tibet.

Location

Located on the southeast face of Chakpo Ri ridge, this secluded hermitage is only a 5-min walk from Dekyi Nub Lam (Xingfu Xi Lu), the main road that goes west from the post office to the Lhasa Holiday Inn. This road cuts between Chakpo Ri and the Marpo Ri ridge of the Potala at a point called Dhaggo Kani, the Gate of Lhasa. Prayer flags link the two spurs and a dirt side road hugs the base of the Chakpo Ri, going south and leading directly to the entrance of the cave monastery compound.

The site

Directly beyond the entrance gate of Dragla Lugug is a one-story building housing the kitchen and the monks' quarters. On the right, at the base of the ridge, is a cave temple called Karshung Phuk. Inside are new religious posters framed within glass cases. Beyond, stone steps lead up to a two-story chapel.

TUNGSHAK LHAKHANG

The first floor is the Tungshak Lhakhang. To the right is the altar with images, from left to right, of Sakyamuni, Jampelyang, Tsepame, Tangton Gyalpo, Drölkar, and the Tselha Namsum. The new murals depict the 35 Buddhas of Confession.

ZHELYE (TSHOKHANG) LHAKHANG

The second floor is the Zhelye Lhakhang, with new murals and a side entrance that leads to the inner sanctum of the grotto monastery. This chapel is dominated by an offering table with a finely crafted wooden prayer wheel at one end. By the far wall, on the left, is a throne for the Dalai Lama (above it is a large photo of the Senior Tutor). Next to it is a row of impressive butter sculptures. The right wall opens into the cave proper; an inscribed history of the monastery flanks the opening.

THE GROTTO

Dragla Lugug was excavated from the living rock of the Chakpo Ri. The dark rock walls of the cave, an irregular rectangle 27 sq m in size, with a width varying from 4.5 m to 5.5 m, glisten with smeared butter offerings. Beautiful multi-colored images in high-relief are carved directly onto the rock walls; much of the workmanship is superb. A central rock column, an irregular rectangle, extends from the cave's floor to the ceiling. Pilgrims circumambulate the narrow passage (0.75–1.3 m in width) formed by the spherical cave walls and the column. Images of deities are also sculpted directly on to the column's four faces. Large stone butter lamps stand before the column near the entrance. Images of Guru Rinpoche and Tsepame are above this 2.5-m high entranceway. The cave has 71 sculptures; all but two are carved from the rock on the south, west, and north walls, and on the central column.

The central column

The four faces of the column have 14 sculptures. Some damaged works were repaired with terracotta and given new garments, thus making it difficult to stylistically assess the originals. Carvings above the main shrine consist of Guru Rinpoche, Tselha Namsum, Tsepame, and Drölkar; all face the window above the entrance. Murals next to the window are recent. The column sculptures are described in clockwise fashion below.

The east face: This is the centerpiece of the cave. Within a glass shrine, the image of Sakyamuni (1.3 m tall) is flanked by his two chief disciples, Shariputra (Sharipu) and Maudgalyayana (Maudgalpu). To the far left and right are Jampa and Chenresi; their crowns were added later.

The south face: The main statue is Mikyöba (Akshobbya), one of the Five Dhyani Buddhas. Two *bodhisattvas* flank this deity, Kuntü Zangpo (left) and Namkhai Nyingpo (right). These statues have been extensively repaired; the heads are probably careful reconstructions.

The west face: Three statues of the Medicine Buddhas. The heads are new but the bodies original. New clay bases, not rock, are apparent.

The north face: Sakyamuni is bracketed by the two *bodhisattvas*: Shariputra (right) and Maudgalyayana (left). Look for the snow-lion hidden under the long garment of Maudgalyayana. It is painted white and has a charming, sleepy posture. This alone of all the cave's carvings seems to have escaped damage over the last thousand years. During the turmoil of the 1960s, a Tibetan woman covered the figure with mud and thus it was overlooked by the Red Guards.

The cave walls

THE SOUTH WALL

This wall has the most statues—32. They can be classified into three rows: the top row has 17 statues, the middle has one, and the bottom has 14.

Top row

The first image, starting from the left, is Drubthob Nyima Ze. He was a *mahasiddha* entrusted with opening and decorating this cave. According to an Indian legend, Nyima Ze was a godly figure who stopped the sun with his bare hands to complete the project in one day. The image's left hand points to a small, round sun. Two gold smears next to the statue represent Yamantaka (Jigje) and the Chögyal (King Songtsen Gampo). Directly below the image is a line of Lentsa script next to two archaic Tibetan numerals of unknown significance. The other sculptures of the top row can be divided into six groups, a small space separating each:

- Group 1. The three images to the right of Nyima Ze are Yeshe Tsogyal, Marma Ze (Sakyamuni), and Jampelyang. Below these three, along the bottom row, are two larger images of Chenresi seated on lotus pedestals (between them is a Lentsa syllable denoting 'Om'). Note that the left image, a representation of Sayi Nyingpo, wears a turquoise necklace. The second Chenresi, a representation of Namkhai Nyingpo, has a lotus on the left shoulder and a white, diagonal scarf. These embellishments are almost certainly from a later period. To the right of the two images are two more gold smears. The left one denotes a *rangjung* Jigje; the Dalai Lama came here in 1958 and personally identified it. The right one is a *rangjung sungma* ('self-manifesting protector') known as Damchen Chögyal. The other top row images, from left to right are:
- Group 2. The main image is Longchenpa, a major Nyingmapa lamas.
- Group 3. Chenresi is flanked by Chana Dorje (left) and Wöpame (right). Chana Dorje's stance is particularly lively.
- Group 4. Sayi Nyingpo.
- Group 5. Sakyamuni is flanked by two attendants, the rather melancholic Kuntü Zangpo (right), and Dripa Namsel. Both are noticeably plump.

- Group 6. Jampa in the center has Namkhai Nyingpo on the left and Yeshe Tsogyal on the right. Due to repeated reconstruction, many sculptural details have been lost.
- Group 7. Sakyamuni's attendant on the left is the same Yeshe Tsogyal from Group 6. The right attendant is Drölma.

Middle row

A single, small image of Sakyamuni rests in the space between the top and middle rows, right of the two gold smears.

Bottom row

This row contains the finest sculptures of the grotto. All are original images carved into the living rock about 1 m above the cave floor. Rendered in the Nepalese style of an early period (perhaps 7th C.), they suffered little damage (noses, ears) during the Cultural Revolution. The top row, clearly of a later period, looks anemic by comparison. Of the statues, 13 represent *bodhisattvas* and buddhas; the 14th is a protector. The crouching posture of the fifth image is one of the most unusual.

To the right of the first two Chenresi statues on lotus pedestals (mentioned above) are the following images (from left to right): Jampa, Kuntü Zangpo, Jampa (crouching figure), Namkhai Nyingpo, Zayi Nyingpo (outstanding). Now find a small hole in the wall with a loose stone inside—according to legend, King Songtsen Gampo, meditating in this cave, communicated with his Chinese wife in a nearby cave by banging this stone against the hole. To its right are the remaining images: Protector Miyowa (wrathful state), Three-eyed Dripa Namsel, Chenresi, Chana Dorje (peaceful state), Drölma (small image), Drölma Rechikma (unusual hand postures), Drölma Ngomo.

THE WEST WALL

This wall has six images. Tradition maintains that the jewels of Songtsen Gampo's Tibetan queen were hidden behind this wall. On the far left is a lively well-crafted Chenresi Karsapani; patterns on its garment are distinct. Next are the Buddhas of the Three Ages (Düsum Sangye). All wear three-tiered crowns and sit on lotus thrones. The center portion of this wall is devoid of sculptures; the rock appears unsuitable for carvings. Further to the right is the clay head of a new Gönpo. Under it is a recent 'Hum' syllable. Finally, Guru Rinpoche sits on a stone platform at the northwest corner of the cave.

THE NORTHWEST CORNER

A free-standing Palden Lhamo, the main figure on the platform, is at the center, flanked by Guru Rinpoche (left) and Chana Dorje and Jigje, all carved on the rock face.

THE NORTH WALL

There are 17 sculptures arranged in two rows.

The upper row

This row has two images: Wöpame (left) and Sakyamuni.

Bottom row

The sculptures, from left to right, are: Jampa, Jampa, Chenresi Lokeshvara (three gold smears above this represent, from left to right, Sengdrongma, Khachöma, and Drölma), Dripa Namsel (Sakyamuni is above this), Chenresi, Thönmi Sambhota (minister of Singtsen Gampo; two gold smears represent Drölkar), Songtsen Gampo and his two foreign queens (Wencheng, left), Gar (minister of Songtsen Gampo), Sakyamuni (flanked by two disciples; notice Sakyamuni's peculiar posture, a uniquely Nepalese interpretation), Jampa and Chenresi (same configuration as the central shrine).

BACKGROUND OF THE SCULPTURES

The authoritative Tibetan text, *Gyalrab Salwai Melong* (written in 1388), mentions that in the 7th C., King Songtsen Gampo built a shrine at Dragla Lugug and commissioned Nepalese artists to sculpt statues on the surrounding walls. According to the 16th-C. historian, Pawo Tsuklak Trengwa, Songtsen Gampo's Tibetan wife, Ruyong Gyalmo Tsün, founded the cave monastery. She probably built it after her conversion to Buddhism, following the arrival of the foreign Buddhist princesses, Wencheng and Tritsun. Thus, a founding date of 645 for Dragla Lugug seems reasonable. The first text documents that during those early times, when salt was precious, the Tibetan queen paid her sculptors in salt. For each measure of rock chipped away, they received an equal amount of salt. The entire work supposedly took 13 years.

Two main types of images exist at Dragla Lugug. The first depicts deities and protectors; the second presents historical figures such as Songtsen Gampo, his ministers and queens, and famous lamas. The latter lived in different periods, indicating that the carvings were not made all at one time. Judging from style and dress, the statues (except for the two, clay free-standing ones) can be classified tentatively into three chronological groups:

Early period, 7th–9th centuries: 47 statues make up this group: 14 of the central pillar; 14 (lower row) of the south wall; the Düsum Sangye of the west wall; 16 (lower row) of the north wall (except the first clay protector).

12th–13th centuries: 19 statues: 17 (upper row) of the south wall; Guru Rinpoche and Chenresi of the west wall.

14th–15th centuries: Three statues: Sakyamuni (middle row) of the south wall; Sakyamuni and Wöpame of the upper north wall.

ICONOGRAPHIC CONSIDERATIONS

Statues of the early period include Sakyamuni and his disciples, Düsum Sangye, *bodhisattvas*, and the court of Songtsen Gampo. Other cave complexes of China (eg Dunhuang, Longmen) depict the Düsum Sangye triad frequently, especially in the late 6th and early 7th centuries. Historical figures like the king and his ministers appear later, after the reign of Trisong Detsen (755–97). Religious personages in the second period (12th–13th centuries) often depict disciples of Guru Rinpoche, who lived in the 8th C.; nevertheless, widespread recognition of his missionary work did not come until much later, and only in the 13th C. did his Nyingmapa sect expand forcefully. These sculptures were probably made at that time.

DRESS

Garments of the *bodhisattvas* flanking the principal buddhas reflect the style of each successive period. Statues from the early period have exposed torsos; short and long skirts (*lungi*) are fastened together with a long belt extending to the feet. Some deities wear ballooning shorts over body-hugging long trousers, while others are completely naked except for a waistcloth and the rear half of a long skirt. Dress of the second period is simpler and less intricate. A distinctive feature is the use of shoulder shawls, unseen in earlier works. Most first-period garments are not found in the second.

LOTUSES AND HALOES

The rock carvings' few lotuses have three configurations: petals carved upwards and downwards, downwards only, and upwards only. Large statues around the center column all sit on the first type while smaller ones are on the second. This arrangement is de rigueur for statues at Dunhuang, Longmen, and Meiji Shan from the Northern Wei Dynasty (386–534) to the early Tang (7th C.). Works from the first period generally have carefully crafted oval or round haloes above the head. There are no back haloes. The second period has no haloes whatsoever, and the third has chörten-shaped haloes behind the deities' heads.

ARRANGEMENT AND WORKMANSHIP

Larger statues (0.5–0.8 m) of the south and north walls are located on the bottom row. The upward curvature of the rock wall forces the upper rows of statues to be smaller (0.5 m or less). These were carved at a later time to make use of remaining space. The middle row of the south wall and the upper row of the north wall are carved between the leftover spaces of the upper and lower rows. They are the most recent works.

Fine workmanship of the early statues shows a mature aesthetic. Proportions of the figures are realistic and the garments meticulously executed. Each figure carries itself in a lively manner, far more dramatically than the clumsy, later works. Carvings of the third period are simplistic, with scant attention paid to the garments. Also, there is considerably less variation between each statue.

STYLE OF THE SCULPTURES

Bodhisattvas flanking central Buddhas provide the most clues to style. Their postures are often more relaxed and charming. The upper body leans to the right, buttocks stick out markedly to the side to concentrate weight on the left leg. This posture, a typical Indian influence, is known as tribhanga. There are major differences in style between these statues and those of Dunhuang. The Chinese ones usually wear long robes that extend down from the shoulders; and the upper torsos are well covered. Furthermore, the vertical pleats of the dresses are sharply pronounced, a characteristic of pre-Tang and Tang art. By way of contrast, those of Dragla Lugug's early works show significant similarities with those of India's famed Ajanta caves. The tribhanga posture and the nearly naked depiction of some bodhisattvas is almost never seen in Tang art, which typically emphasized loose fitting clothing rather than the tight, body-hugging style seen here. Mention of Nepalese artists in the historical chronicles is consistent with Dragla Lulug's stylistic evidence. Nepal, before and during the time of the Yarlung kings, was strongly influenced by artistic currents from India (see page 47).

NETEN LHAKHANG (CHAPEL OF THE 16 ARHATS)

This new (1987), three-story yellow building next to Dragla Lugug has a handsome, classically Tibetan facade. Its main chapel, on the second floor, has a landing that opens on Gyasa

Drubphuk, the meditation cave of Songtsen Gampo's Chinese wife, Wencheng.

GYASA DRUBPHUK

On the altar within the cave is a stone bas-relief image of Chenresi, just under 1 m in height. It is considered to be self-originating (*rangjung*). Along the right rock wall is a cavity. Princess Wencheng, to communicate with Songtsen Gampo below, knocked on the hole with a stone. A natural conduit of sound travels from one cave to the other. Left of the cave, also on the landing, is another rock face. A niche at the top contains the *rangjung* image of Chana Dorje.

THE MAIN CHAPEL

The Yabse Sum, within a cabinet, is on the left upon entering. Turn right through a narrow corridor. On the right wall of this passage are two rows of cabinets. The top one has five statues: two *arhats* on the left, Sakyamuni in the center, flanked on the left by Kedrub Je (a disciple) and another Sakyamuni on the far right. Below them are six statues. From left to right they are Huashang, Darmata, and the Four Guardian Kings. Beyond the passage is the chapel proper. The central shrine along the south wall has the images of Sakyamuni and his two principal disciples. This Sakyamuni is a recent donation from Dharamsala, India. On both sides are two rows of cabinets holding the remaining 16 Arhats. A balcony outside the chapel affords a good view of the Potala and Lhasa. The ground floor has rooms for monks, while the top has quarters for the Dalai Lama. One lama and 20 monks live here.

DRUBTHOB LHAKHANG

The cave nunnery of Drubthob Lhakhang is dedicated to Tangton Gyalpo, the famous bridge and monastery builder (see page 451), and the father of Tibetan opera. It stands above and to the right of the Dragla Lugug complex and is run by four Nyingmapa nuns seconded from Shugseb Nunnery (see page 492). The chapel has red walls with gold line drawings. Dominating the room is the bearded Tangton Gyalpo, with his signature long white hair, inside a glass case. Cabinets on both sides contain many small images of him. The far left-hand corner of the right wall has a new statue of Yutok Yönten Gönpo, founder of Tibetan medicine. The metal *chörten*-tomb (*kudhung*) next to it contains the relics of Khyenrab Norbu, a previous incarnation of the medical master who renovated the chapel in the 1930s. Along the back wall are colored paintings of the Three Religious Kings, Songtsen Gampo (center), Trisong Detsen (left), and Ralpachen (right). In front of these is a Medicine Mandala. At the right corner of the room is a rock wall called Dungkar Rangjung, a 'self-manifesting' rock that resembles a conch shell. Pilgrims have stuck numerous coins on the surface as offerings. Next to it, a tablet with Tibetan inscriptions tells of the shrine's founding.

Tangton Gyalpo came to Drubthob Lhakhang to meditate, and during this time, a black spot formed above his left eye. People believe that for the sake of all sentient beings he undertook to draw all the sins of the world into this point (the chapel's main image depicts it.) Subsequently, a temple was built here to commemorate his selflessness. According to legend, Nyangpa Tenzin Zangpo, another lama who meditated here, was transformed into a 'rainbow body' (*jalue*) nearby. After the turmoil of the Cultural Revolution, Sonam Rinchen, an incarnation of Yutok Yönten Gönpo, rebuilt the nunnery.

RIGSUM GÖNPO: CHAPELS OF THE GODS OF THE GATE

The Jokhang, Lhasa's main temple, is surrounded by four chapels at the four cardinal points. They contain the protective deities of the Three Mystic Families: Gods, Demigods, and Men. These deities, Tibet's most sacred *bodhisattvas*, are Chenresi, Chana Dorje, and Jampelyang. The chapels, also known as Gods of the Gate (*go lha*), have perhaps existed since the 7th century.

SHAR (EAST) RIGSUM LHAKHANG
Located across from the main mosque in Lhasa's southeast corner, this was destroyed and now there is a two-story residence over the site.

LHO (SOUTH) RIGSUM LHAKHANG
This Rigsum Lhakhang, only survivor of the four, stands south of the Jokhang next to a small mosque (see page 201). The chapel appears as an insignificant, one-story yellow building, now a family residence. Apparently it was the first building erected on the Barkhor and was reputed to be one of the homes of King Songtsen Gampo, who stayed here while supervising the Jokhang's construction. Kings Trisong Detsen and Ralpachen also stayed at Lho Rigsum Lhakhang, also known as Chögyal Potrang. Princess Wencheng's stove is said to remain inside.

JANG (NORTH) RIGSUM LHAKHANG
This chapel (destroyed) stood behind (north) the Meru Tratsang and the Dhedruk Labrang (see page 202), at a site diagonally across the street from the Banak Shöl Hotel.

NUB (WEST) RIGSUM LHAKHANG
Located a short distance north of the Yüthok Zampa (Turquoise Bridge, see page 203), the destroyed chapel has been replaced by a government building on the north side of Renmin Lu (Mimang Lam), just west of the Tibetan Hospital.

PABONKA MONASTERY: SONGTSEN GAMPO'S TOWER OF THE TURTLE ROCK

OVERVIEW

Pabonka, 8 km west of Lhasa's center, is an unusual monastery built atop a massive free-standing rock. Locals liken it to a huge *doring* erected on the back of a female turtle. Songtsen Gampo, the 7th-C. king who came here in retreat, was credited with founding the Rigsum Gönpo Lhakhang, one of the original chapels. The principal tower building contains a sacred stone statue of Sakyamuni and next to this structure are 108 *chörtens*, perhaps built in the 7th C. by the king. Thönmi Sambhota, Trisong Detsen, Guru Rinpoche, and Tibet's first seven monks all stayed and practiced Buddhism here. Pilgrims believe a visit to Pabonka equals in merit a trip to Kusinagara in India, site of the Buddha's death.

Also on the site of Pabonka is Gyasa Gonchu Potrang, the residence of Princess Wencheng, Songtsen Gampo's Chinese wife. Within the Rigsum Gönpo Lhakhang are the sacred 'self-manifesting' *rangjung* images of the Rigsum Gönpo deities, protectors of Tibet. These perhaps date back to the 7th C.; Nepalese artists were said to have worked on them. A slab of rock in the chapel has carvings of the Six Syllables, a sacred *mantra* representing the first offerings by Thönmi Sambhota, Songtsen Gampo's minister, who devised the Tibetan alphabet. At the site's eastern side is Pabonka Durtrö, most sacred of eight cemeteries in Lhasa. Nearby is the mountain hermitage of Tashi Chöling and below it the recently rebuilt nunnery of Chupsang. Highed up on the Pabonka ridge is the Tokden cave retreat, one of whose relics is a stone carving representing the third eye of the deity, Demchok. A long, one-day *khorchen* surrounds Pabonka and its associated retreats.

Location

From Lhasa, bicycle or walk 4 km north on Chingdröl Jang Lam (Jiefang Bei Lu) to Sera Monastery. At the end of the paved road is Lhasa Military Hospital. Instead of turning right to Sera, turn left along a dirt road 30 m before the hospital entrance. This road follows the hospital wall around a bluff and then enters a side valley on the right (pass a village on the right, 15 mins after the dirt road turnoff). The path is well defined. Pabonka, with its distinctive truncated tower and inward-sloping white walls, is clearly visible halfway up a hill after rounding the bluff. It is 3/4 hr to Pabonka from the turnoff.

History and mythology

Pabonka is said to be older than the Jokhang and Ramoche. Built in the 7th C., its founding resulted from the need to suppress Tibet's great supine she-demon (see page 43). It was at Pabonka that King Songtsen Gampo and his two foreign wives, in a state of deep meditation, received divine guidance on how to control the demon by establishing temples at strategic points on her 'body' around the country.

Songtsen Gampo went to the Pabonka rock on the advice of goddess Palden Lhamo, and erected a nine-story tower, anchoring it with iron chains. On the seventh day of the structure's consecration ceremony, the Rigsum Gönpo triad (Chenresi, Jampelyang, Chana Dorje) descended from heaven and congratulated the king on his propagation of Buddhism. They told him they would act as witnesses to the success of his mission. After the festivities, the gods dissolved into a rock and left on its surface their *rangjung* images as a testimonial. Later, Nepalese artists embellished the rock. The sacred object now resides in the Rigsum Gönpo Lhakhang.

Thönmi Sambhota spent three years at Pabonka after his journey to India. Here he created Tibet's alphabet from a combination of Sanskrit, Gupta script, and indigenous, spoken Tibetan. In the 8th C., King Trisong Detsen and Guru Rinpoche came to meditate here. They stayed in a cave at the base of the Pabonka rock for ten days; it subsequently took the name Ten-day Chapel. Tibet's first seven monks (*misedun*), ordained by the Samye abbot Santarakshita, also lived here for some time towards the end of the 8th century. In 841, the anti-Buddhist king Langdarma destroyed Pabonka and its 108 *chörtens*. According to a local tradition, Palden Lhamo, protectress of the Ten-day Chapel, became incensed by this wanton destruction and instructed Lhalung Paldhor (see page 340) to kill the renegade king with an arrow in front of the Jokhang.

In the late 11th C., the Kadampa Potowa came here on pilgrimage. Saddened by the devastation, he ordered his disciple, Drakear, to rebuild the monastery. He complied by organizing 200 monks to build a two-story temple on the original site. Later, these Kadampa monks slowly rebuilt the 108 *chörtens*. In the 13th C., the Sakya patriarch Phagpa renovated the chapels.

Four centuries later, the Fifth Dalai Lama (1617–82) extensively restored the monastery and added an extra floor. From that time on, all Dalai Lamas made obligatory pilgrimages here, usually after receiving their Geshe degree; Pabonka hosted the celebration ceremonies. This relationship guaranteed financial support for the monastery from the central government's cabinet (*Kashak*), which appointed Pabonka's abbots (*khanpos*). More recently, Pabonka Rinpoche taught the Dalai Lama's senior tutor.

Pabonka is said to be modeled on Devikota, a temple in Gauhati (Assam). Devikota in turn was inspired by Kusinagara, the Buddha's place of death and second-most sacred of 24 holy pilgrimage sites (*tirthas*) revered by Buddhists. These *tirthas* are often replicated in different locations for the convenience of pilgrims. For example, three more representations of Devikota exist in Tibet: at Ragya (southeast edge of Lhasa), Purmoche (northeast of Tashilhunpo), and Sheldrak (near Tsethang). Each was consecrated with a piece of stone from Devikota itself.

Layout

Built on the lower slopes of Dhok Ri (Precious Umbrella Hill), Pabonka complex is dominated by a three-story, circular building, a truncated tower that sits on top of a 20-m-high granite rock. The rock's flat top is 300 sq m and three of its sides are smooth sheer faces; the north provides the stairways. This giant monolith represents a female turtle, itself a symbol of the cosmos. The tower's floor plan is semi-circular and its northern section squarish. This unconventional structure was badly damaged in the Cultural Revolution; only the lower floors survived. Extensive repairs were made in the 1980s. The Rigsum Gönpo Lhakhang is sited a short distance southeast of the main building. Northwest of this important chapel is a new white chörten (kudhung), next to a ruined one, erected to commemorate a recently deceased lama. Lower down, near the Pabonka Valley entrance, is a large block-like boulder painted white with a red border along the top. Pabonka's protector (sungma), Gönpo Drashe Marpo, is said to live inside.

Immediately north of the tower is a shrine with two stone rangjung images carved on its front face. Drölma is on the left and the Medicine Buddha (Menlha) is on the right. Beyond is a tiny, one-room structure with a door and window. Tsong Khapa, the founder of the Gelugpa, taught here once a year. The remains of Songtsen Gampo's 108 chörtens are to the north. Of these, 18 have been rebuilt. Farther up the slopes stands a new yellow chapel, the Gyasa Gönchu Potrang (Palace of Wencheng). To its right (east) is the sprawling, dilapidated Labrang, residence of the abbot. Nearby are the sites (destroyed) of two chapels, the Tsongkha Lhakhang and the Karthog Lhakhang.

Still further north of these is another large rock, the counterpart of the lower monolith. It is whitewashed, smaller than the other, and represents a male turtle (the two cosmic turtles together are called Rubel Phomo). Far to the left, halfway up the Dhok Ri, are prayer flags at the upper end of a narrow ravine. These mark the Sephuk meditation caves, known for their rangjung images of the 21 Drölmas (1/2 hr). To the right, near the bottom of another ravine, is Pabonka's sacred cemetery (durtrö), marked by a white chörten. Above it, on the slopes of Dhok Ri, is the damaged hermitage of Tashi Chöling. Pabonka is continually being restored and monks have returned to conduct religious services. A large kitchen near the great rock again churns out butter tea and good food.

PABONKA
Ground Floor
Here are storerooms but no chapels.

Second Floor
TSHOKHANG
The main room on the second floor is the Tshokhang which also serves as the dukhang. In the center is a brass pagoda shrine containing Pabonka's important relics. The central image is an original image of Sakyamuni. On a shelf (left) is a rangjung stone statue (dhoku), apparently from Gyama, Songtsen Gampo's birthplace. This archaic statue of Jowo Lokeshvara, overlooking the sacred Pabonka Durtrö, is the most important object in the building. Right of the Sakyamuni, also on an upper shelf, is another stone statue called Chupsang Dhoku Chenresi. This rangjung image came from the nearby Chupsang Nunnery. Below is yet one more Sakyamuni, recently returned from Beijing. Ranged along the north wall, next to the gönkhang entrance, are (from left to right): Santarakshita, the Fifth Dalai Lama, a Kadampa chörten, Songtsen Gampo and his two wives, and the 13th Dalai Lama. By the west wall, right of the Tshokhang entrance, are the images of Trisong Detsen, Guru Rinpoche, and Santarakshita. Old thangkas hang next to the window (east wall); beneath these is the Panchen Lama's throne; he came here twice in the past decade.

GÖNKHANG

Enter this small room through an entrance along the east wall of the Tshokhang. A row of new protector statues line the back wall. From left to right are Lhamo Yudrön, Namse, Damchen Chögyal, Jikje, Sangwa Düpa, Demchok, Palden Makzorma, Gönpa Taksha Marpo (Pabonka's protector), and Lhamo Düzorma.

KAZHIMA LHAKHANG

This chapel's entrance is left of the Tshokhang. Its back wall has new statues of historical personages and high lamas (left to right): Thönmi Sambhota, Lha Thothori, Trisong Detsen, Songtsen Gampo, Ralpachen, Lhopo Gawa, Paljor Lhundrub, Reting Trichen, Tenpa Rabgyal, and Lhatsün Rinpoche.

Roof level
ZIMCHUNG

The Zimchung suite, reserved for the Dalai Lama, is to the right of the stairs. Along the left wall are statues of Demchok, Drölma, Atisha, Yabse Sum, and Chenresi. Neighboring chambers are for the Dalai Lama's attendants.

THE PABONKA ROCK

The short *khora* around the base of the huge rock circles clockwise from the main steps (north). Along the east face is a house inside a cavity. Within a shrine are 1 m-high colored images carved in stone of the Rigsum Gönpo, Sakyamuni, and Mitrukpa. Rock surfaces along the south face reveal indentions, crevices, and lines believed to resemble the buttocks and the sexual organs of the mythical female tortoise.

Beyond is the sacred cave retreat of Songtsen Gampo. This large 8 m by 12 m cavity has a sloping ceiling formed from an impressive rock overhang. Known as the Tshokhang (also Palden Lhamo Potrang), this was where the king performed *tshok* offerings. A square block of rock in the center is said to be his seat of meditation. A big butter tub now sits on top. Along the left (north) wall are bas-relief carvings. From the left, the first is a *rangjung* Palden Lhamo. During Songtsen Gampo's preparation for an offering, the guardian goddess of Lhasa came out of the rock and told him to build a nine-story monastery on the rock, an act that would greatly promote Buddhism in Tibet. This 1m-high image is purported to be the undamaged 7th-C. original. Left of it are some old *thangkas*. The next three wall sculptures represent the king and his two wives. Beyond them is the red-hatted trio of Santarakshita, Guru Rinpoche, and Trisong Detsen. In front of the last is a large painting of Palden Lhamo. Other relics in the cave include an octagonal, lotus-based candlestick and some ancient wood blocks. A caretaker lives here.

Near the rock's west face, stone steps lead to a shrine. Within is a colored bas-relief carving of Trichen Tenpa Rabgyal, a former supreme abbot (*tripa*) of Ganden Monastery, who died here.

GYASA GÖNCHU POTRANG

This new, yellow structure faces east. Inside the ground floor, on the right, is the Zikpa Lhakhang named to commemorate Zikpa Ngadhen, the five forms of Tsong Khapa. Along the back wall are new, 2m-high, garishly decorated statues of Yabse Sum (Tsong Khapa and his two disciples). The left wall has murals of Chana Dorje and Jampelang; the right is dominated by the Drubthob Takzhon and Tamdrin. A room to the left is the Menlha Lhakhang, dedicated to the Eight Medicine Buddhas (all new). Some old *thangkas* hang here.

Upstairs is the building's principal chapel, the Gyasa Gönchu Potrang, consecrated to Princess Wencheng, who supposedly lived here. Cabinet-shrines (left to right) hold images of Drölma, Sakyamuni, Yabse Sum, Songtsen Gampo, and his two wives (all new).

THE WHITE ROCK

This 15m-high rock represents a male tortoise. Tradition records that Songtsen Gampo erected 108 *chörtens* (inside these were *ringsels* belonging to Sakyamuni) between this rock and the female tortoise monolith below, in order to prevent the two creatures from ever meeting. If they met, the country would suffer disaster. Niches on one face make it possible to clamber to the top to an incense burner and depository for *tsa-tsas*. A heavy, iron chain once linked this rock with Pabonka. Langdarma destroyed it and six floors of the tower but spared three floors when a thunderous, admonishing voice boomed down from heaven. (The Chinese finished off the final three floors in the 1960s.)

A rock to the west has a bas-relief sculpture of Tsong Khapa. Two carvings to the east depict Paljor Lhundrub and Gyere Rakawa. In front of the White Rock is an open area for sermons.

LHATSÜN LABRANG

South of the White Rock and east of Gyasa Gonchu Potrang is the Lhatsün Labrang, a complex consisting of a courtyard and other buildings. Next to a narrow, dry ravine (at its head is a white rock with a *rangjung* Chenresi), the main structure is entered through the south-facing courtyard. At its back is a cell where a low, 1m-high passage leads to a cave with a locked door. This is another meditation site of Songtsen Gampo. Above and behind the courtyard are meditation houses (*tsamkhangs*). West of the Labrang is a whitewashed rock with a *rangjung* carving of the Jampelyang *mantra*.

RIGSUM GÖNPO LHAKHANG

This insignificant building south of Pabonka was founded by Songtsen Gampo. Enter through a courtyard with an entrance portico. To the left of the chapel door is an enclosed glass niche containing a stone slab. On its surface is a carving of the Six Syllables. This represents the first offering to the Rigsum Gönpo divinities by Thönmi Sambhota after he created the Tibetan script. Tradition says he carved the syllables himself.

Along the renovated chapel's left wall are new statues of Yabse Sum and Sakyamuni. An 11-headed Chenresi stands inside a glass cabinet at the corner. Enter an inner room. The wall left of the entrance depicts a thousand-armed Chenresi. To the right is a painting of Demchok. A throne for the Dalai Lama, under an umbrella, sits in front of this. The inner *tsamkhang* (no murals) contains the highly venerated stone-carved *rangjung* images of the Rigsum Gönpo. Housed behind glass on a stone platform, these three garish bas-relief works are sculpted on a large piece of flat rock. During the Cultural Revolution, it fell flat on its face and escaped certain destruction. An unusual image of Chana Dorje incorporates two snakes entwined on his forehead. The wrathful figure is virtually naked; only a shawl hangs from his shoulder. His right arm is folded in front of the chest while the left holds aloft a staff. Next to him, the four-armed Chenresi has hair piled in a bun sticking out of his crown. At its very top is a small image of Wöpame. Jampelyang is essentially similar to Chenresi; only the two arms in front of the chest hold a lotus flower. The bas-relief, although covered in thick coats of new paint, is clearly of an archaic design and likely to date from an early period. Chronicles record that a 7th-C. Nepalese artist embellished this remarkable carving.

A small, inconspicuous shrine next to the main north-facing chapel entrance has a *rangjung* image of an eye next to an incense burner. It supposedly belonged to the deity Demchok. Parts of his body were apparently scattered in the hills around Pabonka. His other two eyes can be seen in the Tokdhen Cave (see opposite) and the Ghari Ani Gompa, a center beyond Pabonka with over a 100 nuns.

PABONKA DURTRÖ
This cemetery represents Demchok's skull and surpasses in importance the one at Sera.

TASHI CHÖLING HERMITAGE
A path from the Labrang leads east along the mountain slopes to this complex of ruins and meditation cells. The easy walk to the hermitage, above and right of Pabonka, takes 15 mins. Fronting the complex is a stone courtyard. Its far end tapers into a wide passage that marks the beginning of a trail down to Chupsang Nunnery (see below). The main building, flanking the courtyard's north side, is a two-story structure in fairly good condition. Behind it are ruins.

The entrance passage of the hermitage has charming paintings of a snow-lion, an elephant, and an Indian. On the right is a small room, a makeshift shrine where statues of Drölma, Tsepame, and Namgyalma have pride of place. These works survived the Cultural Revolution (monks with leprosy hid the statues and the Chinese dared not pursue them). Smaller statues of Sakyamuni, Pabonka Lama, the Medicine Buddha, and others deck the altar. Several old *thangkas* are here as well. On the central pillar is a finely carved head of Tamdrin. Small rooms for meditators are to the left after the passage.

CHUPSANG NUNNERY
From Tashi Chöling follow a trail southeast to the floor of a ravine (at its head, prayer flags mark the Tokdhen cave). At a stream marked by stone cairns, follow the path along the left bank; soon the ravine becomes a fairly steep gorge. Cross to the right bank near the nunnery sited in the middle of a village (1/2 hr from Tashi Chöling). Chromatic paintings of deities and lamas decorate rocks to the east.

The first building, on the right, is the enclosed debate courtyard (*chöra*). Next to it is the main *dukhang* and courtyard (completed in 1988). One side of the courtyard is the kitchen, the other an entrance cloister of the assembly hall. The back wall of this hall has two sets of Yabse Sum flanking red-hatted Dawa Gyalpo. Over 80 nuns and a few monks comprise this Gelugpa nunnery, formerly a monastery.

TOKDHEN DRUBPHUK

From Pabonka to this meditation cave takes 3/4 hr. The Pabonka Rinpoche meditated here and one of Demchok's three eyes is carved on a stone enshrined on the altar. A *rangjung* spring (*drubchu*), consecrated to the protectress Dorje Phagmo, wells up from an opening along the back cave wall. Another cave, one of a total of three, was used by Tokdhen Gyaluk, a disciple of the Pabonka Rinpoche. A hermit lives in a nearby stone hut.

THE PABONKA KHORCHEN

Pilgrims undertake the ritual circuit around Pabonka in the following sequence: Pabonka, Tashi Chöling, Tokdhen Drubphuk, Chupsang Nunnery. During the summer, the *khorchen* can be done in a day.

TSAMKHUNG: THE PRINCIPAL NUNNERY OF LHASA

Tsamkhung, one of two nunneries in Lhasa (the other is Drubthob Lhakhang, see page 127), is located south of the Moslem street that runs from the Barkhor's southeast corner to the Gyal Lhakhang mosque. Start from the mosque, then follow a small street west for a few hundred meters. The nunnery is on the right. It consists of a compound dominated by a yellow, two-story building with kitchen and living quarters attached to the perimeter wall. A courtyard is in front of the main entrance.

History

Tsamkhung means 'meditation hollow'. The name and the site derive from the time when King Songtsen Gampo meditated within a hollow near the Kyi Chu to prevent the river from flooding. One day he perceived visions of celestial beings (*dho kham wangmo*) dancing in celebration; later, the body of a woman in Khampa dress floated by. The king then buried the body within the hollow, a set of coincidences that proved to be very auspicious, since the flooding of Lhasa soon stopped. During the first Mönlam celebration of 1419, a sage named Drubthob Chenpo Kuchora used the site as a place of worship and was later followed by Ngari Drubthob Chenpo, one of the 84 Mahasiddhas. Tsamkhung Nunnery was built as a memorial to the famous meditation spot. The first structure, a simple eight-columned chapel, was erected by Tongten (1389–1445), a disciple of Tsong Khapa. The north section contains Songtsen Gampo's meditation hollow, and the south held a black stone statue of the king and a mask used by him. In later years, the Pabonka Rinpoche expanded the premises and added a new second floor to the main building. Tsamkhung's nuns performed various religious activities. They fasted in the name of Drölma and Chenresi on special occasions, ritually turned the *mani* wheels, and lit the butter lamps of the Barkhang inside the Jokhang (see page 62).

Today, Tsamkhung is in good shape with little sign of the damage suffered during the Cultural Revolution. All important relics were lost, however. In 1982, the government paid for its renovation, and Songtsen Gampo's meditation hollow was restored in 1984. The nunnery is very active with more than 80 nuns. It is a veritable oasis of calm in a busy Lhasa.

DUKHANG

The *dukhang*, housed on the second floor and reached by a flight of outside steps, has as its principal image, near the back wall, a thousand-armed Chenresi. Statues to its right are Yabse Sum, Dorje Naljorma (Vajrayogini, the temple's principal tantric deity), Mikyöpa, Sakya Thupa, and Drölkar. To Chenresi's left are Thungwa, Demchok, a statue of the Dalai Lama's Junior Tutor, Pabonka Rinpoche, and Drölma Jang. A 2m by 1.5m *thangka* hangs from the ceiling before the altar. It depicts the Yabse Sum trio—Tsong Khapa and his two disciples—and probably dates to the 18th century.

TSAMKHUNG

A small passage flanks the building on the right (east). The last room at the end is the secret chamber. According to the abbess, it dates back to the 7th C. and is the very place where King Songtsen Gampo prayed to control the Kyi Chu River. Inside is a whitewashed earthen well, dug below the floor: the 'hollow' used by the king. A glass-and-wood pagoda shrine stands over the cavity and simple stylized flowers and stars decorate its sides. Four steps lead down to the well, which is 1.5m deep by 1.5 m by 1.5 m. A glass-enclosed sculpture of Songtsen Gampo, a recent replica of the ancient Ngadrama (true-likeness) image, overlooks the opening. A stone in front of the steps was the king's seat.

CHAKPO RI:
ROCK CARVINGS ON LHASA'S
HOLY MOUNTAIN

The rock carvings of Chakpo Ri (3725 m) constitute an incredible, off-the-beaten-path gallery. Numbering more than 5,000, it is the single largest such collection in Tibet. The carvings are in reasonable condition and their style, subject matter, and date of creation vary greatly. The most valuable, dating back to the 7th C., exhibit distinct Indo-Nepalese influences.

According to literary tradition, when King Songtsen Gampo first set foot on Marpo Ri, site of the Potala, he saw the bright, 'self-originating' image of 'Om Mani Padme Hum' flashed before him. The king immediately bathed and went into retreat. Rainbow colors released by the *mantra* reflected on Chakpo Ri's cliffs opposite Marpo Ri, and *rangjung* images of Sakyamuni, Drölma, Tamdrin, and other deities spontaneously appeared. Songtsen Gampo ordered artists from Nepal to carve images on the rock face according to his visions. For the next thousand years, artists, pilgrims, and believers continued this tradition by engraving images of historical figures and Buddhist subjects on the cliff faces to gain merit. Colors of the early carvings have faded and only etched outlines remain; their style is noticeably primitive and powerful, quite unlike the more refined forms of recent times.

The site

Chakpo Ri, an S-shaped hill, runs more or less from east to west, along the north side of the Lhasa River. Its two ends are anchored by small ridges. Originally, the low east ridge was connected to Marpo Ri but over time, with Lhasa's expansion, the main thoroughfare of Dekyi Nub Lam forced a breach through the low saddle. Chakpo Ri's eastern spur, now the site of a reservoir, was supposedly the place where Wencheng, homesick for China, knelt and made offerings. Beneath cliffs to the east is the cave monastery of Dragla Lugug (see page 121) and near the top of a west spur is Drubthob Nunnery, founded by Tangton Gyalpo (1385–1464), the bridge and monastery builder.

In 1695, under the sponsorship of Regent Sangye Gyatso, Nyingtö Yönton Gönpo relocated the nunnery and built in its stead the Menpa Tratsang. This impressive structure (destroyed) was the only institution in Tibet to combine the study of medicine and Buddhism. Nyingtö Yönten Gönpo was the 14th generation descendant of the original Nyingtö Yönten Gönpo (1126–1201), pioneer of Tibetan medicine and author of the *Gyushi* (Four Medical Tantras), the standard medical text.

The carvings

Most carvings are located in three areas:
• North cliff face of the east ridge. Many of the images are derived from the theme of the Thousand Buddhas. Scattered between these are isolated Buddhas, Chenresis, and protectors. All are in bas-relief and in good condition; they can be divided into two types, according

to size and garments. The first consists of the smaller (10–25 cm) images, while the second encompasses the larger ones (30–90 cm). These latter, unlike the others, are distinguished by their naked torsos and long skirts. At the western end are two large carvings, an 11-faced Chenresi (over 2 m) and a *bodhisattva* (1.5 m); both have similar garments and stance. Below them are two more groups of carvings: the first, from east to west, has four bas-relief images of *bodhisattvas* and protectors; the second consists of three large high-relief images, ranging in size from 0.5m to 1m. West of these two groups is another carving of an 11-faced, thousand-armed Chenresi, over 2m tall. Below it are images of two finely carved *chörtens*, each about 2 m.

- This area is adjacent to the Lhasa Water Company compound, whose main entrance is along Dekyi Nub Lam at the junction of Marpo Ri and Chakpo Ri. To visit Dragla Lugug, you must walk beneath this southern cliff face, over 30m high and 40m wide. Erosion has damaged some of the carvings, which are mostly in bas-relief and small (20–25 cm). Larger images of Sakyamuni, protectors, Chenresis, and Guru Rinpoche are farther up and to the east. These range from 35 to 130 cm.

- South slopes. This western sector of the ridge has the largest, most impressive concentration of images; the cliff face runs for 1 mile and ranges in height from 25 to 50m. The subject matter consists mostly of Sakyamunis and Chenresis. Other carvings include protectors such as Tamdrin, donors, Guru Rinpoche, and Tsong Khapa. Those situated along the upper portion of the cliff are in poor condition, but the general state of preservation is reasonable. Nearly 3,000 images cover this area; most are clustered at a cliff face 50m wide and 27m high, whose lower portion is densely packed with small images (size ranges from 30 to 180 cm). The more accessible of these have been colored by pilgrims. There is also a 2.5-m-high carving of Sakyamuni here, and at the eastern end of the south slopes, a footpath leads up to more carved images, many of which have been damaged (those that remain consist mostly of carved outlines of deities, although there are several images of Guru Rinpoche in the section). Pilgrims have also colored these carvings, whose size varies from 0.5m to 1.5m.

GELUGPA MONASTERIES
AND OTHER MONUMENTS

GANDEN:
THE MAIN SEAT OF THE GELUPGA

Location

Ganden is about 45 km east of Lhasa along the road that follows the south bank of the Kyi Chu to Medro Gongkar (see page 546). From Lhasa, go east past Tibet University, cross the Lhasa East Bridge to the gas station. Continue along the paved road (the main Tibet–Sichuan highway) past the big Dechen bridge at road marker 1545 km, then Dechen Xian (1540 km). The Ganden turnoff is road marker 1529 km (new marker 4591), 39 km from Lhasa. A village is at this junction and a line of telegraph poles goes right from the main road up the Ganden Valley (Medro Gongkar is a further 29 km on the main road). The monastery is 18 km more up a winding road, near the top of the sacred ridge of Wangku Ri.

 Pilgrim trucks go to Ganden from Lhasa every morning, usually at 0730. The points of departure vary. Sometimes the trucks leave from the front of the Jokhang, sometimes from the butter market, Tsomsikhang, on the Barkhor. It costs Rmb 7 for the round trip and takes 3 1/2 hr to go and 3 hr to return. Ganden has a small guest house for overnight visitors. The Lhasa Hotel rents vehicles for the trip, or try other car rentals in Lhasa (see page 1000). The Ganden trip can easily be combined with visits to Tshal Gungthang Monastery (7.5 km east of the Lhasa East Bridge; see page 198), the Lamo Valley (road marker 1519 km, new marker 4582; see page 546), and the Gyalmashing Valley, King Songtsen Gampo's birthplace (road marker 1510 km, new marker 4573; see page 546).

GANDEN TO SAMYE MONASTERY:
A FIVE-DAY TREK VIA THE JOOKER AND SUKHE PASSES

This itinerary (see page 314) linking two of the most important monasteries in Central Tibet crosses the Yartö Drak range of mountains that divide the Tsangpo basin from the Lhasa Valley. The trek provides a superb means of access to Tibet's first monastery, an institution founded in the 8th C. (see page 295).

History

Ganden denotes the Paradise of Tushita and the abode of Jampa, the Future Buddha. The monastery, one of Gelugpa's Great Six (see below) was built on a ridge called Gokpo Ri, the site where Tsong Khapa (1357–1419) first meditated in order to choose a place for the main monastery of the sect. To the left of the ridge is the sacred mountain of Wangku Ri, scene of a celebrated consecration ceremony held at the time of Songtsen Gampo's birth. Next to it is Tsünmo Dingi Ri, favorite picnic ground of Songtsen Gampo's queens. Ganden's foundation was laid in 1409. Legend says the sacred Jowo image within the Jokhang magically confirmed the choice of the site. Six years after the consecration, Tsong Khapa added the outer chapel, Chichökhang, in which he placed jewelled mandalas. Two disciples, Namkha Pelzangpo and Neten Rongyelwa, founded the colleges of Changtse and Shartse respectively. A tantric college (gyürtra), known as Nagyü Tratsang, was founded by Je Sherab Senge, another of Tsong Khapa's disciples. In 1417, Ganden's main chapel, the Tsokchen, was established. Two years later, Tsong Khapa died and the abbotship passed to Gyaltsab Je. At his death, 12 years later, he was succeeded by Kedrub Je, the other major disciple of the Gelugpa patriarch.

Ganden's abbotship, unlike other monasteries, is transmitted neither by heredity nor incarnation. Its highest lama, the abbot (Tri Rinpoche or Tripa), was always chosen from among worthy learned monks, usually from a major monastery in Lhasa. His term of office was generally seven years, although some abbots before the 16th C. had held office longer. A highly revered personage, the Tripa was often a potential candidate for the office of regent, a seat that effectively controlled the country during the minority or absence of the Dalai Lama.

The site

Ganden is the foremost monastery of the Gelugpa sect. It is also the most devastated. Of all the Great Six monasteries (Ganden, Sera, Drepung, Tashilhunpo, Labrang, Kumbum) of the Yellow Sect, none suffered as disastrously as Ganden. The ruins here, a result of the Cultural Revolution when artillery and vast quantities of dynamite where deployed, are the most extensive in Tibet. Over the last

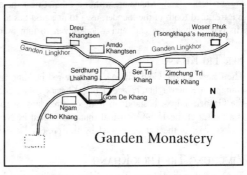

decade, Herculean efforts have gone into the rebuilding. Before the holocaust, over 2,000 monks lived here; now there are 300.

NGAM CHÖ KHANG

This small, very active lhakhang, right of the road after the truck stop, is built on the site where Tsong Khapa gave teachings to his pupils. A small dukhang, with images of Tsong Khapa and his two major disciples, is on the left after the entrance. This is a charming, cosy hall, one of the best at Ganden. To its left is a gönkhang with statues of the protectors, Palden Lhamo, Mahakala, Dharmaraja, and Yamantaka. The second floor contains a private room and throne for the Dalai Lama. Pilgrims and a pack of benign dogs hang about the courtyard and roofs of Ngam Chö Khang. There is tea and food cooking at all times of the day.

SERDHUNG LHAKHANG (THE GOLD TOMB OF TSONG KHAPA)

From the Ngam Chö Khang follow the main road into the heart of the complex. The Depü debating courtyard is to the right, below the chapel-residence, Gom De Khang. Further along on the left is the red Serdhung Lhakhang, distinguished by a recently rebuilt white *chörten* near its entrance. This is Ganden's most impressive restored building, a large fortress with windows on the top floor only. A spacious interior courtyard is reached on entry. Straight ahead is a chapel with black walls consecrated to the protector, Dharmaraja (Tamche Chögyel), a wrathful, bull-headed divinity particularly propitiated within the Gelugpa sect.

Within the second-floor chapel of Yangchen Khang is a new golden *chörten* (*serdhung*) of Tsong Khapa (to the left of this room is a large assembly hall). The original *chörten*, called Tongwa Donden ('Meaningful to Behold'), was the most sacred relic of the monastery. It was made of silver and later gilded by the grandson of the Mongol general, Gushri Khan, during the era of the 50th Tripa. In 1717, when the Dzungars invaded Central Tibet, the *chörten* was enclosed in a special Mongol tent of felt and sandalwood, then placed inside this chapel (built in 1629) with a Chinese-style gilt roof. After its destruction in the 1960s, relics and fragments of skull were saved; these are now entombed within the new *chörten*. In front of the structure are large images of the Yabse Sum, Tsong Khapa, and his two principal disciples. A stone at the left side of Serdhung Lhakhang's back wall is believed to have miraculously flown from the city of Sarvasti (Yangchen), India. Thus this chapel derived its name. More relics of Tsong Khapa are within a cabinet near the *chörten*. Inside a small silver *chörten* is a treasured tooth of the founder, used to make *tsa-tsas* to confer sanctity on the clay images. His begging bowl, tea cup, and a *dorje* given to him by one of his teachers, are also here.

SER TRI KHANG

The Chapel of the Gold Throne, a skinny red building to the right of Serdhung Lhakhang, contains a Kangyur library and Tsong Khapa's gold throne, used through the centuries by the Ganden Tripas. It stands in front of three large statues of the Yabse Sum. The throne is a replica of the 15th-C. original that was crafted by Nepalese artisans. Lying on it, within a cloth bag, is the hat once used by the present Dalai Lama.

ZIMCHUNG TRI THOK KHANG

The Chapel of the Ganden Tripa. Adjacent and to the right of Ser Tri Khang, this substantial building has four main chapels on the ground floor. The Demchok Lhakhang is a dark chamber consecrated to the protector, Demchok, a divinity belonging to the supreme division of the yogic tantra within the Vajrayana tradition. Next to this is the Dzomchen Khang, with statues of Pabonka Rinpoche, Trijang Rinpoche, the late junior tutor of the 14th Dalai Lama, and the Yabse Sum. The next room, left of the courtyard, is the site of Tsong Khapa's death. This spartan chamber contains only the bed and seat of the Gelugpa founder. Murals depict manifestations of Jampelyang, the Bodhisattva of Wisdom. A final chapel on the ground floor is reserved for the Dalai Lamas. The statues within a cabinet represent the 35 Buddhas of Confession.

AMDO KHANGTSEN

A path to the right of the Serdhung Lhakhang leads up the slopes towards the ridgetop. Set among ruins is the Amdo Khangtsen, a chapel used by monks of Amdo, the huge province of northeastern Tibet. The assembly hall is well decorated with brocade hangings and wall paintings of the 35 Buddhas of Confession and the 16 Arhats. On the left side of the altar is a special protector of Amdo called Anima Je. A cabinet supposedly holds the eye of Dharmaraja (Tamche Chögyel), wrathful protector of the Gelugpa.

DREÜ KHANGTSEN

To the left of Amdo Khangtsen, this chapel has images of Tsong Khapa and his two disciples.

THE GANDEN LINGKHOR

The pilgrimage route round the monastery, a highlight of Ganden, starts from near Dreü Khangtsen. If your time is limited, walk the *lingkhor* before all else. It is simply the most spectacular of Central Tibet's monastery circuits. The walk takes 1 hr and along the route are assorted nature-formed objects and man-made shrines that serve to provide essential mythical associations for the pilgrims.

To start, hike beyond Dreü Khangtsen along the topmost portion of the ridge (the parking lot near Ngam Chö Khang is another good place to begin; see Ganden–Samye trek, page 314). The pilgrim's path goes around the back of the hill and encircles the Ganden ridge. A prominent clump of prayer flags indicates the beginning of the walk. First, pass some small rock shrines containing *rangjung* imprints of renowned lamas and divinities. These include images of Dampa Sangye, the Dingri saint (see page 271), the 16 Arhats, Tamche Chögyel (Tsong Khapa's protector), Tsong Khapa's hat, and others. The *rangjung* images of the Rigsum Gönpo—Chenresi, Jampelyang, Chana Dorje—are especially revered.

When the ruins are no longer seen, the trail ascends. A flat, black rock on the right is known as the Vision Rock. Pilgrims stand some distance away and make a hole through their fists—supernatural visions are induced by looking at the rock in this manner. The Kyi Chu Valley spreads below the mountain to the left. Pass more shrines at the highest point of the circuit to find the spot where Tsong Khapa prostrated. Descend to the next place of importance: the sky-burial site (*durtrö*). Piles of bones, old knives, and heaps of clothing represent offerings to this hallowed spot. Pilgrims roll around on the ground to rub off bad *karma* and to simulate death and rebirth. Continue the descent to the so-called Gauge of Sin—a rock with a narrow cleft. The exercise here is to squeeze through the constriction. If you get stuck, it is a sure sign that you are burdened with too much sin. Here are the *rangjung* images of the Yabse Sum (Tsong Khapa and his disciples), 'created' on the rock by Tsong Khapa's fingernail. Further along are more cryptic, spiritually powerful impressions on wayside rocks. These include an image of Senge Dongma, the lion-headed *dakini*, the tongue of Tamche Chögyel (paying homage to this enables the pilgrims to recite *mantras* better) and a rock with a liquid drip (*dütsi*), much prized by believers.

Tsong Khapa discovered on the *lingkhor* the prized conch shell (dungkar ngön chung) of Maudgalyayana, a principal disciple of Sakyamuni. This relic finally convinced him that

Gokpo Ri was the right place to build his monastery. The mythic conch shell has a reverse thread and its emitted tone can supposedly cure diseases and remove strife. (It was enshrined in the Tsokchen.) Near the end of the circuit is Tsong Khapa's Cave of Light (Wöser Phuk) and hermitage. Within are *rangjung* and *sungjönma* ('capable of speech') rock images, all gaily painted. These include Palden Lhamo, Sakyamuni, Tsepame, and a bas-relief sculpture of Tsong Khapa. Above him are the Kadampa lamas of Atisha and Dromtönpa. Far back to the right is a protuberance on the rock wall. Tradition has it that Tsong Khapa grabbed hold of this knob to pull the wall closer to him.

Another shrine, higher up the slopes, is consecrated to Tamche Chögyel, the personal protective deity of Tsong Khapa. Finally, come to Sickness-withdrawing Rock, a black conical rock 1.5m high on the right side of the path. Pilgrims put their stomachs on the top of the smooth stone and then spit noisily. It is considered even more auspicious to vomit! This is an omen that all evil influences within the body are being purged. Contour along the ridge to regain the Ganden complex.

DREPUNG:
TIBET'S LARGEST MONASTERY

OVERVIEW

Dominated by a high ridge known as Gephel Ütse, Drepung was founded by Jamyang Chöje in 1416. This celebrated Yellow Hat lama was born near Samye to a wealthy family (a childhood friend donated large sums for the building of Drepung). First ordained at Tsethang Monastery (see page 518), he also studied at Jangphu and Tsomolung. His prodigious memory and uncommon spirituality made him the leading disciple of Tsong Khapa. Jamyang Chöje benefited greatly from the Phagmo Drupa government. Rich families and feudal lords contributed unhesitantly when he announced plans to create a great monastery. Drepung was thus able to develop very quickly. One year after commencement, the monastery had become home to 2,000 monks.

The Second Dalai Lama, doubling as Drepung's abbot, built the Ganden Potrang in the early years of the 16th century. From this time on, Drepung became the effective center of political power in Tibet. By the time of the Fifth Dalai Lama (1617–82), its population had grown to a staggering 10,000, easily the largest monastic institution in the world. It was renowned as a great center of learning and attracted the best and the brightest. Among these was Jamyang Zhepa, founder of the magnificent Labrang Monastery in Amdo. Of Lhasa's monasteries, Drepung suffered the least during the Cultural Revolution. Most of the important chapels remain unscathed, although prior to this the monastery had been badly sacked three times: in 1618, it was destroyed by the King of Tsang, who invaded Lhasa during the height of his anti-Gelugpa campaign; in 1635, the complex was burned by the Mongols; at the start of the 18th C., the Dzungars of Lajang Khan overran the site.

Drepung means 'rice-heap,' which comes from the Sanskrit Dhanyakataka, the name of a *stupa* in South India where the Buddha first taught the Kalachakra *tantra*. With an area of over 20,000 sq m, its principal buildings are the Tshomchen, the four main *tratsangs*, and the Ganden Potrang. Each of these has its own residential units, *khangtsens*, and other functional buildings. The major structures follow a simple achitectural plan. Each consists of a courtyard, a large hall, and inner chapels. These elements are staggered up the slopes, with the result that the courtyards are always at the lowest level. The *chörten* tombs of three Dalai Lamas (Third to Fourth) are sited at Drepung (only the Potala has more). Since the early 1980s, about 500 monks, many of them young novices, have returned to live at Drepung.

Location

The monastery is located 8 km west of Lhasa. Take the bus west along Dekyi Shar Lam and Dekyi Nub Lam, names of the same main road from the Banak Shöl Hotel. After passing the post office and the Lhasa Holiday Inn, get off at the base of Mt Gephel Ri and walk 1 km north to the monastery. Near to the road, to your right, is Nechung Monastery (see page 165). Cars and mini-buses for the trip can be hired at the Banak Shöl, the Holiday Inn, or other rental agencies. Pilgrims move through the complex in a clockwise sequence from the parking lot fronting the main entrance: Ganden Potrang, Tshomchen, Ngagpa Tratsang, Jamyang Lhakhang, Loseling Tratsang, Gomang Tratsang, and the Deyang Tratsang.

GANDEN POTRANG

Tibet was ruled from here before the Potala existed. A number of Dalai Lamas lived and worked in the Ganden Potrang. The Second, Gedan Gyatso, became the *tripa* (abbot) and in 1530 built this palace. The Great Fifth wielded his enormous and influence over the country from this very building.

Drepung Monastery

COURTYARD

A small courtyard precedes the terrace of the palace. To the right is an ancient tree, sup-posedly as old as the building itself. To the left, a doorway leads into a newly renovated chapel, the Sanga Potrang. Its main image is Jigje. Ascend some steps to reach the main terrace, which is enclosed on three sides by two-story residential quarters. The annual Shotun (Yoghurt) Festival, which includes elaborate Cham dances, begins here before moving to Norbu Lingka. The northern perimeter of the terrace courtyard is bounded by the main structure of the palace. This building is distinctly elevated: its ground floor stands well over 2 m above the courtyard.

DUKHANG

The assembly hall on the ground floor is a spacious, bare room. In the old days monks of the Namgyal Tratsang—the personal monastery of the Dalai Lamas—congregated here. The hall holds two important statues: one is Drölma Sungjönma, one of Atisha's three tutelary deities; the other is Thuje Chenpo (Chenresi), tutelary deity of an Indian master. Beyond is the *gönkhang*. The main statues here are Jigje and his consort. Beside them are Palden Lhamo, Mahakala, and the Fifth Dalai Lama. The Dalai Lamas used the second floor as an office and a left chapel contains the Fifth Dalai Lama's throne, one of the most elaborate and finely designed objects in the palace. Tsong Khapa and his two disciples are the main images. The room is full of cabinet-shrines and *thangkas*.

SANGA POTRANG

This chapel, southwest of Ganden Potrang, was sacked during the Cultural Revolution and not renovated until 1986. Small chapels at the back have some semblance of artistic merit, but the cavernous hall is devoid of the fineries that characterize Drepung's other buildings. The main image here is Dorje Jigje; it is accompanied by a statue of the Fifth Dalai Lama.

THE TSHOMCHEN

The Tshomchen, northwest of Loseling Tratsang and east of Ngagpa Tratsang, is Drepung's most important building. Its abbot held the title of Tripa Khenpo and was an influential personality within the Lhasa government. Near the center of the complex, this large structure, rebuilt in 1735 by Regent Polhane, occupies an area of 4,500 sq m. It is fronted by a spacious terrace, with a magnificent view of Lhasa. In all, 17 grand stone steps lead up to the entrance portico and its massive pillars. To the left is a round stone structure used to store discarded tea leaves.

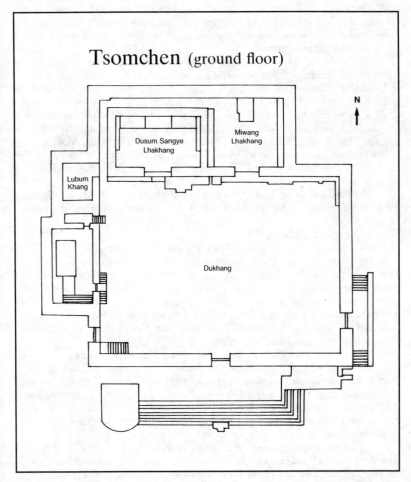

Tsomchen (ground floor)

N

Dusum Sangye Lhakhang

Miwang Lhakhang

Lubum Khang

Dukhang

DUKHANG

The Tshomchen's huge assembly hall measures 50 m (east–west) by 36 m (north–south), and boasts 183 columns. The central portion of the ceiling is dramatically raised to create a light-filled, two-story atrium. A strong sense of pomp derives from the decorative banners, *thangkas*, and brocade hangings that adorn the columns and hang from the ceiling. The *dukhang's* long altar runs outside the Düsum Sangye chapel along the back wall of the hall. Look for a *chörten* containing the remains of Ganden's 95th *tripa*. Next to it is Dhukhar (Chenresi under a white umbrella), a new silver statue nearly one floor high, erected and presented to the monastery in 1951 by a Kashmiri. In front is the Jamyang Chökhorma, a Manjusri in the *mudra* gesture of 'turning the wheel of dharma'; this gilt-copper original rises nearly two floors. The workmanship of both these statues is excellent and their haloes are particularly refined. Notice too the mythical animal figures (*gyendrak*).

To the right of the Dhukhar is another *chörten*, donated by a former *tripa*, and the female deity, Dugkarma. A Sakyathupa sits just behind the Dhukhar. To the east is an image of Tsong Khapa Khamsum Zilnon, a gift of Shatra, a former prime minister. In front of this is the Buddha statue of Thupa Tsultrima. Pilgrims make a point of touching it to feel the sensation of warmth. Statues of the 13th Dalai Lama and Jamyang Chöje, the founder of Drepung (in a finely carved shrine), follow immediately. Next is a series of Dalai Lamas: the Seventh, Third, Fourth, Fifth (on an elevated throne), Ninth, and Eighth. Along the west and east ends of the altar are the 16 Arhats. The wall paintings depict the Lives of the Past Buddha (Dza Gya Paksam Trishing). These were commissioned during the construction of the great hall.

The inner wall of the Tshomchen's western exit has a painting of Khyidra Pala riding a dog. At the time of the British invasion of 1904, it is said that this dog barked a warning.

Düsum Sangye Lhakhang

Positioned at the rear of the assembly hall, the two-story Düsum Sangye Lhakhang (Buddhas of the Three Ages Chapel) is spacious and beautifully illuminated by a skylight over the entrance. Each of the three Buddhas (past, present, and future) is accompanied by two *bodhisattvas*. All are enclosed within unusual *chörten*-shaped cabinet-shrines. The center of the altar holds statues of Sakyamuni and his two principal disciples, Shariputra and Maudgalyayana. They are housed inside three gilt-copper *chörtens*. Behind them, on an elevated platform, are the Buddhas of the Three Ages: Sakyamuni is flanked by Wösum (Kashyapa) and Jampa (Maitreya). These images are inside silver-plated structures.

At the back, on top of a high platform, is an alcove known as Tsenkhang Üma. Here, nine *chörtens* are arranged in a configuration similar to the structures of Dhanyakataka in South India. That site marks the place where Buddha first expounded the Kalachakra teachings to King Dawa Zangpo of the mythical kingdom of Shambala. The central *chörten* represents the throne of Sakyamuni. A festival called Dükhor Düchen is held on the 15th day of the third month in memory of this event. Formerly performed in the Tsokchen (Tshomchen), it now takes place in the Loseling (see below).

Along the western section of the chapel are images of Tamdrin and the Four Spiritual Sons of the Buddha (clockwise from the entrance). The east wall has images of Tsong Khapa, the Four Spiritual Sons, and Chana Dorje (clockwise). Notice the smaller statues of King Songtsen Gampo, his queens and ministers, attached to the columns. All statues and decorative details in the chapel are original. They were not damaged during the Cultural Revolution. Düsum Sangye Lhakhang and the Jigje Chapel (see page 152) are Drepung's only chambers to retain fully the architecture and artistic style of the early 15th century. The chapel is surrounded by a circumambulatory corridor. Although no longer used, it is in reasonable shape. Its northern section has original murals dating from the foundation, and the subject matter relates directly to the main statues inside the chapel. This serves to show that the Düsum Sangye Lhakhang has been preserved intact since the beginning. It is a rare and valuable historical structure.

Miwang Lhakhang

To the west of the Düsum Sangye chapel is the Miwang Lhakhang, erected in memory of Pholha Miwang, who was responsible for the original expansion of the Tshomchen. At the center is a two-story statue of the 12-year-old Jampa (Miwang Jampa). Pholha Miwang's family provided funds for its construction.

Lubum Khang

This small chapel is located to the west (left) and slightly in front of the Düsum Sangye. Its front section has two sunken white *chörtens*, the Lubum Chörtens. Legend says they have been blessed by 100,000 *nagas* (lu). Only part of the *bumpa* of these clay structures is visible, the rest being buried beneath the ground. The rear part of the chamber (usually closed to the public) has three original, undamaged, silver-plated *chörten*-tombs. The center one, 6.2 m tall, belongs to the Third Dalai Lama. To the left is the Fourth's tomb, 6.5 m tall, and to the right is the Regent's, 4.6 m tall. The *chörtens* are all of very fine workmanship; those of the Third and Fourth Dalai Lamas required 740 kilos of silver. In the past, an annual festival, the Lubum Shotun, was performed here on the eighth day of the seventh lunar month. A district magistrate from the Namru Dzong came here specially to preside over the ceremonies, and the dressed effigy of the Nechung Oracle (see page 165) was placed in this room.

Lhamo Lhakhang

As you walk out of the Lubum Khang, proceed a few steps to a partition, the entrance to the Lhamo Lhakhang. Inside, the most important relic is a painting of Palden Lhamo, drawn with blood from the Fifth Dalai Lama's nosebleed. It hangs on the north wall and is always covered by a piece of five-colored silk. In the past, this painting was displayed only once a year. A three-dimensional model of the Paradise of the Palden Lhamo, constructed with five-colored strings, stands on an altar. The high, pyramidal structure was created as a magical cure during an epidemic.

Second floor

JAMPA TONGDRÖLMA LHAKHANG

At the northwest corner is a small, important chapel with a massive statue of Jampa (extending three floors), represents the Future Buddha at the age of eight. Built by the King of Nedong, as instructed by Tsong Khapa, its facial features convey an air of childlike innocence. The name 'Tongdrölma' denotes its supposed power to save believers who propitiate the statue. Its left cheek has a *rangjung* (self-manifesting) sign of 'Ah'. The right has a *rangjung* conch shell. A Chinese plaque over the entrance of the chapel (usually closed) was given to the monastery by the Chinese Amban in 1846. Two gold roofs cover the Tshomchen, one above the Düsum Sangye, the other over the Jampa Tongdrölma Lhakhang. The latter's upper sections are best viewed from galleries on the second and third floors. Of Drepung's many gilded roofs, the one over this chapel is outstanding for its square plan and central peak.

KANGYUR LHAKHANG

Three valuable sets of Kangyur reside in this chapel. One is the Ming-dynasty Litang edition, a gift from Muji, a feudal lord of northern Yunnan. The second dates from the time of the Kangxi Emperor of the Qing Dynasty. And the third, a gold-written manuscript, was a gift from the Depa Lobsang Thudol to commemorate the birthday of the Dalai Lama.

Third floor

ZHELRE LHAKHANG

The face and torso of Jampa Tongdrölma can be seen from the top floor's Zhelre Lhakhang. There are over 400 original bronze sculptures in the chapel. One of the most prized objects is a highly venerated conch shell (*chödhung*), whose anti-clockwise whorls are hidden under white offering scarves. According to tradition, Tsong Khapa asked Jamyang Chöje to build Drepung and afterwards gave this to him as a gift. A verandah in the room allows visitors to see the Tongdrölma from the head down. In front of the face are three statues (from the left): Togme Zangpo, a 12th-C. lama, Tsong Khapa, and Seu Rinzen, the founder of the Drölma Lhakhang in the Jokhang. To their side are Tsong Khapa (left), and Jamyang Chöje. To the rear is the *chörten*-tomb of the Second Dalai Lama. Another *chörten* across the room contains the remains of Jamyang Zhepa, founder of Labrang Monastery in Amdo. Along the walls are 11 statues of various incarnations of Dalai Lamas and Panchen Lamas.

THE DRÖLMA LHAKHANG

The three Drölma statues (in the chapel east of the Zhelre Lhakhang) date from the era of the Fifth Dalai Lama (1617–82). They are all regarded as *rangjung* and *sungjönma* ('spoken'). Brought originally from Tsethang, Yamdrok, and Gyantse, they were previously kept in Ganden Potrang. The first (left), called Nedong Chime Drölma, is regarded as the protectress of Drepung's water source. The second, Yamdrok Drölma, looks after the wealth and prosperity of the monastery, and the third, on the right, is Gyantse Tshechen Drölma, which endows Drepung with its authority. Next to these is a remarkable set of Kangyur, one of Drepung's great treasures. Commissioned by the Fifth Dalai Lama, all 114 volumes are written in gold ink. The sandalwood covers have extraordinarily beautiful carvings of inlaid ivory. Commonly known as the Dzamling Yashak, the faithful believe its value to equal half of the entire world's treasure. Each of the silk ties binding the folios were lovingly made in one day by Andzöm, a pious lady of Lew Dzong. The buckles securing the sets are of solid gold.

There is a magnificent statue of the six-armed Mahakala along the left wall. Previously kept in the Gyarong Khamtsen (in Drepung), this is made from clay tablets left over from the Mahakala statue of the Ngagpa Tratsang. Since the Gyarong Khamtsen was severely damaged, the statue was moved here. Between the Kangyur volumes is a statue of Prajnaparamita, Mother of the Buddhas. On her lap, inside a charm box (*ghawu*) is a tooth relic (*tshem*) of Tsong Khapa.

The roof

CHAPEL OF THE KINGS

This large room contains statues of Tibet's early kings and the Dalai Lamas. At the center of the back wall, on a throne, is the Fifth.

TSHOMCHEN JOWO KHANG

The Jowo statue in this chapel is made of 25 kilos of silver. Flanking it are 13 silver *chörtens*. Above is a gilded roof supported by Chinese-style eaves.

JAMPA KHANG

This chapel is consecrated to Jampa.

Other Sites

JAMYANG DRUBPHUK

A cramped cave-shrine at the eastern base of the Tshomchen, one of the most important pilgrim destinations, attests to Drepung's modest beginnings. Jamyang Chöje, the founder, meditated here in the early 15th century. Inside are bas-relief stone carvings of Tsong Khapa and Jamyang Chöje as well as an old painting of Tsong Khapa. The rear cave wall backs onto the Tshomchen and a small enclosure surrounds the entrance.

JAMYANG LHAKHANG

This small shrine is located immediately behind the Tshomchen. It is simply constructed: a massive rock serves as the northern wall, and the interior space has merely a single pillar. The main image is a stone Jamyang—a *rangjung* image—carved from rock. Wall paintings are of Jamyang Chöje, his first disciple, and Tenma. Jamyang Chöje's walking stick was used by pilgrims to rub their backs to ease rheumatic pains. It disappeared and is now replaced by an iron stick. A few meters east is the white clay *chörten-tomb* of Lama Umapa, founder of Gadong Monastery (see page 674). He was the medium through whom Tsong Khapa communicated with Jamyang, the Bodhisattva of Wisdom. Bumtrak Dhunpa's tomb, containing 100,000 *mantras*, is to the west.

THE TRATSANGS (COLLEGES)

During the early years, seven *tratsangs* were established, each under the control of one of Jamyang Chöje's disciples. During the 18th C., this state of affairs became untenable due to the massive increase of students. The subsequent reorganization created four main *tratsangs*, each institution with its own abbot and syllabus. Three specialized in exoteric disciplines while the fourth, Ngagpa Tratsang, dealt only with esoteric teachings. The Drepung *tratsangs* are noticeably larger than similar institutions at other monasteries, and Loseling is the biggest of them all.

NGAGPA TRATSANG

This structure, west of the Tshomchen, was erected in 1419, three years after Drepung's founding. Consecrated by Tsong Khapa, it is the sole tantric college of Drepung. Before entering this college, aspiring monks first had to master the exoteric disciplines in the other three, then pass an exam. The best pupils from Ngagpa usually gained admission to the Upper and Lower Tantric Colleges in Lhasa. In time, academic excellence became less of an issue and most people who applied were accepted. The institution is situated behind and to the right of the Tshomchen. Its design is dissimilar to the other institutions. Fronting the assembly hall is an enclosed courtyard surrounded by residences.

DUKHANG

The assembly hall was a later addition to the Jigje Lhakhang (see below). Along the side walls are statues of Indian and Tibetan lamas belonging to the Lamrin lineage—the 'Gradual Path to Enlightenment'. The *dukhang* walls are painted with subject matter particular to the tantric disciplines. Images of Tsong Khapa and various Dalai Lamas are on the main altar.

JIGJE LHAKHANG

One of the earliest structures of Drepung, the Jigje Lhakhang, at the rear of the *dukhang*, was erected by Tsong Khapa himself. Its design is simple and the architectural elements crude but massive. The front wall is over 2.5 m thick, and surrounding the chapel is a 1.5-m-wide circumambulatory corridor. Within the chapel is Drepung's most sacred image, Jigje, said to be created by Tsong Khapa. The buffalo-headed sculpture, also known as Chögyal Chaktakma, 'the King with the Iron Rope', is a horrendous, wrathful deity. Inside it is the entire body (minus one finger) of Lama Ra Lotsawa, a major practitioner of the Yamantaka tradition. Pilgrims consider it mandatory to come and seek the blessing of this image. Jigje is the principal tutelary deity and protector of the Gelugpa. Other Gelugpa protectors here include Dorje Drakden, Mahakala, and Palden Lhamo. Also present are the Fifth Dalai Lama and Tsong Khapa. The prayer wheel at the right corner of the room was consecrated by Jigje; it embodies the 'speech' of the protector.

THE LOSELING TRATSANG

Loseling, southeast of the Tshomchen, occupies an area of 1860 sq m. Specializing in logic, it attracted the most monks. The highest official of this *tratsang* was the *khenpo*, who oversaw 23 residences (*khangtsens*) of study. Below the *khangtsens*, in size, importance and status, were the *mitsens*. Several were attached to each *khangtsen*.

DUKHANG

The *dukhang* is elaborate and grand. Its ceiling is supported by 102 columns and along the sides are 60 m of libraries. On the long altar, starting from the left, are the following statues and objects:

- *Chörten* of Legden Rinpoche, first *tripa* of Loseling
- *Chörten* of Kangyur Rinpoche, a lama of the college
- Statues of the Fifth, Eighth, and Seventh Dalai Lamas

- Statue of Jamyang Choje; beneath is a mandala of Jigje
- Statue of Sonam Drakpa, Ganden's 15th *tripa*, forced to commit suicide due to political intrigue. His spirit returned as the Gelugpa protector, Dorje Shukden, seen riding a snow-lion, carrying a sword and human heart.
- Statues of Tsong Khapa, the 13th Dalai Lama
- Throne of Sonam Drakpa
- *Chörten* of Dedrup Rinpoche, a Loseling lama
- Statues of Yabse Sum
- Dugkarma

Along the side walls, enclosed within small niches, are 1,000 images of Tsepame. At the back is a large chapel composed of three chambers whose fronts open to each other.

Neten Lhakhang (left)

The 16 Arhats are arranged in three tiers. At the center is an Enlightenment (Jangchub) *chörten*. The statue in front of it is a former *tripa* of Drepung.

Jampa Lhakhang (center)

Jampa Lhakhang has a large statue of Jampa surrounded by Sakyamuni (left), the 13th Dalai Lama (front), and Yabse Sum (right). Also present is the Kadampa triad of Atisha, Dromtönpa, and Ngok Lotsawa. The last chapel (right) has a small Sakyamuni image flanked by *chörtens*. Along the back wall are glass cabinets containing many small statues. Bookshelves line the walls.

SECOND FLOOR

Only the *gönkhang* is open on this floor. Its main image is Jigje surrounded by the protectors Sangdü, Demchok, and various Mahakalas.

GOMANG TRATSANG

Located east of Loseling, Gomang is Drepung's second largest *tratsang*. Monks from Inner Mongolia, Qinghai (Amdo), and the Nagchu region largely make up this college of 16 *khangtsens*.

DUKHANG

This assembly hall has 102 columns. The statues along the back wall, from left to right are:
- Two six-armed Mahakalas
- Tsangyang Gyatso
- Sixth Dalai Lama
- Tsong Khapa
- Dipankara, a past Buddha
- Two images of Tsong Khapa
- Chenresi
- Tsong Khapa
- Seventh Dalai Lama
  (opening to rear chapel)
- Jampa
- Tsepame

- Jamyang Chöje
- Tsong Khapa
- Chenresi

The murals depict the 108 episodes of the Buddha's life.

CHAPELS ALONG THE REAR WALL OF THE DUKHANG
Tsepak Lhakhang (left)
Within is the longevity triad of Tsepame, Namgyalma, and Drölma.

Mikyöpa Lhakhang (center)
The chamber is crowded with statues of lamas and assorted deities, all ranged on top of three staggered tiers. Mikyöpa, one of the Five Dhyani Buddhas, is at the center of the top tier. He is flanked by Sakyamuni and a smaller Mikyöpa. Below is the triad of Sakyamuni, Chenresi, and Jampa. At their feet is a statue of Tsong Khapa. At the lowest level, are five images, incarnations of Jamyang Zhepa, the renowned Gomang lama who subsequently founded the great Labrang Monastery.

Drölma Lhakhang
The main images are the 21 Drölmas, arranged in tiers along the back wall. The 16 Arhats adorn the left wall.

SECOND FLOOR
Only the *gönkhang* is here, dedicated to Dorje Drakden. Its main image, Mahakala, is flanked by its other manifestations and a statue of Jigje. Other statues are minor local deities, converted to protect Buddhism.

DEYANG TRATSANG
This is the smallest of the four *tratsangs*, dedicated to the Medicine Buddha.

DUKHANG
The main figures of this hall are Tsong Khapa and his two disciples. These are accompanied by female divinities, Dugkarma, Drölkar, and another Drölma. A statue of the Fifth Dalai Lama is significant; Deyang's main text of study was written by him. At two corners of the hall are the protectors, Dorje Drakden (left) and Palden Lhamo.

JOWO KHANG
This chapel at the back of the *dukhang* is much wider than it is deep. Its front wall is made up of a 12-m-long partition rather than a solid wall. The main image is Jampa, flanked on the left by Jangchub Peldan, a lama of the college, and the Seventh Dalai Lama. On the right are Tsong Khapa, Sakyamuni, the Third Dalai Lama, and Yönten Gyatso, first *tripa* of Ratö Monastery (see page 476) and second *tripa* of Deyang. East of the assembly hall are residences and the kitchen. The architecture of this college is one of the most interesting of the complex, being both irregular and haphazard.

THE FIVE MEDITATION CAVES OF JAMYANG CHÖJE

These are:
1) Nyare Barti Chikhang, near Ganden Potrang. Both the *chikhang* and cave seem to have been destroyed.
2) Varti Shobo Khang, near Drepung's western boundary. A small house containing the meditation cave is just above the place where monks get their water.
3) Jamyang Drubphuk (see page 151).
4) Vartsok Khang, on the southern portion of Drepung's *lingkhor*. The cave is at a corner of a willow garden, part of Deyang Tratsang. Jamyang Chöje meditated here on the image of Chenresi and obtained a vision of a *rangjung* 'Om Mani Padme Hum.' This *mantra* can be seen on the cave wall.
5) Gozhima Shamma, near Tewu Khamtsen, south of Loseling.

DREPUNG LINGKHOR

The short *lingkhor* takes 1–1 1/2 hrs to circle the monastery. From the left upper corner of the parking lot in front of the main entrance, follow a wide path up the ridge. Soon turn left (west) to reach a small gully trending north; follow this upwards (the perimeter wall of the complex is now on your right). At a trail junction marked by prominent rock carvings, turn right (east) into a walled corridor (another path zigzags up along the valley to Gephel Ritrö and the top of the ridge). Near the eastern section of the complex, the pilgrim route first turns south towards Nechung Monastery, and then east back to the main entrance. Important sites along the route are:

- Sernya Rangjung, four 'self-manifesting' gold fish imprints on rock faces. The first is behind Ganden Potrang's willow garden (south), the second to the rear of Tashi Khangsar (southwest), the third in the debating courtyard (*chöra*) of Ngagpa Tratsang (northwest), and the fourth above Ghungru Khamtsen (northeast).
- Drölma Kangchakma (Drölma with broken leg), a green *rangjung* Tara southwest of Drepung, below Ganden Potrang. The image is on a rock face.
- Chiri Rizur, southwest of Drepung, at the perimeter of the complex. Here is another green *rangjung* of Drölma, just across from the Chiri Rizur ridge.
- Drölma, inside the *chöra* of Loseling, on a rock face.
- Drölma, an image on a wall inside the courtyard of Lhawang Ling, due south of Ganden Potrang.
- Drölma, at the back door of Tsethang Chikhang, southwest of Ganden Potrang, immediately west of Lhawang Ling.
- Drölma, in a corner inside the Kungara courtyard. This summer residence of the Great Fifth is north of Ganden Potrang.
- Drölma, above Ghungru Khamtsen (north of Gomang). A tiny carving along the *lingkhor*. In front of it is a huge rock with eight hollow holes, created after the mythic Akhu Dhompa struck it with his fists.
- Print of dog's paw. Above the *lingkhor* is the Ngagpa Tratsang's willow garden. Outside the garden (north) is a sunken rock with the paw print. This dog is the same one ridden

by the divinity, Kyidra Pala.

- Near the paw print (north) is a spring called Dzamchu (Zangbala Chu, the God of Wealth's water), marked by prayer flags. Above on a hill 1 km away, is the yellow *rangjung* image of Zangbala.
- Shugtri Chenmo, a stone throne used by the Fifth Dalai Lama, north of the Tshomchen on the *lingkhor*. It stands in front of a pagoda-shaped rock with a *rangjung* Six Syllables. The Great Fifth sat here to compose Drepung's code of conduct.

GEPHEL RITRÖ AND GEPHEL ÜTSE

High above Drepung, visible from the monastery, is this restored retreat founded by Tsepa Drungchen Kunga Dorje in the 14th century. Monks here spend part of their time looking after the yak herds. The curd produced at this hermitage was reserved for the Dalai Lama. A winding trail leads up from the trail junction on the Drepung Lingkhor. Along the way are stone seats, Shugtri Ghong, made especially for the Dalai Lama. The walk takes 3–4 hrs. Gephel Ritrö is 2.5 hrs from the summit (*ütse*) of Mt Gephel Ri, sometimes called Gephel Ütse or simply the Palace (*potrang*). This mountain top, one of the most sacred and accessible in the Lhasa area, is stunning for its innumerable stone cairns erected over the centuries by pilgrims. The ceremony of juniper offerings is held here, and the most auspicious date to be here is Saga Dawa, the Buddha's birthday (the full moon of the fourth lunar month). It is important to note that it takes a solid 6–7 hrs of strenuous hiking to reach the *ütse* from Drepung Monastery, and the altitude gain is some 1500 m. This journey should definitely not be attempted by those who have only recently arrived in Tibet.

Lhalung Ritrö   The hermitage of Lhalung Paldor, assassin of Langdarma, is located 1/2 hr east of the Nechung Monastery (see page 161).

SERA:
ONE OF GELUGPA'S GREAT SIX
INSTITUTIONS

Sera lies at the base of Phurpa Chok Ri (Sera Ütse ridge), a mountain of the Tatipu Range that defines the northern limit of Lhasa City and serves as a watershed for the Kyi Chu and Penpo rivers. A good way to reach the monastery is by bicycle (or get on one of the minibus-taxis that ply between the Barkhor and Sera). From the Banak Shöl Hotel, follow the main Dekyi Shar Lam westward. One block before the post office, turn right and travel north along Chingdröl Jang Lam. At the end of this long road is the military hospital. Sera Monastery is immediately to its right (east).

THE SITE

Sera is one of the Gelugpa's Six Great monasteries (the other five are Drepung, Ganden, Tashilhunpo, Labrang, and Kumbum). It was founded in 1419 by Sakya Yeshe (1355–1435), a principal disciple of Tsong Khapa. But even before this time Tsong Khapa and his disciples, Kedrub Je and Gyaltsab Je, established meditation retreats in the Sera Ütse ridge (see page 164). The complex today, a veritable monastic city, occupies a site of nearly 12 hectares. It is made up of the Tsokchen (Great Hall), three *tratsangs*, and 30 *khangtsens*. A *khangtsen* is a residential compound with chapels reserved for monks coming from different areas of Tibet, whereas a *tratsang* is a college that offers specialized studies, headed by its own abbot (*khenpo*).

Sera, like Ganden and Drepung, was a vital center of religious activity that drew students from the far corners of Tibet. In its heyday, Sera boasted over 5,000 monks and novices. The earliest structures inside the monastery proper are Sera Me Tratsang and Ngagpa Tratsang. Sera Me taught novices and Sera Je, the largest of the *tratsangs*, was reserved for wandering monks from Kham. Ngagpa, the tantric college, gave instructions in esoteric mysticism. A long driveway conveniently divides the complex into east and west halves. To the former are the main buildings of Tsokchen and Hamdong Khangtsen. The three *tratsangs* of Sera Me, Sera Je, and the Ngagpa are to the left (west).

Sera is one of the best-preserved monasteries in Tibet; its principal buildings were inexplicably spared during the Cultural Revolution, and a few hundred monks now live here. One of the most pleasant outings in Lhasa is the 1 1/2-hr hike from the monastery to Sera Ütse, a Tsong Khapa hermitage perched high on the Phurpa Chok. A trail from here contours west to the meditation cave of Tokdhen and to the Tashi Chöling Hermitage. Eventually, it drops to the Pabonka tower at the base of the Sera ridge.

THE SERA KHORA

Pilgrims follow a well-trodden route when they visit the main chapels. The basic clockwise sequence is: Sera Me, Ngagpa Tratsang, Sera Je, Hamdong Khangtsen, Tsokchen, Tsong Khapa's hermitage.

SERA ME TRATSANG

Sera Me, built in 1419 by Sakya Yeshe, occupies 1600 sq m and is south of Sera Je. It has 13 *khangtsens* under its jurisdiction.

DUKHANG

The assembly hall, destroyed by lightning, was rebuilt in 1761 by Kunkhyen Jangchub Penpa. It has a total of eight tall and 62 short columns. The center image is a well-executed copper Sakyamuni, flanked by Jampa, Tsepame, and Jampelyang. Other statues on the long altar are Menlha, Yabse Sum, the Seventh Dalai Lama, Pabonka Rinpoche (in front of Jampelyang), and important Sera Me lamas.

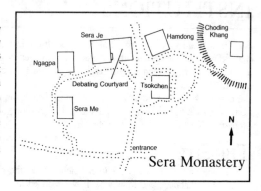

CHAPELS

Five chapels range along the back (north) wall of the *dukhang*. The dark, oppressive, westernmost chapel is Ta-og Lhakhang, containing an image of Ta-og, Dharma Protector of the East. It is housed within a shrine at the left of the chamber. Skeletons and skulls adorn the exterior. Jigje, his consort, and other protectors make up the rest of the images in this unusual chapel. Notice the many old *dorjes* hanging from a beam. Attached to a pillar are a triad of scorpions, whose purpose is to negate the evil influences of the subterranean *nagas*.

The next chapel (to the east) has a *chörten* containing an image of Tsong Khapa. Statues of Tsong Khapa and Sakyamuni flank it. Neten Lhakhang, the chapel of the 16 Arhats, is the next room. Within are statues of the Düsum Sangye and the Buddhas of the Three Ages. Clay images of the 16 Arhats are recessed within stucco wall niches that resemble mountain grottoes. Shelves lining the walls contain the many volumes of the Perfection of Wisdom Discourses (Prajnaparamita). Farther to the east is the Jowo Khang, which once housed Sera Je Tratsang's most sacred statue: the Miwang Jowo Sakyamuni. The Miwang family, influential in affairs of state, and close to Tsong Khapa, commissioned it in the 15th century. At the back is a large statue of Tsepame, and to the sides are the Eight Great Bodhisattvas. Guarding the entrance are the protectors, Tamdrin and Acala.

The last chapel of the *dukhang* is the Tsongkha Lhakhang, consecrated to Tsong Khapa. Surrounding him are important Gelugpa personalities. Among these are the First, Second, Third, and Fifth Dalai Lamas, Sakya Yeshe (founder of Sera), and Gyaltsen Zangpo (the monastery's first abbot). The founder of Sera Me, Kunkhyen Jangchub Penpa, can be seen seated next to the Kadampa patriarchs, Dromtönpa and Atisha.

SECOND FLOOR

The Nyima Lhakhang, on the left after the stairs, is consecrated to Tuwang Tsultrim, a form of Sakyamuni. To its right is a stone image of Drölma (recently moved here), and the most important statue of the Tsang Khangtsen. The Kangyur Lhakhang, opposite the Nyima Lhakhang, once housed the 108 volumes of the Buddhist canon. These were lost or destroyed during the Cultural Revolution. Today this chamber has 1,000 statues of Drölma—and is thus also known as the Drölma Lhakhang. Three statues right of the altar are the longevity triad of Drölma, Tsepame, and Namgyalma. Upstairs are the residential quarters of the Dalai Lama.

NGAGPA TRATSANG

This building is Sera's oldest surviving structure. It was built in 1419 by Sakya Yeshe, just prior to the founding of Sera Me Tratsang, as the main assembly hall. After the installation of the larger Tsokchen, it became the monastery's only tantric college. Ngagpa is the smallest of Sera's three *tratsangs*. The ground floor of the 3-story building consists of a *dukhang* and four chapels.

DUKHANG

This assembly hall has 42 short and four tall columns. The principal statue, of Sakya Yeshe, is the oldest in the *tratsang*. The black hat, inscribed in Sanskrit and worn by the patriarch, was probably a gift from China's Yongle Emperor (1360–1424), who gave a similar hat to the Karmapa Lama. On the left, between Jampa and the Pabonka Rinpoche, is Gyaltsen Zangpo, Sera's first abbot (he can be identified by his goatee). Other famous lamas of Sera sit on either side of Sakya Yeshe. To the far right are statues of Chökyi Gyaltsen, author of an important text on debate and philosophy, and Lodrö Rinchen, founder of Sera Je. Also present are the Yabse Sum and the 13th Dalai Lama. Murals depict stories of Sakyamuni, the Western Paradise, and other themes. The pillars, capitals and entablature of the assembly hall are elaborately carved. At the top of each pillar is a niche containing a tiny image flanked by dragons and floral motifs.

CHAPELS

Neten Lhakhang

The Neten Lhakhang lies left of the back wall, north of the *dukhang*. Within it are statues of Sakyamuni and the 16 Arhats. The latter are noteworthy: a first series, in the Tibetan style, are placed within niches along the upper part of the walls; below these, on a platform, are a second and smaller series made of Chinese-style lacquer—a gift from the Yongle Emperor to Sakya Yeshe. A small figure of Milarepa is to the right of Sakyamuni. Other statues include the Four Guardians and Tamdrin.

Jigje Lhakhang

This chapel, east of Neten Lhakhang, has within it the central image of Jigje, specially commissioned and personally consecrated by Sakya Yeshe. Within the statue's stomach is the thumb of Relö Draya. Other statues portray the various forms of Mahakala and other protectors (Palden Lhamo, Dharmaraja).

UPPER FLOORS

The second-floor chapel of Tsepame (Amitayus) has at its center a statue of Tsepame. Two *chörtens* containing the relics of Gyaltsen Zangpo and Jetsun Chökyi Gyaltsen flank the image. Next to these is another *chörten* paid for by the Lhajang Khan. The Eight Medicine Buddhas surround the altar. The third floor contains the Dalai Lama's chambers.

SERA JE TRATSANG

This is Sera's largest college and the second largest building (1700 sq m) in the complex after the Tsokchen. The founder, Gungyal Lodrö Rinchen Senge, was a disciple of both Sakya Yeshe and Tsong Khapa. During the early 18th C., the college's rapidly increased enrolment required a fourth story to be added and the assembly hall to be enlarged to a room of 100 columns.

DUKHANG

The entrance portico has murals depicting the Wheel of Life (left), and the Indian cosmos and mandala of Mt Meru. Flanking the entrance are the Four Guardians, painted in the Chinese style. The ground floor assembly hall is sumptuously decorated with *thangkas* and brocaded hanging banners. Murals tell the life-story of the Buddha. Along the north wall are statues and *chörtens* belonging to important lamas of the *tratsang*, abbots (*tripas*) of Ganden, and regents. Among the *chörtens* are statues of the Eighth and 13th Dalai Lamas, the Second and the Ninth Reting *tulkus*, and the founder of Sera Je, Lodrö Rinchen (fourth to the right). The Dalai Lama's throne and a smaller throne belonging to the Panchen Lama are here as well.

CHAPELS

These are located west and north of the *dukhang*. Enter the first chapel (west) via a doorway along the hall's left-hand wall.

Düsum Sangye Lhakhang

This chapel is dedicated to the Buddhas of the Three Ages. The Eight Bodhisattvas are also present.

Tamdrin Lhakhang

A passage leads into Sera's most important chapel, which is consecrated to Tamdrin, the chief protector of Sera Je. The statue of the deity is placed within a gilt-copper shrine at the center of the chamber. It was sculpted by the college's founder, Lodrö Rinchen. Known as Pema Yangsang Drakpo, it supposedly spoke out loud, warning of a disaster soon to befall the country. The statue is greatly revered by pilgrims. At the Tamdrin shrine's upper left is a famous, sacred ritual dagger (*phurpa*). In legend, the dagger belonged to the deity, Dorje Shonnü; he empowered the *phurpa*, which then flew from India to a hill behind Sera, where the Phurpa Chok hermitage was built to commemorate the event. The tantric master, Darchapa, rediscovered the dagger within Guru Rinpoche's cave at Yerpa. This relic is on public view during the

15th day of the 12th lunar month. Next to it are statues of various protectors. This dark and eerie chapel also contains numerous wrathful masks that decorate the pillars and walls. Along the blackened upper walls and rafters are hung many suits of chain-mail armor, swords, shields and other weaponry. Tibetan soldiers returning from campaigns gave these as offerings.

Jampa Lhakhang

Within the chapel are statues of Jampa, the 11-faced Chenresi and the Yabse Sum. Library shelves adorn the walls.

Tsong Khapa Lhakhang

Dedicated to the founder of the Gelugpa, this chapel has statues of Tsong Khapa, Yabse Sum, important lamas of Sera Je, the Indian master Nagarjuna, and the protectors Tamdrin and Acala.

Jampelyang Lhakhang

At the northeast corner of the assembly hall, this chapel is dedicated to Jampelyang (Manjusri), the Bodhisattva of Wisdom. The central image of the deity holds the posture of 'turning the wheel of Dharma'; its upper torso is distinctly oriented towards the window, which looks out onto the debating courtyard. According to the caretakers, Jampelyang is raptly listening to the monks' heated discussions. Flanking it are Jampa and Jampelyang.

UPPER FLOORS

There are two chapels on the second floor. Zhelre Lhakhang (west) has a nine-headed Tamdrin as the central image. Also on the altar are statues of Guru Rinpoche and the Fifth Dalai Lama. Above the latter is a row of cabinet-shrines containing wrathful protectors. Jangra Sela Khang (east) is dedicated to Chenresi.

The third floor chapel is named Namgyal Lhakhang. The Dalai Lama stayed in a suite on the fourth floor, which also contains rooms for the abbot.

KHANGTSENS

Sera Je Tratsang controls 17 *khangtsens*, the chapels and dormitories specifically occupied by monks from Tibet's various districts.

DEBATING COURTYARD

This pleasant corner of the complex is well-shaded by ancient trees. The site of the age-old tradition of philosophical debate, at the far end of the open space, is a platform where monks are formally examined. A venerated relic in the courtyard is a large stone under a shrine. Pilgrims make offerings of butter, scarves, and assorted talismans here. According to tradition, Tsong Khapa was writing his great commentary on Nagarjuna's classic, The Middle Way, at a simple mountain retreat overlooking today's site of Sera. Suddenly, the vowel 'A' appeared 13 times in written form above his head. When the master finally finished the treatise, the 'A's' descended from the sky to the valley floor and dissolved into this stone.

HAMDONG KHANGTSEN

This institution is intimately connected with the Sera Je; many of the college's monks stayed at Hamdong. Descendants of the Miwang family built the Khangtsen.

DUKHANG

No central image stands in the assembly hall. The altar statues are Tsong Khapa, Chökyi Gyaltsen (left) Sakyamuni, Drölma, Tsepame and Namgyalma (right).

CHAPELS

There are two chapels at the back of the main hall.

Jampa Khang

The central image is Jampa. To the left is a statue of the recently deceased lama, Thubten Kunga, a man responsible for renovation before the Cultural Revolution. A sacred object here is a Drölma statue placed within a cabinet-shrine, attached to a column on the left. Supposedly the guardian of Sera's spring water, it is said that it spoke aloud on several occasions.

Gönkhang

The central image is Gyalchen Karma Thinle, a manifestation of Tamdrin, Hamdong's special protector.

TSOKCHEN

The Tsokchen is Sera's largest building and administrative center. It was built in 1710 with funds donated by Lhajang Khan, leader of the Qosots who conquered Lhasa. At the northeast portion of the complex, this four-story building (2000 sq m) has a flagstoned terrace, a south-facing assembly hall and five *lhakhangs*. The spacious ten-column entrance portico carries murals of the Four Guardian Kings.

DUKHANG

The impressive assembly hall has 89 tall columns and 36 short ones. A skylight, supported by the tall columns, opens at the center of the ceiling and magnificent appliqué *thangkas* hang from ceiling to floor along the side walls. The principal statue is Sakya Yeshe, founder of Sera. He is flanked by the Fifth and the 13th Dalai Lamas. After the death of the Seventh Dalai Lama, a 5-m-high gilt statue of Jampa was added to the right (east). This particularly fine work shows the Future Buddha seated on a throne supported by two lions. Other images include the

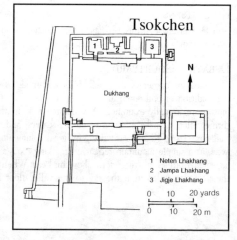

Tsokchen

Dukhang

N

1 Neten Lhakhang
2 Jampa Lhakhang
3 Jigje Lhakhang

0   10   20 yards

0   10   20 m

Yabse Sum and high Gelugpa lamas. To the left is the Seventh Dalai Lama; in front of him are Chökyi Gyaltsen, Tsong Khapa and Regent Sangye Gyatso.

CHAPELS

To the rear of the assembly hall are three chapels.

Jampa Lhakhang

The Tsokchen's principal image is to be found here: a 6-m-high Jampa with an elaborate back halo made up of a *garuda* and other mythical animals. It extends into the second floor and the statue's torso and face can be seen from the upper Zhelre Lhakhang. To the sides are the Eight Bodhisattvas and the guardians, Tamdrin and Acala. Along the south wall are large library shelves containing an important treasure of Sera, a set of the Kangyur embossed with the Chinese royal seal—'Yongle Eighth Year Edition' (1410)—a gift to Sakya Yeshe from the Yongle Emperor. Of 108 volumes, only 105 remain. Each volume has manuscript covers meticulously crafted of red lacquer and carved with gold designs.This Kangyur was the first Tibetan Buddhist work printed from wood blocks. As such, it is a valuable resource for the study of early printing techniques. The wood blocks were sent from Tibet to China and the printed copy returned.

Neten Lhakhang

West of the Jampa Lhakhang is the Neten Lhakhang. It houses clay images of the 16 Arhats and Four Guardian Kings. In the center is an image of Sakyamuni. The original *arhat* statues were made of wood and brought from China by Sakya Yeshe. Later, precise clay molds were made, preserving the Ming sculptural style, and the authentic wooden images placed inside.

Jigje Lhakhang

To the far right (east) of the Jampa Lhakhang is the Jigje Lhakhang. Its main image is Yamantaka and his consort, surrounded by statues of Palden Lhamo and other protectors.

SECOND FLOOR

Zhelre Lhakhang

The two sides of this floor are monks' quarters. To the rear-center is the Zhelre Lhakhang, from where the face and torso of Jampa can be viewed. Notice the small image of Tsong Khapa enshrined within the heart of the giant statue.

Thuje Chenpo Lhakhang

Left of the Zhelre Lhakhang is Thuje Chenpo Lhakhang, containing a refined thousand-armed Chenresi, a sacred image venerated by pilgrims. To receive the statue's blessing, place a staff between your head and Chenresi's heart. The statue was originally hidden in Pabonka Monastery (see page 129), then later discovered and installed at Sera. Images of Drölma and six-armed Nagpo Chenpo (Mahakala) are also here. A final chapel has the main image of Sakyamuni flanked by Gelugpa lamas.

THIRD AND FOURTH FLOORS

These two floors contain the living quarters of the Tsokchen abbot, assembly halls, administrative offices (*lhaje*), and a residential suite reserved for the Dalai Lama.

CHÖDING KHANG: TSONG KHAPA'S HERMITAGE

A path behind the Tsokchen leads along telegraph poles (right) up the slopes of Sera Ütse to this unassuming structure, the sacred site where Tsong Khapa lived and worked. Just behind the Tsokchen are several impressive rocks carved with the images of Tsong Khapa, Jamchen Chöje (below Tsong Khapa), and Dharmaraja and consort. From here, it is possible to enter the Tsokchen at the roof level.

Tsong Khapa's original retreat was destroyed during the Cultural Revolution; a new replica now stands on the site. Within this yellow structure is a simple altar with his image. Just up the slopes is the ancient meditation cave actually used by Tsong Khapa himself. A small shrine has been built over it. The building in front of the hermitage was a retreat for monks attached to Lhasa's Tantric colleges.

SERA ÜTSE

To reach Tsong Khapa's retreat of Sera Ütse (Sera Tse), follow the main tree-lined road inside the compound. After passing Sera Je on the left and Tsokchen on the right, a footpath zigzags up Sera Ütse's ridge at the road's northern end. Follow a ravine with cypresses, passing several white buildings on the left. On the right, near the Tsokchen's gilded roofs, look out for painted rock carvings of *mantras* and *bodhisattvas*. Nearby is the hermitage of Chöding Khang. Continue up the main trail and follow a series of switchbacks that hug the ravine. Sera Ütse is 1 1/2 hr from Sera Monastery.

Founded earlier than the monastery, this hermitage (also used by Tsong Khapa) consists of a chapel (two floors) and the lama's quarters in a small separate building off to the right. A shrine stands farther up the hillside among ruins—this is the *gönkhang* consecrated to Pehar (see Nechung, opposite) and Palden Lhamo. Between the chapel and the lama's quarters is a pleasant courtyard with potted plants and a sensational view of the Lhasa Valley. Several monks live at the hermitage. A flat trail leads to the right (east) of the monastery and goes around the ridge to the ruined hermitages of Raga Chok, Keutsang, and Phurpa Chok (see also Dode Valley, p 193).

SERA ÜTSE TO TOKDHEN DRUBPHUK AND PABONKA MONASTERY

The trail west from Sera Ütse leads to the Tokdhen meditation cave (see page 135) and Pabonka (page 129). Contour along the Sera Ütse ridge, traversing a couple of spurs, to reach a deep ravine (1 hr). The Tashi Chöling Hermitage (page 134) is on the other side. Walk down into the ravine and then switchback up to the Tokdhen cave (1/2 hr). Pabonka, at the base of the Sera Ütse, is a descent of 3/4 hr from here.

OTHER CHAPELS AND HERMITAGES

Sera administers numerous chapels, retreats, abbots' residences, and buildings outside of Lhasa. These are scattered all over the Ü and Tsang provinces and include Reting Monastery (see page 563), Tsomön Ling Monastery (see page 169), and Pabonka Monastery (see page 129). Near Sera are Kelsang Labrang, Phurpa Chok Labrang, Chusang Jantenling Ritrö, Tashi Chöling Ritrö, Kardo Ritrö, Palung Ritrö, Rikatse Ritrö, Tagten Sungpu Ritrö, Jowo Ritrö, Drakri Ritrö, Nebodun Ritrö, Ghari Gongba Ritrö and others.

NECHUNG:
SEAT OF THE STATE ORACLE

The Nechung Monastery in Lhasa is the seat of Nechung, the State Oracle of Tibet. It is also the residence of Pehar, chief guardian-protector of the Gelugpa sect. Known as the 'Demon Fortress of the Oracle King' (Sungi Gyalpo Tsenka), it is a unique institution. Associated with exorcism and retaining remnants of pre-Buddhist rites, Nechung is imbued with a special quality of magic and mystery. It is palpable even upon approach: on the striking monastery doors, against a blood red background, are painted ivory-colored animal and human skins. These are intertwined among ornate, gilt-copper inlay. Macabre, intricate human and non-human heads decorate the metal strips, and the large door rings are elaborate gilt-copper skulls. Two feet with sharp claws grasp the upper corners of the doors.

The Nechung Oracle (Nechung Chöje) was the medium through which the protector Pehar revealed itself to the world. After entering a trance, the oracle became physically and spiritually possessed by a spirit-representative, Dorje Drakden ('The Renowned Immutable One'), Pehar's chief minister and mouthpiece. The Lhasa government undertook no major decisions without first consulting the oracle. Since the Fifth Dalai Lama, Nechung's oracles have had immense influence and power in Tibet's internal and external affairs. Although nominally a Nyingmapa establishment, it has been religiously and politically linked to Drepung Monastery. During important occasions, the State Oracle appeared to 80,000 people in Lhasa, and yet most Tibetans have little knowledge of the monastery's function or secret processes.

The Pehar legend

Guru Rinpoche came to Tibet in the 8th C. at the invitation of King Trisong Detsen and the Indian master Santarakshita (see page 297). To safeguard and spread the new religion of Buddhism, he battled a multitude of indigenous demons. Summoning all his miraculous powers, the guru subdued nearly all of them, at the same time turning them to the task of protecting Buddhism. Five demons, however, proved much stronger than the others. In a series of spectacular magical battles, Guru Rinpoche vanquished them all. He named the five Pehar Gyalpo—the Five Ferocious Kings— and they became the most powerful of the entire hierachy of protective spirits.

Tradition says Pehar originally resided at Zahor in Bengal. He later transferred his seat, as the tutelary deity of the Hor tribes, to the monastery of Bhata Hor in Central Asia. After staying at Samye for several centuries, Pehar was moved to Tshal Gungthang Monastery (see page 198). There arose a conflict between the institution's founding abbot, Lama Shang, and the protector. Through trickery and deception, Pehar animated a painting of a monkey which set the monastery on fire. To retaliate, Lama Shang performed a secret ritual to capture the protector in a box. He succeeded, and the box was thrown into the Kyi Chu River. It was spotted by the abbot of

➡

Drepung Monastery, who ordered a monk to fish it from the river. While walking up to the monastery the monk, overcome by curiosity, opened the box and Pehar escaped in the form of a dove. He flew to a nearby birch tree and then vanished. It was at this tree, just below Drepung, that a shrine called Nechung was built at the end of the 12th century. In time, the protector became manifest within the body and through the voice of a lama. The State Oracle of Nechung was born.

To maintain the tenuous link with Pehar's powerful world, Nechung's monks trained rigorously. Eight hours of practice and ritual, spread over four sessions, was the daily routine. The oracle himself memorized 500 pages of tantric liturgy, and mastered a multitude of intricate tasks. Officials kept meticulous records of the trance sessions and predictions. These were written by employing an inkless bamboo pen on nine two-foot long black boards, which were dusted with limestone powder.

The State Oracle and six of Nechung's 150 monks fled to India in 1959 and now live in exile, but they are still an important part of the Dalai Lama's governing apparatus. East of Nechung is a complex of renovated buildings, presently a debating school for over 100 young monks. They belong to all four major sects, although the texts of instruction are purely Gelugpa.

Location

Nechung, nestled within a grove of juniper and fruit trees, lies 10 min southeast of the monastic city of Drepung. A lane, marked by a water tower, leads to the oracle's residence. Beyond the east main entrance is a courtyard.

The site

COURTYARD

The square, cloistered courtyard, covered with stone slabs, has murals of Pehar's various manifestations and the minor deities of his retinue. Of its three gates, the southernmost is always closed. There is a belief that the Protector Dorje Shugden is constantly waiting outside, biding his time for Pehar's eventual departure. Once this comes to pass, the *chökyong* ('protector of the religious laws') will be allowed to enter the gate and become the chief Protector of Tibet. Visitors can enter the east and west gates. A *doring*, crowned with a pagoda roof and flanked by two incense burners, is consecrated to Pehar but has no inscription. At the courtyard's north end is the main, three-story structure. Steps flanked by Chinese-style lions lead up to a portico. To the sides of the main door are the large paintings of Pehar and Dorje Drakden, his chief minister.

GROUND FLOOR

Nechung's three most important rooms stand behind the dark, bare *dukhang* (sombre murals show demonic deities, mythical palaces, and sacrificial victims).

On the left (west) is the high-ceilinged Jordhung Khang. Its most sacred relic is a tree stump believed to be Pehar's first residence when he became a dove. Flanking this are two images of the deity. A *thangka* depicts his peaceful aspect, as a wise old man, and a statue shows him in the more familiar wrathful form. Other statues in the room include Tsong Khapa and Guru Rinpoche.

A center chapel, the Tsenkhang Üma, has the Buddha Sakyamuni as its main image. It is flanked by pedestals of destroyed statues of the Eight Bodhisattvas. Before the Cultural Revolution, a massive, silver-plated throne dominated the middle of the room; the Nechung Oracle sat here to be possessed. His robes and weighty helmet waited in readiness on top of the throne. A statue of Guru Rinpoche, known as Kushab Rinpoche and purportedly made by the great sage himself, stood behind the throne. This extraordinarily powerful relic contained the life-forces used by Guru Rinpoche to control Pehar. Some valuable *thangkas* depict protectors Relchikma (Ekajati), Gönpo with his consort, and Tsedrekma. The Tsenkhang Üma is considered the monastery's most important room.

The east chapel, *gönkhang* of the monastery, is called Dunkhang Üma. It is consecrated to Magzor Gyalmo, the 'Victorious One Who Turns Back Enemies', a wrathful female manifestation of Palden Lhamo, Guardian of Lhasa and protector of the Gelugpa. A statue of the Dzokchen protectress, Nyima Shönnu, also stands in this room. Formerly, a sacred statue here represented Pehar and all his manifestations combined into a single form (Kundu Gyalpo). This image was paraded around the monastery at times when the seat of the oracle was vacant— when Pehar had not yet entered the body of a new medium. A chapel at the *dukhang*'s right side has stairs that lead to the second floor (usually closed).

SECOND FLOOR

Leave the ground floor and go around to a small door at the building's right to reach the second floor's two restored chapels. The larger one, audience room of the Dalai Lamas, has a throne that was used by the Fifth through 14th. Statues here donated by Drepung Monastery consist of Tsong Khapa, the Great Fifth placed next to Sakyamuni, and Jampa. To the right of the throne are statues of the Yabse Sum and Chenresi. The adjacent chapel, consecrated to Tsong Khapa, holds new statues of the Yabse Sum, Sakyamuni, Chenresi, and Drölma.

ROOF LEVEL

The only chapel on this level is dedicated to Guru Rinpoche. In the center of the room is a large statue of the tantric master as the wrathful 'Suppressor of the Three Realms' (Khamsum Zilnon). Supposedly a Lhasa sculptor completed the image in 1981.

RESIDENCE OF THE ORACLE

The Nechung Oracle's private house stands behind the monastery. Some oracles chose to live in the main building.

NECHUNG'S TREASURES

Nechung Monastery possessed two treasures. One, the Pehar Korzdo, belonged to Tibet's government and consisted of many valuable objects, from gold bullion to Chinese bricks of tea. Pehar supposedly guarded this personally. The second treasure, owned by the monastery, consisted of donations by Sakya Yarphel, a famous oracle, and Phungrab, a warlord who lived at the start of the 20th century. Phungrab also gave a large sum of money to gild the monastery's roof.

THE FOUR ROYAL MONASTERIES

The Four Royal Monasteries of Lhasa, decreed as such by the Fifth Dalai Lama (1617–82), were Gelugpa institutions whose abbots were often chosen to be the Regents of Tibet. They are Tengye Ling, Tsomön Ling, Kunde Ling, and Drib Tsemchok Ling. All were built after the 17th century.

TENGYE LING

Tengye Ling is located 100 m from the Snowland Hotel. A small lane directly across from the hotel runs behind the Tibetan Hospital; follow it to an elaborate entrance portal on the right. Inside the portal is a maze of Tibetan homes within a compound. Keep walking north and ask for directions to the monastery, which is sited towards the back of the compound.

Tengye Ling's western section, once called Seshing, is now occupied by the Lhasa No. 1 Middle School. Many of its chapels were destroyed during the Cultural Revolution. The monastery's large courtyard has been filled with many small, cramped Tibetan houses; and the main entrance is nearly hidden from view by the frenzied overbuilding.

Tengye Ling now consists of only a paved stone courtyard surrounded on three sides by monk's quarters. The three-story main temple, the King's Palace, the treasury, and the secretariat's offices stood on the fourth (north) side. The ground floor of the main temple, divided into east and west sections, contained the most important chapels. In the east is a squarish assembly hall. Behind it, to the north, are three doors leading to a 2-m wide corridor. Three identical doors on the north wall of this corridor open into three *lhakhangs*. This unusual arrangement employs the corridor as a buffer between the main hall and the chapels. During the Mönlam (New Year's) Festival, monks from the Drepung Monastery's Gomang Tratsang used to stay in this part of Tengye Ling. The western section consisted of another assembly hall, about 20 m in width and about 10 m deep. Behind it are large storage rooms. This section, once under the jurisdiction of Sakya Monastery, was used as a printing room. Later it was given over to Samye Monastery.

The *gönkhang*, reached by a flight of narrow stone steps, is on the roof level and consists of a small assembly hall in the front and a raised section, containing the altars and statues, in the back. This is the only renovated, active part of Tengye Ling today. Religious services are held regularly by a few monks and one lama (two of the monks are from Samye). Behind Tengye Ling (north), inside a pleasant garden, is the pretty yellow building of the Demo Labrang. This was the residence of the incarnate lama (Demo Qutuqtu) of the monastery.

GÖNKHANG

The altar at the back wall of this chapel has three wrathful protectors (*sungma*) and a Guru Rinpoche statue. In the center the black-faced Tseumar, the special *sungma* of Tengye Ling. Left of this is Pehar Gyalpo; the Chökyong is on the right. Along the left wall is a statue of Guru Rinpoche, butter sculptures dedicated to Tamdrin, the horse-headed deity, and a library of wood blocks. The right wall has statues of Tamdrin Zungjuk, considered a *terma*, and Phurpa Dorje Zhonnu in *yabyum*. Inside the head of the former is a 'secret support' (*sangten*), a small statue of the deity found in Bhutan and wrapped in red cloth. These new statues are donated by devotees. Affiliated with Samye, Tengye Ling is presently an important Nyingmapa shrine for the cult of the *sungmas*. It is the main temple for the *sungma* Tseumar; a belief states that his essence was preserved here in ancient times.

HISTORY

Tengye Ling was the most important of the Four Royal Monasteries. Its abbots, acknowledged as recurring incarnations, held the Mongol title of Demo Qutuqtu. They became Regents of Tibet three times. The first filled that position from 1757–77 for the Eighth Dalai Lama, the second was regent from 1810 to 1819 for the Ninth and Tenth Dalai Lamas, and the third remained regent from 1886 to 1895. This last Regent was deposed and thrown into prison by the young Dalai Lama who then took control of the government. The monastery remained hostile to the 13th thereafter. In 1912, Tengye Ling was badly damaged by the Tibetan government for its support of the Chinese who occupied Lhasa. It became Lhasa's post office for a while, and ultimately was stripped of its royal authority. Meru Sarpa, across the street from the Kirey Hotel, took its place.

TSOMÖN LING

South of Ramoche Monastery. Tsomön Ling's entrance is north of the junction between the Banak Shöl Hotel street and the Snowland Hotel street. Original pillars survive, and the rooftop is worth a visit. Two-story monks' residences surround on three sides the large courtyard in front of the main building. Lay Tibetans now occupy them. The main building, located at the north end of the complex, consists of two main sections built during two different periods. Karpo Potrang ('White Palace'), the eastern half, was built in 1777 during the regency of the first Nomun Qan Qutuqtu (official title of the Tsomön Ling incarnates). The ground floor housed the main assembly hall, six *lhakhangs* at the back, and the *chörten*-tombs of the second and third Nomun Qans. The second floor contained the *gönkhang*; the third consisted of the abbots' quarters.

Marpo Potrang ('Red Palace'), in the west, was constructed by the second Nomun Qans at the start of the 19th century. The architecture and the decoration showed a significant improvement over the earlier section. Behind the main assembly hall were two *gönkhangs* and a *lhakhang* dedicated to the Eight Medicine Buddhas. The *chörten*-tombs of the third and fourth Nomun Qans were in the main hall. Tsomön Ling's incarnates were twice elected regents, first from 1777 to 1784 for the Eighth Dalai Lama, and finally for the Tenth and 11th Dalai Lamas. This second regent ruled from 1819 to 1844 until he was exiled to China.

KUNDE LING

This monastery is located behind (south) sacred Bhama Ri, to the west of the Potala. From the post office, walk west along the main road of Dekyi Nub Lam towards the Lhasa Hotel. After Chakpo Ri and its cave monastery of Dragla Lugug, come to another small hill, on the left. This is Bhama Ri. Below it is a small, disused gas station (a short distance after the new one). Beyond, a dirt road turns left off the paved road to go around the hill. Follow the dirt road into a small village. Kunde Ling is here. The original complex was large and several chapels stood within a pleasant wooded garden. Kunde Ling's main four-story structure housed an assembly hall with a ceiling nearly the height of the building.

In the back, the principal chapel was dedicated to Tsong Khapa. This room was later converted to house the *chörten*-tombs of the monastery's various Tasak Qutuqtu incarnations. Eight monks and a lama (Tasak Rinpoche) look after a small, rebuilt chapel. The monastery has a special relationship with Eastern Tibet (Kham); its first abbot came from that region. Kunde Ling was the seat of the Tasak Qutuqtu and two of its incarnates became Tibet's regents, the first from 1791 to 1819 for the Eighth and Ninth Dalai Lamas and the second from 1875 to 1886 for the 13th Dalai Lama.

DRIB TSEMCHOK LING

This monastery, a small chapel, lies south of the Kyi Chu across from Lhasa proper. It is located in the picturesque village of Drib, at the entrance of the Tungo La Valley (see page 596). The main building survived the Cultural Revolution; the abbot is the Tsemchok Rinpoche. Tsemchok Ling was built in 1782 by Yeshe Gyaltsen, tutor of the Eighth Dalai Lama. Its construction took only five months. The original 7000-sq m complex faced the Tungo La range to the south. It contained a full set of the Kangyur, printed at Narthang Monastery, and an important copper statue of Tsong Khapa.

THE TRATSANGS: MONASTIC COLLEGES

GYÜRME TRATSANG

Located on Dekyi Shar Lam (Xingfu Dong Lu), Gyürme Tratsang (Lower Tantric College) is directly across the street from the Tibet–Gansu Trade Center, a four-story building immediately west of the Kirey Hotel. East of Gyürme Tratsang, also on Dekyi Shar Lam, is Meru Sarpa Tratsang. Gyürme's entranceway, with a blue-and-white canvas awning, is visible from the street.

History

Gyürme Tratsang was a major religious institution of Lhasa, ranked only below Sera, Drepung, and Ganden. During the 15th C., Je Sherab Senge (1382–1445), one of Tsong Khapa's eight principal disciples, established for the first time a tantric college in Se, Tsang Province. It was then known as Se Gyüpa and specialized in training novices in intricate tantric rituals. Before construction was finished, Je Sherab Senge returned to Lhasa. Sometime later he built another tantric college at Ganden. Demand for enrolment led him to establish one large college at Chumelung, west of Lhasa. This and the one in Se became known as the Upper and Lower Tantric Colleges. Every year, for a period of one and a half months, the monks of both underwent a strict retreat at Yangpachen Monastery (see page 679). Still not satisfied with these tantric institutions, Je Sherab Senge in his later years helped to found more tantric colleges at monasteries such as Tshal Gungthang, Sera, Dechen, and Medro Gongkar. The present structures of Gyürme were built in the 18th C. by Techen Phagtö, principal official (kalon) within the Tibetan cabinet (kashag). According to tradition, only monks from Sera, Drepung, and Ganden were allowed admission.

      The Upper (Gyürto) and Lower (Gyürme) Tantric Colleges of Lhasa were famous for their discipline. No one was allowed to wear shoes during cold midnight assemblies. During recitation of sutras in the debate courtyard, each monk had to dig a small pit, cover the bottom with stones, and sit within. This observance was mandatory, regardless of the weather. Meals were strictly controlled and no food was allowed after midday. The central part of the syllabus contained the four Gelugpa tantras; and the monks were renowned for their depth of learning. They regularly took pilgrimages outside Lhasa. Every year the itinerary was pre-determined and unalterable. These group 'outings' required everyone to carry all their necessities. Only the abbots were allowed to ride horses. High-ranking members of the college went on pilgrimage for only one year; lower ones faced an extended sojourn of nine years. Because of Gyürme's high and enviable reputation for learning, its abbots often were candidates for the abbacy of Ganden Monastery. Some 40 monks are presently attached to Gyürme Tratsang.

DRÖLMA LHAKHANG

Drölma Lhakhang, principal chapel of Gyürme Tratsang, is located on the second floor of the main building. (The ground floor dukhang houses a press for printing the Lhasa Kangyur.)

Reach it via a set of stairs outside and to the right of the main temple entrance. The most interesting objects in the chapel are 30 beautifully-crafted begging bowls, hung by leather straps in the center of the large room. These utensils, held within special cloth coverings, are made of iron with an unusual, black, lacquer-like sheen. In the old days, each of the 575 monks had one of these bowls, which was used to beg alms, make edible offerings (*torma*), and to eat *tsampa*.

Left of the entrance is a cabinet containing a new protector statue (*sungma*). Most of the chapel's objects and relics are lined up on altars along the west and north walls. Starting from the left: a Kadampa *chörten*, statues of Jampelyang, Chana Dorje, Drölma, Tsepame, Sakyamuni, Yabse Sum, Jampa Chökorma, Demchok, Sangwa Düpa, the 13th Dalai Lama, the Dalai Lama's throne, Tsong Khapa, Je Sherab Senge (founder of Gyürme Tratsang), and Jampa. A repainted Green Tara, said to have spoken out loud (and so with *sungjönma* attributes) is behind the Demchok statue. The west wall, across from the entrance, has recent paintings of the Eight Drölmas and Namgyalma. These have been repainted exactly over the originals.

TSANGKHANG

A door at the northeast corner of Drölma Lhakhang leads out to a balcony that opens onto the two-story, inner chapel of the ground floor. Ranged along the back (north) wall of this spacious chamber are three 6-m-high statues of the Yabse Sum (Tsong Khapa and his two disciples). These new works, placed on a 2-m-high dais, were commissioned by an old lama from Amdo. The faithful donated Rmb 30,000 and the work took a year. Left of the three statues is a partition containing a glass cabinet. Within it is a Namse image: it commemorates Gyürme's construction on the site of the mythical Namse Potrang.

KANGYUR LHAKHANG

This third-floor chapel has an old, bronze Sakyamuni as its principal image, centered along the north wall. Flanking it is a new set of the Kangyur. The west wall has statues of Tsong Khapa and the Yabse Sum, inside a cabinet. A stone plaque displays the footprint (*shabje*) of an unknown lama. Opposite this, by the east wall, is another statue of Sakyamuni. All images in the room, except for the central Sakyamuni, are new.

Zhelre Lhakhang

Across the passage from the Kangyur Lhakhang, this chamber looks upon Tsong Khapa's two-story-high upper torso in the north *tsangkhang*.

Zimchung

On the fourth floor, this tiny room with one column is the Dalai Lama's bedroom.

Gönkhang

Located near the side (east) entrance to the *tsangkhang* on the ground floor, this high-ceilinged room with new murals has at the back wall a new statue of Jigje, flanked by Sangwa Düpa (left) and Demchok. The left wall has Gönpo and Lhamo, and the right, Chögyal and Namse.

THE DUKHANG

A large assembly hall (48 columns) on the ground floor. At the back of the hall (now a printing press) is the north inner chapel (*tsangkhang*). Along the eastern wall are three side chapels; no corresponding chapels can be found on the western side. The murals tell episodes of the Gelugpa.

Debate Courtyard

This open-air structure is west of the main building.

SHIDE TRATSANG

Shide Tratsang is located on the north side of Dekyi Shar Lam (Xingfu Dong Lu) near the point where it joins the Snowland Hotel street. Shide is slightly west of the junction. To go: Walk north along the Snowland Hotel street to its intersection with Dekyi Shar Lam. Cross to the north side and walk west. Pass a lane on the right, then turn right at a second lane. This leads straight into an entrance gate and Shide's main courtyard. The courtyard is surrounded on three sides by two-story residences. The fourth side is the central chapel (closed). To enter, return to the entrance gate and follow a perimeter wall eastward, back towards Tsomön Ling (see page 169), then northward along a lane. (Reting Labrang is at the end of this lane.) The imposing three-story building on your left is the Shide Tratsang. Go through a side entrance to the roof, then descend interior stairs to the badly sacked main chapel.

History

According to tradition, Shide was founded by Ralpachen (r 815–38) as one of six principal *lhakhangs* surrounding the Jokhang. It took its present form in the 14th C. as a dependency of Reting Monastery and was the resident chapel of the Reting Tulku. More than ten incarnates (*tulku*) held the abbotship. The first seven confined themselves to religious affairs. Starting from the eighth (late-18th C.), however, the Reting Tulkus exerted a tremendous influence on Tibet's politics. At that time, the college converted to the Gelugpa sect from the Nyingmapa and fell under the jurisdiction of Sera Je Tratsang of Sera Monastery.

MERU SARPA TRATSANG

Meru Sarpa Tratsang stands directly across Dekyi Shar Lam from the Kirey Hotel. It is a large stone building with a typical monastic brown-trim roof. The monastery has been taken over by the Tibet Theater Troupe. The main chapel, located at the rear of the complex, contains a *dukhang* and three small chapels. Former monks residences (three-storys-tall) run along the east, south, and west sides of the compound. The unusual west residential wing consists of two rows of buildings ranged along a north–south axis, separated by a very narrow courtyard. The east wing has only one row of buildings. Recent renovations have kept the monastery in good condition.

History

The abbot of Meru Sarpa used to be the head of Shide Tratsang as well. After 1684, the two colleges separated but Meru's abbot remained powerful and was a contender for the seat of regent. After the disgrace of Tengye Ling (see page 168), Meru Sarpa became one of Lhasa's Four Royal Monasteries in 1912. The present structure was built during the 13th Dalai Lama's reign by the abbot of Nechung, Sakya Ngape, and its architecture reflects prevailing trends of the 19th century. Meru's mendicant monks (grongchog) were associated with the Gyürme Tratsang (buildings are next door; west).

LUKHANG:
THE WATER-DRAGON CHAPEL

Location

From the Tibetan quarter, walking west along Dekyi Shar Lam towards the Lhasa Holiday Inn. Turn right at the post office. After passing the CAAC office, carry on through the first intersection, and enter the gates of Chingdröl Chiling (Liberation) Park. Immediately beyond the gates are the shrines housing the Kang Xi and Qian Long *dorings* (see page 195). Bear left to reach the Lukhang, sited on a tiny artificial island in the middle of a pond. A footbridge connects the Chinese-style shrine to the shore. In days gone by, Dalai Lamas came here by boat.

History

During the time of the Fifth Dalai Lama (1617–82), great amounts of earth were dug from the Chingdröl Chiling to construct the Potala. The resulting cavity became a pond known as the Lake of the Naga King. According to legend, Regent Sangye Gyatso was able to utilize this earth and successfully complete the Potala by making a pact with Luyi Gyalpo, the Naga King. In exchange for the earth, he promised to build a shrine to honor the dragon-like subterranean denizens. After the regent's death, the Sixth Dalai Lama (1683–1706), a pleasure-loving poet fulfilled the promise and built the jewel-like chapel.

The site

The rectangular pond, 270 m by 112 m, is surrounded by trees. In its center is an island with a diameter just over 40 m. The architecture of the three-story, south-facing Lukhang adheres to the strict geometry of a mandala. Its ground floor plan is a precise, symmetrical cross; a *khorlam* encloses the central four-column chapel. The second and third floors are identically enclosed, and the building is crowned by a Chinese-style pagoda roof surmounting a hexagonal room. In 1791, the Eighth Dalai Lama renovated the building and added the Langkhang—a house for elephants—80 m southwest of the pond. The Lukhang was once again restored under the 13th Dalai Lama. Most recently, the chapels were refurbished in 1984.

THE CHAPELS

GROUND FLOOR

Maldro Sechen Lhakhang An entrance porch stands before the entrance. A painting left of the doorway depicts Guru Rinpoche's Paradise of Zangdhok Pelri. The right shows the deeds of Mitrukpa (the Past Buddha). Beyond the entrance is a two-story atrium. At its rear a door leads to the main chapel of the ground floor. A raised stage at the center supports a new *mandala*, a replacement for the original commissioned by the Eighth Dalai Lama. Behind it, on a dais, is a statue of Luyi Gyalpo, the Naga King, riding an elephant. Five snakes of different colors are poised above his head. Also on the dais is an original statue of Drölkar (White Tara).

SECOND FLOOR

The central shrine on this floor encloses in an elaborate glass and wood cabinet, the Lukhang's most sacred object—the Luwang Gyalpo. As supreme Buddha of the subterranean world, he is protected by the nine Naga kings; they can be seen above his head as an umbrella of nine gilt-copper snakes. To the left is a valuable, 11-faced Chenresi. On the right are 21 new Drölmas. In front of Luwang Gyalpo is a *rangjung* stone image of Guru Rinpoche. Also in the cabinet are three dead snakes, now sanctified, found recently near the temple. The front of the chapel, screened off from the rest, is a terrace that was much used as a retreat by the 13th Dalai Lama.

MURALS

The Lukhang's unusual, 18th-C. murals are largely undamaged. Their fine workmanship can be seen on the second and third floors.

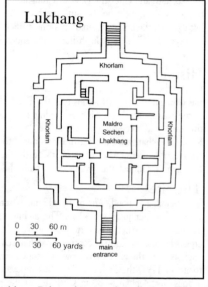

SECOND FLOOR

The south wall on the left tells with strong visual force the story of a well-known opera based on the life of Pema Wöber. The mythical young man came from a family that earned its living by diving in the sea for gems. After the accidental drowning of his father, Pema Wöber became a Buddhist and carried on successfully in his father's footsteps; he came home laden with treasures. News of his good fortune spread and the king of the land confiscated the gems, exiling the young man to a realm of cannibals. The hero survived, was able to convert the region to Buddhism and made his way home, only to be murdered by the evil king. Dakinis, however, brought Pema Wöber back to life and took the king to the land of cannibals, where he was eaten alive.

Most of the west wall and all of the north wall tell the story of India's legendary King Gyalpo Lekkye. The east wall is a continuation of Pema Wöber's story.

THIRD FLOOR

The east wall shows the 84 Mahasiddhas (*drubthob*) of India. Each sage conveys his own unique tantric specialty through a striking, exaggerated pose. Here also are the 25 disciples of Guru Rinpoche (Lakten). At the far end of the wall, near the Dalai Lama's quarters (Zimchung), are paintings of famous monasteries and pilgrimage sites (Mindroling, Samye, Gangri Töker, Sakya, Kailash). The chapel's south side is the light-filled Zimchung, enclosed by ornate Chinese-style windows. Traditionally, the Dalai Lamas came here, especially during the time of Saka Dawa—the anniversary of Buddha's enlightenment. The west wall also depicts the great masters of Buddhism, practicing yoga and meditation. Inscriptions name the yogis and their methods of meditation. Fascinating panels on the left side of the north wall show in great detail life's progression, from birth through death, as seen through Tibetan eyes. Portrayed are alien scenes of conception, death, and sickness (novel examples of how people contract diseases). Depictions of the body's internal organs and energy channels shed light on Tibetan medicinal theory. Images explain how imbalances from planetary motion and other esoteric disturbances cause decay. The wall's extreme left shows the Kagyüpa methods of meditation (Naro Chödruk). The middle section has various Zhitrö, peaceful and wrathful deities encountered along the *bardo*, the intermediate stage between death and rebirth. The themes derive from the Tibetan Book of the Dead. Murals along the western section shows Guru Rinpoche holding a *vajra* to the head of the Nechung Oracle, riding a snow lion. Before the advent of Buddhism, malicious 'protectors' entered the souls of hapless people and controlled them. Guru Rinpoche, having managed to overcome the evil spirits, passed his power to the Nechung Oracle. Left of this panel are curious images showing the proper way to recover from paralysis after prolonged and incorrect meditation.

THE SHORT KHORA

A *khora* along the perimeter of the island circles the Lukhang clockwise. The first object of note is a spirit tree, supposedly the abode of *nagas* (*lu*). It is covered by white offering scarves (*khata*). Behind this is an incense burner; a nearby room is consecrated to the earth spirits (*sadhak*) of the Lukhang. On the island's north side, many trees extend into the water. Next to steps that go up to the temple's north entrance is an empty chapel. It is said that the *nagas* gather here to receive offerings.

GESAR LHAKHANG:
KING GESAR'S CHINESE TEMPLE

Bhama Ri (Bompo Ri) Hill is a little-known sacred hill of Lhasa. It is regarded as a 'life-spirit' or 'soul' mountain of Jampelyang (Manjusri), the God of Wisdom. King Trisong Detsen (r 755–97) built a simple structure on Bhama Ri and Guru Rinpoche came here in the 8th century. In Tibetan cosmography, Lhasa's Bhama Ri, Chakpo Ri and Marpo Ri, represent the glands of the country's supine demoness (see page 43). On top of the hill are 18th-C. Chinese temples with original tiled roofs. This modest complex was dedicated to the Chinese God of War and Justice, Guan Di. For political reasons, the Qianlong Emperor identified the deity with the Tibetan folk hero, King Gesar of Ling, and thus this Chinese temple is called the Gesar Lhakhang. Built after the victory over the Nepalese Gurkhas in 1792, the site retains a stone doring with an inscription dated the 58th year of Qianlong (1793). Chinese officials raised money by subscription for its construction, which took a year.

At the base of Bhama Ri is Kunde Ling, one of Lhasa's Four Royal Monasteries (see page 169). The abbot of Kunde Ling had jurisdiction over the Gesar Lhakhang.

These thoroughly Chinese temples are an anomaly in Lhasa and Central Tibet. They are among the very few reminders of China's 18th-C. presence in Tibet, which was established in Lhasa following the Tibetan civil war of 1727–8. A Chinese observer, the Amban, was sent here by the Kangxi Emperor (1654–1722). Due to political uncertainty, the Amban's power in Lhasa and Tibet grew steadily over the next decades.

Location

Bhama Ri is a small ridge a few hundred meters west of Chakpo Ri. At its north base, next to the main road of Dekyi Nub Lam, is a new gas station. Just west is a public toilet. A path leads up from here to the top of the hill and the west entrance of the Gesar Lhakhang.

The site

The monastery is constructed on two separate levels. The south section is lower and consists of a courtyard flanked by two-story, Tibetan-style buildings (the ground floor comprised monks' quarters,

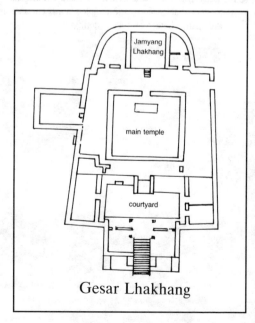

Gesar Lhakhang

the second floor offices and reception rooms). The Chinese-style temple is to the north. Its main entrance is reached by climbing a flight of stone steps from the courtyard, site of the stone doring with the Qianlong inscription. This 2-m doring is similar to the smallpox-edicts stele in front of the Jokhang (see page 70). At its crown is a semicircular stone capital with carvings of two dragons. Only half of the Chinese inscriptions can be made out.

The main chapel (north), with high ceilings, is built completely in the Chinese manner. A porch with a curved ceiling runs along the entire south facade, which is made up of Chinese floor-to-ceiling doors. The interior, partially and poorly renovated, has a near-empty altar (with a new statue of Gesar) and two footprints (*shapje*) of unknown saints. Behind and to the left and right of the altar are shelves containing small images of 1,000 Drölmas. The left (west) and right walls are made of stucco with many rectangular recesses containing 1,000 tiny clay statues of Guru Rinpoche. Among these are larger recesses awaiting the statues of the 16 Arhats. Hidden within the walls are said to be 100,000 small Chana Dorje images. Close to the left wall is a 3-m-high statue of Guru Rinpoche. The right, similar in design to the left, is dominated by a wrathful version of Guru Rinpoche (Gurgyal). Once over 50 wooden plaques with Chinese inscriptions, placed here by Chinese officials, decorated this hall. Only 13 remain and are kept elsewhere.

A perimeter wall surrounds the main chapel. At the center of the north sector is another Chinese-style chapel, a smaller version of the main one. Known as the Jamyang Lhakhang, it was dedicated to Jampelyang. A friendly Tibetan family looks after the largely unkempt site.

NORBU LINGKA: SUMMER PALACE OF THE DALAI LAMAS

OVERVIEW

Norbu Lingka, the Jewel Park, is one of the most relaxing, pleasant parts of Lhasa. The site is a large, 40-hectare enclave on the outskirts of town, full of trees, ponds, gardens, palaces, and pavilions. Since the middle of the 18th C. it has been the official summer residence of the Dalai Lama. The grand palaces and auxiliary buildings were largely built during this century by the 13th and 14th Dalai Lamas.

Norbu Lingka has four major palace complexes; Kelsang, Tsokyil, Takten Migyür, and Chensel. All but the last lie in the park's eastern half. Chensel is the centerpiece of Chensel Lingka, the western half of Norbu Lingka. The palaces consist of no less than 400 rooms and chapels. The Summer Palace's oldest structure, built by the Seventh Dalai Lama, is the Uyab Potrang, part of the Kelsang complex. Takten Migyür, the most ornate palace of the four, was initiated by the present Dalai Lama. Within are his residential quarters, which are left exactly as they were when he fled to India in 1959. Norbu Lingka's recreational section, an artificial lake with charming pavilions built on tiny islands, is at the Tsokyil complex.

Location

Norbu Lingka lies at Lhasa's west end. Its principal entrance is a few hundred meters south of the Lhasa Holiday Inn.

History

Norbu Lingka was started by the Seventh Dalai Lama, Kelsang Gyatso (1708–57). He came to this woodland area each summer to bathe in a medicinal spring; the Uyab Potrang pavilion was erected by him for this purpose. In 1755, he built a palace close by: the larger Kelsang Potrang. At this time, Norbu Lingka consisted only of these two buildings and the bathhouse. The Dalai Lama so loved this peaceful retreat that he established Norbu Lingka as a Summer Palace from which to administer the country. All subsequent incarnates moved here each year on the 18th day of the third lunar month and returned to the Potala in the autumn.

The Eighth Dalai Lama, Jampel Gyatso (1758–1804), spent much time here in meditation and was responsible for one of the Summer Palace's rigorous expansions. He built the Chöra, the Tsokyil Potrang, the Lukhang Lho, Druzin Potrang, and the perimeter walls of the park's southeast section. At the same time, a large numbers of trees and flowers were planted. The next major construction phase came under the 13th Dalai Lama, Thubden Gyatso (1876–1933), who fled to China during the British invasion of 1904 and returned much impressed by Chinese design and architecture. He first upgraded the gardens of the Kelsang Potrang and Chensel Potrang, then expanded and decorated the lake area of the Tsokyil Potrang.

Finally, the Chensel Lingka area in Norbu Lingka's northwest corner was built up in 1930, with the founding of three palaces: Chensel Potrang, Kelsang Dekyil Potrang, and Chime Tsokyil Potrang. The 13th Dalai Lama died in the latter in 1933. From 1954 to 1956, the 14th Dalai Lama built his new palace north of the Chensel Potrang and called it Takten Migyür Potrang. The name signifies that Buddhism is eternal and unchanging. This was the last major construction at Norbu Lingka.

Layout

Norbu Lingka, the park's inclusive name, actually consists of two smaller parks: Norbu Lingka, and Chensel Lingka. Each of these has its own gardens and palaces.

NORBU LINGKA

Norbu Lingka, the park's eastern half, has three major areas: the palace section, the opera grounds, and the government offices. Within the Palace Section are three palaces: Kelsang, Chensel, and Takten Migyür, each with its own grounds. The Kelsang Potrang is at the southeast portion of the palace section and encompasses the Uyab Potrang. North of it are the Chabzhe Khang (bathhouse) and Dhingcha Khang (Debate Platform), both surrounded by gardens. The Khamsum Zilnon, a pavilion for viewing operas, is at the eastern edge of the Kelsang Potrang grounds. It is integrated into the palace walls.

East of this are the opera grounds, an open-air stage and gardens. This area is packed with people during opera performances of the Shötun (Yoghurt) Festival in July. The Takten Migyur Potrang is at the north of the palace section. And to its north is the Loknyen Khang, offices and residences for park workers. The Tsokyil Potrang (Lake Palace) fills the southwest and is the Jewel Park's most dramatic area. In its center is a small lake with three islands: the middle one is the site of the Tsokyil Potrang; the north one has the Lukhang Nub (West Water Dragon Palace). Two bridges connect the middle island with the north and the east shores. The Druzin Potrang is west of the lake while the Chibra Khang (Horse Pavilion) is to its southwest. South of the lake is a row of buildings that held valuable gifts from Chinese emperors and other foreign courts. Lukhang Shar (East Water Dragon Palace) is at the eastern perimeter of the Chensel Potrang's grounds.

CHENSEL LINGKA

The Jewel Park's western half is the Chensel Lingka. It consists of the palace section, the forest section and fields. The first, surrounded by forests, has three palaces: the Chensel Potrang, Kelsang Dekyil, and Chime Tsokyil. Chensel Potrang, located in the east, is the most important structure. Kelsang Dekyil and Chime Tsokyil are further to the west. Southwest of the palaces is the Usil Khang. To the north are compounds for cattle and sheep.

The forest section is east and southeast of the Chensel Potrang. Next to it are the fields, an open area to the southwest that has a platform used by the Nechung Oracle during his divinations. This was also the place for horse races and kite flying.

Norbu Lingka: The Summer Palace

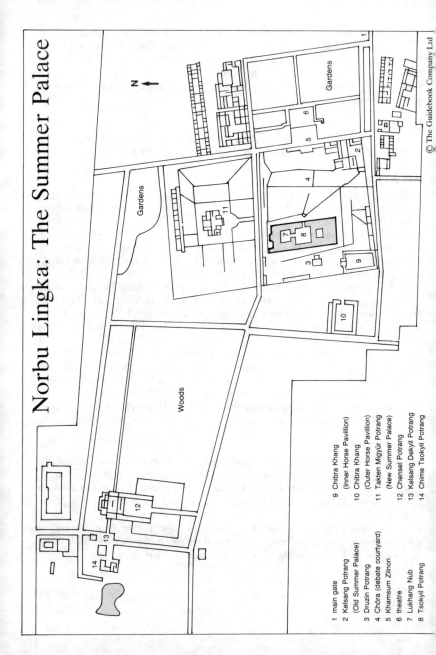

Gardens

Gardens

Woods

© The Guidebook Company Ltd

1 main gate
2 Kelsang Potrang
  (Old Summer Palace)
3 Druzin Potrang
4 Chöra (debate courtyard)
5 Khamsum Zilnon
6 theatre
7 Lukhang Nub
8 Tsokyil Potrang

9 Chibra Khang
  (Inner Horse Pavillion)
10 Chibra Khang
  (Outer Horse Pavillion)
11 Takten Migyür Potrang
  (New Summer Palace)
12 Chensel Potrang
13 Kelsang Dekyil Potrang
14 Chime Tsokyil Potrang

NORBU LINGKA:
THE KELSANG POTRANG COMPLEX

Kelsang Potrang

The Dalai Lamas used this three-story palace to administer affairs of state and religion. Its name derives from the Seventh Dalai Lama, Lobsang Kelsang Gyatso, who built it in 1755.

Tshomchen Nyiwö

The palace's assembly hall lies beyond the entrance cloister (*gochor*). Nyiwö means 'luminous' and signifies the sunlight nature of Buddhism. The hall lives up to its name because of the large skylight at the center; it is bathed in wonderful, warm light during the mornings. The Dalai Lama received visitors of state here and conducted important ceremonies. His throne dominates the assembly hall at the rear. Behind it are statues of the Eight Medicine Buddhas within an elaborately carved cabinet-shrine (*chösam*). The central image is Sakyamuni; also present are clay statues of the 16 Arhats.

    Murals depict Chenresi, Chana Dorje, Jampelyang, the three religious kings (Songtsen Gampo, Trisong Detsen, Ralpachen), 100 forms of the Tushita Paradise, and Jampelyang on a snow lion. A hundred *thangkas* (Drölmas and protective deities) were commissioned by the 13th Dalai Lama and exhibited in Europe in 1986. All the columns are covered with brocade (*kaphen*).

Nechu Lhakhang

A set of stairs at the entrance cloister's southwest corner leads to the second floor. The Nechu Lhakhang is at the building's north end and contains images of the Buddha and the 16 Arhats. The bookshelves have Tsong Khapa's complete works and the murals recount legends of Songtsen Gampo, Trisong Detsen, and other Yarlung kings. This chapel was used for the coronation of the Dalai Lamas.

Tashi Namrol Lhakhang

East of Nechu Lhakhang, this *gönkhang* contains a clay image of six-armed Mahakala (Nagpo Chenpo) made by Tsomön Ling, Regent of the Eighth Dalai Lama. Some Dalai Lamas used this as their bedroom. Murals depict the tantric divinities, Lhamo, Songde Jigsum, Gönkar, Chogyel (*yabyum*), Shinje Phogye, and Moggye.

    Two rooms (Pezoe Khang) at the northwest and northeast corners of this floor store Buddhist texts. Along the corridor facing the Nechu Lhakhang are murals of the Seven Royal Emblems and a complete depiction of the war between the kingdom of Shambala and the barbarians. A Chinese-style painting shows acrobats and a flag, held by a man, displaying in Chinese characters the legend: 'May Tibet enjoy prosperity and long life'.

Thösam Gokyil

This room, south of the *gönkhang*, is the study and library of the Dalai Lama. Its name means 'Paradise for Practicing Hearing and Contemplation'. The west wall is constructed of pretty window screens and the room's interior is cosy and comfortable. Murals depict Sakyamuni, the five different manifestations of Tsong Khapa, and Jampelyang on a snow lion. The corridor mural shows Khyetra Pala, a Mongolian leading a tiger, a Brahmin leading an elephant, and Chinese-style subjects.

Reception Hall

Dalai Lamas used this hall to teach and receive audiences. The 13th Dalai Lama renovated it and added elaborate paintings. At one end are the Dalai Lama's sofa seat and desk. Facing these is a beautifully carved *chösam*, containing life-size statues of the Buddha and Kalachakra. Another life-size, wrathful Kalachakra (gold and copper), known as Trowo Dorje Shuk, complements the other. Both were commissioned by the 14th Dalai Lama and used during his Kalachakra initiations. On the walls are paintings of the Eight Bodhisattvas, surrounded by Wöpame, the Paradise of Chenresi (Riwo Potala), and Khamsum Wangdü, Conqueror of the Three Worlds (men, animals, hell). The central panel depicts the 13th Dalai Lama, his retinue and principal episodes of his life.

Rikne Khang

Rikne Khang means House of Knowledge. The Dalai Lama kept his important books in this inner room of the Reception Hall. On the walls are paintings of Chenresi and his Paradise, the Five Manifestations of Tsong Khapa (Je Zikpa Ngadhen), and the Representation of Ten Powers (Namchu Wandhen).

UYAB POTRANG

The Uyab Potrang, oldest building at Norbu Lingka, is a one-story building west of the Kelsang Potrang, and was used for meditation by the Dalai Lamas. Its half-basement for storage served as a buffer against dampness. The main entrance faces east.

Its architecture reflects the simple but powerful design favored during the first half of the 18th C., a stark contrast to the elaborate palaces of later years. The central room has a large, south-facing window. A golden throne for the Dalai Lama sits before a statue of Sakyamuni. Murals depict the Three Religious Kings, the 16 Arhats, the Potala, Jokhang, Reting, and Norbu Lingka. One interesting scene shows Guru Rinpoche teaching while King Trisong Detsen looks on. Outside this room, two noteworthy paintings depict the origin of the universe and the story of Drime Kundhen, crown prince of India, who sacrificed his wife, children, and his own eyes for the sake of a beggar. A piece of an embroidery contains the Six Syllables: 'Om Mani Padme Hum'. To the west is the Dalai Lama's library-study (Chakpe Khang). The meditation room (Nyenzok Khang) is directly behind the main room.

KHAMSUM ZILNON

The Dalai Lama held court and watched Tibetan operas from this delightful structure, located 70 m northeast of the Kelsang Potrang. It is incorporated into the eastern wall of the palace grounds. The two-story, largely wooden building has multi-level gilded roofs built in the pagoda style. Originally a small wood pavilion built by the 13th Dalai Lama, it was pulled down at the beginning of the 20th C. by the Reting Regent and replaced by a more elaborate structure. A new set of rooms (Zimchung Gyakhang) was added onto the north wing and a new stage was built in front. The entranceway (*gochor*) is enclosed by a low, stone fence, beautifully carved with figures of the Seven Royal Emblems (wheel, precious gem, queen, minister, elephant, horse, commander), known as Gyalsi Nadhün.

The Dalai Lama's chamber, crowned with the highest roof, stands at the center of the second floor. To the north is a room used by his tutors; other officials congregated in a room to the south. The balcony extending from the Dalai Lama's chamber is a beautiful airy space with windows on three sides. Its walls are decorated with symbols of the Seven Royal Emblems, the Four Friendly Brothers and the Six Long-living Beings (Tshering Drukhor).

The Shötun (Yoghurt) Festival
Each summer Lhasa revels in this happy festival; it is a time for family and friends to gather, eat, drink, and sing. Wonderful operas performed by troupes from different parts of the country go on continuously for five days. This festival dates back over 500 years to the time of Tangton Gyalpo (see page 451). He used the festivities to raise funds to build his iron bridges. His statue presides over the occasion at center-stage.

    Lhasa grinds to a halt during these first five days of the seventh lunar month. Picnic tents mushroom all over Norbu Lingka as officials and ordinary citizens join together to watch the operas. This is also the period for yoghurt, which nomads traditionally gave as gifts to the monasteries. Shötun denotes the Feast of Yoghurt.

CHAKPE KHANG (LIBRARY)

The south-facing library north of the Uyab Potrang holds mostly metaphysical texts. Murals depict Sakyamuni, the Six Ornaments and the Two Excellences (Gyendruk Choknyi), Kalachakra, the 16 Arhats, the Eight Medicine Buddhas, and other religious subjects.

CHÖRA (DEBATE COURTYARD)

North of the Chakpe Khang and the Kelsang Potrang and west of the Khamsum Zilnon, situated in a grove of conifers, the Chöra is where the Dalai Lama sat and debated with his tutors. The south-facing structure is semi-enclosed, with windows separating the outer and inner sections (the northern section is a kitchen). A special ceremony called Sachue Bumdrub is held here each year. The vital powers of the Treasure Vase (*bumpa*) are restored during this occasion: rituals are performed whereby treasured objects (precious stones, holy water, grain etc) contained within the vase regain their powers to fend off disaster, disease, and poverty.

NORBU LINGKA: THE TAKTEN MIGYÜR POTRANG COMPLEX

Built by the 14th Dalai Lama between 1954 and 1956, the so-called New Palace (Potrang Sarpa), or Takten Migyür Potrang (Ever Indestructible Palace), stands north of the Tsokyil Potrang. Enclosed within high, yellow walls, the palace is elaborately decorated. A gilded pagoda-roof tops the beautiful second-floor balcony (notice the metal frieze skirting the edges of the roof). On the roof is a *dharma* wheel (*khorlo*) flanked by two deer (*ridak*). Garudas (*khyung*) guard the corners; all are overseen by victory banners (*gyalchen*) and golden ornaments (*sertok*). The south facade is distinguished by many large picture windows (*sheltra*) fronting the ground and second floors. Outside the main entrance, an outstanding carved stone fence (*dramkyor*) encloses the entrance cloister.

Ground floor

A pair of tiger skin whips, denoting power and authority, flanks the main door. The entrance foyer has realistic paintings of a lion and a tiger, which guard the ceremonial stairs.

TSHOMCHEN NELEN KHANG

The Dalai Lama received visitors in this southeast function room. A cabinet-shrine at the room's north end contains a golden statue of Jampelyang flanked by gilt-copper statues of the Eight Medicine Buddhas. Most of the furniture is of European style. A suite of rooms (southeast corner), including a bathroom, was used by the 14th Dalai Lama during his rest periods.

Second floor

TSHOMCHEN LHOMA SIZHI DHO GUKYIL

The South Assembly Hall has striking floor-to-ceiling windows on three sides. Of two entrances (northeast and northwest corners), the northeastern one is flanked by a copper and gold statue of Sakyamuni in yellow robes. An ornate cabinet-shrine along the north wall holds the central image of Sakyamuni, bracketed by Jampelyang (left) and Jampa. Above the Sakyamuni statue, running east to west, is a remarkable embroidered ceiling skirt (*drachi*). This rare work of art has intricate images of Indian Buddhist figures (Atisha, Nagarjuna, Asanga) interspersed with stylized *garudas*. At the bottom of the skirt are tassels (*norbu drakyil*) of different shapes, representing gems. Below the skirt, along the columns, are embroidered brocade hangings (*kaphen*). Atop each is a *garuda*. Murals show Tibetan civilization in 301 famous scenes: its beginning and history up to the time of the 14th Dalai Lama.

ZIMCHUNG DRODREN SEMCHOK KHANG ('ROOM OF EXCELLENT THOUGHT FOR THE EMANCIPATION OF ALL BEINGS')

The Dalai Lama's private quarters consist of two main rooms west of the South Assembly Hall. An outer room (southwest corner) has a sofa-seat with embroidered cushions. The Chinese character on the backrest means 'longevity'. Directly above is an intricate silk appliqué *thangka* depicting Atisha in the center, flanked by his disciples, Ngok Lotsawa and Dromtönpa. Above these Kadampa patriarchs are the four Kadampa divinities: Gönpo, Maksor Gyalmo, Nechung, and Jowo Chingkarwa. A cabinet-shrine by the north wall contains statues of Sakyamuni and Jampelyang. The main altar has silver images of the Rigsum Gönpo: Chenresi, Jampelyang, Chana Dorje. Notice the old Phillips Gramophone with stacks of original 78 rpm records.

The Dalai Lama studied under his two tutors here. The inner room, to the east, is the bedroom. A fine Indian-silver shrine here honors the image of Thuje Chenpo (Chenresi). Flanking this are Wöpame, Drölkar, Dröljang, and Namgyalma. On a *thangka* is Tsong Khapa, portrayed with his disciples and various Gelugpa masters. Incongruous Western items in the suite include an old Russian radio, an art-deco bed, and British plumbing. Apparently, these rooms remain exactly as they were when the Dalai Lama fled Tibet in 1959. Directly north of the outer room is a west-facing chamber with glass picture windows. The shrine has Sakyamuni flanked by a silver statue of Vajrayogini and a gilt-copper Tsong Khapa. The sofa is made of Indian sandalwood.

ZIMCHUNG CHAKPE KHANG

The Dalai Lama's private library (northwest corner) has elaborately carved cabinets along the north wall. The main image within the shrine is Jampelyang. Next to the Dalai Lama's seat are cushions belonging to his two tutors. The west wall has Tibetan murals with Indian influence, painted under the direct guidance of the 14th Dalai Lama. They show the Buddha meditating under the *bodhi* tree of Bodh Gaya. Next to him are his disciples, and landscapes of India's major Buddhist sites: Bodh Gaya, Varanasi, Nalendra, Rajgir.

ZIMCHUNG EWAM GAKYIL

Within the library is this inner meditation room. Above the Dalai Lama's seat is a painting of the three tantric divinities, Yamantaka, Guhyasamaja, and Chakrasambhava, surrounded by their lineage. Other images include Guru Rinpoche, Trisong Detsen, and Santarakshita. A silver shrine contains statues of Guhyasamaja, White Mahakala (Gönkar), and Jampelyang. Bookcases next to the seat have rare manuscripts, topped by gilt-copper statues of Guhyasamaja and Demchok. On a low table is a square cabinet with a pagoda-roof that represents the Potala Paradise of Chenresi. Within it is a solid silver statue of the 11-faced Chenresi, used as a ritual implement during tantric visualizations.

WOKMIN GODHEN CHÖLING

The North Assembly Hall, main reception room of the palace, is devoid of columns. It is dominated by a magnificent gold throne, a priceless gift to the 14th Dalai Lama, made possible by the effusive generosity of the Tibetan people. The shrine behind the throne (north wall) contains the gilt-copper statues of Jampa flanked by Atisha and Tsong Khapa. Opposite are murals of the 14 Dalai Lamas. On both sides of the chamber are large windows, in front of which are splendid religious implements.

   The upper section of the interior walls, from east to west, is painted with the 56 episodes of Buddha's life; the lower section depicts the 202 deeds of Tsong Khapa. Farther along the east wall (north section) are paintings of all the Dalai Lamas. In the center, the Great Fifth holds a gold *chakra* that symbolizes his complete sovereignty. Next to him is displayed the 17th-C. meeting between Regent Sangye Gyatso and Gushri Khan, the Mongol chief. The northern section of the west wall portrays the 14th Dalai Lama shown with the Reting and Takdrak regents and his two tutors. In front of them are ministers and government officials as well as foreign dignitaries: the British officer-in-charge, Hugh Richardson, and the ambassadors of India, Kuomintang China, and Mongolia. Perhaps the most interesting is a Japanese monk (in yellow robes) who stole into Lhasa and studied at Sera for three years. The south wall shows mythical Shambala, the origins of Kalachakra (the complex yogic *tantras*), and the 16 Arhats and Four Guardians.

ZIMCHUNG DHOGÜ PHÜNTSHOK

An interior door along the east wall of the North Assembly Hall opens into this room, used as an office. The shrine along the north wall has golden statues of the Kadampa triad: Atisha, Ngok Lotsawa, and Dromtönpa. Parts of the mural describe Samadhi meditation. Next to Tsong Khapa and his eight disciples are the founders of the most important Gelugpa monasteries.

A bathroom (southeast) adjoins to the south of the Dalai Lama's quarters (where his mother stayed during the daytime). A splendid white sandalwood shrine, crafted at the time of the 13th Dalai Lama, contains sandalwood figures of Sakyamuni, the Six Ornaments, the Two Excellences and Milarepa and Atisha. Notice a painting of the Dalai Lama being driven from the Potala to Norbu Lingka in an Austin car.

ZIMCHUNG JELTRE KHANG

This living room (southeast corner of the second floor), where the Dalai Lama relaxed with his family, has French furniture. The main shrine, an intricately carved white sandalwood cabinet, contains images of Sakyamuni and the 16 Arhats. It was a gift of the Mahabodhi Society to the Dalai Lama, who came to India to commemorate the 2,500th anniversary of the Buddha's *nirvana*. Outside the Zimchung Jeltre Khang, on a landing above the staircase, are the following paintings:

- Kunzang Khorlo (of Tibetan kings)—a square diagram containing many smaller colored squares. Each has a syllable and when they are read either horizontally or vertically, they give the names of all Tibet's kings, from Nyatri Tsenpo to Ralpachen;
- Kunzang Khorlo (of the Dalai Lamas)—a cosmological painting according to the Abidharma text by Vasubhandu;
- Guru Rinpoche, Trisong Detsen, and Santarakshita;
- Domtson Dampa—a painting of hidden symbols. In it are pictures of a lotus (signifying Guru Rinpoche), book (Santrakshita), sword (Trisong Detsen), two-headed duck (8th-C. Indian scholars Khenchen and Karnalasila), and a two-headed parrot (Kawa Peltsek Lotsawa and Chok Lotsawa, 8th-C. translators). This type of painting had a rather archaic origin. During the persecution of Buddhism during King Langdarma's reign, Buddhist personalities were not allowed to be depicted in paintings. Therefore to show, for example, Guru Rinpoche, artists had to paint a lotus instead.
- Namchu Wongdhen—symbols of the Ten Perfections;
- Thunpu Punzhi—symbol of the Four Friendly Brothers (elephant, monkey, rabbit, bird);
- Rikdhen Nyernga—the Twenty-Five Noble Castes;
- Tshering Namdruk—the Six Long-Living Beings (rock, tree, man, bird, deer, water).

In a courtyard behind Takten Migyür are the Dalai Lama's rusting motorcars, a 1931 Dodge (orange) and two 1927 Austins. These were gifts to the 13th Dalai Lama and were carried piece by piece into Tibet on the backs of yaks, then put back together in Lhasa. The 14th managed to get them going!

NORBU LINGKA:
THE TSOKYIL POTRANG COMPLEX

The centerpiece of this recreational lake complex, is the Tsokyil Potrang, sited on a small island in the middle of an artificial lake. It was created in the latter half of the 18th century. There are two other islands: the north one has the Lukhang Nub (West Water Dragon Palace); the south has no buildings. The Lukhang Shar (East Water Dragon Palace) is east of the lake, and Druzin Potrang is to the west.

Tsokyil Potrang (Lhündrub Gatshel)

During the 18th C., the Seventh Dalai Lama came here to bathe in a natural lake fed by a medicinal spring. At the time of the Eighth Dalai Lama, Regent Demo Dhelek Gyaltso built (1784) a house in the middle of the lake (Lhündrub Gatshel) and added the Lukhang to the north. The Chinese design in both buildings is apparent, especially the former with its pagoda roof. Under the roof (south side) is an intricately carved wood skirt (gokhyam).

In 1887, the 13th Dalai Lama (then aged 12) expanded the lake and renovated the building, so that he was able to go around the palace by boat. Animals (including an elephant from Bhutan) were kept nearby, and the area became a resort.

Lukhang Nub

The Lukhang Nub, a square pavilion, has typical Tibetan elements with Chinese overtones. Its pagoda roof, different from the palace, is distinguished by the brown ceiling trim (constructed of pema branches) found in most Tibetan monastic buildings, and a complicated support structure. The pillars and beams are Tibetan and the structure, unlike the Tsokyil Potrang, is stone. Inside, the main shrine is consecrated to the King of the Nagas (Lu Gyalpo) and the murals present the history of Gesar of Ling and the story of Milarepa and Naropa competing with the Bönpos at Mt Kailash. Guru Rinpoche and Tilopa are also figured, as are the main monasteries. Every year a ceremony here propitiated the King of the Nagas and rituals were conducted to divine the future as well as to appease the dragon-serpents of the waters. The Lukhang Shar, east of the lake, stored ritual implements.

Druzin Potrang (Diki Kunga Khyilwe Potrang)

This palace is in an isolated area 30 m west of the central island. The modest, two-story building, facing east, was built by the 13th Dalai Lama as a library and retreat (renovated 1982). Some paintings along the east and west walls have been repainted. During the 13th's retreats, he would circumambulate the palace and, after each circuit, deposit a small stone onto a pile. This pile of pebbles can still be seen outside the building. Nearby is an apple tree planted personally by him. Patterns on the bark allowed him to read the progress of his practice.

The building's plan is a perfect square, 14.5 m by 14.5 m, with a height of 9 m; the proportion of its length to height is 5:3. This accords to rules for temples consecrated to Chenresi, and in this case symbolizes that the occupant and user, the Dalai Lama, is an incarnation of the god. Druzin Potrang is a typically Tibetan structure with no overt Chinese influence.

Tshomchen Chime Gatshal

This assembly hall of the Druzin Potrang once held a life-size statue of the Thousand-armed Chenresi. It was installed by the 13th Dalai Lama in 1903 and later moved to the Dalai Lama's quarters at the Potala. The present wooden Chenresi is surrounded by the Potala Paradise (Riwo Potala Yi Shing) and flanked by Amitayus, divinity of longevity. There is a stone Sakyamuni from Bodh Gaya, India. Near the back wall are statues of the Eight Bodhisattvas. The murals are of Chenresi's Paradise and the 1,000 images of the long-life goddess, Tsepame. Along the walls are bookshelves with books from China and Mongolia and historical, medical, and religious texts.

Second floor Retreat Quarters of the Dalai Lama

These rooms range along the west section of the second floor. The first, outer (north) room is a bedroom with wooden floors. Murals depict the eight male and eight female Yamantaka—manifestations of Guru Rinpoche, the Paradise of Chenresi—and the eight manifestatious of Drölma. The tiny inner room was where the 13th Dalai Lama, in his early 40s, meditated on his personal deity, Yamantaka. The principal statues are Sakyamuni and Tsong Khapa. Murals show Yamantaka (above the seat), Jigje Pawo Chikpa, and Chenresi with a white umbrella.

East of the living quarters is a chapel used by the Dalai Lama for affairs of state. Images of Guru Rinpoche, Tsong Khapa and his two disciples, Chenresi, Jampelyang, Amitayus, and Sakyamuni are in a glass shrine. Above the Dalai Lama's seat are paintings of the Five Dhyani Buddhas (Gyalwa Rigna): Vairocana, Ratnasambhava, Amitabha, Amoghasiddhi, and Akshobhya.

Chibra Khang (Inner Horse Pavilion)

Located 85 m southwest of the Tsokyil Potrang, this structure, measuring 48 m by 28 m, has marvelous murals along the perimeter walls of the stables. They depict various actual and mythical Tibetan stories involving horses including their rearing, feeding, and training. The northern section of the Inner Horse Pavilion is a two-story Tibetan structure. Its second floor was where the Dalai Lama prepared for his outings. The Outer Horse Pavilion, just outside the perimeter walls (west) of the Tsokyil Potrang complex, is surrounded on four sides by stables. An outdoor stage, due east of the Chibra Khang is the focus of the annual Shötun (Yoghurt) Festival.

Chensel Lingka: Chensel Potrang

This principal palace of Chensel Lingka was used exclusively by the 13th Dalai Lama. A path leads west from the entrance gate of the Takten Migyür Potrang to the south-facing palace gates. The compound is enclosed by yellow walls. The 13th Dalai Lama never liked the original structure here so he demolished it in 1926 and started his own construction of an impressive, three-story building, finished in 1928. Fronting the main entrance is a courtyard with two *dorings*. An entrance cloister, supported by six columns, served as a waiting area. The charming, second-floor balcony enclosed by picture-windows, was the viewing stand of the 13th Dalai Lama for *Cham* dances performed by Drepung monks. A west gate has a particularly beautiful carved stone balustrade that flanks the entrance stairs. Above the door is a balcony with wrap-around windows surmounted by a yellow-tiled roof.

Ground floor

Tshomchen Nyiwö

The 13th Dalai Lama held his daily audiences in this assembly hall. Debates and formal examinations for the Geshe (Doctor of Theology) degree were held here, as well as major ceremonies for the monks of Sera and Drepung. The Dalai Lama's throne is on a stage at the rear of the hall. In front of it is a cabinet containing a solid silver statue of the First Dalai Lama. Behind the throne is a statue of the 13th commissioned by the present Dalai Lama. Cabinet-shrines held 36 silver statues of the long-life deities of Amitayus, Tara, and Vijaya. Next to the image of the Dalai Lama is Zangbala, a divinity who promotes conception and children's health. The murals consists of the 100 deeds of the Buddha in his previous lives (*zegya paksam trishing*) and 80 images of Tsong Khapa.

Second floor

The entrance is through the palace's west door.

RABSEL PAKSAM DHOKYIL

North of the central skylight, this room was used as a bedroom and study by the 13th Dalai Lama. Notice the black-and-white photographs on the wall, from a collection taken in India during his exile in 1910. Outside is a cloister partly covered by eaves where officials waited before an audience. The Chinese-style paintings depict Hayagriva (Tamdrin), Jampelyang, and the palace of the Qing Emperor Kangxi. Next to the bedroom are rooms used by the Dalai Lama's attendants.

DHINGJAGANG

The most gracious room of the palace, this south-side balcony is enclosed on three sides by windows.

Third floor

SIZHI PALBAR

In this assembly hall, the Dalai Lama taught tantric initiations, conducted special ordinations for high lamas, and gave sermons. Main images in the room are a Thousand-armed Chenresi (life-size) and Thousand-armed Dugkarma. A cabinet-shrine to the right contains Dorje Drakden, a protector deity who speaks through the Nechung Oracle. Murals show the Dalai Lamas (First to 13th), main Gelugpa monasteries, and the Five Manifestations of Tsong Khapa.

TSUNGDREL TEKSUM JUGIGO
('ENTRANCE TO THE THREE INCOMPARABLE VEHICLES')

An inner meditation and prayer room of the Sizhi Palbar, this was used exclusively by the Dalai Lama for his daily Buddhist rituals.

CHENSEL LINGKA: KELSANG DEKYIL POTRANG (VAJRAKALPA'S 'LAKE OF HAPPINESS')

This two-story building, 60 m west of the Chensel Potrang, was started in 1926 by the 13th Dalai Lama and completed in 1928. It was used to receive important visitors and later became his residence. A pair of snow lions flank the eastern entrance.

Ground floor

ZIMCHUNG TASHI WÖNANG

The 13th Dalai Lama's personal treasure of jewelry, gifts, and cultural relics were kept here.

Second floor

Reach this floor by ascending a set of elegant Chinese marble stairs (east of the building). Over the entranceway is a yellow-tiled pagoda roof. The main room, the reception hall, has a large picture window surmounted by a pagoda roof at the south wall. West of it are rooms, partitioned by carefully crafted wood screens, once used by the Dalai Lama to prepare for receiving visitors. A cabinet-shrine contains statues of Chenresi and Kedrub Je, Tsong Khapa's disciple. The primary statues in the reception hall are of Sakyamuni and Chenresi. Murals display the Paradise of Chenresi, Bodh Gaya, Mt Wutai Shan of China, the Tushita Heaven (residence of the future Buddha, Jampa), and a chörten of Palden Drepung in South India, site of the first Kalachakra initiation.

CHENSEL LINGKA: CHIME TSOKYIL POTRANG

This palace, which means 'Reception Room of the Immortal Body', lies immediately west of the Kelsang Dekyil Potrang. It was the 13th Dalai Lama's favorite building. He built this simple, unassuming structure for himself during his final years and actually died here in 1933. The ground floor is divided into two connected wings. The south, a basement, was used for storage while the north housed the servants and attendants. Its main entrance is tucked away at the side of the south wing. The east and south facades are dominated by an enclosing picture-window of the large, sunny bedroom. Books and clothes were stored in an adjacent room (east). The main statue is Yamantaka.

ÜSIL KHANG

South of Chime Tsokyil Potrang is this dilapidated circular pavilion, the Pavilion for Hairwashing. Its wooden screen walls are topped by a pagoda roof; the pavilion is surrounded by a low, stone fence. Üsil Khang was one of Norbu Lingka's earliest buildings and was used by the Dalai Lamas to wash their hair.

THE DODE VALLEY: MONASTERIES AND CLIFF-TOP RETREATS NEAR SERA

The Dode Valley is due north of Lhasa and its entrance is immediately east of Sera Monastery. It is flanked by Sera Ütse in the west and Jomo Sisi (Chomsi Ri, 5738 m) in the east, highest peak in the range north of Lhasa. The Pembogo La (4975 m), at the head of the valley, is the watershed of the Kyi Chu (Lhasa) River and the Pembo (Phanyul) Chu. (Inside the latter are the monasteries of Nalanda and Langtang; see page 568.) Dode's destroyed hermitages are located at the top of the ridges that flank the valley and most take 2–3 hr on foot to reach. Although in ruins, they are still fascinating and the views from them are unforgettable.

Access

From the Banak Shöl Hotel entrance, walk right (east) to the main intersection. Turn left (north) to the Telecommunications Office and continue north to the turnoff to Sera Monastery. Instead of turning left at this point to go to the sky-burial site and Sera, walk north into the Dode Valley. Keep to the valley's left side. Pass a military camp on the left, then another on the right. Finally, pass a third on the left. Immediately after this, a dirt track goes left (west). Follow it to Taglung Monastery (1/2 hr from the Sera turnoff).

THE VALLEY

TAGLUNG MONASTERY

Most walls still stand. The monastery of medium-sized buildings is peaceful and quiet and it is possible to see its chapels through broken windows. A village is at the base of the monastery.

PHURPA CHOK HERMITAGE

This Gelugpa retreat is on a craggy ridge directly above Taglung; a steep path leads up to it. There are no resident monks.

KIUTSANG HERMITAGE

This hermitage is sited high up on the same ridge as Phurpa Chok, a short distance to its south. Looking up from Taglung, Kiutsang is visible left of Phurpa Chok; it had two main *lhakhangs* (destroyed). Around the corner, southwest of Kiutsang, is the charming, active retreat of Sera Ütse (page 164).

MICHUNGRI NUNNERY

Farther up the Dode Valley (north), this destroyed nunnery is on the slopes of Jomo Sisi's south base, to the right. The nuns have not returned.

KARDO HERMITAGE

The ruins of Kardo are visible from the valley floor. They sit high up on a spur on the right (east) side of the valley, just beyond Michungri. Its impressive position commands the whole Dode Valley.

MONASTERIES OF PHANYUL

Phanyul, the district immediately north of the Pembogo La, centers on the Pembo Chu, which flows southeast along a wide valley to join the Kyi Chu, directly across from Ganden Monastery. The rebuilt monasteries of Nalandra and Langtang are at the valley's south side, due north of the Pembogo La. Beyond them, over the Chak La, are the monasteries of Taklung (see page 566) and Shara Bumpa (see page 567). The Phanyul Valley was a principal area for the growth of Buddhism during the Second Diffusion. Guru Rinpoche practiced here and the important Kadampa sect originated in the valley in the 11th century. The walk to Nalandra and Langtang over the Pembogo La generally takes two days from Lhasa (overnight at Lingbu Dzong).

OTHER SITES IN THE PHANYUL VALLEY

Locations of the following Kadampa institutions are unidentified:

- Potö   This 11th-C. monastery was founded by Potöpa, one of Atisha's five chief disciples and a follower of Dromtön. He is regarded as a patriarch of the Karmapa.
- Nezur   A 11th-C. hermitage founded by Nezurpa, a disciple of Potöpa.
- Nasen Bumpa   This name refers to either a row of chörtens (associated with Potöpa) a short distance northwest of Lhundrub Dzong (see page 567), or to a chapel at Nabu, 6 km north of Langtang.
- Rama Shika   This site is perhaps at Ra, on the south bank of the Pembo Chu (upstream from Langtang).
- Puchung   A chapel founded in the 11th C. by Puchungpa, a disciple of both Atisha and Dromtön.

DORINGS: HISTORICAL STELAE

Dorings are stone stelae whose surfaces usually carry the inscriptions of edicts. Creating *dorings* was one of four common ways for the Yarlung kings to acquire merit (others were building tombs and temples). The erection of a *doring* symbolized the real and spiritual possession of the land. In addition, it served to subdue subterranean demons and to act as a bridge to higher spiritual realms.

During construction, special workers cut the stone and inscribed accomplishments of the king's ancestors and his royal proclamations. The populace attended the consecration ceremony to gain merit and to impart spiritual energy into the earth via the *doring*, which stood at the spiritual center of a consecrated space, usually surrounded by four protective *chörtens* at the cardinal points. This design was used by Tibet's early kings at Samye Monastery (see page 295), Ramagang and Ushang (see page 491). Some *dorings* in Lhasa were commissioned by Chinese emperors to commemorate historical events (see below).

JOKHANG DORINGS

Three *dorings* stand in front of the Jokhang. The main one commemorates the peace treaty signed between China's Tang emperor and King Ralpachen of Tibet in 822. Consecrated in 823, this pillar is about 3.5m high. There is some damage to the surface but most of the Chinese and Tibetan inscriptions are still legible. The text proclaims that both countries have signed a peace treaty, witnessed by God and men, and a peaceful relationship is promised. The second *doring* was erected in 1794 after the outbreak of a smallpox epidemic. Most of the inscriptions are now nearly indistinguishable. Immediately behind this is the third. There are no inscriptions but the platform has bas-relief carvings of a pair of lions (at the back) and an unidentified animal (front). This pillar is probably from the Ming Dynasty.

DZONGYAP LUKHANG DORINGS

Two *dorings* are housed within small yellow buildings inside the main entrance of Chingdröl Chiling (Liberation Park), north of the Potala. Both originally stood in front of the Potala but were moved in the early 1960s to make way for new buildings. The gray *doring* on the left is called the Kang Xi *doring*, commissioned in 1721 by Emperor Kang Xi in rememberance of the victory over Dzungar invaders. 3.5 m high and 1 m wide, the tablet is supported by a beautifully carved stone turtle. The top is a colorful slab of stone with two carved dragons flanking of the emperor's seal. Inscriptions in Manchu, Chinese, Mongolian and Tibetan document in detail the suppression of the Mongol Dzungars by the Manchu armies.

On the right is the Qian Long *doring*. It commemorates the victories of 1788 and 1791 over Gurkha invaders. The stele is nearly 4 m high and once had a turtle as its base (destroyed and replaced by a square stone). Its top is another colored, carved stone and the inscriptions are also in four languages: Manchu, Chinese, Mongolian and Tibetan. The text recounts Tibet's appeal to Emperor Qian Long for help and how China's armies passed through Qinghai and

Sichuan to defeat the Gurkhas by crossing the Himalayas. A peace treaty was forced at Kathmandu.

THE CHIMA AND NANGMA DORINGS

The 8th-C. Doring Chima stands in an enclosure across the road from the Exhibition Hall (Zhanlan Guan), just west of the Post Office. It was created by King Trisong Detsen (755–97) to commemorate Takdra Lukong, his key aide and general. The edict, inscribed on the north, east, and south faces in Tibetan (still legible), praised him for his accomplishments in battle, his intelligence, and his loyalty. This 8-m-tall stele, supported by a small platform, once stood within Zhöl, the village at the foot of the Potala. Doring Chima means 'outer pillar'. Doring Nangma, the 'inner pillar', still resides at the center of Zhöl, below the stairway to the Potala. It is the same size and configuration as Doring Chima but has no inscription.

THE TSHALPA-KAGYÜPA MONASTERIES

History

Founded in 1175 by Lama Shang (1123–94), Tshalpa Monastery was the seat of the powerful Tshalpa Kagyüpa sect. Lama Shang is recognized as one of Tibet's 'Three Jewels' (with Phagmo Drupa and Tsong Khapa), and his teacher was Gompa, a successor of Gampopa. For nearly 200 years (13th–14th C.), during the period of the priest-patron relationship with the Mongols, Tshalpa's abbots and the Tshalpa family were dominant forces in Tibet's affairs. Kublai Khan himself patronized the sect. Later, under Tshalpa Kanga Dorje, the Tshalpas allied themselves with the Sakyapas and Yazangpas against the Phagmo Drupas. They were soundly defeated and lost most of their territories. By the 16th C., they had converted to the Gelugpa sect. A disastrous fire in 1546 destroyed the monastery, and although it was rebuilt, Tshalpa had forever lost its prominence.

Lama Shang began his studies at the age of 13 and was a student of Drogön Phagmo Drupa, founder of Densatil Monastery (see page 635). During his residency there he obtained financial support from descendents of the Gar family (Gar was a minister of Songtsen Gampo) and this laid the foundation for Tshalpa. Most of the funds came from donations, but a significant portion came from the lama's robberies. Since the ultimate goal was to serve the faith, this unorthodox activity, unbefitting for a great teacher, was accepted by the public; he was eventually named one of Tibet's Three Jewels.

Location

The walk from Lhasa to Tshalpa Monastery takes 1 3/4 hrs. From Tibet University, follow the main road east over the Lhasa East Bridge (1.7 km). Turn left at the end of the bridge [the dirt road to the right goes to Drib, (see page 596) along a paved road to a gas station (4 km from the bridge). This is the start of the Tibet–Sichuan highway. Reach a checkpost after 2 km; logging trucks are examined here. Just before the checkpost, a dirt road branches left off the main road. Follow it for 1 km to Tshalpa Monastery, itself surrounded by three smaller monasteries. First reach Gyürme Monastery, then Waling, and Nojin. The houses of the village of Tshal are built around the four temples.

TSHALPA (YANGÖN) MONASTERY

This handsome monastery with beautiful exterior stone work, rebuilt in the mid-20th C., is considerably smaller than the original. The *tshomchen* was once a spacious, 40-column hall; today there are only 12 columns. Chapels run along three sides of the hall. Formerly, there were statues of Sakyamuni, Lama Shang, and the Eight Medicine Buddhas (all destroyed).

GYÜRME (LAMA GYÜRME)

The front section of this two-story building is the *tshomchen*; the back is the Jowo Khang. It was the precursor of Lhasa's Lower (Gyürme) and Upper (Gyürtö) Tantric Colleges. It stands 1 km west of Tshalpa.

Nojin

A one-story structure, 80 m northeast of Tshalpa, it has a statue of the protector Nojin and two other protectors.

Waling (Waling Tratsang)

This two-story monastery, 150 m southwest of Tshalpa, was built by Chungchen Katipa. At the rear of the *dukhang* are three chapels; the center one contained statues of the Buddhas of the Three Ages, Tsepame, and the Eight Medicine Buddhas.

Tshal Gungthang Monastery

Location

After visiting Tshalpa Monastery, the first of the two Tshalpa-Kagyü institutions just outside of Lhasa, continue east past the checkpost on the Tibet–Sichuan highway. 4 km after the checkpost, on the right, is Lhasa's Agriculture Institute. Behind this building are the surviving chapels of Tshal Gungthang.

History

Tshal Gungthang is intimately linked with Tshalpa Monastery. Ten years after the completion of the latter, Lama Shang, with the help of his disciples, built this monastery in 1187. In 1546, the institution was destroyed by fire and the only surviving structures were the Jampa Lhakhang, a *chörten* containing the relics of Lama Shang, and a valuable statue of Drölkar. After three years of preparation, spearheaded by the Tshalpa-Kagyü lamas of Tashi Ritan and Dhundrub Ritan, rebuilding began. Today's structures date from 1549.

The site

The principal building is the Tsuglag Khang. On the ground floor is the large Tshomchen assembly hall surrounded by five chapels and two *gönkhangs*. Only two damaged statues remain, in the inner *tsangkhang*. Most murals in the Tshomchen are destroyed. Remnants depict Sakyamuni, the Dalai Lamas, Tsong Khapa and his disciples. At the rear (north) of the hall is the Jowo Khang (*tsangkhang*). Two chapels open along the Tshomchen's east and west sides. Along the south walls, two *gönkhangs* flank the entrance.

Jowo Khang

The entrance is closed by a chain gate but it is possible to squeeze through a hole. This chamber measures 21 m by 9 m and has four tall columns and eight short ones. The destroyed ceiling exposes the room to the elements. Jowo Khang's central image is a huge 8-m-tall Sakyamuni with a gaping hole in the heart. Its limbs are damaged and the armature exposed. Only one of the Eight Bodhisattvas still survives (on the right). A wall frieze and haloes, backing for the other seven statues, remain as well. Along the south walls, left and right of the entrance, were gilt-copper statues of Tsepame, Drölkar, and others. The roof provides a good view of the Tshomchen.

Northwest Chapel of the Tshomchen (four columns)

Before the monastery's destruction, this chapel contained statues of Lama Shang (1123–93), the founder, as well as his disciple, Dagma Shönnu, the Seventh Dalai Lama, and the Kagyü sages, Marpa and Milarepa.

NORTHEAST CHAPEL

Originally, this (now roofless) hall contained the gold-and-copper *chörten*-tomb of Lama Shang, statues of Atisha, Dromtönpa, Milarepa, and other historical figures, and an uncommon clay, three-dimensional model of Milarepa's mountain cave retreat. A sculpted, clay frieze with background haloes encircles the recessed niches, which once contained the statues.

SOUTHWEST CHAPEL

The main statues here were Tsepame and the Eight Medicine Buddhas. An extensive library has disappeared.

SOUTHEAST CHAPEL

This *gönkhang* has a four-armed Mahakala.

TWO GÖNKHANGS

Next to the main entrance, these dark rooms require a flashlight to see. They contain statues of protectors.

Second floor

This floor contained the chapels of Zhelre Lhakhang, Drölma Lhakhang, Zimkhang (Dalai Lama's quarters), and residences for the abbots.

CHORTENS

Thirteen large stone and earth *chörtens* north of the monastery were said to be built by Lama Shang. One remains a short distance northwest of the Tsuglag Khang, near the main road, just west of the Agriculture Institute. Although little more than a mound, it is ardently worshipped by pilgrims.

OTHER BUILDINGS

Four minor chapels were once attached to Tshal Gungthang; they were built some centuries after the founding of the main temple:

- Zangka Tratsang   southeast
- Zangpo   west
- Chökorling   west
- Chöje   west

CHANGKHANG SHAR PHUK

South of Gungthang is the Yartö Drak range, the divide between the Kyi Chu and the Tsangpo rivers. A day's walk from the monastery brings one to these mountains and the meditation cave of Lama Shang. His cave retreat (known as Changkhang Shar Phuk), a chapel beside the cave, and a 2-hr walk (lingkhor) around the site, are the focus of annual pilgrimage.

200 • GELUGPA MONUMENTS •

OTHER SITES

SHUGTRI AND SUNG CHÖRA

The Shugtri (throne) is the prominent canopied dais located along the Jokhang's southern outer wall. It stands on a large platform made of beautifully crafted yellow stone, which is a focus for important events. The Sung Chöra courtyard (see page 73) encloses Shugtri. During Mönlam, the Great Prayer Ceremony of the New Year, the Dalai Lama preached from here and the site is the venue for the annual *geshe* examination, the Gelugpa equivalent of the Doctor of Divinity degree. The four classes of Geshes are Geshe chung, Geshe chen, Geshe tsog rampa, and Geshe lharampa. The most advanced candidates could participate in the great debates on questions of logic during the Mönlam Festival. Monks from Sera, Ganden, Drepung, and elsewhere poured into Lhasa and the Dalai Lama usually ordained 21 Geshes to the rank of Geshe lharampa. The top five are qualified to head a major monastery, and one might ultimately become the abbot (*tripa*) of Ganden Monastery—a living incarnation of Tsong Khapa, founder of the Gelugpa sect.

JEBUM GANG LHAKHANG

This well-preserved chapel at the junction of the Ramoche street and Dekyi Shar Lam (Xingfu Dong Lu) was dedicated to Tsong Khapa. The north side of the intersection has a yellow Chinese restaurant with public toilets behind. Directly back of it, partially obscured, is the Jebum Gang Lhakhang. Clamber over the rubbish heap next to the toilets. Used as a granary during the Cultural Revolution, the structure is intact and once contained 100,000 images of the Gelugpa founder.

THE KARMASHAR LHAKHANG

Lhasa has three well-known oracles: Nechung (below Drepung Monastery; see page 165); Gadong (above Tolung Dechen; see page 674), and Karmashar. The chapel of the Karmashar Oracle is located a short distance east of the Barkhor.

The oracle-priest (*chöje*) of Karmashar made a prophecy each year concerning the future of Tibet. A few days before this event, the chapel held masked *Cham* dances in its courtyard to propitiate the companion deity of Pehar, the all-powerful possessor of the Nechung Oracle. This companion, Kuyi Gyalpo Monbuputra, manifested itself through the body of the Karmashar Oracle. The performers at the dance were drawn from the corpse-cutters (*ragyabpa*) and the ranks of Lhasa's policemen (*korchagpa*). On the last day of the sixth month, the chöje would travel in procession from his shrine to Sera Monastery in the company of Sera's monks and the corpse-cutters. At the monastery, the chöje entered a trance and became the medium for the spirit-voice of Kuyi Gyalpo Monbuputra. After the prophecy, a copy of it was hung on the door of Karmashar. Citizens made a habit of copying the full text to see which of its pronouncements would come to pass.

KAR NGA DONG LHAKHANG

This small shrine at the southeast base of the Potala, just outside the south entrance of the Chingdröl Chiling (the so-called Liberation Park with its island-shrine of Lukhang; see page 175). Rows of prayer wheels stand outside, and within the cosy chamber are flat stone tablets with relief carvings. Some of these apparently came from the Jokhang and are said to be quite ancient.

THE MOSQUES OF LHASA

Some 2,000 Moslems live in Lhasa and five mosques provide religious focus. Moslem traders from Ladakh and Kashmir first came to Tibet in the 17th C.; they are known as *khache*, Tibetan for Kashmir. Many later migrated south to Lhasa and work as butchers. In the past few years, significant numbers have come from the Sala area (south of Xining) of Qinghai Province and many *halal* restaurants have sprung up. Lhasa has two Moslem areas: Khache Lingka and the Gyal Lhakhang (Main Mosque).

KHACHE LINGKA

Located 3 km west of the Potala on the Drepung road, it has residences, two mosques and a cemetery. Khache Lingka was the original 18th-C. place of settlement for Moslems. A memorial plaque at a grave was erected during the reign of the Qing Emperor Qianlong (1736–95). Chinese annals record that 197 Kashmiri Moslems lived in Lhasa and maintained a mosque at that time.

Khache Lingka's two mosques are less than 100 m from each other; to their south is the cemetery.

GYAL LHAKHANG

Gyal Lhakhang is a short walk from the Barkhor's southeast corner. The Moslem street runs from here, marked by the flagpole of Sharkyaring, to the mosque. Along the street are numerous Moslem restaurants serving noodle dishes (*la mian*), dumplings (*momos*), mutton, and delicious tea. Gyal Lhakhang, constructed in 1716, was initially quite small. After a fire, it was expanded in 1793 to become Lhasa's largest mosque. Destroyed again during the uprising of 1959, it was rebuilt the next year. The site is approximately 2600 sq m and contains the assembly hall, bathhouse, minaret, residences, and a courtyard. On Fridays, as many as 600 people come to worship. Important rituals—marriage, death, circumcision—are performed here.

SMALL MOSQUE

Another mosque stands in the old Tibetan section west of the Gyal Lhakhang in a quiet lane south of the Jokhang. This small, south-facing mosque with minaret is made up of two parts. The north, two-story Tibetan-style building contains the bathhouses (ground floor) and a schoolroom for teaching Koranic Arabic (upstairs). Immediately south is the assembly hall, part of the principal building. The mosque was built in this century to accommodate Moslems from Kashmir, Ladakh, Bhutan, Nepal, and China.

LHASA LABRANGS (RESIDENCES OF ABBOTS)

DHEDRUK LABRANG

The Dhedruk Labrang is east of Meru Sarpa Tratsang on the same side of the street, directly across from the Kirey Hotel. Brown trim encircles its roof; a small Chinese restaurant stands before it. Dhedruk was built on the same plan as Tsomön Ling, Tengye Ling, and Meru Sarpa. Monks lived in three-story residences that form three sides of the complex. A central gate links a courtyard to the street, and the main assembly hall (*dukhang*), with impressive stonework, is at the far side of the courtyard.

DEMO LABRANG

The Demo Labrang is a pretty yellow building within a peaceful garden just north of Tengye Ling Monastery. Enter from Tengye Ling (see page 168) or through a large gate on the Dekyi Shar Lam street's south side. Close by and to its west is a new complex used by the government to receive and house Tibetans returning from abroad. Demo was the residence of the Demo Qutuqtu, abbot of Tengye Ling.

LINGTSANG LABRANG

This two-story *labrang*, now an apartment building, is south of the square in front of the Jokhang, east of the Snowland Hotel street. Enter the building's south side from a street running eastwest. On the landings and corridors upstairs are Chinese-influenced murals. Go to the roof for a good view of the Jokhang.

PABONKA LABRANG

Just beyond the eastern edge of the Barkhor is a building with rounded, exterior walls and a large, open terrace on the second floor. This is the Mönlam building; Pabonka Labrang is just behind it. The three-story complex, now residences, was the home of Pabonka Monastery's abbot (see page 129).

PHURCHOK LABRANG

West of the Ramoche street and Dekyi Shar Lam junction is the three-story building, next to a cobbled street (with traffic barrier) that leads to the Barkhor. No trace remains of its previous function.

RETING LABRANG

Sandwiched to the north between the Tsomön Ling (see page 169) and Shide Tratsang (see page 173) is this attractive building in a garden. The Reting Lama lives here and the place still functions as a *labrang*.

TRIJANG LABRANG

At the southern edge of Old Lhasa, directly south of the Jokhang, is this three-story complex with ironwork balconies. It is now the headquarters of the Lhasa Movie Company. The *labrang* was home to the last Trijung Rinpoche, who died in India in 1981. He was junior tutor to the present Dalai Lama.

Thönpa

An old, dilapidated, three-story building on the south leg of the Barkhor, this is the only structure on this street with brown roof-trim, a mark of palaces and monasteries. Thönmi Sambhota supposedly lived here in the 7th century. Today, it is an apartment building and headquarters of the Barkhor Residents' Committee.

Ngagkhang

A three-story tantric college immediately east of Shugtri; now converted into residences (good views of the Jokhang from the roof).

Yüthok Zampa ('Turquoise Bridge')

This ancient bridge, 300 m west of the Jokhang, is enclosed within the Lhasa Customs Office compound (across the street, west from the new Lhasa cinema). It linked Old Lhasa to the outside, and tradition says the original stone structure dates back to the 7th century. The bridge's span is 28.3 m and the width 6.8 m. 2-m-thick stone walls enclose both sides. Each has five openings with wood barriers. These massive stone walls support a Chinese-style roof with turquoise tiles. Eaves at the north and south ends are decorated with the heads of dragons, although parts of the southern roof have been damaged. Notice the intricately designed tongue-shaped waterspouts. The bridge's superstructure probably dates from the 18th century.

Nangtseshag (Lhasa's prison)

This disused 300-year-old prison stands at the Barkhor's north section; its south wall abuts the Jokhang's north perimeter wall. The square outside its entrance is a lively carpet bazaar and the passage to Meru Nyingba Monastery passes in front of the Nangtseshag. Constructed of stone and wood, the prison occupies 720 sq m. A platform in front of the second-story, east-facing entrance was the site of sentencing and execution, but prisoners were first paraded around the Barkhor. The ground floor was reserved for serious prisoners, while the second floor held women and lesser criminals. In the past, approximately 600 people were imprisoned each year and 40 or 50 of them were executed. Cruel and unusual punishments included gouging out eyes, flaying, and dismemberment.

Mentsi Khang

Mentsi Khang was the original Tibetan hospital of Lhasa. It stands across from the new Lhasa cinema, west of Jokhang plaza, along Mimang Lam. This two-story building, resembling a monastic chapel with its brown roof trim, was built in 1916 by Kalu Norbu and houses an outpatient clinic and the Tibetan Medicine Research Institute. Of five professors, two specialize in Tibetan medicine, two in astrology, and one in eye diseases.

The modern multi-storied building east of Mentsi Khang (directly in front of the Jokhang plaza) is Lhasa's principal Tibetan hospital; it functions primarily as a large outpatient clinic. A room on the top floor is the hospital's shrine. The main images here are Tibetan medicine's three most important contributors. In the center is Yütok Yönten Gönpo (b 729), father of the tradition, trained in both Chinese and Tibetan medicine. He was personal physician to the Yarlung kings, Tride Tsugten and Trisong Detsen. To the left is Sangye Gyatso, Regent of the Fifth Dalai Lama and a renowned physician who wrote two important works on Tibetan medicine. He founded the original medical college on Chakpo Ri in the late 17th century. To the right is Khyenrab Norbu (d 1962), head doctor of Drepung and Tibet's most important 20th-C. physician. An adjacent room holds a superb collection of medical *thangkas*. The 17th-C. originals are kept inside strong boxes while copies hang on the wall. Request to view the originals.

BARKHANG: THE LHASA PRINTING PRESS

Two printing presses survive in Lhasa. Before the Cultural Revolution, the most famous presses for printing Tibetan manuscripts were at Narthang (see page 834), Derge in Kham, and the Potala. Today, the only one that still operates along ancient lines is the one in Derge. The Lhasa presses, both located within the Potala's perimeter walls, have different histories.

THE EAST PRINTING PRESS

The Ganden Phüntsok Ling ('Blessed Garden of Happiness') is situated at the southeast corner of the Potala, adjoining the east perimeter wall. This 600 sq-m structure, the older of the two presses, was built during the time of the Fifth Dalai Lama (1617–82) and is contemporaneous with the Potala's Karpo Potrang ('White Palace').The south-facing, two-story building contains the printing hall, storerooms for wood blocks, living quarters of the keeper, and stables. At the northern section of the ground floor is the printing hall, the site for carving walnut wood-blocks and printing sutras. The south section's east end contains two wood-block storerooms, whereas the southwestern part held the stables (most of which are now residences). At the center of the second floor is the skylight. Ranged around it are nine rooms, the living quarters of the workers and the keeper.

Parts of the wood-block collection, dating from the 17th and 18th C., were transferred to the Mentsi Khang Tibetan Hospital (see page 203) for safekeeping during the Cultural Revolution; the rest were lost or destroyed, and the storerooms now stand empty. Right from the beginning, the tremendous demand for texts overburdened the facilities. As a result, most wood-blocks were worn down and the small press was unable to keep up with the workload. In the reign of the 13th Dalai Lama (1876–1933), a new printing press was constructed at the southwest foot of the Potala. It became known as the West Printing Press.

THE WEST PRINTING PRESS

During the press's construction, new wood-blocks and statues were created at the Norbu Lingka (see page 180). The massive Tengyur, recommissioned at the Kelsang Potrang, followed the old model belonging to Narthang Monastery. At that time, the 91st Tripa (Supreme Abbot) of Ganden Monastery donated a large sum of silver for the statues. After his death, a *chörten*-tomb for his remains was built inside the press. The 13th Dalai Lama named the new complex Gang Gyan Pungtideng Tsünkhang, 'the Great Library of the Blessed Snowland'.

This new six-story press, sited near the west perimeter wall and built along the lower slopes of Marpo Ri, is far bigger than the old one. Its south-facing main entrance, at the second floor, is reached by a flight of stone steps; a pair of stone lions flank the entrance. The ground floor was mainly used for storage, whereas the second floor holds the wood-block library and the printed texts. Printing was done on the third floor, the Jampa Lhakhang, a hall dedicated to the Future Buddha. The east and west sections of the hall contained the complete Kangyur, a wood-block collection of 48,189 pieces. The center-rear section of this hall had images of Jampa, Atisha, and Tsong Khapa. Flanking these were statues of Tsepame, Trisong Detsen, Guru Rinpoche, and Drölkar; all were destroyed during the Cultural Revolution. The third floor, twice the size of the second, is surmounted by the three-story Jigje Lhakhang, which serves as the *gönkhang*. It was built in 1949 to commemorate a temporary retreat of the Chinese army. The sculptures were destroyed, but the murals remain.

The West Printing Press now houses the archives of the Tibet Autonomous Region. It contains many rare and valuable documents on the history, politics, economy, religion, and culture of Tibet. The original collection of over 100,000 wood-blocks is preserved. Of particular importance is the 50,000-piece Kangyur. It is one of only two surviving sets, the other one being at Derge.

PRAYER FLAGPOLES

Four tall flagpoles surround the Jokhang:
• Ganden Darchen, at the northeast corner of the Barkhor, was erected in the 15th century. Supposedly, the top contained Tsong Khapa's bamboo staff.
• Juyag Darchen, in front of the Jokhang's main gate, dates from the 7th C. (the present flagpole is new). Juyag means 'an offering to Sakyamuni.' According to tradition, Tibetan girls came here at age 16 before marriage. As part of a special ceremony they offered sacred scarves (*katas*), burned incense, circumambulated the flagpole, and recited prayers.
• Kesang Darchen is at the Barkhor's southwest corner.
• Sharkyaring Darchen stands at the Barkhor's southeast corner. It was erected at the same time as Ganden Darchen.

Principal Pilgrimages
and
Historical sites

TIBET'S THREE PARAMOUNT PILGRIMAGES

Tibetan pilgrims generally acknowledge that Kailash, Lapchi, and Tsari are the three most important pilgrimages in Tibet. Each place is associated with a holy mountain: Kailash (Kang Rinpoche), Lapchi Gang, Takpa Shelri, all considered palaces of Demchok, the wrathful emanation of the Buddha Sakyamuni. This cult of Demchok was initiated in the early 12th C. by Phagmo Drupa and propagated by the Drigungpa, Drukpa, and later, the Gelugpa. The three sites are identified as the 'body, speech, and mind' of the deity.

Kailash in particular is viewed as the symbolic centre of the world for both Hindus and Buddhists. Milarepa, most beloved poet-saint of Tibet, was strongly associated with the myths and holy places surrounding Lapchi and Kailash, while Tsangpa Gyare, the 12th-C. founder of Bhutan's Drukpa set, spent the most time at Tsari. Guru Rinpoche, the Indian tantric master who introduced Buddhism to Tibet, was ubiquitous in all three. It is worth noting that these foremost pilgrim destinations are all located in extremely beautiful areas of the country.

TSARI: SOUTHEAST TIBET'S MOST CELEBRATED PILGRIMAGE

The Shangri-Las of the Tibet–Bhutan Divide

Location	Southeast Tibet
Map reference	NH46-10 C D, 46-11 C, 46-14 A B C D, 46-15 A B
Trekking days	Route (A) 3 (one-way)
	Route (B) 8 (one-way)
Start–Finish	Route (A) Shobo Qu–Chösam
	Route (B) Nang Xian–Chösam–Migyitun
Passes	Route (A) Baré La
	Route (B) Tangma La

OVERVIEW

Pristine trekking and pilgrimage opportunities exist in the Tsari region of southeast Tibet. It is an area of ethereal natural beauty, lush and green, that retains to this day magnificent stands of ancient silver fir cloaked in heavy veils of Spanish moss. Few places in Tibet can match Tsari's grandeur and sanctity. Most important of all, it is one of the country's three great pilgrimage centers; the other two are Mt Kailash (see page 273) and Lapchi (see page 248). These legendary sites are all consecrated to the divinity Demchok, a wrathful emanation of Sakyamuni. (Once every 12 years, Tsari witnesses a major pilgrimage when Tibetans flock to sacred Mt Takpa Shelri.)

Tradition bans hunting and even cultivation in certain parts of the Tsari Valley. Its few inhabitants used to depend solely on catering to pilgrims from neighbouring Pome to survive. In the first decades of this century only a handful of British naturalists reached Tsari successfully. Among them were the celebrated Frank Kingdon Ward, the botanists Ludlow and Sheriff, and the explorer, F. M. Bailey. They all wrote enthusiastically about the spectacular environment and its unrivaled flora. The Tsari Chu is an upper tributary of the great Subansiri, which flows through the Assam Himalayas into India's Arunachal Pradesh. It then joins the Brahmaputra en route to the Bay of Bengal. Other branches of the Subansiri are the Char Chu, the Loro Chu, and the Nye Chu. They combine to become the Chayul Chu, which in turn merges with the Tsari to become the Subansiri. These river valleys provide fabulous hunting grounds for botanists, and trekkers can easily spend months here hiking from the headwaters of one river valley to the next.

Nineteen itineraries of varying length and complexity are detailed in this chapter. Starting points for pilgrimages to Tsari include Tsethang (Nedong Xian), Nang Xian, Lhuntse Xian, Tsona Xian, Shobo Qu, Sanga Chöling Qu, Chayul Qu, Guru Namgye Qu, Kyimdong Qu, and Chumdo Kyang Qu. The most significant (and easily accessible) begin from the culturally important Yarlung Valley: one starts from Tsethang and goes south to Shobo Qu where the trek to Sanga Chöling Monastery and Tsari's western section begins; another goes from Tsethang to Nang Xian on the Tsangpo, where an idyllic trail leads directly to Chösam in the sacred

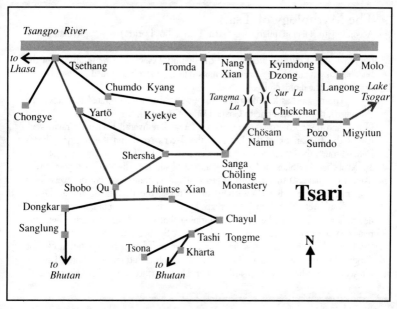

valley. A third goes via the important frontier town of Tsona, situated at the northern fringe of Mönpa territory, and accessible by a road from Tsethang. Monasteries near the upper reaches of the Subansiri lie within the Tsari Chu, Nye Chu, Loro Chu, and Char Chu valleys. The Tsari Kyilkhor pilgrimage, a short circumambulation of the sacred Takpa Shelri peaks, was successfully attempted by Bailey (1913) and Sheriff (1936). No foreigner has done it since, and no outsider has ever completed the long, difficult Tsari Rongkhor pilgrimage, which encompasses the breathtaking headwaters of Subansiri. Only F. Kingdon Ward ever reached holy Tsogar, an ephemeral high-altitude lake above Migyitun at Tsari's eastern end. Also not to be missed is Tso Bunang, a chain of four crystal-clear glacial lakes. The scenery in this secluded valley is among the best in the country.

A two-week optional trek, via the Bimbi La and Kyimdong Dzong, explores the seldom-visited Pachakshiri range, the Assam Himalayas. This itinerary includes a circuit around sacred Tsari Sarpa ('new' Tsari, another renowned pilgrimage in the region). The chapter also suggests treks around Tsona Xian, including the beautiful Dongkar districts and the isolated Nyamjang Chu Valley immediately north of the Bhutan border. Nyamjang borders the eastern extreme of Lhodrak (see page 681), one of the most hallowed regions in Tibet.

Related sections
The Yarlung Valley, p 515
Left bank of the Tsangpo, p 735
Lhodrak, p 681

The Mythology of Tsari

According to Tibetan pilgrimage texts, Tsari (also Tsaritra) is a representation of Devikota in Assam, one of the earth's 24 most sacred places (see page 36). It embodies the physical and spiritual attributes of the divinity Demchok, a wrathful form of the Buddha Sakyamuni. Tsari's principal mountain is Takpa Shelri, a dwelling place of Dorje Jigje, the Lord of Death.

The region has four doorways: the eastern gate is consecrated to Jampelyang (Manjusri), the southern one to Chana Dorje (Vajrapani), the western one to Drölma (Tara), and the northern one to Chenresi (Avalokiteshvara). Four main ravines are named the Human Skin, the Dazzling, the Tiger's Nest, and the terrifying Bear's Den. Through these four flow the four sacred rivers. The four primary passes of Tsari are Kyobchen La, Shakam La, Gayo La, and Shadu La. The valley's topography is likened to a *mandala* that consists of peaceful and wrathful areas. For believers, Tsari is a true, living paradise (Dewachen) of Wöpame, the Buddha of Infinite Light.

Kunkhyen Pema Karpo, the Drukpa Kagyü patriarch of Bhutan, wrote a detailed description of Tsari in the 16th C., affirming that Guru Rinpoche came here and remained seven years in a cave called Zilchen Sangwe Phuk. During the 8th C., the Indian Dzokchen master, Vimalamitra, came to Tibet at the invitation of King Trisong Detsen. He stayed in Tsari at a place called Potrang Kar. Later, Lawapa, a teacher of Atisha, came to Tsari's Eastern Door, reached Chickchar (see page 230) ➡

and then meditated in the caves of Machen Lawa Phuk and Khajor Ri Dorje Phuk. During the Second Diffusion of Buddhism, Tsangpa Gyaré (1161–1211) was in retreat at Jomo Kharak when he received a vision that he would go to Tsari and open a secret valley (*beyul*) for future generations of pilgrims. He subsequently became the first person to thoroughly explore Tsari.

FROM TSETHANG TO TSARI

Different routes lead from Tsethang to Tsari and all involve some hitchhiking before trekking can begin. This section describes two itineraries: (A) Begin at Shobo Qu and finish at Chösam, a village in western Tsari; (B) Start at Nang Xian on the Tsangpo, passing Chösam to reach Migyitun at Tsari's eastern and lower stretches.

(A) Shobo Qu–Chösam

Access: Tsethang to Shobo Qu (Shobo Shar) 121 km

From Tsethang (see page 518), a main road follows the Yarlung Valley's eastern branch (Yarlha Shampo Chu) south to Potrang (17 km) and Yartö Monastery. Cross the Yartö Tra La and Shobo Tu La (Da La), then pass Kadang Monastery to arrive at Shobo Qu. There are road markers in km all along the road.

(Km)	Place	Notes
123	Tsethang	
129	Trandruk Monastery	see Yarlung, page 533
135	Yumbu Lagang	see Yarlung, page 539
140	Potrang	Village with restored monastery; 1 km after this, the valley narrows
163	Yartö	An active Gelugpa center, also called Chöde Gang Monastery (see page 532)
164	Yartö	Ruins
184	Yartö Tra La	Cross the Yarlha Shampo Range; (4970 m) the main peak (6636 m) is southwest. Lake Chim Tso is 8 km northeast. Nomad tents in summer.
194		House and road junction. The left branch goes to Chumdo Kyang, Kyekye, and Tsari (see below); the right is the main road south to Shobo Qu.

(Continues on page 214)

Alternative Route: Yartö Tra La to Tsari via Chumdo Kyang, Kyekye, and the Chartö Valley

Take the left (northeast) road at road marker 194 km for 9 km to Chumdo Kyang (4465 m), a major valley intersection. Here a jeep track leads north to Chusum 44 km away. To the east is a river valley that heads up to the Pu (Kampa) La and Kyekye in the Lhakong Valley. It then makes an abrupt turn southward to follow the upper reaches of the Char Chu (Chartö). Eventually, reach Charme, Sanga Chöling Monastery and the Tsari Valley. This route is an interesting, rarely traveled way to access the sacred valley.

✧ Day 1   Chumdo Kyang–Tratsang   16 km

From Chumdo Kyang head due east (a lake lies 7 km north of this settlement). Cross the Chumdo Kyang River and ascend the opposite bank. Reach the Siri La on a valley spur 6.5 km from Chumdo Kyang. The trail becomes level, narrow, and stony. In 4 km, the valley turns sharply to the right and constricts. It soon opens out again and is joined by a jeep track that takes the longer way from Chumdo Kyang to here. Soon reach Tratsang (4575 m).

✧ Day 2   Tratsang–Kyekye   19 km

Walk up 5.5 km to the Pu (Kampa) La (4630 m). (Before the pass, a large valley on the right goes south via the Tak La to Shobo Qu; this route bypasses the major Yartö Tra La–Shobo Qu road.) After this pass, the Tsangpo drainage is left behind. Continue eastward from the Pu La for 8 km along the valley's right side to Drongshu, on the left bank at a river junction. The river from the Pu La flows past the village before turning south to Sanga Chöling. It is joined by the Lhakong Tö Chu at Kyekye. From Drongshu, climb to the Jatang La. Then walk along a level track for 1.5 km before descending steeply along a rocky valley to a river. Ford it; beyond is Kyekye (4450 m), 2.5 km from the Jatang La.

✧ Day 3   Kyekye–Tengchung   25 km

From Kyekye, the route turns from east to south. Follow the left bank of the Pu La-Lhakong Tö Chu to Charap, then cross a bridge to the right bank and walk 10 km to Pundro. Both Charap and Pundro are administered by Lhuntse Xian. Two routes proceed from Pundro. One goes south over the Tak La to Shobo Qu, the other east to the Char Valley. Take the latter. Cross the Lhakong Tö Chu and follow its left bank down the Char Valley in the district known as Chartö. It is distinct from Charme (farther downstream). Walk east past Kyitö to Tengchung (4270 m).

✧ Day 4   Tengchung–Shersha   22 km

Walk 3 km down the Chartö Valley to a bridge. (Cross it to the right south bank,

➡

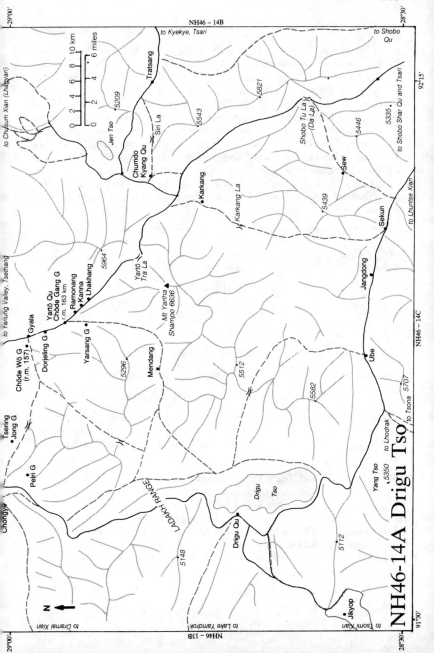

NH46 – 14B

to Kyekye, Tsari

to Shobo Qu

to Chūsum Xian (Lhagyari)

29°00'

28°30'

92°15'

10 km

6 miles

5209

Tratsang

Jen Tso

Chumdo
Kyang Qu

Siri La

5543

5821

Shobo Tu La
(Da La)

5335

5446

to Shobo Shar Qu and Tsari

to Lhuntse Xian

Sew

Karkang

5439

Karkang La

Sekun

5964

Jangdong

Yartö Qu
Chöde Gang G
r.m. 163 km

Ramonang

Lhakhang

Kanna

Yartö
Tra La

Mt Yarlha
Shampo 6636

to Yarlung Valley, Tsethang

Gyala

Dorjeling G

Yarsang G

Chöde Wö G
(r.m. 157)

Mendang

5296

5512

5582

Ube

5707

NH46 – 14C

to Tsona

Tsering
Jong G

Peiri G

LADAKH RANGE

5350

to Lhodrak

Yang Tso

Chongye

Drigu
Tso

Drigu Qu

5148

5112

to Dramal Xian

to Lake Yamdrok

to Tsomi Xian

to Somi Xian

Jikyop

N

NH46 – 13B

28°30'

29°00'

31°36'

NH46-14A Drigu Tso

at Yakshi only if you want to go to Shobo Qu via the Se La and Baré La passes [see opposite].) To continue to Sanga Chöling, stay on the left (north) bank and leave the main valley by climbing 200 m to the small Tsigu La and a further 300 m to the Gyemo La (4575 m). (An easier route that avoids these passes continues along the Char Chu to Shersha [see opposite].) From the pass, descend along the Chegun Valley for 2.5 km to Shosa, then 1 km to Shamda at the entrance to a north-trending side valley (this leads to Ganden Rabden Monastery, near the Tsangpo, via the Gyen La). Continue east from Shamda to Shirap in the Shirap Valley (5.5 km). From Shirap, walk down the Chegun Valley for 5 km to the main Char Valley and Shersha Qu, a short distance west of the valley junction. The journey east from Shersha Qu along the Char Valley to Sanga Chöling is described in the section, Shobo Qu to Sanga Chöling Monastery and Chösam via the Baré La.

(Km)	Place	Notes
196		Nomad tents
205		Nomad tents, house
209		Village
213		House
220	Shobo Tu La	5001 m (also called the Da La)
226		Road maintenance compound (*daoban*)
235	Kadang Monastery	Gelugpa monastery with original mural.
239	Shobo Shar Village	Turnoff to the left leads to Shobo Qu (1 km away), where the trek starts. The main road continues south to Lhuntse and Tsona (94 km further; see below).

Shobo Qu (trail head): Shobo Qu is a district office next to a village. Rooms (mattresses on the floor) and meals are available in the *qu* compound, but it is prudent to avoid prying officials by staying in a village farther up the valley.

The Tsari trek starts from Shobo Qu and goes northeast along a side valley to the Baré La and Sanga Chöling Monastery (82 km). There is very little traffic on the jeep path; pack animals are available 1 hr beyond Shobo Qu at Dzongka Chöde or in villages a short distance before the *qu*. Expect to pay Rmb 35–50 for a donkey and a Tibetan handler for the trip (3–4 days).

Shobo Qu to Sanga Chöling Monastery and Chösam via the Baré La

Time Chart

Day	Place	Hours
1	Shobo Qu–Shersha	10
2	Shobosang	5 1/4
3	Sanga Chöling Monastery	5 1/2
4	Base of Cha La	4
5	Chösam	5

Trail Notes

✤ DAY 1 SHOBO QU–SHERSHA (43 KM) 10 HR

This long section might better be done in two days. From Shobo Qu, walk northeast for 1 hr along the flat side valley to impressive Dzongka Chöde Monastery. Gradually ascend for 2 1/2 hr to the Baré La (4630 m), the last hour being quite strenuous. The pass stands as the divide between the Nye and Char rivers.

Descend to a river (1 hr). The jeep road bears left down the Yesa Valley along the river. Follow telegraph poles along an old trail right of the river. In 1 hr turn right down a narrow side valley to emerge again at the road (1/2 hr). Continue downhill, turning right along the road. Cross the river after 1 hr; the river is now on the right. In 2 hr come to the valley's end. Walk a bridge and bear right into the Char Valley. Shersha Qu is 1 hr further. The administrative center is a mud compound in the middle of the village. Beds are available.

> **Dzongka Chöde Monastery** This large, partially destroyed monastery stands inside a large village. The main buildings have been restored and the main hall, full of old Buddhists texts, has fine murals. Walls of an ancient mud building remain, and behind the monastery is a stone watchtower (unusual in this region) and a fortress-like building.

✤ DAY 2 SHERSHA–SHOBOSANG 5 1/4 HR

Descend the narrow Char Valley (the Char Chu is on the right). Reach Reshue (Reshö), a village with tall watchtowers, after 1 3/4 hr. Walk past Char Tsemo (1 hr) and locate Trip across the river. Reach Shobosang (Sho, Sho Shika) in 2 1/2 hr, a pocket of small hamlets with handsome stone houses. The ruins of Taktse Monastery stand on a conical hill marked by prayer flags.

✤ DAY 3 SHOBOSANG–SANGA CHÖLING MONASTERY 5 1/2 HR

Continue down the valley along a good dirt track. Pass a side valley (1/2 hr beyond Shobosang) across the river, opening to the south. (A bridge here leads to a trail within this south-trending valley that crosses the Mo La [5400 m] to the Nye Valley and Lhuntse Xian.) Beyond this valley junction (1/2 hr) is Gegye (Bung) on a terrace.

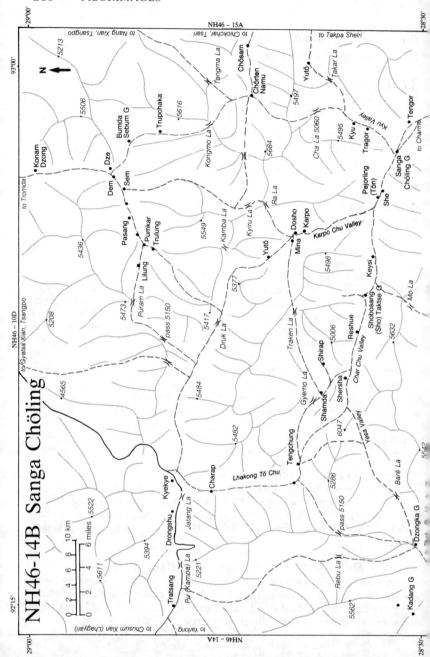

NH46-14B Sanga Chöling

Mo La and the Nye Valley Walk south up the steep, narrow Mo La Valley, and reach the pass in 4 hr. Descend southwest to the Mo La–Nye river confluence. Within the Mo La Valley entrance are the villages of Dikiling and Nyeme. Turn right at the confluence to follow the Nye westward along a dirt road to Lhuntse (turn left to reach Chayul). From Nyeme to Lhuntse is 19 km; from Nyeme to Chayul is 29 km.

Keysi lies 1 3/4 hr from Shobosang and a road maintenance compound is a further 3/4 hr. Enter a narrow gorge and reach a hydroelectric station (1 1/4 hr). Pejorling (Tön), 1/4 hr further, is an army camp with many buildings strung out for 2 km along the road. The village across the Char Chu is She. At the entrance of Sanga Chöling (1 1/2 hr from Ton), buildings belonging to the monastery (on the left) have rooms available. A path zigzags up a ridge to the rebuilt monastery.

For Day 4 of this route, see page 222.

The Karpo Chu Valley

This valley opens to the north a short distance west of Pejorling. Within it are the villages of Karpo, Doshö, and Yutö. The valley divides beyond Yutö. To the left, the main valley ascends the Druk La and the way then follows the Lhakong Chu west to Kyekye, the Pu La, and the Yarlung Valley. The right valley (see below) goes over the Kamba La and follows the Trulung Chu to Trulung, Pumkar, Pasang, Sem, Dem, and Dze. Here the valley divides again; the left branch goes north to Ganden Rabden Monastery and Tromda on the Tsangpo's south bank, the right (described) leads over the Kongpo La to Chösam and Tsari. This roundabout way to Tsari by-passes completely the strategic town of Sanga Chöling Qu and its government offices and Public Security Bureau. It should prove invaluable for accessing the sacred valley with a minimum of bureaucratic fuss. Below is a description of the trek from Pejorling to Chösam.

PEJORLING TO CHÖSAM VIA THE KAMBA LA AND KONGPO LA PASSES
TRAIL NOTES
✧ **Day 1 Pejorling–Karpo 13 km**
Walk back westward from Pejorling (Tön) to the entrance of the north-trending Karpo Chu Valley. A good dirt road follows the river's left (east) bank. (The people of the Char Valley and Sanga Chöling once used this valley as the main route to Lhasa.) The Karpo Valley's first village is Karpo Me and beyond (1 km) is Karpo (3700 m). Sturdy houses on the hillsides above Karpo once belonged to Sanga Chöling Monastery.

✧ **Day 2 Karpo–Kamba La Drok 12 km**
Doshö lies 1.5 km beyond Karpo. (East of Doshö, a trail goes up a side valley over

the Ra La to Ganden Rabden Monastery and Tromda on the Tsangpo.) At Mina, 1.5 km farther, a side valley opens to the west and a trail leads over the Traken La to Shamda on the Chartö (upper Char Chu). 2.4 km after Mina is Yutö, the valley's highest village (2.5 km from Shamda). [The Druk La Pass, 11 km from Yutö, leads west to Yarlung.] The turnoff to the Kamba La is 5.5 km beyond Yutö; the side valley leads from the main Karpo valley northeastward to a nomad campsite (*drok*) at 4800 m (the motor road west to the Druk La is left behind). The Kamba La, Chebo La, and Gyawo La all cross the same range and lead to Takpo District.

◇ Day 3   Kamba La Drok–Pumkar   14 km

The Kamba La (5210 m) is 2.5 km from the *drok*. From the pass, descend 3 km to a valley junction; the large one coming from the left (west) originates at the Gyawo La. On the right is another valley; a trail within it leads east to the Kobo La and Doshö. Continue down the main valley. In 5 km, a side valley on the left (west) leads to the Chebo La. Beyond the valley junction are Kulum, Trulung, and Pumkar (4025 m). At Pumkar, a side valley joins the Trulung Chu at its left bank. A trail up this valley leads to Lilung and the Puram La.

◇ Day 4   Pumkar–Trupchaka   22 km

After Pumkar (2.5 km), another valley arrives from the left. It leads west to the Kye La and Lolen, a valley that joins the Tsangpo at Limda. Continue to Sem and Dem (10 km from Pumkar). On an opposite hill is Tsila Monastery, at the mouth of the Ra La Valley (the Ra La leads to Doshö, just above Karpo). From Dem, cross the river by a bridge and ascend a spur that overlooks the cultivated Trulung Valley. The green fields of Guru Namgye Dzong appear in the far distance. Descend to a side valley that opens to the southeast and follow it to Bumda Sebum, a small monastery 5 km from Dem. Its two large *chörtens* supposedly contain 100,000 demons (*sinmo*), buried there by Lama Tsangpa Gyaré because they impeded pilgrims' progress to Tsari. The valley divides after 2.5 km. Take the right branch south to Trupchaka (4560 m).

◇ Day 5   Trupchaka–Chösam   28 km

The Kongpo La (5340 m) is 10 km beyond Trupchaka. From the pass, descend to a herders' camp (3 km). About 5 km later, the valley reaches the Tsari Chu at a wide plain called Chörten Namu. Looking south and west, locate the valley that leads to Sanga Chöling Monastery via the Cha La. Turn east down the Tsari Valley to Chösam, 10.5 km from the valley junction.

Sanga Chöling Monastery This important Kagyüpa monastery, the most significant in the entire region, was rebuilt in 1986; an exiled monk returned from Darjeeling to supervise the extensive renovations. The monastery's main incarnation is Drukpa ➡

Rinpoche and the central chapel's principal image is Sakyamuni. Some original monastic buildings at village level remain as residences. Stay in rooms next to the monks' quarters. The monastery, constructed of beautifully dressed stones, was sacked during the Cultural Revolution and these same stones were used to build an administration compound for local officials. A Tibetan party secretary is now in charge of Sanga Chöling Qu; he is supported by at least one Public Security officer. They both live in a compound in the middle of the village—avoid it.

The Sanga Chöling to Chayul circuit
Sanga Chöling–Charme–Kyimphu–Nyerong–Chayul–Trön–Lung–Sanga Chöling

This interesting trek from Sanga Chöling to the fortress of Chayul crosses regions with only small villages and monasteries and virtually no traffic. The itinerary traverses the major headwaters of the Subansiri River, the Char Chu and Nye Chu. (To explore the Loro Nakpo and Loro Karpo rivers, follow the Chayul–Kharta trek, see page 242.)

TRAIL NOTES
✧ **Day 1   Sanga Chöling–Charme (3230 m)   17 km**
From Sanga Chöling follow the left bank of the Char Chu to the southeast. The trail passes through a dry, narrow gorge with patches of cultivation and peach trees. Tengor lies 5 km from Sanga Chöling and 8 km beyond Tengor is Chingkar (ruins of defense towers). Below Chingkar, cross the river over a 15-m cantilever bridge. Charme is at the junction of the Char Chu and the Kyimphu Chu (flows from the Le La). To reach the frontier village of Lung, follow the Char Chu southeastward. To go to Kyimphu (4085 m) and Nyerong, follow the Kyimphu Chu southwestward.

✧ **Day 2   Charme–Kyimphu (4085 m)   11 km**
Cross the Kyimphu Chu to its left bank at Charme and walk upstream for 5 km, then cross to the right and cross back again after 0.5 km (take a trail over a cliff on the left bank if the bridge is broken). Reach Gyu (ruined), 7 km from Charme. An optimal trail crosses the river here and goes past Tsi en route to the Drichung La and the Chayul Chu to the south. Eventually reach Kyimphu. An alternative way goes from Charme via the Drichung La for two days and involves camping in the open. This route is impassable for animals. Kyimphu is 4 km beyond Gyu.

✧ **Day 3   Kyimphu–Nyerong (3700 m)   26 km**
Continue westward along the Kyimphu Chu's left bank to the Le La (5240 m), 10 km from Kyimphu. Descend steeply to Gyandro, 8 km from the pass. Further down, the river enters a narrow gorge and flows into the Nye Chu, 5.5 km from Gyandro (24 km from Kyimphu). At the junction, follow the Nye's left bank for 1.5 km to Nyerong.

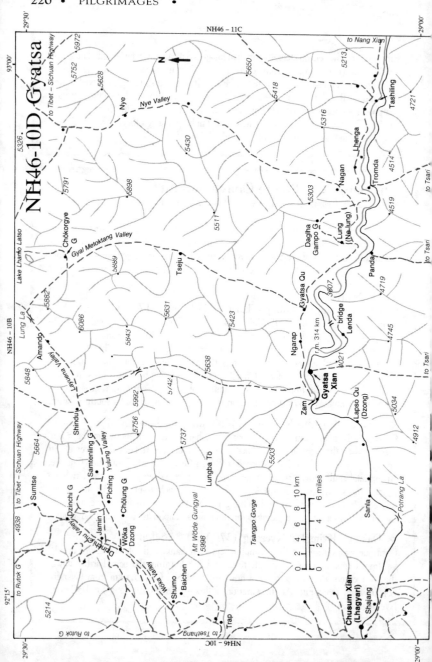

✧ Day 4   Nyerong–Kap (3475 m)   20 km

Continue south down the Nye Chu. Cross to the right bank 1 km below Nyerong and pass Sample after 3 km. Reach a bridge over the Chayul Chu at a point 0.5 km above the Nye–Chayul junction (7 km from Sample). (The village of Chayul Dzong lies 1 km west. The route from here to Kharta takes in the Loro Karpo and the Loro Nakpo rivers, the remaining headwaters of the Subansiri, see page 228). Cross the bridge and head east along the Chayul's right bank to Komlha, a scattered village 1.5 km from the river junction. Kap lies 7 km beyond.

✧ Day 5   Kap–Drotang (3415 m)   26 km

The difficult trail of today at times goes over galleries of sticks and branches along the cliff face. A bridge spans the deep Chayul Gorge 2.5 km after Kap (if broken, the route is impassable). Cross to the right (north) bank and follow the river to the deserted village of Tenzika, 5.5 km from the start. Cross back to the left bank after 9 km, then reach a gorge that must be crossed on a 10-m ladder propped on a 15-m masonry pillar. Reach Trön (Trönta) by climbing 400 m above the river (17 km from Kap). Trön is the last Tibetan village on the Loro Chu. The Assam Lopas are further down the valley. From Trön, descend 400 m and cross a bridge over the Chayul Chu, then ascend to Trön Trip and continue across a steep valley and up a high spur (4.5 km from Trön Trip). Carry on for 5 km to Drotang, 300 m above the river.

The Assam Lopas   Before 1950, Lopas came to this trading center of Trön by three different passes; the Lha La (the route arrives near the bridge 9 km below Kap), the Kashung La (11 km below Trön), and the Chapung La (near Lung, just below the Chayul–Char confluence). Snow usually closes the Kashung La by mid-September, though the Chapung La is passable until November. After that, a roundabout route exists by going up the river.

Tibetans used different names for Lopas who arrived from different passes. Those that came via the Lha La were called Lagongwa; those using the Kashung La were known as Lawa. Below the combined waters of the Char and Chayul is a tribe known to the Tibetans as the Tingwa Lopas. They live within the Ngeshi River valley and trade at Migyitun rather than Trön. In November, however, they come to Lung with rice to trade. A major occupation of Trön's villagers is to help pilgrims on their long walk around Tsari. It takes ten days along the combined rivers of the Char and Chayul to reach the Tsari junction. The route does not actually go to the junction but crosses a spur that runs down to it. Halfway to the junction is a point where the Yumé River joins up with the combined river. Most pilgrims go up the Yumé and finish the pilgrimage via the Rip La but some, those who live in Sanga Chöling and the nearby villages, go up the Char Chu to Sanga Chöling.

✧ Day 6   Drotang–Lung (2900 m)   13 km

Cross a river east of Drotang and walk 1.5 km through a pine wood to Natrampa.

➠

This region marks a transitional zone where the vegetation becomes richer. The trail stays on the right bank; pass three sizeable tributaries before reaching the Char–Chayul river junction. Two bridges cross the river below the junction, the first a few hundred meters away and the second near Lung, 2.5 km downstream (east) from the junction.

◊ **Day 7   Lung–Charme (3230 m)   15 km**
Cross the river to its left (north) bank over the second bridge near Lung. Head back upstream, then follow the left (east) bank of the Char north to Raprang (3150 m), a ruined village. Lopas burned it at the turn of the century and it never fully recovered.

   The trail turns abruptly from north to west; cross the Char Chu 3 km from Raprang, then follow the right (south) for 5.5 km back to Charme.

◊ **Day 8   Charme–Sanga Chöling**
Retrace the route from Charme to Sanga Chöling (see page 219).

✚ **DAY 4   SANGA CHÖLING–BASE OF CHA LA (12 KM)   4 HR**
Go through Sanga Chöling (Sangling) Village, then turn immediately left (north) up the barren Kyu Chu Gorge. (The main Char Valley continues southeast to Charme and the military base of Lung, which stands at the disputed frontier with India. Lung is 3 hr from Sanga Chöling and only accessible with a special pass.) The road keeps to the right (west) bank for the first hour, then crosses by bridge to the left bank. In 1 1/4 hr, it crosses back to the right at the nomad settlement of Kyu. The route up the gorge follows a glacial valley (the entire dividing range between the Char and Tsari rivers is glaciated). Reach a wide, alpine valley farther up. Camp at a spot before the valley divides (12 km from Sanga Chöling). The left valley goes north and the road follows it to the Cha La; the right (northeast) valley leads to the Takar La and the lesser Tsari pilgrimage at Yutö (see page 234). Take the former.

✚ **DAY 5   BASE OF CHA LA–CHÖSAM (20 KM)   5 HR**
Ascend to the broad saddle of the Cha La (5060 m). Although often shrouded in mist, it is usually clear of snow. The Takar La, a few km to the east, is frequently snowed in and impassable. The main Takpa Shelri Range rises to the east. Descend gradually to a wide, marshy plain at Chörten Namu, the junction of three rivers. The Tsari Chu, slow and gentle, is on the north side of the road. (The north–northwest valley leads to the Kongpo La [8 km away] then to Guru Namgye Dzong and Tromda near the Tsangpo [see page 226]. A side valley and trail leads north up the Tangma La; and then to the Tsangpo at Nang Xian [see page 226]. A third valley going due west, leads to the Trorang La.)

   From Chörten Namu, follow the Tsari Valley down east to Chösam, an easy 2-hr walk along a dirt road. Travel along the right (south) bank, then cross over to the left bank and hug the valley's northern slopes. Chösam, a collection of stone houses with shingled roofs, lies below on the valley floor. From Chösam, a trail leads north over the Sur La to Nang Xian on the Tsangpo (see page 229). Another trail goes south over the Rip La to Yumé and Sanga Chöling.

For a continuation of the Tsari Valley itinerary from Chösam, see the Nang Xian–Migyitun section, page 227.

The Tsari Valley

Sacred Tsari is one of Tibet's most beautiful, pristine valleys. The snowy peaks of the Takpa Shelri Range are immediately to the south and seem near enough to touch. And the Tsari Chu, northern branch of the Subansiri, flows majestically through the Eastern Himalayas. Although farther north than Chayul, and separated from it by a high range, Tsari is a much wetter valley by far. The transition from the arid Sanga Chöling Valley to the lush forest of Tsari, within a short 20 km, is a remarkable characteristic of this region of southeast Tibet. Near Chösam, the sheltered, north-facing slopes are densely covered with rhododendron and juniper. Farther downstream, thick virginal groves of tall silver fir, covered with dense veils of pale yellow Spanish moss, line both sides of the magnificent Senguti Plain. The whole effect is mesmerizing.

The Senguti, a wet, marshy expanse (1 km wide, 10 km long) is a virtual sea of *Primula sikkimensis* (yellow bells, long narrow leaves) and purple *Primula alpicola*. Between the primulas and the silver firs is a border of rhododendron, honeysuckle, barberry, cherry, and spiraea. A zone of dwarf alpine flowers exists between the fir forests and the snow fields of the Takpa Shelri. Near Chickchar are the famed sky blue poppy (*Meconopsis betonicifolia*), and yellow *Meconopsis paniculata*.

The Tsari Valley narrows below Chickchar. In small valleys to the south, glaciers hang down from the Takpa Shelri Range nearly to the valley floor; primula, rhododendron, and meconopsis cover the slopes. Further down is a cool, forest zone. Broad-leafed trees next to the swift Tsari Chu include maple, oak, birch, and ilex, interspersed with rhododendron, rosa, and dentzia. Above the valley are large stands of silver fir, hemlock, juniper, and, occasionally, larch.

The Tsari region has plenty of fresh milk and *tsampa*, but because of the valley's sacred status, little cultivation takes place. Fields begin at Migyitun, barley, potatoes, and tobacco being the main crops. The villages of Chösam, Chickchar, Yumé, and Yutö generally forbade farming. Meat, of course, is taboo. Many yaks and horses graze in the valley, especially along its upper reaches. April and May are the birthing months—a good time to see new-born yaks.

Wildlife in Tsari includes the Tibetan stag (*Cervus affinis*), the Sikkim stag, wild sheep (*Ovis nahura*), musk deer, wolves and foxes, and the beautiful Harmon's pheasant (*Crossoptilon harmonii*), a gray, 3-kg bird with red legs and eyes, and a short, dark tail. Down the valley to the east are high, rocky peaks. Beyond them is Kang Pema, a prominent peak of the main Himalayas, about 30 km away.

NH46-15B

NH46-15A Chickchar

NH46-11C

NH46-14B

THE EXTERNAL BOUNDARIES OF INDIA AS DEPICTED ON THE MAPS ARE NEITHER CORRECT NOR AUTHENTIC.

to Molo
to Tsari Sarpa
Gyara Phu Valley
Ne Valley
Tse La 4570
Lang La 4815
Taktsa
Palung
Khama
Kam
Ka Valley
Kyimdong Valley
Kyimdong Dzong
Le 3170
Shu
to Tsangpo
6036
Tsagachi 5050
Flat Plain
Birmba
Pa La 4840
Rimbu
Yu La 4725
Langgang La
Na La La 4660
Lake Tsogar
Kang Pema
HIMALAYA RANGE
Langang
Ola
Migyitun
Subansiri Valley
INDIA
Pozo Sumdo
TIBET
INDIA
Drisam Valley
Kazume
Lapu
Drolma La 4900
Yarap
Chickchar G 3680
Aranjer
Dromzi
Khalip
SENGUTI PLAIN
Tsari Valley
Sur La 4785
Mipa
Mt Takpa 4660
Mt Shein
Shagam La 4900
Taktsang
Tapgyu La 4690
Go La
Potrang
Lador
Beru
Lapu Valley
to Nang Xian and Tsangpo
Zhang
Tso Bunang (3 lakes)
Rip La
4200
Chosam
Gompa Rong
Simoneri
Karkyu La 4570
Tomtsang
Shagyu La 4725
Chakta Trang
Yume
Yuto
Takar La 5090
Kyu Valley
Chorten Namu
Cha La 5060
Tangma La
Kongmo La 5330
Bumda Sebum
Trupbaka
Shibu Valley
Senga Choling
Gomba Leto
Shuteng
Shokar
Kyu Tragor
Tsin

N

10 km
8
6
4
2
0
6 miles
4
2
0

(B) Nang Xian–Chösam–Migyitun

Access : Tsethang to Nang Xian 215 km

From Tsethang (see page 518), the road to Nang Xian follows the Tsangpo's south bank generally to the east, except for one stretch where it leaves the river and heads southeast to Chusum, the main town of a former kingdom known as Lhagyari. It then crosses the Potrang La (5030 m) before returning north to the Tsangpo. Nang Xian is a county seat on the river's south bank. Nearby are Yarlung-era (7th–9th C.) tombs (see page 373).

Hitchhiking out of Tsethang

At the principal intersection (monkey statue), walk east along the main paved road away from Lhasa. Outside Tsethang proper (1.5 km) it turns into a dirt road; start hitching. At Rong (Rongchaka, 27 km east of Tsethang) the road leaves the Tsangpo and heads south. (Zangri is across the river.) The Chagar and Jowo Lhakhang chapels are in a village at this turn. Langkor Dzong stands on top of a hill. The Tsangpo in these parts cuts through a range of hills and descends in a series of rapids through a narrow gorge to Trap.

Below is a description of the road from Rong to Nang Xian; the road markers start at Tsethang.

(Km)	Place	Notes
0	Tsethang	
27	Rong	*Dzong* on hill, road heads south
40	Village	Inside narrow gorge
53		Valley widens
56		Turnoff to Chusum (Qusum Xian, 3 km to the left)
58	Village	Chusum Monastery
61	Shajang (Changra Valley)	Junction at plain; a road goes right (leaving the valley) to Chumdo Kyang (36 km), then to Sanga Chöling via Shobo Qu (see page 211). At Shajang (Shachang), the road enters a 2 km-wide valley; its river has cut a 70 m-deep gorge. This is Lhagyari, a former kingdom associated with Tibet's central government. The palace is at the edge of the gorge.
		There are no more road markers after Chusum.
	Potrang La (5030 m)	Beyond Chusum, the road leaves the main valley. At the pass, a 5915-m peak stands due east, 10 km south of the Tsangpo near Nang Xian. From the pass to Gyatsa Xian is approximately 25 km.
	Gyatsa Xian	Descend a long valley to Zam on the Tsangpo; Gyatsa

Xian is a few km farther. Here lies Dakpo Tratsang Monastery (see page 641). A nunnery at Rapdang is 30 km after Gyatsa Xian.

Tromda

Tromda lies 46 km east of Gyatsa Xian (peach and apple orchards and a hydroelectric station). Daglha Gampo Monastery (see page 352) is across the river (take a ferry) on an unusual-looking mountain. From Tromda, a side valley goes south over the Kongpo La to Chösam in Tsari. The monasteries of Ganden Rabden and Guru Namgye are in this side valley (see below).

20 km after Tromda is Bangrim Chöde Monastery (see page 354) across the Tsangpo. To reach it, go 8 km east to Lu; coracles cross from here to the left bank. Bangrim Chöde is 7 km to the west. 13 km farther to the west is Trungkang, birthplace of the 13th Dalai Lama (monastery here). At Lhenga, 4 km to the west, cross back to the Tsangpo's south bank. Tromda is 5 km away.

Nang Xian

28 km east of Tromda.

From Tromda: an alternative route to Chösam   Ganden Rabden is a picturesque monastery about 7 km south of Tromda in the Trulung Valley. Guru Namgye Dzong is 5 km farther south. The *dzong* (ruined fort) was built spectacularly on a ridge above the valley and administered the entire Tsari district. A new *dzong* sits along the river. Continue up the Trulung Valley for 14 km to a valley junction. (A trail in the right [west] valley goes along the Trulung Chu to the Kamba La [5210 m] and then descends to the Char Valley. From here, Sanga Chöling is to the east.) Take the left (east) valley to charming Bumda Sebum Monastery (5 km from Dem).

(To continue this route along the Karpo Valley to Chösam, see above, page 218.)

Nang Xian (trail head)

28 km from Tromda. At Nang Xian, the Tsangpo turns abruptly north through a deep gorge that forms a horseshoe-shaped watercourse before ending east of Nang Xian at Nye. Rapids in the gorge make it unnavigable. The main road follows the horseshoe along the river; an east–west footpath takes a short cut over the Kongpo Nga La (4440 m) through thick birch and larch forests to Nye.

A barrier checkpost for lumber bars the road just before Nye. A guest house is on the right beyond the barrier and a tea house with noodle dishes is on the left. The rest of the town is farther up the hill. From the guest house look down at the Lapu Chu Valley that leads south to the Sur and Tangma passes and then on to Chösam in Tsari. A jeep track follows the Lapu Chu from a point on the highway just west of (before) the barrier. Begin the trip up the Lapu Valley before the village awakes at 0630 and hire pack animals for the four-day walk to Tsari in a village farther up the valley.

Nang Xian to Migyitun in East Tsari via the Tangma La and Chösam

Time Chart

Day	Place	Hours
1	Nang Xian–Camp	5 1/2
2	Zhang	4 1/4
3	Stone Shelter	3 1/2
4	Camp	5 1/2
5	Khalip	5 3/4
6	Chickchar	4 1/4
7	Pozo Sumdo	2 1/2
8	Migyitun	2 3/4

Trail Notes

✤ DAY 1 NANG XIAN–CAMP 5 1/2 HR

Go through the wooden barrier and enter a gorge-like valley. Walk along a flat jeep road with the Lapu Chu on the left through beautiful countryside. After 1 hr reach a narrow constriction in the gorge; cross a bridge here and continue along the right bank. Reach a compound (1/4 hr), then a village with a small monastery. Come to another bridge in 1 hr. Cross to the left bank, ascend a spur then descend to a bridge (1/2 hr). Go up a rise and follow the river's right bank to Lador, a village on a hill, 18 km from Nang Xian. Beyond, the broken track traverses a region of confused, uncontrolled logging to a bridge; cross to the left bank (1 hr). The valley narrows and habitation ends. Camp at a grassy spot next to the river, 1/2 hr from the bridge.

✤ DAY 2 CAMP–ZHANG 4 1/4 HR

Walk along the jeep track in the narrow valley for 3/4 hr to reach a hollow tree-trunk that irrigates fields, on the left. Beru, a pretty, stone village inhabited by loggers, lies 2 hr from camp at the junction of two valleys (a nearby bluff has monastery ruins). Take the left valley and keep the river on the left. Come to another valley junction in 1/2 hr; a broken bridge crosses the Tambu Chu here at a lovely, grassy area. Ascend a narrow gorge on the right in a series of zigzags (ignore the left and wider valley). After 1/2 hr, reach a grassy glen. The trail initially follows the river's right bank but soon crosses to the left bank over a wooden bridge. Wade back to the right bank at a point where the valley narrows, 1/4 hr from the glen. The jeep track hugs the valley's right side, then crosses a bridge with prayer flags (3/4 hr). A small shrine stands by the roadside. Bear to the left of the widening valley and cross two bridges in 1/4 hr to reach Zhang (Tsang) at a valley junction. A large house marks the village entrance. (The road keeps to the valley's right side and soon ends.) Empty rooms in a storage shed are available for the night and the hospitable villagers will bring firewood for cooking.

Valleys lead left (southeast) and right (southwest) from Zhang. The left one goes to the superb alpine lakes of Tso Bunang, then over the Sur La to Chösam. The right (described) goes over the Tangma La to Chörten Namu at the junction of three valleys. Chörten Namu is 15 km west of Chösam in the Tsari Valley.

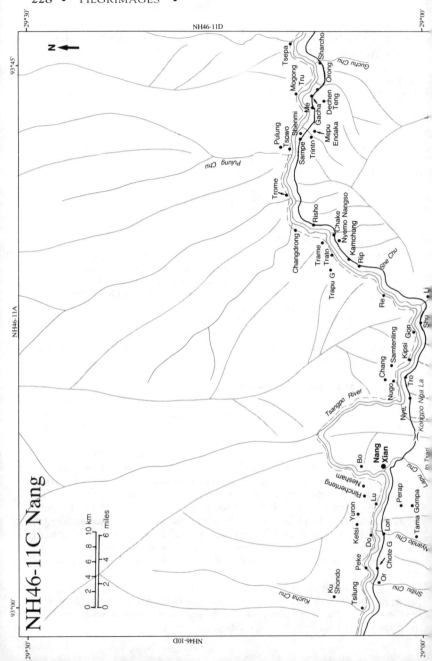

NH46-11C Nang

Alternative route: From Zhang to Chösam via the Sur La
The left valley leads southeast to Tso Bunang (4115 m), a chain of four beautiful, crystal-clear lakes set amidst fir forests. From Zhang, follow the hillsides, then cross to the valley's right and enter fir forests and willow bushes. Five km from Zhang, the first and smallest lake appears. The other three are farther up the valley, each nearly 1 km long. During spring and summer the profusely-flowered glades are perfect places to spend idyllic days of rest. Without doubt this is one of the most scenic spots in south Tibet. After the third lake, the trail crosses a river between the third and fourth lakes, then climbs 200 m through fir, rhododendron, and willow. Pass a yak herders' encampment and continue to ascend fairly steeply for 3 km to the Sur La Pass (4850 m) (2 hr from Tso Bunang, 7 hr from Zhang). Chösam is visible from the pass, less than an hour away but far below.

The Sur La is sometimes closed by snow during the marginal months of April, May, October, and November. However, the Tangma La usually stays open during these times; the Sur La route is more scenic.

✤ DAY 3 ZHANG–STONE SHELTER 3 1/2 HR
The trail to the Tangma La starts from Zhang and goes up the right (south) valley by staying close to its right slopes. Climb up above the village through rhododendron and juniper forests, then follow a level footpath above the river (1/4 hr). After 3/4 hr, descend to the river and cross a small bridge where the valley narrows. Follow the left bank and ascend gradually. After 1/2 hr, a steep side valley can be seen across the river. Ignore. Reach a hut shelter in a further 1/2 hr, then a circular, roofless stone enclosure. This is where the valley splits (1/2 hr). Continue along the main river's left bank. The spur that divides the valleys has stone cairns as a landmark and its slope (100 m away) is covered with rhododendron. Walk over a rock fall to a stone enclosure (1 hr) where the head of the valley appears as an amphitheater enclosed by mountains. The pass is hidden and the area is a confused jumble of rocks with no discernible path up.

✤ DAY 4 STONE SHELTER–CAMP 5 1/2 HR
To find the difficult Tangma La trail, bear to the extreme right of the ring of mountains. The way is often indistinct and the last hour is very steep and involves scrambling on all fours at times. From camp, walk up the valley for 1/4 hr, cross the river (now a stream), and go up to a small plateau to reach a circular stone enclosure on the right bank (1/4 hr). From the enclosure, ascend the right edge of a boulder field and stream bed straight up the valley towards the mountains. After 1/2 hr, cross a jumble of boulders and moraines at the center of the valley, then continue along the valley's left side. Keep on the lookout for stone cairns; follow them to the extreme right of the cul-de-sac. Reach more cairns in 1 hr, and prayer flags on the Tangma La Pass, a hard 2 1/4 hr away, can be seen. The final 3/4 hr is very steep. The descent is short, steep, and straight, only 1 hr on a rocky trail to a bluff near the bottom of a narrow valley. This valley merges with a larger east–west trending valley and the well-defined trail then follows its right slopes. Camp in a rock shelter (no roof) surrounded by stone cairns that mark the southern approach to the Tangma La.

✤ Day 5 Camp–Khalip 5 3/4 hr

The valley opens up into the wide Chörten Namu junction of three valleys (see above, page 222). A small crumbled building marks the middle of the junction. The Tsari Valley, running east–west, lies directly ahead and a jeep road within it clings to the north slopes of the Takpa Shelri Range.

Chörten Namu is a boggy area with slow-moving streams; ford these to get to the road (1 hr). Follow the flat dirt road above the valley floor to the left (east). Cross a bridge after 3/4 hr to follow the Tsari Chu along its left (north) bank. Chösam, a village of stone houses below the road, lies 2 hr from the bridge. It is one of the main halts on the Takpa Shelri pilgrimage (see below). After Chösam, the road zigzags down to the valley floor, to an area known as the Senguti Plain. The Tsari here divides into many branches, and horses and yaks (usually from Sanga Chöling) graze peacefully in this most pastoral of settings. There is considerably more vegetation on the river's south bank and the prominent snow peak downstream is the Kang Pema, which towers over sacred Lake Tsogar (see below).

Continue to Khalip, an infrequently used road maintenance station of 10–12 basic rooms in a long, dilapidated wood building (2 hr from Chösam). Wood-burning stoves for cooking and warmth are in most rooms. The caretaker lives in a house within a stone enclosure and supplies delicious, fresh cheese. This place serves as a good base for exploring the numerous beautiful side valleys that branch southward from the Tsari Valley towards the base of Takpa Shelri.

✤ Day 6 Khalip–Chickchar 4 1/4 hr

Follow the jeep road to Dromzi (1/2 hr from Khalip), a small village with a yellow-roofed monastery on the right. Aranjer, a tiny settlement of crude wooden huts, is 1 1/4 hr farther on the left. The valley now narrows. Thick curtains of Spanish moss woven among silver firs along the southern slopes are a characteristic of Tsari from Khalip on down. Pass three makeshift huts next to a stone enclosure for yaks. Yarap (Yaru, 3 1/4 hr from Khalip) has several stone houses next to the road. Across the river are more huts; a bridge here spans the Tsari Chu.

Further along is Kazume. It has ten houses clinging to the slopes, left (north) of the road (1/2 hr). On the right (south) is a small rise with a shrine and prayer flags. At this point, a trail goes down from the road to the river, crosses a bridge, then zigzags up the mountainside through rhododendron and evergreen forests. Chickchar is at the top, 1/2 hr away, at the beginning of an alpine valley enclosed by stunning snow mountains of the Takpa Shelri Range. This is perhaps the most unforgettable locale in southeast Tibet.

Chickchar is but four stone huts that are usually unoccupied except during the peak pilgrim season (July–September). Wood, water, and campsites are plentiful in this exceptionally pristine area. It was forbidden to ride horses beyond Chickchar; even Dalai Lamas, on pilgrimage to Takpa Shelri, had to dismount at a special stone. The ruined monasteries of Chickchar lie deep within the valley, and the one-week Kyilkhor Pilgrimage around Takpa Shelri's sacred peaks starts from here (see below, page 232). Chickchar has two distinct parts, an inner and an outer valley, separated by low hills, marked by a shrine and prayer flags. It is not possible to see the inner valley from the village. A raised footpath circles the rim of the outer valley to the right to avoid fields of hummocky rhododendron bushes. The main chapel of Chickchar, the Phagmo Lhakhang, is on the valley floor and other chapels are farther up the slopes. Its central images were Dorje Phagmo, the Panchen Lama, and the Drukpa Rinpoche (see Sanga Chöling, page 218). The site is normally deserted until the pilgrimage season.

A trail from Chickchar heads right (west) over a low ridge to a clearing with a hut (milk, turnips available). Further on is the Tsari Chu and the bridge to Yarap. This pleasant side trip can be done in 3/4 hr.

The Great Pilgrimage (Rongkhor) takes place every 12 years in the Year of the Monkey (next in 2004). In former times up to 100,000 people from Kongpo, Pomé, Takpo, and even Lhasa, came for the event (see below).

The Lesser Pilgrimage (Kyilkhor) takes about a week and occurs annually.

For a continuation of this route, Day 7 Chickchar–Pozo Sumdo, see page 235.

The Takpa Shelri Pilgrimages in Tsari

The uncommon sanctity of Tsari Rongkhor, the Great Pilgrimage, attracts crowds of ardent pilgrims who brave dense tropical forests, extreme humidity, and hazardous terrain to reach their distination. No so long ago they used to face the hostile Lopa tribes scattered throughout the forest who attacked with bows and arrows. The Tibetan government had to pay a ransom to the Lopas (cloth, tsampa, and swords) to make them refrain from such attacks during the pilgrimage season. It also sent guides to lead the pilgrims on the treacherous journey. The first 50 people behind the guides were considered lucky and safe; pilgrims threw dice to determine the order in which they would walk. Pomé District alone sent 100 soldiers to guard them.

The pilgrimage proper begins in upper Tsari with its many beautiful and religiously powerful places. Tradition states that a pilgrim who successfully completes the itinerary will be able to travel to any of Tibet's wild, sacred places. The best months to perform the Tsari pilgrimages are July, August, and September; the passes are open but some rain can be expected. May, June, and October are also excellent, though snow might close the passes temporarily. Two main pilgrimages, the Rongkhor and Kyilkhor, circle Mt Takpa Shelri (5735 m).

RONGKHOR—THE GREAT PILGRIMAGE

The pilgrimage season starts every year on the 19th day of the third lunar month and lasts until the 15th of the eighth month. Women are not allowed to complete the circuit and are specifically forbidden to cross the Drölma La (see below, page 232). Formerly, they were sent to Yarap after the close of the pilgrimage season.

From Chösam, the Rongkhor follows the Tsari Chu east to Chickchar, then southeast past Migyitun to where it joins the combined waters of the Char, Nye, and Chayul. For the next seven days or so, the route traverses disputed territory inhabited by the Assamese Lopas, an isolated tribe, which makes its home within mountainous Pachakshiri. It then follows the Chayul Chu west towards Sanga Chöling. At the Chayul Chu–Yumé Chu junction, the pilgrimage turns up the Yumé Chu to Yumé. After crossing the Rip La, Chösam is regained some two weeks later (add another week if you want to go on to Sanga Chöling and other sacred sites). Along the route are shelters (*tsukhangs*) with men who cater to the needs of pilgrims by supplying firewood and hot water, but not food. Pilgrims must carry their own food or pay heavily at places like Chickchar and Migyitun. No Westerners have ever made this journey.

KYILKHOR—THE LESSER PILGRIMAGE

This annual pilgrimage lies entirely within the district of Tsari, once under the jurisdiction of Guru Namgye Dzong near Tromda. The route circumambulates Takpa Shelri (5735 m) by first heading east along the Tsari Valley from Chösam to Chickchar. It then turns south and crosses seven passes between 4550 and 5100 m before returning to Chösam. Before 1950, nearly 2,000 pilgrims left Chickchar annually on the 19th day of the third lunar month to perform the 'snow pilgrimage', a ritual that preceded the full pilgrimage season. Keepers provisioned the pilgrim huts, then returned to their villages until the 15th of the fifth lunar month, the season's official start. They then catered to the needs of the pilgrims until the season finished on the 15th day of the eight lunar month. Before leaving the huts, they collected large quantities of firewood for the next year's 'snow pilgrimage'.

Traditionally, the route is closed after the 15th of the eighth month because of maggots. It is virtually impossible not to step on them after this time. In order not to violate the spirit of the pilgrimage, Tibetans refrain from performing the *khora*.

Women cannot complete the Kyilkhor because they are forbidden to cross the Drölma La. Kinthup, an Indian pandit who went to Tsari at the turn of the century, reported:

> The reason assigned is that formerly a Goddess, named Drölma, who wished to judge the behaviour of men and women, laid herself across the path at the summit of the pass. A man came by and found the road blocked by the Goddess, who was disguised. So he asked her with kind words to get out of the way. In reply, the Goddess said, 'My brother, I am so weak that I cannot stir; if you pity me, please find another road. If not, cross over me.' On hearing this, the man took a different road. After a short time, a woman passed that way and she also saw the Goddess and told her to give way; the same reply was made by the Goddess, but the woman crossed over her and went on. Therefore, from that day, women have been forbidden to pass over, and the pass has been known as the Drölma La.

The route

The pilgrimage goes south from Chickchar, across the Drölma, Shagam, Tama, and

Go passes to a pilgrim rest house (*tsukhang*) called Potrang. From here, the trail turns sharply to the north over the Tapgyü, Shangü, and Karkyü passes to reach Yutö at the east foot of the Takar La. Finally, it makes an abrupt turn southwest to cross the Takar La and reach Sanga Chöling.

Lopa territories

A river rises from the Drölma La to join the Tsari Chu below Migyitun, as does one from the Shagam La. Below the Tapgyü La, the Taktsang and Tomtsang rivers join the Yumé River; their combined waters then flow south to Lopa territory to eventually join the Subansiri. It takes one week to walk along any of these headwaters of the Subansiri to reach the first Lopa villages. The trails are poor and perhaps impassable until September because of the swollen rivers.

TRAIL NOTES

✧ **Day 1   Chickchar–Mipa (4660 m)   18 km**

From Chickchar Monastery, walk south up the Chickchar Valley to Lapü, the first hut, 1 km from the trail. A lake (4510 m) is nearby. Continue for 5 km to the Drölma La Pass (4910 m). Women are forbidden to cross it but are allowed a short pilgrimage circuit around a spur below the pass. The Drölma La is a jumble of sharp rock and fossil shells cast about as offerings. Some 5 km blow the pass is Mipa, a single house on a marshy plain with waterfalls on all sides. The Shagam La is visible from here. A large river from the west eventually flows into Lopa territory. Dwarf rhododendron and primulas are abundant from Mipa to Yumé near the circuit's western end.

✧ **Day 2   Mipa–Potrang (4480 m)   23 km**

This long, 10-hour day begins with the ascent of a steep, occasionally snow-bound path for 2 3/4 hr to the Shagam La (4910 m). Be careful of crevasses in this glacial region. Rivers flowing down the Drölma and Shagam passes join below Mipa to enter a wooded valley. The difficult descent of 3 km passes through snow patches along an ancient glacier, then the trail crosses the tree line and climbs steeply up the valley's right side for 1 1/2 hr to the Tama La (4390 m). The pass (10.5 km from Mipa) has a hut just across its far side. Beyond, the trail follows hilly terrain past many glacial lakes, including Kandro Thang Tso (2.5 km from the hut) where, legend claims, *dakinis* kept mythical cattle (*tsolang*). Continue to the Go La, 7 km beyond Kandro Thang Tso, and descend to the Potrang *tsukhang* (1/2 hr). (A longer, alternative route crosses the range farther to the west over the Keyu La. A short cut from the Tama La heads west to avoid Potrang altogether by going to Taktsang.) Pilgrims here sometimes circumambulate holy Dorje Phagmo Latso, where two houses at the lake provide shelter.

✧ **Day 3   Potrang–Tomtsang (3840 m)   25 km**

The trail from Potrang turns sharply northward on a level path to the lake (4 km), then carries on for 2.5 km to a cliff that must be crossed. Reach the Tapgyü La (4700 m) after 8 km; it is not at the head of the valley, so descend for 1 km to a secondary pass at the valley's top. After this, reach a marshy flat area with a hut (provisioned for important lamas). The short cut from the Tama La arrives here. Continue down the valley's right side into fir forests. Reach Taktsang (4025 m), the next hut, after 4 1/2 hr (13.5 km from Potrang). From here climb steeply to the triple Shangü La (4725 m). A steep 1000-m descent leads to Tomtsang *tsukhang*. The large river here is difficult to ford; a bridge and hut are in the forest. Tomtsang is the limit for women conducting the pilgrimage from this side. Along the trail are many votive cairns, tiny-roofed enclosures built like a house of cards. Stones for the *tsukhangs* are often carved with *mantras*. A direct trail returns to Chickchar from the Shangü La. From Chakta Trang (beyond Tomtsang), a trail heads straight for Totsen, between Chösam and Chickchar on the main road, via the Dorje Drak La. Women are permitted to complete this short pilgrimage.

✧ Day 4   Tomtsang–Yutö (4025 m)   24 km

From Tomtsang, walk 2.5 km down the wooded valley, then turn up a side valley on the right. After another 2.5 km cross the river and climb steeply to Chakta Trang *tsukhang*, a single house, (at 4300 m). The Karkyü La (4570 m) is 1.5 km farther, and beyond appears a large, open valley. Descend steeply to the marshy Lingmotang Plain (3 km by 1 km). The trail runs above the marsh for 4 km to Simuneri *tsukhang*, next to a small lake. Continue down a steep valley for 2.5 km to Yumé (3500 m), a village of 15 houses with a monastery dedicated to Dorje Phagmo. From here a valley to the right (north) leads to Gompa Rong, two houses in a forest (3 km from Yume), and Yutö, a tiny village among dense forests (4 km from Gompa Rong). A trail from here goes directly north to Chösam on the main road, crossing the Rip La along the way. Plan on two days to complete this journey, though it can be done in one long day. Find shelter at the Rip La *tsukhang*, just after the pass. This route is the classic way to complete the Kyilkhor. An alternative route goes to Sanga Chöling, the region's most important monastery.

✧ Day 5   Yutö–Sanga Chöling (3320 m)   29 km

From Yutö, the trail to Sanga Chöling follows the river for 13 km to the Takar La Pass (5090 m), then crosses to Zimsathi, an alpine meadow 5 km beyond the pass. A branch trail on the right (north) leads over the Cha La to Chösam or to the Kongpo La (to Guru Namgye Dzong and Tromda on the Tsangpo). Take the left (southwest) branch along the valley's right side. Cross to the left side 9.5 km from Takar La, just above the first village of Kyu (here cultivation appears). Sanga Chöling lies at the Takar La Chu–Char Chu junction, 6.5 km from Kyu.

A short pilgrimage   A short pilgrimage route goes from Tomtsang to Chakta Trang and follows the standard route to Yutö and Chösam, then back to Tomtsang to complete the circuit.

✤ DAY 7 CHICKCHAR–POZO SUMDO 2 1/2 HR

From Chickchar, return to Kazume (1/4 hr) and then continue east on the dirt road down the main Tsari Valley, here a sheer, narrow gorge. Side valleys join the main valley from both banks, bringing with them large amounts of water. Reach Simigong (1/4 hr from Kazume), a clearing with three logging huts. Walk past three more in another clearing (1/2 hr), then another (1/2 hr). The Tsari Valley now narrows and descends more sharply, and the deteriorating road runs about 40 m above the river. Zigzag down to Pozo Sumdo by the riverside (1 hr), three deserted huts in a clearing noted for its abundance of yellow flowers. Snow peaks rise steeply across the Tsari Chu. To the north is the Bimbi La Valley, and within it a trail leads to Kyimdong Dzong near the Tsangpo River (see page 238). Just beyond Pozo Sumdo a bridge spans the river at an enchanting, lonely spot.

✤ DAY 8 POZO SUMDO–MIGYITUN 2 3/4 HR

Today's walk from Pozo Sumdo passes through the trek's finest stretch for flowers. Both sides of the road are dense with flowers, especially an astonishing variety of rhododendrons. Glaciers from the Takpa Shelri Range come down very close to the road and next to them are groves of silver fir, hemlock, and juniper.The road drops considerably from Pozo Sumdo to Migyitun, the frontier town with an army camp. On the left are slopes lined with bamboo forests and the Tsari Chu is a raging torrent in these parts. The road from Pozo Sumdo follows the Tsari Chu's left bank for 1/2 hr, then crosses a bridge to the right. It zigzags down to the river (3/4 hr) and recrosses it by a second bridge (1/4 hr). Follow the Tsari Valley along its left bank to Migyitun, 1 1/4 hr from the bridge.

Migyitun (Tsari Qu) sits in a clearing at the end of the gorge near the disputed McMahon Line that divides Tibet from India's North East Frontier Agency (NEFA). Half its population is Lopa or part Lopa. A hydro-electric power station is just before the village; and the Oto Chu Valley comes in from the northeast. Avoid this sensitive frontier post if possible. Below Migyitun, the trail follows the Tsari's left bank for 2.5 km to a few houses, then drops rapidly past dense forests on the right and high scrub on the left. Formerly, Lopas came to this area to trade sugar cane, rice, skins, and red dye for woolens, cloth, salt, iron and swords. Many cane bridges, typical of the region, cross the river on the way down, the first one half a day downstream.

Lake Tsogar (2 days from Migyitun)

When pilgrims come to the sacred mountain of Tsari they also make a point to visit this serendipitous holy lake near Migyitun.

To go: Just beyond Migyitun is a glacial river; cross it and walk up its side valley through a maple forest, then forests of silver fir and rhododendron. Ascend steep, grassy slopes to the Na La (Forest Pass), a place with masses of forget-me-nots, then descend to a valley with a deserted hut. At the valley's head is a boggy green slope carpeted with flowers. (Look for a rare primula with tiny, exquisite violet flowers that grows moss-like on rocks.) The steep path skirts the cliffs of a spur, then goes over the Pang La (Turf Pass, 1500 m above Migyitun) before traversing down the spur's far side to a wide, funnel-shaped valley. This is a good place to camp.

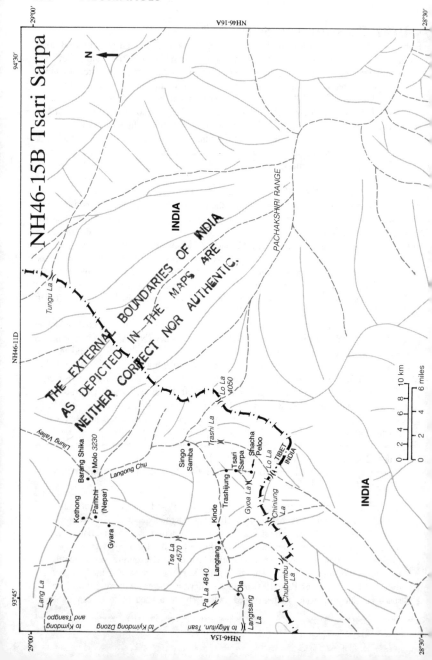

NH46-15B Tsari Sarpa

THE EXTERNAL BOUNDARIES OF INDIA AS DEPICTED IN THE MAPS ARE NEITHER CORRECT NOR AUTHENTIC.

INDIA

PACHAKSHRI RANGE

TIBET

INDIA

INDIA

Tungu La

Lilung Valley

Barang Shika
Molo 3230
Pamchi (Nepar)

Kethong
Gyara

Lang La

to Kyimdong and Tsangpo

Langong Chu

Singo Samba

Trashi La

Tsari Sarpa
Shacha Peloo

Lo La 4050

Lo La

Gyoa La

Chinung La

Chubumbu La

Tse La 4570

Kinde
Trashjung

Langtang

Pa La 4840

Ola

Langtsang La

to Migyitun, Tsari

to Kyimdong Dzong, to Migyitun, Tsari

N

0 2 4 6 8 10 km
0 2 4 6 miles

29°00' 94°30'

NH46-16A

28°30'

NH46-11D

NH46-15A

93°45'

29°00'

28°30'

Ascend again by crossing a difficult moraine on the valley floor, then skirt the foot of a glacier. A herder's hut stands at the start of the final approach to the Ja La (4660 m), the third and most ardous pass. It crosses a major mountain range and offers superb views of the main Himalayan range and the Takpa Shelri to the southwest. The steep descent leads to the alpine zone carpeted with primulas, meconopsis and rhododendrons. (Below the purple-flowered rhododendron bushes are the magnificent *Primula tsariensis*—large green leaves, thick stems, and violet flowers with yellow eyes.) The path descends along a rock ledge; beautiful Lake Tsogar, ringed with glaciers, is straight down. The highest peak above the lake is Kang Pema. A pilgrimage trail goes around the lake and takes one morning to walk; a stone house gives shelter.

OPTIONS FROM MIGYITUN

✛ OPTION 1: BIMBI LA; KYIMDONG DZONG NEAR THE TSANGPO, THE SIYOM HEADWATERS, AND THE TSARI SARPA PILGRIMAGE

Migyitun–Pozo Sumdo–Bimbi La–Kyimdong Dzong–Molo–Singo Samba–Langtang–Kam–Kyimdong Dzong

This option allows two itineraries: the first, the shorter, goes from Tsari to the south bank of the Tsangpo (on Day 4) via the Bimbi La and Kyimdong Dzong. The Tibet–Sichuan highway is regained 49 km east of Nang Xian. From here, hitch back to Tsethang and Lhasa.

The second itinerary involves ten additional days of excellent walking from Kyimdong Dzong to the seldom-visited headwaters of the Siyom River. En route are the interesting villages of Molo and Langtang on the north slopes of the Pachakshiri range, the Assam Himalayas. The short pilgrimage of Tsari Sarpa is included. Kyimdong Dzong is the terminus of this option.

✧ Day 1 Migyitun–Pozo Sumdo–Bimbi La Valley 14 km

From Migyitun, return to Pozo Sumdo and turn north up the spectacular Bimbi La Valley through silver fir and rhododendron forests. The steep trail follows the valley's right side for the first 3 km before crossing to the left and levelling out. Camp in a nice grassy spot.

✧ Day 2 Bimbi La Valley–Tsemachi 13 km

The valley widens into lush meadows and beyond is the junction of two valleys. Take the left (northwest) branch, rather than the right (northeast) one. Ascend through rhododendron forests to alpine meadows and a nomad camp (fresh milk available). Carry on to the Bimbi La (4785 m), 5 km from the camp, then descend for 3 km to a gentle valley and Tsemachi (4175 m, 11 km from the pass).

✧ Day 3 Tsemachi–Sumbatse 16 km

The first 2.5 km pass through fir, rhododendron, willow, and berberis forest. After this stretch, cross to the left bank by a bridge and walk another 2.5 km through junipers to another bridge that leads to the right bank. A short distance downstream is a house overlooking a precipitous valley coming in from the northwest. Continue along the right bank through birch, then larch, for 1 km, then cross again to the left bank. Ascend to avoid a gorge and some sheer cliffs. The trail leads to a steep ravine; descend into it for a short distance and then climb up a spur. Continue along the left bank, 300 m above the river. After 6 km reach Sumbatse; consider camping on a beautiful, grassy plain by the river below.

✧ Day 4 Sumbatse–Kyimdong Dzong 14 km

Beyond the plain below Sumbatse, the river drops rapidly and enters a gorge. Cross by bridge to the right bank, then recross to the left (6.5 km from the start). Pass through thick shrubs and brush for 5 km. Kyimdong Dzong stands on a terrace at the junction of the Kyimdong Chu and a river (east) that descends from the Lang La. The Tsangpo and the main road are 5 km due west. To exit this itinerary, walk to the road and hitch back to Tsethang. Expect a long wait. The remainder of this trek explores the upper reaches of the Siyom, an important branch of the Brahmaputra.

✧ Day 5 Kyimdong Dzong–Taktsa 13 km

The next stretch is a trek east to explore the northern slopes of the Pachakshiri Range; the first section is quite steep. Walk 8 km to Palung, once the center of an independent territory. Ruins of a *dzong* perch on a hillside above the village. This pretty valley has an abundance of flora and birds; and the north-facing slopes are clothed in fir, larch, and birch. Continue to Taktsa.

✧ Day 6 Taktsa–Camp east of the Lang La 16 km

The easy trail leads for 5 km through rhododendron, juniper, and fir forests to the junction of two valleys. Follow the left (east) valley. The trail ascends, then flattens out before the start of a 300-m steep climb to the Lang La (5030 m), a knife-edged pass. From the top, descend southeastward to a herder's camp. The trail then turns almost due east down the Ne (Lang) Chu Valley. Camp on a grassy flat at the junction of Ne and a river coming in from the north.

✧ Day 7 Camp east of the Lang La–Pamchi 16 km

Continue down the valley to Pamchi (Nepar). Here, the large Gyara Phu Chu arrives from the south and the Ne from the east. (A trail leads south along Gyara Phu Chu to Langtang via the Tse La.)

✧ Day 8 Pamchi–Molo 8 km

Molo (3410 m) stands at the junction of the Langtang and the Ne rivers; their combined waters form the Lilung Chu, which flows northward. The Pachakshiris are but a short distance to the southeast. These mountains are difficult to penetrate because the trails are bad and two obscure passes, the Lo and Nyug, must be crossed. North of Molo is the Barang Shika Valley.

✧ Day 9 Molo–Singo Samba 19.5 km

Walk downstream, cross the river by a bridge 1 km below the junction, then skirt some fields and cross to Langong's left bank. The marginal trail leads up the Langtang Chu Valley through fir and birch forests. After 13 km, a large tributary comes in from the southeast. Follow the main valley for 6.5 km to Singo Samba (3460 m), a village with an old *mani* wall. Here, a side river enters the right bank from the Lo La and a bridge spans the main river just above the junction. Cross it and camp on a flat near the Lo La Chu junction.

✧ Day 10   Singo Samba–Kinde   18 km

Walk up the left bank of the Langtang for 4 km then cross to the right bank over a long, cantilever bridge. Here a trail leads south up the slopes to the pilgrimage site of Tsari Sarpa. (To go to Tsari Sarpa, walk past Tashigong [3 km from the bridge]. The circuit starts from the village, taking three days, and crosses five passes.) The trail continues along the right bank for 2.5 km before crossing a bridge (with a pier in mid-stream) to the left bank. The valley widens 3 km farther and has several flat plains along the way to Kinde (3715 m). A large side river enters the right bank from the south (11 km) from the start.

✧ Day 11   Kinde–Langtang   3.5 km

Walk up through extensive grassy meadows to Langtang (3750 m), an idyllic village of 20 houses; wooden structures for animals dot the plain. One bridge is opposite Langtang and one downstream. The Lo La Pass lies to the southwest, another route to Tibet for the Lopas. In this area, any pass used by them is called Lo La. Just before Langtang a side valley leads north over the Tse La to the Gyara Phu Valley and Pamchi.

✧ Day 12   Langtang–Pa La Latsa   14.5 km

The trail continues up the broad valley for 4 km to where it divides and a large side river enters from the south (a trail within this river valley crosses the main range via another Lo La). Go up the wide main river which now turns almost due west. Leave this valley after 5.5 km to turn abruptly northwestward up a hillside. Camp 600 m above the valley at a flat area known as Pa La Latsa (4450 m); from here the Pa La is visible above the tree line.

✧ Day 13   Pa La Latsa–west of Pa La   10 km

Ascend steeply for 1.5 km to the Pa La (4895 m), then descend to the west and camp.

✧ Day 14   West of Pa La–Kyimdong Dzong   35 km

Walk northwestward down the Pa La Valley past a side river that enters from the south (9 km). Cross to the Pa Chu's left bank after another 1.5 km to avoid some cliffs. Travel through fir forest for 1.5 km, then cross a river and continue along a reasonably level track to Kam (14.5 km from the start). Khama lies 8 km farther; a large river enters the right bank halfway between the two villages. At Khama, cross to the Pa Chu's right bank and walk along a level stretch for 4 km. The trail then degenerates until it is joined by another river from the Bimbi La. Cross a bridge to the Kyimdong Chu's left bank at a point 5.5 km above Kyimdong Dzong. The Pa Chu Valley appears insignificant compared to the Bimbi La Valley. At the *dzong*, proceed to the south bank of the Tsangpo and the main Tibet–Sichuan highway. Hitch west to Tsethang and Lhasa.

✦ OPTION 2: KONGPO LA TO TROMDA ON THE TSANGPO

Migyitun–Chösam–Kongpo La–Tromda (on the Tsangpo).

Walk west from Migyitun back to Chösam and follow the Kongpo La route to regain the main road to Tsethang and Lhasa. This is the reverse of From Tromda: An alternative trek to Chösam (see page 226).

✣ OPTION 3: SUR LA OR TANGMA LA: TO NANG XIAN ON THE TSANGPO
Migyitun–Chösam–Nang Xian (on the Tsangpo) via either the Sur La or Tangma La.
Retrace the earlier routes: Tangma La or Sur La, (both page 229).

✣ OPTION 4: SANGA CHÖLING AND TSETHANG
Migyitun–Chösam–Sanga Chöling–Shobo Qu–Tsethang.
To retrace an earlier route to Sanga Chöling via the Cha La, see the reverse of Shobu Qu to Chösam, (see page 215).

✣ OPTION 5: LHÜNTSE XIAN AND THE NYE VALLEY
Migyitun–Chösam–Sanga Chöling–Shobo Qu–Lhuntse Xian–Tsethang.
Below is the itinerary from Migyitun to Sanga Chöling, then south to Lhüntse Xian, a strategic town within the Nye Chu Valley. From Lhüntse Xian, the route returns north to Tsethang.

To Go: Retrace the route from Migyitun to Sanga Chöling and Shobo Qu (page 215). Here, instead of turning right (north) to the Yarlung Valley and Tsethang, turn south along the main road for 3 km. At road marker 242 km, turn left (east) along the broad Nye Chu Valley, a cultivated region with many villages and a few monasteries. Lhüntse Xian lies 21 km east of the turnoff. It is a town of government and army compounds. To return to the Yarlung Valley from Lhüntse Xian, head west along the road back to the road junction, 21 km away. Then follow the main road north to Tsethang, a further 121 km.

Monasteries in the Nye Chu Valley

Chilay Monastery This Kagyüpa center is 2 1/2 hr from Lhüntse Xian. From Lhuntse, walk west along the main motor road to a village below Tebura Monastery (on the north slopes of the Nye Chu Valley), then go southwest on a flat track through cultivated fields and villages to Chilay. The large, impressive monastery is in a village up the southern slopes of the valley (near the old site of Lhüntse Dzong). It was used by the army during the Cultural Revolution and so remains intact. The interior has original murals and *thangkas*, and the *gönkhang* has excellent larger-than-life-size statues. Chilay Monastery is active with over 30 monks.

Tebura Monastery Follow the main road west for 1 hr from Lhüntse Xian. The monastery, once a large center, is at the foot of the Nye Chu Valley's northern slopes. Only one main building remains in good shape.

Trakor Monastery Trakor lies 5 min off the main road between Lhüntse and Shobo Qu, a few km west of Tebura Monastery. Old ruins surround the main building, itself in good condition. A small chapel left of the main hall has good statues and original murals. There are 13 monks living here.

Shangtse Monastery This monastery lies a few km east of Lhüntse Xian halfway up

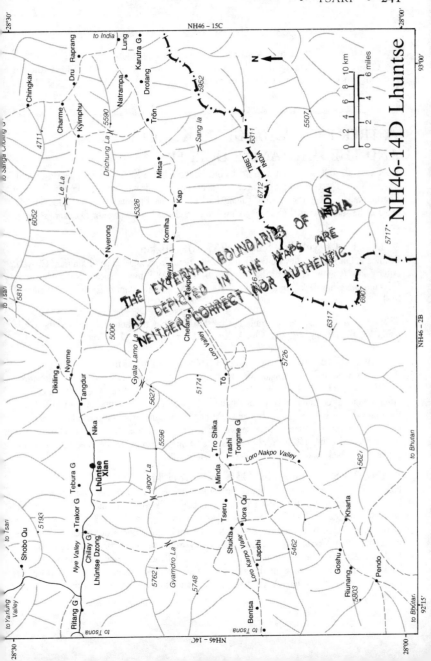

a cliff. A trail from here leads northeast to Dikiling, then crosses the Mo La (5200 m) to Bung in the Char Valley. Sanga Chöling is farther down the valley to the east. (Lhüntse Xian to Sanga Chöling is a three-day walk via the Mo La.)

A TREK FROM CHAYUL TO KHARTA AND THE BHUTANESE BORDER

From Chayul, walk southwest along the Loro Nakpo Chu to Kharta (here a jeep road leads west to Tsona, see below; a number of excursions start from this frontier town). From Kharta, walk a short way to the Tulung La Pass on the Bhutanese border. Alternatively, explore the seldom-visited Nyamjang Chu Valley and the large village of Dongkar (see page 243).

◇ Day 1   Chayul–Tro Shika (3765 m)   30 km

Follow the Loro Chu Valley westward, past Chamchen, Tripa, and Takpa (3 km from Chayul). After 2 km, cross by bridge to the right (south) bank. At Patoyu, beneath Natra Monastery (12 km from Chayul) follow a trail for 8 km to Tro. Within 1 km, cross to the left (north) bank.

Takpa to Lhuntse Dzong   A trail goes northwest within the Lon Valley, over the Gyala Lamo La, then along the Nye Chu Valley, to Lhuntse Dzong (2–3 days).

◇ Day 2   Tro Shika–Shio Shiga (4025 m)   13.5 km

Walk 3 km west to Tashi Tongme Monastery and the Loro Karpo–Loro Nakpo river junction. Together they form the Loro Chu. The Loro eventually joins the Nye to become the Chayul. After the monastery the trail becomes very difficult for animals. The route goes first to Kishung, then crosses the Loro Karpo and climbs 100 m to a plateau. From here it follows the Loro Nakpo for 5 km to a steep, rocky descent to the river and then to a bridge. Cross to the right bank and climb 150 m to Shio Shiga, a charming group of whitewashed houses among poplars. The Nakpo is a narrow valley with steep hills.

◇ Day 3   Shio Shiga–Cha (4360 m)   18.5 km

Follow the river's right (east) bank for one km to a strange, natural bridge over a deep ravine. Cross by bridge to the left bank after 5.5 km, then walk for 5 km more across a plateau and down to the river to Kharta. The village is located on a flat terrace at the junction of two rivers. (Hitch a ride from Kharta to Tsona [60 km] along a dirt road to leave this itinerary.) From Kharta take the right side valley westward along the river's right (south) bank. (The main valley continues to the southwest.) Reach a village and ford to the left bank (7 km). Cha lies a short distance away. (2.5 km downstream is Goshu, a village at the entrance of a side valley. A trail leads up this valley to Tsona [2 days] via the Shangshang [Gunang] La.)

✧ Day 4 Cha–Seti (4875 m) 19 km

Walk southwest up the left bank of the Loro Nakpo to Pendo, the valley's last village (5 km). The Pen La (5282 m) is a further 10.5 km; the snow range to the north divides the Nye and Char rivers. Seti is a camp ground beyond the pass. (A trail goes from Pendo up a side valley to Tsona via the Tra La [two days]. From Seti, a trail also goes up a side valley over the Dzolung La to the same area as the one over the Tra La. Takes two–three days to reach Tsona.)

✧ Day 5 Seti–Goshu Sho (4420 m) 17.5 km

From Seti, follow a trail above the valley on the river's left (opposite) side, then cross the Zangdang La spur at a junction of two valleys (5.5 km). Reach the Chupda Valley at another junction; Chupda is a camp 400 m below the Tulung La (5260 m) used by people going to Mago in Bhutan. A trail climbs steeply to the pass (2.5 km from Chupda), which is closed from December to May. From the pass, walk down steeply for 6.5 km to Goshu Sho at the junction of two valleys. Mago, a small Bhutanese frontier town, is a one-day walk from here.

EXCURSIONS FROM TSONA

A main road from Tsethang links the Yarlung Valley's eastern Yarlha Shampo branch with Ritang (27 km west of Lhüntse Xian) and Tsona (196 km from Tsethang). Hitchhike but expect to spend a good deal of time waiting; most traffic turns from near Ritang to go east to Lhuntse Xian.

✛ OPTION 1: TSONA TO DONGKAR TO THE ME LA (BHUTAN BORDER)

This interesting itinerary heads north from Tsona to Dongkar on the banks of the Nyamjang Chu, a major river through the Himalayas. (A few km south of Dongkar is the Rong Valley; a trail within it leads west to Lhodrak District.) From Dongkar, a trade route between Tibet and Bhutan branches southwest away from the Nyamjang Chu to cross the Chö and Me passes. Me La is on the range that separates Bhutan from Tibet.

✧ Day 1 Tsona–Camp (west of Gorpo La)

From Tsona, the route leads west up the valley to the low Nyapa La Pass (9.5 km). Lake Nyapa Tso (1.5 km long) nestles at its foot. From the pass, travel due north for 3 km past another lake. The trail now heads west and ascends the Gorpo La (5425 m) of the Dongkar Range; to the north is a magnificent range of snow mountains. Expect cold weather. Below the pass, the trail turns after 1.5 km to cross a dividing ridge and reach an adjoining valley to the north. Do not take the obvious route down to the valley floor. Camp before going up the ridge.

✧ Day 2 Camp–Dongkar Qu 9 km

Climb to the Sang La (5210 m) for a magnificent view of the Nyamjang Chu Valley to the north. Immediately below, to the west, lies Dongkar and its *dzong*; descend 1 km to a bridge over the Nyamjang, across from the *dzong*. Dongkar Qu is in a deep gorge, surrounded by cultivated firs and poplars within walled gardens, an altogether enchanting area.

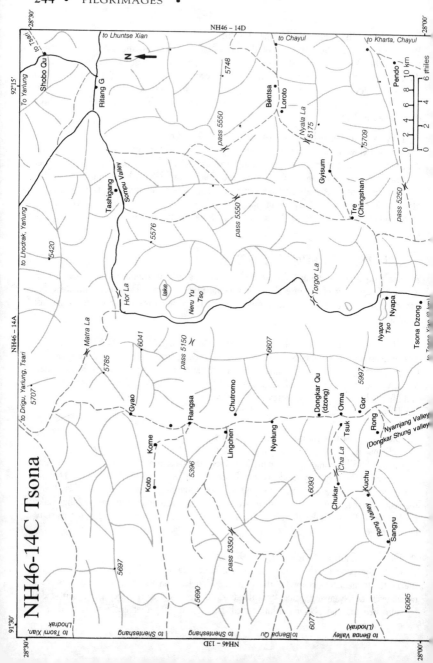

NH46 – 14D

to Lhuntse Xian

to Chayul

to Kharta, Chayul

Shobo Qu

28°30'

92°15'

To Yarlung

to Tsari

Ritang G

5748

Bentsa

Loroto

Pendo

10 km

6 miles

Nyala La
5175

5709

Gyisum

Tashigang

Sompu Valley

pass 5550

pass 5550

5576

Tre
(Chingshan)

pass 5250

to Lhodrak, Yarlung

5420

Hor La

lake

Neru Yu
Tso

Torgor La

Nyapa Tso

Nyapa

Tsona Dzong

NH46 – 14A

Matra La

5785

6041

pass 5150

6607

5997

Nyapa Tso

to Tsona Xian (3 km)

5707

to Drigu, Yarlung, Tsari

Gyao

Kome

Rangsa

Chutromo

Dongkar Qu
(dzong)

Orma

Gor

Rong

Nyamjang Valley
(Dongkar Shung valley)

NH46-14C Tsona

Koto

5396

Lingchen

Nyelung

Tsuk

Cha La

Chukar

Kuchu

6093

Chukar

Rong Valley

Sangyu

to Tsomi Xian,
Lhodrak

91°30'

28°30'

5697

5690

pass 5350

6077

6095

to Benpa Valley
(Lhodrak)

to Benpa Valley

to Shenteshang

to Shenteshang

to Benpa Qu

NH46 – 13D

28°00'

✧ Day 3   Dongkar Qu–Chukar (4145 m)   9.5 km

From Dongkar, follow the left (east) bank of the Nyamjang Chu southward, along a narrow path above the water to Mishi (4 km). Just beyond, cross a bridge to the right bank. The river here flows in a deep, narrow gorge. Follow the Tsuk Chu tributary to Tsuk (1 km), a settlement on the left bank surrounded by barley fields. The village still utilizes stone watchtowers. After Tsuk, turn south up a side ravine and ascend to the Cha La (Hand Pass, 4665 m). Guru Rinpoche apparently passed this way en route to the Rong Valley. At Chukar, the people met him with folded hands to implore him to stay, hence the name Hand Pass. The trail now enters the broad Rong Valley, a region wetter than any north of the Cha La; a forest of fir clothes the south slopes. Reach Chukar, still north of the main Himalaya range, after a descent of 1.5 km.

> **The Rong Valley** This important valley links Tsari with the Lhodrak District (see page 681). Its entrance is 5 km south of Tsuk on the Nyamjang Chu. A trail up the Rong Chu leads due west past Kuchu and Sangyü to the Gomokong La, a few km north of the Tibet–Bhutan border. (A trail before the pass goes due south to Bhutan.) Descend westward to Benpa Qu (see page 689) in Lhodrak. From Dongkar, allow 2–2 1/2 days to reach the pass and another day to Benpa Qu.)

✧ Day 4   Chukar–north base of Cha La (4920 m)   9 km

From Chukar, descend sharply to the Rong Chu and continue west up the left bank for 2.5 km, then cross to the right bank. About 1 km beyond the bridge, turn south up the small Rhe Valley. Camp at a grassy plain 600 m below the Chö La. Guru Rinpoche crossed this sacred pass (*chö* means 'Dharma').

✧ Day 5   Base of Cha La–Karoo (3960 m)   13 km

The Cha La is 3 km south of the camp and the climb to the top is exceedingly steep for the final 300 m. To the west are several glacial peaks and to the southwest, overlooking the Yombu Chu, is another glaciated range. From the summit, descend steeply westward for nearly 2 km to a river that drains from a northern glacier. Follow it for 1.5 km to the Mena Plain, where another large river from a huge hanging glacier comes in from the north. The trail crosses the plain for more than 3 km through a picturesque fir forest rather than follows the Mena Chu to its junction with the Yombu Chu. Eventually arrive at the old customs post of Karoo, 150 m above the Mena–Yombu river junction. The trail now turns nearly due west up the Yombu Chu's left bank.

✧ Day 6   Karoo–Shingbe (3885 m)   19 km

The glacial Yombu Chu Valley has good grazing on the left bank; nearly all the animals are horses. After 3 km, the large Tsesum Glacier appears on the left bank. Continue for 5 km to the campsite of Tsa, then reach in a further 1.5 km a large, glacial river that comes in from high, glacial peaks to the left (north). Walk for another 2.5 km through willow scrub and swamp and ford the main river to the right bank. Ascend immediately southwestward up a series of steep zigzags through otherwise impenetrable rhododendron bushes to the Me La (4555 m). Descend to Shingbe (5 km).

Me La This pass straddles the Tibet–Bhutan border. The Dongkar–Chö La–Me La route is well-traveled by Bhutanese porters who use it, especially during summer months, to carry rice to Dongkar. Other foot traffic goes from Bhutan to Tsona and Dzambuling, a village on the Tsangpo not far from Tsethang.

❖ Option 2: Tsona to Sanglung on the Tibet–Bhutan Border

This route crosses a pass immediately southwest of Tsona and follows the Nyamjang Chu towards the southwest. The area downstream from Shakti is mainly inhabited by Mönpas and the Tibet–Bhutan border at Jangpu lies just beyond Sanglung.

✧ Day 1   Tsona–Trimo   19 km
The trail from Tsona goes southwest for 9.5 km to the Pö La (4540 m), then veers due west to descend steeply to the Nyamjang Chu Valley and Trimo.

✧ Day 2   Trimo–Lepo (2955 m)   6.5 km
From Trimo, follow the left (east) bank of the Nyamjang to the southwest. After descending for 3 km, the trail crosses to the right bank. The trail is good all the way to Lepo.

✧ Day 3   Lepo–Le (2440 m)   9.5 km
Continue down the Nyamjang's right (west) bank through marvelous gorges. Walk up a ridge, then descend steeply. Just before Le, cross to the left bank, then recross to the right immediately after the village.

✧ Day 4   Le–Pangchen (2130 m)   16 km
Shoktsen appears across the river 13 km from Le. Cross to the left bank here, then travel for 3 km downstream to Pangchen at the north end of a beautiful plain. The Nyamjang Chu meanders slowly by. Camp near here.

✧ Day 5   Pangchen–Shakti (2200 m)   14.5 km
Cross by bridge to the right bank 1 km below Pangchen, then walk 1.5 km to Gorsum Chörten, a massive structure, about 50 m on each side; 120 *mani* wheels line each side. This *chörten* (present condition unknown) has the same design as Chörten Karra in the Tashiyangsi Valley. From here, continue down the river's right bank for 9.5 km, then cross by bridge to the left bank. Ascend 500 m to Shakti.

✧ Day 6   Shakti–Gyipu   8 km
From Shakti, walk around a spur to the next valley, then go up to Gyipu on the right bank. The area downstream (south) is inhabited by Mönpas; their houses are distinguished by their bamboo roofs. All their villages stand above the Nyamjang River and are linked by a trail.

✧ Day 7   Gyipu–Sanglung   13 km
The next village is Shabrang, 1.5 km from Gyipu. Drop 300 m to the river, then climb to Karteng (just before Karteng a trail leads east to Tawang in Bhutan). From Karteng, descend steeply to a bamboo suspension bridge; cross it to the west bank and ascend to Sanglung. The Bhutan–Tibet border is at Jangpu, a further 4 km.

❖ Option 3: Tsona to Chayul Dzong and Tsari via Sanga Chöling

One of the best things about this trek from Tsona to Chayul is that it stays away from the dirt roads except for a short section. From Chayul, hike to Sanga Chöling to begin the Tsari pilgrimage. For a description of this portion, see the Sanga Chöling–Chayul circuit, page 219.

◇ Day 1   Tsona–Tre (4325 m)   13 km

From Tsona walk northeast up the valley behind the *dzong*, past Tsolung. Cross the easy Doko La (4725 m), then descend 6.5 km down a broad valley to Tre, a village of three houses. Above the village is a campground called Tang.

◇ Day 2   Tre–Gyisum (4725 m)   9.5 km

Today's an easy walk, gradual all the way up to Gyisum.

◇ Day 3   Gyisum–Loroto (4325 m)   11 km

Continue up the wide valley for 3 km, then turn up a side valley for 3 km to the Nyala La (5175 m), the watershed between the Manas and Subansiri rivers. Descend for 5 km to Loroto.

◇ Day 4   Loroto–Jora (4050 m)   14.5 km

An easy trail leads down the valley past many villages. Jora and its picturesque monastery stand on a hill 100 m above the river's right bank.

Jora to Lhuntse At Jora, a foot-trail leads north along the Tanning Chu via the Gyandro La to Lhuntse Dzong (Lhuntse Xian is farther east). This stretch takes three days.

◇ Day 5   Jora–Tro Shika (3765 m)   11 km

From Jora, descend through dry country for 8 km to Tashi Tongme, where the Loro Nakpo Chu joins the Loro Karpo Chu to create the Chayul Chu. During April, low water allows the Chayul Chu to be forded easily. An impressive monastery is perched on a rock at Tashi Tongme. Walk 3 km along the left bank of the Chayul (Loro) to Tro Shika. Looking south to the Assam Himalayas, locate 18 peaks over 6000 m.

◇ Day 6   Tro Shika–Chayul Dzong (3500 m)   29 km

Below Tro Shika the valley narrows and the trail keeps well above the Chayul's left (north) bank. Pass Trolungka. Cross to the right bank by a cantilever bridge (8 km from Tro Shika), then continue for 2.5 km to Tro. Follow the right bank through barren country for 5 km to reach another bridge; cross the Moga Lengye Chu. (A pilgrimage route up to the Moga Lengye Valley leads to Takpa Shelri, not to be confused with the Takpa Shelri of Tsari.) Sanga Shika lies 3 km beyond the bridge. Continue down the right bank past several villages. Just after Takpa, cross a cantilever bridge to the left bank, then pass Trip and Chamchen to reach Chayul Dzong, an impressive place with a ruined fortress and small monastery. (A farther 12 km from Chayul is Hordoryu, a castle-like house at the mouth of a ravine.)

Chayul to Tsari See the Sanga Chöling–Chayul circuit, page 219.

LAPCHI:
MILAREPA'S MAGICAL HERMITAGES

A journey through the Valley of the Roses deep in the heart of the
Tibet–Nepal Himalayas

Location	Southwest of Dingri; east of the Nyalam Valley
Map reference	NH45-14 B D C
Trekking days	11 (one-way)
Start–Finish	Dingri–Tashigang (Friendship Highway)
Passes	Seven moderately difficult passes

OVERVIEW

This pilgrimage is among the very finest that Tibet has to offer. Lapchi, after Mt Kailash and Tsari, is the most sacred destination in the Himalayas. The beloved Buddhist master, Milarepa (1040–1123), lived and died in this region, and the devout from all over Tibet visit Lapchi to come into contact with the cave hermitages and monasteries associated with this illustrious poet-saint. They

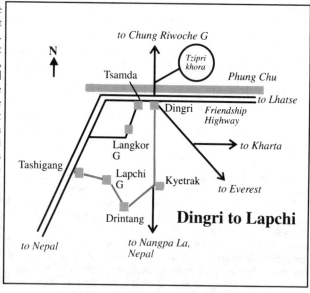

are also drawn here because Lapchi is related to the important tantric cult of Demchok (Chakrasamvara). In some long ago time, this wrathful manifestation of the Buddha Sakyamuni subjugated demons in the area. Demchok subsequently transformed this secluded enclave into a Buddhist sanctuary. Milarepa was the first to explore and 'open' this pilgrimage for ordinary people; to achieve this he had to overcome a second echelon of local gods and goddesses.

Many of the legends concerning the caves and temples of Lapchi are derived from these magical encounters.

The fabled retreats of Tashang, Chuwar, Drin, Drakmar, and Lapchi are all found within the mountains of the Lapchi Kang range. Despite the ravages of the Cultural Revolution, these sites and the surrounding countryside still preserve a magical quality. Their great beauty and discernible spirituality are matched by only one or two other places in all Tibet. And the abrupt transition of terrain from the arid, high-altitude desert of Dingri to the lush green valleys of Lapchi is breathtaking. It is difficult to imagine a more powerful contrast.

The pilgrimage begins in Dingri (Tangger), center of an important district dotted with 54 monasteries and retreats. Langkor, a holy mountain 10 km west of Dingri, is closely linked with Padampa (Dampa) Sangye, an Indian saint who lived at the end of the 11th century. The Tzipri range, immediately to the northeast of Dingri, has a complex of 12 small monasteries and hermitages strung out along its *khora*, and each year many pilgrims come to circumambulate the holy peak. Dzarong Monastery, better known as Rongphuk, was built in 1902 at the southernmost limit of the Dingri Plain. Standing at the foot of the Rongphuk Glacier, it is one of the main monasteries of the region and one of the highest in Tibet.

The charming villages of Drintang, Drubden, and Chuwar, nestled beneath sacred Mt Tseringma (Gaurishanker), are situated in the Rongshar Valley. Dubbed 'The Valley of the Roses' by members of Britain's first Everest Expedition (1921), Rongshar is a haven for naturalists and plant hunters. Thousands of rose bushes line the entire valley as a celebration to life; the killing of animals is strictly forbidden here. Chuwar Monastery, the place where Milarepa died at the age of 84, is located in this splendid area.

Drin (Drintang), further down the Rongshar Valley, is a sublime village in a superb setting. Nearby is Drakmar, a complex of cave retreats consecrated by Milarepa. Mt Tseringma is the prominent high snow peak that straddles the Rongshar and its knife-edge profile is visible for a long stretch of the pilgrimage walk. Most Sherpas living in the Himalayan region consider it their most sacred mountain. From Chuwar, the beautiful Menlung Valley leads up to the mountain's high reaches. Within it are glacial lakes and more hermitages associated with Milarepa.

After Rongshar, the approach to the holy Lapchi Kang range (via the Kangchen La Pass) begins. The Lapchi monastic complex, with its many cave retreats used by Milarepa and his disciples, stands on the Tibet–Nepal border. Surrounded by forested mountains and perpetually veiled by swirling mists, Lapchi, without question, is one of the most memorable pilgrimage sites in Tibet. Before 1959, this haven drew pilgrims from as far away as India. Nowadays, Tibetans and Nepalese Buddhists still arrive regularly. It is easy to spend a few days here exploring hidden pathways and tucked-away shrines. Be sure to budget sufficient time to savor the mystical atmosphere of this pilgrimage-trek, especially in the Rongshar and Lapchi areas.

The route crosses a total of seven passes. None of them is especially difficult unless there is snow. The walk starts from Dingri and ends at Phegyeling Monastery and its Milarepa cave, both situated within the Nyalam (Nyanang) Valley. From here, head either to Nepal or to Lhasa via the Friendship Highway. An alternative itinerary via the Thong La is included at the end of this chapter.

Related Sections
Friendship Highway, p 987
Mt Everest, p 895
Mt Shishapangma, p 940

Access
The Lapchi retreats are best approached via Dingri on the Friendship Highway. From Lhasa, hitch or take a bus to Dingri (at road marker 544) along the Friendship Highway, a distance of 637 km. From Zhangmu on the Nepal border, hitch or bus to Dingri, 194 km. (See Friendship Highway, as above.)

When to go
The best seasons for this region of the Tibet–Nepal Himalayas are spring and autumn. However, the passes here close earlier and open later than in Nepal, and there may be times in November and April when it is not possible to make the complete circuit. Avoid the area in winter. Few people trek in Nepal during the summer monsoon: from mid-May through mid-September. For this pilgrimage, however, July and August are good months. There is rain, but not as much as south of the Himalayas, and the flowers are superb at this time. For a short stretch after Drintang, before the Sobje La Pass, expect leeches during the wet season.

Food and lodging
Bring a tent for this trek, especially during the potentially rainy summer season. Three long stretches have little habitation except for random nomad camps: Sharto Tö–Tashang; Drintang–Lapchi; Lapchi–Tashigang. It is difficult to complete any of these within one day. Having a tent and adequate winter gear give peace of mind. Food is not a problem. *Tsampa* is readily available and supplies can be replenished every one or two days. Only Dingri and Chungmoche have stores along the way but there isn't much by way of choice. Bring food from Lhasa or Nepal if you want more than the usual Tibetan fare. Pack animals are available along the entire route. However, if you use animals to carry packs, tent and food, plan for extra time; there are inevitable delays with animals. From time to time you may lose a day or two because the yaks or horses are out in the pastures and not available immediately.

Horse carts for the first leg are available in Dingri (Rmb 20–30 to Shoto Tö). One cart can carry the gear of six or more persons.

Time Chart

Day	Place	Hours
1	Dingri–Sharto To	4 1/2
2	Drakmar	8
3	River junction	7 1/2
4	Tashang	2
5	Chuwar	5 1/4
6	Drintang	3
7	cave shelter	5 1/2
8	stone marker	4 1/2

9	Lapchi	3 3/4
10	Jamgang	5
11	Friendship Highway	5 1/2

Trail Notes

✤ Day 1 Dingri–Sharto To 4 1/2 hr

From the south end of Dingri, head south towards a low, brown hill. (Beyond is the main Himalaya range: Everest is the insignificant small triangle far to the left; the wide gap in the horizon is Nangpa La, sandwiched between Cho Oyu [left] and Melung Tse.) An abandoned cave monastery, Gonda Phuk, is at the north end of the hill, 1 1/4 hr from Dingri.. Skirt west around the hill and bear to the southwest. Ford some streams and cross two small wooden bridges, following a distinct cart track, to reach Shoto Me and Gulung Monastery (2 1/4 hr). Gulung is a small Nyingmapa monastery, 15 min from Shoto Me. Behind the small *dukhang* is a chapel decorated with color photos taken from a Tibetan calendar. A couple of small murals still remain. From the village turn east, go around a spur, to Sharto To (1 hr), a traditional stopping place between Dingri and Kyetrak. There is a wonderful sense of space here. Nangpa La is due south. *Dzos* and yaks are available; Rmb 30–40 for a *dzo* and a man to go to Tashang and back.

✤ Day 2 Sharto To–Drakmar (via Laiya La) 8 hr

After Sharto To the trail crossing the southwest portion of the Dingri Plain is faint and difficult to follow. Aim generally for a distinct gap in the low hills to the southwest. Cross a dry, stony riverbed at a place marked by five vertical stone columns (1 1/4 hr); then wade across a river just beyond. Continue towards the low hills in the distance. Round the corner of the hills and bear to the right at a spot marked by two stone corrals that serve as animal shelters (1 hr). A more distinct trail from here crosses a small plain to join a well-defined tractor track. Follow it to the right, over the low Laiya La (4787 m) (2 hr). The top of Mt Everest rises just above the mountain range to the east. To the southeast is a great jumble of mountains; Cho Oyo is the highest.

Descend from the pass onto a moon-like, desolate valley. Expect a strong head wind. At the bottom, turn right along the left bank of the river. Pass, but do not cross, a bridge constructed of tree trunks anchored by stones (1 1/2 hr). Just before a nomad camp at the Drakmar Valley entrance is a swift river with many channels (1 1/4 hr). Find a safe point to cross. (Increased snowmelt causes these glacial streams to rise significantly in the afternoon.) After the crossing, turn right into the valley of the Drakmar nomad camp (1/2 hr). Four or five black tents are usually here and donkeys are available. Glaciers, close and impressive, loom at the head of the main valley.

✤ Day 3 Drakmar–River Junction 7 1/2 hr

From Drakmar continue up the side valley. Go past a small pond and a stone corral to join a tractor track (1/2 hr). An abandoned Chinese military outpost is halfway up a hill on the right. Chinese characters across the slopes proclaim: 'Long Live Chairman Mao' (1/4 hr). Kyetrak, a bleak, deserted village east of the multi-channeled Kyetrak River can be seen across the river. The pilgrimage route runs along the west (left) bank.

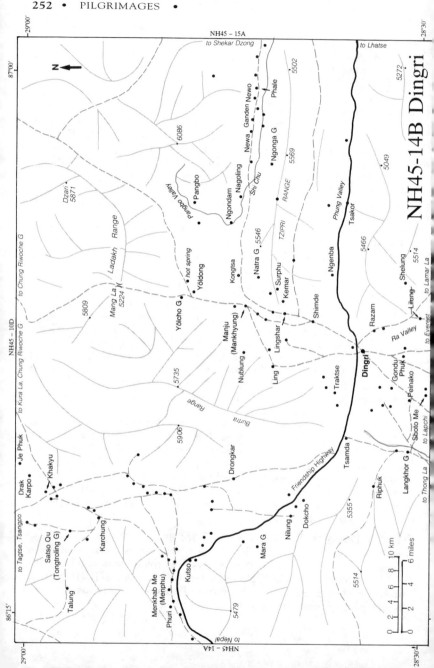

NH45 - 15A

to Shekar Dzong

to Lhatse

NH45-14B Dingri

NH45 - 10D

to Kura La, Chung Riwoche G

to Chung Riwoche G

to Tagtse, Tsangpo

to Nepal

NH45 – 14A

N

5502

5272

6086

Pangbo

Phale

Newa Ganden Newo

Ngonga G

5569

Nagoling

Ngondam Nagdoling

Shi Chu

Dzari 5871

Pangbo Valley

Ladakh Range

hot spring

Yöldong

Kongtsa

Natra G 5546

Surphu Kemar

TZIPRI RANGE

5049

5466

Phung Valley

Tsakor

Ngenba

5514

Shelung

Lharng

Mang La 5224

Yölcho G

Manju (Mankhyung)

Lingshar

Shimde

Razam

to Lamar La

5809

Nublung

Ling

Ra Valley

to Everest

5735

Burtra Range

Dingri

Gondu Phuk

Peinako

Traktse

Shoto Me

5906

Drongkar

Langkhor G

to Lapchi

Je Phuk

Khakyu

Friendship Highway

Riphuk

to Thong La

Drak Karpo

Tsamda

5355

Satso Qu (Tongtroling G)

Karchung

Nilung

Dokcho

5514

Talung

Kutso

Mara G

Menkhab Me (Menphu)

Phuri

5479

10 km
6 miles

0   2   4   6   8
0   2   4   6

The Nangpa La   This high, difficult pass (5800 m) leads from Tibet to the Solo-Khumbhu region of Nepal by way of Thame and Namche Bazaar. Nangpa La is normally only open from May to August, and the Cho Oyu Base Camp is very near the pass. From Kyetrak Village a trail follows the east bank of the Kyetrak Glacier past the deserted villages of Palung and Japawa, then crosses ice fields and large crevasses. The pass is beyond Tapawa. Sometimes whole caravans of Tibetan traders are wiped out by sudden blizzards—the fine powdery snow blasted into the men's faces causes slow suffocation. Unless you are highly experienced, hire a competent guide and bring top-notch gear.

Continue up the valley past a waterfall on the left to reach another stone corral and a *mani* pile (1 1/4 hr). Climb up low hills and through a ravine (follow the stone cairns that serve as trail markers) to a small plateau (3/4 hr). The vista of the surrounding mountains is tremendous, with excellent views of Cho Oyo and its glaciers on the left. The tractor track, following the land's contours, goes off to the right for 1/2 hr. Take the footpath shortcut that climbs a steep spine. This is the approach to the Pozé La—also called Drin Pozé La—at 5200 m. Rechungpa, the principal disciple of Milarepa, flew to this pass from Loro Dol Monastery upon hearing of his master's death. He reached here at sunrise, thus the name of the pass: *po* is summit and *zé* is a shaft of light.

Alpine flowers, dwarf forget-me-nots, and many white and yellow saxifrages cover the wide open area just before the pass. Reach the pass in an hour. At the top, Cho Oyu, Nangpa La, and the Kyetrak Glacier are all to the left. The trail down is gradual. Pass a glacial lake on the left and a boggy area where some streams need wading. A stone corral stands to the right (3/4 hr). A tractor track joins the trail at the entrance to Rongshar Gorge, which is guarded by dramatic cliffs. Follow it into the gorge to begin the long, steep descent into the area named the Valley of the Roses by early British mountaineers. At about 4880 m the barren slopes give way to junipers and dwarf rhododendron bushes. Further down are berberis (barberry), loniceras (honeysuckle), white and pink spiraes, primulas, anemones, geraniums, and white roses.

Pass corrals on either side of the trail (1 1/2 hr) then continue to a spot marked by prayer flags on stones (3/4 hr). At this point, leave the tractor track for a zigzagging shortcut downwards, rejoining the main track by the bank of the Rongshar River. Here is a junction of two rivers; the combined waters flow south to become the Rongshar (1/2 hr). Cross the big wooden bridge and follow a motorable track along the west bank. The descent from now on is much more gradual.

Rongshar: The Valley of the Roses   Rongshar is a modern name. The old one, as mentioned by Milarepa, is Drin. This Himalayan valley is considered sacred for many reasons. One is the large number of juniper bushes (used as offering incense) that grow here. Another is the legacy left by Milarepa and other hermits who lived here for prolonged periods. Their spiritual ambience still lingers in caves and hermitages; the killing of animals is strictly forbidden in the valley. Rongshar is more Nepalese ➠

than Tibetan in character and receives far more rain than the dry, arid Dingri Plain. During the monsoon season, warm winds from Nepal and the Indian subcontinent carry a great deal of moisture through the Himalayan gorges; much of this comes through Rongshar. In June and July the valley is a wondrous profusion of blooming white and red roses and large (3–4 m) gooseberry bushes. The powerful, unforgettable scent of roses throughout the region is a hallmark of the pilgrimage.

✤ Day 4 River Junction–Tashang 2 hr

This is an easy day. Follow the right bank of the upper Rongshar (also known as the Shung Chu), which in these parts is a fast-moving glacial torrent. The track is quite stony. Barley fields appear after a roofless stone building (left) is passed. Great clumps of white roses are everywhere, marking the beginning of the narrow, ever-fragrant Valley of the Roses. A side valley opens to the right. Cross a bridge here (1 1/2 hrs). Go past large piles of beautifully and meticulously carved *mani* stones, each the size of a large pumpkin, on the left next to the river (1/4 hr). The dramatic hermitage of Luma Dzog Dzog, high up on the impressive cliffs (right), blends imperceptibly with the rock face.

Just beyond is Tashang (4030 m), a pretty village at the junction of three river valleys: Rongshar, Salung, and Shung. Tashang is short for Takpa Shantsen, 'the limit of birch trees'; it stands at the upper fringe of the forest zone. An idyllic campsite is over a bridge, across the Rongshar, on the left bank. *Dzos* are available in Tashang: Rmb 20 each, including the handler, to go to Drubden.

Luma Dzog Dzog: A Congregation of Lu (Water divinities)

Known also as Dzakar Drubphuk (White Rocky Mountain Cave), this retreat center is set among the sheer cliffs of the upper Rongshar (Drin) Valley. It was here that Milarepa met Zessay Bum, his former fiancée, Khujuk and other lay followers. The trail leading to the hermitage is first marked by large piles of beautifully carved *mani* stones by the right bank of the river. From here, looking up, a chörten on a flat ledge outside the hermitage can be seen. Colored frescoes decorate the cave entrances. The climb up is short, about 1/4 of an hour. Within the main cave chamber is a tall white burial chörten (*dhungbum*), which holds religious relics. Along the walls are carvings of the Six Syllables, 'Om Ah Hum' and Vajraguru *mantras*. Below the chapel, a level path hugs the slopes and goes south to a white chörten. Further along is a vertical cleft in the mountain side. Inside, at its base, is a ruined building, originally a three-story meditation retreat. Continue left, towards Tashang, to another chörten and the last meditation cave. A difficult path leads from here to Tashang, or retrace your steps.

✤ Day 5 Tashang–Chuwar Monastery 5 1/4 hr

Follow the Rongshar south. Barley and potatoes grow on one side, birch and willow forests on the other. Handsome wild gooseberry bushes and cream-colored roses predominate here (lower down the roses are red). Masses of anemones and yellow primulas appear from time

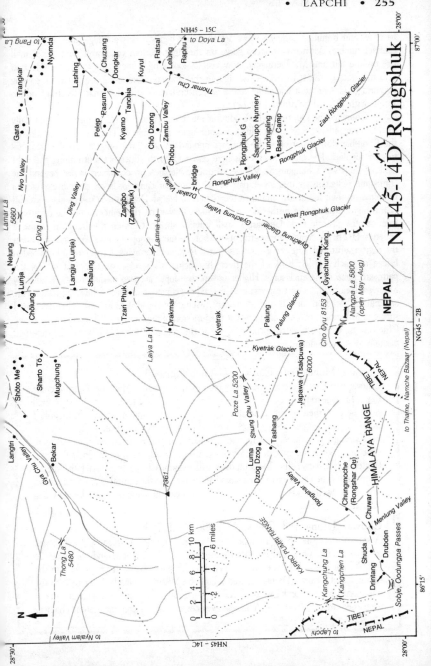

NH45-14D Rongphuk

to time, and beguiling camping spots dot the river banks. Cross a bridge after 1 1/4 hr; a cataract tumbles down from a steep gorge on the right. Further on, prayer flags top a small rise on the left and Mt Tseringma, now visible, looms high above the valley. A side trail (1/2 hr), goes to the right over a rise. Ignore this and continue along the dirt road, passing two bridges (1/4 hr) to a side valley and a broken bridge over the Rongshar. Reach a roadside shrine with defaced paintings (3/4 hr).

Chungmoche Qu, the region's administrative compound, is 1/2 hr further. Don't dally in this area; officials might make life uncomfortable. A couple of Tibetan cadres administer the Rongshar district out of a new stone compound. A store, the only one in the area, has meager supplies. The motor track ends here and a footpath continues south along the right bank of the river. Chungmoche Village, distinctly Nepalese in character, is just beyond the compound. Tibetans in this lower part of the Rongshar carry loads on their backs with a tumpline on their foreheads, similar to the porters in Nepal. Don't miss a spectacular waterfall (25 m-high) inside a cliff further down. It is tucked away, on the right, within the cavernous interior of a gigantic rock. Go past a small wayside shrine, Chörten Karchung, in honor of Milarepa (1/2 hr). It commemorates the place where he met a group of ghosts (dre) and symbolizes the fight against evil. The chörten is consecrated to Jomo Tseringma. Cross over a big wooden bridge to reach the left bank of the river. Just before the bridge, on the right side of the path, are some stone enclosures. Higher up on the slopes are two meditation caves used by Milarepa. Nearby, dramatic near-vertical cliffs and the constricted gorge of the Rongshar provide a stunning backdrop for Chuwar Monastery (Menlung Chuwar) (3300 m). This celebrated shrine of Milarepa is perched on a ridge at the junction of the Rongshar Chu and the Menlung Chu valleys. It is possible to spend a night at the school compound next to the deserted, partially destroyed monastery.

Chuwar Monastery (Chuwar Gephel Potrang)

Chuwar and Lapchi are the two most prominent retreats of Milarepa. Pilgrims come to pay homage to the poet-saint's monasteries and caves; the former is specially revered since he died there at the venerable age of 84. Chuwar's architecture, distinguished by its pagoda design, shows a marked Nepalese influence. Together with the shrines in Kyirong (see page 924), it represents a radical departure from traditional Tibetan structures. Some Indian-style paintings on wood panels and a few slightly damaged (bullet holes), larger-than-life sculptures still remain. Chuwar was under the special protection of the Drigungpa and Phagmo Drupa, as well as the central Lhasa government. The main dwelling cave (zimphuk) of Chuwar, near the monastery, is Khyung Gong (Garuda Egg) Phuk.

Chuwar Dzong and Chuwar Drejik Drubphuk

A short distance north of the monastery is a trail junction marked by a red chörten and mani walls. One trail goes down the Menlung Chu Valley and the other up the Chuwar ridge. Take the latter, ascending the slopes between prayer flags to the hermitage of Chuwar Dzong, reputedly built by Milarepa himself. Next to it is the important Chuwar Drejik Drubphuk (Ghost Vanquishing) meditation cave, built within a recessed area of the ridge. A lower level contains the secret meditation chamber where Milarepa subdued ghosts and ultimately died. Legend tells how Milarepa carried a large stone all the way from Lapchi; it is here, marked with a hand-print of the poet-saint on its surface. To some pilgrims, this cave is known as Driche (Dzo's Tongue) Phuk, so named because a stone outcrop resembles the tongue of a dzo. Just beyond Chuwar Dzong is a tiny cave. Constant dripping from the ceiling has created a small pool in the cave floor. This is the Mila Terchu—the sacred Water of Milarepa.

Menlung Chu Valley (Valley of Medicinal Herbs)

The beautiful Menlung Chu Valley leads to the basecamp of Menlung Tse (7181 m) and the difficult snowy pass of Menlung La that provides access to Nepal. A high-altitude glacial lake, La Tso Ogma, is at the head of the Menlung Chu. In the vicinity are several caves. The eastern side of the valley conceals Thom Phuk (Bear Cave); it was here that Milarepa transformed into a bear. Near the pass there are more lakes; they are associated with Tsering Ringa, one of the Five Goddesses of Long Life, and are said to be filled with a fluid 'like turquoise or lapis lazuli'. Menlung Tse (Jowo Guru), situated entirely within Tibet, was climbed in 1987 by Chris Bonington, the British mountaineer.

✤ Day 6 Chuwar–Drintang 3 hr

From the monastery descend a short distance to the Menlung Chu and cross to its left bank by a bridge. Pass a small house under a big rock (right, 1/4 hr).

Khyung Gong Phuk

This cave, inside the house, is one of Milarepa's first meditation caves in the area. On the rock are carvings of mantras and the Six Syllables. According to a local legend, the Five Goddesses of Long Life came here to seduce and threaten Milarepa, to try to keep him from enlightenment. The cotton-clad saint simply subdued and converted the temptresses. An old man now lives here.

Beyond the cave is a flat and pleasant stretch of path, along which are specific sites of the foot, hand, fist, and penis (sangwa drubtak) prints of Milarepa. The path soon rejoins the Rongshar Chu, crosses to the right bank by way of a festooned bridge, and heads southward (3/4 hr). After Shuda, a tsampa mill near the bridge, leave the Rongshar Valley to turn up to Drubden, a large village halfway up the right slope of the valley (1/2 hr). From Chuwar to Drubden there are beautiful pockets of natural flower gardens, carpeted with irises, roses, and dwarf rhododendrons.

Drubden (Center of Ascetics)

Cave retreats in or near Drubden (also Dinma Drin) are Dakpo Phuk, a cave of Gampopa, and Kyi Phuk Dzong, a Milarepa cave. A flat path goes from the south

➠

end of the village to Chushing (Water-Wood) Dzong and the Shel Phuk; both marked by prayer flags. The stone retreat of Chushing Dzong is named for the thin ribbon-like waterfalls that cascade nearby and the local bamboo groves. Beyond is the meditation cave of Shel Phuk. These two sites are usually considered as one—Shel Phuk Chushing Dzong (Water-Wood Crystal Cave)—and they are among the Six Unknown Caves of Milarepa. At the time of his retreat here a horrendous drought struck the area. The inhabitants of the Drin Valley, embroiled in conflicts over water rights, came to the master for a judgement. He was reluctant to do so, saying that hermits don't know much about secular affairs, and anyway, the rain would eventually come by itself. He believed that those who want to be free should remain silent and refrain from taking sides. A local named Rechungpa, however, continued to urge Milarepa to help. He relented and started to pray. Soon there was a heavy downpour and all disputes were forgotten.

Drubden to Nepal A trail along the Rongshar Valley continues south from Drubden to Nepal. The route: Drubden–Shokta (2 houses) 3 hr; Shokta–Nyalu (border with a bridge but no peremanent habitation) 4 hr; Nyalu–Choksam (Lamabager) 6 hr; Choksam–Charikot 18 hr; Charikot–Kathmandu, bus, 113 km. The entire walk takes three–four days. The Rongshar River drops 425 m in 10 km between Drubden and the Nepal frontier (approx. 2750 m). Some trade exists between the two countries, mainly butter, salt, and tea.

From Drubden to Drintang (Drin) is a 1 1/2 hr stiff though beautiful walk up the range that flanks the Rongshar Gorge on the right. (Tibetans are sometimes reluctant to take their dzos up and you might have to carry your own packs.) Drintang, one of the loveliest villages in Tibet, is often shrouded in mist, caused by the warm air of Nepal's Bhote Kosi Valley interacting with the cold air mass of the Tibetan Plateau. Dzos are available to go on to Lapchi from Drintang: Rmb 40 for dzo and handler for the two-day journey.

Drintang (Drin)

Drintang occupies a small enchanting glen 500 m above the Rongshar River. The setting is dramatic: across the valley is the twin-peak of Mt Tseringma, one of the Himalaya's most inspiring mountains; secluded in a lush, hidden valley full of alpine flowers are grey stone houses and half-forgotten shrines. Some 400 m below is Drubden, the winter residence of Drintang's populace.

Two Kagyüpa chapels, the Mani and Changkha *lhakhangs*, are in the village. The former has a big prayer wheel inside the main hall and is much used by the villagers. Well-preserved murals of the Kagyü Sertreng (lineages of Kagyüpa lamas) decorate the inside walls. The founder of the monastery was apparently a Bhutanese lama, Drukpa Topche. Changkha is on top of a nearby rock. Guru Rinpoche, the main image in the chapel, is flanked by his consorts, Yeshe Tsogyal and Mandarawa. On the sides is a set of Bum, an 18-volume summary of the Kangyur and the Tengyur.

➠

Many small bas-relief images of various saints are carved on framed slates—relics that are not commonly seen. The chapel, also called Yatse, is used for communal services on the 8th, 10th, 15th, 25th, and 30th of each month, when monks present *tshok* (a form of edible offering made primarily of *tsampa*) and chant liturgies. On the slopes of the rock, to the rear, is a large *mani mantra*.

The large rock and the chapel are considered to be a representation of Zangdhok Pelri, the paradise of Guru Rinpoche, and the benign and wrathful divinities, Zhitrö, reside within the nooks and crannies of the rock. The rock, a mandala of Zhitrö, has a number of 'self-manifesting' signs—the Six Syllables, various tantric syllables, a hand and footprints—on its surface. These two chapels appear to have avoided the destruction of the 1960s. Religious activities are at a low ebb, however, because the small population is unable to easily sustain the monks. Semkye Phuk (Contemplation Cave) is 1/2 hr due north from Drintang.

Söduk Drangsa (The Place Where Poison was Given)

To one side of the Drintang Valley, between the village and Mt Tseringma, is a spectacular jumble of strangely shaped rocks, darkly somber and covered with moss. Guru Rinpoche pronounced each of the rocks as 'self-manifested' and affirmed that the whole represents the complete environment of Pemakö, a fabled pilgrimage site at the great bend of the Yarlung Tsangpo (see page 717). Furthermore, he told of a secret valley (*beyul*) that exists beneath. Söduk Drangsa, located at the edge of the rock formation, is the most sacred site of Drintang: Milarepa's ruined house is on top of Rekpa Dukchen (Poisonous to Touch), a rock shaped like the hood of a snake, where the great teacher was given poison. An adjacent pond is the Duk Tso (Poison Lake). According to legend, it was created when Milarepa vomited some of the ingested poison. To this day, the villagers do not use the water from the small streams that enter and leave the pond.

Tsakpuwa Drubphuk Cave

Geshe Tsakpuwa was the Drin lama who poisoned Milarepa. His cave, at the base of a reddish hill, is on the other side of the Changkha Lhakhang, away from the village proper.

The Death of Milarepa

Geshe Tsakpuwa, a well-to-do lama who lived at Drintang, was jealous of the widespread respect accorded to Milarepa. During a wedding reception, he pretended to honor the master by prostrating to him just like the other villagers. When the gesture was not returned (Milarepa had never prostrated to anyone except Marpa, his teacher), the *geshe* was furious and tried to engage Milarepa in debate. The teacher declined—he preferred the practice of meditating in mountain retreats over arguments about pedantic textual obscurities.

Ostracized by the Drintang community, the *geshe* decided to kill Milarepa with poison curd. This he gave to his mistress to give to Milarepa, promising her a large piece of turquoise in return. When she took the curd to him, he refused to accept it. He already foresaw the situation and, out of concern for the girl, wanted to make sure she received her reward. Milarepa asked her to come back later. The girl sensed that Milarepa knew what was going on and refused to return a second time. The *geshe* finally managed to persuade her, giving her the precious stone right away and promising that he would marry her and that she would have all his treasures.

This was a period in Milarepa's life when his foremost disciples had achieved enlightenment; it was time for him to leave the world. When the girl appeared a second time, he agreed to drink the curd. At this, she was overwrought with shame and guilt and begged him to allow her to drink it instead. Milarepa replied that he had tremendous compassion for her and he would take the poison to satisfy the *geshe* and her. The poison and death were of no consequence as his work on earth was now complete. He then drank the curd.

Milarepa asked all his disciples and followers to come together at Chuwar and taught for many days on the doctrine of *karma* and the essential nature of reality. After blessing everyone, Milarepa went back to Drintang and stayed at his house on Söduk Drangsa, where the symptoms of the poison started to develop. His disciples tried to give him medicines but he refused, telling them that it was now the proper time to die. The *geshe* came and gratuitously asked Milarepa to transfer the poison to him, knowing that this was impossible. The saint refused, but said he would transfer it to some inanimate objects. He pointed his finger at the door of the house and the rock upon which the house stood. Large cracks immediately appeared. Part of the poison was vomited out to create Duk Tso (Poison Lake).

The *geshe* thought these feats an illusion created by a magician and asked again that the poison be transfered to him. Milarepa then decided to give him a small dose by taking a portion from the door. Geshe Tsakpuwa collapsed and was on the verge of death. Having had a dose of his own evil, the *geshe* repented and asked for forgiveness. Milarepa removed the poison and the *geshe* renounced his greed by giving all his riches to the teacher's disciples. He became a devout disciple himself and his money was used each year to commemorate the death of Milarepa.

Milarepa then went to Driche Phuk in Chuwar. As his last rite, he distributed his belongings (the black aloe-wood staff, his robes, wooden bowl, and skull cap) among his foremost disciples—Rechungpa, who became the lineage holder, Gampopa, Ngandzong Tönpa, and Calm Light Repa. Others got pieces of his cotton robe. After some final instructions, at the age of 84, at sunrise on the 14th day of the 12th month in the year of the Wood Hare, under the ninth lunar constellation, Milarepa passed into *nirvana*.

Mt Tseringma (Gaurishanker, 7148 m)

The Tibetans have various names for this sacred mountain: Jowo Tseringma, Jowo Tsering, or Tashi Tsering. It is the westernmost of a group of five holy peaks known

➠

as Tsering Tse-nga (Tsering Five Peaks). The other four are: Tinki Shalzang, Miyo Lobsang, Chöpen Drinzang, and Tekar Drozang. Tseringma is revered by both Buddhists and Hindus. Shanka, northernmost of the twin peaks, represents the Hindu god, Shiva, who is married to the goddess Gauri, the southern peak. It is the holiest mountain for the Sherpas, who call it Jomo Tseringma. In old Tibetan guidebooks, this mountain is the 'snow triangle reaching to the sky'. On its left is the palace (*potrang*) of Tseringma.

A combined US–Nepal team led by Al Read succeeded in climbing Mt Tseringma for the first time in 1979 via the west face. The South Summit was conquered by a British team in the same year. To the east, and higher, is Menlung Tse, known to the locals as Jowo Garu. It is entirely in Tibet. Four sacred mountains in this region merit the title of *jowo*. From east to west they are: Jowo Uyog (Cho Oyu) (8153 m), Jowo Razang (6666 m), Jowo (Jobo) Garu (7181 m), and Jowo Bamare (5927 m)—due south of Lapchi Monastery, its Nepalese name is Kukuraja.

Drakmar Khyunglung Cave Hermitages

This important complex of caves and retreats, associated with Milarepa, is 3–4 hrs from Drintang. To reach them it is best to hire a guide in Drintang.

To Go: Walk up the trail west of Drintang towards the Sobje La (see page 263). After 1/2 hr, there is a fork. The right path goes to Sobje La and Lapchi; the left crosses a small stream to head southwest up a ridge. Take the latter, which follows a water pipe. The trail soon leaves the pipe, goes off to the left and crosses a river valley. It ascends gradually, passing some prayer flags, a cave, and a *shabje* (footprint) on top of a small rock. A 4000 m pass is reached after two hours from the trail fork. This spot, marked by a *lhatse* (cairn), is visible from Drintang. At the bottom of a steep descent are the Drakmar Khyunglung cave hermitages (Red Rock Valley of the Garuda). The following are some of the principal sites:

Rechung Phuk (Kusum Drubphuk)

This hermitage is situated within a rock overhang some distance above the main sites of Drakmar Khyunglung. It is reached by a precarious, rather rotten bridge. The rock cavity has small compartments, which serve as individual meditation chambers (*tsamkhangs*). Close by is Khandro Drora (*dakini* dancing place), where Milarepa sang some of his joyful songs. This grassy area is graced by a sacred spring, known as Mila Terchu, which emerges from beneath a stone slab.

Potho Namkha Dzong (Mountaintop Sky Fort) 3800 m

This is one of Milarepa's famous Six Dzongs (retreats). Basically a simple stone hut, it is the dwelling of a monk, Lama Shenrab, who has been staying here for the last few years. Villagers from Drintang make the long trek up here to bring him supplies. Behind the building, inside the woods, is a spring consecrated to Karmapa. An inscribed ➠

slab testifies to the fact. A short distance away is Kyi Phuk Nyima Dzong (Sun Fort of Joy), marked by the *shabje* of Milarepa, created when he flew from here to Tse Phuk. A delightful story is associated with these two sacred sites: Milarepa and Rechungpa were on their way to Potho Namkha Dzong via Drintang after the latter's return from India. He had traveled to study and was now laden with books. The younger man wanted to stop to rest and pay respects to villagers. Milarepa, however, didn't want the villagers to disturb their planned retreat, so the two went straight up to Drakmar. Rechungpa was miffed by this. At Potho, Milarepa sent Rechungpa to fetch water while he started the fire. On the slopes overlooking the hermitage Rechungpa was sidetracked by the enthralling spectacle of wild mountain goats frolicking and giving birth. In the meantime, Milarepa had burned all the books from India, considering them worthless magical texts, mere distractions and hindrances to one's proper practice.

Rechungpa was livid on his return. He had spent a great deal of effort and money to acquire the library. He now wanted nothing more to do with his teacher. To assuage and entertain him, Milarepa began to perform miraculous transformations. Marpa, appearing as Dorje Chang above Milarepa's head, was surrounded by the Gurus of the Lineage; suns and moons appeared on either side of Milarepa's eyes; five-colored light rays spewed from his nostrils. The disciple, too upset to be impressed, demanded that the books be restored. Meanwhile, the show continued. Milarepa became transparent. He walked through rocks, walked and sat on water, generated and threw flames from his body, and flew through the sky. As an encore, he walked to the main Drintang path and proceeded to slice a large rock into tiny slivers with his bare hands. All to no avail. Rechungpa was still sulking and wanted his precious books back. Milarepa then soared up the sheer cliffs of Drakmar like an eagle and disappeared.

All of a sudden Rechungpa was struck with grief and realized the folly of losing his great teacher over some books of dubious value. He was saddened that Milarepa, in his effort to please him, had gone to such amazing lengths. Anguished, he threw himself down the cliffs. He landed on a rock ledge below and was miraculously unharmed. On the other side of the mountain, Milarepa waited in a cave. Rechungpa managed finally to reach the place and was overjoyed. Afterwards the two went back to Potho. Milarepa then told him that most of the books from India were harmful and only some, like those that discourse on the formless Dakini Teachings, were truly beneficial. Rechungpa then made a prayer and the appropriate scriptures reappeared. At this, Rechungpa made a vow, which he kept all his life, to serve Milarepa with total devotion.

Drakmar Khyunglung

Most of the retreat caves and *tsamkhangs* of Drakmar are situated here, some distance below Potho along a twisting path that circles around a ridge to the north. The ruins of the stone meditation cells dot the front slopes of the mountain. A table-sized rock, with *mani* stones to mark its base, was the platform where the poet-saint sang. These *tsamkhangs* were used by Milarepa's family and his 108 disciples.

Mila Durtrö

Descend from the ruins to a small valley, cross its floor and ascend to Milarepa Durtrö.

➠

This small burial ground is one of the most hallowed spots of Drakmar; Tibetans come long distances to cremate their dead here.

Drakmar Khyunglung Dzong

Further to the south, along the western ridges of the Rongshar Valley, a trail leads to the base of a large hill. This landmark, 'shaped like a *garuda*', gives rise to the name Drakmar Khyunglung (one hour from Potho Namkha Dzong). The hermitage, exquisitely sited, is superb for its absolute seclusion. One of Milarepa's songs pays homage to it:

> *The sky keep of Red Rock Heights*
> *Is where Dakinis meet,*
> *A place of delight that brings*
> *Much inspiration to me.*

Take care when visiting the Drakmar caves. This area, with its steep slopes and near-vertical rock faces, can be treacherous. The Rongshar River rushes 1/2 km below, but there is no obvious way down.

✤ DAY 7 DRINTANG–CAVE SHELTER (VIA SOBJE-OODUNGPU LA) 5 1/2HR

Sobje (3 1/2 hrs from Drintang), the first part of a double pass, is visible from Drintang looking to the northwest: the prayer flags of the pass fly next to a rockslide at the top of the range. The walk up along a well-defined path is wonderful—there are good views of Drintang beneath Mt Tseringma and the entire mountainside is alive with wild flowers during spring and summer. Descend from the pass for a short distance, passing a glacial lake in 1/2 hr. Then walk up the second half of the pass, Oodungpu La (1/2 hr). Sobje and Oodungpu are both knife-edge passes with steep sides near the top. This makes it difficult for snow to accumulate. Crossing them is relatively easy most of the year but the descents are steep.

Some distance below the pass is a flat plateau. At its far end, just before the final approach to Kangchen La, is a narrow corridor hemmed in by rocky mountains, a protected area to spend the night. Be sure to camp before the pass. Some caves offer shelter as well (3/4 hr from the top of Oodungpu). A jumbled rockfall on the right is a habitat for the rare *primula wollastonii*. To some naturalists, the flower's deep purple bells, the size of a thimble and frosted with silver inside, represent the most beautiful primula in the world.

✤ DAY 8 CAVE SHELTERS–STONE MARKER
(VIA THE KANGCHEN-KANGCHUNG LA) 4 1/2 HR

Follow the stone cairns up a well-defined trail along a grassy spine. The trail goes through a rocky area for an hour before reaching the Kangchen La (Big Snow Pass, 4940 m). Kangchung La (Little Snow Pass, 5060 m) is 2 1/2 hr further. These passes straddle the crest of the Karro Pumri Range. Between them is a long amphitheater of glacial lakes, moraines, glaciers, subterranean rivers, and snow fields, all ringed by high rocky mountains. A rewarding place to spend some time. The walk up to Kangchung La is gradual but the descent, through snow, is steep. After the slopes flatten out, walk through a rocky area to reach the flat valley floor. This is the beginning of a long stretch of verdant but uninhabited land. The ground is marshy and wet, and at various points along the trail, wading across diverse streams is necessary. A stone cairn on the west (left) bank of the river signifies the end of the trail on this side (2 1/2 hr from the Kangchung La). Ford to the east (right) bank to continue. Find a dry spot nearby to camp for the night.

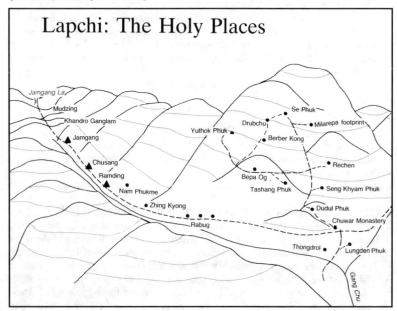

Lapchi: The Holy Places

✤ DAY 9 STONE MARKER–LAPCHI 3 3/4 HR

Wade back to the left bank in 1/2 hr. The river continues along this valley until it drops steeply down into the Lapchi Valley, which runs perpendicular to it. Leave the river before the drop and ascend some low hills to the left. A cave shelter, marked by cairns, is near the summit (1/2 hr). Traverse gradually along grassy slopes to the west, then descend towards the Lapchi Valley, the eastern tributary of the Lapchi Kang Chu. A bridge over a boulder spans the river (3/4 hr).

On the other side is Gidu Phuk, cave shelters and stone corrals for animals, and a good place to spend the night if necessary. Walk southwest (turn left after crossing the bridge) along the right bank of the river. Wade across a swift tributary coming in from the right from a steep side valley (1/4 hr). Continue down the main valley. Across the river, ribbon waterfalls drop vertically. This eastern tributary of the Lapchi Kang Chu is a foaming cataract along here. The well-defined and well-used trail clings to the right slopes some distance above the water.

Go through a rhododendron forest to a spot marked by prayers flags (1 hr). Zigzag down to Lapchi Monastery at the confluence of the east Lapchi Kang Chu and the Takialing

Chu (the western tributary), which comes in on the right from the Jamgang La (3/4 hr). The Milarepa shrine is located practically on the Tibet–Nepal border, nominally under Nepalese jurisdiction. Both of the two valleys trending northwest and northeast from the monastery are in Tibet: the western one leads up to Jamgang La and contains the Nan Phuk cave of Ramding.

(continues on page 268)

Lapchi

Lapchi, the short form of La Rinpoche (Precious Hill), is the celebrated home of Milarepa and the most sought-after pilgrimage site in the Himalayas after Mt Kailash. Pilgrims equate it with Godavari, one of the 24 tantric *tirthas*, or pilgrimage sites, on the subcontinent (most of these have been 'copied' and transferred symbolically to Tibet [see page 130]).

The monastery is built on a forested spur overlooking the junction of the Kang Chu (Lungden Tsangpo) and the Takialing Chu, which originates from Jamgang La— the watershed between the valleys of Lapchi and Nyalam. The entire area is wrapped under a thick mist in the mornings, and in winter, heavy snowfall can pile up as high as the top of the monastery's *darchog* (flagpole).

The architecture of the monastery's main building combines Tibetan and Nepalese styles. The pagoda roofs are similar to those of Tengboche Monastery in Khumbu (Nepal), Chuwar, and Kyirong. A stone wall completely surrounds the temple and its inner courtyard. The monks' quarters stand along the perimeter walls. A long, impressive row of *mani* stones with multi-colored *mantras* are outside the main gate. Pilgrims and traders are welcome to stay in the empty rooms to the right of the main entrance. An ancient, jewel-like stone *chörten*, the Thongdröl Chörten, tops a small hill close by. The lama-in-charge often comes here to circumambulate the monument and to admire the serene setting, surrounded by rhododendrons and medicinal plants.

According to the lama, the monastery, also called Chura Gepheling, is nearly 400 years old. The hermitages used by Milarepa further up the Lapchi Kang Range are even older and date back to the 11th century. The peaks surrounding Lapchi, which are considered sacred by pilgrims, represent the deities of Chana Dorje, Jampelyang, Demchok, and Chenresi. To the southeast is a snow peak called Karpo Bumri.

Inside the main hall (*dukhang*), at the back wall, is a row of seven bronze sculptures enclosed in glass and wood cabinets. Milarepa is the central figure. This image, consecrated by the sage, was supposedly made personally by Rechungpa from Milarepa's nosebleed. It is called Mila Nyikyi Ku Tshal Trakma. A second sacred relic is a stone taken from the site of Milarepa's death. It is believed to be imbued with his vital essence. A *rangjung* image of a *garuda* marks the stone. The walls are panelled in wood and painted with frescoes that show distinct Nepalese influence. Original, exotic *cham* masks are scattered about with sacks of grain. It is fortunate that the monastery was virtually untouched by the Cultural Revolution; both the exterior and interior are in remarkably good shape.

➡

THE CAVE HERMITAGES OF LAPCHI

These ancient cave hermitages represent an even more direct link to Milarepa than the monasteries. Most are only a short hike up the ridge.

Dudul Phuk Some 10 min from Chura Gepheling, across a daisy field, are huge, distinctive boulders. Dudul Phuk (Dudul Phukmoche) cave monastery is under one of them on the right. Milarepa's biography lists it as one of his 'four great caves'. At the base of the Bempo Drakri Ridge, the abode of Demchok, pilgrims identify the cave as the sexual organ of the female goddess, Vajravarahi. A large rock immediately west of the cave entrance is distinguished by its carvings of 'Om Mani Padme Hum'. This *mantra* miraculously 'self-manifested' during Milarepa's cremation on top of the rock.

A small building is outside the cave entrance and its interior is wood-paneled. Look for a small tunnel that leads to a dark inner cave; this is the *drubphuk* where Milarepa meditated. After the sage's death, a transformation of his body was cremated here. At the time, a rainbow appeared and there was a shower of blossoms. In the air was the fragrance of perfume and the sound of music.

Rechung Phuk Behind Dudul Phuk is another daisy field with a few small bamboo shelters built low to the ground. Go through this field, follow a zigzagging path up the hillside (bearing to the right) and pass a stream. Here a big rock with prayer flags marks Rechung Phuk (20 min), which contains a footprint of Milarepa.

Rechen The Rechen hermitage is a bit further to the right of Rechung Phuk, along a level path. Within the hermitage walls, next to a rock, is a cave chapel (*lhakhang*). A meter-tall, wood-carved *chörten*, placed near the back wall, has painted eyes on four sides and bears a striking resemblance to the famous temple of Bodhnath in Kathmandu. Surrounding it are 20 or more wooden sculptures with lovely faded colors. The inside of the cave has wood panels all around, some with paintings. Rechen has been in use since the 11th century. Above this hermitage was another chörten also called Thongdröl.

Milarepa was meditating in Drakmar Khyunglung when he received a vision of a ray of light shooting out from a crystal *chörten*. This was a sign that his disciple, Rechung, was having trouble with his practise—having acquired some black magic tricks from the heretics, he was experiencing difficulty with his breath-control. Milarepa flew from the top of Drakmar and landed at the Rechen cave, leaving his footprints on the rock. He again went into meditation and saw that the younger man was in no imminent danger, that only unwarranted thoughts were intruding on his practise.

Bepa Og Coming up the hillside from Dudul Phuk, instead of turning right at the stream to Rechen, take a left (west) to the two-roomed Bepa Og cave, sited at the base of some cliffs (a short distance before this is the trail to Takshang cave).

➡

Bepa Gong Another of Milarepa's 'four great caves', Bepa Gong is some 50 m above Bepa Og. A small meditation hut has recently been built here. To the west, within a high cliff, is the cave of Yuthok Phuk.

Se Phuk One of Milarepa's 'four great caves', Se Phuk is situated near the top of the Lapchi Kang Range (at the foot of a massive rock wall), highest of the cave temple retreats. Reach it by following a steep trail behind the big rock of Rechen (1/2 hr from Rechen). Se Phuk cannot be seen from Rechen but eight prayer flags high up the range mark the location. The site is a three-room chapel at the base of a cliff face. Near the retreat, to the west, is a sacred spring with many flags. Coming from Rechen, look for a side trail on the right that leads to Milarepa's footprint, also liberally marked with flags; this is the spot where he flew off to Chuwar.

Lungden Phuk This meditation cave, under a large rock, is near the junction of the Kang and Takialing rivers. From the main monastery, a trail skirts the small *chörten* on the hill to follow the Takialing Chu down towards the junction (10 min from the monastery).

Ramding Nan Phuk About 2 hrs up the Lapchi Valley (beyond the Lapchi Village), 200 m to the right of the path, this cave holds an image of Milarepa. During the time that Milarepa stayed at Ramding Nan Phuk with his disciples, some wealthy patrons arrived from Nyalam. They were horrified that Milarepa was sitting with his penis fully exposed. Finally, one of the patrons approached him and offered him a piece of cloth. The saint then stood up naked and sang a song. In this he told the patrons that he traveled so much he had forgotten his native land, that having spent so much time in hermitages, all diversions were forgotten. Likewise, his manners, worldly shame, clothing, and propriety were all cast away. There was no need for him to follow any earthly customs. Buddhahood is spontaneity, he sang.

> Caring for nought, I live the way I please.
> Your so-called 'shame' only brings deceit.
> And Fraud. How to pretend I know not.

Lapchi to Nepal The main Lapchi Kang Chu flows to the south and enters Nepal at a place with no visible frontier and no checkpost. Lapchi was ceded to Nepal by the Chinese in 1962 in exchange for other territorial concessions along the Himalayan watershed. The boundary stones stand very near the monastery. Pilgrims from both countries regularly visit the sacred monastery without undergoing border formalities. The first Nepalese villages, when going south from Lapchi, are Thangchemo and Numu Nagmo. The latter is mentioned in Milarepa's *Gurbum* (Book of 100,000 Songs). At Hom, the Rongshar Chu meets the Kang Chu to become the Bhote Kosi of Nepal. Further down is the Lamabager checkpost and the roadhead at Charikot (see Day 6, page 258).

✤ Day 10 Lapchi–Jamgang 5hr

From Lapchi, the route goes northwest across the Lapchi Kang Range before dropping down into the Nyalam Valley. Pack animals are available at Lapchi Village, on a bluff above the Takialing Chu, 15 min northwest of the monastery. The first section, from Lapchi to the nomad camp of Chusang, is relatively flat and easy. Immediately after Lapchi Village is an area with many stone cairns by the river. Further on, 3/4 hr from the village, a landslide has destroyed parts of the track. Take a short, sharp detour up the slopes on the right. Descend and pass some stone corrals on the right. Here the path becomes level with the river again (3/4 hr). Chusang, the second of the three summer pastures, is 1 hr further at the entrance of a large side valley on the right. It is the biggest nomad camp (over ten tents) on the pilgrimage, a good place to observe and interact with the nomads. Butter and superb yogurt are available.

Chusang It was here that Milarepa was attacked by the king of demons, Bina Yaka, who transformed himself into many Nepalis. They rolled large rocks to try to crush the master, but his powerful meditation protected him. Perceiving Milarepa's immense grace, the demons gave up trying to prevent him from opening Lapchi to pilgrims and became his sponsors. From here, Milarepa went on to Chura Gepheling Monastery at the heart of Lapchi.

After the nomad camp, continue up the main valley for 1/4 hr, then, bearing to the right, go over a low ridge and turn into a narrow side valley. At the turnoff, a bridge spans the main river and a stone corral can be seen on the other side. The trail now starts to climb steadily and the landscape changes dramatically—lush forests are replaced by desolate moon-like scenery. A rock shelter is 1/4 hr from the turnoff. Wade across two swift rivers, coming in from the right, to reach Jamgang, a single stone hut on a narrow spine about 100 m above the river (1 3/4 hr). Campsites are down by the river.

Jamgang At Jamgang, Milarepa meditated on *bodhicitta* ('enlightened mind of compassion'). Jamgang is the Ridge of Compassion, the highest of three summer grazing areas used by the villagers of Lapchi. The path from Jampang up to the Jamgang La, where it follows a gully and ridge, was named Khandro Ganglam by Milarepa, because *dakinis (khandromas)* provided this safe passage for him when he was attacked by rock-throwing demons. The small cave of Shingzang Phuk, used by Milarepa, is on the right side of the trail at its beginning. Notice a large depression enclosed by a terminal moraine wall. Pilgrims identify this as the lake bed of Mudzing (Demon Lake), formed to block Milarepa's way. Beside the trail, look for a rock perched on the moraine. Its deep cavity was supposedly created by Milarepa's walking stick (*chakhar*), which he used to drain the lake.

✤ Day 11 Jamgang–Friendship Highway (via Jamgang La) 5 1/2 hr

Cross the Lapchi Kang Range via Jamgang La (5275 m), also called the Zullekang La.

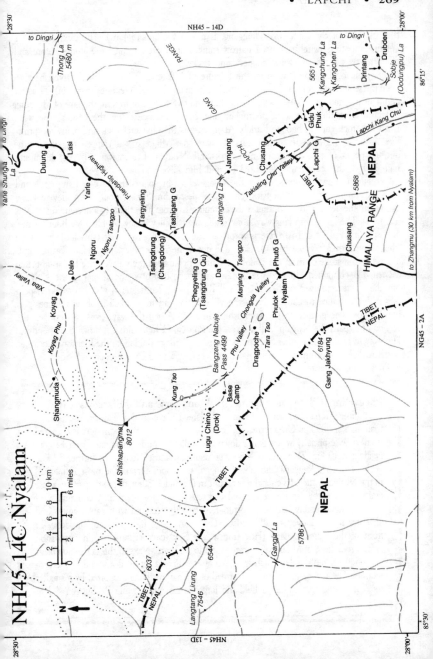

the first part of the route, from Jamgang, is a steady climb (3/4 hr). The next section, 1 1/4 hr, is a steep switchback up a narrow spine. Snow patches and loose stones before and after the pass make the going slippery and tricky.

Jamgang La is renowned in the folklore of Milarepa. When he first arrived here to open the secret valley of Lapchi he was attacked by many demonic creatures (*mimayin*). Thunder and lightning caused avalanches all around him and rivers collided to form the lake of Mudzing. After subduing them, he went on to Jamgang. Some distance below the pass, to the west, is a white rock called Phabong Karleb. At its base is the character Om, and many footprint-like depressions are on its surfaces. It was here that Milarepa was trapped for six months during a period of unusually heavy snow. A disciple, Nyanang Tsangmawa, believing the master had died in the storm, was delighted to find him alive and well.

Further down the pass, before the village of Tashigang, is the cave of Sang Phuk and a chapel founded by Dhuldzin Rinpoche. After descending for an hour, the valley makes a dogleg to the left to join another valley coming in from the right (good camping at this junction). The Friendship Highway along the Nyalam Valley is now visible. One hour further, at a spot marked by cairns, there is a fork in the trail. Ignore the left (this leads to Chura Phegyeling Monastery; see below). Continue down the main valley. Just before Tashigang is a pond with a stone cairn in the middle (1/2 hr). A chapel in the village once had a Jangchub *chörten* that contained Milarepa's relics. An avalanche destroyed the chapel in the 19th C., but the *chörten* survived until the Cultural Revolution. Tashigang is also known as Lapchi Nego, the 'entrance to Lapchi'. From the village (you might be asked to show your passport here) follow a jeep track to the Friendship Highway. Along the way, cross two bridges, the second one spans the Nyalam Valley river, the Pö Chu (1 hr). Turn left down the Friendship Highway to reach road marker 680 km. (Changdong Village is 2 km up the highway. Continue north to Yalep to return to Dingri via the celebrated Thong La, see opposite). South of this is Phegyeling Monastery.

Phegyeling (Place of Expansion) Monastery and Milarepa's cave

Phegyeling Monastery, with its famous Milarepa Cave, is 3 km down the road at road marker 683 km. On a terrace below a roadside village, the monastery is obscured from view, especially when going down the valley towards Zhangmu. From here to Nyalam is 10 km. Zhangmu (Chinese immigration and customs) is a further 30 km.

Formerly Kagyüpa and now Gelugpa, this monastery is the most influential in the Nyalam Valley. Its chapel was rebuilt in the mid-1980s with the help of Nepalese craftsmen. Nearby are the residential quarters for a once flourishing community of monks. The assembly hall is, unfortunately, newly decorated with garish colors and an entry fee is charged to all tourists. The main image here is Guru Rinpoche. In front of the Namkha Ding (Hovering in the Sky) cave entrance is an impression on the rock floor of Milarepa's buttocks and lower limbs. Next to this is the hoofprint of Palden Lhamo's mule, which appeared after Milarepa received a vision of the protectress. The low-ceilinged cave is formed of a large overhang supported by a smaller rock. It is told that Milarepa held the large slab in place while Rechungpa slid in

➡

the other piece. As a result, his hand-print remains. The principal statues in the cave are: Milarepa, Tsong Khapa and his two disciples, and Palden Lhamo. Above and behind the chapel is another cave. This cavity, serving as the *gönkhang*, has as its main image Yamantaka. Also present are masks of the wrathful deities Yamantaka, Mahakala, and Shukden.

Further up is Rechung Phuk with damaged images of Chenresi and Sakyamuni. A bamboo stick, said to belong to Rechungpa, hangs on the cave wall.

Alternate pilgrimage: Dingri to the Nyalam Valley (via the Thong La) 3–4 Days

Dingri–Tsamda–Langkor–Thong La–Tulung–Yalep

After Phegyeling Monastery, instead of exiting to Nepal, it is possible to walk back to Dingri by going over the Thong La, the site where Milarepa had a memorable encounter with Dampa Sangye, the Indian sage. There is no backtracking involved in this option (described in reverse). En route is Langkor, the important pilgrimage center associated with Dampa Sangye. Before the Friendship Highway was constructed, the Thong La was the main pass for trade between Nepal, India, and Tibet. This itinerary provides a nice alternative to the Everest Base Camp excursion.

TRAIL NOTES
✧ Day 1

Tsamda, at road marker 555 km, is 14 km (2 1/4 hrs) west of Dingri along the Friendship Highway. Here the Phung Chu narrows for a few km before broadening out on the wide Sutso Plain. Heading east and then south after penetrating the Himalayas, it becomes the mighty Arun in Nepal. The village is known for its hot spring, which emerges from some unusual rock formation. From Tsamda, a flat tractor path leads south along the wide Dingri plain for 12 km to the monastery and village of Langkor (2 hrs). (Head towards a range of low hills slightly to the right.) Near Langkor, a handsome village appears on a hill to the left. Beyond this, the path reaches a low spur and curves clockwise towards the monastery. The village backs on to the Langkor mountains; the derelict monastery is on a small rise.

Langkor Monastery and Meditation Caves The monastery's ground floor *dukhang* has new statues of Dampa Sangye and Machik Labdrönma, the Indian sage's principal student, one of the few *yoginis* in Tibet to gain prominence. Walk to the back of the monastery. A trail descends the Langkor hill and then, hugging the base of the mountain range, heads to the west. Near the monastery (1/4 hr) is a cave at the edge of a hill. A spring emerges from the grotto, through a tunnel. The water, said to be created by Guru Rinpoche, is considered beneficial for a variety of diseases.

➡

Pilgrims also try to divine their future by looking into the water.

Dudul Drubphuk Continue along the trail to Dudul Drubphuk (Demon-subduing Cave), where Machik Labdrönma meditated secretly to pursue her special practice. She did not allow even her guru, Dampa Sangye, to know her whereabouts.

Dampa Drubphuk From Langkor Monastery, walk along the left bank of the river in front of the Langkor hill. Go past the entrance of a small side valley, then ascend a hill on the right to Dampa Drubphuk, Dampa Sangye's meditation cave (1/2 hr), where the lama's hand-print is on the back wall.

Guru Drubphuk A short distance to the right of Dampa Drubphuk is Guru Drubphuk, a meditation cave of Guru Rinpoche. Between the two caves, a well-used trail continues to the top of the hill (1 hr). Here are ruins of the residential quarters for Dampa Sangye's students and a cemetery (*durtrö*) marked by *tsakhangs* (reliquary for *tsatsas*).

Machik Drubphuk Cross the river in front of Langkor by a bridge. A trail heads towards a range of mountains in the distance, then skirts its edge clockwise to reach Machik Drubphuk (4–5 hrs). Pass several large villages en route. All the villagers know the cave; just ask if you are unsure of the trail. In front of Machik Drubphuk is a footprint, on a rock, known as Machik Trulma Nakmo Shabje. It is deep and obvious. People say when Machik emerged from her retreat, she became her wrathful incarnation, Machik Trulma Nakmo, and left her print here. Within the cavity are the footprints of Guru Rinpoche and Karmapa.

◊ Day 2
Continue southwest from Langkor, hugging the mountainside, by following the Gya Chu; the river is on the left. After 4–5 hrs the trail turns northwest (right) into a side valley that leads to the Thong La. Camp at the valley's entrance.

◊ Day 3
From the valley turnoff to Thong La (5482 m) is 2 1/2 hrs. Pretty blue dwarf poppies (*Meconopsis horridula*) grow around the pass, which offers fine views of the Himalayas. Here, at the top of the pass, is where Milarepa met the Indian master, Dampa Sangye. Follow a steep track down. Large colonies of long-tailed marmots scamper about. Below the pass the valley bottom widens into a plain. Steep, bare limestone hills rise on both sides. The settlements along the way, elaborately irrigated, produce crops of barley and mustard. Oil from the mustard seeds is used in lieu of butter for votive lamps. It is about 4 hrs from the pass to the Friendship Highway.

KAILASH:
THE MOST SACRED OF MOUNTAINS

Ultimate destination for Buddhists and Hindus in Tibet's far west

Location	West Tibet
Map reference	NH44-3 C, 44-7 A
Trekking days	3 (circuit)
Start–Finish	Darchen
Passes	Drölma La

OVERVIEW

Mt Kailash (6714 m), Asia's most sacred mountain, is located in a high and isolated enclave of West Tibet (see page 943 for access). It is one of three pilgrimage sites in the area, known collectively as Kangri Tsosum; the other two are Pönri Ngaden and Lake Manasarovar. All are said to be at the heart of the ancient Shangshung kingdom, the supposed land of origin of the pre-Buddhist Bönpos. Mt Kailash is their soul-mountain (*lari*), which they also call Yungdrung Gu Tse, the Nine-story Swastika Mountain. This is the very place where the sect's legendary founder, Tönpa Shenrab (see Bönri, page 741), descended from heaven to earth.

In the 11th C., with the revival and ascendancy of Buddhism in Tibet, Milarepa, the poet-saint and patriarch of the Kagyüpa sect,

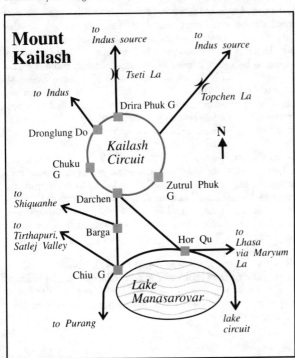

was the dominant influence in the area. This came to pass when he defeated his Bönpo arch rival, Naro Bönchung, in a series of magical contests. Relic traces of this epic battle can be seen from time to time along the ritual circuit (khora) around Mt Kailash. From the 12th C. onward, the Kagyüpa flourished around the mountain and sacred Lake Manasarovar. Monasteries and retreats sprang up and pilgrims arrived in large numbers to pay homage to Kang Rinpoche, the Precious Snow Mountain, holiest of Tibet's peaks. To Buddhist believers, it is the abode of Demchok, the wrathful manifestation of Buddha Sakyamuni. For Hindus, Kailash is the dwelling of Shiva the Destroyer and, according to the Sanskrit tradition of Vishnu Purana (200 BC), it is a representation of Mt Sumeru, cosmic mountain at the center of the universe.

Four major rivers of Tibet, India, and Nepal have their sources near Kailash. These are the Indus, the Satlej, the Tsangpo (Brahmaputra), and the Karnali. The holy Ganges also originates in the general area. Joined by the Karnali, it flows across north India to the Bay of Bengal at Calcutta. The Tsangpo wends its way across the length of Tibet, turns abruptly at Mt Namche Barwa (7756 m), and drains through the Assam Himalayas to enter the Bay of Bengal. To the west, the Indus and the Satlej eventually merge south of the Punjab and empty into the Arabian Sea near Karachi. Tibetans consider all these rivers sacred and their sources even more so.

Leaving aside the mythological and devotional aspects, Mt Kailash is by any measure a stunningly beautiful mountain that stands completely alone in all its glory, with no other peaks near it. Its rounded cone is symmetrical, its distinctive horizontal and vertical striations give it the name Swastika Mountain (the swastika is a Buddhist symbol signifying spiritual strength). Deep valleys along its base allow pilgrims to circumambulate the entire mountain in one long day, a rare possibility in Tibet's high mountain world. The circuit around Mt Everest, by comparison, takes three weeks. Many Tibetan pilgrims attempt more than one round and most do three. The more devout circle the mountain 13 times and from time to time one meets the true ascetic who is hell-bent on performing a staggering 108 circumambulations. Conventional wisdom says a single circuit wipes out the sins of a lifetime, 108 guarantees enlightenment.

This chapter describes the 53-km pilgrim path around Mt Kailash. It begins and ends at Darchen, a small settlement at the mountain's south base and in the process visits four monasteries and crosses the high Drölma La Pass (5636 m). Like its counterpart, the Bönri ritual circuit (see page 741) in southeast Tibet, the Kailash khora is punctuated at intervals by numerous religiously significant nature-formed icons. Over the centuries, diverse rock outcrops, glacial streams and assorted boulders have been imbued with potent spirituality—a result of their frequent contact with saints and holy men. The most important of these are described.

Three days is perhaps the minimum time required to walk leisurely around the mountain: spend two nights in or near Drira Phuk and Zutrul Phuk Monasteries. If conditions permit, try to stay four or five days, which would allow time for short trips to the inner regions of the area. The pilgrimage to the source of the Indus River begins near the Drira Phuk Monastery; for a description of this trek, see page 983.

Although it is not uncommon for hardy pilgrims to come to Kailash in the winter, the best months are between May and October.

Related chapters
West Tibet, page 943
Manasarovar, page 614
Tsaparang, page 430
Tholing, page 425

Access
Darchen, West Tibet (see page 957)

Accommodation and pack animals
Darchen, 6 km off the main Shiquanhe (Ali)–Purang road, is the point of departure for the pilgrimage around Mt Kailash. A basic guest house here was built expressly to accommodate Indian pilgrims (Rmb 15 per bed) but now a more recent Indian Pilgrim (IP) Guest House has better facilities (12 rooms, 5 beds each, hot water, quilts; Rmb 20 per bed). A restaurant serves adequate food and a store has limited supplies. Food in general is a problem at Darchen; it is expensive and limited. During the summer's peak pilgrimage months, food tents cater to pilgrims and travelers. A market opens on the full moon of the fourth lunar month (Saga Dawa, the day of Buddha's birth, enlightenment, and death) and lasts for 2 1/2 months. This is the best time to visit Mt Kailash.

On the pilgrimage circuit, it is possible to stay at one of the six recently rebuilt monasteries; sleep on the floor in a room set aside for pilgrims (leave a small donation in the morning). A good sleeping bag makes the retreat caves associated with the monasteries another possibility. The Darchen Guest House sets up tents for Indian pilgrims every summer near Drira Phuk and Zutrul Phuk. It is sometimes possible to stay in these tents (for a nominal fee). Try to get prior authorization in Darchen. Nomad tents stand near the eastern and western bases of the Drölma La and have a tradition of offering hospitality to travelers (bring your own food). They are seasonal and the number of tents varies. At the IP Guest House, it is usually possible to arrange for yaks but this is by no means certain. Expect to pay Rmb 20 per day for one yak and Rmb 20 per day for a handler. Chöyü Dorje of the guest house can usually have something ready within two days. For the trek, bring a very warm sleeping bag and warm clothing, food for three days, and rain gear during the peak monsoon months of July, August, and September.

Darchen Gön Monastery
This two-story monastery (Drukpa sect) in the center of Darchen largely provides shelter for pilgrims and serves as a trading post. Within the *dukhang* are old and new *thangkas* and a few statues. The main image is Sakyamuni; the murals are defaced and poor. West of Darchen Gön is the small Mani Lhakhang with a large, new *mani* wheel. This site marks the location of the old flagpole (*darchen*) of Darchen. Before starting around Kailash, pilgrims often circumambulate Darchen Monastery and the Mani Lhakhang.

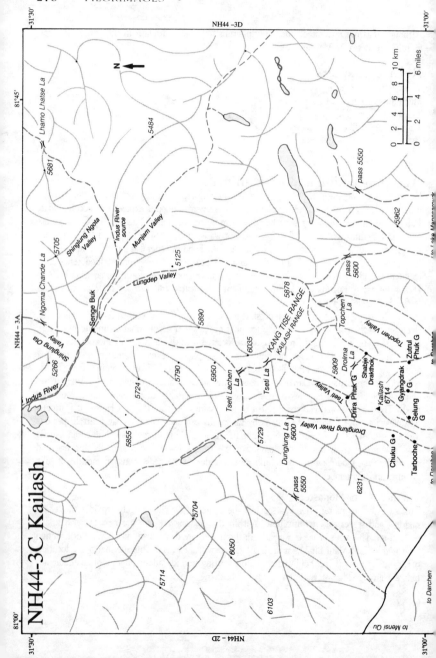

NH44-3C Kailash

THE PILGRIM ROUTE AROUND MT KAILASH

Time Chart

Day	Place	Hours
1	Darchen–Drira Phuk	5 3/4
2	Zutrul Phuk	6 3/4
3	Darchen	2 1/2

Trail Notes

❖ DAY 1 DARCHEN–DRIRA PHUK MONASTERY 5 3/4 HR

Stage 1: Darchen–Chaktsal Gang 1 1/4 hr

From Darchen, the wide pilgrim path leads northwestward, skirting the base of an outlier ridge of Mt Kailash. It is well marked with stone cairns. The peak's south side (Sapphire Face) is visible in a few locations and there are splendid views of the Barga Plain between Mt Kailash and the lakes of Manasarovar and Raksas Tal. The spectacular Gurla Mandhata massif rises to the south and beyond is the great Himalaya Range near the junction of Nepal, Tibet, and India. Clearly defined peaks are Nampa, Api, Saipal, and Darchula. From Darchen to the first of four chaktsal gang (sites of prostration), on a low ridge, is 6 km (1 1/4 hr). At this point one encounters the first good view of Kailash's south face; pilgrims perform their first prostrations here. Soon, rounding the mountain's southwest corner, one turns north to enter the Lha Chu Valley. The view upstream is remarkable. Cliffs take on wild, fantastic shapes, slopes and terraces of scree give rise to myriad gigantic steps, and stone pinnacles soar to great heights. The canyon of red rocks, interspersed by orange, rose, and blue-green strata, appears jagged and irregular. An eerie, haunted feeling hangs over this stretch of the *khora*, among the most memorable on the circuit.

Chaktsal Gang

This spot is marked by a big pile of stones, many carved with *mantras* and images. Surrounding it are cairns and prayer flags hung between rocks. Pilgrims customarily do the following prostrations: the first three towards Kailash, the next three towards Lake Manasarovar, the third set to Tirthapuri (southwest, a sacred site on the Satlej), and a final set to Darchen. After prostrating, pilgrims hang prayer flags and offer incense (*sangchö*) to invoke the region's protective spirits to bless the forthcoming journey around the mountain. The local incense is a shrub called *khenpa*; a red flowering plant known as *shangpe* is also used. Other incense like juniper (*shukpa*) and red and white sandalwood (*tsenden*) is brought to the area.

Stage 2: Chaktsal Gang–Tarboche 3/4 hr

Descend from Chaktsal Gang in a northerly direction along the Lha Chu with Kailash on the right. The valley trail leads to Sershung (up the slopes on the right is Drachom Ngagye Durtrö, the cemetery of the 84 Mahasiddhas), and Tarboche.

Tarboche

Saga Dawa is the most important annual festival of Mt Kailash. During this time, the giant flagpole is ritually taken down and the prayer flags along its length replaced. Tibetans from all over Tibet pour into the area, most of them two or three weeks before the actual date,

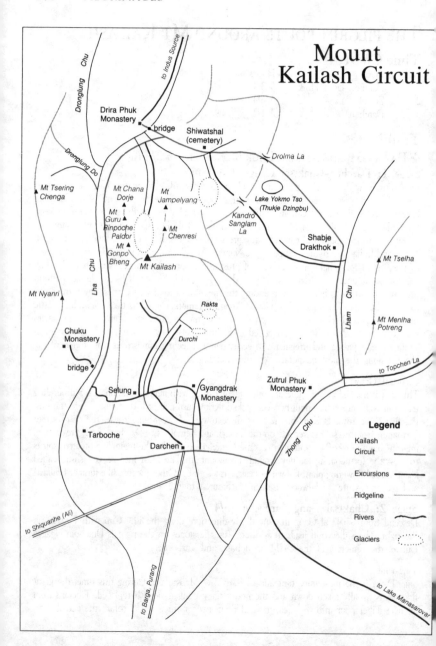

Mount Kailash Circuit

Dronglung Chu

to Indus Source

Drira Phuk Monastery

bridge

Shiwatshal (cemetery)

Dronglung Do

Droíma La

Mt Tsering Chenga

Mt Chana Dorje

Mt Jampelyang

Lake Yokmo Tso (Thukje Dzingbu)

Mt Guru Rinpoche Paldor

Kandro Sanglam La

Shabje Drakthok

Mt Chenresi

Mt Tselha

Mt Gonpo Bheng

Mt Kailash

Lha Chu

Lham Chu

Mt Nyanri

Rakta

Mt Menlha Potreng

Chuku Monastery

Durchi

bridge

Zutrul Phuk Monastery

to Topchen La

Selung

Gyangdrak Monastery

Zhong Chu

Tarboche

Legend

Darchen

Kailash Circuit	
Excursions	
Ridgeline	
Rivers	
Glaciers	

to Shiquanhe (Ali)

to Barga, Purang

to Lake Manasarovar

the full moon of the fourth lunar month. Many bring products to sell and the result is a remarkable carnival. During the flagpole ceremony, as the pole's tip is raised and pointed east towards Gyangdrak Monastery (see below), monks of that monastery perform a special ritual. A cacophony of music from long trumpets, conch shells, and other instruments welcomes the rising flagpole. After the Tarboche is fully upright, Tibetans scrutinize its position for omens. If the column is ramrod straight, all will go well: diseases will abate, livestock will be healthy, and everyone will prosper. If the pole leans towards Kailash, local inhabitants will suffer famine, disease, and perhaps untimely death. If the flagpole tilts away from the mountain, great alarm is generated.

Tarboche's importance is linked to the sanctity of the nearby cemetery of Drachom Ngagye Durtrö, situated on a ridge east of the flagpole. Götshangpa, first explorer of Kailash, and Guru Rinpoche are known to have blessed the site. The latter predicted that the trunk of an exceptionally tall, 'self-originating' (rangjung) tree would serve as the flagpole. The present one is a replacement and lacks the original's vital power (neupa), but pilgrims still chip off pieces of wood to take home as sacred relics.

Drachom Ngagye Durtrö

This cemetery of the 84 Mahasiddhas is noted for a special site reserved for deceased monks and lamas, a spot sanctified in the distant past by the mahasiddhas; some supposedly were cremated here. In the vicinity are caves where the great masters stayed. Devout pilgrims spend hours meditating in them to absorb their special power. Rock outcrops of the durtrö are considered sacred and worthy of worship, and there are piles of abandoned personal belongings—clothing, tsampa bowls, hair, bones, saddles. Pilgrims detour here to leave hair, a piece of clothing, fingernails as offerings. By these devotions, a pilgrim increases his chances for rebirth in the Paradise of the Dakinis (Khachö Zhing Kham) or the Western Paradise of Wöpame (Nubchok Dewachen). Pilgrims sometimes lie down and visualize their death and most have a desire to be cremated here. The stench here is strong due to countless 'sky-burials' over the centuries and the horrendous smell has its own epithet, shendri; it has acquired the sacred characteristic of 'self-origination'. Horses were often used to carry the deceased and thus saddles, saddle blankets, and other effects imbued with the stigma of the dead were sometimes left behind. Significant sites in the area are:

Drubchu

Near the cemetery's base is a tiny spring with crystal clear water, the Miracle Spring (Drubchu) of the Mahasiddhas. Tibetans believe people with proper merit can see straight through it into a subterranean lake.

Khandro Drora

Near the cemetery is an area known as Khandro Drora (dakini dancing place) where the masters stayed to receive visions and vibrations. They held communion with the dakinis and prayed for predictions on the future of their spiritual activities. It is widely believed that this spot is most auspicious during Saga Dawa and that proper religious attributes allow one to perceive these female divinities.

Naro Bönchung Phuk

Along the slopes bordering the cemetery, overlooking the Lha Chu Valley, is the Naro Bönchung

Phuk, cave of Naro Bönchung, the celebrated Bönpo master who competed with Milarepa for dominance over Kailash. Outside the cave, above the opening, is a footprint of Milarepa. During one of many magical demonstrations against Naro Bönchung, Milarepa put one foot here and another at Chuku Monastery (a few km away) simultaneously.

Tshokzhung
Left of the cave, beyond some outcrops, is the Tshokzhung, a large cauldron-like rock believed to be the pot for edible offerings (*tshok*) used by *dakinis*.

Tshechu
Near the bottom of the cemetery is a stream that runs into the Lha Chu. It is the Water of Longlife; pilgrims splash water three times onto their heads and take ritual drinks.

Chörten Kangnyi
Descend from the cemetery to the main *khora*. A short distance north of the Tarboche site is Chörten Kangnyi, a large white *chörten* with a long *mani* wall. Its base consists of two legs and the path leads through the archway. Walking through nullifies past sins. This monument has been recently rebuilt.

Chörten Kangnyi to Selung and Gyangdrak monasteries
From the *chörten*, a side path leads due east to Selung (Seralung) and Gyangtrak monasteries (see page 293) via the Tugsum La. The latter is on the banks of the Gyangdrak Chu, which flows south from the base of Kailash to Darchen (it is also possible to reach Gyangdrak from Darchen by following the river through a gorge due north of the village). From Gyangdrak, a trail leads east over the Shapje La and Gevo La to a point just south of Zutrul Phuk Monastery on the eastern half of the Kailash circuit. From Selung, a trail goes north (after the bridge) to Tso Kapala, the black and white twin lakes, then on to the *chörtens* of Serdung Chuksum. This difficult walk takes 8 hr for the round trip.

Sershung (Gold Pot)
The area around Tarboche is known as Sershung. Once a wealthy trader named Norbu Zangpo hired a pilgrim at Tarboche to circumambulate Kailash on his behalf. A pot of gold, loaded on a mule, was the reward. After the deal was struck, the man and the mule started off. However, not far from Tarboche, the mule laid down and refused to proceed. It finally dawned on Norbu Zangpo that it was a mistake to equate the spiritual value of Mt Kailash with earthly treasures, and he promptly cancelled the agreement. However, the pilgrim still got his gold. From this time on, the place has been called Sershung.

Stage 3: Tarboche–Chuku Bridge 1 hr (bypass Drachom Ngagye Durtrö)
The new bridge to Chuku Monastery is 1 hr north of Tarboche. Simply follow the Lha Chu's left (east) bank, staying close to the slopes on the right. Chuku Monastery is visible from the trail but easily missed; it stands on the flanks of Nyanri Ri, west of the Lha Chu. The path up to the monastery is clearly seen from the wood bridge. Lha Chu Valley in this region consists of near perpendicular ridges of green and brownish sandstone and conglomerate. The

landscape becomes more spectacular as one ascends and the Nyanri cliffs rise like a vertical wall above the monastery. At the turn of the century, a giant block fell and crushed the meditation retreat. After Chuku, paths continue up the Lha Chu Valley along both sides of the river.

Stage 4: Chuku Bridge–Chuku Monastery   20 mins

A steep trail goes up through a maze of boulders carved with *mantras* to this Drukpa Kagyu monastery, considered the dwelling place of Gangri Lhatsum, protector deity of the Kailash region. It was restored in the mid-1980s and now houses a lama and five or six monks. A nearby rock has a rangjung image of a conch shell believed to have fallen from the sky and dissolved into the rock.

Chuku Monastery

Inside the *dukhang*, along the left wall, are small, metal *chörtens* on a platform, statues of Tsepame, and three different forms of Sakyamuni. The center of the back wall is dominated by a highly unusual, original image of Nangwa Thaye. The squat statue, known as Chuku Rinpoche, is made of solid white marble and widely believed to be the most important statue of Kailash. One source claims that this *rangjung* image was discovered at Wöme Tso (Milk Lake), a sacred lake southwest of Tirthapuri. Another version asserts it came from Wöme Tso of Lahoul, India, where seven such images were naturally formed; one of these ended up at Kailash. One popular story tells of an invisible cave near the monastery that once concealed the statue. An old lady on pilgrimage to Chuka chanced to enter the cave and, on discovering the statue, wanted to bring it to the monastery where everybody could receive its blessings. It proved far too heavy to move but in the end the statue spoke out, saying it was willing to relocate. It then moved into her basket and thus became Chuku's central deity. Flanking the statue are peacock feathers and a pair of antique elephant tusks from the sacred elephant, Sala Rabten.

In front of the Nangwa Thaye is a silver-inlaid conch shell called Chödung Thongwa Kundröl. This supposedly has the power to generate a sense of well-being in the penitent pilgrim and can also remove bad *karma*. Legend says it flew magically from Bodh Gaya, India. Behind the central statue are bookcases with a set of 108 brocade-wrapped volumes of the Kangyur. The skylight above gives an auspicious reflection of Mt Kailash in the glass panes; a mirror below provides the same image. Notice the large copper vessel here, an important relic reputedly brought from India by Tilopa. The Chuku Rinpoche statue, the conch shell, and the copper vessel represented the body, speech, and mind of the Buddha.

A *khorlam* surrounds the *dukhang*. Walk along it to a small ochre building overlooking the cliff, the monastery's *gönkhang*. The central image (new) is Kailash's protector, Gangri Lhatsum, a wrathful male divinity and incarnation of the White Indra (Tsangpa Karpo). This being manifests itself in the bodies of oracles and speaks through them. On the left and right are images of Palden Lhamo and Mahakala.

Götshang Phuk

Chuku was founded by Götshangpa Gompo Pel (1189–1258), a Drukpa Kagyü disciple of Tsangpa Gyaré, the sect's original guru and celebrated discoverer of the great Tsari pilgrimage (see page 208). His cave is near the back of the monastery.

Caves of the Mahasiddhas (Drubthob)

South of the Götshang Phuk are more caves supposedly used by the great Mahasiddhas. The middle one was perhaps used by Milarepa; the ceiling was too low for him and in raising it he left behind his hand-print.

Langchen Phuk

At the base of Chuku's large rock is (perhaps) the Elephant Cave that housed the elephant Sala Rabten, whose tusks now reside in the *dukhang*. This cave is consecrated to Guru Rinpoche.

Stage 5: Chuku Monastery–Chuku Bridge–Tamdrin Dronkhang   1 1/2 hr

Go back down from the Chuku Monastery, recross the Chuku Bridge to rejoin the main *khorlam*, and continue north along the Lha Chu's east bank. To the west are the three peaks of Tselha Namsum—Three Goddesses of Longevity (Drölma, Tsepame, Namgyalma). Between the first two is a ribbon waterfall known as Ta Gyangpu Ngama (Tail of King Gesar's Horse). Along the trail, look for a squarish platform of stones. On the top are three votive cairns, small three-sided stone enclosures housing the rangjung images of the long-life divinities. Pilgrims rest here and make offerings of grain, incense, and water.

Drölma Nyishu Tsakchik (Rock of the Twenty-one Drölmas)

Farther to the north is a large rock on which is carved the complete text of the prayer of the 21 Drölmas. It is believed the inscription, a representation of their divine power, appeared miraculously when the 21 goddesses dissolved into the rock.

Kyiki Tapho (Horse of Happiness)

On the right side of the path is a rock with an unclear *rangjung* image of a horse. Milarepa considered this rather insignificant rock very important; it is believed that by riding this horse, one can attain peace and happiness. He left instructions that only those who have completed 12 rounds of Kailash and are now on their 13th are qualified to mount the rock.

Chaktsal Gang

Near the Kyiki Tapho is the second prostration point of the Kailash *khora*. To the east rise the peaks of Gönpo Bheng and Guru Jator; the latter is a squat, dome-shaped outcrop considered Guru Rinpoche's *torma*. Across the Lha Chu Valley, on its west side, are the four peaks of Tselha Namsum and Gesar Tega (Gesar's Saddle). Pilgrims prostrate first to Kailash, then to Gönpo Bheng and Guru Jator, and finally to the Tselha Namsum. Gönpo Bheng (more southerly) has a belt-like band near its base. According to legend, when the mountain arrived here to be with Kailash, *naggas* (*lu*) tried to drag the mountain down into their subterranean world. Palden Lhamo, the protectress of Tibet, came to the rescue by looping a rope around the mountain to prevent it being towed under; the rope mark remains. This is also the spot to discern Mt Kailash's West Door (Nubgo), one of four mythic entrances. Multi-colored lights are said to emit from this opening from time to time. Between Gönpo Bheng and Guru Jator (below and closer to the latter) is a small ridge that represents the *rangjung* saddle of King Gesar's queen, Sengchang Drukmo.

Tamdrin Drönkhang

Upstream from the Chaktsal Gang is Tamdrin Drönkhang. Here a black rock, marked with prayer flags, has a small *rangjung* image of Tamdrin, the horse-headed divinity and wrathful emanation of Chenresi. It is thickly smeared with butter and pilgrims have stuck many coins and paper money to it. They customarily put their heads to the image, rub dirt from the rock, and apply it to their heads. A boulder nearby holds a vivid footprint of Milarepa; it also is studded with coins and smeared with butter.

Stage 6: Tamdrin Drönkhang–Drira Phuk Monastery   1 hr

Beyond the Tamdrin Drönkhang is Dronglung Do, a valley junction where the Chamo Lungchen Chu, flowing from the northwest, and the Dronglung (Wild Yak Valley) Chu, from the north, drain into the main Lha Chu that forms the eastern valley of the Kailash *khorlam*. Granite is on both sides and from here Kailash's peak resembles more than ever a tetrahedron.́ Drira Phuk Monastery, up the valley, is visible. North of this junction, in a green and pleasant area, are the tents of Indian pilgrims. Some distance below the monastery, cross the Kangjam Chu stream (which drains north from Kailash); follow its west bank upstream (due south) for 500 m to find an exquisite, unobstructed view of Mt Kailash's north face.

To reach Kailash's north temple, cross the Drölma La Chu (this flows from east to west into the Lha Chu from Drölma La) by way of a bridge. Then backtrack and ford the Lha Chu (flowing from the northeast) by stepping stones. The monastery can also be visited by means of a trail on the west side of the Lha Chu: cross to its west bank after the monastery comes into view.

The south-facing monastery is on the side of a steep narrow valley near the base of Kailash's sheer North Face. Two huge rock peaks flank the face on the east and west and a prominent ridge connects the east peak to the mountain's East Face. Good views can be had from a flat area just before Drira Phuk, a place littered with cairns and stone enclosures to keep out the chilly wind. Three peaks flanking Kailash are known to pilgrims as Chana Dorje, Jampayang, and Chenresi. The first peak is in the west while the other two are to the east, all clearly visible from the monastery.

Dikyi Drönkhang

Beyond Kangjam is a stone enclosure (*lhaera*) known as Dikyi Drönkhang. Near it are three rocks that contain the imprints of three jackals (*changku*), transformations of Drölma. Seven came to the Kailash area, three dissolved into these rocks, and the rest disappeared into rocks on the Drölma La.

Kusha

From Dronglung Do, the North Door (Chango) of Kailash supposedly can be seen. Below and to the left of the 'opening' is a tall rock that represents a *rangjung chörten*. After the mandatory 12 rounds around the mountain, pilgrims gain enough merit to proceed to the North Door. Underneath the North Door is a soft, malleable clay known as Kusha (Flesh of Kailash). Its sacred, unusual properties inspire pilgrims to dig it out and ingest a chunk, said to have a combination of flavors.

Kar Wöma

Also at this spot is the Kar Wöma, a stream that issues from the heart of Kailash. Pilgrims typically stick their arms into the water and, if they have sufficient merit, might fish out a precious relic. If animal objects, like yak hair or a horse's tail are salvaged, the penitent clearly has far to go spiritually and is liable to be reborn in the animal realm. If special attention is given, one might see Milarepa, Palden Lhamo on a mule, Maitreya, or other divinities emerging from the depths of the mountain.

Drira Phuk (Cave of the Female Yak's Horns)

The Drukpa Kagyü monastery, built around the cave of Drira Phuk, was renovated at the end of 1986. Beyond the south-facing main entrance is an open-air courtyard where pilgrims make tea and rest. Straight ahead is the *dukhang*, within which is the Drira Phuk Cave. It is consecrated to Götshangpa who, according to Kagyü literary records, practiced in the Kailash region from 1213 to 1217. Its ceiling has a *rangjung* imprint of a *dri* (female yak). Götshangpa was the first master to circumambulate and explore Kailash. Local tradition states that he went to Lake Manasarovar on pilgrimage and passed the Lha Chu Valley entrance. Wishing to make tea, he picked up stones as supports for his kettle and was surprised that all had imprints of a *mantra*; every stone in the area was imbued with spiritual significance. A heavy rain started but a *dri* eventually came to the rescue and led him to this cave. She turned out to be a manifestation of the *dakini*, Senge Dongpa (Lion-Faced Celestial Angel). At the rear wall of the cave is a new doll-like statue of Götshangpa (the original destroyed in the Cultural Revolution). It is possible to stay in a pilgrim rest house below the monastery.

The short *khora* around Drira Phuk

The sacred sites along the monastery's ritual circuit are:

Kunlek Drubtak Along the *khorlam* beyond the main building, look for a pile of cairns in front of a large rock. On this rock is an unknown image, which one source claims to be the *lingam* imprint of Drukpa Kunlek, the crazy, lovable yogi who adored many women.

Götshang Drubphuk Above the slopes, within a confusing jumble of large and small rocks, is Götshangpa's most secret cave. It is not visible from the *khora* and even knowledgeable pilgrims may not know of its existence. Ask the monks for directions.

The long *khora*

This 3-hr circuit takes in the ridges and valleys behind the monastery. The route begins near the penis-print rock and proceeds to weave in and out among the rock-strewn slopes of the Drira Phuk Range. Along the way are carved images and *mantras* on rock faces on either side of the path; they serve as trail markers. Regain the monastery at the end of the circuit.

Excursions from Drira Phuk

To the source of the Indus River (see page 983) From the monastery, cross the Kang Tise Range by the Tseti La to reach the source of the Indus, an important place of worship for Tibetan pilgrims.

To the north base of Mt Kailash This 3-hr round trip goes south from the monastery across the Lha Chu and ascends steeply towards Kailash. After some *chörtens*, follow the Kangjam Chu upstream (it flows south from Kailash into the Lha Chu). Near

➠

here, look for a hole with more white clay of *Kusha* (Flesh of Kailash). Scramble over boulders, sometimes following an indistinct trail, to the source of the Kangjam, a dome-shaped glacier with many icicles. Continue up loose glacial debris, along a stream, to reach the spine of the glacier. Clamber up over moraines to an ice field, then ascend 100 m over ice and snow to the top of the Kangjam Glacier. The vertical wall of Kailash is straight ahead, separated from the glacier by treacherous crevasses. And the view is stupendous.

✦ DAY 2 DRIRA PHUK–ZUTRUL PHUK 6 3/4 HR
Stage 1: Drira Phuk Monastery–Drölma La 3 hr

This steep, strenuous, sometimes frigid hike goes from Drira Phuk Monastery to the Drölma La. The altitude gain is some 500 m; plan to spend 3–4 hrs to cover a distance of about 7 km. From the monastery, recross the bridge and follow the right (north) bank of the Drölma La Chu. The trail zigzags up the slopes past innumerable cairns, offerings to Drolma, lining the path. Pilgrims recite the Drölma *mantra* 'Om Tare Tu Tare Ture So Hah' along the way. The last stretch to the pass is very steep.

(Stage 1a) Drira Phuk–Siwatshal 1 1/4 hr

Shama Ri

On the steep ascent eastward up the pass, Shama Ri, east of Kailash, appears to the south. The peak's full name is Shama Ledri Dhongpo, the Eighteen Hells (Eight Cold Hells, Eight Hot Hells, Two Trial Hells), but a more familiar name is Shama Liyi Dhongpo (Tree of Pure Li; *li* is a precious metal used to cast statues). The north side of this sharp, jagged ridge is covered with snow and scarring the snow fields are striated rocks and moraines that give the face a distinctive, furrowed appearance. Cataracts tumble down along the snow and ice fields. In front of Mt Kailash is a short, truncated glacier within a trough-shaped basin. It has small but distinct terminal, lateral, and medial moraines. Immense masses of granite protect Kailash in the north and, to the left, farther north, are amazing pyramidal peaks consisting of fissured granite. Shama Ri is an important spiritual landmark in the circumambulation of Mt Kailash. Its treacherous appearance serves as a sober reminder to pilgrims that hell exists and perhaps looks like this. The devout prostrate towards the mountain and pray that they escape the hellish realms. To the north is Jarok Dhongchen, a peak shaped like the face of a crow. Jarok Dronkhang, a stone shelter, is found after Dhikpa Karnak (see below).

Khandro Sanglam (Secret Way of the Dakinis)

The path climbs to a trail junction called Tangyü from where the route to the Khandro Sanglam La starts. The Senge Dongpa, the same fierce *dakini* who led Götshangpa to Drira Phuk, guard the pass. Only pilgrims who have completed 12 circuits around the mountain are allowed to traverse it. From here the path drops down to the third Chaktsal Gang, situated between Shabje Drakthok and Zutrul Phuk Monastery (see below). Pilgrims walk this route to obtain, near the pass, a piece of sacred Khandrome Kusha ('Flesh of the Dakini'), believed to be effective against many diseases. Rainbow-shaped and multi-colored trails along the hillsides are said to be paths traversed by *dakinis*.

Siwatshal

Beyond the Tangyü trail junction is Siwatshal Durtrö, said to be a replica of the fabled burial ground at Bodh Gaya, India. Here pilgrims undergo ritual death and enter into the horrific presence of Dorje Jigje, Lord of Death, before being reborn on top of the Drölma La. On the ground is an incredible assortment of clothing, bones, saddle bags, hair, shoes, and endless other objects. All who pass leave something, even offerings of blood (cut a finger or scrape the gums). Many lie on the ground and visualize their after-death journey through the *bardo*. A few brave ones stay overnight. Above the cemetery is a red footprint of Milarepa on the surface of a rock.

(Stage 1b) Siwatshal–Drölma La   1 3/4 hr

After the burial ground, the trail flattens out and zigzags between granite boulders. In 1/2 hr, it veers to the right to continue its ascent along a glacial ridge. Numerous cairns and assorted stone piles line the route. And a number of spiritually significant sites are sought out by knowledgeable pilgrims. The main ones are described.

Above Siwatshal reach an area marked with hollows dug by pilgrims who seek the earth as a relic. Small amounts of it are taken home in pill form. A test authenticates whether the soil is special or not: a statue made of *li* metal is held above the pills; genuine ones behave like iron shavings to a magnet and leap to the bottom of the statue. They are then put inside statues.

Shinje Melong

At this point, towards the Drölma La, is a peak to the right of the pass. At its base is a large, reddish outcrop known as Shinje Melong (Mirror of the Lord of Death, Yamantaka), the judgement mirror of Shinje. Its contemplation reveals the amount of sin a person has accumulated. Pilgrims prostrate towards the rock and some perform tantric rituals and recite prayers in the name of Guru Rinpoche's paradise, Zangdhok Pelri.

Bardo Trang

A short distance further is Bardo Trang, a large rock with a narrow tunnel underneath. To be stuck crawling through it is an indication of too much sin. Strictly speaking, pilgrims should perform this test only after completing 12 rounds of the mountain, but most people do it the first time.

Drubtak Shabje

Beyond Bardo Trang are three large rocks piled upon each other. Next to them, closer to the path, is one more rock. According to legend, Naro Bönchung and Milarepa competed here. The Bönpo master first lifted a large boulder to this spot. As an encore, he tried to place another on top of it (his hand-print is on this one). Due to Milarepa's invisible intervention he failed, and the rock rolled down next to the path. To make sure it stayed down, Milarepa stepped on it and thus left his footprint. Next he lifted a large rock on top of Naro Bönchung's and then, to cap it all, placed a third one on top of the pile. Between the top two is Milarepa's head-print. Drubtak Shabje means Sign of Miracle.

Pugu Rangjung

Beyond Drubtak Shabje is a large rock near the path; on its surface is the *rangjung* image of an eight-year-old boy. Apparently the youngster tried to go through the sin gauge of Dhikpa Karnak (see below), got stuck, and starved to death. This serves as a grim warning to pilgrims.

Dhikpa Karnak (White and Black Sin)

Also known as Dhikpa Sigong, this site above Pugu Ranjung is distinguished by a white rock with a red sword-like mark. Here boulders interconnect to create sin-gauging tunnels between them. The first has the narrowest passage. This symbolizes the journey through hell (*nyalwa lam*) and pilgrims within the opening try to experience the sensation of being in hell and then being elevated out of it. This exercise helps remove sin and improve prospects for a better rebirth. They then crawl into the second and third tunnels, which represent passages through the higher realms (*dhe lam*). Within these, the devout concentrate on performing the ritual on behalf of others.

Phame Drilen Tasa (Parent Indemnity Test)

Continue to climb and reach a rock marked by stone cairns. Locate three small holes on the rock's surface. These holes, smeared with butter, are designed to test a pilgrim's devotion to his parents. With closed eyes, try to put a finger in one of them. If a finger connects with a lower hole, it means one must try harder to repay one's parents' love; insertion into the top hole indicates admirable filial piety.

Shenpe Dhiklak (Sinful Butcher's Hand) Chu

Shenpe Dhiklak Chu is a small glacial stream that crosses the *khora* path. Butchers who spend their lives slaughtering animals come here to try to cleanse themselves of bad *karma*. This is customarily done after they have successfully completed 12 circuits of the mountain. Also at this spot, on a rock, is the hand-print of Shenpa Jithuk Gyalpo, one of the 84 Mahasiddhas who worked as a butcher for King Gesar of Ling. He accompanied Gesar to Mt Kailash and on his 13th *khora* washed his hands in the stream and left this hand-print. Pilgrims put their arms into the shallow water to search for a small, black, pill-like substance (*mendrub*) that has powerful medicinal properties.

Guru Buram

Beyond the stream is a round, yellowish rock beside the trail where Guru Rinpoche made offerings to the 21 Drolmas. Rock chippings, supposedly quite sweet, are considered valuable.

Mila Shugtri

This large rock has the syllables 'Om Mani Padme Hum' carved on its surface. Beneath the *mantra* the rock is smeared with butter and has many coins stuck on it. At its base is a natural stone step where Milarepa rested. Pilgrims believe they will be blessed by the poet-saint if they sit here.

Tsechu

After zigzagging up the steep path, reach the stream of Tsechu, Guru Rinpoche's Long-Life River. It appears and then disappears under rock slabs. Pilgrims splash water on their heads, take a drink, and collect water to take home.

Drölma La (5636 m) and Phawang Mebar (Burning Flame Rock)

The actual crossing of the Drölma La, a broad saddle, represents the transition from this life to a new one. Here the pilgrim is reborn and all sins forgiven because of the compassion of Drolma, the Goddess of Mercy. At the pass pilgrims traditionally shout aloud the verbal offerings, 'Lhaso!', 'Kiki Soso Lha Gyalo!', 'Kiki Soso Lasolo!'.

Every stone here is looked upon as representing the Three Jewels, (Buddha, *dharma*, and *sangha* [monkhood]), and each is considered to be imbued with the three qualities of the Buddha: mind, body, speech. In the center of the pass is a gigantic, cubic rock called Phawang Mebar. On top of it are smaller stones piled into a pyramid to support a flagpole. From its top, long ropes with prayer flags are tied to other poles fixed in the ground. Clothing, hair plastered onto butter on the rock, horns, skulls of animals, and countless other objects are piled on and around the rock. Its surfaces are inscribed with *mantras* in yellow and red and there is a *rangjung* 'Om' some distance above the ground. Beneath it, pilgrims gather to rest and celebrate at this high point of the *khora*. Strangers become intimate friends and here, under the Phawang Mebar, vow to become brothers and sisters for life. At the rear, an outcrop is the sacred rock of Drölma Neri, where the 21 Drolmas—after leading Götshangpa to this point—dissolved as wolves into the stone.

More so than other sacred spots on the circuit, pilgrims here daub large amounts of butter on the rock surfaces as offerings and then leave behind something of themselves (a lock of hair, a loose tooth to prevent further dental problems, clothing, *tsampa* bowl, shoes). In return they may take some momento from the pass. They believe such objects, having been in such a powerful spot, have accrued protective properties. Notice the carved *mantras* on the animal skulls. These were brought here in the hope that the slaughtered animals would soon be reborn into a better existence. Pilgrims perform long rituals, apart from circumambulation, on top of the Drölma La—protracted recitation of sacred texts, prayers, *mantras*. The main rituals are the Sangchö (incense offering) and Serkyem (offering of *chang*, tea etc). Personal items like hair, clothing are offered together with the wish that when one dies, this would be the most appropriate place for the occasion. By performing the proper rites here, it is hoped that the subsequent rebirth would occur at a higher plane. It is also customary for pilgrims to eat their best meal on the *khora* here. This observance might further one's prosperity and help to ensure bountiful food in times to come.

On the pass, the savvy pilgrim would look for omens to tell him something of the future. An important indication is offered by the black crows that appear from time to time. The manner in which the bird lands is significant. If the process is smooth and accompanied by a sweet-sounding cry, it is likely that there would not be any obstacle during the remainder of the trip. If the landing is botched and a discordant cackle is emitted, this would imply a treacherous journey and it is then necessary to perform long rituals to try to dispel the bad influences. The burning of incense is another way to look for forewarnings. For positive indications, the fire should catch quickly and then burn strongly with a good crackling sound. If the smoke goes straight up, this is taken to be very auspicious. The reverse of these would presage an uncertain future.

A most compassionate tradition is that of *tshetar*. Animals subject to slaughter (yaks, *dzos*, sheep etc) are rescued and brought up to the pass. After completing the *khora*, these animals are not killed but are well taken care of until they die a natural death. To indicate that they have made the Kailash circuit, colorful braids are tied around their necks. Sometimes a red tassel is affixed to their ears.

Ngödrub Terdho (Treasure Rock that Confers Spiritual and Material Benefits)
One corner of the Phawang Mebar has a number of hollows on its face. Pilgrims take a stone to strike and deepen these depressions. During the process, they visualize leaving their sins in the rock and, in return, receive good *karma* and vitality. This spot is known also as the Dom (Bear) Shabje. Perhaps these hollows were regarded in earlier days as the footprints of bears (mountain spirits).

Stage 2: Drölma La–foot of pass   1 hr
Descend southeastward from the Drölma La. The trail, one of several parallel ones all leading to the eastern foot of the pass, is rocky and steep. In 3 km reach the floor of the Lham (Lham Chukir) Chu Valley, 600 m below the pass. Quite a few grassy meadows are here. (The Lham Chu's upper reaches flow from the north and are called Tselúng. At the river's head is the Tsemo La, not far from the Tseti La that leads to the source of the Indus. Tseti was the old name of the region in which these two passes sit.)

Yokmo Tso
Below the pass on the right is sacred Lake Yokmo Tso (also Thukje Dzingbu, Lake of Compassion; Indians call it Gourikund), which is 50–60 m down from the trail. At 5608 m, it is one of the highest lakes in the world. Yokmo means 'Maid Servant'. Once upon a time, the maid of a rich family had an illicit affair and bore a baby boy. She took him to Mt Kailash and by the lake took a drink. Through carelessness, the baby slipped into the water and sank without a trace. The maid stayed here for days, heartbroken, and spent all her waking hours watching the lake's surface. Finally, a message appeared on a rock next to her. The baby was in fact a deity and he asked his mother not to worry but to perform the 13 circuits around the mountain and then go home a new woman. This small rock, smudged with butter, is still here. Pilgrims circumambulate the lake, but unlike Indian pilgrims, Tibetans do not immerse themselves. In general, they consider immersion a defilement of the sacred water. Instead, they perform ablutions—rituals called *trusol*—to purify and consecrate. Pills that are previously sanctified are thrown into the water and a purification *mantra* repeated. After this, pilgrims take some lakewater and splash it over their heads. In order to make it easier to take some of the water home, they might mix it with earth and then shape the mixture into small balls.

Mt Takgo
A mountain southeast of the lake is Mt Takgo (Tiger Head); some say it resembles a tiger's head with an axe. This axe was used by Shinje, Lord of Death, and the mountain represents one of Shinje's many messengers.

Shabje Drakthok
Near the base of the Drölma La is a large rock close by a stone hut. Ringing its base are numerous stones deposited by countless pilgrims who also clamber to the boulder's top to make offerings of prayers. A *rangjung* Six Syllables and the footprint of the Buddha are on its surface. On a nearby rock are the footprints of Milarepa and Naro Bönchung, the place where the two met as they circled Kailash in opposite directions.

Mila Drubphuk

To the rear of the rock is Milarepa's meditation cave. On its back wall are *rangjung* symbols of a swastika (*yungdrung*), the letter 'Om,' and three thumb-prints of Milarepa. According to tradition, Götshangpa transformed himself into a bird and landed on top of the rock when Milarepa was meditating inside the cave. He then returned to human form and congratulated the poet-saint on his victories over Naro Bönchung; he confirmed Milarepa to be undisputed master of Mt Kailash.

Stage 3: Foot of pass–Zutrul Phuk Monastery 2 3/4 hr

To continue south along the Lham Chukir valley, most pilgrims follow a trail west of the river. An alternative is to walk along the drier east bank, where Kailash can be viewed more prominently. Either way, the going is downhill and easy. The valley, with its rounded sides, is considerably less dramatic than its counterpart, the Lha Chu, to the west of the Drölma La.

Tsering Chenga

Five-peaked Mt Tsering Chenga stands to the east. It is the abode of five sister protectresses, who were entrusted by Milarepa to guard Mt Kailash.

Chaktsal Gang

This prostration site (third on the *khora*), 1/2 hr from the foot of the pass, affords a rare glimpse of Kailash's East Face. The Khandro Sanglam Valley opens to the right (west). A trail within it leads close to the East Face, crosses the Khandro Sanglam Pass, and heads north to rejoin the main *khorlam* at a point east of Drira Phuk Monastery.

Menlha Shabje

South of the Chaktsal Gang, reach the entrance of the Menlung Chu Valley, which opens to the right (west). In the vicinity is a rock with a *rangjung* footprint of the Medicine Buddha (Menlha Shabje). Nearby is another stone known as Men Khuk, the medicine bag of the Medicine Buddhas. Pilgrims circumambulate the area and chip off pieces of the rock to take home. It is said that a strong medicinal smell pervades the vinicity. Tibetans believe the water of the Menlung Chu has potent medicinal qualities, especially good for stomach ailments. Within the valley are many medicinal herbs and minerals and at its north wall rises the sacred peak of Sangye Tongku Potrang (Palace of 1,000 Buddha Images). In the river junction area of Menlha Shabje another river flows in from the east to join the main river. It has its source at the eight-peaked mountain of Menlha Tsengye (Menlha Potrang).

Kunlek Drubtak

A table-sized rock, beyond Menlha Shabje, has *rangjung* penis-prints of Drukpa Kunlek. These shallow depressions have been dabbed with butter.

Zutrul Phuk (Cave of Miracles) Monastery 4863 m

The Zutrul Phuk Monastery is on the right bank of the Zhong Chu (name of the Lham Chukir Chu in these parts). Around the monastery is a large collection of *mani* stones and piles of stones and rocks carved with *mantras*. Also in the vicinity are destroyed *chörtens* and, along the slopes, many meditation caves. On the valley floor are a number of long, finely crafted *mani* walls. And during the summer, Indian pilgrims pitch tents along the grassy meadows.

The Topchen Chu Valley is east of here. Below the monastery is a pilgrim rest house.

Suspended in rows above the monastery entrance are many sheep bones with *mantras* written over them. Beyond is the *dukhang*. On the altar are stone relics, each with a *rangjung* footprint. These belonged to Götshangpa, Karmapa, and Milarepa. Here also is a trident called Mile Changkha, which supposedly belonged to Milarepa. This and Milarepa's stone statue (within the Zutrul Phuk cave) are the monastery's most venerated objects. The trident is carved of a single piece of stone and perhaps dates to the 11th century. Its top was damaged during the Cultural Revolution. Mile Changkha is considered to be a rediscovered treasure (*ter*) and as such contributes to the survival and well-being of Buddhism and the prosperity of the area.

The Zutrul Phuk Cave was the site of the celebrated magical contest between Milarepa and Naro Bönchung, a competition to determine who had the greater power to build a shelter. It was agreed that Milarepa would build the ceiling and Naro Bönchung the walls. Milarepa proceeded to a huge rock and with his bare hands sliced it in two. One part, designated as the roof, he suspended in mid-air to allow the walls to fit underneath. Naro Bönchung, overwhelmed by this performance, was unable to produce the side walls and Milarepa finished the cave-shelter alone. A final test was held to see who could fly to the top of Mt Kailash first. Bönchung started before sunrise, mounted on his drum. Milarepa was relaxed at the base of the mountain, totally unconcerned with the Bönpo's progress; he was waiting for the morning's first light. By catching a ride on a ray of sunlight he reached the top instantaneously, thus beating Bönchung handily. Subsequently, the Bönpos relinquished their hold on Kailash and were given the small mountain of Pönri to the east as compensation.

The cave's most important object is a Milarepa statue made of the precious metal *li*. According to tradition, it was created by the sage himself before his death. The *Jangchub chörten*, next to it, belonged to him. Near the altar is a round protuberance in the cave wall, called Ngödrub Terbur (Gift of Treasure). Milarepa claimed it had great powers to bless and protect. The black ceiling has the hand-prints and head-print of Milarepa; pilgrims imitate him by putting their heads into the depression. These impressions were created when Milarepa used his head and hands to push the roof up. He miscalculated and the ceiling was raised too high. He then climbed on top of the stone to stamp it back down with his foot and left behind his footprint. Near the Ngödrub Terbur is another hand-print of Milarepa, supposedly an exact match of the one on Chakje Drak outside.

Khorchen, the long *khora* around Zutrul Phuk

This ritual circumambulation takes in the religiously significant sites in the vicinity of Zutrul Phuk. The path from the monastery passes a long *mani* wall and some large *chörtens*. It then winds up the mountainside towards the southwest along a well-defined path marked with stone cairns. Allow 3 hr for the circuit. The highlights of this walk are:

Zhalkar Durtrö

This unusual burial ground is known as the White Face Cemetery. Milarepa coined this name when he received a vision of the white-faced Chenresi here. The rocky site has deep fissures, the bottom of which serve as meditation cells. At one end of the cemetery are boulders piled one upon the other, a creation of Milarepa; butter offerings cover the stones. Pilgrims assert that the surface of the cemetery resembles the flayed skin of a human. A short distance away are some small meditation caves within the hillside.

Aphuk Chengak Drubphuk (Eye-shaped caves with *rangjung* 'Ah')

This cave complex once had a monastery (destroyed) at its entrance. The roof of the *dukhang* has collapsed but the walls are intact. At the rear of the building is the first of a series of interconnected caves. The innermost ones, used as meditation chambers, are very dark. In one is the *rangjung* image of the letter 'Ah'. According to tradition, Guru Rinpoche discovered the 'Ah' letter and meditated here for some time with his disciples. Before the chapel was built, these caves looked like so many eyes, thus the name of the complex. Follow the path back to Zutrul Phuk.

✤ DAY 3 ZUTRUL PHUK–DARCHEN 2 1/2 HR

Continue southwest along the Zhong Chu. Cross a footbridge over the Gedhun Lha Chu, regarded by pilgrims as the urine of Kailash. Beyond is the footprint of Milarepa on top of a rock marked by stone *mandals*. Then come to an oval, fissured rock. According to a legend, Dhenma, King Gesar of Ling's general, lay in ambush here for Tselha Dorje of Tazik (Persia). As the latter advanced, he spotted the general and threw his sword at him. It missed but sliced the rock. Dhenma then killed the Persian with an arrow.

Later, ford several small rivers issuing from Mt Sangye Tongku Shugtri to the northwest. About 1 1/4 hr from the monastery is Trangser Trangmar (Gold and Red Cliffs), an amazing canyon of bright mineral colors. Beyond lies the fourth and final Chaktsal Gang. The Zhong Chu now leaves the gorge to enter the wide Barga Plain. Reach a trail junction. The main khora goes west towards Darchen, another trail to the southeast leads to the *khorlam* of Manasarovar, and the south-trending path goes to Barga and Purang. Regain Darchen after crossing a wood bridge over the Darchen (Üma) Chu.

Trangser Trangmar

The gorge of the Gold and Red Cliffs. Go past a *mani* wall and rock carved with the Six Syllables. Next to a cluster of *mandals* is a table-sized rock with the hoofprint of Gesar's horse. Another hoofprint is farther to the west, some distance away (the super horse flew from the first spot to the second). Near the first print are rocks, all marked by stone *mandals*, with imprints of Gesar's hat, Milarepa's foot; and finally the hoof of a wild yak, the soul-yak (*la drong*) of Hor Ghokar Gyalpo, the evil King of the Changtang. This king, the devil incarnate, has a tremendous battle with Gesar. Ghokar Gyalpo was protected by 18 different soul-beings, one of which was the soul-yak that lived in the Dronglung Valley near Tamdrin Drönkhang, west of Drira Phuk. Gesar killed the wild beast at this spot with an arrow; its body disintegrated and the vital organs were scattered around different parts of the *khorlam*. At the same time, vast quantities of blood colored the surrounding valley and this red, contrasting with the yellow earth, gave rise to the gorge's name.

Yokmo Langar Je

Farther along this gorge, the trail curves to the right. A short distance beyond, a 2 m-high rock leans against another rock. Here is the forearm-print of the maid servant who lost her baby at Yokmo Tso. She rested against this rock and left the print called Yokmo Langar Je. Next are a series of rocks that supposedly resemble the liver (Chinpa Rangjung), lungs (Lowa Rangjung), and intestines (Gyuma Rangjung Rimo) of the wild yak. West of Trangser

Trangmar is a range of multi-colored mountains, the Dzam Sernak Rangjung, representations of Zangbala, the God of Wealth.

Jinlab Drubphuk
Beyond the organ rocks is a large rock at the base of which is a tiny hollow. This is the Jinlab Drubphuk (Cave with Consecrated Matter). It contains miraculous earth (*sana*) and water (*chuna*). The stones have different hues, and a bluish one supposedly cures eye diseases.

Nedho Nyungsa (Site for Sacred Stones)
The *khora* path now climbs to Nedho Nyungsa, an area pock-marked with holes dug by the devout in their search for sacred pebbles. Pilgrims, on finding one, put a hole through the center and wear it as a necklace or keep it in the family treasure box (*yangyam*). They believe that the rare stones prevent strokes, epilepsy, and other diseases. Some rub off parts of the outer layer to put into drinks as an antidote to poison.

Chaktsal Gang
This is the last prostration site on the *khora* and represents the southern limit of Trangser Trangmar. Here the Zhong Chu leaves the gorge to enter the Barga Plain. Just beyond is a trail junction, where paths lead on to Lake Manasarovar, Barga, and Darchen. This site has a beautiful view of the wide Barga Plain, with the massive profile of Mt Gurla Mandhata in the background and Raksas Tal in front.

Darchung Marka
Some distance west of the Chaktsal Gang, reach an area of *mandals* and cairns, offerings to Mt Kailash. This is Darchung Marka (Path to the Darchung Flagpole). Pass long *mani* walls to reach Darchung River, flowing north–south from the southern ramparts of Kailash. A flagpole once stood here. Wade across the small river and pass more *mani* walls.

> **Darchen** Cross the Darchen River on a wood bridge to reach Darchen Monastery, the end of the *khora* around Mt Kailash.

The Gyangdrak and Selung monasteries
North of Darchen, within the Gyangdrak Gorge, is the renovated monastery of Gyangdrak. To its west is the Selung (Seralung) Monastery. These two institutions lie within the inner *khora* (*nangkhor*), generally attempted only by pilgrims who have completed 12 standard Kailash circuits. Beyond Gyangdrak and Selung, at the eastern base of Mt Neten Yelakzung, are the twin lakes of Tso Kapala. The water of one is supposedly black and the other is white like milk; the latter contains the mystic key that can open the secret door of Mt Kailash.

Gyangdrak Monastery
From Darchen, cross the Darchen Chu to its east bank. Due north is the Gyangdrak gorge, festooned with prayer flags. Follow a wide path that trends steeply east up a ridge flanking the gorge. The path levels out and eventually the river divides ➡

(3/4 hr from Darchen). Follow the left bank of the eastern tributary; the trail later crosses to the other bank. Finally, reach a grassy plain—Gyangdrak is on top of a ridge. The walk from Darchen takes 2 1/4 hr.

The complex's recent renovation was completed by monks of the Drigung Kagyü sect. Consisting of three main buildings, it was and still is Kailash's largest monastery. The primary structure contains the *dukhang*. West of it is a one-story residence for the monks. To the south is the kitchen. Clay *chörtens* near the monastery entrance receive the *tsa-tsas* of pilgrims. A tall, white Jangchub (Enlightened Mind) *chörten* is at the rear of the main building, and a footprint of Karmapa Rangjung Dorje or perhaps Drigung Kyopön is on a rock near its northeast corner. The main image in the *dukhang* is a clay statue of Drigung Kyopön. Next to it is Apchi, the special protectress of Drigung Monastery, a manifestation of Palden Lhamo, and a statue of Guru Rinpoche. Upstairs is the private residence of the Gyangdrak Lama.

Selung Monastery

This monastery lies 1 1/2 hr from Darchen. From Darchen go north up the Gyangdrak Gorge. At the point where the river divides, take the western branch and follow it north along its left (east) bank. Travel through the Selung Valley, which trends initially to the northwest before turning due north. The ruins of Selung Monastery, smallest of Kailash's five monasteries, can be seen on the valley's western side. It can also be approached from Gyangdrak (a trail goes due west from Gyangdrak, crosses a ridge, then descends to the Selung River and the monastery). From Selung, a trail continues west via the Tugsum La to Tarboche. Another leads to the base of Kailash's South Face (Serdung Chuksum), beyond a field of treacherous moraines. A row of 13 *chörtens* that once contained relics of Drigungtil Monastery's lamas has been rebuilt here. This route essentially circumambulates the pyramidal peak of Neten Yelakzung, south of Kailash. Hindus know it as Nandi, after the sacred bull that kneels in front of Shivaist temples.

THE SAMYE MANDALA

The 8th-C. Samye was the first and most important monastery founded in Tibet by the Yarlung king, Trisong Detsen, and it formally inaugurated Buddhism as the state religion. As the royal chapel of the early kings, Samye is one of the most fascinating architectural showpieces in the country, even more so because of the unusual way in which it was configured. Uniquely designed temples and *chörtens* were placed in specific sites surrounding the cathedral (Ütse) thus creating a large structural mandala. This arrangement, which can still be seen today, replicated the Buddhist cosmological order. Conceived by the renowned Indian masters, Guru Rinpoche and Santaraksita, the Ütse is the only surviving temple in the country whose three floors were constructed in the different styles of Tibet, India, and China.

SAMYE: TIBET'S FIRST MONASTERY

Established over 1,200 years ago, Samye with its unique mandalic architecture was the most impressive monument in Tibet throughout the Yarlung Dynasty (7th–9th centuries). Ranged around this central institution are the important pilgrimage sites of Samye Chimpu (page 631), Hepo Ri (page 629), Drakmar Drinzang (page 628), and the five Surkhar Chörtens (page 312).

Samye is widely recognized as the first monastery of Tibet, the place where monks were trained and ordained for the very first time. The ancient shrines of Jokhang, Ramoche, and Trandruk have earlier foundations but they are temples of worship and not, strictly speaking, monasteries with an attached community of monks. Samye's inception began in the second half of the 8th C., when King Trisong Detsen invited to Tibet the Indian Buddhist masters, Guru Rinpoche, Santarakshita, and Karmalasila, as well as Chinese monks from the Tang Court. The king personally laid the foundation for the monastery at this time; Buddhism steadily gained strength—in 779 it was proclaimed the state religion.

Access
See pages 625, 630 (Map reference NH46-9 B)

HISTORY
Samye played a pivotal role in the advancement of Buddhism in Tibet. It served as the royal temple of Tibet until the end of the Yarlung Dynasty, the 8th C. being the most critical time for the fledgling religion. Although it had the support of King Trisong Detsen and the royal court, Buddhism encountered fierce opposition from the entrenched feudal aristocracy,

who held to the indigenous Bön religion. The ensuing struggle resulted in tremendous hardship for the country. Only through the establishment of an unparalleled monument and center of focus could the new religion from India put down permanent roots. Samye's contribution to Tibet's political, economic, and cultural development also cannot be overestimated. From the beginning of the 8th C. until the late 10th C., it emerged as a major political center of the country.

By the mid-10th C., the effective ruler of the Yarlung Valley was the abbot of Samye. This governing structure became so developed that later dynastic powers were able to exert total control over both church and state affairs. However, the civil wars that were routinely waged in central Tibet at that time began to take their toll on the monastery. Added to this confusion was sectarian feuding over the ultimate control of Samye. Bitter infighting led to the destruction of many chapels and relics, and for the next 100 years, Tibet's first monastery suffered tragically. In the middle of the 11th C., Samye's fortunes changed. The famous translator, Ra Lotsawa, came to the monastery with a few thousand disciples. They banished the incompetent monks and embarked on extensive renovations. From this time on, Buddhism again thrived on the north banks of the Tsangpo.

In the latter half of the 14th C., the Sakyapa lama, Sonam Gyaltsen, wrote an historical classic at the monastery—*Salwai Melong*, an indispensable reference for later historians—and initiated a major program of reform at Samye. Historically, the monastery had always been strongly linked with the Nyingmapa tradition, mainly because of Guru Rinpoche and his close association with Samye's founding. All this changed with the arrival of important Sakyapa lamas like Sonam Gyaltsen. They took control during the Sakyapa ascendancy (15th C.) and confined the Nyingmapas to the background. Later still, Samye came under the influence of the newly powerful Gelugpas. The Dalai Lamas fluctuated between supporting the Nyingmapas and advocating a mixture of doctrines, but in times of calamity and panic they have tended to favor the Nyingmapa lamas' depth of practice and their mastery of the esoteric. In any case, the great institution of Samye has always been an eclectic mix of sects and doctrines. Even today, the number of both Nyingmapa and Sakyapa monks in residence indicates that Samye does not belong to any particular school.

In the mid-17th C., much of the Ütse—the principal structure—was damaged by fire and full restoration did not begin until the reign of the Sixth Dalai Lama (1683–1706). In 1770, in accordance with the will of the Seventh Dalai Lama, a large program of restorations and additions, perhaps the most extensive since Samye's founding, was initiated. The restored chapels were the Ütse, the Lingshi, the Lingtren, and the three buildings attributed to the queens of Trisong Detsen. In 1816, however, an earthquake wreaked havoc on the complex. Ten years later, Samye was again devastated, this time by fire. Scenes of the incident are vividly depicted in some of the later murals. They show the complex being enveloped by flames, the monks' vain attempts to put out the fire, the Ütse being burned, and the subsequent restorations. In 1849, the Kashag (cabinet) authorized more repairs, which took five years to complete.

In the early 1960s, the Chinese Communist Party declared Samye a protected cultural site. Unfortunately this did not stop Red Guards from savaging the monastery; the gold roof and the third floor of the Ütse were completely destroyed. The red, white, black and green *chörtens*, ancient structures of the complex, were leveled. Finally, irreplaceable statues and ritual implements destroyed or stolen amounted to a staggering 40,000 kilos. Yet, by comparison, Samye has suffered far less than most religious centers in central Tibet. Despite wholesale looting and destruction, many of the important temples of the Lingshi and Lingtren still stand, albeit in a sorrowful state of disrepair. Some temples and a large part of the town have been lost beneath encroaching dunes—Guru Rinpoche himself prophesized that the monastery would eventually be buried by sand. Before his death in 1989, the Panchen Lama put aside a large sum to restore the Ütse to its former glory. Construction started in earnest in 1987 and this superb building, complete with gilded roofs, was fully rebuilt in 1989.

EVENTS PRIOR TO THE FOUNDING

In 756, when the young Trisong Detsen began his rule of Tibet, he inherited a coterie of ardently anti-Buddhist advisers. As he grew older and more confident, he began to surround himself with people he had chosen himself. One of these was the Buddhist minister, Ba Salnang, who was keen to learn more about Buddhism directly from its source. Sent by the king to India, he visited the great Buddhist universities of Nalanda and Mahabodhi. From there he went to Nepal where he invited Santarakshita (c 700–760), the renowned abbot of Vikramasila University, to teach in Tibet. After four months of teaching dogma and liturgy within the king's palace, Santarakshita was reluctantly sent back to Nepal because he was unable to thwart the power of the Bönpos.

Continuing his efforts to establish Buddhism in Tibet, the king turned to Guru Rinpoche (Padmasambhava). This celebrated tantric master from present-day Swat was known for his prowess in magic and the mystical arts. His practice was quite different from Santarakshita's formal, academic Buddhism but to a certain extent the two overlapped. On entering Tibet, the great teacher immediately encountered the aboriginal forces residing in the earth and waters of the high plateau. Using his powers of exorcism, he subdued the primordial demons, converted them to Buddhism and transformed them into protectors of the faith. Tibet's local spirits thereby joined the established Buddhist pantheon, becoming full-fledged members of the unique array of deities that characterize contemporary Tibetan Buddhism.

Although presented in mythic form, this story of Guru Rinpoche's spiritual victory symbolizes the coming of the new religion and its determination to conquer the entire land. After an exhausting journey, filled with displays of his thaumaturgic powers, Guru Rinpoche came face to face with King Trisong Detsen in Surkhar, a village just west of Samye. Unmoved by the sage's reputation, the young king stood haughtily and refused to pay homage. Only later, seeing his entire entourage fall to the ground in reverence, did the king perceive the guru's extraordinary aura and prostrated fully. Five stone *chörtens*, known as Chörten Rigna, were erected to commemorate this auspicious meeting.

Guru Rinpoche, the king, and Santarakshita all acknowledged that the most crucial task in propagating Buddhism was to build a truly great monastery in the tradition of Nalanda and Mahabodhi. According to the *Barshed*, a historical chronicle of the time, a pivotal debate ensued between the Buddhists and the Bön adherents—one that was to determine the future course of religion in Tibet. The outcome favored the Buddhists, and the establishment of Samye proceeded.

FOUNDATION DATE OF SAMYE

Tibetan and Chinese sources present a bewildering number of dates for the founding of Samye.

According to Butön, the Shalu scholar (see page 409), construction began in 787 and finished in 799. Demieville's research, however, places the date of the Great Debate between Indian and Chinese Buddhists, which took place after Samye's completion, between 792 and 794. Some sources assert that the building began when King Trisong Detsen was 20 years old, thus giving a starting date of 763. The authoritative Tang Annals support this version by stating that the inception of Buddhism and the building of temples in Tibet began just before the fall of the Tang capital, Chang'an, ie in 763. At present, consensus for Samye's foundation appears to settle around the year 779.

CHOOSING THE SITE
To find an appropriate site for the monastery, Guru Rinpoche and the king climbed Hepo Ri to survey the surroundings. To the west was a large tract of flat land distinguished by pretty white shrubs and herbs; the master confirmed the auspiciousness of the location by geomantic calculations.

CONSECRATING THE FOUNDATION
The king, Guru Rinpoche, Santarakshita, and high officials all gathered for Samye's consecration. Wearing a white robe, the king started to dig at a spot specified by Guru Rinpoche. Three times he dug, followed by his four offsprings, who did exactly the same. Within the shallow cavity, white, yellow, and red earth was seen, a very good omen indeed. In order to suppress the demons of the soil, the king drove four stakes in the form of *chörtens* into the ground.

After the ceremony, Santarakshita drew up the plans for the monastery. The *cubit*, a unit measure used in the blueprints, was the length of the king's arm. Trisong Detsen thus symbolically projected and multiplied himself into the sacred structure. Identified with the Ütse, the central temple, he 'became' the axis around which the entire country revolved. Trisong Detsen wanted an extremely large monument to reflect the glories of Buddhism, so he decided to define the limits of Samye's outer walls by the range of his arrow-shot. His ministers thought this unrealistic, but were afraid to contradict the king. They managed, however, to devise a way to temper the monarch's enthusiasm by injecting mercury into the hollow of his arrow, thus effectively reducing its flight.

CELEBRATING THE COMPLETION OF SAMYE
Trisong Detsen, Santarakshita, and Guru Rinpoche presided over the completion ceremony, an event of great joy and dazzling festivities. A record of the occasion exists in murals along the side walls flanking the Ütse entrance. They show large numbers of citizens crowding into the complex on opening day, singing, dancing and feasting. Between small *chörtens* on top of the perimeter wall, numerous leather sacks containing food and sweets are being presented to participants. Another memorable scene depicts a man racing around the entire Ütse, carrying seven sandalwood pillars on top of his head. At the south entrance, he throws the logs into the air one at a time. so that they land unerringly on top of a door frame. Another vignette shows a man climbing a post and then setting himself on fire!

Tibetans from all over the country celebrated the auspicious occasion for days on end. At times, the huge numbers of umbrellas, flags, and birds around the monastery completely blanked out the noonday sun; the crush of people took up so much space there was no room left for the animals. The citizens sang and danced, hanging on the tails of yaks, imitating the cries of lions and tigers, and putting on animal masks.

The Plan of the Complex

Samye's magnificent complex was constructed in mandala form and based on the Odantapuri *mahavihara* (great temple) of south Bihar, India (Pala Dynasty, 9th–11th century). Ütse, the main structure, has a symmetrical arrangement; its four sides are oriented to the four compass points. It was construed as a representation of Mt Sumeru, the axis mundi of Indian cosmology. At the center of the mandala, Ütse is the mythical palace of the Buddha, the very core of the universe.

Furthermore, it is surrounded by four major and eight minor temples. The first four, known as the Lingshi Lhakhangs, symbolise the major continents situated in a vast ocean to the north, south, east, and west of Sumeru. The smaller eight are satellite islands (Lingtren Lhakhangs). Accompanying each Lingshi on either side are two Lingtrens. Two additional structures represent the sun (*nyima*) and the moon (*dawa*) which revolve around the sacred mountain. A large oval-shaped wall topped with 1,008 small *chörtens* once enclosed the complex. It symbolized the Chakravala, a ring of mountains that surrounds the universe. There were four entrance gates, each a different color—red, green, black, white—and each marked by a large *chörten*. These gates stood facing the southwest, northeast, northwest, and southeast corners of the main temple; their primary function was to suppress demons and prevent calamities. Only a fraction of the 108 buildings in the complex survive.

Samye was once famous throughout Asia for its magnificent library, founded by King Trisong Detsen. More important Indian Buddhist texts resided here than in all the leading Buddhist centres of India. The collection was destroyed by fire.

Sami Dün (The Seven Test Cases)

An event of fundamental importance was the first ordination of Tibetan monks towards the close of the 8th century. After Samye's completion, Buddhist leaders invited 12 Sarvastivadin monks from Kashmir to visit Tibet. The reason for this was that proper ordinations demanded at least ten highly advanced monks as witnesses. Seven young Tibetans were selected to become the first indigenous monks. Ordained by Santarakshita himself, these became known as the sami dün, the 'seven test cases' or 'seven examined men'. They represented an experiment to see if Tibetans had the ability and aptitude to immerse themselves whole-heartedly in the rigors of Buddhism. The seven proved successful, thus becoming holders of the first Vinaya lineage in Tibet.

This pivotal occasion is charmingly recorded on the gallery wall surrounding the Ütse, left of the east entrance. A panel shows the bald Santarakshita sitting cross-legged inside a temple, discoursing to four raptly attentive monks. To the side, two other monks are ordaining a long-haired Tibetan. One cuts his hair and the other holds new monastic robes. In the following years, 300 more Tibetans were ordained as monks and nuns, including two of Trisong Detsen's wives. The king decreed that the state would henceforth be responsible for their livelihood. Practice of Buddhism thus began in earnest at Samye, and renowned teachers came from abroad: these included Santigarbha, Visuddhasimha, and the Kashmiri masters, Jinamitra and Danasila. Due to their efforts, many Buddhist texts were translated into Tibetan. From 781, Trisong Detsen also invited monks from China to teach in Tibet.

THE GREAT DEBATE

Both Indian and Chinese monks were invited to expound Buddhist doctrines at Samye. According to Butön, the Chinese masters taught meditation within the Miyo Samten Ling and lived in the Jampa Ling; the Indians resided in the Aryapalo Ling. Monastic disipline was taught in the Namdak Trimkhang Ling. Grammars and dictionaries were written in the Dajor Tshangpa Ling, and treasures stored in the Kordzo Pehar Ling.

In time, however, a simmering conflict arose between the Indians and Chinese regarding doctrinal interpretation. The king, forced to decide which faction to follow, called a public debate to settle the issue. Pre-eminent teachers of both sects expounded their philosophies within the Jampa Ling in the year 792. Karmalasila, a disciple of Santarakshita, was specially invited to represent the Indian position. He called for a religion centered on the traditional Mahayana teachings. The attainment of *bodhisattva*-hood and enlightenment must be gradual and consist of a systematic program of study and a firm adherence to ethical rules. According to this school, it was necessary to patiently accumulate—over innumerable ages—the required quantities of wisdom and merit to achieve the ultimate goal of buddhahood. No miraculous short cuts to the process exist. This method argues for conventional intellectual and moral training, thereby ensuring the stability of monastic institutions and the orderly propagation of Buddhist doctrines.

The Chinese, represented by Hoshang, concentrated on the absolute nature of buddhahood. They asserted that anyone in an authentic state of quietude, achieved through intensive meditation, can achieve spontaneous enlightenment within a single lifetime. Intellect and morality, the twin pillars of the Indian school, are not necessary prerequisites and in fact can sometimes be a hindrance to liberation. The Chinese method (Ch'an) favors a direct breakthrough to the ultimate nature of consciousness and existence.

The Indians won the debate. Morality and mind triumphed over contemplation and freedom. Nevertheless, many Tibetans, even at that early time, adhered to a Buddhism that emphasized meditation without the need for conventional moral discipline. This state of affairs continues to the present day.

THE SAMYE COMPLEX

ARCHITECTURE OF THE ÜTSE

The main chapel of Samye is the Ütse, also known as Tsuglag Khang. The design was a synthesis of Tibetan, Chinese, and Indian sensibilities. Some sources even believe there was a fourth: Khotanese. Artisans and builders from all the regions participated in constructing Samye. This type of sharing and cooperative construction was rare in Tibet.

South-facing, the three-story structure has a total area of 6,000 sq m. Each level is unusually high, about 5.5–6 m. Fronting the second and third floors are large terraces placed lower than their corresponding main halls. This arrangement allows more light into the interior spaces while simultaneously making the south facade imposing and more elaborate. Because of the unconventional placement of the terraces, it is easy to think the building has five storys. The floor area of each level decreases with height in order to create something of a pyramid effect. For a pilgrim, this gives the impression of ascending a sacred mountain.

The bottom half of this pseudo-pyramid—the cloister, the eastern entrance and the first two floors—is quintessentially Tibetan. This is apparent from the slightly inwards sloping exterior wall, trapezoid windows and doors, and the decorative band at the top. The ground floor is built of stone, the most common construction material in Tibet. This use of a traditional medium at the foundation level symbolizes the country's pre-Buddhist roots. The middle floor, of brick, has Chinese themes. Its ceiling structures and consoles on top of the columns show the considerable contribution of Chinese Buddhist architecture. Some texts attribute a Khotanese style to the original second level and this may well be the case at the time of the Ütse's foundation. Khotan was an important Central Asian Buddhist center and its influence was pervasive even in far away Tibet. Over the centuries, however, it is probable that this floor was badly damaged. Later architects, unfamiliar with the Khotanese/Chinese style and the Silk Road monuments, probably simply substituted a more indigenous interpretation. Thus it is possible that the second level, remodelled in the Tibetan style, was a late addition. The top floor, constructed of wood, is Indian and—as the monument's apogee—it pays homage to India as the source of Buddhism, symbolizing the triumph of the Indian school in Tibet. At the center of the floor is a stepped structure often seen in Indian monuments. The design, known as *prasada panchayatana*, is crowned by a pinnacle in the form of a lotus. Indeed, the architecture of Ütse can be compared with the *mahavihara* of Vikramasila Univeristy or with the Somapura *mahavihara* in Pahapur, India. These edifices have the same cloisters enclosing central temples. The entrances are all oriented to the four cardinal directions, with the main one a structure of monumental proportions. Samye is smaller than the other *mahaviharas* but is unquestionably built along the lines of the Indian models: its central structure, Ütse, represents Mt Sumeru, and the rest of the complex laid out as a mandala. Alone of all the great monasteries of Tibet, Samye retained characteristics unique to the early Pala monuments of India. No others possessed—at least, not to the same extent—the following important architectural features: the close interpretation of the mandalic plan according to Indian cosmology; the incorporation of diverse artistic currents and the use of craftsmen from foreign lands; the uniquely Tibetan idiom of superimposing different design styles on each floor of the Ütse. These three considerations are eloquent testimony to Samye's Yarlung-dynasty origins. In all likelihood, the Ütse and some of its associated buildings were founded at the time of the First Diffusion of Buddhism in the 8th century.

THE BUILDING

Ütse is surrounded by two walls. The outermost is almost a perfect square, and has large entrance gates on the east, north, and south sides, the first being the most important. In lieu of an entrance, the central part of the west wall has a rectangular protrusion. This preserves the overall mandalic symmetry. A damaged section at the south wall clearly shows its construction. Layers of earth and sand are interspersed with layers of *pema* twigs (these form the red roof fringe seen in most monastic and royal buildings). An outer envelope of stone, a later addition, serves to strengthen the wall. Attached to the inner face of this perimeter wall is a two-story wood building. Its lower level is a wide gallery, used as a circumambulatory corridor, and supported by two rows of pillars whose stone supports have fine, carved designs. Splendid murals left of the east entrance depict the festivities following Demo Ngawang Jampel Delek Gyatso's restorations of Samye. Before and after aerial plans of the complex are also shown. Other panels illustrate the mythical world of Shambala. The 35 Buddhas of Confession are spaced at regular intervals along the gallery. Monks quarters are on the upper floor.

The inner wall surrounding the Ütse is considerably smaller than the outer. Two-story

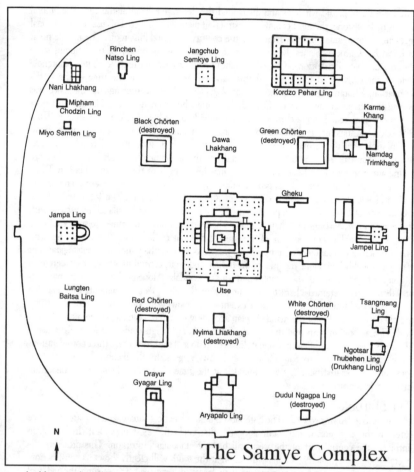

Rinchen
Natso Ling

Jangchub
Semkye Ling

Nani Lhakhang

Mipham
Chodzin Ling

Miyo Samten Ling

Black Chörten
(destroyed)

Dawa
Lhakhang

Kordzo Pehar Ling

Karme
Khang

Green Chörten
(destroyed)

Namdag
Trimkhang

Gheku

Jampa Ling

Jampel Ling

Utse

Lungten
Baitsa Ling

Red Chörten
(destroyed)

Nyima Lhakhang
(destroyed)

White Chörten
(destroyed)

Tsangmang
Ling

Ngotsar
Thubehen Ling
(Drukhang Ling)

Drayur
Gyagar Ling

Aryapalo Ling

Dudul Ngagpa Ling
(destroyed)

N

The Samye Complex

buildings with galleries, each oriented to the cardinal directions, are attached to the west, south, and north sides of the wall. (The east is closed off by the main structure.) Each has a ground floor storeroom that forces the inner wall to make a pronounced extension along three sides. Since the *dukhang* extends to the east, the floor plan of the Ütse is cruciform. The eastern side is composed of an impressive entrance portico and the assembly hall. Flanking the hall are a pair of two-story buildings designed to project monumentality.

Ütse, the central temple, stands within these two outer walls. The ground floor is partitioned into two parts, the *dukhang* in front and the Jowo Khang in back. Outside the main entrance are two stone lions and a *doring*, relics from the Yarlung period (7th–9th century). The Dalai Lama's throne is also here.

Near the main east gate, outside of the Ütse, are the remains of a nine-story structure called Gheku Khang, used to display huge *thangkas* (*gheku*). These embroidered works, depicting Sakyamuni, were shown to the public on the fifth day of the first lunar month and the 16th day of the fifth lunar month.

GROUND FLOOR OF THE ÜTSE
Dukhang

The *dukhang* is the main assembly hall for monks. At the front of the right row of seats is a life-size statue of Guru Rinpoche. On each side of the stairs leading up to the inner chapel are double rows of statues representing the most important personalities in Samye's history. To the left are five statues (L to R): Vairocana (Guru Rinpoche's disciple and one of the first seven Tibetan monks to be ordained), Santarakshita (founding abbot), Guru Rinpoche (this statue is called Guru Ngadrama, 'true likeness of the master'; a stone with his footprint rests in front), Trisong Detsen, Songtsen Gampo.

Right of the stairs are the founders of the Kadampa school: Dromtönpa, Atisha (this Indian master visited Samye in the 11th C.), Ngok Legpai Sherab. These statues are followed by the Manjusri triad: Longchen Rabjampa (a great Nyingmapa scholar), Sakya Pandita (13th-C. Sakya patriarch) and Tsong Khapa (founder of the Gelugpas).

These groupings democratically represent the major figures of the principal sects. The *dukhang* murals (early 20th C.) are a mixture of Nyingma, Sakya, and Gelug styles and themes. Between the *dukhang* and the Jowo Khang are three tall, magnificent entranceways. Symbolizing the Three Doors of Liberation—emptiness, signlessness and wishlessness—they are among the most distinctive features of the monastery.

Jowo Khang

At the back of the *dukhang* is the Jowo Khang, Samye's most sacred and impressive chapel. Surrounding this inner chapel is a circumambulatory corridor with wall paintings that include life episodes of the historical Buddha and some Jataka tales. The chapel's floor is raised and the ceiling, sumptuously decorated with mandala designs and murals displaying the 1,000 Buddhas, is supported by ten eight-cornered pillars resting on stone foundations.

The Jowo Khang has architectural features that date back to Samye's earliest age. Its extraordinary stone walls are more than 2 m thick. According to a well-informed monk, the architects of the monastery at the time of construction asked a well-known *lotsawa*

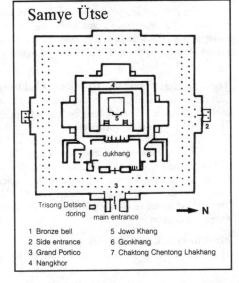

Samye Ütse

1 Bronze bell
2 Side entrance
3 Grand Portico
4 Nangkhor
5 Jowo Khang
6 Gonkhang
7 Chaktong Chentong Lhakhang

Trisong Detsen doring
main entrance

→ N

(translator) to indicate the necessary thickness of the walls. He obliged by fully extending both arms. These walls extend throughout the three floors, showing clearly the brute strength and fortress-like qualities of the early structure.

The principal focus of the Jowo Khang is a 4-m-high stone statue of Sakyamuni decorated with *bodhisattva* ornaments. This image is called Jangchub Chenpo. On each side are five tall standing statues and one protector, all recent works that depict the Buddhas of the Ten Directions in their *bodhisattva* manifestations. In essence they are the Eight Great Bodhisattvas, accompanied by Drimamepa and Kawai Pe. The two giant protectors (*chökyong*), Tamdrin (Hayagriva) and Miyowa (Acala), are the personal guardians of King Tride Tsugten. When Tucci, the Tibetologist, came to Samye in 1949, he reported that the ten *bodhisattva* statues were Chinese in style. Behind the main Sakyamuni statue are vast quantities of texts, including a set of Kangyur and Tengyur. To the right of the entrance is the Dalai Lama's throne.

The Gönkhang

Located at the north side (right hand wall) of the *dukhang*, this dark and sinister chamber contains some of the most important statues of Samye, rescued from the Lingshis and the Lingtrens. They are difficult to identify because of the many scarves—offerings by pilgrims—draped across them. An outstanding statue is the Tamdrin, formerly the principal image of the Aryapalo Ling.

To the right of the *gönkhang* entrance are the statues of Reting Rinpoche and Karmalasila, the Buddhist teacher who represented the Indian school at the Great Debate. At the back wall are images of King Trisong Detsen and Pehar. The latter is the main figure of the room, reputedly made by Guru Rinpoche himself. It is said that anyone who dares unveil the statue will die immediately. At the very back is a stone called Do Padma Je, upon which Trisong Detsen said his prayers.

The *gönkhang* also holds statues of Tseumar, the divinity who succeeded Pehar as the protector of Samye's treasures, and Begtse. Secured to one of the pillars is a huge stuffed snake; next to this is another pillar with a musket and a sword. Look out for the statue of Peldon Masung Gyalpo, easily identified by a stuffed fox dangling from his belt, and a horn and lasso above him.

The Chenresi Chaktong Chentong Lhakhang

This chapel, located to the left of the *dukhang*, is entered via a separate entrance at the front of the building. It is a shrine built by Sonam Gyaltsen in memory of his deceased mother. The central image here, sculpted in relief, is the repaired statue of the thousand-armed Chenresi. To its left are Vairocana (one of the *sami dün*) and Dzokchenpa. At the right corner are statues of Guru Rinpoche and Songtsen Gampo. The remains of Kunga Zangpo, a student of Tsong Khapa, reside within a glass reliquary. Here also is the walking stick of Vairocana. On the day of the full moon, pilgrims come here specifically to receive the blessings of the staff. Stone slabs carved with the images of Atisha, Milarepa, Guru Rinpoche, the Green Tara and others are items salvaged from the destroyed White Chörten. The murals depict the principal lamas of the four sects.

SECOND FLOOR OF THE ÜTSE

The second floor consists of a main chapel and the *tsangkhang*, an upper extension of the

Jowo Khang. This latter is enclosed by the same massive stone walls, a hallmark of early structures. In front of the chapel is an entrance foyer with eight eight-cornered columns. The entrance is flanked by two 1.5-m-thick walls.

The south (left) wall murals depict episodes from Guru Rinpoche's life while the north panels show how Samye looked during its early days. The west wall has a series of portraits of the Seventh and Fifth Dalai Lamas surrounded by Tibet's early kings and Guru Rinpoche. Basically, the second floor chapel mirrors the ground floor Jowo Khang, with a variation in ceiling structures. The highly complicated ceiling design of this room is strongly influenced by early Chinese temples.

At the center of the spacious chapel is an imposing statue of Guru Rinpoche in his semi-wrathful state. As the 'Suppressor of the Three Worlds by means of Inner Light', he holds a nine-pronged *dorje* on his knees and a skull-bowl to his chest. To the left are Jigme Lingpa and Sakyamuni, and to the right Longchenpa and Wöpame, the Buddha of Infinite Light. These two Nyingmapa lamas are among the most important sages to follow Guru Rinpoche. The two Buddhas are of an early vintage and undamaged. The murals show the Buddhas of the Ten Directions, and the circumambulatory corridor is decorated with images from the Buddha's previous lives.

Quarters of the Dalai Lama

A suite of three rooms used by the Dalai Lama whenever he visits the monastery is to the left of the main chapel. Beyond the entrance is an ante-chamber, which leads to the throne room. A noteworthy object here is the jewel-like mural of the Samye complex, in excellent condition and protected by a piece of silk. On the walls of the third room, the bed-chamber, are depictions of Sakyamuni, Jampa, and Drölma.

THIRD FLOOR OF THE UTSE

This floor, built according to Indian design, was destroyed in the 1960s and then rebuilt recently at the instigation of the late Panchen Lama. The main image propitiated is Nampa Nangse (Vairocana).

LINGSHI (THE FOUR CONTINENTS)

At the four cardinal directions of the Ütse are the four 'continents': east—Jampel Ling; south—Aryapalo Ling; west—Jampa Ling; north—Semkye Ling. These four temples are still structurally sound; only the interior was gutted during the Cultural Revolution.

Jampel Ling

This east-facing chapel, only 15 m from the east gate of the Ütse, is dedicated to Jampelyang (Manjusri), the Bodhisattva of Wisdom. It served as the commune office during the early 1980s. An entrance portico fronts the main door, beyond which is the *dukhang* housing a large *mani* wheel. On the walls are paintings of Jampelyang. At the back of the hall is a long passage leading to the back door, which faces the main entrance of the Ütse. Within the passage is a platform. This was where the Dalai Lamas alighted from their palanquins before walking to the central temple. The second floor is a chapel surrounded by a *khorlam* painted with images of the 1,000 Buddhas. Wall paintings in front of the chapel mostly depict Jampelyang.

Aryapalo Ling

The Aryapalo Ling was the first temple to be built at Samye, even before the Ütse, and is the most important of the four *lings*. It was damaged in the early 1960s but has been restored. Located due south of the Ütse, about 15 m from the south gate, this south-facing structure occupies 600 sq m. At the entrance is a courtyard bordered to the east, south, and west by a two-story gallery whose walls are decorated with images of the Buddha and various mythical creatures.

The ground floor of the chapel consists of the *dukhang* and the *tsangkhang*. The latter once had statues (now destroyed) that stood away from the wall. As a result, there is a 1-m-wide space that serves as a circumambulatory corridor. The *tsangkhang's* interior walls are made of 6-cm layers of earth and sand reinforced with layers of *pema* twigs. This is a typical detail of early construction that shows the chapel's roots. Along the sides of the *tsangkhang* are two more chapels.

The second floor chapel is a low-ceilinged room with four pillars. Its wood ceiling has paintings of the Eight Treasures. Two small rooms stand adjacent to the chapel. There are no wall paintings except for the balcony; here are mythical creatures (*devas*) on the backs of dragons, elephants, scorpions, and other animals. Some steps to the right of the main room lead to the Lukhang, temple of the divinities of the underworld. The main statue here is Chenresi.

Jampa Ling

This temple is dedicated to Jampa (Maitreya). The Great Debate between the Indian and Chinese Buddhist factions took place here.

The west-facing, 2-story structure (only the ground floor is intact) is located west of the Ütse, about 30 m from the west gate. The old Samye walls are just behind it. Jampa Ling, a reddish building is made up of an entrance portico, *dukhang*, *tsangkhang*, and a *khorlam*. Murals of the Four Guardians decorate the portico, while the *dukhang* has paintings of Jampa, the 16 Arhats, Guru Rinpoche, Trisong Detsen, and a plan of the Samye complex (left of the entrance).

The *tsangkhang* is the most unusual of Samye's chapels, perhaps unique in all Tibet. Tucci remarked that it resembles one of the sun temples of Taxila, center of the great Gandharan civilization of India. It is semi-circular, with a ceiling supported by four eight-cornered pillars. The main statue is a new Sakyamuni. Murals display large images of Sakyamuni, with small *chörtens* superimposed on the foreheads. Surrounding the interior space is a semi-circular *khorlam*, with paintings of Jampa. All murals are of 19th-C. vintage, painted after a devastating fire.

Jangchub Semkye Ling

Due north of the Ütse, this building has a north-facing entrance and is used as a storeroom for timber. It houses a model of the newly renovated Ütse. Parts of the original walls can still be seen along the inner surfaces of the new, outer stone wall. The ground floor is made up of an entrance portico and a *dukhang* with well-preserved murals. One of the central images, showing only the upper torsi, portrays Bodhicitta, the mother of the Buddha in preaching posture. Her headdress is remarkably similar to that of King Songtsen Gampo. These one-of-a-kind paintings belong to quite an early period, and are rare, little-known treasures of Samye.

THE LINGTRENS (EIGHT SUBCONTINENTS)
Each of the four main 'continents', located at the four directions, are flanked on the left and right by smaller lingtren.

Namdag Trimkhang Ling
Located to the north of Jampel Ling, this was where monastic discipline was taught in the early years. Only two of the original three floors survive. South-facing, the ground floor *tsangkhang* was consecrated to the Buddhas of the Three Ages. The second floor is important for being the residence of Santarakshita.

Tsangmang (Tsenmai) Ling
South of Jampel Ling, the ground floor was Samye's printing press.

Dudul Ngagpa Ling
This temple was dedicated to the Tantrists subduing Demons. Lying east of the Aryapalo Ling, the structure was completely destroyed.

Dragyur Gyagar Ling
A yellowish south-facing chapel to the west of the Aryapalo Ling. Only the ground floor remains. King Trisong Detsen established the chapel for the sole purpose of translating *sutras* from Sanskrit into Tibetan.

Beyond the front entrance is an idyllic courtyard planted with trees and bamboo. A small stream runs through the open space, which is surrounded by a cloister supported by pillars. On the walls of the cloister are numerous scenes depicting translators at work, two to a group, cross-legged and facing each other. One recites while another translates the passage verbally into Tibetan. A third, older monk, sitting at a higher level, makes sure there are no mistakes. Finally a young monk transcribes the work onto paper with a bamboo brush.

The translators came from both India and China; the Chinese worked not only on Buddhist texts but also on treatises on astronomy and medicine. A number of outstanding Tibetan translators emerged from this workshop, including Vairocana, one of the country's three great translators.

Lungten Baitsa Ling
South of Jampa Ling, this chapel, dedicated to Vairocana the translator, was a three-story structure whose top floor was lopped off during the 1960s. The T-shaped temple has a west-facing entrance. A courtyard within the gates is surrounded by a running two-story gallery. The upper-story murals depict scenes from the life of the Buddha. Most of the paintings of the lower level are ruined, but those that remain tell the story of Vairocana.

Miyo Samten Ling
North of Jampa Ling, this destroyed chapel was the site where Chinese masters taught meditation to the first Tibetan monks.

Rinchen Natsö Ling
The Rinchen Natsö Ling (Temple of Multiple Jewels), a two-story chapel and one of the smallest structures of the complex, lies west of Semkye Ling. The ground floor consists of the *dukhang* and an inner *tsangkhang*, and the murals are of large Sakyamuni figures.

Kordzö Pehar Ling

This important north-facing building, to the east of Semkye Ling, is the chapel where Samye's famed protector-deity, Pehar, resided in ancient times. His mandate was to watch over the monastery's treasures.

According to literary accounts, Pehar originally resided in the meditation school of Bhata Hor, east of Kokonor. After the school's destruction, Pehar was brought back to Tibet and enshrined here at Samye. A number of sacred objects, looted from Bhata Hor, accompanied him. These included a marvelous turquoise image of a wooden bird, a lion of crystal, and a leather mask. The mask, called *sipai muchung*, was an object of veneration. Tibetans relate that it was made of congealed blood and possessed powerful magic that enabled the features of the mask to come alive—the bulging eyes would roll suddenly and traces of blood appeared in the whites. Only a few very high officials have ever seen it.

Pehar remained at Samye for many centuries, but finally ended up at Nechung, where he became protective deity of the State Oracle (see page 165).

Nyima Lhakhang

Nyima Lhakhang, the Chapel of the Sun, stood at Samye's southeast edge. The original building is destroyed and in its place is a clinic. This chapel, known also as Tseumar Chok, was dedicated to Tseu Marpo, the red-colored protector of Samye, who took over the job after Pehar moved to Nechung. Tseu Marpo thus became the Samye Oracle.

Before its destruction, Tseumar Chok's upper floor was the residence of the oracle-priest, the Tseu Marpo medium. Next to the *gönkhang* on the ground floor was a legendary and horrifying room. Opened only once a year, it was the home of Tseu Marpo, who sat in judgement of the souls of men. He forced the judged souls to squeeze their way through an extremely narrow window in the middle of the night; the struggle of the anguished was so violent that they left their fingernail marks around the window's tiny opening. A powerful stench of coagulated blood accompanied them—for after Tseu Marpo pronounced judgement, the unfortunate souls were chopped to pieces on a wooden block. Elderly monks recalled that during the night it was possible to hear dull thuds coming from the direction of the chapel. A regular duty of the monks associated with the Nyima Lhakhang was to change the wooden block once a year, the old one being completely worn down.

Dawa Lhakhang

The Dawa Lhakhang, Chapel of the Moon, is north of the Ütse. It is in a fair state of preservation, although usually closed. The chapel is small but important from an archaeological standpoint. The surviving walls date the *Lhakhang* to the Yarlung period (7th–9th century) and are formed of varied, uneven stone pieces, the construction being reminiscent of the early Yarlung tombs. Within are murals of the 1,000 Buddhas. The entrance portico is a much later addition.

The Four Chörtens

Located at each corner of the Ütse, these magnificent *chörtens* (destroyed) were 40–50 m from the central building, and were built after the completion of the Lingshi and Lingtren. Performing a clockwise *khora* from the main gate, the *chörtens* encountered were: white, red, black and green. It is a great pity that none survived the turbulent 1960s; they constitute some of the most architecturally imaginative structures in the complex.

THE PERIMETER WALL

The long, 1.2-m-thick perimeter wall that encircles the Ütse is still largely intact. Its circumference is over one km long and its height averages 3–4 m. Old paintings show the wall to be square, with many right angles, and not oval. Thus the existing wall was built after Samye's foundation in the 8th century.

KHAMSUM SANGKHANG LING

Located 15 mins by foot southwest of Samye, this is the only surviving temple built by the three queens of Trisong Detsen. It is a replica, on a smaller scale, of the Ütse. According to the *Pawo Tsuglag Trengwa*, the Tibetan historical text, the queen built this after giving birth to a son, and the structure was a model of the top part of Ütse. It is likely that the original foundation was initiated just after Samye, towards the late 8th century.

The Khamsum Sangkhang is a west-facing, four-story temple second only to the Ütse in size (4000 sq m). Encircling the main building are two-story monk's residences with four gateways; the one to the west is the principal entrance. Beyond it is a spacious foyer. Fronting the building is a courtyard paved with egg-shaped stones.

The *dukhang* is a high-ceilinged hall with tall pillars extending to the second floor ceiling. The entablatures are elaborately decorated. Two small storerooms stand at each side of the hall. The Jowo Khang lies beyond the *dukhang*. As with the Ütse, the two halls are separated by an entranceway with triple doors. Surrounding the inner chapel is a circumambulatory corridor whose walls are painted with images of Sakyamuni and various protectors. Murals on the Jowo Khang's walls show the 16 Arhats. The rear portion of the second floor is simply a high extension of the ground floor chapel. In front of this is a terrace.

The main chamber of interest on the third floor is a small chapel surrounded by a *khorlam* whose murals depict the celebratory scenes honoring Samye's reconstruction after the great fire of the early 19th century. Other sections of the corridor have paintings of Sakyamuni, Tsepame, Wöpame, and other *bodhisattvas*. Within the chapel are murals of Guru Rinpoche.

The fourth story is the site of the *gönkang*, an ancient, unusual piece of architecture simply and cleverly designed. A *khorlam* surrounds the chapel. Along the outer walls of each of its four sections are two small windows. The chapel itself has four

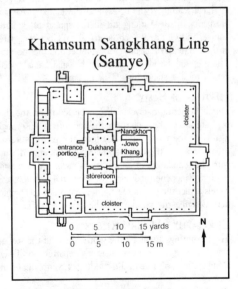

Khamsum Sangkhang Ling (Samye)

entranceways and two large windows along the west wall. Additionally, near the top of each of the four walls are two more windows. Chapels in Tibet rarely have so many openings.

The rationale: this ensures that the circumambulating pilgrims can easily see the terrifying images inside. Also of note are the chapel's ceiling and wood structures. The capitals and entablatures above the four square columns, the ceiling supports above the walls and columns at the four corners of the room, are all distinct and finely carved. Colored mandalas and inscribed Sanskrit *mantras* are outstanding features. The fact that no large ceiling beams are used reflects a strong Indian influence. It is interesting that the Ütse's destroyed third floor was probably quite similar to this chapel.

The *gönkhang* murals consist of Sakyamuni, Tsepame, Wöpame, and various protectors. Those of the surrounding corridor depict protectors, Guru Rinpoche, King Trisong Detsen, and divinities in the *yabyum* position. The unusual architecture of the *gönkhang*, its surprising ceiling and wall support structures, are some of the most impressive in the entire complex.

THE SAMYE MURALS

Samye's murals are noted for their breadth of subject matter and technical expertise. Though not particularly early works, they are valuable for their vividness and their depiction of rare historical scenes. The murals were repainted during the restorations of the mid-18th century. Below are some of the highlights:

HISTORY OF TIBET

These paintings are located along the middle gallery attached to the inner perimeter wall surrounding the Ütse. The first ones cover the very beginnings of Tibetan civilization: the mythical mating of the ogress and the monkey. After these are panels showing the rise and prosperity of the Yarlung tribes, the spread of Buddhism, the building of the Jokhang and Samye, and Guru Rinpoche's arrival in Tibet. The later history, comprising the rise and fall of the Sakya and Phagmo Dru dynasties and the inception of Dalai Lama rule, is also depicted. These episodes end with the Ninth Dalai Lama's deeds. The works, filled with astonishing detail, total a staggering 92 m in length.

HISTORY OF SAMYE

Murals depicting Samye itself can be found on the first and second floors of the Ütse. The best are along the gallery to the left of the east (main) entrance. These detail the entire history of the monastery; they form the pictorial version of the *karchag* type of informative literature about the chapels, their contents, and the monastery's history. The paintings start with the foundation of Samye, then move on to the main personalities and their feats, such as Guru Rinpoche subduing demons by magic before the construction could begin. Numerous panels depict the glorious festivities that followed completion of the complex. Further paintings here describe the building of the other great Tibetan monasteries.

BIOGRAPHY OF GURU RINPOCHE

These paintings are along the south gallery of the second level of the Ütse. They show events before and after the Indian master's departure for Tibet, how he was able to subdue demons along the way, his role in the building of Samye, and portraits of Guru Rinpoche in his wrathful forms.

DANCE, ACROBATICS, AND ATHLETICS

Look for these delightful scenes of celebration in two places: left of the east (main) entrance of the Ütse, along the gallery; in the galleries of the second floor. Some scenes show the lifting of heavy stones, horse racing, archery, wrestling, and archaic contests seldom seen today.

IMPORTANT RELICS OF SAMYE

STONE DORING

This reasonably well-preserved stone *doring* is located to the left (south) of the main entrance of the Ütse. A stele about 5 m tall, it is composed of three parts: the base, the pillar, and a crown. The base, a double-faced lotus, is largely obliterated, although a short Tibetan inscription, deeply etched in the stone surface, can still be read. It reflects on the historical state of the time, the heated struggle between the pro-Buddhist royalty and the entrenched feudal lords who continued to support the Bön religion. The edict upholds Buddhism as the state religion and exhorts the signatories—King Trisong Detsen and his family, the royal houses of various principalities, the queens, the high officials, and all their descendants—to preserve and defend Buddhism at all costs. The *doring* dates back to the foundation of Samye. A stone lion once stood on the top to symbolize strength and power.

BRONZE BELL

This famous bronze bell hangs over the Ütse's main entrance. Inscribed on its surface is a text in ancient Tibetan characters, dedicating the bell to Trisong Detsen and his family and eulogizing him for adopting Buddhism. Gyalmo Tsün of the Phoyong family and her son offered the bell as a tribute to Trisong Detsen. She was the king's third queen and an ardent Buddhist. Bronze bells from the Yarlung period are extremely rare; only three are known to exist. Tradition holds that this one was the work of a Chinese Buddhist master. In recent years, paleo-musicologists discovered that Samye's bell is capable of sounding nine separate notes.

According to the *Barshed*, a work detailing Samye's history, eight small bells were cast. The two now in storage belonged probably to this group. They have approximately the same shape as the larger Samye bell and are also constructed of bronze. On their surfaces are ancient Sanskrit inscriptions and some unidentified designs. The bells (35 cm high, 24 cm diameter) are well crafted and exhibit distinct Yarlung-era features; they were probably created at the same time as the large bell.

LIONS AND THE ELEPHANTS

Two stone lions placed within wood enclosures beside the main entrance of the Ütse date from Samye's earliest years. The animals' inherent power and strength are cleverly captured by the artist. These early works are distinguished by pronounced muzzles and receding foreheads. Two elephants, finely carved from single stones, stand at the front entrance. Their surfaces have been polished to a jade-like finish by the hands of myriad pilgrims.

STONE SCULPTURES

The stone sculptures of Samye are a well-kept secret. In numbers, breadth and quality, the carvings are probably without parallel in Tibet. A preliminary inventory has revealed 1,500 individual works. Most of the statues are stored within two rooms attached to the south side of the inner perimeter wall of the Ütse. Many are carved on oblong slabs of stone measuring between 0.4–0.8 m in length. Pigments were added in later years. Many damaged pieces are haphazardly piled up outside the storerooms, and the remaining collection stored within the

Chenresi Chaktong Chentong Lhakhang. These works are in high-relief and mostly depict historical figures: Guru Rinpoche, Atisha, Milarepa, Tangton Gyalpo and others. The earliest works portray the Sakyamunis. Their simple, unembellished style points to the 15th century. The rest of the collection, mostly high-relief carvings, were created later, during and after the 18th century.

TILES

A fascinating collection of roof tiles purportedly date back to the monastery's foundation. The tiles, red, black and green, correspond to the colors of three of the four original *chörtens*. They are surprisingly varied in shape and the surfaces are inscribed with intricate designs and Tibetan writing.

ENVIRONS OF SAMYE
THE FIVE CHÖRTENS OF SURKHAR

A few km west of Samye are five *chörtens* of differing sizes sculpted out of five huge rocks. (The village of Surkhar is a short distance west of the *chörtens*; on the west side of the Surkhar valley entrance is the ferry plying both shores of the Tsangpo.) These monuments commemorate the spot where King Trisong Detsen met Guru Rinpoche, and are among the most unusual in Tibet for their elongate, archaic design. They align east to west along a single axis and are visible from the south bank of the Yarlung Tsangpo. According to tradition, these works were initiated by Santaraksita.

Each *chörten* has a base, a bell (*bumpa*), and a spire. There are two types of bases—square and multi-sided. The westernmost *chörten* is the largest. Its height of nearly 6 m is unusual for Tibet. A multi-sided base (about 4 m per side) supports a *bumpa*. Its tall spire extends 3 m and is topped by a sculpted sun and moon. The four other *chörtens* extend eastward at varying distances from each other. During the Cultural Revolution the long spires of all five were destroyed. In recent years, villagers used clay to remodel the damaged portions but were unable to duplicate the original lines. Nearby rocks are carved with many figures and deities. Most are of Tsepame. The rest are *bodhisattvas*, Guru Rinpoche, the Rigsum Gönpo, and the Six Syllables. These images and *mantras* were carved at a very early stage, perhaps at the same time as the *chörtens*.

DHO NGAKLING MONASTERY

This monastery, located near the Surkhar *chörtens*, is unprepossessing but highly unusual; secreted in its sanctum sanctorum is the founding lama's mummy, an extremely rare relic in Tibet. Dho Ngakling, a branch of the Gomang Tratsang of Drepung Monastery in Lhasa, is located at the upper end of the Surkhar Valley, a 2 1/2-hr walk north of the Surkhar ferry. It rests on top of a small hill by the banks of the Surkhar River's western tributary. Nearby is Karu Shang Commune situated 1 1/4 hr northwest of Nekar, a village 1 1/4 hr north of the Surkhar ferry.

The small south-facing monastery, a two-story building, was founded in 1438 by Jangse Kunga Sangpo (1366–1444), one of the eight major disciples of Tsong Khapa. Beyond the entrance portico lies the *dukhang*; at the southwest corner is a small *gönkhang* with simple black and white paintings clearly executed by experts. The inner *tsangkhang* holds the mummy, the dessicated remains of the first abbot. It was recovered from the copper burial *chörten* of

Jangse Kunga Sangpo, which was destroyed during the Cultural Revolution. This remarkable relic is still well preserved; only small parts of the body have been torn away by fervent believers. Enclosed within a yellow satin bag made from his monastic robes, the parched lama sits with his head and shoulders between his knees—a typical burial practice in old Tibet.

GANDEN TO SAMYE: A TRAVERSE OF THE KYI CHU–TSANGPO DIVIDE

Location	East of Lhasa
Map reference	NH46-9 B D, 46-10 A
Trekking days	5
Start–Finish	Ganden–Samye
Passes	Jooker, Sukhe

OVERVIEW

Similar to the trek from Dechen to Samye via the Gökar La (see page 625), this itinerary has a rich variety of scenery: from high snowy passes to lush alpine meadows to the desert-like environs of Samye Monastery. Camping along the way is excellent. En route, near the passes, are secluded valleys whose only inhabitants are the high-altitude nomads and their yaks. This pilgrimage route is well used by Tibetans, who find it convenient to combine a visit to Ganden, the principal monastery of the Gelugpa, with a reasonably direct, albeit hard walk to Samye, Tibet's 'first monastery'. The trek, if taken slowly and spaced out with one or two rest days, is wonderfully pleasant. Its two passes are not exceptionally onerous; new visitors to Lhasa should be able to attempt the walk without undue worry about physical conditioning (acclimatize in the city for at least a few days before starting). However, expect foul

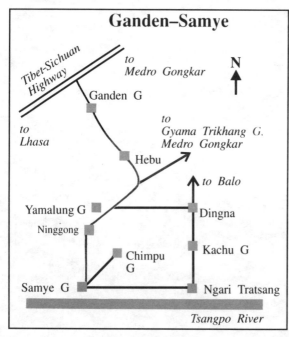

Ganden–Samye

N

Tibet-Sichuan Highway

to Medro Gongkar

Ganden G

to Lhasa

to Gyama Trikhang G. Medro Gongkar

Hebu

to Balo

Yamalung G

Dingna

Ninggong

Chimpu G

Kachu G

Samye G

Ngari Tratsang

Tsangpo River

weather on or near the passes at any time of year. It is best to take along a tent, even though shelter can be found inside a nomad tent or under a rock. The direct return to Lhasa involves crossing the Kyi Chu–Tsangpo Divide once more, from south to north. This can be accomplished via the following passes: Gökar, Tungo (page 597), Tseb/Kampa (page 550), and Se (page 627).

Related sections

Samye, p 295
Ganden, p 140
Lhamo Latso, p 623
Upper reaches of the Kyi Chu River, p 544
Drak Yerpa, p 338
Yön, p 510

Access

Ganden Monastery (see page 140)

Time Chart

Day	Place	Hours
1	Ganden–nomad camp	5 3/4
2	South base of Jooker La	5 3/4
3	Valley junction	7 1/4
4	Ninggong	3 3/4
5	Samye	3 1/2

Trail Notes

✤ DAY 1 GANDEN–NOMAD CAMP 5 3/4 HR

The trek begins just before the Ganden complex at the truck stop. From the road, make a left turn past small stone houses to reach a track going up the slopes. This is also the beginning of the Ganden *khora*, the ritual circuit which encircles the Ganden ridge. In 1/4 hr, it forks. Take the lower left (the upper right continues along the *khora*), which contours along one side of the Wangku Ri. Pass a stone cairn (*lhatse*) and then reach a saddle on the ridge (1 1/4 hr from Ganden), also marked by a *lhatse*. The upper Hebu Valley can be seen below, left of the ridge. It branches into two side valleys; a village stands near the entrance of the nearer one. The path down from the saddle passes this village. Another landmark to look for is a distinctive cliff that borders the far side valley. Head generally towards it along a distinct trail. Walk 3 hr from the saddle to Hebu Village on the right bank of a river, takes three hours. Pack animals can be hired here.

Wade to the left bank (during the summer the river is 1 m deep), then walk up the far branch of the Hebu Valley. (Do not go up the side valley closest to the village.) After passing the steep cliff face, watch out for a large cave on the left and other suitable camping spots (1 hr). Nomad tents on the right (1/2 hr), at the entrance of a tributary valley, might also be a source for horses or yaks. Have a good rest here before tackling the pass.

✤ Day 2 Nomad Camp–South Base of the Jooker La   5 3/4 hr

This is the day of the pass. Make sure to start early for the strenuous day. From the nomads, continue up the Hebu Valley. The path heads due south by following the river's right (east) bank. Pass the entrances of two side valleys opening to left and right. Ignore these and continue the ascent. The trail climbing to the Jooker La is indistinct at times and the going can be quite steep. From the nomad camp to the pass (tucked away to the left) takes 4 hr. Look back from the top to see a grand panorama of mountain ranges stretching away to the north. Ahead is a long waterfall.

From the pass, walk down scree slopes strewn with rocks. The start of the trail down is indistinct and may take effort to find. It follows the scree slopes, bearing to the left. Zigzag along the higher stretches of the ridge before straightening out once the trail becomes distinct. Reach the floor of a river valley in 1 1/2 hr. Follow the right bank southward. This pleasant valley has excellent camping sites along the river. Next to the entrance of a side valley are nomad tents and, across the valley, stone enclosures for animals. They provide some relief from the unsettled weather in these parts. The path to Samye turns right up this side valley, following the west bank of the river. (A second, wider valley is a short distance further to the east; it contains a lake. At the head of this valley is Kampa La, which allows access either north to the Gyama Valley or south to Samye [see page 550].)

✤ Day 3 South Base of Jooker La–Valley Junction   7 1/4 hr

Walk up this first side valley to the Sukhe La, lower and easier than the Jooker La (3 hr from the valley floor). The climb is gradual except for a short, steep section near the top. Descend past two glacial lakes, ringed by large rock formations, in 1 hr (the path skirts their western shores). 1 hr beyond them is a nomad settlement. The valley then narrows into a short gorge before opening to grassy meadows, a lovely section of the walk. Pass more nomad tents to reach a rocky valley junction. Camp near here. From the last lake to the junction is 3 1/4 hr.

✤ Day 4 Valley Junction–Ninggong   3 3/4 hr

Head southwestward by descending the valley to the right of the junction. Cross a log bridge and follow the left bank of the river. This valley is distinguished by spindly trees. (Grassy clearings and ample firewood make the area quite suitable for camping.) Pass a deserted house on the right, then a *lhatse* and a village (2 1/4 hr). 1 hr further, a path goes up the slopes on the right (across the river) to the renowned Yamalung hermitage (see page 627). Ninggong Village, 1/2 hr further, is at the Gökar La–Samye Valley junction. A right (north) turn at this point leads to Dechen and Lhasa via the Gökar La Pass.

✤ Day 5 Ninggong–Samye   3 1/2 hr

Turn left (south) at Ninggong to walk down the easy Samye Valley. Samye Monastery is 3 1/2 hr from the Yamalung turnoff (see page 627 for more details on this section).

GURU RINPOCHE'S INCREDIBLE CAVE COMPLEXES

Drakyul and Jinka contain unusual hermitages sited within elaborate cave systems of small and large grottoes, all linked by convoluted passages. Legends ascribe their discovery and initial exploration to Guru Rinpoche, the Indian tantric master who introduced Buddhism to Tibet. Inside the labyrinths of Drak Yong Dzong, Dzong Kumbum, and Jinka are shrines, assembly halls, and wonderful arrays of natural images and icons formed by the erosion of limestone. Many colorful myths are associated with these peculiar stone formations, all held in great esteem by pilgrims.

DRAKYUL: TWO LABYRINTHINE HERMITAGES

A hidden world of cathedral-like grottoes, subterranean rivers and mythical valleys

OVERVIEW

Drakyul is an ancient district sited on the north bank of the Yarlung Tsangpo. Centered between Samye in the east and Dorje Drak in the west, it extends from the Tsangpo Basin north to the Yartö Drak range of mountains. In spite of its proximity to Lhasa (30 km south), Drakyul is surprisingly isolated. Locals usually depend on ferries to enter and leave the area.

The two cave systems of Drakyul are archaic Buddhist centers imbued with otherworldly

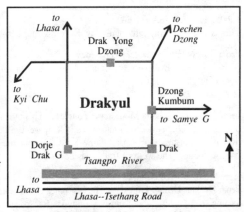

power and a palpable aura of mystery; their labyrinthine complexes are among the most fascinating and unorthodox religious monuments in Tibet. Simple man-made shrines merge with nature's own intricate creations to form these secret sanctuaries. The very simplicity of Drakyul's unembellished caves confers upon them a primordial potency. Vast limestone structures, they are a maze of small and large grottoes, narrow twisting tunnels, subterranean lakes and rivers, and bizarre structural formations. Although there are few sculptures and paintings, the interiors—often hidden behind unassuming cave openings—are surprisingly rich in natural iconography. The caves' own morphology—cracks, designs, and patterns—takes on tantric and organic significance, thus becoming an integral part of the sacred.

During the reign of Songtsen Gampo, Drakyul was identified with Karchen, one of seven petty kingdoms that later formed part of unified Tibet. Because of their association with Guru Rinpoche, Tibet's first tantric master, the Drakyul caves are considered a premier holy site, one of five principal 'power places' in Tibet. The famed yogini Yeshe Tsogyal, consort of Guru Rinpoche and princess of Karchen, was born near Tsogyal Latso, a sacred pond near the entrance of Drakyul Valley. Pilgrims visit this site, known as 'the soul-lake of the consort', to divine their past and future on the water's surface. They also claim that Drakyul's two systems, Drak Yong Dzong and Dzong Kumbum, are 'hidden valleys' (beyuls), inviolate sanctuaries for the Tibetan people in times of crisis. Other highlights of the region include an intact fortress, one of the very few in Central Tibet, petroglyphs, and hermitages.

The climate and geography of Drakyul do not permit extensive habitation. The land is rugged and inhospitable. Its lower reaches, near the north bank of the Yarlung Tsangpo, are severely encroached by sand. Drakyul's forests have long been decimated by indiscriminate logging over the centuries and the mountain sides are irretrievably eroded. Despite these harsh features, a journey to this region is one of the more rewarding in central Tibet.

Access
Drakyul can be approached from the north (via Lhasa), from the south (by crossing the Tsangpo River) or by way of the monasteries of Samye, Dorje Drak, and Shugseb. Map reference NH46-9 B D.

From the Lhasa Area
This is the hard way; all routes involve crossing passes over 5000 m.

From Tsecholing Monastery: Four days South of Lhasa, on the south bank of the Kyi Chu, is the village of Drib (site of Tsemchok Ling, one of Lhasa's Four Royal Colleges). A trail from here goes south over the Tungo (Trango La) Pass to Dorje Drak and the Drak Valley (see page 595).

From Tshal Gungthang Monastery: Four days This monastery is located 13 km east of Lhasa on the main Lhasa–Medro Gongkar road (see page 198). A trail behind the monastery leads over the watershed that separates the Kyi Chu from the Yarlung Tsangpo. After crossing a pass, it divides. The western trail leads down the Dorje Drak Valley; the eastern one enters Drakyul.

From Dechen Dzong: Four days The first portion of this itinerary is identical to the pilgrimage leading to Yamalung and Samye monasteries (see page 625). From Dechen, travel 1 1/2 hr to Shingjang. Here the valley divides: the left route goes over the Gökar La to Samye; the right trail leads over a 5200m-high pass into the Drak Valley.

FROM THE TSANGPO RIVER

Most Tibetans prefer these easy access routes that involve no more than crossing the river by ferry and hiking up the Drak Valley. Begin by taking the main Lhasa–Tsethang road.

Ferry to Dorje Drak About 22 km east of the airport and next to the Lhasa–Tsethang road is Chitishio Village. West of here, at road marker 48 km, is a ferry that plies between the south bank and Dorje Drak Monastery. From the monastery, walk east to the Drak Valley entrance.

Ferry to Drak This is the quickest way to the Drakyul caves. The Yangkar ferry stands at road marker 73 km, 3 km west of Dranang (Trathang) and 24 km east of Chitishio on the main Lhasa–Tsethang road. A hydroelectric station is a landmark. The ferry crosses to the north shore; Ngadrak village is 10 km beyond (find a horse-cart) and Drakda, site of the sacred lake of Tsogyal Latso (see below), is 4 km from the ferry dock.

FROM SAMYE: ONE DAY

Simply walk west from Samye along the north bank of the Yarlung Tsangpo to Drakda. This long day's walk passes the five *chörtens* of Surkhar (see page 312).

FROM SHUGSEB: TWO TO THREE DAYS

A faint trail leads east from this hermitage (see page 493), crosses a 5050 m pass, and descends onto an east-trending valley that merges with the main Dorje Drak Valley. These two valleys 1 km north of Trango Cho (Pusha) Village. From here walk south to Dorje Drak, then east to Drakda.

THE DRAKYUL PILGRIMAGE

(Map Reference NH46-9 D)
The description of the pilgrimage starts from the confluence of the Drak River with the Tsangpo and goes north up the valley. This approach is the one most commonly used by Tibetan pilgrims. Bring a powerful flashlight and sufficient batteries for exploring the two labyrinthine cave complexes of Drak Yong Dzong and Dzong Kumbum.

TSOGYAL LATSO

The walk from the Tsangpo ferry at Drak to Tsogyal Latso takes 1 hr. West of the village is the Drak Chu River.

Tsogyal Latso is the name most widely used for the pond consecrated to Guru Rinpoche's consort, Yeshe Tsogyal. The others, Palden Lhamo Latso and Makzor Gyalmo Latso, are usually invoked by Bönpo adherents. Surrounded by the houses of Drakda and tall trees, this is the first sacred site in the valley. Tsogyal Latso is 4 m deep (its water issues from an underground spring) and a rectangular stone wall encloses it. Villagers recount that their ancestors caught rare glimpses of mythical lake oxen (*tsolang*) and lake sheep (*tsoluk*) rising from within its depths. These ethereal creatures, manifestations of divinities, conferred sanctity on the water. Tibetans come here to learn about their past and future by studying patterns on the water's surface. This exercise becomes difficult in early spring due to strong, ruffling winds from the Tsangpo.

KAZHIMA LHAKHANG

A small Nyingmapa chapel called Kazhima Lhakhang stands on the north side of the sacred pool. The *Lhakhang*, once occupied by villagers, was saved from the Cultural Revolution. Under the jurisdiction of Samye Monastery, its founding probably dates back to the 8th century. Some old paintings remain on the porch. The west wall has images depicting Tsepame and the White Drölma. Below these is Dorje Neljorma. Chenresi and Jampelyang are to the east. Images of Guru Rinpoche and Dorje Neljorma, a female tantric deity considered a representation of Yeshe Tsogyal, adorn the shrine. At its center is a richly clothed clay statue of Yeshe Tsogyal's mother (in a wood cabinet). Outside the chapel is the soul-tree (*lashing*) of Yeshe Tsogyal.

Yeshe Tsogyal

Tsogyal Latso is one of the most important places associated with Yeshe Tsogyal, the famous consort of Guru Rinpoche. She was born at Seulung (in the palace of Karchen) and recognized as the incarnation of Yangchenma (Sarasvati), the Indian goddess of music. A legend recounts that when Guru Rinpoche and Yangchenma were performing a mystic ritual, a garland of red and white syllables suddenly pierced the sky and fell to earth. Simultaneously, the king of Karchen and his wife had a vision of a lovely girl playing the guitar divinely. The sky burst with light and the earth moved—nine months later Yeshe Tsogyal was born. The lake by the Karchen palace grew dramatically, thus causing the king to call his newborn 'Queen of the Lake'.

At the age of 16, Yeshe Tsogyal married King Trisong Detsen and later became a companion to Guru Rinpoche. During teachings, she would carefully note down the essence and principles of Tantrism as expounded by the master. This she achieved by rendering the discourse into a special code inscribed on yellow parchment. Over time, a large number of these texts were collected. Under Guru Rinpoche's direction, Yeshe Tsogyal meticulously wrapped and hid the sacred documents, setting into motion the unique Tibetan relationship of *terma* (hidden texts) and *tertön* (discoverers of *terma*). In this way, posterity had access to Guru Rinpoche's words and deeds at the appropriate time. Yeshe Tsogyal did not die but dissolved into a rainbow to join Guru Rinpoche in his paradise of Zangdhok Pelri.

NGADRAK MONASTERY

This Karma Kagyü monastery, on the west (right) bank of the river, is 1 1/4 hr north of Tsogyal Latso near Ngadrak village. The name Ngadrak (Jowo Ngadrak) denotes the Monastery of Five Yeshes. It was founded by Khenchung Pema Zangpo during the period of Pönpo Wang. The original building had four storys but a major renovation in 1955 converted it to three storys. Ngadrak once had more than 30 monks in residence and was administered by Tsurphu Monastery (see page 671) before being transferred to the Pawo Rinpoches of Nenang. Today, there are four monks who conduct services from time to time.

A large courtyard flanked by residences is in front of the *dukhang*. Five chapels, including the *tsangkhang* (to the right of the entrance) and the Jowo Khang (at the back) open onto the *dukhang*. Elements of the original architecture are discernible—note in particular the capitals and cornices of the pillars. Next to the chapel are the monks' houses. One belongs to the caretaker (*konyer*) of Drak Yong Dzong, one or the Drakyul cave complexes. (The *konyer* of Dzong Kumbum lives on the east side of the river.) Check in with them before going to the hermitages.

PEMA DZONG

This fortress, dating from the Phagmo Drupa Dynasty, was founded by Jangchub Gyaltsen (1302–73). It was sacked by the Dzungars in the early 18th C., but is surprisingly intact. Most ancient forts in Tibet were thoroughly and systematically destroyed during the turbulence of recent decades. The geographic isolation of Drakyul somehow saved Pema Dzong from certain destruction, making it a rare archeological find. Straddling Jönmo Ri (Dzong Ri), 2 km north of the Ngadrak,

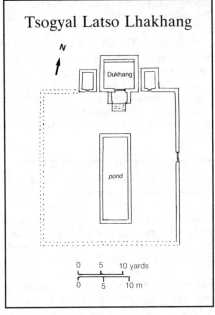

it commands a strategic site overlooking the valley. Surrounded by sheer cliffs and the only access is up a steep, 60-degree path. The fortress is 200 m long from east to west and 10–25 m wide from north to south. Its height varies between 4 m and 20 m. A defense tower, partially destroyed, sits on the easternmost rise and commands the entire complex. Below, to the west, are small defense-related houses. In the north is an 8m-high perimeter wall.

DRAK YONG DZONG (RENOWNED FORT, REPOSITORY OF TREASURES)

Follow the right bank of the river from Ngadrak for 1 3/4 hr to a point where the Drak Valley divides at a village. Take the left branch towards the west (the right leads over a 5250 m pass to Dechen, 21 km east of Lhasa; see page 625). After 1 hr come to Chasi Nunnery, sited in a peaceful side valley west of Pema Shang Village. The main two-story structure has been completely destroyed; only the walls and minor buildings remain. Enter through the south wall and the kitchen is on the right. To the left are the nuns' residences. A small chapel and *gönkhang* are across the courtyard. The nunnery is approximately 400 years old. Walking to Drak Yong Dzong from here is pleasant, especially during autumn. Ample vegetation, wild roses and small waterfalls liven the way. Stone cairns (*lhatse*) erected over the centuries clearly mark the way. The turnoff to Drak Yong Dzong (4500 m), the first cave system, follows a hard climb of 2 1/2 hr beyond the nunnery. Caves and *mani* walls are visible on the mountainside before the hermitage. The final approach traverses a white limestone cliff called Shinje Rolpa

Potrang (Palace of the Dancing Lord of Death). Drak Yong Dzong has three principal caves. Their entrances all open to the south and two of the caves are joined.

THE ROCK CARVINGS OF DRAK YONG DZONG

Scattered near the entrances are bas-relief images. Going east from the second cave towards the first are the following: Guru Rinpoche, Milarepa, a Buddhist patron, a small, vivid galloping horse. A cliff west of the second cave has over 30 carvings. These include Guru Rinpoche, Tsepame, Milarepa, Sakyamuni, and assorted animals. To the east are six elaborately crafted images. All have animal heads (deer, lion, tiger, ox, dog, *garuda*) and human bodies. Although created over the centuries, some of these carvings may well date back to the late Yarlung Dynasty.

SHINJE DRUBNE SHÖ, THE FIRST CAVE

High stone walls form a passageway leading to the entrance of Drak Yong Dzong. The first, easternmost grotto is a cavernous chamber about 15 m high and over 10 m wide. Its interior, over 100 sq m in floor space, houses a small rebuilt chapel that was damaged under the Dzungar invasion of the early 18th century. The front wall has a good painting of Mindroling Monastery. Beside it are paintings of the Minling Terchen Lamas. The altar's primary statues include a bronze, semi-wrathful Guru Rinpoche (original but restored) and his two consorts, Yeshe Tsogyal and Mandarawa. Painted fragments of Guru Rinpoche, Sakyamuni, and the Samye complex are barely recognizable. An unusual *thangka* depicts a four-armed Guru Rinpoche surrounded by Buddhas and *bodhisattvas*. One intriguing figure is naked from the waist up and wears a long skirt; the clothing and jewelry show a marked Indian Pala (9th–11th C.) influence. Along the cave's perimeter are ruined meditation cells and lesser caves. Nine monks still practice here under the jurisdiction of Dorje Drak Monastery.

SHINJE ROLPE DRUBNE, THE SECOND CAVE

Guru Rinpoche, Yeshe Tsogyal, and Vairocana used this cave as a retreat. Its opening is 5 m west of the first cave and about 8 m above the ground. To enter, climb a tall ladder and then crawl through an opening into a rock chute. This long, narrow interior passage inclines upwards and is barely wide enough for one person. A thick rope helps you propel yourself along the polished surface on your belly. Near the end is a small hole that opens downwards. It represents Hot and Cold Hell (*Nyalwa Tshanyal Drang Nyal*); pilgrims make a point of throwing coins and *khatas* down it. Reach a large, deep opening and climb down to its bottom via an ancient sandalwood ladder.

Guru Drubphuk

The first of two possible *khora* routes in the second cave circles to the back to the Guru Drubphuk chamber, notable for its collection of rocks. Jampa is represented by a large, dominant one; smaller ones are 'manifestations' of the internal organs of a demon (*sinpo*).These include its lungs (*sinbu lowa*) and heart (*sinbu nying*). A flat area is the Khandro Drora (*dakini* dancing place) where female divinities, personifying the wisdom of enlightenment, performed a dance of offering for Guru Rinpoche after he subdued a demon here.

The guru and the demon Legend recounts how Guru Rinpoche spent a long time trying to vanquish this cunning, protean demon. Whenever close to defeat, it would simply change form and escape. Finally, as a pigeon, the demon arrived at Drak Yong Dzong, which in those early times was nothing but a rock cliff. Hotly pursued by Guru Rinpoche, now transformed into a vulture (*jago*), the two tunneled into the rock. An epic struggle ensued, during which the supernatural squirmings and diggings inside the mountain created the intricate complex of caves we see today. At one point, Guru Rinpoche turned himself into seven suns. The tremendous heat and energy held the demon in captivity for seven days but somehow it again managed to escape. Finally, after further pursuit, the demon became exhausted and revealed its true form as a human. Guru Rinpoche pounced and killed it with his thunderbolt (*dorje*).

Guru Sangwa Drubphuk (Guru Rinpoche's Secret Cave)

The second route, opposite the sandalwood ladder, leads via stone steps to Guru Sangwa Drubphuk, sanctum sanctorum of the Drak Yong Dzong complex. This cave is the main reason Tibetan pilgrims come to Drakyul. Guru Rinpoche spent three years, three months, and three days in meditation here. His last will and testament designates this place as the personification of his body (*Kuyi Wenne Drak Yong Dzong*). Pilgrims prize the cave's earth, as it represents Guru Rinpoche's *tsampa*. Sacred pearl-like relics (*ringsels*), actually small pebbles of crystalline rock, are found within a hole in the rock wall. A ledge in the cave holds stone *manis* and photos of various lamas, and an opening in the floor leads to a cavity large enough to permit sitting meditation.

The Yogins of Drak Yong Dzong Three of Guru Rinpoche's 25 disciples stayed and meditated here. Sangye Yeshe of Nub, west Tibet, was one of the 108 translators sent to India by Trisong Detsen. The yoga adept acquired wizardly powers, enabling him to pierce rocks with his sacred dagger (*phurpa*). He once intimidated Langdarma, the Yarlung king infamous for banishing Buddhism, by balancing on his fingertips a huge scorpion, larger than a yak. The nightmare monster then emitted a thunderbolt that pulverized nearby rocks into sand. Dorje Dudjom, another disciple, went to India to invite Guru Rinpoche to Tibet. He could walk on air and travel to remote continents with the speed of thought. During the period of great spiritual activity surrounding Samye's consecration, Guru Rinpoche sent 100 monks into retreat here. Fifty-five of them became known as 'The Yogins of Drak Yong Dzong' after they had achieved enlightenment.

A long tunnel leads out of Guru Sangwa Drubphuk to reach a terrace directly above the first large grotto, Shinje Drubne Shö.

Jago Rangjung Drubphuk ('Cave of the Vulture'), the Third Cave

Known also as Luyul Drubphuk (Cave of the *Nagas'* Paradise) or Ne Phuk (Nego Sarpa), this pilgrimage site is located 40 m west of the second cave, Shinje Rolpe Drubne. The main path from the Drak Valley passes below the cave's mouth. At this point it is joined by another one to the left, which leads up to the cemetery (*durtrö*). The Cave of the Vulture is 8 m wide, 50 m deep and in places more than 10 m high. It was first opened by Rigdzin Pema Trinle, a venerated lama of Dorje Drak. Above the entrance is a large imprint of a vulture, Guru Rinpoche's demon-vanquishing transformation. Beyond is the convoluted interior of one of Guru Rinpoche's 'hidden valleys' (*beyul*). Limestone outcrops with special religious symbolism and fantastically shaped stalagmites and stalactites line the surfaces of the grotto. Hidden valleys, the phenomenal notion of *beyuls*, are found in only a handful of regions. They are secret, paradisaical places established by Guru Rinpoche, particularly in the Himalayas. When wars and doom threaten mankind's existence, these valleys will serve as safe refuges for Buddhism and its followers. Different sources say there are between seven and 20 *beyuls*. Pemakö, at the Great Bend of the Yarlung Tsangpo, is one of the most best known but rarely visited *beyuls* in the Himalayas (see page 717).

Once inside the Jago Drubphuk, look out for a small rock with a depression at the top. The liquid paste contained within is believed to be the milk (*wöme chöpa*) offered to Guru Rinpoche by Lu Gyalpo, King of the *Nagas*. On the walls are faint *rangjung* images of a lion, a tiger, and the 16 Arhats. One side of the *beyul* wall is distinguished by roughly-formed bumps that represent begging bowls (*lhungze*) of the 84 enlightened ascetics (*Mahasiddhas*) from India. Across the tunnel, a hollow contains a dry powder known as *tsamter* (*tsampa* treasure), another offering given to Guru Rinpoche by Lu Gyalpo. Soon come to a quartz-crystal pillar attached to the rock wall. Pilgrims say this *rangjung* object, Shel Gyi Kawa, was created miraculously by Guru Rinpoche. The begging bowls and pillar were gifts given by the tantric master to the king of the netherworld. Finally, three small holes on the tunnel floor hold water that is considered the elixir (*dutsi*) of Guru Rinpoche. It supposedly has potent curative powers.

Further on, the tunnel floor begins to drop. Most pilgrims stop here, stand on a rock and throw offerings into the void below. If you have a good flashlight, it is possible to slide and scramble down the slope to a pool of water. This represents the Paradise of the Nagas (Luyi Potrang). A story is told that the water level has decreased since the Chinese invaded Tibet in 1959. If the lake dries up altogether, Tibet will come to an end.

Siwatsal Cemetery

From the entrance of Jago Rangjung Drubphuk, a path leads west up a ridge to Drak Yong Dzong's cemetery known to pilgrims as Siwatsal (Cool Garden). Beyond and above are ruins of meditation rooms. Below the ridge, on the right, is a small Yeshe Tsogyal cave.

From Drak Yong Dzong to Dorje Drak via the Kur La A path leads west from the Siwatsal ridge to the Kur La (Kugu La), a 5050 m pass 1 3/4 hr away. The trail is indistinct, overgrown and difficult. Try to engage a guide from the cave complex. Descend due west from the pass to Pusha Village in the Dorje Drak Valley (2 hr), then walk south down the valley to Dorje Drak Monastery (see page 598).

NGAR PHUK

Ngar Phuk retreat, in a side valley north of Drak Yong Dzong, was established in the 13th C. by Melong Dorje, a disciple of Trulshik Senge Gyalwa. From the main valley turnoff to Drak Yong Dzong, continue north to the next side valley, then turn west (left) to Ngar Phuk.

DZONG KUMBUM, FORT OF 100,000 IMAGES

The second major cave system of Drakyul is best reached by starting from Ngadrak Village. Dzong Kumbum is usually uninhabited and it is thus wise to ask the caretaker (konyer) to come along. He lives in a house east of the river, near Ngadrak. A trail from the village's eastern edge (left bank of the Drak River) heads due east along a side valley. It takes 3 1/2 hrs to the limestone ridge (4800 m) of Dzong Kumbum. The route is straightforward (ignore a small side valley on the right) and in time an enormous cave opening appears within a cliff (Karchen Drak). The tall peak flanking it is 5199 m tall. Below the 30m-high cave mouth are ruins of a chapel. To the right, a rock face has a number of obscure colored paintings and carvings. Beneath the ruins, a trail goes southeast (right) and then divides into two branches: one leads to either the Surkhar or Samye valleys; the other goes to Samye Monastery and crosses two low passes in the process. To the left of the ruins can be seen stone hermitages along a cliff face. A trail from here leads to more ruined tsamkhangs on a plateau.

> **The rock carvings of Dzong Kumbum** A total of 73 carved images embellish the face of a cliff south of Dzong Kumbum's entrance; most are less than 1 m high. The top image is Guru Rinpoche and Amitabha (Wöpame) is below him to the right. Two identical sets of Guru Rinpoche and his consorts follow. Tangton Gyalpo, the bridge builder, can be seen below to the left. Naked from the waist up, he holds iron chains in his right hand. Wrathful protectors and images of Sakyamuni are common. The carvings, all created within the same period, date back to the 15th and 16th centuries. Pilgrims probably painted the images during the past few decades.

The gigantic, west-facing entrance leads into a tapering cave approximately 30 m high, 35 m deep, and 25 m wide. At its back are a series of twisting tunnels, most of which end in culs-de-sac. A legend tells of an unopened beyul within the Dzong Kumbum complex that ostensibly will be revealed one day by a deserving lama. The first tunnel, the shortest, opens to the right and leads to a small cave halfway along the left. A second requires some care— a number of small holes are along the tunnel floor. These are known to pilgrims as Shinje Torong, the deep cauldrons where the Lord of Death cooks his victims in Hell. Within these one can hear the sound of running water. A short distance from the entrance is a small cavity on the ceiling, supposedly created when Guru Rinpoche accidentally stood up after meditating. Further is a long rock wall whose surface is studded with pearl-like limestone nubs. Beyond is a sculpted pillar that looks remarkably like a large fish hanging from its mouth. Its scales are vivid. The ceiling and tunnel then expand into a large cavity, noteworthy for its eerie stalagmites and stalactites. One represents a sacred lingam, another the sword of Jampelyang. Some distance further is a medium-sized cave. At its entrance is a small hole; the faithful say that every so often music of drums and cymbals, produced by an unseen assembly of monks, emanates from it.

A third tunnel, opening to the left, is distinguished by a subterranean river that runs the entire length of the tunnel. Towards its end, the tunnel widens to reveal a phantasmagoria of rock and limestone shapes. Some resemble wild animals—lions, tigers, and elephants. Others hang from the ceiling, taking the forms of flying *garudas* and mythical birds. Further on, at the far end of the passage, are two pools, sources of the subterranean river. Be very careful reaching the second pool. Locals tell of careless pilgrims who have disappeared without trace after falling in. According to tradition, these pools are the female complement, or *yoni*, to the *lingam* in the other tunnel. For some, they are the soul-lakes of Guru Rinpoche.

Go back to the main cave to enter the fourth tunnel. Near its end, the passageway opens to a large multi-tiered rock formation that represents a *rangjung*, three-dimensional mandala (*kyilkhor rangjung*). On one side, a stone has the 'imprints' of Guru Rinpoche's head and hands. These were created when he prostrated to the mandala, an icon of Zangdhok Pelri, his Paradise. The last section of the tunnel terminates at Guru Rinpoche's secret meditation cave, Guru Sangwa Phuk. It contains the *rangjung* mantra 'Om Ah Hum' and his handprint. Outside the entrance is a hollow with holy water, the elixir (*dutsi*) of the master.

For the fifth tunnel, go back out to the main Dzong Kumbum entrance, then follow a trail up the cliff. It soon branches: one fork goes to some ruined *tsamkhangs*, the other circles up above the gigantic opening to a tiny entrance. Go through this to enter a constricted passage that wriggles and turns as it penetrates into the innards of the limestone peak, passing stupa-like rock sculptures (*chörten rangjung*). Some sections of the tunnel are very narrow, making ingress difficult. At the end, small openings break through for a glimpse of the outside world.

JINKA:
THE SIX-TUNNELED MANDALA CAVE

Tantric topography and a medicinal hotspring

Location	South of Gyantse and Shigatse
Map reference	NH45-16 B
Trekking days	8 (one-way)
Start–Finish	Gyantse–Kala
Passes	Pongong, Lama, Selung, Kesar, Do, Langu, unnamed

OVERVIEW

The first foreigner to visit the amazing cave complex of Jinka Dradruk was the celebrated pandit, Lama Ugyen Gyatso, sent by the British Raj in 1883 to secretly map and explore Tibet. He wrote the following in his report:

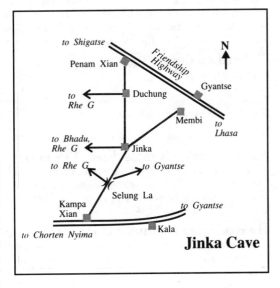

Jinka Cave

> ... *a rock-cut cave or hermitage of considerable celebrity. We took lighted lamps and after going 120 paces inside the cavern, we reached an open flat area, from which a rock-cut ladder led us up to another open space; 30 paces further brought us to a stone seat, said to be the seat of Guru Pemajungnet (Guru Rinpoche). Behind this seat was a small hole drilled through the rock; through this hole a wooden spoon about two feet long was passed by the sister of the lama who accompanied us, and a small amount of reddish dust was extracted which is said to be the refuse of the Guru's food. This we ate and found very sweet to the taste ...we descended another flight of steps to a place where a stream issues from the face of the rock. The total length of the cave from the entrance to the stream is about 1/4 mile. There are ascents and descents, and many turns and twists through narrow passages where only one man can go at a time, and many people are afraid to risk exploring the place. If the lamp were to go out there would be no finding the way back again.*

The complicated hermitage, cleverly concealed within dramatic cliffs south of Shigatse, sees a steady trickle of pilgrims who come to honor the cave where the Indian master, Guru Rinpoche, meditated. Beyond the outer grottoes, deep within the mountain, are secret passages and hidden chambers consecrated to Guru Rinpoche and his two consorts, Yeshe Tsogyal and Mandarawa. The labyrinthine interior has many natural rock formations that appear as 'self-manifesting' religious icons to test and inspire the pilgrims' progress through the dark tunnels. Legends associated with these have been handed down for generations.

Near Jinka is a hot spring believed to be created miraculously by Guru Rinpoche, and one which Yutok Yönten Gönpo (8th–9th C.), the famed first physician of Tibet, endowed with potent medicinal properties. A neighboring *chörten* is consecrated to him and a short pilgrims' walk (*khora*) circumambulates the base of the hermitage's cliffs.

A four-wheel-drive vehicle can reach the cave complex from Gyantse or Shigatse via Penam Xian. Trekking into the area from Gyantse takes three easy days and passes through an area essentially untouched by the Chinese. An extension of the itinerary, an old trade route, goes south from Jinka to Kala near the Tibet–Sikkim border. In the process, seven generally easy passes are crossed. Various nomad encampments lie along this little-known route.

An option at the end of the trek is to continue on to the Sikkim Himalayas by joining the superb Chörten Nyima pilgrimage at Kampa Xian (see page 809).

Related sections
Chörten Nyima, p 801
Gyantse, p 412
Chumbi Valley, p 787
The Rhe and Ku valleys, p 831

Two dirt roads connect Jinka to the Lhasa–Nepal Friendship Highway:

By road from Gyantse direct (35 km)
At the center of town, go west along the main road past the Gyantse Hotel to a T-junction. Turn right towards Shigatse. After approximately 1 km, turn left on a dirt road that leads to Jinka via Jangra (Changra). Beyong Jangra is the Nabru La Pass. Further on is Gazhi (Jinka Qu), a short walk from the cave.

By road from Gyantse via Penam Xian (90 km)
A better road to Jinka starts from Penam Xian, a county seat 44 km northwest of Gyantse on the Friendship Highway. Below are points of interest along the way from Gyantse to Penam Xian. Numbers correspond to road markers.

87   Ruins of Tsechen Monastery (seat of Rendawa, Tsong Khapa's principal teacher) on the left atop a steep hill. The road follows the left bank of the Nyang Chu.

71   Drongtse Monastery, halfway up a hill on the left. A Guru Rinpoche shrine stands by the roadside.

> **Drongtse Monastery** This monastery was founded in 1442 by Rinchen Gyatso, an ascetic who received Tsong Khapa's blessings. The complex consisted of the yellow

> *dukhang* and two colleges specializing in philosophy and tantric rituals. The former, rebuilt in the mid-1980s, has a back chapel with an image of Sakyamuni. Behind the building is a *lhakhang* built over a rock with carved images of Guru Rinpoche, Drölma, Chenresi, and others. Next to the chapel are fine relief images on slates.

65   Tsi Nesar Monastery is in a small ravine 100 m from the left side of the road. Its superb 11th–12th-C. sculptures and murals (destroyed) were similar to those of Yemar (see page 390) and Dranang (see page 393). New south-facing white buildings have been built since the Cultural Revolution. Pökang Monastery, directly across the Nyang Chu from Nesar, is 7–8 km up a side valley that opens to the north. At the valley entrance is Lhachung. Pökang was founded by a disciple of the Khache Panchen Sakyasri in the early 17th century.

56   Sera Drubde hermitage is on the Nyang Chu's right bank, perched up a side valley across the river, 1 km from the road. Fronting the hermitage, to its left, are two earth *chörtens*, and farther up the mountain are retreat caves.

54   The Jinka turnoff. Turn left off the Friendship Highway, cross a narrow bridge and follow the dirt road past villages to Duchung Qu.

52   Concrete bridge

50   Penam Xian

Penam Xian to Jinka

Two dirt roads head southwest within the Penam Valley. The first one starts from the 55 km road marker, the other from Penam Xian at the 50 km road marker. Take the first. The following itinerary starts at 0 km. No road markers indicate the way; plot the mileage (in kms) on the vehicle's odometer. The drive to Jinka takes 3 1/2 hr in a Landcruiser.

5.5   Village on the left

7.5   Side valley on the left. Up this valley is Dechen Monastery (functioning). Continue straight.

9   Duchung (Dochung) Qu, a compound left of the village, has lodging. The valley's river is the Danshung Chu.

14.5 Junction of three valleys. The left one leads to Jinka, the middle one goes to Wongdan Qu (28 km from the Friendship Highway turnoff) along the Danshung Chu, and the right (west) valley leads over a pass to Bhadu Monastery (see page 836) via the villages of Madha, Maphu, Tsego, and Bending. From the pass, an alternate trail goes north to Shigatse.

17   Village

22   Village. Beyond are two *chörtens* below a small hill with a *lhatse*.

25.5 Ruins and *chörten* on the valley's right side.

27.5 Village

29 Side valley on the left, village at its entrance.

31 Zumilu Drubphuk, a prominent Bönpo cave retreat, sits within sheer cliffs (on the valley's right side). A zigzagging path leads up to the cave, named after a local lama.

33 Valley splits to the left and center. Take the center valley, following telephone poles along its left side (the left valley's trail leads east to Gyantse).

38 Side valley on the left, with a trail to Gyantse. The main valley narrows.

40.5 Broad, flat plain and junction of valleys. The center valley leads to Jinka. Ahead is Jinka Qu. The left valley (Lhakhang at its entrance) leads to Jangra and Gyantse via Nabru and the Nabru La along a dirt road (35 km to Gyantse).

42 The road crosses a narrow bridge.

43 Gazhi (Jinka Qu) has a two-story government building.

45.5 Jinka Sheng. The road peters out. Walk along the left valley towards a narrow gorge flanked by cliffs. It takes 1/2 hr from the end of the road to Jinka (paths run along either side of a river bed). Right of the flat plain is the white *chörten* of Yutok Yönten Gönpo under Neri (Sacred Hill). The valley next to this leads to Wongdan; at the valley entrance is a sacred hot spring and the village of Chutsen (Hot Spring).

TREKKING FROM GYANTSE TO KALA (VIA JINKA)
Time Chart

Day	Place	Hours
1	Gyantse–Membi	3
2	Camp 1	5 3/4
3	Jinka	1 1/2
4	Shanjung	5
5	Camp 2	4
6	Camp 3	4
7	Nomad camp	3
8	Main road	5
9	Kala (42 km)	hitch

Trail Notes
✤ DAY 1 GYANTSE–MEMBI 3 HR

From the center of Gyantse, walk southwest along the main motor road (part of the Friendship Highway) towards Shigatse. Cross a concrete bridge over the Nyang Chu, pass the Gyantse Hotel and arrive at a T-junction (1/2 hr). Go right. After ten minutes, turn left onto a dirt road heading west. Pass the villages of Manga, Pala (on the right), and Surta (on the left,

1/2 hr from the T-junction). Just before Surta, a trail branches off to the left. Do not take this. After Surta, the dirt road curves northwest, around a low ridge, to reach a *mani* wall on the right (1/2 hr). The road forks around a bluff; take the left branch (south-southwest) to Membi (1 1/2 hr). (The right path goes to Tuchung and the Nabru La.) Camp in woods near here and hire donkeys if necessary for the trip to Jinka (Rmb 10 per day, with handler).

✤ DAY 2 MEMBI–CAMP 1 5 3/4 HR

Continue along the dirt road following the telegraph poles, passing ruins of an old fort on the left. Do not take a side road to the left. Reach See in 20 mins; the road curves to the right around this village, then starts to climb. Pass a reservoir and a side valley on the right. Continue to a ruined house on the left (3/4 hr from Membi) and on to a destroyed *mani* wall (1/2 hr). The road hugs the left (south) side of the valley; the Dara Tza Monastery (destroyed) is high up on the mountain slopes to the north. Under the ruins are an animal shelter and two small houses. A broad dirt road leads to the left after 15 mins (do not take it). Farther along, on the right (north) side of the valley, a large rock protrudes from the mountainside (1/2 hr). At this spot, take a short cut along a path south of the road. Rejoin the road after 15 mins and follow the telegraph poles. Pass a sheep shelter and a small house on the right and continue to the southwest. Reach the gradual Pongong La (4938 m) in 1 1/4 hr. Descend and pass a sheep shelter and house, then another shelter (1 1/2 hr from the pass). Reach a grassy campsite next to a river in 3/4 hr. An animal shelter and house stand on the valley's north side.

✤ DAY 3 CAMP 1–JINKA 1 1/2 HR

The river is on the left. Walk southwest past fields on the right to Jinka Tarmar (on the right) at a junction of valleys. To the north of the wide north–south trending valley is Chendro. Walk south, along the valley's eastern perimeter. An inscribed *mantra* can be seen high up the mountainside on the right (west) (1/2 hr from camp 1). Further on, a side valley opens to the left (east); Chokpay is near its entrance. Ignore this. Continue to Gazhi (1/2 hr), the last village before the Jinka cave complex. At Gazhi the road and telegraph poles stop. The peak due west of Gazhi is 5130 m high.

> **Gazhi** Gazhi is the village's original name and means 'pleasant valley'. Since the communist takeover of Tibet, it has been upgraded to *qu* status and is now commonly known as Jinka Qu. Jinka is a phonetic corruption of *kyilkhor* ('mandala') and refers to the cave hermitage of Khilkhor Trangdruk (local pronunciation: Jinka Dradruk), the region's most important cultural monument. The administrative offices are housed within a compound. To its left (east) flows the river, and the motor road curves to the right around the *qu* to go up towards the hermitage. An extension of Gazhi farther up the valley is known as Jinka Yadrong (the village around the *qu* is also known as Jinka Madrong, the 'lower Jinka').

The valley, with its head to the south, terminates near Gazhi to become two small side valleys. Trending to the southwest, the right has Chutsen (Hot Spring) at its entrance and leads west to Bhadu, Tramo, and Rhe monasteries (see page 836). The left one heads south-southeast; follow this valley along a trail to two flagpoles (*darchen*) at the base of cliffs on your right (west). They mark the entrance to the dramatic cave hermitage of Jinka Dradruk. From Gazhi to Jinka takes 1/2 hr.

Note: For a continuation of the Trail Notes from Jinka to Kala, see page 336.

KYILKHOR TRANGDRUK (SIX TUNNELS OF THE MANDALA)

Near the flagpoles is a bridge that leads to the far side of the valley. Cross it for an excellent view of the cliffs and hermitage. To the left of the cave hermitage proper, on top of a rock, are two damaged meditation cells (*tsamkhangs*) along the cliff face. Jinka's main entrance, flanked by high white walls, leads to a courtyard and the spacious outer cave (*dukhang*). An entranceway on the left leads into the Guru Lhakhang.

Guru Lhakhang

This round cave, 6 m in diameter, has an altar (cups, butter lamps, Dalai Lama photos) at the far wall. Next to the photos are wrathful and peaceful divinities carved on stone tablets. Above the altar on the rock wall is a painting of Guru Rinpoche. Beneath it are faint remains of an original Guru Rinpoche sculpture, known as Guru Ngadrama. According to tradition, this was created by Guru Rinpoche as an exact likeness of himself. It had a metal mirror fixed to its heart, a powerful relic with the uncanny ability to predict the future.

Along the right wall is a new, garish statue of Guru Rinpoche within a cabinet. Next to it is a stone with the small footprint of Yeshe Tsogyal, imprinted when she was eight. An opening in the ceiling illuminates the room.

Gönkhang

Adjacent to the Guru Lhakhang is another cave (5 m by 7 m), a *gönkhang* for rituals to propitiate the wrathful divinities, Gönpo and Pehar. These rituals (*nangso*) served to exact confession and atonement before the terrifying guardians. In the ceiling is a long, narrow shaft that extends 20 m or more into the rock; it is known to pilgrims as the *sanglam* of Yeshe Tsogyal, the secret passage of Guru Rinpoche's consort. Beyond the *gönkhang* is a 10m-long low tunnel that leads to an inner cave. Right of the entrance is a sacred spring known as Guru Tsechu; the water benefits crops, cattle, and humans. Between the Guru Lhakhang and *gönkhang* is an incense burner with an image of the protector (*sungma*), Chakpa Milen. On top of it are prayer flags with attached clumps of wool and old clothes. Pilgrims swap their clothes with those here, believing that some of the powerful energies of the hermitage have been transferred to them.

Dukhang

The large outer grotto, just outside the *gönkhang* and Guru Lhakhang, has an earth and stone altar at its far corner. On top of this are *zhitrö* (wrathful and peaceful) images carved on stone slabs. An L-shaped earthen platform on the right is used for sleeping. Above this is a shallow depression in the rock known as Tergo ('Treasure Door'). It is believed that a sagacious lama will one day open this imaginary door to reveal a treasure of animals (*zokter*) immensely beneficial for all livestock. Owners of yak and sheep make a point of coming here to touch the rock face with their heads to receive blessings for their animals. On the walls to the right and rear of the cave are obscure 'self-manifesting' (*rangjung*) images, which can only be perceived by the worthy.

Immediately behind and to the left of the main entrance leading to the *dukhang* is a set of narrow stairs that leads to an enclosed terrace (12 m by 3 m) above the ground floor. Bounded by low walls and a high, rock ceiling, the terrace has a wide front with good views of the valley and river below. A large rock up the hill and across the river denotes a *rangjung* Tamdrin (tantric protector). The terrace's rear looks down on the *dukhang*. It was once a two-story structure and remnants of the floor partition remain. The upper floor was perhaps a meditation room. Return to the *dukhang* and go through the long low tunnel at the rear to enter an inner grotto.

Inner Grotto The bare, oval chamber with a high ceiling contains the recessed meditation cave of Yeshe Tsogyal. This was the home of the *yogini* during Guru Rinpoche's three-year, three-month, three-day sojourn at Jinka.

Guru Tsechu A stream issues from a crack near the wall beyond Yeshe Tsogyal's cave and flows along a shallow channel at the grotto's side. It disappears into the ground, only to reappear within the *dukhang*.

Mandarawa Drubphuk Opposite Yeshe Tsogyal's cave is the meditation cave of Mandarawa, another consort of Guru Rinpoche.

The rear cave wall left of Yeshe Tsogyal's cave makes a sharp concave thrust into another, smaller, cavity. Inside is a 6-m-tall wood ladder with 13 rungs that leads up, with a rope, to an opening. This is the entrance to the Jinka Dradruk complex. Ranged along the wall, clockwise from the entrance, are the following:

- Langpoche (Langchen Rangjung). After a pronounced corner of the wall is an abstract *rangjung* image of the front of an elephant.
- Rayi Rangjung. After Langpoche, at the junction of the large outer grotto and inner one, is a piece of rock that protrudes out from the wall to resemble the head and neck of a goat. This *rangjung* goat represents the guide that led Guru Rinpoche to Jinka when he was lost in a storm.
- Milarepa statue. Beyond the goat image is a narrow horizontal shaft in the rock. A few meters within is a small image of Milarepa. (Use a flashlight.)
- Beyul Nego. High above the ground is a cave opening blocked by a stone. According to legend, the space beyond is the 'Door to the Secret Retreat'; Guru Rinpoche personally sealed it with a rock carried from a river near Tsang.
- Senge Rangjung. Go past the ladder back to the grotto entrance to find this *rangjung* image of a lion's head.
- Ladder and rope. A stout, near-vertical wood ladder rests on a stone at the grotto's back wall. The end of a rope dangles near the top of the ladder. Here is a small ledge for resting. To its right a grooved incline reaches a tiny cave. At the back is a rock with a hollow at its top that holds a powdery substance known as Guru Soltsam. This *tsampa* of Guru Rinpoche is highly valued by pilgrims.

Left of the ledge is a Guru Rinpoche handprint; to the right is one of Yeshe Tsogyal.

Grasp the rope and inch carefully up an inclined tunnel. At the top of the rope is an opening that leads into a narrow passage. Squeeze through, then slide down to reach the beginning of a tunnel called Bardo Trangchen Chobgye.

Bardo Trangchen Chobgye ('Tunnel of the 18 Bardo stages')

The tunnel, uneven and littered with obstacles, symbolizes the progress through the 18 stages of Bardo, the 49-day intermediate phase between death and rebirth. Some of the nature-formed icons near the entrance are:

• Neten Chudruk. Beyond the passage are *rangjung* images of the 16 Arhats on the left wall.
• Sernya Rangjung. Opposite the Neten Chudruk on the right wall are *rangjung* images of four goldfish, one of the eight auspicious symbols in Tibetan Buddhism.

Yaknyal Dorje Drak Further along the tunnel, on the right, is a rock close to the wall. Walk clockwise around it and at its rear enter a narrow tunnel beneath it. Crawl to the far end. Pilgrims do this three times to symbolically reciprocate their parents' love and care for them as children. Halfway through the tunnel is a hollow. Inside, a brownish, earthy substance with the smell of herbal medicine is much prized by pilgrims for the curing of sores and colds. Its bitter taste becomes sweeter after chewing.

Dhikpa Ratsa (Scorpion) Legend says Guru Rinpoche detected a demon that had become a poisonous scorpion. He dissolved it into the rock and its imprint remains on the ground next to the left wall. Pilgrims make a point of treading on it.

Cave Beyond the scorpion imprint is the opening to a cave near the ceiling on the left. Pilgrims throw barley grains (*neh*) inside it as an offering and the cave floor has become a carpet of dwarf barley.

Langchen Dropa (Elephant Stomach) After this cave, the ceiling and walls close in. Wriggle through a short, narrow tunnel to a cavity whose surrounding walls appear to be formed of a white marble. The moist, slippery surface resembles the stomach of an elephant. Enter another grotto and look for the following:

• Je Phagmo Drupa image. This obscure *rangjung* sculpture stands next to the left wall near the grotto's entrance.
• Sangchab. At the crux of the sculpture is a thimble-sized hollow where water accumulates. It is said to be the secret water, or urine (*sangchab*), of Phagmo Drupa. Pilgrims use a spoon to collect this highly prized liquid.
• Yeshe Tsogyal and Mandarawa. *Rangjung* images of Guru Rinpoche's two consorts are on the right wall.
• Chuwo Yanlak Gyedhen (Water of the Eight Qualities). Beyond the consorts, water drips down from the ceiling. Many pilgrims visit Jinka during the auspicious full moon, half moon and tenth lunar day to wash beneath this Water of Purification.
• Zokter (Treasure of Animals). On the right wall is a round depression in the right wall. The *zokter* once held holy objects beneficial to animals.
• Choter (Religious Treasure). A circular depression next to the Zokter.
• Guru Tsechu. Guru Rinpoche's long-life water accumulates in a bowl-like depression on the surface of a rock ledge at the bottom of the left wall. A copper spoon is used to ladle it out.

• Yeshe Tsogyal Sangchab. The 'Secret Water' (urine) of Yeshe Tsogyal stands in another hollow next to the Guru Tsechu. Embodying the power of universal medicine; it can supposedly cure everything. The color of the Tsechu and Sangchab changes from time to time, from clear to milky to yellowish. Both have a slight medicinal taste.

Return to the rope and ladder, descend to the inner cave and exit by way of the *dukhang*.

SURROUNDINGS OF JINKA
The populated valley west of the Jinka Valley (the Chutsen hot spring is at its entrance) eventually leads to the monasteries of Bhadu and Rhe (see page 836). It has a number of interesting sites at its beginning.

Yutok Yönten Gönpo Chörten
This white *chörten* stands near the river's right bank. It was supposedly built by Yutok Yönten Gönpo (b 729), Tibet's first physician, who attended the two Yarlung-dynasty kings, Tride Tsugtsen and Trisong Detsen. Guru Rinpoche blessed the site and Yutok Yönten Gönpo deposited essences of 108 medicines and the Treasure of Medicine (*menter*) within the *chörten*. Pilgrims circle the *chörten* up to 100,000 times and believe it has mystical curative powers. Parts of the base have been chipped off and used as medicine.

Chutsen
Across the river from the *chörten* is a hotspring, believed to be created miraculously by Guru Rinpoche. A single pool (1 m deep) is in the first building on the left. Yutok Yönten Gönpo imbued the spring with medicinal properties; there is usually a congregation of men and women who stay in the small complex for extended periods.

Neri (Sacred Hill)
Near the *chörten*, down the valley, are two connected hills. According to local tradition, these hills contain 108 sacred caves and 108 sacred cemeteries. Guru Rinpoche first sanctified the site, then practitioners of the Kagyüpa lineage, seeking an ideal retreat, came here in droves. Eventually, they were displaced by an influx of Bönpos. Today, only deserted caves and ruined buildings remain. Locals affirm that Neri, with its different rocks and earth strata, resembles a rainbow at auspicious times. The nearby *chörten* derives much of its power from the sacred mounds.

Jinka khora
Allow one day for the ritual circumambulation of Jinka (start early in the morning). The *khora* starts at the two flagpoles below the cave hermitage. Follow the river's left bank along the base of the Jinka spur up the valley. The flat path passes, on the right, Kyilkhor Tsamkhang, an unusual meditation complex that is mostly in ruins. The lower portion consists of stone-and-earth meditation cells. Directly above them are more cells, progressively smaller, that lean precariously to one side against a rock wall. Near the base, a path circles up and around to the back of the rock face to reach a large meditation cave, the Kyilkhor Drubkhang. The pilgrim path continues up the valley. In a short while, enter a side valley to the right and follow the left bank of its river. Cairns mark the route. Reach a pass at the head of the valley (the first of a double pass), then follow the trail to the right to the second pass. Take

the right branch of a fork to descend, keeping a ridge to the right. Reach a river that flows east of Neri, wade across it, and walk up to the *chörten* of Yutok Yönten Gönpo. Finish the *khora* by circling Neri's smaller half and exploring caves, sacred springs, and cemeteries.

Return to Jinka to continue the trek to Kala.

✤ DAY 4 JINKA–SHANJUNG 5 HR

Note: Pack animals It is possible to rent horses at Jinka's villages (Rmb 15 for two horses and handlers to the Lama La Pass).

From the hermitage, follow the left valley south-southeast (the right [west] valley goes to Bhadu and Rhe). The path hugs the slopes on the right above the valley floor. The river is on the left. After 1 1/2 hr, reach a valley junction and two side valleys. These two side valleys go left (east) and right (west). The right one leads over the Wongde La to Rhe Monastery in the Rhe Chu Valley (see page 836), and the left one goes over the Nabru La to Tuchung and Gyantse or the Gyantse–Yatung road at a point 20 km south of Gyantse.

Ignore the side valleys and continue south-southeast along the main valley. At the top of a hill on the right are the ruins of Shekar Monastery. In 1/2 hr, another pair of side valleys. The more distant right valley has at its entrance the ruins of a fort. The left valley leads east to Sakang (28 km south of Gyantse) on the Gyantse–Yatung road. Again, ignore these two valleys. Farther south, the main valley ends abruptly. Turn right (west) to follow a faint path southwestward. Cross a spur to drop down to a nomad camp (1/2 hr). Side valleys lead to the east and west; three animal shelters stand in the eastern one.

Continue southwest along the main valley, which narrows. Stock up at the last water source before the pass (1/2 hr from the nomad camp). The path zigzags for 1/2 hr to the easy Lama La Pass (5120 m). Beyond is a wide plateau that stretches to the southwest. Descend it and then cross a river to four square animal shelters (1/2 hr). Reach Sapshi (1 hr from the pass), then Shanjung (Sangye Rabjung) after another 1/2 hr. Camp near a river east of the village. Tumbe Monastery is visible to the south.

✤ DAY 5 SHANJUNG–CAMP 2 4 HR

Continue southwest close to the broad valley's eastern side, and pass a *mani* wall 1/2 hr from Shanjung. In a further 1/2 hr, turn westward towards a horseshoe-shaped ridge. Tumbe Monastery, on top of the horseshoe's southern portion, consists of a fort-like main building surrounded by destroyed houses, living quarters for the monks. (A trail leads south to the Kampa Dzong–Kala road along a broad valley.) After the horseshoe ridge, cross the easy first half of the Selung La, then walk southwest over the pass' flat second half (1 1/2 hr after the ridge). Carry on past a side valley with a small river to the left and three animal shelters. The river flows southwest into the main valley and the trail follows its western bank. Camp near an animal shelter (1 hr from the Selung La).

✤ DAY 6 CAMP 2–CAMP 3 4 HR

Go southwestward on the left (east) side of the valley. Cross the easy Keser La in 1/2 hr. Descend to the southwest, then south-southwest, to Pamo (1/2 hr). The locals can be a bit shy and suspicious. Pass a square animal shelter; the trail now starts to ascend the Do (Lamo)

La, a double pass separated by a saddle. After the second ridge, turn left (east) before continuing south. Camp near a river with clean water (from Pamo to here is 2 hr).

❖ DAY 7 CAMP 3–NOMAD CAMP 3 HR

South of camp is a valley junction (1/2 hr). The right branch (going towards the northwest) leads to Tramo and Rhe monasteries; the nomad camp of Ru is near its entrance. The left one is the broad Langu Valley with nomad camps and many yaks. Straight ahead (south) is Langu Tso, a freshwater lake (1/2 km by 2 1/2 km). Skirt the lake by going right (west) around it. The muddy area east of the lake is a labyrinth of green islands and watery hummocks; the west route is easier and safer. The settlement of Langu is near the west shore and a nomad camp lies at the lake's southeastern tip (friendly nomads). From the lake, the trail goes southwest up to the easy Langu La (4877 m). At the pass, five or six high snow peaks appear to the southwest (from the valley junction to the pass is 1 1/2 hr). After the pass, turn southeast, then south down a main valley to a nomad camp (1 hr) called Chogshe (other camps are in the neighborhood). The valley north of here leads to Tramo and Rhe monasteries; the one trending west leads to Kuma and Kampa Dzong.

❖ DAY 8 NOMAD CAMP–MAIN ROAD 5 HR

Walk southwest along the valley. After 1 1/2 hr cross a steep pass (5200 m) with good views of the Himalayas to the south. Several valleys lead from the pass. (A well-traveled one on the right [west-southwest] leads to the nomad settlement of Neratogo [1 1/2 hr]. From here to the main Kampa Xian–Kala road is 2 hr.) Walk east from the pass along a ridge, then turn right (south) down a steep valley. The tricky descent along scree slopes passes some animal shelters. Eventually, the valley broadens and the trail meets a tractor track. In 1 1/2 hr from the pass, reach a grassy area with a stream on the west side of the track (first and only water all day). Follow the tractor track to the main Kampa Xian–Kala road. Camp near an animal shelter on the left (east) side of the track, next to the main road.

> **Chörten Nyima pilgrimage** Kampa Xian is a jumping-off point for the important Chörten Nyima pilgrimage on the Tibet–Sikkim border (see page 801). For the pilgrimage to the Rhe and Ku valleys, see page 831.

❖ DAY 9 MAIN ROAD–KALA (HITCH)

The road from camp runs east for 42 km to Kala. On the way, pass villages and a large area of ruins—forts, monastic buildings and unusual structures. From Kala, find a ride back along the Gyantse–Yatung road to Gyantse (94 km). The other option is to continue south along the Gyantse–Kala–Yatung road to the Chumbi Valley sited at the Nepal–Sikkim border (see page 787).

RITRÖ: MOUNTAIN HERMITAGES AND MYSTICS' HAUNTS

Described in this section are several mountain retreats endowed with remarkable spiritual power. These lesser-known hideaways were favored by serious meditators, who valued them for their heightened religious ambience and special geomantic qualities. All were consecrated by illustrious Tibetan Buddhists like Songtsen Gampo, Guru Rinpoche, Milarepa, and others. The small caves where the great Buddhist masters first meditated embody the essence of these *ritrös*. Intended for solitary practice, they are invariably located in secluded places.

DRAK YERPA: A RETREAT FOUNDED BY KING SONGTSEN GAMPO

The hermitage of Drak Yerpa (ancient name: Thogyal Lhunpo Yerpa) ranks with Samye Chimpu (see page 631) and Yarlung Sheldrak (see page 522) as one of Tibet's three principal cave retreats. Its natural beauty and spiritual ambience have attracted illustrious kings, saints, and ascetics since the Yarlung Dynasty (7th–9th century). King Songtsen Gampo's wife, Mong Tricham, built the first chapel and the monarch meditated in a cave known as Chögyal Drubphuk. The other two Religious Kings, Trisong Detsen and Ralpachen, and many well-known visitors — Guru Rinpoche, Lhalung Paldhor, Atisha, Vairocana, Padampa Sangye, Gedun Gyatso — practised within its many cave sanctuaries. Because of Atisha's three-year sojourn here, Drak Yerpa is considered a place of great sanctity for the Kadampa; the sect's second largest institution, Yerpa Drubde, was established here. Before the holocaust of the Cultural Revolution, Drak Yerpa had over 300 monks. Today, with ongoing renovations, the cave complex is again a powerful spiritual magnet for recluses and pilgrims from far and wide.

Related sections
The Ningchi road, p 707
The upper reaches of the Kyi Chu River, p 544
Lhamo Latso, p 623
Ganden, p 140

Access (Map reference NH46-9 B)

It takes 7 hr to walk from Lhasa to Drak Yerpa. Five roads intersect at the Telecommunication Office across from the Plateau Hotel in Lhasa's northeast section. The gravel road due east leads to Yerpa. Follow it over a tributary of the Kyi Chu, then past a rock quarry and a hydro-electric station. Reach Kawa, 3 hr from Lhasa. Beyond this village the road forks. The left branch ascends the mountainside in a series of switchbacks to a low pass. From here the village of Yerpa Da appears below within the Yerpa side valley, which trends south–north from the Tsangpo. Descend to the village (Lhasa to Yerpa Da is 4 1/2 hr) where a road goes north along the Yerpa Valley to its head, along the left (east) bank of the Yerpa Chu. Walk uphill for 2 hr, past a number of villages within the cultivated valley. After a reservoir, the white cliffs of the Yerpa complex can be seen. Leave the road (the valley veers northwest) at a village to hike northeast up the slopes. Arrive at a *chörten* guarding the entrance to the hermitage, then cross a side valley to finally reach the ruins of Yerpa Drubde Monastery (1/2 hr).

This large Kadampa institution was founded by disciples of Atisha in the tenth century. It later converted to the Gelugpa and in modern times served as the summer residence of Lhasa's Upper Tantric College (Gyurtö). The ruins are on a flat terrace at the base of high white cliffs. Some 100 m above are the main caves of Yerpa. The round trip from Lhasa can be made in one day by vehicle (2 hr each way). On foot, two days is the minimum. Bring sleeping gear and food if possible. Tibetans along the way and at Yerpa are generous but resources are scarce.

DRAK YERPA: HISTORY AND MYTHOLOGY

Drak Yerpa's importance as a pilgrimage site is made most clear by the long line of historical figures and prominent teachers who chose it as a retreat of choice. Below is a description of these people and their involvement with Yerpa.

SONGTSEN GAMPO

The 7th-C. king divined that mysterious and harmful occurrences in Tibet were caused by the ill-will of intangible beings (*asuras*). To suppress them, temples needed to be built at an auspicious site. In a vision, Songtsen Gampo saw that Drak Yerpa was the designated place.

The king and his queens, Tritsun and Wencheng, came to this mountain and found a number of 'self-manifesting' (*rangjung*) objects. At Rangjung Dorje Drak Lhakhang, they discovered that the chapel contained a *rangjung* image of Mahakala (Gönpo). Below this, the *rangjung* Trewu Marser Gyi Lhakhang (Red and Yellow Monkey Temple) had within it an image of Vairocana, symbol of the Buddha Body. Two other objects were a *rangjung* 'Om Mani Padme Hum' and a *chörten* containing 100,000 *tsa-tsas*. Nearby stood many juniper trees, a natural environment for mountain protectors (*zhidhak*). From this propitious beginning, Songtsen Gampo and his wives devoted themselves to developing the powerful site. The king spent much time at the cave of Chögyal Phuk (see page 342).

GURU RINPOCHE

After helping to lay the foundation of Samye Monastery in 779, Guru Rinpoche came to Drak Yerpa to meditate. He spent 7 months in Dawa Phuk, a cave he considered to be one of three major Places of Realization (*drubne*; the others are Sheldrak and Samye Chimpu). Considered one of his most profound actions, Guru Rinpoche hid many religious treasures (*terma*) within the caves of Yerpa. Here is a partial list:

Cave	Terma
Khandro (*dakini*)	Dakini chörten
Ja (bird)	Confers the ability to recognize parents of prior incarnations
Dawa (moon)	White Drölma; bestows long life
Senge (lion)	Gold mandala
Drilbu (bell)	Crystal water
Yönten (learning)	Old and new Nyingma text
Naljor (ascetic)	Bestows spiritual and material wealth
Zang (copper)	Gold vase
Namkha (sky)	Power to vanquish demons

Guru Rinpoche also hid the relics and begging bowl of Shariputra, a chief disciple of Sakyamuni, in the nine-pointed Chörten Tsegu. This magnificent *chörten* contained a clay pot with texts written by the 84 Mahasiddhas. Guru Rinpoche predicted that these would one day prevent famine and diseases of cattle. The *chörten* was completed in the 9th C. by Lhalung Paldhor (see below) and his brothers. Later, on the day of a full moon, a government minister discovered the structure and its treasures and moved them to Samye; from then on, the monastery prospered spiritually and materially. Guru Rinpoche blessed three chapels at Drak Yerpa, known collectively as the Jumo Ling Sum. They took the names of two of the consorts of Guru Rinpoche and one of Trisong Detsen. The guru then created a holy *chörten*, the Chörten Karchen, from the Samye's excavated foundation material (*phue*) and placed within it relics from sacred sites in Tibet and India.

LHALUNG PALDHOR

Lhalung Paldhor, the celebrated assassin of King Langdarma (see page 704), spent 22 years at Drak Yerpa in the 9th century. According to him, the area was at first a nest for vultures, then a trading zone for the Hor nomads of the Changthang. In time, scholars and ascetics arrived, including himself. Before becoming a monk, he commanded an army against the Chinese and took part in the most horrible atrocities. Later, he repented, quit the army and went to Samye, where he took religious vows under Santarakshita, Vimalamitra, and Guru Rinpoche. To further his practice, he came to Drak Yerpa, choosing the highest peak for a retreat and digging a cave under a rock for shelter. Lhalung Paldhor built *chörtens* at Naljor Phuk and Chok Khang and created the Karu *chörten* to the right of Drakla Sinlak (Mountain Resembling a Demon's Hand.) He also founded a monastery at Khyam Tramo.

LUME

Tibetan Buddhism declined seriously under Langdarma and many sacred objects at Drak Yerpa were destroyed. After his assassination by Lhalung Paldhor, practitioners gradually drifted back. One of these was Lume, who eluded Langdarma and saved many precious manuscripts. He spearheaded the Second Diffusion of Buddhism and revitalized Drak Yerpa by building 108 temples. The most famous was the Nampa Nangse (Vairocana) Lhakhang, which had the central image of Vairocana, statues of the Eight Spiritual Sons of the Buddha, and Chenresi.

MARTÖN CHÖKYI JUNGNE

Martön Chökyi Jungne escaped Langdarma's persecution by fleeing to Kham. He returned at the beginning of the Second Diffusion and contributed much to Buddhism's resurgence. He founded the Jampa Lhakhang and the Mani Lhakhang with its large prayer wheel.

ATISHA

The famous teacher from Bengal came to Drak Yerpa ca 1047 and introduced the Dheno Sum (Tripitaka) doctrine into Tibet. He also expounded on the tantric doctrines of Phachö, Buchö, and Khuchö over a period of three years. A chapel called Kyormo and a large library were built by him. Chö Khang chapel was built by Drom, Ngok, and Naktso Lotsawa, Atisha's three main disciples. It contained a statue of Atisha that held a tooth of the master. Atisha's long tenure at Yerpa endowed the hermitage with immense importance for the Kadampa, who considered it more sacred than Reting Monastery. Many of them came to Yerpa to die.

OTHERS

Nub Nyima Nyingpo astounded his fellow meditators by hanging his orange robe on a beam of sunlight. He once rode into the sky on another beam and returned from a distant snow mountain with a snow lion. Nyizer Phuk and Senge Phuk were caves named after his exploits. Dawa Drakpa, another memorable ascetic, went to the top of Mt Lhari Nyingpo and rode down to Drak Yerpa on a moonbeam; he stayed in Dawa Phuk. Namkhai Nyingpo (see page 807) meditated in Namkhai Phuk and there perfected his ability to fly.

THE CAVES OF DRAK YERPA

Approach the site from the south and pass on the left the last village before the complex. Several trails lead to the major caves. The most direct way heads to a knoll crowned with ruined *chörtens* between the village and a steep ascent. This knoll gives the best view of Drak Yerpa's extent. To the left, up an inclined plateau, are the ruins of a cave chapel dedicated to the Rigsum Gönpo, Tibet's three principal protectors (Chenresi, Jampelyang, Chana Dorje). To the right is the stone throne of Atisha. To the northeast (immediately ahead) is a sacred pyramidal peak, Yerpa Lhari, abode of Yerpa's special protective deity. Near its base, in white rock, is inscribed the six-syllable *mantra* 'Om Mani Padme Hum.' Along a ridge that leads to Yerpa Lhari are two ruins sited just below a saddle. The far one was Atisha's own monastery, the near the residences of his disciples. Two damaged *chörtens* stand to the left and right of these sites. On the left (west) is a phallic peak known popularly as mythic Mt Meru. Beyond the plateau are the sheer cliffs that contain Yerpa's celebrated caves. They are connected by trails that crisscross each other at different levels. The caves below are described from west to east.

TENDREL DRUBPHUK (ATISHA'S MEDITATION CAVE)

Within a spur far to the west (left of a tall cleft) is the Tendrel (Relativity) Drubphuk, heavily embellished with the paraphernalia of religious devotion. Two narrow trails, one within the cave through a stone arch and the other leading outside the entrance, take one to a larger cave, Atisha Zimphuk (Atisha's Sleeping Cave). It is bedecked with prayer flags and an altar inside once displayed clay images of Atisha, Drokmi Lotsawa, and Ngok Lotsawa. Two nuns live here.

CHANA DORJE PHUK

This grotto next to Tendrel is comprised of four simple caves with terraces in front. The principal one has a number of *rangjung* images of Chana Dorje. Inside the caves are beds and altars carved from stone.

JAMPA LHAKHANG

The trail now turns more directly east and divides into branches at different levels. Slightly above and to the east of the Chana Dorje group is Jampa Lhakhang, the largest cave of the complex. It has a square internal structure that once contained a 13th-C. statue of Jampa, considered one of Tibet's four most important statues. According to Tucci, the Tibetologist, it also had statues of the Eight Bodhisattvas, Drölma, Namse, all commissioned by Martön, the 9th-C. lama. Below the Jampa Lhakhang are walled ruins. Inside, on a red rock face, are ornate, well-executed bas-relief carvings of the Rigsum Gönpo, the best by far at Yerpa.

DRUBTHOB PHUK

Small caves within two large ones are dedicated to the 84 Mahasiddhas who stayed at Yerpa in the 9th century.

CHÖGYAL PHUK

Songtsen Gampo meditated in this large cave in the 7th century. After the entrance, walk through a corridor to an interior cave chapel. On the left, at the junction of the corridor and the chapel, is a *rangjung* white lion face (Senge Dongma) on a rock surface. A sacred rock protrudes from the center of the chapel. Pilgrims say that the merit gained by circling this rock equals a full circumambulation of the fabled Tsari (see page 208).

Along the left wall is a shrine with a statue of Dorje Chang. Next to it are *rangjung* images of a horse's head and the Rigsum Gönpo (not located). To the right of the rock is a window. On the ground between the rock and the window are traces of 'milk', supposedly secreted by the goat that helped create the original site of the Jokhang. At the back are fragments of murals (Gönpo, Drölma, Sakyamuni) that probably date back to the 16th century. The chapel's inner part is a meditation cave with a shrine on the left. Within it were the true-likeness (*ngadrama*) statue of Songtsen Gampo and a statue of Palden Lhamo, erected by Lhalung Paldhor.

DORJE PHUK

This cave (west and below Chögyal Phuk) is the place where Guru Rinpoche left his *dorje*.

DAWA PHUK

Dawa Phuk (Moon Cave; east below Chögyal Phuk) is an overhang now rebuilt as a chapel. Guru Rinpoche meditated here during the day of each full moon. A rock near the center has the *rangjung* image of a *mahasiddha*. At the far end of the cave's first section is a *rangjung*, red-faced Relchikma (Ekajati), wrathful guardian of the Nyingma Dzokchen tradition. The second section has a shrine with footprints of Guru Rinpoche and Lhalung Paldhor. Next to these is a new Guru Rinpoche statue. Outside the cave entrance is a *rangjung* image of Guru Rinpoche's trident (*khatram*). Near Dawa Phuk is Trewu Marser (Red and Yellow Monkey Temple), the *rangjung* chapel used by King Songtsen Gampo upon arrival at Yerpa.

LHALUNG PHUK

Below Dawa Phuk and Chögyal Phuk stands a rebuilt chapel, hiding place of Lhalung Paldhor. He stayed here for several years and then moved to a higher cave. After the entrance is the small Palden Lhamo Lhakhang. Right of the shrine in a low, recessed niche are carvings of Guru Rinpoche and his two consorts on a rock pillar. This pillar once had statues of four of the Five Dhyani Buddhas (Akshobhya, Amitabha, Amoghasiddhi, Ratnasambhava). The pillar is positioned exactly below the sacred rock in Songtsen Gampo's cave. To circumambulate it carries the same benefits as circling the rock above. To the right of Guru Rinpoche is a statue of Songtsen Gampo; behind him is a *rangjung* Jampa on the rock surface. To the left, behind Guru Rinpoche, are c. 15th-C. paintings of Tsepame, Thousand-armed Chenresi, and Drölkar (White Tara). Lhalung Paldhor's private meditation cell is behind the Guru Rinpoche carving. Within it are faint traces of early cave paintings.

NETEN LHAKHANG

This chapel (destroyed) lies below and east of Dawa Phuk. Reputedly one of the oldest chapels in Tibet (built by Lume and his disciple Ngok Jangchub Jungne in the 11th C.), this site saw the start of the cult of the the the 16 Arhats. Inside was a one-story-high statue of Sakyamuni surrounded by 16 magnificent Chinese-style Arhats (probably 11th C.).

DORJE AND DRILBU PHUK

The last caves of Yerpa are east of Lhalung Phuk and considerably farther up the mountain. They are Dorje and Drilbu, caves of the thunderbolt and bell, the commonest ritual instruments of Tantric Buddhism.

ATISHA'S THRONE (JOWO JE SHUGTRI)

Stone seats on a flat ledge below the Neten Lhakhang were used by Atisha and his chief disciples. Nearby is Nyamgakor Durtrö cemetery.

Note Many other caves dot the hillside. They, too, have names and legends associated with past masters. Some major Yerpa chapels from the original Yerpa complex (destroyed) are Lama Lhakhang, Yerpa Labrang, Madhor Lhakhang, and Bara Lhakhang.

TERDROM:
AN 8TH-CENTURY NUNNERY
AND ITS MEDICINAL HOT SPRING

Location	See Upper Reaches of the Kyi Chu, page 544
Map Reference	NH46-6 C

Terdrom means 'Hidden Treasure Casket,' a reference to the many concealed treasures (*terma*) supposedly discovered here. It is a Kadampa nunnery that perhaps dates back to the 8th century. The larger complex was developed in the 11th century. Like neighboring Drigungtil, Terdrom suffered little destruction during the Cultural Revolution. A guesthouse is built around the wonderful Chutsen Chugang hot spring baths and many pilgrims come here to immerse themselves in the medicinal waters. Nearby is a sacred spring called Sindhura Chumik. The monastery has 30–40 nuns and a few monks. To the north, a few hours' walk away, is a sacred Guru Rinpoche cave. This and the nunnery are the most important religious sites of the Zoto Valley.

Approximately 30 buildings stand at the entrance of an extremely narrow gorge with near-vertical cliffs—an arresting, idyllic spot. Nuns and lay workers have been rebuilding the lesser chapels since the mid-1980s. The main assembly hall is well decorated with images, *thangkas*, and brocades, and is the scene of daily services. On the altar are statues of Guru Rinpoche and his two consorts. Above the many buildings that constitute the nuns' dwellings and retreats are numerous meditation caves, hollowed out of the base of a small plateau. The main one was used by both Guru Rinpoche and his consort, Yeshe Tsogyal. A rebuilt hermitage now stands in front of it and a young nun, considered the reincarnation of Yeshe Tsogyal, lives within.

History

According to popular tradition, King Trisong Detsen in 772 offered one of his queens, Yeshe Tsogyal, to Guru Rinpoche, the Indian tantric master who introduced Buddhism to Tibet. This was an unpopular act for the Bönpo members of the king's court and the situation became untenable for the tantric teacher. He and Yeshe Tsogyal then sought refuge in a cave at Terdrom. After the guru's departure, his consort stayed on for a number of years. The nunnery is built on the site of her historic retreat. Two renowned Dzokchen masters stayed in this isolated hermitage as well. In the 11th C., Dzeng Dharmabodhi, a disciple of the Indian sage, Padampa Sangye of Dingri, made this his home. Later, the second of the 'text-discoverer kings', Tertön Dorje Lingpa (1346–1405), came here and recovered hidden texts.

Pilgrimage sites

Above the nunnery are the caves of Dhudul Phuk and Sang Phuk. A trail leads from them up to the peaks of Zophu Terdrom Drakar and Dhechok Khorlo Drakri. Within the latter is a cave called Phukdrang Ngu, where Lama Drigung Phowa meditated for five years. Below this is the small chapel of Rinchen Phüntshok Zimkhang, consecrated to Guru Rinpoche. Beyond it, on the *nangkhor* path (see below), is Tshokhang Chenmo, a vast grotto also called

Kiri Yongdzong. Guru Rinpoche supposedly spent seven years here preaching to the *dakinis*. In the surroundings is the five-peaked mountain that represents the five sisterly divinities called Tsering Chenga. Halfway up it is the cave of Tamdrin Phuk consecrated to Tamdrin, the horse-necked divinity and wrathful emanation of Chenresi. Half a day from here is Rinchen Pungpa, from where Kunzik Sherab Wöser discovered the sacred mountain of Ri Rinchen Pungpa.

THE TERDROM NANGKHOR

The Terdrom Nangkhor (Inner Circuit) is a pilgrimage route that links the nunnery to the famed Guru Rinpoche cave in the higher reaches of the Zoto Valley. Many naturally occurring sacred sites along the route have mythological significance; hire a guide from the nunnery who can show the way and explain the religious import of these obscure icons. The following description follows Keith Dowman's *The Power Places of Central Tibet*.

The *nangkhor* starts at the hot spring baths. Directly below them is a limestone ridge that spans the river next to the complex; water tunnels through the ridge within a 15-m-long cavity. Local legend says this ridge once dammed a poisonous lake whose fumes were so deadly that birds were brought down by the vapors. Within its depths lived evil spirits. When Guru Rinpoche came to meditate in this area, he threw his *dorje* at the ridge and a tunnel was created, thus draining the lake. As a testimonial to the miracle, the shape of his *dorje* can still be seen inside the tunnel. To placate the spirits he gave them as a residence a red rock that now stands on the right (west) bank of the river. To make the place a comfortable sanctuary for future practitioners, he created the medicinal hot springs.

The *nangkhor* leads from the springs to the nunnery. Cross a bridge north of the complex and climb a trail up a ridge to the west. At its top is a *chörten*; from here the plateau above the nunnery and the mountain behind it resemble the head and trunk of an elephant. Beyond is a spring that supposedly flows from Guru Rinpoche's cave, and after it is a ruined monastery called Tinkye. The trail ascends sharply to the Norbu La and then skirts a steep ridge around a large cirque. A *chörten* marks the point of descent from the pass down into a valley to the north; a nearby rock has a hole in which a treasure was hidden by Guru Rinpoche. Within the descending valley is a sacred cave and a ruined hermitage called Bugung Sumdo. The path then climbs up the valley's south side to a sky-burial site and continues along and up the valley's side to the crest of the ridge.

The next stage involves traversing the face of a large limestone rock by following natural hand and foot holds on the surface. At the other end is Khandro Kiri Yongdzong, a large grotto inside a tall limestone pinnacle. This is the Assembly Hall of the Dakinis, and the sheer size of the cavern—50 m high—merits the name. Inside are two hermitages (some nuns live here) and the ruins of a temple. Climb by ladder to a passage that leads to a cave high in the limestone tower. This is the Tsogyal Sangphuk, the Secret Cave of Yeshe Tsogyal. A small altar commemorates the site where Guru Rinpoche and his consort meditated. Here, Yeshe Tsogyal received her three Khandro Nyingtik initiations from the master. Over the years she returned to this cave to deepen her spirituality and, towards the end of her life, performed her last Dzokchen retreat in the cave. The Tsogyal Sangphuk is a major site associated with the *yogini*.

To continue the *nangkhor*, return across the limestone rock face and descend 500 m down one of the steep scree slopes that drops from the ridge to a gorge. A trail within the gorge leads to the ruins of Drang Monastery, sited on the river's left bank. (At this point, a side valley opens away from the main one.) Within the ruins is the hermitage of Rinchen Phüntshok, a Drigungpa tertön who discovered some of Guru Rinpoche's treasures within Khandro Kiri Yongdzong. A trail leads down the gorge back to the hot springs.

THE CHIKHOR

This long pilgrimage route completely encompasses Drigungtil Monastery (see page 553) and Terdrom. It also goes north from the nunnery to Khandro Kiri Yongdzong, but instead of returning south to the hot springs along the gorge, it continues east along an east–west trending valley. At the end of it, after a relatively easy 4-hr descent, make a right turn down another valley. A trail within it goes due south to meet eventually the Zorong Valley. This takes another 4 hr. At the junction, head west back to Drigungtil along the Zorong Chu on a good, level track. Menpa Qu, the village below the monastery, is regained in 4 more hours. Budget four–five days for a leisurely exploration of this circuit, and try to find a qualified guide from either Terdrom or Drigungtil. Many meditation caves are scattered along the route, some associated with Guru Rinpoche and other famous Dzokchen practitioners.

RECHUNG PHUK:
THE YARLUNG CAVE TEMPLE
OF MILAREPA'S DISCIPLE

Location	See Yarlung, page 525
Map Reference	NH46-10 C

Rechung Phuk was once a large Kagyüpa complex with 1,000 monks. Today, its striking ruins stand out clearly on the Mila Tse spur that divides the two branches of the Yarlung Valley. A few small chapels, some of them cave shrines, have been rebuilt. Supervised by lamas transplanted from East Tibet, this place is on its way to regaining some of its illustrious past.

The site

The first structure is a new, two-story building on the right. Its ground floor is a storeroom and kitchen; the upper floor houses the monks. Beyond is a rebuilt, one-story chapel with an entrance portico. The principal images here (all new) are Guru Rinpoche, his two consorts, and Tsangnyön Heruka. Behind this chapel is the all-important Rechung Phuk, the meditation cave of Rechungpa, trusted disciple of Milarepa. A narrow stairway leads up to the cave, itself fronted by a new building under a rock overhang. (Below is a tiny *gönkhang*.) Noteworthy objects in the chapel are the footprints (on stones) of Karmapa, Rechungpa, and Milarepa. Next to these is the imprint of Guru Rinpoche's boot (*zhabchak draku*). Within the cave is the stone seat (*shugtri*) of Rechungpa and on the altar are images of Marpa, Milarepa, and Rechungpa. A rock has the footprint of Tsangnyön Heruka. The most outstanding piece of art in the cave before the destruction of the complex during the Cultural Revolution was a statue of Tsangnyön Heruka, made personally by Götshangpa. It was decorated with a rosary of silver skulls.

Above and to the left of the path is the *dukhang*, a new one-story building. Further up the slopes, resurrected from extensive ruins, is another two-story building. Overlooking all the new buildings are the meditation caves (*drubkhang*). This row of retreats, perched on a narrow ledge, is entered through the first cell. A *khorlam* path circles the complex from the *dukhang*. It ascends a small pass and then goes down to a renovated *chörten* before doubling back to the monastery (1 hr).

Rechungpa (1083–1161)

Rechungpa was Milarepa's most illustrious disciple. Born in Kab, Gungthang, the district north of Kyirong, he began studying with the master at the age of 11 and twice went to India for teachings. Many credited him with Milarepa's biography (*Mila Khabum*) and *Mila Gurbum*, the famous 'Hundred Thousand Songs of Milarepa'. (In fact, these two texts were probably written by Tsangpa Gyare Yeshe Dorje; see below.)

Tsangpa Gyaré Yeshe Dorje (1161–1211)

Born in Nyangtö and known as the Mad Monk of Tsang, Tsangpa Gyaré was the disciple of Phagmo Drupa (1110–70), himself the student of Gampopa, Milarepa's chief disciple. Tsangpa Gyaré founded Longdhöl (near Ratö) and Ralung monasteries as well as the Phurdruk Gompa of Choknam. One of Tibetan Buddhism's most colorful personalities, he and Rechungpa, following the ascetic example of their teacher, traveled throughout Tibet as pilgrims. He became the first person to explore and to open the Secret Valley of Tsari (see page 208). Tsangpa Gyaré had many devoted disciples, and he died here at Rechung Phuk.

NYANGTÖ KYI PHUK: WHERE MONKS WERE TRAINED IN THE ARTS OF LONG-DISTANCE RUNNING AND LEVITATION

The Nyangtö Kyi Phuk hermitage, easily accessible from Gyantse, contains a number of meditation cells once used by practitioners of the Maha Ketongwa cult. They would seal themselves in utter darkness for long periods of time in order to develop specific yogic powers. One specialty was *lungom*, an integrated discipline of meditation and yoga, whereby the adept learned to run very long distances in a trance without tiring and at unusually high speed. This site was the premier institution in Tsang to teach and promote these esoteric disciplines.

Location (Map reference NH45-16 B)

Nyangtö Kyi Phuk is located on the right bank of the Nyang Chu, 16 km from Gyantse. Head out of town and follow the eastern banks of the river northwestward for 3 1/2 hr to reach the hermitage.

THE CULT OF MAHA KETONGWA ('GREAT CALLER')

Before the Cultural Revolution, 200 monks under the guidance of a *tulku* underwent training at Nyangtö Kyi Phuk. Novices entering the program went through courses similar to those of other monasteries. After an initial period, they immersed themselves in a practice called *losum chösum* (three years, three doctrines). which concentrated almost exclusively on yoga. If a student desired to proceed further, he enrolled in courses lasting six, seven, or 12 years; senior monks provided the closely guarded instruction.

The two most accomplished masters from the hermitages of Nyangtö Kyi Phuk and Thalchok Ling (see below) received the title of Maha Ketongwa. This ranking had to be officially confirmed by oracle-priests and the Tibetan government. Every 12 years (Year of the Rooster), one of these Maha Ketongwas went for a remarkable run. Accompanied by two yogic adepts, he followed a circuit around central Tibet known as the Yuldruk Barkhor. The route started at Shalu Monastery (see page 400), went to Lhasa via Shigatse, then continued to Samye and the districts of Yarlung and south Tibet. It turned back to Nethang near Lhasa, and finally headed west back to Gyantse and Shalu. The Maha Ketongwa were obliged to finish the trip within two weeks, a seemingly impossible feat.

The tradition of the run started in the 13th C. with Butön, the historian and renovator of Shalu, and the prominent yogi, Yungtön Dorje Pal. Once every 12 years, the yogi performed an elaborate ritual of appeasement for Shinje, the Lord of Death, to prevent the deity from ingesting a person every day. Butön and three other lamas journeyed to visit the magician and to witness the event. On arrival, they found that Shinje had appeared, huge and terrifying. Yungtön told the four that the conclusion of the rites involved a human sacrifice. The three lamas invented excuses but Butön offered himself. Yungtön then told the historian that an alternative was available. If Butön promised to perform the same ritual every 12 years and hold his descendants to the same oath, he could escape. Butön agreed and Yungtön miraculously created in his stead innumerable doves that flew into the gaping mouth of Shinje.

Since that time the abbots of Shalu have propitiated the deity. Over the centuries, other lesser deities had to be appeased as well and swift runners were needed to summon them from various parts of the country in a very short time. For centuries, Shalu vigorously trained monks in the practise of *lungom*, a collective term for a large number of disciplines integrating mental concentration with heroic physical feats. The best-known discipline, however, is the long-distance run, a test for Tibet's premier yogis.

To prepare for the Yuldruk Barkhor, three yogis went into strict retreat for 11 years. In the company of the abbot and other high lamas, they would enter a cave on an auspicious day. The entrances would then be walled up and only a tiny opening left for food. Within the cell, each adept concentrated on perfecting two esoteric practises. The first was *thumo*, a breathing and meditation technique to generate extraordinary body heat. As a final test, a yogi took 12 huge sheets and a large pot of half-boiled wheat flour to a snow-covered mountain-top. After undressing, he wrapped a wet sheet around his body and at the same time ingested a cup of the dough. Focusing his concentration, he would dry the sheet thoroughly in a short time and concurrently digest the dough. The cycle was repeated until all sheets were dried and all the dough consumed.

The second technique that would absorb the inmate for the duration of 11 years was levitation. This consists of the person sitting cross-legged on a thick cushion. After doing a number of very vigorous breathing exercises, he then tries to leap up without the use of his hands. This cycle was repeated innumerable times. After long periods of practise the body supposedly becomes very light and the truly advanced person can float a few feet above the ground. At the very least, the accomplished can sit on a barley stalk without bending it. When the time was up, the cells were broken open and the yogis journeyed to Shalu to be tested in public. The chief adept, the Maha Ketongwa, entered a bare room below ground. The ceiling, twice his body height and level with the ground, had a square hole in its center. After a week of intense meditation he took a final examination in the presence of two government officials from Shigatse. The date was usually the 11th day of the tenth lunar month. Large crowds of monks and laymen sat around to watch the Maha Ketongwa levitate and squeeze through the hole. If successful, he went on to another test. A yakskin coat, soaked in icewater, was wrapped around his body and he was required to dry it completely by means of *thumo*. After the feat, the coat was passed around to judges and onlookers.

Before starting off for the Yuldruk Barkhor, the chief yogi was elaborately dressed. On top of his robes was bound a broad sash. A *phurpa* was stuck into the sash and a rosary placed around his neck. Part of his long hair was piled into a bun and decorated with a *dorje*. He wore huge earrings made of white conchshell and over his eyes were put screens endowed with magic and made from the hairs of a bear. His left hand held a thigh-bone trumpet and the right a trident. The governor from Shigatse attached seals along the sash to prevent the yogi from taking off his clothes for a proper rest. After these elaborate preparations, the three embarked on the arduous Yuldruk Barkhor.

In the meantime the governors sent a report to Lhasa informing the cabinet of the results of the test. According to those who witnessed the event, the pace of the three was not particularly fast and there was nothing special in the manner of their walk. Some informants insisted that the three were in a trance; others denied this. A few young men invariably tried to keep up with them but they usually dropped out after some time, unable to maintain the pace. During the journey, the three were not allowed to take long rests or to lie down. As the three yogis approached each settlement, the populace turned out *en masse* to receive the blessings of the Maha Ketongwa, which he dispensed by touching the person with his trident. At the same time he would purify the locale by scattering rice and barley seeds into the air.

When the three eventually reached Lhasa, they proceeded directly to the Potala. At the base of the palace, within the village of Shöl, are two stone *dorings* erected in front of the long stone ramps leading up to the formal entrances. Here, the Maha Ketongwa blew on his bone trumpet once to signify his arrival. At this the servants of the Dalai Lama immediately opened all the rooms and lit incense inside them. There was only a short time for this to be done before the Maha Ketongwa reached the bottom of the steps, where he blew the instrument once more; the third and last time it was blown was at the entrance. Then the chief yogi, in a great frenzy, went into every room, scattering rice before him to rid the premises of evil influences. Finally, he went into the personal chambers of the Dalai Lama, where he sat in front of the god-king and was given two cups of tea. All this was conducted in total silence. At the end, without a single word being spoken, the three visitors were invited into the houses of the noble families. Sitting on a high dais, the Maha Ketongwa blessed each member of the household by putting his two hands on their bowed heads. The patriarch, similarly blessed, had his forehead touched by that of the yogi. As part of the ritual, each room was purified by the same scattering of rice. Finally, after regaining the monastery of Shalu, the three spent a few months in rest and relaxation before continuing the practise of meditation, yogic exercises, and other aspects of monastic life.

SHALU, NYANGTÖ KYI PHUK AND THALCHOK LING

It should be noted that Shalu Monastery (page 400), besides being a respository of some of the most spectacular wall paintings now in existence in Tibet, was well-known in former times as an advanced center of esoteric yogic instructions. The most celebrated among these was that of the *lungom*. Shalu, together with Nyangtö Kyi Phuk and the Thalchok Ling, was the most renowned institution for the teaching of fringe dsiciplines. The forte of all these monasteries was that the student achieved high-leveled physical prowess not by the development of muscles but by means of a remarkable concentration of mind.

DAGLHA GAMPO: PRINCIPAL RETREAT OF THE KAGYÜ SECT

Daglha Gampo, the Dakpo (part of southeast Tibet) district's most significant hermitage, was a powerful Kagyüpa institution. With Tsurphu, it was the major retreat center of the Kagyüpa. It was founded in 1121 by Milarepa's pupil, Gampopa, patriarch of the lineage known as Dakpo Kagyü, which eventually became the thriving Karma Kagyü. Over the centuries, Daglha Gampo became famous far and wide for its cave hideaways; many pilgrims came to undertake long, arduous retreats. The center was destroyed by the Dzungars in 1781 and subsequently rebuilt. Some 60 monks lived here before the Cultural Revolution—now considerably less. Since the late 1980s, chapels and monks' residences have been rebuilt. An old lama, Konchok Chöphel, preserved some original statues and *thangkas*. He lives in a house overlooking the monastery; inside are two precious statues, Chenresi (12 heads and eight arms) and Demchok in *yabyum*. The latter supposedly came from India during Tilopa's time. A small chapel houses about 30 bronzes and ten *thangkas* saved from the Cultural Revolution.

Find a guide from the monastery to help explore the many meditation caves, some very high up on the mountain. A sacred walk circumambulates the monastery and surrounding caves. Allow 3–4 hr. The *khora* route starts from the one-room chapel and heads northwest, past the Sewa Phuk caves of Gampopa's three main disciples. Then the path curves and heads east. At the eastern end of the *khora* the path all but disappears. A gangway of rickety wood planks serves as a catwalk along the sheer face of the cliff. Within imposing ridges are numerous meditation caves. The *khora* finally swings to the southwest, and then back down to the monastery.

THE CAVES

The six major caves of Daglha Gampo are:

- Sewa Phuk—the Three Caves of the Three Khyenpas (Gampopa's first disciples): Düsum Khyenpa (the First Karmapa), Phagmo Drupa, Sagom Shatopa.
- Dremba Phuk—the cave's name is a contraction of *dremo* (female spirit) and *phurpa* (ritual dagger). Both Gampopa and Phagmo Drupa stayed here. A headprint of the latter is on a rock. A natural spring called Chime Namo flows nearby. In the cave, pilgrims squeeze through a small passage and circumambulate a rock.
- Salongten—this *lhakhang* is in ruins.
- Namkhading—Gampopa's main meditation cave, attached to a *lhakhang*.
- Chime Phuk.
- Shago Gompa—a small ruined monastery with a *chörten* made by Gampopa. Legend says ten flying Indian *siddhas* delivered the material for the *chörten*.

Access (Map reference NH46-10 D)

There are several ways to reach Daglha Gampo. The easiest route is via Gyatsa Qu and Lung (described below), which begins immediately after the Lhamo Latso pilgrimage (see page 623).

Alternatively, pilgrims often start from Bangrim Chöde (see below), Dakpo Rinpoche's mona-stery, located 10 km east of Nang Xian on the north bank of the Tsangpo. From here it takes 1 1/2 days to reach the hermitage.

GYATSA QU TO DAGLHA GAMPO MONASTERY

The route follows the north (left) bank of the Tsangpo, where the river's course is twisted and complicated. From Gyatsa Qu, a dirt road heads east, then south-southeast, to follow the river bank. Finally it makes a sharp turn to the northeast to reach Lung (Nelung), where the walk to the monastery starts. Lung, 20 km southeast of Gyatsa Qu, can be reached by a motorable dirt road; trucks take one hour to cover the distance.

From Gyatsa Qu, follow a dirt jeep-track which branches east from the main road. It clings to the edge of the Tsangpo River; some very narrow sections are difficult to negotiate by truck—one slip and it's into the river. Avalanches during the rainy season are common. In fact, few trucks run from Gyatsa to Lung and it is a good idea to walk (4 hrs).

Lung is located up a small side valley that trends to the northeast. A side road leaves the river road to make the final zigzag approach to the settlement. (The dirt road continues past Lung for about 10 km more.) At the truck stop in Lung, walk east along the dirt road for five minutes to join a trail going north. (Ask a villager for directions.) Its beginning, along sand, is quite steep (1/4 hr). Then it levels off, follows a river on the left, and reaches a meadow in one hour. The trail then divides: the right branch returns to Lung; take the left to reach the big village of Ruka Nyipa (1/2 hr). The path to Daglha Gampo skirts the village. It is not obvious; ask a local. In a short time, the now distinct trail becomes very steep. Aim for a small saddle between two peaks in the north. Reach the first part of a double pass after 1 1/2 hrs. There are no prayer flags, only stone cairns. Beyond the pass is a sloping plateau. At its end, marked by a juniper incense burner, is the second half of the double pass. Do not go as far as the second pass (the trail returns to Lung).

After the first pass, look carefully for a side trail that goes to the left. (Small, low bushes in the area make it difficult to see the beginning of the trail.) Follow it across the hillside to a ridge. After 1/2 hr from the first pass, come to a point on the ridge with many prayer flags. The monastery appears here for the first time. Carry on along the ridge, then descend to Ngakhang, 1 1/2 hrs from the pass. The village is situated in a small meadow and a river runs through the center. The monastery is not visible from here. From Ngakhang, looking north, two prominent peaks stand out, one in front of the other. A huge, prominent rock protrudes from the first. Go steeply up from Ngakhang towards this rock along an indistinct trail (ask the villagers for directions). Later, the trail becomes more well-defined. Reach the rock in 1/2 hr. Skirt it from below, traverse the hillside, and then drop down to a river and bridge (the river runs between the two peaks). Cross the bridge and start ascending the second peak, away from the river. The path is clear. Reach a trail junction and a stone cairn in 1/2 hr. The right path is very good. Do not take it. Take the left, less obvious one. Continue to climb the steep mountainside in a northerly direction, passing small meadows along the way. The monastery, on a flat plateau, finally appears after 1 hr. All around are superb views.

DAGLHA GAMPO: MYTHOLOGY AND SACRED PLACES

The site of Daglha Gampo is ancient. King Songtsen Gampo embarked on a program of building monasteries at the cardinal points outside of Lhasa to subdue the she-demon of Tibet (see page 43). One of these, according to tradition, was Daglha Gampo, which is geomantically located at the head of the monster. To hold down the demon, the king concealed a book, a statue, and a *chörten*, denoting mind, body and speech, at carefully selected sites. Later, King Trisong Detsen, Guru Rinpoche, and his consort, Yeshe Tsogyal, came here to meditate in the caves of Norbuchen, Shel Phuk Lhayi Drak, and Drak Penzha. They also visited a sacred lake, Tso Mendel Nakpo, and a sacred peak, Zanglung Drak. Songtsen Gampo had hidden important sacred relics at these five sites as well. Guru Rinpoche also stayed and meditated on nearby Dargyi Ri; his footprint (*shapje*) is still there. Other holy places in the area include: Khandro Truekyi Zingbu, a lake to the west; a *rangjung chörten* called Drepung Chörten Rangjung to the northwest; a holy peak, shaped like a stack of five mandalas, in the north.

THE FOUNDING OF DAGLHA GAMPO

Daglha Gampo, originally known as Dhensa, was founded in the early 12th C. by Gampopa (Nyame Dakpo Lhaje Sonam Rinchen, 1079–1153). He was taken with the physical shape of Mt Daglha Gampo, which to him resembled a king sitting on the throne. The seven associated minor peaks around it represented ministers before the monarch. Gampopa first meditated at Namkhading (Garuda Peak), a nearby ridge. From his cave he taught and converted the aboriginal inhabitants. In the vicinity he established three chapels: Jakhyil, Gomdhe Zimkhang, and Chökhang Nyingma. Over the years, due to the spiritual presence of diverse masters, a number of meditation caves on Mt Daglha Gampo became highly sanctified. The most important are: Zanglung, Numo Rinchen, Dredrang Dheshek, Sa-en, Atshang, Shei, Sewa, Ghurteng, Jakyib, Layak, Thatsa, Chöje, Wösel, Tachu Dham Gyi, Men, Ngo Thong, and Jamyang.

Bangrim Chöde Monastery This Gelugpa monastery is located on the north bank of the Tsangpo, 12 km west of Nang Xian (see Tsari Pilgrimage, page 226, for location details) and 63 km east of Gyatsa. A ferry landing, called Cherter, is across from the monastery. Pilgrims sometimes start from here to Daglha Gampo.

From the main Tibet–Sichuan highway walk 1/2 hr along a stone and sand path to the ferry. The boatmen live in a village on the north bank, a little distance east of the monastery. The crossing takes 1/4 hr. After reaching shore, walk 20 min to the monastery complex. Dakpo Rinpoche, abbot of the monastery, has his residence in a large *dukhang*. More than ten functional buildings (80 monks and several old lamas) form the rest of this thriving complex. The *dukhang's* interior is new and holds a statue of Dakpo Rinpoche's previous incarnation. Fine old *thangkas* and small original statues are kept in the abbot's private room upstairs. He returned to Tibet from Paris in 1987. A two-day pilgrimage route goes west from here to Daglha Gampo Monastery.

NECROPOLISES OF THE 7TH AND 8TH CENTURIES

Ancient Yarlung-era burial grounds have been found not only in the Valley of the Kings at Chongye but at other sites in central Tibet. In addition to the characteristic earth tumuli associated with the tombs of early kings, unusual *chörten*-tombs, stone coffins, sacrificial chambers, and ritual platforms have all been unearthed. Located in tributary valleys near the Tsangpo–Lhasa River confluence, these finds—discovered mainly in the 1980s—contribute significantly to the scant body of archeological knowledge in the country.

CHONGYE:
COLOSSAL TOMBS
OF THE YARLUNG KINGS

These colossal Yarlung-dynasty tombs, burial chambers of ancient kings, are unique in Tibet. They represent a rich source of information about life and society between the 7th and 9th centuries. The structures, some measuring close to 200 m per side and up to 30 m in height, consist of funeral cavities topped up and protected by large earthen tumuli.

As is well-known, at death, the bodies of most Tibetans are disposed of by the so-called sky-burial method, in which the body is dismembered and fed to vultures. Lamas usually are embalmed inside *chörten*-tombs called *dhungbums*. Only in the Yarlung period and earlier were important people buried in the ground. According to a 17th-C. Tibetan text (*Tamsig Gyatso*), the interiors of the huge tumuli were sometimes partitioned into five quadrangular chambers. Within was placed a statue of the deceased king, made especially of earth, silk, and paper. Many precious objects were also buried as well, and in some cases, living humans and animals were entombed with the monarch.

Songtsen Gampo's tomb, supposedly containing a silver coffin, is located at a site known as Chongpuda, close to Chongye Xian. (All Yarlung tombs had a secret name; this one is Murimug.) Five chambers (chapels) within it held priceless, mythic treasures: five kinds of divine gems, five kinds of gems of the *nagas*, five kinds of human gems, and earthly substances that bestow life and induce happiness in all living things. The chapels represented a complete cosmology that corresponded to the Five Mystic Families of the Buddha.

For the construction, special earth was taken from Tregi Ri and mud from the Nyang River. The tomb entrance, like that of the Jokhang in Lhasa, faces west to Nepal. At the center, a representation of Dorje Tsug served to subdue the *damsi*, intangible spirits created by violent deaths. Near the top of the cavity was a verandah made of sandalwood. The principal object here was Songtsen Gampo's garment, encrusted with innumerable gems and jewels. Over this was a sandalwood umbrella. Accompanying these objects were tributes from Tibet's neighbors. From India came a coat of armor made of gold and wrapped in copper, concealed in the west chapel. China sent the right hand of a coral statue of the queen, placed in the north. The king's most treasured object, a quantity of precious glass wrapped in silk, was in the middle together with a volume of gold, also wrapped in silk. The gold figures of a man and his horse,

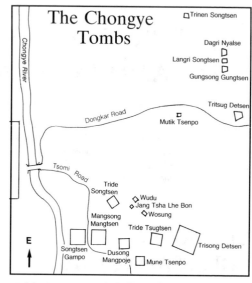

a gift from the King of Hor, were hidden in the east. From the Kingdom of Yartse came a heavy weight of pearls wrapped in the skin of a young deer, which was buried in the south. Many statues also stood in the five chapels (not all were Buddhist deities). Songtsen Gampo's grandson, Mangsong Mangtsen, led the processions of ministers and subjects during the burial ceremony. Each person carried a load of priceless funeral offerings. In this way they entrusted the tomb of their great king to the gods charged with protecting the country. Looting long ago stripped the monument of these many treasures.

Description of the Chongye tombs (Map reference NH46-10 C)

The Chongye Yarlung tombs are scattered across a large area along the lower slopes of Mt Mura and the entrance of the Dongkar Valley. The site extends along a east–west axis for about 2 km and measures 1 1/2 km from north to south.

Two main groups of tombs, 800 m apart, can be identified. The larger one, consisting of ten tombs, is located south of Chongye Xian and the Chongye River. Scattered along the valley floor and the lower slopes of Mt Mura; they include the major tombs of King Songtsen Gampo and Trisong Detsen. A lesser group of six, farther to the east, is at the entrance of the Dongkar Valley. The tombs lie on the east side of the dirt road that leads from Chongye Xian south into the Dongkar Valley. As the main Chongye Valley road heads southeast to Tsomi, it bisects the larger cluster, isolating Songtsen Gampo's prominent tumuli to the north. The rest of this group is south of the road. It is possible to identify 16 tombs, although research indicates there should be 19. One of the missing three, belonging to the semi-mythical King Drönyang Deru, is situated near Sangda, half-way between Tsethang and Chongye. The other two have probably disappeared through centuries of erosion.

THE GROUP OF TEN

SONGTSEN GAMPO

King Songtsen Gampo's tomb (Bangso Marpo, the Red Tomb; also Songtsen Bangso), closest to the main Chongye Valley road, is 1 km south of the Chongye Bridge. The most sacred of the entire group, its square tumulus measures 129 m per side and has a height of 13.4 m. A small, rebuilt Nyingmapa chapel, on the top of the huge earth mound, is reached by a steep flight of stone steps that begins immediately right of the road. From the top, it is possible to see all the Yarlung tombs except Trisong Detsen's. The original chapel was built by the Nyingmapa lama, Ralpachen Nyima Wösel (1124–92). Its main room is consecrated to King Songtsen Gampo, his two wives, and his two principal ministers, Gar and Thönmi Sambhota. Murals depict Guru Tsengye (Eight Manifestations of Guru Rinpoche), the 35 Buddhas of Confession, Eight Drölmas, and the protectors Palden Lhamo, Mahakala, and others. Behind this room is another small chapel. The main images here show the Past, Present, and Future Buddhas. They are flanked by Tsepame (left), Guru Rinpoche, and the two protectors, Chana Dorje and Tamdrin. Surrounding the temple is a *khorlam*.

The tomb, badly eroded at the base, is open to an *in situ* examination of its construction methods. Its tumuli, built from the ground up, is composed of many individual layers. Each is a combination of earth, wood, grass, and stone. Along the south side, the earth and stone layers are generally 10–20 cm thick. The structure is further reinforced by round wooden poles that pierce through the layers vertically. Small pebbles, packed tightly together to form a sheath, in turn protect the wood. Time, however, has caused these wooden elements to disintegrate completely. As a result, only the cavities remain. On top of each layer is a secondary layer of *pema* branches, the material used to strengthen monastery roofs.

MANGSONG MANGTSEN

The tomb of Mangsong Mangtsen, grandson of Songtsen Gampo, is directly across the main road from the Bangso Marpo. Its tumulus is square and each side measures 136 m. Within the exposed south wall (4.5 m in height) are layers of stone slabs, each about 30 cm thick; *pema* branches provide support for the earth fill. A large cavity at the top was dug long ago by grave robbers.

DUSONG MANGPOJE

Dusong Mangpoje succeeded Mangsong Mangtsen. His square tomb is 100 m behind his predecessor's, on the left of the main road after it makes a sharp left turn and then a right to continue down the valley. The sides of the tumulus are each 90 m long and its height 8.9 m. Erosion has altered the physical appearance significantly. Parts of the base reveal the tomb's structure; various earthen layers bound together by a stone wall (1 m thick, 1 m high). Grave robbers also created the hole at the top.

MUNE TSENPO

Mune Tsenpo was a son of Trisong Detsen; he abdicated in 797. His tomb is at the base of Mt Mura near the road's sharp right turn. Each of its sides is 75 m long, and the earth mound is 12 m high. There is again a cavity at the top. The exposed north side shows a long stone wall, 22 m in length and 9 m in height, within the tumulus. The earth and *pema*-branch layers are clearly visible here.

TRIDE TSUGTSEN (ME AGTSHOM)

Tride Tsugtsen and his Chinese queen, Jincheng, founded the 8th-C. Kachu Monastery (see page 378). His tomb, on the slopes of Mt Mura, is directly behind Dusong Mangpoje's and further up the hill from Mune Tsenpo. Each side is 99 m long and its height is 13 m. The tomb blends naturally into the hillside. Grave robbers had entered the center of the south side and left a large hole. Another triangular hole is on the top. The north side has suffered the most from erosion. Some of the walls have round cavities that once held wooden structural posts. Layers of thin stone slabs separating each individual layer of earth are clearly seen.

TRISONG DETSEN

Far up the slopes of Mt Mura, this is the highest of all Chongye's tombs and the most difficult to reach (about an hour's walk from the valley floor). Trisong Detsen's tomb overlooks the mound of his father, Tride Tsugtsen, and they are separated by a distance of 100 m. Literary sources claim the king erected this tomb himself before his death. A *doring* once stood at its side.

The tomb is the largest and most impressive in the Chongye area. Its sides are each 180 m long; its height nearly 15 m. The north side is honeycombed with peculiar round cavities. On closer inspection it is evident that the holes are precisely patterned. Three rows have a total height of 4.5 m. Each opening, 20–40 cm in diameter, is separated from its neighbor by 0.5–1.5 m. A distinct layer of thin (20-cm) stone slabs reinforces the rows. The west side also has a belt of exposed holes which are similar but slightly larger than those of the north. Here the largest cavity measures 0.7 m in diameter and is nearly 2.5 m deep. All, at one time or another, held wooden supports, now rotted away. Openings on the west side have been reworked by pilgrims into veritable shrines, with *tsa-tsas* and other offerings. Some were even used as kilns to fire the *tsa-tsa* moulds. The south side is more or less parallel to the mountain slope and its construction is simpler. The layered composition of the earthen tumulus is similar to Songtsen Gampo's tomb. A deep, 4.5-m cavity at the top indicates the handiwork of tomb robbers. Rain and mountain streams have created many small gullies along the tomb's surfaces; the west side is particularly damaged.

Two stone lions once guarded the east and west corners of the tomb. The western one, buried by debris over the years, reveals only parts of its badly damaged body. The other, though damaged, can still be largely made out. It is 1.5 m high and sits on a platform. Its right front leg is destroyed and the rear left leg is missing a piece. Notice that the curly mane is beautifully crafted with intricate details. This lion is certainly one of the most valuable relics of the Yarlung Dynasty.

The tomb's *doring* was moved in recent years to Chongye Xian's hospital, presumably for safekeeping and research. Its height (including base) is 5.2 m. The sides of the *doring* display two carved dragons; the one on the right is faint. A single stone forms the base and it is shaped into a large tortoise. Most of the inscriptions are eroded and very difficult to make out. Hugh Richardson, the last British envoy to Lhasa, managed to secure a rare copy of the original and made a translation by comparing it to the *in situ* inscription. It is essentially an eulogy to the deeds of the king, praising his contribution to the Dharma and his domination of foreign lands.

TRIDE SONGTSEN (SENELEK)

This king, a son of Trisong Detsen, ruled from 800 to his death. His tomb is east of the tombs of Mangsong Mangtsen and Dusong Mangpoje, some 230 m from the latter. Looking down from Songtsen Gampo's chapel, this tomb is to the far left (east) near the Dongkar road. Its rear is a stone *doring* enclosed within a temple-like enclosure. Its inscription records the main events of the king's rule, lauding the empire's size and referring to political troubles at the beginning of his reign. The stele uses Bönpo terminology in the inscription, possibly indicating the residual influence of the pre-Buddhist religion in the royal court.

The dimensions of the tomb are 84 m per side and 11 m in height. A platform on the top attests to the efforts of grave robbers, and a nullah along the south side continually contributes to the problem of preservation. South of the *doring*, away from Senelek's tomb, is a group of three smaller tombs. The center one belongs to Jang Tsha Lhe Bön, son of Me Agtshom and Jangmo Tritsun. To the east (left) is Wudu; Wösung's tomb is to the west (right) and set back.

JANG TSHA LHE BÖN

This tomb is considerably smaller than the tombs described so far. Its sides are only 30 m long and the tumulus 4 m high. Three of the sides have sloped noticeably over time; only one is still vertical. Historical accounts say this tomb was built in the ground, but this is definitely not the case.

WÖSUNG

Wösung was the son of Langdarma, the renegade king who persecuted Buddhism at the close of the Yarlung empire. According to one literary source, the Yarlung Dynasty's custom of entombing kings within gigantic tumuli ended with Wösung. His 5 m-high tomb is about 100 m southwest of Wudu's. A rare exception among the Chongye tombs, it was designed in the trapezoid rather than the square. The long side measures 36 m, the short 24 m. The two equal sides are 39 m. This tomb was also sacked, as is evidenced by the large cavity in its top.

WUDU

This square tomb, the smallest of all, is about 100 m south of Senelek's. Each side is 39 m in length; the height is 4.3 m. The monument is noticeably humbler than the others and local tradition claims it to be an unfinished tomb.

THE GROUP OF SIX

Five of these tombs are on the far side (east) of the Dongkar road and not visible from the top of Songtsen Gampo's tomb. The one closest to the larger group, and the only one sited to the west of the road, belongs to King Mutik Tsenpo.

MUTIK TSENPO

This tomb is located along the left bank of the Dongkar River near its entrance to the Chongye Plain. Houses stand on top of the tumulus and severe erosion makes it difficult to discern the original shape. Its north side is 30 m long and 2.5 m high.

TRITSUG DETSEN (RALPACHEN)

Tritsug Detsen's tomb, 1/2 km from Mutik Tsenpo's, lies further within the Dongkar Valley on the east side of the road. The site is below the Dongkar Shang Village at the base of the slopes. This sizeable tumulus is, like Wösung's, trapezoid in plan. The two equal sides are 78 m in length, the long side is 87 m and the short one 54 m. Its height is 4.7 m. A cavity at the top was dug by grave robbers.

Farther east of the Dongkar road is a group of three tombs. The one closest to the road belongs to Gungsong Gungtsen.

GUNGSONG GUNGTSEN

This king reigned for only five years and died at the tender age of 18. His tomb, at right angles to the road, aligns with those of Langri Songtsen and Dagri Nyalse. It also is trapezoid, measuring 63 m by 48 m by 7 m (desecrated by robbers).

LANGRI SONGTSEN

This tomb is sandwiched between the tombs of Gungsong Gungtsen and Dagri Nyalse. Its sides are approximately 36 m long and its height 5 m. There is an enormous hole on the top.

DAGRI NYALSE

Historical sources insist there were two small tumuli below this trapezoid tomb and within within them were buried two of Dagri Nyalse's wives. The earth mound measures 75 m by 54 m by 48 m (sides) and 3.8 m (height). Stone reinforcing is clearly visible where the earth structure has collapsed. Robbers raided this tomb as well.

TRINEN SONGTSEN

This tomb is farthest from the Dongkar road, 200 m northeast of Dagri Nyalse's tomb. Sited below Dongkar Shang, the trapezoid mound measures 51 m by 33 m by 36 m (sides) and 4.7 m (height). Three sides have collapsed considerably; only the north wall is still vertical. Grave robbers have left behind two holes, although supposedly the tomb had no buried treasure.

OTHERS

LHA TOTORI

The tomb of this legendary king is supposedly located at the northeast base of Mt Chingwa Taktse (see page 528), below the ruins of Chingwa Taktse Dzong. Lha Totori received Tibet's first sacred scripture from the sky at Yumbu Lagang (see page 539).

DRÖNYANG DERU

This tomb is located in the village of Sangda. Alone among the Yarlung tombs, it is round. According to literary sources, this semi-historical king was entombed alive, perhaps a form of ritual regicide. The diameter of the much eroded tumulus is 35 m and its height is 4 m. Ancient ruins lie next to it.

YALA SHAMPO: FOUR YARLUNG-VALLEY TOMBS

Tsantang, Dongkar Me, Phu Nublung, Ri Mar

(To get your bearings for these Yarlung-valley sites, see Yarlung, page 515.)

The Chongye tombs of Tibet's early kings are the best known burial ground in Tibet. Below is a description of little-known tomb sites of approximately the same antiquity, in the general area of the Yarlung Valley. Most have been discovered and chronicled only since 1984 by the Lhasa Wenwu Institute. Scholars have not yet studied the tombs in depth and no historical record pinpoints their foundation and background. The majority of these sites are in the lower Yarlung Valley between Yumbu Lagang and the Tsangpo River, along both banks of the Yala Shampo River.

> More Yarlung-dynasty tombs exist in the nearby valleys of Dranang, Drachi, and Yon; see below.

TSANTANG VILLAGE TOMBS

Tsantang Village (site of Tsantang Yuyi Lhakhang, see page 522), 3 km southwest of Tsethang, sits on a wide alluvial plain at the Sheldrak Valley entrance. To the west, a trail leads up to the celebrated Guru Rinpoche cave of Sheldrak Drubphuk (see page 522). The plain, sloping from west to east, is surrounded on three sides by mountains; the fourth fans out widely towards the Yarlung River. Spread across 2 sq km are 233 tombs but only a few are in good condition. A millennium of flooding and erosion has done its damage. These trapezoid tombs can be classified in three general categories:

1) Earth mound. This type of tumulus conceals the burial chamber under a large structure of tamped earth. There are two methods of construction. One consists of horizontal layers of earth built up to the requisite height. The other involves a series of thick earth walls, each abutting the adjacent one. Tombs of this type vary between 10m and 15 m in length. A few are larger, their length being more than 20 m.

2) Earth mound with stonewall. These tumuli have two main types. One has an earth mound enclosed by a stone wall; the space between the wall and mound is filled with stones and earth. The tombs are usually trapezoid. The second type is made up of concentric stone walls. Over the centuries, stones have been removed by villagers making it virtually impossible to recognize the original shape. Most of these tombs are less than 10 m per side.

3) Stone and earth mound. The mound above ground is constructed of a mixture of large stone pebbles and earth; the majority of this type are small.

A typical trapezoid tomb faces east. Its sides from west to east measure some 15 m. The burial chamber, a round, vertical shaft 3 m deep lies underneath the mound. The bottom section of the shaft's wall is made up of two circular layers of stone. This constitutes the coffin. Two more layers of stone cover the top. Within the cavity are parts of the skeleton. It appears the corpse was bound up by ropes to form a compact bundle and then placed inside the shaft.

DONGKAR ME VILLAGE TOMB

Lower Dongkar Me is part of the Nedong Commune, near Tsethang. About 2 km southeast of the village, on the west alluvial slopes of Mt Bomchen, lies the largest, most impressive tomb of the Nedong Xian district. This rare, solitary structure has no satellite tombs. A portion near its center was damaged by the construction of a sheep shelter during the first part of this century.

This tomb is trapezoid with its front facade wider and taller than the rear; this in order to conform to the slope. The dimensions of its walls are: 45.5 m (west), 42 m (north), 42 m (south). The side walls slope slightly inwards. Consecutive layers of earth and stone, each 20 cm thick, lie one upon the other to create the tomb, which reaches a height of 5 m. Reinforcement for this large structure is provided by two stone belts, one 2.3 m wide, the other 1 m, which encircle the mound from top to bottom. Between this double wall are more stone slabs, arranged at right angles for additional strength. This bulwark was added in part to dissuade thieves. The Dongkar Me Tomb, similar to the carbon-dated Nang Xian (Lishan) tombs (see page 373), most probably dates to the Yarlung Dynasty.

TOMBS OF THE PHU NUBLUNG VALLEY

The Phu Nublung Valley, 10 km south of Nedong Xian and 2 km east of the Sangdrub Dechen Commune, has a typical alluvial, fan-shaped entrance bounded on the south by the Yumbu Lagang ridge. This valley holds a total of 323 tombs, divided into 12 main groups. 105 of these are sited on seven hillocks, which form the northern edge of the alluvial fan. The rest are scattered along the fan's north half. Virtually all have been vandalized. However, small pieces of pottery, ornaments, metal implements, and other artefacts have been discovered within the tombs. All of them, in varying stages of disrepair, consist of an earth mound enclosed within a stone wall. The better-preserved ones are 2 m high and their stone perimeters clearly discernible. It is likely that the Phu Nublung tombs belonged to a clan that settled here in the Yarlung Period. Below are the main features of these tumuli.

1) A stone perimeter wall frames an internal cavity, which is filled with stones and earth.
2) The trapezoid tombs become taller as their size increases.
3) The placement and orientation of an individual tomb is determined only by the lay of the land; the widest facade of the trapezoid faces down the slope.

There are three types of burial chambers:

1) Vertical shaft, single-stone coffin. Most of these chambers are small with sides 0.5 m long and a height of 1 m or less. The vertical shaft is round, with a rectangular coffin constructed of stone pieces at the bottom. In some cases, two skeletons may lie within a single coffin.

364 • NECROPOLISES •

2) Vertical shaft, stone multi-cavity coffin. Below the stone and earth mound are multiple shafts containing many stone coffins. In one excavated tomb, beneath the mound are three shafts containing three separate coffins.
3) Vertical shaft, stone slab coffin. The sides of the coffin are made of whole stone slabs. Some of the bodies were cremated before interment.

TOMBS OF RI MAR

Ri Mar (Red Hill) is a ridge of the Gönpo Ri Range, east of Trandruk Monastery. Peppered on the gentler parts of its slopes are 38 tombs. Eight of these are south of a narrow gully that effectively cuts the ridge in two. The rest are to the north. All tombs have been vandalized.

The methods of construction here resemble those of other tombs found in the Nedong Xian district. A trapezoid stone perimeter wall encloses a cavity filled with stones and earth. The thickness of the wall increases with the dimensions of the tomb. Small and medium-size tombs array themselves around and below the bigger ones. A large, elevated, well-preserved tomb lies south of the gully; its facade measures 40 m and its back 20 m; the two equal sides are 22 m. This 6 m-high tomb differs in construction from most. Its four sides are bounded by a thick (2-m) red earth wall, built of many earthen layers. Occasionally, some of the layers are reinforced by *pema* branches. This feature, peculiar to some of the Yarlung tombs, is a precursor to the typical roof construction of monasteries. A staircase of five wide stone steps leading to the front is another anomaly.

DRACHI:
THE TOMBS OF KHONGCHA,
CHANGRA, AND DHOKU RI

(To get your bearings for these Drachi Valley sites, see Drachi: The Valley of Mindroling Monastery, page 495.)

KHONGCHA VILLAGE TOMBS

Khongcha Village is a short distance south of Tsongdü Tsokpa Monastery (see page 495) on the east slopes of a ridge near the east bank of the Drachi River. Three squarish, west-facing tombs lie near the village. The sides of the tumuli vary between 16 and 38 m, and their heights are some 6 m. All have been ransacked. Two of the tumuli are enclosed by a double wall, each 1 m thick. Within the two walls is a mixture of earth, sand, and pebbles. This design is unusual. The third, the largest, is surrounded by a stone wall. These tombs, similar in shape and construction to the Yarlung-dynasty tombs of Nang Xian and Chongye were probably built by members of the nobility.

CHANGRA VILLAGE TOMBS

About 16 km south of Drachi Qu, the Drachi Valley divides. At this junction is Changra; nearby is an unusually large collection of tombs, built on a west-facing, fan-like alluvial plain surrounded on three sides by mountains. The site is effectively cut into three sections by two east–west trending gullies. Most of the tombs, all facing west, lie in the southern section. The larger tombs are surrounded by the smaller ones. Unfortunately, most have been badly damaged and atop some of the more substantial ones are dwellings (now in ruins). The majority are step-tombs: the front facade is taller and wider than the back and the sides slope inwards as they rise.

The largest tomb measures approximately 30–40 m per side with a height of 10 m. Its interior has wood beams and stone walls for support. Some tombs have an additional layer of stone slabs beneath the wood beams. All are constructed of a stone outer wall that encloses a mixture of earth and stones. Usually only the bottom three or four layers are intact. A few tombs are *chörten*-shaped. Clearly these were for high lamas and wealthy landowners. It is likely that these tombs were the precursors of true *chörtens*. A small number of tombs, also step-shaped, are constructed entirely of earth and sand with no inner support. A few have sandwiched stone slab layers. The Changra site has 43 tombs. Others have disappeared due to the expansion of villages and cultivation.

The configuration of the surviving tombs is identical to those of Nang Xian (see page 373). All three types of tombs (stepped, *chörten*-shaped, and stepped with no retaining walls) are represented in both places. Using carbon 14 tracers, the Nang Xian tombs have been dated to the Yarlung-dynasty era. It is probable that the Changra tombs also date from that period.

THE DHOKU RI TOMB

The Yarlung-dynasty tomb of Dhoku Ri lies 150 m east of Drachi Qu, near the right bank of the Yarlung Tsangpo. This round earth tumulus, 10 m in diameter and 2.7 m in height, has been pillaged over the centuries. A ruined stone wall, less than 1 m high, surrounds the tomb. Below and to the left are two trenches; their surmounting earth mounds have eroded completely. One is well preserved. Its oval opening is 0.7 m by 0.6 m and the depth of the cavity 1.5 m. The trough has two parts: an upper drum-like cavity (0.9 m in diameter, 0.9 m in height) bounded by small stones; and underneath, a coffin-like, irregular oblong chamber (0.5 m–0.7 m long, 0.7 m wide, and 0.6 m high) with stone slab sides. There is no cover. Pottery pieces and skeletal remains of sheep and rabbits were discovered within. One of the clay urns, unique in shape and design, has circular patterns on its surface.

These two trenches served as companion burial chambers. It was at one time common for attendants, valuable possessions, horses and other animals to be buried alongside the deceased. Apparently, this custom was phased out at the end of the dynasty and only minor animals were used.

DRANANG:
THE SERKHUNG TOMBS AND THE
STONE COFFINS OF DHELEKLING

(To get your bearings for these Dranang Valley sites, see Dranang: Valley of the 13 Buddha-lamas, page 501.)

In a land where the dead are cut up and fed to vultures, ancient tombs are surprising and unexpected. The Yarlung-dynasty Serkhung tombs (7th–9th C.) are exciting and significant recent discoveries. Chongye's tombs of the Early Kings are well known; Tucci published a study on them in 1950 (see above). Only since 1984, however, have the historically rich districts of Dranang, Drachi, and Nedong been systematically investigated.

At the southern outskirts of Dranang Xian (see page 502), where the main dirt road divides, is a satellite dish (on the right) within a compound. The left branch goes to Jampaling Chörten (see page 465). Take the right branch. Walk across a stone bridge, which spans the dry Dranang River bed, to reach the other side of the valley and some villages. Follow the dirt road south to the entrance of a side valley, the Serkhung, leading west. A red shrine is on the right, 10 m above. Walk west within the valley to Serkhung Village. The large tombs are nearby. From Dranang Monastery to the shrine is 3/4 hr; the tombs are 1/2 hr further.

The site

Serkhung's 12 squarish tombs form two groups 1 1/2 km apart; ten to the north and two to the south. Eight of them are large with sides varying from 30 m to 90 m in length. All but one is trapezoid. The tombs incorporated natural hillocks and their interiors were dug out of the hard bedrock. In general, the large tumuli sit on prominent sites overlooking the smaller ones. Local oral history claims the tombs twice suffered desecration, once at the end of the Yarlung Dynasty, and again under the Dzungar Mongol.

THE CHÖRTEN-SHAPED TOMB

This rare 10 m-tall tomb has only one other counterpart in Tibet: in the necropolis of Lishan (see page 373) at Nang Xian. Situated at the northeast edge of the north group near the base of the largest tumulus, its plan is square, each side being 11 m long. The foundation consists of 0.5-m-thick layers of stones, above which are two square platforms of tamped earth and sand. These are now so eroded as to appear circular. On top of the platforms is a large solid bell, nearly 5 m in height. Its center holds a cruciform cavity supported by stone slabs. This provides rigidity and allows for the leeching of moisture. A 3m-deep hole has been carved out of the bell by local villagers to form a rudimentary shrine, a depository of *tsa-tsas* and small clay *chörtens*.

THE LARGE TUMULI

The largest, most impressive Serkhung tomb sits on a hillock to the northeast. Its dimensions are 87 m (rear) by 92 m (front) by 96 m (sides), and the front facade reaches a height of 20 m (7 m at the back). This structure, made of earth and reinforced by stone-retaining walls, was once completely surrounded by a stepped stone wall, now unfortunately collapsed. The imposing size and commanding positioning of this tomb can easily be compared to any of the Yarlung kings' tombs in the Chongye Valley. The person buried here was in all likelihood a member of the royal family.

THE TRAPEZOID TOMBS

Two types of trapezoid tombs are categorized according to size. The eight large ones have sides between 30 and 90 m long. Three smaller ones have sides 10 to 25 m long (one is located to the south). The tumuli of these tombs are basically constructed of layers of earth and sand, each 0.1–0.2 m thick. Criss-crossing stone walls provide reinforcement. The burial chambers are generally located deep within living rock. Exceptions are large tumuli in relatively flat areas, which have theirs constructed within the man-made mounds. The two similar-sized tombs east of the largest tumulus are separated by a distance of 23 m. Both are well preserved. A pronounced depression caused by robbers is on the flat top of the second. Some 100 m southwest of the biggest tomb is another tumulus built on gradually sloping ground. Half of the earth mound has been destroyed by a small river coming through from a side valley. The exposed cross-section shows clearly the basic internal structure: the top of the mound consists of a stone wall framework; beneath is a large quantity of stones overlaying the burial chambers.

350 m southwest of the main tomb is a grave located on a hill. The tumulus' measurements are: 40 m (front), 30 m (rear), 35 m (sides), 8 m (height). Stone foundation walls of a former monastery stand on top of the mound. At the right front of the tomb is a square stone *chörten*. Along the four sides are cavities that served as meditation cells. Three more tombs lie along the south side of the Serkhung Valley. One, at the west end of this group, faces north. Its measurements are: 30 m (front), 24 m (rear), 9 m (sides), and 3 m (height). The naturally steep slope dictates its configuration: the front and rear are significantly longer than the sides, and its burial chamber is within the slope rather than inside the earth mound. This plundered tomb has a 5-m-wide chasm at its center.

AN EXCAVATED TOMB

One of Serkhung's tombs has been excavated to reveal a well-preserved interior. It is the only Yarlung-era tomb in Tibet to allow of a complete study of its passages and burial chambers.

Located on a hillock in front and to the left of the largest tomb, this trapezoid tumulus measures: 15.5 m (front), 12 m (rear), 12.5 m (sides), 4.1 m (height). Its interior is reinforced by criss-crossing stone walls located 0.3–0.5 m below the surface. The tomb chambers, dug into the original bedrock of the hillock, consist of four parts: an entrance passage, entrance cavity, tomb chamber, and extension chamber. The entrance passage and the entrance cavity begin 0.8 m below the top of the mound. Measuring 2.3 m by 1.2 m, the rectangular passage reaches a maximum depth of 2.7 m. It has nine steps of dressed stone slabs that form narrow treads. Human bones and pieces of pottery were found among the stones. Below the ninth step is a stone platform (0.7 m wide, 1 m long). To its right is the tomb cavity, made of variable stone pieces. It also is rectangular: 2.3 m (long), 1.3 m (wide), 4.8 m (deep). Within are seven more stone steps similar in construction to the other set. 1.55 m above the cavity

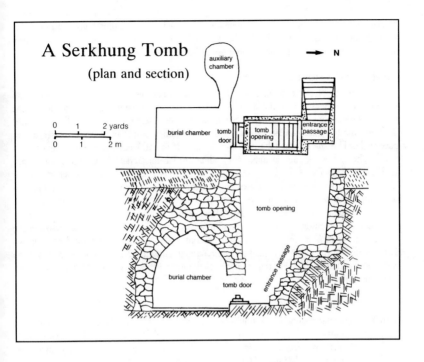

A Serkhung Tomb
(plan and section)

auxiliary chamber

N

burial chamber   tomb door   tomb opening   entrance passage

0   1   2 yards
0   1   2 m

tomb opening

burial chamber   tomb door   entrance passage

opening, along the sides of the stone walls, is an encircling two-tiered platform of 0.1–0.15 m wide, built to support the entrance slab (now collapsed). The distinctive walls enclosing the passage and cavity are made of meticulously laid out stone pieces; empty spaces are filled with earth.

At the bottom of the steps is the tomb chamber proper. It rests at the lower portion of the cavity's front wall. Fragments of ancient pottery and a pigeon bone were found within stone cracks of the cavity. The constricted chamber entrance had a door made of a single stone slab (now removed); the frame and sill are of carefully polished slabs. Three more stone slabs, one atop the other, make up the threshold. The entrance, low and narrow (0.75 m high, 0.55 m wide), requires one to inch in horizontally. Within is the totally dark tomb chamber: its rectangular floor plan measures 2.5 m by 1.8 m; the walls, made of stone pieces, curve upwards to converge at a point 2.75 m above the soft earth floor. Below this 0.1m-thick earth layer is bedrock. A thin, uniform surface of earth covers the walls; it was created by many hands (ancient handprints are still visible). On the floor is stone rubble. Human bones and a small pile of 1,000-year-old *tsampa* were found here.

Along the right wall, near the opening, is the entrance to a small extension chamber, similar in shape and construction to the tomb chamber. The two are linked by a narrow passage, 0.8 m long, 0.4 m wide, 0.6 m high. Its floor is littered with loose stones that once blocked the entrance. Part of a pelvic bone was discovered here. This tiny chamber was probably used to store objects and valuables of the deceased. The tomb was constructed for one person and evidence points to the body being deposited directly into the cell without a coffin.

SOME CONCLUSIONS

The positioning of the Serkhung Valley's 12 tombs indicates a well-defined hierachy that corresponds to the status of the deceased. All the tombs are large, further evidence of the important social rank of the occupants. Serkhung's tumuli closely resemble the well-documented Yarlung-dynasty tombs of Chongye and the less well-known ones of Nang Xian (see below, page 373). The *chörten*-tomb has a Tang Dynasty (618–907) counterpart in China.

The excavated tomb is an important landmark in Tibetan archeology. Of special importance is the way the walls of the burial chamber curve inwards and upwards to taper at a point in the center of the ceiling. The existence of the extension chamber, whose sole function is to serve as a depository for the personal effects of the deceased, is also an important clue for establishing a tenable foundation date. Other unique features include: the very steep stone-step entrance passageways (each flight containing an odd number of steps, a definite correspondence to the number of *khora* repetitions within the context of Buddhist pilgrimage doctrine); two stone platforms; the extremely small and narrow tomb entrance; and the predominantly stone wall construction. It is likely that that the Serkhung necropolis was established in the 8th and 9th centuries.

STONE COFFIN TOMBS OF DHELEKLING

Two Yarlung-dynasty stone coffin tombs have been discovered near Dhelekling Village. (For Dingboche Monastery, higher up to the west, see page 505.) The burial chambers, exposed by the river's corrosive effect, lie within a rock face close to the riverbed. The larger, southernmost tomb is oblong-shaped, 1.1 m by 0.65 m by 0.18 m high. Its southern portion is ruined. The walls are formed of stone slabs but the top consists merely of wood (now decayed). Within was the skeleton of a young man. During burial, his limbs were bent back to accommodate the narrow coffin. The other tomb is similar, although empty.

TWO MORE TOMB SITES IN THE DRANANG VALLEY

After Dhelekling and Serkhung there are at least two other early burial sites in the Dranang Valley. One is near Pedrong Shang, below Nyingdho Monastery (see page 504). It has ten tombs constructed of stone, all in poor condition because the local villagers have appropriated the stones for construction. The second site, near Gasa and Samyul Drong villages, contains six dilapidated tombs. The biggest tomb has sides of over 30 m in length; the smallest is round, with a 3 m diameter.

YÖN:
THE LARGEST YARLUNG BURIAL
SITE IN CENTRAL TIBET

There are three particularly notable Yarlung-era burial sites in the Yön Valley (see page 511 for its sacred sites). Among these little-known archeological finds is Chimlung Tsemo, the largest necropolis discovered in central Tibet. For location details of the Yön Valley, see page 510. Map reference NH46-10 C.

CHIMLUNG TSEMO TOMBS

Chimlung Tsemo ('Falcon Spreading Wings') is a range of mountains due west of Yön Qu. Over 80 tombs have recently been discovered along its foothills near the village that serves as district center. Mountain streams have cut through the slopes creating natural divisions among the dispersed sites. Unlike the compact tomb clusters of the Lower Yarlung Valley, these tombs stretch from Kelsang Commune in the north to the Tsalung Valley entrance, opposite the Jeba commune (north of Yön Qu), a distance of over 10 km. Along the slopes, the width of the burial band varies from 100 m to 500 m. No other necropolis in central Tibet occupies such a large area.

The exposed tumuli of these tombs are of uniform construction, a trapezoid earth mound enclosed by a stone wall. Underneath the mound, vertical shafts as burial chambers have been dug out. The size and depth varies. Usually a stone coffin with a stone slab cover is at the bottom of the shaft. Personal belongings of the deceased have been unearthed. One large tomb has sides of nearly 30 m. The smallest tomb measures only 2 m by 3 m. This dramatic disparity reflects the unequal social status of the buried.

An important, rare discovery is two sacrificial burial sites, the only ones found in Tibet. They are near the Songka Village of Jeba Commune. At least nine horses were destroyed and buried near the tombs of their owners. Small pieces of pottery were also found. The burial chamber of the horses is 10 m long, 0.5 m wide, and 1.5 m deep. From analysis of the skeletons, the horses seem to have been chosen for their youth and strength.

GYALZANG VILLAGE STONE COFFIN TOMBS

Gyalzang Village, about a 1-hr walk north of Yön Qu, is part of Kelsang Commune. On the slopes of the Chimlung Tsemo Range, 100 m north of the village, are 15 recently discovered (1984) stone coffins. Most of the tombs along a north–south axis are medium or small in size; many have no tumuli. The burial trough of one, already partly exposed because of the lack of a protective mound, has a coffin constructed of large stone slabs. One of these partially covers the coffin's top and the floor is a mixture of stone and earth. The head of the coffin points westward.

At another excavation is an oblong burial trough that also lacks a tumulus (perhaps eroded). Its stone coffin is small and simple—only the head of the cavity is enclosed by stones. The skeleton is in the foetal position, a typical feature of Tibetan burials. In general, the cavities of the smaller Gyalzang tombs are rectangular, quite unlike the round, vertical shafts found elsewhere in Yarlung. The heads of the stone coffins are aligned towards the west and usually the stone slabs were used only as sides, with no cover or floor. Some of the larger tombs have surface tumuli and their internal cavities, although similar in shape and construction to the smaller ones, can be between 4 and 10 m long. The small tombs are usually less than 3 m long. Few personal effects have been found.

Jasa Ri Tombs

Menchung is on the Yön Chu's west bank, halfway between Chermen in the south and Yön Qu in the north. A ridge, 1 km to the southwest of the village, is known locally as the Jasa Ri. The tombs are grouped along the gentler parts of the slopes. East of the tombs the Yön Chu flows gently north–south into the Tsangpo.

The site contains 52 tombs in an unusual cruciform configuration. The largest tomb, epicenter of the cross, sits high up the slope. Ten small tombs in a straight line extend from it to the west. Three extend similarly to the south and four to the north. The eastern arm, composed of ten small tombs, has a pronounced curve to the southeast. In the angle between the north and east arms, a group of tombs fans down the northeastern slopes. Every tomb is trapezoid and they all face downhill. The method of construction is similar to the graves of the Lower Yarlung Valley. There are essentially two types, one of earth and the other of earth enclosed by a stone wall. The larger tombs are generally built of earth only.

During the Dzungar invasion of the 18th C., most of the larger tombs were ransacked. The biggest one, supposedly belonging to the Yarlung general, Muwangpo, was severely damaged— a large trough over 20 m in diameter was dug out of its center. The Jasa Ri tombs are very similar in style and construction to the Nang Xian (Lishan) tombs. Both sites date back to ca 740.

LISHAN: ANCIENT TOMBS IN SOUTHEAST TIBET

The exciting archeological finds at Lishan reveal a necropolis that, according to carbon-dating analysis, dates back to AD 700. This group of tombs can be favorably compared to that at Chongye, formerly believed to be the only, and the most ancient, burial site in central Tibet. Many of the Yarlung-dynasty kings were entombed beneath gigantic earth tumuli in Chongye. Lishan's centrally placed, large tombs overlook numerous smaller tumuli, which may perhaps be burial chambers for sacrifical animals. Many of the mounds are trapezoid. The tumuli are constructed of individual layers of stone, earth, and wood. Each layer is sometimes reinforced by further layers of stone slabs and logs. The actual cavities under the mounds are made of stone pieces that form crude coffins.

The site (Map reference NH46-11 C)

The Lishan tombs of Nang Xian county are located within the entrance of the Kyimdong Valley, 52 km east of Nang Xian, near the Tsangpo River. From the prefectural headquarters at Nang Xian (staging post for the Tsari pilgrimage; see page 226), follow the main Tibet–Sichuan road east along the Tsangpo's south bank. Reach Dungkar Qu after 33 km, then Shu after a further 16 km, at the junction of the Tsangpo and Kyimdong rivers. Cross a bridge over the Kyimdong to reach Li, on the right bank. The Yarlung-era tombs, scattered along the south slopes of the Lishan ridge, are 1.5 km northeast of the village. (A farther 2 km northeast of the tombs is the government compound of Kyimdong Qu.)

The necropolis is sited in two main areas, east and west, separated by a deep ravine and a distance of 1.5 km. By far the largest is the eastern site, with 163 tombs. It has an area of 780,000 sq m, 1.2 km long (east–west) and 650 m wide (north–south). In addition to the tombs, there are early dwellings, sites for ancient rituals, and the base of a stone *doring*. The western site has 21 tombs over an area of 35,000 sq m. These Yarlung relics were discovered in March 1982.

The tombs

The 184 tombs can be classified into three types according to floor plan: trapezoid, square, and round.

1) Trapezoid. This type of tomb is the most common and numbers 133 in the east and 20 in the west. The largest is 14 m high with a ground plan of 2725 sq m; the smallest covers a protuberance and has a surface area of only 11 sq m. There are 23 large (over 700 sq m), 74

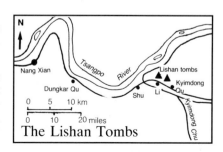

The Lishan Tombs

medium (90–700 sq m), and 56 small (under 90 sq m) tombs.

2) Square. There are only two square tombs, both large and near the center of the west site. About 7 m high, their elevation is *chörten*-like, with four distinct levels. In the south section of the eastern site are three incomplete *chörten*-tombs.

3) Round. Twenty-seven round tombs are scattered over the eastern site. An additional one is located 450 m northeast of this. There are two large, four medium and 22 small tombs.

Dwellings, ritual sites, *doring* base

One example of an early dwelling survived at the base of the eastern site. It occupies an area of about 30 sq m and parts of the walls still stand. Two rectangular sites for burial rituals (animals perhaps were sacrificed during the final rites) are on a terrace along the southern section of the eastern site. This flat ground measures 300 m (east–west) by 160 m (north–south). One site measures 70 m by 26 m, the other 51 m by 29 m. The surviving walls, formed of stone pieces, are about 2 m thick. One stone *doring* base has been discovered at the northwest part of the eastern site. It is round with archaic carvings of a lotus.

CHÖGONG:
NEOLITHIC RELICS IN LHASA

The ruins of Chögong Village, discovered in November 1984, are the first Neolithic relics unearthed in the Lhasa area and the third Neolithic site within the Tibet Autonomous Region (the others are Karu near Chamdo and Ningchi in southeast Tibet.) Major finds here include two limestone trenches or pits, a cave, a stone-coffin burial ground, and various Neolithic implements.

Location

Chögong Village is about 5 km north of Lhasa's center, behind the large compound of the Lhasa Military Hospital (Sera Monastery is east of the hospital). The archeological site runs along the base of the ridge due north of Chögong and the hospital. Measuring 150 m from east to west and 30 m from north to south, much of it has been damaged by rivulets and a dirt road.

The site

Only a small part of the site was excavated. One of the two limestone pits is small, only approximately 1 sq m. The larger one measures 18 sq m. These two cavities yielded a quantity of Neolithic relics and implements, including quite a few pottery shards, bone needles, a bone hammer, and primitive stone tools. A small cave north of the two pits has an external platform; within it were stone and bone implements, pottery shards, and animal bones. Chögong is probably the same age as the Ningchi site, both later than Chamdo's Karu.

STONE-COFFIN TOMB

This tomb, in very poor condition, was created later than the limestone pits. The burial chamber, constructed of round stone pieces, probably dates back to the Yarlung Dynasty (7th–9th centuries). Human skeletal remains were found.

Tibet's Pre-eminent Monuments of Art

THE EARLY MONASTERIES

The following chapters describe in detail the monasteries that house Tibet's most important paintings and statues. Some, such as Kachu and Dranang, are exciting new discoveries holding special interest for serious students of Tibetan art.

The monuments cover a wide span of time, from the 8th to 15th centuries. Kachu is the earliest Yarlung-dynasty temple extant in Tibet. Its magnificent statues (8th–9th C.), although somewhat damaged, have no parallel in the entire country. Dranang contains unique Pala-influenced murals and Shalu is an astounding art gallery full of gloriously detailed paintings. The West Tibet sites of Tsaparang and Tholing, twin capitals of the ancient kingdom of Guge, still retain paintings and statues dating back to the 15th century.

Over the centuries, cosmopolitan and sumptuous art styles from Tibet's diverse neighbors—Kashmir, Central Asia, Nepal, China—made lasting contributions to the arts of Tibet. Their superb influences are dramatically showcased within the walls of these temples.

KACHU: TIBET'S SOLE SURVIVING YARLUNG TEMPLE

A recent discovery showcasing statues from two separate and distinct epochs of the Yarlung Dynasty

OVERVIEW

Kachu Lhakhang is the only Yarlung-dynasty temple in Tibet known to have survived. Its original statues are almost completely intact. More ancient than Samye, widely considered to be Tibet's first monastery, Kachu was built in the first half of the 8th C. in the reign of King Tride Tsugtsen (705-55), father of the Trisong Detsen who first designated Buddhism as the state religion. Karchu symbolized the first tentative efforts of a monarch to foster Buddhism after its embryonic inception at the court of Songtsen Gampo.

The most exciting finds within the small monastery are 13 monumental statues, including Kachu's most important—a huge Sakyamuni created by Khotanese artists in the first half of the 8th C. With the possible exception of a few statues in the Potala's Chögyal Drubphuk (see page 110), these are the earliest, best-preserved statues in Tibet. Other outstanding relics include four archaic columns, their unusual capitals, and many ancient handwritten manuscripts.

The monastery was renovated by one of King Ralpachen's ministers in the mid-9th C., a period when the Eight Great Bodhisattvas and other standing figures were sculpted. Although damaged, they remain the only extant statues from the era of Ralpachen. They exhibit a rare combination of 9th-C. Nepalese and Central Asian influences, moderated by the sensibilities of indigenous Tibetan artists. These works thus represent the earliest known example of an autonomous Tibetan sculptural style, and the discovery of the chapel in the mid-1980s gave a major boost to the study of Tibetan culture.

Location (Map reference NH46-10 C)

Kachu (known popularly as Keru) is located about a third of the way up the north–south trending Yön Valley, on the north bank of the Tsangpo 35 km east of Samye. The main village of Yön Qu (formerly Gyalkang Dzong) lies 15 km north of the valley entrance. Kachu itself is in Kelsang, about 1 km beyond, on the west side of a dirt road behind some farm buildings.

Access

VIA TSETHANG 6 HR

From the center of Tsethang (the big crossroads with its stone sculptures of monkeys), walk east along the main paved road. Shortly, the paved portion ends and a good dirt road begins. There are plenty of tractors and trucks, but it may not be easy to get a ride. Be prepared to walk 1 1/2–2 hr to the Nyango ferry, left of the road beyond a small rise. The landing is unmistakable. Next to the river are three large piles of stones and, in the middle of the river, another gigantic one (support for the destroyed bridge). All have prayer flags on top. Next to these are the ferry and a small compound. The boats are long wooden barges that can carry tractors to the north bank. Service is efficient and frequent (0900–1800) and the dirt-cheap crossing takes only 5 min.

Nyango Druka Chaksam

The Nyango Druka chain bridge (destroyed) was famous among bridges over the Tsangpo. For the past five centuries, this engineering marvel served as a vital link between Lhasa and Yarlung. The bridge (chaksam) was built by Tangton Gyalpo (1385–1464), the celebrated architect, who is also considered the inventor of the Tibetan opera. He used this fund-raising entertainment to finance over 100 bridges; the best known ones are at Chusul, Lhasa, Nyango, and Chung Riwoche.

The Nyango Bridge had a span of between 150 and 250 m. Five major bridge supports extend across the river from north to south. These oval, stone structures are highest (about 8 m) and largest (15 m in diameter) near the north bank. Perhaps 30 stone supports were needed to span the wide Tsangpo; nearly all have been washed away by the current. Defense towers stood at the tops of the supports at either end of the bridge and ruins at the river's south edge are obviously the foundation of such a structure. This place has become a shrine to Tangton Gyalpo and pilgrims honor the celebrated bridge-builder with periodic offerings. A few original iron links are preserved in the basement of Dongmen commune at the river's edge.

Once on the north side, follow a tractor track north up the wide Yön Valley (see page 510). After 10 min, wade across a small river. The valley is wide; in its lower reaches it measures 2–3 km across. Follow the valley's western perimeter and pass the village of Chermen on the right. To its east is a prominent hill with the ruins of Ngari Tratsang Monastery on top. Another track hugs the valley's eastern side and between the two flows the Yön Chu River. Cross a bridge 2 1/4 hr from the ferry. A more substantial one lies just beyond. Between the two, on the right, is a path that traverses the valley from west to east. It leads to Tashi Doka Monastery (3/4 hr from here; see page 511). Continue north along the river's right bank for 2 hr, passing Menchung, to Yön Qu (Songka). This large village, serving as the nerve center of the valley, is dominated by a conspicuous two-story building. (From here another path leads east across the valley.) A quarter hour from Yön Qu, on the right, is a compound, the district school. A small village just beyond is partially hidden by trees. The Kachu Lhakhang is inside it. From the ferry to here is a relaxing walk of 4 1/2 hr. Arrange for a donkey at Chermen (Rmb 5–10) to carry packs if necessary.

FROM BALO ON THE TIBET–SICHUAN HIGHWAY 2 1/2 – 3 DAYS

Start at Balo (Tashigang) near road marker 1480 km, 21 km east of Medro Gongkar (see page 550). From the main road, walk south up a side valley to Sephuk (1 1/4 hr) and a trail junction. The right branch leads to Samye via the Sephuk Chu Valley. Take the left to go due south past Sephuk Sango and Sephuk Na (3 1/2 hr), near the valley's head. Ascend to the Takar La (6 hr). After the pass, descend east, then turn sharply to the south to Dingna village at a valley junction (4 hr from the pass). (The west valley contains within its upper reaches the pilgrimage site of Yönpu Taktsang, a Guru Rinpoche cave retreat, 1 1/2 days from Dingna.) Follow the main Yön Valley south past Dingna Qu (formerly Songju) on the Yön Chu's east bank (2 1/2 hr). Cross to the west bank to reach Kachu in a further 1 1/2 hr.

FROM SAMYE 3–4 DAYS

From Samye, go up the Drakmar (Samye) Valley (see page 627) to Ninggong (3 1/2 hr) and take the right, side valley (the main one straight ahead leads to the Gökar La) towards Yamalung Monastery. In 3 1/2 hr the valley divides. Take the right branch. This splits again after 1 1/4 hr. Take the left branch. After 1/2 hr, go up a side valley on the right. This east-trending valley leads to a 5250-m pass (1 hr). After the pass, in the upper reaches of the Yön Valley, look out for Yönpu Taktsang, Guru Rinpoche's hermitage high up on the cliff face that flanks the valley to the south (see page 513). Continue due east to Dingna (8 hr); pass Chigong (Jangdo) 1 3/4 hr before the village. Dingna to Kachu is 4 hr more.

Combine a walk to Samye Monastery (from Dechen, Ganden, or the Gyama valleys) with this itinerary to Kachu (via the Yönpu Taktsang cave) to explore two ancient sites in one circuit.

Layout

The east-facing monastery, about 30m wide and equally deep, has an area close to 1,000 sq m. Its main entrance is at the east compound wall, near the southeast corner. Straight ahead is the *dukhang* entrance; the inner Jowo Khang opens from the *dukhang's* rear wall. The temple courtyard is around the corner to the right, and the east and north walls of the complex are bounded by two-story monks' quarters, with porches running along the ground floor. At the west end of the courtyard are the empty, roofless Namla Lhakhang and Katang Chugong Lhakhang. Steps outside the former lead to the roof.

Kachu can be conveniently classified into five sections, each one built in a different period:

1) Namla Lhakhang. This is the most ancient part of Kachu, built perhaps in the time of Tride Songtsen (676–704) or even earlier. It collapsed in September 1984.

2) Jowo Lhakhang and *khorlam*. These were built in the first half of the 8th C. during the rule of Tride Tsugtsen. The present monastery was enlarged over the centuries from this modest building.

3) Katang Chugong Lhakhang. This early 11th-C. chapel was once occupied by Atisha.

4) Dukhang, the *dukhang khorlam*, second-floor monks' quarters and the two-column entrance porch. These were all constructed ca 16th–17th century.

5) Three chapels, two *dukhangs*, and more monks' quarters. The more recent structures (the new Namla Lhakhang and Netang Chugong) were completed in 1957. Some of this group are north of the complex; the older ones south.

JOWO LHAKHANG AND KHORLAM

This most ancient surviving structure of Kachu is at the southwest corner of the main complex (see plan). It is reached through the *dukhang*. The one-story, flat-roofed chamber measures 8.8m (width) by 7.6m (depth) by 6.5m (height) and the floor area is 67 sq m. Its unusually high ceiling is more exaggerated than any other temple in Central Tibet, and it is likely that this peculiar design was meant to accommodate the tall, monumental Buddha, a creation of Khotanese artists (see below).

The 1m-thick walls are constructed of rough stones and lime, and the uneven workmanship is indicative of an early era. These construction materials are typically Tibetan; it is most likely that Tibetan architects and craftsmen designed and built this chapel, not foreigners. Four ancient, round columns each about 0.4 m in diameter and 5 m in height, were cut from whole trees and shaped minimally by simple implements. All exhibit cracks at the top and iron corsets have been added later. The unusually large capitals have miraculously survived from the first half of the 8th century. They are made of three separate wood blocks. The top and longest (2.05 m) is separated from the middle by three cushioning wood pieces. Supported by the capitals and columns is a wood frame (north–south), built of six square-sectioned planks. Above these are 15 ceiling beams. These are large, round logs (30 cm in diameter); three joined end to end are needed to span the chamber from west to east. The whole ceiling structure evokes strength and durability, and the arrayed timbers are quite extraordinary. Originally the room had no windows, but later a small opening over the entrance was added for illumination. it is best to see the Jowo Khang in the morning.

In earlier times, a *khorlam* encircled the chapel along its north, west, and south walls. Its relatively low walls were intended to set off the high, spacious depository of Sakyamuni's image. Later expansion dismantled most of the structure; only the eastern part of the south segment survives (access to the former corridor is provided by two blocked doors along the *dukhang's* north and south walls).

THE CAPITALS

The four round columns are valuable 8th-C. works, as are the capitals. Surfaces of the latter have individual designs, three of which depict mythical animals with a simple flourish. The carvings were painted, but earlier colors are lost beneath today's red coat. It is notable that there is no art work on the back of the capitals.

Right front	*Norbu* (wish-fulfilling gem)
Left front	A lion in full stride flings its head back in a highly spirited movement; the artist accomplished this with just a few deep knife strokes
Rear left	An S-shaped dragon with horns, wings, and clawed feet in a crouching pose; its rear is raised as if on the verge of flight
Rear right	A winged tiger has much the same configuration as the dragon

In ancient Tibet, these four figures were royal emblems. One implication is that Kachu was a royal temple sponsored personally by King Tride Tsugtsen. The animals were inspired by Chinese mythology. Although there is no evidence that Tibetans in the early Yarlung period produced sculptural or painted works, some had mastered minor crafts like woodwork and silversmithery. In producing these carvings on the capitals, the artist followed fairly closely the Chinese Sui and Tang models that were in vogue throughout Central Asia and Tibet. The technique and expression of the dragon, for example, resemble others attributable to the early Tang Dynasty (7th century). It is also similar in style to a dragon carved on the 9th-C. stone *doring* on top of the tomb of Tride Tsugtsen (799–815). These comparable designs contribute towards establishing Kachu's foundation date as that of the first half of the 8th century. One motif of the Kachu capitals has survived to recent times—the cloud pattern boldly executed in relief with a few masterful strokes.

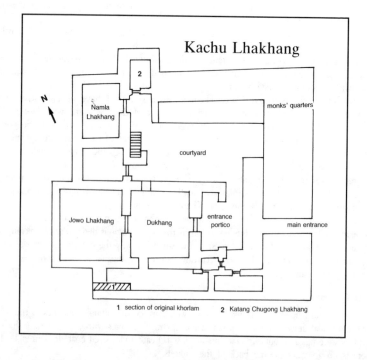

Kachu Lhakhang

2

N

Namla Lhakhang

monks' quarters

courtyard

Jowo Lhakhang

Dukhang

entrance portico

main entrance

1 section of original khorlam   2 Katang Chugong Lhakhang

THE STATUES

A total of 13 painted clay statues dominate the dark chamber. They are Kachu's most important relics. The features of the eight standing *bodhisattvas* are distinctive: aquiline, aristocratic, and a general impression of haunting other-worldliness. Remarkably composed, these statues exhibit a spiritual serenity reminiscent of India's fabled Gupta art (3rd–6th century). All possess an understated power and originality that is rarely encountered elsewhere in Tibet. Some faces have been damaged but the disfiguration somehow makes them more evocative.

The central Buddha figure (Jowo), with its stern but compassionate visage, is perhaps the most memorable statue in the country. Its face is fuller and the nose more prominent than the surrounding statues. Its chest is massive (fully 1 m thick), an important stylistic trait useful for dating the image. The clay body is painted dark brown and clothed with robes. Seated on a lotus atop a stone-and-earth platform protected by a new wood scaffold (a small painting of a lotus mandala, rendered below the front of the throne, can be seen through a crack), this 3.2-m-high figure is the best-preserved in Kachu. Over its head are the sacred Six Ornaments (*garuda*, conch, goldfish, lotus, pillar, vase), sculpted here in a highly unusual archaic design. The throne originally was covered with detailed, white line-paintings on a black background, but now only traces remain.

The Eight Great Bodhisattvas and two guardians are ranged along the two side walls, five on each side. These 3 m-high standing statues are fixed by wooden pegs to heavy library shelves. Two additional figures, supported by pegs inserted directly into the wall, are placed along the left wall immediately adjacent to the entrance. These images face the Jowo square on and, according to the monks, they depict Trisong Detsen's parents, Tride Tsugtsen and Princess Jincheng.

The *bodhisattvas'* faces contrast strongly with other Tibetan monumental statues. Their pronounced flat planes reflect non-indigenous ethnic features: higher cheek bones, more slanting eyes, smaller noses, and thinner, more refined lips. Notice the exceptionally thin eyebrows. The proportions of the figures are pleasing and elegant. They hold themselves rigidly with a slight bow of the upper body. All these traits suggest a strong Central Asian influence that originated from the desert oases of the Taklamakan.

Another departure from the norm is that although the images' arms and chests are naked, the shoulders are wrapped in blue or green shawls. Flowing, floor-length red skirts subtly reveal the shapes of the bodies. The four disciples nearest the door and the 'royal couple' have, in addition, short blue skirts over the long ones. Adorned with ornaments, all these works proclaim a high degree of artistic achievement.

The ferocious guardians, Tamdrin and Chana Dorje, have astonishing musculature, a rare expression that attests strongly to their Central Asian provenance. They are dressed similarly in tiger skirts and long boots. Curled around each upper torso are five snakes. The contrast between the demure, effete disciples and these strapping demigods is striking. The 'king' and 'queen' are dressed similarly to the eight *bodhisattvas*, but she has an expression almost of shyness and, alone among all the statues, has well-defined breasts. Although the faces are undamaged, their crowns are destroyed. A new coat of paint was probably applied to all in the last 50 years, during the tenure of Yungje Wangchak, Kachu's last abbot.

No statues stand right of the entrance, an incongruous feature of Kachu (most Tibetan chapels have symmetrically placed divinities). Behind the disciples and along the north wall next to the entrance are exceptionally strong library shelves that serve to provide a stabilizing framework for the large statues. They were carefully designed to permit integration with the statues. Vertical supports and the spacing between them correspond precisely to the number of statues. The L-shaped shelves along the chamber's north portion compensate for the lack of statues right of the entrance.

SOME ARCHITECTURAL CONSIDERATIONS OF THE JOWO KHANG

The architecture of Kachu's inner sanctum is both archaic and simple. Notice in particular the unusually heavy-duty ceiling beams and the outsized capitols, which were clearly shaped by early and primitive implements. In less ancient monasteries, these architectural elements are generally much less substantial. The ceiling of the Jowo Khang is striking: a uniform row of massive timber is arrayed across it. Iron corsets at the top of the pillars were added at a later date to contain the cracks that have developed.

Originally, the side and rear walls were enveloped by a completely enclosed *khorlam* and the chamber was in effect isolated from the rest of the complex. The corridor was narrow, windowless, and relatively much higher than it was broad—all design characteristics of the Yarlung Dynasty.

OTHER YARLUNG-DYNASTY RELICS IN KACHU

1) An ancient *thangka*. Discovered at Kachu in 1984 and now stored in the Cultural Relics Office in Tsethang. Measuring 79 cm by 23 cm, the painting depicts a standing Chenresi rendered in the Pala (9th–11th C.) style. The face of the deity is rather full and his exposed torso is decorated with a string of precious gems. Dressed in the Indian style, the image wears short pants and behind his legs, hanging from the waist, is a long piece of cloth. Below him are two donors. The one on the left sits on the floor with hands in front of his chest; the other is clothed in markedly Chinese garments. On the back of the *thangka* are Tibetan inscriptions—a phonetic transliteration of Sanskrit. They resemble those used after Ralpachen's modification of the alphabet, and perhaps date from between the 9th and 11th centuries.
2) Palm-leaf folio of a *sutra*. This and the *thangka* are kept by the local Lhoka (Shannan) government.
3) Fragments of tree-bark folios, inscribed in ink, which are visible within the damaged head of a disciple (third on the left).
4) Handwritten manuscripts with over 100,000 folios, many on high quality paper. Some date from the Yarlung Dynasty (7th–9th C.), others from the 16th century.

OTHER CHAPELS

NAMLA LHAKHANG

North of the Jowo Lhakhang is a small room. The severely damaged Namla Lhakhang, located adjacent to and due north of this, is Kachu's oldest part, perhaps from the late 7th century. Its present configuration, derived from the renovation of 1957, is approximately twice the size of the original. The chapel was thoroughly rebuilt and lost much of its historic significance. Its only indication of antiquity is a short, dilapidated wall. Within it is a layer of *pema* branches, typically used to reinforce monastic roofs. The chapel contained statues of Sakyamuni and the eight *bodhisattvas*, all lost during the Cultural Revolution.

KATANG CHUGONG LHAKHANG

This cramped chapel is diametrically opposite to the Namla Lhakhang. Faint murals on the center wall depict Atisha; he is flanked by his disciples, Dromtönpa and Ngok Legpai Sherab, both along the side walls. In 1957, the Tibetan government issued strict orders that these paintings not be retouched. Although popular tradition holds that they were painted by Atisha himself, a recent examination shows that the style is late, probably not earlier than 18th century. The Chörten Karchung (destroyed), contained Atisha's relics. Only faint traces of the base remain. Atisha stayed at Kachu for one month (ca 1047–48) before going to Samye. Tsong Khapa is also said to have stayed here; his meditation retreat, Tashi Doka, is nearby. The Katang Chugong in all likelihood dates from the first half of the 11th century.

DUKHANG

The dimensions of this chamber, built ca 16th–17th C. are similar to those of the Jowo Lhakhang. Its stone walls are 1.3 m thick and its ceiling is staggered (the skylight is at the interface). The chapel has four square columns with ornate woodwork similar to that of the 17th-C. Mindroling Monastery (see page 496); the walls are covered with murals (early 20th C.) that depict Nyingmapa subjects.

West	Sakyathupa
South	Guru Rinpoche at center
North	Dorjedrak Rinchen Chenpo
East	(and parts of north and south walls) Four Guardians

Kachu Lhakhang changed allegiances in the 16th century. Previously, it belonged to the Kagyü sect and was appended to the Drigung Monastery. It was subsequently transferred to Dorje Drak, principal seat of the Nyingma. The Nyingmapa-related paintings of the *dukhang* indicate that its founding coincided with its association with Dorje Drak. It is thus reasonable to assume it was built no earlier than the 16th century. At the time, a *khorlam* was added around the *dukhang* to join with the old one to complete a circuit.

HISTORY AND ART OF KACHU LHAKHANG

The following section is a summary taken from Roberto Vitali's ground-breaking book, *The Early Temples of Central Tibet*.

EARLY HISTORICAL RECORDS

The earliest reference to Kachu are found on stone pillars (*doring*) from the Yarlung period. One such *doring* was erected at Samye by King Trisong Detsen at the time of the monastery's founding. The inscription essentially proclaims Buddhism to be the state religion. It also mentions two documents related to the inscription. One is a sworn account (*katsig*) of the edict and the other the annotated text (*kachi*) of the inscription. Both survive. The *kachi*, the earliest description of Buddhism in Tibet (ca 779), states that Kachu was built in the time of Tride Tsugtsen—Trisong Detsen's father (Me Agtshom). This fact is corroborated by another *doring* at Karchung Monastery.

Tride Tsugtsen acceded to the throne in 712, and was essentially controlled by his powerful grandmother, Dro Trimalod. She sent her chief minister to the Tang court in 709, and the relationship between China and Tibet entered into a short period of stability when he succeeded in arranging a marriage between the Chinese Princess Jincheng and Tride Tsugtsen. She arrived in Lhasa in 710. In 712, the moderate Emperor Zhongzong was deposed by the more militant Xuanzong, and the border situation between the two countries became tense once more. Jincheng was cut off from the Tang court and found that she now had little sway over Chinese diplomacy. In Tibet, one of her principal achievements was to give refuge (probably in 728) to the Khotanese Buddhist monks who were trying to escape persecution by the Khotanese king. They and the princess consolidated Buddhism at court and helped found Kachu. Historical sources mention that Tride Tsugtsen sent two trusted ministers to India to invite Buddhist masters to come to Tibet to teach. En route, they learned that two eminent teachers, Sangye Sangwa and Sangye Zhiwa, were in retreat at Mt Kailash. They made a detour to extend the king's invitation, but the sages had no desire to travel to Central Tibet. Instead, they gave five sacred texts to the emissaries, and these were successfully brought back to the king. Tradition says he and Princess Jincheng built five temples to house the texts; Kachu was one of them (the others were: Chimpu, Drinzang, Lhasa Khardrak, and Masa Gongi Lhakhang).

Just as Tride Tsugtsen failed to bring Indian Buddhist masters to Tibet, no Indian artists practiced in the country during the early 8th century. Equally, no Chinese religious teachers or artists served at court. Thus the temples of Tride Tsugtsen were devoid of influences from both China and India. However, early Tibetan texts recounting the religious history of Khotan—probably written during the latter part of the Yarlung period—provide valuable insights into other missionary activities during the reign of Tride Tsugtsen. The expulsion of the Khotanese monks and their arrival in Tibet figure prominently in these historic accounts, along with the establishment of perhaps five monasteries for them. On of the texts, however, is more reserved: it states that only one temple was built for the monks, and that they stayed in the country for only 12 years.

In any case, there is documentary confirmation that the only religious masters present in Tride Tsugtsen's Tibet were from Khotan, and they lived in the country fully half a century earlier than the onset of the First Diffusion of Buddhism. It may well be that only one temple, Kachu, was built for the Khotanese monks; examination of the monastery certainly shows stylistic influences directly attributable to Khotan.

THE FIRST ART PHASE

Kachu Monastery is located in the Yön Valley, a district of the ancient principality of Drakmar and main seat of the Yarlung kingdom. According to the Dunhuang documents, this area was important for Tride Tsugtsen, and from 704 to 746 it was his winter residence. The strategic Yön Valley borders on Üru (the area centering on Lhasa) and Yöru (the Yarlung area), regions considered to be the cradle of Tibetan civilization. When Lumé returned to Central Tibet from Kham (see page 27), in order to revitalize Buddhism after Langdarma's suppression, he was asked to re-open disused temples in Drakmar. It is significant that he only chose Kachu, both for its historical and geographical importance. The most ancient chapel in the monastery is the Jowo Khang. One of the most unusual aspects of this room is the height of the ceiling in relation to the floor space. The chamber, more than any other in Central Tibet, is exaggerated vertically. It is most likely that the reason for this is that the room was specifically designed to house the tall monumental Buddha that was the product of the Khotanese artists. Another notable feature is the set of capitols that act as an interface for the four pillars and the ceiling. As mentioned earlier, these are works dating back to the beginning of the 8th century.

THE BUDDHA

The single most striking object in the Jowo Khang is the central Buddha image. Pronounced Khotanese influences, essentially derived from Tang China and post-Gupta India, can be discerned. Unique among Tibetan statues, this statue combines the spirituality of the Gupta with the solemnity of the Tang. The Khotanese artists that produced the work successfully synthesized both genres and at the same time infused it with a distinctive vision that is all their own. The amount of extant Khotanese art is rather small, but fragments of murals recovered from the Silk Road oasis of Domoko and adjacent Farhad-Beg-Yailaki show marked similarities with Kachu's sculpted Buddha. A distinguishing feature of the image is its smooth, rounded head. There are no sharp angles or planes; all lines are in a continuum and the features merge imperceptibly and naturally. This is also the case with the Domoko paintings. To instil vigor into the works, the eyes in both mediums are exaggerated horizontally and slightly closed. The Buddha's upper lip is arched but the lower is straight, and there is a ghost of a smile at the edges of the lips. These traits mirror the Domoko fragments. The statue's chin is small and rounded, fitting perfectly into the overall design.

A remarkable feature of the Kachu figure is the monumentality of its upper torso. The chest and shoulders are massive and contrast vividly with the willowy Chinese models of the period. It is likely that the Domoko oasis, part of Khotan's cultural orbit, provided artistic inspiration for the Kachu Buddha. King Trisong Detsen stated in the *Samye Kachi* that Kachu was founded by his father and that the deities and religion of Khotan were imported to Tibet. It would seem that this is further corroborated by the artistic evidence.

THE LOTUS FRAGMENT

The only painting within the Jowo Lhakhang is a small lotus medallion on the front face of the throne underneath the Buddha (hidden by a wood scaffold). Its archaic design has the shape of a bud with a double set of inner joined petals surrounded by an outer circle of more petals. Lotuses are used profusely at Dunhuang but are rare at Khotan. The Kachu lotus is similar in design to one on the vest and the throne of the Silk God at Dandan-uiliq, another Tarim oasis. However, the Kachu lotus decorates the throne and was not conceived as part of a mural; the artist was probably a sculptor, not a painter. The absence of murals in the chapel indicates that wall painting in the 7th and 8th C. was an autonomous function in the design of temples, not an integrated and indispensable component.

THE SECOND ART PHASE

The striking dissimilarity in style between the central Khotanese Buddha and the standing *bodhisattvas*, guardians, and the 'royal couple' by the entrance points to the likelihood that the statues were created at different times. The latter grouping has no remotely similar counterparts in Tibet. The Buddha was conceived in terms of mass. Its head and torso are much larger and more impressive than most Tibetan Buddha figures. There is an absence of angles and planes in the features, and the head is distinguished by its smooth roundness.

The secondary figures, on the other hand, stand with solemnity and rigidity. Their heads and faces are characterized by flatness rather than three-dimensionality; the chins are well defined and lack the roundness of the Buddha. Their eyes, however, have been recently painted and artificially elongated in order to conform more to those of the Buddha. Their mouths, too, have been painted to appear wider (the originals are considerably smaller and the edges did not curve upwards). Although significant, the torsos of the standing figures lack the Buddha's massiveness. The long limbs of the *bodhisattvas* are exceedingly stiff and the lower bodies are dressed in floor-length skirts with heavy, vertical pleats; all wear jewelry.

The two guardians are unique in Tibet for their well-defined musculature. One powerful trait is the open, cubic mouths and jaws and the artists' profound attention to anatomical detail. Strength and menace are conveyed through the rippling muscles and exaggerated stance. Their rigor and liveliness provide a strong contrast to the stiffness of the *bodhisattvas*.

The two standing figures by the left door wall are an anomaly. Their style is identical to the *bodhisattvas* but they are placed outside the sacred cycle of statues. At the same time, the guardians, which normally stand by a door, are grouped in with the *bodhisattvas*. No corresponding statues stand along the right door wall. These two images near the entrance are clothed in saintly garments but are said by the monks to represent Tride Tsugtsen and Jincheng, his Chinese queen. The king is depicted as a *bodhisattva* and his wife as a Tara. No precedents exist that explicitly show kings and queens as divinities. Songtsen Gampo and his wives, for example, are portrayed in the Potala and Jokhang as royal figures. They do not wear heavenly clothings. It is uncertain which deities are represented here by the king and queen.

These are the only extant examples of a provincial idiom. Local artists responsible for the images must have absorbed foreign ideas; their primary inspiration probably came from 8th-C. Newars of Nepal (the post-Gupta arts from India also penetrated Nepal, finally finding their way to Central Tibet). Bronze statuettes, sculpted in Nepal, were well established in this post-Gupta idiom. It is possible that they provided a direct stimulus for local artists working at Kachu.

A special aspect of Kachu is its very substantial wooden bookshelves. The wood used is surprisingly thick and solid, and the frames were obviously able to sustain much more weight than mere volumes of text. The design is an extension of the ceiling beams and the columns and capitals that support them. All are characterized by the use of far more material than is strictly necessary.

HISTORICAL CONTEXT

In 755, King Tride Tsugtsen was assassinated and two of his most trusted ministers were accused of murder. A state of siege was proclaimed at court and the entire Bönpo faction began to make its presence felt. As a result, Buddhism was banned and all religious institutions, including Kachu, were allowed to fall into decay. To maintain continuity, young Trisong Detsen was proclaimed king, although he did not effectively rule the country until he was 20. In the intervening years, there was no record of events linked to Kachu—until the reign of Rapalchen, who became king in 815. In the text of *Den Chöjung* a list of eight temples was given, together with the names of persons who built or renovated them. Kachu apparently was rebuilt by Dro Trisumje, one of the principal ministers of Rapalchen.

THE DUNHUANG CONNECTION IN THE SECOND ART PHASE

The Dunhuang cave temples, repositories of so much invaluable art and so many ancient texts, were under Tibetan control from 787 to 848, and a group of banners with images and Tibetan inscriptions of the period have been found in the caves. Some of the images are remarkably similar to the standing *bodhisattvas* of Kachu. Those from Dunhuang have the same head and facial structure as those from Kachu, with similarly shaped eyes. The main difference between them is Dunhuang's more faithful adherence to the original inspiration of the 8th-C. Newar art style. Compared to those of Kachu, these figures are more sinuous and slender, their stance more fully expresses the tripartite curvature of the body (*tribhanga*), and the clothing descends directly from the Indo-Nepalese style. It appears that these characteristics were modified or abandoned altogether by the local artists of Kachu. There is consensus that the banners were produced during the time of the Tibetan occupation. Perhaps they were the work of a community of Tibetan painters who moved there at the time. After all, their presence in this oasis was sustained for nearly a hundred years.

Considerable interchange certainly existed between the Tibetans at Dunhuang and those in Central Tibet, and thus Kachu. Tibetans in the north absorbed influences particular to Chinese Central Asia and transferred them to their counterparts in Drakmar. The frontal posture of the *bodhisattvas* is a definite trait from Central Asia, as are the floor-length garments. The unusual guardians with their muscular bodies clearly originate from Central Asia. In general, the Kachu *bodhisattvas* follow the established idiom of Nepal and are modified by Central Asian sensibilities. The guardians, however, were modeled entirely on the Central Asian genre, and they depart radically from the Nepalese solution.

Historically, there is conclusive evidence that Dunhuang and Kachu maintained artistic links. It seemed that Trisumje had a residence in the oasis and he even built a temple there. This probably happened before 810, while he was still a lower-ranked army officer and before his promotion to chief minister. Between his sojourn on the Silk Road and his dharma activities in Kachu there is a span of some 20 years. During this time, the Tibetan art school of the north probably absorbed stylistic elements of Central Asia. Thanks to Trisumje and his retinue, the result was transmitted to Kachu, and it is likely that the second art phase of the temple—the period when the *bodhisattvas* and the guardians were created—happened not long after the 822 peace treaty.

YEMAR:
CENTRAL ASIAN-PALA STATUES
IN A DERELICT ROADSIDE TEMPLE

Yemar's insignificant appearance and forlorn location belie its true magnificence. Within the derelict temple splendid sculptures, the last of their kind in Tibet, have somehow survived. Founded during the first decades of the 11th C., its life-sized statues exemplify a unique synthesis of the East Indian Pala style and the Buddhist Xixia style of Central Asia (see page 51). Since the 7th C. Tibet had significant cultural interaction with the independent Xixia Kingdom (now part of northwest China). Tibetan artists, already versed in the potent Pala idiom of the subcontinent, thus gained valuable artistic insights that are part of the Silk Road heritage. The statues of Yemar were the product of this rich and diverse mixture, in which emotive Tibetan sensibilities also played their part.

Dranang Monastery (see page 393) was the only other site to contain murals and sculptures of this genre. The former, painted in the style of Pala and Xixia still exist, but the statues are all gone. Yemar is thus the only known temple in Tibet to retain sculpture of this type.

Location (Map reference NH45-16 D)

Yemar, known locally as Iwang, stands on the Gyantse–Yatung highway that links southern Tibet with Sikkim. To reach the monastery from the center of Gyantse, walk 1 km west to the main highway junction (road marker 255 km). The right branch goes to Shigatse, the left south to the Chumbi Valley (see page 787) and Yatung.

Go left along the west bank of the Ralung Chu. At road marker 265 km is the Gelugpa Nenying Monastery (see page 790). Yemar, further to the south, is at road marker 315 km. The deserted, one-story monastery sits 200 m on the right up a small incline. It is easy to miss. From the road, it appears as a reddish, square building minus its roofs. Further to the south is Kyangphu Monastery (ruined), at road marker 323 km.

The following summary follows Roberto Vitali's *The Early Temples of Central Tibet*.

THE FOUNDATION

During the Second Diffusion of Buddhism, Indian, Kashmiri, and Nepalese pundits supervised Tibetan translators. Their translations of texts and *sutras* inspired new thinking and doctrinal innovations that had long-lasting effects. At the same time, obscure lamas established monasteries that became important regional centers for learning and practice. Most of these, founded in the pivotal years after the 11th C., did not survive. Neglect, wars, and sectarian strife destroyed institutions and relics inspired by the religious fervor of men like Atisha and Lume.

Tsongtsun Sherab Senge was a lama active in the district of Myangtö in Tsang. His untiring efforts to revive Buddhism after Langdarma's reign of terror produced the monasteries of Khule, Goyul, Gyangro, and Kyangphu (Samada). Another focus of Tsongtsun's energies was in the area of Tsi, where the monastery of Tsi Nesar (founded 1037) became particularly important. Both Tsi Nesar and Kyangphu survived until recently; Tucci studied and chronicled their relics in his *Indo-Tibetica* (see Bibliography, page 1064). The other monastery thoroughly researched by him in the Gyangro District was Yemar.

Yemar's founding is attributed to Lharje Chöjang, a lama and a physician considered a previous incarnation of Khache Panchen, himself a Kashmiri who came to Yemar in 1204. By comparing Yemar's murals with similar ones at Tsi Nesar, it is possible to say that those at Yemar are earlier. Thus the monastery was probably founded in the first decades of the 11th century.

THE SITE

When Tucci visited this south-facing temple during the 1930s and 1940s, it was already badly neglected. More recently, the flat roofs have collapsed and the murals lost due to exposure. Despite these ravages, Yemar (called Iwang by Tucci and the local population) is one of the few temples from the Second Diffusion that retains its original structure. Kyangphu and Tsi Nesar, sites with invaluable images and paintings, were completely demolished by the Red Guards in the 1960s.

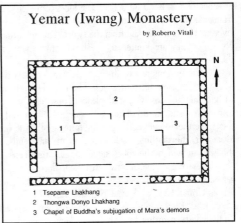

Yemar (Iwang) Monastery
by Roberto Vitali

1 Tsepame Lhakhang
2 Thongwa Donyo Lhakhang
3 Chapel of Buddha's subjugation of Mara's demons

A *khorlam* enclosed three chapels. Its external crenellated wall is also the perimeter wall of the entire monastery. Yemar's central chapel runs along the entire northern wing, directly across from the entrance. It is dedicated to Thongwa Dönyo (Amogadarshin) whose image is flanked to the left and right by a row of seated Jampas, three on each side. All are costumed in heavy, densely pleated stucco robes. Once 16 *bodhisattvas* stood here, but all are destroyed except for a few severed heads.

The chapel left of the entrance is consecrated to Tsepame. There are 16 standing *bodhisattvas* robed in heavy medallioned garments arranged along the chamber's four sides and two guardians defend the entrance (destroyed). It is gratifying that the complete cycle of images still exists here. Right of the entrance is an empty room that contained a three-dimensional sculpture of 'The Attack of Mara's Demons'. Only the paintings of two donors' faces remain, hidden under the altar.

THE STATUES

All the statues retain their essential features—details that can be examined more carefully now than previously due to the loss of paint. Photos of the monastery and its contents taken several decades ago exist in *Tibet in Pictures* by Li Gotama, whereas Roberto Vitali's *The Early Temples of Central Tibet* shows them as they are today.

According to Tucci, the stylistic features of Yemar's statues are very similar to those (all destroyed) of Kyangphu, Tsi Nesar, and Dranang (see page 393). This is particularly evident in the hands and heads, parts not covered by the stucco robes. All works are Pala-inspired and moderated with unmistakable Central Asian influences. This Pala idiom (9th–11th C.) is evident in the elongated eyes with heavy lids, wide, protruding foreheads, broad cheeks, and tall, thick hair buns (*ushnishas*) atop flat skulls. Another tell-tale Pala trait is in the hands. They have larger than average palms and the fingers are hooked.

The Central Asian element comes across in the relative heaviness of the images; they are devoid of the lightness that characterizes Pala statues. Individual details also confirm the presence of Silk Road influence. The lobes of the crown are large and leaf-shaped rather than triangular. Eyebrows are straight rather than arched, chins are square, and the hair is highly stylized. The halos deviate from the typical Pala rendition by being small, hollow, and upwardly pointing. They are limited to the heads only; there are no corresponding nimbuses behind the bodies.

The most impressive, distinctive characteristic of the Yemar statues is their bulky garments, which are of two different types. Thongwa Dönyo and the six Jampas have flowing robes with numerous closely spaced pleats. Those of Tsepame and the *bodhisattvas* hang straight to the floor and are decorated with rare medallions. Although the bodies are well concealed, they nevertheless evoke strength and form, another departure from the standard Pala treatment. Moreover, the clothing itself shows no Indian trends. A typical Central Asian signature is the way in which the robes slope towards the feet.

The use of medallions as garment decoration is intriguing. It is possible to trace its genesis to the Iranian Sassanid empire (3rd–7th C.), whose artistic heritage reached all the way to China, Central Asia, Tibet, and India. This medallion motif was widespread and works of art from Khotan and Kashmir to China have made use of the popular design. A famous Tang-dynasty painting by Yan Liben depicts Gar, King Songtsen Gampo's minister, at the royal court of China wearing medallioned robes. Tibetans seemingly associated this particular style of garment with divinities, nobles, and high officials—contradicting the notion that the design is more indicative of ethnicity.

Tibet's strong link with Central Asia after the 7th C. and its overlordship of a large territory centered on the Silk Road created the conditions for a close absorption of local Xixia influence and its integration into Pala-inspired works. A clear example of the Pala style altered by Central Asian sensibilities exists in the two guardians. Furthermore, the artists who modeled these works added a third and final component: a peculiarly Tibetan interpretation of the Xixia-Pala style. The statues of Yemar, Kyangphu, and Tsi Nesar all embodied this unusual genre. Those at Dranang took on more overt Tibetan characteristics.

From documentation provided by Tucci, Yemar's murals show a strong affinity to the traditional Pala style and closely resemble paintings in Bengali and Bihari manuscripts. Tucci discovered inscriptions (now destroyed) inside the Thongwa Dönyo chapel, which stated that the murals in that chapel were executed in the Indian manner, whereas those of the Tsepame chapel followed the Khotan tradition. After a close reading of the text, Vitali concluded that the latter actually referred to Xixia rather than Khotan. The artists are also identified: the two painters of the different chapels were in fact Tibetans who followed both Indian and Xixia idioms.

DRANANG:
XIXIA-PALA MURALS LONG
THOUGHT LOST TO THE WORLD

An uncommon synthesis of two early and seminal art-styles

OVERVIEW

Dranang, although virtually unknown to the outside world, is a monastery of paramount importance. Its ancient wall murals are unique in all Tibet and the Indian subcontinent. If Kachu Monastery (see page 378) is the repository of the country's earliest monumental sculptures, then Dranang is its counterpart in painting.

Miraculously preserved 11th-C. murals within the Tri Tsangkhang chapel were inspired by the Pala art style that flourished in east India from the 9th to 11th centuries. The Tibetan interpretation of this genre was further moderated by artistic currents from the ancient Xixia Kingdom of Central Asia. On Dranang's walls, therefore, one finds an uncommon synthesis of two seminal styles, both of which retained their vitality in the early stages of the Second Diffusion of Buddhism. The site (near Yarlung Valley) was visited by Tucci, the pre-eminent Tibetologist, in 1949. (No foreigners returned until October 1988.) He wrote of the paintings:

> (They are) as expressive as portraits, yet set in a hieratic collectedness remindful of Byzantine paintings. There might have been more than a casual coincidence of spiritual attitude to that resemblance. The Hellenistic-Roman painting school drove with slow waves into the heart of Central Asia and left traces of its advance up to the threshold of China. The Dranang frescoes may be the indirect echo of that influence, which crossed Asia and tailed off in the Land of Snows.

These paintings are perhaps the earliest and only extant example of their kind in Tibet. The Jokhang's Pala murals were probably irreparably damaged when the authorities brutally removed them from the walls for 'restoration'. Shalu is the only monastery that has remotely comparable paintings of major significance, and no Pala *thangkas* or murals survive in India, their country of origin. (The genre can best be seen in the early manuscripts of Bengal and Bihar.)

The highly unusual architecture of the original monastery was heavily influenced by Samye and its Indian precursors. Dranang, like Tibet's first monastery, was designed as a mandala. Also similar to Samye are architectural features from indigenous Tibetan designs complemented by influences from China and India. These can be seen in the capitals, roof tiles, and the essential layout of the complex.

History

Dranang was founded in 1081 by the Nyingmapa *tertön*, Drapa Ngönshe (1012–90), one of the legendary 13 Buddha-lamas of the Dranang Valley. Born in a neighboring village, he reputedly built 128 chapels in Central Tibet among which Dranang was the most important. Thought to be initiated at Samye by one of Lume's disciples, he later became a student of the Indian sage, Dampa Sangye (founder of the Chö tradition at Langkor near Dingri; see page 271).

Drapa Ngönshe was also a master of the Ngagpa tradition as well as an adept of the Abhidharma (Ngongpa), a systematization of ideas on Buddhist psychology and metaphysics. His most impressive accomplishment was the discovery at Samye (1038) of the *Gyüshi* (Four Medical Tantras). This has become the standard text for every Tibetan doctor since the 11th century. Later, he developed a separate sect, called the Drapa, and is credited as its founder.

The monastery took 13 years to complete and was finally finished in 1093 by Drapa Ngönshe's two nephews. Dranang became the main tantric school within the monastic tradition re-established by Lume; Sonag Tangboche (see page 527) was the principal shrine to study Vinaya, the rules of conduct of Buddhist order. During the mid-13th C., the predominant spiritual and political power in Tibet rested with the Sakyapa. Many monasteries were converted to that sect; Dranang was one of them. Later, in the 18th-C., the Dzungar did untold damage to the complex. Under the Reting Regent (r 1922–41), Dranang underwent a grand renovation that restored the second and third floors of the Tsuglag Khang. When the Chinese sacked Tibet's religious monuments, the all-important ground floor was spared in order to make room for a granary for the Dranang government.

Location (Map reference NH46-9 D)

Dranang Monastery lies 2 km inside the Dranang Valley, whose entrance is at road marker 76 km on the Lhasa–Tsethang highway (see page 501), about half-way between Gongkar airport and the Yarlung Valley.

THE MONASTERY

The main building, the Tsuglag Khang, was originally surrounded by three imposing sets of concentric walls. Only the elliptical outer wall remains. This trait of having a protective perimeter is similar to Samye (see page 295). It was also a personal tendency of Drapa Ngönshe who built, for example, Chengye Monastery in like manner. The central building is irregularly sited, not at the center of the circle but near its north end. Drapa Ngönshe's successors contracted the north wall to bring it closer to the Tsuglag Khang. The stone construction of the 2 m-thick south wall differs from the rest and clearly shows a much later technique, which was developed only in this century. The west wall is the best preserved, then the east, followed by the damaged north and south walls. Their heights vary between 3 and 5 m. A moat outside these three sets of walls added further protection. Within the inner wall were the principal chapels. Between the inner and middle walls were the kitchen, storage buildings, and debating pavilion. A large chörten rose beyond the middle wall.

TSUGLAG KHANG

The floor plan of this east-facing building resembles an irregular cross. To the east is the *dukhang* and the porch; adjacent to them in the west is the Tri Tsangkhang, the chapel with the wonderful paintings. South and north of the *dukhang* are two chapels; the former, a *gönkhang* survives. Residences have been added to the south-facing second floor of the west wing whose outer wall has three high windows that provide illumination for the *tsangkhang khorlam*. Garages with living quarters above are north of the courtyard, in front of the main entrance.

The long, narrow entrance porch of the Tsuglag Khang has two doors at its north and south ends, a rare design feature. On the walls are paintings of the Four Guardian Kings, an elephant and deer. Above the aluminum-plated front entrance are two inconspicuous, archaic wood lions. The meticulously carved sculptures depict only the front half of the lions, which are distinguished by their porcine noses and large ears.

DUKHANG

The empty *dukhang* has 20 octagonal and square columns. The older (octagonal) ones lack refined carvings, while the square ones are more elaborate and ornate. Some murals survive on both sides of the entrance. They depict the Four Guardian Kings, Tsepame and others. Near the ceiling, the walls of the skylight have late Sakyapa paintings in good condition. They portray principal Sakyapa lamas, Guru Rinpoche, the founder of the monastery, and other historic figures. All are oriented to the west to face the sacred Tri Tsangkhang (Jowo Lhakhang).

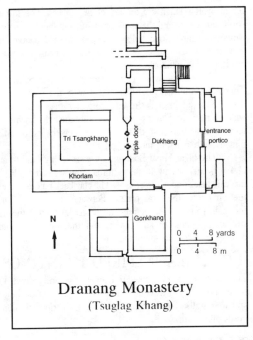

Dranang Monastery
(Tsuglag Khang)

The only surviving *gönkhang*, entered from the left (south) wall of the *dukhang*, has eight columns but no paintings or objects. Next to it were chapels dedicated to Tara and Kalachakra. On the north side of the hall was a chapel of the 11-faced Chenresi. The assembly hall is still being used for storage and is littered with grain sacks and oil drums. It only opens briefly for the movement of goods. The authorities generally refuse entry to outsiders and photography is strictly forbidden.

TRI TSANGKHANG

This most important chapel has an impressive entranceway consisting of three large doors with paintings of *bodhisattvas* and the Four Guardian Kings on the lower panels. Above them are three pairs of metal lions. Surrounding this inner chamber is a surprisingly wide circumambulatory corridor with murals in good condition. In places, broken walls reveal early construction techniques: the stone walls, layered in a primitive way, resemble the 7th-9th-C. stone coffin tombs unearthed in Yarlung. The corridor murals tell the life story of Sakyamuni. Other subjects include the Four Guardians, Tsepame, and Chenresi. An unusual figure is the protector with a red face and white beard. Next to him are various mythical creatures with animal heads and human bodies.

There is no formal entrance into the Tri Tsangkhang proper beyond the *khorlam* entrance and exit. The chapel floor is higher than the corridor and its ceiling supported by eight simple 11th-C. octagonal columns (6.6 m)—the first and second rows are unusually close, less than

0.5 m apart—which are formed of two pieces. The lower sections have been shaped with considerable care and the upper ones only minimally. Crude implements were used. The capital carvings of simple cloud designs were probably added later. Originally, the room had no windows; in later years, two were added along the west and north walls. Limited light enters from the *khorlam*'s high windows.

The central image in the Tsangkhang was Sakyamuni, a 3.4-m-high statue known as Thupa Jangchub Chenpo. Flanking it were the Eight Great Bodhisattvas and two guardians. These have all been destroyed except for their elaborate haloes; Sakyamuni's is fully 3 m wide at one point. Flame patterns decorate the haloes, which have archaically designed *gyendruks* (Six Ornaments) above them. Surrounding the head and body haloes is another large, oval nimbus with a flame motif.

The Eight Great Bodhisattvas were as high as the main image. Their elongated haloes (1.4 m), enclosed by flame patterns, consist of red, blue and green rings intertwined with intricate black and white designs. The clay back haloes of the guardians are also flame-patterned; the left one is the most ornate. Between the statues, floral decorations similar to those of the main paintings, cover the wall spaces. Although the statues are missing, the high chapel still exudes grandeur and power, and the unique monumental haloes provide a dramatic counterpoint to the sumptuous murals.

THE PALA-INSPIRED PAINTINGS

The paintings adorning the Tri Tsangkhang can be divided into two periods. Those belonging to the 11th C., which comprise nearly 90 per cent of the collection, are on the south, north, and west walls. Those of the later second period are along the easternmost sections of the north and south walls.

THE FIRST PERIOD

Most paintings of the first period consist of Sakyamunis surrounded in semi-circles by smaller male and female *bodhisattvas*, monks, and laymen. A distinguishing feature of these portraits: all have dissimilar facial features and all are clearly of foreign ethnic origin. The clothing, jewelry, and ornamentation are radically different from those in most Tibetan paintings. Many have head and back haloes. Between the images are floral motifs that completely cover the walls. These early works show a marked Indian (Pala) and Central Asian (Xixia) influence and can be divided into ten main groups. Those on the back (west) wall are the best preserved. Some along the north and south walls have suffered water damage. Paintings along the upper sections (above the statues' haloes) require a ladder to be seen properly.

- Group 1. In the center of the south wall, above the destroyed guardian king, is Sakyamuni flanked by 10 male and 20 female figures. Only the upper bodies are depicted and they all face the central image. The men are hatless and the women all wear crowns.
- Group 2. West of group 1, this group is similar to the first (poor condition).
- Group 3. South wall, upper west section. Sakyamuni is surrounded by 38 kneeling male and female figures, the males above the females. The hand positions of the devotees are all different. Below the central image are two squatting lions. Three smaller females, perhaps attendants, are below the right group.
- Group 4. West wall, upper south section. This group is essentially similar to group 1.
- Group 5. Below group 4, these paintings are in excellent condition and, being closer to

the ground, most details can be seen distinctly. The central Sakyamuni, like the others, sits on a lotus pedestal above flower pots entwined with floral motifs. The lotuses are particularly impressive. Enclosing the figure are head and back haloes of blue, green, and red circular bands.

Arrayed around the Buddha are 35 male and female figures; the males are on top. As in the other paintings, only their upper bodies are shown. The physiognomy is strongly Central Asian. Many have large noses, beards, and mustaches. Over their wide-sleeved inner garments are typical Buddhist robes. The females all have high, floral crowns (three-flower and five-flower forms arranged in three levels) and long shoulder-length hair. Protruding from the tops of the crowns (with triangular elements rather than the elongated ones of the Pala genre) are unusual pleated turbans, similar in style to the one used by King Songtsen Gampo. The skin color of the females varies among seven colors: white, yellow, red, brown, black, green, blue. Their faces are either square or triangular. Thin, delicate eyebrows frame eyes with distinctive upturned corners. Circular double-earrings sandwich each earlobe. The long dresses, draped with shoulder shawls, have large turned-out collars. Below Sakyamuni are two vivid crouching lions, which are placed above four female figures whose faces are fuller than the others. Behind their heads are haloes.

- Group 6. West wall, upper north section, this group is similar to group 5.
- Group 7. Below group 6, this and group 5 are the best preserved and the most accessible. Flanking the Sakyamuni, which differs from that of group 5 in only minor details, are 31 figures (19 males), some full-length. Representing different nationalities, their clothing and hand gestures are very similar to the portraits of group 5. The patterns of the garments, however, are considerably richer and more complex. Especially outstanding are the female figures—the clothing, bodies, and facial features are more noticeably Indian. The varied crowns consist of six distinct types. In front of the piled hair buns are painted small *chörtens* and, outside the head haloes, are complex flame patterns.

  Below Sakyamuni, next to the flower pots, are two seated female figures. Their exposed upper bodies, complete with flame-patterned head haloes, are bedecked with ornaments and jewelry. Each wears a short skirt with horizontal stripes. Above them are two ferocious lions.
- Group 8. North wall, upper west section. Sakyamuni is surrounded by 31 male and female figures. All have oval head haloes. Their clothing and postures are similar to those of group 3. Two lions are below the main image. A green square frame encloses the paintings.
- Group 9. East of group 8, these paintings are in very poor condition. Only four female heads remain.
- Group 10. East of group 9, Sakyamuni is flanked by 35 figures, the males above the females. Below the main image are two lions and four females. A 30-cm horizontal band runs along the lower part, near the floor of the west wall. Within it are different, indistinct lions. Above this is another band decorated with floral patterns.

The iconographic program of these early murals is consistent. At the center of each group is invariably a bejeweled, diademed Buddha closely surrounded by many male and female *bodhisattvas*. This arrangement is also found in other early Kadampa monasteries (Yemar, see page 390; Samada). At Dranang, the number of *bodhisattvas* significantly exceeds the conventional scheme. Instead of eight, ten, 12, or 16, combinations here vary from 30 to 38. Only a few full-length *bodhisattvas* are shown, thus blunting the full force of the Pala tradition with its hallmark svelte and languorous figures. The repetitive composition tends toward aesthetic monotony, despite the great technical virtuosity. Although classic, the figures lack the palpable spirituality that permeates great art—for example, Gupta painting and sculpture (4th–7th century.). Nevertheless, these are some of Tibet's most beautiful images.

An outstanding feature of the paintings is their deep, smooth, vibrant colors, especially apparent in portraits of the groups 5 and 7. The skin tones of the 16 female *bodhisattvas* run the spectrum of the rainbow. Red predominates, but it is harmoniously complemented by glowing yellows, greens, and blues. The outlines are carefully drawn and there is a distinct elegance to the half-figures. Feelings of effortless grace and animation permeate the paintings, and indeed these are remarkable examples of early Tibetan portraiture. The realism and fluidity in the round, full faces are simply not found elsewhere.

The distinct Central Asian current in Dranang's paintings can be clearly seen in the physiognomy and garments of the figures. Some of the faces are radically different from those in a standard Pala rendering. Note in particular the male *bodhisattvas* with balding pates and mustaches. The wide lapels of their comfortably loose, wide-sleeved costumes are especially telling. This Central Asian influence on the otherwise typical Pala-derived paintings is intriguing. It parallels the artistic traditions of other Central Tibetan Kadampa monasteries like Yemar, Samada, and Tsi Nesar.

Dranang's destroyed statues were similar to those of Yemar. This is especially apparent in the long garments with open necks and wide lapels. Both show distinctive medallion motifs with enclosed animal designs. These patterns were widely used throughout the Islamic world, including Central Asia, and the garments were probably worn by Persian, Turkish, Kashmiri, and Afghan royalty. It is thus difficult to pinpoint the exact origin of these features.

THE SECOND PERIOD

The paintings of the second, later period are in two groups along the easternmost sections of the north and south walls. Each group consists of three Tsepame figures, aligned vertically. The 1-m-high images are surrounded by head and back haloes. Their upper torsos are bare and all have long skirts (*lungi*) and body ornaments. The style, clothing, coloring, and lotus thrones are easily recognizable as later works.

AN ASSESSMENT OF DRANANG'S PAINTINGS

The following is a summary from Roberto Vitali's *The Early Temples of Central Tibet*.

The paintings of Dranang are intended to convey an overwhelming sense of devotion. All the scenes repeat the same motif: numerous secondary figures in postures of supplication crowd around the central Buddha. A remarkable aspect of the paintings is the number of lesser figures the artists succeed in grouping around the Buddha images. This configuration continues an ancient Indian tradition not necessarily confined to the Pala genre. Dranang's artists took the liberty of depicting more freely the postures of individual figures, a striking departure from paintings of other monasteries. Here is less emphasis on iconographic correctness. In fact, it was the sole intention of the artists to portray pure, unadulterated devotion to the master, and this required deviation from the precise placement of each image. The source of inspiration of these works is the Central Asia (Xixia) Pala style. In the paintings the basic characteristics of Pala are retained. These are the same ones that can easily be seen in Bengal and Bihar manuscripts.

The orthodox Pala style is defined by a number of unifying elements: shading to give the illusion of a third dimension, volume in the depiction of human figures, disproportion of the bodies (large hands, oversize torsos, disarticulated legs), and curvaceousness. In later periods, shading fell out of fashion and the proportion of the figures became more balanced, with smaller hands and slimmer torsos. Two-dimensionality of the images was the rule and outlining was used more frequently.

Although strongly Pala-inspired, Dranang's paintings show a number of distinctive deviations from this standard. For example, chiaroscuro was used to give an added dimension to the figures—a technique not generally used in Tibetan Pala art after the 11th century. The secondary figures that display Central Asian characteristics, are distinguished by their small eyes, large noses, and narrow dark beards. There is also a marked squarishness to the images' heads and jaws. This seems to be a local interpretation of the Central Asia-Pala style, revealing a wish to exaggerate the foreignness of facial features. Another noticeable aspect of these countless faces are the noses, distinguished by their solidity and prominence; the bases are large, the bridges aquiline. In profile, the foreheads are elongated back towards the temples. The triangular crowns, a typical Pala feature, are aligned in a single row, to enable turbans to be painted inside the crowns and thus establish a popular Tibetan signature. These turbans resemble the ones worn by King Songtsen Gampo and other Yarlung kings.

Most of the garments also deviate from the orthodox Pala tradition—there is little Pala influence evident and the ubiquitous *dhoti* is lacking altogether. Rather, the imaginative clothing design shows a pleasure in ornamentation that borders on fantasy. Medallions, arranged in a loose, creative manner, are often used and rich, brocaded patterns are *de rigueur*. Even the haloes depart from the typical Pala idiom. They are formed of polychrome bands and closely follow body contours (Pala haloes are usually monochromatic and less spatially restrictive). Lotuses in the Dranang paintings are simple, with blue and green leaves, while Pala lotuses usually have plain petals colored with contrasting tones. Lions are also liberally used; they decorate the lotus bases and reside among the figures in unlikely stances. Here again, Tibetan sensibilities infringe on Pala characteristics. The animals are white with green manes, this combination being a favorite among later Tibetan painters. In general, the palette of colors used in the paintings is decidedly un-Pala-like: the dominant colors are deep blue, red, and green; the faces of the Buddhas are orange.

In Dranang, interpretation based on sensibilities particular to the Xixia kingdom in Central Asia modified the essentially East Indian conception. That the artistic tradition of Xixia was at work in Central Tibet during the advent of the Second Diffusion of Buddhism can be shown by an inscription at Yemar (see page 390). It can also be established that Yemar was intimately connected with Dranang through artistic influences—both borrowed from and inspired by the Pala and Xixia genres. A well-known site where Xixia-modified, Pala-style works have been unearthed is Karakhoto. Relics at neighboring Dunhuang can also be ascribed to the Pala idiom. During the downfall of the Yarlung empire (9th C.), Xixia was a leading power in the northeast, and since the Xixia (Minyag) in Tibetan were culturally and ethnically akin to the Tibetans, it is likely that many Tibetans fled there during the reign of Langdarma. When they finally returned to Tibet in the late 10th and early 11th C., they brought back many artistic ideas from that region.

SHALU:
A 14TH-CENTURY ART GALLERY

Yuan-dynasty-influenced, Newar-style wall paintings

OVERVIEW

Shalu is the only monastery in Tibet known to possess a significant collection of 14th-C. Newari-style murals, moderated and enhanced by the artistic sensibilities of the Yuan Dynasty of China. Arniko, a master painter from the Kathmandu Valley, pioneered this unique art form that later came to full flower in the Chinese capital. Shalu's paintings inspired generations of artists and played a seminal role in the development of a truly Tibetan style of art.

Although Shalu's foundation goes back to the 11th C., it rose to prominence in the 14th C., when the temple came under the jurisdiction of Drakpa Gyaltsen and Butön Rinpoche. Patronage by the Mongol emperors allowed for extensive rebuilding from 1306 onwards, when outstanding artists of the Yuan court arrived. Butön, a renowned scholar who compiled and edited the monumental *Tengyur*, finished what Drakpa Gyaltsen started; he supervised the creation of the large painted mandalas still seen today in the top chapels. Next to the complex is the small chapel of Gyangong, a pivotal site founded in 997 that predates Shalu. Some consider it the first temple of the Second Diffusion of Buddhism (10th–12th centuries).

Many of Shalu's most spectacular murals are in the great processional corridor (*khorlam*) of the Serkhang, the principal, three-story building. Others can be found in the Kangyur Lhakhang and the *khorlam* of the Yumchenmo Lhakhang. The *gönkhang* contains rare Pala-style murals (restored in the 14th C.) that follow closely the 11th-C. East-Indian prototype. Within the Dedan Lhakhang are two relics: an unusual stone statue of Chenresi and a vase of sacred water that supposedly remains forever constant.

The architecture of Shalu is a rare combination of Chinese and traditional Tibetan elements, most strikingly represented in the multi-level Chinese palace roofs, with brilliant turquoise tiles, that surmount a Tibetan temple design. Shalu was also well-known as a center of esoteric yogic instruction. Disciplines included long-distance travel in trance (*lungom*) and the generation of internal heat (*thumo*). Riphuk, Shalu's cave hermitage, is on a hillside 1 1/4 hr to the southwest of the main complex.

Location (Map reference NH45-12 C)

The walk from Shigatse to Shalu takes 4 hr. From the main department store in the center of Shigatse, wak past the truck depot (on the right) and the Shigatse Hotel (on the left) to get out of town. The road (the Friendship Highway leading southeast to Gyantse) passes brick kilns and a gas station, then a hill on the right, just before a large bridge. (This bridge is a good starting point for the walk west to Narthang Monastery, see page 834, and Ngor Monastery, also page 834; the dirt track leading due south from here goes to sacred Tromo Tretung Lake and to the Chörten Nyima pilgrimage; see page 801.) Continue southeast along the main road, which is soon flanked on the right by an aqueduct. Reach a hill with a white building. Just beyond, on the right, is a roadside village, called Tsungda, with a large black rock and many prayer flags hanging from trees. This is the entrance to the Shalu Valley, near road marker 18 km (16 km from Shigatse). The monastery is 4 km inside the valley and clearly visible from the main road. Head south along a dirt road to the Gyangong Lhakhang, a two-story building on the right, 150 m before the village of Shalu. An alternative to walking is to catch the Shigatse–Gyantse–Lhasa bus, which leaves the bus station (near the Shigatse Hotel) at 0830. Be sure to look for road marker 18.

Gyangong Lhakhang

This is considered by some scholars to be Tibet's earliest temple of the Second Diffusion. Known formally as Gyangong Jangchub Gi Gene, it was founded by Lotön Dorje Wangchuk in 997, and predates Shalu by 30 years. Atisha's disciple, Dromtönpa, believed Buddhism's rejuvenation began with this small chapel. The rebuilt Gyangong is dedicated to Rabtenma, a form of Palden Lhamo, Tibet's protectress. She also looks after Shalu.

The Serkhang, Shalu's principal complex, is surrounded by houses, themselves enclosed by an old village wall. A main gate east of the monastery and another at the southern perimeter lead into the community. The east-facing edifice is essentially a square with pavilions, or wings, oriented to the four cardinal points. Its classic Chinese-inspired pagoda roofs are unmistakable. Outside, east of the main entrance, is a large enclosed courtyard that can be entered via a gate along the east wall. An elevated terrace on the first floor is enclosed by chapels of the four pavilions. Reach the terrace by a flight of stairs at the north side.

History

In 997, Lotön Dorje Wangchuk, oldest disciple of Lachen Gongpo Rabsal (the lama who spearheaded the Second Diffusion of Buddhism), came to the village of Gyangong (next to Shalu) and built a small temple here. Its full name was Gyangong Jangchub Gi Gene and was in effect Shalu's precursor. The Shalu (Small Hat) complex was begun in 1027 by Chetsün Sherab Jungne, member of a noble family that originated in Shangshung, West Tibet. In a reversal of fortunes, he fled a rebellion and found refuge here with Lotön Dorje Wangchuk. Lotön ordained him; he was considered an incarnation of Mahakala and Chenresi.

The first phase of construction took 18 years and ended with completion of the Yumchenmo Lhakhang just prior to Atisha's visit. Shalu's inner sanctum, the twin chapels at the back of the assembly hall, is the oldest structure. These served as repositories for the sacred statue of Chenresi (in the south Lhakhang Lhoma) and a *chörten* that contained Chetsun's relics (in the north Lhakhang Jangma). In 1045, the great Bengali master, Atisha, came to Shalu for three months after his sojourn in West Tibet. He undertook to consecrate the Yumchenmo Lhakhang, and this auspicious event was witnessed by the clay Chenresi, who, legend says, spoke out loud.

The second phase of Shalu's development came at the hands of Drakpa Gyaltsen who was appointed abbot of the monastery in 1306 by the Yuan Emperor Oljadu (1265–1307), successor to Kublai Khan. Shortly after, he began a great renovation, utilizing resources from the Yuan court (during the 1290s, Gönpo Pal, a predecessor, built the Gosum Lhakhang along the Serkhang north wing). According to literary sources, Drakpa Gyaltsen conceived the overall architectural plan and proceeded to build the four pavilions of Serkhang. The ground floor was significantly enlarged and every square inch of its walls covered with glorious murals. At this time, the south wing, housing the Segoma (Kangyur) Lhakhang, was also completed. This chapel was distinguished by a treasured rhinoceros skin door (*segoma*) painted with images of the Buddhas of the Golden Age. Although the door is lost today, the murals are preserved.

The architectural and artistic marvel of Shalu, built by Drakpa Gyaltsen in the early 14th C., is the monumental *khorlam* that surrounds the *dukhang* and its four interior chapels. Its copious murals of the 100 deeds of Sakyamuni are among the most outstanding in all Tibet. In the same period, the east wing was renovated and the entrance corridor converted into a multi-room *gönkhang* that houses Shalu's main protective deity, Namthose (Vaishravana). To do this, the north and south parts of the 11th-C. walls built by Chetsün Sherab Jungne were utilized. They still retain the 11th-C., Pala-style murals that were meticulously repainted by Drakpa Gyaltsen's artists in the early 14th century. The middle story of the east wing, consisting of the Yumchenmo Lhakhang and its *khorlam*, was also renovated. Finally, four top-floor chapels in each of the four pavilions were added, but the completion of their interiors and the complex as a whole was left to Drakpa Gyaltsen's son, Kunga Döndrub, and Butön Rinpoche between 1333 and 1335.

To decorate Shalu, Drakpa Gyaltsen invited artists of diverse nationalities from the Mongol court. These were, in fact, disciples of Arniko, the Newari master from Nepal, whose work so charmed the Mongols that he became a confidant of Kublai Khan. His school, the 'Western Style of Image-making', was based on Newari artistic precepts and was centered at the Yuan capital.

Architecture

The Shalu Serkhang was conceived as the Paradise of Chenresi and represented a religious haven from all hunger and poverty. In execution, it has obvious Chinese influences, especially the magnificent turquoise roof tiles supported by distinctive tongue-and-groove wood structures. The central rafter has vertical enamel panels decorated entirely in the Chinese style: the motifs are floral patterns and intricate zoomorphic and divine figures. Along both ends are coiled, open-mouthed dragons. At the corners, heads of mythical sea creatures (*makara*) serve as rain spouts. Charming figures of lions, tigers, *apsaras*, and humans sit astride this central divide. It is likely that Chinese artists, familiar with Lamaist themes, produced the molds for these tiles at the Yuan court. Most of the roofs have been badly damaged and haphazardly restored (reach them by a series of ladders).

Each architectural module of the temple is topped by a separate roof. The main (east) three-story facade has a simple first roof supported by a console. The more elaborate second roof is upheld by wooden columns, and the third, at the apex, is a true roof similar to those of Chinese palaces. This successive, symmetrical configuration of roofs of different dimensions and heights was a favored design of the Yuan.

The Serkhang's architecture has traces of Indian elements that go back to its foundation in the 11th century. Most important is the inner sanctum of twin chapels at the back of the *dukhang*. The precursors of this configuration were perhaps Indian temples (*viharas*). When viewed in elevation, the components of the east wing, the entrance extension, the *dukhang*, and its inner chapels can be seen to fit tightly together as an integrated and compact whole.

The principal Chinese and Indian elements, each embodying its own heritage, came together at Shalu to create a striking, unique Tibetan shrine. The most outstanding result of this congruence is the monumental *khorlam*, a typically Tibetan concept wrapped around an Indian-inspired inner sanctum.

THE SERKHANG CHAPELS AND THEIR WALL MURALS

The art-historical analysis of Shalu's magnificent murals is a summary from Roberto Vitali's *The Early Temples of Central Tibet.*

Ground floor

A large courtyard is immediately outside the main east-facing entrance. The façade of the Serkhang's east wing is particularly pleasing from here, because of the three distinctive Chinese-style pagoda roofs. A stone plaque with Tibetan inscriptions and four carved *chörtens* is in front of the entrance; it reputedly survives from Shalu's founding in the 11th century. South of the entrance extension is a garden with prayer wheels. Beyond is another entrance that leads to the pilgrimage route around the entire monastery. Stairs immediately north of the entrance extension lead to the inner terrace and the four top-floor chapels. Along the north perimeter walls of the courtyard are new monks' quarters, a kitchen, and workshops. The Serkhang's unusual floor plan first leads one through the main entrance to an extension building made up of the multi-roomed *gönkhang*. Only after this is the main assembly hall reached.

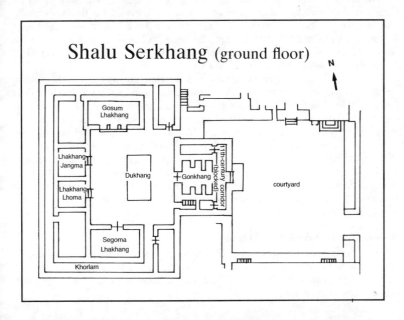

GÖNKHANG

The design of the *gönkhang* extension is basically a narrow T-shaped space with three sets of doorless chambers opening along its central east–west axis. The north–south axis, closest to the entrance, runs the breadth of the extension. This part of the Serkhang was built during the time of Drakpa Gyaltsen who modified the original entrance corridor built by Chetsün Sherab Jungne. Parts of the *gönkhang* walls, the north and south sections of the north–south axis, thus date back to c 1045. Murals commissioned by Chetsün were repainted during the renovation of the early 14th C. and the outcome was a unique juxtaposition of styles that represented diverse artistic sensibilities. The Yuan court artists repainted the main Buddhas in the style they were most familiar with, namely Yuan-influenced Newari. The surrounding secondary images of worshipping *bodhisattvas*, princes, monks, foreign figures, and others remained unaltered; the artists were content to follow the originals precisely. What remains is a faithful preservation of the classical East-Indian Pala style of the mid-11th century. There is a close affinity between these secondary figures of the Shalu *gönkhang* and ones in the *tsangkhang* of Dranang Monastery (see page 396). Notice, for example, the turbans of the princes (similar to those of the Yarlung kings depicted at Dranang) and the foreign figures with short, trimmed beards. The existence of these Pala-style works shows that Shalu was in the vanguard of an artistic milieu that took much of its inspiration from Pala India.

The north section of this north–south axis (north and east walls) also contains surprising murals not encountered elsewhere at Shalu. These depict the Four Guardian Kings in a background filled completely with clouds unlike any others found in Central Tibetan temples. The style is quintessentially Yuan Chinese, with no trace of Newari influence whatsoever. Both the kings' warrior attire and facial features are pure Chinese, as are the clouds that float geometrically. The considerable difference between the Yuan style and Arniko's Yuan-influenced Newari style is easily appreciated here. Simply compare the image of Chana Dorje (next to the superbly rendered Chinese dragons and phoenixes), painted in the latter style, with the Four Kings. Notice also the realistic throne in the background.

Towards the entrance of the assembly hall along the east–west axis of the *gönkhang* are six chambers that open to both sides of this central corridor. They have no doors or outer walls. The first four lack paintings, but on the walls are large stucco haloes with heavy lotus bases. Wood struts protrude from their centers, obviously supports for the now destroyed statues. These works supposedly were devoid of Tibetan motifs and closely followed Chinese-Central Asian forms. Radiating outward from these oval haloes are unusual wavy lines, reminiscent of the famed haloes of Tapho (Tabo) in Spiti, India. The last two chambers have late, unimportant murals painted in the Indian style. Goddesses riding on animals are rendered on parallel bands that encircle the rooms. Outside the openings of these six chambers are clay pots buried up to their necks in the ground (the significance of which is uncertain). At the western end of the axis is a door to the main assembly hall.

TSHOK KHANG (ASSEMBLY HALL)

The large assembly hall has four interior chapels along the west, north, and south walls. An unusually wide and high circumambulatory corridor (*khorlam*) encircles the whole. The hall, lit by a skylight, retains murals along the back (east) wall; formerly covered with whitewash, they are now being restored.

Segoma (Kangyur) Lhakhang (south chapel of the Tshok Khang)

This was the library of Shalu. An iron lattice curtain closes off the entrance. Stacks of forgotten texts and manuscripts lie on the floor, part of the complete sets of the *Kangyur*. Along the west and east walls are shelves with still more volumes. The back wall has well-preserved, large paintings of the Five Tathagatas (Gyalwa Rigna). Classically 14th-C. Nepalese, these were executed by artists faithful to the Newari idiom of the Kathmandu Valley. Notice the use of frames around the medallion decorations and secondary images ranged around the principal deities. This device is typically Nepalese. Note also the Newari depiction of the thrones. Some aspects of the murals, however, diverge markedly from the traditional. The colors used imply a more imaginative approach; in addition to deep, rich tones, brilliant bold hues seldom seen in Nepalese works of that time are employed. Most unusual of all is the shading used on some of the Buddhas, a technique virtually absent in Newari art, although adopted in the Pala genre.

Lhakhang Lhoma

The Lhakhang Lhoma is the southern chapel of Shalu's dual inner sanctum. It opens from the back wall (west wing) of the assembly hall. This unusual, archaic design dates from the 11th century. No paintings or sculptures have survived, but along the wall's surfaces are numerous small, painted *tsa-tsas* attributed to Atisha. Attached to a column in front of this chapel is an antique *rinchen dharu*, held by an old, lion-shaped lock.

Lhakhang Jangma

This empty room north of Lhakhang Lhoma has several stucco haloes on the walls, similar to those of the *gönkhang*.

Gosum Lhakhang

Unlike other side chapels of the Tshok Khang, this locked chamber has an elaborate entrance with three wooden doors (*gosum*). The interior is full of damaged statues, broken *chörtens*, parts of walls, and dismembered bronze and copper statues. Murals from 2 m down have been badly defaced, but higher up are 14th-C. Nepalese paintings in quite good condition, rendered predominantly in blue and dark red. The images are surrounded by semi-circular haloes. Unused spaces of the panels are filled with myriad flowers and trees, a typically Nepalese habit of cramming meticulous detail into the fringes of the paintings. East of the chapel entrance is perhaps the monastery's earliest mandala painting, unfortunately covered with whitewash.

GREAT KHORLAM OF THE SERKHANG

On the walls of the Shalu *khorlam* are stupendous murals, some of the most dramatic works of art in Tibet. The long corridor, consisting of five segments, is an inspired gallery of Tibet's religious and secular life. Scenes are packed with vivid images and uncounted, enchanting details. Most are in good condition, but a small portion have been damaged irreparably by rain and neglect.

Enter the corridor via the southeast corner of the main hall, east of the Kangyur Lhakhang. Along the corridor's outer walls are two horizontal bands starting from a height of about 2 m. Each has an extraordinary number of paintings. Under each band are Tibetan inscriptions translated from Indian texts such as the *Ratnakuta* and the *Jatakamala*. Scenes depict the 100 episodes of the Buddha's life. Tibetan literary sources attribute the *khorlam* paintings to the

Newari style. They are divided into frames that contain fantastic arrays of architecture, diverse ethnic types, mythical flora and fauna, and religious subjects, all co-existing in splendid harmony.

Two cultural influences are at work here. Newari elements are readily seen in the subcontinental facial features. Much of the landscape is also Newar-inspired, particularly the tell-tale geometric rocks, the gorges, and the banana trees. Also Nepalese are the *chörtens* and the quaint trees. For Nepal's religious heritage look for brahmins and dark-skinned *sadhus* meditating in caves. Distinctive elements from China are sprinkled here and there and provide startling contrast. The obvious ones are Chinese nobles and scholars with long flowing robes and small black caps, Yuan-style palaces with latticed windows, and Mongol warriors. In spite of the cross-fertilization, however, it is quite apparent that the Newari component dominates and that the Yuan sensibilities merely lend support, adding minor details. The artists clearly were intimate with both the Nepalese and Chinese artistic mediums but there is little doubt that their grounding and emphasis were in the Newari tradition.

The inner walls of the corridor hold quite different paintings, mostly large Buddhas of the Golden Age. There are also rows of lamas and deities enclosed in frames in the typical Nepalese manner. Some panels depict figures wearing Central Asian clothing, and numerous Indian ascetics and holy men are gathered amidst lovely landscapes. The best and the most impressive murals are framed below the large Buddha figures. Pilgrims have gouged out red background coloring to take home as a precious relic.

These 14th-C. *khorlam* paintings were created by the greatest masters of the day, trained disciples of the Arniko school that garnered so much influence at the Yuan court. The massive scale of the murals transformed Shalu into an unparalleled treasure trove of art.

Rooms of the *khorlam*

Three small rooms, to the south, west and north, are entered through doorways along the inner walls of the long corridor. The last room along the *khorlam*'s north leg has well-preserved murals that depict Chenresi, Tamdrin, and other deities. The wall above the entrance has paintings of mandalas.

Intercultural Links at Shalu

In the 13th C. a special link developed between the Sakyapas, the artists of the Kathmandu Valley, and the Yuan Mongols. In 1260, Kublai Khan and the Sakya patriarch, Phagpa, initiated the *yöncho*, a spiritual master–imperial patron relationship that was to elevate the sect to one of undisputed dominance in Tibet. In that year 80 Newar master artists, led by the great Arniko (1244–1306), were invited by Phagpa to work on his monastery at Sakya. Three years later, Arniko was summoned to the Yuan capitals of Dadu and Shangdu to display his legendary skills before the emperor. During his sojourn there he established his famed art school, the Western Style of Image Making, and took on a number of disciples. Later, when Emperor Oljadu succeeded Kublai Khan, he received Drakpa Gyaltsen at court in 1306. At that meeting, the patron and the monk made arrangements for Shalu's renovation and followers of Arniko's school were sent there to work on the murals and statues of the Serkhang.

Middle floor (barkhang)

The present Yumchenmo Lhakhang is not the original founded by Chetsün Sherab Jungne in the 11th century. It was renovated by Drakpa Gyaltsen in the early 14th century.

THE YUMCHENMO LHAKHANG KHORLAM

The paintings of the *khorlam* surrounding this chapel are among the most important in Shalu. Traditional images of deities are included and their study provides an authentic, accurate understanding of Yuan-influenced Newari art of the early 14th century. The murals are also forerunners of the distinct Tibetan style that first found expression in the Gyantse and Riwoche *kumbums* (see pages 447 and 451), and thus they help to document the evolution of Tibetan art during the 14th century.

The most notable feature of Yuan-influenced Newari art is the use of elliptical lines to render the heads and bodies of the divinities. This makes the body parts more heart-shaped, imparting understated dynamism to the images, and yet preserving the peaceful nature of the Buddhas. Their faces are noted for long, subtle noses and small mouths. Different hues of light blue and red, cream, and pale green are used. These contrast sharply with the traditional Newari prototypes, which emphasize rich and deep tones. Creativity and experimentation appear in the landscapes and scenes of everyday life, showing marked attention to detail. Trees are painted in a voluminous and rounded way; the foliage is massive but intricate, and a three-dimensionality is hinted at by the use of thin black contour lines. Clouds, a predominant motif in Chinese landscape painting, are adopted wholeheartedly by these Yuan court artists, who render them freshly and imaginatively; the clouds have diverse shapes and extraordinary patterns. Another influence from the Yuan court is the richness of the Buddha's robes. Their edges are distinctly decorated in geometric or brocaded patterns.

Traditional Newari elements, of course, are also evident: in particular, the use of frames to effect a narrative progression. Other traits include Pala-type crowns, medallioned decorations that fill the entire background behind deities, and simple lotus designs with petals in contrasting colors.

The *khorlam's* inner surface was probably painted by a Tibetan. These panels consist of a series of individual deities (Drölma, Tamdrin, Chenresi, Jampa) surrounded by *bodhisattvas*. A few are signed by the name 'Chimpa Sonambum'. Comparing technique and detail, it can be shown that the entire internal wall was most likely painted by this single artist. This means that Tibetan artists were present at the Yuan court, studying Newari painting traditions in the workshop established by Arniko.

The *khorlam's* outer wall has paintings mainly of Buddhas and their paradises. These are surrounded by secondary images arranged in a semi-circular pattern. All are characterized by superb attention to detail and human form. Lower segments of the wall depict fascinating Indian and Nepalese subjects, surprising for a Tibetan Buddhist shrine. There are scenes of the Kathmandu Valley, human and animal sacrifice, the Hindu god Ganesh, and assorted naked ascetics (the faces of some Hindu gods are defaced). One unusual panel shows a female Indian ascetic offering the head of a goat to a black lingam.

The small chapel of Yumchenmo Lhakhang (locked) has masks, costumes, and trunks displayed around the floor; the chamber served as a storehouse for the paraphernalia of Cham dances.

Four top-floor chapels

Most original statues commissioned between 1333 and 1335 by Butön and Kunga Döndrub are now lost. The only relics from that time are the large mandalas painted in the four chapels and the murals within the *khorlam* of the Tengyur Lhakhang. Butön himself supervised the creation of the mandalas.

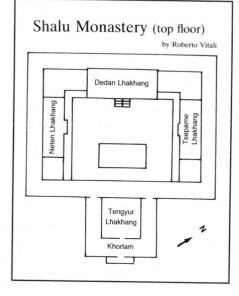

Shalu Monastery (top floor)
by Roberto Vitali

[Floor plan showing: Dedan Lhakhang, Neten Lhakhang, Tsepame Lhakhang, Tengyur Lhakhang, Khorlam, with compass indicating N]

BUTÖN'S MANDALAS

These 14th-C. mandalas have survived in poor condition. Many essential iconographic details are difficult to make out and only the bare outlines remain clear. These works represent a major change in concept from the Yuan-influenced Newari art found elsewhere in the monastery. However, elements of the Newari style can be seen in the deep, rich colors and medallions that copiously embellish the minor images. During the last decades of the 13th C. and the early 14th C., many mandalas were painted at Sakya Monastery, which in those days exerted a strong influence on Shalu. The Newari artist, Arniko, worked at Sakya; it is likely that Shalu's mandalas closely followed the Sakyapa models.

DEDAN LHAKHANG (SUKHAVATI CHAPEL, WEST)

This principal chapel, located directly in front of the second-floor terrace entrance, contains poorly preserved mandala paintings that are obscured by many rather ordinary 18–19th C. *thangkas*, which depict (left to right) the kings of Shambala, the 35 Buddhas of Confession, and the 16 Arhats. Many high-quality bronzes decorate the altar along the back wall. To the left are two fine gilt-bronze *chörtens* that supposedly contain relics of Atisha and Butön. In the center is an image of Chenresi Karsapani, carved from a large piece of black stone. This is the most important religious relic of Shalu (see below). Other statues include Butön (large), the Eight Medicine Buddhas (left), Jampa, Tsepame, Guru Rinpoche, and Dorje Sempa. On the altar is a vase sealed with red cloth, called Bumchu Nyongdröl (see below). Next to it is a leather bag containing 108 pieces of sandalwood mandalas, which fit together like a jigsaw puzzle. It is said that, once taken apart, the pieces can never be put back together again. The monks maintain that this relic is over 700 years old and pilgrims make a point of touching their foreheads to the bag.

Within a glass cabinet on the altar is a conch shell dating back to the 14th century. Tradition claims that it emits musical notes by itself. On the column nearest the altar, a small thangka in very good condition depicts Virupa. Near it is a 1-m-high 14th-C. statue of Chana Dorje with an unusual crown. At the room's northwest corner, there is another statue of a wrathful Chana Dorje (1/2 m tall). The murals consist of large 4-m-high, 14th-C. mandalas, painted in accordance to the personal guidance of Butön, who also wrote the index and inscriptions that explain the mandalas. They represent cycles of deities associated with the Yoga Tantra, one of four systems of tantra. The mandalas on the back wall were restored (19th C.) while those of the side and front walls are originals, albeit in poor condition.

South of the Dedan Lhakhang is a room full of statues, thangkas, porcelain, and other valuable objects. In front of the chapel, near the skylight, is a stone basin, an important 11th-C. relic of the monastery. Rain water accumulates here and the monks assert it never overflows. The founder of Shalu, Chetsün Sherab Jungne, washed his face in it and later Sakya Pandita, one of the Five Great Masters of the Sakyapa sect, used it when shaving his head. Pilgrims today use a twig to splash water from it in the four directions and on their heads.

The stone Chenresi Karsapani According to literary tradition, Shalu's principal image was a clay Chenresi Karsapani, made personally by Chetsün. Within its center was the heart of Gelong Ma Palmo, a monk considered the manifestation of Chenresi. Its back has a 'self-originated' (rangjung) image of Dorje Jigje (Yamantaka, Lord of Death), though it cannot easily be seen, as the statue would first have to be turned.

Bumchu Nyongdrol This sacred vase was brought here by Virupa (Birupa), the Indian mahasiddha who pioneered the Lamdre teachings of the Sakyapa and whose lineage gave birth to the Sakyapa tradition. It was used by him during the ritual transfer of power (wang) to Tibetan monks. The vase changed hands a number of times among various Indian mahasiddhas. Finally, Gayadara took it to Tibet and gave it to Drokmi Lotsawa, a translator who transfered the Virupa system of tantric teachings from India to Tibet via the Sakyapa. Drogmi in turn presented it to other learned lamas and eventually the Sakyapa patriarch, Sonam Gyaltsen, gave it to Butön as a gesture of respect for his insights on the Kalachakra. Due to the blessings of so many illustrious masters, believers affirm that the vase's sacred water need never be replenished; its level remaining perfectly constant. Those who have the good fortune to set eyes on the vase will be saved from damnation and those who drink the water will obtain spiritual perfection. Once every 12 years, the seal is removed and pilgrims can drink from it.

Butön (1290–1364) This celebrated lama lived at Shalu for most of his life and founded the Butönpa lineage, a sub-sect derived from Kadampa and Sakyapa traditions.

Later he started the Shalupa school and sect, and created the architectural and iconographic design of the Gyantse Kumbum.

Butön came to Shalu from Tröphu Monastery (between Shigatse and Pindsoling Monastery) when he was 31, becoming abbot in 1320. He was responsible for the iconographic and artistic content of the Serkhang's four top chapels. His greatest accomplishment, however, was the revision and reorganization of the *Tengyur* and *Kangyur*, compendia of all sacred Tibetan texts. The final product ran to 227 volumes. Unfortunately, the originals of this prodigious work were all destroyed during the Cultural Revolution.

Butön also wrote prolifically on nearly every subject connected with Tibetan Buddhism. Tantrism was his forte and he completed three great treatises (26 volumes) on the subject. He described in exacting detail the mandalas of various tantric cycles, which were taken as the foundation of the complicated iconographic laws that govern all tantric paintings. It is fair to say that Butön exerted a tremendous influence on Tibetan painting, its iconographic structure and development. The murals within the Gyantse Kumbum are good examples; the stupendous organization of the cycles of various deities follows precisely the rigorous set of rules laid down by the master. He once constructed a huge mandala nearly 20 m in diameter. Butön was also interested in the design and construction of *chörtens*.

Neten Lhakhang (South)

The outer walls of the Neten Lhakhang, protected by an awning supported by pillars, have 18th–19th-C. paintings depicting the life of Butön. He is near the top with his two disciples. Below them are pictorial representations of monastic rules. On the left, a painting shows the circuitous upwards progress of an elephant and a monkey. These symbolize the stages of meditation on the way to *nirvana*. The monkey (excitement) and the elephant (inertia) are captured by a monk to show that these obstacles of the mind are tamable through perseverance. The monk finally rides off into the sky with the elephant. Another panel shows an astrological chart conceived by Butön to explain the relationship between the movement of the stars and the lunar calendar.

Neten Lhakhang's interior is also dominated by 14th-C. mandalas (cycle of Palchok). The three behind the altar (mandalas of the yogic *tantra* cycles of Doying, Tsemo, and Kamsum Namgyal) are in reasonable condition (probably restored). Notice the Tibetan inscriptions—these are Butön's commentaries. Butön supervised the narrative paintings, which depict previous lives of *bodhisattvas* and the deeds of the Buddha. The altar has a 1-m statue of Butön with copies of 26 volumes of his treatises beside him. To the left is his chief disciple, Rinchen Namgyal. Right of the texts is a 14th-C. Kalachakra image beside two Kadampa *chörtens*.

Tsepame Lhakhang (North)

The mandalas here (cycle of Kunrig), some obscured by *thangkas*, are better preserved than those of the Neten Lhakhang. Along the back and side walls are more than 20 statues (most

0.5 m tall); some are early Tibetan and Nepalese bronzes. The back wall has an insignificant gilt-copper statue of Butön; behind it is a beautiful 14th-C. Nepalese-style *torana* (halo). On the right wall is a fine painting of Dorje Sempa (Vajrasattva), the *bodhisattva* who personifies the purity of enlightenment.

TENGYUR LHAKHANG (EAST)

Butön's *Tengyur* was kept in this room (now locked). In 1335, when he and Kunga Döndrub finished the Serkhang's four top chapels, this final edition of the text was installed with much pomp and ceremony. Mandalas here (cycle of Jampa) are dusty and dirty, but generally in good condition. On the north wall is a portrait of Butön and paintings of Chenresi and *chörtens*. These 14th-C. works retain a strong Newari influence. Surrounding this chamber is a *khorlam* with murals that are particularly interesting (see below). The chapel's floor plan and its processional corridor is a close replica of the Yumchenmo Lhakhang, directly below. The western leg of the *khora*, however, is absent; there are only three sections.

Murals of the Tengyur Lhakhang *khorlam*

The main subjects are a group of Lokeshvaras and the eight types of *chörtens*. All are enclosed by a profusion of floral and vegetal motifs. The style of these intriguing works is a later, local derivative of the Yuan-influenced Newari style. Although Newari roots are evident, they are unmistakably tempered by local interpretation. The ornate *chörtens* are a good example. They exhibit indigenous features that served as prototypes for the next generation of Tibetan paintings in the Tsang Province. The Lokeshvaras have tiny noses and angelic faces, characteristics found also in the Yumchenmo Lhakhang *khorlam*, the work of Yuan artists. Tibetan forms are expressed in the crowns and the lotuses; other traits distinct from the earlier phase are the exceptionally large flowers and clouds. Local artists probably painted these; Arniko's master painters had left Shalu by the time Kunga Döndrub and Butön worked on the top chapels.

RIPHUK

This cave hermitage of Shalu is in the mountains southwest of the monastery. To walk there will take 1 1/4 hr. It was a retreat established mainly during the time of Butön. Atisha meditated here in a cave and consecrated a spring and pond at the site. He also personally made a large number of clay tablets (*tsas-tsas*) with images of a *chörten* and deities. Some of the meditation caves were built underground and hermits were at times sealed inside for 12 years. Disciples of the Shalupa studied here to acquire the esoteric skills of levitation, long-distance running, and voluntary regulation of body temperature (see also Nyangtö Kyi Phuk, page 349).

Hidden from view from Shalu, Riphuk was a surprisingly large monastic center. Housing over 300 monks. it once included several sizeable chapels and two large assembly halls. A modest chapel has now been restored. To get to the hermitage, walk due west from Shalu to locate the distinct trail that zigzags up a gully to the ruins.

Jampaling Nunnery

The ruins of the Jampaling Nunnery are 1 1/2 hr's walk north of Shalu, halfway up a steep side valley. In the vicinity are the remains of several *chörtens*.

GYANTSE:
AN INTRODUCTION TO ITS
ART AND ARCHITECTURE

by Roberto Vitali

Although it has suffered badly from the ravages of time and man, Gyantse retains even today a deeply Tibetan character. It is still possible to step back in time here and have a glimpse of an irretrievably lost era. Despite destruction of some old sections, the town has maintained its architectural homogeneity; the typical cubic houses of Tibet are the rule. Gyantse is timeless and, as witness to the potential combination of nature and human genius, manages to convey a rare sense of wonder. Its principal structures consist of a castle on a ridge overlooking the town and a walled monastic complex by the far hill. The monastery includes the massive temple of Palkhor Chöde and the great multi-chapel Kumbum Chörten. These religious monuments, part of Gyantse's ancient monastic town, contain some of the most extraordinary works of art in Tibet.

Gyantse suffered a devastating flood in the early 1950s, which washed away some of its old structures but fortunately did not touch the ancient temples. The reconstruction of Gyantse has shown respect for the style and flavor of the old town. Some differences from the old plan can be ascertained. In particular, notice the principal old road and the much narrower lane that parallels the present main road on its northeast side. The construction of this new main road changed the entrance to the monastery. A new monumental door has been opened in the boundary wall just in front of the wide motor road. At the end of the ancient lane the old entranceway can still be seen.

Gyantse's monastic town stood inside the walled area which was once crowded with religious colleges (none have survived). They belonged to three different sects: the Sakyapa, Shalupa, and Gelugpa. All made contributions to the construction and all have existed in the monastery since the 15th C., a rare case of sectarian tolerance in Tibet. This is just one example of Gyantse's many peculiarities. Apart from the Palkhor Chöde and the Kumbum, only one of the major structures built inside the compound remains. This is the ancient residence of the abbots (*Labrang*), the derelict white building just above the great *chörten*. It is devoid of relics.

Gyantse, formerly a rich settlement, is strategically sited at the confluence of a number of major routes significant for cultural, political, and commercial reasons. These were the Route of Wool from nearby Gyangro (southeast) and more distant Jang (northwest), the Route of Wood from the Bhutanese border (an active trade route today), the trade routes from Nepal through the Himalayan passes, and the Route of Religion that connected Sakya to Lhasa. All found their way through the town.

EARLY HISTORY

In its surviving form, Gyantse dates from the 14th century. Yet the site most likely goes back to the distant past and must have attracted the attention of the early, pre-Buddhist cults.

One of Gyantse's hills, the higher castle peak, is among the 13 inauspicious mountains that Guru Rinpoche subjugated in order to give them a distinctly Buddhist orientation. It is possible that ancient Gyantse was a stronghold of the Bön religion. During Langdarma's persecution of Buddhism in the 9th C., Gyantse was never mentioned in historical accounts; it must be presumed that it played a minor role during the period. At the end of the 9th C., Langdarma's nephew, Palkhortsan, the rightful heir of the kingdom, founded a castle on the hill of Gyantse. This fact was recorded, centuries later, in the inscriptions accompanying the Kumbum murals. The castle was named 'Crystal Castle on the Peak'. It is said that Palkhortsan used it as his residence, since he could not rule in Central Tibet (Ü), having been overpowered by a branch family. He died young, assassinated during the political struggles for dominance in those troubled years of Tibetan history. No other record of his castle has survived and archeology has failed to prove its existence.

There is little information on Gyantse until well after the Second Diffusion of Buddhism in Central Tibet (early 11th century). The reintroduction of religion was accompanied by the founding of many new temples, but Gyantse did not figure in this phase. Soon after, the ancestors of the Gyantse lineage of princes, claiming ancestry from King Gesar of Ling, started to encroach in the area. They left northeast Tibet, where the family had its roots, because a prophecy promised them a new land. One generation after the other, they moved towards their final destination and eventually settled in Nyangtö, the area where Gyantse is located, in the 13th century. At that time the Sakyapa, under Yuan patronage, were controlling most of Tibet. The ancestors of the Gyantse princes originally followed the Nyingmapa tradition, but serving new masters in southern Tibet resulted in their conversion to the Sakyapa faith. After Phagpa Pal Sangpo's birth, the fortune of the Gyantse lords changed dramatically. It was Phagpa who established the genealogy of the Gyantse princes.

RISE OF THE GYANTSE PRINCES' LINEAGE

The Gyantse princes became powerful very quickly. Between 1342, when Phagpa Pal Sangpo received his first major title, and 1440, when the monuments of Gyantse practically reached completion, they built one of Tibet's greatest cultural artefacts. Their political consolidation was based on a small but highly important part of southern Tibet, at a time when new political orders were substituting old ones in both Tibet and China. The princes' ascent to power was connected with the rule of the Sakyapa over Tibet—and in particular, over Tsang. They created and enhanced their authority as part of the old Sakyapa alliance. A policy of intermarriage with the Shalupa, who had close family relations with the Sakyapa, also helped.

When the Phagmo Drupa, and in particular Jangchub Gyaltsen (1302–64), caused the downfall of Sakyapa-Yuan rule in Tibet, the princes of Gyantse—far from being displaced—managed to increase their sphere of influence. After the Mongol Yuan Empire collapsed in 1368, the princes succeeded in gaining the favor of the new, entirely Chinese Ming Dynasty; at the same time, they wisely maintained a policy of balance between the Sakyapa and the Phagmo Drupa. In religious matters, the princes were fortunate in having outstanding and charismatic spiritual masters. Together they put into effect their great program of establishing Gyantse as one of the main centers of Buddhism in Tibet.

In order to build their temples and open colleges, the Gyantse princes taxed their subjects and relied on donations from the nobles (inscriptions in the Kumbum faithfully record the names of the donors). In 1440, a Gyantse prince concluded the task of making Gyantse a masterpiece. He issued an edict that exempted all subjects from taxes for the following three years. This formal act constitutes the official aknowledgement that the long building efforts were over. Since Gyantse had become an especially sanctified spot, the edict also forbade acts against Buddhist ethics, such as hunting and fishing.

THE GYANTSE PRINCES (14TH–MID-15TH CENTURY)

Phagpa Pal Sangpo (1318–70) was the first great patron prince of his lineage. This brilliant student went to Sakya for his education and was attached to the Sharkha class of Sakyapa dignitaries. At the age of 17, he invited the religious master, Chal Phag Gyalwa, to bless his family home, Danyul. Since then, he adopted the appellation Phagpa (noble) to honor his teacher. He became a member of the Lhakhang Labrang branch of Sakya and fought for them so successfully that, when his old Sakya mentor died in 1342, he was appointed head of the class. He was then only 25. After that, his family—the future princes of Gyantse—became known as the Sharkhapa family. He mediated successfully between the Sakyapa and the rising Phagmo Drupa.

In 1350, he married the daughter of the powerful lord of Shalu and as a dowry received the fief of Changra, southwest of Gyantse. Later on, he founded another seat at Phagri, a castle near the Bhutanese border. He made Changra a center of Buddhism by building a temple and inviting to it Butön Rinpoche (1290–1364), possibly the greatest Tibetan master of his time. The connection with Butön Rinpoche proved important for Gyantse. Butön consecrated a chapel at Changra, which remained for some time the main religious center of the Sharkhapa. Phagpa Pal Sangpo went from success to success, culminating in his being awarded the title of Nangchen by the Sakyapa in 1364. Subsequently, in 1365, he built a great castle on the peak of Gyantse's mountain. At the same time, he obtained permission from the Yuan Emperor, Togon Temur, to build a castle and a magnificent new religious institute on the nine-peaked mountain at the entrance of the Gyantse Valley. The complex was called Tsechen and its ruins can still be seen today southwest of the town. It was first devastated by the British expedition of 1904, and its final demise came in the recent past. Tsechen supplanted Changra as the main seat of the Sharkhapa and retained this role until Phagpa Pal Sangpo's son, Kunga Phagpa, vigorously expanded Gyantse at the end of the 14th C., thus beginning Gyantse's rise to its ultimate grandeur.

In 1367, Nangchen Phagpa Pal Sangpo achieved his highest rank from the Yuan court—Tai Situ. In the following year the Yuan Dynasty crumbled and, in 1370, the Tai Situ died in his private room at Tsechen. His younger brother, Phagpa Rinchen (1320–76), became the new ruler of Gyantse. The Ming court awarded him the same title of Tai Situ, thus proving that the fall of the Yuan did not harm Gyantse and the Sharkhapa.

Phagpa Rinchen's short reign was succeeded by that of Phagpa Pal Sangpo's son, Kunga Phagpa (1357–1412). Although his father's rule had been marked by a dramatic expansion of power and aggressive military campaigns, Kunga Phagpa's reign brought stability to the fief. He transferred the lay rule of his family's main branch from Tsechen to Gyantse, and must therefore be considered the Sharkhapa prince who established Gyantse as the principality's capital.

His son, Rabtan Kunsang Phag (1389–1442), was the Gyantse prince who did most for the town and its religious edifices. His architectural boldness matched his will to assert independence from the Phagmo Drupa, and he seriously clashed with them on two occasions. Rabtan Kunsang Phag brought Gyantse to its apogee, but after his reign, the center rapidly lost momentum. This decline was caused largely by the rise of the Rinpungpa, whose fief was near Gyantse. They established themselves as ministers of the Phagmo Drupa and were their main allies in Tsang. Their progressive rise to power, which ended with the conquest first of Tsang and then Lhasa in 1498, limited and ultimately ended the Gyantse princes' power.

THE LAMA–EMPEROR RELATIONSHIP AND ITS EFFECTS ON ART

The appointment of the Gyantse princes had to be made directly by the Chinese emperor. Such acts were part of an entrenched Mongol system for controlling the country, being based on the special relationship (*yöncho*) between the lama as spiritual master, and the emperor as enlightened patron.

The alliance between Tibet and the Ming emperors was critical for the development of Gyantse's art. The uncanny similarity between the works of the Kumbum and the Yongle and Xuande relics of China points towards the existence of a single school of art that spanned Central Tibet and the imperial court. This is further suggested by the copious production of movable bronzes in China at this time. The close contacts between the spiritual masters of Tibet and their royal patrons in Yuan and Ming China assured an equally uninterrupted flow of teachings between the two territories. Emperors Taizu (r 1368–99), Yongle (r 1403–24), and Xuande (r 1426–35) showed great interest in Tibetan Buddhism and their contacts with Tibetan masters of the leading sects caused a number of Tibetan delegations to visit China. Many Lamaist religious objects were created and used at the Chinese court. It is highly probable that delegations coming from Central Tibet supplied the Chinese with iconographic and iconometric models, works popular in the most important monasteries of Ü-Tsang, and that Chinese ateliers then adopted them. The Ming court artists were thus very familiar with the art of Ü-Tsang, to which they added their own interpretation.

THE RELIGIOUS PANORAMA

The monuments of Gyantse were built when the power of the rising Phagmo Drupa superseded that of the Sakyapa. Yet the former did not exercise a religious influence on the Sharkhapa, whereas the Sakyapa did. In broad terms, the religious institutions of Gyantse must be considered part of the Sakyapa tradition. Complicating this relationship, however, is the important role played by Butön Rinpoche and the Shalupa. The mystical systems expressed in the various chapels, depicting the cycles of gods, owe much to this master and his sect.

The Shalupa, which was basically a sub-sect of the Sakyapa with Butön Rinpoche as its recognized founder, began at roughly the same time as the Sharkhapa rise to splendor. Butön Rinpoche was by far the most charismatic master of his time, and Shalupa teachings—which annexed important doctrinal elements from the Kagyüpa tradition—were strongly influential. They had a major effect on the princes of Gyantse, who entertained marital relations with Shalu as well.

Inscriptions in the Gyantse Kumbum record that the organization of the cycle of deities within the chapels into a complete mystical system was based on Butön Rinpoche's dictates. This is an important sign of the cultural and religious milieu of those times. Also relevant for Gyantse was the emergence of the Gelugpa, founded by Tsong Khapa (1357–1419). The Yellow Hats played a major role in the monuments of Gyantse, particularly from 1418 to 1425, when the Palkhor Chöde was constructed. Around that time the Gelugpa established their most important monasteries: Ganden in 1409, Drepung in 1416, Sera in 1419, and Tashilhunpo in 1445.

Rabtan Kunsang Phag, the Gyantse prince responsible for the Palkhor Chöde and almost all of the Kumbum as well, was assisted as spiritual advisor for these constructions by Gedrub Je (1385–1438), one of Tsong Khapa's best disciples. He became Rabtan Kunsang Phag's guru in 1413 by acceding to the abbotship of Changra, the old Sharkhapa see. Gedrub Je played a leading role in the Palkhor Chöde enterprise, but not in that of the Kumbum, since he left Gyantse before the foundation of the great *stupa* was laid. His sculpted image is to be found on the Kumbum's fourth floor, seventh chapel.

GYANTSE CASTLE: RARE NEWARI-STYLE PAINTINGS

By Roberto Vitali

The inception of Gyantse Castle (*dzong*) is attributed by some sources to Phagpa Pal Sangpo (1318–70), who established his residence on the same cliff where the last Yarlung-dynasty king, Palkhortsan, built his palace. After receiving the seal and permission to build from the Yuan Emperor Togon Temur, he laid the foundation of a settlement in 1365. It had secular functions and no mention exists of temples.

Details of the original structure are difficult to ascertain. It went through a number of renovations and major damage occurred during the British expedition of 1904 and the Cultural Revolution. As a result, some of the complex's edifices no longer exist. Also, no archeological remains can be traced back to the original foundation. The castle, though less extensive than just a few decades ago, has preserved its scenic character. If the view of the *dzong* is aesthetically rewarding, the panorama of the walled city of Gyantse from here is one of the most breathtaking views of any settlement in Tibet.

The castle was initially conceived for lay occupancy. Kunga Phagpa (1357–1412) established a great temple (*tsuglag khang*) near the palace in 1390. It was completed in 1397. The complex, named Samphel Rinpoche Ling, included an inner chapel (*tsangkhang*), to which a *shalyekhang* (top-most chapel) and a *gönkhang* (Chapel of the Wrathful Deities) were added. The temple has suffered through the ages; the *gönkhang* no longer exists, and only a few murals have survived. Yet they are important ones; they exemplify the style popular in Gyantse at the end of the 14th century. In present-day Tibet, murals are usually in far better condition than statues. The latter, in the great majority of cases, were the first to suffer at the hands of intruders and were usually substantially altered during restoration.

THE TEMPLE WITHIN THE CASTLE

The temple complex, midway up the hill, is centered around a courtyard enclosed by a gallery on three sides. The west side of the ground floor is the *tsangkhang* (inner chapel), which is surrounded by a processional path in the rear. Its interior is devoid of objects (above it is the *shalyekhang*, also empty). Modern, extremely mediocre murals are on its side walls. The rear wall, however, still has ancient works. Being superimposed, the *tsangkhang* and *shalyekhang* both open to the east. The *tsangkhang* was dedicated to a statue of the Buddha as an eight-year-old boy, whereas the *shalyekhang* was an initiation room with mandalas on its walls.

The remaining ancient works of art amount to faded traces of murals inside the *tsangkhang*, along its processional corridor, on the external walls of the gallery at the temple's entrance and in the *shalyekhang*. The painted deities in the Gyantse castle are listed in Tibet's traditional literature. In the *tsangkhang* are images of the 35 Buddhas of Confession, the Goddess of Retreat (Ritröma), Marici, Vaishravana, the God of Wealth, and lineages of high Sakyapa lamas. Most of them have disappeared, except for a few that are still in fair condition.

The paintings on the processional path include the Five Dhyani Buddhas and the Three Protectors of the Buddhist Doctrine (Rigsum Gönpo), Gods of the Planets, and manifestations of Tara, amidst numerous repetitions of the Buddhas of the Golden Age (Bhadrakalpa). The *shalyekhang* still has three large painted mandalas among esoteric divinities on the rear wall. These cycles are dedicated to Kalachakra, whose initiation was evidently obtained in this chapel. The murals were executed in 1408.

Paintings in the gallery consist of Sukhavati (Western Paradise), a complete set of the Medicine Buddhas, Abhirati (Eastern Heaven), Sakyamuni surrounded by the Arhats, events of the Buddha's life, the Previous Buddha's Births, the Story of Norsang, an image of Vijaya, and the Four Guardian Kings. The majority of the latter images have been irremediably lost and others, in faded condition, are covered by a thick layer of soot. The most legible subjects are Sakyamuni and his retinue of Arhats. They are in poor condition, however; the panel depicting the Abhirati heaven is the gallery's best-preserved mural.

ART STYLES

Dates in Tibetan sources for the construction of the temple in Gyantse Castle help to confirm that, by 1390–1397, an early local style—feasibly executed by Tibetan artists—was fully developed in Tsang. The role of Nepalese Newar artists, critical to the Tibetan artistic milieu from the mid-13th C. onwards, was one of the major fruits of the patron-priest relationship between the Yuan Dynasty and the Sakyapa. A Newari style that absorbed Chinese influences was developed in China, and this found its way to the Sakya temples of Central Tibet. The paintings in the *tsangkhang*, the processional corridor, and the castle's gallery are a local interpretation of this style. Eminently Newari in conception and rendering, it had, however, already undergone an initial process of local adaptation before reaching Gyantse. The main gods of the Abhirati heaven, religious scenes, and flanking *bodhisattvas*, are unmistakably Newari. Likewise, the use of trilobated arches over the deities, the heavy, intricate jewelry (crowns, necklaces, earrings, bracelets) rendered in gold relief, the medallions, and the registers of minor images. Details like the flowing curvilinear clouds are part of the Chinese contribution that found its way into the style before it was executed in Tibet.

Yet the paintings are more than faithful replicas of modified Newari prototypes. Increasingly confident of themselves, Tibetan artists began to create their own indigenous solutions within the Newari context. This is evident in the physiognomies, no longer strictly Newari; in the choice of colors; and in a freer arrangement of the painted space. One particular departure is the attention to landscape, a feature never adapted in the original Newari prototypes. Hence, by 1390–97, a Tibetan style born of the Newar existed at Gyantse. Its dependency on a foreign idiom, however, remained extremely strong—a common characteristic of Tibet's ancient art styles.

The case of the *shalyekhang* murals is somewhat different. In the paintings of mandalas and esoteric deities, the style is definitely Newari, with no contributions from a local hand. Hence, these represent exceptionally rare Newari murals of the early 15th century. This type of monumental work is no longer extant in Nepal itself.

PALKHOR CHÖDE:
THE GREAT TEMPLE OF GYANTSE

by Roberto Vitali

Cosmopolitan art-styles of the Gyantse school

THE GREAT TEMPLE

The Palkhor Chöde, built by Rabtan Kunsang Phag between 1418 and 1425, is an imposing, severe building whose outer walls are painted a customary red. Within it are superb works executed during one of the most creative periods of Tibetan art; a time before the Tibetan styles became stereotyped and ubiquitous. The temple also is seminal from historical and icono-graphic points of view. It has two floors, with an additional single chapel superimposed on the second. Its main entrance opens to the south.

Ground floor

The temple's verandah at the entrance has modern statues of the Four Guardian Kings; they are of little interest. The wide assembly hall (*dukhang*) is reached through a large, canonically red door in the antechamber. Left of the chamber is a diminutive door with the painted face of a wrathful god. The image guards the inner secrets of the room, a chapel (*gönkhang*) dedicated to the wrathful deities.

ASSEMBLY HALL (DUKHANG)

The assembly hall has 48 columns and contains long rows of seats where the monks perform their daily rituals. On the walls, damaged murals depict paradises with larger-than-life deities. On the left side of the hall's entrance, next to the door, Acala with a sword is followed by the paradises of Vairocana, Manjusri (Jampelyang), Avalokiteshvara (Chenresi), Sakyamuni, and Ratnasambhava.

On the right wall outside the inner chapel's entrance (in the *dukhang*) is a painted paradise of Vairocana. The style of this mural differs somewhat from that of the murals in the assembly hall and is similar to most of the painted works in the Kumbum. On the walls of the right side of the assembly hall, starting after the processional corridor's exit, are painted images of the King of Snakes (*Nagas*) (smaller than other painted themes in the hall), the heaven of Green Tara (Dröljang) and her other manifestations, Brikuti, Vijaya, Namgyalma, Sakyamuni, and his disciples. Finally, right of the assembly hall entrance is Tamdrin, the other door guardian. These murals convey an impression of antiquity because of their imposing solemnity. Recently, a huge clay statue of Maitreya (Jampa) has been built in the assembly hall to the right of the inner chapel's entrance. This rather garish statue contrasts dramatically with the hall's ancient relics, but is a good sign of the local populace's renewed devotion to its temple.

DORJE YING CHAPEL

On the left side wall, going clockwise, is the entrance to the Dorje Ying chapel, dedicated to the Five Tathagatas (Dhyani Buddhas) according to the mandala of Dorje Ying. Their

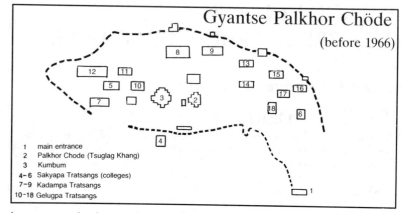

1   main entrance
2   Palkhor Chode (Tsuglag Khang)
3   Kumbum
4~6 Sakyapa Tratsangs (colleges)
7–9 Kadampa Tratsangs
10-18 Gelugpa Tratsangs

clay statues are placed against the rear wall among 20 minor representations (in clay as well) holding mainly musical instruments, also part of this mystical cycle. These secondary gods, inserted into lobated arches, extend to three sides of the room.

The paintings on all the walls portray a proliferation of diminutive images depicting the Five Tathagatas; the author of the ancient guide to the temple has counted them—249 for each Dhyani Buddha family. A volume of the *Perfection of Wisdom Discourses* (*Prajnaparamita*), unusually large with intricately carved wood covers, is placed on the shrine dedicated to Vairocana in the center of the room. The book is the object of particular veneration.

Near to the door, a monumental *thangka* of patchwork and embroidery is kept inside a leather bag. This is the extraordinary *thangka* ordered by Rabtan Kunsang Phag in 1419. It has Sakyamuni (Tongwa Dönda) as the main subject, surrounded by Jampa, Mitrukpa, and Mahakala. This kind of *thangka* (*gheku*) is meant for outdoor display and is hung from tall, rectangular walls built exclusively for the purpose. In Gyantse, the *gheku* tower can still be seen, massive and severe, high up on the hill. The paintings and statues in this chapel are all of exceptional quality and artistic relevance.

INNER CHAPEL (TSANGKHANG)

The central or inner chapel (*tsangkhang*) faces the *dukhang* entrance and opens on the rear wall of the assembly hall. Within it are colossal statues of the Buddhas of the Three Ages (Dipankara, the past Buddha, on the left; Sakyamuni, the present Buddha, in the middle; Jampa, the future Buddha, on the right). Sakyamuni is flanked by the standing sculptures of Jampelyang and Jampa. They are lit by a skylight on the upper level above the sculptures. The room is also filled, for consecrational purposes, with a stunning array of portable statues and holy relics. On the walls, although in poor condition, are traces of murals portraying *bodhisattvas*. Minor shrines are located in front of the main statues. Of much interest are two banners made in slit tapestry technique of Chinese origin, commonly called *kosu* in the West. They hang from the columns in front of the colossal triad. The works of art in this room are not as important as in other Palkhor Chöde chapels. They are, with the exception of the above-mentioned painted fragments, later substitutions.

PROCESSIONAL CORRIDOR

Around the inner chapel runs a long a processional corridor *(khorlam)* with murals. The Buddhas of the Golden Age (Badrakalpa) are painted in endless repetition, while life-size images of Tsepame, Sakyamuni with his disciples, Mitrukpa, Jambhala, Chana Dorje, Wöpame, Amoghasiddhi, Vairocana, White Tara (Drölkar) and others are the main deities presiding in this area.

THE ROYAL CHAPEL (CHÖGYAL LHAKHANG)

Another chapel, the Chögyal Lhakhang (Royal Chapel), opens on the assembly hall's right side wall. It was dedicated to the 11-faced Chenresi whose clay statue is in the middle of the rear wall, flanked by clay images of the most eminent Sakyapa lamas on the right, and Chana Dorje and the Kashmiri master, Sakyashribhadra, on the left. Along the side wall, right of the entrance, are clay statues of the three Tibetan religious kings—Songtsen Gampo, Trisong Detsen, and Ralpachen—all wearing distinctive flowing robes and turbans. They are among Tibet's most artistically relevant portraits of the Yarlung-dynasty monarchs. The chapel probably derives its name from these images. A Jampa statue stands in the center of the room. The chapel was dedicated to this divinity at a later stage.

On the walls are images of Tsepame and Dorje Sempa. A mural depicting an imposing and beautiful image of the 11-faced Chenresi is on the wall left of the door; the chapel is dedicated to this deity. Of special interest is a small and graceful painting of Chenresi sitting on a lion (above the door).

Wrapped in a huge leather bag is another monumental appliqué *thangka (gheku)* near the entrance. It was ordered by Rabtan Kunsang Phag in 1432 and portrays a Sakyamuni amidst bodhisattvas. The existence of these huge, early *thangkas* of extraordinary quality, to be displayed during special occasions, is part of Gyantse's uniqueness. Present-day Tibet has no other *thangkas* comparable to these two. The painted and sculpted works in this chapel resemble those of its twin chapel, Dorje Ying, located symmetrically on the left side of the assembly hall. They both were the product of the same artistic milieu. Libraries occupy parts of the chapel's left and right side walls. A little door in the latter wall leads to a small room. Within it are shelves containing the canonical texts, *Tengyur* and *Kangyur*, begun during Rabtan Kunsang Phag's lifetime and continued by his successors. In the middle of the room is a *chörten*.

CHAPEL OF THE WRATHFUL DEITIES (GÖNKHANG)

The last chapel on the ground floor is dedicated to the wrathful deities. As mentioned above, its access is near the Palkhor Chöde entrance. A short corridor, whose walls show menacing protectors, some with animals' heads, leads to the room. Mahakala, Lord of the Tent (Gur Gönpo), is the main statue. It is flanked by Ekajati (Relchikma) and Lhamo, all in clay. A shrine stands in front of them. On it is a butter sculpture of the Five Assembled Senses. Almost directly in front of the main statues hang a bow and leather bag (ostensibly containing diseases) from a column. Murals show scenes from cemeteries with wild animals, severed human parts, Indian *sadhus*, and ritual objects. This Palkhor Chöde *gönkhang* is particularly interesting because it is the earliest chapel of its type to have survived in Central Tibet. Its sister chapels in the Gyantse Kumbum, much reduced in size, served the same function.

Upper floor

The upper floor has three ancient chapels, while all others on this story have undergone different degrees of renovation. These rooms are reached through an open gallery with late murals (substitutes of the originals). Religious dances were staged in the open space in front of this gallery.

CHAPEL OF THE SAKYAPA LINEAGE

The first chapel, going clockwise, is on the left side of the open gallery. Dedicated to the lineage of the Sakyapa Lamas, it is called the Lamdre Lagyü Lhakhang. The main statue is Dorje Sempa flanked by Dagmema, on the left, and Birwapa, on the right. Other statues depict Sakyapa teachers and ascetics, the supreme masters of the sect. All are in clay and sit on Chinese-style thrones. In the center of the room is a three-dimensional bronze mandala, dedicated to Samvara, a rare relic contemporary to the

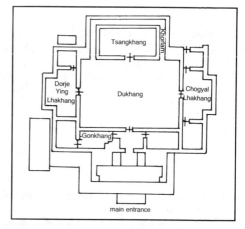

chapel's sculptural and pictorial cycles, but in my view, less inspired than the conspicuous masterpieces located in this chapel.

On the wall, left of the entrance, are images of the Goddess of the Sun and Moon (she holds the southern continent in her hand), Lhamo, and another wrathful deity called Durtra Dagpo, presiding over cemeteries. The left wall has a painting of Sakya Pandita, portrayed defeating heretics in a religious contest. On the rear wall and adjoining sides are the 84 Mahasiddhas, drawn with an inventiveness and liveliness almost unequaled in Tibetan art. The *siddhas*, accompanied by their naked consorts, are shown in yogic, acrobatic postures in the act of displaying their magical powers. Each is unique and all have realistic, distinctive bodies, yet all retain slight hints of idealization. The result is fantasy meeting reality in the best tradition of Tibetan religious painting. The right side wall from the entrance illustrates the dominant episodes of the great Sakyapa lama Phagpa, the guru of Kublai Khan. These are followed on the left door wall by paintings of the paradises of Vaishravana (the God of Wealth), Lhamo, and Mahakala.

SHALYEKHANG

The top-most *shalyekhang* is reached by a short flight of stairs. The room, as with its counterpart in the Gyantse Castle, was meant for initiations. It still contains a great number of painted mandalas. The main ones (15) of remarkable size are dedicated to the highest and the most esoteric deities in the Lamaist pantheon. The identification of all major and minor diagrams is contained in detail in the ancient sources. This *shalyekhang* once housed collections of sacred texts but is today almost empty, and the few objects inside are modern. The chapel's murals are an intricate showcase of early Tibetan mandalas and a meaningful example of the diffusion of these diagrams during the 14th–15th centuries.

CHAPEL OF THE ARHATS

Return to the upper floor. On the right side of the open gallery is a chapel dedicated to the 16 Arhats. These statues are displayed together with Sakyamuni, within three-dimensional caves amidst sculptural representations of mountains with hermitages and wildlife. This arrangement complemented well the lively realism employed by the artists in the depiction of the 16 saints. On portions of the two side walls left free by the Arhat sculptures are statues of Jampelyang on his lion (left) and Tara (right). On both door walls are the chapel's only paintings, the Four Guardian Kings (life-size). These murals are good examples of a Tibetan interpretation, in the typical Gyantse style, of a Chinese theme.

LATER CHAPELS

Carrying on along the *khorlam*, two chapels of no particular antiquity follow. The first houses a number of ancient objects, in particular bronzes, and a collection of manuscripts. The other one, on the side of the open gallery where the main door stands, is entirely renovated. This was done recently and the room has images of the 16 Arhats.

The upper floor chapels mentioned above all open to the south side of the open gallery. Two more rooms open to its north side. The first is a completely renovated space, used as a printing press and for other monastery activities. Its entrance is almost directly in front of the one leading to the chapel of the Sakyapa lineage. The second is more hidden. It allows pilgrims to view the main Palkhor Chöde images, the monumental triad of Sakyamuni, Dipankara, and Jampa, which are installed inside the ground floor's inner chapel. This is nothing more than a tiny balcony suspended on Sakyamuni's face. The entrance to this small space, called the Shelre Chapel, is through a small door below the *shalyekhang*. Palkhor Chöde's abbot can often be found here.

ART STYLES

The works of art in Gyantse's great temple are executed in a remarkable variety of styles and influences. The earliest relics are the murals in the assembly hall and its adjoining processional corridor. They are derivative of the Gyantse Castle's works and similarly have their roots in Newari art, which reached Central Tibet in the second part of the 13th century.

Although Newari insemination must be acknowledged during the preceding and following centuries, it was particularly influential during the period of the Sakyapa-Yuan domination of Tibet, when the Newari style absorbed Chinese elements. However, the hand employed here is definitely Tibetan and the style's general characteristics are already a more marked local adaptation of the foreign idiom.

Particularly remarkable are the decorations in gold relief, a technique popular in Tibet even in earlier times, as proved by other Central Tibetan temples. Gyantse's monumental examples (especially now that Sakya's early relics are gone) use gold in relief more lavishly, in the crowns, necklaces, earrings, bracelets, and robes, than any other centers. The same technique is employed in the murals of the Gyantse castle. As for the colour palette, although drastically darkened by human contact and smoke from innumerable butter lamps, it mainly consists of light hues of blue, red, green, full orange, and cream.

The art style of Gyantse has undergone a significant evolution from an earlier time.

There is a precise and decisive shift in favor of an indigenous expression, ample proof coming from the overwhelming number of chapels in the Kumbum. Its stylistic origins are indebted to the artistic expressions of the castle. The years 1418–36 witnessed notable variations in the works of the Kumbum and the Palkhor Chöde, all descendents of a single style that is now fully Tibetan. Although it retains Newari art as its fundamental basis, it has absorbed influences from late-Yuan and early-Ming China. Below is a classification of the variations:

1) The predominant style at Gyantse can best be seen in the Palkhor Chöde's Chapel of the Sakyapa Lineage, dating to 1425. The paintings of the 84 Mahasiddhas and the statues of the Sakyapa masters are among the most accomplished exhibits of this style. This very same artistic expression is also found in a great number of chapels in the Kumbum. Thus it is not only the dominant style but also possibly the most inspired. It has to be regarded as the most typical achievement of Gyantse art. For clarity, I define it as the 'Gyantse main style'.

A confirmation of this order of dating is offered by the Palkhor Chöde *shalyekhang*, another chapel of the great temple in which all the mandalas (executed in 1425) are painted in this manner. That the style was firmly established by then is proved by the fact that the builders of the Chapel of the Arhats again employed the 'Gyantse main style' in 1425. The statues of the Arhats are an example of this style as well and their iconography is thoroughly Chinese (the Four Guardian Kings are commonly depicted in Chinese warriors' outfits and their depiction in Tibet has consistently shown Chinese traits). However, their style is remarkably similar to that employed for the mural of Durtra Dagpo in the Chapel of the Sakyapa Lineage.

The Gyantse main style is an evolution towards an independent Tibetan expression of the idiom adopted at the castle. Autonomy from the latter can be seen, for example, in the withdrawal from the gold-relief technique. The colors are strong, bold tones of red, blue, green, and white. Emphasis is on the use of full, rich colors from an unrestrained, broad palette. Finally, the Gyantse main style found its apogée in the years when the Kumbum was built (1427–36).

2) The Dorje Ying and Royal Chapels, whose works of art were made in 1422–23, are similar. They constitute a transition from the old styles represented by the castle art to the Gyantse main style. The physiognomies of the images tend towards those peculiar to the Gyantse main style. Yet the color palette, being more vibrant and brilliant than at the castle, does not yet reach the boldness and complexity that is a defining characteristic of the mature Gyantse expression. For simplicity, I call this idiom the 'Gyantse transitional style'.

3) The stylistic variation adopted in the Chapel of the Wrathful Deities (*gönkhang*), dating not later than 1425, has notable qualities of essentiality and restraint. These add significantly to the immediacy and boldness of the images. They reinforce the ferocity of the Wrathful Deities, and yet the very same treatment is adopted for purely decorative elements like flames. This variation used to portray wrathful divinities is close to the 'Gyantse main style' but its underlying forcefulness and simplicity, both uncharacteristic traits, make these paintings a unique sub-style. This can be called the 'Gyantse *gönkhang* style'. The few peaceful images in the *gönkhang*, in corners and high up near the ceiling, share with the wrathful images the same simplified treatment. Palkhor Chöde's *gönkhang* is similar to a chapel dedicated to the same wrathful god, Mahakala, on the Kumbum's ground floor (19th chapel). The statues are credited to Dorje Gyaltsen, a Tibetan artist.

THOLING:
A ROYAL TEMPLE WITH
GUGE-STYLE PAINTINGS

An 11th-century Rinchen Zangpo shrine

OVERVIEW

Tholing, at the center of Zanda Xian, was the greatest and historically the most important monastery of West Tibet, and its influence extended all the way from Kashmir in the west to Assam in the east. It was built in the 11th C. (1014 or 1025) by Rinchen Zangpo (985–1055) who, together with Atisha of India, led the revival of Buddhism in Tibet. According to the lama's biography, Tholing was one of three major monasteries founded by him (the others are Khachar at Purang and Myarma in Maryul, Ladakh). Although Rinchen Zangpo is credited with the creation of 108 temples in West Tibet (including the Indian territories of Spiti, Lahul, and Ladakh), few have survived; Tholing was badly damaged by the Red Guards.

The monastery's surviving murals from the 15th–16th C. are stylistically very close to the paintings within the Lhakhang Karpo and Lhakhang Marpo chapels of Tsaparang (see page 430). Painted in the Guge style, they represent a splendid synthesis of Kashmiri and Nepalese styles. Tholing and Tsaparang are, in all likelihood, the only places in Tibet with a meaningful collection of this distinctive art form. Tholing's architecture was strongly influenced by designs from the Yarlung era (7th–9th century). These in turn were modeled on Indian prototypes, in particular, the religious buildings of the Pala-Sena style of northeast India. Tholing follows the basic plan of a typical *mahavihara* and can be favorably compared with Samye, the acknowledged first monastery of Tibet.

Location (Map reference NH44-2 C)

To reach the Tholing complex from Zanda Xian (see page 953), West Tibet, head west from the large store (beyond the guest house), at an intersection. The entrance to the monastic compound is at its east end, while the centerpiece, the badly damaged Yeshe Ö Chapel, is to the west, adjacent to a school. Only two buildings of six (Yeshe Ö, Serkhang, Lhakhang Karpo, Neten Lhakhang, Dukhang, Tongyü) remain in good condition. They are the Dukhang, on the left (south), and the Lhakhang Karpo, on the right.

YESHE Ö CHAPEL

This central edifice was named after the king of Guge who invited Atisha from India. Yeshe Ö was also the patron of Rinchen Zangpo, the emissary sent by him to Kashmir to study Buddhism. Many important Buddhist works were translated into Tibetan here during the religion's decline in India, and from this chapel Buddhism emanated throughout Tibet. Tholing supported 500 monks in its heyday.

The distinctive floor plan of the chapel corresponds to a mandala. Around this structure are 7 m-high walls and within, massive red chapel walls enclose a maze of corridors and roofless chambers. The large sculptures that lined the main hall are all destroyed, although their silhouettes remain. Rubble fills the courtyard and corridors. Four elegant *chörtens* shaped like minarets survive on top of the perimeter walls. Beyond the Yeshe Ö Chapel, on a field on the banks of the Satlej, are two rows of over 100 conical *chörtens*. Other oddly shaped *chörtens* are scattered about the vicinity.

DUKHANG

The one-story assembly hall at the south side of the complex has dark murals that require a powerful flashlight to see them (no statues). An altar and posters of *thangkas* are all that remain in the high-ceilinged chapel. Find a caretaker in a building south of the chapel walls to let you in. Along the entrance walls are paintings of the Buddhas of the Golden Age. To the left of the entrance is a long series of paintings that describe the history of Sadaprarudita, contained in the *Prajnaparamita* texts. Paintings of these episodes are accompanied by explanatory inscriptions. Other interesting murals in the main room depict the history of Tibet and West Tibet, showing major monastic centers that propagated Buddhism. The historical figures of Yeshe Ö, Chang Chub Ö, Ziwa Ö, Trisong Detsen, and Ralpachen are represented; the period costumes worn by kings and monks are noteworthy.

The *dukhang's* Guge-style paintings are similar to those of Tsaparang's chapels (its founding is roughly contemporaneous with them, 15th–16th centuries; for a description of Tsaparang's art, see page 436). These works, highly influenced by the Sakyapa style, which had thoroughly assimilated the Nepalese tradition, still retained strong elements from the golden age of Kashmiri paintings. Sumptuous color and intricate detailing are the main characteristics. The murals of the Tholing Dukhang are perhaps more provincial and less refined than those of Tsaparang, although in feeling and spirit the works are very close.

LHAKHANG KARPO (THE WHITE CHAPEL)

This chapel, normally closed, is north of the Dukhang. Its distinguishing feature is an unusual entrance which has two large archaic columns (of deodar trunks) in front of the main doors. This is intriguing because of the general absence of timber in the area; the trunks were probably brought over high Himalayan passes from India. The entrance design shows an early Indian influence and the carvings, rough and unrefined, were executed with a heavy hand.

Lhakhang Karpo is a large hall with an indented niche along the back wall that accommodates the main, damaged image. The walls are covered with splendid paintings dating back to the 15th–16th centuries. Those on the right wall are in excellent condition; the ones on the left are somewhat damaged. The former depict life-size male images of peaceful, tantric *yidams* whereas the principal figures on the opposite side are the female counterparts. There are also portraits of Tsong Khapa, Sakya Panchen, Vijaya (Namgyalma), Drölma, and Prajnaparamita (the female deity who personifies wisdom). Among the most striking images are cemetery scenes that show various stages of a sky-burial: improbable figures representing the spirits of the dead, wild beasts devouring corpses, ascetics in meditation, and deities presiding over the cemetery.

THE SUMMER RETREAT

These crumbled ruins on the top of a ridge outside Zanda Xian are reached by following the road to Tsaparang for 11 km. A path leads first to a complex of ruins halfway up the mountain. Unlike Tholing, most of the dwellings here suffered neglect and decay well before the Cultural Revolution. During the 11th C., the entire monastic community would move here in summer to escape the warmer plains below. Monks lived in multi-layer rows of caves dug out of the soft clay, each cell large enough for one person. Shelves carved in the back walls served as altars and held the monk's belongings. The slopes are dotted with these caves. Near the decayed walls of the main chapels is a 15-m natural pillar that functions as a multi-story dwelling. A path from here leads farther up the slope. After a steep, tricky 1/2-hr climb, reach a cave. A stepped tunnel goes from here through the innards of the mountain to its flat top. Here another monastic complex (ruined) provided accommodation for monks and palaces for Guge's royal family. Andrade, the 17th-C. Jesuit monk, came here to pay respect to the king's mother.

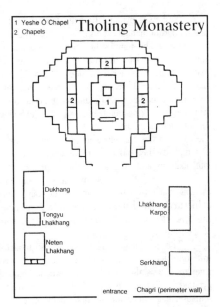

ARCHITECTURE

Constructed at the start of the 11th C. by the Guge King Yeshe Ö and the translator, Rinchen Zangpo, Tholing exemplified the prosperity of the West Tibet kingdom. One measure of this was the large amount of timber imported from northwest India. This principal shrine was strongly influenced by two architectural currents. Yarlung (7th–9th C.) sensibilities are evident in the basic design, which was copied faithfully from Samye Monastery (see page 295). The second theme came from India, specifically from the temple of Odantapuri.

The complex is oriented to the four cardinal points, with the sacred precinct enclosed within a rectangular perimeter wall (in later times, monks' residences were added inside this enclosure). There are three entrances, two minor ones at the north and south sides, and a monumental one in the east. On top of this major entranceway was a surmounting structure resembling a stepped crown. This emulated the motif and profile of the stepped, or terraced *prasada*-type central temple typical of Indian architecture.

Within the perimeter walls, the Yeshe Ö chapel is aligned with the main entrance along a central axis. To the left (south) are three chapels, two rectangular—the Dukhang and the Neten (Nechu) Lhakhang—and a third, the Tongyü. There are only two chapels on the right. The rectangular Lhakhang Karpo, with its unique entranceway, is one and the other is the square Serkhang (only the Dukhang and Lhakhang Karpo have survived). The Yeshe Ö chapel, a series of concentric structures, is similar in design to the Samye Ütse. Its outer parts, consisting of the temple walls, are less monumental than the central structure, which has a cruciform plan. Multi-angled walls retain the essential characteristics of the Indian model. Their lengths were conceived as a series of zigzags that give the overall plan its distinctive appearance.

Yeshe Ö's pyramidal architecture was elaborated as a three-dimensional representation of a *vajradhatu* mandala. This conception was reinforced in the interior chambers by the murals and statues. The temple, like Samye Ütse and its Indian prototype, is distinguished by its emphasis on the eastern (main entrance) wing. This part of the complex is considerably more massive than the other three sides. The building itself, however, is less grand and impressive than the Samye Ütse. It also has less space between the external wall and the cruciform central edifice. The primary difference between the two is Yeshe Ö's uniformly Tibetan construction. A striking architectural signature of Samye is its use of different motifs for the decoration of each floor. For example, its ground floor was completed in the Tibetan style while the topmost was conceived in the Indian tradition. The only foreign element in the Yeshe Ö temple is the gold and bronze roof, made in the Chinese manner. This was probably a late addition and not part of the original.

From a distance, Tholing's most prominent characteristic is four slender pinnacle-like *chörtens* that crown the roofline at the four corners. These are the only surviving examples of Indian *chörtens* that adorned the *prasada*-type monasteries of that country. Outside of Tholing, this type of *chörten* exists only in 11th-C. illuminated manuscripts and in the Guge murals of Tsaparang.

The Serkhang of Tholing was also modeled on Indian architecture. This Temple of Initiation, located at the northeastern corner, was considered the most sacred chapel of the complex. It was also Tibet's earliest wooden building designed entirely on Indian motifs. The pyramidal structure consisted of three progressively smaller floors, each reached by an external staircase. Each floor was surrounded by an external wooden portico surmounted by a roof. This configuration gave the temple the religious significance of a mandala: the floors symbolized the three bodies of Buddha and represented the different stages on the path to enlightenment. The chapel walls were richly decorated with images of divinities linked intimately with advanced consciousness; they augmented the pilgrims' actual and symbolic ascent through the Serkhang. A most distinctive architectural element was the S-shaped consoles that adorned the tops of the wooden columns conceived in the Central Asian manner.

The entrance doors and portals of the Lhakhang Karpo are unique in West Tibet. Much admired by Tucci, the Tibetologist, they were closely linked to early Indian design elements. The most noticeable features of the entrance are the ponderous columns with heavy bases. They are of Gandharan origin and can be compared to those of the Ali Masjid stupa near the Khyber Pass. Small beams of the portal are arranged to resemble a stylized stepped pyramid, a repetition of the *prasada* motif encountered in the Yeshe Ö chapel and main entranceway. This *prasada* theme, clearly originating from Indian architecture and iconography, is echoed in the background decoration of many divinities in West Tibet. It also exists in the 11th-C. illuminated Nepalese manuscripts. Symbols on the columns are associated with the Buddha's first sermon at Sarnath. These are the Wheel of Law flanked by two deer. This design was widely copied throughout Tibet and became a most common feature on monastery roofs.

Outside the central complex, four monumental *chörtens* stood at the four corners at unequal distances from the Yeshe Ö Chapel (only the two southern ones have survived). These are similar to those that once stood at Samye. Of the Lhabab type, characterized by stairs on each of the four sides, they represent Buddha's descent from the Tushita heaven where he went to preach to his mother. According to tradition, the relics of Rinchen Zangpo were contained within the northwestern *chörten* (destroyed). The features that most distinguish these 11th-C. West Tibetan structures from their Central Tibetan counterparts are the almost spherical cupolas and tall, massive pinnacles.

WEST TIBETAN ARCHITECTURE

Two major artistic currents characterize the architecture of West Tibet. One is the Kashmiri style, epitomized by the monasteries founded by Rinchen Zangpo. The other is the Pala-Sena style of northeast India (Bihar and Bengal). This latter was introduced by Atisha, who began the Second Diffusion of Buddhism in West Tibet at the beginning of the 11th century.

Ladakh was the territory most influenced by the Kashmiri idiom in West Tibet. Typical elements included distinctive three-lobed arches, the particular dressing of wood structures, and lantern ceilings. In Guge, the architectural signatures of Pala-Sena were more evident. Principal temples, like Tholing, followed the *mahavihara* plan of the Pala Dynasty (9th–11th centuries). The major monuments are of the *prasada* type, palace-style buildings with graduated, stepped floors. *Chörten* pinnacles are a distinguishing mark as well. The Central Asian city-states of the Silk Road also exerted considerable influence. These traits came to West Tibet either via Kashmir or directly from pilgrims and traders (examples can best be gleaned from temple carpentry). There was no trace of Chinese infiltration at this time.

The temples of West Tibet are usually located on plains and within the protection of castles. Most are oriented along an east–west axis. The complexes, surrounded by walls, generally consist of several principal buildings arranged symmetrically. Their ground floor plans sometimes resemble the monastic complexes of the Yarlung kings, who derived their inspiration from Indian models. One significant difference, however, is that the edifices of West Tibet generally lack monumentality. Linear decoration on the external walls is pure Tibetan. Only the internal wooden support elements display echoes from Central Asia, Kashmir, or Pala India. The contrast between the stark, monochromatic outside walls and the sumptuous, polychrome images that decorate all surfaces within is the most striking aspect of these monasteries.

In the 12th C., many West Tibetan monasteries switched to the Kadampa sect pioneered by Atisha and Dromtönpa. At the beginning of the 13th C., other schools exerted their influence. The Kailash area, for example, was dominated by the Kagyüpas, specifically the Drigungpas. In Gungthang, the Sakyapa held sway. By the 15th C., because of this influx of new idioms, religious buildings started to exhibit some Central Tibet attributes. Complexes were now being built on top of mountains or along ridges. The kingdom of Guge, with Tsaparang as its capital, is an example of this genre, with royal castles, temples, and common dwellings erected on a crest. The prototype may have been the Yumbu Lagang (see page 539) of the Yarlung Valley. Other complexes were located near the base of a mountain. They were the precursors of the great monastic cities of Lhasa and Shigatse.

Some of the most remarkable religious structures in Tibet are found in Guge. These are the troglodytic communities at Tsaparang, Khyunglung, Dungkar (the most impressive), and elsewhere. Entire mountainsides are dotted with cave dwellings and cave temples. These natural and man-made cavities have attracted yogis since early times. The practice of living in caves, especially during severe winters, may well have started in Paleolithic times. Simple in structure, the cave complexes are radically different from the elaborate ones of India (e.g. Ajanta) and Central Asia (e.g. Dunhuang). Most are semi-circular or quadrangular, and many are painted and decorated with statues placed within rock niches.

TSAPARANG:
LOST CITY OF THE GUGE KINGDOM

Kashmiri- and Nepalese-inspired art treasures

OVERVIEW

The kingdom of Guge in West Tibet was established in the 9th C., after the assassination of the anti-Buddhist King Langdarma and the breakup of the Yarlung empire. One of the king's sons, Wösung, traveled west to the upper Indus and Satlej valleys and founded Guge, establishing Tsaparang as its capital. In the 10th C., King Yeshe Ö, and the translator, Rinchen Zangpo, reinstated Buddhism in this part of Tibet and over 100 monasteries were built—the most important being Tholing and Tsaparang. A further expansion of the religion occurred in the 11th C., when Atisha, the renowned Indian master, came to Tholing to teach. Tibetan Buddhism gained a foothold in the country from that time on.

Antonio de Andrade, a Portugese attached to the Jesuit mission in Goa, was the first European to visit the isolated kingdom in 1624. He was well received by the King and succeeded in setting up the first Christian church in Tibet the following year. Later, a second mission was founded at Rutok, 398 km to the north. Buddhist lamas at Tsaparang, upset by the spread of Christianity, enlisted the help of neighboring Ladakh to overthrow the Guge kingdom in 1630. Andrade's church was driven out. Ladakh briefly absorbed Guge but eventually Lhasa took over the territory.

Lama Govinda (a German) and his wife, Li Gotama, prepared ten years for a two-year pilgrimage to West Tibet. Determined to see the remains of Tibet's magnificent religious art, they reached Tsaparang in the autumn of 1948. Lama Govinda later wrote in *The Way of the White Clouds*:

> *After the Valley of the Moon Castle and the awe-inspiring canyons on the way to Tholing, we feared that Tsaparang would perhaps come as an anticlimax or at least something that could not compete with the natural wonders through which we had passed. But when, on the last lap of our journey—while emerging from a gorge and turning the spur of a mountain—we suddenly beheld the lofty castles of the ancient city of Tsaparang, which seemed to be carved out of the solid rock of an isolated, monolithic mountain peak, we gasped with wonder and could hardly believe our eyes.*

Tsaparang sprawls all over the slopes and the top of a ridge bounded to the north by the Satlej River. Mountains surround it to the east, south, and west, providing a natural and impregnable fortification. The entire ridge is covered with temples, *chörtens*, houses, cave dwellings, all in varying degrees of ruin. Remains of the royal castle and its temples stand at the top, 170 m above the valley floor, and can only be reached by a secret tunnel dug within the innards of the mountain.

Tsaparang is one of the most important art-historic centers in Tibet, the repository of stunning West Tibet-style murals and statues. Within the Lhakhang Karpo and Lhakhang Marpo (White and Red chapels) are resplendent Kashmiri-inspired works of art, interpreted in the local artistic idiom. Concurrently, the foundation of this uncommon genre was provided

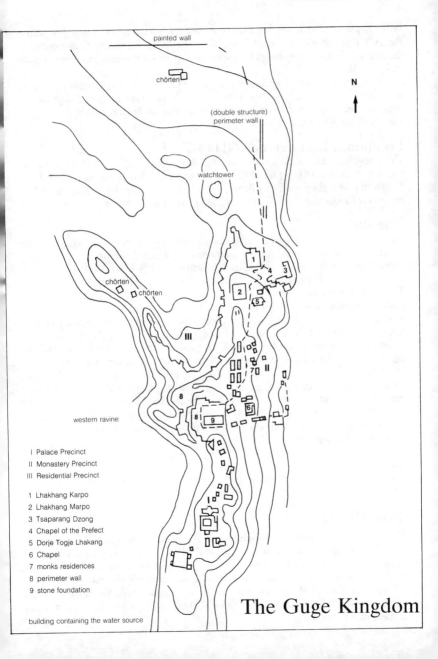

painted wall

chörten

N

(double structure)
perimeter wall

watchtower

chörten   chörten

III

western ravine

I   Palace Precinct
II Monastery Precinct
III Residential Precinct

1 Lhakhang Karpo
2 Lhakhang Marpo
3 Tsaparang Dzong
4 Chapel of the Prefect
5 Dorje Togje Lhakang
6 Chapel
7 monks residences
8 perimeter wall
9 stone foundation

building containing the water source

The Guge Kingdom

by the Nepalese tradition, which derived from the Sakya dominance of Central Tibet during the 14th–15th centuries. In the Lhakhang Karpo are life-sized terracotta statues crafted in the unique Kashmiri style. Although badly damaged, they represent some of Tibet's most visually striking images.

Tsaparang was spared annihilation during the Cultural Revolution perhaps because of its advanced state of decay from the 17th C. onwards. Its artistic treasures thus stand as a remarkable anomaly of modern Tibet; they are relics of an astonishing museum that contains some of Asia's most beautiful murals.

Location (Map reference NH44-2 C)

The geographic center of the kingdom of Guge is near the small village of Tsaparang, 13 km west of Zanda Xian (see page 953). Reach it simply by following the road out of Zanda Xian to the west along the Satlej River gorge. Climb up a steep slope behind the village and proceed south along a wide, flat plain for 3 km to reach the site.

The site

Tsaparang's appearance has changed little since its abandonment in the 17th century. Inside the chapels, however, statues have been destroyed and damaged and vandalism has marred its irreplaceable paintings. In its heyday, 500 families lived here; nowadays only ten do.

Left of the Tsaparang ridge, a river runs along the eastern base to join the Satlej. Across it is a *chörten* next to the roofless Lotang Lhakhang, a temple dedicated to Vairocana, a deity particularly revered in West Tibet. On the far right are two *chörtens* and a colony of about 300 caves at the lower portion of nearby slopes. Northeast of the mountain are more tall, standing *chörtens*. Nearby are earth and mud watchtowers. The caretaker lives in a house in front of the complex, outside a new wall. A path leading to the temples and dwellings zigzags up the hill behind a locked door set into the wall. Beyond the entrance are two chapels left of the path, one above the other. The lower is the Chapel of the Prefect of Tsaparang Dzong; the upper is the Dorje Jigje Lhakhang. Lhakhang Karpo is the first large temple encountered, right of the path, soon followed by the Lhakhang Marpo. From the base of the ridge, paths and secret tunnels lead up to the mountain's middle sections. Here are 300 mud and clay houses and other large structures. In general, only walls remain. At the very top are ruins of the Guge palace.

Layout

The main components of Tsaparang are the royal palace, civilian dwellings, monastic structures, buildings of the Dzong government, and defensive structures.

THE PALACE

The palace precinct extends north–south for over 200 m and its east–west axis measures some 80 m. Most of the structures are destroyed and difficult to identify. Four groups can be made out, however. To the north are the residences (probably) of the Summer and Winter Palaces. Many buildings, some two-story high, are clustered close together. Within this area is a square hall with 6-m sides. Flanking it on two sides are three smaller cells. On the walls of this hall are remnants of niches for statues. This was likely the king's personal chapel and part of the Summer Palace.

Directly underneath this northern group of buildings, within the mountain itself, is the Winter Palace, which extends north–south 12 m below the surface. It is linked to the Summer Palace by a flight of steep stairs. Running the length of the underground palace is a corridor with small chambers along its sides, three on the west, and one on the south. All have windows that look out over the plains far below. East of the corridor are three more chambers. All the rooms are bare except for shelves in the walls. About 7–8 m from the surface entrance, a tunnel extends to the rear of the ridge and links up with a water tunnel, an escape route for the royal family in emergencies.

The three palace chapels are in the middle of the complex, two above ground and one a cave chapel. The Mandala Lhakhang (good condition) is a squarish chamber (6 m by 6 m) with no columns and an east entrance (see below). A smaller chapel, perhaps the Jowo Lhakhang, is 30m south of the Mandala Lhakhang. Its inner chapel, repository of the Jowo, is along the west side. The two side walls had statues of the Eight Bodhisattvas. Surrounding this building are the red walls of a *khorlam* corridor. Some literary sources identify this as the Guge king's principal chapel. The cave chapel is 5 m south of the Mandala Lhakhang. Its square cavity has 4-m sides and the north wall has a recess for an image. The murals are intact.

South of the Jowo Lhakhang is a group of administrative buildings considerably larger than the rest. The northern part is dominated by a 9 m by 8 m assembly hall. To the south is a square, open plaza (19 m per side) surrounded by buildings. Its function was similar to the Deyang Shar of the Potala: the venue was used for assemblies, masked dances, and festivals. East of this group is the water tunnel

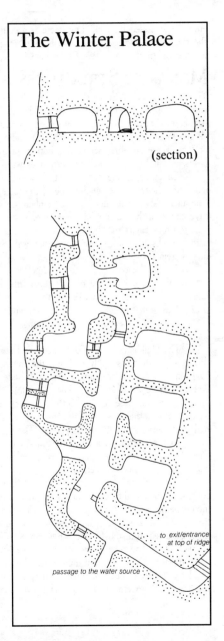

The Winter Palace

(section)

to exit/entrance at top of ridge

passage to the water source

entrance, enclosed by a building. Here is a courtyard with an attached room. Buildings at the rear of the ridge top were probably kitchen and storehouses, and close by are chambers for storage. In the early 1980s they held armor, arrows, shields, and other objects.

MONASTIC STRUCTURES

These are on the northeast slope near the base of the ridge and comprise a long *mani* wall, various chapels, *chörtens*, and monks' residences. The unique *mani* wall at the ridge's north base consists of numerous large, oval stones carved with deities, *chörtens*, inscriptions, *mantras*, all cemented near the top of the wall. Extending for over 100 m, it has an average height of 3 m. There are three sections, a bottom of oval foundation stones, a middle of earthen layers, and a top embedded on both sides with the carved *mani* stones.

Cave chapels are common at Tsaparang. A well-preserved one sits above the main monastery, halfway up from the base of the ridge. The walls of this cavity are covered with colorful murals and it once stocked bamboo arrows and wood saddles. Near here is another cave chapel with a man-made extension. It faces east and is divided into two parts. The west is a rock cavity that housed an image (destroyed), while the east is a one-story building with two cells dug into the north mountain wall. Some rather simplistic murals, mostly *yabyum* images, remain.

The Lhakhang Marpo (Red Chapel) and Lhakhang Karpo (White Chapel) are the two main chapels. Near the base of the north slope, the former is the higher of the two. Lhakhang Marpo is 22 m wide, 19.4 m deep, and has 30 closely placed columns. These unusually thin columns are typical of Guge. The entrance is set in the east wall and its door frame is the finest carved wood relic at Tsaparang. 380 sq m of murals are painted on the inside walls.

The Lhakhang Karpo, 10 m below and north of the Lhakhang Marpo, has two parts: the large, southern assembly hall and the inner, northern Jowo Khang. The hall is 21 m by 19 m with 32 slender columns. Along the side walls are 18 statues, the only ones of their type to survive in West Tibet. The inner Jowo Khang is 7.6 m by 7.8 m, and the main image's platform, close to the north wall, occupies half the space of the recess. Lhakhang Karpo's main entrance is along the east wall. The distinctive lantern ceiling of the assembly hall is the most beautiful in Tsaparang. There are 500 sq m of murals.

At the southeast corner of the Lhakhang Marpo is the Dorje Jigje Lhakhang (Yidam Chapel). Facing east, the building has an entrance cloister, a main hall, and a high inner chapel along its western section.

Tsaparang also has numerous large *chörtens*. One at the foot of the north slope has collapsed and it is difficult to make out its original shape. At the northwest slope are two more, one in reasonable condition. In the Guge area, long rows of *chörtens*, known as Chörten Ringmo ('Long Chörtens'), are a common feature and consist of over 200 identical small *chörtens* ranged in a straight line. They can be 100–200 m long. Tholing (see page 425) has six such rows. The base of one of the *chörtens* at the northwest slope has a pair of lively lions in bas-relief. At the top are terracotta tiles decorated with images and floral designs. Monk's residences consist of three main types: individual houses, cave dwellings, and caves combined with external structures. The first usually has room for 6–7 monks.

THE DZONG

Buildings belonging to the *Dzong* (district government) are at the base of the northeast slope, adjacent to the monasteries. After the fall of Guge at the beginning of the 17th C., the Ganden Potrang government of Lhasa established a simple administrative headquarters here. Most of its structures have collapsed but the Chapel of the Prefect (property of Tsaparang prefecture) is in reasonable condition.

CIVILIAN DWELLINGS

Lay dwellings generally were built around the north and northwestern slopes. Most consist of single caves excavated from the soft earth, although some have multiple cavities. The majority face east to escape the prevailing western wind and their interior walls often have small niches. The second type of civilian dwelling is a combination of cave and building. This form of architecture is still popular in Tholing and Purang.

DEFENSIVE STRUCTURES

Many rings of defensive walls, from the foot of the ridge to the top, protect Tsaparang. Around the palace, adjacent to the sheer cliffs, is one such wall constructed of two levels. The bottom is a double wall with a 1-m-wide corridor where soldiers can be stationed. Its ceiling is made of timber and designed to bear loads. Above this level is a single wall. Both sections have openings for archers. The northwest slope, from top to bottom, has no less than seven different walls. Watchtowers stand at strategic points.

SECRET TUNNELS

THE PALACE TUNNEL

The ridge's top portion, 40 m in height, is a citadel with sheer sides. The only way to ascend it is through the interior of the mountain by a secret tunnel whose entrance is at the topmost part of the northeast slope, 120 m from the valley floor. Immediately

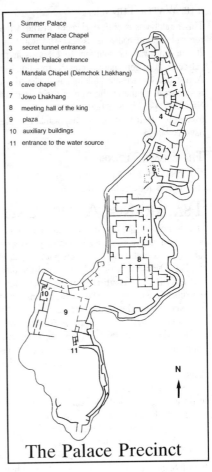

1   Summer Palace
2   Summer Palace Chapel
3   secret tunnel entrance
4   Winter Palace entrance
5   Mandala Chapel (Demchok Lhakhang)
6   cave chapel
7   Jowo Lhakhang
8   meeting hall of the king
9   plaza
10 auxiliary buildings
11 entrance to the water source

N

The Palace Precinct

above this opening is a balcony laden with stones. In case of attack, these were used to block the tunnel. Inside the entrance, stone slab and timber stairs lead southwestward for about 15 m, then turn sharply to the south, then southwest and southeast, and finally southwest again to reach an upper exit, guarded by a door. The entire tunnel (1.3 m wide by 1.8 m high) is 45 m long and has a height differential of 35 m. In some sections, openings to the outside provide light.

THE WATER TUNNEL

This tunnel was a critical element in the defence of Guge. The palace, 165–170 m above the valley floor, badly needs access to water in the event of a siege. A secret tunnel, over 200 m long was the solution. One end is at the junction of the mid-south section of the palace. A 10-m-long natural crevice, trending east–west, leads to the tunnel's entrance proper. Above this crevice are buildings that cleverly conceal the passage. The water tunnel's exit is at a small ravine at the base of the western cliffs. Water comes from a river and a spring. Near the opening is a house on a flat terrace among trees; the camouflage for the secret passage is effective. It is now impossible to traverse the entire tunnel because some sections have collapsed.

THE ESCAPE TUNNEL

This connects the Winter Palace with the water tunnel. In times of crisis, the royal family and retinue retreated via this tunnel to canyons and mountains south of Tsaparang.

TSAPARANG: ARTISTIC CENTER OF WEST TIBET

Stylistically, in spite of indigenous modifications, the murals of Tsaparang consistently follow-ed basic Indian (particularly Kashmiri) prototypes. This West Tibet art style was further rein-forced by its multifarious contacts with Nepal, whose paintings were strongly influenced by the Pala Dynasty of eastern India. Until the domination of the territory by the Dalai Lamas in the 17th C., the artists of West Tibet contented themselves with artistic currents from the subcontinent and showed little inclination or necessity to adopt other trends. Kashmir and Nepal were the major external influences that shaped Guge's paintings.

The murals of Tsaparang are stylistically close to those of the fabled 11th-C. temples of Alchi (Ladakh, India) and Tapho (Spiti, India). They are distinguished by the same brilliant, luminous colors; sensuous figures with large bosoms and slender waists; and wondrous costumes, all derived from typical Kashmiri paintings. This influence can be traced back to Rinchen Zangpo (958–1055). After his religious studies in Kashmir, he returned to King Yeshe Ö's capital with 32 artists. The entire heritage of Kashmiri painting, with the exception of minor works in Gilgit, would have been completely lost were it not for Tsaparang's surviving murals and a few others in West Tibet. They represent interpreted extensions of the Kashmiri-Tibetan style of the 11th-C., however, rather than perfect derivatives of Kashmir.

A second characteristic apparent in Tsaparang's paintings is their surprising similarity to the Newari murals of the 15th-C. Gyantse Kumbum (see page 447). The colors used in both monuments are subdued and subtle and have pronounced leanings towards the Nepalese style. Notice the palette of the physiognomies, the scarves, decorative items on the bodies, and especially the lotus pedestals. A fundamental component of Tsaparang's murals was influence from the Sakyapa style, traced ultimately to Nepal and predominant in Tsang during the 14th-

15th centuries. The paintings were created by a group of artists intimate with the Sakyapa tradition of south-central Tibet. On the other hand, the paintings are virtually devoid of Chinese influences, probably the only ones in Tibet without such elements. A few extremely minor exceptions include cloud formations in the paintings of the Mandala Lhakhang.

The murals of Tsaparang, though obviously linked to early Kashmiri art (10th–11th C.) were probably not painted until the 15th–17th centuries—an understandable fact. Tsaparang was tied to the Guge royal family and its political machinations. As a palace and monastic center at the heart of an empire, its structures and art invariably underwent many renovations and redecorations. Thus early murals had almost no chance to survive unaltered.

However, Tsaparang's geographic isolation led to unusually slow stylistic changes. The Indian artistic foundation can be seen, for example, in the miniature paintings on the Lhakhang Karpo walls. Notice the shading, a non-Tibetan element. Another Indian trait is the presence of half-profiles. Also, the grouping of figures is free and fluid and no haloes are present. In typical Tibetan works, figures with haloes predominate. Contrast these paintings with those of the Mandala (Demchok) Lhakhang at the top. The Buddha figures have lost their shading and sense of relief. They look flat compared with the Lhakhang Karpo figures. Yet some angularity in the faces, a typical Indian form, remains. The faces are less full than those in most Tibetan paintings and the Indian triangular crown is still in evidence. But in this topmost chapel, early Indian Pala artistic sensibilities were losing ground, a change that coincided with the decline of the Guge. Not long after, the kingdom was conquered first by Ladakh and then taken over by Lhasa. This artistic shift before the kingdom's downfall was dramatic: the painted figures took on conspicuously awkward proportions, as if the heart of the painter was no longer in his work. Artists concentrated more on elaborate jewelry, clothing, and ornaments rather than on portraying the essence of the person or deity. The paintings were technically proficient but sadly lacking in spirit. After the demise of Guge, Central Tibetan styles dominated and by the end of the 18th century the West Tibet (Guge) idiom was completely lost.

Tsaparang's murals were based on the precepts and doctrines of Tantric Buddhism that were brought to West Tibet by Rinchen Zangpo and others. All the figures and themes were carefully presented in strict accordance to tantric mandalic cycles; these were prescribed in minute detail in sacred texts, most of which depict aspects of the Vairocana cycle.

LHAKHANG KARPO (WHITE CHAPEL)

Artistically, this is the most important and magnificent chapel in West Tibet; its paintings are Tsaparang's oldest. The chapel's exterior walls are actually grey, not white, and the entrance door, unlike the original one of the Lhakhang Marpo, is ordinary and gives no clue to the riches inside. A large hall with a high ceiling dominates the interior space. Along the center of the rear wall is the smaller Jowo Khang (Tsangkhang) chapel, completely open to the assembly hall.

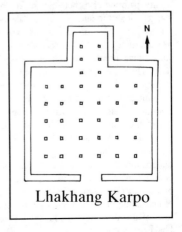

N

Lhakhang Karpo

The beautiful ceiling is supported by many thin and narrow columns with carved and painted capitals. Divided by parallel cross beams, the ceiling is made up of panels, each painted differently. These predominantly geometric designs resemble patterned textiles. In the center of each panel is a circular mandala and the colors used on the wood are exceptional.

Formerly, 22 gilded life-size statues on finely crafted bases lined the side walls. Only 16 remain (excluding the two guardians); all are damaged. These statues, the epitome of Tsaparang's artistic expression, were commissioned by the three Guge princes under the Second Dalai Lama, Gedan Gyatso (1476–1542). As late as the latter half of the 1980s, chunks of shoulders, arms, and torsos lay in the hall. The broken pieces, however, show clearly the construction of the statues: essentially stucco mixed with an internal filling of wood, cloth, paper from books, and straw. Fortunately, the murals behind the images are intact and compare well with the documentation provided by Tucci and Li Gotama half a century earlier.

On each side of the entrance is a 5-m-tall guardian; these two are Tamdrin (red) and Chana Dorje (blue). The torsos (significantly elongated; a typical West Tibetan trademark) have been broken open and the arms are missing. Notice the wall of red flames behind Tamdrin; usually only a ring of flames is shown. The smaller figure of Shinje, right of the guardian within the field of flames, shows distinct stylistic elements from Central Tibet. This trend of incorporating artistic ideas from the central provinces is common in the Lhakhang Marpo. Tamdrin's scepter, normally held in the right hand, is missing. Its left arm and the horse head protruding from the head are broken. To the left of the statue, along the upper parts of the wall, are many painted images, a principal characteristic of the Lhakhang Karpo. The pictorial composition relies heavily on arrays of small divinities rather than large, central, dominant figures. Each is portrayed in isolation.

> The description of the hall follows a clockwise direction along the walls.

Beyond the red Tamdrin is the pedestal of a four-armed Chenresi (destroyed). Behind it is a large painting of a thousand-armed Chenresi flanked by smaller images of the same deity. Ranged along the left wall are six fabulous, unique statues. Each of the first three represents a three-headed Vairocana (the right wall also has a similar set). The six figures together form a meditation cycle of Vairocana. Originally they were each enclosed in a richly decorated stucco frame (torana), an arch, usually depicting foliage and animate designs above the divinity's head. The torana represents a celestial paradise. Small holes in the wall secured them around the images. These magnificent works were dismantled and are scattered on the floor. The only intact torana is at the far corner of the left wall, a canopy of leaves above the image. Stylistic models of these structures apparently derived from Nepal or Central Tibet, after the fall of the Pala empire at the end of the 11th century.

Two figures along the left wall are undamaged except for knees and hands. Notice especially the thin, elongated torsos (a trait present also in the guardians). The faces are also molded in a similar, elongated manner. Distinctive stomach cleavage, slight abdominal bulge, and extremely slender waists are all characteristic traits of Kashmiri art. The ushnishas (hair protuberances), a sign of Buddhahood, resemble toupees. Behind the figures are painted haloes of emanating rays, another Kashmiri characteristic. The lotus pedestals vary and the painted rows of divinities next to the statues are of different sizes, both recognizable trends of the Lhakhang Karpo.

An interesting feature is the integration of the statues with their surrounding murals. The paintings flanking a statue are directly complementary and related to the image. Deep, dark blue background allows the rich reds and browns to stand out vividly. Notice the triangular border that delineates the mural's lower extremities, a device typical of West Tibet. The murals around the sculptures are created with great richness, intricacy, and precision. According to Tucci, the eminent Tibetologist, the artists of Tsaparang had backgrounds in manuscript painting and they transferred this punctilious skill to the walls of the Lhakhang Karpo. The paintings are extraordinarily busy; every space is filled with *bodhisattvas*, animals, flowers, trees, and temples.

Particularly striking are the detailed garments and lovely ornaments adorning the *bodhisattvas*. A cloth covering the knee of a deity, for example, depicts two females practicing yoga on a bed of nails. The deities are wrapped in swirling, beautifully designed scarfs; the deep reds and blues are stunning. Female figures are characterized by bulging breasts, narrow waists, and full, slightly bloated, faces. Throughout these works, Kashmiri influence is obvious. In other respects, however, the paintings have much in common with the 15th-C. Sakyapa works of Gyantse. A good example are the lotuses on which the deities sit. Each petal is curled and more elaborately divided at the edge than the single, united whorl typical of Kashmiri lotuses.

The unusual iconography of the fourth Vairocana (heavily damaged) displays eight arms instead of the usual two. On the wall behind it are paintings of animals, trees, wrathful and peaceful divinities, and Indian gods. The last represent the Hindu pantheon absorbed by the Tibetans, and include Ishana (Master of Knowledge), Vishnu and his retinue, Brahma and Shakti, Ishwara (female Lord of the Earth), Ganapati (God of Wealth), and Agni (God of Fire).

Farther along the left side wall are painted mandalas of the Five Tathagatas. In the center is Saravid Vairocana, the All-Knowing, surrounded by 36 divinities. The last figure is Sakyamuni, flanked by Jampa and Jampelyang, meditating under the Tree of Enlightenment. Toward the recessed inner chapel at the hall's rear is a seated Jampa flanked by two *bodhisattvas* (left of the inner chapel entrance). To the right is a painting of Tsong Khapa and his two disciples (badly damaged). The presence of Gelugpa figures with yellow hats affirms that these paintings postdate the 15th century.

All statues within the inner Jowo Khang chapel have been destroyed and only their pedestals remain. The back of the chamber once had a gigantic, gilt-bronze statue of Sakyamuni on a massive stand, flanked by Jampa and Jampelyang. Parts of the Buddha's *torana* survive. Each side wall has four rows of tiny, sculpted divinities, and each of these is supported on its own console. Some of the gilded clay images in the higher series are still intact. These unique statues mostly represent Sakyamuni with different *mudras*.

In the chamber's lower part is a 0.5-m-high band of paintings. One wonderful register shows the construction and consecration of the Lhakhang Karpo. The scenes, full of life and rendered in rich details, give a valuable glimpse into the lives of ordinary citizens. Another panel, starting from the left wall and moving to the right, depicts the legends and life of Sakyamuni. The narrative, in the manner of a long scroll, proceeds clockwise along the walls. One delightful detail in the *nirvana* scene shows little *asparas* with wings. Next to them are little *nagas*. The depiction of flames and polychrome mountains is unusual. Along the top portions of the walls are paintings of myriad rows of tiny monks. Like the murals of the main hall, these are strongly influenced by the Kashmiri style. Legible inscriptions describe the contents of the paintings.

Compared with the paintings of the Lhakhang Marpo (similar iconographic themes), the works of the Lhakhang Karpo are slightly earlier (mid-15th C.) and more primitive. Lhakhang Marpo's paintings are more Central Tibetan in expression.

Although the statues of the Jowo Khang are destroyed, noteworthy relics still exist. The ceiling capitals and beams are among the most accomplished in Tibet. Their typical West Tibetan design is characterized by intricate, serrated palmette outlines. At the top of each of the four slender columns is a small wood-carved Sakyamuni. Extremely few examples of this type of ceiling structure survive; it can also be seen in the Lhakhang Marpo. Notice the lantern-style architecture of the ceiling. The structure is directly above the central Buddha and the skylight is placed at the other section. In effect, this creates two ceilings. The assembly hall has no windows, so all the light for the chapel comes from this inner chamber. Slender columns are another characteristic of West Tibetan architecture. Their fragility requires that many be used to support the ceiling.

After exiting the inner Jowo Khang, continue the clockwise progression around the main hall of the Lhakhang Karpo. Along the back wall, right of the inner chapel, are two more stucco statues (torana and throne destroyed). The first one (badly damaged) is a learned monk, probably Rinchen Zangpo, in elaborate robes. This work is conserved from the navel down, and the left arm, shoulder, and portions of the red robe with large, gold bands and blue interior lining also survived. On the walls high up behind the monk, in series of threes, are painted images of the Guge kings. Each, surrounded by his retinue, is seated on a throne. Gold inscriptions for each king are placed so high as to be practically unreadable.

Right of Rinchen Zangpo, also clothed in the robes of a monk, is a statue of another Vairocana. Its head and most of the seated body are intact, but the torso has a large hole and the two hands are missing. This statue's halo and body aureole are significantly reduced. Unlike other bodhisattvas in the hall, this image, instead of displaying the Indo-Tibetan style, has elements traceable to Central Tibet. This influence is also found in the paintings behind the statue, which show the cosmos of a multi-level mandala framed within a deep blue celestial background. In the lower third, just above Vairocana, are miniature paintings of exquisite, intricate scenes, with haloed figures of saints and bodhisattvas amidst shrines, trees, and mountains. A charming object is the multi-hued, conical mountain, a generally unknown form in Central Tibet. Here perhaps is a touch of influence from China (similar to Gyantse). The temple roofs in the paintings do not follow an Indian design but rather are based on indigenous Tibetan models. Notice the faces of the diverse figures: they are chubby and bloated; a clear departure from the Kashmiri treatment and a peculiarity of this region. The clothing, too, is late Tibetan. In general, there is a surprising lack of Indian stylistic signatures in this wall panel. The art style is very close to that of the inner chamber, the life episodes of Sakyamuni. These are all good examples of the so-called Guge style, which strongly absorbed ideas from Sakyapa Tsang. It evolved by means of inventive local interpretation and transformed the Kashmiri idiom into a distinct genre of its own. Above the delightful miniature paintings of the world is a seemingly infinite repetition of tiny Vairocanas. The top part is a dreamy representation of diverse celestial figures.

The first statue along the right side wall of the Lhakhang Karpo is Ratnasambhava. Drölkar, the White Tara, is at the extreme right of the wall. The other statues are Amogasiddhi and three of Vairocana. Two of the latter are fairly well preserved. The base of one is superb and unique, a rounded, columnar stand, expanded in its top portion (mushroom-shaped) to support the image. This surprising innovation probably originated at Tsaparang and is seen also at Tholing Monastery, but nowhere else in West Tibet. The floral motif on its curvilinear surface is striking and the use of colors original. The wall directly behind the statue is blue and purposely unpainted because of the large, complex *torana* (destroyed) that masked it.

LHAKHANG MARPO (RED CHAPEL)

A short distance above the Lhakhang Karpo is the Lhakhang Marpo, built ca 1470 by Queen Döndrubma of Guge. It is perhaps 30 years older than the Lhakhang Karpo. However, its murals are later, due to repainting just before the downfall of the Guge kingdom in 1630.

The interesting Lhakhang Marpo entrance has a wood frame of three separate, concentric sub-frames. The inner two are carved with floral motifs, while the outer one is made of individual panels. Within each panel are carvings of various subjects. The transverse element of this sub-frame depicts Sakyamuni in meditation, and to his left are two angelic figures with long trumpets. The smaller, single panels have carvings of Sakyamuni, meditating ascetics, the king of Guge, elephants, etc. Most likely, the design of the frames originated from Kashmir. There is no precedent for this in Tibet and the three sub-frames make it all the more unusual. The carvings, however, are not Kashmiri but indigenous to West Tibet. Notice the two standing *bodhisattvas* at the bottom of the inner frame. Their rendering is similar to the chapel murals. The two deodar doors enclosed by the frames are original. Each door has three circular medallions inscribed with the *mantra* 'Om Mani Padme Hum'. This feature is unique in Tibet.

The large assembly hall has very high ceilings. All the beautiful statues seen by Tucci and Govinda were destroyed by the Red Guards and portions of the magnificent murals were damaged by water and vandalism. Nevertheless, they remain stunning works of art. Like the Lhakhang Karpo, this chapel is distinguished by the many slim columns used to support the roof. At one time, monumental gilt-bronze statues of Mitrukpa and Sakyamuni stood one in front of the other; Sakyamuni was the temple's central image. This type of alignment is not found in the Lhakhang Karpo. A *chörten* still exists at the right rear corner of the hall. Similar to the *tsangkhang* of the Lhakhang Karpo, the assembly hall's rear wall is decorated with small stucco figures of the 35 Buddhas of Confession. These have been cemented onto the wall and some of the higher

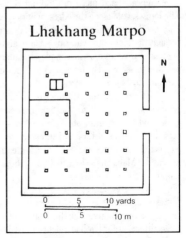

ones are intact. Most of the lower ones have been destroyed and some have only lotus bases. This state also applies to the stucco images next to the murals of the Eight Medicine Buddhas. The well-preserved ceiling has a skylight at the center rear of the hall. Its panels have painted mandalas in the center, but compared to those in the White Chapel, the decorative patterns are less geometric and more imaginative. This floral design was also used for the bases of statues.

Generally well-preserved and extremely fine murals dominate the assembly hall. The Lhakhang Karpo's indigenous West Tibet genre is considerably more stylized than this temple's noticeably more rigid works. This, however, is to a certain extent ameliorated by the use of floral decorations and lively representations of animals around the main figures. The *toranas*, haloes, and thrones of the divinities consist of a striking combination of flames, flowers, and mythical animals. A noticeable anomaly is empty space between the paintings reserved for inscriptions. Their absence perhaps indicates the repainting stopped just before disaster overtook the kingdom. In Tsaparang's other temples, inscriptions always accompany the murals. The content of the paintings reveals the religious preferences of Guge's royalty: the lion's share of wall space is given to the large Medicine Buddha and protective deities. (stucco figures of the favored 35 Budddhas of Confession are destroyed.)

The huge images of the principal divinities have the same arrangement: all flanked by two *bodhisattvas*. Elaborate floral and mythic animal *toranas*—beautiful, foliated arches— enclose the figures and have the same basic design as the stucco superstructure of the throne in the Lhakhang Karpo. Notice the convoluted tail of the mythical Kinnara bird, perched on a column, which blossoms into amazing, multi-colored whorls to become the *torana*. Other *toranas* are derived from the tails of the mythical water elephant and *makara*. This inspiration clearly came from Indian prototypes, found typically on Pala manuscript covers. Floating above the divinities are flying *apsaras*.

The artists of the Lhakhang Marpo paid outstanding attention to detail. For example, the halo and its subtle but elaborate red background all have different, individual motifs that never repeat. Each piece of clothing is painted different colors and with different designs. The lotuses, gold along the edges, are finely rendered to give the illusion of three-dimensionality. Subjects that show the artist's skill to advantage are the *dhotis* and scarves worn by the flanking *bodhisattvas*. Notice the paintings of animals under Mitrukpa. Their representations are extremely lively and inventive, each completely different from its neighbor. All are enclosed by vegetal mandala structures. The intricacies of these diverse elements and the execution of the monumental portraits are simply staggering.

The style of the paintings is quintessentially West Tibetan, derived from the Nepalese genre first propagated to the Sakyapa monasteries of Tsang. After its assimilation by local artists and the infusion of distinctive local traits, it traveled all the way to Tsaparang. Only very slight echoes of Kashmiri influence remain. The faces of the divinities are West Tibetan; Nepalese sensibilities are seen but the treatment is distinctly that of Guge. In some instances, such as the Mahakala's elongated torso, there is a similarity with the earlier style of the Lhakhang Karpo.

At the entrance, a panel depicts an epic battle between male and female protective deities and the forces of evil. Another portrays the figures of Vajrapani, Pratisara (female protector, one of five Pancharakshas), Dröljang, Chenresi, an unusual red Mahakala, an especially beautiful Drölkar (eight-armed Ushnishavijaya, who in Tibet is associated with the Buddha's mother), one more Drölkar, and Arapacana Manjusri. These paintings have not dete- riorated since Tucci's visit in 1933.

The registers below the large portraits have brilliantly colored scenes from the life of Sakyamuni (north side wall) and the construction and consecration of the Lhakhang Marpo (left of the entrance). The iconography and content here are similar to those of the Lhakhang Karpo. Life of the Buddha is a common theme throughout Tibet, but the ones here are among the most mature and accomplished. The composition is extraordinarily dense with tremendous wealth of details, movement, and richness of content; the colors are breathtaking. The narrative proceeds clockwise and progresses clearly and logically like a long scroll. This segment is not large and thus easy to miss. It is only 1 m high but in very good condition; an outstanding work of art.

The last panel (right of entrance) is a beautiful illustration of the eight *chörtens* that contained the Buddha's relics. Next to this are paintings of the auspicious symbols. Murals depicting the construction of the Lhakhang Marpo reveal the society and mores of the Guge court in the 16th century. One frame shows the king and queen in rich robes, seated on thrones under a canopy, surrounded by princes and nobility. By their feet, in a row, are gifts from foreign dignitaries (Kashmir, Garhwal). To the side are Kashmiris and Moslems, distinguished by their turbans. Caravans and pack animals carry construction material (huge tree trunks) to the site. There are charming scenes of dancing and festivities after the temple's construction and these include a Chinese-style lion dance, a tiny orchestra, and musicians. In the midst of the festivities sits the crowned Sakyamuni of the Amitayus. The style of these panels, basically derived from Tsang, is the same as the large divinity portraits. A perfect unity of artistic sensibilities exists between the diverse paintings of the chapel. They are noteworthy for exhibiting no Chinese or Indian stylistic influences, and for being indigenously Tibetan.

DORJE JIGJE LHAKHANG

The Dorje Jigje Lhakhang is a small doorless chapel, left of the path above the Lhakhang Marpo. Since the mid-1980s, the walls have been cleaned and the paintings are more legible than before although smudges and streaks remain. The statues have all been destroyed, and the capitals and columns are similar to those of the larger temples. Geometric patterns predominate in the ceiling panels but are less accomplished than those of the Lhakhang Marpo.

This iconographically complex temple has every inch of its walls covered with wrathful tantric figures like Guhyasamaja, Samvara (Demchok), and Hevajra (Kye Dorje). The central image is the famous, wrathful, buffalo-headed Dorje Jigje (Yamantaka). Left of the door is a huge painting of Mahasuvarna-Vaishravana, protector of the north and God of Wealth. He rides a roaring snow lion and in his left hand is the mythical animal that imparts wealth. The room is dominated by four life-size tutelary deities (*yidams*), the tantric deities with whom practitioners have a special relationship. In West Tibet, every fortress had a chapel dedicated to its *yidam*; Tsaparang's protector is Demchok.

On the right wall are two tantric forms of Heruka, an emanation of the Dhyani Buddha, Mitrukpa. Chakrasamvara is the four-headed, 12-armed figure. His two crossed arms embraced his consort, Vajravarahi. Next to him is Hevajra, five-headed, 16-armed, holding Nairatmya. The left side of the room consists of Guhyasamaja, a tantric form of Aksobhya and Guhyasamaja-Manjuvajra, central figures of the Guhyasamaja *tantra*. Surrounding the *yidams* are many smaller figures of Tara, Vajrapani, various *bodhisattvas*, and lamas. All eight forms of Tara are depicted and Vajrapani is shown in its many varieties. The most interesting is a *garuda* with golden wings. Next to Tara is the historical figure, Tilopa, and the yellow God of Death, Dorje Jigje. Below each figure is a black panel with gold inscription.

Unlike the Lhakhang Karpo and Lhakhang Marpo, the murals in the Dorje Jigje Lhakhang are closely related to the Central Tibetan style of the 15th and 16th centuries and similar to those of Gyantse (see page 412). The tantric figures are rendered in a bold manner; features and bodies are characterized by heaviness, even fatness. Heads are conspicuously oversized and the faces, bloated with circular, bulging eyes, have angry, snarling expressions. The red background haloes of flames (*prabhamandalas*) are very similar to those in the murals of the Gyantse Kumbum, consisting of complicated floral designs to represent tongues of fire. This type of halo is also found in the Nepalese paintings of the 15th and 16th centuries.

The figures in this chapel and Gyantse have much in common, although the facial features here are distinguished by round, full lines, and heavy folds. Dimensionality is created by the use of different color tones and the paintings appear vigorous and assertive. In Gyantse, the faces are flatter and more schematized. In some cases, macabre graveyard scenes are inserted randomly into the area immediately around the *prabhamandala*. This creates a sense of disorganization and breaks the unity, an aspect found only in this part of Tibet.

The paintings here are inferior to those of the larger temples; the small, minor figures that surround the large, principal ones are painted in considerably less detail and more crudely, as if the master painters, having dealt with the main deities, let their less accomplished apprentices work on the supporting elements. This simplification of the side images is pronounced and confined only to the Dorje Jigje Lhakhang. These somewhat less sophisticated murals were painted after the Lhakhang Marpo. In this chapel, it seems that the golden years of the Guge style had passed. The freshness and inventiveness are gone and the paintings become increasingly stereotyped. The amazing attention to detail, the vibrant colors, and the shaded, contoured figures that characterized the murals of the Lhakhang Marpo are to a significant extent lost. Depiction of the facial features is a striking example: the features and expressions in the larger temples are vital and strong, but here they lack perspective and depth. Nevertheless, the murals still convey a sense of power not found in many Central Tibet monasteries.

CHAPEL OF THE PREFECT

This small chapel near the Lhakhang Karpo, above the entrance to the ruins, belonged to the Tsaparang Dzong (prefecture). It is the first temple after the compound walls, to the left of the path.

Tsaparang was once one of Tibet's four prefectures (the others were Purang, Dawa Dzong, and Rutok) and the prefect lived here in the winter. During the summer, he moved north to Shangtse, a higher and cooler place. This chapel was his private shrine; his home was close by. By tradition, its proximity to the protector chapel of Dorje Jigje meant it was usually locked to avoid disturbing one of the most terrifying and powerful of deities. The red of the outside walls has faded and the door to the building is missing. Inside, the bare room of four columns has murals nearly completely blackened by fire and smoke. Some cleaning has been successful; the lower walls are considerably brighter than the upper.

This chapel's paintings are from the late 16th century. In the center of the rear wall is a portrait of Sakyamuni. Flanking him are Atisha (right) and Tsong Khapa (left), both wearing the typical Gelugpa headdress. Four figures, in the robes of learned lamas, surround the Buddha. The spaces between and beneath them are filled with bands of paintings that depict ascetics, supplicants, lamas, elephants, lions, and *bodhisattvas*. Some inscriptions can be seen in the lower level. Although nearly a century later than the larger chapels, they stem from the same stylistic source and are based on the same artistic developments current in 16th-C. West Tibet. Compared with those of the Lhakhang Marpo, the facial features of the principal figures are broader and rounder. There seems to be an overall flattening and stiffening of the forms. The large, elaborate Sakyamuni throne is spacious enough to allow two flanking *bodhisattvas* to stand on it. This throne treatment can be traced back to Nepalese art of the 15th–16th centuries. Flowing robes of the principal figures drape over the tops of the thrones and the folds fall vertically into multiple, stylized, schematic pleats. The fabric's geometric design resembles the famous Dege inlaid metal of some Central Tibetan monastery entrances. On the side wall right of the entrance is a beautiful painting of an emerald green horse with many arms. Its muzzle is particularly delightful. In the center of the capitals (different and cruder than the ones of the Lhakhang Marpo and Lhakhang Karpo) is carved the sacred six-syllable *mantra* 'Om mani padme hum'.

Compared to the beautiful works of the Lhakhang Marpo and Lhakhang Karpo, the paintings of this chapel are relatively uninspired. Guge's robust artistic powers had passed and the awesome creativity of the fallen kingdom had degenerated into mannerism and displayed a marked lack of vitality.

MANDALA (DEMCHOK) LHAKHANG

This small, red chapel is in the center of the palace precinct on top of Guge's ridge. It was a site of initiation rites and was dedicated to the Tsaparang protector, Demchok (Chakrasamvara), depicted in his 12-armed form in *yabyum* with his consort, Dorje Phagmo. Together they denote the union of emptiness and bliss. The king and his ministers came here to ask for protection and guidance in difficult times.

The chapel's entrance door frame is carved with images, vegetal designs, and mythical animals. (Another chamber, of later vintage, opens along the east side.) Four main beams span the ceiling, each with charmingly carved lions underneath. The round platform in the middle of the room has a three dimensional mandala (destroyed), consecrated to Demchok, that measured 2.5 m per side. This was the most outstanding object of worship. Constructed of wood and stucco, its top, forming part of the mandala, had 32 stucco statues of deities, eight in each cardinal direction. Now only the base of the structure remains.

On the walls are paintings of all divinities, and their wrathful incarnations, related to Demchok. The front wall depicts the two forms of the tantric protector, Nagpo Chenpo (Mahakala), and the *dakinis* of the mandala. The left and right walls show the cycles of Demchok and Kye Dorje (Hevajra), respectively. Towards the back, opposite the door, is the cycle of Sangdü (Guhyasamaja). Here are the Five Tathagatas garbed in rich *bodhisattva* ornaments and crowns. The deep blue Mitrukpa is at the center, left are Vairocana and Ratnasambhava, and right are Wöpame and Amogasiddhi. Along the side walls are five *dakinis*, each the same size as these figures. Each holds in tantric *yabyum* a Heruka of four faces and two arms. On the right side wall are the wrathful aspects, on the left the peaceful. The *dakinis*' bodies are very skinny and elongated—a rare characteristic.

The principal row of Tathagatas displays the same meticulous, minute details as the paintings of the Lhakhang Marpo. Gorgeous costumes and fabulously rendered fabrics are *de rigueur*. Treatment of the lotus petals is exceptional and the schematic cloud forms are painted in a Chinese manner. The faces and bodies are elongated, not as rounded as those in the Lhakhang Marpo; the waists are very narrow, the abdomens slightly bulging with a characteristic cleavage similar to the Lhakhang Karpo statues. The Five Tathagatas have well-developed, almost breast-like pectoral muscles, although their multiple arms are thin and spidery. These typical Kashmiri traits have been fully absorbed by indigenous Tibetan painters.

The style of these works, predominantly West Tibetan (Indian-derived), shows little influence from Sakyapa Tsang. Some art historians, notably Tucci and Huntington, concluded that the paintings here were probably later than those of the Lhakhang Marpo. This may not be correct. The works of the two temples represent only a variation on the same style; the details of both are essentially the same.

Along the central band of paintings is the deep blue figure of Candarmaharshana, a wrathful and important image in the mandala of Mitrukpa. Supposedly, only the initiated were allowed to see this deity and it was usually propitiated in secret. Its inclusion here is an indication of the temple's esoteric sacredness. The arrangement of the upper register of Tathagatas and *dakinis* is similar to that of the Lhakhang Karpo. A 0.5-m-high band of paintings runs beneath the murals. The panels depict the eight great cemeteries of India, which correspond to the four cardinal directions and four intermediate directions. There are macabre scenes of disembowelment by lions, tigers, and other wild animals and a striking image of a long-haired man impaled on a pole. These extraordinary works extend around the walls and the illustrations are copious; depictions of cemeteries are not all that common in Tibet's monasteries. Here also are images of the Eight Chörtens, the Eight Holy Mountains (including Kailash), the Eight Holy Trees, and the Eight Holy Waters. Meditators use these for visualization.

From top to bottom, the murals can be divided into five bands. The top one, just below the ceiling, is a decorative frieze. Below this is a narrow band of small figures of lamas, *mahasiddhas*, and ascetics. Then comes the main, large images of Tathagatas and *dakinis*. Immediately below them is another narrow row of small, naked *dakinis*. At the bottom is the register of India's sacred cemeteries

The interesting ceiling is constructed of a modified lantern style that encompasses the entire room. Its square, wooden panels are exceptionally beautiful and the cross beams are painted with various mythical animals. All are wonderfully preserved. The chamber has no windows and unless the door is open the room is in complete darkness.

Near the chapel are more than 10 small caves, the royal storehouses for weapons, ammunition, daily utensils, and Tibetan texts. At the southern end of this hilltop plateau is an open terrace with four walls, once the town square and entertainment center, and the palace kitchen is in a ruined courtyard. Near the terrace is a pile of stones to be hurled at enemies. The eastern slopes are protected by a long wall that encircles this portion of the complex; the western side is sheer and inaccessible. A 2-km-long stone aqueduct at the bottom of the mountain provided drinking water via a secret tunnel.

LOTANG LHAKHANG

The Lotang chapel, on the plain across a small river from the Tsaparang ruins, is sited close to the eastern base of the Guge ridge. It was known locally as the Lotsawa Lhakhang, the *lotsawa* (translator) feasibly being Rinchen Zangpo. This interesting monument can be traced directly to the great translator himself; like most temples built by him, it is not on a hill or slope but rather on a flat plain. The plan and design are typical of Rinchen Zangpo, although the damaged structure postdates the 11th century. It has an atrium and niche-like inner chapel. To reach it, ford the river and walk up its right bank to the plain. The roofless chapel has no paintings or sculptures left. Its walls used to be covered with 15th-C. paintings and the statues consisted of Sakyamuni, Vairocana, and the Medicine Buddhas.

GREAT MULTI-CHAPEL CHÖRTENS

Until recently, the magnificent Gyantse Kumbum was thought to be the sole large multi-chapel *chörten* in Tibet. In 1987, however, the Chung Riwoche *chörten*, strikingly located on the banks of the Tsangpo, was discovered to be intact. Within its myriad chapels are 15th-C. paintings considered the forerunners of the Tibetan style of art that dominated the country's artistic sensibilities in the following centuries. Jonang and Jampaling, two other monumental *chörtens*, have now been renovated; the former still retains important murals in its chapels.

GYANTSE KUMBUM: A MONUMENTAL SHOWCASE FOR 15TH-CENTURY PAINTERS

By Roberto Vitali

The Gyantse Kumbum is a monumental *chörten* whose architecture is peculiar to Tibetan Buddhism. Constructed of multi-leveled rows of superimposed chapels, this pyramidal structure is of a type called Tashi Gomang. Kumbum denotes 100,000 images and the term derives from the proliferation of divine images in the myriad chapels.

Gyantse Kumbum is perhaps the most important *chörten* of this kind ever built in Tibet. Others have survived (Jonang, Riwoche, Gyang, Jampaling), but most have been irreparably damaged and none can compare to the majestic Gyantse Kumbum in terms of design and artistic contents. The only exception is perhaps the Chung Riwoche *chörten* (see page 451), located on the Tsangpo's north bank, west of Lhatse.

Within Gyantse's eight-story *chörten* are innumerable murals in excellent condition. Its statues, however, have suffered recent damage, and having been restored (some drastically), they have less artistic significance. The *kumbum* has 64 chapels in its four lowest floors. These give shape to its steeped architectural foundation (*bangrim*), the distinguishing characteristic of this type of *chörten*. Each story of the *bangrim* has chapels organized in rows along every side. Central chapels at each point of the compass are much larger than the others. They take up two floors instead of one and usurp the space of the corresponding central chapels on the level immediately above. Hence, only the first and third floors have two-story chapels, while the second and fourth lack them. Moreover, because the *bangrim* is tapered, the chapels decrease in size in successive levels. Thus, for example, on the fourth floor, because of insufficient space, some closed doors are in fact nonexistent chapels. The number of chapels per story varies. Additionally, each story's flight of stairs, considered a sacred space, equals one chapel.

The *bangrim*'s 68 chapels are arranged as follows:

First floor: 20
Second floor: 16
Third floor: 20
Fourth floor: 12

The fifth floor has only four chapels, each similar in size to the central rooms of the first and third storys. This level constitutes the *chörten's bumpa*, or bell—the spherical section of the monument. On each of the sixth and seventh floors, a corridor runs along all four sides around a central cubic structure, thus forming a four-winged chapel. Finally, a single chapel on the eighth floor (with an open terrace above it) crowns the whole. The seventh and eighth storys are bound in their exterior by an umbrella, the metallic, conical part of the *chörten*.

All central chapels have a shrine against the rear wall opposite the door; the flanking minor chapels almost always have theirs against a side wall. Some chapels, especially at the *bangrim*'s higher levels, are quite small. Access to each is by an external walkway. The fifth floor's four large chapels are reached either by passing internally from one chapel to the other or externally by a platform.

The *kumbum*'s main entrance opens to the south, the same direction as the Palkhor Chöde (see page 419). Internal stairs of the first four storeys are located on the eastern side at its south corner. Above these levels, the stairs move away from this specific coordinate, following an irregular pattern. The conception of the *chörten* implies a customary clockwise circumambulation, yet the very location of the first story's stairs does not allow a complete tour of all chapels in a single circumambulation; it is necessary to perform two rounds.

ART STYLES

The art styles adopted in the *kumbum* do not generally differ from those of the Palkhor Chöde. However, there is one important departure. In the *chörten*, no works of Newar origin exist. The Newar-style relics in the Gyantse castle's top-most chapel (Shalyekhang) were painted prior to the *kumbum*'s founding. The Palkhor Chöde's Dorje Ying and royal chapels contain Newar-influenced paintings executed during the construction of the great *chörten*. It is quite feasible that the artists of Palkhor Chöde did not work on both monuments; the *kumbum* thus was an exclusively Tibetan artistic endeavour. Inscriptions in the individual chapels testify in all cases that the artists were Tibetans. Four art styles can be identified:

(For more information on these four styles, see Palkhor Chöde, page 423.)

1) The most common style in the *kumbum* is the 'Gyantse main style'. Most chapel murals on the first four floors and all of those in the three storys directly above the *bangrim* are exclusively painted in this dominating idiom (the topmost floor has no pictorial or sculptural traces attributable to the 15th century).

2) The 'Kumbum narrative style', dating from after 1427, can be seen within the central chapels on the *kumbum*'s ground floor and nowhere else. This style is well adapted to

the conception of paradises where deities inhabit diverse heavens made up of naturalistic landscapes. Murals depicting paradises are housed exclusively in these chapels. This narrative sytye has close links, in its essential features, to the 'Gyantse main style'. The images are outlined with rounded, fluent lines, and the palette of the narrative murals is characterized by a more restrained, softer use of shades. This variation embodies an idyllic impression absent in the bolder 'Gyantse main style'.

3) A third sub-style, the 'Kumbum variation', dating to after 1427 and before 1431, is unique to this *chörten*. Found especially on the ground floor, its characteristics include the use of a darker, more simplified palette than the 'Gyantse main style'. The deities are less profusely ornamented and their physiognomies leaner and more nervous. The general feeling is that these murals are slightly less exuberant than those of the 'Gyantse main style'.

4) In the topmost floors of the *kumbum* (seventh and eighth), the painted and sculpted works of art were executed in 1472–73 by a successor of Rabtan Kunsang Phag. Their style reveals a simplification in both the composing traits of the images and the choice of tonalities. This in turn holds the first seeds of decadence, since its main features reveal a subtle, yet evident degree of stiffness and mannerism. This idiom can be aptly called the 'Kumbum late style'.

OTHER BUILDINGS AND RELICS

A spectacular feature of Gyantse is the imposing walls and fortifications that encircle the monastic complex. Although large boundary walls were common in ancient Tibet, no other town has anything comparable. The walls were built in 1425, when Rabtan Kunsang Phag completed the construction of the Palkhor Chöde. It is not known why the fortifications are so substantial; the natural configuration of the castle's cliff constituted adequate protection and there was no need for such massive walls.

The prince of Gyantse not only paid special attention to the construction of holy edifices but also tried to give Gyantse a properly organized lay structure. He erected a bridge, described as magnificent, on the Gyantse River. Its loss deprives us of an important clue to 15th-C. lay architecture, as the bridge seems to have had a *chörten* incorporated in it. Religious colleges (recently

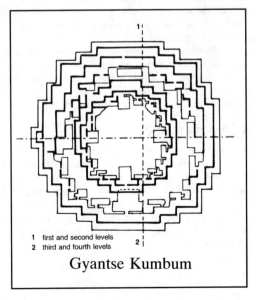

1 first and second levels
2 third and fourth levels

Gyantse Kumbum

destroyed) once stood inside the huge walls. They belonged to three sects active at Gyantse: the Sakyapa, Shalupa, and Gelugpa. Their presence gave a crowded look (missing today) to the Palkhor Chöde Kumbum complex.

THE ARTISTS

Literary sources and inscriptions in the temples help identify Gyantse's artists. Some Newar artists may have worked here, but their contribution must be considered marginal. The main building and its decorations were a purely Tibetan affair and inscriptions in the *kumbum* prove this point: names of the artists and their place of origin are given, and there is no doubt that during the Kumbum's construction (1418–27), a local art school flourished here. Except for a few isolated cases, no names are given in the Palkhor Chöde inscriptions, but it is reasonable to deduce that the artists responsible for the *kumbum* also helped with the Palkhor Chöde chapels. This conjecture is based on the similarity of styles, especially in the case of the 'Gyantse main style'.

The art of the Gyantse Castle is more complex and mysterious. In this earliest building phase at Gyantse (1390–97), when the first religious art of the Sharkhapas' main seat appeared, the artists' identity is obscure. Inscriptions imply that they were local.

According to epigraphical evidence in the *kumbum*, the 'Gyantse main style' penetrated and took hold in the following places: Nenying (southeast of Gyantse), Nyemo (northeast of Gyantse) and, more than anywhere else, Lhatse. Epigraphy proves that many artists originally from Lhatse came to Gyantse to practise their style. In the region centered on Lhatse, the Latö style, aesthetically more provincial, was very popular and well diffused during the same period. The concomitant presence of the two styles (Gyantse and Latö), and in particular the fact that the Latö style was less accomplished, serve to underline the cosmopolitan nature of the Gyantse idiom.

Newari art at Gyantse was of marginal importance. The paintings of the Shalyekhang (Gyantse Castle) represent a close rendering of the fundamental, undiluted Newari style. It stood apart from the rest of Gyantse's artistic production and shared little with the innovative 'Gyantse main style', a form also popular at the Ming court. The obvious intersection of the two styles derives from the fact that the original source of inspiration at Gyantse was Newar.

CONCLUSION

The Gyantse styles, although stemming from a limited area, reveal a high degree of cosmopolitanism. They were a direct result of contacts with the Chinese court, which enabled Gyantse's indigenous artists to operate in an international milieu. Whether the masters actually traveled to China to work on Lamaist subjects is not known, although their own iconographic models (bronzes, paintings) almost certainly made the trip with Tibetan delegations. The art of Gyantse is a rare case of Tibetan idioms influencing foreign art; during almost all periods in Tibetan art history, the reverse is true. This is probably the greatest legacy of Gyantse's art.

CHUNG RIWOCHE:
A TANGTON GYALPO CHÖRTEN

Vestiges of extant Latö-style murals

OVERVIEW

The Chung Riwoche Kumbum, an impressive multi-chapel *chörten* on the Tsangpos' north bank, is a one-week walk north of Dingri. It was founded by the celebrated bridge builder, Tangton Gyalpo, in the mid-15th C. and, because of its isolation, miraculously escaped destruction by both the Mongols in the 18th C. and the Red Guards in the 1960s. Examples of early Tibetan painting still survive within the many chapels, representing the very beginnings of a distinctive Tibetan genre. With influences from China and Nepal, these works are the first tentative attempts by Tibetan artists to achieve a mature art style, now called the Latö school. It co-existed with the art of Gyantse (see page 412) between the mid-14th and mid-15th century.

Chung Riwoche's paintings were significantly inspired by the murals of the Yumchenmo Lhakhang at Shalu Monastery (see page 407). However, the artists were no longer content merely to imitate masters from other lands. They forged a new synthesis, a local interpretation of foreign concepts that at the same time provides valuable insights into the genesis of Tibetan art. From these modest beginnings at Chung Riwoche and other similar *chörtens* (Gyantse, Jonang, Gyang Bumoche), a uniform style of painting spread throughout Tibet.

Access (Map reference NH45-10 D)

There are two principal ways to reach the *chörten*. One is by road from Lhatse (there are no buses), the other by foot from Dingri (see page 456). The Landcruiser or jeep trip from Lhatse to Chung Riwoche takes 5 hr or longer; the uncertain Tsangpo ferry schedule might add 2 1/2 hr if you happen to arrive during the sacrosanct lunchtime. It is difficult to hitchhike from Lhatse; the route after Kaga (near Ngamring Xian) is especially troublesome. Very few vehicles ply this section, so expect a long wait in Kaga before catching a ride. In general, to get to Riwoche, there is little option but to rent a car from Lhasa.

The route

Lhatse–Tsangpo ferry	8 km	ferry rarely operates between 1230 and 1500 and after 1800
Ferry–Kaga	51 km	
Kaga–Dorbai	60 km	
Dorbai–Chung Riwoche	20 km	

The indistinct dirt road turnoff to Chung Riwoche goes left 0.5 km before Kaga. It is necessary to pay close attention so that the driver will not miss the turn. (If the road is in good shape, it takes 3–3 1/2 hr to the *chörten* from the turnoff by Landcruiser.) From here the road immediately ascends the range. Reach a low pass in 13 km (nomad tents before the pass), then another one in 8 km more. Look out for a large red rock and shrine with prayer flags just beyond.

The few modest dwellings en route are built of bricks of turf cut from the earth. Soon the road bears sharply left to enter a narrow gorge, 28 km from the turnoff. A pretty, prominent village is at the entrance. In 6 km, the gorge widens and its eroded sides are reminiscent of the fantastic canyons of West Tibet. Beyond the gorge flows the Tsangpo, here only 50 m wide. Follow the north bank west for 5 km to an iron-chain bridge.

Cross the bridge and head west along the Tsangpo's south bank. Another dirt road follows the north bank; it is in poorer condition than the southern one. Pass villages along the way, each 5–10 km apart. Reach Dorbai Qu, 60 km from the turnoff. 6 km further is the village of A and 6 km beyond is a ruined *chörten*. The Tsangpo here is wide with many channels. About 2 km after this are prayer flags and unusual stone dwellings only 1 m high— perhaps the superstructures of subterranean shelters. At this point, Chung Riwoche's large, striking *chörten* can be seen across the river. The road climbs a rise and then descends to a village. Here the Tsangpo turns dramatically to the north. Follow it to an iron-chain bridge and cross the swaying structure to the bright-yellow (newly painted) Chung Riwoche *chörten*.

To visit Chung Riwoche by car, go during the dry months of spring and autumn. Flooding of the Tsangpo and its tributaries in the summer can make the journey considerably more difficult. Along the way, there is primitive accommodation in Dorbai Qu, A, or Chung Riwoche. Bring a warm sleeping bag.

The site

The *chörten* is at the base of a craggy hill called Pal Riwoche, crowned by the ruins of the Chung Riwoche Monastery. Its surviving walls give a good idea of the complex's unusual architecture and layout. Near the *chörten*, spanning the Tsangpo, are two iron-chain bridges. The closest one is newer and can handle vehicles; the far one is a rare, authentic Tangton Gyalpo bridge. About 1 km east of Chung Riwoche on a rocky hill is Chukenda Monastery (destroyed). A side valley here leads north to Sangsang, a staging post on the main Lhatse–West Tibet road.

THE CHÖRTEN

The Chung Riwoche Kumbum stands at the north end of Riwoche Qu (formerly Chung Dongzhur). In the village center is the *qu*'s small compound. If the upper chapels of the *chörten* are locked, appeal here to the commune secretary (*shuji*) for permission to enter. The *chörten* is slightly smaller than the Gyantse Kumbum. Its top, consisting of round bell and gilded spire, was destroyed during the Cultural Revolution. The bottom half suffered some damage but the structure is essentially intact. In 1988, the bell was restored. Four sets of huge, painted eyes look out in the four directions from each of the first four floors. The *chörten* has eight storys (nine with the basement). An unusual feature: along the eastern base is a double wall that served as the encircling *khorlam*; the outer wall has niches at regular intervals that once held images. The other three perimeter walls lack this enclosed path; they were probably built at different periods.

Enter the *chörten* through a door at the northeast corner that leads into the basement via a narrow flight of stone stairs. This floor serves as an interior *khorlam* along the entire circumference of the base. This design is unique. There are no chapels here, and the corridor walls are painted with three rows of Buddhas of the Golden Age, most of them faded and in poor condition.

Another flight of narrow stairs leads to the second floor. This and the next three constitute the *chörten's* lower section, known as *bangrim*. An open-air platform encircles the floor and gives access to each of the 20 chapels, five per side. Most are of uniform size, measuring approximately 3 m wide, 1.5 m deep, and 2.5 high. Typically, in the center of the rear wall is a cubic niche and on its three side faces are painted three figures (usually standing) of divinities. Flanking the niche, and on the chapel's side walls, are six intricate Mandalas. These are all painted about 0.5 m from the ground and extend to the ceiling. Mandalas are typical of Sakyapa monasteries founded between the 14th and 16th C. and are rarely seen in temples of other religious orders. The Sakyapa Mandalas are excellent examples of the so-called Sakyapa style of painting, which developed largely through the efforts of Newari artists invited to Tibet by the great Sakya lamas of the 14th century. Most of the Mandalas and painted figures in the *chörten* exhibit some damage. Only rarely have entire Mandalas or whole figures survived and, in some chapels, all walls have been rebuilt and no vestige of old painting remains.

Three of the second floor chapels are locked. One, located within the third room, contains the interior passage to the third floor. Once this is unlocked, all the other floors can be reached. The positioning of the stairways, each within its own room along the *khora* of each floor, is unique: individual stairways are configured along different points of the compass. The third, fourth, and fifth floors of the *bangrim* all have 20 chapels each, the chambers becoming progressively smaller on ascending.

Within the large dome-like bell (*bumpa*) are two circular floors, the sixth and seventh levels. Each of these is surrounded by a circular *khorlam*. Many of the walls have been rebuilt and only the bottom circular floor has original murals. At the four directions of the lower circular floor, inset within the inside walls, are the remains of lotus pedestals of large clay statues destroyed during the Cultural Revolution. Each image must have been at least 2 m tall. The renovated upper story probably contained large sculptures as well. No paintings survive on these two floors, except fragments on the lower *khorlam's* internal and external walls. On top of the bell is another level with four small chapels at the cardinal directions. An open, circular roof terrace with a low perimeter wall constitutes the eighth floor and the *chörten's* apex. From here are good views of the Tsangpo Valley.

ARCHITECTURE AND ART

The following section is a summary from Roberto Vitali's *The Early Temples of Central Tibet.*

Before their destruction in the Cultural Revolution, multi-chapel *chörtens* similar to Chung Riwoche and Gyantse included Tröphu, Narthang, Tshal Gungthang, Jonang, Gyang Bumoche,

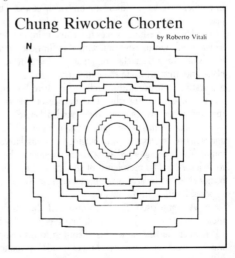

Chung Riwoche Chorten

by Roberto Vitali

N

and Jampaling. The architecture of Jonang (restored) and especially Gyang Bumoche (destroyed) is very close to Riwoche. An unusual feature common to all three is the existence of an internal *khorlam* that encircles the floors within the bell (*bumpa*). Another characteristic is the organization of the chapels within the *bangrim*. The four floors of Chung Riwoche's *bangrim* retain the same number of chapels on each floor despite the *chörten's* progressive upward tapering; the chapels simply diminish in size. However, this reduction of floor space as the building gains height is most dramatically shown at Gyantse. Chung Riwoche and Jonang are also distinguished by the central chapel on each floor of the *bangrim* having only one story. At Gyantse and Gyang Bumoche, the central chapels have two storys. The intimate connection of the master bridge builder, Tangton Gyalpo, with these *chörtens* is certainly a factor in their similarity.

Mandalas dominate the murals of the *bangrim* chapels. Their style, although more provincial and less accomplished than that of Gyantse, is similar to the Sakyapa mandalas. Some of these retain a shiny outer coat and have the same deep, bright underlying colors (reds, blues, greens) of the Sakyapa. Others, lacking this protective coat, have soft pastel colors, the hallmark of Chung Riwoche's paintings.

Perhaps the most exciting works are the paintings within the chapels' central niches. The rear panel of the niche usually depicts a Buddha, while *bodhisattvas* and other secondary images adorn the flanking sides. Most of these are characterized by a fresh and charming simplicity. The sparse brush strokes are executed rapidly to produce an impressionistic effect. This is well demonstrated in the depiction of trees and clouds, for which there are no strict iconographic rules. Elaborate details are forsaken in favor of imagination and spirit. Thick black lines enclose many of the peripheral objects next to the principal figures, which are painted in a more traditional Sakya style. Oval faces of the seated Sakyamunis generally lack shading. Their eyes and lips are small but the shoulders are big and rounded and over the heads are double haloes, treated with different tones. In contrast, lamas accompanying the Buddhas are shown in profile, have large bodies, and unshapely gowns. The few *bodhisattvas* have unusual crowns placed high on their skulls, necessitated by their protruding foreheads.

These refreshing, somewhat naive paintings differ from the common murals found in so many Tibetan monasteries, with their intricate, mind-numbing details. Exceptions are the murals of Gyang Bumoche and Jonang. Another feature common to these three are the thick, black lines that delineate the minor figures and ornaments. However, the device of portraying a narrative sequence within individual square frames exists at Jonang and Gyang Bumoche but not at Chung Riwoche. The absence of this ancient technique here perhaps indicates that the other two *chörtens* were founded before Chung Riwoche.

Jonang's images are quite similar to those of Chung Riwoche—stocky, full-bodied monks and elongated *bodhisattvas* with bulging foreheads. However, there are differences. At the former, minor figures are grouped in semi-circles around the main deities. This trait can be traced to India. Also, the prevalence of shading and the distinctive construction of the heads and bodies of seated *bodhisattvas* imply a post-Pala/Newar inspiration. This style in Tibet is usually associated with 14th-C. murals.

A comparison of the paintings of the three *chörtens* supports the authenticity of their founding dates. Jonang, built by Dolpopa (d 1361), was probably constructed just before 1354, when he bequeathed his abbotship to his disciple, Chogle Namgyal. Gyang Bumoche was the work of Sonam Tashi (1351–1417); young Tangton Gyalpo was in attendance during its construction. This puts its foundation date within the first 15 years of the 15th century. Chung Riwoche, latest of the three, was started in 1449, but only completed in 1456.

SOURCE OF THE STYLE

The genesis of the art style of Jonang, Gyang Bumoche, and Chung Riwoche goes back to Shalu Monastery. Within the Shalu Yumchenmo Lhakhang's *khorlam* are the superb paintings that provided the original inspiration. They were created by seasoned masters and appear far more accomplished and imaginative in their use of colors and depiction of details than anything at Chung Riwoche. There is no doubt, however, that underlying traits link the *chörten* murals here with those of Yumchenmo. The physiognomy of Sakyamuni and the monks graphically illustrate how the genre developed from its inception at Shalu to its final stage at Chung Riwoche. The Yumchenmo Lhakhang was built in the first decade of the 14th C., and the source of its paintings is primarily Nepalese Newar. The facial features of the images and the distinctive use of colors are quintessentially Nepalese. However, Chinese influence is apparent in the clouds, the Four Guardian Kings, and the landscapes. In the early 14th C., China was under Mongol rule and Newar artists were sent by the Sakya patriarchs to the Yuan court to decorate imperial monuments. The most famous of these was Arniko. After immersing themselves in Chinese sensibilities, these artists returned to Tibet and slowly developed a new art form. Shalu was its first manifestation. Later it appeared at Jonang; its images, painted by local artists, were the closest to Yumchenmo's chapel. Still later, the genre moved to Gyang Bumoche and finally to Chung Riwoche. With each move, the original became increasingly modified by local interpretation. At Chung Riwoche, the departure was so great that it is possible to identify an independent style—one that nevertheless retains Shalu characteristics.

THE LATÖ STYLE OF PAINTINGS

The location of Chung Riwoche, Jonang, and Gyang Bumoche in the same district of Latö gives credence to the possible existence of a local art school at the time of Tangton Gyalpo. This supposition is reinforced by an action of Sonam Tashi, builder of Gyang Bumoche. Instead of drawing on the expertise of Sakyapa painters, he used local artists familiar with the genre. They and others probably formed an indigenous school in Latö. Tangton Gyalpo's biography also mentions that artists from Lho and Byang (identified with parts of Latö) came to Riwoche to decorate the *chörten*.

The founding of Jonang, Gyang Bumoche, and Riwoche more or less coincided with the completion of the Gyantse Kumbum (erected between 1390 and 1417) and Gyantse Dzong (completed 1390). Jonang's foundation ca 1350 implies that the Latö art school, on the borders of Tsang, flourished before the Gyantse school (Gyantse, Nenying, Narthang, Lhatse). Thus, two separate idioms existed in central and western Tsang between the mid-14th and mid-15th centuries.

The Latö school, represented by the paintings of the three *chörtens*, was not the forerunner of the Gyantse school, but rather a separate and fully autonomous body that worked independently of Gyantse. The style of Gyantse, basically derived from Nepal, was more cosmopolitan and open to influences from Ming China, whereas the Latö school, although initially Nepalese-Yuan in inspiration, was strongly modified by local traits.

Chung Riwoche: A nine-day trek from Dingri

Location	North of Dingri
Map reference	NH45-14 B, 45-10 D
Trekking days	9
Start–Finish	Dingri–Chung Riwoche–Sangsang (one-way)
Passes	Mön, Kura, Sangsang Pay

This route, an old trade artery, goes north from Dingri to the ancient multi-chapel *chörten* of Chung Riwoche. Traversing the gap between the mountains of Burtra (west) and Tzipri (east), the route then crosses the gentle Mön La Pass, which straddles the lower reaches of the Kang Tise Range. Beyond the pass are nomad settlements with their characteristic black yak-hair tents. Chung Riwoche is further, on the north bank of the Tsangpo. After leaving the monastery and its large *chörten*, a good trail continues north to the roadhead at Sangsang via the low Sangsang Pay La. From here, hitch a ride east to Lhatse and then to points east or west. Settlements along the way have food and water, but it is best to take along a tent for this trek, since one small section is quite isolated. However, most people should have no difficulty in completing the trek by staying in villages.

Related sections
Lapchi, p 248
Mt Everest, p 895
Dingri, p 918
Tzipri, p 921

Access
Dingri on the Friendship Highway (see page 250)

Time Chart

Day	Place	Hours
1	Dingri–Camp 1	3 1/2
2	Camp 2	5 1/4
3	Camp 3	4
4	Camp 4	3
5	Camp 5	3 1/4
6	Camp 6	4
7	Chung Riwoche	1
8	Camp 7	2 3/4
9	Sangsang	6 3/4

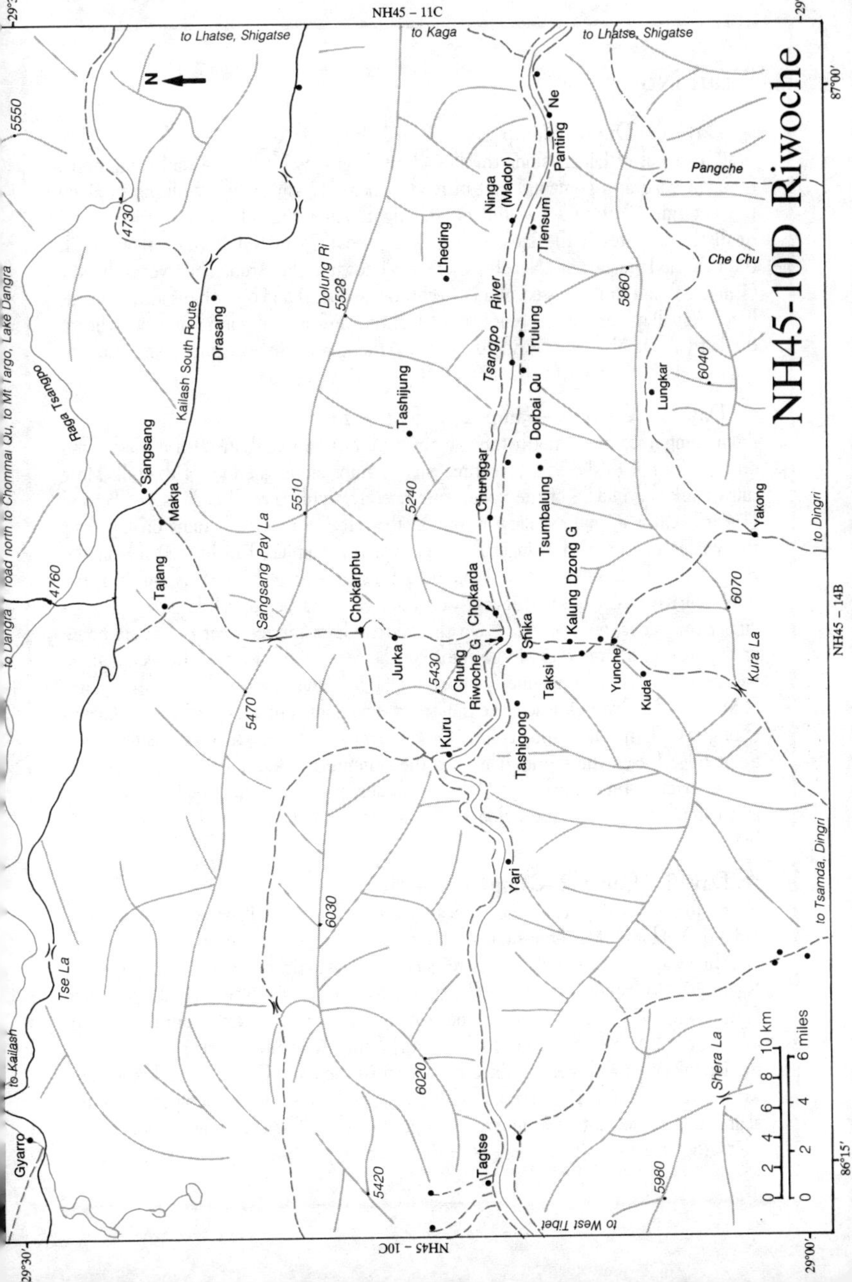

NH45 – 11C

to Lhatse, Shigatse

to Kaga

to Lhatse, Shigatse

N

29°30'

29°00'

87°00'

5550

4730

Dolung Ri 5528

Kailash South Route

Drasang

Lheding

Ninga (Mador)

Panting Ne

Pangche

Che Chu

Tashjung

Tsangpo River

Trulung

5860

Lungkar

6040

Raga Tsangpo

Sangsang

Makja

Tajang

Sangsang Pay La

5510

5240

Dorbai Qu

Chunggar

Tsumbalung

Kalung Dzong G

Yakong

to Dingri

to Langra | road north to Chommai Qu, to Mt Targo, Lake Dangra

4760

5470

Chökarphu

Jurka

5430

Chung Riwoche G

Chökarda

Shika

Taksi

Yunche

Kuda

6070

Kura La

NH45 – 14B

Kuru

Tashigong

Yari

6030

to Kailash

Tse La

Gyarro

6020

to West Tibet

5420

Tagtse

Shera La

5980

to Tsamda, Dingri

NH45 – 10C

29°00'

86°15'

NH45-10D Riwoche

0 2 4 6 8 10 km
0 2 4 6 miles

Trail Notes

✧ Day 1   Dingri–Camp 1   3 1/2 hr

Walk east out of Dingri along the Friendship Highway. Look for a trail going north from the road at a point just east of road marker 539 km (1 hr). Walk north along the flat trail, skirting a low hill on the right. After the hill, wade across several small rivers to reach the large Phung Chu (about 75 m wide) which flows south through the Himalayas to Nepal—where it is known as the Arun. The river is shallow (1 m deep) and easily crossed. Water fowl (orange ducks) and other birds are numerous here. A valley entrance appears straight ahead and a cold spring and pool lie to the left (west). Above the spring is a rock overhang with three distinct compartments; a good place to camp (1 1/2 hr).

✧ Day 2   Camp 1–Camp 2   5 1/4 hr

From camp 1 continue north through the valley entrance. Ruins of a fortress stand on top of a hill to the east, and three smaller ruins are at the foot of the hill. More ruins mark the middle of the valley entrance. The village of Shimde is just beyond (1/4 hr). Cross a small, shallow river. On the left is a rock with ruins on top. Pass the village of Lingsharr (Lingcha) to reach a reservoir (200 m by 300 m) on the right (1 1/2 hr from camp). Jagged, rocky hills lie east of here. This valley of the Lobo Chu River cuts through the east–west Tzipri Range (a sacred, well-known pilgrimage circles this range, see page 922). On the north side of the reservoir is a single house at the base of a large rock. More ruins can be seen to the west of the well-defined path. Go through a commune (compound) (1 hr), and beyond it reach the village of Manju (Mankhyung), where the trail splits. The right path goes northeast to Khansa (Kongtsa). Do not take this. Follow the one straight ahead, which begins to ascend a flat ridge (reach the top in 1 hr from the commune). Descend the ridge and cross a river over a 4-m-long bridge (1 hr). Bear left past some ruins lying in a valley, and camp next to a house belonging to a friendly old man named Rinchen (1/2 hr).

✧ Day 3   Camp 2–Camp 3   4 hr

Soon after this camp, continue to bear left to reach the village and monastery of Yölcho (Yöldong). Mountains encroach on both sides. A cave lies west of the village (1/2 hr away). A side trail near here goes northeast (right) to the Tsangpo River, Ngamring Monastery, and Lhatse. Follow the main trail, which now climbs gradually. Further on, to the left, is a cave and a house (1/2 hr). The trail continues north, following the Lobo Chu along its left (east) bank. A mountain cave on the left is the landmark for a cluster of ruined houses across the river. One is a small monastery with statues of Tara (Drölma) and Mahakala. (It appears that the inhabitants of the abandoned settlement have moved to larger villages.) The trail now detours to the west around a hill with several caves (a side valley opens to the northeast of the

➧

hill). Continue north. A row of six *chörtens*, each 1 1/2 m tall, appears on the left perimeter of the valley. The valley now narrows and the trail meets a spring which emerges from the rocks on the right (1 hr). The Lobo Chu now veers northwest, flowing from a side valley to the left. Do not follow the river any more, but rather continue due north. The valley becomes very narrow and the approach to the Mön (Me) La begins (the ascent is gradual). Keep to the trail, which follows a small river (1 m deep); ford it easily. The Mön La (5224 m) is reached in 2 1/2 hr from the spring (a 5809-m peak rises 10 km northwest of the pass). This pass traverses the Kang Tise, also known as the Ladakh Range, and its far side is dry and barren, consisting mostly of rolling hills. Water is available, however. A camp, 1/2 hr below the pass, has a tiny river on the right (east).

✧ Day 4   Camp 3–Camp 4   3 hr
Below the camp, pass some nomad settlements. The entire valley is a parched tableland covered with grassy hummocks and sand. Cross the river to its right (east) bank after 1 hr, then reach a stone and sod animal shelter. Black tents rise west of the river and near the trail. A range of mountains looms straight ahead and a side valley goes off to the left. Continue to follow the river. At the northern end of the broad valley, where it is blocked by mountains, the trail splits. One goes left and the other goes right to the northeast. Take this second trail to follow the Pardrok River. Camp within the entrance of the valley (2 hr after crossing the river).

✧ Day 5   Camp 4–Camp 5   3 1/4 hr
In 1/2 hr cross a solid stone-and-earth bridge to the river's left bank. Chakpa Village is left of the trail (1/2 hr). Pass piles of *mani* stones. Ahead, a saddle-shaped spur forces the river and trail to the left (north-northeast). Reach a village with nine houses (1 3/4 hr from Chakpa). Here the valley splits in three: one branch goes north-northeast, one goes northwest, and one to the west. Take the middle valley and camp at its entrance (1/2 hr). From here on, habitation and cultivation increase. If you are not sure of the route, ask for directions to Chung Riwoche *gompa*. Everybody knows it.

✧ Day 6   Camp 5–Camp 6   4 hr
The trail ascending the middle valley stays close to the right (east) slopes above the valley floor. In 1 hr reach the Kure La Pass (5498 m). On its far side, a secondary valley goes to the right. Do not follow this valley, but descend the one to the left. Cross over a hill, then drop steeply to the west. In 1 hr the trail turns north. Pass an animal shelter west of the trail, then another large, square shelter in 3/4 hr. The village of Pua, in three sections, lies west of this second shelter at the valley's west side. Here verdant green fields can be seen once again. A mountain west of the village has a long, thin waterfall. Continue north. About 3/4 hr after the square animal shelter, two *chörtens* appear near the eastern wall of the valley. Pass ruins and a cave to the right of the trail. In 1/2 hr reach a scattered settlement. Yunche

Village is further west of the valley. Camp beyond this village (a side valley goes left). The local children can be overly curious and obnoxious; stay some distance from the houses. The main valley is populated and cultivated with barley fields. It is possible to hire donkeys here.

✧ Day 7   Camp 6–Chung Riwoche Monastery   1 hr

Continue north along the main valley. Kalung Dzong (locked) stands on a hill on the valley's left side. Further along are ruins on the slopes to the left. About 1 hr from camp reach Taksi Village on the west slopes. Beyond, the valley opens up to join the east–west trending Tsangpo Valley. Shika Village lies west of this junction. The Tsangpo flows from northwest to southeast at this point. The trail now turns slightly to the north–northeast to cross the Tsangpo on a wide, wood bridge able to support motor vehicles. The dramatic Chung Riwoche *chörten* is sited across the bridge and to the east. A large village and district office (*qu*) lie at its base. One of the very few original Tangton Gyalpo iron bridges (see page 379) spans the Tsangpo near the *chörten*. The surroundings are delightful; plan on staying at least a day to see the *chörten*, bridge, and the very interesting monastery ruins atop a ridge. Try to get a lift east to Ngamring (see page 947) and the main road if you do not want to continue walking to Sangsang. Expect a long wait, as traffic is sparse.

✧ Day 8   Chung Riwoche–Camp 7   2 3/4 hr

Walk northeast from Chung Riwoche to a rounded ridge with striking ruins on top. Turn left (west) around it to enter a narrow valley running north. The constricted valley entrance is only 75–100 m wide (a separate valley leading to an open plateau goes right, to the northeast). A river flows left (west) of the trail, yet the valley is arid. In 1 3/4 hr, the village of Nanse appears on top of a hill west of the river. Pass ruins west of the river, then reach a larger ruin above a cave with a brick wall in front. Look out for three tsampa mills (1/2 hr). The river now curves to the right to flow through the village of Galung (four houses). Cross it before the village to reach Chögar (1/2 hr). A hill rises immediately west of the village and a small river runs along the west side of the hill. (A side valley goes west before Chögar. A trail follows this valley for a while and then loops southwestward back down to the Tsangpo at a point 15 km from Chung Riwoche.) Camp between the river and the hill near an animal shelter; a good place to stop before crossing the Sangsang Pay La.

✧ Day 9   Camp 7–Sangsang   6 3/4 hr

After Chögar, the trail climbs towards the pass. From camp, bear left towards the village of Pari (2–3 houses) at the west side of the valley. Then swing right (north) to cross a small river. A mountain spur is ahead and two valleys lead to its top from either side. Take the left (1/2 hr). The trail crosses the top of the spur, then drops down into a north-northwest trending valley. A river is on the west side of the trail. Cross it to the right bank, then recross it soon again. Ford the river once

➡

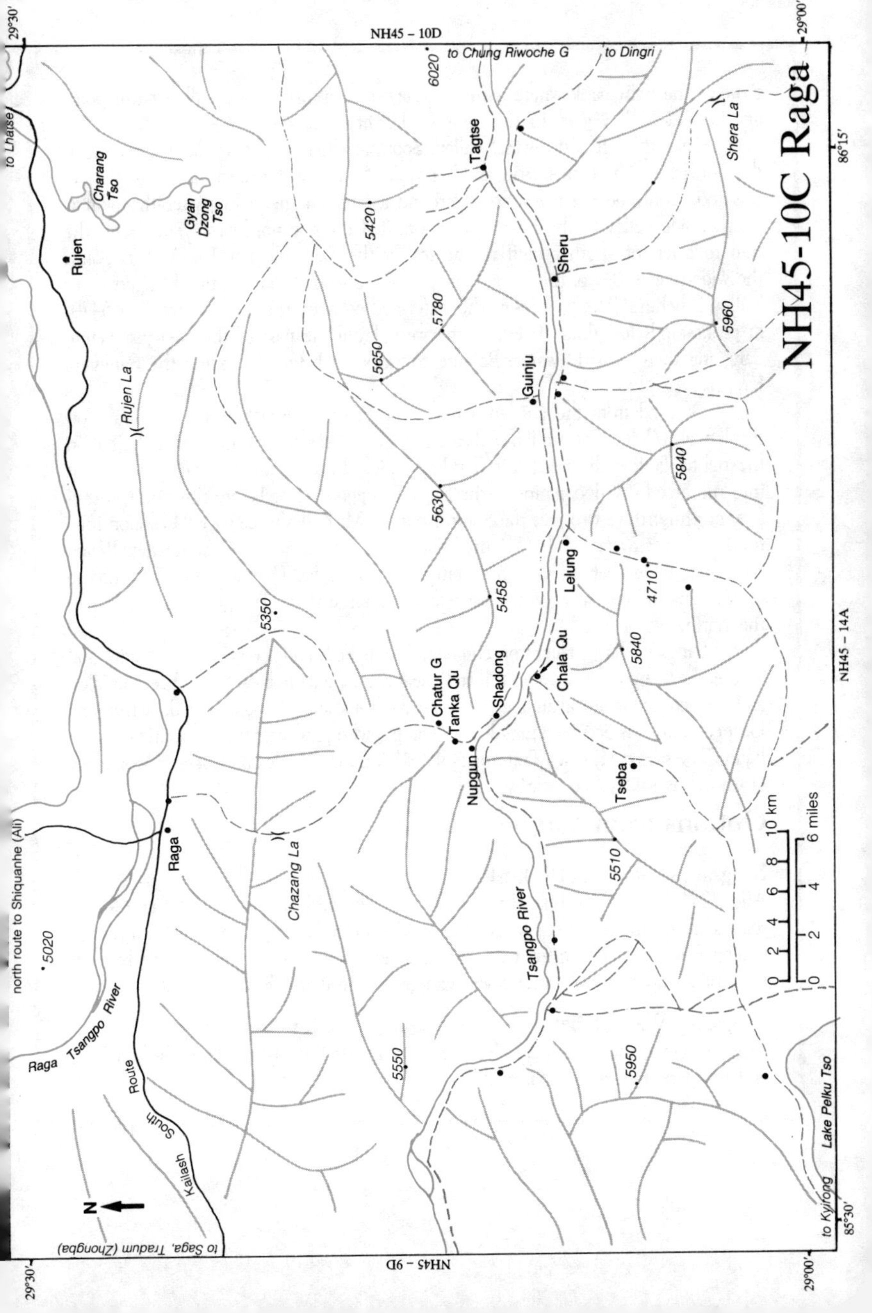

NH45 – 10D

to Chung Riwoche G   to Dingri

NH45-10C Raga

Shera La

Tagtse

6020

5420

Sheru

5780

5960

5650

Guinju

5840

5630

5458

Lelung

4710

Chala Qu

5840

5350

Chatur G

Tanka Qu

Shadong

Nupgun

Tseba

Rujen

Charang Tso

Gyan Dzong Tso

to Lhasa

Rujen La

Chazang La

Raga

5020

north route to Shiquanhe (Ali)

Raga   Tsangpo River

South Route to Kailash

5550

Tsangpo River

5510

5950

Lake Peiku Tso

to Kyirong

to Saga, Tradum (Zhongba)

NH45 – 9D

NH45 – 14A

N

10 km

8

6   6 miles

4   4

2   2

0   0

29°30'

29°00'

86°15'

85°30'

29°00'

29°30'

more to the right bank where it runs through a man-made stone wall. At this point another side valley goes to the right (1 1/2 hr).

Take the left (northwest) valley. Soon, another small side valley turns off to the northeast. Ignore this. Still another valley bends to the north-northeast. Ignore this too. Continue northwest to go around a bluff on the right. After the bluff is another side valley to the northeast; ignore it. Continue northwest. After 1 hr, the trail runs left of another bluff to the top of the Sangsang Pay La. At this point, the wide river valley of the Raga Tsangpo can be seen ahead and the Tsangpo River Valley is behind. The pass forms the watershed between these two systems. A 5470-m peak stands less than 10 km to the west. From the pass to the area just before Sangsang there is little water. Be sure to stock up before ascending the Sangsang Pay La.

Descend from the pass in a northerly direction. Reach three *mani* walls on the left in 1/2 hr. The trail now bears right (northeast); pass an animal shelter on the right. Follow the northeast trending valley. In 1 1/2 hr, the valley peters out into the broad dry floodplains of the Raga Tsangpo (1/2 hr before this point, a trail goes north-northwest to join the South Route to Mt Kailash; see page 945). Continue northeast over a small hill (3/4 hr). The village of Makje is 1/2 hr further. Reach Sangsang, hidden behind some hills, after another 1/2 hr. The main road from Lhatse to Mt Kailash runs west of the settlement and the Raga Tsangpo is a few km to the north.

Sangsang has a truckstop compound with beds and food, an army camp, and a store, the first encountered on this trek, near the Tibetan houses. Sugar, beer, noodles, and canned goods are available. Beds are Rmb 4 each. The compound, within the local commune, is occupied mainly by Khampas who pass their time drinking Chinese liquor. The sacred Mt Riwo Tratsang is about 7 km west of town and Nerang Monastery (13th-C.) is said to be nearby.

Options from Sangsang

Sangsang–Lhatse (119 km)
Allow 2–4 days to hitchhike this stretch. Kaga lies 60 km east of Sangsang. (A side road leads north from here to Ngamring Monastery [7 km]; another, southwest to Chung Riwoche.) The main road continues east from Kaga to Lhatse (59 km) on the Friendship Highway, where you can either head to Lhasa or Nepal.

Sangsang–West Tibet
From Sangsang the main road also goes west to Mt Kailash, via both the northern and southern routes (see page 945).

THE JONANG, GYANG BUMOCHE, AND JAMPALING KUMBUMS: THREE RUINED ARCHITECTURAL WONDERS

Currently, Tibet's best-preserved multi-chapel *chörtens* are the huge *kumbums* of Gyantse (see page 447) and Chung Riwoche (see above). Before their wanton sacking at the hands of the Red Guards, those of Jonang, Gyang Bumoche and Jampaling were considered their equal. During the past few years, both Jonang and Jampaling have undergone extensive renovations and their former glory has been partially restored.

The wall murals of Jonang (main seat of the Jonang-Kagyü subsect) and Gyang Bumoche (destroyed) were painted by Tibetan artists in the 14th and 15th centuries. They were strongly influenced by the prevalent Nepalese style, itself tempered by artistic elements from Yuan China. Jonang's surviving works are unique in Tibet. Architecturally, the Jonang *chörten* is one of the best of its genre and can reasonably be compared to the Gyantse Kumbum. The Jampaling *chörten* at the entrance of the Dranang Valley was Tibet's largest *chörten* before its near-total destruction in the 1960s. Within its many chapels were murals painted by the famous Tibetan artist, Khyense Chenmo, founder of the Khyense school of painting.

To reach the Jonang *chörten*, near the Pindsoling Monastery on the south bank of the Tsangpo, see page 864 (map reference NH45-11 D).

JONANG KUMBUM

The Jonang *chörten* is nearly as large as the Gyantse Kumbum. This octagonal, seven-story edifice is 20 m tall, and each level has chapels arranged in a circle. Within some are surviving murals consisting of series of small, painted squares, which depict scenes rather like the ones at Kizil, a famed Silk Road oasis west of Dunhuang. This unusual device is rare in Central Tibet. It is an attempt by artists to present stories through a carefully structured progression within different squares. Each sub-plot has its own frame.

Pilgrims from all over Tibet came to Jonang to honor the *kumbum* and to celebrate auspicious events. The pleasant surroundings include large trees and a stream, ideal sites for picnics and quiet contemplation. Near the castle-like building on a precipitous slope are shrines and meditation caves hidden by trees. Other caves in nearby hills on this side of the valley are splashed with red paint and festooned with prayer flags. These are the hermitages of the Jonangpa school; the most important is the retreat cell of Dolpopa Sherab Gyaltsen, its founder. Also here are the Kyiphuk Ritrö and Dhochok Phuk hermitages.

The *chörten*, known as Thongdröl Chenpo (Liberation on Sight), was the spiritual centre of the Jonangpa sect, a sub-sect of the Kagyüs founded by Dolpopa Sherab Gyaltsen

(1292–1361). He was an eminent Sakyapa lama who came to Jonang to practice tantric meditation. At the age of 35, he became abbot. He collated and edited the Kalachakra *tantra*, which others translated into Tibetan from Sanskrit. Construction of the great *chörten* began under Dolpopa before 1354, the year he handed his mantle to his disciple, Chogle Namgyal. The *chörten* was restored by Taranatha (b 1575) in 1621. Thus, two stylistic periods were involved in its decoration. The architecture, called *tashi gomang* (multi-chapel design), is similar to the great *chörtens* of Gyantse (see page 447), Gyang Bumoche, Jampaling, and Chung Riwoche (see above).

The Jonangpa doctrine was derived from the last Indian teachers of Buddhism, who held views similar to the Shivaists. They maintained that the nature of the Buddha is identical with that of all creatures, and for this they were considered heretics. After the death of Taranatha, the Fifth Dalai Lama (1617–82) converted all Jonangpa monasteries to the Gelugpa. In 1990, this superb structure underwent extensive restoration. Many of the *chörten*'s chapels are preserved and some murals have survived. The only other multi-chapel *chörtens* in Tibet in such a good shape are those at Gyantse and Riwoche.

ARCHITECTURE AND ART

The following section is a summary from Roberto Vitali's *The Early Temples of Central Tibet.*

Some of Jonang's murals can be traced to the Indian Pala style that was absorbed by the Newars of Nepal. This is particularly evident in the portraits where the central deity is surrounded by a group of lesser figures. Shading and the design of the heads and bodies of the seated *bodhisattvas* are unmistakable signatures of post-Pala painting. These attributes are found in many 14th-C. Tibetan murals. On the other hand, elements of the Jonang paintings link them to the Chung Riwoche *chörten* —stocky, muscular monks contrast with the elongated *bodhisattvas* noted for their prominent foreheads.

These combined characteristics came to full fruition in the murals of Shalu Monastery (see page 400), where the vibrant, sumptuous paintings of the Yumchenmo Lhakhang *khorlam*, painted around 1310, epitomize the genre. The Jonang *chörten* is an early example. Wall paintings of Jonang and Shalu are in fact very similar. This is most evident in the seated *bodhisattvas* and associated figures, their physiognomy, and shading. Other characteristics of the Jonang paintings are the thick, black outline of minor figures and ornaments, fewer brush strokes, and bolder colors. When compared with their Central Tibet counterparts working at Shalu, however, the Jonang artists are clearly provincial.

The art of Jonang is derived from the Newars of Nepal. This is apparent in the figures' features, their configuration within and outside the boxes, and the choice of colors. But the Newari imprint is tempered by a Chinese influence; Newar artists worked at the Yuan court during the second half of the 13th C. (the most famous was Arniko, founder of the style). Later, when Drakpa Gyaltsen began his renovation of Shalu at the beginning of the 14th C., he used artists familiar with this Sino-Newar school. By the time Jonang was being built, its muralists were probably Tibetans who used the work of Shalu's Yumchenmo Lhakhang as a model. Their work announced the beginning of a Tibetan school of art now known as 'Latö' (named after the region that encompasses Jonang, Gyang Bumoche, and Riwoche). It flourished for 100 years, from the mid-14th to the mid-15th century. Of the three similar Latö *chörtens*—Gyang Bumoche, Riwoche, and Jonang—the last is the oldest, followed by Gyang

Bumoche and Riwoche. Gyang Bumoche was probably built in the first or second decade of the 15th C., whereas Riwoche was founded in the mid-15th century.

The Latö school (see page 455) existed in conjunction with the Gyantse school (Gyantse Kumbum and Palkhor Chöde; see page 419) and should not be considered a precursor to it. Gyantse was a product of strong Nepalese and Yongle Chinese influences. Compared to the Latö school, it is more cosmopolitan and characterized by distinct elements from both countries. Unlike Latö, it was not markedly altered by indigenous sensibilities. Jonang, Gyang, and Riwoche all owe a debt of varying degrees to Shalu.

Jonang has an internal *khorlam* (circumambulatory corridor) housed within the *bumpa*, the bell-shaped top of the *chörten*—an unusual feature found in only two other *chörtens*, Gyang Bumoche and Chung Riwoche. Another similarity between Jonang and Riwoche is that they both lack two-story chapels and thus each floor has the same number of chambers. The *chörtens* of Gyantse and Gyang Bumoche both have central chapels—in the four cardinal directions on the lower floors—that are two storeys high. The configuration of Jonang's many small chapels within the *chörten* is distinctly different from that of the Gyantse *chörten*. All the chapels on all levels have approximately the same floor space. Those of the Gyantse Kumbum, however, decrease in size as one progresses upwards.

GYANG BUMOCHE KUMBUM

To reach Gyang, near Lhatse on the Friendship Highway, see page 867 (map reference NH45-11 C).

This *chörten* was built in the first or second decade of the 15th C. by the Sakyapa master, Sonam Tashi (1352–1417), with the help of the famous bridge builder, Tangton Gyalpo (see page 379). Shortly after its completion, the Sakyapa declined in influence just as the Phagmo Drupas became more powerful. Later, the Gelugpa took over the territory and built a monastery and summer palace for the Panchen Lama. Before its destruction in the 1960s, the Gyang Bumoche *chörten* was important for the study of Tibet's artistic and architectural heritage. The design of this multi-chapel monument is very similar to Chung Riwoche and Jonang, the other *chörtens* in the Latö district.

Gyang Bumoche's paintings strongly resemble works in these other *chörtens*. All were executed by local Tibetan artists now recognized as part of the Latö school. The result was a quintessentially Tibetan style of painting that incorporated distinctive elements from China and Nepal. The paintings, an immature absorption of these foreign influences, show comparatively primitive and rough interpretations and are less sophisticated than their counterparts at Shalu.

JAMPALING KUMBUM AND MONASTERY

To reach Jampaling, near the Yarlung Valley, see page 502 (map reference NH46-9D).

Jampaling, 1 km south of Dranang Xian, lies halfway up the slopes, to the left of the main Dranang Valley dirt road. From the road, go up the stony slopes to the first ruins (numerous houses have been rebuilt). A small *gönkhang* has three eyes painted on the door; beyond is the destroyed *chörten* of Jampaling (3/4 hr from Dranang Xian). Below the main gate of Jampaling is a large, painted eye on a rock. It 'monitored' the faithfulness of monks and pilgrims and 'discriminated' robbers among the hordes. Three such painted eyes exist in the vicinity.

Before its destruction in the 1960s, the 13-story Jampaling was the largest *chörten* in Tibet. Similar to Gyantse's Kumbum (see page 447) it had a multi-chapel (*tashi gomang*) design. The murals were painted by Khentse Chemo, a Sakyapa lama who founded the Kyenri style of paintings and created the Gongkar Chöde murals (see page 479). Partial reconstruction of the huge complex has been going on for the last few years. The site is deceptively large, comprising three main building groups along the ridge and covering over 137,000 sq m. Thönmi Lhundrub Tashi (Jampalingpa), a 12th-generation descendent of Thönmi Sambhota, Songtsen Gampo's famous minister, founded this religious center in 1472. Jampaling once had 200 monks.

Layout

The main site is surrounded by an irregular rectangular wall, 1 1/2 km long, built along the contours of the ridge. Parts of the destroyed watchtowers are sited at the northern perimeter. A substantial, well-built flight of stone steps leads up to the main entrance (west) and auxiliary buildings are grouped in two large clusters some distance above and below the *chörten*. Nine main structures once existed in Jampaling: Jampa Lhakhang, Jampaling Labrang, Jamtang Lhakhang, Kumbum, Jampaling Tratsang, Bhutanese Shops, Nepalese Shops, Thangka Wall, and Jungden Monastery. The *chörten* is west of the monastic buildings.

JAMPALING LABRANG

This destroyed building, south of Jampa Lhakhang (now rebuilt), was the *tripa's* (abbot's) residence. Built to commemorate Panchen Jamling Sonam Namgyal (1400–75), younger brother of the founder, it housed all subsequent abbatial incarnations. Jampalingpa's 3-m-high *chörten*-tomb, to the west, has a square base, round body, and is still in reasonable condition. This is one of seven small *chörtens* surrounding the main one.

JAMTANG LHAKHANG

Situated directly in front (south) of the Kumbum, this partially destroyed chapel is now the new Jampa Lhakhang.

JAMPALING TRATSANG

This *tratsang* (monastic college), near the Jampa Lhakhang, was built by Thönmi Tashi in 1472. Its 16-column *dukhang* has been levelled.

BHUTANESE AND NEPALESE SHOPS

Two groups of two-story shops stood directly in front of the Jampa Lhakhang. The eight in the west belonged to Bhutanese merchants and the Nepalese controlled the eight to the east. Built slightly later than the Kumbum, they developed and thrived with Jampaling's fame and influence. This symbiosis of shops and trading depots with a major monastery is very rare in Tibet.

THANGKA WALL

Southeast of the Kumbum is a large building constructed of stone slabs. Used to display a huge, cloth *thangka* (16 m by 8 m), it is the best preserved and tallest (18 m) structure of the complex. Interior stone stairs connect the four floors. The *thangka*, depicting Jampa, was taken out of storage and affixed to the face of the wall on the 30th day of the fifth lunar month each year.

KUMBUM

The Kumbum (Kumbum Thongdröl Chenmo), southwest of Jampa Lhakhang, is surrounded by a square stone wall (7 m high, 1 m thick) with watch towers at the corners. Jampalingpa and Lochen Sonam Gyaltso were the builders. A yearly festival, from the 24th to the 30th day of the fifth month, commemorated the *chörten's* completion. The first six days of the sixth month marked a fair that became the central focus of trade in Central Tibet.

JUNGDEN MONASTERY

This Sakyapa monastery, situated 200 m east of Jampa Lhakhang, consists of an entrance porch, the *dukhang* and the Jowo Lhakhang. It was founded shortly after 1472.

NEW JAMPA LHAKHANG

This three-story structure, rebuilt on the original site of the Jamtang Lhakhang, consists of a ground floor *dukhang* and a courtyard, flanked on one side by a two-story residence for monks. Some archaic, faded murals, part of a series depicting the life of Buddha, remain along the back walls of the *dukhang*. The entrance porch has new, elaborately designed columns and capitals, and the workmanship is surprisingly good. A pleasant room upstairs in the monks' quarters acts as an interim shrine. It holds texts, small sculptures and *thangkas*. One brass-plated toe, 1/2 m long, from the original Jampa statue, is venerated. The Serkhung Tombs (see page 367) across the Dranang Valley are visible from the courtyard. Notice the distinctive white *chörten*-tomb next to a large tumulus.

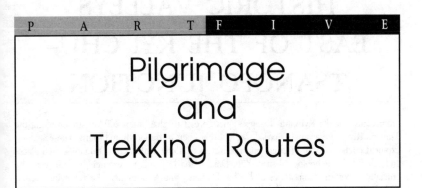

Pilgrimage
and
Trekking Routes

HISTORIC VALLEYS EAST OF THE KYI CHU– TSANGPO JUNCTION

From Chusul at the Kyi Chu–Tsangpo junction east to Lhagyari, a 200-km stretch along the Tsangpo River, are a number of side valleys that open to the north and south. These seldom-explored enclaves, close to Lhasa and the historic Yarlung Valley, contain many sacred places and 7th–9th C. archeological sites. Yön, Drachi, and Dranang, for example, are home to the crucially important monasteries of Kachu, Dranang, and Mindroling. The following section includes a pilgrimage along the Kyi Chu's left bank to its junction with the Tsangpo, and on the way the Nyingmapa nunnery of Shugseb, Dorje Drak Monastery, and the holy mountain of Gangri Tökar are visited.

HOLY PLACES ALONG THE LHASA–TSETHANG HIGHWAY

OVERVIEW

Culturally rich and fascinating, some of Tibet's outstanding monasteries and religious monuments are sited near the Lhasa–Tsethang highway. The first part of this itinerary follows the west (right) bank of the Kyi Chu (Lhasa) River to its junction with the Tsangpo; the second heads east along the south (right) bank of the Tsangpo to Tsethang, Tibet's fourth largest town.

Many sacred places exist on both banks of the Kyi Chu. In this section, only the right bank will be treated. (For details of a pilgrimage from Lhasa along the left bank of the Kyi Chu to its junction with the Tsangpo River, see page 487.) The most important monument is the virtually undamaged Nethang Drölma Lhakhang, chief residence of Atisha in the 11th century. This jewel-like chapel contains monumental sculptural works, created in the rare Xixia-Pala art style. Namkading Hermitage on sacred Mt Chuwo Ri, located at the Tsangpo–Kyi Chu junction, is an age-old pilgrimage site. Footpaths from the nearby Nam and Chusul valleys lead to the Tölung Valley, site of Tsurphu Monastery, the important main seat of the Karmapas. Beyond the river junction, six principal side valleys, all easily accessible, lead south from the east–west trending Tsangpo Valley. These are Gongkar, Namrab, Drib, Dranang, Drachi, and Yarlung. The most important—Dranang, Drachi, and Yarlung—are treated separately elsewhere. Many monasteries in these six valleys belong to the Sakyapa sect. Noteworthy ones include: Gongkar Chöde in Gongkar, Rame in Namrab, Dungpu Chökor in Drib, Dranang and Gyaling Tsokpa in Dranang, and Tsongdü Tsokpa in Drachi. They all suffered little structural damage in the Cultural Revolution and, compared to other monasteries in Central Tibet, are very well preserved. These Sakyapa institutions survived by becoming party offices and grain storehouses.

For those who feel like a short trek, the route from Chitishio on the south bank of the Tsangpo to beautiful Lake Yamdrok (via the Drib La) is a good choice (see page 595).

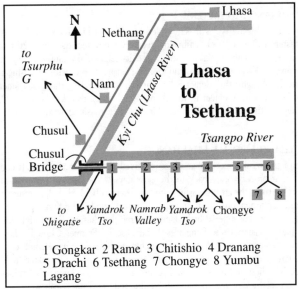

Another superb diversion is to take the ferry across to Drak, on the north bank of the Tsangpo, and then explore on foot the amazing cave complexes of Drakyul (see page 317).

For information about the valleys and monasteries on the north bank of the Tsangpo, see pages 295, 510, 623. Most sites can be reached by ferries from the main Lhasa–Tsethang highway or by simply trekking south from Lhasa.

Related sections
The Yarlung Valley, p 515
Lhasa to the Yarlung Valley, p 595
Lhamo Latso, p 623
Drakyul, p 317

THE LHASA–TSETHANG HIGHWAY

Starting from Lhasa, the sacred and significant places along the Lhasa–Tsethang highway are presented below. They are preceded by a number that corresponds to the road marker in km from Lhasa. There are two sets of numbers: the first from Lhasa to Gongkar Airport, the second from the airport to Tsethang.

Lhasa to Gongkar Airport road markers

(11) ROCK CARVING

A large and colorful Buddha is carved onto the base of a cliff on the right side of the road. (It is not easily noticeable while driving towards Lhasa.) Prayer flags mark the site.

(15) TASHIGANG MONASTERY

The turnoff for Tashigang is 2 km before Nethang Drölma Lhakhang. A dirt road leads left to the monastery (20-min walk). Tashigang, recently renovated, has about 20 monks. In the *dukhang*, the central image is Sakya Pandita. To its left is Sakyamuni and to the right are a small Chenresi, a Kadampa *chörten*, and Gönpo (*sungma* or protector of Tashigang). Recent murals adorn the skylight; they depict Sakya Pandita with the 16 Arhats, Sakyamuni, Drölma, and Atisha. A noteworthy object in the chapel is a 17th-C. *thangka* above the Dalai Lama's throne. It depicts the Medicine Mandala. Upstairs is a *gönkhang* with remnants of original murals.

(17) NETHANG DRÖLMA LHAKHANG

This is one of the most important and best-preserved monasteries in Tibet. It contains relics and artwork that probably date back to the early days of the Second Diffusion of Buddhism (11th century). Atisha, the great Bengali master, died here in 1054. He helped resurrect Buddhism in Tibet and Drömtonpa, one of his principal disciples, founded the Kadampa sect, a precursor of the Gelugpa. Nethang suffered little damage during the Cultural Revolution due to a direct request by East Pakistan (now Bangladesh). Supposedly, Premier Chou En Lai intervened personally to protect the chapel. Small but richly detailed, it is a welcome contrast to the monastic towns of Drepung and Sera. Despite the rather insignificant exterior, Nethang has some of Tibet's earliest and finest relics. The monastery was also known as Drölma Lhakhang; Atisha was especially devoted to the cult of the goddess Tara (Drölma).

History

Nethang Drölma Lhakhang probably dates from the mid-11th century. It all started with Atisha. Abbot of the celebrated Vikramasila Monastery in Bengal, he was one of the most revered Buddhist teachers of his time. Invited by King Yeshe Ö of Guge, West Tibet, the Indian monk came to Tibet in 1042 and spent the rest of his life in Ngari, Tsang, and Central Tibet. He taught Mahayana Buddhism and his writings, *The Lamp of the Path to Enlightenment*, became the central treatise for the Kadampa. Three centuries later, the Sakya Lama, Sonam Gyaltsen also resided at Nethang. After conversion to the Gelugpa (15th C.), its religious community grew and Dewachen Monastery was established in addition to the original chapel. This was destroyed during the Cultural Revolution.

The site

This ancient, unassuming monastery is set back a little from the main road. Go through two sets of doors into the main courtyard. In the center is a stone used by the Dalai Lamas to dismount. Next to it is a stone grinder where Yutok Yönten Gönpo, Tibet's first physician, used to prepare his medicines. To the left is an incense burner. Steps on the left lead to a covered terrace fronted by a stone balustrade. To the extreme left of the terrace is the entrance to the *khorlam*, which surrounds the chapel. Next to this is a rather unusual wooden

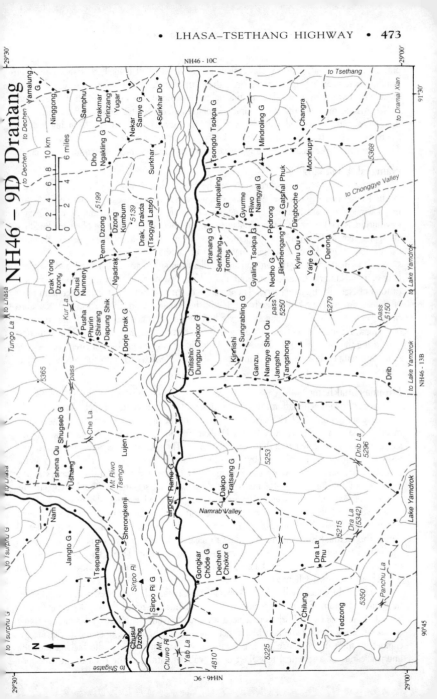

NH46 – 9D Dranang

NH46 - 10C

to Tsethang

to Dramai Xian

NH46 - 13B

to Lake Yamdrok

NH46 - 9C

to Shigatse

N

Lake Yamdrok

10 km

6 miles

to Lhasa

to Dechen

to Tsurphu G

to Tsurphu G

to Lhasa

to Lhasa

to Chonggye Valley

prayer wheel. Here also are two clay archaic Guardian Kings. It is likely that they have been standing here guarding the entrance since the 11th century. The *khorlam* exit, also with two Guardians and a prayer wheel, is to the right. New murals on the rear wall of the terrace depict Atisha, his two principal disciples, Dromtönpa and Naktso Lotsawa, Sakyamuni, and the *bodhisattvas*, Jampa and Jampelyang. Two white sunken *chörtens* (2 1/2 m high) adorn the terrace. The left contained the sheep-skin robe of Dromtönpa; the right has Atisha's robes. The entrance proper leads into the Namgyal Lhakhang, first of three interconnecting chapels.

Namgyal Lhakhang

The center of this chapel is dominated by the large, white Namgyal Chörten. It was built by the Reting Rinpoche in the 1940s and contained *tsa-tsas*, supposedly handmade by Atisha. In its window is a small image of Namgyalma. The *chörten*, untouched during the Cultural Revolution, is flanked by two bronze Kadampa *chörtens*. In front are the Eight Medicine Buddhas, all approximately 1/2 m in height, perhaps brought by Atisha from India. Among them, in the center, is an old, clay portrait (*ngadrama*) of Atisha.

On a platform along the left wall are excellent statues of Drölma, Chenresi, and Tsepame. Left of the Namgyal Chörten are four more Kadampa *chörtens*, two large and two small (a total of eight in the monastery). These were brought to Tibet by Atisha and contain relics of Naropa, one of the 84 Mahasiddhas. Right of the Namgyal Chörten is a 3-m-high Kadampa *chörten* known as Narope Dhungten. It was built during Atisha's lifetime and holds the skull of Naropa, Atisha's books, and his begging bowl. Behind this are stacks of old manuscripts comprising the entire *Kangyur*. The Namgyal Lhakhang has no murals—a mystery, considering relics and sculptures have survived intact. A side door leads north into the second (center) chapel.

Drölma Lhakhang

A U-shaped, two-tiered platform runs along three sides of this center chapel. On it are 17th-C. bronze statues of the 21 Drölmas. At the center of the upper tier is a statue of Sakyamuni, made in India in 1288. To its left is a Drölkar Sungjönma ('Spoken White Tara'), which supposedly communicated with the 13th Dalai Lama. The right statue is Serlingpa, the teacher visited by Atisha during his sea voyage to Sumatra. To the left of the Drölkar is a statue of the 13th Dalai Lama. Along the extreme right of the upper tier are old statues of the Five Dhyani Buddhas. Tradition holds that these were consecrated in the 11th C. in the presence of Atisha. A number of important relics associated with Atisha reside within an ornate wood and glass case at the center of the bottom tier. Having pride of place is a white conch shell (*dungkar*). This replaces an original Drölma Sungjönma statue that disappeared during the Cultural Revolution. According to legend, this was the very image that spoke to the Indian master, instructing him to spread his knowledge in Tibet. The conch shell was brought from Nalanda, India; Atisha used it liturgically. Behind the shell, inside a small cabinet, is a Thousand-armed Chenresi.

Left of the conch shell is Atisha's own Drema Chörten (1/2 m), taken with him wherever he went. It contains Serlingpa's remains. In front of this is a rolled *thangka* depicting Gönpo Chakdruk. It is said that Atisha's nosebleed was used to paint the image. A 1/2-m-high statue of Sakyamuni is right of the conch, another relic brought by Atisha from India. Outside the cabinet, in front of the conch shell, is a small stone *rangjung* statue of the Buddha with the unusual feature of a spherical base. Left of the cabinet, sitting at the bend of the U-shaped platform, is a round urn, nearly 1 m in diameter, known as Jowo Je Kudhung Shugsa. Originally inside a *chörten*, the urn (*bumpa*) containing some of Atisha's bones was saved when the structure collapsed.

Nearby, inconspicuous among the Drölmas, is a 1 1/2-m-high standing statue of Jampa from Nalendra. When the Mongols invaded Tibet they sacked monasteries and destroyed statues. This statue apparently cried out '*A-tsa*' ('Ouch!') and was thus spared. It is one of the finest pieces in the monastery. Another fine statue is Avalokiteshvara Karsapani, located at the right elbow of the U, behind the eighth and last Kadampa *chörten*. The statue, cast in bronze in India in 1275, is distinguished by a prominent halo (*torana*). Pilgrims believe it helps cure leg swellings. Go through a side door to reach the Tsepak Lhakhang.

Tsepak Lhakhang

This chapel of the Buddha of the Three Ages and the Eight Great Bodhisattvas is a religious and artistic paragon. Atisha taught here, and the clay statues, all huge, monumental works, 4–5 m tall, date back to ancient times. It is likely they were crafted in the 12th C., after Atisha's death, at a time when the monastery was restored. These works represent rare and fascinating resources for art historians.

At the center of the rear wall is Tsepame, the room's principal image, sitting on a large throne flanked by two snow-lions. When Atisha died here in 1054, his disciple, Dromtönpa, cremated the body and installed some of the remains at Reting Monastery. He mixed the remaining ashes with earth to create 100,000 small lumps which were used to construct the Tsepame statue, a commemoration of Atisha for his years of dedicated teaching at Nethang. Marmaze is at the center of the left wall, Wösung at the right. The Eight Great Bodhisattvas are placed between the three Buddhas, an uncommon configuration. Perhaps the size of the statues and lack of space dictated this arrangement. Immediately left of the chapel's west entrance is a 3-m-high Tamdrin Marpo statue (enclosed within chicken wire). To the right, in line with Wösung and the three *bodhisattvas* along the north (right) wall, is a 3-m-high Chana Dorje. The *bodhisattva* next to this lacks a halo and its eyes are rendered peculiarly. Most statues in this room have undergone minor repairs.

Stylistically, the statues show a marked evolution of the Xixia-Pala style that characterizes the art of Dranang (see page 393) and Yemar monasteries (see page 390). Tibetan sensibilities show up much more vigorously here in Nethang. The statues are a product of local artists; although well versed in the Xixia-Pala style, they were also partial to Tibetan motifs. Notice the use of a single row of decorative medallions on the sleeves of two *bodhisattvas*. (The now-destroyed statues of Dranang had garments liberally decorated with these same medallions.) The rendering of the guardians is also distinctive. There can be no doubt that these traits bear a well-defined correspondence to those of the Yemar statues. Drölma Lhakhang's statues must have been created soon after those of Yemar and Dranang, most likely in the 12th century. The Nethang style carried a subtle hint of what was to come in the mature monumental sculpture of Central Tibet.

In the center of the chapel is the massive clay throne of Atisha. Only the solid slab of the back remains. In front is a 1-m-high image of Atisha, grafted inseparably to the throne. Protecting the image is a cabinet with pagoda roof. Tradition relates that the statue was built by Atisha himself before his death. It was one of two such images. Remnants of paint (part of a halo) can be seen on the front of the throne, flanking the cabinet.

RATÖ MONASTERY

Access

From Nethang Drölma Lhakhang, walk south along a dirt road up the west-trending side valley. Reach Ratö Monastery in 1 hr. It is located within Ratö Village, part of the extensive monastic complex that once housed 400 monks.

History

Ratö was founded in the late 11th C. by Takshang, a lama born in 1045. He founded the Taktsangpa, an obscure sub-sect of the Kagyü. The monastery was known for its study of Tshanipa, a metaphysical school of thought that specialized in logic. Celebrated figures sojourned here, among them Tsong Khapa and Ngok Loden Sherab, the famous translator. The monastery now belongs to the Gelugpa and has 50 monks.

Dukhang

This is the monastery's principal chapel. Close to the back wall, in front of the long altar, are three statues of Yabse Sum (Tsong Khapa and two disciples) and nearby, a revered old statue of Drölma enclosed within a glass case. This supposedly is one of Atisha's three personal Drölmas, the only one to survive, and thus the monastery's most prized object. To its right is a pillar adorned with clothing and boots (kuseb) of the protector (chökyong) known as Sidrup Kundhen. His attire is used in lieu of a proper statue for ease of transport. The sungma (protector) of the monastery is obliged to accompany the monks everywhere. Behind the pillar is a brass plate, brought here by the Longdhöl Lama. This mirror-relic (melong) is the dwelling place of the sungma known as Gyalpo Drukdzin. Another set of kuseb dangles left of the altar.

The statues ranged along the back altar are: Lukchok Dorjechang, Ngok Loden Sherab, Manga Draksang, Shakya Thupa, Atisha, Chokla Wözer, Ngok Legpai Sherab, and Gewe Shenyen Yönten Phüntsok. Most are images of illustrious lamas associated with the monastery. Between the third and fourth statues is a Lhabab Chörten. The Eighth Dalai Lama carried this with him at all times. A Jangchub Chörten stands between the sixth and seventh statues. Along the upper shelves are numerous Kadampa chörtens and brass images. At the end is one more Lhabab Chörten. Right of the altar is another sungma, an original, called Tsedrakpa. It is an image of a Bön god transformed into a mainstream Buddhist deity, specially revered in Ratö. Along the right wall are statues of the Fifth and Eighth Dalai Lamas, Panchen Lobsang Chögyal and Lobsang Gönpo. Behind the altar, an entranceway leads into the tsangkhang. In the old days, the principal images here were the Buddhas of the Three Ages and the Eight Great Bodhisattvas. Now the central image is a Tsong Khapa statue called Je Tshedzinma.

Dukhang Murals Lining the walls of the dukhang are surprisingly well-preserved murals. They probably date from the 17th and 18th C., though the monks claim they come from the 13th or 14th centuries. To the left of the entrance are images of the protectors, Yamantaka, Dharmaraja, and Tsedrekpa, the special sungma of Ratö. The last is covered by a cloth. The left side wall has Drölma, Chenresi, and Jampa. On the back wall of the dukhang are paintings of the lamas belonging to the Lamrin lineage. Here also are early kings and the architects of the Gelugpa: Tsong Khapa and the Fifth Dalai Lama. The far end of the right wall has an image of Sangye Gyatso, followed by the 35 Buddhas of Confession, the Sangye Menlha, Jampelyang, Chenresi, Dugkarma (a female deity with a white parasol), and Chana Dorje. Next to the entrance are Drölma, Namthose (God of Wealth), Palden Lhamo, and Drongdzin, a protector.

Ratö Nyetri Lhakhang

This two-story chapel is behind and left of the main building, at the back of a two-story quadrangle. On the altar of the ground floor chapel are statues of Ngadhak Gyalsum, Atisha, Yabse Sum, and Dröljang. The walls are adorned with new *thangkas*. Upstairs is the *gönkhang*, with original gold-line paintings on a black background. The Dalai Lama's Zimchung (bedroom) is one more floor up.

Jamkhang

Behind Ratö, near the top of the village, is a yellow building called the Jamkhang. Inside is a new one-story statue of Jampa. A small shrine on the way to the chapel is the dwelling place of Tsedrakpa, the protector of Ratö.

Retreat Caves

Gormo Ridruk Drakphuk and Khedrup Chungnam are the two main caves associated with Ratö, about 2 hr from the monastery, high up in the mountain ranges to the north. One can be seen as a small dot near the top.

Rinchenling Ritrö

West of Ratö Village are two large white *chörtens*. Nearby is Rinchenling Ritrö, a retreat associated with the Longdhöl Lama.

(29) Nam Village

This village, at the entrance of the Nam Valley, is the point of departure for a visit to Druk Sewa Jangchub Chöling (Jang Chöling) Monastery, a 1 1/2-hr-walk from Nam up the slopes of the valley. After Nam, on the main road, are the villages of Jangtö (Gelugpa Jangtö Monastery is here) and Jangme.

Nam to the Tölung Valley and Tsurphu Monastery (see page 671): three–four days From Nam, a trail goes northwest up the Nam Valley. Reach Baimutang Village at the head of the valley in 4 hr. After spending the night here, cross the 5500-m Lungsang La (4 1/2 hr), then descend due north to Nampa, a village in the Tölung Valley (3 3/4 hr). Follow the valley westward for 4 1/2 hr to Tsurphu Monastery.

Druk Sewa Jangchub Chöling

This monastery was the founding institution of the Drukpa sect of Bhutan, begun in 1189 by Tsangpa Gyare, the wandering ascetic and Root Guru of the Drukpa Kagyü sect. Followers of the Tshanipa sect came here especially for winter teachings.

(40) Sakyaling Monastery

A small, dilapidated Sakyapa monastery stands across from the village of Tsepanang on the left side of the road.

(52) Chusul

This town on the right near the Kyi Chu–Tsangpo confluence has a two-story guest house with a restaurant.

> **Chusul to Tsurphu Monastery: three days** A trail from Chusul goes north up the Chusul Valley. In 1 3/4 hr, walk past Chuphu, then Sarje (1 1/4 hr). Continue due north; cross the 5500-m Nampa La in 7 hr. Descend, also due north, from the pass to the Tölung Valley at Nakar Village (4 hr). Tsurphu (see page 671, the principal monastery of the Karmapa, is 2 1/2 hr west of Nakar near the head of the Tölung Chu River.

(60) (NEW MARKER 4703) CHUSUL BRIDGE

A modern bridge spans the Tsangpo. Soldiers guard both ends.

MT CHUWO RI

Sacred Chuwo Ri, located at the Kyi Chu–Tsangpo junction, exists to confer prosperity on Tibet. According to tradition it had 108 holy springs and 108 monasteries. In the 8th C., King Trisong Detsen founded a hermitage here that later served as a retreat for Tsangpa Gyare and the First Karmapa. Seven centuries later, Tangton Gyalpo built a famous iron-chain link bridge across the river. Known as the Chaksam Bridge, it was ruined in the mid-20th century. It is possible to circumambulate Mt Chuwo Ri in 4 hr by crossing the low Pab La (4250 m), south of the peak. On the north (left) bank of the Tsangpo, a little to the west, is Yöl Rigong Monastery.

Tsechu Köpa Lhakhang

There was once a thriving monastic complex at Chuwo Ri, now totally destroyed. A holy stream flows from the Tsechu Phuk meditation cave; nearby is the ruined Tsechu Köpa Lhakhang founded by Tratshang Manlung Lochok Dorje. This chapel was administered by monks from Mindroling Monastery (see page 491) and contained statues of a one-story Sakyamuni and the Eight Great Bodhisattvas.

Namkading Hermitage

Namkading is a recently restored cave retreat near the top of Mt Chuwo Ri. According to some sources, it is considered one of Guru Rinpoche's 'eight great caves.' The retreat had statues of him and his two consorts. Another retreat consecrated to the master is Guru Drubne, located below Namkading in a difficult-to-reach site.

(69) CORACLE CROSSING

Across the Tsangpo, on the north bank, is Mt Sinpo Ri. At its base is Drongnak (Black Village), which supposedly has a rock sculpture of Demchok made by the Nepalese artist, Archarya.

(72) GONGKAR DZONG

Gongkar chieftains ruled from this fortress (now damaged), on a hill to the right. Their domain, an ancient tract of territory stretching from the Kyi Chu–Tsangpo junction to the Namrab Valley, was an important center of Sakyapa power until the rise of the Phagmo Drupas in the 15th century. At the base of the hill is a small chapel. Coracles also cross the Tsangpo at this point.

Gongkar Dzong to Lake Yamdrok: one day   Gongkar Dzong is situated at the entrance (western perimeter) of the Gongkar Valley. A trail from here (it is also possible to start from Gongkar Chöde Monastery, 3 km to the east) follows the valley to the south, passing Dechen Chökor Monastery. The trail forks 2 3/4 hr from Gongkar Dzong. Take the right fork. (The left one also goes to the lake but takes an extra day. It crosses the 5342-m Dra La Pass and meets the lake at its eastern end.) In 3 hr cross a 5000-m pass, then descend for 1 hr to Chilung Village by the lake.

(75) GONGKAR CHÖDE MONASTERY

This impressive, well-preserved monastery lies a few hundred meters off the main road. Its 16th-C. Kyenri murals are a rare and important find. This particular style of Tibetan painting was pioneered by Khentse Chemo, a 16th-C. native of Gongkar. According to tradition, the master personally painted all the murals in Gongkar Chöde. Not all survived but those that did are grouped in small pockets within the 64-pillar main hall, along the circumambulation corridor and in small rooms on the second floor. They are characterized by a pronounced Chinese influence. All the murals were whitewashed by the Red Guards and have only recently been cleaned.

The paintings in the assembly hall show the life of Sakyamuni according to the text of Paksam Trishing. Flanking the entrance of the inner chapel (tsangkhang) are two murals. The left one portrays the Sakya patriarch, Kunga Nyingpo, surrounded by Drakpa Gyaltsen (left) and Sonam Tsemo. To the right are Sakya Pandita and his nephew, Phagpa. The altars carry new statues of Dorje Denpa (center), the founder, Sakya Pandita, together with Guru Rinpoche (left), and two Buddhas (right). Opening on the back wall of the dukhang is the high-ceilinged inner tsangkhang, surrounded by a circumambulatory corridor. On the walls are lively paintings of the main lamas of the Sakya lineage: Sonam Gyaltsen, Sakya Pandita, Phagpa, Drakpa Gyaltsen, Kunga Nyingpo, Sonam Tsemo, and scenes from their lives. These are freer and less rigid than paintings from other monasteries in Central Tibet. On the altar are images of Dorje Denpa and Sakya Pandita. Formerly, the main statue here was a three-story Sakyamuni; inside it was the skull of Gayadhara, the 11th-C. Kashmiri Pandita. The inner wall of the corridor has Kyenri-style paintings depicting Sakyamuni's 12 deeds. On the outer wall are images of the Thousand Buddhas. The gönkhang, left of the main hall, has paintings of gruesome 'sky-burials'. There are 12 divinities, Gönpo Ghur's retinue (a form of Mahakala highly revered by the Sakyapa), in an inner room.

Two rooms on the second floor have fine paintings by Khentse Chemo. The room directly above the front porch of the assembly hall has charming oval paintings; one shows the original monastic complex. The other room, Kyedhor Khang, has excellent paintings of principal deities (yidams) propitiated by the monastery. These include Kye Dorje (the main image), Demchok, Kalachakra, and others. Other chapels on this floor are the Lamdre Lhakhang, Kangyur Lhakhang, and Barkhang. The third floor Lama Lhakhang is consecrated to Kunga Namgyal, founder of the monastery in 1464. His tomb was here.

Behind the main building is the Lamdre Lhakhang (ruined). Its architecture was unusual. The first floor had four load-bearing columns, the second eight, the third 16, and the top floor had 32. Gongkar Chöde had four colleges (tratsangs); Drepung Tratsang (behind and to the right) and Keutsang (left) still stand but are in bad condition. The monastery's atmosphere is friendly and purposeful. Young novice monks spend a great deal of time chanting sutras on the upper floors. Previously, Gongkar Chöde was renowned for its school of Cham (Lama Dance).

History

The monastery, founded in 1464 by Kunga Namgyal, belongs to the Zung tradition within the Sakyapa sect. Kunga Namgyal was a disciple of the Sakyapa master, Sonam Gyaltsen. He also studied under Jampalingpa, founder of the magnificent Jampaling Kumbum (see page 465) in Dranang.

Kyenri: Tibetan paintings with Chinese influence

Murals in most monasteries of Central Tibet depict a central divine figure, a god or incarnation of some well-known saint, surrounded by other divinities. Scenes are painted in rigid symmetry on a large wall. Chinese influence, however, produced paintings in which the most important figures stand to the side, away from the center. Landscape enlivened and permeated the whole composition. This freer style avoided the traditional stiffness of typical Tibetan temple paintings.

The Kyenri style is most apparent in Sakyapa and Karmapa monasteries of Kham (East Tibet), and it is unusual to find it in the Lhasa area.

DECHEN CHÖKOR MONASTERY

Follow the dirt road in front of Gongkar Chöde southward for 5 km to reach Dechen Chökor, an important monastery of the Drukpa Kagyü sect. It can be seen halfway up some slopes to the left; it takes 1 hr to walk from the road. Most of the complex is destroyed. A large chapel on the right has been rebuilt and houses 20 monks.

The Dechen Chökor abbots served the king of Ladakh and the monastery was popular with hermits and ascetics. In early times, 80 monks followed the Drukpa tradition of Drukluk. The monastery's principal lhakhang, dedicated to the Bhutanese teacher, Yongdzin Jampal Pawo, had Demchok in yabyum as its main image. Lama Yongdzin founded a hermitage here in the 13th century. There was also a nunnery in the vicinity.

GONGKAR AIRPORT TO TSETHANG ROAD MARKERS

(35) NAMRAB VALLEY AND DAKPO TRATSANG MONASTERY

The monastery is 6 km south of the main road; turn off to the right at road marker 35 km and follow a tree-lined dirt road that goes up the Namrab Valley (Namrab Lungpa), known formerly as Zung Trezhing.

Dakpo Tratsang is a sizable, preserved Sakyapa monastery in the middle of Namrab Qu. Used as a grain depot, it was spared during the Cultural Revolution. What little damage it sustained was repaired in 1983, and now the place is religiously strong and vigorous. Over 35 adult monks and 40 very young ones live here. The assembly hall, renovated in recent years, retains some original murals. On the altars are images of Sakya Pandita flanked by Tashi Namgyal (left), the founder of the monastery, and Gorampa Sonam Senge, a renowned

15th-C. lama. The *gönkhang* is left of the *dukhang*; its protector is Pangboche. The deity's image resides in a red enclosure, next to the courtyard's incense burner.

History

Dakpo Tratsang's founder, Tashi Namgyal (1398–1459), came from Nalanda Monastery (see page 568) in the Phanyul Valley north of Lhasa. A disciple of Rongtönpa, he was steeped in the Kadampa tradition. He later crossed over to the Sakyapa to head a college at Sangphu Monastery (see page 490). Eventually he founded this monastery. A Guru Rinpoche cave lies within the nearby mountains. Dakpo Tratsang, a Sakyapa institution, should not be confused with the Gelugpa Dakpo Tratsang located in Gyatsa Xian, east of Tsethang (see page 641).

Dakpo Tratsang to Dungpu Chökor Monastery: one day A trail from here follows a side valley to the east. Cross a 4650-m pass, then descend northeastwards to the entrance of the Drib Valley to reach Chitishio (road marker 52 km) next to the Lhasa–Tsethang road. Dungpu Chökor stands within the village.

Dakpo Tratsang to Yamdrok Tso: two days A trail goes south from Dakpo Tratsang to follow the western side of the Namrab Valley. The trail splits 1 3/4 hr from the monastery. Take the right fork (the left one also goes to the lake). In 5 hr, cross the 5342-m Dra La Pass and descend to the northeastern shore of the lake (2 3/4 hr). Drayul village is here.

ZUNG TREZHING

The important Kagyüpa center of Zung Trezhing (Lhakhang Serpo) is a few km southeast of Dakpo Tratsang, high up the eastern slopes of the Namrab Valley. Founded in the 12th C., it stood for 800 years but was leveled in the 1960s. Below the ruins is a Milarepa cave that had images of Ngoktön Chökyi Dorje (1036–1102), a disciple of Marpa and founder of the monastery. Zung Trezhing was the main seat (*dhensa*) of Ngokton; he met Milarepa here and also died at this site. A *chörten*-tomb in one of the chapels supposedly contained Marpa's skull. His teachings dominated this monastery for several centuries. Below the Zung Trezhing is a cave once used by Serwa Drubpa, a yogi capable of causing hailstorms. Dungpu Chökor Monastery (see below) is situated within Chitishio Village in the Drib Valley, down a side valley from Zung Trezhing.

(36) RAME MONASTERY

This Sakyapa monastery, also known as Thubden Rawame, was founded by Rawa Laepa (1138–1210). It is situated 200 m north of the main highway at the end of a short dirt road. Rame, surrounded by houses and the government compounds of Gongkar Xian, has an imposing TV antenna on the top of its roof. The chapel is intact but run-down, its murals dilapidated. Monks and young novices roam about. Close by is a government restaurant serving rice and vegetables at set hours. A guest house is on the east side of the dirt road.

(47–48) Ferry to Dorje Drak Monastery

The Dorje Drak monastic complex (see page 598), one of the most important Nyingma institutions in Tibet, is visible across the river.

(52) Drib Valley and Dungpu Chökor Monastery

Chitishio stands to the right of the Drib Valley entrance, and the ruins of Chitishio Dzong can be seen high above to the east. The large village is known for its colorfully striped woolen aprons (panden), created with dyes from Bhutan. This cottage industry still thrives. Go through the settlement for 1/2 km to Dungpu Chökor Monastery.

Dungpu Chökor Monastery

A large courtyard flanked by monks' quarters precedes the main entrance of the monastery. Paintings of the Wheel of Life and a diagram of Buddhist cosmology decorate the porch. Within the handsome main chapel are murals in good condition. The wall to the left of the entrance has paintings of four protectors. The first is Pekor She, a Bön deity converted to Buddhism; the next is Gönpo Ghur, the principal protector of the Sakyapa, followed by Mahakala and Palden Lhamo. Along the left wall of the main hall are murals depicting the 12 main episodes of the Buddha's life.

The Tri Tsangkhang chapel at the rear wall has before its entrance a portrait of Kunga Nyingpo, the renowned Sakya patriarch. This room has old sculptures studded with coral; the most important one is an original Drölma Sungjönma (Talking Tara), placed in the center of the altar. The wall on the other side of the chapel entrance has images of the five principal Sakyapa lamas: Kunga Nyingpo, Phagpa, Sakya Pandita, Drakpa Gyaltsen, and Sonam Tsemo. The complete Sakyapa Lamdre lineage, the 16 Arhats, the Eight Medicine Buddhas, Guru Rinpoche and his lineage are depicted under the skylight of the main assembly hall. A room left of the hall is used as a printing room; one on the right is dedicated to Vairocana. (The deity is flanked by Drölma images, and there are impressive frescoes of Yamantaka.) The right wall of the main hall has murals of Kye Dorje and Dugkarma. Just before the hall entrance are images of more protectors: Namthose, Shalo, a local deity, and Chana Dorje. The present Dalai Lama stayed in a room on the top floor during his flight to India in 1959. Here are a few good statues, including one of Guru Rinpoche.

According to Tucci, the Tibetologist, the only objects of note in the monastery are the plinth of a pillar with carved arabesques and a Chinese inscription of the Guangxu period (1875–1908) on the entrance door of a chapel. About 30 monks reside here.

History

Drapa Ngönshe, disciple of the Indian master, Dampa Sangye (see page 271), founded this monastery in the 11th century. The chapel was taken over and expanded by the Sakyapa in the 15th C., under the guidance of Chökyi Gyalpo.

Dungpu Chökor–Yamdrok Tso trek. From Dungpu Chökor, trek south along the Drib Valley over the Drib La Pass to Tangda at the eastern end of Yamdrok Tso. The itinerary then closely follows the north shore of the lake to the main Tibet- ➡

Nepal highway at Nakartse or Tamalung. Dungpu Chökor to Yamdrok Tso (part of the Lhasa–Dorje Drak–Yamdrok trek, page 595) is a three- or four-day walk. From Tangda, another trail goes east to Chongye in the Yarlung Valley.

SURULING (SUNGRABLING) MONASTERY

From Dungpu Chökor go 3 km south on a dirt road, along the Drib Valley. The Gelugpa monastery of Suruling is halfway up the eastern slopes of the valley. The walk up from Kinnishi Village takes 3/4 hr. Renovated in 1985, the monastery now has about 55 monks, most of them quite young. A large, white, fortress-like chapel has been built among the extensive ruins. Three new *chörtens* are on its right. The tallest one (15 m), closest to the chapel, sits on a base of wood columns. A porch with murals runs around this base. The entrance to the rebuilt *dukhang* is beyond two consecutive courtyards, flanked by monks' rooms and a kitchen. It is possible to stay the night in the monastery.

History

Suruling was founded by Nyakwön Sonam Zangpo in the early part of the 14th century. He was the elder brother of the celebrated Sakyapa lama, Kunga Lhodro Gyaltshen Pal Zangpo.

Suruling to the Dranang Valley This pleasant 7–8 hr walk over a range of mountains east of the Drib Valley starts from Suruling and heads east to the head of the Sungrabling Valley. Cross a 4750-m ridge before dropping down to Dranang Xian and the entrance of the Dranang Valley.

(59) PYRAMIDAL ROCK

On the north bank of the Tsangpo is a huge pyramidal rock beneath the Yartö Tra mountain range, a good landmark.

(61) DRAK

Across the Tsangpo on the north bank is Drak (Drakda) Village. Within the Drak Valley are the amazing cave complexes of Drak Yong Dzong and Dzong Kumbum (see pages 321, 325). The latter can be made out just beneath the top of the range, on the right ridge below the green mountaintop.

(65) GAKTSA

This village stands at the entrance to a wide valley, on the right. A ferry goes across the Tsangpo to Drak.

(76) TRATHANG AND THE DRANANG VALLEY

Trathang Village is on the right side of the road at the entrance to the south-trending Dranang Valley. A tea house and Tibetan restaurant are next to the road. Tsethang is 47 km further to the east.

DRANANG XIAN

This administrative center, 2 km south of Trathang and inside the Dranang valley, has a few large Chinese-style compounds and a place to spend the night next to the cinema.

DRANANG MONASTERY

Dranang is perhaps the sole repository of rare 11th-C. Pala-style paintings in Tibet. For art historians, it is one of the most exciting destinations in this part of Asia. An entire section is devoted to this remarkable site (see page 501).

(82) DRACHI VALLEY

This broad valley leads south from the road and jeep tracks follow both sides of the Mindroling River. For a description of the cultural sites of Drachi, including the pre-eminent Mindroling Monastery of the Nyingma sect, see Drachi: page 495.

(89–90) TONGSHOI

The ferry to Samye Monastery runs from this point; a ferry house is on the left side of the road. The crossing takes 1–1 1/2 hr and costs 1 yuan. A new ferry, for the sole use of tourists and therefore considerably more expensive, is located at road marker 112, further to the east.

(95) NAMSELING ZHARMA GONSAR (NAMSELING)

Some 16 km east of the Drachi Valley is a south-trending valley directly across the Tsangpo from Samye Monastery (see page 295). From the highway, a tall seven-story structure, the most unusual in the region, is clearly visible within the valley (4 km away). It is one of the tallest buildings in Tibet.

The precursor of Namseling was Drachi Rudan, a four-story estate located nearby in Drachi Lhakpa Village. Its founder, Tashi Rudan, was patriarch of a feudal family that produced two abbots for Dorje Drak Monastery and the important writer, Panchen Lobsang Yeshe. With the rise of the Phagmo Drupa, this building was deemed insufficient. Namseling was thus begun in the broader part of the valley to the north and was completed at the end of the 14th century. In 1959 this site saw much fighting between Chinese and Tibetans.

Namseling is not a monastery. It served as the estate of prominent noble families during the Phagmo Drupa era and its extensive grounds include agricultural areas, orchards, gardens (*lingkas*), and threshing yards. Although the building still stands, its interior and structural walls were badly damaged during the Cultural Revolution. Nevertheless, it is possible to go up through the different levels. A tall (10 m) double wall constructed of stone and earth enclosed Namseling. Watch towers stood at the corners; within the two walls is a 5-m-wide moat. The main gate opens along the center of the east wall and the large gardens (no longer existing) lie outside these walls, south of the complex. To the north is an unusually large threshing ground for barley. Stables, staff quarters, and animal shelters (all destroyed) once clustered next to the principal south-facing structure.

Namseling's main building stands 22 m tall and the stone foundation wall is fully 1.4 m thick and 1 m tall. The eastern façade is constructed entirely of stone. Two sets of stairs lead to the elevated entrance foyer which is in fact on the third floor! (The first floor was for animals, the second and third for storage.) All rooms are small and low-ceilinged, and the interior stairs narrow and steep. The third and fourth floors once contained chapels. The fifth consisted of the Kangyur Lhakhang (it still has paintings of Sakyamuni, Tsepame, and others) and the *gönkhang*. Living quarters occupied the eastern section of the sixth floor; the western half was another Kangyur Lhakhang. A chapel on the top floor held Namseling's principal image, Karma Pakshi (1204–83), second patriarch of the Karma Kagyü sect. The tradition of incarnated high lamas originated from him. A noteworthy object within this room was a three-dimensional mandala intricately carved of stone.

(105) JING

Just before the road marker, a big sand dune rises to the right. West of the dune is a tractor track that goes south into a small valley to Jing. After the village, the track continues west to a destroyed monastery on the left. It then crosses a gully and ascends to the deserted Wökar Drak ('White Light Rock') hermitage under a prominent overhang. Tsong Khapa studied the Cycles of Samvara and the Kalachakra here. Wökar Drak cannot be seen from the road. The walk up takes 2 1/2 hr.

JINGDHA WÖKAR DRAK

The Wökar Drak ridge contains Phukpa Götshang and Guru Drubphuk, celebrated meditation caves of Guru Rinpoche. Above them is Bairo Drubphuk where Vairocana discovered the treasure of Dorje Sempa. This cave was also occupied by Tsong Khapa for three months. Some distance below is Tsogyal Drubphuk, with a small, difficult entrance. Towards the top of the ridge is Namring Drubphuk, a favored site of Namkhai Nyingpo. Nearby is Yönten Palzang Chapel with a handprint of Guru Rinpoche. From the top of Wökar Drak, a trail along the ridge leads to Sheldrak (see page 522), a renowned hermitage high above Tsethang.

   After their exile from Samye, Guru Rinpoche and Yeshe Tsogyal were escorted by 12 goddesses to Terdrom Nunnery (see page 344) near Drigung along this route. Nyingma practitioners thus consider Wökar Drak a place of pilgrimage and many hidden treasures were found over the centuries in the area. One cave, consisting of a hollow protected by an overhang, is marked by prayer flags. Dorje Lingpa, the Third Discoverer King (1346–1405), and Terdak Lingpa, founder of Mindroling, both uncovered treasures here.

(112) NEW TOURIST FERRY

This crosses the Tsangpo to Samye Monastery. 25 yuan per person.

(119–120) JASA LHAKHANG

This destroyed chapel, close to the south side of the highway, west of Jasa Village, was one of Tibet's earliest chapels. It probably dates back to the end of the 11th C., during the Second Diffusion of Buddhism. Before the destruction, its statues exhibited the seldom-seen Xixia (Central Asia)-Pala style, similar to statues at Yemar (see page 390) and Nethang Drölma Lhakhang. Jasa was inspired by Gongpo Rabsal (832–915 or 855–939) and his disciple, Lume. Literary sources attribute its initial foundation to Pel Kortsen, grandson of Langdarma. This man, son of Wösung, ruled eastern Tsang at the end of the 9th C. after the breakup of the Yarlung empire. He is said to have founded eight temples. Two centuries later a local lord, Yuchen, constructed the main building (Ütse). Both his son and grandson expanded the complex and the latter, Jasa Lhachen, erected the main image during the first half of the 12th century.

Jasa was a Kadampa establishment until the Sakyapa took it over during their ascendancy in the 13th century.

The temple's name perhaps derives from the cuckoo (*ja*), considered the king of birds. These birds migrate from India and Nepal each spring, an auspicious time of year. The Lhasa government held a special celebration, called Jatön, to honor the occasion. Pel Kortsen laid the foundation of the Yasa Lhakhang on the spot where cuckoos congregate. A modest chapel was rebuilt here in 1988.

(124) TSETHANG

Tibet's fourth largest town stands at the entrance of the historic Yarlung Valley (see page 518).

LOWER KYI CHU: A PILGRIMAGE TO SHUGSEB NUNNERY

Location	Kyishö, lower left bank of the Kyi Chu
Map reference	NH46-9 B D
Trekking days	8 (one-way)
Start–Finish	Lhasa–Dorje Drak Monastery
Passes	Che

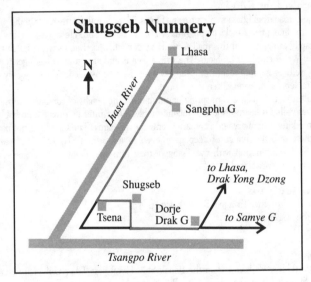

OVERVIEW

This eight-day pilgrimage follows the rarely visited left bank of the lower Kyi Chu. It is one of the journeys in this book that begins directly from Lhasa and is therefore very easy to access. Simply put on a pack and walk out of your hotel.

Although close to the capital, few outsiders have ever visited this area, known as Kyishö. One of those who did was the eminent Tibetologist, G Tucci, who came to the left bank of the Kyi Chu to study early temples of the Yarlung Dynasty (7th–9th centuries). A number of ancient sites are along the river and within nearby valleys, just two or three days' easy walk from Lhasa. Two royal temples built by 9th-C. Yarlung kings are outstanding examples. Sadly, these monuments are now in ruins. Also in the area is the Second Diffusion monastery of Sangphu Neutok, an institute of higher learning founded by the Kadampa during the era of Atisha (11th century).

The surroundings of the royal temples are especially sacred to the Nyingmapa tradition: the holy mountains of Gangri Tökar and Riwo Tsenga are here. Shugseb Nunnery, at the base of the former, is one of the most important Nyingmapa nunneries in Tibet. Today the place fairly hums with fervent religious activity. The historic Guru Rinpoche cave hermitages, high up in the ridges above the nunnery, are still used by nuns and ascetics. Longchenpa, the famed 14th-C. mystic and text-discoverer (*tertön*), spent years in these caves meditating and composing his epic works on the Khandro Nyingtik tradition.

At the end of this itinerary is Dorje Drak, an important Nyingmapa monastery. It is set among the undulating sand dunes of the Tsangpo Valley and is reached by the little-known Che La which straddles the western tip of the Yartö Drak Range, the watershed between the Tsangpo and the Kyi Chu.

A jeep road from Lhasa to Shuntse and Shugseb largely follows the route of the pilgrimage. From time to·time a truck picks up pilgrims at Lhasa's Banak Shöl Hotel to go to the nunnery. There is rarely any traffic on this road so walking, generally level and easy, is much the better alternative. Water can be a problem. The whole area is arid and most villages get their supply from deep wells or mountain springs. Tsangpo water is to be avoided. A good supply of water-purifying tablets or a water filter is essential.

Walk this trek in the cool spring or autumn. In the height of summer, the route along the flat river valley is far too hot and uncomfortable. The winter months are probably alright, although trekking in January and February is only for the hardy. The Che La is not particularly high, so there is little chance of deep snow even in mid-winter. To avoid the pass, follow the Kyi Chu to its junction with the Tsangpo, then turn east along the Tsangpo's left bank. This stretch is very isolated.

Related sections
Historic Valleys of the Tsangpo River Basin, p 470
Lhasa to the Yarlung Valley, p 595
Drakyul, p 317

Access
From central Lhasa, walk east from the Banak Shöl Hotel past Tibet University (across from the Sunlight Hotel and the Lhasa City Bus Station). At the end of the university street, turn right to cross the large East Lhasa Bridge. After the bridge, turn immediately right onto a dirt road (do not go left to follow the paved road, the Tibet–Sichuan highway) and walk west along the Kyi Chu to a military compound and the village of Drib (Selingbaton). In the vicinity is Tsechok Ling Monastery, one of the Four Royal Monasteries of Lhasa (see page 170).

Time Chart

Day	Place	Hours
1	Lhasa–Sangphu Valley	7
2	Sangphu Monastery	3
3	Namgyal Gang	7
4	Shugseb Nunnery	5 1/2
5	Nomad camp	5 1/4

6	Nomad camp	5
7	Tsangpo River	5
8	Dorje Drak	5

Trail Notes
✤ DAY 1 LHASA–SANGPHU VALLEY 7 HR
Walk west from Drib past the military compound and Tsechok Ling Monastery. Lhasa is across the Kyi Chu to the right. The jeep road forks at a point when the Potala is visible. Take the left fork that ascends from the river flats. Winding its way up and around a few hills, the track flattens out along a wide riverbed. After rounding a couple of spurs on the Kyi Chu, reach Lushon Village at the mouth of a green valley (1 1/2 hr from Tsechok Ling). The ruins of Sangda Karchung Monastery are in the hills to the left, as is Ramagang Village. Drepung Monastery can be seen from the ruins, a short hike from Lushon.

> ## Sangda Karchung Monastery
> One of the most ancient temple foundations in the Lhasa area, this monastery was built by King Tride Songtsen (Senelek), who ruled the Yarlung Dynasty from 804 to 814. Sangda Karchung was probably founded before 810. The king erected an inscribed stone *doring* proclaiming the allegiance of himself and his subjects to Buddhism. It also mentioned Songtsen Gampo as the first religious king, founder of the Jokhang, and Me Agtshom (Tride Tsugtsen), the Yarlung king who sponsored Kachu (see page 378) and Samye Chimpu (see page 631).
>
> Tucci, the Tibetologist, came here in 1948 and saw four *chörtens* marking the four corners of the temple with the stone column to the northeast. The *doring* has now disappeared but some accounts claim that fragments are in Lhasa. Ramagang is a village that has grown up on the site in recent times. On a ridge between the village and Sangda Karchung are the ruins of Neudzong Palace. The Lang family of the Phagmo Drupa Dynasty ruled much of Tibet from this spot.

Walk past a final few scattered houses. A steep path over a saddle is now visible. This is a short cut to the road that goes around another spur. The road soon turns sharply left, leaves the river behind and enters a side valley of dry plains and spectacular mountains. Further up this side valley are ruins, a white *chörten*, and a few painted rocks on a hillside to the left. Walk past this side valley. The road, curving into a second side valley, now forks at a row of trees. Its left branch goes to Sangphu Monastery, the right to Sangda Village.

✤ DAY 2 SANGPHU VALLEY–SANGPHU MONASTERY 3 HR
From the fork to the monastery is 3 hr. The route goes past houses and ruins. A barley mill is on the right bank of the river, a dam and a lake on the left. Continue past more houses up the increasingly steep valley. After a bright yellow-orange pipe, Sangphu Monastery appears high up the slopes. Eventually, the road becomes a path that leads to the grounds. A grove of trees next to a stream below the monastery is perfect for camping. Sangphu, the first functioning monastery on this itinerary, is a mass of ruins, but a few buildings have been restored in recent years.

Sangphu Monastery

The main chapel on the ground floor, a tiny chamber, has an image of Setrabpa. This wrathful divinity on horseback is one of the special protectors of the Gelugpa, especially for the Shartse Tratsang of Ganden. Upstairs is a larger room with new *thangkas*. These depict Atisha and his two main disciples, Dromtönpa and Ngok Lotsawa. One of Sangphu's most important treasures, now perhaps forever lost, is the set of over 100 volumes of rare texts that belonged to Ngok Lotsawa, original founder of the shrine. Higher up the valley is an area called Lingtö Dhokpa. Here is a sacred meditation cave of Rongtönpa, the 15th-C. founder of Nalendra Monastery.

History

This 11th-C. monastery was among the most important in Tibet and functioned as a unique nonsectarian center of Buddhist studies. Its founding was closely associated with Atisha, who strongly influenced the direction of the teachings. Ngok Legpai Sherab, one of his foremost disciples, began the Buddhist institute in 1073. He was succeeded by his nephew Loden Sherab (1059–1109), a respected scholar and translator who studied Buddhism in Kashmir. His tomb (present condition unknown) is located below the monastery at Sangda Village.

The monastery was originally called Neutog, 'the Source of Learning'. Between the 12th and 15th C., it attracted thousands of students from all over the country and Karmapa Dusum Khyenpa, Lama Shang, and Longchenpa, all illustrious figures, made use of its facilities. Later it split into two separate Kadampa institutions, Lingtö and Lingme. In 1152, however, the monastery came under Sakyapa control and its first abbot was Chapa Chökyi Seng (1109–69), a renowned Sakya scholar. He renamed it Sangphu and it thrived greatly, expanding into 14 colleges. By the end of the 18th C. this once great center had declined to a summer retreat (May and June), known as Yarchö, for Sakyapa and Gelugpa monks. Sangphu was reputedly renovated by the 13th Dalai Lama at the start of the 20th century.

✤ DAY 3 SANGPHU MONASTERY–NAMGYAL GANG 7 HR

Come back down the Sangphu Valley to Sangda (2 hr from Sangphu), site of the Sangda Kumbum Chörten (destroyed). It is located at the junction of the Sangda Chu and the Kyi Chu where the large, earth *chörten*-tomb of Loden Sherab once stood inside Lhakhang Yujochen Chapel. This small, neglected building still stands but all the sacred objects are gone.

Turn left at Sangda and follow the road along the Kyi Chu. Walk along a row of trees and cross the remainder of the side valley. Go around another long spur. The ruins of a house are immediately after this point on the banks of the river. Binge Village is visible up a side valley. The road now divides. The left branch leads up this valley to Binge, the right continues along the Kyi Chu Valley towards Sherong Village. Follow the latter to a small side valley. Walk past this valley and another spur. The road now goes inland to Chegay and the large village of Namgyal Gang.

✤ DAY 4 NAMGYAL GANG–SHUGSEB NUNNERY 5 1/2 HR

From Namgyal Gang follow the road past two side valleys. A short distance after Tshena

Qu is Tshena Sha (2 hr from Namgyal Gang. From Drib to here is 38 km). Look for the coracle that crosses the Kyi Chu from Tshena Druka (south of Drölma Lhakhang) and docks at the small village of Gyenbe (nearby is Ushang), which is part of Tshena Qu. This is one way to exit the itinerary and to reach the Lhasa–Tsethang road.

Riwo Tsenga This Mountain of the Five Peaks is a rocky ridge southwest of Mt Gangri Tökar (and south of Ushang). It is the Tibetan counterpart of China's famous Mt Wutai Shan, consecrated to Jampelyang, Bodhisattva of Wisdom. The easiest way to reach the peaks is simply to walk south from Ushang. This is also the start of a one-day *khora* around the western flank of the mountain (1 km from the village). One sacred site, Zangyak Namkha Drak, is believed by pilgrims to be the depository of many treasures (*ter*). It is accessible via an adjacent ridge distinguished by a set of natural steps. A meditation cave of Guru Rinpoche (Guru Drubphuk) is in the vicinity. Other caves were reputedly used by Yeshe Tsogyal (Guru Rinpoche's consort) and Guru Jotse, the 13th-C. text-discoverer, an incarnation of the Yarlung king, Senelek. Another important site of Riwo Tsenga is the cave called Lharing Longchen Drak.

At Tshena Sha, take the track that leads up the side valley of Nyephu. Cross a dry, hot plain, ascend gradually and pass the villages of Nyendha and Nyephu. Ruins of the 9th-C. Ushang Tower are near Nyendha (see below). Continue uphill through terraced barley fields to the last settlement of Ratö, located just below the junction of two upper valleys (Tshena Sha to this valley junction is 2 hr).

Ushang (Onchangdo) Temple

A 9th-C. monument located at the southwest corner of the Shuntse Valley entrance (beyond Tshena Sha and near Nyendha), was built by King Ralpachen (r 815–38). This extraordinary shrine, the monarch's most important, consisted of a nine-story pagoda with a Chinese-style turqoise dome. Ushang probably looked very much like a Nepalese temple. Its main image was Jowo (Sakyamuni). The three lower floors, used by the king and his ministers, were made of stone. He assigned the middle three to translators and pandits, and these were constructed of brick. The top three floors, a depository of images, were apparently built of wood and leather. According to the *Nyangral Chöjung* texts, Ralpachen invited master artists from China, Nepal, India, Kashmir, Khotan, and Tibet to decorate the monument. The Lhasa area, even at this early time, had a cosmopolitan artistic milieu. Ushang was destroyed in the 1960s. On nearby hills are traces of ancient walls, possibly elements of the royal castles. These might well have been built by King Senelek.

Across from Ratö in the right-hand valley is a good campsite beside a river, a picturesque and pleasant spot where herders and their yaks and goats pass by. To reach the path leading to Shugseb Nunnery, cross barley fields to the left-hand valley (Ratö Phu). Walk up its right side past a stone dam (note that the area leading up to the nunnery is also referred to as Shuntse). The nunnery is visible from the bottom of the valley as a rectangular white structure halfway up the mountain. Two smaller white buildings stand above the main structure; these are cave retreats and small shrines. From the dam follow the track up to the nunnery's large complex. The view from Shugseb is spectacular with snow ranges reaching out across the horizon. Across the Shuntse Valley is Gangri Tökar (dam to nunnery takes 1 1/2 hr).

SHUGSEB NUNNERY

80 nuns live in a veritable village of clay huts that make up this potent religious center. The nunnery proper consists of just one building with the ruins of a *chörten* and other collapsed structures beside it. Inside the courtyard is a kitchen on the right and an assembly hall that holds 20–30 people. New *thangkas* and a new statue of Guru Rinpoche are in the hall, and the altar bears an image of Machik Labdrönma, the female *yogini* intimately associated with this place. Upstairs, directly above the hall are living quarters for Shugseb Jetsünma, the incarnate lama-in-charge.

Before the Cultural Revolution, Shugseb was a major Nyingmapa center for nuns. Nowadays, even after the destruction, the tradition of retreat and practice (Dzokchen Nyingtik) is still very much alive. Some nuns take a respite from the rigors of the retreat and go down to Lhasa to stay at Tangton Gyalpo Nunnery (Drubthob Lhakhang, see page 127). A few live and meditate in the caves above the nunnery. One of these can be reached by following the trail past the nunnery, ascending through the living quarters of the nuns. This hike is worthwhile to see the cave and shrine and for the great views.

History

Yogini Machik Labdrönma (1055–1149) recognized Shugseb's remarkable geomantic properties and stayed here to pray, meditate, and teach. She was a student of Dampa Sangye, the famed Indian sage who took up residence at Langkor near Dingri (see page 271) and became one of the foremost masters of the Chöyul tradition, the esoteric teachings which require practitioners to spend a great deal of time meditating in cemeteries. The retreat of Shugseb was formally established by Gyargom Tsultrim Senge (1144–1204), student of Dorje Gyalpo, the founder of Densatil Monastery (see page 635). He is considered the originator of the Shugseb Kagyü lineage. Longchenpa is another important lama who spent time here while expounding his Nyingtik teachings.

GANGRI TÖKAR (WHITE SKULL MOUNTAIN, 5336 M)

This holy mountain is located behind Shugseb. A steep walk through scrub is required to reach its ridge (1 hr). Gangri Tökar's fame is largely tied to Longchenpa (1308–63), the pre-eminent Dzokchen lama who meditated here and wrote down his unique system of religious practice. He was the author of a commentary on the *Khandro Nyingtik* as well as the *Lama Yangtik*, and he subsequently achieved a high level of spiritual insight.

Not much snow accumulates on Gangri Tökar, a phenomenon that local tradition likens to a person who has gone to India and contracted a feverish disease called *gyagar tshaepa*. Because of the fever, little snow can stay on the mountain. It is supposedly shaped like the Gangtö La Ridge, itself a reflection of the deity, Dorje Phagmo. Her nipples generate streams of milky water and her *yoni* is the source of the principal river that drains the ridge's north side. Shugseb is sited at her left knee.

A noted pilgrimage site on the Gangri Tökar is the cave hermitage called Orgyen

Dzong (Gangri Tökar Monastery) or Lhakhang Kazhima. Longchenpa meditated here while his manifestations visited other caves. Outside the hermitage were two juniper trees (now only stumps), the homes of two tantric divinities called Za and Ngaksung Yudrön. These two were invaluable to Longchenpa when he immersed himself in writing. Nearby is the *rangjung* image of Khyabjuk, an efficacious protector for strokes and paralyses. Here also is a large rock, marked by prayer flags, believed by pilgrims to be the residence of Dorje Yudrönma, Gangri Tokar's protectress, who first enticed Longchenpa to visit this sacred area. Within the rock chapel of Lhakhang Kazhima is Dawa Chushel Phuk Cave, the Paradise of Kuntu Zangpo (Nangwa Thaye, a Primordial Buddha). Inside its inner chamber occasional murmurings can be heard. Some say these come from the Nechung Oracle (see page 165), wrathful incarnation of Kuntu Zangpo. To the east is Melong Phuk Cave, abode of Melong Dorje, where Longchenpa meditated. Shar Zimphuk Cave, farther to the east, is visible from here. Although difficult to reach, pilgrims consider it a prime site for practice. Other meditation caves associated with the nunnery are Ter Zimphuk, near Shugseb, and Dolung Zimphuk, a long way off.

✤ DAY 5 SHUGSEB NUNNERY–NOMAD CAMP 5 1/4 HR

Leave Shugseb and go back down to the valley junction above Ratö (1 1/4 hr). Follow a goat path up the canyon of the right-hand valley. The trail climbs gradually along the left side of the valley floor. A nomad camp is at the head of the valley (4 hr from valley junction) and the Che La Pass is visible from here.

✤ DAY 6 NOMAD CAMP–CHE LA–NOMAD CAMP 5 HR

Head towards the pass, angling towards the saddle to avoid a long, steep climb. The trail is clear most of the way. Che La is marked by a cairn and prayer flags; locate another cairn and a well-defined path to the left. From the second cairn, another nomad camp is visible in the valley below. Walk down to it. (Nomad camp to the pass, 4 hr; pass to second nomad camp, 1hr.)

✤ DAY 7 NOMAD CAMP–TSANGPO RIVER 5 HR

After the second nomad camp, a path follows the left bank of a long valley that leads down to the Tsangpo. The path crosses to the right at some mud structures on the left. After this it crisscrosses back and forth over the river. Herder trails on both sides all lead down the same valley. On approaching Lujen, the path works its way down to the right bank. Beyond the village, follow the left bank of the river to the Tsangpo. At this junction, turn east (left) for Dorje Drak or west (right) for Sinpori. Be sure to get water at Lujen before going down to the river. The stretches along the Tsangpo are exceedingly dry and no water is available unless you have means to purify the river water.

Sinpori Sinpori is the westernmost ridge of the Yartö Drak Range, which divides the Tsangpo from the Kyi Chu. Sinpori Village, at the tip, is at the very junction of the rivers. This village and a monastery of the same name are directly across from the Gongkar Chöde Monastery (see page 479) on the other side of the river. Sinpori Monastery, founded in the 13th C., belonged to the Sakyapa and was dedicated to Demchok. Its present condition is unknown.

✤ DAY 8 TSANGPO RIVER–DORJE DRAK 5 HR

Follow the Tsangpo River east along a track that leads up and around a spur. The landscape is dry and barren with no habitation whatsoever. Continue across the sand dunes. Keep close to the mountains to avoid pools of water formed between the dunes, unless you want a swim. Progress along the Tsangpo involves crossing side valleys and going over or around sand dunes. There are no clear paths; just follow the river. After crossing the entrance of the second and longest side valley (leading north), reach a nomad camp next to a cluster of trees at the foot of the mountains. Walk past more sand dunes, then round a final rocky point after bypassing the lower reaches of three more side valleys. Dorje Drak Monastery now appears as a large, partly ruined, partly rebuilt complex with striking red walls.

Dorje Drak Monastery One of two principal seats of the Nyingma sect; see page 598.

Excursion from Dorje Drak
Dorje Drak–Samye Monastery, 2 days, 42 km. This rather onerous route crosses an empty expanse of desert and sand dunes. Despite the large river, most settlements along this part of the Tsangpo Valley are set back inside more hospitable side valleys. They depend on mountain streams rather than on the river for their water.

Dorje Drak to the Lhasa–Tsethang highway
Cross the Tsangpo by the Dorje Drak ferry (see page 599) then follow a trail upstream towards some trees where prayer flags mark the path. Cross a bridge over a stagnant waterway to reach the main road at the road marker 47/48 km. Hitch to Lhasa or Tsethang. Another option is to connect with the Lhasa–Dorje Drak–Yamdrok itinerary in order to head to Lake Yamdrok and the Yarlung Valley (see page 595).

DRACHI:
THE VALLEY OF MINDROLING MONASTERY, A PRINCIPAL SHRINE OF THE NYINGMAPAS

OVERVIEW

The Drachi is one of six principal valleys that open southward from the Tsangpo, between the Tsangpo–Kyi Chu junction and the Yarlung (see page 515). Immediately east of the Dranang Valley (see page 501), this broad valley—whose entrance is between road markers 78 and 83 km—leads due south from the Lhasa–Tsethang road. Tracks lead south on both sides of the Drachi River. The western one goes to Mindroling, one of two principal Nyingmapa monasteries and one of the largest religious institutions in the country (Lume, the celebrated pioneer of the Second Diffusion of Buddhism, founded a small chapel on this site towards the end of the tenth century). At the Drachi Valley entrance is Tsongdü Tsokpa,

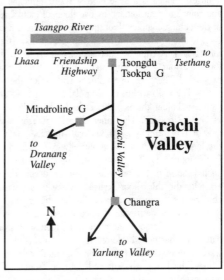

a 13th-C. Sakyapa monastery, and within the valley are a number of recently discovered Yarlung-dynasty (7th–9th C.) archeological sites. These include the ancient burial sites of Khongcha, Changra, and Dhoku Ri. Changra's large necropolis has nearly 50 tombs, and Dhoku Ri contains rare burial chambers where small animals were entombed to accompany the deceased. See page 365 for further information.

TSONGDÜ TSOKPA (JIZING TSOKPA) MONASTERY

Tsongdü Tsokpa Monastery, at the eastern limit of the valley entrance, is 250 m south of the main road near road marker 83 km. The large village here is called Drachi (Tsongdü). This Sakyapa center was founded in the early 13th C. by Khache Panchen Sakyasri (b 1127), a renowned teacher from Kashmir. As the last abbot of the legendary Nalendra Monastery in India, his fame earned him an invitation to teach in Tibet in 1204, when he was nearly 80 years old. In ten years he founded four lineages known as the Tsokpa Shi; one of them began here. Gyaling Tsokpa (see page 504) and Tsongdü Tsokpa were two of four Sakyapa *tsokpas* (monastery) founded by Sakyasri. The other two were in the Yarlung Valley and Shigatse area. A number of illustrious lamas practiced in Tsongdü Tsokpa through the ages: Lume, who first explored the Drachi Valley, established two chapels here; Go Lotsawa Shonnu Pel, the compiler of the *Blue Annals*, a valuable compendium of religious history; Khyungpo Neljorpa, the 12th-C. Bönpo lama who founded the Shangpa Kagyü School at Shang Shong. The monastery initially followed the Kadampa tradition but later, when the Sakyapas dominated the region in the mid-13th C., it converted to that sect.

THE SITE

Tsongdü Tsokpa is a large monastery. Its principal south-facing structure is four-storys high and completely surrounded by two floors of monks' residences, which also form the perimeter of the oblong complex. Fronting these quarters is a corridor for circumambulation. The main gate, to the south, passes below the second floor (the first floor of the main building is used for storage). A triple wooden staircase leads up to the main entrance, framed by a spacious foyer and four grand, intricately carved pillars. Remains of paintings show two four-headed, two-armed Chenresis, one riding a white swan, the other a black horse. The style is unusual.

The walls within the 20-pillar *dukhang* have all been whitewashed. The only surviving paintings border the skylight: Eight Medicine Buddhas and Guru Tsengye, the Eight Forms of Guru Rinpoche. The inner chapel, Tri Tsangkhang, is a small, two-column room with most of its paintings—1,000 Buddhas—intact. A lower section, adjacent to the entrance, displays the Eight Bodhisattvas, all beautifully executed. These are, without a doubt, the best works in the monastery. The southwest corner has a secret passage that leads to the bottom floor, an indication of the prevailing paranoia during the era of Mongol overlordship. A *khorlam* encircles the third floor skylight. Along its south wing is a spacious, light-filled room, the chamber for the incarnate lama. Within this are a *gönkhang* and a Kangyur Khang. The fourth floor has been destroyed; it once housed the Neten Lhakhang.

A major restoration of the monastery took place in the 19th C. and all paintings date from that period. However, their contents closely follow the originals. Tsongdü Tsokpa was spared total destruction in the Cultural Revolution because it was used as a grain storehouse. Chöne Lhakhang, adjacent and right of Tsongdü Tsokpa, is a small two-story chapel with a courtyard enclosed by a *khorlam*. The paintings within the ground floor chapel are destroyed.

MINDROLING MONASTERY

About 8 km south of Drachi, near the head of a side valley, is the large and impressive monastery of Mindroling. Situated above Mondrup Shang Village, this famous institution, together with Dorje Drak Monastery (see page 598) across the Tsangpo River, are the two major Nyingmapa centers in Central Tibet. Most of the vast complex has been destroyed and part of the main chapel's west wing was blown up by dynamite in the 1960s. Despite the damage, its handsome buildings constructed of beautifully dressed stones are among the finest in the country. Four hills surround the site: Miyo Ri to the east, Drepo to the west, Gyaldan to the south, and Danma to the north. The east-facing complex looks down towards the flood plain of the main Drachi Valley.

HISTORY

Towards the end of the 10th C., Lumé Tsultrim Shenrab (see page 27) came here and built a very modest chapel, the earliest foundation of Mindroling. This renowned lama (c 950–

1025), with Atisha, Rinchen Zangpo, and others spearheaded the restoration of Buddhism—Tibet's Second Diffusion—during the early 11th century. He was a disciple of Gongpa Rabsal and one of ten monks who fled Tibet for Kham in 970 to study Buddhism. His influence spread quickly upon his return to Central Tibet in 978 and he was instrumental in re-establishing monasteries that proved pivotal in the religion's development: Neten Lhakhang at Yerpa, Lamo, Dranang, Tsongdü Tsokpa, and Sonak Tangboche (see Place Name Index for further information).

In 1677, Terdak Lingpa (Pema Garwang Gyürme Dorje, 1646–1714), alias Minling Terchen (Great Treasure-finder of Mindroling), vigorously expanded the monastery. To this day he is popularly considered the founder rather than Lumé. He 'rediscovered' important texts (Rigdzin Tutrik cycle, Dzokchen treatises, etc) that were incorporated into the Nyingmapa teaching known as Lhoter (Southern Treasure). Mindroling became the head monastery of the Southern Nyingmapa. Dorje Drak, across the river, is the seat of the Northern Nyingmapa, whose teachings are based on the Jangter (Northern Treasure). Terdak Lingpa taught both the Great Fifth Dalai Lama and Lochen Dharmashri, a monk well versed in medicine, poetry, and painting. He also compiled the *Nyingma Kama*, Guru Rinpoche's 13-volume exposition on the methods of enlightenment.

Mindroling's four principal buildings were largely destroyed during three traumatic periods. The first was the Dzungar invasion of 1718, when parts of the Jowo Lhakhang and its main statue were severely damaged. Polhane Sonam Tobgyal (1689–1747), a nobleman and minister who effectively ruled Tibet from 1728 to 1747 with the support of the Chinese, contributed large sums for restoration. The second occurred in 1959 when the Chinese invaded. But

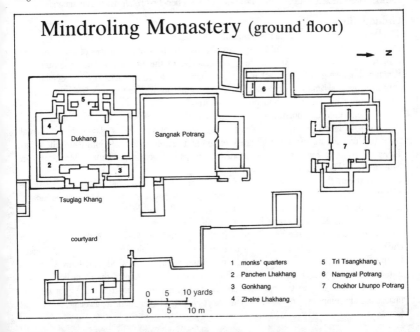

Mindroling Monastery (ground floor)

N →

Dukhang

Sangnak Potrang

Tsuglag Khang

courtyard

1 monks' quarters
2 Panchen Lhakhang
3 Gonkhang
4 Zhelre Lhakhang
5 Tri Tsangkhang
6 Namgyal Potrang
7 Chokhor Lhunpo Potrang

0   5   10 yards
0   5   10 m

perhaps the most destructive phase was the Cultural Revolution, when this vast site, including a 13-story *chörten*, was razed. Only a fraction remains of the untold treasures accumulated over the centuries. Mindroling had over 300 monks before the Chinese came.

THE SITE

Mindroling, one of the largest monasteries in Central Tibet, encompasses an area of over 100,000 sq m. Two entrance gates lead to the complex. The main one, opening to the east, is now blocked and disused. A similar north-facing gate, located at the south corner of the east wall, is in better condition and now functions as the main entrance. Some murals remain along the stairway inside the gateway. Two different layers of paint represent earlier and later works; the latter includes Guru Rinpoche and various animals.

TSUGLAG KHANG

This three-story, east-facing structure on the west side of the courtyard is the principal building of Mindroling. One of the most impressive in Tibet, its brown stone walls were meticulously constructed by master craftsmen. The building's exterior is in reasonable condition. Its interior, however, was gutted and is recently restored. The original stone entrance has been replaced by a wooden one; flanking it are two stone structures. Recessed cavities near their tops contain images of the main figures of the various sects. The walls of the entrance foyer have paintings of the Four Guardian Kings, the Wheel of Life (*sipa khorlo*), and inscriptions on the north and south walls describe Mindroling's history as well as the benefits of offerings and circumambulation.

Ground floor

The large *dukhang* (20 columns) is surrounded by chapels. Its walls have paintings of Tsepame, Drölma Jang (Green Tara), and Guru Rinpoche. The south wall has images of the eight Guru Rinpoche manifestations. Around them are episodes in the life of the tantric master. The Panchen Lhakhang (six columns) is the first chapel to the south (left) of the assembly hall entrance; the *gönkhang* (two columns) is to the right (north). The latter's inside walls have line paintings depicting wrathful protector deities.

Zhelre Lhakang, opening from the south wall of the *dukhang*, is a four-column chapel. Its principal objects are a silver *chörten* of Dechen Chokdrub and a clay statue of Terdak Lingpa. Along the west (right) wall are another eight manifestations of Guru Rinpoche (Guru Tsengye). A set of *Kangyur* and ten *chörtens*, perhaps salvaged from Dranang Monastery, are here as well. The murals show Jampelyang.

Between the fourth and fifth row of columns in the *dukhang* is a 1.5 m-tall statue of Terdak Lingpa (white hair and beard) enclosed in a glass case. A gold and silver *chörten*-tomb to the right contains his remains. The throne in the hall belongs to the incarnate lama (*tulku*), Kunsang Wangyal, now living in India.

Tri Tsangkhang, the most important chapel, stands at the back of the *dukhang* (west end). The room, over 6 m high, has as its main image a 4-m-tall Sakyamuni, ornately backed by the Six Ornaments (*gyendruk*): *garuda*, fish, vase, pillar, conch shell, and lotus. Only the statue's head is original. Flanking the Buddha are his two main disciples; the Eight Bodhisattvas are to the sides. Next to the entrance are the two protectors, Tamdrin and Vajrapani, and images of Sakyamuni are on the walls. This inner chapel is larger than the *dukhang*, an unusual feature.

Second floor

Six principal chapels constitute this floor.

Tersar (New Treasure) Lhakhang, East-center, eight columns: This large chapel, considered the most important, contains the *chörten* tombs of Garje Desi Chuding and the Ninth Tulku Tripa Kunsang Wangyal. A set of *Kangyur* is also stored here. The east wall is made up of a broad series of picture windows.

Dechenling Lhakhang, Southeast corner, six columns: Dechenling (Migyur Paldrön Lhakhang) is dedicated to Migyur Paldrön, the daughter of Terdak Lingpa. Her silver *chörten*-tomb, two-storys high, is studded with precious jewels. On the altar are numerous small bronzes and several Kadampa

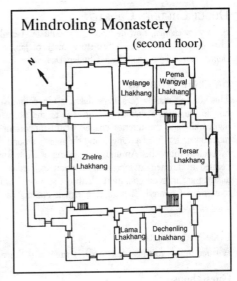

Mindroling Monastery
(second floor)

chörtens. Some are finely crafted, especially those from the Pala period (8th–12th century). The library contains the voluminous works of Terdak Lingpa.

Zhelre Lhakhang (Neten Lhakhang), West-center, six columns: This chapel has clay statues of the 16 Arhats.

Pema Wangyal Lhakhang; The main relic here is the two-story silver *chörten* of Pema Wangyal, the fifth incarnation of Mindroling's founder. Gilt statues are here as well.

Welange Lhakhang, North-center, six columns: This chapel contained silver *chörtens* and several gilt statues.

Lama Lhakhang, (Dechen Buk), South-center, six columns: The walls of this chapel have good paintings of the lamas in the Nyingmapa lineage. In the past, the principal relic here was the silver tomb of Pema Tenzing, a past abbot. A powerful object was the statue of Kuntu Zangpo (Samantabhadra), a Primordial Buddha of the Nyingmapa pantheon. It has now been replaced by a wall painting that shows the deity with its consort. To the right of the altar is a rock with supposedly the hoofprint of Terdak Lingpa's horse. Notice the unusual *thangka* of Terdak Lingpa—his handprints and footprints are meticulously depicted at the four corners. It was commissioned by the Fifth Dalai Lama.

Chökhor Lhünpo Potrang

This three-story stone building is located north of the Tsuglag Khang beyond the courtyard. Behind the *dukhang* is the Jowo Khang, which once contained the gold-plated statue of Terdak Lingpa, murals of the 100,000 Buddhas, and a huge Sakyamuni statue made of a precious alloy (*zhikhyim*).

DUDUL CHUDHEN CHÖRTEN

A 13-story *chörten*, now destroyed, was built by Terdak Lingpa. Its first floor was the Jampa Lhakhang and contained a two-story image of Jampa, the Future Buddha. Surrounding the *chörten* were eight small Desi Chuden *chörtens*.

SANGNAK POTRANG

This consists mainly of a large *dukhang* (36 columns) and a Jowo Khang. The three-story building, used as a granary, is adjacent to the north end of the Tsuglag Khang. Both the main walls and the interior chapels of this important structure were heavily damaged. The main image was Terdak Lingpa and the murals around the upper walls were said to be painted by Lochen Rinpoche. An unusual painting of Guru Rinpoche stands near the entrance. Also painted by Lochen, it represents a vision of Terdak Lingpa. Most of the paintings in the *dukhang* are in good condition. Within the inner Jowo Khang was a two-story statue of the four-armed Chenresi Chakzhipa. Sangnak Potrang can be reached via the top floor of the Tsuglag Khang.

NAMGYAL POTRANG

A three-story structure (destroyed) is sited near the northwest corner of Sangnak Potrang.

Guest house

The two-story guest house and monks' quarters is on the north side of the monastery courtyard. Its rooms are pleasant and cosy with cushions and Tibetan carpets on the floor. Chinese quilts are provided for overnight guests. The food is adequate and the monks hospitable. Mindroling is a good place to stay for a couple of days.

Ritrö Kyipo Shing Tshal Chen Once a sizeable and influential hermitage high up and across from Mindroling, it contained an important statue of Mahakala (Gönpo Jingdhen). Nearby are five other retreats.

Treks from Mindroling A path from Mindroling leads south to the head of the Drachi Valley. After crossing a 5250-m pass (one day to reach the base), it descends to a populous east–west trending valley that leads east to Chongye. This route is an interesting, alternative way to reach the Yarlung Valley. Allow two days to cross the pass and two more to reach Chongye. Another trail from the head of the Mindroling Valley goes due east over a 5050-m pass to Chongmoche Monastery in the Chongye Valley (three days).

For The Yarlung Dynasty tombs of the Drachi Valley, see page 365.

DRANANG:
VALLEY OF THE 13 BUDDHA–LAMAS

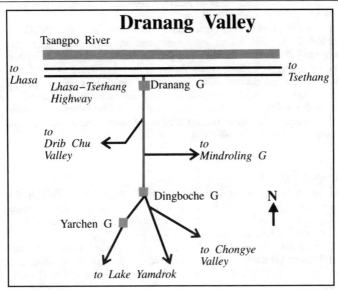

Dranang Valley

Tsangpo River

to Lhasa

Lhasa–Tsethang Highway

Dranang G

to Tsethang

to Drib Chu Valley

to Mindroling G

Dingboche G

Yarchen G

N

to Chongye Valley

to Lake Yamdrok

OVERVIEW

The Dranang Valley is popularly known as the Valley of the 13 Buddha-lamas (Dranang Kyebu Dampa Chusum). Some of Tibet's best-known religious masters were born here: Drapa Ngonshe, founder of the Dranang Monastery; Longchenpa of Derong Monastery; Terdak Lingpa, the patriarch of Mindroling; Tsangpa Gyare, the first explorer of Tsari; and Orgyen Lingpa, founder of Yarchen Monastery. Dranang Monastery is doubtless the most important institution in the valley. Its stunning collection of 11th C. Pala-style murals is perhaps the earliest and only extant example of its kind in Tibet. Because of its artistic and historical significance, Dranang Monastery is treated in a separate chapter (see page 393).

Jampaling Kumbum (see page 465), the largest *chörten* in Tibet before its destruction by the Red Guards, still has extraordinarily imposing ruins. It was one of the few monastic institutions to integrate commerce and religion by having traders on the premises. Both Nepal and Bhutan had trading missions here. The Yarlung-dynasty (7th–9th C.) tombs of Serkhung (see page 367) were discovered in the valley recently; the largest rivals in grandeur those of the Valley of the Kings at Chongye. A rare *chörten*-shaped tomb is also found here. But perhaps the most exciting discovery is the completely intact interior of a Yarlung-era burial chamber, the only one excavated in Tibet. Overlooking the necropolis are the extensive ruins of Pema Chuling, one of Tibet's largest nunneries.

Further up the valley is the large Gelugpa monastery of Riwo Namgyal, the birthplace of Tsangpa Gyare, an ascetic who first explored the important pilgrimage site of Tsari. At the county seat of Gyaling Qu is the 13th-C. monastery of Gyaling Tsokpa. Early architectural elements have survived and its notable collection of *thangkas* has been transferred to a charming hideway chapel a short distance away. Nearby is Nyingdho Monastery. Here the principal object of veneration is a pillar of uncommon powers.

Dingboche is sited at the upper reaches of the Dranang Valley. This 16th-C. monastery, perched high in the cliffs, has an unusual *chöra*-cum-hermitage; meditators practice inside numerous small pits dug into the soft earth. The Dra Yugang Drak is a Guru Rinpoche cave complex just around the corner and near the top of the ridge. Within Dranang's side valleys are other nunneries and monasteries, including Derong, birthplace of Longchenpa, and Dargye Chöding, birthplace of Terdak Lingpa. The chapel of Yarchen has preserved archaic structural elements and a nearby Yarlung-dynasty burial site is noted for its rare stone coffins.

The Dranang Valley offers a rich mix of archeology, religion and art, making it a rewarding destination for a two- to three-day visit.

Access
TRATHANG VILLAGE

Trathang lies at the entrance of the south-trending Dranang Valley, on the right side of the Lhasa–Tsethang highway (at road marker 76 km). A tea house and Tibetan restaurant next to the road cater to travellers. Tsethang is 47 km further east. For more information on the Lhasa–Tsethang highway, see page 472.

Dranang Xian, the district seat for the Dranang Valley and neighboring areas is 2 km south of Trathang. The government occupies several compounds in the village center, and accommodation is available in the one next to the cinema. Dranang Monastery is sited within the village.

DRANANG XIAN TO DINGBOCHE MONASTERY

The walk from Dranang Xian to Dingboche follows a level dirt road that runs along the eastern rim of the valley. It takes most of one day, without allowing for rest stops. Only the final stage, a steep ascent to the monastery along zigzagging trails, is strenuous. Bring sleeping gear and spend the night in Dingboche.

From Dranang Monastery, walk along the wide dirt road towards the Jampaling Chörten. Pass two large government compounds flanking the road. A satellite dish is on the right where the road divides. The left branch goes up to Jampaling. Take the right fork, which leads first to the valley's eastern side and then south to Jurme (Gyürme) Village. This is the birthplace of Gyürme Yeshe Dorje (Tsangpa Gyare) the ascetic who first explored and popularized the premier pilgrimage site of Tsari. A side trail goes left up the mountain to Riwo Namgyal Monastery (see opposite). 1 hr beyond Jurme, on the left, is an archaic-looking *chörten* known simply as Chörten Karpo ('White Chörten'). Continue along the main road to a shrine on top of a hillock, overlooking the road from the left. Called Gyürme Tsen, it commemorates Gyürme Yeshe Dorje. Just beyond is Gombu Ba Village. Further on, to the left, is a wide side valley (a footpath along its left perimeter leads in 1/2 hr to Gatshal Phuk Monastery, see page 505). At the center of the valley entrance is Gyaling Qu Village, 1/2 hr from Chörten

Karpo. Here is the disused Gyaling Tsokpa Monastery (see page 504). Continue south up the Dranang Valley, past several villages, to another wide side valley off to the left. Astride the road at this junction is the village of Rinchen Gang. A small Mani Lhakhang chapel, with a *mani* wheel, is at the village's south end. From Gyaling Qu to here is 1 1/2 hr.

Rinchen Gang to Mindroling Monastery From Rinchen Gang, a trail leads east up a wide, gentle valley. At the head of the valley, cross a ridge (4700 m); the important monastery of Mindroling lies below (4 1/2 hr).

Follow the main road south to Kyiru Qu (3/4 hr), where a government compound stands amidst finely built stone houses. Overlooking the village is a small ridge with a line of colorful prayer flags leading to the top. Yellow-walled Kyiru Lhakhang, recently renovated, is in the village. Its *gönkhang* has new, life-sized clay statues.

Ruins crown a ridge across the valley to the west. Below them is a white *chörten*, site of Dingboche Monastery. Towards the head of the Dranang Valley, further to the south, it is possible to see it dividing into two branches. Near the beginning of the right (west) branch are some tin-roofed buildings. Beyond that is the important Yarchen Lhakhang. Quite a few villages are scattered around this junction area. To reach Dingboche, walk from Kyiru Qu to the western edge of the valley, wade a river, and carry on to Dhelekling Village. From here a trail and a rudimentary jeep road climb to the monastery. (A path also leads south, curving to the right, to Yarchen Monastery.) From Kyiru Qu to here is 1 hr of hard climbing, but the reward is a superb view of the valley.

PEMA CHULING NUNNERY

This south-facing nunnery (destroyed) is located on the north slopes of a hill above Serkhung Village. Pema Chuling was one of the few large nunneries in Tibet. Its site occupied an area of 5,000 sq m and consisted of one principal building surrounded by ten smaller chapels and residences. Only one floor of the main building still stands.

RIWO NAMGYAL MONASTERY

This recently rebuilt Gelugpa monastery, under the Namgyal Tratsang of the Potala, sits within Gyaling Qu district, 4 km south of Dargyaling in the Dranang Valley. Below, on the valley floor, is Jurme (Gyurme) Village. The extensive ruins and new structures, at an altitude of 3900 m, occupy an area of 11,000 sq m.

The badly damaged Tshomchen, a large two-story stone structure, is surrounded by chapels, monks' quarters, and a long, stone perimeter wall. Like most houses in the Gyaling Qu area, these secondary buildings have walls made of stone for the base and topped with walls of earth. On the south slopes, 20 m below the monastery, is a large rock carved with the 'Om Mani Padme Hum' *mantra*. Above it is a square platform with a lotus pedestal. Some inscriptions are still legible. A conspicuous white *chörten* on the valley floor stands below and west of the monastery. Originally built in the 15th C., it is known simply as Chörten Karpo ('White Chörten'). Destroyed, together with Riwo Namgyal, in the 1960s, the *chörten* was rebuilt according to the original design. Riwo Namgyal was founded ca 1470 by Gönten Gyalpo, one of Tsong Khapa's disciples. In its heyday 60 monks and nine *khenpos* lived here.

Jurme is a celebrated site within the Dranang Valley because of its association with Gyurme Yeshe Dorje (Tsangpa Gyare). Yeshe Dorje spent his whole life on pilgrimage and did not associate with monastic establishments.

NYINGDHO MONASTERY

About 5 km south of Gyaling Qu, a dirt road leaves the Dranang Valley and goes west up a branch valley. Another 5 km west of this junction is Pedrong Shang, where ruins of three 17th-C. Nyingma monasteries and an early burial site can be found in its vicinity. Nyingdho is a further 6 km west on a south-facing cliff. This Nyingmapa monastery was built during the first part of the 13th C. by Panchen Rinchen Lingpa. The second abbot, Nyingdho Thamche Khyenpa (1217–77), another of Dranang's 13 Buddha-lamas, was born here. Towards the end of the 17th C., the center was absorbed by Mindroling (see page 496), a main seat of the Nyingmas. When the Dzungars invaded, Nyingdho, like most Nyingmapa temples, was sacked. It recovered with the help of Mindroling. Rotting interior columns required the entire monastery to be rebuilt in 1958, only to be again destroyed in the 1960s! The monastery is now being restored.

Interestingly, Nyingdho's most sacred relic was a short column. It came originally from Khyungpo Tengcheng, a Bön stronghold in East Tibet, and was believed to prevent droughts and hailstorms, and to control epidemics. Once a year, on the 29th day of the 11th month, this pillar was displayed to the public; at all other times it was carefully hidden. Some say this pillar still exists, kept secretly in the neighborhood.

GYALING TSOKPA MONASTERY (GYANGLING TSOKPA)

The monastery, 7 km south of Dranang Xian within Gyaling Qu Village, is used as offices and remains in reasonable condition. One of four celebrated *tsokpas* (monasteries), it was founded in 1224 by a disciple of Kashmiri Pandita Sakyasri (1127–1225). Sakyasri followed in Atisha's footsteps, spreading Buddhism throughout Tibet. He travelled around the country between 1204 and 1213, visiting all the principal pilgrimage sites, and founded four new monasteries known as the Four Tsokpas (see page 495). Many important personages from all sects were taught by him. Gyaling Tsokpa became a Nyingmapa monastery, although it maintained strong ties with the Gelugpa and Kagyüpa. In the 15th C., Go Lotsawa Shonnu Pal, author of the encyclopaedic *Blue Annals*, made this his residence.

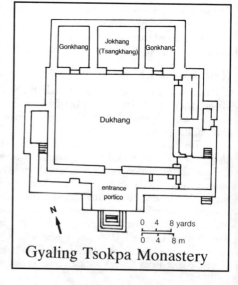

Gyaling Tsokpa Monastery

The architecture of this monastery resembles Tsongdü Tsokpa. Its large south-facing, three-story building is surrounded by a rectangular wall and a 5 m-wide moat. The ground floor, sunken like a half-basement, retains parts of the original stone foundation. The second floor, reached by a flight of stone steps, contains the main assembly hall (*dukhang*). Notice the two types of columns here: one is colorful and ornate; the other, square and short, is carved with simple scroll, floral, and lotus patterns. The latter is the earlier.

Most paintings were whitewashed during the Cultural Revolution but some remain. These show Sakyamuni, Tsepame, Guru Rinpoche, Trisong Detsen, birds and animals. A painting left of the main entrance depicts the founders of Tibetan Buddhism: Guru Rinpoche flanked by Trisong Detsen (left) and Santarakshita (right). Above and below them are the 25 disciples of Guru Rinpoche, each demonstrating a special skill. Some are in full flight, others eat rocks; the motifs are enchanting. Along the side walls of the *dukhang* are two tiny chambers.

The inner Jokhang has four square columns, similar to the older ones of the *dukhang*. At the southwest corner is a secret passage, used by the monks to escape during times of strife. The murals are in good condition. They depict images of Sakyamuni (two peculiar lions flank his throne), Chenresi, Tsepame, the Four Guardians, and various animals. West and east of this inner chamber are two *gönkhangs*, a layout characteristic of Gyaling Tsokpa. The left one has four round columns painted with wrathful human heads. A third floor corridor encircles the skylight of the second floor. Small rooms open onto the passageway and its badly damaged paintings.

Important relics of Gyaling Tsokpa have been removed to Gatshal Phuk Monastery (see below). These include 17 *thangkas* (from the 17th, 18th, and 19th C.) and a small *rangjung* statue of Sakyasri. The latter, only 0.15 m high, was made in the early 13th C. by the great teacher himself (one of four made by him). It is a fine piece of early Tibetan statuary.

GYALING GATSHAL PHUK

This charming, hidden monastery is located halfway up the north edge of the Gyaling Tsokpa Monastery side valley. Two foot trails lead to Gatshal Phuk, one along the northern perimeter of the valley, the other from Gyaling Tsokpa. Both take 1/2 hr; large fields of stone cairns are passed en route. Gatshal Phuk, a complex of new buildings, nestles behind a lovely grove of trees. Restored in 1986, it was originally a meditation retreat for the monks of Gyaling Tsokpa. Now, a dozen old, friendly monks remain.

The assembly hall has front and rear sections. Its front room contains some 20 original *thangkas* (18th and 19th C.), still in good condition. The rear portion has a row of recent statues. Guru Rinpoche is at the center. To his right is Longchen Rabjampa, one of the 13 Buddha-lamas of the Dranang Valley (born at Derong Monastery), and statues of Rabjam and Konchok Pal Gyatso. Left of Guru Rinpoche are Sakyamuni and Jigme Lingpa, principal disciple of Longchenpa. Towards the front is a small *rangjung* statue of Khache Panchen Sakyasri (see page 495). Near it is a noteworthy Nepalese-style bronze image of an early period.

Dingboche Monastery

Dingboche, a recently restored Drukpa Kagyü monastery, sits halfway up the west ➡

slopes above Dhelekling Village, which is located on the west side of the Drathang River, 15 km due south of Dranang Xian. The extensively fortified monastery was founded in 1567 by Rinchen Pelzang (1529–1611), a disciple of Pema Karpo (1526–92), the most prominent lama of the Drukpa Kagyü lineage. At that time, only a one-story chapel existed. The second abbot, Chokdra Nyendrak Pelzang (1613–82) vastly expanded Dingboche. It was twice destroyed, by the Dzungars and during the Cultural Revolution, and twice rebuilt. The Lhasa Government has funded the recent reconstruction, begun in 1984.

TSUGLAG KHANG

The centerpiece of the complex is a huge four-story Tsuglag Khang (severely damaged), which sits on top of a 2.5-m-high stone platform. Its design is a representation of the Demchok Kyilkhor mandala. The main statues were Sakyamuni and his two chief disciples, Shariputra and Mandgalyayana. This Buddha image contained the heart, tongue, and eyes of Rinchen Pelzang. To the left, outside the perimeter wall (parts of which reach a height of 15 m) is the rebuilt Namgyal Chörten. This round two-story structure, sitting on a square base, was built by the Third Chokdrak Tulku in the early 18th century.

JANGCHUB CHÖRTEN

About 70 m southeast of the main building is another, larger *chörten* (8 m) called Jangchub Chörten. Its top has been destroyed but the rest is in good condition. Two oblong cavities (3 m) lie along the west and north walls.

THE COMPLEX

The Tsuglag Khang sits at the north end of the complex. In front of it is a large flagstone courtyard. To the west (left) are most of Dingboche's rebuilt chapels. Preceding the courtyard is a communal kitchen to the right of the entrance passage, and above it the Zimchung Lhakhang. A sheltered porch outside

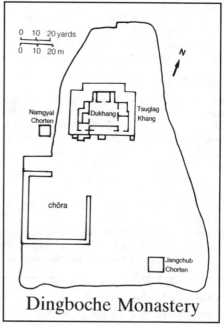

Dingboche Monastery

this chapel provides accommodation for visitors. From the spacious courtyard, the rebuilt buildings with the extensive ruins as a backdrop provide one of the most dramatic vistas in the Dranang Valley.

The monastery's two main chapels are to the west of the Tsuglag Khang. The south Jokhang, fronted by an entrance porch with a large *mani* wheel, is the first one reached. Within the ample room are three new statues: Jowo, in the center, is flanked by Rinchen Pelzang and Drölkar (White Tara). The left and right walls contain a complete set of the *Kangyur*. North of the Jokhang is the Guru Lhakhang, reached by a small flight of steps. Clay images of Guru Rinpoche and his two consorts are inside. Along the left wall, a door opens into a cramped *gönkhang*. The center image is a four-armed Mahakala (Gönpo). Flanking it are the Chökyong (protector) of Dingboche (left) and Palden Lhamo (right).

Fronting the ruins to the east, near the kitchen, is a new *dukhang*. The south side of the *dukhang* courtyard is taken up by one-story monks' residences. Between these and the Jokhang is a narrow passage that leads south to the *chöra* (courtyard). Here is one of the more unusual monastic institutions found anywhere in Central Tibet.

CHÖRA

The *chöra* is a square, grassy site (50 m by 50 m) enclosed by a low double wall. These two walls, separated by a distance of 3 m, contain between them numerous cavities dug into the earth, called *chöku*. Each one is about 1 m deep and 1 m distant from its closest neighbor. Stone slabs line the bottom and sides, while miniature blue and white tents canopy the *chökus*, providing shelter for a single person. Monks in retreat seclude themselves inside these cavities. There are 22 *chökus* running along the west side of the field, 20 along the south, and 10–11 along the east and north sides. Near the center of the *chöra* is the principal *chöku*, reserved for the supervising lama. Named Chokdra Chokzhung, this remarkable little structure is enclosed by low stone walls with colored *mani* stones on top. This unusual hermitage has existed for more than 400 years.

At the southern edge of the square field is a long row of finely carved *manis*. Most are images of deities and famous lamas. Beyond is a hillock topped by three singular, virtually undamaged *chörtens* built of stone pieces and slabs. They stand 3–4 m tall. The center one, the tallest, has three sections, each with a glass window at the center. Standing on a stone base, it resembles a charming miniature pagoda. To its sides are similarly designed *chörtens*, although with two sections only. The tall *chörten* contained the relics of Lobtsen Jangme, a Dingboche lama; the right one is consecrated to the protector Zhidhak Dorje Drakdul. These *chörtens* were built to commemorate the site where Dingboche's first stones were quarried. Many white stone cairns litter the area. Approximately 20 monks now live at the monastery.

➡

THE STONE CARVINGS OF DINGBOCHE

Dingboche is known for its 16th-C. carved stone images. Before the Cultural Revolution over a thousand existed; today, there are only a fraction of that total. Most of the collection consists of relief carvings. The rest are small statues (5–10 cm) carved in the round.

Typically, the artwork is impressive and the details intricate. The subject matter includes divinities (Sakyamuni, Chenresi, various protectors) and historical figures (Guru Rinpoche, Tangton Gyalpo, the Fifth Dalai Lama). Many have inscriptions to identify the image. *Mantras* are written in Tibetan, Sanskrit, Nepali and Phagpa script, derived from the Mongolian alphabet in the 13th century. The Sanskrit and Phagpa texts usually carry a Tibetan translation. Most carvings are 10–50 cm tall. Perhaps the finest are Songtsen Gampo, Jambala, an 11-faced Chenresi, the Fifth Dalai Lama, and *mantras* rendered in the seldom-seen Phagpa script.

DRA YUGANG DRAK

A meditation cave of Guru Rinpoche, this retreat is located within a sheer cliff behind Dingboche. A fairly level path heading northwards reaches the cave in an hour. The tantric master supposedly spent a month here. Terdak Lingpa erected an image of him, and Minling Terchen Gyürme Dorje (founder of Mindroling) and the Seventh Dalai Lama, Kelsang Gyatso, came for retreat. The hermitages and *tsamkhangs* around the cave were damaged in the 1960s but devotees have returned to meditate in seclusion. This little complex is visible from the valley floor.

DRAPHU TÖDRONG (DERONG) NUNNERY

Here is the birthplace of Longchen Rabjampa (1308–64), the famous Nyingmapa scholar who compiled the Dzokchen Nyingtik text (see page 492). The nunnery, located within a large side valley southeast of Dingboche, perches on the northern slopes above the village of Tashiling. A ruined house some distance below the nunnery is the actual site of Longchen Rabjampa's birth. Nearby is the Lhakhang Shukdongchen, a chapel erected by Padro Chowang Lhündrub.

YARCHEN (YARJE) MONASTERY

This Nyingmapa monastery is sited within Yarje Village, 5 km southwest of Dingboche. Originally a three-story structure, the monastery was largely spared during the Cultural Revolution;

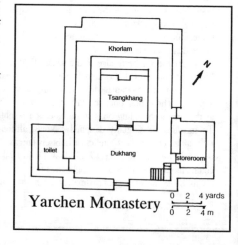

Yarchen Monastery

only the third floor was badly damaged. Unfortunately, no paintings or statues have survived.

The ground floor south-facing entrance is only 1.4 m wide. Inside is a small two-columned *dukhang*. The back wall has three openings: the center one leads to the inner *tsangkhang* while the other two act as entrance and exit to a *khorlam*, which encloses the *tsangkhang*. This configuration is reminiscent of other early structures, such as Lhasa's Meru Nyingba (see page 119), Dranang (page 393), and Samye Utse (page 300). It is likely that the foundation of Yarchen dates back a long way.

Stone steps leading up to the second floor are situated in the southeast corner of the *dukhang*. Behind the skylight is a chapel, enclosed by a 1.6 m-wide *khorlam*, dedicated to Chenresi Senge Drak (Chenresi seated on a lion). There are still some original stone carvings remaining at Yarchen, bas-relief works on rectangular slabs. The subjects include Sakyamuni, Tsepame, the Medicine Buddhas, Guru Rinpoche and his two consorts, and a *chörten*. Among the most noteworthy are:

• Two *bodhisattvas*—the two images are identical, both have naked torsos and long *dhotis*, and both sit on lotuses.

• Guru Rinpoche and his two consorts—the two consorts, dressed similarly to the *bodhisattvas*, kneel and face the master.

• *chörten*—the top and bottom of the body are narrower than the middle.

Orgyen Lingpa The Nyingmapa *terton*, Orgyen Lingpa (1323–ca 1360) was born in Yarje. He discovered many 'hidden' texts, the most important being the *Katang Denga*, the five treatises describing the historical era of Trisong Detsen. These were discovered near Samye (see page 295).

DARGYE CHÖDING (DARGYE CHÖLING) MONASTERY

This mid-17th-C. Nyingmapa establishment (now destroyed) is situated on a ridge west of the Yarje Lhakhang, 4 km from Dingboche. Terdak Lingpa, patriarch of Mindroling Monastery, was born here. The monastery was begun by Natshök Rangdröl, a noted follower of the Longchenpa tradition, and as a precursor of the mighty Mindroling, it was an important institute for the practice of the Dzokchen Nyingtik.

YÖN:
THE TEMPLE OF KACHU, TSONG KHAPA'S HERMITAGE, AND PRINCESS KARCHEN'S RETREAT

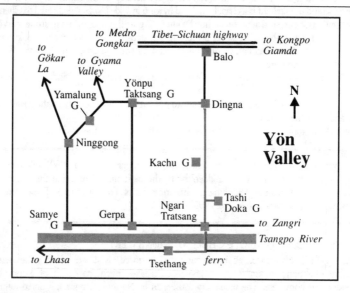

OVERVIEW

The jewel within the fertile Yön Valley across the Tsangpo from Yarlung is undoubtedly the recently discovered 8th-C. Kachu Lhakhang. Perhaps Tibet's oldest monastery (see page 378), it is the repository of monumental statues created in the 8th and 9th centuries. Due to its proximity to the Yarlung Valley and Samye Monastery, Yön is an exciting area of early archeological finds as well. At least three ancient Yarlung-era burial sites have been unearthed. Jasa Ri is a complex of over 50 tombs arrayed in an unusual cruciform configuration. Chimlung Tsemo is an even larger site with nearly 100 large and small tombs spread over a 10-km area, the largest necropolis in Tibet and the only one with sacrificial chambers. At Gyalzang are stone coffins in graves that have no protective tumuli, a deviation from most Yarlung-dynasty tombs.

At the entrance of the Yön Valley is Ngari Tratsang, once an important Gelugpa institution. Near the Kachu Lhakhang, a short distance north of Yön Qu, is Tashi Doka Monastery, a charming rebuilt hermitage founded by Tsong Khapa in the 15th century. His meditation cave of Zimphuk is a sacred spot for pilgrims. Farther up the valley are the 12th-C. Tshezik *chörtens* built by Lama Shang, the founder of the Tshalpa Kagyü sect.

At the head of Yön is Yönpu Taktsang, an important pilgrimage site consecrated to Guru Rinpoche and associated with Yeshe Tsogyal (Princess Karchen), his consort. This was the main seat of the Taktsangpa, a sub-sect of the Kagyü, who followed closely the ascetic precepts of Milarepa. Its illustrious lamas were spiritual advisors to the Ming emperors of China. Near the retreat, side valleys radiate north and south. The former lead to the historic Gyamo Valley, birthplace of Songtsen Gampo, and the Medro Gongkar Valley; the south ones lead to the Tsangpo Valley.

After reaching Yönpu Taktsang from the Tsangpo Valley, consider completing a loop of this seldom visited region by crossing the 5350-m Le La Pass. This itinerary, one of the best in Central Tibet, explores the entire Yön Valley, connects with the Yamalung and Samye valleys, and takes in the ancient monasteries of Kachu and Samye. The entire trek can be done in six days; but take more time to explore other monasteries along the way.

Related sections
Historic Valleys of the Tsangpo, p 470
Kachu, p 378
The Yarlung Valley, p 515
Lhamo Latso, p 623
The Ningchi Road, p 707
Upper Reaches of the Kyi Chu River, p 544

TASHI DOKA MONASTERY

This early 15th-C. monastery is on the left bank of the Yön Chu, up the slopes of an alluvial fan some distance north of Chermen (see Kachu, page 379 for a route description). The idyllic monastery is surrounded by willow trees and is auspiciously sited next to a magical spring (*drubchu*). From the floor of the Yön Valley, nothing but a *chörten* and small retreat buildings are visible. The thriving, self-contained nature of the complex is evident only upon arrival.

The first and largest building is the *dukhang*. In front of it is a courtyard, flanked on the right by the kitchen. An entrance porch is in front of the assembly hall which has images of Tsong Khapa, Chenresi, the Eight Medicine Buddhas, Tsepame, Drölma, and the 16 Arhats.

On the two side walls are new paintings of the 21 Drölmas. There are a few original *thangkas*, but most are new. Upstairs are rooms for the head lama. West of the *dukhang* is a debating courtyard (*chöra*).

Zimphuk

This is the cave where Tsong Khapa meditated in 1415. He stayed for two months and it was here that he met his disciple Gedundrub, the future First Dalai Lama. Up the hillsides from the *dukhang* is the small retreat, built around the cave. The entrance terrace is lined with flower pots and affords a great view of the Yön Valley and the Tsangpo. A corridor leads from the terrace into the cave. On both sides of the passage are small, cosy rooms for meditators. Farther along, on the right, a cabinet contains statues of Tsong Khapa and his two disciples. The cave has a painted yellow wall decorated with floral motifs, exactly like the design used on veils for *thangkas*. A statue of Tsong Khapa is at the center of the rear wall. About 30 m to the right of the Zimphuk is another cave (no building outside) known as Dhungden Jampel Gyatso Zimphuk. To the east is a grove of trees surrounding the holy spring.

Chörten

West of the Zimphuk was a large stone *chörten* founded prior to the monastery, before Tsong Khapa's arrival. Only the base survives. Beyond it is a new *chörten*, a landmark visible from the Yön Valley floor. Next to this is Tamdrin Phuk, a third meditation cave.

History

Tashi Doka was founded by Tsong Khapa (1357–1419), the celebrated scholar who reformed the Kadampa school and institutionalized the Gelugpa. Chime Sonam Wongyal provided much of the funding for the building of the monastery. The name 'Tashi' of Tashi Doka comes from a legend: One day a saint named Tashi descended to this site from the sky while Tsong Khapa was meditating in his cave. Being an expert sculptor, he asked permission to create a statue of the Gelugpa founder. In one day Tashi made seven statues and Tsong Khapa shaved his head seven times in order to provide hair as a relic for each. Immediately after the shavings, his hair grew back. The life-like statues greatly impressed Tsong Khapa and he built the monastery in commemoration of them. According to local tradition, the statues are now scattered at important Gelugpa institutions—such as Kumbum in Amdo, and Tashilhunpo (see page 808) in Tsang.

CHÖDING MONASTERY

This was Yön's largest Gelugpa monastery, and in its heyday it dominated the politics and economics of the valley. The complex was destroyed during the Cultural Revolution; its ruins (in a side valley to the east) can be seen from Kachu Lhakhang.

Chöding was founded as a Nyingmapa institution during the 12th century. Its roots can also be traced back to the Kadampa, who were active north of Lhasa during the early period of Buddhism's Second Diffusion. The Gelugpa took over the monastery in the 15th C. and in the 18th C., when the Dalai Lama fled to the Chinese border, the abbot of Chöding became Tibet's regent.

TSHEZIK CHÖRTEN

This unusually designed *chörten* is located north of Kachu Lhakhang, near the valley's upper reaches. Before the valley branches into three is the village of Dingna Qu. The *chörten* is within a gully 5 km west of Kadong Commune, a part of the *qu*. Left of the *chörten* is Tshezik Monastery. The monument consists of five interconnected 12th-C. *chörtens* laid out in an L-shape. Four are along one axis and the fifth is at a right angle to the others. All are on a 30 m-long stone platform and each *chörten* is 2–3 m high. The spires have all been broken. Tshezik was built by Lama Shang (1123–94), founder of the Tshalpa Kagyü sub-sect (see page 197). He was renowned as the disciple of Gompo, the third of Gampopa's successors. The fifth, unaligned *chörten* is consecrated to Lama Shang. It was probably constructed after the other four by his disciples, following his death.

ÜTSE TENG MONASTERY

This destroyed monastery, on top of Mt Utse Teng (4600 m) near Kadong Commune, was a branch of Lhodrak Lhalung Monastery. It was founded by Drubthob Kunga Ngonshe. Various buildings are spread irregularly across the top of the ridge, with the principal chapels at the bottom of the complex. A distinctive feature is a small, beautiful garden (*lingka*) near the front. The monastery declined after the rise of the Gelugpa, a situation made especially acute by its isolation.

YÖNPU TAKTSANG

Yönpu Taktsang is one of three *taktsangs* (tiger-den hermitages) associated with Guru Rinpoche. The other two are Paro Taktsang in Bhutan and Kham Taktsang near Katok Monastery in Kham. Yönpu was also the site of a Kagyü monastery, where the little-known sub-sect of the Taktsangpa flourished after 1405. Its practitioners followed the teachings of Milarepa and were inveterate ascetics; it is the most spiritually powerful site within the Yön Valley.

It takes three days to walk here from the Tsangpo River (2 days from Kachu). The Guru Rinpoche cave is located high up within a cliff face; since its destruction in the 1960s only a small chapel has been rebuilt. Yeshe Tsogyal, Guru Rinpoche's consort, spent considerable time here. A princess of the Karchen kingdom, she arrived in upper Yön to escape the attentions of a prince who had won her hand in marriage through an athletic contest. She was found and taken back to Surkhar, but in later years, she returned and was initiated by Guru Rinpoche into the Dorje Phurpa ritual. After visiting Yönpu Taktsang, most pilgrims continue west over a 5350-m pass to Yamalung and Samye monasteries.

KACHU LHAKHANG TO SAMYE MONASTERY VIA YÖNPU TAKTSANG

From Kachu Lhakhang (Keru Lhakhang), head north up the Yön Valley. In 1 hr arrive at Gyalzang, part of Kelsang Commune. Near this village are rare, ancient relics of Yarlung-era stone coffins (see below). Continue to Kadong (Chadang) and Surdu. Cross the Yön to its east bank by a bridge before Dingna Qu (Sangdrub) and continue to the village of Dingna (not to be confused with Dingna Qu, further south). From Kachu to here is 2 3/4 hr.

The Yön Valley divides at Dingna. The north-trending branch goes up to the Takar La (5150 m) and then drops down to Balo (Tashigang), 20 km east of Medro Gongkar at road marker 1480 km on the main Lhasa–Chengdu highway. Take the left branch west and follow power lines that go all the way to Chigong (1 3/4 hr). In 3/4 hr, reach Ahor. A tractor track follows the Yön Valley all the way to here. Beyond Ahor, motor traffic is impossible on the footpath.

Walk past yak shelters with traces of murals in 1/2 hr (shelter is available here if necessary). Soon there are more roofed ruins. Uphill from here is a nunnery known simply as Ani Gompa, with a dozen buildings (destroyed) and retreat caves in the rocks above. The place is deserted; spend the night here before the next stage to Yönpu Taktsang.

After the Ani Gompa, the path degenerates into a yak trail that climbs to the west. In 3 1/4 hr reach a broad side valley on the right. Do not take this. Just after this valley is another yak shelter. Further on is a field, sometimes with nomad tents, and after 1/4 hr Yönpu Taktsang is reached. The hermitage is destroyed but there are two main retreat caves. The larger one has a pile of carved *mani* stones and a shrine for offerings. From the Ani Gompa to here is 4 hr; the last hour being quite strenuous.

Beyond Yönpu Taktsang, the trail climbs steeply to another side valley that trends north. In another hour, a side valley goes off to the left (south); this leads to Kaipa on the Tsangpo's north bank. At this junction is a large nomad tent. Continue to the 5350-m Le La Pass (1 1/2 hr), then descend steeply along scree slopes. The path levels off to head west to another nomad encampment (1 1/4 hr). Here, another side valley goes south to the Tsangpo Valley along yak trails. In 1/2 hr reach a village at a valley junction. A trail within the north-trending valley crosses the Kampa (Bama) La and Tseb La passes to reach the historic Gyalmashing Valley (see page 549), birthplace of Songtsen Gampo.

The next easy stretch follows the river southwestward for 2 hr. Walk along rocks in the middle of the river for the first hour, then through brush next to the river, and finally on a more distinct trail, to rock overhangs that can serve as a shelter. After 1 1/4 hr, reach a house on the side of the path, then continue for 3/4 hr to a valley junction and cross a wooden bridge (4 hr from the Gyalmashing Valley turnoff). Follow the south-trending valley for 2 hr to the turnoff for Yamalung Monastery (see page 627). Then, 1 hour further is a principal trail junction that meets the large valley south to Samye (see page 295).

For the Yön Valley's burial sites, see Necropolises, page 627.

THE YARLUNG VALLEY: FOUNTAINHEAD OF TIBETAN CIVILIZATION

YARLUNG: THREE SANCTUARIES, THREE CHÖRTENS, AND OTHER SACRED SITES

OVERVIEW

The Yarlung Valley is known as the cradle of Tibetan civilization. It was here, within a cave on Gönpo Ri, that a monkey mated with a demoness to create the first Tibetans. This myth parallels the findings of historians and archeologists. The great Yarlung empire (7th–9th C.) was home to Tibet's early kings. Their colossal tombs, located at Chongye, testify to the region's grandeur and antiquity.

Two valleys, Chongye and Yala Shampo, make up Yarlung; within them are an

Yarlung Valley

Tsangpo River

to Lhasa

to Nang

Tsethang

Trandruk G

Gönpo Ri circuit

Rechung Phuk G

to Drachi Valley

to Lhagyari

Potrang

Chongye

to Yamdrok Tso

Yartö G

N

to Drigu Tso, Lhodrak

to Shobo Shar, Tsari

uncommonly rich and varied concentration of religious and historical centers, some superbly located. Pilgrims can explore a large number of monasteries, hermitages, *chörtens*, and other sacred places. Many were destroyed during the Cultural Revolution of the 1960s, but a good proportion survived to this day.

Tsethang, at the junction of the Yarlung and Tsangpo rivers, dominates the valleys. Immediately south is Nedong, Tibet's capital during the Phagmo Drupa Dynasty. The foremost pilgrimage sites in Yarlung are known as the Three Tensum (*chörtens*) and the Three Nesum (sacred places), all founded between the 7th and 9th century. The former: Göntang (Kundan), Tsechu, and Takchen; the Three Sacred Places: Trandruk Monastery, Sheldrak Hermitage, and Yumbu Lagang castle. Most pilgrims walk a ritual clockwise circuit along the valley to take in all these monuments. Tsethang is the usual starting point. After visiting the monasteries of the old town, the devout head east to circumambulate the sacred Gönpo Ri. Near the peak is the Monkey Cave, fabled place of origin of the Tibetan people. After the mountain is the 7th C. monastery of Trandruk, founded by King Songtsen Gampo. Then come Yumbu Lagang, the first castle erected in Tibet, Takchen Chörten, and various minor sites. Particularly interesting is a remarkable row of *chörtens* at Gyatsa Gye. Beyond Yumbu Lagang, to the south, are a number of well-preserved but rarely visited monasteries. These include Yarzang, Chöde Gang, and Chöde Wö.

The next major site after Yumbu Lagang is Rechung Phuk Monastery, strategically located on top of a ridge that effectively divides the Chongye Valley from the Yala Shampo Valley. Nearby are the archaic Göntang Chörten and the 8th-C. Bairo Phuk Cave-shrine. (In the vicinity, a trail leads up to Sheldrak Hermitage, one of Guru Rinpoche's most sacred caves; this is a hard 5-hr hike.) The pilgrim then circles south to Lhabab Ri, most prominent peak of the Sheldrak Range. This sacred mountain received Nyatri Tsenpo, the first mythical king of Tibet, when he descended from heaven.

The last leg of the circuit takes in the holy places of the Chongye Valley: Tangboche Monastery and its well-preserved murals; the monumental tombs of the Yarlung kings; and ancient Chingwa Taktse, castle of the early kings and birthplace of the Great Fifth Dalai Lama. Archeologists will also be interested in the recently discovered Yarlung tombs on both banks of the Yala Shampo River.

The best way to properly explore the Yarlung region is to walk—some of the most fascinating sites are high up in the mountains and difficult to reach. Allow a few days to visit all the major holy places of Yarlung, if you wish to do so at a comfortable pace. If you come with a group and have transport, budget one or two days.

Related sections
The Historic Valleys of the Tsangpo River Basin, p 470
Lhodrak, p 681
Tsari, p 208
Lhasa to the Yarlung Valley, p 595

Access from Lhasa
A major road from Lhasa goes south to the Chusul Bridge. After the bridge, one branch goes right to Shigatse, another left to the airport at Gongkar. Take this left road along the south bank of the Tsangpo to Tsethang (Lhasa–Tsethang is 183 km). Try hitching from the gas station west of Drepung Monastery or take a bus from the Lhasa bus station next to Norbu Lingka (or the bus station one block east of the central post office). Buses leave Lhasa at 0830 daily and arrive in Tsethang at 1230. Alternatively, try to get a free ride to the airport from the CAAC office behind the Post Office and then hitch. Note that most drivers are reluctant to give rides to foreigners, the exception being those who drive tractors. For more details on the route, see Holy Places along the Lhasa–Tsethang Highway, p 471.

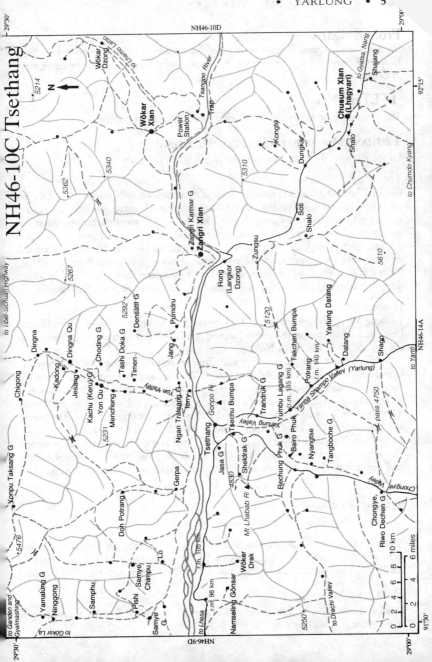

NH46-10C Tsethang

Shigatse

No direct buses go from Shigatse to Tsethang. Take the bus to Lhasa, get off at the Chusul Bridge and then hitch east to Tsethang. Buses leave every morning from the transport depot in Shigatse.

TSETHANG

The following is a description of culturally significant sites in Tsethang.

TSETHANG MONASTERY (GANDEN CHÖKORLING)

Location Left of the main square in the center of the old town

The site

Ganden Chökorling was badly damaged. Most of its surrounding walls, residences, and chapels are in ruins and the main building's second floor was nearly obliterated. Extensive renovations, in stops and starts, have been going on for the last few years. Entrances to the square complex are along the east and west walls. The principal structure is at north-center. To its left is a *labrang* (abbot's residence) with a debating courtyard, and between the main building and the courtyard is an open area. The *dukhang*, located on the ground floor of the main building, has murals that are in bad condition. The ceiling of the second floor is dominated by a large skylight overlooking the assembly hall. Behind the *dukhang* is the Jowo Lhakhang.

History

Tsethang Monastery was founded in 1351 by Jangchub Gyaltsen, an abbot of the Phagmo Drupa sect, which had as its centers Tsethang and Densatil monasteries. The Phagmo Dru family once ruled Tibet from Nedong.

The present Gelugpa monastery was rebuilt on an earlier Kagyü foundation from the time of the Seventh Dalai Lama, Kelsang Gyatso (1708-57). Since the Kagyü institution opposed the rule of Polhane, who had the support of China during the mid-18th C., it was abolished for insubordination and replaced by a new Gelugpa monastery, built 30 m to the west of the original site. The existing structure of Ganden Chökorling went through a phase of restoration and expansion in 1900 but the lack of funds severely delayed the process and the complex was not completed until 12 years later. 145 monks lived here before the Cultural Revolution. The army took over the premises from 1960 to 1968 and thus spared the monastery from total destruction. However, all statues, *thangkas*, and decorations have either been destroyed or stolen.

NGACHÖ TRATSANG

Location A short distance east of Ganden Chökorling

A rebuilt monastery in fine condition, this was formerly an important institution dedicated to Sakyamuni, Wöpame, and Jampa. Jangchub Gyaltsen erected its statues. Wars of the 16th and 17th C. badly damaged the structure and in 1718 it was sacked by the invading Dzungars.

TREBULING MONASTERY

Location About 200 m northeast of Ngachö Tratsang, Trebuling stands within the compounds of the Shannan Diesel Factory.

The monastery originally belonged to the Sakyapa sect. By the 20th C. most of its buildings had collapsed. However, the *tshomchen* and the monks' quarters, dating back to a 1940 reconstruction, still remain. The two-story *tshomchen*, next to oil tanks, is in reasonable shape. Its most sacred statues were Drölma and Thupa Ngadrama, 'True Likeness of Buddha'. This last supposedly was formed of over 70 precious gems and alloys. The murals have all been destroyed. One small room on the west side of the second floor was used by the present Dalai Lama.

SANG NGAG ZIMCHE NUNNERY (SAMTENLING)

Location This charming nunnery, close to Tsethang Monastery, stands at the foot of Gönpo Ri.

A path leads up the slope from the Tsethang Monastery square directly to the nunnery. Sang Ngag Zimche is built around a cave, meditation site of Kyerong Ngawang Trakpa. According to tradition, it was among the first Gelugpa nunneries in Tibet, built during the life of the Seventh Dalai Lama (1708–57). Both monks and nuns live in this two-story center which, with Ngachö, is the most religiously active in Tsethang. Courageous nuns saved their home from the Red Guards and certain destruction by completely sealing up the nunnery with massive stone walls The main entrance faces south and within it is a small chapel. A *dukhang* to the right houses an ancient 11-faced Chenresi, supposedly one of four such statues personally crafted by Songtsen Gampo. Flanking it are statues of Tsong Khapa, Drölma and Tangtong Gyalpo. Behind these is the unusual construct of the 16 Arhats and the 35 Buddhas of Confession (clay) placed within tiny caves inside the stucco model of a mountain. Old *thangkas*, in good condition, hang from the wall. At the back, beyond the kitchen, are two small chapels. One has as its central image the founder, Kyerong Ngawang Trakpa. He is flanked by Chenresi (on a lion) and Jampelyang. The other chapel has images of Tsong Khapa and his disciples, Tangton Gyalpo and Atisha. Behind and west of the nunnery are two sacred springs, Guru Rinpoche *terchus*. Sonam Gyaltsen (1312–75), a great Sakyapa teacher and tutor of Tsong Khapa first lived and meditated in the area.

Map labels:
Tsethang Commune No. 9 (Zorthang)
monkey statue
to Lhasa
hospital   bus station
to East Tibet
dep store
Tsethang Monastery
truck depot
bank
Old Town
Tsethang Guest House
cinema
market street
shop
Monkey Cave
Tsethang Hotel
Public Security Bureau
Nedong Bridge
Nedong Government
post office
Nedong Guest House
water tower
army compound
Trandruk Monastery
Yumbu Lagang
to Chongye
to Tsona
Tsethang

GÖNPO RI

Gönpo Ri, one of four sacred mountains in Central Tibet, is the abode of Yala Shampo, an ancient mountain god. A delightful two-day pilgrimage circuit (*khorlam*) around the mountain starts in Tsethang and ends at Trandruk Monastery.

The khorlam

From the center of Tsethang, at the large intersection marked by a monkey monument, walk east along the main road (towards Gyatsa Xian and Ningchi), by following the south bank of the Tsangpo. After 1 hr, leave the road and walk south, following stone cairns, up a side valley that flanks the eastern perimeter of Gönpo Ri. The valley entrance is nearly 3 km wide and prayer flags strung halfway across the Tsangpo define the valley's western limit just before the south (right) turn towards the mountains. Here a motor ferry crosses the river to the north bank and the entrance of the Yön Valley (see also page 510).

Hug the valley's right side, pass a sacred spring (terchu) on the right, then a site marked by stone mandals. At this point, across a small gully to the right, is the Bego, the Door to the Secret Valley of Gönpo Ri. Faint indentations and cracks on the rock face suggest a door-like opening. A qualified lama will supposedly one day open this entrance to Gönpo Ri's secret paradise. A local story tells of an old woman on her way to Thongdröl Nunnery, further along the walk. She chanced to look back and saw a monk following her. At a turn, she sat down to wait for him, but after some time went back to see why he still had not arrived. The monk has disappeared. She then continued up to the nunnery to make tea for herself and the monk. Then the old woman began to search for him in earnest. At the spot marked by the stone mandals was a dog, tied to the entrance of the Bego. As she approached the dog barked ferociously. She shared her food with it and managed to comfort it. After this gesture of kindness, the dog, a transformation of the monk, led her into the Secret Valley. The old woman thus became the first person to glimpse the hidden paradise and its three glorious monasteries. This crone, now 130 years old, supposedly lives at Tsethang.

Further up the valley is Thongdröl Nunnery (destroyed). No one lives here and there are no present plans for restoration. East of the complex is another terchu (consecrated to Lama Yeshe Dorje), the second of three on Gönpo Ri. Beyond the nunnery, on top of a hillock, is a cemetery (durtrö). Near here is a large rock with rangjung images of the 21 Drölmas. The trail winds towards the Gönpo La (4750 m) and the third sacred spring is near the pass. The renowned Monkey Cave of Gönpo Ri and other grottoes are near the top. Thubpa Serlingma is a cave once used by the monks of Ngachö Monasteries.

The Monkey Cave of Gönpo Ri

According to legend, the Tibetan race originated here. A simian incarnation of Chenresi, the Bodhisattva of Compassion, mated with Sinmo, a white ogress. From this union came six offspring, founders of the six original clans of Tibet. The first plot of cultivated land in the country, known as Zorthang, is at the base of the Gönpo Ri.

The Monkey Cave, at a height of 4060 m, is located some 70 m below Gönpo Ri's summit. A sheer drop of 500 m falls from the cave mouth to the floor of the Yarlung Valley. Just within the entrance, on the surface of a crack, is an image of the monkey. This 'self-manifesting' figure is much venerated by pilgrims. On the southeast wall is a colored painting of the monkey sitting on rhododendron flowers. Next to this is another painting of a baby monkey. Nearby are a few stone slabs, each carved with figures of divinities. Prayer flags and carvings of the Six Syllables are everywhere. Outside the cave is a grape vine, revered by pilgrims as the monkey's source of sustenance.

ZORTHANG

Tradition points to this as the first cultivated area of Tibet. Some sources believe the site to be half an hour's walk north of the People's Hospital at Tsethang Commune No 9. Others assign it to the base of Yumbu Lagang, near Lharu Mengye Monastery.

Cross the Gönpo La from east to west and descend westward towards the main Yarlung Valley. Some distance from the top is a sacred, powerful site marked by two white *chörtens* and *manis*. Pilgrims and monks spend days and weeks here in meditation, performing Chö rituals, practices pioneered by Dampa Sangye and Machik Labdrönma. Practitioners of these esoteric rites measure themselves in the dark of the night against the intangible spirits of the holy mountain. Below, on the valley's right slopes, are extensive ruins of a large monastery. The *khorlam* ends at Trandruk Monastery.

The entire Gönpo Ri *khorlam* can be done in one long day but it is better to do it in two. Spend the first night at Thongdröl (or a nearby village east of the ruins) before going over the pass.

TRANDRUK MONASTERY

A contemporary of the Lhasa Jokhang, this most ancient monument (located at road marker 129 on the Tsethang–Yumbu Lagang road) of the Yarlung Valley was founded by King Songtsen Gampo, the First Religious King of the Yarlung Dynasty. For a description, see p 533.

IMPORTANT SITES OUTSIDE TSETHANG

NEDONG XIAN

Two km south of Tsethang, a short distance beyond the Tsethang Hotel on the eastern side of the Yarlung River. During the 15th C., Nedong and its fortress, Nedong Dzong, was the civil capital of Tibet, administered by the Phagmo Drupa family. At the end of the 15th C., the Red-hat princes of Tsang wrested political control from the Phagmo Drupas and the fortunes of the town slowly declined.

YARLUNG BRIDGE

This 14th-C. bridge, called Namo Zampa, spans the Yarlung River near Nedong Xian. Its surface is made of nine huge logs. Beneath them is a layer of square logs, providing the overlay for nine more round logs. Large wood buttresses reinforced by stone walls provide support at the two ends. The bridge has four spans; the widest covers nearly 10 m.

TSE TSOKPA MONASTERY

This Sakyapa monastery was located on the south slopes of a side valley at the back of Nedong Xian. Tse Tsokpa (destroyed) was one of four famous religious communities in Tibet (*Tsokpa Shis*). The other three are Tsongdü Tsokpa in Drachi (see page 495), Gyaling Tsokpa in Dranang (see page 504), and Chölung Tsokpa north of Gyantse. All were founded by the Kashmiri Sakyasri (1145–1243). Tsong Khapa's ordination took place near here as well. Only one very valuable embroidered *thangka* survives from the monastery. It dates to the Ming Dynasty (1368–1644) and is certainly not the personal handiwork of Princess Wencheng, as local legend states. The *thangka*, displayed to the public for one day each year, has as its central image a red-robed Sakyamuni against a dark blue background. It is now at Trandruk Monastery, as is another relic, the Mutik Thangka, made of 29,000 pearls. The earliest foundation of Tse Tsokpa is located along the west edge of Nedong Dzong's hill. Known as Baija Kunpa, it gave rise to Tse Tsokpa Tratsang, the monastery's precursor.

TSECHU BUMPA CHÖRTEN

Across the Yarlung River from Nedong, near Tsantang (Kato, or Kadu). This archaic *chörten*, one of the Three Tensums of Yarlung, is now partially destroyed. Supposedly, during the full moon, water of longevity flows from it and locals still believe the *chörten* contains King Songtsen Gampo's armor. It is also known as Chokro Tsechu Bumpa. A legend relates how the translator, Chokro Lui Gyaltsen, gave King Trisong Detsen a crystal statue from India which later was concealed within the monument.

TSANTANG YUYI LHAKHANG

This destroyed monastery is 3 km east of Nedong Xian in the village of Tsantang, east of the Tsechu Bumpa. It was one of Three Nesum (sacred places) of Yarlung; only ruins remain. Some accounts attributed the temple's foundation to one of King Songtsen Gampo's queens. However, according to Keith Dowman, the author of *The Power Places of Tibet*, Tsantang Yuyi Lhakhang, also known as Kanden Lhakhang, was founded by Ngangtsul Jangchub, mother of King Trisong Detsen. She met Guru Rinpoche here at the end of the 8th century. The temple's style was heavily influenced by the Chinese and considered one of the handsomest in Tibet. During the middle of this century it underwent a major renovation but was totally destroyed in the turbulent sixties. Today, only the perimeter walls are left.

SHELDRAK DRUBPHUK, THE CRYSTAL CAVE OF GURU RINPOCHE

The Sheldrak cave is one of the most significant pilgrimage destinations in Tibet. Sited high up the Crystal Mountain, it is a long, tough climb from the Yarlung valley floor. The retreat is most certainly worth the effort.

Sheldrak was Guru Rinpoche's first meditation cave in Tibet. From here he exorcized demons and the influences of Bön from the land. Later in the 13th C., Orgyen Lingpa, discovered the *Padma Katang* within the cave. This text, vitally important to the Nyingmapa, is Guru Rinpoche's biography as recorded by his consort, Yeshe Tsogyal. It states that Sheldrak, one of the five most sacred hermitages in all Tibet and Bhutan, is a representation of the guru's virtues. The other four are Drak Yong Dzong, his body, Samye Chimpu, his speech, Lhodrak Karchu, his mind, and Monka Senge Dzong in East Bhutan (see Index of Place-Names for further information).

Tibetan pilgrims believe there are no better places to go than Chimpu, Yerpa, and Sheldrak to achieve significant spiritual progress.

It is at the three great places that one will have the best
Attainment;
If an invocation is made in those places; there
Is nothing one cannot attain.
The Knowledge Bearers associated with those places are there
In all their ranks,
And the inhabitants of heaven who have rejected their bodies
Make their way there also.
Especially this Crystal Cave of Yarlung,
Where the incantation with special substances and with
Ambrosia is carried out,
And which has, like Uddiyana, achieved the limit of what is
Possible with the Secret Formulas;
This very noble cave is a temple of marvelous evocations.
One finds there many celestial palaces of calm, of anger,
And others.
At this rock of rejoicing for the Tibetans,
Those who possess the hundred virtues make speeches which
Are inconceivable.
And there Turks do not come to settle.
Although in the White Snows, at Kailas, at Tsari, at
Zambulung, and at other places virtues may abound,
Nothing approaches the Crystal Cave in accomplishment.

From The Life and Liberation of Padmasambhava (Padma Katang),
(Dharma Publishing, Berkeley)

Sheldrak is a consecrated replication of Devikota and Kusinagara, site of the Buddha's death. (For details on Devikota and the concept of replication, see page 126.) The cave was repaired in 1981, after the desecration of the Cultural Revolution and a new statue of Guru Rinpoche was added in that year.

Access

To reach Sheldrak, it is necessary to start from Tsethang at the entrance of the Yarlung Valley. The trail to the cave retreat (4550 m) leads from Tsechu Bumpa Chörten up the Crystal Mountain, a stiff 5–6 hr climb. It heads west up the Sheldrak Valley with the river on the right, passing mandalas and ruined chörtens. The path is gradual and wide; a jeep can go far up the valley. Continue to Serkhang Zhika, a cluster of houses atop a ridge. Sheldrak's caretaker (konyer) lives here sometimes. Follow a path from Serkhang Zhika, up the spine of a spur to Lumo Durtrö (Female Naga Cemetery), a place marked by a restored chörten consecrated to the horse-headed deity, Tamdrin. A rock next to the cremation ground has a Guru Rinpoche footprint (shabje). This is the only cemetery, in the Sheldrak area, created by Lama Rechen. From here, an obvious path leads north along the Sheldrak Ridge. (Another path crosses a pass and loops back down to the Yarlung Valley at Göntang Bumpa.)

From the base of the Serkhang Zhika ridge, the path bears right. Go past a chörten on a ridge to the left to Sheldrak Monastery (Sheldrak Labrang Ütse) at the base of the ridge. Dedicated to Rinchen Lingpa (Sangye Lingpa, 1340–96), a Nyingma *terton*, the main chapel was known as Sharling Gya (1000 Eastern Continents) and Nubling Tong (1000 Western Continents). Monks have restored it and they hold the keys to the caves above. Continue to the right across a narrow ridge. At the ridge's base is the Terchu (Rediscovered Water), a sacred spring of Guru Rinpoche. It flows within a natural amphitheater hemmed in by ridges. To the north (right) is a prominent, isolated peak—Kritkita Dzong, Sheldrak's main mountain— and Guru Rinpoche's limestone grotto lies 70–80 m below the top. Its entrance faces northwest.

Sheldrak Drubphuk (Somdrub), incorporated into a two-story cave-chapel built into a cliff, is the most important Nyingmapa shrine in Tibet. Originally, the three principal images were a gold-alloyed Guru Rinpoche and his two clay consorts. In 1962, the Panchen Lama brought them to Lhasa for safekeeping and now the central Guru Ngadrama resides at Trandruk Monastery. A new clay Guru Rinpoche statue sits within the second floor. Next to it is an image of Drölma. On the ceiling, to the east (left), is a small depression, purportedly the footprint of Yeshe Tsogyal. The cave's small altar has a large collection of photos, mostly of the Dalai Lama. On one side are offering implements. Along the rock wall are unidentified *rangjung* imprints. Guru Rinpoche's footprints and handprints, on stones smeared with butter, lie on the side walls. Near the cave is a small one-story *tsamkhang* whose outer chamber serves as a kitchen. The inner room is a walled-in cave with new images, butter cups, and a throne for visiting lamas.

Other sacred sites of Sheldrak

TSOGYAL SANGPHUK

This was the secret cave of Yeshe Tsogyal (unidentified).

PADMA SHELPHUK (CRYSTAL CAVE)

One of Sheldrak's most sacred sites, this cave is located at the end of a trail that goes around Sheldrak Peak to the north and northeast. Guru Rinpoche left behind a number of hidden texts (*terma*). Orgyen Lingpa later discovered them within a statue and unearthed the celebrated Padma Katang.

LHABAB RI

This hill is just south of Sheldrak Peak. Foottrails lead to it from the south and west. After visiting Sheldrak, pilgrims continue on the sacred circuit to Lhabab Ri, then descend southeastward to regain the Yarlung Valley at the Göntang Bumpa. Legend has it that the first king of Tibet, Nyatri Tsenpo (identified with the Indian prince, Rupati), descended from heaven to this mountain. *Lhabab* in Tibetan means 'The Hill Where God Descended'.

YARLUNG ROUTES

The following is a series of short hikes designed to take in most of the culturally relevant sites in the Yarlung Valley. If time permits, these itineraries can easily be linked together to form a fairly complete pilgrim's circuit. The routes are:
- **Tsethang to Rechung Phuk Monastery and the Bairo Phuk**
- **Bairo Phuk to Chongye**

- Trandruk Monastery to Yumbu Lagang and Potrang
- Potrang to Yartö (Upper Yarlung)

Tsethang to Rechung Phuk Monastery and the Bairo Phuk

THE ROUTE

From Tsethang follow the main road south to Trandruk Monastery (see Trandruk, page 533) at roadmarker 129 km (1 1/4 hr by foot). It is the most important temple in the Yarlung Valley. After Trandruk, continue south to road marker 132 km (1/2 hr). Turn right onto a dirt road just before the main road curves right around a rock spur. A village flanks the start of this side road. Follow it to a village on the left at the foot of a ridge, then walk up the steep trail up to Rechung Phuk Monastery (1 hr from the main road turnoff).

Rechung Phuk Monastery: For a full description of the monastery, see page 347

After visiting this hermitage founded by Rechungpa, the most famous of Milarepa's disciples, follow the trail down the western side of the spur to descend onto the Chongye Valley (the western branch of the Yarlung) and to the ruined Göntang Bumpa Chörten (45 min). Then cross the dry river bed of the Chongye River to reach the main road leading south to Chongye. Walk south along this for 15 min to the village of Bairo Drong (Baichung), part of Karmay Commune. Bairo Phuk lies 500 m west of the village, halfway up the slopes of Shema Ridge.

MILA TSE TOWER

Mila Tse is the ridge that divides the Yarlung and Chongye valleys. Halfway up it is Rechung Phuk Monastery and a strategic observation tower at the top has unimpeded views towards Chongye (west), Potrang (south), and Tsethang (north). The tower is built on top of an oval, earthen platform and steps lead up to it from the south. A moat surrounds the base. The round stone tower (about 3 m diameter) is largely destroyed and its remaining stub is only 3 m tall. It probably dates back over 600 years to the wars between the Phagmo Drupa chieftain, Jangchub Gyaltsen, and the forces of the Tshalpa and the Drigungpa.

GÖNTANG BUMPA CHÖRTEN

This *chörten* is one of the Three Tensums, principal sites of pilgrimage in the Tsethang, Nedong, and Chongye areas. It is also known as Kundan or Kunphen Chörten. It is sited at the entrance of the Kundan Village (part of Katok Commune), close to the western base of the (Mila Tse) ridge. The Yala Shampo River runs north of the village.

The rulers of Nedong and Chongye had a serious land dispute in the mid-8th century. Vairocana, King Trisong Detsen's great translator, was meditating nearby within Bairo Phuk Cave (see below). Upon hearing of the problem, he mediated between the two leaders and helped them resolve the border issue. To prevent similar problems in the future he persuaded the two districts to build the Göntang Bumpa, consecrated by Mitipa, as a memorial to the everlasting settling of the dispute. Therefore, another name for the Göntang Bumpa is Sichö (Mediator) Bumpa.

The 6 m-high chörten is today in a bad state of repair but much of its original shape remains. It has a square base, measuring approximately 18 m per side. The top is designed to resemble, by means of earthen constructs, rays of light shooting forth from the 'sun', a cavity nearly 2 m in diameter at the chörten's centre. The 12 short walls made of earth radiate outward like spokes of a wheel, creating a unique pattern. A short distance west of the chörten is a two-story chapel, in good shape, called Tamdrin Lhakhang. The principal image within the ground floor chamber is Tamdrin flanked by Guru Rinpoche and Lhodrak Longka Geling.

BAIRO PHUK

Bairo Phuk, consecrated to Vairocana, is one of the three most important caves in the Yarlung region. The other two are Sheldrak and Rechung. Vairocana, son of Nyemo Ganjakpa, was a contemporary of Trisong Detsen and one of Guru Rinpoche's 25 principal disciples. This sacred site, a must on any pilgrim's route around the Yarlung Valley, is usually visited together with Rechung Phuk. Bairo Phuk was also one of the 13th Dalai Lama's favorite places.

Just below the cave is an area marked out by votive shrines constructed over the centuries by visiting pilgrims. They are made of stone slabs, four for the sides and one on top, and represent symbolic sanctuaries of the soul. The devout has hopes that the spirit of a dead person will reside within one of these stone cavities for a while, to recoup his energies before embarking on the difficult, intermediate journey (bardo) between death and rebirth.

The south-facing cave has a high, 8-m entrance. Inside the 6 m-deep cavity, to the left, is a nine-petaled copper lotus seat above a stone platform. Also on the left is Vairocana's handprint on stone. Along the walls are carved inscriptions. Difficult to make out, they are likely to be mantras of the Six Syllables. A narrow passage, less than 1 m wide and 0.2 m high, leads into the mountain from the cave. The Karu Lhakhang Chapel (destroyed) once existed near the cave. A difficult trail leads from here directly to Rechung Phuk and, above, Gorgon (Pagor) Nunnery (not located).

Bairo Phuk to Chongye

THE ROUTE

After visiting Bairo Phuk, return to Bairo Drong Village and the motor road. Follow this south for 3/4 hr, then head east (left) through cultivated fields and wade a stream to reach a small village at the bottom of the hills (1/2 hr). In the center of the village is a big, yellow building, part of Tangboche Monastery. To go on to Chongye Xian, the Chongye Valley's main town, return to the main road and walk south for 2 1/4 hr. Alhough once the capital of Tibet, the town itself is unremarkable. However, the fascinating surrounding area includes Riwo Dechen Monastery, the Chingwa Taktse Fort, and the famed Yarlung Tombs. One possible trek leads from Chongye to Yamdrok Tso and then returns to Lhasa by crossing the Yartö Range (see page 595). Another goes south to Tsomi Xian, then on to the important pilgrimages in Lhodrak (see page 681).

TANGBOCHE MONASTERY (SONAG TANG, 'PLAIN OF COALS')

History

Tangboche was founded in 1017 by a group of eight monks and played an important role during the Second Diffusion of Buddhism. It became the seat of a school of philosophy called Tangkor. Atisha, the great Indian teacher who exerted a seminal influence on the development of Tibetan Buddhism from the 11th C. onward, came here at the invitation of the abbot. He stayed in a small retreat northeast of the monastery. (Tsong Khapa also visited in the 14th century.) Two important objects associated with Atisha, his statue and a set of 12 texts brought by him from India, precious and irreplaceable, disappeared during the Cultural Revolution.

The site

Tangboche, miraculously, was not completely destroyed in the 1960s. The main building stored grain and remains largely intact. Most of its murals, commissioned in 1915 by the 13th Dalai Lama, survive in good condition and are reason enough to visit the monastery. A few small sculptures (Atisha, Sakyamuni, Jampa Kesang, the incarnate lama of Tangboche, now in exile in Germany) and a few *thangkas* remain. A *gönkhang* opens from the *dukhang*; most of the interior chapels of this Gelugpa monastery have been recently redecorated and restored.

CHONGYE XIAN

This small town, 28 km south of Tsethang, is the birthplace of the Great Fifth Dalai Lama. It was capital of the early Tibetan kings before Songtsen Gampo made his move from Yarlung to Lhasa. The Chongye Guest house stands in the middle of a Chinese compound, the local *xian*-level government of Chongye. A movie theatre dominates the town square, which has a few shops.

Chongye

Important sites in the Chongye area

RIWO DECHEN MONASTERY

Directly above Chongye Xian (1/2 hr). This 15th-C. Gelugpa monastery was founded by Lodro Pelsang (disciple of Kedrub Pelsang, in turn disciple and biographer of Tsong Khapa) and subsequently expanded by the Seventh Dalai Lama in the 18th century. Restored since the mid-1980s, it is now very active with close to a hundred monks and two lamas. The new main chapel (dedicated to Jampa) was built in 1985 and is located 100 m from the site of the old destroyed monastery. The original complex, under the shadow of the Chingwa Taktse Dzong, was built along lines of the Ganden Monastery.

CHINGWA TAKTSE DZONG

The ruins of this ancient castle straddle the Chingwa Ri ridge above Riwo Dechen Monastery. Chingwa Taktse was one of the most powerful castles in central Tibet, home of the early kings who preceded Songtsen Gampo. A large building, below and behind the knife-edged ridge, belonged to the Chongye chieftains, whose ancestors reputedly came from the royal family of Sahor (today's Mandi, within the Kulu Valley in Himachal Pradesh, India). The clan strongly supported the Nyingmapa, but switched allegiances to the Gelugpa during the era of the Fifth Dalai Lama. The Great Fifth was born here in 1617; a chapel commemorates this auspicious event.

TSERING JONG NUNNERY

From Chongye Xian, follow the Dongkar side valley eastward for 2 hr to the hermitage of Tsering Jong (Wösel Thekchok Ling), located at the base of some brown hills emblazoned with white Tibetan script. (Further up the valley, a trail crosses a 4750-m pass to drop down into a side valley; at its junction with the main Yarlung Valley road is Chöde Wö Monastery; see page 531.) The walk takes 7 1/2 hr.) The nunnery sits above the village of Tsering Jong (Long-life Valley) and its main building, totally destroyed in the 1960s, has been rebuilt. A nearby Meditation Spring (*drubchu*) has willow trees said to be derived from the hairs of Jigme Lingpa, founder of this center. West of this site are five *sungkhangs* (residences of protective divinities), consecrated to the Five Long-life Sisters of Tseringma.

History

Jigme Lingpa (1729–98), founder of Tsering Jong, was born near the Pelri Monastery, south of Songtsen Gampo's tomb. He transcribed, in a vision, the Nyingtig of Longchen Rabjung. This seminal treatise formed the basis of the entire Dzokchen meditation system. Jigme Lingpa spent years at Tsering Jong's hermitage, part of the meditation center called Namdröl Yangtse. He died here at the age of 69. The Zimchung Lhakhang (destroyed) once held the tombs of Jigme Lingpa, Losal Drölma, and Khyentse Yeshe Dorje.

CHONGYE PELRI MONASTERY

This rebuilt Nyingmapa monastery is located a few km south of Bangso Marpo, the tomb of Songtsen Gampo (see page 357), on the north slopes of a southeast-trending valley. To walk from Chongye Xian to here takes 2 hr. Pelri was founded in the 16th C. by a lord of the Chingwa Taktse Dzong. Its principal abbot was Trengpo Terchen Sherab Wöser (1518–84), an incarnation of Vairocana.

CHENGYE LHAKHANG

Chengye lies southwest of Chongye, within a large west-trending valley. This old, relatively well-preserved Gelugpa institution was founded by Geshe Drapa and expanded by Geshe Kache prior to the 14th century. It was the seat of the once flourishing Vinaya school. The name Chengye derives from the most important relic of the chapel, the right eye of Sariputra, one of Sakyamuni's two principal disciples.

Chongye: Colossal tombs of the Yarlung kings
See page 355 for a description of these unique archeological relics.

Yala Shampo: Four Yarlung-valley tombs
See page 362 for a description of the Tsantang, Dongkar Me, Phu Nubling, and Ri Mar tombs.

Trandruk Monastery to Yumbu Lagang and Potrang

THE ROUTE

From Trandruk Monastery (road marker 129 km), follow the main road south to spectacular Yumbu Lagang (1 1/4 hr), located on the crest of a ridge next to road marker 135 km. (Along the way pass the turnoff for Rechung Phuk hermitage at road marker 132.) On the west side of the Yala Shampo river, close to Yumbu Lagang at the foot of a hill in the middle of a grove, is the ruined Sakya monastery of Tashi Chöde. The Gelugpa Riwo Chöling Monastery is to the north.

From Yumbu Lagang, a path southward leads to Lharu Mengye Monastery. Nearby are the *chörtens* of Mendrub Kongsar. Farther south from Yumbu Lagang (1 hr) along the main road is Potrang Qu (road marker 140 km), one of Tibet's most ancient villages. A side valley opens from here to the west and a foot trail leads over a 4750-m pass and descends to Chongye Xian (7–8 hr). Immediately south of Potrang Qu a dirt road leads east within a side valley. Near its head is Takchen Bumpa, one of Yarlung's Three Tensums. Just before this sacred monument is Gyatsa Gye, an amazingly long row of *chörtens*.

YUMBU LAGANG: FIRST PALACE OF THE YALUNG KINGS

See page 539 for a description

RIWO CHÖLING MONASTERY

Riwo Chöling was one of 13 monasteries (*lings*) built by the Gelugpa south of the Tsangpo. It is situated on a low spur a short distance east of Charu Village, south of Tradrak Qu. The monastery is to the north of Yumbu Lagang and its monks traditionally looked after this early kings' castle. Although destroyed, the ruins of Riwo Chöling are still impressive. The staggeringly large complex (50,000 sq m) was founded by Tsong Khapa's principal disciple, Kedrub Je, a prolific temple builder. This relatively little-known institution had as its principal buildings the Tshomchen and Nguldhung (Silver Chörten) Khang. The latter housed the two-story silver tomb of Dakmar Dode. Since the time of the Great Fifth, all successive Dalai Lamas made obligatory visits here. It was rebuilt by the Seventh Dalai Lama, Kelzang Gyatso, and destroyed in the 1960s.

LHARU MENGYE MONASTERY

This monastery is reached by means of a steep path a short distance south of Yumbu Lagang. It is also called Lhakhang Nyenru (present condition unknown). An old Tibetan pilgr' nage guide recommends it as one of the holiest places of the Gelugpa in the Yarlung Valley. The two-story temple was dedicated to the Eight Medicine Buddhas.

MENDRUB KONGSAR CHÖRTENS

The *chörtens* are next to Mendrub Kongsar Village (part of Sangdrub Dechen commune), 5 km north of Potrang Qu (road marker 140 km). Yumbu Lagang is nearby. To the east of the main road are nine scattered *chörtens*, built during diverse periods from the 11th to 17th centuries. Only two of the nine are in reasonable shape. The largest, with a remaining height of 5 m, has a complicated, almost haphazard construction and is one of the earliest of the group.

TAKCHEN BUMPA

The Takchen Bumpa is Tibet's first *chörten* consecrated to Guru Rinpoche, and is the first of the Three Tensum *chörtens* in the Yarlung Valley. Immediately north of Potrang Qu (road marker 140 km), a side valley heads east. Follow a flat, motorable road up to the monument. (This also is the old route leading to the Eyul (Lhagyari) district.) First come to the Gyatse Gye *chörtens*, a remarkable row of ancient *chörtens* mounted on a long wall (see below). Then comes a village (Shangyang Commune). On a nearby slope is the Takchen Bumpa, facing south over the Yarlung Valley (1 1/4 hr by foot from the main road).

The site consists of a small Drukpa Kagyü monastery, Takchen Bumoche, as well as the *chörten*. Near the monastery entrance is a small *chörten* that marks the subterranean site of the Paradise of the Nagas (Luyi Potrang). Next to it is the soul-tree of Guru Rinpoche (Guru Lashing). Villagers come here to divine their fortune: the tree's health indicates the well-being of crops and livestock. The courtyard is flanked by residences now occupied by laymen. Guru Rinpoche is the principal image within the chapel.

The Takchen Bumpa's unusual shape reflects the antiquity of its design. It stands 6–7 m high and is made up of three parts: the base, the *bumpa*, and the spire. (Only the first two remain.) The large, dome-shaped base has steps leading up to a window, and the upper portion has three oval cavities that represent eyes. Takchen Bumpa was erected by Lama Dewachen in the second half of the 8th century. Within it were his relics, a constantly weeping left eye, a crystal *chörten*, and his ritual and personal effects. After the *chörten*'s completion, many auspicious signs began to appear. Legend recounts how the divinities, Tashi and Wöbar, came from the sky, accompanied by rainbows and flower showers. They cleaned and washed the *chörten* and finally dissolved into it. Thus the structure is also called Tashi Wöbar Chörten. In the old days three one-story Namgyal *chörtens* stood nearby.

CHÖRTEN GYATSA GYE (108 CHÖRTENS)

Immediately north of Potrang Qu (road marker 140 km), a secondary road follows a side valley to the east. The Gyatsa Gye row of *chörtens*, 1 km southwest of Purin Village (part of Shangyang Commune), extends from east to west and is the most prominent landmark in the valley.

The stone base of the row measures 360 m long and is 3 m wide by 14 m tall. 119 *chörtens*, each nearly 2 m high, surmount the wall. The main body of each *chörten* is square and each has four levels; all were once topped by spires. The fine stone slab construction is clearly the work of excellent craftsmen. This unique, impressive monument was apparently initiated by a 17th-C. doctor. Profoundly disturbed by civil wars and epidemics, he built this massive structure with the hope of eradicating both evils. The *chörtens* did not completely escape the ravages of the Cultural Revolution. A section in the east, about the length of nine *chörtens*, was completely demolished. The original structure was over 400 m long.

Potrang to Yartö (Upper Yarlung)

THE ROUTE

To go to the monasteries of Upper Yarlung, from Potrang Qu continue south along the main road. The valley begins to narrow 1 km after the village. Walk to the entrance of a side valley (1 1/4 hr) that opens to the east (left). Some distance later, reach the village of Shago at the beginning of a broad west-trending valley (1 1/2 hr further). Going further up the range, come to another side valley that opens to the west (road marker 157 km, 1 3/4 hr). Just within it is Chöde Wö Monastery. Further along the main road is Chöde Gang (Yartö) Monastery at road marker 163 km (1 1/4 hr). Yarzang Monastery is inside a side valley 1 hr more to the south.

Yartö to Tsari Tsari, with Kailash and Lapchi, is one of the three principal pilgrimage sites in Tibet. From Yartö, the main road crosses the Yartö Tra La to descend to Shobo Qu, which is one of the access points to Tsari (see page 211).

YARZANG MONASTERY

Yarzang Monastery is on the left bank of the Yarzang Chu, a western tributary of the Yala Shampo River. The main road splits at Yartö Village (road marker 164 km). The main branch (left) goes to the southeast; take the right fork to Yarzang Village, 3 km beyond the junction. Halfway up a ridge above the village, the superbly located, east-facing monastery has excellent views towards sacred Mt Yala Shampo.

Yarzang is the main seat of the Yarzang Kagyü sect, founded by Gheden Yeshe Chengye (d 1207), a Mönpa shepherd who eventually became a disciple of Phagmo Drupa. His disciple, Gyürme Long (1169–1233), built the monastery in 1206 and from here he actively disseminated the sect's doctrines. The monastery, although mostly destroyed, still has impressive chapels and broken walls. Its site extends from north to south for nearly 1/2 km and its east–west axis is about 250 m. A long zigzagging ramp leads up to the ruins from the foot of the ridge, an effect reminiscent of ascending the Potala in Lhasa. Locals nicknamed the monastery 'Little Potala'.

CHÖDE WÖ MONASTERY

Chöde Wö Monastery (Lower Chöde) stands next to the Chöde Wo Commune. It backs onto a hill and looks north down the Yala Shampo Valley. The Fifth Dalai Lama (1617–82) founded this monastery and taught here during his sojourn in the Upper Yarlung (Yartö) Valley. Later, the Seventh Dalai Lama, Kelsang Gyatso (1708–57), expanded the institution. Despite damages, the central three-story building, its murals, pillars, and beams are intact. A room next to the *dukhang* has a large quantity of moldy *sutras*. A perimeter wall and monks' residences (destroyed) surround the main structure. The main assembly hall and inner chapel dedicated to Sakyamuni (flanked by disciples, 16 Arhats, and Eight Medicine Buddhas) are on the second floor. On the third floor are the living quarters of the Dalai Lamas, who routinely spent time here during the winter.

CHÖDE GANG MONASTERY

Chöde Gang (Upper Chöde) Monastery is a large, handsome 11th-C. structure on the east side of the main Yarlung Valley road, near road marker 163 km. In earlier times it was the residence of Ra Lotsawa. What we see today survives from early 20th-C. reconstructions.

The monastery is similar though smaller than Chöde Wö. Its principal structures consist of a four-story main building and two-story monks' residence. One interesting feature: the central area of the main building's ground floor is sunken, and within are thick, twisting stone walls that create a series of narrow subterranean passages. Perhaps the function of this unusual design is to distribute the heavy load posed by the four-story building. The spaces between the walls serve as living quarters as well. Up one level are the *dukhang* and the Jowo Lhakhang. The main images in the former are Tsong Khapa and his two disciples, the 13th Dalai Lama, and Sakyamuni. On the sides are the Buddhas of the Three Ages and the Eight Bodhisattvas. The Dalai Lama's living quarters and three *lhakhangs* are on the third floor. Dedicated to Dorje Chang, the central chapel has a large statue of Lobsang Chudrak, personal physician of the Fifth Dalai Lama, and his *chörten*-tomb. The western one has the Thousand-armed Chenresi while the last has statues of the 21 Drölmas. The murals at Chöde Gang are in good condition and accompanied by written commentaries on the wall.

In front of the main building is a large courtyard completely enclosed on three sides by two-story residences. Its eastern perimeter consists of two rows of buildings. The other sides, west and south, have only one row. It is surprising that these structures are all in good shape.

Above the monastery, on the east slopes, is a long wall for displaying the monastery's huge *thangkas*. This ceremony usually takes place on the 25th day of the fifth month. Many monks now live in Chöde Gang and the monastery is returning to life.

TRANDRUK: YARLUNG VALLEY'S MOST ANCIENT MONASTERY

Principal shrine of the Yarlung Valley, Trandruk is located at road marker 129 km of the main north–south Yarlung Valley road. It is 7 km south of the Tsethang Guest House (map reference NH46-10 C).

MYTHOLOGY

Trandruk was conceived and built in the 7th C. as a small-scale copy of the Jokhang in Lhasa. Together with the Jokhang and Samye, it was one of Trisong Detsen's three royal temples, as well as one of the 12 monasteries built by Songtsen Gampo to subdue Tibet's mighty she-demon (see page 43). According to legend, King Songtsen Gampo's Chinese wife, Princess Wencheng, decided on the basis of geomancy to build a monastery southwest of Gönpo Ri. The site corresponded to the left shoulder of the legendary supine demon. At that time, the area was a lake inhabited by a five-headed dragon. To clear the region of evil influences, Songtsen Gampo went into retreat. Upon emerging, he had sufficient power to summon a great falcon (tra) that managed to subdue the dragon and suck up all the lake water. In this way, the foundation of Trandruk was prepared.

Another legend relates that Guru Rinpoche turned into a falcon while meditating on the Lord of Death on Gönpo Ri. He then flew to Trandruk, at that time a lake with no human habitation. The bird, liking the geomantic properties of the region, sucked up all the water to make it liveable. It was named Trandruk (Falcon-Dragon) due to the fact that when the bird first saw the lake it uttered the strange cry of a dragon.

After Guru Rinpoche founded a settlement and the modest beginnings of a monastery, he created eight statues of himself (Guru Tsengye), on Gönpo Ri, which later were taken to Trandruk. These partly destroyed images, purported to be the originals, still remain in a chapel.

THE MONASTERY

Trandruk was badly sacked during the time of Langdarma (r 838–42) but made a comeback in the 11th century. From modest beginnings, Trandruk achieved prominence through three major expansions. According to its karchag (monastery guide), the first was in ca 1351. Buildings and chapels were added to the original chapels of Tsuglag Khang and Neten Lhakhang. This construction basically defined Trandruk's ultimate layout. In the 17th C., the Fifth Dalai Lama embarked on another program of renovation and addition. A golden roof and an entranceway were built for the Tsuglag Khang; the Sang Ngak Potrang, south of the courtyard, was constructed. The last restoration was carried out under the Seventh Dalai Lama (1708–57). Trandruk had 21 lhakhangs and was an obligatory annual stop for all the Dalai Lamas from the Great Fifth onwards. After the Cultural Revolution, the faithful rebuilt the Tsuglag Khang in 1988, re-establishing the complex as an important pilgrimage site.

⌐ (16 ARHAT) LHAKHANG

...gtsen Gampo's first chapel (two storys), the Neten Lhakhang, is located directly across from the Tsuglag Khang in a small, dirt lane near the front courtyard. Partially visible murals remain. The ground floor (Neten Shöl) is a six-column room measuring 10 m by 7 m. Songtsen Gampo was the principal image. Above this chamber is another chapel called the Neten Dong, which also had a Guru Rinpoche statue. In its early days, this building was constructed predominantly of *pema* shrub twigs. The present structure, made of stone and wood, reflects a later restoration.

LAYOUT AND ARCHITECTURE

Trandruk's unusual layout is divided into two sections. The front centers on a courtyard surrounded by a cloister. To the rear is the Tsuglag Khang; its principal chapel is the Tshomchen assembly hall. To reach the entrance, go through part of Trandruk Village and then the main gate to reach the courtyard. On the right is the Mani Lhakhang, with a large prayer wheel and old murals. Beyond is the Tsuglag Khang. An ancient, inscribed bronze bell (lost), similar to Samye's bell, once hung in the entrance passage. This 8th-C. relic was donated by a wife of Trisong Detsen.

The ground floor plan of Trandruk is similar to the Jokhang in Lhasa. Both temples have concentric rectangular structures surrounding a central courtyard. Monumental entranceways are oriented to the west. In both complexes, inner temples are enclosed by chapels with the most important ones located at the extreme east end of the principal axis. The entrance, diametrically opposite, is at the other end. Trandruk's premier chapel, the Drölma Lhakhang, is flanked by two small but important chapels. This arrangement is repeated in the Jokhang. These many similarities between the two monasteries support the premise that Trandruk was founded during the Yarlung Dynasty (7th–9th centuries).

SANG NGAK POTRANG

Right (south) of the courtyard is the 17th-C. Sang Ngak Potrang, used mainly by monks of the southern Nyingma (Mindroling) sect. In 1938, its ground floor was converted into the Ngak Khang, a shrine to Yamantaka and other major protectors. A secret passage with two narrow storage cells leads from within the southern part of the west wall to an external point southwest of the building.

TSUGLAG KHANG
Ground floor

Beyond the courtyard is the Tsuglag Khang's entrance. Immediately within the high, spacious foyer are two passages (left and right) leading into the Barkhor *khorlam*, which surrounds the spacious Tshomchen assembly hall. In the foyer, outside the door, are statues of Chana Dorje and Tamdrin. Inside are the Four Guardian Kings. A spacious enclosed courtyard (*khyamra*) adjoins the rear of the assembly hall. Another *khorlam*, the inner Nangkhor, surrounds the *khyamra* and the Tshomchen's interior perimeter.

Opening along the four legs of the square Nangkhor are 12 *lhakhangs*. The chapels are asymmetrical and uneven in size. For example, the south-central Orgyan Lhakhang is a complex chapel comprising an inner and outer room. Its counterpart on the north side, the Thuje Lhakhang, is smaller and less complicated. This is a result of the many additions to the monastery through the centuries; the original configuration has been lost. The Nangkhor has two types of columns: the older ones have stone platforms carved with lotus petals as their bases; more recent columns have no carvings. Murals on the north and south walls show episodes from the Buddha's life. The west wall depicts the Fifth Dalai Lama, Gushri Khan, and Sangye Gyatso (see page 71). These unremarkable paintings belong to the 19th or early 20th centuries.

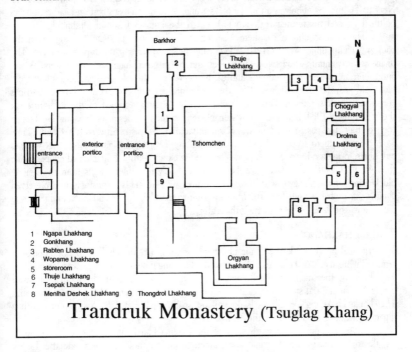

Barkhor

2
Thuje Lhakhang

3 4

1
Chogyal Lhakhang

Tshomchen

Drolma Lhakhang

exterior portico
entrance portico

5 6

entrance

9

8 7

N

1 Ngapa Lhakhang
2 Gonkhang
3 Rabten Lhakhang
4 Wopame Lhakhang
5 storeroom
6 Thuje Lhakhang
7 Tsepak Lhakhang
8 Menlha Deshek Lhakhang   9 Thongdrol Lhakhang

Orgyan Lhakhang

Trandruk Monastery (Tsuglag Khang)

DRÖLMA LHAKHANG

The Tshomchen's most sacred chapel is the Drölma Lhakhang, located at the center of the east wing, facing west (the Jowo Lhakhang in Lhasa's Jokhang has a similar configuration). On its left and right are the Chögyal Lhakhang and Thuje Lhakhang, all facing west. Enclosing these three chapels is another small *khorlam*. Between the Drölma Lhakhang and the courtyard is a foyer. The left and right columns flanking the entranceway each have a wooden statue of Gönpo. These unusual images are short and fat with engaging stances and expressions.

The Drölma Lhakhang is larger than the other chapels and has as its principal images, along the back wall, the Five Dhyani Buddhas. One tradition claims the stone statues are 7th-C. creations from Khotan. These masterpieces were badly damaged during the Cultural

Revolution and partially put back together. Two Kadampa *chörtens* stand in front of them; a standing Jampelyang is by the left wall. Right of the entrance is the sacred statue of Drölma Shesema, the Tara who consumed her offerings (the monks call her Drölma Sungjönma, the 'speaking' Tara). This chapel's name comes from the image.

CHÖGYAL LHAKHANG

The Chögyal Lhakhang (north of Drölma Lhakhang) has new statues of Songtsen Gampo with his Chinese and Nepalese wives, and his two principal ministers, Gar and Thönmi Sambhota. Next to Thönmi Sambhota is an image of Tsepame. Note that Tibet's best and earliest images of the king and his retinue (8th–9th C.) are in the Potala's Chögyal Drubphuk.

The most striking object here is an unusually large brocade *thangka* hanging on the back wall. This impressive work is undoubtedly the finest *thangka* on display in Tibet. The image is Sakyamuni, which wears red robes and has a green halo of lotus flowers. A sun and moon are at the upper corners and in the center is a three-legged, golden bird. A rich, blue field provides the background for the figure, and six horizontal, finely brocaded stripes constitute the lower limit. This spectacular work of art was returned to the authorities at the beginning of 1984. It was the most valuable relic in the now-destroyed Nedong Tse Tsokpa (one of four Tsokpas founded by the Kashmir Pandita, Sakyasri, between 1204 and 1213).

According to Roberto Vitali, author of *Early Temples of Central Tibet*, this work is of Chinese origin and it resembles murals of paradise extant within a dilapidated chapel inside the 14th-C. Gyantse Fort (see page 417). It also closely resembles images from the Beijing block prints of the Tengyur and Kangyur, executed in 1410. This surprisingly well-preserved *thangka* was probably a gift from the Ming emperor to the Phagmo Drupa family, and therefore dates from the late 14th or early 15th century.

THUJE LHAKHANG

The principal image inside the Thuje Lhakhang (south of Drölma Lhakhang) is a Thousand-armed Chenresi, one of Trandruk's earliest works. Flanking it are Chana Dorje and Jampelyang. The three together made up the Rigsum Gönpo trio. Tucked away in the room's southwest corner is a substantial stove, supposedly used by Princess Wencheng. Murals cover the walls. The Thuje Lhakhang's smallness is due to lost space appropriated by a storeroom, with a separate entrance (south) from the Nangkor.

Along the north and south sides of the Drölma Lhakhang's foyer are four chapels. On the right (north) are Wöpame and Rabten, while on the left (south) are the Tsepak and Menlha Deshek chapels. This unusual architectural feature is not found in the Jokhang. Around the corners from the Rabten and Deshek chapels are two white *chörtens;* one (nearer Rabten) is a Namgyal *chörten* and the other is a Jangchub *chörten.*

Wöpame Lhakhang Here a statue of Sakyamuni is shaded by a peacock feather umbrella. Flanking him are Chana Dorje and Tamdrin.

Rabten Lhakhang The Rabten chapel has an 11-faced Chenresi flanked by statues of Trandruk's lineage holders. On the walls are paintings of variform *chörtens.*

Tsepak Lhakhang The principal image is Tsepame, flanked by two protectors (right) and three *bodhisattvas.*

Menlha Deshek Lhakhang A clay Medicine Buddha has pride of place here, one of nine such Buddhas in the room.

Thuje Lhakhang At the center of the north wing, facing the courtyard, is another Thuje Lhakhang. The main image is an archaic, well-executed 11-faced Chenresi. To the left is a *bodhisattva*; Guru Rinpoche is on the right. Murals depict Tsong Khapa, his two disciples and Gelugpa lamas.

ORGYAN LHAKHANG

Across the courtyard from the Thuje chapel (south side) is the Orgyan chapel, built in the first half of the 18th C. by the first Reting Rinpoche. The room has front and back sections. Inside the small front room are statues of Tsepame and Gönpo. The large rear chamber is consecrated to a one-story-high image of Guru Rinpoche; he is flanked by his two consorts. Vestiges of late paintings are on the walls. Unlike its counterpart, Thuje Lhakhang of the north wing, this double chapel has a long north–south axis that extends well beyond the usual boundaries of the Tsuglag Khang's rectangular plan. The Barkhor, the circumambulatory corridor that encloses the central Tshomchen, makes a U-shaped adjustment to accommodate this anomaly.

NGAPA LHAKHANG AND THONGDRÖL LHAKHANG

These two chapels of the west wing flank the Tshomchen's main entrance. They face east and were built in the 17th century. The left (north) Ngapa Lhakhang contains a one-story-high statue of the Fifth Dalai Lama. Next to him are Tsong Khapa, Gelugpa lamas, Dalai Lamas, and Atisha. The Thöngdrol Lhakhang (right) has for a central image Tsong Khapa, surrounded by high ranking Gelugpas.

GÖNKHANG

North of Ngapa Lhakhang is the south-facing *gönkhang*. Its location at the perimeter of the central courtyard is asymmetrical to the rest of the chapels. Sited at the northwest corner of the rectangle, it has no counterpart in the southwest. At its rear wall is a black, seated statue of Gönpo. The other walls have shelves with protector statues, some of the monastery's earliest works.

Second floor

The Tsuglag Khang's second floor consists of a large terrace that surrounds a central skylight. To the south are a kitchen (west) and chapel. The latter, above the Menlha Deshek Lhakhang, has statues of the tantric protectors, Tshangpa Chok and Seku.

DRUBTHOB LHAKHANG

In the east, above the Drölma and Thuje chapels, are the outer and inner rooms of the Drubthob Lhakhang. The outer room is dedicated to Guru Rinpoche, the inner to Tsong Khapa. The most treasured statue is Guru Ngadrama, a 'true-likeness' image of Guru Rinpoche at the age of eight. This statue was originally the main image of Sheldrak (see page 522), but after a long period of concealment during the Cultural Revolution, it came to Trandruk in the early 1980s. Few Guru Rinpoche statues are as well loved by Nyingmapa pilgrims as this one. Next to Guru Ngadrama is a famous *thangka* called Wencheng Gonju Mutik Thangka. It is made entirely of pearls and depicts Princess Wencheng, incarnation of White Tara (Drölkar).

The chapel once contained statues of the 84 Mahasiddhas (now lost). Near the extant statues are the 18 volumes of *Bum*, a summary of the Kangyur and the Tengyur. Pass through an entrance along the north wall to the Khaja Lhakhang, sited above the Chögyal Lhakhang. Inside were 100 clay statues of the Nyingma pantheon (lost). At one corner is a throne (*shugtri*) for the Dalai Lama. The room is distinguished by fine *thangkas* hanging on the north wall. One is a brocade *thangka* of Chenresi; the other depicts Naropa. The center of the west wing, directly above the entrance portico, is the private suite of the Dalai Lama. Noble families used the two rooms north of the suite.

Outside the Tsuglag Khang

At the southeast corner of the Trandruk compound is a disused Guru Lhakhang consecrated to Guru Rinpoche. Although a late addition to Trandruk, most of the religious activities were centered here before the Tsuglag Khang's recent renovations. Along the perimeter wall right of this chapel are a row of colored bas-relief images carved on slate slabs. The workmanship is outstanding. Within the Zokhang chapel (unlocated) was Songtsen Gampo's kitchen. Outside it were the sacred Six Syllables, supposedly written personally by Thönmi Sambhota, the 7th-C. creator of the Tibetan alphabet.

YUMBU LAGANG: FIRST PALACE OF THE YARLUNG KINGS

For location, see page 529.

BACKGROUND AND LEGENDS

Yumbu (Mother Deer) Lagang (Lakhar, Lhakhang) is a distinctive and easily recognizable tower-like structure. The monastery, unlike any other in Central Tibet, appears as a fairy castle on the crest of prominent Mt Tashi Tshe Ri. This ridge is said to resemble the hind leg of the mother deer and overlooks the Rechung Phuk Ridge (Mila Tse) and much of the Yarlung Valley.

The original Yumbu Lagang may well be the oldest building in Tibet (the present structure is practically a new reconstruction). According to legend, it was founded by a mythical king, either Nyatri Tsenpo or Lha Totori Nyentsen. When Nyatri Tsenpo first descended from heaven to the Yarlung Valley, 12 Bönpo shepherds (representations of the 12 demon-chieftains of prehistoric Tibet) saw him and asked where he came from. The king pointed his finger heavenward. Deeply impressed, the shepherds bore him aloft on a wooden throne to their village and elected him king of Tibet. He received the epithet Nyatri, 'Neck-enthroned'. Another source claims Nyatri Tsenpo reached Yarlung in 127 BC and built the palace of Yumbu Lagang at that time. If the claim were substantiated, the foundation would be over 2,100 years old. An additional legend states that Lha Totori Nyentsen, 28th king of Tibet, resided at Yumbu Lagang at the end of the 4th century. This was also the place where Buddhist texts fell from heaven in 446. A voice accompanying this event proclaimed the scriptures would remain unknown until five more kings succeeded to the throne. Thus it fell to Songtsen Gampo to reveal and spread the Buddhist doctrine.

The Tibetan text, *Gyalpo Kathang*, asserts that Lha Totori's tomb is in the red rocks of the Yumbu Lagang Ridge. Indeed, an 11 m by 6 m crypt has been excavated beneath the complex. Another tradition attributes the foundation of Yumbu Lagang to Trewu Jangchub Sempa, the monkey *bodhisattva*, incarnation of Chenresi, who mated with the ogress, Madrak Sinmo, an incarnation of Drölma.

In later times, Songtsen Gampo supposedly established a pair of two-story chapels next to the original palace-fortress. From this time on, the king's residence also became a monastery and the modest *lagang* expanded with each successive king. The Fifth Dalai Lama added a four-cornered gold roof to the tower and in the 15th C., Tsong Khapa's disciple, Kedrub Je, established the monastery of Riwo Chöling north of Yumbu Lagang. Its monks were charged with looking after the palace.

ARCHITECTURE

The present Yumbu Lagang is a reconstruction (1982) of the original building, which was almost totally destroyed during the Cultural Revolution. Its tower was damaged so badly only the stub of a base remained. All interior details that showed Indian influence have been lost. However, the foundation probably dates back to the time of the religious kings, Songtsen Gampo and Trisong Detsen. Tell-tale signs of its ancient origin are the construction technique and the material used to build the external walls. They are made of roughly-cut stones cemented together by a simple earth filler. This feature is similar to the construction method mentioned in Chinese sources. It is also a detail noticed by Tucci, the Tibetologist. He remarked that this method is the same one used for another ancient building, the Chingwa Taktse Dzong in Chongye (see page 528). Richardson, the last British envoy to Tibet, came to the conclusion that it was the earliest building method in the country.

P M Vergara, an Italian scholar, compares Yumbu Lagang to Mazar Tag, a Khotanese fortress. Both complexes consist of box-like modules thrown together in a seemingly random manner. This was dictated by the nature of both sites, along the irregular slopes of a ridge. Asymmetrical entrances, located in the minor sides of the edifice rather than along the central axis, are not immediately obvious to the first-time visitor. One has to walk around the buildings before stumbling across them. It is also difficult to determine which side is the main facade, a fact further complicated by the modular design. These two forts are also distinguished by their tall towers. Both have square plans placed off-center from the rest of the complex (see plan opposite). Since the founding of Yumbu Lagang, subsequent fortresses probably used it as a model and they consequently retained some early architectural characteristics.

DESIGN OF TIBET'S EARLY STRUCTURES

During the Yarlung Dynasty, it was the custom to build heavily fortified structures because of strife and warfare. The *Tang Annals* report one fortress for every 100 *li* (50 km) of territory. Religion induced the royal families to erect monuments as well. Founding temples earned the builder tremendous amounts of merit (*gechö*). At that time four main types of structures other than common dwellings were built: tombs, royal castles and palaces, temples, and dorings.

Tibet's prototypic architecture had its entrances facing east or west. This preference probably came from ancient megalithic complexes put up by the pre-Buddhist inhabitants of the country. As a result, the plans took on magico-religious overtones associated with early animistic beliefs. At ground-breaking, an elaborate set of rituals accompanied the laying of the foundation. Tibetans believed that a specific deity lived within each part of the edifice, thus there were gods of the entrance, the pillars, the stairways, the rooms, etc. Buddhism and cultural influences from India created and codified architectural principles. Buildings were oriented to the cardinal points and axial symmetry was a main element in the plans. These ideas were almost certainly borrowed from Indian cosmology, whereby religious structures conformed to a mandala. Three basic forms exist:

1) *Garbhagriha*. A central cell with an entrance foyer and a circumambulatory corridor. Examples are the Kachu Chapel in Yön Valley and Katsal Monastery in the Maldro Valley.
2) *Vihara*. A square courtyard with monks' cells attached to the inner face of the perimeter

walls. The principal temple faces the main entrance, preceded by an entrance portico or an entrance hall. The Jokhang and Trandruk Monastery are good examples of a *Vihara*.
3) *Mahavihara*. Great complicated monuments, whose plan is similar to the *Vihara*, designed to symbolize the cosmic mountain at the center of the universe. Samye is a good example.

Tibet's early religious architecture was influenced not only by India but also by the Buddhist countries of China, Central Asia, and Nepal. (Quintessentially Tibetan were the castles and fortresses.) Most temples were built on plains where there was sufficient space to allow unhampered interpretation of the Indian cosmology as it translated into architecture. Indian temples often served as prototypes. Some early structures around the Yarlung area had innovative design features, such as multi-story buildings whose individual floors were decorated in different styles. A prime example of this technique is the Samye Ütse (see page 300). Complexes built as mandalas generally lost their viability from the time of the Second Diffusion onwards; resources simply failed for such monumental, extravagant edifices. The one exception is today's great *chörtens* (Gyantse, Chung Riwoche), some of which are still erected to represent mandalas. Funeral mounds (tumuli) and *dorings* disappeared at the end of the royal period.

YUMBU LAGANG

The faithful reproduction of the complex consists of three separate components:

1) The tower. This highly conspicuous, unusual structure, located at the east end of the complex, has sides of 4.6 m and 3.5 m, and is 11 m high. From the outside there appear to be five storys. In fact, there are only three. The first is low, only 1.2 m tall. A narrow passage leads west into the first floor chapel and enters it from behind the main statue. A small door on the second floor leads to the upper part of the second floor chapel. The third floor was once topped by a gold roof, commissioned by the Fifth Dalai Lama. The tower's very thick walls result in extremely constricted interior spaces. The first floor has only 2.3 sq m, the second and third only 4.2 sq m.

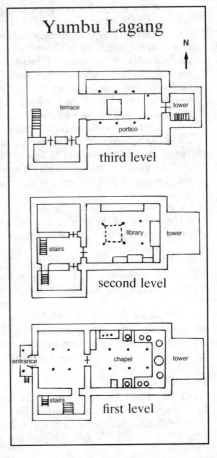

Yumbu Lagang

N

terrace · tower · portico

third level

library · tower · stairs

second level

entrance · chapel · tower · stairs

first level

2) The chapels. Tradition maintains that Songtsen Gampo built this part of the complex. Only two of the original three storys have been rebuilt. The ground floor chapel is dedicated to the historical kings of Tibet. The front half of this floor is the entrance foyer. Outside the entrance door is a small platform protected by an overhead portico. Once four pillars stood in the foyer; now there are only two. Beyond is an eight-pillar chapel. At the center of the altar is a statue of the Buddha, called Jowo Norbu Sampel Gulyendho. The original, erected by Songtsen Gampo, held within it a precious gem large as an egg. It is flanked on the left by King Nyatri Tsenpo and on the right by Songtsen Gampo. Along the left wall are Thönmi Sambhota, Songtsen Gampo's minister, Trisong Detsen, and Lha Totori Nyentsen. On the right are Ralpachen, Wösung, the 9th-C. king of West Tibet, and Lompo Gar, another minister of Songtsen Gampo.

The second floor has two parts. The first consists of a terrace enclosed on three sides by low walls; the second is a chapel surrounded by a circumambulatory corridor (balcony). This chapel, the Phakpa Lhakhang, affords good views of the kings' statues below. The altar holds the main statue of Chenresi (Phakpa), similar to the important image within the Potala's Lokeshvara Lhakhang (Phakpa Lhakhang). This sandalwood statue, supposedly mutilated, has been patched together. The other statues are Tsepame and Sakyamuni. To the left are new murals depicting lives of the early kings. Nyatri Tsenpo descends from heaven to Yumbu Lagang; the first Buddhist text falls from the sky at the time of King Lha Totori; Guru Rinpoche meditates in Sheldrak Hermitage. Other murals show the eight manifestations of Guru Rinpoche, Sakyamuni, the 21 Drölmas, and the 16 Arhats. A small cell (*drubkhang*) under the roof, at the back, was supposedly the meditation room of Nyatri Tsenpo. His tomb was said to be here.

The third floor remains unbuilt. It consisted of a front terrace and a rear chamber with a passage linking the tower to the chapels.

3) The monks' quarters. South of the chapel building are the Nyingmapa monks' rooms. The southeast corner of the entrance foyer has a door that leads into this building, and the second floor, adjacent to the second floor chapel, has quarters for the Dalai Lama.

GAR CHU

Some 400 m northeast of Yumbu Lagang, in a small gully, is a spring discovered by Gar, Songtsen Gampo's minister. Pilgrims make an obligatory trip here to drink its curative waters.

Six natural elements, all symbolizing longevity, are associated with Yumbu Lagang: mountain, water, deer, bird, human, and tree. The mountain is Tashi Tshe Ri, the water is a small pond at the southwestern base of the mountain. Even in the driest years, it always has water. The other four elements have not been identified.

YARLUNG ZORTHANG

Next to the Yumbu Lagang Village, by the motor road, is a plot of land shaped like a scythe when viewed from the air and enclosed by low walls. This is known as Zorthang, Scythe or Sickle Plain, the first cultivated field in Tibet. It is a tradition for pilgrims and farmers alike to collect soil from this place and sprinkle it on their own plots to ensure a good harvest. Each year at sowing time monks conduct rituals to propitiate the earth spirits. Some sources, however, consider a plot of land near Tsethang to be the actual Zorthang (see above, page 521).

UPPER REACHES OF THE KYI CHU RIVER

THE DRIGUNG, JANG, AND PHANYUL DISTRICTS

Great Monastic Centers of the Kadam and Drigung Sects

Location	North-east of Lhasa
Map reference	NH46-6 C, 46-5 D
Trekking days	17 (circuit)
Start–Finish	Lhasa–Lhasa
Passes	Chak

OVERVIEW

This pilgrimage explores the sacred places of Kyitö, the Upper Kyi Chu (Lhasa River). The first stretch heads east from Lhasa to the Drigungpa monasteries of Drigungtil and Terdrom.

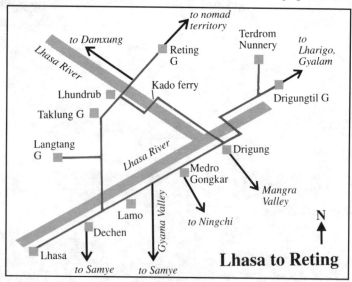

Lhasa to Reting

Along the way, explore the Gyalmashing, Mangra, and Zorong valleys, regions that saw the founding of early monastic institutions. The itinerary then swings northwest after the small town of Drigung Qu to follow the Upper Kyi Chu. After traversing the Lungshö Valley, beyond the strategic town of Lhündrub Xian, is the important Reting Monastery. The final section goes due south from Reting to Lhasa. En route, visit the Pak (Taklung) and Phanyul valleys with their Kadampa monasteries.

A short distance out of Lhasa is the Gyalmashing Valley, the birthplace of Songtsen Gampo; the future king was born in a house near the Gyalpo Kongkar Monastery. From Rinchengang (Rinjigon), a seldom-traveled trail leads south over the Tseb and Kampa passes to Samye (see page 549), the first monastery of Tibet.

Beyond Gyalmashing, at a junction of rivers, is the large town of Medro Gongkar and the 7th-C. Katsal Monastery, one of Tibet's earliest temples. Also in the vicinity, inside the Mangra Valley entrance, is Zhayi Monastery, founded at the beginning of the 9th century. Two original stone pillars survive there. Near Drigungtil is the Terdrom Nunnery, a stunning site with a fine hot spring and a one-day pilgrimage route that explores the amazing Guru Rinpoche grotto of Kiri Yongdzong, one of many retreat caves in the area.

Drigungtil, the largest of the Drigungpa monasteries, is a large complex of chapels and hermitages. Two highly respected incarnations, one in his late 80s, are in residence. A primary site of worship here is the Drigung Durtrö, a burial ground famous all over Tibet. The *Chikhor* (circumambulatory path) encompasses both Terdrom and Drigungtil. At the head of the Zorong Gorge, a trail leads north and east to the Gyalam, an ancient trade route that linked Tibet with China.

The Drigungpa sect, founded in the 12th C. by Rinchen Pel, is one of four major Kagyü schools; it exerted a powerful influence for centuries on the religious landscape of Tibet. Unlike the doctrines of the present-day Gelugpa, the sect emphasized solitary retreat and its monasteries are thus characterized by their isolated, remote hermitages. Both Drigungtil and Terdrom are dotted with retreat cells and caves. In its heyday, Drigungtil was a match for Sakya for religious and secular domination. Its influence was most noticeable at Tibet's pre-eminent pilgrimage sites: Kailash, Lapchi, and Tsari are well-known for their Drigung-Kagyü shrines. Because of the sect's intimate relationship with the Nyingmapa, holy places associated with Guru Rinpoche are commonly sited within Drigung's valleys.

The second leg involves walking from Drigung Qu to the 11th-C. Reting Monastery, founded by Atisha's chief disciple, Dromtönpa. This itinerary follows the upper reaches of the Kyi Chu, a rarely-visited stretch noted for its isolated nomadic encampments. Along the way are a number of Drigung-Kagyü monasteries and small villages. Reting, the first Kadampa temple ever built, is located in a strikingly scenic valley a stone's throw from the snow peaks of the Pangtö Range. In recent centuries, Reting became a key Gelugpa center and its abbots were occasionally appointed regents of Tibet.

Finally, after Reting, the pilgrimage heads south to enter the Pak and Phanyul valleys, strongholds of the Kadampa sect and areas where the Second Diffusion of Buddhism found its warmest reception. Atisha came here in the 11th C.; he and his disciples, notably Dromtönpa, spearheaded the development of vital monastic institutions.

The Kadampa's founding is attributed to Dromtönpa, whose principal disciples were Potowa, Chenga, and Puchungwa. Kadampa monks were widely respected for their ascetic vows and, unlike other sects, they shunned political involvement. Many important monasteries in Jang and Phanyul—Nalanda, Langtang, Reting—began as Kadampa institutions but were subsequently taken over by the Sakyapa and Gelugpa. One rare exception is the Taklung Monastery. It started life as a Kadampa center but later became the seat of the Taklung-Kagyü school.

Related sections
The Ningchi road, p 707
Drak Yerpa, p 338
Ganden, p 140
Lhamo Latso, p 623
Gyalam, p 570

Access
Take the daily 0830 Medro Gongkar bus from the Lhasa City Bus Station (across from the Tibet University's main gate, near the Sunlight Hotel). Buses also depart in the afternoon. Go early as the bus is crowded. Pass Dechen and Ganden Monastery to reach the village of Lamo (tell the driver you want to get off at Lamo) 49 km east of Lhasa on the south bank of the Kyi Chu. Hitchhiking this stretch should not be too difficult; there are quite a few tractors whose drivers are amenable to giving short rides.

LHASA TO DRIGUNGTIL MONASTERY

Time Chart

Day	Place	Hours
1	Lamo–Rinchengang (Rinjigon) Monastery	4 3/4
2	Katsal Monastery	4 3/4
3	Drigung Qu	6 1/2
4	Drigungtil Monastery	9
5	Terdrom Monastery	2 3/4

Trail Notes
✤ DAY 1 LAMO–RINCHENGANG (RINJIGON) MONASTERY 4 3/4 HR
Lamo Monastery is sited west of the roadside village while Sizhi Monastery is an easy 1-hr walk up the small south-trending valley. After visiting the latter Gelugpa institution, return to the main road and head east along it. This portion of the trek between Lamo and Medro Gongkar (19 km) is on the most important artery between Tibet and Sichuan. Try to hitchhike and get off this heavily-traveled, dusty highway as fast as possible. Do not, however, miss Gyalmashing Valley. The village of Jimicher (1/2 hr from Lamo) with its ruined monastery is near road marker 1514 km. Walk another 1/2 hr to road marker 1510 km (new marker 4573) and a wide side valley to the right. This is Gyalmashing, which contains three Kadampa monasteries—Dumburi, Gyamo Trikhang, and Rinchengang. The valley used to be a stronghold of the sect before the rise of the Gelugpa. Turn right (south) from the road into it. Follow the valley's western slopes with the river on the left. Cross an elevated grassy platform, then descend to two villages near the Gyalmashing River. Cross the river by a bridge after the second village and then climb to the small Gelugpa monastery of Gyalpo Kongkar (3/4 hr)

NH46-10A Medro Gongkar

NH46 – 10B

to Tibet – Sichuan Highway   to Ningchi

to Tibet-Sichuan Highway

pass

pass

5513

5510

5218

5346

5310

5314

5226

5246

5052

5081

Yarigon G

Zhayi Lhakhang

Drigung Qu

Mangra G

Mangra Chu

Mangra G

Yuhe

Pungda

Kangchen G

Tankya G

Jungne

Mochung

Katsal G

Gyata G

Medro Gongkar

Xian

Takpa G

Talung

Ngonda

Nangda

Tagtse Dzong
(Tongka Qu)

Gyalpo
Kongkar G

Sizhi G

Lamo G

Kyi Chu River

to Lhasa

to Lhasa

r.m. 1510 km

5214

4936

N

to Ganden G

Hebu

Lamo Ri
5511

Rinchengang G

Dumburi G

Gyamo Trikhang G

Gyalmashing

Valley

Thugcha

5018

5218

5531

Jooker La

Kampa La
(Sukhe La)

TsebLa

to Samye / to Tsangpo

5476

5350

5518

5341

to Yön valley

to Yön Valley

NH46 – 10C

Sephuk Valley

Kalwa Valley

Sepuk

Tashi Gang, Balo

Rinchenling

Sibuktsango

Sibukna

5513

5521

5536

5536

5576

5310

r.m. 1446 km

Rutok G

Usekiang

Tibet-Sichuan Highway

r.m. 1481 km

to Dzinchi G

r.m. 1443 km

r.m. 1436 km

r.m. 1431 km

Damxung La

Magon La

to Dzinchi G,
Lhamo Latso

to Tsangpo

to Tsangpo

5261

5100

5536

5050

5326

5318

Takar La

10 km

6 miles

0 2 4 6 8 10 km

0   2   4   6 miles

92°15'

29°30'

29°30'

91°30'

92°00'

on the other (east) side of the valley. King Songtsen Gampo was supposedly born near here.

Return to the valley floor and cross a bridge farther south to continue up the left (west) bank of the Gyalmashing River. The track is jeepable. About 1/2 hr from Gyalpo Kongkar is the Gelugpa monastery of Gyamo Trikhang. On the valley's western hills near Gyamo Trikhang is the ruined monastery of Gyamo Dumburi (1/2 hr). The remains of five large *chörtens* are here. Continue upstream along the jeep track. The valley soon divides and the larger branch curves to the right. At a bend of the western slopes, on the right and set above a village, is Rinchengang (Rinjigon) Monastery (1/2 hr from Gyamo Trikhang).

Gyalmashing to Samye (see below). From Rinchengang (Rinjigon), the Gyalmashing Valley continues southward. By following it and crossing 2 passes (east of the Gökar La), one eventually reaches Samye Monastery—in four days—to connect with the Lhamo Latso trek.

Lamo Monastery

Lamo sits on the west side of the main village path, across from a white building. A small *chörten* marks the beginning of the path, which starts from the main road. The handsome monastery, facing a large enclosed courtyard, is still in good shape and retains some small murals.

History Lamo was among the first monasteries founded during the early days of the Second Diffusion of Buddhism in Tibet. The movement was led by the exiled lama Lume, who returned to Central Tibet in the beginning of the 11th century. This illustrious teacher founded Lamo in 1009. The site, together with Sonak Tangboche, Yerpa Neten Lhakhang, Tsongdü Tsokpa, and Dranang (see Place-Name Index), was a major center in this part of Central Tibet during those heady days. Lamo was the principal seat of the important protector, Tsangpa Karpo (the 'White Brahma'), and his oracle. Setrabchen, the wrathful form of this deity, resides at Trandruk Monastery in the Yarlung Valley.

Sizhi Monastery

Sizhi is 1 hr up a side valley south of Lamo, at the entrance of a smaller side valley to the right. Pass a few *chörtens* on the way. The monastery's two main buildings are large; the first one is used for storage. Across from it is a neglected chapel with a restored room on the top. Monks are now in residence (this Gelugpa monastery once had 50–60 monks).

Gyalpo Kongkar Monastery

Originally called Tashi Migyur Jampe Potrang, this restored monastery is well built and quite charming. King Songtsen Gampo reportedly was born in a house nearby. The small, well-appointed chapel contains images of the king and his two foreign wives and a continuous row of small prayer wheels are built around the outside walls.

Gyamo Trikhang Monastery

The monastery is at the center of a large village noted for its thick surrounding walls. Three large *chörtens* once dominated the monastery. They were earth *chörtens* (*sabums*) consecrated to Gyar Gomchenpo (Tsultrim Senge, 1144–1204, a member of the powerful Yarlung clan and disciple of Phagmo Drupa Dorje Gyalpo), Sangye Wanton (see below), and Khuwon, the uncle of Sangye Wanton. Only one of them still stands. The main hall has been renovated and the two side chapels are Chökhang Ghongma and Chökhang Wökma. Gyamo Trikhang was founded by Sangye Wantön, abbot of Rinchengang (Rinjigon), and controlled by the Horkang clan, an influential noble family.

Rinchengang (Rinjigon) Monastery
This monastery was founded in 1181 by Khuwön, a disciple of Neuzurpa. Later it was rebuilt by Sangye Wanton, second abbot and nephew of the founder. Rinchengang (Rinjigon)'s importance was highlighted by two visits of the Khache Panchen Sakyasri. A small chapel, rebuilt on the roof of the ruined monastery, has new paintings and clay bas-relief sculptures. Six *chörtens* marked the approach to the monastery, but now only stubs remain.

Gyamo Dumburi Monastery
This Kadampa shrine was founded in the 12th C. by lama Dumburipa Dawa Gyaltsen, a disciple of Neuzurpa and Jayulpa.

A walk from the Gyalmashing Valley to Samye Monastery
This is a wonderful alternative to either the Dechen–Samye (see page 625) or Ganden–Samye (see page 314) routes. One principal advantage is that the terrain is comparatively less inhospitable than the other two. Except for the first and last days, there are no villages en route. Nomad camps, however, are encountered near the passes.

✧ Day 1
From Rinchengang (Rinjigon) Monastery
Rinchengang (Rinjigon) is situated at a valley junction. The path to Samye leads up the right valley, one which trends to the southwest. Walk up this valley through fields and scattered villages, past interesting ruins. In 1 1/4 hr, the valley divides again. This time go left, nearly due south, and climb gradually through the narrowing valley. The peak on the right, only 5 km away, is 5511 m high. Reach the valley's last village 1 hr after the fork. Here the jeep road gives way to a footpath. A good campsite is right by the river just beyond the village. This is the first encounter with the Gyalmashing Chu since it was crossed lower down near Gyamo Trikhang.

✧ Day 2
Cross the river and walk up the valley along the right bank for about 1 hr, then cross back to the left. Beyond are nomad encampments, all on the left bank (1 3/4 hr). Continue up; the river is now well below and the path zigzags up. Camp at the foot of the Tseb La (2 3/4 hr) inside a stone enclosure situated on the right side of a large meadow at the head of the valley. The area is hemmed in on all sides by 5500-m peaks.

➡

❖ Day 3

Continue up the meadow's right side at the head of the valley, then turn right into the first side valley that leads out of the meadow-bowl. Reach a small plain after a steep ascent. Follow the trail across it, walking nearly due west. After the plain, ascend sharply for 2 hr to the Tseb La. Descend from the pass into a bowl at the head of another valley that trends to the southwest. The path goes across the head of this valley with little view, though it is a very pretty region skirted by the Ganden–Samye trek (see page 314). The clear trail from the Tseb La leads to another pass, the Kampa La. After coming down from the former, cross a plain at the head of the descending valley to reach this second pass without making another ascent (1 hr between the two passes). From the Kampa La, descend for 2 hr along the Langsang Chu to reach a valley junction. Camp here.

❖ Day 4

Take the right valley, which leads to the Yamalung Valley (see Lhamo Latso, page 627). The river in this valley must be crossed and recrossed several times. Reach the village of Ninggong at the Samye–Yamalung valley junction (3 hr from the start), passing the turn-off for the Yamalung Hermitage. The latter valley is lush and bordered by large grassy meadows and forests. From Ninggong to Samye is an easy walk due south along the Samye Valley (2 3/4 hr).

(Tom Laird of Kathmandu contributed the above information.)

✤ DAY 2 RINCHENGANG MONASTERY–KATSAL MONASTERY 4 3/4 HR

Return to the main Tibet–Sichuan highway in 2 hr from Rinchengang (Rinjigon). Medro Gongkar is 10 km away at road marker 1500 km (new marker 4564), a 1 1/2–2-hr walk. This important town at the Kyi Chu–Metoma river junction has tea shops, stores, and a big Public Security Bureau. The dirt path to Katsal Monastery starts from near the center of town and goes off to the left (northeast) at a right angle to the main road. Continue to a hospital on the right, cross a bridge, then pass a large walled compound on the left. Go over a bigger bridge to follow the Kyi Chu (on the right) to Katsal, 3/4 hr from Medro Gongkar. Nomads camp here along the wide plains bordering the river. They have traveled large distances from the Nagchuka area of North Tibet with their herds of yak.

Katsal Monastery

The architecture of this 7th-C. Drigungpa monastery is among the more unusual in Tibet. Its exterior façades are full of surprising angles and sloping walls and its two storys contain recent but good quality murals. An inner corridor enclosing the entire ground floor hall still has original paintings depicting the patriarchs of the Drigung lineage. There is also a recent painting of Apchi, protectress of the Drigungpa. The inner chapel that opens off the outer assembly hall has images of the Past, Present, and Future Buddhas. At the back is a chapel known as the Lukhang, consecrated to the subterranean deity that was subdued in the 8th C. by Guru Rinpoche.

Katsal was rebuilt in 1980, although it did not suffer badly during the Cultural Revolution. It is religiously vigorous under the incarnate lama, Tulku Nedar, who is likely to provide visitors with accommodation under a porch on the second floor. This is a gem of a monastery, a beautiful and friendly place. A village next to Katsal used to house the monks.

History The original construction is attributed to King Songtsen Gampo, who built it at the behest of his Nepalese wife. Katsal and three other monasteries in Central Tibet were designed to keep down the demoness that generated catastrophes in the country; these are known as the Tandul monasteries (see page 43). Katsal's function was to hold down the right shoulder of the demoness at a point northeast of Lhasa. One local tradition holds that Guru Rinpoche was involved in the construction. According to Hugh Richardson, last British envoy in Tibet during the 1940s, Katsal's Tugdam Tsuglag Khang chapel was 'the only building in Tibet which struck me as really ancient and untouched'. This is the chapel that dates back to Yarlung times, but unfortunately, it is difficult to find anything of antiquity in it now.

✤ Day 3 Katsal Monastery–Drigung Qu 6 1/2 hr

Katsal backs on to a small hill. Follow its contours up the Kyi Chu Valley, which curves to the right, to a village with five or six large ruined *chörtens* (1/2 hr). Continue along the valley to a big bridge that crosses the Kyi Chu on the left (1 hr). Tankya Monastery is on the other side, 15 min away in the middle of Tankya Qu. From the bridge continue to ascend the valley, passing nomad caravans and encampments along the way. Men with long braided pigtails and heavy sheepskin robes bring tea down to Lhasa and return to their pastures with *tsampa* and other staples. From November to February large groups of these nomads make pilgrimages to Lhasa's major monasteries (especially the Jokhang) and to the towns of Gyantse and Shigatse.

Occasional villages dot this route. About 4 hr from the bridge at Tankya is a white *chörten* left of the road. A village is nearby and the valley now widens. Continue to the small town of Drigung Qu, built on the ruins of Drigung Nyima Changra, a famous Nyingmapa college (*shedra*), at the junction of three valleys (1 hr). Zhayi Lhakhang, a historically important monastery, is 15 min away inside the Mangra Valley, which opens to the southeast. From Medro Gongkar to Drigung Qu is 25 km.

Tankya Monastery

Tankya's main building was closed at the time of visit and the villagers were reluctant to get the keys. (The administrative compound is next to the monastery.) Its exterior is in reasonable shape. The interior contained ancient clay sculptures from the original shrine (destroyed) and Kadampa-type bronze *chörtens*.

History Tankya Monastery, like Katsal, was built by Songtsen Gampo in the 7th C. to 'tame the frontiers' and to subdue Tibet's destructive demoness. The original chapel, destroyed some time ago, was sited on the slopes north of the present chapel. After the collapse of the Yarlung Dynasty, it fell into disuse and was later resurrected by Lume, the exiled lama responsible for the Second Diffusion of Buddhism. In the 12th C., the monastery was under the Taklung Lama and Taklungpa precepts were practiced. Later, the Jonangpa controlled Tankya until they too were displaced by the Gelugpa, who associated this site with the Potala's Namgyal

Tratsang. From Tankya return to the bridge and road. (This road is a secondary route in Tibet and carries little traffic; consider it a good trekking trail.)

Drigung Qu

Drigung Qu, a town of Chinese compounds and old village houses, lies on the Kyi Chu's left bank. At a pronounced turn in the river is the junction of three valleys. The northeast one leads to Drigungtil Monastery along the Zorong Gorge. Lungshö, the second valley, bears to the left (northwest) and leads along the Kyi Chu to Reting Monastery. The third, the Mangra, trends to the right (southeast). Within it, near Drigung Qu, is the important monastery of Zhayi Lhakhang. The town is on one side of a narrow gap where the Zorong Chu, coming from beyond Drigungtil Monastery, emerges from the Lungshö Valley. On the other side of the gap is Yuena Monastery, now in ruins. Cross a bridge to reach Yuena.

Drigung Qu is a recent settlement. The original site was the Drigung Dzong, perched on the Kyi Chu's left bank where the river cuts through a low spur before joining the Mangra and Zorong rivers. It was strategically important in the early history of Tibet; later it functioned primarily as an administrative headquarters of a district governed by the Drigungtil Monastery. A monastery associated with the Dzong was one of the principal seats of Geshe Jayul, founder of Mangra Monastery (see below). Overlooking the fortress was a chapel called Zhika Saten Dorje Potrang. Stay at a government guest house in Drigung Qu.

Zhayi Lhakhang

Zhayi Lhakhang (Uru Zhayi Lhakhang), sited at the southwest corner of a village, is on the left (south) bank of the Mangra Chu, 15 min east of Drigung Qu. The principal building was the Ütse. Next to it was the Guru Tsengye chapel and the Rigna Chörten. All these structures were leveled during the Cultural Revolution. A newly restored chapel contains images of Longchenpa and the three Dzokchen protectors: Ekajati, Dorje Lekpa, and Rahula.

Surviving cultural objects of major importance are two stone *dorings* that stand outside the Ütse. The left pillar with a carved swastika, a traditional Yarlung design, is in good condition; only the stub remains of the right one. Both pillars have inscriptions that praise Lama Tingedzin Sangpo, Trisong Detsen's selfless minister who later focused his attention on young Senelek until he acceded to the throne in 804. The proclamation records the rewards Tingedzin Sangpo received from the grateful king. One of the minister's major accomplishments was his success in persuading Trisong Detsen to invite the Indian master, Vimalamitra, to Tibet. In the 14th C., Zhayi was headed by the famous Dzokchen master, Longchenpa, who restored the chapels.

Across the river from the monastery is Zangyak Drak; high up on it is a Guru Rinpoche cave and a hermitage used by Tingedzin Sangpo. Beyond is the peak of Karpo Drak, a place where Guru Rinpoche supposedly transformed into a *garuda* and subdued wild demons. A cave within Karpo Drak, the Nub Phuk, has the *rangjung* images of a *garuda* and a conch shell. Tsurung Monastery, near Zhayi Lhakhang, is said to be sited in quite beautiful surroundings. Also nearby is the restored Kadampa monastery of Mangra (2 hr beyond Zhayi, farther along the Mangra Valley). Within the chapel is the footprint in stone of Geshe Jayul (1075–1138), founder of the monastery. During the first part of this century, Mangra was under the jurisdiction of Ling Rinpoche, the senior tutor of the Dalai Lama.

History Zhayi Lhakhang, built during the reign of King Trisong Detsen in the early 9th century, was founded by Tingedzin Sangpo, an illustrious member of the powerful Nyang clan.

He was allied strongly with Trisong Detsen and led the king's efforts to promote Buddhism. Later he became the first Tibetan abbot of Samye. This site was a principal center of the Nyingma Dzokchen tradition. In modern times, it was subject to the Sera Je Tratsang of Sera Monastery. Both Gelug and Nyingma tantric deities were propitiated. During the time of the 13th Dalai Lama's trip to India, the monastery was renovated by Chuzang Rinpoche of Dorje Drak.

✤ DAY 4 DRIGUNG QU–DRIGUNGTIL MONASTERY 9 HR

From Drigung Qu, continue along the main road. Cross a bridge, turn left and pass a Chinese compound. A small village is beyond on top of a rise. The road now enters the Zorong Gorge. An army compound is on the right, 1/2 hr from Drigung Qu. This level road is passable by jeep but has little traffic. Reach Yangri Gön Monastery in another 2 1/2 hr, now mostly a Chinese army compound with some fine houses in the village. The monastery, founded by Trinle Kyapgön, the eighth incarnation of the Drigung Kyapgön (founder of Drigungtil) was completely leveled. There used to be 500 monks here. The clear Zorong Chu runs on the left in a deep gorge. Beyond is a small side valley on the right and the rebuilt monastery of Yamure is on its left slopes.

After 2 hr the road crosses a bridge and begins a gentle ascent of the valley (the river is now on the right); a side valley branches off to the left (a dirt road goes north up this) and a village is next to the road. Continue to the northeast along the Zorong Valley and travel on an elevated plateau above the river, which extends all the way to Drigungtil Monastery. The road climbs gradually along this pleasant valley. Reach another side valley on the left after 3 1/2 hr. A village is at the entrance and a dirt path branches off from the main road to cross a small bridge to go up this side valley (Terdrom Monastery [see below] is 2 1/2 hr up this). Continue along the main valley. After 1/2 hr a few villages appear on both sides of the road. Drigungtil Monastery can now be seen halfway up a steep cliff overlooking the valley.

The administrative compound of Menpa Qu, directly below the monastery, is on the left. There is accommodation but no cooked meals. Beyond the compound, the road stops and a track leads up to the snow mountains at the head of the valley. It eventually joins the Gyalam (the old Tibet–China Trade Road, see page 570) after passing the village of Tantuk Sumdo.

Note This long walk from Drigung Qu to Drigungtil is perhaps best tackled in 1 1/2–2 days.

Drigungtil Monastery

Drigungtil and Terdrom are two outstanding monasteries in the region east of Lhasa and should not be missed. Drigungtil, greatest of all Drigungpa monasteries, is a fascinating and extensive complex, so be sure to have at least a day to explore the buildings, hermitages, and chapels, and to visit the two incarnate lamas who reside here.

History A small hermitage was first established here in 1167 by Minyag Gomring, a disciple of Phagmo Drupa Dorje Gyalpo, the renowned abbot of Densatil Monastery. In 1179, the site passed to another disciple, Rinchen Pel (Jigten Gönpo, 1143–1217), who was instrumental in starting an influential Kagyü lineage here. Due to his efforts, the monastery rapidly acquired a high reputation as a sanctuary for the contemplative tradition. A large following resulted

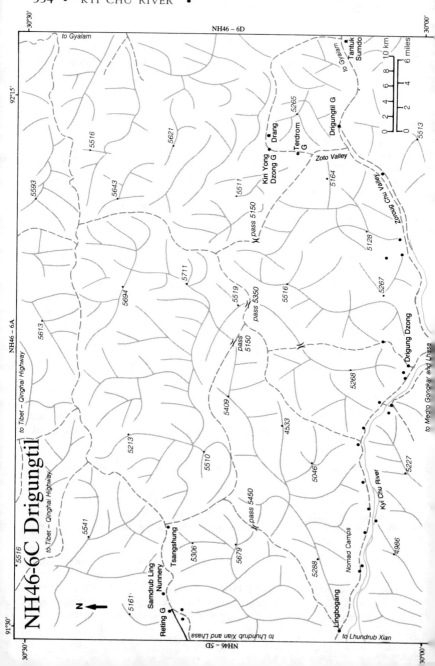

NH46-6C Drigungtil

NH46 – 6D

NH46 – 6A

NH46 – 5D

to Gyalam

to Tibet – Qinghai Highway

to Tibet – Qinghai Highway

to Lhundrub Xian and Lhasa

to Lhundrub Xian

to Medro Gonokar and Lhasa

to Gyalam

Tantuk Sumdo

Drigungtil G

Drang

Terdrom G

Kiri Yong Dzong G

Zoto Valley

Zorong Chu Valley

pass 5150

pass 5350

pass 5150

pass 5450

pass 5450

Drigung Dzong

Kyi Chu River

Nomad Camps

Lingbogang

Samdrub Ling Nunnery

Tsangshung

Reting G

5516
5621
5593
5643
5511
5265
5513
5164
5128
5267
5711
5519
5516
5694
5613
5409
5268
5213
4533
5510
5046
5541
5679
5288
5306
4986
5227
5161

and it became one of the most important monastic centers in Central Tibet. The 13th C. was a time of great change and expansion for Drigungtil and at one time it rivaled Sakya for political and religious domination. This hostility came to an unfortunate head when the Sakyapa, with the help of a Mongol army, burnt the monastery down in 1290. Although this main Kagyü center was destroyed, its teachings had taken root firmly in other monasteries and hermitages throughout the region.

The Drigungpa, one of the three major Kagyü lineages derived from Phagmo Drupa, essentially followed the ascetic tradition of Milarepa. Many practices particular to the Nyingmapa were incorporated as well. In fact, there is not that much distinction between the Drigungpa and the Nyingmapa. A peculiarity of the monastery was that an abbot presided over spiritual matters while an administrator handled day-to-day matters. The latter also oversaw the large Drigung district. This form of monastic organization was based on the Sakya model.

The site The monastery is built on a steep ridge that resembles a yak's back; hence the name—*dri* is a female yak. To reach Drigungtil, return along the valley from Menpa Qu to a small village at the bottom of the ridge (10 min away). From here a trail zigzags up sharply to the monastery complex (1/2 hr). Another path goes directly up from Menpa Qu, but this is a much steeper climb. A wide jeep track also goes to the monastery from the valley's eastern end.

The most striking aspect of the complex is its distribution of chapels, monks' quarters, and colleges on various levels along the upper part of the ridge. Steep trails, stone steps, and sometimes simple tree trunks with notches, provide access. There are 50 buildings and three or four main chapels. The principal halls were modeled on Sakyapa architectural characteristics, even though the two sects were antagonistic. Over 100 monks now live here, quite a few in small hermitages at the top of the ridge. Pilgrims and worshippers from nearby villages come here regularly. About ten of the buildings were badly damaged in the Cultural Revolution. The main chapels are connected by a wide, open-air gallery that serves as an outdoor courtyard for services and informal gatherings. The architecture of the gallery is unusual but functional. Providing a natural focal point for the whole complex, it is the unifying element for all the main monastic halls. Most days it is crowded with pilgrims, traders, and monks. The atmosphere can be festive when the entire community gathers for teachings. The view of the Zorong Valley and beyond is unforgettable.

The most impressive building in Drigungtil is the assembly hall (*tshokhang*), the first substantial structure encountered before reaching the gallery. It has been destroyed and rebuilt many times—the worst sacking came in 1290 at the hands of the Mongols and the Sakyapa. Despite its precarious history, this building still retains design features that can be traced back to the early architecture of India and West Tibet. The *dukhang* has the external form of a stepped pyramid, an unusual configuration, further reinforced by a wooden portico that supports the open-air terrace. It is clear that the basic scheme owes its genesis to the great temples (*mahaviharas*) of India and the 10th- and 11th-C. monasteries of West Tibet, such as Tsaparang (see page 430) and Thöling (see page 425). The floor above contains a lion figure in the corner that resembles very closely the one found in ancient Sani of Zanskar. The roof, made of bronze and decorated with a high cornice, is of more recent Chinese derivation.

The main hall is well appointed with sculptures, *thangkas*, and all the paraphernalia of worship. It was restored in the early 1980s and has been used actively since. The main image here is Rinchen Pel (Drigung Kyapgön, the Saviour of Drigung). This is flanked to the right by Apchi, the protectress of Drigung, in her incarnation as Palden Lhamo and Dorje Chödron. Before their destruction, there were large statues of Dorje Chang and a one-story-high Jampa. Sacred objects on the altar include the founder's footprint on a stone (below Rinchen Pel's image) and his conch shell and trumpet.

Drigungtil's most important relic is a small *chörten* that contains the mummified body of Rinchen Pel. It is next to the footprint. According to tradition, the 12 *rangjung* images of the Demchok family were imprinted on the founder's tongue, heart, and head. Within the *chörten* are relics of the Karsapani Buddha, a gift from King Amshuvarma of Nepal. Other sacred objects were brought by Atisha and the monks claim that the fire of 1290 was unable to damage the *chörten*.

Two incarnate lamas (*tulkus*) live at the monastery. One is Pachung Rinpoche, an ancient man who lives in a cosy room at the gallery's eastern perimeter. Monks who look after him live in a small room just outside. Among this cluster of cells is the original hermitage first built by Rinchen Pel in the 12th century. Here, a short distance above Pachung Rinpoche's room, is the *gönkhang* consecrated to the goddess Apchi. There are two images of the protectress; the white one is the peaceful form of Palden Lhamo, the gold one the wrathful Dorje Chödron. Other statues in the room include Guru Rinpoche and Sakyamuni. Beneath the former is another stone imprinted with the founder's footprint. A historic object in the chamber is a pair of horns hung on a column, supposedly from the original yak that inspired Rinchen Pel to build his hermitage here.

West of the assembly hall are large, striking ruins, site of the *labrang*, the residence of the abbot. Within the complex are a number of retreat centers called *drubdra*. One was founded by Dharmaraja Rinchen Phüntshok, another by Kunga Rinchen. A cave here, called Drubphuk Karchungma, was used as a retreat by Rinchen Pel, and a small hole within it contains his footprint. In front of it is a tree that supposedly grew from one of his teeth. The younger of the two *tulkus* of Drigungtil, Sordruk Rinpoche, has a room in this part of the monastery.

Drigung Durtrö

Near the monastery complex is a sacred site used for sky-burials. It is a particularly hallowed place and Tibetan families have for centuries traveled long distances to bring their dead here. This burial ground is supposed to be the Tibetan counterpart of Siwatshal, the famed cemetery near Bodh Gaya considered first among the Eight Great Cemeteries in India. The site is located at the far western end of the Drigungtil ridge and the *khora* path that encircles the entire complex leads west from the monastery to here. It is marked out as a circle by prayer flags, shrines, and large rocks, designed to resemble the mandala of Demchok. Behind is a shrine with paintings of wrathful and peaceful divinities. Next to this shrine is a room with the shaven hair of the dead. The *chörten* on the right represents the throne of Rinchen Pel; his footprint can be seen on the surface of a rock.

Drigungtil Monastery to the Gyalam: a one-week walk

The Gyalam is the centuries-old trail that linked Tibet with China. It traverses the remote districts of Lharigo, Penba, Shopado, and Lhorong and crosses the great Nyenchen Tanglha Range, watershed of the Salween and Tsangpo rivers. From Central Tibet there are two main routes to Atsa Monastery and the Gyalam: from Drigungtil and from Giamda on the Tibet–Sichuan highway. The former is briefly sketched below; the times given are a rough approximation only. For a detailed description of the Gyalam and its access from Giamda, see Gyalam, page 570.

Continue east up the Zorong Valley to the nomad encampment of Tantuk Sumdo (3 1/4 hr from Drigungtil). Ignore a side valley to the left (north) but continue up the main valley (northeast) and pass another side valley, also trending north, after 4 1/2 hr. Turn left (north-northeast) into a side valley after 2 hr and reach a pass in another 2 hr. Descend into a north-trending valley. After 9 1/2 hr along it, come to a junction of four valleys. The three main ones go west, north, and southeast. A small, narrow one leads east (the main path leads due west from the junction).

Continue up the north valley. After 2 1/2 hr, come to another junction. A side trail goes off to the left (northwest); follow the main trail to the northeast. The valley soon widens into a broad plain and the route reaches the nomad camp of Shag Paserat (Chakpatang) in 4 hr. Proceed for 6 hr to the northeast to an important dirt road and turn right (if you go left for 157 km you will reach the large town of Nagchu, on the main road between Lhasa and Golmud). A small village is 1 1/2 hr away. 3/4 hr later the road loops left (north) for a few km, crosses the river, and loops back to continue in an easterly direction; this detour takes 2 1/2 hr. After 10 hr more, a trail branches right (southwest) along the south shores of Lake Atsa (this leads via either the Trö La or the Draksum Kye La to Giamda; see the Lake Draksum Latso trek, page 656). Do not take this, but rather follow the dirt road that continues east to Atsa Monastery (1 1/4 hr). For the itinerary from here along the Gyalam to the Bön enclave of Khyungpo Tengcheng, see Gyalam, page 574.

✤ **DAY 5 DRIGUNGTIL–TERDROM NUNNERY   2 3/4 HR**

To reach Terdrom, go to the village below Drigungtil. From here walk up a path to a bluff west of the Drigung ridge. On the far side of the bluff is the Zoto Valley that leads to Terdrom. (Another way is simply to walk back down the Zorong Valley along the road. In 1/2 hr reach a side valley that opens to the right [north]. The dirt track within it leads to the nunnery.)

The trail along the left bank of the narrow Zoto River is wide (trucks come through occasionally). Along the valley are dwarf rhododendrons and other shrubs. Cross a bridge after 1 3/4 hr from the village; the road now becomes quite stony and the river is on the right. Continue to a village where the valley splits. Follow the right branch by fording a stream. The path, difficult for vehicles, now climbs along the valley's right side. Reach Terdrom (Repna is the local name; the river flowing past the nunnery is the Rep Chu) after 15 min. It is set at the dramatic confluence of two rivers

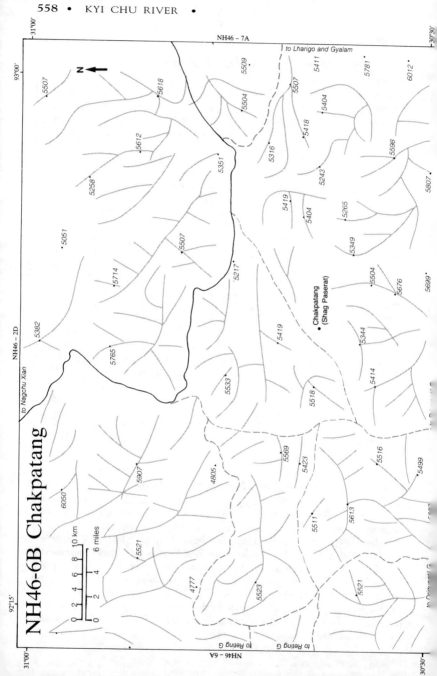

NH46-6B Chakpatang

NH46 – 7A

to Lharigo and Gyalam

to Nagchu Xian

NH46 – 2D

Chakpatang
(Shag Paserat)

to Reting G

to Reting G

NH46 – 6A

10 km

6 miles

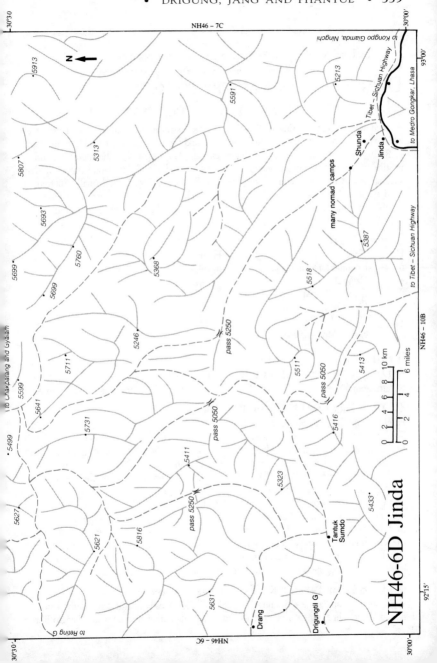

NH46 – 7C

30°30'

93°00'

to Kongpo Giamda, Nyingtri

Tibet – Sichuan Highway

to Medro Gongkar, Lhasa

· 5913

N

· 5213

5591

· 5313

Shunda

Jinda

· 5807

many nomad camps

to Tibet – Sichuan Highway

· 5693

· 5387

· 5760

· 5368

· 5699

· 5518

· 5699

pass 5250

to Chakpatang and Gyalam

· 5246

· 5711

· 5511

pass 5050

· 5413

· 5599

· 5641

· 5416

· 5731

pass 5050

10 km

6 miles

· 5499

· 5323

· 5411

NH46 – 10B

· 5627

pass 5250

· 5433

· 5621

· 5816

Tantuk Sumdo

to Reting G

· 5631

Drang

Drigungtil G

NH46-6D Jinda

92°15'

30°00'

NH46 – 6C

> **Terdrom Nunnery** See Ritro: page 344 for a full description

DRIGUNGTIL MONASTERY TO RETING MONASTERY ALONG THE UPPER KYI CHU

A good way to reach Reting is via the Upper Kyi Chu from Drigungtil and Drigung Qu. This avoids the hassle of hiring vehicles in Lhasa and bypasses the motor road from the capital to Reting via the Pembo Valley and Chak La Pass. The Upper Kyi Chu route goes through pristine valleys with isolated monasteries and villages and virtually no motor traffic. Monastic sites along the way are Pardu (destroyed), Tsa, Batsak (destroyed), and finally Sherteng, in good shape with a new *chörten*. The first part of the walk is along a jeep road; the second involves crossing the Kyi Chu by ferry to its right bank before heading to Lhündrub Xian and Reting.

Time Chart

Day	Place	Hours
6	Drigungtil–Drigung Qu	6 1/4
7	Camp 1	5 1/4
8	Drigung Tsa Monastery	6
9	Kadö ferry	5 1/2
10	Lhündrub Xian	2 1/4
11	Reting Monastery	6

Trail Notes

✤ DAY 6 DRIGUNGTIL–DRIGUNG QU 6 1/4 HR

Return from Drigungtil to Drigung Qu by walking back down the Zorong Chu Gorge.

✤ DAY 7 DRIGUNG QU–CAMP 1   5 1/4 HR

From Drigung Qu, walk down the road towards Medro Gongkar. In 1/2 hr reach a road junction. Take the right dirt track which leads north and crosses the river confluence formed by the Kyi Chu, Zorong Chu, and the Mangra Chu by means of a bridge. Follow it up the left (east) bank of the Kyi Chu; the valley here is called Lungshö. Reach Drigung Dzong in 1 1/4 hr at the eastern perimeter of a valley entrance. After the Dzong, walk northwestwards along the flat Lungshö Valley, which slowly widens. Pass a number of villages and in 1 1/2 hr a side valley can be seen to open to the southwest across the Kyi Chu. Here villages on both sides of the river are linked by a bridge. Continue along the left bank to the northwest and in 2 hr come to a major river junction. A large side valley trends from the left bank of the Kyi Chu to the north. Within it, a trail leads north to the secondary ranges of the Nyenchen Tanglha and many nomad encampments. At this point, the Kyi Chu makes a bend to the left and the valley heads due west. Stop here for the night.

✤ DAY 8 CAMP 1–DRIGUNG TSA MONASTERY 6 HR

Walk due west along the Kyi Chu's left bank. Villages, mostly on the left (north) bank, are spaced about 1 hr from each other. Pass short side valleys that lead up to the Pangtö Range.

In 6 hr reach another side valley opening to the northeast. Follow a dirt track within it to the village and monastery of Drigung Tsa.

Drigung Tsa Monastery

This institution was founded by the Drigung lama, Thinley Sangpo, the eighth incarnation of Rinchen Pel, the 12th-C. founder of Drigungtil. He also established Yangri Gön Monastery. Drigung Tsa was destroyed and a modest chapel has now been rebuilt. Within it are images of Apchi Drölma, female protective deity of the Drigungpa, Tsong Khapa, Guru Rinpoche, and others. Drigungtil, Terdrom, and Drigung Tsa (*tsa* means 'root') are the three most important Kagyüpa monasteries in the area.

✤ DAY 9 DRIGUNG TSA MONASTERY–KADÖ FERRY 5 1/2 HR

Continue to the west past a large roadside *chörten*. Reach a large side valley, with a wide estuary, that opens to the northeast in 3 hr. The village here is Lingbogang. (A dirt track leads up this side valley to the Pangtö Range, crosses it via a 5500-m pass, then descends north to Tsangshung, a village within the Reting Valley that is only 4 hr east of Reting Monastery.) In 2 1/2 hr, reach a ferry landing called Kadö and cross over to the right bank of the Kyi Chu.

✤ DAY 10 KADÖ FERRY–LHUNDRUB XIAN 2 1/4 HR

Continue up the Kyi Chu's right bank along a dirt track. In 2 1/4 hr reach the small town of Lhündrub Xian (formerly Phongdo Dzong).

Lhündrub Xian

This capital of the Jang district sits in a strategic and beautiful area, marred only by unsightly Chinese compounds and military camps. An amazing sight here is the perfectly conical mountain that towers over the far end of town. A suspension bridge spans the Kyi Chu, out of town to the east. Three rivers converge here to form the Kyi Chu: the Rong Chu, which flows east from the Nyenchen Tanglha Range, the Taklung (Pak) Chu from the south, and the Miggi from the north, which flows past Reting.

Routes from Lhündrub Xian radiate in four directions: northwest to Damxung and the Lhasa–Golmud highway; northeast to Reting Monastery and the Gyalam; southeast to Drigung Qu and Drigungtil Monastery; southwest to Taklung Monastery, the Chak La, and Lhasa. A rare and ancient iron-chain bridge, built by the master engineer Tangton Gyalpo (see page 379), still exists next to a modern bridge below the old fort and village. The Chinese compounds are located north of this bridge. Stay at a military truck stop located among the compounds. There is a regular but infrequent bus service to Lhasa.

Chom Lhakhang

This restored monastery is located in the old part of Lhündrub Xian. It was founded by Polhane, member of a noble clan, who with the support of the Chinese was *de facto* ruler of Tibet from 1728–47.

✤ DAY 11 LHÜNDRUB XIAN–RETING MONASTERY 6HR

From Lhündrub Xian follow the road northeast up the beautiful Miggi Valley, with the river on the right. In 2 3/4 hr the road turns up a side valley to the left. Within its entrance is a village and here a bridge spans the tributary. Cross it to the left bank to follow the road that now loops back into the main valley.

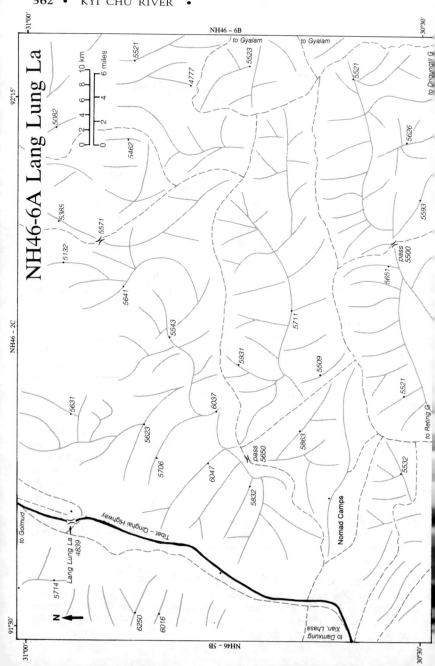

NH46-6A Lang Lung La

NH46 – 6B

NH46 – 2C

NH46 – 5B

to Gyalam

to Gyalam

to Drigungti G

to Golmud

to Reting G

to Damxung
Xian, Lhasa

Tibet – Qinghai Highway

Lang Lung La
4839

Nomad Camps

pass
5650

pass
5500

pass
5650

N

• 5521
• 4777
• 5623
• 5521
• 5082
• 5626
• 5462
• 5385
• 5571
• 5593
• 5132
• 5641
• pass 5500
• 5543
• 5651
• 5711
• 5931
• 5509
• 5631
• 5521
• 5623
• 6037
• 5863
• 5706
• 6047
• 5532
• 5832
• 5714
• 6250
• 6016

10 km
6 miles
8
6
4
2
0

To Damxung: two days (48 km)

A trail within this side valley ascends due north for 1 1/2 hr to a valley junction. Take the right one to continue north. Reach the head of the valley in 3 hr; the trail now veers to the left to approach the Lanji La, which is reached in 2 1/2 hr. After the pass, descend to the north to reach the Lhasa–Golmud highway at the village of Natung Kamu (5 hr). Turn left (west) at the road to Damxung. Buses from here return to Lhasa. The trek to Namtso Lake (see page 657) starts here.

Continue northeast up the Miggi Valley. Reting Monastery, sited on the slopes of a hill amidst a remarkable grove of juniper trees, is reached in 2 3/4 hr.

Reting Monastery

A path through the junipers leads up from the road to the monastery ruins. Reting is in a striking area of Jang, a region of pristine valleys and high ridges north of Lhasa. Sadly, the scale of destruction here is second only to Ganden. The nearly 100 monks now in residence live in stone buildings salvaged from the extensive ruins near the main structure. To the left of the complex are the stubbled remains of many *chörtens* that once contained relics of important Kadampa lamas. Everywhere is rubble and shattered walls.

According to tradition, Reting is surrounded by four sacred mountains: Sheldhen (crystal) in the east, Serdhen (gold) in the south, Zangdhen (copper) in the west, and Yudhen (turquoise) in the north. Supposedly, the area has 20,000 juniper trees and springs. Dominating the site is a large restored chapel, pieced together from the vast, once magnificent Chökhang Chenmo. The spacious assembly hall has new, impressive murals depicting Tsong Khapa, lamas of the Kadampa and Gelugpa sects, and Gelugpa tantric deities. At the back is an inner chapel called Ütse Ngö, consecrated to Sangdü Jampel Dorje, an aspect of Sangdü (Guhyasamaja), a deity of the Supreme Yoga *Tantra*. It is considered Atisha's most important personal deity. This small statue, the most famous at Reting, is Indian in origin and supposedly constructed of pure gold. Legend says the image was derived miraculously from the Dorje Chang Yabyum, the mythical union of Dorje Chang (tantric manifestation of Sakyamuni and primordial Buddha of the Kagyüpa) and Yumchenmo, the deity's consort. It is said to have the property of granting wishes. Another account attributes the statue to the famous artist, Khamsum Zowo. Over 300 nomad families supported Reting in dedication to this image: in the past, one thousand *dri* (a cross between a yak and a cow) were required to produce sufficient butter for the monastery. The other important statue in this chamber is Drölma Sungjönma, a 'speaking' Tara.

Higher up, in Drak Senge—a ridge overlooking the monastery—is a restored chapel known as Gyalwa Dromgi Zimphuk Lhakhang (next to the *gönkhang* dedicated to Damchen Garwa Nagpa, a local deity converted to Buddhism by Guru Rinpoche). It contained Dromtönpa's meditation cave of Dromgi Drubphuk. In a courtyard outside the cave is the sacred spring, Dhütsi Chumik Ringmo, the soul-tree of Dromtönpa, and the willow believed to be the embodiment of the red and black Mahakala. In this area above the complex, behind a quadrangle of ruins, are Wöbarwa hermitage and the Yangön Chapel. Dromtönpa lived here in the 11th C. and the Taklung Kagyüpa used it as a retreat. A juniper tree called Shugpa Yudhen is here and in front of it are the remains of Dromtönpa's stone seat, where he sat and preached. Tsong Khapa also expounded his 'Foundation of All Excellence' from this stone. Three other thrones to the left have statues of Atisha, Dromtönpa, and Jampa. A red painted rock in the vicinity is the residence of Reting's protector divinity, Chingkawa, introduced to Tibet from Nalandra, India, by Atisha.

Below Reting is Pabong Tang ('Rock Plain') located between the road and the river. A large rock, surrounded by smaller ones, is considered the abode of Khandro Sangwa Yeshe, a female protective deity. Pilgrims circumambulate the site. About 4 km to the east of Reting is the small nunnery of Samdrub Ling.

History Reting, Tibet's first Kadampa monastery, was built in 1056 by Dromtönpa, the sect's founder. It was intimately associated with Atisha, the Indian Buddhist teacher who spearheaded the revival of Buddhism in Tibet in the 11th century. Dromtönpa, born in 1005 in upper Tölung district northwest of Lhasa, went to see the master in West Tibet and the two then traveled together to Central Tibet and Phanyul. After Atisha's death in Netang in 1054, Dromtönpa, his spiritual son, stayed on in Tölung and then went to Reting in 1056, where he stayed until his death in 1064. The master was considered an incarnation of Chenresi and thus the progenitor of the Dalai Lamas. He had three famous disciples: Potowa, Puchungwa, and Chenga.

Dromtönpa's successor was Neljorpa Chenpo, who expanded the monastery vigorously. Potowa was appointed abbot for a period of three years in the late 11th century. In 1240, the Mongols invaded and sacked Reting severely. Tsong Khapa came here in 1397 and received a vision of Atisha; this prompted him to compile his great work, the *Lamrin Chenmo*. After Tsong Khapa's reform of the Kadampa school, the monastery became an important Gelugpa institution. The Seventh Dalai Lama appointed his tutor, Ngawang Chokden, as abbot. From then on the abbots were eligible for the post of regent, the powerful position that oversaw affairs of state before the Dalai Lamas reached their majority. There were two periods when Tibet's regents came from this monastery: 1845–55 and 1933–47.

RETING MONASTERY TO LHASA

From Reting head due south along a dirt road to 12th-C. Taklung Monastery, main seat of the Taklung-Kagyu school, located within the Pak Valley. After crossing the Chak La, follow the fertile Phanyul Valley to small, charming Ganden Chungkor Monastery. A secondary track from here leads west to the centers of Langtang and Nalanda and the Shara Bumpa, a well-known *chörten* of Phanyul. The valley eventually merges with the Tsangpo and the main Tibet–Sichuan highway is rejoined. Follow it west to Lhasa.

Time Chart

Day	Place	Hours
12	Reting–Lhündrub Xian	6
13	Taklung Monastery	2 1/2
14	Langma	5 3/4
15	Ganden Chungkor Monastery	6 1/4
16	Dechen Xian	9
17	Lhasa	Hitch 21 km

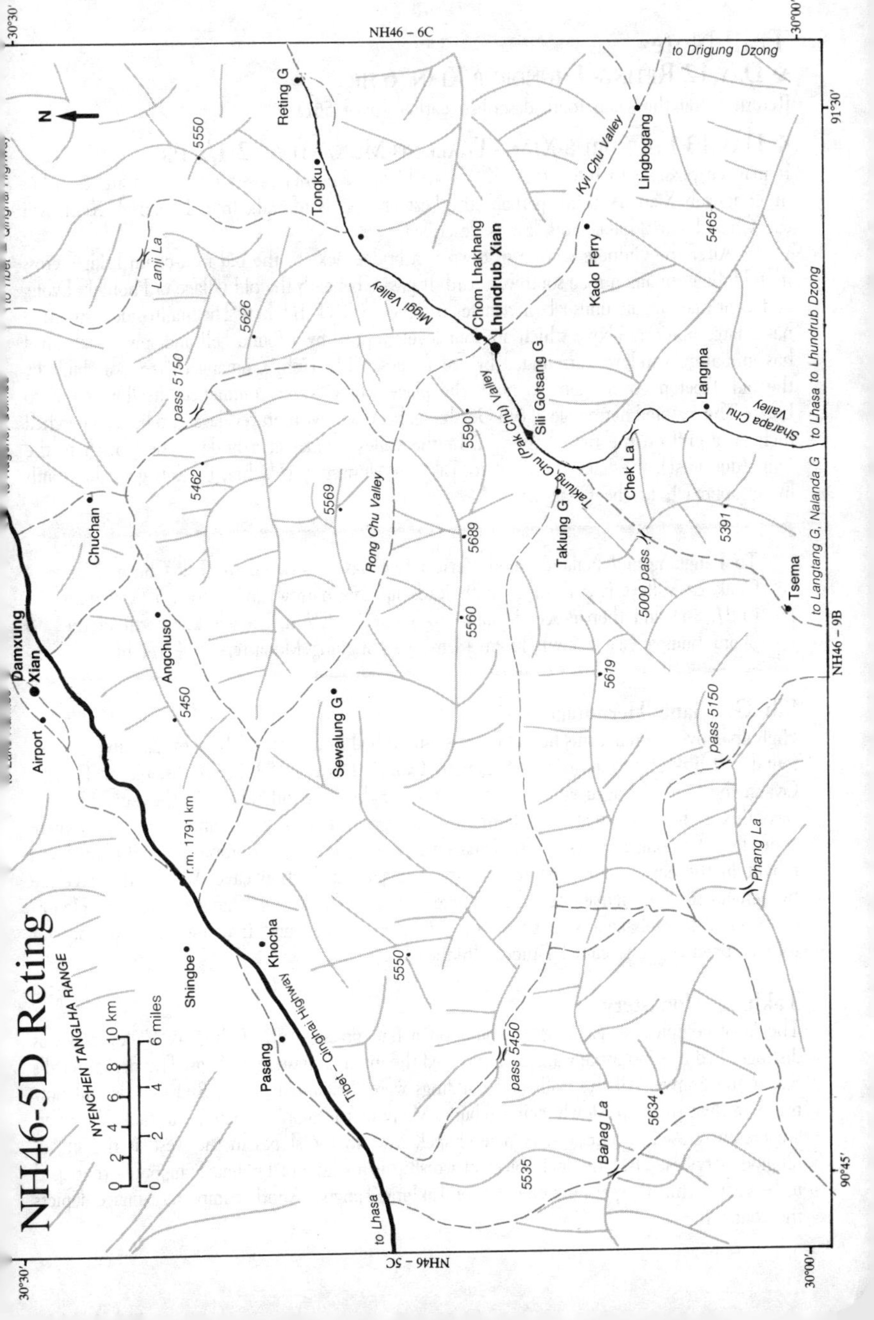

NH46 – 6C

NH46-5D Reting

NYENCHEN TANGLHA RANGE

0 2 4 6 8 10 km
0   2   4   6 miles

to Drigung Dzong

Reting G

Tongku

Lanji La

Maggi Valley

pass 5150

5550

5626

Chom Lhakhang
Lhundrub Xian

Kyi Chu Valley

Lingbogang

5465

Kado Ferry

Sili Gotsang G

Langma

Sharapa Chu Valley

to Lhasa to Lhundrub Dzong

5462

5569

5590

Taklung Chu
(Pak Chu) Valley

Chuchan

Rong Chu Valley

5689

Taklung G

Chek La

5391

to Langtang G, Nalanda G

Angchuso

5560

5000 pass

Tsema

NH46 – 9B

Damxung
Xian

5450

Sewalung G

5619

pass 5150

Airport

r.m. 1791 km

Phang La

Shingbe

Khocha

5550

Pasang

Tibet-Qinghai Highway

pass 5450

Banag La

5634

5535

to Lhasa

NH46 – 5C

Trail Notes

✤ DAY 12 RETING–LHÜNDRUB XIAN 6 HR
Return along the same route described earlier (page 561).

✤ DAY 13 LHÜNDRUB XIAN–TAKLUNG MONASTERY 2 1/2 HR
It may be possible to hitch the 150 km to Lhasa. Another possibility is to wait for a bus in Lhundrub Xian. A third, perhaps the best choice, is to walk from Lhundrub Xian over the Chak La to Lhasa. This last is described.

After the Chinese section of town is a bridge next to the old iron-chain bridge; cross it and follow the main road southwestward. It passes beneath the old village of Phongdo Dzong and continues to an unusual *chörten* left of the road (1 1/2 hr). The multi-sided structure has a large platform above which are four levels topped by a round bell and spire. Each level has miniature windows surrounded by red frames. This Tashi Gomang *chörten* was built by the old Tibetan government to mark the place where water commences its flow south to Lhasa. The restored hermitage of Sili Götshang, bedecked with prayer flags, can be seen perched high on a cliff on the right. After 1/2 hr the valley divides at a bridge. The branch to the right (due west), the Pak Chu, goes to Taklung Monastery (1/2 hr); the left goes due south in its approach to the Chak La.

> **To Langtang and Nalanda monasteries: two days** Between the Pak Chu and the Chak La valleys is a third. A path leads up this narrow ravine to a 5000-m pass (3 1/2 hr) and then descends south to Tsema (3 1/2 hr), a few km north of the Shara Bumpa (see below). From Tsema to Langtang Monastery is 4 1/4 hr.

Sili Götshang Hermitage
High up above the road, this hermitage was established in the late 12th C. by Taklung Tangpa, founder of Taklung Monastery. Götshangpa Gompo Dorje (1189–1258), disciple of Tsangpa Gyare, the Drukpa Kagyü lama who first explored the Tsari pilgrimage in the early 13th C., used this as his main seat. The hermitage is appended to Taklung and monks from there come here for long retreats. Badly damaged in the Cultural Revolution, a small chapel was rebuilt in the early 1980s next to Taklung Tangpa's meditation cave. Within the cave are two chambers, one above the other. There is also a Chökyong Khang (Protector's House) consecrated to Mahakala. On top of the cliffs is a vultures' nest that used to be a place for solitary practice; it is called Drubpa Zhidhe.

Taklung Monastery
The large complex of Taklung was built on a flat, grassy plain of the Pak Valley and was distinguished by substantial walls that enclosed the main monastic buildings. This design recalls Sakya and Samye. All the walls and buildings were dynamited by the Red Guards and now the extensive ruins are slowly being rebuilt. Many of the monks' quarters, towards the river, are presently used by villagers. A new chapel, next to the slopes in the west, is the site of religious services. The principal object of worship is a statue of Drölma Sungjönma that used to be kept within the personal chamber of Taklung Tangpa. Another important image depicts the founder.

Taklung's most impressive structure was the Tsuglag Khang (also Markhang, the Red Temple). Its massive walls still stand. The main statue, within the inner Tri Tsangkhang chapel, was a huge two-story Sakyamuni with an umbrella—an unusual iconographic form. Taklung Tangpa's bedroom was on the top floor. There are plans to restore this large building. The 5391-m peak south of Taklung Monastery is known for its many alpine willows, used to cure fever and female diseases.

History Taklung, main seat of the Taklung Kagyü, one of the four chief Kagyü schools, once had over 600 monks and an incarnate lama (*tulku*). It was founded by Taklung Tangpa Tashi Pel (1142–1210) in 1180 over the dwelling of Potowa, the Kadampa disciple of Dromtönpa. Taklung Tangpa was a Khampa, and studied under the great Phagmo Drupa in Densatil and Potowa. He was strongly influenced by the Drigung Kagyüs, and developed the monastery along strict monastic discipline. His fame spread throughout Central Tibet and at its height he could claim 3,000 disciples.

Later, his nephew enlarged the monastery and built the impressive Tsuglag Khang, which was completed in 1228. At one time Taklung had 7,000 students. It was one of the few major monastic centers in Central Tibet to escape the Mongols. In the 17th C., the Gelugpa took over and the tradition of incarnate *tulkus* was inaugurated, but the period also saw the decline of the Taklung Kagyü and their seat of power eventually shifted to Riwoche in Kham.

✦ DAY 14 TAKLUNG MONASTERY–LANGMA 5 3/4 HR

From Taklung return to the bridge and valley junction. Ascend south along the main road to the Chak La Pass (4825 m), a fairly steep climb of 3 3/4 hr. The scenery on the far side is magnificent, with ranges of mountains spreading to the horizon. This is the beginning of the Phanyul Valley, where Buddhism gathered strength in its march across Tibet. Follow the zigzagging road down, taking shortcuts from time to time. The valley floor is 2 hr from the pass. A side valley to the left has the small village of Langma.

✦ DAY 15 LANGMA–GANDEN CHUNGKOR MONASTERY 6 1/4 HR

Continue due south from Langma for 1 hr. Here the road forks: the right branch follows the right bank of the Sharapa Chu (this route goes to Shara Bumpa, an important Kadampa monument; see below); the left follows the main road on the left bank. Go south along the latter. In 1 3/4 hr come to where a large side valley opens to the left (east). The village at the junction is the old Lhündrub Dzong, and the valley is known as the Lhündrub (Sharapa). Continue south for 1 1/4 hr to Kusha, where another dirt track goes right (west) to Shara Bumpa (2 1/2 hr) and on to Langtang and Nalanda monasteries within the Phanyul Valley.

The main road makes a sharp left turn to the east after 1 hr. Follow it to Phanpo Lungcheung (1 1/4 hr), a small town with the active monastery of Ganden Chungkor. Original murals are still on the walls and the monastery escaped irreparable damage in the 1960s and 1970s. The ambience here is good and it is well worth a visit. The town stretches along the main road with large fields on either side; this valley is one of the most fertile in the Lhasa area.

Shara Bumpa

Shara Bumpa, a large *chörten* west of Kusha, is particularly revered by pilgrims. They believe it can cure blindness if they perform enough circumambulations. The typical Kadampa design has a two-tiered square base surmounted by a porticoed bell, itself topped by a spire. Numerous lesser *chörtens* of this type are in the vicinity. A rebuilt chapel, serving as a nunnery, is nearby. Sharapa Yönten Drak (1070–1141), a Kadampa lama who followed Potowa for many years, founded this monument.

Langtang Monastery

Location A dirt track from Ganden Chungkor goes south over the southern side of the east–west trending Phanyul (Phanpo Chu) Valley (3/4 hr). It then makes a sharp turn to the right (west) to follow the valley's southern perimeter to Langtang (3 hr), sited on the flat plains south of the Phanpo Chu. Behind the monastery, up the south-trending valley, is the old trade route that leads over the Pempogo La to Lhasa.

Much of the original Kadampa monastery has been converted into a farming commune and the main chapels are surrounded by village houses. One chapel with an assembly hall has been renovated and there are over 20 monks in attendance (before the Cultural Revolution, Langtang had 85 monks). Part of the upstairs, still with old murals, is used for religious services. Two buildings around the main courtyard are used as monks' quarters.

On the altar of the chapel are the principal objects of worship: a new statue of Langtangpa, the founder, and an original Drölma Sungjonma: the Talking Tara, one of Langtang's most sacred relics. On the walls next to the *dukhang* entrance are faded murals depicting the protective deities of the Sakyapa—a direct result of the Kadampa institution's takeover by the Sakyapa during the height of its power. Ruins of the Lhakhang Chenmo, Langtang's principal structure, are below the courtyard. Beyond this is a Kadampa *chörten* that contained relics of Langtangpa. According to tradition, the famous Dingri lama, Dampa Sangye, was buried here as well.

History Langtang's founder was Langri Tangpa Dorje Senge (Langtangpa, 1054–1123), a disciple of Potowa and Neuzurpa, both important Kadampa masters of the 11th century. He established the monastery in 1093 and in a short time assembled over 2,000 students.

Nalanda Monastery

Location Nalanda lies 1 1/2 hr southwest of Langtang. To reach it, simply follow the Phanpo Chu's south bank within the Phanyul Valley. Nalanda is at the entrance of a south-trending side valley; within it is a path that leads over a pass west of the Pempogo La. The monastery was named after the legendary Nalanda temple near Bodh Gaya, India. Ruins of the formerly imposing walled complex are extensive, though renovation in recent years has been carried out. A principal chapel (*dukhang*) has as its main image that of Rongtönpa, the founder. It dates back to the 15th century. Next to it is his footprint on stone. Two colleges (*labrangs*) for the abbot are restored as well. Outside the monastic walls is a large, rebuilt *chörten* in the typical Kadampa style. Additional ruins on a hill overlook the main grounds. The present Sakya Trizin, now in the West, trained as a monk at Nalanda.

History As with other monasteries of the Phanyul, Nalanda started as a Kadampa institution and was considered one of the most prestigious centers of learning in Central Tibet. It was founded in 1435 by Rongtön Chenpo Mawai Senge (1367–1449), a master of the sect who was initiated at Sangphu Neutok Monastery (see page 490) near Lhasa. Rongtönpa was a prodigious scholar who wrote over 300 works; the Sakyapa recognized him as one of the Six

Jewels of Tibet. After his death, Nalanda's influence declined, and at the close of the 15th C. the Sakyapa took over.

✤ DAY 16 GANDEN CHUNGKOR MONASTERY–DECHEN XIAN 9 HR

From Ganden Chungkor the flat main road goes east along the left (north) bank of the Phanpo Chu to its junction with the Kyi Chu (4 1/4 hr). Here is the village of Pingchö and a large earthen plaque marking the entrance of the Phanyul Valley (Ganden Monastery is directly south across the Kyi Chu). The road now turns sharply right (south-southwest) to follow the Kyi Chu's north (right) bank. In 4 1/2 hr reach Bomtö (Dromtö) and its cave of Nyen Gomphuk. Immediately after, cross a large suspension bridge to follow the main Tibet–Sichuan highway on the south bank. Dechen Xian is 1 km beyond.

Bomtö

Bomtö, near the north end of the Dechen suspension bridge, is a village marked by a new *chörten* on the side of the road. This was the birthplace of Lhalung Paldhor (see page 704), the ascetic who assassinated Langdarma during the last days of the Yarlung Dynasty. On the slopes is the hermitage of Nyen Gomphuk, a cave retreat once used by Nyen Lotsawa Darma Drak, who went with Ra Lotsawa to India and Nepal to study Sanskrit.

✤ DAY 17 DECHEN XIAN–LHASA, HITCH 21 KM

Hitchhike westward from Dechen Xian back to Lhasa or continue to follow the Kyi Chu's north bank to Lhasa (4 hr).

Lhasa direct to Reting To reach Reting directly—skipping the extended trek from Lhasa to Drigungtil Monastery—simply reverse the route.

GYALAM: THE OLD TIBET–CHINA CARAVAN ROUTE

The Gyalam, an ancient trade route between Tibet and China, begins from the Tsangpo Basin in the south and then traverses the high mountains of the Salween Divide (eastern Nyenchen Tanglha Range), via the notoriously difficult Nub Gong and Shar Gong passes. After crossing the range, the caravan road continues east to Lhorong and Chamdo, capital of Kham Province. The itinerary below turns north after Shopado to the Salween River and Khyungpo Tengcheng, a district renowned for its pre-Buddhist Bönpo shrines.

A TREK FROM KONGPO TO THE BÖN ENCLAVE OF KHYUNGPO TENGCHENG THROUGH THE SALWEEN–TSANGPO DIVIDE

Location	East Tibet
Map reference	NH46-7 A B C, 46-8 A B C, 46-4 D
Trekking days	19 (one-way)
Start–Finish	Giamda–Tengcheng
Passes	Trö, Nub Gong (Nubghang), Shar Gong

OVERVIEW

Much of this itinerary explores the little-known Salween Divide, the huge range of high snow peaks that forms the eastern section of the Nyenchen Tanglha. These mountains are pierced from west to east by the magnificent Po Yigrong River, the only course to cut through the landmass.

Before 1950, the Gyalam was the main artery of trade and communications between Tibet and western China. Nowadays, the Tibet–Sichuan highway carries most of the traffic between the two regions. Along the Gyalam, at Lharigo, Atsa, and Alado, side valleys opening from these small towns provide the main access into the Po Yigrong Valley. Towards the east, valleys south of Pemba and Shopado also lead over the mountains into the Yigrong and Pomi (Poyul) districts. There are a number of important monasteries (Pemba, Shopado, Zitho) and isolated Guru Rinpoche retreats (Urgyen Tamdha) along this eastern part of the route. The trek described below ends at Khyungpo Tengcheng, a predominantly Bönpo area with a number of significant Bönpo sanctuaries. From the town, a main motor road heads east to Chamdo, the second-largest city in Tibet.

Two main points allow entry into the Gyalam and the Nyenchen Tanglha range; one from Drigungtil Monastery (see page 557), the other from Giamda on the Tibet–Sichuan highway. The latter is described.

Note: The major passes of Trö, Nub Gong and Shar Gong are infamous in Tibet for their difficulties and ruggedness. Be sure to bring along top-notch gear, and it would be wise to hire a guide for the crossings.

Related sections
Upper Kyi Chu, p 544
The Ningchi road, p 707
Draksum Latso, p 647

Access
Take the Lhasa bus to Bayi or Ningchi on the Tibet–Sichuan Highway (see page 709) or rent a vehicle. Pass Medro Gongkar (road marker 1500 km, new marker 4564), then turn east up the Maldro Valley. After crossing the Kongpo Ba La, get off at road marker 1317 km. A suspension bridge leads to the village of Giamda, not to be confused with the large town of Kongpo Giamda, 23 km further. The settlement sits above the confluence of the Jya Chu (from the north) and the Sia Chu (from the west). These two rivers join the Nyang Chu, which flows southeast to the Tsangpo. This area is very pleasant in September and October, when the sun is out most days and there is no rain.

Time Chart

Day	Place	Distance (Km)
1	Giamda–Laru	30

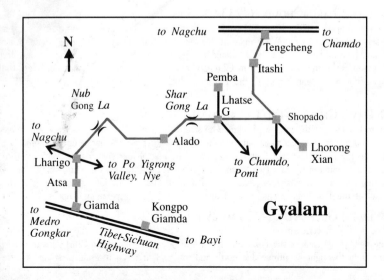

2	Chomdo	25
3	Gole	20
4	Atsa	29
5	Lharigo	17.5
6	Tsachuka	28
7	Arong Dhothok	29
8	Ala Jagung	30
9	Alado	35
10	Namgye	38.5
11	Urgyen Tamdha	33
12	Pemba	26
13	Lhatse	24
14	Parinang	37
15	Shopado	39
16	Rua Tung	30.5
17	Zinda	31.5
18	Itashi	38
19	Tengcheng	38

Trail Notes

✤ DAY 1 GIAMDA (3580 M)–LARU (3780 M) 30 KM

From Giamda, walk north up the Jya Valley with the river on the left. Pass Miki, Za, Sangar, and Anpa (here a side valley opens to the east). Laru is above the confluence of the Niem (upper Jya) and Buri Chu. The latter flows in from the east. A monastery once stood at Laru. The Jya Valley is about 200–400 m wide and the peak flanking it is about 700 m higher.

✤ DAY 2 LARU–CHOMDO (4233 M) 25 KM

Continue up the river's left (east) bank; flowing from the Trö La, it is known in its upper reaches as the Trö Chu. Wade many streams and pass the village of Buchung Kamo. After 2 km, halfway between Laru and Chomdo, is pretty Toro Monastery on a hill at a valley junction. Take the right branch to Chomdo, which is also at a valley junction. Here the right (northeast) branch goes to the Trö La. A high snow peak (5819 m) can be seen due east.

✤ DAY 3 CHOMDO–TRÖ LA (4890 M)–GOLE (4404 M) 20 KM

From Chomdo to the pass is 14.5 km. The steep, winding ascent first goes through a gorge with huge, perpendicular mountains on the left and glimpses of snow mountains through a gap on the right. The trail is stony. Trö La is the first of four great passes on the way to Chamdo, capital of Kham. (Two others are crossed on this itinerary, the Nub Gong La, worst during autumn, and Shar Gong La, worst in winter.) Descend to Gole, a tiny village at the head of the Pok Valley, which trends due north between steep flanking ridges.

✤ DAY 4 GOLE–ATSA (4175 M) 29 KM

The gradual descent through uninhabited countryside (except for a few nomads) goes along the right (east) bank of the Pok Chu. In 1 1/4 hr, a lateral valley (Jien Chu) joins the main one from the right. Continue due north and in 1 3/4 hr reach the southwest tip of Lake

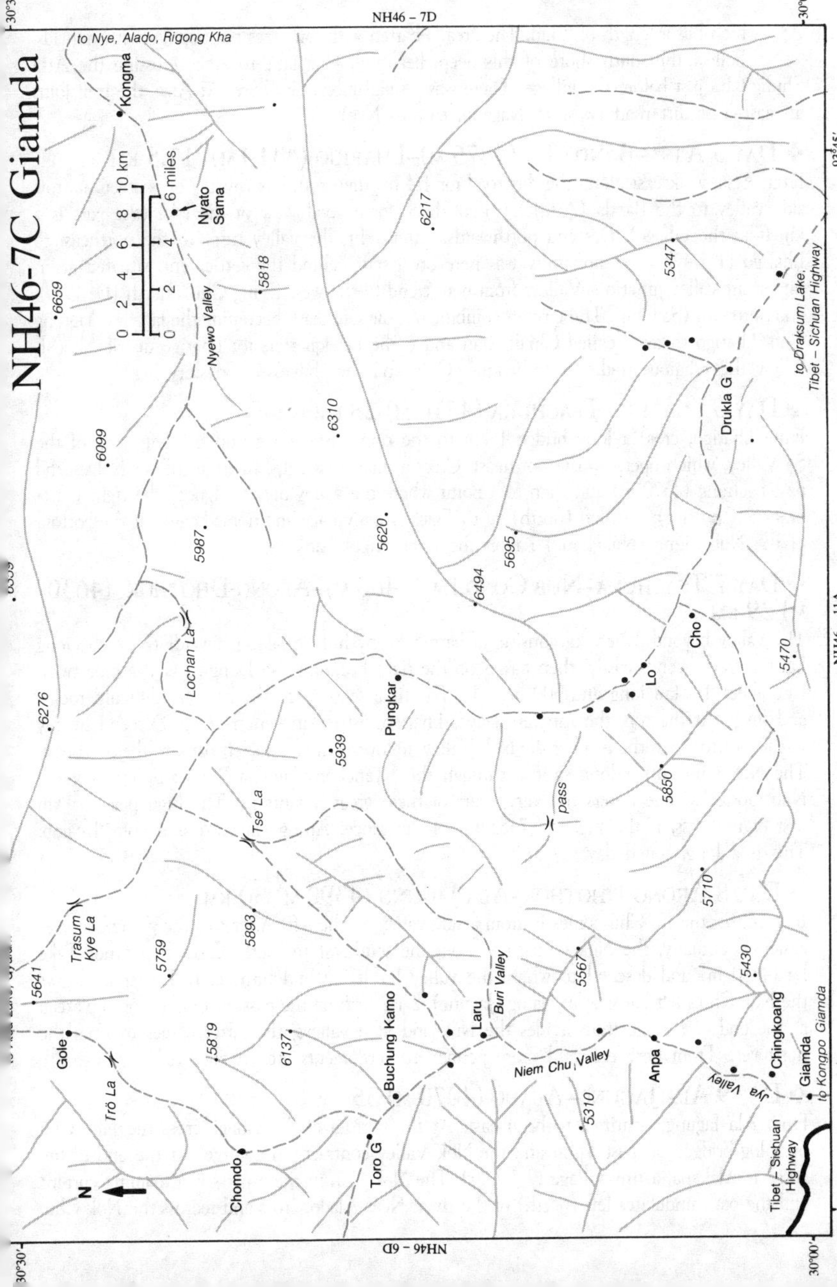
NH46-7C Giamda
NH46 – 7D
NH46 – 6D
NH46 – 11A
30°30'
30°00'
93°45'
93°00'
to Nye, Alado, Rigong Kha
Kongma
0 2 4 6 8 10 km
0 2 4 6 miles
Nyato Sama
Nyewo Valley
6659
5818
6217
5347
to Draksum Lake, Tibet – Sichuan Highway
Drukla G
6099
6310
5987
5620
5695
6494
Lochan La
Cho
Lo
Pungkar
6276
5939
pass
5850
5470
Tse La
Trasum Kye La
5759
5893
5710
5641
5567
5430
Buri Valley
Laru
Buchung Kamo
Chingkoang
Gole
5819
6137
Niem Chu Valley
Anpa
Jya Valley
Giamda
to Kongpo Giamda
Trö La
5310
Toro G
Chomdo
Tibet – Sichuan Highway
N

Atsa which has a length of 5 km. The area is barren with few trees but popular with nomads.

Follow the south shore of this deep, beautiful, blue lake to Atsa, crossing the Atsa Shung Chu just before the village. There was a small monastery here. At Atsa, the trail joins an east–west dirt road (west to Nagchu, east to Nye).

❖ DAY 5 ATSA–BANDA LA (4875 M)–LHARIGO (4310 M) 17.5 KM

From Atsa, walk east along the dirt road for 1/4 hr, then turn left (north) up a steep, narrow side valley to the Banda (Atsa) La. Look back for a good view of the lake (the pass is 5 km from the village). Descend northwards. After 1 hr, the valley turns to the northeast to Lharigo (1 1/4 hr). A monastery was here on a spur behind the settlement, situated at an important valley junction. Valleys from here trend to the west (Song Chu), north (De Chu), and northeast (Sa Chu). These rivers combine to flow southeast, becoming the large Po Yigrong Chu. Lharigo today is called Chiali Xian and is the headquarters for Lharigo district. Locals follow the religious tradition of Nyidrak Chö, and they have a monastery here.

❖ DAY 6 LHARIGO–TSACHUKA (4510 M) 28 KM

From Lharigo, cross a long bridge 1 km to the northeast, and go up the left bank of the Sa Valley, which opens to the northeast. Cross a small pass 2 1/2 hr from the town. Descend past Lachung (4570 m) and then to a point where the valley divides. Ignore the right (east) branch (Chu Jige); turn left (north) up to Tsachuka, a village and nomad camp at the bottom of the Nub Gong (Nubghang) La on the river's right bank.

❖ DAY 7 TSACHUKA–NUB GONG LA (5468 M)–ARONG DHOTHOK (4630 M) 29 KM

The valley beyond Tsachuka consists of barren, stony hills. Snaking towards the Nub Gong La, the trail ascends easily, then passes on the right beautiful Tso Dungwu Ngi, a blue twin-lake about 1.5 km long and 300 m wide. The final sections to the pass are difficult, rocky, and steep. At the top, the itinerary leaves Lharigo district and enters Arig. Descend steeply to the east to reach the head of the Nok Valley, following the river's left bank to the southeast. The Nok Chu cuts a long swathe through the Nyenchen Tanglha Range; by crossing the Nub Gong La, one enters the very heart of these great mountains. The high peak 15 km east of the pass, is the highest (7353 m) of the range. Arong Dhothok is a nomad camp. This is a long, tough day.

❖ DAY 8 ARONG DHOTHOK–ALA JAGUNG (4390 M) 30 KM

In 1 1/2 hr, the Ifu Chu comes in from a side valley on the left. After this the going becomes easier. Eventually, the Nok Chu turns from the southeast to south. Cross the minor Také La (4650 m) and descend to where the valley levels out and turns east. The trail follows the Nok Chu's left bank. Ala Jagung (Jagung), 2 1/2 hr from the pass, is a village on a plateau at the end of a ridge that divides the Nok and Jabu valleys; the latter comes in from the northwest. From here eastward more permanent settlements are encountered.

❖ DAY 9 ALA JAGUNG–ALADO (4070 M) 35 KM

From Ala Jagung, continue to head east. At the bottom of the village cross the Jabu Chu by a log bridge. Go past Yulin and the Nok Valley contracts to a gorge. At the end of the gorge is Alakapa, a tiny village (2 1/2 hr). The Nok Chu in these parts is a foaming current and the path undulates left (north) of the river. Near Alado, cross and recross the Nok Chu.

The valley turns south before the village, located at a valley junction within a narrow, winding valley. Here the east-flowing Nok Chu meets the west-flowing Sia and the combined waters, known as the Dakson (Alado) Chu, flow south to join the Po Yigrong at a point 8 km east of Nye. (The Po Yigrong Valley divides 6 km east of Nye and the left branch, trending west-southwest, is known as the Nyewo Valley. At its head is the high Lochen La; its west side forms the upper reaches of the Drukla Valley.)

Optional trip: Alado to Draksum Tso.

Draksum Tso (see page 647) is a sacred pilgrimage site in Kongpo. Guru Rinpoche, Gesar of Ling, and Sangye Lingpa, illustrious figures in Tibetan history, all spent time in the area. The lake lies due south of Alado on the southern side of the Nyenchen Tanglha, the high Salween Divide. This itinerary from Alado is a difficult one, particularly the stretch west of Rigong Kha in the Po Yigrong Gorge. Do not attempt this trip unless you have adequate equipment and experience in the wild.

From Alado, go due south along the Dakson Chu to its junction with the Po Yigrong (24 km). (6 km west of the junction is Nye and beyond it, the valley's left branch leads to the Nyewo Valley.) Turn left (east) down the Po Yigrong to Rigong Kha (25 km). The rough track besides the river goes through a sheer rocky gorge, nearly impossible for pack animals. Beyond here to the east the track worsens. Negotiate a high, vertical cliff with few foot holds (a good rope would be invaluable). At the top is a narrow ledge and a sheer drop. Descend a long, rickety ladder of tree trunks to a rock in the river. From here, a makeshift bridge of more tree trunks crosses rocks to the far bank.

After this, the trail is no less easy; it continually climbs up cliff faces more than 300 m in height, sometimes with only foot holds cut in the rock. Rigong Kha is an isolated, friendly village with a small monastery high up on the north slopes above the turbulent Po Yigrong. To reach the south side, slip into a harness attached to a pulley that tracks along a long rope slung between the two banks. Some 6 km south of Rigong Kha, the Tsophu Valley divides into three:

1) The right (southwest) branch goes 9 km to another valley division. From here, go due south along the left branch. Cross a 6000-m pass after 15 km and descend southwest for 14 km to reach a main valley which trends due south to Tsogo, a village at Draksum Tso's northeast end (18 km).

2) The left branch goes southeast then southwest to the Tsophu La. Pass two side valleys on the right before reaching the pass (30 km). Descend southwest past beautiful glacial lakes to reach Je on the south shore of Draksum Tso (34 km).

3) From the Tsophu La, a rough trail descends due east for 48 km to Paka (see page 655).

DAY 10 ALADO–NAMGYE (4420 M) 38.5 KM

From Alado, walk northeast up the Sia Valley and cross a couple of log bridges. A peak (6683 m) to the southeast is visible 10 km away. The trail follows the right bank, past Je (Cha) before reaching the Arig Monastery (2 1/2 hr). The trail climbs above the river, then descends to the upper Sia Chu (Chara Chu). Continue northeast past Ngödrok, Wokchu,

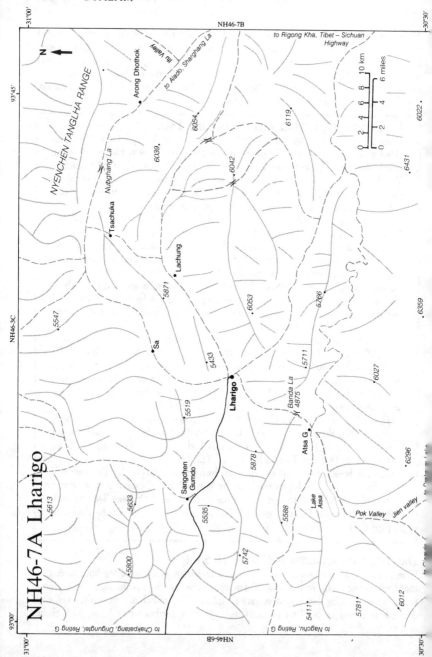

NH46-7B

to Rigong Kha, Tibet – Sichuan Highway

NYENCHEN TANGLHA RANGE

Arong Dhothok

Ibi Valley

to Alado, Sharghang La

to Chakpatang, Drugungtel, Reting G

6054

6039

6119

6042

6431

6022

Nubghang La

Tsachuka

Lachung

6053

5871

5766

5547

NH46-3C

Sa

5433

6359

5711

Lharigo

Banda La
4875

6027

Sangchen
Gumdo

5519

Atsa G

5878

Lake
Atsa

Pok Valley

Jien valley

6296

5535

5588

6359

5742

NH46-7A Lharigo

5613

5633

5800

5411

5781

6012

to Nagchu, Reting G

NH46-6B

10 km

6 miles

93°45'

93°00'

31°00'

30°30'

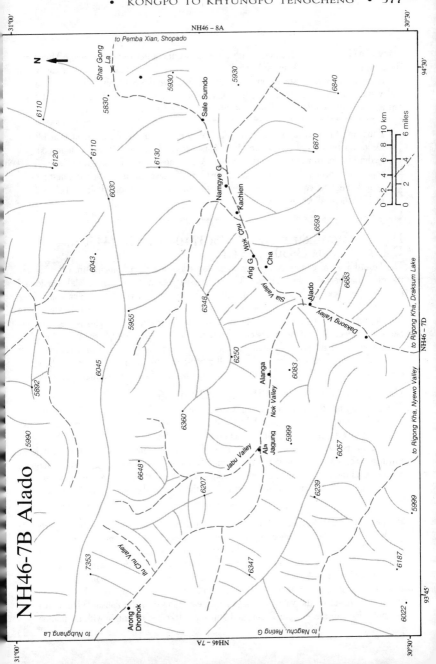

NH46 – 8A

to Pemba Xian, Shopado

NH46-7B Alado

Shar Gong La

Sale Sumdo

Namgye G

Kachien

Wok Chu

Arig G

Cha

Sia Valley

Alado

Daksong Valley

to Rigong Kha, Draksum Lake

NH46 – 7D

to Rigong Kha, Nyewo Valley

Alanga

Nok Valley

Ala Jagung

Jabu Valley

Iiu Chu Valley

Arong Dhothok

to Nubyhang La

to Nagchu, Reting G

NH46 – 7A

5990
5892
7353
6648
6207
6045
6360
6043
5955
6030
6110
6120
6110
6130
5830
5930
5930
6840
6870
6593
6348
6250
6347
6207
5999
6083
6187
6239
6057
5999
6022
6663
6110

0 2 4 6 8 10 km
0 2 4 6 miles

N

Jamtsoling Gong, and Kachien on a path 200 m above the water to reach Namgye Monastery, the northern limit of the Tsangpo Basin. Beyond this, over the Shar Gong La, is the catchment of the Salween. Namgye stands on a plateau 200 m above the Sia Chu. (At Kachien, a side valley turns north, then northwest; the main valley continues northeast to Namgyal 5 km further.) On the south side of the last stretch, is a range of 6500-m peaks.

> **Phugyang Phuk cave** High up the Sia Valley is a Guru Rinpoche retreat near Mt Dedra Lhatse (here is the Puwo Drage Changki Pass), abode of the mountain god, Dedra Lhatse. In the vicinity is Ghyangra Mukpo and near it is the cave. The guru apparently spent a long time here and within the cave are many 'self-manifesting' images. Pilgrims come here in droves in the summer as the sacred site is believed to be beneficial for assorted ailments.

DAY 11 NAMGYE–SHAR GONG LA (5037 M)–DORJE LA (4450 M)– URGYEN TAMDHA (3930 M) 33 KM

The beautiful gorge east of Namgye goes on for 4 km and then branches into two. Ignore the right that opens to the southeast. The northeast valley leads to Chara (Sale) Sumdo and then a steep, rocky trail ascends to the difficult Shar Gong La. (At Chara Sumdo are three valleys; take the middle one to the north-northeast; Namgye to the pass is 26 km.) From the top, high 6100-m peaks, 20–30 km away, rise in all directions. The pass is the Tsangpo–Salween Divide. After a steep descent, the trail ascends again through snow, to the Dorje La. It then drops steeply to Urgyen Tamdha (8 km from the Dorje La) in a narrow valley facing a high snow peak to the west. A small monastery with a famous Guru Rinpoche statue once stood here. West of the Shar Gong La is the district of Arig; now enter that of Pemba.

DAY 12 URGYEN TAMDHA–PEMBA (3828 M) 26 KM

Zigzag east up the Roka La (4 km from Urgyen Tamdha), 200 m above the flanking valleys. To the left, pretty Barjung (Bargo) Monastery perches on a 300-m-high spur. (100 monks once lived here.) Descend to a valley junction (the north branch leads up to Panger Monastery in 1 1/2 hr; beyond this, the valley trends northeast to the important Bönpo stronghold of Khyungpo Tengcheng after four days of walking). Follow the Me Chu east to Chakra Monastery, 3 km beyond the junction. There were 50 monks here. Along the route are villages surrounded by cultivation—Rata, Yung, Doshu, Denka. At the end of the day's walk is Pemba.

> **Pemba (Palbar) Monastery** Pemba (Palbar) Monastery was a large government monastery with 200 monks, surrounded by 100 houses. It consisted of a *labrang, dukhang,* and two chapels—Dhechok Tratsang and Dramang Lhakhang. The chapels contained over 200 statues, a big courtyard above the monastery had 1,000 Buddha images on the wall, and the Jowokhang held a magnificent Sakyamuni statue. The founder of Pemba was a Ngakpa and thus the Nyingmapa influence was very strong.
> Higher up the valley is Chögar, a retreat founded by the Palbar Tulku. Other holy places in the area are Tinang and Shinang, a lake and mountain with meditation ➡

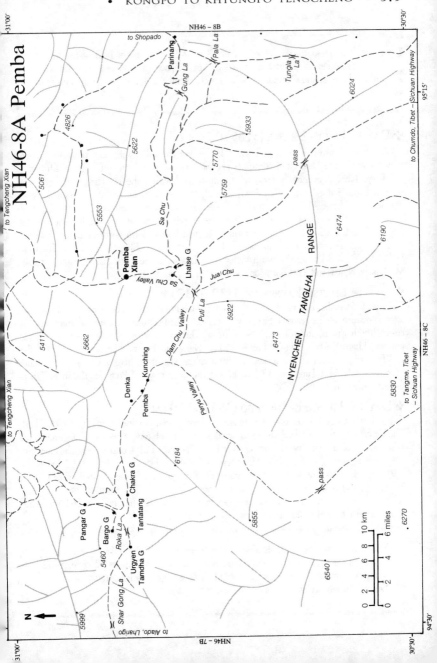

caves. To the south-southwest is sandy Riwo Ma, a mountain held sacred by the locals. From Pemba, a dirt road travels east to Shopado (now more commonly called Zitho), Lorong, and Chamdo. Traffic between Pemba and Shopado (3 days on foot) is scarce.

✤ Day 13 Pemba–Lhatse (3765 m) 24 km

2 km east of Pemba is Kunching. Then, 5 km further the valley splits and the main branch, now known as the Dam Chu, continues eastward. (A side valley to the right, southwest, is the Peryu Chu; it eventually leads to the main road within the Po Yigrong Valley.) The dirt road inside the Dam Valley slowly ascends the easy Puti La (4160 m), then descends northeast to Lhatse Monastery, situated at the junction of two valleys. Cross the Jua Chu 3 km before the junction. (The river from the east is the Sa Chu and it is joined by the Jua Chu from the south. Together they form the Sa, which flows north-northeast to the Salween.) Once, 30 monks resided at the monastery. From Lhatse east to Shopado is 92 km. The town of Pemba Xian, 8 km up the north valley from Lhatse, is the main district capital. Sacred Mt Lhatse Nyipa and Dzakhol Monastery are in the area.

✤ Day 14 Lhatse–Parinang (3730 m) 37 km

The road follows the right bank of the Sa (Gatung) Chu to the east. Traverse a belt of grassland after going through the beautiful Sa Chu Gorge, sandwiched between fantastic mountains thickly covered with woods, and reach the Seme (west) Gung La, part of a 4050-m double pass (25 km from Lhatse). About 3 km further is the East Gung La. Descend steeply to the Baré Valley and Parinang, a small village in another little valley. (South of here, a trail goes due south over the Pa La and Tung La to Chumdo and the large town of Pomi on the main Tibet–Sichuan highway.)

✤ Day 15 Parinang–Shopado (3565 m) 39 km

The valley divides 1.5 km out of Parinang. Take the right to the steep Tra La (3.5 km). The descent to the east leads to the nomad settlement of Jung Ying Do (Tungsing Koto) at a valley crossing (the north-flowing river is the Jangpu Chu). Continue straight, due east. The path zigzags up to Puti Gön Monastery and a short distance beyond (1 1/2 hr) is the U (Ode) La. Walk down for 1 hr to reach a valley that trends southwest–northeast. Turn left (northeast) and descend the Do Chu to Shopado (2 hr). The town consists of narrow cobbled streets and the mud houses are generally two storys. At the northeast end were three large chörtens in which important lamas were entombed.

Shopado Monastery This sizeable institution once had 300 monks, eight one-story statues of Jampa, and over 2,000 volumes of scriptures. Within its 12 chapels were many old thangkas. It was the main seat of Martsang Kagyü, a school started by Phagmo Drupa. Two other small monasteries existed at Shopado.

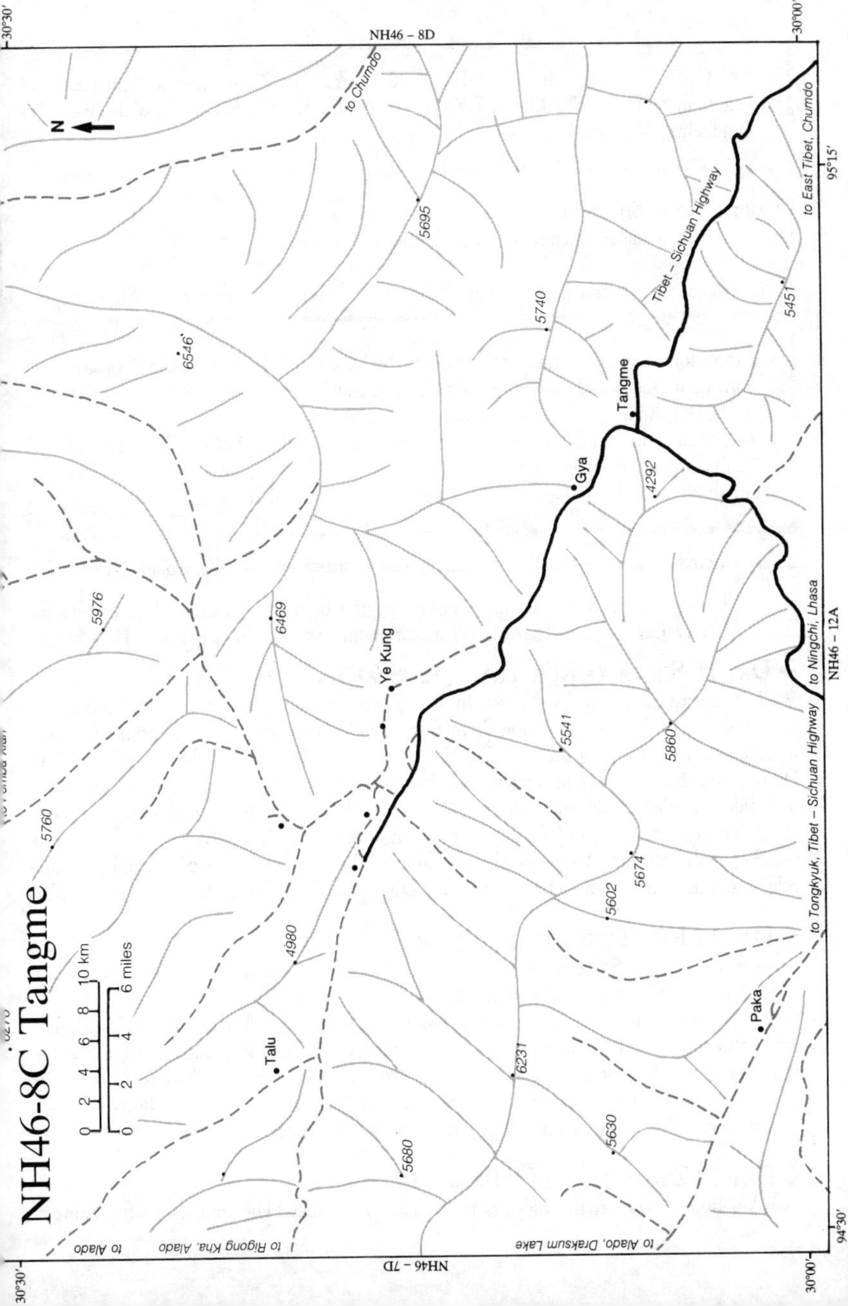

NH46-8C Tangme

NH46 – 8D

to Chumdo

N

to East Tibet, Chumdo

30°30'

30°00'

95°15'

Tibet – Sichuan Highway

5695

5740

5451

6546

Tangme

Gya

4292

5976

6469

Ye Kung

to Ningchi, Lhasa

NH46 – 12A

5541

5860

5760

5674

5602

to Tongkyuk, Tibet – Sichuan Highway

4980

6231

Talu

Paka

10 km

6 miles

5680

5630

to Alado

to Rigong Kha, Alado

to Alado, Draksum Lake

NH46 – 7D

30°30'

30°00'

94°30'

> **Puti Gön** There were five chapels and 30 monks here. This center and Shopado were founded by Kundhe Lingpa Tatshak Tshang, the Kundhe Regent, who also built Kundheling Monastery in Lhasa in 1794.

Options from Shopado
Shopado is at a major intersection with interesting options.

1. To Chamdo (district capital of East Tibet) via Lhorong Xian and Zitho Monastery.

> **Zitho Monastery** Descend northeast down the Do Chu Valley (6 km from Shopado). Turn right (southeast) along the main Tibet–Sichuan road. The district headquarters of Lhorong Xian is 19 km further. Zitho Gön and Nyiseb Gön monasteries are here. The former had over 300 monks and was the main seat (*dhensa*) of the Demo Regent. Dodhu Monastery, higher up, was a branch of Chamdo with over 100 monks. Ten km south of Zitho is Ngödru Monastery, another dependent of Chamdo.

2. To Chumdo and Pomi via Zitho and Ngödru monasteries and the Chamdo La.

3. To Khyungpo Tengcheng, the main Bönpo pilgrim destination in East Tibet, along the Salween River (see below). There is no motor traffic between Shopado and Tengcheng.

✤ Day 16 Shopado–Rua Tung (3298 m) 30.5 km
Walk northeast along the Do Valley. In 1/2 hr, pass a side valley on the left; ignore this. Continue to a main valley junction (1 hr from town). The main road to Lhorong Xian and Chamdo turns right, along the Dze Chu Valley, to Zitho Monastery, 19 km to the southeast. Do not take this but continue straight ahead to the northeast. In 3/4 hr, turn left (northwest) up a side valley and climb steeply for 2 3/4 hr to the Batou La (3688 m). Descend northwest along the beautiful Yimda Valley to its junction with the mighty Salween (1/2 hr). Follow the Salween's right bank to the northwest and cross the Chungke La (3660 m) and two more ridges to Rua Tung Monastery (Dadye Monastery and Shapathang are on the left bank).

✤ Day 17 Rua Tung–Zinda (Singka) 31.5 km
Cross by ferry to the Salween's left bank. Tashi Gön Monastery, on the opposite shore, once had 60 monks. Climb gradually along the river to the Pragar La (3745 m), then descend to the Tungkar Chu Valley and up its opposite ridge to the Tungkar La (also 3745 m). The gray Salween on the left has many twists and turns and the path stays high above the water. Pass the tiny village of Unk, then cross the Jukua La (3593 m) to Chatung. Beyond lies Zinda, a village near the junction of the Salween and the Zinda Chu, which flows west into the big river. Zinda stands on a ledge 30 m above the water.

✤ Day 18 Zinda–Itashi (3508 m) 38 km
One km from Zinda, on the right, is the Zinda Chu Valley. The trail leaves the Salween

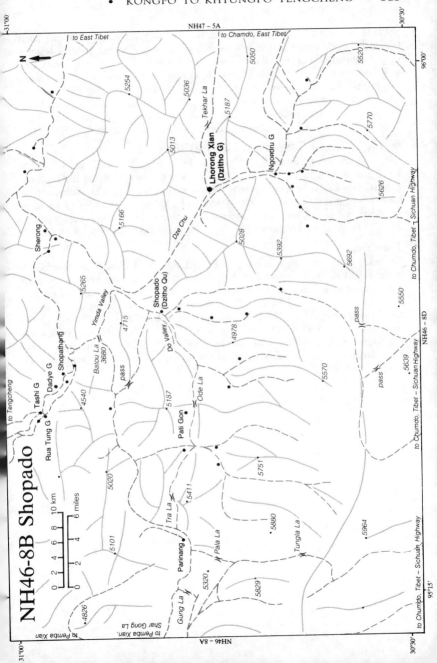

NH46-8B Shopado

and heads up the ridge that guards the north slopes of the valley entrance. Go past Juwaki (Kanwachi) to Dola Ruhung, both villages high on the slopes. Beyond, the trail begins its steep ascent to the Do La (4373 m) by following the Do Chu's right (west) bank. The excellent view from the pass takes in mountains in all directions and one snow-covered range that runs north-northwest. Descend due north down the Dola Yung Valley with the river on the left (west). Itashi, at the junction of the Do Chu and narrow Lachin Chu (northeast–southwest), is a village on the Lachin Chu's north (right) bank surrounded by four or five other villages. Many stone cairns are found within the Lachin Valley, next to the path.

✤ DAY 19 ITASHI–TENGCHENG (4084 M) 38 KM

Follow the Lachin Chu along its right bank, to the northeast. Pass a side valley in 1/2 hr; a trail goes along it to Tengcheng as well, but ignore this and follow the Lachin Chu to its head at the Lachin La (4510 m). From Itashi to the pass is 22 km (6 hr). Descend steeply between bare, grass hills along the narrow Kwom Chu Valley. A few km before Tengcheng is the large village of Chalung Kuo, the first permanent settlement since Itashi. Cross the Zok Chu by bridge to Tengcheng. Khyungpo Tengcheng Monastery is 5 km to the west.

Tengcheng

The town, mostly one-story mud houses at the end of a 30-m-high spur, is a major Bönpo center. Zok Chu River flows down from Nagchu District in the west and the Zong Chu drains from Jyekundo in the northwest. The picturesque Tengcheng valley is bounded by red sandstone hills covered with grass and colorful fields. Between the Zong Chu and the town is a fertile plain 3 km long by 1 km wide. To the south is the Ri Ma Hill, about 1000 m high. Six routes radiate from this regional center. The main roads go to Chamdo in the east (248 km) and Nagchu in the west (via Bacheng and Zok Xian). Traffic is infrequent, so expect to wait a few days for a ride. This offers an opportunity to explore on foot the Bönpo holy sites in the district.

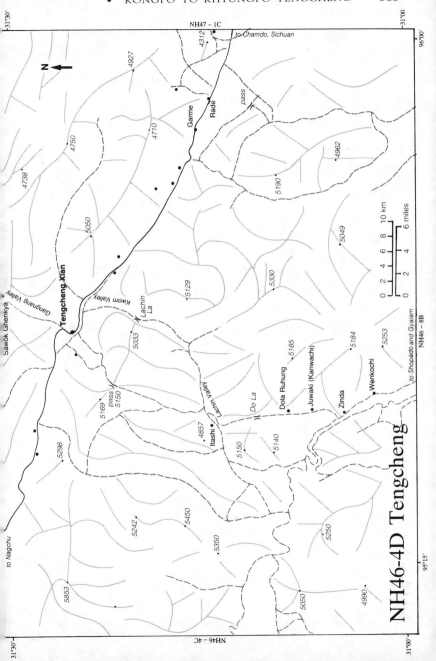

NH46-4D Tengcheng

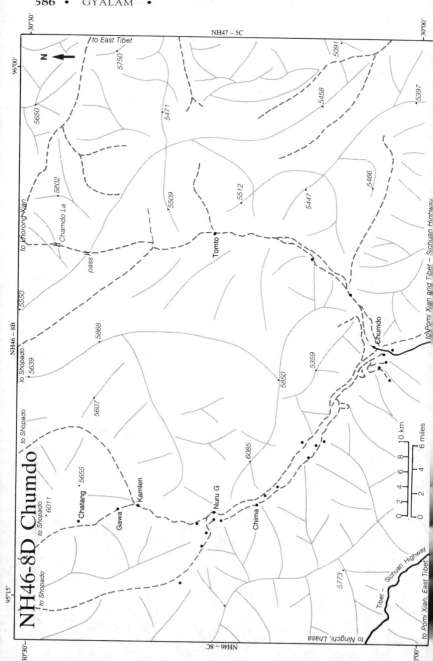

NH46-8D Chumdo

SACRED LAKES

Like many holy mountains, a number of lakes in Tibet are believed to be endowed with unique spiritual powers. Lhamo Latso is the most important oracle-lake, known for its remarkable divinative properties. Believers from the Dalai Lamas down made obligatory pilgrimages to it in order to have their futures foretold; Regents came here to look for clues to the whereabouts of future Dalai Lamas. It is considered to be the dwelling of Tibet's protectress, the goddess Palden Lhamo, and its waters contain her soul or life-force.

Lake Manasarovar is intimately associated with Mt Kailash, the holiest mountain for Buddhists and Hindus. Pilgrims gain religious merit by circumambulating its 100-km shoreline. Far to the north of Central Tibet, the inhospitable Changtang Plateau also has a number of sacred saltwater lakes. One is Nam Tso, which has various monasteries located within its superbly scenic environs. Remote treks exist in the vicinity of Lake Yamdrok: a one-week circuit goes around its arms; a long walk proceeds from the lake to Lhodrak, South Tibet, then—after visiting the unknown south shores of Lake Phurma—on to Ralung Monastery.

YAMDROK:
A ONE-WEEK CIRCUIT
OF THE SCORPION LAKE

Location	Yamdrok Tso
Map reference	NH46-13 A B, 46-9 C
Trekking days	7 (circuit)
Start–Finish	Nakartse–Nakartse
Passes	None

OVERVIEW

This easy trek visits the remote portions of Lake Yamdrok (Yamdrok Tso; 4408 m) and skirts holy Tönang Sangwa Ri, a mountain consecrated by Guru Rinpoche, a founder of Tibetan Buddhism. A highlight of this itinerary is the unusual island monastery of Yönpodo, now a reviving monastic community. The best-known monastery of Yamdrok Tso is Samding, an institution that welcomes men and women; its abbess, Dorje Phagmo, was the only female incarnation in Tibet. This idyllic walk has the dramatic, contrasting scenery of expansive water and high mountains. Outside of the occasional valleys habitation is sparse. Peace and quiet permeate the whole circuit. The trek starts from Nakartse, situated between the Kamba La and the Karo La, next to the Friendship Highway. East of Nakartse is Lake Dumo Tso (Jem Tso, 15 km by 5 km), neatly enclosed within the arms of Yamdrok Tso. Southeast of

Dumo Tso is the Tagla Range running northeast–southeast. Interesting, relatively easy walks lie within the area ringed by these two lakes. The locals live partly by fishing, an unusual occupation in Tibet; the scaleless fish found here is reportedly quite delicious. Near Nakartse are unusual, little-known prehistoric caves.

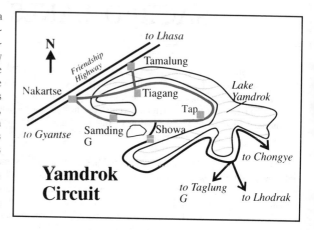

Yamdrok Circuit

Related sections
Lake Yamdrok to Lhodrak, p 606
Lhasa to Yarlung Valley, p 595
Rinpung Dzong, p 841

Access: Nakartse
Nakartse is 154 km southwest of Lhasa and 100 km east of Gyantse near the westernmost part of Yamdrok Tso. The daily bus from Lhasa arrives between 1300 and 1500; the one from Shigatse pulls in between 1200 and 1400. This substantial Chinese town has a Tibetan enclave (just a cluster of houses) below the old fort. A monastery south of the fort overlooks the truck stop-guest house and restaurant. Nakartse is a common stop on the Friendship Highway when traveling between Lhasa and Nepal.

Nakartse dzong
The ruined fortress (dzong) of Nakartse stands on a ridge overlooking the lake and the town. Nakartse was a small feudal state that became well known when one of its princesses married into the Chongye family of Yarlung. She gave birth to the Fifth Dalai Lama in 1617. The ruins of Lhündrub Lhakhang are 1/4 hr from town on a craggy hill. This monastery belonged to a branch of the Kagyüpa known as the Potöpa.

Time Chart

Day	Place	Hours
1	Nakartse–Samding	1 1/2
2	Showa	6
3	Tap	5 1/4
4	Ne	4 3/4
5	Tiagang	7
6	Mekpa	5
7	Nakartse	8 1/2

✤ Day 1 Nakartse–Samding Monastery 1 1/2 hr

From Nakartse follow a tractor trail east towards a ridge on top of which are the toppled walls of Samding Monastery. Cross three bridges to reach the base of the ridge (3/4 hr) and Dsamje (Dsamjo), site of a monastery (destroyed). Continue east following the contours of the ridge to reach a second village, Guju, (1/2 hr). After this (10 min) is a junction; the left path goes up the slopes to Samding; the right leads to Lingme and another path up to the monastery.

✤ Day 2 Samding–Showa 6 hr

From the monastery, descend to Lingme and continue east along the base of the ridge. In 1/2 hr the path diverges. The left branch heads east along the north shore of the Dumo Tso to Tap (Tapé). Take the right branch southward along the Dumo Tso's west shore. Wade across two rivers. After the second one, walk along a narrow strip of land marked by three large rocks, between a small lake on the right and the Dumo Tso. An island is in the latter. Beyond, a finger of the Dumo juts to the south. At the tip is a hut. On reaching this, go up a side valley to the right (southwest) to a saddle (a second hut is within the valley). On the other side, the trail leads southeast, then east, to Kham. Another (northwest) branch goes to Gado near Nakartse.

From the saddle, follow the top of the ridge southward for a short distance (1/2 hr from the second hut), then drop down into a valley that trends to the south, following the trail that leads towards Kham. On the descent, Dumo Tso is on the left (east) and Yamdrok Tso on the right (southwest). Head south across the saddle of another ridge, then walk down to the southernmost tip of the long south-pointing finger of Dumo Tso. Follow the shoreline for 1/4 hr to some houses here. (Lingme to here is 3 1/4 hr.)

The trail forks and the left branch turns north to Tsim. The right (east) goes over the Dugu La to Kham. Take this second choice. Yamdrok Tso appears to the right (south and southwest), and for a moment Samding can also be glimpsed. Some distance to the east of Dumo Tso's finger, the path zigzags up to the Dugu La, a double pass. After the first saddle, continue for 10 min to the second. On the far side, descend eastward into a valley. Stay on the main path along the valley to Showa. From the southernmost tip of Dumo Tso to here is 2 1/2 hr. Showa, only 10 min east of Yamdrok Tso, has a school useful for shelter and plenty of food is available from the hospitable villagers. Ruins of a watchtower stand to the north; the village of Kham is beyond that. Other ruins of a watchtower are at the lake's north shore.

Nakartse

to Lhasa

Lake Yamdrok

marsh

restaurant

guest house

Nakartse Village

guest house, restaurant

Samding Monastery

The monastery is 8 km east of Nakartse on top of a ridge that divides the southern extreme of Yamdrok Tso's north arm from Dumo Tso (Devil Lake). According to legend, Samding was built here to assure the lake water did not overflow and inundate the whole of Tibet. In 1716, a female incarnation (*tulku*) of the monastery supposedly transformed herself and the nuns into sows during the Dzungar Mongol invasion. When the commander entered the monastery by force, he was astounded by the sight. They turned themselves back into nuns and the impressed Mongols made profuse offerings to the monastery. Samding suffered near total destruction during the Cultural Revolution. Dynamite was used to bring down the thick stone walls. Some buildings and an assembly hall have been rebuilt and religious activities resumed.

History One source asserts that Samding was founded in the 13th C. by Khetsün Zhönnu Drub. The lama most intimately linked with the monastery, however, was Bödong Chokle Namgyal (1306–86), founder of the obscure Bödongpa sub-sect whose teachings are a combination of Sakyapa and Nyingma precepts (see page 33). Bödong was also the tutor of Tsong Khapa, patriarch of the Gelugpa. After the rapid rise of the Gelugpa, his small sect almost died out. Samding, and a few minor temples along the lake, practised the Bödong discipline until the Cultural Revolution. The abbess of Samding, Dorje Phagmo, was considered the incarnate consort of Bödong.

✦ Day 3 Showa–Tap 5 1/4 hr

Walk away from the lake to follow a side valley northward. Near its head, the path splits. The trail continues along the valley while a tractor track leaves the valley to the right. Both ways lead to the same ridge over different saddles (150 m above the lake) and go on to Kham. The tractor route is slightly longer. Showa to Kham is 3/4 hr. From Kham, continue down the valley along its north side via a footpath (do not follow the tractor track). In 1/4 hr reach a house, then leave the valley to go up the slopes on the left. After crossing a north–south ridge (100 m above the valley), descend to some ruins by the shore of Yamdrok Tso. (Kham to here is 1 hr.) The lake is on the right (east).

Follow the shoreline for 1 hr. The path then veers to the left (northwest) and leaves the lake. Cross a small ridge (100 m high) and descend into a valley with a house on its left (west) flank. From the ruins to here is 1 1/4 hr. Beyond the house are the villages of Nga (Ngadrak Qu) and Tankya (Dongkya Monastery is reported to be here). Both are close to the eastern shore of Dumo Tso. At the house, follow a tractor track right (east) towards Tap. (Another track goes left [west] from the house, along the northern shoreline of Dumo Tso, to Samding and Nakartse.)

Cross another small ridge and again walk down to the shoreline of Yamdrok Tso. Follow the water closely to the east to Tap (Tabe). Just before the village, the path detours to the north, then east, to negotiate a northern finger of the lake. From the house near Ngadrak to Tap is 2 1/4 hr. Tap is a tiny village. Nearby is a ferry landing for the boat to Yönpodo Monastery (Rmb 2 round trip; the schedule is unreliable). One of the few island monasteries

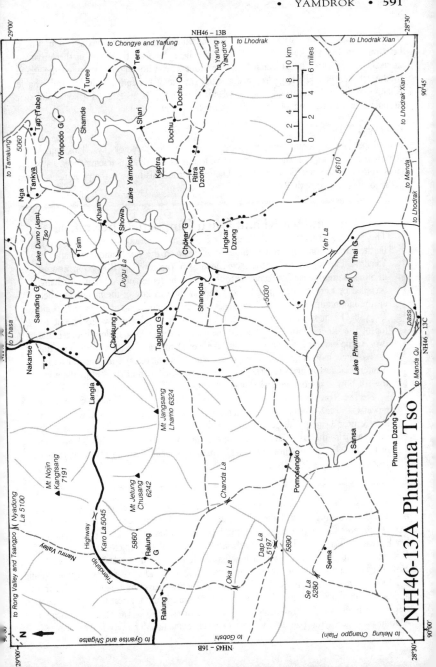

NH46-13A Phurma Tso

in Tibet, Yönpodo was destroyed during the Cultural Revolution. Some of the buildings have been renovated and quite a few monks now live here. Sleep at the house of the ferryman-monk. The monastery is consecrated to Guru Rinpoche, who supposedly visited the island in the 8th century. His huge 'self-manifesting' (*rangjung*) handprint, called Zutrul Chakje Khangchen Tsam, is the wonder of the island. It is said to be as large as a house and that its reflection can be seen on the lake surface from a great distance.

✤ DAY 4 TAP–NE 4 3/4 HR

From Tap, start northward along the long, curving arm of Yamdrok Tso. This remarkable, elongated hook of water is the most distinctive feature of the lake. Its resemblance to a pincer gives Yamdrok the name Scorpion Lake. Enclosed within this hook is the prominent, sacred massif of Tönang Sangwa Ri.

Tönang Sangwa Ri and Guru Rinpoche's hermitage

The Tönang (Inside Rocks) Peninsula is the mountainous mass that projects northeastward from Nakartse to insert itself between the north and south arms of Yamdrok Tso. It is probably the sacred mountain Yamdrok Dza Rongbo mentioned in Situ's pilgrimage guide. According to the guide, the retreat of Drubkhang Yakhang, occupied by Karmapa Rangjung Dorje, stands at the east face of the mountain. High up the mountain are the cave hermitages of Guru Rinpoche and his consort, Yeshe Tsogyal. The master's footprints are above the caves. Nearby are two rocks, one on top of the other. Guru Rinpoche hid medicinal treasure in a hollow between the two. At the summit is the *rangjung* stone castle of Menmo Potrang. Here are wonderful views of great mountains: Yala Shampo and Wöde Gungyal (east), Kula Kangri (south), Samten Gangwa Zangpo (west), and Nyenchen Tanglha (north). Within these are the six holy lakes of Yamdrok Yutso Dhodruk.

The Tönang range has two main peaks. In the west is Tönang Sangwa Ri proper (5150 m). Guru Rinpoche's secret hermitage, Sangwa Ne of Tönang, is within a ridge near Dutong Village and Duila Hill (location unknown). The second peak (5336 m) is to the east. Circumambulate both mountains by following the inner shore of Yamdrok Tso, starting from Samding Monastery. Tönang Sangwa Ri is almost always visible.

The trek north from Tap skirts numerous bays and inlets that make up the western shores of the lake's arm. In general, follow the contours of the lake and cross small ridges to avoid the westernmost fingers of land. Follow the beach if you are unsure of the way. The largest bay lies east of Tap. From Tap walk northeast up a valley along a tractor track. After a ridge (150 m above the lake) reach a trail junction. Follow either the track or a footpath (short cut). The two join later at the bottom. Continue crossing low ridges to Yalung. (Tap to Yalung is 2 hr.) The next village is Deng, 1 1/4 hr away. Pass two bays and finally reach Ne (Nen), a settlement of about 20 houses (1 1/2 hr). The Lonjok meditation retreat lies up the mountain slopes north of Ne. (A trail from Ne goes southwest into a valley. At its head is a 4950-m pass. Cross the pass to the west to reach Samding Monastery.)

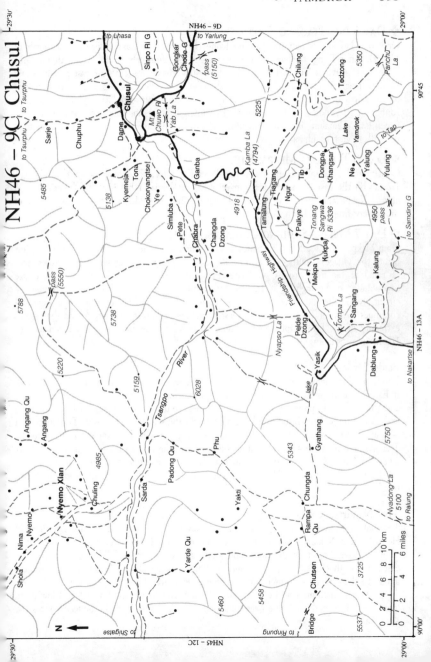

NH46 – 9D

to Lhasa
to Yarlung
Sinpo Ri G
Gongkar
Chode G
pass
(5150)
Chusul
Dana
to Tsurphu
Sarje
Chuphu
Mt.
Chuwo Ri
Yab La
Chokoryangtse
Ye
Kyemela
Tona
Ganba
5225
Chilung
Tedzong
5350
Panchu
La
90°45'
29°00'
Kamba La
(4794)
Dongpa
Khangsar
Ne
Yalung
Yulung
Lake
Yamdrok
to Tap
5485
5138
Similuba
Pete
Chabra
Changda
Dzong
4918
Tamalung
Hagang
Ngur
Tib
Palkye
Tonang
Sangwa
Ri 5336
4950
pass
to Samding G
pass
(5550)
5788
5738
5220
5159
River
6028
Tsangpo
Friendship Highway
Nyapso La
Pelde
Dzong
Kupka
Mekpa
Tompa La
Sangang
Kalung
Yasik
Dablung
to Nakartse
NH46 – 13A
Angang Qu
Angang
4985
Chuling
Nyemo
Nyemo Xian
Sarda
Padong Qu
Phu
Yakti
Lake
5343
Gyathang
Chungda
Rampa
Qu
5750
Nyadong La
5100
to Ralung
Shola
Nima
Nyemo
Yarde Qu
5460
Chutsen
Bridge
to Rinpung
5458
3725
5537
to Shigatse
NH45 – 12C
29°00'
90°00'

0   2   4   6   8   10 km
0   2   4   6 miles

N

29°30'
29°30'

✤ Day 5 Ne–Tiagang 7 hr

Only one bay stands between Ne and Dong (Dongpa), the next village to the north (2 1/4 hr). After Dong, the great arm of water curves definitively to the west. After passing three bays, arrive at Tib (2 hr). Then walk west-northwest for 2 3/4 hr past four bays and Ngur to reach Tiagang, a village on the shoulder of a valley. Here is a ferry to Tamalung on the north shore. The ten-person coracle usually leaves between 1700 and 1800 and costs Rmb 3–10, depending on the ferryman. In winter, it is possible to simply walk across the frozen lake. Tamalung is on the Friendship Highway. To leave this itinerary, hitchhike from the village east to Lhasa or west to Gyantse.

✤ Day 6 Tiagang–Mekpa 5 hr

Continue west from Tiagang for 1 hr. Ascend a ridge, then drop down to Palkye (1 1/2 hr) on the east shore of a long finger of water. Kukpa (1 hr) is at the finger's tip. Go around Kukpa and then turn north to Dongkar, Kura, and Mekpa, at the western base of the watery finger (1 1/2 hr).

✤ Day 7 Mekpa–Samding–Nakartse 8 1/2 hr

From Mekpa, turn southwest to Sangang (3 3/4 hr); cross the low Tompa La, 4620 m, just before the village). South of Sangang (3/4 hr) is a bridge that crosses the narrowest part of Yamdrok Tso from east to west. The Friendship Highway is on the far side (the bridge to Dablung on the highway is 1/2 hr). Either hitch to Lhasa or Gyantse or continue the circuit around the lake. The latter option, from the bridge (do not cross it to the highway) continues south for 1/4 hr, then turns east to Kalung (2 hr). It contours around the eastern extremity of the lake's arm before heading westward to Samding (4 hr) and Nakartse (1 1/2 hr from Samding).

Pelde Dzong

The Friendship Highway passes through this picturesque fishing village 24 km north of Nakartse. It has fortress ruins next to Yamdrok Tso. Some 6 km southwest of Pelde, between Pelde and Yasik, is a rocky promontory. Rock outcrops next to the road are painted red and decorated with prayer flags. This shrine to a local deity marks the spot for the unusual Tibetan custom of water burial. From Pelde, a trail behind the village crosses the Nyapso La (3 hr) to the Tsangpo at a point west of the Chusul Bridge. From the pass to the Tsangpo's south bank takes 3 1/4 hr. (Across the river is Pindu Monastery.) From here to the Chusul Bridge is a 6 1/2-hr walk to the east. Hitch along a new road (built 1987–88) to the bridge and then to Lhasa.

The Nakartse caves

The Nakartse caves are located southwest of Nakartse in an area called Tatang (Plain of Horses). From Nakartse, follow the main road south for 1 1/4 hr on foot. On the left is a village. Bounding it on the north and south are two old walls. Within a canyon to the east is a river that cuts through conglomerate strata to expose about 40 caves. (Certain sources allude to these as possibly prehistoric.) Some extend over 10 m deep into the rock cliffs.

The southernmost wall of these straddles the river by means of a bridge. Below it are four caves. Ten more caves are near some houses 1/2 hr away from the bridge, towards the Karo La.

LHASA TO THE YARLUNG VALLEY VIA LAKE YAMDROK

Location	South of Lhasa
Map reference	NH46-9 B D, 46-13 B, 46-14 A
Trekking days	14 (circuit)
Start–Finish	Lhasa–Chongye
Passes	Tungo, Drib, Gonzo, Shanda

OVERVIEW

This itinerary follows one of Tibet's ancient trade routes, from Lhasa southward over the strenuous Tungo La, watershed of the Lhasa and Tsangpo rivers. At the north base of the pass are nomadic yak herders with their characteristic black tents and a rare bird's-eye view of Lhasa and the Potala. On the other side is a branch valley that leads to the amazing Guru Rinpoche cave complexes of Drak Yong Dzong and Dzong Kumbum (see pages 321, 325). Further to the south, at the left bank of the Tsangpo, is the important monastery of Dorje Drak, one of the two principal Nyingmapa centers in the country. Situated in a striking and remote location amidst sand dunes, it is seldom visited by outsiders.

After crossing to the Tsangpo's south bank, the route leads to several obscure monasteries in the large Drib Valley. Beautiful Lake Yamdrok Tso is then reached after negotiating the easy Drib La; this retraces the footsteps of the present Dalai Lama during his escape to India

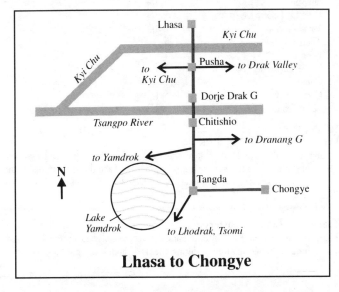

Lhasa to Chongye

in 1959. Beyond the lake are old caravan trails that lead to the district of Lhodrak and then on to Bhutan and India. The eastern shores of Yamdrok Tso have a number of superb campsites; good places to spend a couple of rest days. Finally, the trek heads east to Ache Dzong and Tragtse, then crosses the Shanda La to descend into the Chongye and Yarlung valleys, the cradle of Tibetan civilization.

Related sections
Holy places along the Lhasa–Tsethang highway, p 515
The Yarlung Valley, p 470

Access
From the center of Lhasa, walk east past the Banak Shöl Hotel and Tibet University (across from the Sunlight Hotel and the Lhasa City Bus Station). At the end of the university street turn right across the large East Lhasa Bridge. After the bridge, turn immediately right onto a dirt road (do not go left to follow the paved road, the Tibet–Sichuan highway) and walk west along the Lhasa River to a military compound and the village of Drib (Selingbaton). The route to the Tungo La starts from here.

Time Chart

Day	Place	Hours
1	Lhasa–Camp 1	3
2	Camp 2 (via Tungo La)	7
3	Pusha	2
4	Dorje Drak Monastery	5 1/2
5	Sungrabling Monastery	4
6	Jangshö	3 1/4
7	Drib La (south base)	5 3/4
8	Yamdrok Tso	2 1/2
9	Touree	5
10	Bengar	4
11	Stone enclosure (via Ache Dzong)	3
12	Camp 3	4
13	Camp 4 (via Shanda La)	5 1/2
14	Seda Tronzu	3 1/2

Trail Notes
✤ DAY 1 LHASA–CAMP 1 3 HR
From Lhasa, cross the East Lhasa Bridge and turn right along a dirt road that follows the south bank of the Kyi Chu to Drib (Selingbaton), 3/4 hr. Take the left fork out of the village (Drepung Monastery stands out across river) to Tsemchok Ling (1/4 hr), walking south along the valley floor.

> ### Tsemchok Ling Monastery
> This was one of Four Royal Monasteries of Tibet established by the Dalai Lama's regents under Chinese patronage during the 18th and 19th centuries. The regents
>
> ⟹

were ostensibly chosen from one of these four monasteries. Tibetans, however, never respected this rule and they were sometimes chosen from a monastery outside Lhasa, such as Reting. The other three Royal Monasteries are Tengye Ling, Kunde Ling, and Tsomön Ling, all in Lhasa proper (see page 168). Tsemchok Ling, located in Drib Qu, was destroyed as recently as 1979 when villagers were invited to pillage the monastery by the Chinese. A few monks are presently in residence in a rebuilt chapel.

Beyond Drib, keep to a trail on the east (left) side of the valley. This entails crossing several deep gullies. At the head of the valley is a distant pyramidal peak and just below it are well-defined paths to the pass. A dry river bed is to the right. Reach a third village, Driba, in 3/4 hr. (All three villages thus far answer to the name Drib.) Continue along the east bank; the trail makes an exaggerated curve to the left to bypass a western spur. In 1 1/4 hr reach a grassy campsite on the left bank of the river (the trail continues up the valley along the right bank). This is near the point where a dry river bed joins the main one from the west. A deserted village stands further up the valley, also on the right bank. The Tungo La can be seen below and to the right of the pyramidal peak. Looking back towards Lhasa, the Kyi Chu and the Potala are still visible. Yak herds pass through the camp every morning and evening en route to the west side valley; it is possible to hire yaks for transport.

✤ DAY 2 CAMP 1–TUNGO LA–CAMP 2 7 HR

This is a difficult, strenuous day. Having pack animals to carry gear will help a lot. From the camp wade back to the right bank and follow the well-marked trail on the left side of the valley. Cross a wide gully. The trail divides at a point where a second river comes down the valley on the left. Take the higher route up. Cross a wide, dry riverbed, then turn left up towards parallel goat tracks (an obvious landmark) that traverse from left to right below the pyramidal peak. Commence a steep climb by following the trail up the left bank of a small stream. Halfway up the valley the trail crosses the stream to its other bank. Distinct outcrops of rocks appear on the left. Follow the valley due east to a goat track, then traverse the mountain along it. This will lead you directly to the summit of the first pass (camp 1–pass, 3 hr).

Follow the trail over the pass to a gentle, rocky valley. The pyramidal peak is left behind. Stay on the right side of the valley (the river flows northward towards Lhasa). After 2–3 km, the rocky valley ends at a ridge. Continue along a flat, swampy plain which curves to the right just below the second pass (first pass–second pass, 2 1/2 hr). This second pass, marked by prayer flags and a large cairn, is the Tungo La (4977 m). Follow another rocky valley southward after the pass. From this point on until the village of Phurin, the trail is gravelly and overgrown with thorny bushes. After 1/4 hr bear right and descend a steep gully. Turn left at a ridge and descend into a bowl-like valley, leaving the trail. Follow this lush valley downward along the right bank of the river. Camp along this stretch of the route (Tungo La–camp 2, 1 1/2 hr).

✤ DAY 3 CAMP 2–PUSHA 2 HR

Continue down the valley. During the next few km, two small valleys from the east join the main one. Good camping is possible near the second. After this second side valley a trail appears on the left side of the main valley. Cross the river and follow it. Later recross to the right bank by a bridge. The valley narrows to become barely wider than the river; prayer flags hang from two outcroppings (second pass–prayer flags, 3 hr). The valley widens and the trail immediately crosses another bridge to the valley's left side. Here a side valley (with a small monastery on the left) comes in from the east (left) just before the village of Pusha. This valley leads to the Guru Rinpoche cave systems of Drak Yong Dzong and Dzong Kumbum (see pages 321, 325). A large, ancient tree stands left of the junction (prayer flags–Pusha, 1/2 hr). Pusha (50 families) is on the left side of the valley about 70 m above the river. Cultivated fields increase in frequency from this point. A campsite lies just below the village on the grassy right bank of the river. Walk through fields of brambles to get to it.

✤ DAY 4 PUSHA–DORJE DRAK 5 1/2 HR

Return to the main trail and continue down the left bank of the valley past another settlement (1/4 hr from Pusha). On the right is a disused hydro-electric power station. The trail now curves south-southwest. Fine views of the Tsangpo Valley appear for the first time. Pass Nangasone, 3/4 hr from Pusha, then Phurin, 1/2 hr from Nangasone. After a small shrine just outside Phurin, the trail becomes easier and the valley wider.

Pass the following villages:

- Sherang (Shirang, 1 hr from Phurin). The valley flattens and the track widens.
- Tschora (1/4 hr from Sherang). Hemp is grown here for rope.
- Shena (3/4 hr from Tschora). Willow trees line the trail.
- Chukapa (1/4 hr from Shena). A bridge crosses to the right side of the valley. Chukapa has a population of about 100 people.
- Thurshirak (1/2 hr from Chukapa). This small settlement on the left precedes an old, Tibetan-style army barracks on the right.
- Dapung Shika (1/2 hr from Thurshirak). This is the last village before Dorje Drak Monastery.

After Dapung Shika cross a deceptively long stretch of desert to reach the monastery. The mouth of the valley, near the Tsangpo, is wide. Bear right and follow a poorly defined path towards a conspicuous sandy mountain. Dorje Drak Monastery, on a rocky hill overlooking the Tsangpo, stands below this mountain at the far right of the valley (1 hr from Dapung Shika). A cave with inscriptions below it is to the left. There are sandy camping spots by the riverbank. Swim in the river but watch out for the strong current.

Dorje Drak Monastery

The monastery is located at the bottom of a ridge said to resemble a *dorje*, thus its name. A path encircles the complex and goes up to Dorje Drak Ütse, a ruined meditation retreat to the west. Footprints of various saints and lamas, and also rock paintings enliven the path. The monastery has suffered badly under the Chinese. In 1960 it

➠

was disbanded and 300 monks forced into the fields. By 1965, numerous sacred objects had been thrown into the river and the buildings levelled. Only a fraction of the extensive complex remained. The hills and the surrounding areas are littered with old foundations and ruins. Rebuilding started in 1985 and monks slowly trickled back. Local villages helped with donations; over 15 young novices, ten senior monks, and one lama now live at Dorje Drak. The former abbot, Taglung Tsetul, went into exile and stayed in Ladakh from 1959 to 1983. He now lives in Simla, India. Rigdzin Pema Trinle is the present abbot; he occasionally spends time here.

Enter the main assembly hall via the courtyard, which is flanked by monks' quarters. New murals depict Nechu, Guru Tsengye (the Eight Manifestations of Guru Rinpoche) and the personal tutelary deity of the Jangter Lama, Godemchen. A new statue of Guru Rinpoche, brought from Lhasa in May 1986, is the Tri Tsangkhang Chapel's centerpiece (notice the skulls painted on the chapel's entrance doors). The original (destroyed) was supposedly made by Pema Thinle, the founding abbot. In former times, statues of Sakyamuni and the Eight Great Bodhisattvas resided in this chapel. To the left of the *tsangkhang* is a *gönkhang*, its central image Dorje Zhonnu. A printing room has been installed on the second floor.

History Dorje Drak was founded at the end of the 16th C. by Tashi Tobgye, one of five incarnations of King Trisong Detsen. The originator of this illustrious Nyingma lineage was Rigdzin Chenpo Ngödrub Gyeltsen (1337–1409), also known as Godemchen, 'the one with the eagle feather'. He was born in Tsang to a family with links to the Mongolian royalty. Godemchen 'discovered' a body of sacred texts known as Jangter (Northern Treasure), and the essential teachings of Dorje Drak derive from this. Mindroling, across the river, primarily uses the Lhoter (Southern Treasure).

Rigdzin Pema Trinle (1641–1717), abbot and fourth incarnation of Godemchen, brought fame to Dorje Drak by adopting a clear method of instruction that incorporated precepts of the Jangter, thus providing a rational, practicable model for meditation. He immured himself in solitary retreat within the Nego Che Cave inside Drak Yong Dzong. Near the monastery is Nepu Chölung, a retreat of Lingrepa, founder of the Drukpa Kagyü sect that today flourishes in Bhutan and to a lesser extent in Ladakh. Mor Monastery is sited near the Che La, a pass that crosses the Yartö Drak range (watershed between the Tsangpo and Lhasa rivers) north of Dorje Drak.

✤ DAY 5 DORJE DRAK–SUNGRABLING MONASTERY 4 HR

A ferry crossing the Tsangpo is directly below the monastery. Departure is 0900 but delays, due to ridiculous overloading, are frequent. Two motor ferries travel up-stream and dock between road marker 47 and 48 km on the Lhasa–Tsethang road, about 5 km west of Chitishio (road marker 52 km). The crossing takes 50 min. There is an afternoon ferry as well. Hitch a ride or walk (1 hr) into Chitishio, a large village with shops and a teahouse-cum-restaurant. This community was known for its colorfully striped woolen aprons dyed with a special substance from Bhutan. It still does a certain amount of weaving today. Renovated Dungpu Chökor

Monastery (Sakyapa) is at the south end of town (see page 482). Follow the dirt road south along the Drib Valley. Take the left fork to Kinnishi (3 km, 2 hr from Chitishio). Sungrabling (Suruling) Monastery, 1/2 km from Kinnishi, is above the village (see page 483). The monks are friendly and it is possible to spend the night here.

✦ DAY 6 SUNGRABLING–JANGSHÖ 3 1/4 HR

Continue south along the main Drib Valley. The dirt road follows the valley for a long way; if preferred, ride a tractor or get a donkey at Kinnishi. Susha is 1/4 hr from Kinnishi. Ganzu, a long, strung-out village, is 3/4 hr further, with a square building on the right (it takes 1/2 hr to walk through Ganzu; at the end is a small lake on the right). Soon come to Namgye Shöl Qu, administrative compound for the entire valley (15 km from Chitishio). It is a collection of prosperous villages with fine houses, and was once the residence of the Gongkar Dzongpon, governor of the Gongkar Dzong (fort).

Continue along the jeep road that branches near the village's south end. Take the tree-lined left fork. In 3/4 hr cross a dry riverbed that originates from a valley on the left. The valley narrows as the path approaches Jangshö (13 km south of Namgye Shöl Qu). Cha Monastery, halfway up the valley wall on the right, is a small, square white building with a white *chörten*. One monk lives here. Jangshö is on the left, 10 min up a cliff. Just after the village is a dry side valley on the left; Tse-o-na Monastery is said to be up this valley.

✦ DAY 7 JANGSHÖ–DRIB LA (SOUTH BASE) 5 3/4 HR

After Jangshö, the path crosses to the right side of the valley over a red bridge (1/4 hr from Jangshö). Take the left fork immediately after the bridge to follow the Drib Chu to the south. A stone wall and patch of woods are on the right. Cross a dry riverbed coming in from the right. Tangshong, on the right up a short cliff, is 1/2 hr from the red bridge. The track now joins the riverbed and is less defined. It forks at a tiny village with a small stone mill on the left (1 hr after Tangshong). Take the right fork up the valley along the river's left bank. The track, now rocky and dusty, ascends above the river. Before this point the main valley has been gentle. Drib is visible on a hill and the Drib La looms directly above the village on the left. Drop down to the river, cross to the right bank, then follow a path 40 m above the water. The valley forks and the river veers to the west (right). Take the left fork. The well-defined path narrows and crosses a gorge just below Drib (2 1/2 hr from Tangshong). It then traverses the right slopes of the valley and climbs steeply to the pass (Drib La is 1 1/2 hr from Drib) where majestic views of Yamdrok Tso's northeast corner and the surrounding country can be had. The snowy Himalayas provide a shimmering backdrop to all this grandeur. Follow a path south into a valley. Camping spots, on the river's left bank, can be found 1 hr below the pass.

✦ DAY 8 DRIB LA (SOUTH BASE)–YAMDROK TSO 2 1/2 HR

Continue down the valley. The path curves southeastward around a hill at the bottom of the valley. (A high, brick dam is a landmark.) The path goes left of the dam, then bears right into a large valley behind the hill. Tangda (Dromda) and Yamdrok Tso appear in the west. Cross the river, then a long wall along the foot of the valley, heading in the direction of Tangda (2 hr from Drib La). The village, on top of a hill near the lake, is formed of two settlements, one on each side of the valley (the path heads left). Yamdrok Tso is 1/2 hr away. The area is ideal for camping and rest.

Tangda and vicinity Shabshi, 1/2 hr south of Tangda, lies behind a range of hills on the lake's left side. The path goes from Tangda southeastward along a dry river, up a small valley, and passes a sheep pen on the right. It leads to a wide flood plain that stretches eastward as far as one can see. The path cuts across the plain to its southern edge, where it is joined by a rocky valley. Shabshi is at this spot. Partö is a small village on the lake 2 hr southwest of Tangda. Good campsites exist by the lake, between these two communities.

Alternative route : Tangda (Dromda) to the Friendship Highway

Instead of heading east to the Chongye and Yarlung valleys, this alternative route explores the seldom-seen northeast regions of Yamdrok Tso, the Scorpion Lake. It is an easy walk with little gain or loss in altitude. The journey generally follows the contours of the lake along a good dirt road. Tamalung Village, at the end of this walk, is next to the Friendship Highway.

Day 1 Tangda–Kangmar 4 hrs		Walk along the shore, occasionally going inland, and cross a small pass to a yak herder's stone shelter. Around the corner is Kangma, a short distance off the road. The village of Tsayu is further to the west. It is possible to hire pack horses at Kangma.
Day 2 Gongar	4 1/2 hrs	Walk 1/2 hr to the Tsayu turnoff, but do not take it. Carry on to the turnoff for the Puchu La (4725 m); it is marked by ruined foundations. (The Puchu La trail, a shortcut, joins the jeep track between Tongra Dzong and Gongar.) Gomba is 2 hr after the Tsayu turnoff. Offshore from here is a small island, site of Peto Monastery. Further on (1 hr) is Tongra (59 km from here to the Friendship Highway at Tamalung), a large village with over 100 houses overlooking a bay. The village produces sun-dried bricks. Occasional transport goes between Tongra and Tamalung. Gongar, with three wind mills and a large Chinese compound, is 1 hr from Tongra. The road is good from Tongra onward and replaces the old trail over the Puchu La. The terrain is gradual. ⟾

| Day 3 Shuju | 7 1/2 hrs | From Gongar, walk southwest up an easy pass, then descend to Telong (Tedong), keeping to the north side of the valley. A river is on the left— Tseno and Noori are across from it. From Telong, follow the road along the shore to reach a large inlet; three villages can be seen to the north. To the east, a valley ascends to the Puchu La. Shuju is next. (Gongar to Telong is 4 hr; Telong to Shuju, 3 1/2 hr.) |
| Day 4 Tamalung | 4 hrs | After Shuju, some white Chinese characters can be seen on a hill. Pass through the villages of Tilung, Pema (Dema), Rama, Sa-o, Yoga, Se, Se-u; take occasional shortcuts. Above Yoga is a radar station. Tamalung is a village adjacent to the Friendship Highway. From here hitch back to Lhasa over the Kamba La or go west to Gyantse and Shigatse. (Nakartse is 54 km west of Talmalung; Lhasa is 102 km to the northeast.) |

✤ Day 9 Yamdrok Tso–Touree 5 hr

Follow the short valley immediately south of Tangda which opens onto the flood plain. (Alternatively, go to Shabshi and turn left before the village onto the plain.) Head east, keeping to the north (left) side of the plain. Campsites are available up the slopes, but below, the area has stagnant, muddy pools of water. The path is well-defined along the green valley. Reach a ridge after 1 1/2 km. Here a river enters the valley from the left, then later disappears underground. The broad valley turns south 3 1/2 hr from Tangda and the path crosses a low ridge marked by a cairn. Hagan Gushu is on the right at the head of a smaller valley (4 1/2 hr from Tangda). Further along is Touree (1/2 hr from Hagan Gushu).

✤ Day 10 Touree–Bengar 4 hr

Touree stands at the valley wall left of the path. A river flows from the left just before the village; cross it and continue down the south-trending valley which divides 1/2 km after Touree (the main river flows west). Take the eastern branch, which has good camping spots. After a few km, cross to the left bank and walk east (right) up a shallow and wide valley for 3/4 hr to its apex. Follow the path down to a north-south valley. Cross this to another north–south valley (three such valleys parallel one another; their rivers all flow south). Turn south (right) here to reach a lovely camping area and a deep river. Bengar, 1 hr from the top of the valley, lies below.

✤ Day 11 Bengar–Ache Dzong–Stone Enclosure 3 hr

From Bengar, follow an ill-defined path along the southeast trending valley by staying on the river's left bank. Pass several valleys on the left. Reach Chedaka (1 hr from Bengar) on the valley's right side. Continue until the valley narrows (do not turn up a steep valley at Chedaka), then follow it to Ache Dzong (1 hr from Chedaka). The approach to the impressive fortress, 150 m high on a rocky hill, is from the back of the village. A Gelugpa monastery, on top of the hill, is in excellent condition but the buildings' interiors are largely destroyed. Some old murals remain above the main shrine, and a few monks live here. This community seems to be under Chinese influence; the atmosphere is rather cold and suspicious. Continue along the north (right) bank of the river over flat, boggy land (mosquitoes can be bad). The walking is difficult. Then, 1 hr from Ache Dzong, is a stone enclosure and hut on the valley's left side. Try to hire yaks from here.

✤ DAY 12 STONE ENCLOSURE–CAMP 3 4 HR

After the stone enclosure, cross the river to its left bank and continue east. A long, semi-circular stone wall runs across the width of the valley. Cross back to the right bank and head towards a hill at the valley's center. The path becomes more distinct at the hill's base, while the main valley narrows and disappears to the right. Follow the path upward to Tragtse. Another path, much clearer, joins from the left near the settlement. (Tragtse is 4 hr east of Ache Dzong and 3 hr from the stone enclosure.) Tragtse is a large village with a store and basketball court. Continue through the village taking the left fork twice. Climb steeply out of the settlement for 1/2 km to a rocky, quarry-like summit. Here are good views of the Shanda La (left) and several snow-covered peaks (right). (The main valley heads east, eventually reaching Lake Drigu after 45 km along a good dirt road.) After the summit, drop down to the left side of the valley. Good campsites lie next to small streams 1 hr from the village. Yak caravans amble through this spot in the morning, going to the Shanda La and the Yarlung Valley.

✤ DAY 13 CAMP 3–SHANDA LA–CAMP 4 5 1/2 HR

Cross the valley floor to a gentle gully leading up to the valley wall. The path is clear, although it changes direction a few times—head towards a point left of a large scree peak. Below this peak is the Gonzo (Dromda) La (4 hr from Tragtse). The pass is marked with cairns. Descend to a stony valley coming in from the left. Cross its river to the left side along an obvious path. The valley drops steeply to the right (the river originating from the Gonzo La veers to the right as well). Do not follow this valley. Stay left. The path to the Shanda La can be clearly seen traversing the valley wall on the left of another high scree mountain (Shanda La is 1 hr from Gonzo La). Descend steeply from the pass into a north-trending valley. The path is obvious and follows the right side of the valley wall. (The valley is too steep and rocky for good campsites.) Cross to the river's left bank, then to the right, finally reaching a marginal campsite (1 1/2 hr from Shanda La). Dramai Xian in the Chongye Valley is visible below.

✤ DAY 14 CAMP 4–SEDA TRONZU 3 1/2 HR

Follow the valley's right side along a well-marked path. Drop down steeply and turn east (right) at the bottom of the valley. Dramai Xian, a government town, is next to the jeep track that runs along the south side of the valley. Follow it to Dramai Qu, 20 min further. (Tragtse to Dramai Qu is 15 km; from the Shanda La to the valley bottom is 2 1/2 hr.)

Good camping spots appear after Dramai Qu on the right side of the river. The road crosses to the left bank of the river 1 hr after Dramai Qu, and Seda Tronzu is 2 hr from Dramai Qu. Motor traffic appears from this point on. Hitch a ride to Chongye and the Yarlung Valley or walk for 3 hr (Dramai Qu to Chongye is 25 km).

The Yarlung Valley See page 515 for details on this historic region of Central Tibet.

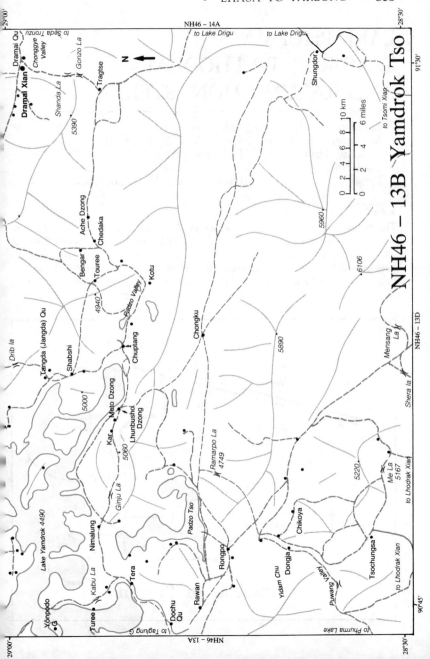

NH46 – 13B Yamdrok Tso

LAKE PHURMA: YAMDROK TO LHODRAK AND RALUNG MONASTERY

Location	South Tibet
Map reference	NH46-9 C, 46-13 A B C D
Trekking Days	14–21 (one-way)
Start–Finish	Tamalung–Ralung
Passes	Turee, Tera, Me, Nga, Tsay, Chanda

OVERVIEW

This trek explores the territories between Lake Yamdrok, Tibet's southern district of Lhodrak, and Lake Phurma (Phurma Yutso). Yamdrok, a beautiful, surrealistic lake has seen numerous visitors on its northern shores. It is an obligatory stop for those plying the Lhasa–Gyantse–Shigatse road. Few, however, have travelled amongst its many arms and bays largely accessible only on foot. One of the gems is Yönpodo, a rare island monastery. This rebuilt center, consecrated to Guru Rinpoche, was visited for the first time by an outsider in 1987.

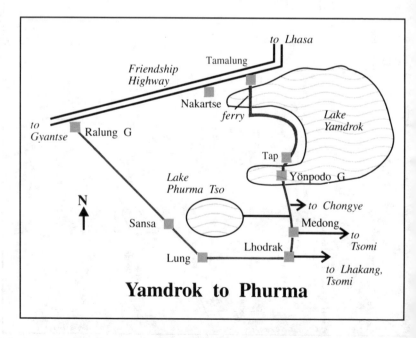

Yamdrok to Phurma

Lhodrak is a rugged region of high snow peaks and isolated hermitages. To its south is Bhutan and the main range of the Himalayas. The district's major town is Lhodrak Xian; nearby are two 8th-C. inscriptions attributed to King Trisong Detsen. This South Tibet enclave is home to the important monasteries of Serkhar Guthok (Milarepa's Nine-story Tower), Lhalung, Guru Lhakhang, and others. Mt Kula Kangri (7538 m), one of the highest peaks in Tibet, casts a long shadow over them all (see Lhodrak, page 701). From Lhodrak the route swings west to a remote, isolated region and skirts the south side of Phurma Yutso (5040 m). The lake is too high for year-round pastoralism and thus has few villages on its shores. Local herders live by the lake for about seven months of the year and then migrate to the lower regions. Even in mid-summer the environs of Phurma Yutso can be freezing.

From the lake the route continues north over the Chanda La Pass to Ralung Monastery, main seat of the Drukpa Kagyü sect that now flourishes in Bhutan. The route from Lhodrak to Ralung follows an old pilgrim trail, today used only by yak herders. Most traffic from Lhodrak to Central Tibet has been diverted to the Manda–Taglung–Nakartse motor road (see page 706).

This trek requires a minimum of 14 days; 18 or 21 days is a more realistic estimate. Few facilities for food or lodging exist except at Lhodrak Xian, and it is necessary to be entirely self-sufficient. Even in mid-summer, expect sub-zero temperatures on the passes and at Phurma Yutso. As in most places in Tibet you should be able to obtain *tsampa* from nomads and villages along the way, but do not count on such availability in a few isolated stretches.

Related sections
Lhodrak, p 681
Yamdrok, p 587
Lhasa to the Yarlung Valley, p 595

The trek
THE TAMALUNG START
Travel by bus or rented vehicle from Lhasa (or Gyantse) to the southern base of the 4794-m Kamba La, the pass on the Friendship Highway between Chusul and Yamdrok Tso. Here is Tamalung, a small village, adjacent to the Lhasa–Shigatse portion of the highway. At this spot, leather coracles make the crossing across Yamdrok Tso every day or so (Rmb 3–5). Be patient; set up camp below Tamalung and wait. In winter, it is possible to simply walk across the lake.

TAMALUNG TO YÖNPODO MONASTERY
After the crossing, arrive at a mountainous peninsula connected to the southern mainland by two narrow strips of land. Head east on a motor road along the jagged lake shore, skirting three coves, to where the lake bends to the south. (5 hr from the ferry landing to here. Villages are sited behind each of these coves; the locals are as much pastoralists as agriculturalists due to the short growing season.) Continue along the lake shore, taking short cuts to circumvent the inlets. Between the second and third cove, after turning southward, is a small pass that cuts across a cape. The view from here is memorable. After the rise come to two villages in a lakeside dale. One is called Yarlung (Yulung), 4 hrs from the southern bend. Beyond the village the motor road leaves the lake. Do not follow it; rather, stay along the lake shore.

If uncertain about the route, ask the locals for the way to Yönpodo Monastery. Stay near the the lake for 2 hr. Go around some inlets to a grassy meadow. Now leave the shore temporarily: a clear trail leads southwestward to a small pass 350 m above the lake (1 hr). The top is marked by cairns and looks down on the southern arm of the lake. Head down to the water (1 hr). Before the lake are houses flanking the trail. On the left is the tiny hamlet of Tap (Tabe), an important way station for travellers. From Tap, a coracle ferry goes to the island monastery of Yönpodo (the timing of the service is haphazard).

> **Yönpodo Monastery** Yönpodo, remote as it is, was attacked by Red Guards during the Cultural Revolution. A kitchen, chapel, and chanting hall have been rebuilt and there are now about 15 monks in residence. The Demikhang shrine (rebuilt) is also here. Yönpodo is consecrated to Guru Rinpoche; his footprint (*shapje*) is enshrined within a stone cubicle by the shore. Guru Rinpoche's hand in *mudra*, with index and little finger extended, is said to be represented by two long spurs that jut into the lake. West of Yönpodo is impressive Mt Nojin Kangtsang (7191 m). Although the monastery is small and only regionally significant, its unique natural setting makes it one of the most enchanting in Central Tibet.

Yönpodo to Lhodrak Xian via the Me La

Two ferries lead to the mainland from Yönpodo island. Wait for the one that departs from the island's eastern side. Ask for the way to the village of Turee. Once on the mainland, follow the shoreline southward. An hour from the ferry landing is a sandy saddle inland from the beach. Cross it to another bay; in the distance is Turee, less than 1 hr from the saddle. A steep, 350-m climb to the top of the range behind Turee leads to a pass with an excellent panorama of the lake. Go down the south side towards an extremity of the lake. At the lake shore, continue to Tera, the route's next settlement (4 1/2 hr from Turee to Tera). From here, walk southwestward, parallel to a range of mountains south of the lake. The range gradually recedes and along the lake is a grassy plain. About 2 hr from Tera are two gaps in the range, both of which are suitable for traversing. Beneath the first gap are ruins. The second one, though not clearly marked, is obvious. Trails lead to both passes (300 m above the lake) and then to the village of Rawan (4 hr from Tera to Rawan). If you miss these passes, continue southwest for several km to a break in the ridge at the villages of Dochu (large) and Sadue. Here the Kurkhyim Chu River, flowing from the Lhodrak–Central Tibet Divide, debouches into Yamdrok Tso. Ask for directions to Rawan.

> **Dochu–Taglung–Nakartse**
> The dirt track from Dochu leads west to Taglung Monastery by following the southern shores of Yamdrok Tso. Dochu to Taglung is two days on foot (11 hr). Taglung to the Friendship Highway takes 3 hr more. Turn right at the highway to reach Nakartse (2 hr).

From Rawan continue upstream (east–southeast). About 1 1/2 hr from Rawan is a pyramidal mountain dedicated to Guru Rinpoche. Its base is marked by hundreds of stone cairns. (Beyond Rawan is Rongpo, at a major trail junction. A track goes east to the southeastern tip of Yamdrok and then connects with the dirt track to the Chongye Valley. About 2 1/2 hr past this mountain the valley turns south. Continue for 1 hr to Dongja. 2 hr south of Dongja is the first side valley to the left. (From this junction, the main valley of the Puwang Chu leads southwest, for 8 hr, to the southeast corner of Phurma Yutso. Follow this side valley southeast to the Me La Pass (5167 m; 4 hr) on a wide trail. The ascent is gradual. Leave Nakartse County and enter Lhodrak after the pass. The first village is Mendong (1 1/2 hr). The narrow valley continues to a convergence with the main Lhodrak Valley (4 hr from Mendong). [Travel downstream after the valley junction to reach historic Serkhar Guthok (Milarepa's tower, see page 698)] Walk upstream (west) on the Lhodrak Valley's south side to Lhodrak Xian (2 hr). Do not linger unneccesarily in this government town.

LHODRAK XIAN TO PHURMA YUTSO

The Lhodrak Valley, trending east–west, parallels the Tibet–Bhutan Himalayas. It is a continuous patchwork of villages and fields. About 4 hr upstream from the town, along the Lhodrak River, is the extensive complex of Lhalung (see page 704), accessible by crossing a bridge. The monastery, one of the most important in South Tibet, stands in the middle of a village. An almost continuous series of villages and cultivated fields connect Lhalung with Manda Qu (Monda), 3 hr upstream on the main road. From Manda, the road crosses the Manda La (north) and goes on to Nakartse; do not follow this road.

Manda is home to the once famous Guru Lhakhang (ruined) (see page 705). West of here, the Lhodrak river's upper reaches are called the Manda Chu. Kula Kangri (7538 m), a major peak of the Eastern Himalayas, is a glittering companion for this stretch of the trek. After Manda, the Manda Chu River departs from its westerly course and swings southward. Leave the river here and follow its northern tributary. Near this confluence is Lung; a motor road connects Monda with Lung, but beyond are only footpaths. Follow the tributary north–northwest all the way to its headwaters and ascend the Nga La (5 hr from Lung). (A major lateral valley along the way opens to the west and leads to the Tsay La; a path from this pass goes west to Nyeru and Kangmar on the Gyantse–Yatung road.) This pass has a double summit, separated by a ridge. Exquisite Phurma Yutso, visible from the top, is a steep, 2–hr descent from the pass. Before the lake are the settlements of Tala, Shasok, Terma, and Jangri. Beware of the dogs. At the lake shore turn left (west). Proceed for 1 hr, then find a low pass that circumvents a spur extending into the lake. (If you miss the pass continue along the shore.) From the rise the western end of Phurma Yutso can be seen.

> ### Phurma Yutso (Flying Turquoise Lake)
>
> According to a legend, this enormous saltwater lake flew here from the oceans at the end of the universe. Guru Rinpoche initially thought the lake embodied evil spirits, but then the waters sent him a distinct message of benevolence and well-being. The guru then blessed it and declared it an important place of pilgrimage. The lake's guardian deity (tsodhak) is Phurma Yutso Drölma, whose image is kept

➡

at the Potala. Senge Gön Monastery (perhaps the unusual maze-like complex sited on a peninsula at the eastern tip of the lake near the Yeh La; see page 706) is one of eight important sites frequented by Guru Rinpoche. Sometimes a heavy mist rises from the center of the lake and spreads outwards. At auspicious moments, a rainbow appears over the water and remains for long periods.

Local inhabitants take horses and perform a springtime (April, May) pilgrimage around the lake. The journey takes 8–9 days. Villages (*pokhang*) and black nomad tents scattered around the lake shore assure shelter and food. Hire horses at Pomo (Phurma), Drong and other villages near the lake's western tip. It is prudent to take supplies for trekkers and horses for several days.

The hike from the pass to the lake's end takes 4 hr. The second half of this section crosses a vast swamp so expect to get confused from time to time following indistinct trails. Walk generally in a westerly direction. A crude bridge spans Phurma Yutso's largest tributary near the western shore. Beyond the bridge is the village of Sansa (also Shanjang, Phurma Jangtang). Bear north from Sansa past the western tip of the lake.

Phurma Yutso to Ralung Monastery

Watch for a valley opening northward from the Phurma Yutso Basin, 3 km west of the lake's northwestern tip. Enter this valley, which soon splits in two. Follow the larger, westerly branch along the valley's watercourse that ascends to the the Chanda La. Just before the pass, the tiny stream bends to the south. Continue westward onto a gravelly incline and follow an obvious route. From the stream to the pass is 15 min (4 hr from Sansa). Descend northwest from the Chanda La along the valley on the other side of the pass. A distinct trail begins after a few hours; follow it to the first cultivated fields (6 hr from the Chanda La). At the farms locate the turnoff to Ralung Monastery. Do not proceed up a valley that merges with the one from the Chanda La. Keep going downstream for a few hundred meters to a place with 'Om Mani Padme Hum' made out of white stones above the trail. Another trail leads to a saddle above this landmark. Follow it over the top and drop down to a basin on the other side. Cross this to join a dirt road leading to Ralung Monastery which stands at the foot of giant Nojin Kangtsang (7191 m). For information on Ralung Monastery, see below. From Ralung, backtrack to the path leading to the saddle. Then just keep on the road for 2 hr to the village of Ralung, located next to the Shigatse–Lhasa highway. From here, hitch east to Lhasa or west to Gyantse and Shigatse.

Ralung Monastery to Lhodrak

It is possible to reach Lhodrak by simply reversing the course of this itinerary. From Ralung near the Friendship Highway (see below), traverse a large tract of idyllic nomad territory en route to Phurma Yutso. Beyond the Nga La are Lung and Manda Qu within the Lhodrak Valley. This route is particularly interesting, since it avoids

➡

entirely the main arteries that connect the Lhodrak district with the Yarlung Valley (page 515) and with Nakartse on the Friendship Highway (page 588).

The above section was contributed by John Bellazza.

RALUNG MONASTERY: A DRUKPA KAGYÜ CENTER

Ralung Monastery (12th C.), a major center of the Drukpa Kagyüs, lies halfway between Gyantse and Nakartse near the Friendship Highway. Its setting, directly beneath the Nojin Kangtsang snow range (7191 m), is gorgeous. A number of excursions start from the monastery. One goes south to Lake Phurma (Pomo) to connect with the Lhodrak pilgrimage (see above); another heads north, via the Nyadong La, to the Rong Chu (Rinpung) Valley, and finally to the small town of Nyemo, on the north bank of the Tsangpo.

Access to Ralung Village

From Gyantse Go east along the Friendship Highway towards Lhasa. The road follows the right bank of the Chure Nyeru Chu to the river's headwaters near Ralung. Ralung Village (4510 m) is 51 km east of Gyantse at road marker 200 km.

From Lhasa Go west along the Friendship Highway to Nakartse (see page 588) next to Yamdrok Tso (154 km). Ralung Village is 49 km west of Nakartse at road marker 200 km. The Karo La (5045 m) is crossed 16 km before the village.

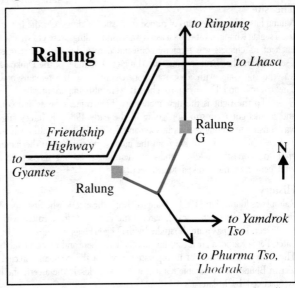

RALUNG VILLAGE TO RALUNG MONASTERY

The monastery is 2 hr by foot east of the village. Along this route are some of Central Tibet's highest snow peaks. To the north, 15 km away and close to the main road, is 7191-m-high

Nojin Kangtsang. Immediately to its east is a 5860-m peak, 7 km south of the Karo La. A farther 7 km west is a 6242-m peak, Mt Jetung Chusang. Its glacier descends close to the road, just a few km east of Nojin Kangtsang's glacier. About 10 km east of Jetung Chusang is Jangsang Lhamo, a handsome, 6324-m peak.

At road marker 200 km of the Friendship Highway, follow a trail south across a bridge to reach Ralung Village. (A cluster of houses to the right, on a small bluff, can be reached by crossing another bridge over the Shak Chu.) From Ralung Village, head southeast along the Shak Chu (Ralung) Valley. After passing a red shrine with prayer flags on the left, reach a flat, open area with cultivated fields on the left. Here the trail splits. One fork continues southeast (right) towards a hill with white Tibetan writing on its slopes. Don't take this. Follow the northeast (left) fork. After a short distance, walk under a distinctive rock outcrop halfway up a brown hill on the right.

Soon Ralung Monastery appears beneath a range of high mountains. The prominent snow peak on its left (northeast) is sacred Nojin Kangtsang. The walk between village and monastery through rolling hills and a prosperous valley is pleasant and easy. Plan to spend some time near the monastery, exploring the high alpine landscape of the Nojin Kangtsang range.

The site

Ralung has two main groups of ruined monastic buildings. On the left is a huge central chapel, the Tsuglag Khang; most of its massive walls and ceilings were blown apart by Chinese dynamite. Each of its chapels was formerly consecrated to a different deity: one was a huge statue of Tsepame; another Drukpa Rinpoche (Lingrepa), founder of the Drukpa sect. The oldest chapel was the gönkhang, with a central chörten containing the remains of Choje Shonnu Senge. The Drölma and Dorje Sempa chapels were also important.

To the right is the new monastery. Government funds and contributions by villagers and monks got reconstruction going in the early 1980s. Ralung's large kumbum (destroyed) was constructed along the Tashi Gomang design similar to, although smaller than, Gyantse's. The chörten ruins are 1/2 km from the monastery. Further up the mountain slopes is another group of monastic buildings and cave hermitages. Ralung has seen a rebirth and is again a vital center of the Drukpa Kagyü sect.

History

Ralung was founded in 1180 by Tsangpa Gyare, the ascetic who first 'opened' the great pilgrimage site of Tsari. His teacher was Lingrepa, the famous siddha credited with founding the Drukpa Kagyü sect. Tsangpa Gyare also studied with Drögon Phagma Drupa, founder of Densatil Monastery. Later, Pema Karpo, a great Kagyüpa master, lived here and wrote a guidebook on the monastery. The Drukpa Kagyü school incorporated much of the Nyingma precepts and is the principal sect in Bhutan. One notable feature: it followed closely the asceticism and solitary meditation as practiced by Milarepa.

According to tradition, Ralung's modest beginnings involved a sacred goat. When it was milked, some of the liquid splashed on a rock. Later, when it dried, the words 'Om Ah Hung' appeared, symbols of the physical, verbal, and spiritual planes of existence. Lingrepa heard of this miracle, recognized it as an important omen (lungtsen) and called the area Ralung, 'the Goat's Omen'. He went into a long retreat in a nearby cave and his disciple eventually built the monastery on this site.

Two excursions from Ralung Monastery

RALUNG TO LAKE PHURMA AND LHODRAK

One trek goes southeast to the western shores of Lake Phurma. From the lake continue southeast to join the Lhodrak pilgrimage at Manda, then carry on to Lhalung Monastery, sacred Lake Pemaling Tso, and Serkhar Guthok (Milarepa's tower, see page 681).

RALUNG TO NYEMO

The second trek goes north over the Nyadong La (5105 m) to the Rong (Rinpung) Valley (see page 841), then continues across the Tsangpo to the Nyemo Valley.

✧ Day 1 Ralung Monastery–Camp 4 1/4 hr

A trail from the monastery heads north away from Ralung Village and hugs the base of the mountain range immediately to the east (right). Reach the Friendship Highway in 2 hr at a point just west of the Karo La. Turn right along the road for 1/4 hr. A trail to the left of the road goes due north up a side valley, following the western flank of Mt Nojin Kangtsang and the left bank of the Namru Chu. Ascend the valley. After 2 hr the gradient increases on the approach (north-northeast) to the Nyadong La. Camp here.

✧ Day 2 Camp–Rampa 7 1/4 hr

Reach the Nyadong La (5105 m) in 3 hr, cross it, and continue north down a narrow valley. Arrive at the Rong Valley in 2 1/2 hr. Turn west (left) to follow the Rong Chu to Rampa (1 3/4 hr). (About 1/4 hr before the village, a trail turns right towards the south bank of the Tsangpo. Ignore this.)

✧ Day 3 Rampa–Yarde Qu 5 3/4 hr

West of Rampa (1/4 hr), a dirt road goes north to the Tsangpo. Follow this up a small valley. In 1 hr, a side trail splits off to the right. Ignore this and continue north. In 1 1/2 hr cross a small ridge, then descend gradually to Yarde Qu (3 hr from the ascent of the ridge).

✧ Day 4 Yarde Qu–Nyemo Xian 5 3/4 hr

Continue north. In 2 hr come to the Tsangpo and meet a dirt track along its south bank. Cross the river by coracle and walk east along the north bank for 1/4 hr to a dirt road that goes north to Nyemo Xian (3 1/2 hr). From Nyemo, one option is to trek north to the important Karmapa monastery of Tsurphu (see page 671). The other is to head east along the north shore of the Tsangpo to reach the Chusul bridge after 63 km, a two-day walk. Lhasa is a further 60 km to the north on a paved road.

MANASAROVAR: RITUAL CIRCUMAMBULATION OF MT KAILASH'S HOLY LAKE

Location	Kailash region, West Tibet
Map reference	NH44-7 A
Trekking days	4 (circuit)
Start–Finish	Tseti–Tseti
Passes	None

OVERVIEW

Sacred Lake Manasarovar (4588 m) is located in West Tibet between Mt Kailash (6714 m) and the Gurla Mandhata Range (Memo Nani, 7694 m). For Hindus, Manasarovar floats beneath the shadow of holy Kailash (see page 273) as the lake formed in the mind of God. It was created to show the omnipotence of Brahma's mind, *manas*. Tibetans know it as Mapham Tso, 'the Unconquerable Lake'. In any language, this is the holiest, most famous lake in Asia. The Hindu poet, Kalidasa, wrote in the 3rd C.:

> When the earth of Manasarovar touches anyone's body or when anyone bathes therein, he shall go to the paradise of Brahma, and who drinks its water shall go to the heaven of Shiva and shall be released from the sins of 100 births. Even the beast that bears the name of Manasarovar shall go to the paradise of Brahma. Its waters are like pearls.

West of Manasarovar is Lake Raksas Tal (Langak Tso), named after the flesh-eating demons of Hindu mythology believed to lurk within its waters. A representation of dark, malevolent forces, this lake is generally shunned by pilgrims. In contrast to the eight monasteries that dotted the shores of Manasarovar, Raksas has only one temple, Tsegye. According to legend, the water of this smaller lake was poisonous. This condition changed when a gold fish from Manasarovar tunneled through a narrow isthmus to let sacred water flow into Lake Raksas Tal, thus neutralizing the poison. The channel created is known as Ganga Chu, and Tibetans carefully watch its level to divine the state of the country. High water augurs well for Tibet and its citizens. During much of this century, the salt-encrusted channel was virtually dry and led explorers like Sven Hedin to doubt its existence. Only in the last few years has water flowed between the two lakes again; some say this coincides with the resurgence of religious practice in Tibet.

The eight monasteries of Manasarovar were destroyed during the Cultural Revolution but recently most have been rebuilt. With snow mountains and turquoise lakes as a backdrop, the setting of these shrines is otherworldly. The monastery of Gossul was visited by Hedin in 1907–8 and he wrote, 'Did fate compel me to pass my life in a monastery in Tibet, I would without hesitation choose Gossul Gompa.' The monasteries once again provide spiritual and physical refuges for pilgrims who perform the 90-km circumambulation of the lake. Most Tibetans, however, simply opt for an offering by the lake's northwestern shore and forego the full circuit.

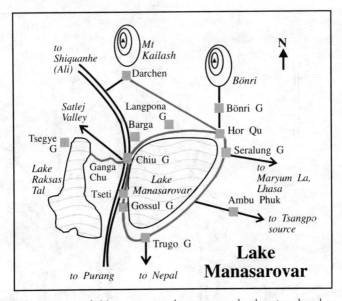

The best time to circle Manasarovar is in late autumn and early spring when the streams and rivers flowing into the lake are low (some Tibetans actually prefer to come in winter when everything is frozen, including the lake). It is then possible to walk very near the shoreline. During most of the year, be prepared to wade across small and large streams.

The spectacular environment of Manasarovar, sandwiched between two high snow ranges, is one of the most dramatic in Tibet. To the north is Kang Tise, the crescent-shaped mountain range that sweeps from West to Central Tibet. Within Mt Kailash (6714 m), its crowning jewel, is the mythical palace of Demchok, the powerful tutelary deity, and his consort, Dorje Phagmo. The two together symbolize compassion and wisdom, making Kailash and Manasarovar the perfect complement: father and mother of the earth.To the south is the Gurla Mandhata Range and Memo Nani (7694 m), the third highest mountain entirely within Tibet's borders (after Shishapangma, 8012 m, and Namche Barwa, 7756 m). Known also as Memo Namgyal ('Son of Victory'), it is considered the abode of Lhamo Yangchen, a female divinity particularly propitiated by the area's farmers.

The Manasarovar *khora* is intimately linked to the Mt Kailash pilgrimage; the two chapters should be read together. The author wishes to thank John Bellazza for his contributions to the trail notes.

Related sections

West Tibet, p 943
Kailash, p 273
Tholing, p 425
Tsaparang, p 430

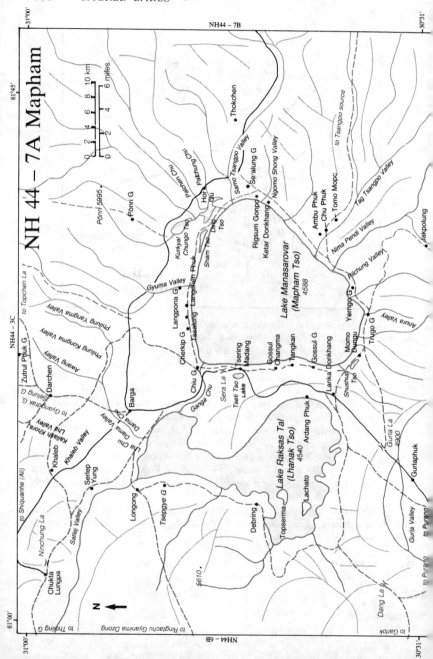

NH 44 – 7A Mapham

Access

From Darchen (see page 275, 957) at the base of Mt Kailash, a dirt road leads south to Barga to join the main Shiquanhe (Ali)–Purang Road. Follow it to Lake Manasarovar's western shore and Chiu Monastery. After the lake, this road continues south to Purang (Taklakot) and the western frontier of Nepal (Barga–Purang is 104 km). Start the sacred circuit around Manasarovar from either: (a) Chiu Monastery or the Tseti Guest House; or (b) Hor Qu.

FROM CHIU MONASTERY OR
TSETI GUEST HOUSE

When hitching a ride from Mt Kailash to Lake Manasarovar on a truck bound for Purang, get off at Chiu Monastery or the Tseti Guest House. The former is above the Ganga Chu water course, 32 km from Darchen and 16 km from the small settlement of Barga. It is the only significant river (30 m wide) to be forded. To begin the *khora* here, remain north of the Ganga Chu. Alight at the ford, and walk east along the river for nearly 1 km to the lakeshore below Chiu, sited on a craggy hill. From here, keep the water to the right and walk northeast. (Sleep at the monastery, or camp next to a hot spring by the river or a cave below the monastery.) The second staging post is 5 km south of the Ganga Chu, a convenient place to be dropped off by truck. This area, easy to recognize because the lake is plainly visible 300m from the road, is called Tsering Madang. The Tseti Guest House (1 1/2-hr walk from Chiu Monastery) is here.

TSETI GUEST HOUSE

The guest house compound has five rooms, each with four beds. There are no mattresses and practically no food (Rmb 3 per bed). The Tibetan caretaker will make fire and bring hot water; he reportedly has circled Mt Kailash and the lake more than 100 times. The main road to Purang and Barga is 15 min from the guest house.

FROM HOR QU (HORER)

This is the traditional starting point for the circumambulation of the lake. Hor Qu is a small village near the lake's northeast corner, 28 km east of Barga along the Kailash–Zhongba–Lhatse route (Kailash South Route; see page 945). Nearby is the sacred Bönpo mountain of Pönri (5995 m). According to legend, it was bequeathed by Milarepa to his defeated Bön enemy, Naro Bönchung, as a consolation prize. Barga, a village of compounds and a military post, is at a junction of roads; the southern branch leads to Purang and Shiquanhe.

Hor Qu has rooms (Rmb 5 per bed) and a movie theater. Horses and yaks are available, for Rmb 20–30 per day (for horse and handler). Reaching Hor Qu by truck from Darchen is relatively easy during the peak pilgrim months. An Indian pilgrim bus leaves Darchen once every four days during the summer (Rmb 10). When starting the *khora* from Hor Qu, do not be misled by a lake to the south. This is not Lake Manasarovar. Walk southwest and keep this small lake to the right. On reaching Manasarovar's northeast corner, look out for 'Karmapa's stones'. From here, head south along the lakeshore to Seralung Monastery (3 hr).

Pönri Monastery Hor Qu is a convenient staging point to visit Pönri (Langpöna Monastery is also close by). Horses can be hired to do the round trip. It takes 3–4 hr to reach the destroyed monastery, high up a valley at the base of the Pönri peak (5960 m). The site, 300 m above the lake, had 10–12 monks before the Cultural Revolution. This location, at 4872 m, has the best views of Manasarovar and Raksas Tal.

Time Chart

Day	Place
1	Tseti–Langpöna
2	Seralung
3	Trugo
4	Tseti

Trail Notes
✦ DAY 1 TSETI–LANGPÖNA

The following description of the clockwise pilgrimage route around Lake Manasarovar starts from the Tseti Guest House. For the first few km, head north along the lake's western shore. A rocky headland then forces the trail 100 m above the water; the low Sera La is crossed. A place of prostrations (*chaktsal gang*) is here, opposite Seralung Monastery at the lake's eastern extreme. After rounding a reddish ridge, the trail gradually descends to the Ganga Chu and Chiu Monastery, at the lake's northwest corner. En route, pass the exhausted gold field of Serka Khira.

Chiu (Bird) Monastery

The monastery, with three *chörtens*, is marvelously situated on top of a low, craggy cliff overlooking the lake. It was a branch of Mt Kailash's Drira Phuk Monastery (page 284), itself under Dingboche Monastery (page 505) near the Yarlung Valley. The Ganga Chu, marked by prayer flags, is near the bottom of the cliff, and a village of compounds and houses is across the water channel. A storehouse in the village sells tinned food, beer, sweets, and assorted goods. The hot spring on the other side has a stone compound enclosing a pool with very hot water. Walk up to the monastery (1/4 hr). The main chapel, at the second level of the small complex, is only 8 m by 10 m. A new stucco Guru Rinpoche statue is the only large statue of note, the rest being small. The topmost room of the monastery is the *gönkhang*. A small Guru Rinpoche cave, most sacred part of the complex, is below the main chapel and houses a statue of the Indian master. The walls are covered in cloth. According to local tradition, the guru spent the last seven days of his life here. Walk to the crest of the hill to get bearings of the surroundings.

The trail beyond the Ganga Chu inlet climbs again to avoid the headlands that drop to the lake (it is also possible to follow a narrow trail along the shoreline). The cliffs here are dotted with caves dug out by Hindu and Buddhist hermits over the centuries. Stay above the lakeshore, where the route is marked by stone cairns. The trail remains on the headlands for 5 km and is quite level. Mt Kailash is a constant companion during this stretch. The trail then descends to a short, open valley bordering the lake. Here, at the site of Cherkip Monastery on a terrace, is a *chörten* and *mani* wall. The ruined center, consecrated to Guru Rinpoche, is at the water's edge at the mouth of a dry stream. It was the smallest of the eight lakeside monasteries. Near here in the hills are disused meditation caves with a warm southern exposure.

Finding the trail from here is a bit tricky. From the Cherkip Valley, the trail climbs back onto the headlands. (It is also possible to follow the lake shore during the low-water season (winter, spring); the strip of land by the water is very narrow and steep cliffs drop to the lake's edge.) Pass Tasalung, a *mani* wall at the mouth of the valley, and the retreat cave of Langchen Phuk, near the shore. Small trails lead north up the headlands back to the main pilgrim path at Langpöna Monastery. To locate this trail, keep in mind that it parallels the lake on top of the ridge. After reaching a high point, descend gradually to Langpöna Monastery (5 km from Cherkip). The monastery, consecrated to Sakyamuni, is on the right (west) bank of the Gyamo Chu and was under the control of Hemis Monastery of Ladakh. The site is surrounded by pastures where nomads from Hor Qu and Purang graze their animals in winter.

✤ DAY 2 LANGPÖNA–SERALUNG

After Langpöna, do not return to the lake shore but rather cut inland; a broad plain extends north to the Kailash range. Look out for three small lakes 12 km east of the monastery. Near Manasarovar's shore, Sham Tso is the most westerly. Lake Kurkyal Chungo is northeast of Sham and Ding Tso is due south. Stay to the north of these lakes. The trail is clear, flat, and easy from Langpöna to the east side of Manasarovar. It would be attractive to stick to the lake shore east of the monastery, but such a route only leads to a river, the outlet of the waters of the last two lakes. It empties into Manasarovar via the Gugta River, which is quite difficult to ford, especially in the summer. Following the lake shore might well require backtracking 20 km.

Lake Kurkyal Chungo According to tradition, this lake represents the head of Manasarovar and is the site where *dakinis* take their ritual baths. Some consider the *khora* of Manasarovar to be incomplete unless this lake is also circumambulated.

Ding Tso About 0.5 km east of the lake's eastern tip is a cairn (*lapcha*) of *mani* stones on the banks of the Palchung Chu, a point where pilgrims cross directly from the Kailash *khora* (from Zutrul Phuk Monastery) to the Manasarovar *khora*. They usually leave Zutrul Phuk late in the morning to arrive at Kyo, a campground with pastures, in the evening. Seralung Monastery is reached the next day.

Manasarovar's east side is embraced by a range of hills that rise from its edge. A trail along the shore fords the Samo Tsangpo shortly after rounding the lake's northeastern corner. North of the river entrance is an inlet surrounded by swamps and pastures. Between the lake and the inlet is a narrow neck of land with a 3-m wall of gravel. The inlet and swamps are fed by water from the Palchen and Palchung valleys. About 7 km south of the Samo Tsangpo is Seralung Monastery, well-hidden at the mouth of a side valley.

Seralung (Hailstone Valley) Monastery

This simple, rebuilt (1984) Drigung Kagyü monastery is on the right side of a side valley next to a spring. It has a chapel flanked by a kitchen and the lama's quarters. The original, up the valley to the east, was destroyed in the Cultural Revolution. Guru Rinpoche and Sakyamuni are the main images and colorful masks adorn the shrine. Seralung, together with Silung and Gyangtrak (both on Mt Kailash), were branches of the Drigungtil Monastery (page 553) east of Lhasa.

Along the lake shore, west of the monastery, is a ruined pilgrims' shelter (*dharamsala*), with *mani* walls, called Söra Drönkhang. About 1.5 km south of this, also next to the lake, is a sacred site consisting of three hills known as Rigsum Gönpo. They represent the deities, Chana Dorje, Chenresi and Jampelyang. At the lake, look for a narrow strip of violet sand called Chema Ne Nga, found in thin layers over the white sand. Supposedly, grains of five different colors exist: yellow, white, green, red and black. Tibetans believe they represent gold, silver, turquoise, coral, and iron. They eat a few grains as *prasad*, relics from a sacred place that impart blessings and help cure ailments. Also, growing wild in the area are medicinal and fragrant herbs greatly prized by pilgrims. The lake water is thought to be imbued with the most potent curative properties of all.

✤ Day 3 Seralung–Trugo

Look carefully for the trail a few km south of Seralung. The hills bordering the lake recede and a plain develops southeast of the lake. Traverse it and move inland for about 1/2 km; ford a stream and cross a wood bridge festooned with prayer flags over the Tag Tsangpo.

Excursion to Ambu Phuk A nice side trip follows the Tag Tsangpo southeast to Ambu Phuk, a site on the right (east) bank. Across the river, on the left, are several hot springs at Nyomba Chutsen ('Mad Hot Springs'). Some are also on the right bank. Large pools and spouting geysers have temperatures that vary from lukewarm to boiling. Several big caves at Ambu Phuk are part of an ancient monastery complex (ruined) consecrated to Guru Rinpoche. Farther up the Tag Tsangpo is a site called Tomo Mopo with more hotsprings and geysers (1 km).

Beyond the bridge, the trail returns to the lake's southern portion 18 km past Seralung. About 7 km along the southern lake shore, look for the ruins of Ningo (Yerngo) Monastery (destroyed). Atisha visited this monastery, consecrated to Guru Rinpoche, en route from India to Tibet.

Before it, on top of a hill, is a *chaktsal gang* (prostrations site) and a large *mani* wall. The monastery site, near water, is a good place to camp; the Richung River flows into the lake east of here. 4 km further is Trugo (Thugolho), an active monastery. Seralung to Trugo takes 7 hr. Most Tibetan pilgrims walk from Hor Qu to Trugo in one long day. Several *mani* walls are passed between Yerngo and Trugo.

Trugo (Trugolho) Monastery

The name of this monastery is the Head-washing South Gate Monastery; it was rebuilt in 1984. A large center next to the lake, it is the most important of the eight Manasarovar monasteries. Hindus at this auspicious site perform their ablutions by immersing themselves totally in the icy water. Most Tibetan pilgrims simply splash water on their heads and drink the water. Both Atisha and Ra Lotsawa spent time here. The monastery's principal image is Dorje Chang (Vajradhara), the tantric manifestation of Sakyamuni and the primordial Buddha of the Kagyüpa. Trugo and Gossul were branches of the ruined Simbiling Monastery (ruined) of Purang. In front of the complex, along the lake shore, is a long row of *mani* stones each carved with a *mantra* and parts of sacred texts. The site affords a grand view of Lake Manasarovar and Mt Kailash. A government guest house with 10 rooms stands behind the monastery. There are no beds—sleep on the floor. The monastery consists of a pair of two-story buildings left and right of the entrance. Pass an interior courtyard to reach the main one-story *lhakhang* straight ahead. Most of the decorations and furnishings are new, but nevertheless a warm, cosy atmosphere prevails. Recent murals include one of Mt Kailash.

An old lama and a few monks live here. A certain amount of trading between Tibetans from the north and Nepalese from West Nepal goes on within the grounds. Wool and salt are purchased by the latter, then shipped to Darchula (West Nepal) and Kathmandu. Nepalese Hindus come to the lake on pilgrimage but seldom continue to Kailash. Trugo is the only one of the five rebuilt monasteries sited on the lake shore; the others are set into hillsides. The Gurla Mandhata massif, rising to the south, protects the monastery from the furious storms that buffet the lake from time to time.

About 1 km west of Trugo, the Anura Chu flows into the lake from the south. In early summer, there are swarms of black insects here on the southern shore. They do not bite but are a nuisance and it is necessary to cover the nose and mouth.

✤ Day 4 Trugo–Tseti

From Trugo, there is a crude motor road that connects with the Purang–Darchen–Shiquanhe (Ali) road. A pilgrim trail parallels the lake 100 m away. Much of the southern shore is swampy and the trail skirts the wettest areas. This tract, nesting place for wild geese, is also the haunt of wild ducks, yellow-billed swans and cranes. The best time to visit this sanctuary is in August and September.

Around Manasarovar's southwest corner is Shushup Tso, a narrow body of water separated from the main lake by a 20-m strip of shingle. No detour is required as Shushup Tso has no outlet. A *chaktsal gang* is at the south tip of the small lake and another at nearby Momo Dungu, a giant pile of strange rocks. Tibetans offer *chang* and *khatas* to commemorate a lama who supposedly transformed cakes of brown sugar into these unusual rocks. *Shushup* means 'bow'; the small lake is bow-shaped and runs almost parallel to the main shore. Proceed between the lakes. After Shushup Tso, hike 7 km to Gossul Monastery along the shore. Nearby are several shallow blackened caves within tall cliffs.

> **Gossul Monastery** Sited on a prominence, the monastery is reached by foot trails from the lake. A ritual circuit surrounds the rebuilt monastery and retreat caves still used by monks. Bönpo pilgrims stay at a grotto at the bottom of the cliff. A courtyard is in front of the entrance and the lama's room is to the left. A large chapel at the rear has new statues of Thuje Chenpo (Thousand-armed Chenresi). Tremendous views of the lake below can be had from a window on the right. Beyond the altar, a cloth hides the entrance to an inner meditation cave consecrated to Gombo Sedhup. Overlooking the monastery and two chörtens is a hillock. On the top are four poles planted in a square. In the middle is a tall trident draped with prayer flags, a ritual Bönpo implement. Indian pilgrims begin their circuit of the lake at Gossul.

South of the monastery, a trail follows a ravine and climbs rounded, steep hills to reach the highest point between Raksas Tal and Manasarovar. This site, 285 m above the the latter, has an outstanding view of the entire region. It is a 6-km walk from Gossul Monastery to the Tseti Guest House at Tsering Madang. Simply follow the edge of the lake. From Trugo to Lake Tseti is one long day. From the Tseti Guest House to the Chiu Monastery is another 2 hr.

Raksas Tal (Langak Tso)

The 130-km circumference of the lake takes six days to negotiate. There are two islands: Topserma and Lachato. Small Lachato, in the south, close to a peninsula, is rocky and hilly with a few stone shelters for egg collectors from Kardung (south of the lake). They usually come in the first week of April, when the lake is still frozen, and during two weeks they manage to collect between them 2,000–4,000 large eggs of the *nyangba* swan. Topserma is the larger island to the west, near the tiny settlement of Debring.

LHAMO LATSO:
A PILGRIMAGE TO TIBET'S
PREMIER ORACLE LAKE
VIA SAMYE MONASTERY

Location	Southeast of Lhasa
Map reference	NH46-9 B D, 46-10 C D
Trekking days	16 (one-way)
Start–Finish	Lhasa–Tsethang
Passes	Gökar, Lung

OVERVIEW

This pilgrimage to Samye Monastery and Lhamo Latso is richly varied and has much to offer: high snow mountains, a magnificent monastery, seldom visited cave hermitages, nomads and their black-tent culture, and a sacred 'oracle lake'. The itinerary starts at Dechen, a small town only 21 km from Lhasa, so there are no messy transport problems. Along the route, stay in monasteries and village houses. At higher elevations, the black yak-wool tents of nomads

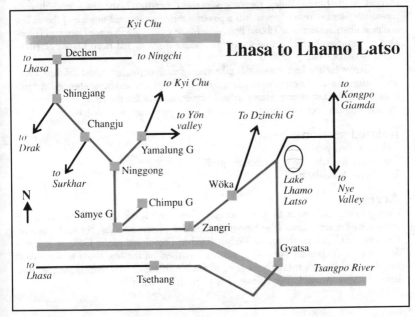

make welcome and surprisingly cosy shelters. Small jewel-like retreats, such as Chölung and Yamalung, are especially good places to spend the night. They are friendlier than the bigger monasteries and give an insight into Tibetan religious life in isolated areas.

The terrain of the pilgrimage varies from easy to moderately difficult and involves crossing two high passes. These pose no special difficulties unless there is heavy snow. Most of the walking takes place along river valleys with gentle gradients. After crossing Mt Yartö Drak reach Samye, the so-called First Monastery of Tibet. Beyond its celebrated *mandalic* complex, the trail follows the flat Tsangpo Valley with its sand dunes and myriad freshwater pools (excellent for swimming). Small, untouched villages and monasteries dot the way to the Yulung Chu Valley. Near its head, close to high snowcapped peaks, are the delightful nomad settlements of Shindu and Amando. Being at the radiant oracle lake of Lhamo Latso is a high point of this journey. It is the foremost 'vision' lake in Tibet and sitting Dalai Lamas were obligated to come here at least once in their lifetimes. In nearby valleys are the cloistered monasteries of Dzinchi, Chökorgye, Dakpo Tratsang, and Daglha Gampo. The last is a particularly hallowed pilgrimage center. Hermits regularly spend long periods in retreat, staying in the many meditation caves that dot the top of a high ridge. The return leg of the Lhamo Latso pilgrimage follows the beautiful wooded valley of Gyal Metoktang (Valley of Flowers), with its crystal clear river and superb campsites, back to the Yarlung Tsangpo River.

Samye on the Tsangpo, is perhaps the most important and ancient monastery in Tibet. Founded in the 8th C., it is noted for its expansive, Indian-inspired architecture (see page 300). Nearby is Samye Chimpu, a remarkable monastic cave complex, high in the mountains overlooking the Tsangpo Valley. Yamalung is another cave retreat in the Samye area. Although considerably smaller than Chimpu, it is a powerful shrine consecrated to some of the earliest and most illustrious names in Tibetan Buddhism. In the vicinity are Drakmar Drinzang (Trisong Detsen's birthplace), Surkhar (the site of five ancient *chörtens*), and Hepo Ri, one of Tibet's sacred mountains (see page 629).

Except for the high passes, this pilgrimage goes through areas noted for their warm, dry climate. Rain can be expected in July and August, less in June and September, and virtually none during the rest of year. Heavy snow, however, can blanket the passes from December through February. For nine months of the year this pilgrimage is a good bet.

Related sections
Yarlung Valley, p 515
East of the Kyi Chu–Tsangpo Junction, p 470
The Samye Mandala, p 295

Access
Getting to the trailhead at Dechen is an easy 45-minute bus ride (21 km) from the Lhasa city bus station across from Tibet University. (Ganden Monastery is just beyond Dechen on the same road.) Ask for the bus to Dechen (Dechen Dzong) and Medro Gongkar; it leaves daily at 0830. Tickets are not sold in advance; get them on the bus. If you miss the 0830 bus, there are other short-haul buses going to Dechen during the day. Arrive early, as these buses are quite crowded. The alternative is to hitch or take a taxi.

Dechen A small town on the south bank of the Kyi Chu (Lhasa) River, Dechen was once the site of a powerful fortress (its ruins can be seen on top of a hill, to the left, as you enter town.) Nearby is a small monastery built by Kedrub Je, Tsong Khapa's disciple, and dedicated to Jampa. In Dechen, on the right side of the road when coming from Lhasa, is a two-story white building (the new road market 4612 is further along) where milk tea and noodle soup (*thukpa*) are available. The track to Gökar La starts from the right side of this building.

Time Chart

Day	Place	Hours
1	Dechen–Changju	4
2	Base of Gökar La	7
3	Three valleys	6
4	Samye Monastery	4 1/2
5	Gerpa Ferry	7
6	Ngari Tratsang	7
7	Zangri Karmar	8
8	Chölung Monastery	6 1/2
9	Nomad camp	4 1/2
10	Amando	7
11	Chökorgye	6 1/2
12	Lake Lhamo Latso;	4
	return to Chökorgye	3
13	Tseju Village	5
14	Gyatsa Qu	6
15	Dakpo Tratsang	2 1/2
16	Tsethang or Lhasa	hitch

DECHEN TO SAMYE

Trail Notes
✤ DAY 1 DECHEN–CHANGJU NOMAD CAMP 4 HR
From Dechen follow a straight, tree-lined path due north. Pass the handsome Ninga Dzong to the right. At the junction of two valleys is Shingjang Commune, where it is possible to rent horses or donkeys.

> **Shingjang to Drakyul** The right branch of the junction leads to the Drakyul Valley, with its fabulous Guru Rinpoche cave system, via a 5250 m pass. Three days

Follow the left valley, along a well-used trail, for 4 hrs to Changju, a grassy campsite with nomad tents and stone buildings. Tea, cheese (*chura*), and potatoes are available. There are many grazing yaks in the area. Be careful of mastiffs at night.

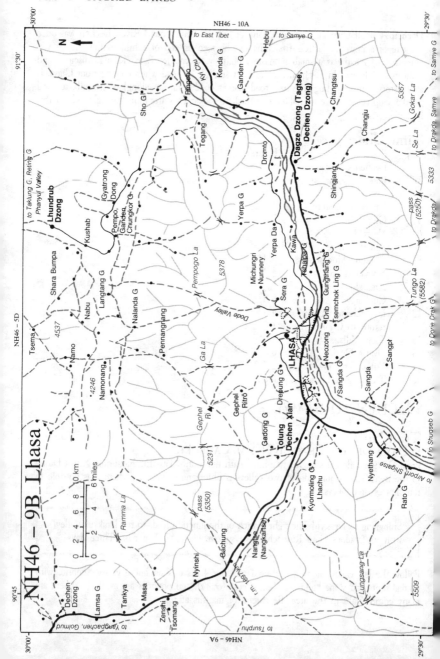

✤ DAY 2 CHANGJU–BASE OF GÖKAR LA 7 HR

The main valley forks again at Changju.

> **Changju to Surkhar Do** The right branch goes due south over the Se La (5150 m) to Surkhar Valley and Surkhar Do's five historical *chörtens*. Three days.

Wade across the river left of the nomad camp where the current is weakest. Follow the left valley along the west bank of the river. The trail is obvious and the gradient gentle. After 5 hr the valley divides again. Turn to the right. The climb now becomes more strenuous as the path zigzags to the foot of the pass (2 hr). The Gökar La is difficult to discern from its base; a solid wall of peaks rises up from here. A good camp site for the night is right (left bank) of the small river. This area below the pass is always cold; it is important to have a good sleeping bag and perhaps a tent.

✤ DAY 3 BASE OF GÖKAR LA–THREE VALLEYS 6 HR

The path from camp, bearing to the right, is a series of steep switchbacks. Altitude makes this a strenuous 2-hr walk to the top. At the pass, prayer flags decorating a stone mound (*lhatse*) mark the watershed between the Lhasa and Yarlung Tsangpo rivers. The famed translator, Vairocana, was so impressed by the height of the pass he named it Gökar, 'White Eagle', implying that even eagles struggle to cross it. The expansive view reveals the Samye Valley directly ahead. A conspicuous peak to the north belongs to the great Nyenchen Tanglha Range. To the southeast is sacred Mt Yala Shampo at the head of the Yarlung Valley.

The route of descent is not obvious. To locate the path, bear left from the *lhatse*. Walk down for 2 hr along an ancient, wide stairway constructed of large stones, to a stone bridge. These stone stairs are unusual. Unlike the Nepalese, Tibetans rarely pave mountain paths with stones. This was done for the comfort and security of high officials commuting between Samye and Lhasa in the old days. This trail was also an important trade route between the Tsangpo and Lhasa river valleys. Follow the narrowing valley. After 2 hr, three valleys converge at an idyllic place. Cross two bridges here, very close to each other, then bear left, continuing with the river on your left. Good campsites pepper this entire area, but some spots can be swampy in the summer.

✤ DAY 4 THREE VALLEYS–SAMYE MONASTERY 4 1/2 HR

Reach a single house on the left after one hour. Barley and potatoes are grown here. The village of Ninggong, 1/2 hr further along, is the point of departure for the famed hermitage of Yamalung.

Yamalung Hermitage

Classified as one of Guru Rinpoche's Eight Supreme Sanctuaries, Yamalung is an obligatory stop for Tibetan pilgrims. From Ninggong follow a trail skirting the western perimeter of a ridge that stands at the junction of the Gökar La and the Ganden Monastery valleys (see the Ganden–Samye trek, page 314). Walk up the latter; your route south from the pass now tracks to the northeast. Cross a bridge to follow the east (left) bank of the river in 1/4 hr. Cross back to the right by means of a small makeshift bridge festooned with prayer flags to the base of a cliff (1/2 hr from Ninggong). The hermitage of Yamalung, reached in another hour, is perched high up among cliffs above the river. Look out for the mythical tent of King Gesar (see below) near the base of the cliffs.

The trail to the right goes up the steep mountain slopes to first a cemetery (*durtrö*) on top of a rock, then to Guru Rinpoche's Long Life Water (*tshechu*), a small trickle issuing from a rock. Spring water collected here is valued highly by the pilgrims. Nearby is a tree with many prayer flags. This represents the soul-tree (*lhashing*) of Guru Rinpoche to some pilgrims. Others claim the tree materialized when he stuck his trident into the ground. Continue up the ridge to reach the Bardo Trang, a tunnel formed by two rocks. Pilgrims crawl through the narrow space to test their preparedness for passing the after-death Bardo state. If they fail here they need to acquire more merit in this life. The cave hermitage (Guru Drubphuk) of Guru Rinpoche is further up the slopes, and in the vicinity ruins of meditation cells.

The Yamalung cave chapel is a walled-in space under a rock overhang. Outside, above the entrance, is the guru's handprint. Within the cavity, on the left, is an outcrop with a number of *rangjung* prints, including those of Guru Rinpoche, Karmapa, Yeshe Tsogyal, Drölma, and Phurpa, an important Nyingmapa divinity. The right wall has the *rangjung mantra* of 'Om Ah Hum', created by the guru's finger. On the altar are religious implements and a new statue of Guru Rinpoche. Further up the slopes is the meditation cave (Bairo Phuk) used by Vairocana.

History Guru Rinpoche, the most important figure of the Nyingmapa sect of Tibetan Buddhism, supposedly concealed hidden treasures (*terma*) in the caves here. Vairocana of Nyemo, the chief Tibetan disciple of Guru Rinpoche and one of the first seven monks to be ordained in Tibet, meditated at Yamalung for three years. In the 17th C., Terdak Lingpa, an incarnation of Vairocana and founder of Mindroling Monastery, discovered the hidden text *Rigdzin Tuktik* here.

Luba Thingshok Gung Gu ('White Tent with Nine Windows') An unusual monument lies at the base of the cliffs of Yamalung near the makeshift bridge. It is a low-profiled structure (low walls formed of stones and earth) which represents King Ling Gesar's mythical nine-windowed tent. It commemorates the meeting place of Gesar and Guru Rinpoche. The outlines delineate the entrance, the anchor ropes, the windows, and other elements of the palatial quarters used by the epic king while traveling. The structure blends imperceptibly with its surroundings and is easily overlooked.

After returning to Ninggong, follow the level, well-defined trail to the next village (1/2 hr). To the right of the path are ridges that make up the west wall of the Samye Valley. Continue for another 1/4 hr, then take the right fork to Pisay (1 hr from Ninggong). 1/4 hr further is Drakmar Drinzang, a site of ruins on the right.

DRAKMAR DRINZANG: THE PALACE OF TRISONG DETSEN

This ancient palace, located on a small hill close by the village of Sangpu Shang,

➥

was built during the early 8th C. and became a residence of King Tride Tsugtsen and his wife, Queen Jincheng. Their son, Trisong Detsen, was born here. Guru Rinpoche stayed in the palace on arrival from Uddiyana and plans for Samye Monastery were drawn up at this spot. Drakmar Drinzang (destroyed) was surprisingly small for a palace, only about 200 sq m. The walls, neatly constructed of large stone pieces interspersed with thin stone slabs, reflected the typical techniques of early Tibetan construction. To the south are extensive ruins. According to the locals, these were once buildings contemporaneous with the palace, perhaps additional housing for the king and his family.

Follow the trail from Drakmar Drinzang to Yugar (1/2 hr), a village on the left, and soon the gilded roofs of Samye appear. A tree-lined trail leads to the monastery complex (1 1/4 hrs).

Samye Monastery Samye is one of the most important monasteries in Tibet. For a description, see The Samye Mandala, page 295.

Environs of Samye
HEPO RI

Hepo Ri is one of the four sacred mountains of Central Tibet. The others are Lhasa Chakpo Ri, Gongkar Chuwo Ri, and Tsethang Gönpo Ri. Located a short distance east of Samye, the top of Hepo Ri takes about one hour of easy walking from the monastery to reach. It has a north–south length of about 1 km and a height of only 60 m. The name *Hepo* means 'panting' in Tibetan and implies that some effort is needed to reach the top. In the 8th C., Trisong Detsen and Guru Rinpoche ascended Hepo Ri to scout out an appropriate site for Samye. Three early translators of Buddhist scriptures had their remains enshrined within burial *chörtens*.

Kawa Paltsek Chörten Kawa Paltsek was one of the three principal translators during King Trisong Detsen's reign. As a small boy he was sent to India to study Sanskrit and Buddhism. His *chörten*, located at the north end of the hill, is nearly 11 m high and has a large stone base. This monument, with five levels, was damaged during the Cultural Revolution and the top was lopped off. Locals recovered a gold-painted box containing the ashes of the translator, but this has since disappeared.

Chögro Lugyaltsen Chörten This native of the Yarlung area helped translate a number of important works. His *chörten* stands at the south end of Hepo Ri.

Yong Yashede Chörten Yong Yashede was born in Tölung Dechen, west of Lhasa.

➠

His family descended from Yong Zhungza, one of Songtsen Gampo's five queens and his *chörten*, the largest of the three, sits at the extreme south end of the ridge. Its sides are over 16 m long and its height 11 m. Built of earth, the structure is reinforced by an outer sheath of stones.

Santarakshita Chörten The Indian teacher who designed Samye and invited Guru Rinpoche to Tibet also had his *chörten* located on the east slopes of Hepo Ri.

HEPO RI LHAKHANG

This small, restored chapel on top of the hill was built in ancient times to commemorate the principal architects of Samye: Trisong Detsen, Guru Rinpoche, and Santarakshita. Throngs of pilgrims come here during auspicious days and religious festivals to burn juniper incense and make offerings. Northeast of the chapel is the meditation cave of Guru Rinpoche. A tablet with Tibetan inscriptions and a rock where Guru Rinpoche sat in meditation are inside. On the rock surface is a carved image of the tantric master.

The Samye Chimpu Cave Complex Together with Yamalung, Samye Chimpu is one of Guru Rinpoche's Eight Supreme Sanctuaries. This very vital hermitage now has a flourishing colony of assorted hermits and ascetics, and without doubt is the most colorful and vibrant of all mountain-top hermitages in Central Tibet. For route direction and a description, see below.

Samye Guesthouse is a graceless utilitarian Chinese-style compound next to the monastery. A small kitchen and dining hall function occasionally. (The monastery turns away overnight visitors.) An alternative to the guest house is a local house in the village of Samye, but expect cramped, dirty surroundings. A small Chinese restaurant is near Samye's entrance gate. Potatoes, *chang*, and *tsampa* can be bought in the village; there is also a store near the guest house.

Samye to Lhasa by the Surkhar ferry

From Samye, walk 9 km (2 hr) westward along the north bank of the Yarlung Tsangpo to Surkhar Valley. Surkhar Do, 5 km west of Samye, is the site where King Trisong Detsen met the Indian teacher, Guru Rinpoche. This place is marked by five ancient *chörtens* (see page 312). The ferry, at the valley's western edge, crosses to the south side of the river at road marker 88–89 km (a new tourist ferry docks at road marker 112). [Hitch from here to Lhasa or the Yarlung Valley.] It is also possible to ride a tractor or truck from Samye. The ferry has no fixed schedules, so it is best to go early in the morning; the first crossing is usually at 0900. It takes 1–1 1/2 hrs.

Lhasa to Samye: alternative trekking routes

Below are two alternative trekking routes that lead from the Gyalmashing and Ganden valleys to Samye.

Lhasa to Gyalmashing Valley to Samye Take the Lhasa–Medro Gongkar bus from the station in front of Tibet University. After passing Ganden (see page 140) and the village of Lamo, get off the bus at road marker 1510 km (new marker 4573). The side valley to the right is Gyalmashing. A trail leads from here over a pass to Samye. The walk takes three or four days. (For more details, see page 549).

Lhasa to Ganden Monastery to Samye The trek from Ganden Monastery direct to Samye entails walking south from the Ganden ridge, crossing the Hebu Valley and two passes to reach the trail junction leading to Yamalung. A short distance from here is the village of Ninggong and the main valley to Samye (see page 314).

Lhasa to Samye by road

Hitchhiking Start in Lhasa from, say, the big gas station just west of Drepung Monastery. The ride follows the paved main road, crosses the big Chusul Bridge (road marker 59 km) and then turns left (the right turn leads to Shigatse). After passing the airport, get off at the 88–89 km road marker, for the Samye ferry (or go a little further, to road marker 112, for the new and more expensive tourist ferry). On the north bank of the Tsangpo there are usually horsecarts, tractors, or trucks waiting to go to Samye, 9 km to the east.

Bus Take the Lhasa–Tsethang bus from the main bus station next to the Norbu Lingka, or from the station near the post office (at the entrance of Lhasa's No 2 Guest House). Get off at the 88–89 km road marker for the Samye ferry.

THE SAMYE CHIMPU CAVE COMPLEX

Chimpu, one of the most amazing pilgrimage sites in Tibet, is a must for any visitor remotely interested in Buddhist pilgrimage culture. The stiff 5-hr hike from Samye Monastery (see below) is most certainly worth the effort. Since 1983, Chimpu has become perhaps the most vital hermitage center of Central Tibet. Upwards of a hundred highly dedicated hermit-meditators create a strong magnetic and magical atmosphere for others who are serious about the practice.

Established by King Trisong Detsen in the 8th C., Chimpu is a fine example of a *gomdrak*, a meditation cave monastery. According to legend, these cave retreats near the top of a high ridge were used by Guru Rinpoche and his consort, Yeshe Tsogyal, while Samye was being built. Chimpu represents the 'speech' essence of Guru Rinpoche and is one of his celebrated Eight Supreme Sanctuaries. Since its foundation, it was an obligatory place of retreat for aspiring Nyingmapa practitioners. Over the centuries, a veritable who's who of the Old Sect came here to meditate. *Chim* is the name of the original clan who lived in this valley in ancient times; *pu* denotes the head of a valley.

The caves, located near the top of a range of mountains northeast of Samye, are visible from Hepo Ri as white dots high up the end of the Chimpu Valley. Tibetan pilgrims usually set off from Samye at 0500 to reach the site, where they would stay three or four hours before returning to Samye around 1800. An alternative to this long, tiring day is to take a sleeping bag and spend the night in one of the small chapels or caves, or better yet, take a tent. There are wonderful camping spots. It is important to keep in mind that the elaborate complex takes time to explore properly. There are remote meditation caves near the top of the range; these by themselves take a couple of hours to reach from the Chimpu chapel. It is best to reserve at least a couple of days for this fascinating area.

The route to Chimpu

It is possible to hire a monk from Samye as a guide or join a group of Tibetan pilgrims heading up in the chill, pre-dawn darkness. Bring a flashlight. The route, quite easy in the day, is tricky in the dark. Getting a guide is a good idea; he can also point out places of religious importance along the way.

To reach the Chimpu Valley, go north from Samye Monastery up the tree-lined road. Just outside the village, take the path that branches to the right into the fields. After half an hour cross a little bridge over a canal, then another small bridge over the river. Climb a low stone wall, turn right, and follow the contours of a small ridge until you reach the mouth of the next valley. This is the Chimpu Valley. Follow the clear track towards two white dots near the top of the mountain, left of a big rock slide. Pass a group of deserted houses among ruins. Further on, to the right, are more ruins. These formed part of Chimpu Village. In 1982, the main stream dried up and most of the surrounding fields became too dry to irrigate. The village was then abandoned and the inhabitants moved to Chogasa in the Samye valley. Beyond this, the trail starts to climb steeply. A pond is on the left and more ruins are a little further on the right. The setting is idyllic and the sweet smell of herbs is in the air. Next to a clear stream are many good places to camp.

The first signs that you have arrived at Chimpu are trees decorated with many small stones tied to branches. Pilgrims do this with the hope that their sins may be left behind with the stone. Small cave dwellings on the left are known as Lhamo Drubphuk and Chupo Pasang. A white burial *chörten* stands by the side of the path. Next to it is a black butter smear on a rock. The hermits living here explain that the strange designs were painted by Guru Rinpoche.

The Chimpu Complex

ZANGDHOK PELRI

Directly above the first cave dwellings is a huge pyramidal rock called Zangdhok Pelri, the 'Copper-colored Paradise' of Guru Rinpoche. Most of Chimpu's caves and cells are clustered around this astonishing boulder. Some 50 to 100 monks and nuns live here in caves or small wooden huts. Most have names associated with great masters: Guru Rinpoche, Vairocana, Longchenpa, Nyang Tingzin Zangpo, and their disciples. Guru Rinpoche spent three months in a cave (*phuk*) called Longchen Gurkar Phuk, near the top of the range.

THE KHORA

The following is a description of the pilgrimage route around the Chimpu complex.

At the base of Zangdhok Pelri, towards the east, is a big cave with a sign written in red in the *U-chen* script. It names the cave as Sangchen Metok ('The Great Secret Flower') Phuk, the residence of an 18th C. *terton* called Jigme Lingpa, the principal disciple of Longchenpa. Inside is a stone bed covered in deer skin, and a stone shrine of Guru Rinpoche. A rock outside is carved with an image of Jampelyang, supposedly incised by Guru Rinpoche's finger. In front of the rock is a tree, known as Trowa, growing out of a cleft. According to legend, the celebrated Nyingmapa lama, Gyalwa Longchenpa (1308–63), who completed the 102 volumes of Nyingma doctrine, put his walking stick here and it grew into the tree. Nearby are the Dronme (Butter Lamp) Phuk and Nyang Phuk Wökma (the lower cave of Nyang Tingzin

Zangpö). King Trisong Detsen stayed in the latter. Along here, many *chörten* images are carved into rock faces. Below these is a small shrine that marks the rock headprint of Guru Rinpoche.

Higher along the *khora* circuit is a shrine with Guru Rinpoche's inscription. Here the guru elucidated the doctrines of 'the heart-blood of the *dakinis*'. The *khora* then divides near a huge rock known as Guru's Horse. On its surface is an outsize footprint left by Guru Rinpoche when he transformed himself into a giant. Below the upper path is the cave of Nyang Phuk Gongma (the upper cave of Nyang), also used by Longchenpa. Within it is a handprint of Guru Rinpoche and his personal inscription of 'Om Ah Hum'.

Towards the western end of Zangdhok Pelri lies a peaceful little burial ground (*durtrö*) among a grove of trees. Human hair left by pilgrims hangs from branches to express the hope that they won't die prematurely. Immediately above Zangdhok Pelri is the retreat cave of Ma Rinchen Chok, the translator, and above that is the cave of Shubu Pelseng, which is east of Tsogyal Drubphuk, the meditation cell of Yeshe Tsogyal. The latter contains a handprint of the female *yogini*, the consort of Guru Rinpoche.

The northeast side of Zangdhok Pelri contains more caves. One of them is Tamdrin Phuk whose entranceway provides a superb view of the Chimpu Valley. Within are two small chambers, connected by a short tunnel. A shaft in the ceiling provides some light. On the wall of the inner room is a butter-smeared carving. The faithful believe it to be a *ranjung* ('self-originating') image of Guru Rinpoche. Tamdrin Phuk was formerly occupied by Gyalwa Chökyang, one of Guru Rinpoche's 24 disciples. A couple of young Khampa nuns now live here.

DRAKMAR KEUTSANG

Drakmar Keutsang, the principal and most sacred meditation cave (consecrated to Guru Rinpoche) of Chimpu, is located less than 100 m above Zangdhok Pelri. A new two-story temple has been constructed outside; the cave is located at the rear of the ground floor *dukhang*. Along the back wall, the guru's image is flanked by Yeshe Tsogyal and Mandarawa, his two consorts. It was in this cave that Trisong Detsen, Yeshe Tsogyal, and the first seven disciples of the guru received instructions on the precepts of *Drubpa Kagye*, the Eight Logos Deities. At the cave entrance is a *ranjung* print of a mandala belonging to the tantric cycle of Palchen Drubpa Kagye.

In the *dukhang* is a raised flagstone, surmounted by a small pillar enclosed by cloth. Pilgrims have attached many safety pins and bangles as offerings to a remarkable legend. When King Trisong Detsen's daughter, Pemasel, died at the age of eight, her body was brought up to Chimpu and placed on the flagstone. Guru Rinpoche, meditating inside the cave, revived the young princess in order to initiate her into the secrets of the Khandro Nyingtik. As a result, she achieved ultimate liberation, and the flagstone raised her small body heavenward. Pemasel was then offered to the vultures. This spot has been known ever since as Pemasel Durtrö. The caretaker performs a large number of prostrations in front of the stone and pillar each day, and his forehead has developed a large callous as a result. Above the ground floor is a large open-air terrace, a wonderful place to rest and take in the wonderful views of the Tsangpo Valley. Inside a room at the west end of the building is the small empty cave of Vairocana, the lama-translator associated with Yamalung. The cave, known as Bairo Phuk or Zim Phuk, is reached through a short tunnel.

Mountaintop Cave Retreats

A number of meditation retreats are close to the top of the range. Among them are:

- Gurkar ('White Tent') Cave—Guru Rinpoche and Trisong Detsen's chief minister stayed here.
- Tsogyal Zimphuk—resident cave of Yeshe Tsogyal. Above it is the cave of Atsara Sale, Yeshe Tsogyal's Nepalese consort.
- Longchen Phuk—another cave used by Longchenpa.

Below Drakmar Keutsang is a small cave called Zhuphuk Pasang. Near it, east of the two-story chapel, are a few small stone buildings. These are retreat centers (*drubkhang*) consecrated by the *tertons*, Jigme Lingpa—the 18th C. Nyingmapa lama, compiler of the liturgical text, *Nyingma Gurbum*—and Drime Lingpa. A lama lives in the far building; this holy man is enormously hospitable and fun-loving.

The *khora* path from here winds its way downward, bearing east past a holy spring (*drubchu*). A tall white *chörten* (Longchen Bumpa) stands level with Zangdhok Pelri, near the rockslide, and contains the remains of Longchenpa, the Nyingma lama who classified and made available the *Dzokchen Nyingtik* texts. A *doring* at the side commemorates his deeds; nearby is his meditation cave. An unusual twin-*chörten* is beneath Longchenpa's *chörten*. The path continues its descent to the west to join the main trail below Zangdhok Pelri. It takes four hours to return to Samye.

Samye to Lhamo Latso

Trail Notes
✤ Day 5 Samye–Gerpa Ferry 9 hr

The pilgrimage now heads east from Samye along the north bank of the Yarlung Tsangpo to the village of Lo, located at the entrance of the Chimpu Valley. Along this stretch, the expansive Tsangpo Valley is several km wide and its north (left) bank consists of a broad belt of scrub and undulating sand dunes. During the rainy season (July and August), this sandy area can be flooded, making the going difficult. After Lo, the trail disappears. Stick close to the river and walk towards the low bluffs that come down to the water. The area here is delightful with many small and large pools, collected between the dunes; good for swimming. (Take along iodine or other water purifiers during this isolated stretch.) It takes 5 hrs from Samye to reach the entrance of the Doh Valley, running north–south. (The village and monastery of Doh are up the valley.) From here stay close to the Tsangpo for four more hours to Gerpa Ferry, a small landing by the river. The going can be muddy along the trackless north bank.

✤ Day 6 Gerpa Ferry–Ngari Tratsang 7 hr

After Gerpa, wade across a small river that flows south into the Tsangpo. The region is barren. A more distinct trail following the Tsangpo starts east of here and makes the going easier. The riverbank consists of three or four rounded bluffs that reach down from the northern mountains and the trail, appearing and disappearing, generally follows the water closely. From the ferry to the last bluff takes 4 hr. This is a good place to camp. The snow peak to the south is Yala Shampo; across the river is Tsethang, the largest town in South Tibet.

The trail now heads north, veering left just before another ferry. Eventually it crosses a small bridge and after 3 hr reaches the village of Chermen (Timen) at the entrance of the Yön Valley (see page 510 for more information about this important valley). Tagka Shö is a short distance to the east. Donkeys can be hired here, and tinned goods and staples are available at a store. Totally destroyed Ngari Tratsang Monastery, on top of a craggy hill at the entrance of the Yön Valley, is 1/2 km further. It was built during the reign of the Second Dalai Lama, in 1541, to serve as a Gelugpa monastic academy for West Tibet (Ngari).

✚ Day 7 Ngari Tratsang–Zangri Karmar 8 hr

Follow the well-defined track 1 km north of the river, to Jang (2 1/2 hrs). Goats, sheep, and donkeys abound in this obviously prosperous area. The commune headquarters (Jang Gungsher) are at the east end of village. Basic accommodation is available, as are plenty of eggs, potatoes, and apples. The friendly villagers will help you procure donkeys if necessary. From Jang walk 1/2 hr to a small village next to the main path. At this point a track on the left zigzags up a range of mountains to the northeast. A three-hour walk along it leads to the ruins of the Densatil Monastery, a monument of renown in Central Tibet.

Densatil Monastery

Densatil (Densatil Drakri Karpo) is perched high up in the mountains at a site surrounded by wild roses, rhododendrons, and other flowering bushes. Its juniper trees, like those of Reting Monastery, are justly famous. Meditation caves within cliffs can be seen to the west. Densatil's most sacred relic is a tooth said to belong to the Buddha. The Maharaja of Bodh Gaya presented it to Phagmo Drupa, who founded the monastery in 1158. Its principal chapel was the Red Cathedral (Tsuglag Khang Marpo), built into the cliffs by nearly a thousand ascetics in the late 12th century. In the 14th and 15th C. it was one of the richest monasteries in Tibet, known for its stupendous holdings of finely crafted ritual objects. Today there is nothing left of the monastery except the broken red walls and a newly rebuilt chapel under the caves.

History Founded in 1158 by the well-known ascetic, Phagmo Drupa Dorje Gyalpo, a disciple of Gampopa, Densatil was originally nothing but a simple meditation shelter. Later it became the see of the Phagmo Dru family, which in the 14th C. conquered nearly all of Tibet, wresting political control of Central Tibet from the Sakyapa. (The Phagmo Drupa belonged originally to the Kadampa sect but with strong leanings towards the Kagyupa. Later they were assimilated into the Gelugpa.) Among the many illustrious lamas who studied here with Dorje Gyalpo were: Taklung Tangpo Tashi Pel, the founder of Taklung Kagyü; Drigung Rinchen Pel, who started up the Drigung Kagyü sect; and Lingrepa Pema Dorje, the founder of the Drukpa Kagyü.

After Dorje Gyalpo's death in 1170, internal strife grew between the Taklungpa and the Drigungpa. The latter eventually gained control and Densatil became attached to Drigung Monastery. Increasingly involved with politics, the Phagmo Dru family slowly emerged as one of the most powerful in Tibet. This culminated in the 14th C., when Tai Situ Jangchub Gyaltsen took over as ruler of the country and established Nedong in Yarlung as his capital. In the process, the Phagmo Drupas allied themselves with the Gelugpa. In the coming centuries, Densatil benefited greatly from the ascendancy of the family and accumulated fabulous wealth. The decline of the dynasty and monastery occurred in the 16th C., when the ministers in Rinpung (Tsang) revolted openly against the family.

After returning from Densatil, continue along the river to Pumdru (3/4 hr from the Densatil turnoff), where the track widens and becomes passable for jeeps. The track divides 3 hr from Jang. Leave the main track that continues along the river, and follow a side trail, lined by transmission towers, up the hill to the left. Cross over a small rise and then descend towards Zangri. Follow a motor road for 10 min to where wooden posts block the road. Take a side road to the left, skirting the large Chinese administrative compound of Zangri Xian (*xian* means 'county seat' but frequently refers to the office building), where there is a guest house and a restaurant. At the back of the Xian, cross some fields and a bridge to Zangri Qu.

Zangri Qu to the Tibet–Sichuan highway A dirt track goes north from Zangri Qu up a north-trending valley. After crossing a 5050-m pass, it descends to road marker 1457 km, 11 km west of Rutok Monastery on the Lhasa–Medro Gongkar–Ningchi road, which eventually leads to Chengdu. It takes three days to walk this section from Zangri Qu to the highway.

Samdrub Potrang

This large and impressive three-story building, within the Qu, is one of the few noble houses in the region. It was the palace of the ruler of Zangri and it servès as a prime example of a genre of Tibetan architecture distinct from monasteries and common houses. Within it is a store.

Zangri Karmar ('Red Castle on the Copper Hill')

Ten minutes further along the main road is a small hill on the left. From Jang to here is 5 hr. Climb for 15 min to the badly sacked Gelugpa monastery of Zangri Karmar, once a dependency of Ngari Tratsang Monastery. Stay in the village or at the monastery. A few monks live in a rebuilt chapel near the cliff face. To the west is the meditation cave of Machik Labdrönma, a powerful female *yogini* of the 11th C. She was a disciple of the Indian guru, Dampa Sangye, and lived at Langkor, near Dingri (see page 271). After receiving instructions in the Chö tradition, a discipline practiced within isolated cemeteries, she came to Central Tibet. Zangri Karmar and Shugseb Nunnery (see page 492) were her two principal sites of retreat.

✤ DAY 8 ZANGRI KARMAR—CHÖLUNG MONASTERY 6 1/2 HR

A scenic motor road runs north for 22 km from Zangri Karmar, along the east bank of the Tsangpo River, to a power station. Hitching is possible; this will save 5 hr of walking. (Do not take photographs near the power station.) After the station follow the wider of the two valleys to the left. (Ignore the narrow river gorge directly ahead of you.) Carry on along the valley for 1 3/4 hr to a small bridge. Here the valley divides again. The motor road continues to the left. (The road crosses a 5050-m pass, then descends to the Lhasa–Medro Gongkar–Ningchi road at road marker 1443 km; a 2- or 3-day walk.) Take the dirt track to the right through a side valley (vehicles are rare). This is the Wöka Valley, trending to the northeast. After 1 1/4 hr on a level path, the valley widens, with good views of sacred Wöde Gungyal ('Old Man Mountain') to the right.

Wöde Gungyal

Worshipped by both Buddhists and Bönpos, this is one of Tibet's holy mountains, named after a king of the second Tibetan dynasty, son of King Drigum Tsanpo. Wöde Gungyal is also the name of a mountain divinity, father of the Nyenchen Tanglha, Mountain God of the West, a towering range that divides the northern boundaries of Central Tibet from the Changtang.

Ignore the small bridge that crosses the river on the right. Continue for 15 minutes to good campgrounds, then follow the jeepable track to Wöka. From the camping area to Wöka is 3 1/2 hrs. There are no villages along the way but a couple of km before Wöka, there is extensive cultivation; at Wöka, the narrow valley opens wide into a flat plain. Wöka (Wöka Taktse) is dominated by the ruins of a fort on top of a ridge, destroyed by the Mongols in the 18th C. Tinned goods and some staples can be had at the store near the ruins. Stock up here for the next five days of trekking.

The ruined monastery once contained an important faculty of theology, founded by Setsun, teacher of the three chief disciples of Atisha. The two branches of the Wöka Valley meet here. The left (north) branch goes to Dzinchi and Rutok monasteries via the Magön La (see page 642 for a description of a trek to this region) and the right (east) goes to the Lung La and Lhamo Latso. Take the latter. From Wöka, cross a small bridge and head east towards the mountains along the right side of the Wöka Valley. Cross a range of low hills, to reach Chölung Monastery (1 1/2 hr).

Chölung Monastery

Chölung, built by Tsong Khapa, the founder of the Gelugpa sect, commands a beautiful site overlooking the Wöka Valley. It is the premier retreat on the west slopes of Wöde Gungyal. Destroyed in the Cultural Revolution, the monastery was one of the first to be rebuilt in Central Tibet (1982). The workmanship is surprisingly good and it is most difficult to find any sign of past atrocities. Chölung has 20–30 monks and one lama, a most hospitable man. The guest house has plenty of food (rice, eggs, potatoes) and the friendly monks can help obtain horses or yaks to go up to the pass. Without a doubt, Chölung is one of the mellowest stops along the pilgrimage.

✤ Day 9 Chölung Monastery–Nomad Camp 4 1/2 hr

With the river on your left, follow the wide valley northward to the tiny monastery of Chusang (1/2 hr). The trail hugs the slopes and overlooks the valley floor. Chusang has two chapels, one above the other. Tsong Khapa stayed here, and his footprints and handprints are treasured relics. From here, walk down to the valley floor past the village of Yergo Tib on the left. A large, handsome religious building (Bilung) appended to Sera Monastery stands across the valley to the left.

Garphuk Further along, within a side valley (north of Chusang and opening to the east) are the ruins of Garphuk, a cave hermitage of Guru Rinpoche. It is an early sacred site of the region. Guru Rinpoche concealed texts (terma) here and later, in the 12th C., Gampopa, Milarepa's foremost disciple, resided and taught here. Tsong Khapa was another illustrious visitor.

Back on the main trail, the Wöka valley divides. The ruined Gelugpa hermitage of Samling (Samtenling) can be seen in the range of hills straight ahead. Gampopa and Tsong Khapa both spent time there. Follow the river to walk up the right valley. Cross a small hill to the northeast, then drop down into a side river valley called Yulung. (The district from here on is known as Loyul.) Do not cross the bridge on the left at the valley entrance.

Continue along the flat east side of the main river valley. Good campsites are plentiful.

Four hours from Chölung, the valley (now called Yulung) abruptly becomes a narrow gorge flanked by sheer cliffs. Climb a small bluff, bearing to the right. Cross a bridge at the top and descend to a small lateral valley with nomad tents (1/2 hr). It is possible to stay with the herdsmen, surrounded by yaks and snowcapped mountains.

✤ Day 10 Nomad Camp–Amando 7 hr

Cross a small hill on the north side of this valley and descend back down to the Yulung. Continue for 1 1/2 hrs to another side valley opening to the right. Black tents sometimes mark the spot. Bypass this valley and walk for 2 hrs to a broad open area with many black tents; this is Shindu nomad camp. (Wade across the river to reach the tents.) Ignore a side valley left of Shindu. Follow the west bank of the main river for one hour to a stone hut enclosed by a low stone wall. The valley divides here. Take the left branch, known as Layuena. Glorious high snow mountains dominate the valley on the right. After 1 hr reach another stone hut and shortly afterwards a couple of black tents. Continue for 1 1/4 hrs to a clearing with about ten tents. This is Amando. A small side valley trends to the left; the Lung La is straight ahead. So far the path has been obvious and easy, although melting snow and meandering streams can make the going quite wet. Edelweiss and small blue flowers grace these high pristine valleys, empty save for small pockets of nomads. Pilgrims, going up or coming down the pass, traverse this area on horseback. Yaks are available in Amando for crossing the pass to Chökorgye Monastery. Snow goggles are a good idea from November to April.

✤ Day 11 Amando–Chökorgye 6 1/2 hr

Walk up to the Lung (Gyelung) La (4968 m), 1 1/2 hrs from Amando. Only the final 1/2 hr is strenuous. At the top, to the left, is a field of thick snow covering the sides of a prominent peak, with a small lake at its base. This is one of 21 sacred lakes in the area, consecrated to Drölma. Beyond the pass is the district of Dakpo. Descend steeply, curving to the right. After 1 1/2 hrs cross the river on stone steps to the east (left) bank. Follow the river for 3/4 hr, then wade back to the right bank at a point marked by stone cairns (lhatse). Reach Chökorgye Monastery (destroyed) after a further 2 3/4 hrs of easy, pleasant walking. There is no habitation throughout this stretch from the pass; not even black tents. There are, however, good camping sites along the way. At the monastery, camp or stay with nomads.

Chökorgye Monastery

This large ruined monastery complex, about half the size of Ganden, sits dramatically in the middle of the wide, grassy plain of Gyal Metoktang. Three valleys converge at this point; the one to the northeast goes to Lhamo Latso. Chökorgye, from a bird's eye view, has an unusual shape, rather like a truncated pyramid. The broad base is oriented to the southwest while its blunted apex points north, up the Gyal Metoktang Valley. Local terrain largely dictated this configuration. It was built in 1509 by the Second Dalai Lama, Gedan Gyatso, and was once one of the most important monasteries in Tibet. It was destroyed in 1718 by the Dzungars and rebuilt shortly afterwards by the regent, Kangchena. The 1960s brought wanton destruction, including the use of dynamite to bring down the thick stone walls. Unlike Ganden, restoration has been slow.

According to Keith Dowman, author of *Power Places of Central Tibet*, Chökorgye is enclosed by three mountains. The white mountain to the north is the abode of Shidak, Bönpo protector of the earth. To the south is the blue mountain consecrated to Palden Lhamo, site of Chökorgye's cemetery (*durtrö*) and a place where the trees are supposedly derived from the deity's hair. The protector Chamsing lives in the red mountain to the east. Nyingsaka Monastery (ruined) was built on its west-facing slopes. According to legend, a square rock on the valley floor holds the key to a hidden treasure. When times are bad, the treasure will activate the three mountains, causing them to close in and form a hidden valley (*beyul*). Here the Tibetans will have a secure refuge. Dowman also mentions the site of Shinje Melong (Mirror of Yamantaka, Lord of the Death), a piece of grey polished granite south of Chökorgye that purportedly reveals the past, present, and future.

Below the white mountain are handsome ruins, former living quarters of the Dalai Lamas and the regents when they came to the holy lake of Lhamo Latso on pilgrimage. Quite a few nomads live in the area. Pilgrims from the Gyatsa, Yarlung, and Lhasa areas regularly pass by on their way to Lhamo Latso, camping in cheerful blue and white tents among the ruins. Chökorgye is a lovely spot to spend a rest day.

✤ DAY 12 CHÖKORGYE–LHAMO LATSO 4 HR

From the east wall of the monastery, follow a path over a bridge to the entrance of the northeast valley. As you walk through the entrance, the trail passes below ruined chapels on your right. This was Nyingsaka Monastery. Follow the valley for an hour, along the left bank of the river, to an area marked by many cairns. Cross the river here on stepping stones to a nomad camp. Then climb abruptly and steeply north to reach a side valley that runs perpendicular to the main river. A small turbid pond, on the left, is reached in one hour. This is Yoni Lake. Follow the river (on your left) for one hour to a flat plateau. (Look behind for a close, dramatic view of Mt Lhamo Nying.) Directly ahead is an amphitheater of seemingly impassable mountains. It is just possible to make out the prayer flags on top of the ridge. The trail up to the saddle is steep and lined with numerous cairns. Snow can make the climb difficult and sometimes it is necessary to scramble on all fours.

Reach the pass overlooking Lake Lhamo Latso after 1 hr. This spot, crammed full of prayer flags and stone cairns, is known as Shugtri, the Dalai Lama's Throne. Pilgrims usually stay here for several hours, chanting prayers, meditating, and making offerings. The path to the lake is difficult and pilgrims rarely descend. However, a *khora* circles the lake and includes a chapel, consecrated to Magsorma, at its eastern end. The return to Chökorgye from the pass is a 3-hr walk.

LHAMO LATSO, THE ORACLE LAKE

Known as the Latso (life-force lake) of the Dalai Lamas, this is the most important 'vision lake' of Tibet. Every Dalai Lama came here at least once in his life to look for clues, usually on the lake's surface, concerning his future and the circumstances of his death. The regents pilgrimaged here to divine the location of the Dalai Lama's next incarnation. In 1933, at the death of the 13th Dalai Lama, Regent Reting Rinpoche came and clearly saw the countryside of Amdo, where the present Dalai Lama was eventually discovered.

According to Tibetan belief, every person, family, and country has a life-power. It resides in humans and in such places as lakes (*latso*) and mountains (*lari*). If something untoward happens to the environment, such as the drying up of a lake, misfortune will befall a person, his family, or the country. Lake Lhamo Latso is the *latso* of the Dalai Lamas. Tibet's *latso* is Lake Yamdrok Tso (see page 587).

LHAMO LATSO KHORCHEN

This long pilgrimage circuit takes in the lake, Daglha Gampo Monastery, Demchok Tso, and the Nye Valley, which is drained by a river originating in Lhamo Latso. It is a 4–5 day journey regularly undertaken by pilgrims and monks.

To go: From the pass, carefully walk down the scree slopes to the lake shore. After paying homage to the lake and the small chapel, continue to the lake's north end and descend a small valley. After 1 1/4 hr, reach a larger valley, perpendicular to the small one. Turn right (southeast) and descend to the southeast. In 5 hr come to a major intersection of valleys. The north–south trending valley, paralleling the Gyal Metoktang Valley to the east, is the Nye. Turn right and follow it south. Nye Village is reached in 2 1/4 hrs. Then proceed for a further 10 1/2 hrs to the north bank of the Tsangpo. (Nagan is 3/4 hr before the river.) Walk westward up a ridge to the powerful Daglha Gampo Hermitage (see p 352). Across the Tsangpo River, a short distance to the east, is Tromda.

LHAMO LATSO TO TSETHANG

Trail Notes
DAY 13 CHÖKORGYE–TSEJU VILLAGE 5 HR
From Chökorgye walk south across the grassy plain. Cross a small bridge and continue south down the beautiful Gyal Metoktang, Valley of Flowers, with the river on the left. The trail is wide, easy, and straight. Keep to the western perimeter of the valley. For the first three hours, cross several streams and some swampy terrain. Look out for an unusual plant known as 'winter-worm, summer-grass' (*yatsa gambu*). It is in fact a caterpillar that burrows under the ground in winter. A fungus (*cordiceps militaris*) sometimes invades the larva and grows 3–6 cm above the surface. The fused entity is a valuable, highly sought after medicine in Tibet and China. Chökorgye to Tseju takes five hours. Tseju is a village of some 20 stone houses with thatched and shingled roofs. Accommodation is available in the headman's house. The village has potatoes, eggs, *momos* and fresh Tibetan bread.

DAY 14 TSEJU–GYATSA QU 6 HR
Follow the track (now motorable) south. This is not as swampy as the previous stretch and is infinitely more enjoyable. Occasional loggers and nomads inhabit this area. Leave the road from time to time to take shortcuts. Some enchanting small islands with grazing yaks stand in the middle of the crystal-clear river. Black tents on the bank mark places of good campsites. Pass a hydro-electric station, on your left, to reach Gyatsa Qu 5 hr later. The official compound (*qu*), a Tibetan-style building, is at the far end of town. It might be possible to spend the night here. A small store nearby has some meager provisions. The Tsangpo River is a short walk from the village. This region, at the mouth of the Gyal Metoktang Valley, is extensively cultivated and has a large number of mature walnut trees, as well as willows and apricot trees.

The Daglha Gampo Hermitage Gampopa, Milarepa's principal disciple, founded this very important retreat center in the early 12th century. Many of the Kagyü sect's patriarchs stayed in meditation caves here. See Ritrö, page 352, for a description.

✦ DAY 15 GYATSA QU—DAKPO TRATSANG MONASTERY 2 1/2 HR

From Gyatsa Qu follow the motor road that hugs the hills on the right side of the valley. It makes a big curve to the right around a bluff, passing villages along the flat valley floor. To the left is a beautifully wooded ridge, below which the Tsangpo flows. The main Tibet–Sichuan highway follows the other (right) bank of the river. After 2 hr of easy walking, cross the river on a big and modern suspension bridge. Follow the main road (road marker 314 km) west for 1/2 hr to Gyatsa Xian, a large district headquarters. A side road on the right leads to the town and monastery of Dakpo Tratsang.

Dakpo Tratsang Monastery (Dakpo Shedrubling)

This Gelugpa monastery stands at the town entrance of Gyatsa Xian. In the 16th C., it was a stronghold of the Sharmapa; the Sixth Sharmapa was invested here in 1589. (Near Lhasa airport is another monastery of the same name.) The monastery survived the Cultural Revolution largely untouched. Its chapels and a debate courtyard, recently restored, are home to quite a few friendly monks. Food and lodging are available here.

✦ DAY 16 DAKPO TRATSANG–TSETHANG (139 KM) AND LHASA (322 KM). HITCH

Very little traffic uses this main road to Tsethang. For hitching, start around 0800 and hope for the best. Dakpo Tratsang to Tsethang takes about 7–8 hr in a vintage Chinese truck.

Shortly after leaving Dakpo Tratsang the road turns away from the Tsangpo River into a side valley, within which is the fortress of Lapso Dzong. This detour is necessary because of a range of mountains, the Palung Ri, that comes down precipitously to the water. Once in the side valley, the road zigzags steeply up the mountain to the Potrang La (5020 m). After the pass, the route passes a steep canyon, on the right, and enters a broad plain. A side road to the left leads to Tsona (see page 243) and the south end of the Yarlung Valley. This flat region is called Lhagyari (also Eyul), one of the original petty kingdoms of Tibet. The noble families who live here today can boast a direct link to King Songtsen Gampo. After Lhagyari, go through a narrow gorge to finally emerge along the southern bank of the Yarlung Tsangpo at Rong (across the river is Zangri; there is a motor ferry). Here are the ruins of Langkor Dzong. Below there is Chagar Monastery and a short distance to the west is Jowo Lhakhang. Chagar was built in the 16th C. by the Third Dalai Lama, Sonam Gyatso. It has some good murals but is not active. From Rong, the road hugs the south bank of the Tsangpo River for 35 km to arrive at Tsethang and the Yarlung Valley, the cradle of Tibetan civilization.

Tsethang For information on this large South Tibet town and the Yarlung Valley, see page 518.

AN ALTERNATIVE ROUTE TO LHAMO LATSO VIA RUTOK AND DZINCHI MONASTERIES

Location	East of Lhasa
Map reference	NH46-10 A B C D
Trekking days	4 to Wöka Dzong; 4 more to Lhamo Latso
Start–Finish	Rutok Monastery–Wöka Dzong–Lhamo Latso
Passes	Damxung, Magön, Lung

OVERVIEW

This pilgrimage con-stitutes the northern route from Lhasa to the sacred oracle lake of Lhamo Latso, via Dzinchi Monastery and the Wöka Valley. The first part of the journey requires traveling by bus, truck, or hired car for 122 km along the Tibet–Sichuan highway: from Lhasa to Rutok Monastery and its hot springs. From here, trek south for four days along foot-trails to Dzinchi and Wöka by crossing the easy Damxung and Magön

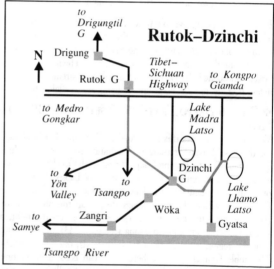

passes, meeting several nomad encampments along the way. Dzinchi, a 10th-C. institution, is the Wöka Valley's principal shrine and birthplace of the 11th Dalai Lama. Its lamas claim descent from Gyaltseb Je Dharma Rinchen, Tsong Khapa's main disciple. Hallowed meditation caves lie near the monastery.

A trail leads north from here to the soul-lake of Madra Latso. Beyond Wöka, the four-day trek to Lhamo Latso follows the itinerary described in the previous chapter (see page 637).

Related sections

Lhamo Latso, p 623
The Ningchi road, p 707
Upper Reaches of the Kyi Chu River, p 544

Access: Lhasa to Rutok Monastery

Take the bus from Lhasa to Medro Gongkar (buses leave daily at 0830 from the station opposite Tibet University; buy tickets on the bus). Medro Gongkar (road marker 1500 km; new marker 4564) is 68 km from the capital. After alighting, hitchhike along the main Tibet–Sichuan highway to Rutok Monastery (road marker 1446 km; new marker 4510), 54 km east of Medro Gongkar. The trailhead is at roadmarker 1443 km (new marker 4507).

An easier way to reach Rutok is to take the Lhasa–Bayi (or Lhasa–Ningchi) bus that passes in front of the monastery. (For details, see page 709.)

RUTOK MONASTERY TO WÖKA DZONG

Time Chart

Day	Place
1	Rutok–Camp 1
2	Farmhouse
3	Dzinchi
4	Wöka

Trail Notes

✤ DAY 1 RUTOK–CAMP 1

From Rutok Monastery, sited halfway up a low ridge on the road's north side, walk east to the Rutok hotsprings, past *tsampa* mills and a road maintenance compound (*daoban* 145). Continue to some large red rocks; a bridge spans a side river near here, site of the springs. Beyond is a stone bridge. Cross it to the road's south side to enter a south-trending valley (road marker 1443 km) that leads to the Damxung and Magön passes. Follow a trail hugging the valley's west slopes (the trail begins between the two bridges). On the left is the Magön La River. Reach a side valley that opens to the right; within it is a village. Ford a stream and continue up the main valley, passing a second side valley (also on the right with a village) opposite ruined walls next to a hill. Wade across another side stream, then reach a nomad camp. After passing one more side valley opening to the right, wade to the right bank of the Magön La River. On the left are gentle grassy hills.

Continue to a valley junction; two side valleys open on both the right and left banks (at the end of the left valley is a red hill crowned with a distinctive square rock). Beyond this junction the path steepens and passes two *chörtens*. Wade to the stream's left bank again; the gradual, grassy slopes make for a good campsite. The area south of here becomes more barren.

✤ DAY 2 CAMP 1–FARMHOUSE

Continue up the main valley steeply at first, then more gradually. The path goes south past three nomad camps to a barren plateau, where the way becomes indistinct. At its head, the valley splits. Take the right branch to the Damxung La, a pass marked by prayer flags and a *chörten*. Descend gradually towards the south, then walk past nomad tents and a side valley with a *chörten* on the right. The path stays on the right side of the grassy main valley. A round peak is on the left. Come to a T-shaped junction with a deserted hermitage on the right. Turn into the right-hand valley (nomad camps within stone fences lie inside the left valley); just beyond the hermitage, hike gradually upward, following stone cairns to the Magön La; the pass is marked by cairns but no prayer flags. Descend a steep ledge into a broad stony area. Further to the south, the scenery improves.

Come to two side valleys open to the left and right; a *chörten* and nomad tents stand at the junction. The short right valley has some houses and a yak pen, while the left has one house at its entrance. Continue south down the main valley, which narrows. A small river runs left of the path and along the way are springs. Reach another valley junction and follow the branch that turns abruptly eastward. Follow this long, narrow, sloping valley to eventually reach a large farmhouse surrounded by fields.

✤ DAY 3 FARMHOUSE–DZINCHI MONASTERY

After the farmhouse, the valley widens. Cross the river on a log bridge. The path, reaching the base of some southern slopes, follows them to the east. Further on, the valley makes a dogleg to the south and becomes narrow with steep, rocky sides. Suddenly, grassy meadows give way to a terrain of huge boulders. After some time a valley opens to the left. At its entrance is Dzinchi Monastery. A large bridge stands just before the village.

Dzinchi Qu

Dzinchi is separated into two parts. A grand stone house dominates the western section; located just before the monastery, it was the birthplace of the 11th Dalai Lama. The village's main section is mostly within a side valley that trends to the northeast. A trail, starting from the final houses near the ruins of a nunnery, ascends steeply to Dzinchi's three meditation caves. Tamdrin Drubphuk contains the hoof-prints of a goat that appeared before Gyalwa Jampa, Dzinchi Monastery's mythic founder. In front of another cave, also used by Gyalwa, is a tall, sacred juniper, said to be his soul-tree (*lashing*).

Dzinchi to Garphuk, Lake Madra Latso, and Rutok Monastery

Another trail from this same side valley continues northeastward to the village of Sumtse (1 1/2 hr), then north to Madra Latso (2 3/4 hr), soul-lake of the protectress Madra. At its southern end is Gongdeling Monastery and Garphuk, a Guru Rinpoche cave. The cave is an ancient shrine where Guru Rinpoche meditated and concealed sacred texts, and also where Gampopa, disciple of Milarepa, spent a year. The Madra La is 2 1/4 hr north of the lake. From the pass, descend due north to a valley junction (3 1/2 hr). Turn left (west) at this point to regain the Tibet–Sichuan highway at road marker 1431 km (3 1/4 hr); Rutok Monastery is 15 km to the west.

A well-defined foot-trail starts immediately after the village school and goes around a hill. This route is a shortcut to Lake Lhamo Latso. It heads east to the Yulung Chu Valley, then to the Lung La (page 638), a pass leading to Chökorgye Monastery and Lhamo Latso. From Dzinchi Monastery, a dirt track goes southwest to Wöka Dzong and Zangri (see below), after skirting the house of the 11th Dalai Lama.

Dzinchi Monastery Garmiton Yönten Yungdrung founded Dzinchi in the 10th century. He was a disciple of Gongpa Rabsel (see page 27), a celebrated monk who helped revive Buddhism in Tibet. Tsong Khapa, founder of the Gelugpa in the 15th C., ⇒

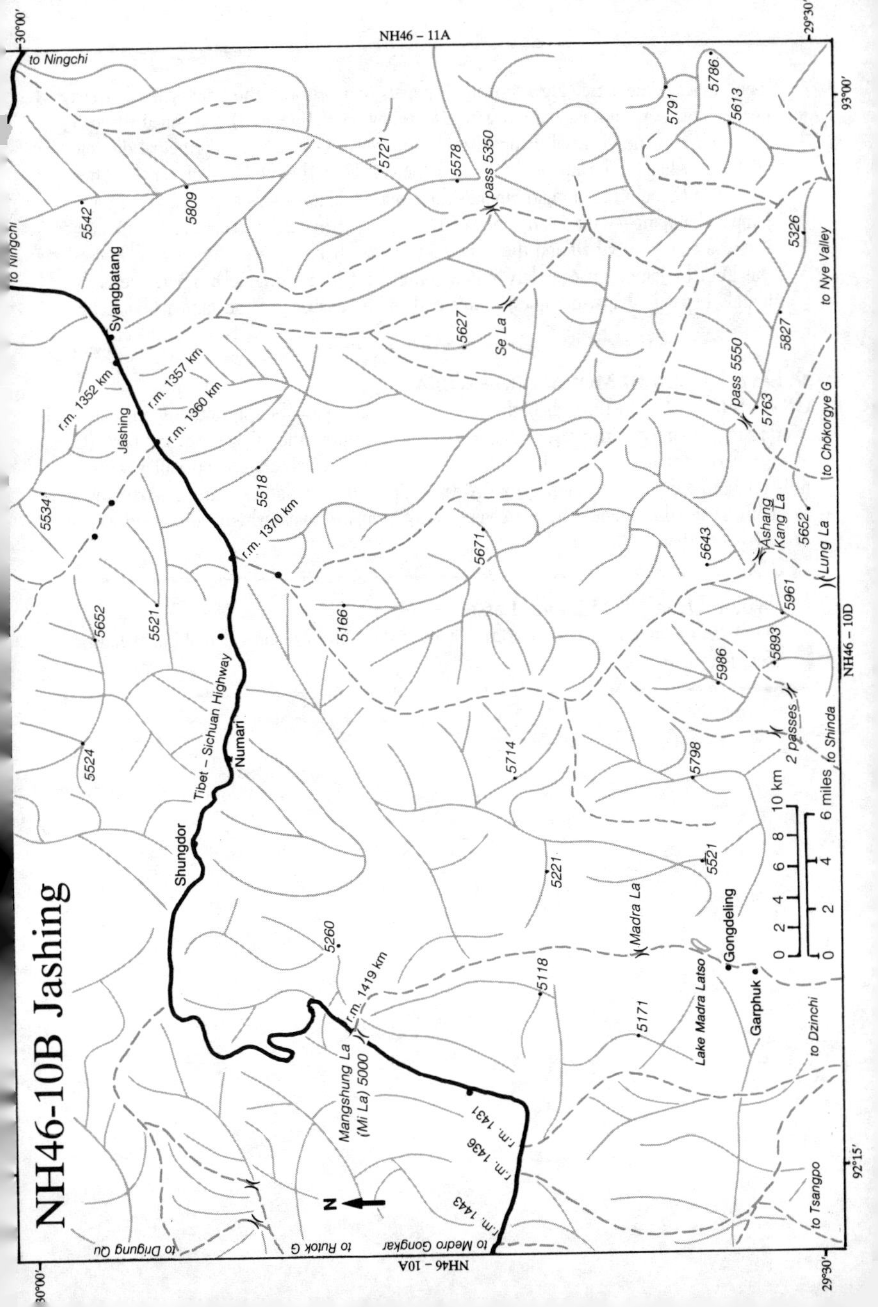

NH46-10B Jashing

Map labels (as shown):

NH46 – 11A

to Ningchi
to Ningchi

5786
5791
5613
5721
5578
pass 5350
5326
5542
5809
Syangbatang
5627
Se La
pass 5550
5827
5763
r.m. 1352 km
r.m. 1357 km
r.m. 1360 km
Jashing
Ashang Kang La
to Chökoryé G
to Nye Valley
5518
5534
r.m. 1370 km
5671
5643
Lung La
5662
5521
5652
5166
5961
5893
Tibet – Sichuan Highway
5986
Numari
5714
5798
NH46 – 10D
5524
Shungdor
2 passes
to Shinda
5260
5221
Madra La
5521
Gongdeling
5118
Lake Madra Latso
Garphuk
to Dzinchi
5171
Mangshung La (Mi La) 5000
r.m. 1419 km
r.m. 1436
r.m. 1431
N
r.m. 1443
to Medro Gongkar
to Rutok G
to Drigung Qu
to Tsangpo
NH46 – 10A

Scale: 0 2 4 6 8 10 km / 0 2 4 6 miles

spent much time here. He renovated chapels and restored the principal Maitreya image. This powerful association with the Yellow Hats (Gelugpa) continued through the lineage of the Gyaltsab Rinpoches, incarnates of Gyaltsab Je, a principal disciple of Tsong Khapa. The abbots of Dzinchi helped keep the Wöka Valley rich. They resided in Dzinchi's Labrang. Dzinchi's three main buildings—Tsokhang, Labrang, and Jampa Lhakhang—have been renovated or replaced in recent years. The Tsokhang is now a community hall and the important Jampa Lhakhang, with a new roof, houses the Dzinchi Jampa, a legendary statue (only the feet are original). There are early murals (Tsong Khapa, disciples, protectors) in the *dukhang* of the Jampa Lhakhang.

✤ DAY 4 DZINCHI MONASTERY–WÖKA

Go south from Dzinchi through both parts of the village past the big house. Continue south over a bridge marked with prayer flags, a short distance from the village's second part. (Camp along the river if necessary.) The path, now a motor road, enters a deep valley with rocky hills on both sides. Cross another bridge (negotiable by car), and continue along the river to Jamin. After the village, the path veers away from the river, which flows southwestward. Wöka is less than 2 hr from Dzinchi.

Wöka Dzong to Lhamo Latso

From Wöka, a trail goes east-northeast over the Lung La and on to Lhamo Latso. For details, see page 637.

DRAKSUM LATSO: AROUND THE SOUL-LAKE OF KING GESAR

Location	Kongpo, Southeast Tibet
Map reference	NH46-7 D
Trekking days	2 (circuit)
Start–Finish	Draksum Latso
Passes	None

OVERVIEW

The area around Lake Draksum Latso, in the heart of scenic Kongpo, was the domain of King Gesar of Ling, Sangye Lingpa and Guru Rinpoche. These towering figures of Tibetan Buddhism appear prominently in the legends and folklore of the lake. Draksum is considered the soul-lake (*latso*) of Gesar, the natural environment in which the king's life-spirit resides. Sangye Lingpa, the renowned 14th-C. Nyingma lama founded the idyllic Tsosum Monastery on an island in the lake. Guru Rinpoche traveled throughout the Himalayas in the 8th century. Intimately connected with secret caves and hermitages, his presence transformed these simple sites into important places of pilgrimage. Such is the case with Draksum Latso. Ling Gesar is well known to all Tibetans for his epic battles and conquests of renegade kings and hostile territories. He lived in the area of Draksum (*Pasum* in the local Kongpo dialect), and one

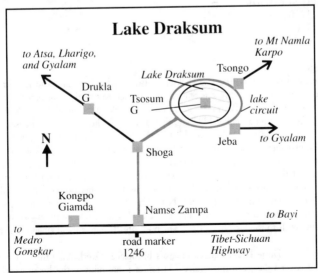

Lake Draksum

account tells of his nine-year sojourn at Pibang Monastery on the lake's north shores. A considerable number of stone relics in the region are attributed to these three sages. This section describes a short, two-day pilgrimage which circles the lake and includes a visit to Tsosum Monastery, the region's most sacred shrine.

Draksum Latso is located in Kongpo, a heavily forested district quite unlike the barren plateau landscape of much of Tibet. Besides the walk around the lake, other options for exploration exist in the region: the Po Yigrong Range that serves as the watershed between the Tsangpo and Salween rivers, beautiful Mt Namla Karpo (7315 m), the Ama Chömo Taktse peak, superb glacial lakes, and hermitages built over the years by meditation masters. The Draksum Latso area is also a place to come into contact with the Kongpopa, a people with their own customs and habits. One macabre practice worth noting: the Kongpopas are—or at least were—renowned for poisoning unwary outsiders in order to imbibe their essence. Around Draksum Latso are tall defense towers, regarded by the locals as demon houses built not by men but by *duds* (black demons). The ancestral kings of Kongpo figured strongly in Tibet's early history; some of the Yarlung-dynasty kings came from a branch of Kongpo's rulers.

This chapter includes two optional treks: one, via Tongkyuk on the main Tibet–Sichuan highway, is an excellent alternative itinerary of one week to the Draksum Latso area, a journey bordered on the north by the mighty Po Yigrong Range; the other is a two-week exploration of the Salween Divide via the Draksum Kye La, a trek that also serves to access the Gyalam, the old China–Tibet caravan route (see page 570). It is quite possible to spend a month or more in the enchanting lake district of Kongpo Draksum with its many small villages and monasteries. There should be no problem finding accommodation and food.

Martin Brauen and Sylvie Grand-Clement both contributed to this section.

Related sections
Mt Namche Barwa, p 712
Bönri, p 741
Gyalam, p 570

Access
The easiest and fastest way to get to Draksum Latso is by bus from Lhasa to Bayi or Ningchi (see page 708). The Lhasa City Bus Station is one block east of the post office; a bus leaves every morning at 0830 for Bayi, a large town 19 km before Ningchi. Kongpo Giamda is 274 km east of Lhasa at road marker 1293 km. Spend the night here in a guest house. The next day, continue past Ngapé (road marker 1281.5 km), Shiri, and Langa (road marker 1254 km). The bridge of Baher (Namse Zampa) is 8 km further at road marker 1246 km. Get off here. This point is 48 km east of Kongpo Giamda and 85 km west of Bayi. The large Baher Valley left (north) of the Lhasa–Ningchi road leads to Draksum Latso; a dirt track just before the bridge gives access to the valley. At this junction are restaurants (wood shacks) and a guest house, a long stone building with a few beds. The dirt road enters a forested area almost immediately. A river—the combined waters of the Drukla and Draksum rivers—is on the right. It flows due south to the big Nyang Chu, which eventually enters the Tsangpo near Ningchi.

Draksum Dorje Drak: Sangye Lingpa's birthplace Overlooking the entrance of the Baher (Ba) River valley, is a small ridge. On top of it are ruins of the house where Sangye

Lingpa was born. Known locally as Jetsün Nyingpo (or Dorje Drakpa), he lived in the 14th C. and rose to fame as a discoverer of sacred texts. Across from the main road is a small chapel that contains the handprints of Guru Rinpoche and Sangye Lingpa.

SANGYE LINGPA'S MONASTERY

The main monastery of Sangye Lingpa is a one-day walk from the Baher Bridge. Near the bridge's south end, two trails zigzag up a ridge. Take the right, easier trail. Along the way are handprints and footprints of the *tertön*. At the top, the trail continues through an isolated region to the destroyed monastery. His meditation cave is in a chapel behind the *dukhang*. Farther up the thick forest are lakes, caves, and peaks associated with the lama. Four lakes, each a different mythical colour (black, white, red, blue) are in this area; a local legend says their waters boil spontaneously at midday.

From the Lhasa–Ningchi road to Draksum Latso

Logging trucks sometimes ply the dirt road between the lake and the main Lhasa–Ningchi road; try to catch a ride. It takes 5 hr to walk to Muba at the lake. First pass Shinshasa, a lumber mill with wooden houses, on the left (1 hr by truck). Look out for the interesting 12-corner stone defense towers (south of the village) and the monastery of Len. The road then forks at Djokar. The left branch goes northwest to Drukla Monastery, the right continues to the lake. Shoga Dzong (Shoga Qu), with a hydro-electric station, shops, and restaurants is next. The Drukla Chu runs through the town from the north. Continue along the main river's right bank. Transmission towers are on the right. Pass Lingthang, a small logging depot, on the left, then cross the river by bridge and follow the Draksum Chu's left (south) bank. Farther along are the settlements of Kala, Gyara, Bimathang Monastery, Shi Dzong, and Muba (15 min by truck from the bridge). Tsomchuk, on the far side of the Draksum Chu, can be reached by crossing a bridge. The road now hugs the south shore of Draksum Latso and winds through forests. A short distance east of the Tsomchuk Bridge, trucks stop at a place with many prayer flags on the right. Pilgrims descend from here to the island monastery of Tsosum (Tso Dzong).

THE DRAKSUM LATSO KHORA

The clockwise pilgrimage around the holy lake starts at Tsosum Monastery and takes approximately 10 hr to complete. Allow two days for a leisurely pace. A big wooden boat, capable of carrying ten people and attached to a cable, links the island monastery with the mainland. The crossing is free and takes 5 min. Tsosum (see below) consists of a two-story temple and a house that contains the lama's quarters and kitchen. Sleep in the kitchen or on the temple's empty second floor.

After visiting the monastery, return to the mainland and walk west along the motor road that skirts the lake. At its southwestern tip, the road descends to a bridge that spans the Draksum Chu which flows southwest out of the lake (3/4 hr). Cross the bridge and walk up to Tsomchuk. Continue northeast along a flat path along the lake, then cross a meadow (follow the lake shore). The path splits; one branch goes north and another east. Take the latter across fields to a village (Puru). After this, descend through forests to a gorge. Find a bridge on the right and cross the swift river. Beyond are the ruins of Pibang Monastery, a Gelugpa center that once had 100 monks (1 1/4 hr).

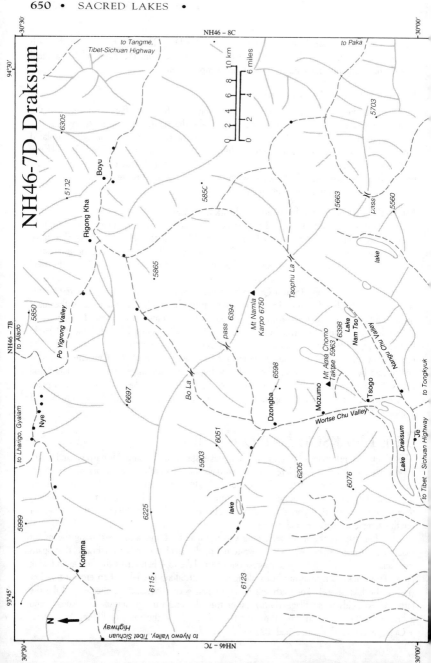

NH46-7D Draksum

Continue along the distinct path that goes northeast through thick forests. Reach the Dorje Phagmo Cave (1 hr) which is marked by prayer flags and offerings left by pilgrims—pieces of clothing, hats, scarfs, painted and carved stones.

After the cave, the path winds upward along the slopes. Pass a village with chalet-like dwellings on the right, on a hill. Ama Chomo Gyamo, some distance further, has prayer flags and a *mani* wall (1 3/4 hr). This site alerts pilgrims to holy Mt Ama Chomo Taktse to the north; prostrations are performed here.

Continue through thick forests. The path skirts the lake, alternating between the shoreline and woods. Near the northeast end of the lake, the path traverses a sandy area. After this, come to one of two biggish rivers, the Wörtse Chu, that drains into the lake's eastern section. (Before this is a smaller river; ignore it.) Cross a bridge and continue to detour around the head of the lake (another island and a cable ferry is here). Walk past a white *chörten*, on the left, which commemorates sacred Dorchen Ri and Dorchen Monastery (ruined) at its base. Stay on the path and cross the second larger river, the Nangu Chu, by bridge. Tsogo (Lake-head) is on the east bank; the path goes through the village. The river divides in this vicinity: one branch comes from Mt Namla Karpo, a holy mountain visible from Tsogo; the other, the larger branch, flows from the north. Between river valleys is sacred Mt Amo Chomo Taktse. Tsogo, near a lagoon, can be very wet in the summer; the fields are usually flooded (3/4 hr).

The trail now rejoins the motor road. Walk southward along the road above the lake. Reach Jeba in 1 1/2 hr, a village with large wooden houses. The Penam Chu, a glacial river from Mt Namla Karpo, flows into the village; spend some time in this pleasant place. To complete the *khora*, follow the road to the truck stop just above the island monastery of Tsosum (1 1/2 hr).

THE SACRED PLACES OF DRAKSUM LATSO

The beautiful lake, about 16 km by 3 km (at the widest point), lies in a long, narrow valley between steep mountains. Locals liken it to a dragon: the rivers flowing into its northern end constitute the ears and flames issuing from the dragon's mouth. The most prominent peaks to the north are Namla Karpo and the Ama Chomo Taktse. To the northeast is the Po Yigrong range of mountains, the divide between the Salween and the Tsangpo. Two large rivers draining the range enter the lake from the north.

THE TSOSUM MONASTERY

This important Nyingma monastery, known properly as Draksum Tso Dzong, is one of 100 monasteries traditionally ascribed to King Trisong Detsen (8th C.). Before it was burned in the Cultural Revolution, it had a college (*shedra*) with four monks and the monastery proper was home to one lama and ten monks. Presently, Tsosum is under Dudjom Rinpoche and the rebuilt chapel now has a young lama and three monks. In front of the main entrance is a round, black stone, about 0.5 m in diameter. On it is the imprint of a horseshoe that belonged to Ling Gesar's horse. Within the chapel look for an old text with a red seal. This document supposedly confirms that the seal belonged to Guru Rinpoche and that he received the text personally from King Trisong Detsen.

Behind and left of the shrine is a 14th-C. statue of Sangye Lingpa. The image, in wrathful form, holds a scorpion and *dorje* in its hands. (To the sides are two stone *chörtens*: the left one is said to be 'self manifesting'). Tradition says the head was made by Guru Rinpoche himself. Sangye Lingpa, riding a tigress, brought the head to Tsosum and installed it on the body. The tigress, impressed with its death-defying leap across the water, danced with joy and left its imprint on a rock on the island's western side. The original foundation of the monastery probably dates back to the 8th century. An ancient tree on the island is said to have grown from the hair of Yeshe Tsogyal, the consort of Guru Rinpoche. Supposedly, signs of snakes and sacred syllables actually appear on individual leaves. A tree trunk jutting onto the water is believed to be Gesar's tree of life (*lashing*), a site where the hero's soul resides. Surrounding the temple is a short *khora*. Ruins of the *shedra* are on a hill at the islands's southeast end.

Pibang Monastery
It is generally believed that Gesar of Ling lived here for nine years. This Gelugpa monastery is now totally in ruins.

Dorchen Monastery
This small Kagyüpa monastery now has only ruined walls and a white *chörten*. Behind it is Dorchen Ri, a sacred mountain associated with Guru Rinpoche.

Muba
Between this village and the lake is a rock with a small shrine. This polished rock, in the form of a seat, was where Gesar shot the demon (*dud*) known as A Chung.

Jeba
A hill close to Jeba Village was the site of King Shingtri Tsanpo's palace. (Some claim he was the son of Langdarma.) Between Jeba and Tsogo is a stone column with faint engraved inscriptions. Villagers claim that the height of the column represents precisely the height of Gesar.

Mt Namla Karpo
Namla Karpo, the White God of Heaven, is a sacred mountain of the Po Yigrong Range that towers over the Draksum Latso region. Hor Gunka, a demon, lived on top of this mountain ages ago and ruled over his kingdom in the north. Ling Gesar passed by on his famous horse and persuaded the demon to get off his mountain, stop his evil ways, and become a protector of the world. Hor Gunka did so and changed his name to Gyajin Namla Karpo. This is one of the few instances in which Gesar subdued his adversary by persuasion rather than by force. Two other sacred mountains in the region are Ama Chomo Taktse and Dorchen Ri.

Gesar and Draksum Latso
Gesar of Ling left many relics, real and mythic, in the area:
- A column of stone, between Jeba and Tsogo
- A stone imprinted with the horseshoe of Gesar's horse (at Tsosum Monastery)

➡

- Gesar's tree of life on Tsosum Island
- An imprint of Gesar shooting the demon, A Chung, on a rock between the lake and Muba
- A light band running the length of the lake, believed to be the trace of Gesar's horse
- Rocks associated with Gesar near Muba (destroyed during road construction)

Dud Khang: demon houses Tall stone defense towers exist in the Kongpo region, centering on the Nyang Chu. Some are near Bayi (see page 743), clustered in groups of four. Others stand near Len, south of Shoga Dzong at Draksum Latso's southwest tip, and near Drukla Monastery on the banks of the Drukla Chu. Rising as high as 15 m, the ground plan of these towers consists of a large square with the center of each side opening outward to form smaller squares. The result resembles a 12-corner mandala. The insides of most towers are bare; some, however, have interior wood frames that allow defenders to climb up to small openings. (Stone and mud defense towers also exist in Kham and Lhodrak; especially at Zhe, site of Milarepa's Tower [see page 698].) These structures are known locally as *dud khang* (demon houses) and are believed to be built not by humans but by A Chung, the king of demons mentioned in the Gesar epic.

The Kongpo kings Research about the pre-Yarlung kings of Tibet is scant and rather incomplete. According to the Dunhuang documents, the kings of Kongpo originated in Tibet's northeast corner, a loosely administered area occupied by Chinese and Tibetans. They later settled in the Kongpo area. The reigning dynasty belonged to King Drigum, but there was a major dispute between him and his general, Lo Ngam. Drigum was killed and the kingdom fell into disarray. A myth states that the umbilical cord connecting the king to heaven was severed in battle and thus all future kings would be unable to ascend back to heaven. Their burials from now onwards would be on earth, hence the beginning of the Yarlung tombs. One son of Drigum stayed on in Kongpo while others went west to establish the Yarlung Dynasty (7th–9th C.). Throughout the centuries, there were many conflicts between these two branches.

The poisons of Kongpo A cautionary tale is heard in Kongpo—stay away from the local food and drink because the Kongpopas poison unsuspecting travelers. The tasteless, odorless poisons are usually added to rice and *chang* and considerable time is necessary for them to work through the system. Death is said to be inevitable. This rumour is heard not only in the Kongpo/Draksum Latso area. Even as far east as Metok in the Pemakö region (see page 717) and certainly in the nearer districts like Takpo and Nyang, one is warned to be careful. The practitioners believe the essence and vitality of the poisoned person will transfer to them. Takpo, Nyang, and Kongpo are collectively called 'the Land of the Very Harmful'; the shape of the territories supposedly resembles a black demon (*dud*). The Kongpo people are considered the worst offenders, and they suffer from the resultant stereotypes: their black wool capes are said to resemble witches' coats, and the distinctive Kongpo caps with upturned corners are likened to the horns of demons.

ALTERNATIVE ITINERARIES
1 Tongkyuk to Draksum Latso and the Salween Divide: five–seven days

This itinerary starts from Tongkyuk (86 km northwest of Ningchi) on the main Tibet–Sichuan highway. Sited at the Rong Chu–Tongkyuk Chu confluence, this small town is 14 km southwest of Tongme and 130 km west of Pomi. The trek heads generally west along the Tongkyuk Chu, which is bordered on the north by the Po Yigrong Range. It explores Draksum Latso and offers optional hikes into the seldom visited Salween Divide, which in this region is dominated by beautiful, sacred Mt Namla Karpo.

ROUTE SUMMARY

Place	Distance (km)	Trail notes
Tongkyuk–Temo	2	Along the Tongkyuk Chu's left bank through a narrow pine-forested valley.
Paka	7	The path hugs the steep mountain side. Paka is an attractive village with wooden houses surrounded by peach trees. Beautiful view of the Po Yigrong Range. A trail leads north along the Paka Phu Chu to Sobhe La; cross the Po Yigrong Range to the Po Yigrong Valley (see below).
Lokmo	8	Cross the Paka Phu Chu to Lokmo, a village of much cultivation, at the Nambu Chu–Nunkhu Phu Chu junction.
Nambu Monastery	30	Follow a long gorge along a narrow trail. Continue along the river, then up a cliff (4200 m) by stone steps. Reach a level, boggy valley with a small lake in a side valley. Nambu Monastery (destroyed) is surrounded by a wide valley with plenty of good pastures.
Nambu La	20	Pass a glacial lake at the head of the (4560 m) Nambu Chu Valley before the pass. Cross the Nambu La which, when approached from Tongkyuk, is so gradual as to be barely noticeable.
Lopa	24	Descend past a glacial lake. Cross a bridge over a glacial river coming from Mt Namla Karpo. Nam Tso, another glacial lake surrounded by fir trees, is up this valley. Descend to a boggy meadow, then reach Lopa in a more arid region.
Je	14	Cross a large glacial river coming from the (3658 m) north; ascend a ridge with Draksum Latso below, and descend across a gravel fan to reach Je (Jeba) by the lake.
Tsogo	5	Tsogo, wet and swampy in summer, is situated on an inlet.

OPTIONAL SIDE TRIPS FROM PAKA AND LOKMO

Paka (near Tongkyuk) to the Sobhe La on the Salween Divide

This trip allows one to cross the Po Yigrong Range and access the Po Yigrong Valley. From Paka (see above), follow the Paka Phu Chu's left bank northward to the Sobhe La (8 km). The route along the river goes through thick willow and rhododendron shrubbery; wade across several streams. After a silver fir forest, ascend due north through overlapping moraines, then follow a valley to the left and cross the Sobhe La of the Po Yigrong Range (cross from west-southwest to east-northeast). The trail then descends precipitously from the pass. Head north down to the Po Yigrong Valley. The giant yellow rhubarb, *rheum nobile* (see page 732), can be found near the top of the range in early summer. Sobhe La, a difficult pass, is usually open only during July, August, and September.

From Lokmo along the Nunkhu Phu Valley

This short excursion from Lokmo (see above) goes along the Nunkhu Phu Chu's left bank in a valley scoured out by a glacier long ago. The level path goes through a forest of buckthorn under the mountains of the Salween Divide. Reach the nomad camp of Bachumo after 22 km. Another camp, Lisum, is about 20 km further. A glacial lake lies 17 km from Lisum.

2 Draksum Latso to Kongpo Giamda via the Draksum Kye La: two weeks

From Draksum Latso, walk northwest to the Drukla Monastery, then turn up the Salween Divide, via the Draksum Kye La, before heading south to Kongpo Giamda on the main Tibet–Sichuan highway.

ROUTE SUMMARY

Place	Distance (km)	Trail notes
Draksum–Gyara	24	Travel to Draksum Latso's southwestern tip. Cross a bridge over the Draksum Chu, a river that has cut a channel through a moraine at the lake's end. Pass Tsomchuk at the foot of the moraine. The valley broadens; follow the river's north bank to Shi Dzong and Gyara.
Shoga	10	Continue along the right (north) bank past Kala Qu to Shoga, situated between the Draksum and Drukla rivers. Their combined waters flow south to the Nyang Chu near Namse Monastery on the Tibet–Sichuan highway. [From Shoga to the highway is 15 km along the left bank. At road marker 1246 km, hitch either west to Kongpo Giamda (48 km) or east to Bayi (85km).]
Drukla	12	Follow the Drukla Chu's left bank past Nola to Drukla Monastery. Ancient, ruined villages and defense twers (15 m high) can be seen here and there. The river divides before the monastery. Cross the smaller branch by bridge.

Pungkar	40	Continue northwest along the Drukla Chu into the heart of the Salween Divide. From Drukla to Chao, go along the left, then the right bank.From Chao, walk to Lo, then follow the left bank to Pungkar. Cross three bridges between Drukla and Pungkar.
Draksum Kye La	28	The glaciated upper Drukla Chu Valley has numerous hanging valleys. Cross the river twice by wooden bridge. (A branch valley leads over the Lachen La, 4875 m, to the Po Yigrong Valley. The pass is open most of the year.) Near the Draksum Kye La (5250 m) are nomads and their black tents. Cross the Salween Divide by this pass.
Atsa	37	Descend to a nomad camp. After a few km, join Gyalam, the old China–Tibet caravan route (see page 570). Then reach Lake Atsa (4553 m), 1 km by 5 km. Continue along its southeast shore and cross a river to Atsa Monastery, a place known for its strong winds and sudden storms. To the north is a low range crossed by the steep Banda La (5550 m). This pass leads to Lharigo and Chamdo. The Salween River can be reached in about ten days from Atsa Monastery (see page 574).
Trö La	37	Retrace the route from Atsa Monastery to the valley junction, then take the wide valley to the right (the left one goes back up the Draksum Kye La). Pass Kolep (nomad tents and cabins) and climb steeply to the Trö La.
Loru	29	The trail from the pass descends to a wide, grassy valley. A river flows due south and has nomad camps along its banks. Pass Tramdo and Ko Monastery (across the river) and follow the left bank to Loru.
Giamda	25	Villages are now more frequent. Continue due south along the left bank past Onpa Dzong and Chingnga to Giamda (road marker 1317 km) on the main Tibet–Sichuan highway. From here, hitch west to Lhasa (251 km) or east to Ningchi (169 km) or walk to the Tsangpo via the Se La from road marker 1352 km near Jasing.

NAMTSO:
A PILGRIMAGE TO SKY LAKE AND THE BIRD SANCTUARY OF TASHI DORJE HERMITAGE

Location	North of Lhasa
Map reference	NH46-9 B, 46-5 A B C D, 45-8 D, 45-12 B
Trekking days	Damxung–Tashi Dorje; 3
	Tashi Dorje–Shang Valley; 21
Start-Finish	Lhasa–Namtso–Shang Valley
Passes	Lhachen, Kiang, Kalamba

OVERVIEW

Namtso (Sky Lake) is one of Tibet's renowned holy lakes. Despite its isolation on the Changtang (Northern Plateau), pilgrims visit regularly and a few hardy ones perform the full ritual circumambulation (18 days). The lake, at 4718 m above sea level, is 70 km long, and 30 km wide. It is the second largest saltwater lake in all of China and Tibet; only the Kokonor (Qinghai Hu) in Amdo is bigger. Tibet has over 1500 lakes; the most expansive are Namtso, Siling Tso, and Zhari Namtso. Most have no outlet.

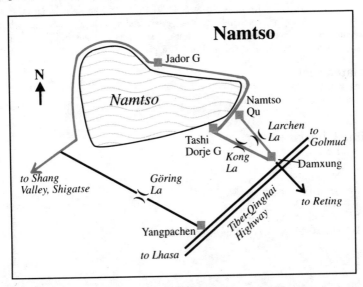

The southeastern end of Namtso is easily accessible from Lhasa. Namtso Qu, the district administrative center of the lake, (191 km from Lhasa), is linked to the capital by road. En route from Lhasa, pass the Yangpachen Monastery and a geothermal power station that provides much of Lhasa's electricity. Interesting short excursions from the former include walks to Dorjeling Nunnery and Tsurphu Monastery, main seat of the Karmapa sect. Damxung, a *xian*-level town on the Lhasa–Golmud road, has cave monasteries nearby and a horse festival each summer.

A visit to the lake requires crossing the Nyenchen Tanglha, Tibet's magnificent median range, which extends 500 km from east to west. Its snowcapped mountains flank Namtso on the south and its highest peak, Mt Nyenchen Tanglha (7088 m), towers over the lake. A bird sanctuary, home to great flocks of migratory birds and assorted water fowl, is at Namtso's southeast corner. At the tip of a nearby peninsula is Tashi Dorje, a deserted cave hermitage. Rugged cliffs contain dozens of limestone caves, some with unusual, primitive cave paintings. Without a doubt, this part of the lake, with its unsurpassed sense of space, is among the most breathtaking places of Central Tibet.

A popular sacred route (*nekhor*) circles the promontory and one of Tibet's longest, most impressive *mani* walls is here. The lake shore, graced with lovely pebble beaches, is superbly serene and untouched. Try to spend at least a couple of days here.

Optional trek:
Tashi Dorje–Namtso north shore–Shang valley

A track encircling the lake anti-clockwise heads north and then west from Namtso Qu. Along the way are isolated nomadic settlements and monasteries. Jador Monastery once had large mysterious mounds of unknown function. A trail from the northwest tip of the lake goes to the southwest, traversing an empty land with only rare nomads. (This portion of the route has an Exploratory Trek advisory, see page 669.) After crossing the Kalamba La (5240 m), pass wonderful hot springs, powerfully gushing geysers, and a number of monasteries before descending the prosperous Shang Valley to Shigatse. A side excursion joins the Zabso pilgrimage, widely regarded as the most sacred in Tsang (see page 877).

Related sections
Shang Valley, p 869
The Lhasa–Shigatse north route, p 815
Tsurphu, p 671

Time Chart

Day	Place
1	Lhasa–Damxung
2	Namtso Qu
3	Tashi Dorje Hermitage
4	Namtso Qu
5–12	Namtso Qu–North Shore
13–24	Namtso–Shang Valley (Exploratory Trek)

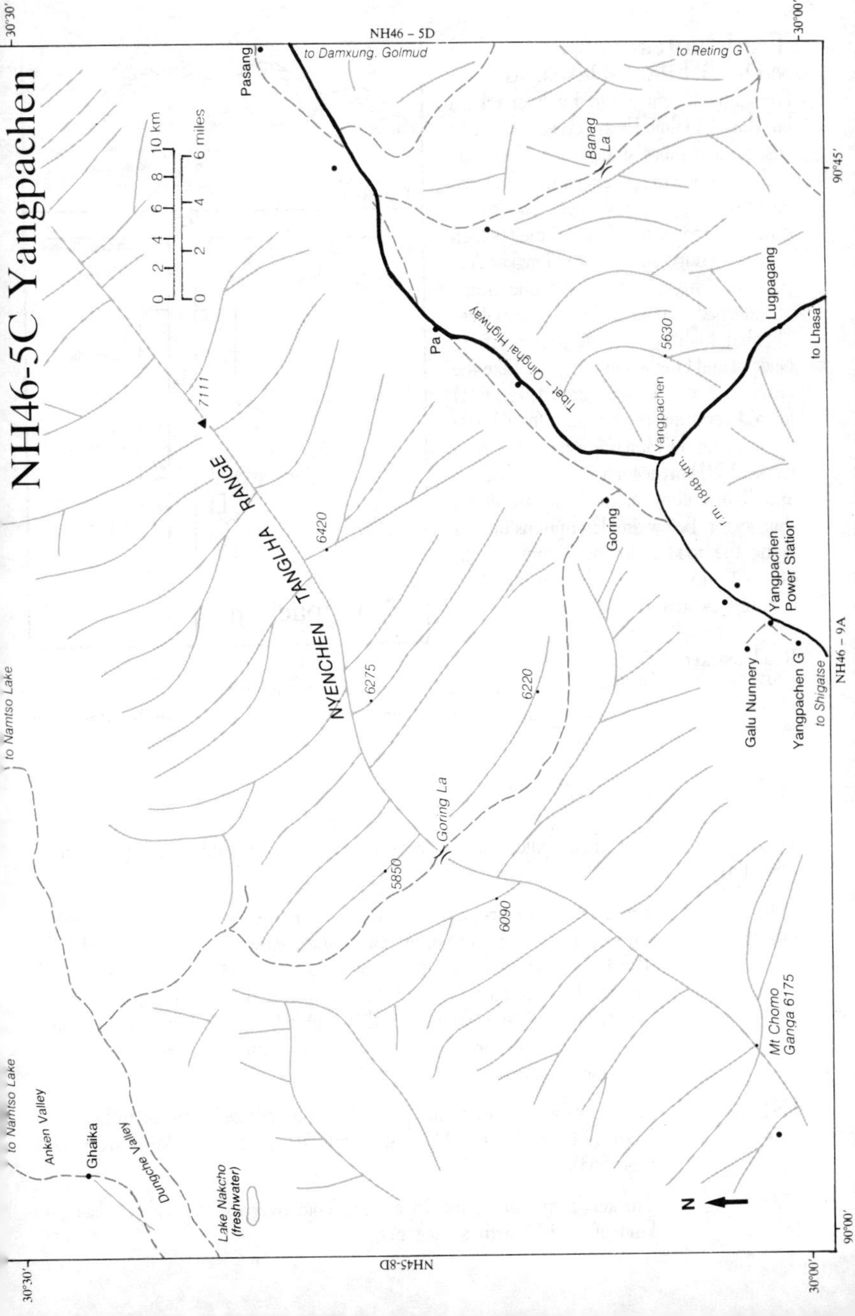

NH46-5C Yangpachen

NH46 – 5D

to Damxung. Golmud

to Reting G

Pasang

Banag La

Tibet – Qinghai Highway

Pa

Lugpagang

to Lhasa

5630

Yangpachen

7111

NYENCHEN TANGLHA RANGE

6420

f m. 1848 km.

Goring

Yangpachen Power Station

6275

Galu Nunnery

Yangpachen G

6220

to Shigatse

NH46 – 9A

Goring La

5850

6090

to Namtso Lake

Mt Chomo Ganga 6175

to Namtso Lake

Anken Valley

Ghaika

Dungche Valley

Lake Nakcho (freshwater)

N

0   2   4   6   8   10 km
0   2   4   6 miles

30°30'
30°00'
90°45'
90°00'
90°30'

NH45-8D

Trail Notes
✤ DAY 1 LHASA–DAMXUNG

From Lhasa, rent a car, hitch or take a bus (Lhasa-Golmud bus or Lhasa–Damxung bus, from the bus station one block east of the post office) past Drepung Monastery. After the big Lhasa Western Suburb gas station, the paved road forks. The left branch crosses a bridge and goes to Gongkar Airport and Shigatse. The right one (starting at road marker 3879) is the Tibet–Qinghai highway, which goes north to Nagchu and Golmud in Qinghai. Take the latter. See the Tsurphu trek (page 671) for a description of the route from Lhasa to the Tsurphu Monastery turnoff at road marker 1897 km (new marker 3853). Gadong and Kyormolung monasteries are along that sector. Below are descriptions of sites along the road from the Tsurphu turnoff to Damxung. (Numbers in brackets denote new road markers.)

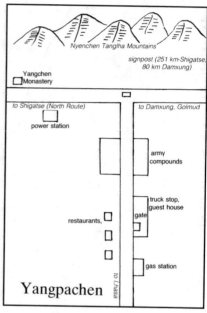

Road marker	Notes
1897 (3853)	A blue metal bridge on the left side of the road. (Cross the bridge into the Tölung Valley. This leads to Tsurphu Monastery, main seat of the Karmapa sect.)
1869 (3825)	Roadside tents, tea shacks.
1850 (3806)	The broad valley narrows into a gorge and the road begins to climb.
1848 (3804)	Yangpachen (Yangbejing). A desolate town with gas station, truck depots, Chinese restaurants, and army compounds. After the town the road forks. The left branch goes over the Shogar La (5300 m) to Shigatse (251 km). Yangpachen Monastery is 18 km after the turnoff (see page 679 for details on Dorjeling Nunnery and Tsurphu Monastery). The right branch continues to Damxung (75 km). Take this. After Yangpachen, the valley is flat and wide.
1791 (3746)	Settlement and valley to the right. This valley leads southeast to Lhündrub Xian (14 hrs by foot), then northeast to Reting Monastery (see page 563).
1785 (3740)	Truckers stop here to fish in a clear, cold river for the scaleless *huang* (a kind of catfish) with a long net.

1782   Suspension bridge, village, and side valley entrance are on the right. Incense
(3737)   burners mark the beginning of a tractor track into the valley.

1781   New monastery on top of small hill on the right. Beautiful pastures with many
(3736)   yaks.

1773   Damxung Xian, a government center with houses and compounds on both sides
(3729)   of the river. The Lhasa–Damxung bus stops here. Cross a concrete bridge left
of the main road and go for 1 km to the main government compound (cinema,
army station, Public Security Bureau, offices, restaurant, guest house; Rmb 5).
A solar bath house is just outside the guest house gate. A dirt track in front
of the compound goes to the right and on to Namtso. Moslem and Sichuan
restaurants are on the side of the main highway.

✤ Day 2 Damxung–Namtso Qu (via the Lhachen La) 38 km, 9 1/4 hr

If you came by bus from Lhasa, you can either walk this portion (dirt track) or hitch a ride
on the tractors that infrequently ply between the lake and Damxung. Given the choice, and
if you have sufficient time, the first option is by far the better. There are several nomad
campsites along the route; in their vicinities are good places for setting up tents. As this
is a particularly long day, it is a good idea to camp near one of the nomad settlements before
the pass. Cross the Lhachen La to reach Namtso Qu on the second day. Start the walk from
Damxung's main government compound.

Walking Time (Hr)

1   Jangra, a Gelugpa monastery with over 20 monks, is built inside cliffs on the
left side of the valley and has about ten cave dwellings. (Kangwa Monastery,
with over 40 monks, is in the valley behind Jangra 90 min away.) From the
main dirt track, turn left to Jangra (20 min).

Jangra to Namtso   A separate trail goes up the Jangra Valley, crosses a pass, and
then descends along scree slopes to Lake Namtso. Ford several easy rivers in the
first two days. Cross the pass on the third, then descend to the lake on the fourth.
There are no shelters. This is a viable option to following the dirt road, but only
if you are equipped and well-supplied.

---

1   Small village on the right. Cross a stream, then follow a river up a side valley
bearing to the right.

1/2   Nomad tents.

1/2   Valley narrows, cross a small bridge; the river is now on the left. Cross the river
again in 10 min, cross back in another 10 min; keeping the river to your left.
The valley opens up again.

NH46-5B Namtso Qu

1/2	Nomad tents.
3/4	Nomad tents.
3/4	Nomad tents.
1 3/4	Lhachen La Pass (5150 m; 25 km from Damxung); good view of Lake Namtso.
1/4	Nomad tents.
1	Walled mud compound on right.
1/4	Village on left.
1	Namtso Qu (4590 m) is a nondescript compound with mud houses and a basketball court near the lake. A guest house and a couple of shops are here. It is possible to hire yaks or horses here for the trip to Tashi Dorje Monastery.

✤ Days 3–4 Namtso Qu–Tashi Dorje Monastery–Namtso Qu

From Namtso Qu, walk west along the south shore of the lake. The faint track is 2–3 km from the shore and runs parallel to it. The Nyenchen Tanglha Range rises 25 km away to the south. Head southwest for 4 hr to some black tents sited near a trail junction (north to Tashi Dorje, south to Kong La; see below). The nomads here rent horses and a tent for travelers (usually a clean, white canvas tent big enough for six people, with blankets and carpets on the floor). A daily fee is charged for the horse, the tent, water, and fire (yak dung). Bargain but expect to pay Rmb 10–15 per person per day. Take the north track towards the lake; skirt a swampy, hummocky area by going west of it. Reach the western shore of a large inlet in 1 1/4 hr. Bird life teems here. April to November is a good time to view the large flocks of migratory birds that use this as a base. In early summer, it is possible to get glimpses of the rare black-necked cranes. In the distance to the northwest are two distinct, low brown, flat-topped hills, separated by a narrow gap. They border Namtso and take 1 1/2 hr of easy walking along a flat, grassy plain to reach. Deserted Tashi Dorje Hermitage is built inside caves at the base of the low hill, called Tashi Dor Chungchung, on the left.

Tashi Dorje Hermitage

About seven cave chapel-dwellings comprise the hermitage, known to pilgrims simply as Tashi Dor. Most caves are walled in by low enclosure walls and all are empty, with no artefacts or evidence of religious activities (over 30 monks once lived here). Some of the caves have built-in mud stoves. The far ones, to the extreme left and right, have faint traces of murals. It is quite possible to stay in any one of these cave dwellings for an extended period. With the vast deserted lake close by and a few nomads camped half a day's walk away, this hermitage is as remote and splendid as any in Tibet. Farther to the left, by the lake, are two phallic towers of rock, standing dramatically against the expansive turquoise waters.

Nekhor

An idyllic pilgrimage circuit (2 hr) surrounds the hill of Tashi Dor Chungchung but does not extend to the one on the right (Tashi Dor Thuje). Starting from the cave hermitage, follow the base of the small ridge clockwise past more empty caves. Reach a place where the path makes a sharp left to follow the contour, going through a corridor defined by the hill on the right and an eroded mound of rock on the left. Here is a meditation cave, a small *mani* wall, and a water hole situated well above the lake level. Continue along the base (the lake is now on the left); the path is marked occasionally by votive cairns. The next cave is a so-called 'booming cave'. It has a low 1.2-m entrance but its interior is high enough to stand. The ceiling and side wall have a number of shafts that penetrate into the rock strata. Pilgrims make a point of making loud noises in order to hear the echoes.

After exiting, walk past a concavity to reach the Gesar Drubphuk. Over the centuries, pilgrims have left talismans and junk inside. There are pieces of wool, bits of Khampa headdresses, cloth, hair, etc, all affixed to the walls by globs of butter. Some crude drawings, including reversed swastikas (religious symbol of the Bönpos), are also on the wall. At the back, on the floor, is a protruding piece of rock polished to a shine by the foreheads of innumerable pilgrims. It has an imprint attributed to Gesar of Ling, the epic hero of Tibetan folklore.

The path now strikes off towards the lake shore at the tip of the promontory. Pass eroded rock shutes. The hill's extremity is marked by many votive cairns and one stone mound festooned with prayer flags. Some *mani* stones are even submerged beneath the lake's surface. Walk back to the base of the hill to round the tip of the promontory. Here a narrow chasm extends into the rock; pilgrims crawl through this to light candles within a small cavity. Coming back out to a patch of grass dominated by a cairn at the promontory's tip, they perform their most meticulous prostrations to the west. After skirting the hill, the path follows its long side with the lake on the left. Cairns mark the way. Reach another cave at the promontory's other end. It is larger than the rest and its walls have simple ochre paintings. The strange, somewhat prehistoric style depicts scenes of hunting and schematic drawings of people and animals. Pilgrims perform a test here. With eyes closed and right arm extended, they try to negotiate the length (10 m) of the rubble-strewn grotto. The object is to touch a couple of coins, with index and middle finger, stuck on the far wall. Invariably most fail amidst loud hoots of laughter. To arrive within a few inches of the coins is considered respectable and a sign of good luck to come.

After this, pilgrims walk to the edge of the water and bless each other, their chattels and animals, by throwing water over all. This ritual usually begins in earnest, but soon degenerates into a protracted water fight, much to the dismay of the horses. Between the two low-slung brown hills is a spectacular wall of *mani* stones. The workmanship of the carvings is excellent and the number of tablets astonishing. Nomads and pilgrims continue to bring new *mani* stones to the wall but quite a few are also added to the spring or lake. A path near the *mani* wall goes up to the top of the ridge (1/2 hr), which is marked by more carved stones. This is a superb vantage point to take in the grandeur of the lake and the Nyenchen Tanglha. The valley due south provides an alternative return route back to Damxung (via the Kong La). The other low hill, not on the *khora* proper, has several caves at a point nearest the *mani* wall. About five of these also have primitive, ochre paintings. A pristine pebble beach is between the lake and the hills. The water is crystal clear and the swimming cold but wonderful. Though slightly brackish, it is quite alright to drink; pilgrims, however, maintain that it is bad for their stomachs and will only drink from the water hole on the *khora*. Two low islands to the northwest are visible from the summit of the hills. Birds at a certain time of the year retreat to these islands. The sense of space and solitude in this enormous basin is stupendous. Try to camp here for a few days to enjoy the magnificent surroundings.

Kong La: Optional return from Tashi Dorje to Damxung (three days)

Instead of retracing your steps to the Lhachen La, it is possible to cross an adjacent pass on the Nyenchen Tanglha range, the Kong La, to return to Damxung.

✧ Day 1 Tashi Dorje–nomad camp 5 3/4 hr

From Tashi Dorje, walk north back to the nomad camp located near the track junction. The opening of a valley can be seen to the south. Do not enter this. Instead, walk to the southwest across grassy plains and into the mouth of another valley immediately to its west. Follow a trail on the right (east) bank of the river. After passing a solitary nomad encampment (4 1/2 hr from Tashi Dorje), skirt the base of the east valley wall to reach a flat plateau with another nomad camp (1 1/4 hr).

✧ Day 2 Nomad camp–Kong La–south base of Kong La 3 1/2 hr

Beyond the nomad camp, the valley first trends to the left, then right. 1/2 hr from start, ford the river to its left bank. In quick succession, recross it twice to begin the final ascent of the Kong La (1 3/4 hr from nomad camp). From the broad saddle of the pass, descend south along the right (west) bank of a river. In 1 hr ford to the other side. Continue down to an expansive valley floor, the site of several nomad camps (3/4 hr). Four side valleys merge at this tremendous amphitheater.

✧ Day 3 South base of Kong La–Damxung 5 3/4 hr

From the valley floor, descend the valley by following the base of the east valley wall. Ford the river to its west bank in 1 3/4 hr. After 1 hr, trek up a low ridge in order to bypass a ravine. From the top, the town of Damxung and its airstrip can be seen. Descend along grassy slopes and then angle left (southeast) across the wide valley for Damxung (3 hr).

Lake Namtso *nekhor* Pilgrims completely circle Lake Namtso in about 18 days.

DAY 5–12 NAMTSO QU–NORTH SHORE (EIGHT DAYS)

This portion of the itinerary follows the northern shore of Namtso westward, after rounding the lake's northeast corner. Nomadic settlements, not more than 15 km apart, punctuate the route. Along the way are Jador and Dargye Lugudong monasteries, and several hermitages sited on off-shore islands. The terrain is easy, with the exception of a tract of land immediately north of Namtso Qu. Here, the broad Nai Chu must be forded and the vicinity is swampy in summer. The north shore is prime pasture land, so there are plenty of animals, especially during the warmer months. Avoid winter travel because of severe cold. Tibetans, however, sometimes use the route in this season to take advantage of the frozen rivers.

Below is a summary of the north shore route.

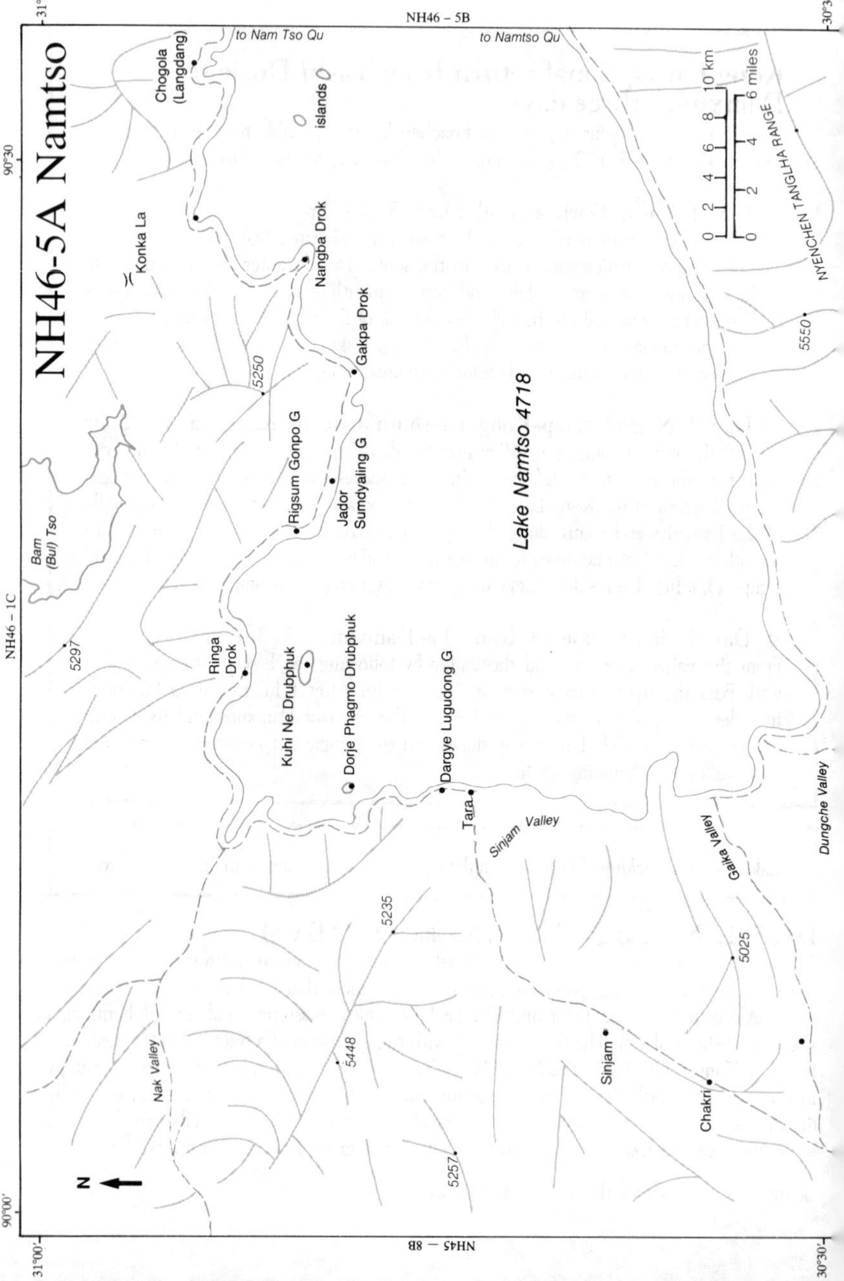

NH46 – 5B

NH46-5A Namtso

NH46 – 1C

to Nam Tso Qu

to Namtso Qu

Chogola (Langdang)

islands

Konka La

Nangba Drok

5250

Gakpa Drok

Rigsum Gonpo G

Jador
Sumdyaling G

Bam (Bul) Tso

5297

Ringa Drok

Kuhi Ne Drubphuk

Dorje Phagmo Drubphuk

Lake Namtso 4718

Dargye Lugudong G

Tara

Sinjam Valley

Nak Valley

5235

5448

Sinjam

Galka Valley

Chakri

5025

Dungche Valley

5550

NYENCHEN TANGLHA RANGE

5257

N

10 km

6 miles

NH45 – 8B

❖ **Day 5 Namtso Qu–Chang Phang Chuja (hot springs)**

Go north from Namtso Qu along the eastern shore. The going is wet and swampy near the Nai Chu, largest of the rivers that drain into the lake. Cross several tributaries and pass the settlement of Thugo Sumna (Shana). The snow peaks of Nuchin Gasa are to the east (right).

❖ **Day 6 Chang Phang Chuja–Dakmar**

Immediately after Chang Phang Chuja is the Thugo Sumna Monastery. Dakmar is located at the eastern shoulder of a peninsula that juts south into the lake.

❖ **Day 7 Dakmar–Langdang (or Chogola)**

Juniper (*shugpa*) bushes abound at Langdang. On a low hill is a monastery consecrated to a divinity called Chogola.

❖ **Day 8 Langdang–Nangba Drok**

After passing a village called Dakmar, the coastline turns southwest to Nangba Drok on a peninsula. Approximately 25 km to the northeast is Bam (Bul Tso), a large borax lake. Borax is a salt used as a spice for meat and tea and also for washing.

❖ **Day 9 Nangba Drok–Jador Sumdyaling Monastery**

Walk past Gakpa Drok to Jador, an interesting monastery described by the pandit Kishen Singh as having three large pyramidal structures made of sun-dried mud. The perimeter of each base was 150 m and all three were impressively tall. Passages led to central chambers, probably the tombs of high lamas. A carving of a gigantic doorway is on a nearby rock and tradition says the divinity, Nyenchen Tanglha, passed this way. Fossils here are greatly valued.

❖ **Day 10 Jador Sumdyaling Monastery–Ringa Drok**

Pass Rigsum Gönpo en route to Ringa Drok. An island with a cave retreat called Kuhi Ne Drubphuk, across from Ringa Drok, is 6 km from shore.

Alternative routes from Ringa Drok

1. Ringa Drok–Nagchu Xian on the main Tibet–Qinghai highway (288 km)

A major river, the Nag Chu, drains into the northwest tip of Namtso from the west. From Ringa Drok, follow its left bank to a dirt jeep track which goes northeastward to Chinglung (73 km). After 27 km come to Sailung; 18 km further is the settlement of Jangchö at the junction with the North Tibet Route (from Nagchu to West Tibet). From here the track goes east to the important town of Nagchu Xian (160 km). Tsomi Ri (5178 m) is near Sailung.

2. Ringa Drok–Banlung on the North Tibet Route

From the crossroads near Ringa Drok, follow a dirt track north to Baoji (12 km). Go past Mt Sangri (5445 m) on the right of the track to Banlung (52 km). From here, either go east to Nagchu (262 km) or west to Nyima, Gerze, and Shiquanhe (Ali), the capital of West Tibet.

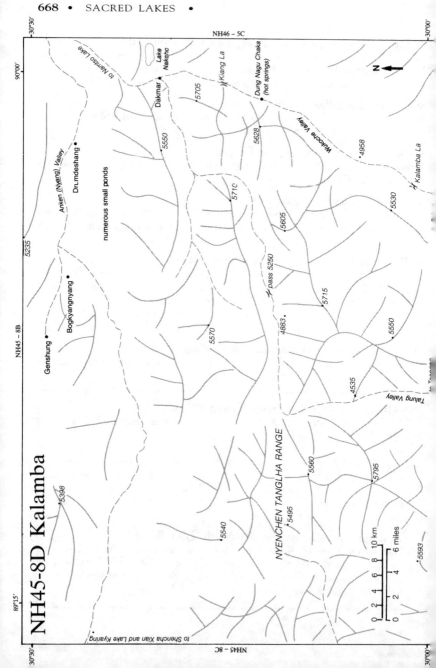

NH45-8D Kalamba

❖ **Day 11 Ringa Drok–Dargye Lugudong Monastery**

The trail rounds the lake's northwest corner and heads south (see alternate routes below). Snow mountains stand out to the southwest and the scenery is memorable. Another island close to shore has a small monastery and cave consecrated to Dorje Phagmo. Continue to Dargye Lugudong.

❖ **Day 12 Dargye Lugudong Monastery–Tara**

Tara is the last settlement on the lake. The trail after Tara veers away to the southwest. Retrace your way to Namtso Qu if you do not want to tackle the arduous route described below.

DAY 13–24 LAKE NAMTSO–SHANG VALLEY (12 DAYS)

The first section of the route from Namtso Qu to Shang Valley (gateway to the main town of Shigatse and the Tsangpo Basin) traverses Namtso's north shore. The next is an extremely isolated stretch of 10–12 days (Exploratory Trek). There are few permanent settlements and the route crosses the Kiang and Kalamba passes as well as a number of rivers. Spring and autumn are therefore good times to undertake this difficult walk. Summer is problematic; this is the time when the rivers are the most swollen. Attempt this journey only if you have adequate wilderness experience and gear and are used to handling severe weather conditions.

After Tara on Namtso's west shore, there are no villages until Nako at the beginning of the Shang Valley (see page 869). Small nomad camps, however, may be found. South of Salung Sumdo, more substantial ones can be expected. After crossing the Kiang and Kalamba passes, the trail descends into the Labu Valley, one of the tributaries of Shang. The region is noted for its amazing geysers and hot springs. Winter is a particularly good time to see these. Then, 10-m-high jets of water freeze into spectacular ice towers and the river is generally free of ice due to the large volume of thermal water.

❖ **Day 13 Tara–Sinjam**

Sinjam usually has over 50 nomad tents. Cross the Sinjam Chu, which flows into Namtso.

❖ **Day 14 Sinjam–Chakri**

At Chakri are ruins of a large mud compound with several houses of sun-dried bricks.

❖ **Day 15 Chakri–Gaika camp (4904 m)**

Cross the Gaika Chu, which flows into Namtso's southwest corner. The wide river, difficult to ford in the summer, is 1 1/2 km north of Gaika nomad camp. Namtso is now visible from Gaika. The Dungche nomad camp is a few km to the east. (A trail from here cuts through the Nyenchen Tanglha Range via the Göring La to Yangpachen Monastery (see page 679), 18 km west of Yangpachen.)

❖ **Day 16–17 Gaika camp–Dakmar camp**

After Gaika, follow the Dungche Chu south. Pass the west shore of Lake Nak Cho (fresh water). Continue along the Dungche Chu's left bank to Dakmar, a place full of nomads and their herds in the summer.

❖ **Day 18–19 Dakmar camp–Dung Nagu Chaka camp (hotsprings)**

Cross the easy Kiang La, then follow the left bank of the Wukoche Chu south to the nomad camp of Dung Nagu Chaka.

❖ Day 20 Dung Nagu Chaka camp–Kalamba La (south base)

Follow the left bank of the Wukoche to its source near the north face of the Kalamba La. From the pass (5240 m), parts of the Nyenchen Tanglha range can be seen to the east. The highest peak is Jomo Ganga (6175 m), a sacred mountain similar in shape to Mt Kailash. Crossing the Kalamba La is fairly difficult; the north side is steeper, as with most passes in this region. Camp at the southern base of the pass.

❖ Day 21 Kalamba La (south base)–Dungchaka

The Labu Valley begins after the pass. Follow the left bank of the Labu (Jomo) Chu and travel west to the hot springs at Dungchaka.

❖ Day 22 Dungchaka–Naisum Chuja

Naisum Chuja, a great pilgrimage site, is only 8 km from Dungchaka. Cross small rivers coming down from the Nyenchen Tanglha. Hot springs dot both sides of the Labu Chu. On the right bank are geysers, which become frozen ice columns in the winter.

❖ Day 23 Naisum Chuja–Korlung

A permanent nomad encampment is at Korlung (Phusum).

❖ Day 24 Korlung–Salung Sumdo

Another permanent camp is at Salung Sumdo (Labuphu).

Shang Valley and the Zabso pilgrimage For a description of the route south from the Kalamba La and Korlung along the Labu and Shang valleys to Shigatse, see the Shang Valley chapter, page 869. The important Zabso pilgrimage is also described.

TÖLUNG VALLEY: STRONGHOLD OF THE KARMA KAGYÜ

The upper Tölung Valley is the site of Tsurphu, supreme headquarters of the Karma-Kagyü tradition. Consisting of both the Black Hat and Red Hat factions, this ancient sect derived directly from the spiritual lineage of Milarepa in the 11th century. A pivotal force in affairs of state and religion in the 15th–16th C., the Karma-Kagyü patriarchs were favored by the emperors of Yuan and Ming China, receiving substantial political and financial support. The grandeur that was Tsurphu was a direct result of this special patron-priest relationship. Allied with the king of Tsang, the Karma-Kagyü became the principal force blunting the rise of Gelugpa power in Central Tibet. In the 17th C., the sect was irrevocably suppressed by the Fifth Dalai Lama and his Mongol partners. A number of excursions start from the Tölung valley. The one to Yangpachen Monastery is particularly worthwhile.

TSURPHU: PRINCIPAL TEMPLE OF THE BLACK HAT LAMAS

Location	Northwest of Lhasa
Map reference	NH46-9 A B
Trekking days	1
Start–Finish	Lhasa–Tsurphu
Passes	None

OVERVIEW

The journey from Lhasa to Tsurphu is essentially a pilgrimage to the historic stronghold of the Karma Kagyü, once one of the most powerful religious orders in Tibet. Tsurphu, the main Karmapa shrine, lies within Drowolung Valley, an upper tributary of the large Tölung Valley. Not far from here is another center of the sect, the Shamarpa (Red Hat) Nenang Monastery, which belongs to the Pawo Rinpoche lineage. A 4-day optional trek from Tsurphu leads to Yangpachen Monastery, chief temple of the Shamarpa.

The Tsurphu itinerary heads northwest out of Lhasa to enter the Tölung Valley. At its entrance, on the right bank of the river, is Kyormoling Monastery, an institution blessed

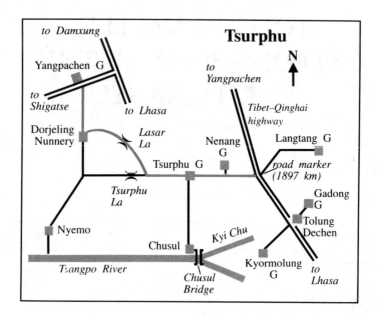

with surprisingly well-preserved architecture and murals. Next to this is the sacred spring of Lhachu, a renowned site consecrated to Guru Rinpoche. Side trails from here lead south to the Nam and Chusul valleys. (The latter, near the junction of the Kyi Chu and Tsangpo valleys, provides an optional way to reach Tsurphu.)

On the left bank of the Tölung is Gadong, formerly an important seat of a renowned oracle. One route leads north from the monastery to the summit of Mt Gephel Ri, a holy mountain overlooking Lhasa, and then circles back down to the capital. Another goes to the Phanyul temples of Nalanda and Langtang (see page 568). (A superb way to arrive at these celebrated monuments is via a footpath that begins at the confluence of the Drowolung and Tölung rivers and leads northeast over a pass to the Phanyul District.)

After visiting Tsurphu's rebuilt chapels and circumambulating Jampa Ri, home to several meditation retreats of past Karmapas, an interesting option is to cross the Lhasar La (5300 m). After the pass, descend to the prosperous Lhorong Chu Valley and either trek north to Dorjeling Nunnery and Yangpachen Monastery or south to the Nyemo Valley and the north bank of the Tsangpo. Between the Lhorong and the Tsangpo basin farther south are virtually untouched monasteries and hermitages with very little contemporary information.

Related Sections
Lhasa to Shigatse, p 815
Namtso, p 657

Access

Hitch or walk out of Lhasa past Drepung Monastery on the Tölung Dechen Xian road to the large gas station just west of Drepung. Here is a major road junction. Take the right, paved road (with new road markers starting at 3879; old marker 1941) that leads to Golmud in Qinghai Province (the left goes to the airport and Shigatse). It might be difficult to get a ride; be prepared for a long wait. The alternative is to take the Damxung or Golmud bus (see page 660, Namtso; the bus is the same one that goes from Lhasa to Nagchu Xian, departing the station located one block east of the post office). Get off at road marker 1897 km (new marker 3853). This is the Drowolung (Tölung) Valley entrance.

Time Chart

Day	Place	Hours
1	Lhasa–Drowolung	hitch or bus
2	Tsurphu Monastery	5 3/4

Trail Notes
✤ DAY 1 LHASA–DROWOLUNG VALLEY (LUNGPA ZAMPA BRIDGE)

Hitch or walk out of Lhasa past Drepung Monastery to reach the large gas station and road junction. (A side trip of 1 1/4 hr from the junction leads to Kyormoling Monastery (see below).) At the junction, to begin the journey to the Tölung Valley and Tsurphu, take the right, paved Golmud road to Tölung Dechen Xian at road marker 1921 km (new marker 3877), a bustling town with several Chinese compounds. From here, a short side trail leads up the slopes on the right for 2 km to Gadong Monastery (see below). Continue from Tölung Dechen Xian along the main road, with the large Töbing (Tölung) River on the left, to road marker 1897 km. Cross the river on a blue iron bridge called Lungpa Zampa (ignore an earlier, similar bridge). This is the entrance of the wide, flat Drowolung Valley, an upper branch of the Tölung (from here to Tsurphu Monastery is 28 km). Consider stopping at the first village for the night. On the eastern side of the river, near the turnoff for Tsurphu, is the village of Gachung. In its vicinity is Tragtse Monastery.

Gachung to Nalanda and Langtang monasteries: three days.

A trail from Gachung leads northeast to the monasteries of Nalanda and Langtang. Cross a 5350-m pass (4 hr), descend north, then east to the Pempo (Phanyul) Valley. Nalanda Monastery (see page 568) is 8 hr further. Close by is Langtang monastery.

Kyormoling Monastery and the sacred pond of Zhongpa Lhachung

Location At the large gas station at Lhasa's western suburbs, turn left (rather than right to Tsurphu and Golmud) and follow the paved airport road. Soon after the junction is the big concrete Dongkar Bridge. Immediately beyond it is a dirt road on the right that drops sharply from the paved road. Walk along this tree-lined track following the right bank of the Tölung (Tobing) Chu northwestward, for 1 1/4 hr to Kyormoling (7 km from the turnoff, 16 km from central Lhasa), a monastic complex beneath a low bluff. ➡

Kyormoling Monastery

Kyormoling was founded by Balti (1129–1215) of the Tsarong Vinaya school in the Yarlung Valley. Tsong Khapa studied here and a pupil of his converted the monastery to the Gelugpa. There were three colleges: Jampa, Pukhang, and Tsangnipa. The present incarnation of the Balti Rinpoche is the Dalai Lama's younger brother. Here are three handsome stone buildings. The stone work is nicely finished and there is little structural damage. The main building, at one end of a courtyard, has empty, cavernous halls containing some of the best-preserved murals in Central Tibet.

Zhongpa Lhachung

Near Kyormoling is the walled compound of the Zhongpa Lhachung chapel (also simply called Lhachu, 'Water of the Gods'). Inside the entrance is a courtyard. (To the left is a one-room chapel consecrated to Guru Rinpoche.) This is an active place where pilgrims and monks congregate. The right side opens onto another compound. Within is a small pond with prayer flags and trees marking a sacred spring. Pilgrims drink, collect the water, and circumambulate the pond.

Lhachu is a natural water spring, believed to be created by Guru Rinpoche when he inserted his walking stick into a seven-headed river called Chab Kago Dhunpa. Water from this river subsequently flowed into the Lhachu via a tree. It is said that even in the height of winter, fish swim here. Lucky pilgrims sometimes see the temple of the Eight Manifestations of Guru Rinpoche (Tsengye Lhakhang) inside the pond.

Kyormoling–Chusul: three days. Continue along the right (west) bank of the Tölung Chu. After rounding a ridge, a dirt track heads west up a side valley. Follow it to a valley junction (4 hr from Kyormoling). Take the left branch to go up to the Lungsang La (5 1/2 hr). Descend southward to Chusul Xian (6 1/2 hr) at the junction of the Kyi Chu and Tsangpo rivers. Another trail from the pass, the left branch, goes southeast down the Nam Valley to the Jang Chöling Monastery (see page 478).

Gadong Monastery

A dirt trail goes to the right from the center of Tölung Dechen Xian (at road marker 1921 km). Gadong Monastery, in the middle of a village, is 1/4 hr up a gentle slope. Once the seat of a famous oracle, it was founded by Zingpo Sherapa, probably in the 11th century. Tsong Khapa lived here for a time in a meditation cave. The handsome main building still stands but is usually locked. Inside are original murals and decorated beams and pillars. Beyond the monastery is a chapel with recent sculptures and old murals. One monk with a hearing-aid lives here.

Gadong–Mt Gephel Ri and Lhasa

A trail continues up the Gadong Valley to the north then northeast. It leads to the summit of sacred Mt Gephel Ri (page 156), 5 1/2 hr from the monastery. From the top, a footpath leads back to Lhasa in 4 hr. This forms an interesting circuit of two days. Another option from the top is to head northeast to Nalanda (5 1/4 hr) and Langtang monasteries in the Phanyul Valley (see page 568).

✤ Day 2 Drowolung Valley–Tsurphu Monastery 5 3/4 hr

Walk along an unpaved road up the Drowolung Valley due west. There is little traffic. A village is on the right at the valley entrance, and after 1 1/2 hr, the valley divides. (Here are two villages; the one to the left [south] is Nampa.) The main road continues straight ahead and then turns south to go up either the Nampa La or Lungsang La (from the junction to the latter is 6 3/4 hr; descend south to Chusul Xian, a further 6 1/2 hr). Do not take this. Follow the side road to the right (west). Soon reach an earth plaque (3 m by 2 m) on the roadside, then cross a small bridge 4 km from the turnoff. Continue up the valley for 2 1/2 hr (from the turnoff) until it divides again. Before this junction is Nakar, on the right on a terrace above marshy land. Above the village, over a small ridge, is rebuilt Nenang Monastery (1/2 hr from the road) in a grove of trees.

> ### Nakar–Chusul Xian via the Nampa La
> A side valley at the Nakar junction goes due south (acute left) towards the Nampa La. In 3 hr, the valley branches; take the left route to the pass (3 hr). Descend south to Chusul Xian (6 3/4 hr) at the junction of the Kyi Chu and Tsangpo rivers.

From the valley junction, follow the left valley straight ahead. Immediately cross a bridge and then another one in 10 min. 1 3/4 hr further is Tsurphu Monastery, on a slope north of the river. An old, active monastic compound, left of the road 1 km before Tsurphu, was the summer residence (Linka Wök) of the Karmapa Lama. Due west, beyond the monastery at the head of the valley, is a range of snow mountains and the Tsurphu La Pass.

Nenang Monastery

This rebuilt monastery now has about 20 monks. Its main buildings are the Jampa Lhakhang and Lhakhang Chenmo.

History Nenang is a Shamarpa (Red Hat) monastery that looked to Yangpachen Monastery, the sect's main seat, for spiritual guidance. One of its past abbots was Pawo Tsuklak Trengwa, an acclaimed historian. The monastery was founded in 1333 by Tokden Drakpa Senge (1283–1349), the first Shamarpa. With the establishment of the Shamarpa sub-sect, the Karma-Kagyü effectively was divided into two branches, the Black Hats of the Karmapa and the Red Hats. After Yangpachen's founding in 1490, the abbots of Nenang came from the line of Pawo Rinpoches. The first one was the ascetic, Pawo Chöwang Lhündrub (1440–1503).

Tsurphu Monastery

Tsurphu Monastery, sited in the upper reaches of the Drowolung Valley, was an impressive complex, one of the most handsome of Central Tibet. The ravages of the 1960s badly damaged most of its buildings. Today, among extensive ruins, are huge, cavernous shells with walls reaching to 10 m. Before the devastation, the 16th Karmapa, Rangjung Rikpai Dorje (1924–81) escaped to Sikkim with many of Tsurphu's treasures. A new Karmapa center was founded in Rumtek.

The rebuilding of Tsurphu was spearheaded by Lobsang Yeshe. He and others requested permission to renovate the site; reconstruction of the Zhiwa Tratsang, retreat centers, and

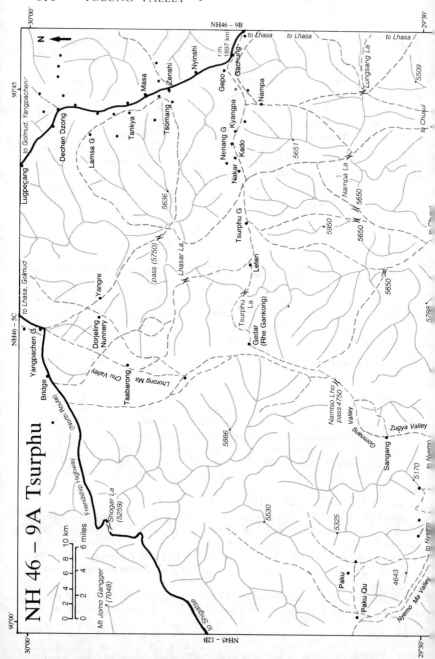

the palace of Gyaltsab Rinpoche began in 1983 with government funds. Later, extensive work continued under Drupön Dechen Rinpoche, a disciple of the 16th Karmapa, who returned from Ladakh to Tibet in 1984. In its heyday, the principal buildings of the monastery were the Lhakhang Chenmo, main chapel and palace of the Karmapa, the palace of the Gyaltsab Rinpoches, and two smaller chapels, the Zhiwa Tratsang and Zuri Lhakhang. The present assembly hall is within the Zhiwa Tratsang, noted for its Chinese-inspired *thangkas*. In the center of the spacious chamber is a throne reserved for the Karmapa. Flanking it on the right is an old statue of Nugu Rinpoche, tutor of the Eight-Karmapa, Mikyö Dorje, who in turn taught Pawo Tsuklak Trengwa, the historian. To the left are statues of the First, Second, and 16th Karmapas.

Upstairs is the monastery's *gönkhang*, dedicated to the protectors, Mahakala, Palden Lhamo, and Tamche Chogyel. The murals here are new. Also on this floor is an ornate bedroom reserved for the Karmapa Rinpoche. Within a glass cabinet are small images of the various Karmapas. Jamgön Kongtrul Rinpoche and Tai Situ Rinpoche, both incarnate lamas of the sect, stayed here when they visited Tsurphu in 1984. The former ordained over 30 monks and at that time met with officials in Beijing and Lhasa to request permission to rebuild the main chapel. This was granted and work started in 1985. Another residential chamber contains images of Kagyü patriarchs, Marpa, Milarepa, and Gampopa. A statue of the 16th Karmapa is to the right of Marpa.

A new assembly hall, the *tshokhang*, has been constructed on its original site right of the Zhiwa Tratsang. Behind it are impressive ruins of two major buildings. One, with a very high wall, was the palace of the Karmapa, the Lhakhang Chenmo (Drowolung Tsuglag Khang). Installed here was Tsurphu's most sacred statue, a huge 20-m brass Buddha called Lachen Dzamling Gyenchik ('Ornament of the World'), which supposedly contained relics of Sakyamuni. Built by the Second Karmapa, Karma Pakshi, after his return from China (ca 1265), it was widely known as Tibet's largest Buddha statue constructed from one mold. According to tradition, after the statue was forged, Karma Pakshi simply lay on his side in the posture of the statue. He then righted himself and by exercising his considerable vital powers (*lung*), he caused the statue also to rise into place. Within the Zimchung Chime Dhedhen Wöselkhyil, an upstairs room, the famed Karmapa black pills (*rilnak*) were secretly manufactured. These were greatly prized for their potency against a multitude of diseases.

Overlooking these principal buildings are ruins of the five-story Gyaltsab Potrang Chökhang, palace of the Gyaltsab Rinpoche, incarnates of an important Karma-Kagyü lineage whose head lamas served as regents of the order. They held power over their own institutions within the Tsurphu complex. This building is sometimes called Chögar Ghong, 'the camp above'. A large rebuilt white hermitage, Drubtra Samtenling, is high up on a steep ridge behind the main chapel (the path up takes 3/4 hr). To its left is Pema Khyung Dzong, a renowned retreat of Karma Pakshi, the Second Karmapa (1204–83), and Rangjung Dorje, the Third (1284–1339). Just above this was Muntsham, a cave where Karma Pakshi meditated in complete darkness. A statue of him here was said to have spoken out loud during his sojourn in Mongolia. West of Pema Khyung Dzong are more retreat cells distinguished by their lack of windows: only one window for each building of four chambers. Retreats usually lasted for three years; practitioners were locked in.

The Tsurphu khora

A pilgrim path (nekhor) around the monastery takes in the retreats and meditation complexes above Tsurphu. It first leads west (from the western perimeter of the complex) along the road, passing mani walls, to the confluence of two valleys and a ridge called Jampa Ri. To its south is a summer residence of the Karmapa. Farther to the north, the path passes Tsurphu Durtrö, the cemetery. After making its way east to the hermitages of Samtenling and Pema Khyung Dzong (3/4 hr), the circuit begins its descent after passing two rebuilt shrines consecrated to Palden Lhamo and Tamdrin. Regain the main road and Tsurphu by zigzagging down a small ravine (3/4 hr). Budget 2–3 hr for the khora. Across the river from the monastic grounds is a large, conspicuous wall built in steps into the hillside. This displayed a huge thangka (gheku) during the tenth day of the fourth lunar month.

History

Tsurphu was founded in 1187 by Düsum Khyenpa (1100–93) whose birthplace was Treshe in Kham's Sharda district. At 20 he traveled to Central Tibet and studied at important institutions like the Sangphu Monastery (see page 490) near Lhasa. Known as the First Karmapa, at age 30 he became a follower of Rechungpa and Gampopa, the two principal disciples of Milarepa. The monastery's founding was first predicted by the latter; then Düsum Khyenpa had a vision of Tsurphu appearing as the mandala of Demchok. He is credited with the founding of the Karmapa sect. The movement began in 1147 in Kham near Riwoche and Derge, two renowned monasteries. In 1155, the Karmapas built Tshur Lhalung Monastery and in 1187, Karma Lhadeng Monastery. Tsurphu became the Karmapa headquarters at the end of Düsum Khyenpa's life.

  A major practice instigated by him was the establishment of tulkus, incarnates of a particular lineage. Shortly before his death, he predicted he would soon be reborn in Tibet and gave clues for the identification of his coming incarnation. This phenomenon was adopted by the Gelugpa and accounts for the uninterrupted succession of Dalai Lamas and Panchen Lamas. Düsum Khyenpa was reborn as Karma Pakshi, the Second Karmapa, who was well known for his magical powers. These so impressed the Mongol-Yuan court of Kublai Khan that he was accorded the title of Pakshi and given a black hat decorated with gold. With new wealth from his patrons, he greatly expanded Tsurphu during the 13th century. Subsequently, the Karmapa patriarchs maintained strong ties with the Yuan and Ming dynasties in China.

  In the 15th C., during the decline of the Phagmo Drupa empire in Central Tibet, the Karmapas became very close to the princes of Rinpung (an influential principality in Tsang) and were deeply embroiled in Tibet's politics. The princes and the Karmapa led the fight against the Gelugpa—essentially a power struggle between the rulers of Tsang and those of Central Tibet. Finally, in 1642, the Fifth Dalai Lama, with help from Gushri Khan and his Mongolian army, devastated the Tsang princes and the Karmapa once and for all. Tsurphu was sacked by the Mongols and the sect's involvement in politics ended.

Tsurphu to Dorjeling Nunnery and Yangpachen Monastery on the Lhasa–Shigatse road

This is a four-day trek from Tsurphu to the Shamarpa main seat, Yangpachen Monastery. It involves crossing the 5300-m Lhasar La, one of several passes straddling the Tsurphu range. From Yangpachen it is possible to hitch southwest along the Friendship Highway (see page 817) to Shigatse, or to return to Lhasa by following the Tibet–Qinghai highway.

✤ Day 1 Tsurphu–Leten 3 hr

Follow the dirt road west from Tsurphu. It soon divides; take the right fork. After going through a narrow valley, pass some nomad tents to reach another valley junction. More nomad tents are here (1 1/2 hr). Take the left branch, fording to the river's right (south) bank. In 1/2 hr, a trail leaves the road to go up the slopes on the left. Take this to ascend to Leten (1 hr), sited near the top of a ridge. (A trail traversing the south side of this ridge leads to the Tsurphu La and then to Lhorong Valley, from where the Tsangpo basin can be reached in two to three days.)

✤ Day 2 Leten–valley junction 4 1/2 hr

The Lhasar La is due north of Leten. From the village, descend to the north, cross a small tributary stream, and hike up the ridge on the other side. Continue north, negotiating another ridge in the process. On the far side of this, follow a river to the northwest; it is necessary to ford it in a couple of places. 2 1/4 hr from Leten, come to a small valley junction with rivers coming in from left and right. Walk up between them (due north) to the Lhasar La (3/4 hr), marked by stone cairns. Descend along the west wall of a valley. After passing some nomad tents and stone enclosures, reach a valley junction (1 1/2 hr).

✤ Day 3 Valley junction–Dorjeling Nunnery 5 hr

From the valley junction, take the left, crossing its river to the north bank and following its course to the west. In 1/2 hr, come to a nomad encampment. Continue west along the base of the valley's north wall. A small river comes in from the right 1/2 hr beyond the nomads. Cross this and then climb the slopes to the north. Cross the low saddle and then drop down the other side to an east–west valley (1/2 hr). Follow this due west, reaching the large Lhorong Chu Valley (north–south) in 1/2 hr. From this point on, more settlements are met along the way. Walk north along the Lhorong Chu to Dorjeling (2 hr), a recently rebuilt nunnery with over 30 Kagyü nuns. It is sited at the base of vertical cliffs.

✤ Day 4 Dorjeling–Yangpachen Monastery 4 hr

Take the dirt road that trends west from the nunnery, passing houses and fields. In 1 1/4 hr, reach the large river of the Lhorong Ma Chu. Ford this to its left (west) bank, then follow it north to the north route of the Friendship Highway (2 1/4 hr). A bridge is crossed just before this main road. Turn right to Yangpachen Monastery (1/2 hr), located near road marker 18.

YANGPACHEN MONASTERY

This monastery was the main seat of the Shamarpa sect; the first Shamarpa was a student of the famed Third Karmapa, Rangjung Dorje (1284–1339). Shamarpa denotes Red Hat, the better to distinguish it from the Black Hat Karmapa, which has its headquarters at Tsurphu. Its teachings, derived from Milarepa, stress severe asceticism and meditation. An actual red hat became the trademark of this sub-sect and was bestowed upon the first Shamarpa by a Mongolian emperor. The monastery was founded in 1490 by Muran Jampa Thukje Pal under instructions from the Fourth Shamarpa and financially supported by the Rinpung princes. The Shamarpa ruled the Yangpachen district for three centuries until the Gelugpa wrested it away;

the Gurkha invasion of 1792 triggered the transition. Nepal's adventurism was stopped short by a Chinese army; the Emperor perceived the Shamarpa to be too closely allied with the Gurkhas. The Tenth Shamarpa was stripped of his title, his lineage terminated, and the Gelugpa took over. The 13th Shamarpa now lives in Nepal and his rights have been finally reinstated. Yangpachen was rebuilt in 1986 and is a thriving center with nearly 100 monks.

LHODRAK: THE PILGRIM SITES OF SOUTH TIBET

FROM YARLUNG TO MILAREPA'S NINE-STORY TOWER, A GURU RINPOCHE CAVE, AND A WALK AROUND LAKE PEMALING

Location	South Tibet
Map reference	NH46-13 A B C D, 46-14 A
Trekking days	10 (one-way)
Start–Finish	Tsomi–Manda Qu
Passes	Drum La

OVERVIEW

Home to mystic hideaways, Lhodrak—just north of the Bhutan border—is a vast district encompassing much of southern Tibet. Getting to the trail-head requires patience and luck, but the effort is worth its while. This pristine, unspoiled enclave includes six first-rate sacred sites: Mawochok, Benpa, Karchu and Lhakhang, Serkhar Guthok, Lake Pemaling, and Lhalung. Important masters of Tibetan Buddhism spent a great deal of time in retreat within these hermitages. Foremost among them were Guru Rinpoche, Milarepa, and Marpa. Others, including famous text discoverers (*tertöns*), were Nyima Wösel, Pemalingpa, Guru Chuwang, and Ratna Lingpa.

      The route to Lhodrak begins from the southern end of the Yarlung Valley near Yumbu Lagang, the castle of early kings (see page 539). Near Tsomi is Mawochok, an important but little-known pilgrimage site consecrated to the Rigsum Gönpo, the divine trinity of Chenresi, Chana Dorje, and Jampelyang. Outside of the three greatest pilgrim centers—Kailash, Tsari, Lapchi—it is among a handful of Tibet's most powerful places of worship. From Tsomi, the route then follows the Lhodrak River south to the Benpa Valley. En route are a series of stone watchtowers, unique to this part of Tibet and considered by some scholars to be the prototypes of Tibetan architecture. Sacred places with hidden religious treasures (*terne*) are cloistered within the valley; also here are the mystic claw-prints of the she-devil, Drak Sinmo Barje, and a number of Guru Rinpoche caves.

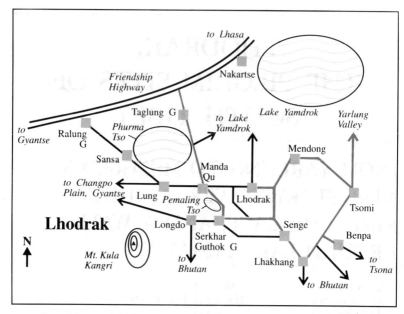

Beyond Benpa is Lhakhang, a village superbly situated at the confluence of three rivers, immediately north of the Bhutan border. Khothing, within the village, is one of King Songtsen Gampo's four famed Tandul monasteries (see page 43) built in the 7th C. to suppress Tibet's demoness. Nearby is Karchu Monastery built on a beautiful pine-clad ridge and hemmed in by magnificent snow peaks. Mt Chakphur Chen, a secret retreat in a side valley, was where Guru Rinpoche meditated for seven years. Other sites include Pal Gi Phuk Ring, the cave where Namkhai Nyingpo achieved enlightenment; and Lhamo Kharchen, a replica of Devikota, one of India's 24 most sacred places. If time allows, it is highly worthwhile to spend a few days in the Karchu area.

After Lhakhang, the pilgrimage makes an abrupt turn northwest to Serkhar Guthok Monastery, built personally by Milarepa (1040–1143), Tibet's most famous poet-mystic, as an offering to his teacher Marpa. This unusual, nine-story tower stands at the base of Mt Kula Kangri (7538 m), one of the highest peaks in Tibet. Despite its fame in Tibet, few Westerners have visited the shrine since Hugh Richardson, head of the British Mission in Lhasa, did so in the 1940s. Near the tower is Marpa's own Drowolung (Valley of the Birches) Monastery, and Taknya Lungten Phuk, supposedly Milarepa's first cave retreat. This part of Lhodrak is noted for a splendid hot spring, set in a secluded section of the valley.

From Serkhar Guthok, the route continues to Pemaling Tso, a high-altitude lake widely considered one of Tibet's most sacred. Within easy reach of the glaciers of Kula Kangri, it is a sublime Shangri-La of the Tibetan–Bhutan Himalayas. After crossing the Drum La Pass, with its stupendous views of Kula Kangri's snowpeaks, reach the Lhalung Gompa, a substantial monastic complex and main seat of Pemalingpa, a distinguished 15th-C. discoverer (*tertön*) of 'hidden texts'. Nearby are the monasteries of Guru Lhakhang (Guru Chowang's main seat), Lhatag, and Kyichu, reputedly also built by King Songtsen Gampo. Finally, a good road returns to Lhasa via Nakartse. An optional trek goes from Lhodrak to the isolated nomadic region of Phurma Tso, a large seldom-visited lake. From here the route veers north to Ralung Monastery near the Friendship Highway. (For this itinerary, see page 606.)

Related sections
Lake Yamdrok to Lhodrak, p 606
Yarlung Valley, p 515
Lhasa to the Yarlung Valley, p 595
Tsari, p 208

Access: Tsomi Xian
LHASA TO TSETHANG
The Lhodrak pilgrimage is intimately linked with the Yarlung Valley and is best done after an exploration of its principal shrines. If time is limited, start from Lhasa and take buses or hitch to Tsethang on the south bank of the Tsangpo.

TSETHANG TO TSOMI XIAN
From Tsethang, hitch or walk along the west branch of the Yarlung Valley along the Chongye River to Chongye (see page 527). Then walk south (on the main road) past a cinema in the town square, the bridge, and King Songtsen Gampo's tomb (20 minutes from the beginning of town). From here, hitchhike to the town of Tsomi, 96 km from Chongye, 5 hr away by a slow Chinese truck. The road heads south through a long, narrow valley, crosses the Yasang (Cheya) Pass (5200 m), then descends to a wide, stony plain. Lake Drigu (4725 m) is here; along the shore are countless water birds, and a few herds of yaks and sheep. A lone village, Drigu Qu, stands at the northwestern end of the lake, one of the windiest places in Tibet; nearly every house has a windmill. On its outskirts is the rebuilt one-room chapel of Namgyal Tratsang. After crossing a desert-like plain, the road goes over the Shar Khalep Pass (5129 m) and enters a dramatic canyon. Its steep ravines are so eroded as to resemble the labyrinthine canyons of Tholing and Tsaparang in West Tibet. Ruins line the side of the road. The first village after the canyon is Haide. Between here and Tsomi (3825 m), one of Lhodrak's two main towns, are the ruined monasteries of Rimon, Tashi Chöling, and Churli; all are off the road in side valleys.

Lake Drigu
Drigu is a sacred lake (and bird sanctuary) consecrated by Guru Rinpoche. The locals believe it possesses divinatory powers: before the Chinese occupation of Tibet in 1959, the birds disappeared, the lake's color deepened, and the surroundings took on a haunting eeriness. According to the villagers, these omens foretold an impending disaster. The rise and fall of the lake's level provides other clues about the future. When it drops, diseases increase and crops fail. Abundant water brings well-being to man, animals, and crops. The strong convergence of Drigu's waves towards Drigu Dzong (Drigu Qu) is taken as an auspicious sign.

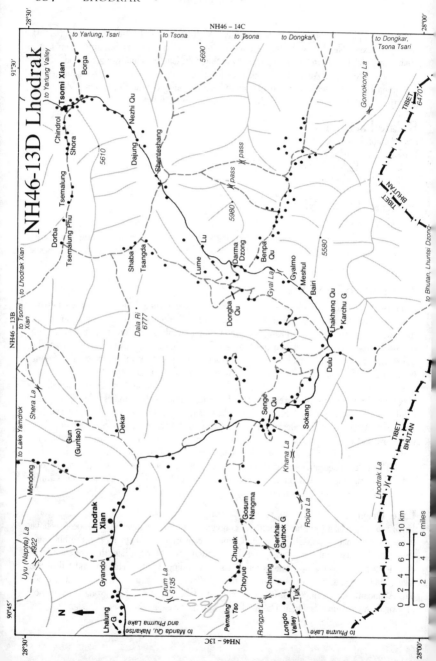

NH46 – 14C

NH46-13D Lhodrak

to Yarlung, Tsari   to Tsona   to Tsona   to Dongkar   to Dongkar, Tsona Tsari

Tsomi Xian
Borga
Chindrol
Shora
Tsemalung
Dorba
Tsemalung Phu
Nezhi Qu
Dajung
Shenteshang
Shaba
Tsangda
Lume
Lu
Darma Dzong
Benpa Qu
Gyalmo
Meshul
Bairi
Dongba Qu
Gyal La
Lhakhang Qu
Karchu G
Dala Ri 6777
to Tsomi Xian
to Lhodrak Xian
Shera La
Gun (Guntso)
Dekar
Dulu
Senge Qu
Sokang
Khana La
Mendong
to Lake Yamdrok
Uyu (Napra) La 4922
Lhodrak Xian
Gyando
Lhalung G
Chupak
Gosum Nangma
Choyue
Chating
Serkhar Guthok G
Tuk
Roipa La
Lhodrak La
Pemaling Tso
Drum La 5135
Rongpa La
Longdo Valley
to Manda Qu, Nakartse and Phurma Lake
to Phurma Lake

TIBET 6470
Gomokong La
TIBET / BHUTAN
to Bhutan, Lhuntsi Dzong
5690
pass
pass
5980
5580
5610
TIBET / BHUTAN
5560

N

0 2 4 6 8 10 km
0   2   4   6 miles

NH46 – 13B

NH46 – 13C

Tsomi Xian

Tsomi, the most fertile and productive town in the region, sits in a plain surrounded by extensive cultivation. The setting is dramatic: wonderfully eroded mountains and canyons with their many subtle hues tower over a broad expanse dotted with villages. Flowing past the town is the Lhodrak Shar Chu, the major river running south from the watershed of Shar Khalep. Tsomi has a sizeable contingent of Chinese cadres who live in three large compounds next to the old village of Tamshul. Most transport coming south from the Yarlung Valley stops in the town centre near the cinema; the government compound (with the Public Security Bureau inside) is just around the corner. The best plan to avoid potential bureaucratic hassles is to walk 1/2 hr farther south along the valley and stay in one of the many small villages. After Tsomi there are no major government offices until Lhakhang.

Mawochok (Chökhorpal) Monastery

Location Mawochok is situated on top of a hill east of Tsomi and can be reached either by a dirt road or a footpath that zigzags up the hillside. It takes 1 1/2 hr to walk from a village (1/2 hr south of Tsomi) to the monastery. Most of the buildings of the complex were destroyed during the Cultural Revolution. The main building with a big front hall has been rebuilt. In front of it are two large renovated *chörtens*, and the *gönkhang* is to the left. From Mawochok, the ruined monastery of Churli is visible back up along the Lhodrak Shar Chu Valley. The chapels are on a hill, to the right of the road, which has large white Chinese characters ('Long Live the Communist Party') on its slopes. Reach the monastery in an hour from the road.

Background Little-known Mawochok is a Nyingmapa monastery and an important pilgrimage site. According to legend, its name was given by the *bodhisattva*, Jampelyang, in a prophecy revealed at China's sacred mountain of Mt Wutai Shan. In his *Ter Yig*, Guru Rinpoche called it Orgyan Sangphuk Pema Dzong, and the renowned Panchen Sakyasri named it Nyung Gu Drak. Mawochok's principal mountain is Drak Mar Dorje Tsenga ('Rocky Mountain with Five Peaks'), similar in appearance to Riwo Potala in South India. Its interior is said to be a replica of Zangdhok Pelri, Paradise of Guru Rinpoche, with a representation of Chenresi, Jampelyang and Chana Dorje, the Rigsum Gönpo trinity. Mawochok's importance derives primarily from its association with these deities. Guru Rinpoche wrote a commentary on Mawochok's significance as a site of pilgrimage. He identified Nyalme Geridrak (a mountain near Lhüntse Xian; see page 240), Chuwo Ri (near the Chusul Bridge: see page 478), Drak Yerpa (see page 338), and Mawochok as Tibet's four primary places of religious practice. It was supposedly built miraculously (*tsulpa tsuglag*), by Nakpo Dzumme, one of the 84 Mahasiddhas. It was the main seat of Nyima Wösel who, with Guru Chuwang and Longchenpa, was one of the three most famous *tertöns* of the Nyingmapa.

According to tradition, the prominent *chörtens* in front of the main building, Thukten Chörten and Tashi Wöbar Chörten, were miraculously created and housed within separate buildings. It is likely they existed before the monastery proper. The reverence accorded these receptacles, considered rediscovered treasures (*ter*), is fervent; pilgrims and monks regard them as the centerpiece of the Mawochok pilgrimage and believe their emanations to be so strong they can cure leprosy, rheumatism, and nervous disorders. Mawochok was consecrated by the illustrious Sakyasri. During the Mongol invasion, its all-important statues of Chenresi, Chana

Dorje, and Jampelyang, were brought to Sakya Monastery for safe keeping and later restored. A gold statue of Drogön, founder of Densatil Monastery, was once here; this was one of the monastery's most treasured objects.

The khora A Tibetan monk provided the following information. The beginning of the *khora* (ritual circuit path) starts below the monastery. *Mani* cairns and stone path markers (*lamtaks*) mark a trail junction; one way goes to the main building, the other leads to the *khora*. The well-worn trail gradually climbs up the hillside to reach the cemetery of Khandro Durtrö, a sacred site considered to be consecrated by *dakinis*. Continue to another trail junction. The right path zigzags up the steep slope to a cave once used by the monastery's founder. The left continues along the *khora* to a sacred spring (*terchu*), hidden in a recess. Thus its other name, the Sang Chu ('Secret Water'). A short distance above, after a steep climb, is the pass. Along the way, look out for the colorful pebbles on the sides of the path. These are considered as 'long life pills' (*tsheri*) and are highly prized.

To the left of the path, in the distance, are the three holy peaks of Tselha Namsum, recognized by Guru Rinpoche as the abode of the long-life deities. At the pass is a *lhatse*, surrounded by *mani* stones and prayer flags. To the right is a cemetery sanctified by Guru Rinpoche. Clothing, hair, bones, and diverse talismans commemorate the site. Beyond are the snow peaks that form the Tibet–Bhutan border and, closer to Mawochok, the high reaches of the Benpa Valley to the south. (A trail goes east along this valley to Tsona Dzong [see page 243].) The path from the saddle desends to a large rock surrounded by *mandals*. Look for the *rangjung* body-print of Yeshe Tsogyal, consort of Guru Rinpoche, on the rock's surface. Legend has it that she played a joke on him by dissolving herself into the rock. When he arrived here during his circuit of Mawochok, she came out of hiding and they completed the *khora* together. After passing some ruins on the left, the *khora* terminates at the monastery.

Nyima Wösel (1124–92)

Nyima Wösel (Nyangral, Ngadhak Nyang Ralpachen), first of the Five Discoverer Kings (Terton Gyalpo Nga), was born in Jesa Sergon, near Mawochok. At the age of eight he had a vision of Guru Rinpoche riding a white horse whose legs were supported by four *dakinis* (*khandroma*). The guru bestowed on the child four empowerments (*wangkur*) by using an elixir from his ritual flask (*bumpa dudtsi*). During this event, the sky opened and the earth quaked. Later he came to Mawochok, and started his life's work of unearthing hidden texts. Supposedly, a list of places with such texts (*terne*) was given to him by Wangchuk Dorje, an incarnation of Guru Rinpoche. He discovered hidden treasures at Khothing Monastery (see below), and in the Drag Gi Lhakhang of Samye Chimpu (see page 631). Nyima Wösel, Guru Chuwang (1212–73), and Longchenpa (1308–63) were the three major *tertöns* of the Dzokchen school of the Nyingmapa. Longchenpa translated the most famous Dzokchen text, the commentary on the *Nying Thig*.

An alternative trek from Tsomi to Lhodrak Xian

Instead of going southwest from Tsomi to Nezhi and Lhakhang (see main trek), this alternative route goes west over the Mensang and Shera passes before turning south ▸

to reach Lhodrak Xian, the principal town of Lhodrak. This option goes through seldom-visited territory devoid of motor traffic.

✧ Day 1 Tsomi–Tsemalung Phu 4 1/2 hr

Due west of Tsomi is the large Shoralung Valley. Walk along a jeep road past the villages of Tsinga, Chindrol, Drimpa, Padma, Shora, and Gangsu, and many ruins. Obtaining pack animals (horses are the most suitable for this trek) should be easy. In 2 hr, reach the entrance of a gorge where two vertical cliffs (visible from Tsomi), constrict the valley in the west. Go through them to follow a well-defined path upstream in a narrow valley that quickly widens. Cross a low pass (4380 m) to reach the village of Tsemalung (Tsema), a settlement of two parts. In the east is Tsemalung Tö (the first group of houses) and in the west, 1 hr away, is Tsemalung Phu (2 1/2 hr from the gorge entrance). Consider camping just after Tsemalung Tö—plenty of space and water. A strong wind blows here after 1600 and dies down at night.

✧ Day 2 Tsemalung Phu–Camp 1 5 hr

After Tsemalung Phu, the trail enters gorge-like country again; wade across three rivers before passing a monastery on the valley's right side. After this point, follow the trail that stays above the valley floor. The fourth ford is 3/4 hr after the third. Just after this the valley divides. Follow the left (west) branch. (The right branch leads to Taglung Monastery at the southwest corner of Yamdrok Tso.) Soon come to a grassy terrace with a stone wall along its north side, an ideal camping site at the base of the Mensang La. Beyond this, fodder for horses is difficult to find.

✧ Day 3 Camp 1–Camp 2 7 1/2 hr

This long, tiring day entails the crossing of two passes; start by 0730. After passing some large rocks, the path veers to the right and ascends the easy Mensang La (3 1/2 hr from camp). Descending, follow a river (trending to the right) to begin the ascent of the second pass, the Shera La. It is possible to take a short cut by wading across to the river's left bank and then proceeding to the left to follow a trail between two ridges (one of these has two peaks). The Shera La is more difficult than the Mensang La because there normally is more snow (1 1/2 hr from the first pass to the second). From the pass, one trail goes northwest to Yamdrok Tso. Walk down the far side to follow a rocky valley that trends to the southwest. Stay close to the Guntso Chu to avoid detours. Camp at a gorge-like point or walk for another 1 1/2 hr to the first village of Guntso.

✧ Day 4 Camp 2–Lhodrak Xian 5 1/2 hr

Descend along the beautiful gorge to Guntso, a charming village with friendly people. All around are ruins and cultivated fields. The houses are of stone and most courtyards have stockpiles of firewood for the cold months. The trail then descends and again enters a superb gorge. Pass another village, then reach a major valley junction with tower ruins and a village. Turn right, now following the Lhodrak River upstream

➡

(west) along the main Lhakhang–Lhodrak–Manda road which traverses the Lhodrak Gorge. In 1 hr, reach another valley junction with the lesser Mendong Valley opening to the north. Reach Lhodrak Xian in another 1 hr. The town has a strong Chinese presence and is dominated by the ruins of a monastery and a round tower. On the right, before the town, is Karpo Qu Village. Here the gorge opens up.

See Day 8, page 702, for rejoining the Lhodrak pilgrimage.

TSOMI TO LHASA VIA SERKHAR GUTHOK
Time Chart

Day	Place	Hours
1	Tsomi–Nezhi	3
2	Lu	6
3	Benpa Chakdhor	5 1/2
4	Lhakhang	5 1/2
5	Senge	6
6	Serkhar Guthok	6 1/2
7	Pemaling Tso	5 1/2
8	Lhasa road	9
9	Manda Qu	3
10	Lhasa	1 1/2 days (hitch)

Trail Notes
✤ DAY 1 TSOMI–NEZHI 3 HR

From Tsomi, follow a level jeep track along the Lhodrak Shar Chu Valley, which makes a dogleg to the southwest. Pass ruins of watchtowers and forts. The valley trends right and narrows; dramatically eroded cliffs rise sharply on both sides. Walk past a large earth *chörten* called Nawokyok on the far side of the river (1/2 hr). Continue to Lethang (2 hr), then cross the river on a stone bridge (a village and school are before the bridge). Nezhi (1/2 hr from Lethang) stands on an escarpment over the river. Its houses cling to the slopes right down to the water and a monastery is within the village.

Nawokyok ('Crooked Nose') Chörten This monument stands at the 'nose' of Mt Nawokyok. Founded by Phagmo Drupa (see page 635), it is said to contain his relics. Originally, the site had a stone with the handprint of the *siddha*, Drukpa Kunlek. Phagmo Drupa, after receiving a vision of Guru Rinpoche, decided to built a *chörten* over it. The mountain on the river's east side is believed to be the abode of 1,000 Buddhas. A trail parallels the pilgrimage route on the right (west) bank of the river (this should be a good alternative to walking on the jeep track).

Nezhi Zhitrö Monastery The exterior of this monastery is well preserved, although its interior was gutted during the Cultural Revolution (restored 1987). This Nyingmapa monastery, a branch of Mindroling (see page 496), was noted for its many life-size clay sculptures, including eight ferocious, wrathful deities (*zhitrö*), the Eight Doorkeepers of the World. Their remains are in an inner hall. The monastery's principal images are Guru Chuwang and a Nepalese statue of Guru Rinpoche. A chapel once held Guru Chuwang's gold tomb, surrounded by eight holders of his lineage.

✤ DAY 2 NEZHI–LU 6 HR

Follow the road south to Dajung (1 hr). Soon reach Tair (Ti), site of two beautifully preserved stone watchtowers, each 15 m high. After Tair the valley narrows to a barren gorge. The track climbs up the hillside with the river on the left. Pass steep terraced fields across the river. At the end of the gorge, the path descends to the river. Cross a bridge (4 hr from Tair; the river now bends to the right) and follow a steep trail up the mountain to the left to Lu (3/4 hr) on top of the ridge. This sizeable village can provide accommodation and pack animals.

Guru Drubphuk Before Tair, a trail leaves the motor road to the left towards the river at some stone markers. A Guru Rinpoche cave near the water has his footprint and handprint on the back wall. Supposedly, the sage spent three years here.

Stone Watchtowers Along the route from Lu to Serkhar Guthok are many tall, stone towers. Varying from 15 to 20 m in height, they are usually grouped in threes or fours. Unique in this part of Tibet (more common in eastern Tibet), these defensive structures first appeared in the 6th C. south of the Koko Nor in the land of the Qiang. Chinese scholars maintain that the proto-typical Tibetans came from a Qiang tribe. Today, the Qiang can still be found in the mountains between Tibet and China, their language and customs being similar to the Tibetans. The watchtowers, perhaps designed on the Qiang model, are considered by some to be the forerunners of Tibetan architecture. The 9-story Serkhar Guthok is a fine example (see page 698).

✤ DAY 3 LU–BENPA CHAKDHOR 5 1/2 HR

A footpath climbs gradually from Lu to the low Shang La Pass (1 1/2 hr; the rocky, jeep track winds below), then descends to Darma Dzong (3/4 hr), an area distinguished by ruins, watchtowers, and an intriguing crenelated walled compound. Darma Zimkhang Monastery once stood here, residence of Darma, a noted teacher of the Nyang Kingdom. Across the river is Dongba Qu. The trail flattens to follow the mountain's contours; the river is far below on the right. Spectacular ruins and towers enliven the way. The trail curves left around a large rocky spur in the middle of the river, then enters the side valley of Benpa. Follow this (the Benpa River on the right) to Benpa Qu, an administrative compound. More stone towers stand near the village entrance. The substantial Benpa River flows into the Lhodrak Shar Chu from the Karmo Gong La watershed in the east (beyond is the Dongkar Valley and Tsona, see page 243). Numerous settlements lie within the prosperous valley. Benpa Chakdhor Monastery is 1 km past Benpa Qu (3 hr from Darma Dzong).

Zangdhok Pelri According to Situ's pilgrimage guide, a Tibetan text detailing sacred sites, a beautiful stretch of narrow gorges and high, wooded mountains exists near the Benpa Valley, an area said to represent Guru Rinpoche's Paradise of Zangdhok Pelri. Sites described include the following. Rongsha Mongsul is a sacred spot consecrated to Drak Sinmo. This ogress, mother of the Tibetan people, mated with the monkey-transformation of Chenresi. Her clawprint (*barje*) is visible on a cliff face. Guru Drubphuk is a Guru Rinpoche cave near the Chona Chukha River. Mensham (Menshe) encompasses an area formed of eight peaks and eight rivers, the embodiment of the Eight Medicine Buddhas. (Perhaps identified with the village of *Meshul*, some distance south of Benpa on the main road to Lhakhang.) Finally, there are two Gelugpa monasteries: Botö Gön and Dhemik Gön.

Benpa Chakdhor Monastery This handsome, three-story structure is home to several monks who have trickled back in recent years. Inside the large *dukhang* are well-preserved murals with overt Indian influence. On the altar are stones with footprints of Karmapa, Milarepa, and Götshangpa. Behind the *dukhang*, on the left, is the Drölma Lhakhang. A side entrance leads into a central chapel, which has a large renovated statue of Chana Dorje. Flanking it are statues of Marpa and Guru Rinpoche. Right of this chapel is the *gönkhang*, which was once the repository of Dawa Gyaltsen's *chörten*-tomb. A *khorlam* surrounded the monastery. According to tradition, the monastery is sited over the Paradise of the Nagas (Wök Luyul). A sacred spring bubbles up in front of the monastery entrance, its water considered a 'rediscovered treasure' (*terchu*).

Monasteries near Benpa Chakdhor

Benpa Drukral Monastery The Drulue Lhakhang had a huge copper and gold statue of Guru Rinpoche erected by Chokden Gönpo.

Nab is downstream from Benpa Chakdhor. It was the birthplace of Chokden Gönpo. Near here was a house with a juniper tree that belonged to the assassin of Tertön Namkha Gyaltsen.

Drowa Gön is located above the Benpa Valley. The headquarters of Lhodrak Drubchen Lekyi Dorje, it was visited and converted to the Gelugpa by Tsong Khapa in 1395.

Samdrub is above Drowa Gön. This Nyingmapa monastery was founded by Serkyimpa, a lama who initiated the tantric Serkyimpa tradition, which allows its monks to marry and have homes.

Lhakar Gön is near Samdrub. These ruins are of an ancient Nyingmapa monastery founded by Je Karam Lhakar.

Dröshul lies across the Karchu River. The main seat (*dhensa*) of the renowned Tertön Ratna Lingpa consisted of the monasteries of Dröshul, Jangchubling, and Dhokhar Lhündrub Potrang. Beyond Dröshul, following the Karchu River to its upper reaches, is the Mönka Senge Dzong of Bhutan.

Ratna Lingpa (1403–79) This Nyingma *tertön* collected the important 'Hundred Thousand Tantras' (*Nyingma Gyubum*) at Zur Ug Pa Lung, west of Shigatse. He was born in Dröshul and, when 27 years old, had a vision of Guru Rinpoche, who told him of the many treasures (*ter*) he had hidden. By the age of 30, Ratna Lingpa had embarked on his career as a *tertön* in earnest. His first discovery was at Khyungchen Drak (Khyungpo, Kham). Within Lhodrak, Ratna Lingpa found hidden texts at Namkhachen and the cave of Pelgyi Phuk Ring near the Karchu Monastery (see page 693). His most important achievement was the compilation of the *Nyingma Gyubum*, the esoteric *tantras* of the Vajrayana. Much of the text was located at Zur Ug Pa Lung, the rest obtained from the oral transmissions of his teacher, Megom Zangpo of Tsang. Ratna Lingpa's work on the *Gyubum* was done at the Dhokhar Lhündrub Potrang of Dröshul.

❖ Day 4 Benpa Chakdhor–Lhakhang 5 1/2 hr (34 km)

Walk from the monastery back to Benpa Qu, then follow a tractor path that hugs the left side of the valley. It zigzags steeply up to the Gyal La, the Pass of Kings (1 1/2 hr from Benpa Qu). Descend to Gyalmo Village using shortcuts (1/2 hr). The area is memorable for its many stone towers, which stand at strategic locations.

The Gyalmo Mizen ('Queen Man-eater') and her palace The following information is provided by a Tibetan pilgrim. A short distance from Gyalmo Village is Gyalmo Mizen Potrang on the top of a hill. The decayed complex is a fort-like structure surrounded by unusual structures, some pyramidal with spy-hole windows, others with circular bases. Scattered among them are tall, stone towers. All are unoccupied. According to the villagers, these strange buildings and towers were used in some long ago time to store the corpses of the Queen Man-eater, and to lodge her retinue. The devil queen's reign came to an end when Guru Rinpoche, wielding his powerful *dorje*, vanquished her. She fell from the mountaintop to the river below and a rock by the bank still has the imprint of her brain and the *dorje*. A remarkable feature of the palace is a tall, multi-level tower that clings to the mountainside. Each level has its own spy-hole, used to repel enemies. The palace surroundings are beautiful but nobody lives here—the locals still fear the monster and believe that the houses are haunted. The stone defence towers in the area are known as Dhukhar Shomo Gudrik (dice-shaped, nine-in-a-line devil houses).

To go: Start from the Gyal La before Gyalmo and follow a trail up to the palace. Another route goes via Gyalmo Village itself. Near the village's entrance is a trail junction. The way down the mountain goes to Lhakhang; the other two paths lead to Gyalmo Mizen Potrang.

From the far side of Gyalmo, follow the tractor path down the mountain, taking short cuts from time to time. Eventually reach the bottom of a narrow gorge with the river on the right. Follow the level path along the river until the gorge opens, then climb gradually until the path levels again, 50 m above the water. Beyond Gyalmo is Meshul (3/4 hr), then Bairi at the entrance of an east-trending valley that leads to the Karchu La straddling the Tibet–Bhutan border (1 hr from Meshul). Cultivated fields and peach tree orchards are on the left, snow mountains straight ahead. The river's far side is strangely barren. Lhakhang and the red walls of Karchu Monastery (500 m above the village) now appear, 3 1/2 hr after Gyalmo. Accommodation and food are available, but be cautious and circumspect in this border town (Bhutan is only a day's walk away).

From Benpa to Karchu Monastery: sacred sites The Situ pilgrimage guide describes the following:
Meditation caves After Drowa Gön and Dröshul, go past Gya Tshoka, Yerchen, and ➠

Dujomling. Near the last are four caves known as Nyima, Dawa, Dorje, and Drilbu, the meditation caves of Rechungpa (see page 347) and Vairocana, one of the first seven ordained monks in Tibet (8th C.).

Karchu Tadhong Karmo ('White-Horse Face of Karchu'). Beyond the four caves is the 'self-manifesting' (*rangjung*) print of the horns of the tantric deity, Damchen. This area, the abode of many divinities, supposedly had 108 caves and many soul-lakes and soul-forests with 108 flowering plants. Götshangpa (see page 281) used two of these caves, and nearby are the footprints of this famous Drukpa Kagyü *yogin* and a lingam.

Mt Chakpur Chen (see page 694) A mountain like a conch shell, it contains the fabled Guru Rinpoche cave where he spent seven years in meditation. The mountain's face supposedly has images of the eight different forms of Guru Rinpoche (Guru Tsengye). Above the cave is Guru Lhakhang, where Guru Chuwang (see page 705) discovered a concealed thunderbolt. Chakpur Chen had five white *chörtens* (to prevent war with the Mongols), and footprints of Guru Rinpoche and Namkhai Nyingpo, an 8th-C. Tibetan master of the Chinese Ch'an (Zen) School. A trail leads from the upper reaches of Chakpur Chen to Khandro Dro, then along a precipice to the Karchu Monastery.

Lhamo Kharchen A replica of the Devikota, one of 24 holy sites in India (see page 130).

Lhakhang Lhakhang (3000 m), at an important junction of river valleys, is superbly sited. The south-trending valley once was a main trade route into Bhutan (the border is only 15 km away), to Thunkar and Lhüntsi Dzong. Lhodrak Nub Chu Valley, to the northwest, leads to Lhodrak Xian, the Manda La Pass, and Lhasa. The third follows the Lhodrak Shar Chu River northeast to Tsomi and the Yarlung Valley. High snow peaks of the Tibet–Bhutan range are seen to the south and, at the center of the village, is Khothing Monastery, founded by King Songtsen Gampo in the 7th century. Close by is Lhakhang Qu, the administrative center where rooms and meals are available (it is best to sleep at charming Karchu Monastery, however). A store has tinned foods and staples.

Khothing Lhakhang Khothing, a yellow building with red trim around the peaked wooden roofs, was reputedly built by King Songtsen Gampo as one of four 'Subduers of the Border' (*Tandul*) monasteries (see page 43). It served to pin down the left elbow of Tibet's demoness. Beautiful painted columns and line paintings survive inside. The building had been neglected for a long time and not used for anything other than a store house. Before the destruction of the 1960s, Khothing's main image in the *dukhang* was a huge Vairocana surrounded by Vajrasattva (east), Ratnasambhava (south), Amitabha (west), and Amoghasiddhi (north), the last supposedly erected by Songtsen Gampo himself. All were two storys high. Upstairs was the Tshedhak Gönkhang, containing images of the Five Dhyani Buddhas. Four huge trees planted by Guru Chuwang (see page 705), one for each direction, surrounded the monastery.

Karchu Monastery

This Nyingmapa monastery, once one of Tibet's richest, stands in the midst of an enchanting alpine meadow. Snow mountains encircle the complex and a clear glacial stream flows between tall pines. Camping here is as close to Shangri-La as any place in Tibet. To reach Karchu, follow a narrow path behind Lhakhang Qu up the hill. After 15 min the trail branches; take the left branch up. In 1 hr, it forks again (before the fork, notice a large rock with the red image of Jambala, God of Wealth). Take the right path. From here on, small puffs of wool hang as trail markers from the tree branches beside the path; follow them closely. Reach the top in 1 1/2 hr. The monastery, although badly damaged, is being rebuilt. At the back of the complex is a *chörten* and a charming building with a 2-m-high prayer wheel driven by a stream. Valuable *thangkas* and sculptures decorate the little chapel of an old lama farther down the slopes. Karchu was sacked during the civil war after the Yarlung Dynasty, but was rebuilt by Lorepa (1187–1250). Principal chapels were the Drölma Lhakhang and the Tri Tsangkhang, the latter built by Pema Karpo, a famous scholar and *tertön* of the Drukpa Kagyü sect. Its main images were a copper and gold Mitrukpa (Akshobhya), Marpa and Milarepa.

Karchu khora A short *khora* circles the monastery. Begin at the north from an area in front of the main entrance known as Khandro Drora (*dakini* dancing place). Four Khandro Droras surround the monastery. Circle clockwise to the second in the east. This open space has a ruined stone enclosure and within are three stone seats used by Karmapa Düsum Khenpa, Guru Rinpoche, and Namkhai Nyingpo. The third Khandro Drora, at the complex's south, has *mani* stone piles. Beyond is the Mani Lhakhang, housing a water-driven *mani* wheel. A white *chörten* beyond it is an important relic built by Namkhai Nyingpo and consecrated by Guru Rinpoche. The last (west) Khandro Drora is small, and in one corner on a stone is a *shabje*, perhaps of Drukpa Kunlek or Namkhai Nyingpo. At this spot, look out for a small spring. This used to provide water for the monastery, but since its destruction during the Cultural Revolution, its output has become significantly less.

Below the path, on the left, is a cemetery (*durtrö*) consisting of a flat rock with a hollow indentation. Legend has it that this hollow was created by intangible spirits, which continue to come and deepen the hollow by beating on it. The souls of the deceased are supposedly deposited here and laid to rest within the depression. It is said that sometimes hair, personal belongings, and a watery liquid mysteriously appear from out of the hollow. Pilgrims make a practice of scraping their gums until they bleed and then spitting on the stone in gesture of an offering. This cemetery is said to be a powerful, highly blessed place populated by *dakinis* and spirits of the mountains and earth.

Karchu khorchen

The following information was provided by a Tibetan pilgrim. This remarkable, long *khora* surrounds Karchu Monastery and takes in the important pilgrimage sites of Lhamo Kharchen (Lhamo Karchu) and Mt Chakpur Chen, site of Guru Rinpoche's seven-year retreat. The *khorchen* starts at the white *chörten* near the Karchu's south end. An obvious trail descends down the side of the ridge.

Note Allow at least one day to walk the *khorchen*. To properly explore Lhamo Kharchen and Mt Chakpur Chen, spend a night at each place. ⟱

Tsamkhang Below the *chörten* are two wooden meditation houses (*tsamkhang*), still used occasionally by hermits.

Namkhai Nyingpo Drubphuk Below the *tsamkhangs*, watch for a side trail to the right of the main path. This leads to Namkhai Nyingpo's meditation cave. Above the cave entrance is a footprint of the lama and his handprint is on the cave's back wall. Return to the main path, pass a *tsampa* mill, then turn sharply left and down to a trail junction marked by a stone cairn. Take the left fork to a long wooden bridge over the Karchu River. Cross it, go along a flat, obvious path and then, at a point marked by another cairn, wind steeply up the valley side to some stone steps. While ascending these steps bear left to enter, then crawl through, a narrow tunnel. This is the Bardo Tranglam, a physical representation of the after-death (*bardo*) passage of the soul. Beyond the tunnel, turn back onto the trail. Here a rock has the butter-smeared footprint of Namkhai Nyingpo. Climb to the top of the steps to reach the hermitage of Lhamo Kharchen.

Lhamo Kharchen is the three-story retreat of Phagmo Drupa. Along the back wall of the bottom floor is a rock with Phagmo Drupa's footprints. Inside the second level are stone slabs with carved images. A notched tree trunk leads to the empty top story. To the rear of the Lhamo Kharchen, situated on the flat top of a ridge (believed to be the abode of Dorje Sempa, Vajrasattva), is an incense burner (*sangkhung*). This renowned hermitage is considered a replica of sacred Devikota, the temple of Kamakhya near Gauhati in Assam and one of the 24 most revered sites in India. Pabonka Monastery, near Lhasa is another replica of Devikota (see page 130). Continue along the *khorchen* by returning to the bottom of the stone steps. Turn right to follow a trail flanked by trees. On the branches are trail markers made of small, multi-colored pieces of cloth. En route pass sacred waterfalls consecrated by Guru Rinpoche, Phagmo Drupa, and Namkhai Nyingpo, respectively. Tibetans know these as 'long life water' (*tsechus*) and pilgrims stand below them for a good wash. After the last waterfall, the trail descends to the ridge's base, then skirts around it to rejoin the main *khorchen* at the junction marked by a stone cairn. (Here began the ascent to Lhamo Kharchen.) Recross the bridge over the Karchu River, then go past the trail junction. One trail leads back to Karchu Monastery. Follow the other.

Khandro Drora Beyond the junction, the trail leads steeply up to a tall, wood ladder. Go up this rickety contraption to a trail that winds among rocks on a terrace to reach the Khandro Drora. At the center of this level ground is a stone *doring* with illegible inscriptions (perhaps Sanskrit). One source claims this relic came from Bodh Gaya. A short distance further is a large rock with the footprint of Namkhai Nyingpo. Beyond, the trail squeezes through two rocks to reach a set of stone steps. Descend to a long, unstable wooden bridge suspended high above an abyss. Across it is the entrance to Mt Chakpur Chen.

Mt Chakpur Chen ('Iron Dagger Mountain') Inside the bowels of this mountain is a huge cavern, within which is a multi-story wooden hermitage on stilts. Each of the floors has an opening that serves as a window. A ladder leads up to the first floor which has murals depicting episodes from the lives of the main Kagyü lamas. At the back wall is a cave with damaged clay *chörtens* built to prevent war with the Mongols. The other floors, similar to the first are reached by interior ladders. The top floor, like the first, has an attached cave with ruined *chörten*-tombs of the Kagyü lamas. Back on the ground floor of the cavern, walk to the left side wall to locate a disc-like protuberance on the wall's surface. This is the Door to the Hidden Treasure (*tergo*). Guru Rinpoche apparently used his finger to delineate this mythical opening. When the time is ripe, a knowing lama will come here to retrieve the treasure.

Inner Chakpur Chen Climb to the top of the hermitage to reach a path that follows along the inclined, top portion of the cave into the heart of the mountain. The undulating path zigzags along and becomes progressively darker. Be careful, use a rope if possible and do not go alone. A bright flashlight is essential. The passage finally ends in a low, pitch-black cave: Chakpur Chen's most sacred spot. Meritorious pilgrims are supposed to see the *rangjung* image of Guru Rinpoche's iron dagger on the cave wall. To the right is a 'long life spring' (*tsechu*), a trickle of water that drips from a hole. Pilgrims collect soft earth from between two rocks at the cave's back wall. It is believed to be the sacred food of Guru Rinpoche. Along the left wall is a crack and beyond it another cavity; inside are parts of a *mani* wall with *tsa-tsas* on top. According to tradition, Guru Rinpoche discovered this remarkable hermitage and spent seven years in solitary meditation. He first flew from Mt Lhodrak Namkha Zumo ('the Mountain that Penetrates the Sky') to the summit of Chakpur Chen, then tunneled into the very stomach of the mountain where he created this secret cavern which conforms precisely to the shape of his outstretched body. Namkhai Nyingpo also spent three months in retreat here. After the Chakpur Chen pilgrimage, recross the perilous bridge to the stone steps, then turn left along a clear, level trail. Soon come to Namkhai Nyingpo's meditation cave.

Namkhai Nyingpo Drubphuk First come to the lower of the two caves. A wall divides the cavity; the left side is a kitchen and the right a meditation room. An altar supports a few stone slabs carved with *mantras* and damaged stone statues. Turn left out of the cave to climb a trail to a notched, tree trunk ladder that leads to the second cave. Over the entrance is the *rangjung mantra* 'Om Ah Hum.' This cave is known as the secret cave (*sangphuk*) of Namkhai Nyingpo.

Return to the *khorchen* by going back down the stone steps towards the Khandro Drora. Watch for a trail junction a short distance before it. Take the left branch, an obvious path up the mountainside. Soon reach a cluster of stone *tsamkhangs* (meditation huts) above the path. Here the path splits. The left goes up to a rock imprinted clearly with the hand, feet, and body of Namkhai Nyingpo. According to tradition, the lama flew from this spot to Lhamo Kharchen and then to Chakpur Chen, circling the Karchu *khorchen* as he did so. Return to the main path and go back up the mountain to Karchu Monastery.

Karchu Pelgyi Phuk Ring ('The Long Cave of Karchu') Namkhai Nyingpo achieved his ultimate enlightment here. Within the cave he hid Chinese Buddhist texts, later discovered by Ratna Lingpa and incorporated into the Dzokchen doctrines. He also left behind his foot- and handprints. The mountain facing this sacred cave resembles a jumping snow lion and the castle (*dzong*) of Senge Zangpo stands on a high cliff. Above the castle is a cemetery (*durtrö*) and, beyond, a temple that contained three white earth *chörtens* (*sabum*) belonging to Melong Dorje, his consort, and his son. Supposedly the scholar, Kumarazi (344–413) of Khotan, stayed here. In the area was the Melong Lhakhang, built by Melong Dorje, and the Lhamo Gönkhang. The journey to this hermitage goes directly from Lhakhang and takes 2 hr.

Tselam Pel Ri This Guru Rinpoche site, with a sacred spring, lies south of Lhakhang. From Lhakhang, the 3-hr journey first crosses the Lhodrak Shar Chu, then the Lhodrak Nub Chu, before turning south to follow the right (west) bank of the river. Guru Rinpoche meditated within a large cave, which retains his footprints and those of Yeshe Tsogyal, Guru Chuwang, and Namkhai Nyingpo. Guru Chuwang built three war-preventing *chörtens* here. Below the Tselam Ngo Pass is a Yeshe Tsogyal cave containing her clay statue. Above it is another cave, used by Guru Rinpoche. Nearby are more caves used by Drigungpas in earlier days. The Nyingmapa monastery of Pelri Gön stood near Gontsam, and Sang Phuk cave, further up the mountain, supposedly contains long-life pills and a magic elixir.

✤ Day 5 Lhakhang–Senge 6 hr

A path behind Khothing Monastery leads down the slopes to the Lhodrak Shar Chu. Cross a bridge, then turn left down the river to a valley junction (the south valley leads to Bhutan). Cross another bridge and turn right up the northwest-trending Lhodrak Nub Chu Valley, follow-ing a flat jeep path with the river on the right. Pass a hydro-electric station and a military compound along this prosperous valley. Infrequent trucks from Lhasa and Tsethang bring sup-plies to the army compound. Senge, in Mönkar District, appears after 6 hr of easy walking from Lhakhang. Senge Qu is on a rise just above the road and has rooms, meals, and a store.

Senge Drubphuk From Senge Qu, a side valley goes off to the west, leading eventually to Serkhar Guthok (see below). A trail follows the valley to the cave hermitage of Senge Drubphuk. Founded by Guru Rinpoche, it was visited by Milarepa and Yeshe Tsogyal. Today, nuns come to perform services.

An alternative route to Serkhar Guthok

An alternate, mountainous trail goes to Serkhar Guthok via the Khana and Roipa (4815 m) passes. The villages en route are Tag, Lungna, Tur, So Kong, Kyema, Mu Gyab, Mu, and Sishing Zhika. Cross two more passes to the west before descending to a hot spring just before Serkhar Guthok. Religious sites along this way include:
• Tashiling. This is a monastery near Lhodrak Guchu founded by Khuyung of Gangshok Lekpo.
• Mu Gön Kar. This monastery, near Dolter, was built by a disciple of Sangye Lingpa.

➟

Within were 108 *chörtens* surrounding the tomb of Sangye Lingpa (1340–96) and four rare replicas of the Mahabodhi Temple of Bodh Gaya.
• Lhadro Namgyal Khangzang. This monastery of Amye Ngak lies across the river from Mu Gön Kan.
• Trowo Ritrö. A hermitage above Gangmen, within Mt Sinmo Drak.

✤ **DAY 6 SENGE–SERKHAR GUTHOK 6 1/2 HR**

From Senge Qu, follow the winding road down to the Lhodrak Chu (1 hr). Turn left and walk northwest along the river valley to a bridge (1/2 hr). The Lhodrak Nub Chu Valley, with its main road, now bears right. Turn to the left and follow the narrow, left-hand Zhe Chu Valley, keeping the river on the left.

Khandro Jewa Bum Drubphuk About 1 1/2 hr from the turnoff, wade across the Zhe Chu to its opposite bank. A narrow gorge branches off here. The Khandro Jewa Bum Drubphuk cave, festooned with prayer flags, appears high above. Follow a well-used footpath up the gorge, keeping the river to the left. It takes 2 1/2 hr to reach the meditation cave (wade across two rivers to their right banks just before it).Within the cavity, to the right, is a restored clay *chörten* containing relics. Behind the *chörten* is an altar said to be a sacred site and frequently visited by *dakinis*. Return to the Zhe Chu Valley, turn left and continue along the dirt track towards Serkhar Guthok.

Reach, but do not cross, a small bridge 2 1/2 hr after leaving the Lhodrak Valley. The path along the river is flat and pleasant.

Ngok Chöku Dorje Monastery A side trip to this monastery crosses the small bridge to enter a branch valley. A winding trail leads to a pass at its head. Descend to a village, then cross another pass. The distinct trail crosses a river by a bridge, then goes over a third ridge to reach the Ngok Chöku Dorje Monastery after passing a village and crossing a river. Reach the monastery in one day of hard walking. The destroyed site, founded by Ngok Chöku Dorje in the 11th C., is empty except for some broken statues.

Return to the Zhe Chu Valley. Continue to a black tent below a rock (3/4 hr). Soon the valley divides around the huge cliff of Gosung Nangma.

Gosung Nangma Known as the Protector of the Inner Entrance, this arresting, impressive rock face is a symbolic opening into the sacred realms of Serkhar Guthok, Drowolung, and Pemaling Tso. An almost inaccessible meditation cave sits high up in the cliff. Cross a bridge and follow the left dirt track along a line of electricity poles with the river on the left. (The footpath heading up to the right leads directly to Pemaling Tso [see page 701].) Reach a hot spring parallel to the river on the left after 3/4 hr, an ideal place for a good, serene soak. This medicinal hot spring, blessed by Guru Rinpoche and called Menchu, is renowned for its curative powers over skin and rheumatic diseases. Some pilgrims stay as long as four months. From here, cross a bridge after 15 min, just beyond some stone baths and arrive at Serkhar Drong 20 min later. Serkhar Qu government compound stands at the village's beginning on the left. Beds and sometimes meals are available. Buy and cook food if necessary; soldiers billeted in the village sometimes sell instant noodles and other provisions. About 5 min from here is Milarepa's tower of Serkhar Guthok.

> **Serkhar Guthok to Lhasa** The pilgrimage continues from Milarepa's tower to the holy lake of Pemaling Tso, then over the Drum La (5135 m), to rejoin the Lhasa road (description follows). To go directly to Lhasa from Serkhar Guthok, backtrack along the Zhe Chu Valley to the main road and bridge at the valley's entrance. From here, the Lhasa road goes left (north) to Lhodrak Xian and Nakartse via the Manda La Pass.

Serkhar Guthok

Milarepa (1040–1123) built this tower-monastery for the son of his teacher, Marpa. Serkhar Guthok means 'nine-story son's house'. Milarepa, to prove himself worthy of the undertaking and to expiate sins, was forced to build the nine-story monastery by himself. In its heyday, Serkhar Guthok housed 100 monks and a large collection of Tibetan texts, sculptures, and wood blocks. Today one lama looks after the two-story monastery at the base of the slender, stone tower. Steep wooden stairs lead up the entire length, which actually has only seven internal floors, each 2 m high. Three still retain original murals and Marpa's chapel has a fine *thangka* depicting Marpa and Milarepa. A pagoda roof, with a ledge and chains for pilgrims to circumambulate the apex in the open, was destroyed and has been replaced by a simple, flat roof with a ledge. Near the tower, in the village, is a chapel (the lama has the key) whose *gönkhang*, to the left of the main hall, is crammed full of looming clay sculptures of terrifying deities. Of excellent workmanship, most of these are still in good condition. Bring a powerful flashlight.

Serkhar Guthok's architecture The tower-monastery retains architectural features found in West Tibet in the 11th C., particularly at Tholing (see page 425). Above the main entrance is a design motif resembling a stepped pyramid, a stylized symbol of an Indian temple (*prasada*), which was Tholing's model. This pyramidal element can also be found in other monasteries built in the early years of Buddhism's Second Diffusion (11th–12th century). Examples are Yemar and Nethang. More recently the entranceway of the Norbu Lingka used this device. Serkhar Guthok consisted of a series of low, white buildings with dark cornices. The tower has a square plan, similar to the multi-story Chapel of Initiation (Serkhang) at Tholing, and it is likely that it has a link with the defense towers of the Yarlung era (7th–9th C.). A good case in point is the Yumbu Lagang (see page 539); both structures are crowned by Chinese-style roofs.

Drowolung Monastery

This was the favorite residence of Marpa (teacher of Milarepa) and main seat of the Kagyüpa

Its founding was first predicted by Naropa. A Sakyapa monastery was later founded here by Kongchok Gyalpo in the 12th century. Drowolung sits on a hill southeast of Serkhar Guthok, 1 hr along a clearly defined trail. The deserted site, resembling Uddyana, Guru Rinpoche's birthplace, has many fragrant herbs.

To reach Drowolung, walk from Serkhar Qu towards the village. Before the village entrance, look for a trail on the left which leads to the bluffs above Serkhar Guthok. Follow it to a rise marked by a white *chörten*. From here, a wide, distinct path continues up the hillside to Drowolung. A less obvious trail provides a short cut to the monastery, past an irrigation pond. Drowolung's main building, Potrang Marpa, was Marpa's personal residence; it is now empty and in ruins. The central image here was Marpa and to the right was his son, Darma Dhodhe. The *drubkhang* contained the monk's meditation cells. At the back of the complex is the *dukhang*. Between it and the *drubkhang* are large rocks, some with caves. Surrounding the main buildings are the smaller monks' residences. Sections of the perimeter wall still stand. To the left of Potrang Marpa, near some *mani* walls, is the stone seat of the First Karmapa Lama, Karmapa Düsum Khenpa (12th century). Beyond the monastery on a hill is a renovated *chörten*. A short distance to the left is the Khandro Drora, a level site marked by stone *mandals* and prayer flags.

Beyond the *chörten* is Marpa's meditation cave, Sangwa Phuk. Milarepa came here to meditate on the image of Yamantaka, Lord of Death. The cave is atop a large rock marked by prayer flags. Below are other caves. The central one was used by Marpa, Milarepa occupied the cave on the left, while the right one was used by Gampopa (1079–1153). 'Long life' water (*tsechu*) drips from cracks within the caves and is much prized by pilgrims. A cemetery (*durtrö*) is in the vicinity.

Serkhar Guthok khorchen The pilgrimage circuit goes from Milarepa's tower to Drowolung, visiting the important sites of the area before returning to Serkhar Guthok; budget half a day.

Taknya Lungten Phuk: Milarepa's first meditation cave

This obligatory stop for pilgrims is the site of Milarepa's first one-year retreat after completing his studies under Marpa, who divined the precise location of this powerful cave. Milarepa was completely sealed inside, and during the entire period he meditated with a butter lamp balanced on top of his head.

The cave is difficult to find—if possible, take a guide from Serkhar Guthok. Allow 2 1/2 hr to reach it from Marpa's cave. (Taknya Lungten Phuk can also be reached directly from Serkhar Guthok in 3 1/2 hr.) Cross a stream west of Sangwa Phuk and follow a trail west over a low pass (4250 m). A nomad tent is before the top. Descend due south, pass another nomad camp, then go over one more ridge. Detour to the east to bypass a stream that flows from east to west into a north-flowing river that ultimately drains into the Longdo Chu. Head back to the southwest, cross a ridge (4400 m), then zigzag southward and ford a stream to reach Milarepa's first meditation cave (4300 m). Prayer flags mark the site. A one-room temple has been rebuilt around the cave; a stone wall is across part of the opening. The interior has an altar and *thangkas*, and a bare inner cell contains Milarepa's footprint and carved *mantras*.

Zhe: Marpa's birthplace

Across the river (north) from Serkhar Guthok is a phallic mountain in the distance, holy

Mt Tashi Dhenga ('Auspicious Five Groups') flanked by four minor peaks. Near its base is Zhe, said to be the birthplace of Marpa and site of his first monastery, now in ruins. To reach Zhe, continue up the valley from Serkhar Guthok. Cross a bridge to the river's left bank (north). A well-defined trail zigzags up the mountain sides past several villages. Reach Zhe in 2–3 hrs from Serkhar Guthok; the trail is visible from Milarepa's tower.

Marpa, Milarepa, and the Kagyüpa

Marpa, Milarepa's teacher, was a tyrannical man with a violent temper. He was born in Lhodrak to wealthy, land-owning parents. His wife, Dakmema, had considerable influence over him, especially during the period of Milarepa's schooling. Marpa received his teachings from the Indian saint, Naropa, who in turn was the student of Tilopa. He became the first Tibetan in the Kagyüpa lineage, a sect whose teachings were transmitted orally from master to pupil through a series of initiations. These teachings are secret doctrines that are supposed to confer mystical powers to initiates. Tantric in nature, they employ symbolic gestures, words, images, and ritual music to heighten awareness. These elements gave rise to Tibet's colorful tradition.

The Kagyüpa line is often called the White Sect, perhaps because of its monasteries' white walls. Buddhism flourished at the time of Marpa and Milarepa. Milarepa had 21 disciples, including his biographer, Rechung (1084–1164), and Gampopa (1079–1153). Many schools were founded after Milarepa, and by the 13th C. the history of the Kagyüpa becomes quite complex. Milarepa was very different from Marpa. He was a true ascetic who rigorously renounced the material world to become Tibet's greatest poet and song writer. His love for poetry probably came from Marpa, who introduced a new, essentially religious form, similar to Indian poetry but with deeply personal observations and feelings. Milarepa's poetry and songs were immensely popular with all classes of society.

✤ DAY 7 SERKHAR GUTHOK–PEMALING TSO 5 1/2 HR

To follow the main itinerary, retrace the way from Milarepa's tower back to the Zhe Chu Valley and the stone bathtubs (3/4 hr). At this point, take an indistinct, small path on the left up the side of the valley to a low saddle (3/4 hr). This shortcut avoids the valley junction with the huge cliff. Descend to a side valley and cross a bridge (next to some ruins, 1/2 hr). Walking upstream with the river on the left to Chupak (1 1/4 hr) with glaciers looming large at the head of the valley. Continue to Chöyue (1/2 hr), passing on the left a handsome stone house and stone tower. Chöyue is distinguished by stone pillars forming an entrance gate, then come the villages of Sheega and Wongguo. Impressive Mt Cham stands at the valley's head; Mt Kula Kangri is to its left.

After Wongguo the path forks: one way clings to the valley's right side and continues straight ahead. Do not follow this. Take the left. Walk over a stony riverbed, cross a bridge, and climb to a grassy plateau on the left side of the valley. Follow the stone cairns along the way as the trail parallels the river, crosses the plateau, then descends again to the valley. Cross another bridge to the right (west) bank of a side river. The path carries on in the same direction as the plateau, curving to the right around a bluff. Immediately, it crosses another bridge over the main river to follow its left bank. The path is now more distinct. Further on, a path branches right; ignore it and follow the main path up the valley for 10 min. Cross the stream and follow cairns to the top of a rise marked with prayer flags. Below is holy Pemaling Tso.

Note   A more strenuous direct route to Pemaling Tso leads across the Rongpa Pass.

Pemaling Tso

This turquoise-colored, glacial lake is dramatically ringed by glaciers and tall, snow mountains. According to one classification, it is one of four major holy lakes in Tibet (the others are Tsomo Dretung, near the Sikkim border; Yamdrok, next to Nakartse; and Namtso, north of Lhasa). Three or four nomad tents can usually be found at the edge of the lake.

The Guru Rinpoche cave of Lake Pemaling Tso

A pilgrim trail leads clockwise around the lake to Guru Rinpoche's cave and Pemaling Monastery (destroyed). From the nomad tents, the trail follows the lakeshore to a narrow neck of land that divides the lake in two (a channel connects the two halves in summer). The trail climbs the precipitous mountainsides (be careful) and eventually descends steep slopes to the lake and monastery. A courtyard fronts the building where pilgrims stay. The roofless main building has empty chapels and behind the monastery are ruins of meditation cells (*drubkhang*). A 'rediscovered' image of Vajrapani was the most important object here. A clear trail from the monastery's rear leads up Mt Damchen Gara Nakpo ('Subdued Blacksmith') to Guru Rinpoche's cave (3/4 hr). The master supposedly spent three years, three months, and three days meditating here and subduing the demon blacksmith (Gara Nakpo) in the process.

Within the cave, imprints of Guru Rinpoche's trident and hand are visible on the ceiling, and one shows where he traced the *mantra* 'Om Ah Hum' on a rock face. An altar has butter lamps, photos of the Dalai Lama, and carved pieces of stone. Pilgrims sometimes stay here for months. The Lhachu waterfall near the cave has a pool at its bottom, a wonderful place for a good wash. Some believe the cave to be the opening to a secret, hidden valley (*beyul*), prophesied by Guru Rinpoche to exist within Mt Kula Kangri. In the future, a lama with the right knowledge and attributes will formally open it. Lhama Kangri, a nearby peak, also has a Guru Rinpoche cave. Locals sometimes see Mt Damchen Gara Nakpo quake and hear a great noise resembling a blacksmith striking his anvil. Supernatural emanations from Pemaling Tso include ritual music, as if produced by a full assembly of monks playing trumpets, conch shells, bells, and drums. The mythical ox-of-the-lake (*tsholang*) appears at times as does the sound of barking dogs. Reports tell of sheep, yaks, and horses emerging from the water to graze by the shore, then disappearing back into the depths. These occurrences suggest to the Tibetans that the bottom of the lake is in fact Luyi Potrang, Paradise of the Nagas. Guru Rinpoche himself stated that the vicinity around Pemaling Tso was ideal for uninterrupted meditation, completely isolated from any hustle and bustle.

Kula Kangri khora

A little-known pilgrimage of eight or nine days circles this beautiful, pristine mountain. It involves the crossing of two high, although not difficult, passes and a detour into Bhutan. A monk at Lhalung Monastery (see below) supposedly possesses a rare copy of the Kula Kangri pilgrimage guide.

> **Pemalingpa** (1450–90) was the fourth of the Five Discoverer Kings (Terton Gyalpo Nga). Legends recount that he obtained a list of hiding places (*khajang*) of the 108 ➧

Great Concealed Treasures when he was 27 years old. Some treasures, such as a chest (*terdrom*) shaped like a clay jug, he recovered from Mewar Tso, near Mt Nering Drak, by entering the water with a burning torch. At Samye Chimpu (see page 631) and other places he located hidden texts, 'liberation-pills' and other potions that can set people spiritually free. Pemalingpa even revealed the sacred monastery of Lho Kyechu, which had somehow become invisible. The incarnations of Pemalingpa kept Lhalung Monastery as their center.

✤ DAY 8 LAKE PEMALING TSO–LHASA ROAD (VIA DRUM LA, 5135 M) 9 HR

A stream flows down an eroded ravine at a point opposite the black tents at the tip of the lake. Follow the trail along the right slopes of this ravine to eventually join the main path coming up from a lower part of the valley. Using stone cairns as path markers, come to a point above a long, narrow lake (1 hr). At its head is the broad face of Mt Gawa; an impressive glacier descends left of the Drum La.

Continue to a third lake, then pass a final tiny glacial lake at the glacier's base which is only 1/2 hr away. Follow the clearly defined path for a hard climb to Drum La (3 1/2 hr). (The pass, marked with prayer flags, is 700 m above the second lake, and 5135 m above sea level.) From the top, Mt Kula Kangri can be seen as a thin wedge of a triangle. To the northwest is the domed peak of Mt Kula Cham, the female accompaniment of male Kula Kangri. Next to it are Mt Chenresi and Mt Gawa (closest to the pass). The view is awesome.

Follow a difficult, slippery trail down from the pass. Be very careful and take your time. Descend to a flat plain (1 1/2 hr from the pass), then follow a trail north down the valley for 1/2 hr. The path is poorly defined and stony. Reach a bridge marked with two large stone cairns (*tsakhang*) and prayer flags (1 1/2 hr). The path now divides; both branches lead to the Lhasa (via Nakartse) road. Take the left, a more direct route to the monasteries of Lhalung and Guru Lhakhang near Manda Qu. It meets the main, flat Lhasa road in 1 hr. (A right turn leads to Lhodrak Xian, 2 hr on foot.) Turn left to Manda Qu and Lhalung Monastery.

North of Lhodrak Xian Minor trails lead north from Lhodrak Xian to the southern shores of Yamdrok Tso. From the lake, go west to Nakartse on the Friendship Highway or east to Chongye in the Yarlung Valley (see page 355).

Rock of Chenresi After turning left, near the turnoff, there is a huge rock on the left. Carved *mantras* decorate its face and signs of the sun and moon are near the top.

✤ DAY 9 LHASA ROAD—MANDA QU 3 HR

Walk west along the main road to a village on the left (1 hr). The monastic complex of Lhalung surrounded by fields and houses, can now be seen across the river. About 1/2 hr further is another village with houses on both sides of the road. A side dirt road on the right leads down to a bridge and Lhalung (1/4 hr).

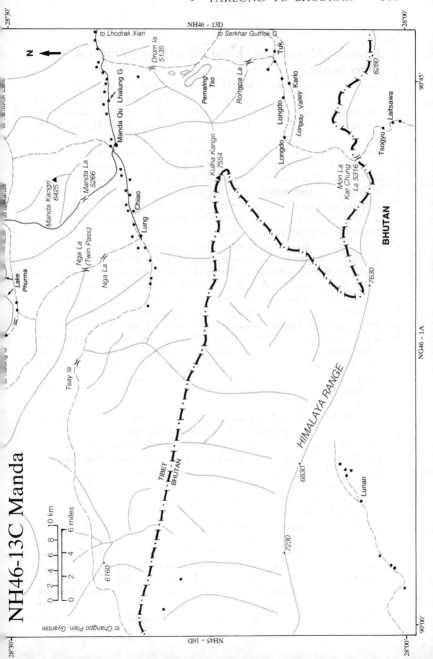

NH46-13C Manda

NH46 – 13D

to Lhodrak Xian

to Serkhar Guthok G

Drum la 5135

Pemaling Tso

Rongpa La

Tuk

Longdo

Longdo Karlo

Longdo Valley

Longdo

6280

Laitsawa

Tsogyu

Manda Qu Lhatung G

Manda La 5266

Manda Kangri 6425

Chiao

Lung

Kulha Kangri 7554

Mon La 5316

Kar Chung La

BHUTAN

Nga La (Twin Pass)

Nga La

Lake Phurma

7630

Tsay la

HIMALAYA RANGE

TIBET

BHUTAN

6830

6160

Lunan

7230

to Changpo Plain, Gyantse

0   2   4   6   8   10 km

0   2   4   6 miles

NH45 – 16D

NG46 – 1A

Lhalung Monastery (Lhodrak Lhalung Zimkyal Dhechenling)

Lhalung was founded officially in 1154 by Karmapa Düsum Khyenpa. However, locals call the monastery Lhalung Paldhor Gompa, so perhaps Lhalung Paldhor (see Yerpa, page 340), the 9th-C. assassin of King Langdarma, built the original foundation. Later, the historian, Pawo Tsuklak Trengwa (1503–66), became abbot. Lhalung was the seat of several important incarnate lamas (*tulkus*), including Pemalingpa. His followers formed the the Lhodrak Lungpa, a Nyingmapa sub-sect. At the time of the Fifth Dalai Lama (1617–82), the monastery was converted from the Karmapa to the Gelugpa, hence its teaching was a strange mixture of Drukpa (Bhutanese school), Kagyüpa and Nyingmapa. Lhalung had many branch monasteries, including Yardrok (Yamdrok), Yönpodo (Yamdrok's island monastery; see page 608), Yangdhing, Dhongkya, Nye Nae Lhakhang, Wön (two monasteries), Dra (two nunneries), Pemaling at Bumthang and Bhutan, and Gangdhing in Bhutan.

The site of Lhalung, its red monastic buildings scattered about the central temple, was constructed as an octagonal mandala. It was surrounded by 108 *chörtens* (destroyed) and 108 willow trees. Outside of the high exterior wall, with entrances in the four directions, were three, three-story-high *chörtens*. The large central building, the Tsuglag Khang, has original painted beams and columns, and it houses 20 monks. Previously, within the main entrance, were paintings of Peling Phurpa (a tantric teaching) and a diagram of Tshedrub Dorje Trengwa (tantric teachers). A chapel with fine original murals, to the right of the Tsuglag Khang's entranceway, has become a store selling clothes, food, and daily necessities. The adjacent Mani Lhakhang has a new *mani* wheel, constantly used by villagers. A knowledgeable old caretaker saved many valuable objects during the Cultural Revolution, including the footprints (*shabjes*) of Düsum Khyenpa, Marpa, and Milarepa, now kept in the second floor *zimkhang* of the Tsuglag Khang.

Within the ground floor *dukhang* of the Tsuglag Khang were 8-m-high clay statues of the Seven Past Buddhas (*Sangye Rabdün*). The hall has unusual branching pillars of wood not found in other chapels. Other statues included the Long-life Divinities, Guru Rinpoche framed within a mandala, and the seven statues of the Pemalingpa lineage. Inside the *gönkhang* was a statue of Gönpo Bernak. The inner *tsangkhang* had three large statues of the Primordial Buddhas and a silver *chörten* of Tenzin Chökyi Nyima, whose son, Tenzin Gyürme Dorje, painted the eight *thangkas* in the chapel. At the back of the *dukhang* is the Zhitrö Lhakhang, a double-chapel that houses the monastery's peaceful and wrathful divinities. The statues are new and the chapels are in daily use by the monks.

The second floor *zimkhang* contains the bedroom of Lhalung Paldhor, Langdarma's assassin. At one end of the room is his throne and to one side an altar. The large room next door was used by Karmapa Düsum Khyenpa, the founder. Behind his throne is an altar with the stone footprints of the First Karmapa, Marpa, and Milarepa. Dilapidated

➡

murals adorn the walls. At the rear are chapels used as an artisan's workshop. The top floor, in poor condition, still has some interesting murals, and chapels around the central skylight are being renovated. A large collection of wood block texts did not survive the Cultural Revolution.

After visiting Lhalung, return across the bridge to the main road. Manda Qu, the area's administrative center, lies to the west (1 1/4 hr from Lhalung). Layak Guru Lhakhang is in the vicinity of Manda Qu.

Layak Guru Lhakhang This main seat of Guru Chuwang is a recently restored, one-story monastery. It was rebuilt in 1949 on the design of India's Nalendra.

Guru Chuwang (Chökyi Wangchuk) (1212–70)

Guru Chuwang was Tibet's Second Discoverer King after Nyima Wösel (see page 686). He was a precocious child, able to read and write at age four. At 13, he had a vision of Drölma, who led him to a crystal castle. Here he received a vision of Vajrasattva (Dorje Sempa) and met a *dakini* with four faces, who exhorted him to embrace Buddhism and spread the faith. Guru Chowang was given a ceremonial arrow (*dakar*) with five feathers, and from this time on he began the search for hidden treasures.

His life was punctuated by magical and outlandish adventures, culminating in a heroic tale. A rock-sized vulture appeared and flew him to the 13th stage of Heaven where, within a rainbow-tent, Guru Chuwang saw Vajrasattva, the Buddha of Undiminished Being, and received power and a ritual flask of elixir. He found two copper chests with the concealed treasures (*terjang*) of 108 Advices. After this discovery, he managed to locate a further 18 treasures and one concealed teaching. A worthy event in Guru Chuwang's life was his prophecy of the Mongol invasion. In 1239, Godan and his Mongols did actually penetrate into Tibet as far as Reting and Gyal Lhakhang. His prowess as a *tertön* and teacher and his performance of miracles gained him the reverence of the Nyingma. He is remembered for building the monasteries of Tsongdü Gurmo and Samdrub Dewachen.

Lhatak (Lhatok) Monastery Near Layak Guru Lhakhang is Lhatak, in a valley west of Manda Qu. It was founded by Tsangpa Gyaré Yeshe Dorje (1161–1211), a disciple of Pemalingpa. An adept of the Drukpa sect, he discovered the hidden valley (*beyul*) of Tsari (see page 210). The ascetic revealed texts originally concealed by Rechungpa (1083–1161) at Narphu and also founded the Longdhöl retreat on the Kyi Chu right bank, near Nethang Drölma Lhakhang (see page 472).

Kyichu Lhakhang Some sources claim this to be one of King Songtsen Gampo's Tandul Monasteries (see page 43), placed on the borders of the country to suppress Tibet's mighty demoness. Its location (unconfirmed) is at the junction of the Kyi Chu and Lhodrak Nub Chu, near Lhodrak Xian.

✤ Day 10 Manda Qu–Lhasa: 1–2 days (hitch)

Traffic through Manda Qu can be as sparse as one or two trucks per day. Most come from Lhodrak Xian. Settle down by the side of the road with a good book.

Manda Chu–Nakartse (102 km) 3 1/2 hr by Chinese truck

After Manda Qu, the road climbs steeply to the Manda Pass (1 1/4 hr). Later it follows the wild, uninhabited eastern shores of Phurma (Pomo) Tso, a large lake with three islands. An unusual maze-like complex of buildings (a monastery, perhaps Senge Gön, consecrated by Guru Rinpoche) stands at the edge of a peninsula at the lake's eastern end. After an hour, cross the low Yeh La. The first of many villages in a wide plain appears 3 hr after Manda Qu. Then Taglung Village with its ruined fort appears, as does Yamdrok Tso. The Friendship Highway is ahead. At a road junction, turn right along the main road to soon reach Nakartse. A guest house in a Tibetan building is just off the road and a restaurant nearby serves rice, vegetables, and tea.

Nakartse to Lhasa (154 km)

After Nakartse, the road follows Yamdrok Tso. Before Pede, a road goes left to historic Rinpung (see page 841). The main road ascends the Kampa La (4556 m), then drops down to the Tsangpo. After crossing the Chusul Bridge, follow the Kyi Chu to Lhasa.

Optional Excursions in Lhodrak

Serkhar Guthok to Pemaling Tso via the Rongpa La

A direct, more strenuous route to Pemaling Tso leads from Serkhar Guthok westward up the Zhe Chu (Longdo Chu) Valley. Cross the Longdo Chu to its left (north) bank and walk west to Droka (1 1/4 hr). Here the jeep track narrows to a footpath. Reach Tuk after an hour; ruins of Bentsa Serki Monastery are nearby. One hour west of Tuk is Yuro Dzong, and beyond it (west) is a treacherous bridge and Longdo. From Longdo, a trail leads south along the Kanang Chu to Bhutan (Jakar Dzong) via the well-known Mönla Karchung La. (This is one of the main Tibet–Bhutan trade routes.)

Just beyond Tuk, a trail goes north up the Tuk Chu Valley to the 5050 m Rongpa La (1 1/2 hr). After the pass, descend to a plain with a stream running through the middle. Cross a low ridge and pass three small glacial lakes on the left. Go over another low ridge (3 hr from the Rongpa La). Descend to the eastern tip of Pemaling Tso and to a nomad camp (1/2 hr). This route takes you very close to the spectacular Mt Kula Kangri. (Another trail up the Rongpa La from the Longdo Chu Valley heads north before Tuk and leads to Chating [north of Tuk].)

Lhodrak from Yamdrok Tso

This itinerary follows a little-known route from Yamdrok Tso to Lhodrak district. En route, visit the remarkable island monastery of Yönpodo (see page 608) . From Lhodrak Xian, the district capital, the route swings west to Phurma Tso, then north to Ralung Monastery (see page 611).

MT NAMCHE BARWA AND THE TSANGPO GORGES: A BOTANIST'S PARADISE

Near Mt Namche Barwa, until 1992 the world's highest unclimbed mountain, is the 'hidden valley' of Pemakö, long considered one of the most sacred and mystical regions of Tibet. According to legend, if there comes a day when Buddhism is on the verge of collapse, this special enclave will provide a sanctuary for all. At this eastern extremity of the Himalayas, the mighty Tsangpo makes an abrupt turn onto itself. The uncommon congruence of high mountains and Tibet's most powerful water course creates one of the deepest gorges in the world. Pristine and botanically sans-pareil, it is a superb area for pilgrims and plant-hunters. The beautiful Nyima La links the Tsangpo Valley with the heavily forested Rong Valley.

THE NINGCHI ROAD: LINKING LHASA WITH KONGPO

OVERVIEW

Lhasa to Ningchi is a major section of the vital Tibet–Sichuan highway, the link between Tibet and China. Ningchi, properly called *Nyingtri* in Tibetan, is a principal town of Kongpo, a large district of southeast Tibet. It is a staging post for a number of sacred pilgrimages. Foremost among them are Bönri, the holy mountain of the Bön sect, and Pemakö, one of Tibet's premier hidden sanctuaries (*beyul*). Included in the latter area are the 7756-m Mt Namche Barwa, and the unexplored Tsangpo gorges.

The main stages of the Tibet–Sichuan highway are:

Lhasa–Kongpo Giamda	174 km
Kongpo Giamda–Ningchi	146 km
Ningchi–Baxoi	435 km
Baxoi–Chamdo	265 km
Chamdo–Sichuan border	313 km
Border–Chengdu	977 km

The northern route from Lhasa to Ningchi is a surprisingly rewarding artery for the exploration of central and southeastern Tibet. It is possible to stop off at numerous points along the way and start hiking to various pilgrimage and trekking destinations. Below is a brief guide.

LHASA TO NINGCHI

The first part of this itinerary heads northeast from Lhasa and follows the south (left) bank of the Kyi Chu until Medro Gongkar. It then makes a sharp turn to the right and goes up the Medro Valley to the east. After crossing the Mangshung (Mi) La, the road drops southeast to Kongpo Giamda, Bayi, and Ningchi. Km stones mark the whole way.

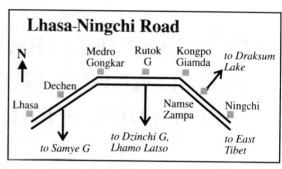

Lhasa-Ningchi Road

Map reference   NH46-9 B, 46-10 A B

Sector	Distance	Area accessed
Lhasa– Medro Gongkar	68 km	Gyalmashing Valley: birthplace of King Songtsen Gampo (page 546)
		Samye, via Gökar La or Ganden (page 295)
		Taklung, Reting, and other monasteries of the Phanyul Valley (page 544)
		Zorong Valley: Drigungtil, Terdrom, Katsal monasteries. Beyond Drigung to Lharigo, Alado, Shopado along the Gyalam (old Tibet–China road; page 570)
Medro Gongkar– Kongpo Giamda	206 km	Medro Valley (page 550)
		Wöka Valley and Lhamo Latso, via Rutok Monastery (page 642)
		Yön Valley, via Takar La (page 510)
		Lake Atsa, from Giamda (page 572)
		Yigrong Range, from Giamda (page 655)
		Gyalam, from Giamda (page 572)
		Tromda on the Tsangpo, via Ashang Kang La (from road marker 1362 km; page 710)
		Tromda, via Sho La (from road marker 1352 km; page 710)

Kongpo Giamda– 127 km Bayi	Draksum Lake and Nambu La, via Shoga Dzong (page 647)
	Atsa Lake, via Drukla Gompa (page 655)
	Yigrong Valley, from Namse Zampa (page 655)
	Gyalam, from Namse Zampa (page 570)
	Bayi Pelri, from Bayi (page 743)
	Bönri, holy mountain of Bön (page 741)
Bayi–Ningchi 19 km	Mt Namche Barwa and Pemakö Tsangpo gorges (page 712)
	Rong Chu Valley, via Nyima La (page 729)
	Po Yigrong Valley, via Rong Chu (page 734)
	Tsangpo (Pe) to Dihang, via Doshang La (page 716)
	Pomi, via Su La from Metok (page 717)
	Chimdro, Zayul, from Metok (page 717)

Access
Bus
The bus station in Lhasa for the Ningchi-Kongpo area is at the Tibet Autonomous Region (TAR) No 2 Guest House (one block east of the post office). Buses leave every morning at 0830 (Rmb 20). An extra bus sometimes runs if demand is great; it usually leaves between 0900 and 0930. Bring food and drinks for the trip.

Hitch
From central Lhasa walk past the Banak Shöl Hotel and Tibet University, cross the East Lhasa Bridge and continue for 4 km to the large gas station, a good place to start hitching. Chances of getting a ride are not good, however, because truck drivers are reluctant to pick up foreigners for fear of being fined.

Car rental
Negotiate a price at any of the car rental offices in Lhasa, based on the 420-km tariff between Lhasa and Ningchi.

Lhasa–Medro Gongkar 68 km
For a detailed description of this sector, see Upper Kyi Chu, page 544.

Medro Gongkar–Kongpo Giamda 206 km

Road marker (km) **Notes**
In brackets are new road markers.

1500 (4564) Medro Gongkar. Start of trek to Drigungtil and Reting monasteries.

1496		Takpa. A handsome monastery and village are on the right. Here Medro Valley is wide and fertile.
1484		The Medro Valley narrows.
1481	(4545)	Balo (Tashigang) A trail at the entrance of the Sephuk Po Chu Valley leads south to the Yön Valley (see page 510) via the Takar La. Another trail goes southeast via the Le La to Yamalung and Samye monasteries (see page 627).
1474		Rinchenling. A small monastery is on the right, next to ruins. A larger monastery also stands in this valley to the left, 1 1/2 km from the road. The road starts to climb gradually.
1466		Rock carving on the right. The land becomes wild and desolate.
1464	(4528)	Jenju Valley. A side valley on the right has 10 nomad tents; a trail leads south to the Zangri Valley (see page 636).
1446	(4510)	Rutok Monastery. This renovated monastery is halfway up a hill on the left. The pilgrimage to Dzinchi Monastery and Lhamo Latso (see page 642) starts near here (see road marker 1443 km). Hot springs are nearby. A walled village (145 *daoban*: road maintenance compound) is below the monastery.
1443	(4507)	The road crosses a stone bridge. The Medro River is now on the right side of the road. A side valley here leads south to Dzinchi and Lhamo Latso. The Medro Valley, with nomad tents, begins to widen.
1436	(4500)	Trails south to Magön La and Madra La passes. The latter leads to Lake Madra Latso (see page 644) and Dzinchi Monastery.
1431	(4495)	A wide junction of valleys. The road turns into the left valley and climbs gradually to the Mangshung (Mi) La, passing a lake. A trail on the right heads southeast, then turns south to Dzinchi Monastery and Wöka Dzong.
1419	(4483)	Mangshung La (5000 m).
1391		Unusual sod huts.
1390		Shungdor. Truck stop and restaurant.
1370	(4434)	A major valley heads right over a bridge and leads south to the Ashang Kang La (see map, page 645), then to Tromda on the Tsangpo. A trail from this pass goes via the Lung La to Lake Lhamo Latso.
1360		A trail within the valley on the left leads to Nagchu (nine-day walk).
1357	(4421)	Jashing. Chinese compounds next to a village.

1352	A valley on the right leads to the Se (or Shö) La, (4416) then Tromda.
1350	Syangboteng.
1339 (4403)	Jinda Qu. Tap Monastery is nearby.
1337	Double bridge leads left to a river valley.
1326	Songtsen Monastery. Villages on both sides of the road.
1317 (4381)	Giamda. Suspension bridge. A valley leads to the Yigrong Valley and the Gyalam caravan route.
1316	Ruined monastery.
1294 (4358)	Kongpo Giamda (3200 m). A major town of Kongpo with a watchtower, two bridges, and wood inspection station. Guest house and restaurant are near the gas station.

Kongpo Giamda–Ningchi 146 km

Road marker	Notes
1281	Ngape Dzong.
1254	Langa.
1246 (4310)	Ba River. Namse Zampa bridge at the entrance of a large valley. Small wood shacks with shops and lodging. A route leads northwest to the seldom-traveled Po Yigrong Valley and a track goes northeast to sacred Draksum Lake (Pasum; see page 647). The Ba River is formed of the Drukla and Shoga rivers, which meet at Shoga, then flow south into the Giamda (Nyang) Chu. Nearby is Namse Monastery.
1240	15-m-high polygonal, brown, stone, defense towers on the left.
1224 (4288)	Baiba.
1203	Charming village; a valley comes down from the right.
1196	Town.
1189	Village on a knoll.
1164	Guncang. Gas station on the right.
1161 (4225)	Bayi (see page 743). Large town with textile factory.
1142 (4206)	Ningchi (see page 758).

MT NAMCHE BARWA:
THE GREAT BEND OF THE TSANGPO

Location	Southeast Tibet
Map reference	NH46-12 A B C D, Heart of the Tsangpo Gorges
Trekking days	10 (round-trip)
Start–Finish	Lusha–Gyala–Lusha
Passes	None

OVERVIEW

Pemakö is the region of southeast Tibet whose northern limits are defined by two great ranges: Namche Barwa and Gyala Pelri. Across the Tsangpo River from Mt Namche Barwa (7756 m) is Gyala Pelri (7151 m)—only 21 km separates these two, and between their peaks is an awe-inspiring gorge some 5000 m deep. In the process of tunneling through the ramparts of the Eastern Himalayas, the mighty Tsangpo makes a stupendous bend upon itself to flow through northeastern India as the Brahmaputra before entering the Bay of Bengal. Within a distance of 45 km, the Tsangpo, quantum-leaping from the Tibetan plateau to the Indian plains, loses 7000 m in altitude. This is even more dramatic than the Kali Gandaki in Nepal or the Grand Canyon in the United States. Botanists have long considered the Namche Barwa area one of the most spectacular in the world. Britain's renowned flower-hunters explored here in the early 20th century.

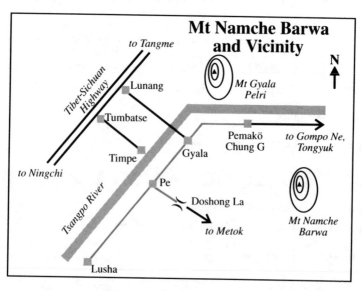

Mt Namche Barwa and Vicinity

Beyond Namche Barwa, the Tsangpo River enters the highly sacred region of Pemakö or Metok ('Flower Country'). The incredible flora, with habitats ranging from the alpine snow belt to the verdant subtropics, is regarded as the richest in Tibet. For Tibetan Buddhists, Pemakö is among the most important 'hidden valleys' (beyuls), and perhaps the most legendary in their country. The area is so remote that currently no road links it with the rest of the country. It is best reached by crossing the 4115-m Doshong La and then descending a long, long way to Metok Xian, the main settlement. Renowned pilgrimage sites in the area are Buddha Tsepung, Pemakö Chung, Rinchenpung, and Kondü Dosem Potrang.

The trek takes ten days from Lusha to Gyala and back. This itinerary is a continuation of the Bönri pilgrimage (see page 741), which circles the sacred mountain of the Bönpos. To explore Namche Barwa and the Tsangpo gorges, begin at the little village of Lusha on the south bank of the Tsangpo near its junction with the Nyang Chu (Giamda River). The walk is easy; simply follow the river downstream. No passes need be crossed unless an attempt is made to enter Pemakö via the Doshong La, or to reach the pilgrimage monastery of Pemakö Chung in the heart of the river gorges.

A noted enclave for plant enthusiasts is the Doshong La, a relatively low pass south of the river. The famed botanist, Frank Kingdon Ward, dubbed it 'Rhododendron Fairyland'. Another enchanting locale is between Tripe and the base camp of Namche Barwa. This side valley offers fine views of the region's mountains; near Tripe is a sacred circuit around a ridge of the massif. One of the trek's loveliest destinations is a beach of pristine white sand set on the banks of the Tsangpo and surrounded by lush forests. Gyala Pelri towers over it, while across the river, accessible by Tibetan canoes (drus), is the temple of Sinje Chögyal—where the carved image of its most important deity can be viewed from behind a waterfall (although only between the months of November and June).

Beyond Gyala is the monastery of Pemakö Chung, a sacred pilgrimage site within the Tsangpo bend. This difficult journey requires four or five days to cover a distance of less than 60 km. The overgrown trail is only passable when the Tsangpo's water level is low (avoid July and August). Near the monastery is the transcendent Rainbow Falls, also named Kinthup Falls, after the Indian pandit who first discovered it. One optional, arduous journey follows the footsteps of Kingdon Ward and Lord Cawdor who, in 1924, succeeded in reaching Gompo Ne, a sacred site at the Tsangpo–Po Tsangpo junction. Five weeks of extremely rugged gorge country places high demands on outback experience, preparation, and equipment. This route has an Exploratory Trek advisory, see page 17.

After visiting Gyala or Pemakö Chung, a worthwhile alternative to retracing one's route is to cross over to the Tsangpo's north bank and return westward.

Related sections
Bönri, p 741

Access
Lusha (see Bönri, page 761)

Time Chart

Day	Place	Hours
1	Lusha–Pungkar	5

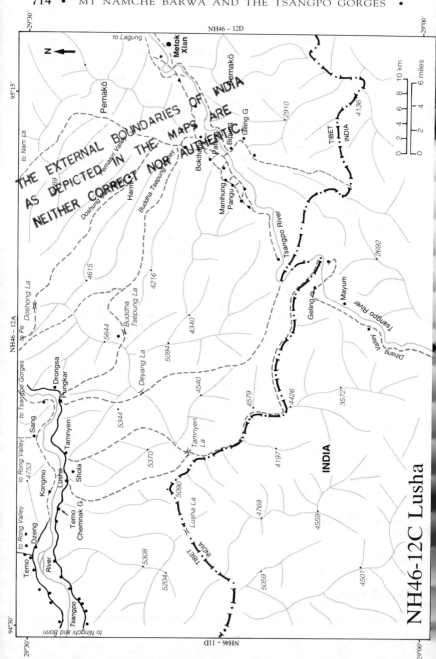

THE EXTERNAL BOUNDARIES OF INDIA
AS DEPICTED IN THE MAPS ARE
NEITHER CORRECT NOR AUTHENTIC

NH46 – 12D

NH46 – 12A

NH46-12C Lusha

NH46 – 11D

2	Pe	3
3	Tripe	5
4	Beach camp	3
5	Gyala	4 1/2
6–10	Gyala–Lusha	

Trail Notes

The trek basically follows the south bank of the Tsangpo, along a dirt road with hardly any traffic.

✤ DAY 1 LUSHA–PUNGKAR 5 HR

A jeep track skirts the north end of Lusha; from the ferry walk through fields to get to it, then head east along the Tsangpo. Shola is reached in 1/2 hr. Across the river is the deserted village and monastery of Kongmo, whose villagers have all moved here. A bit further along is a school on the right at Langa and some fields cultivated by Lopas. After Langa, pass a side valley on the right, which leads to the Giga La, then a small hill (Drölma Ri) with prayer flags on the right (1 hr). Tamnyen is a further 5 min on the left, home of the important Gelugpa monastery of Kongpo Aki Gyalpo (smashed during the Cultural Revolution). An army camp stands across the road and Dokong Valley, leading to the Dokong La, is to the

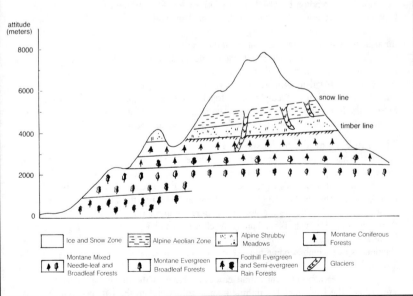

Mt Namche Barwa (7756 m)

right. Continue east along the main road. Wade across several channels of an ice-cold river coming down from the Dokong La. The current is fast and strong—be careful. Carry on and cross over a wood bridge in 1 1/2 hr. The Tsangpo here is wide with islands in the middle. Pungkar, a village with a store, is 2 hr from the bridge. The river crossings, today's and tomorrow's, are very difficult, although trucks and Beijing jeeps make it through regularly.

✤ DAY 2 PUNGKAR–PE 3 HR

Drongsa (Gyakateng), 1/2 hr from Pungkar, marks a start of the Tsangpo's sweeping turns. Just after the village is another fast, ice-cold river coming in from the right. Choose a point of crossing carefully. Walk 1/2 hr from the river to a wood gate on a small rise. Pe Qu (Doshong), the admin compound of the district is 1 hr beyond. Here are Chinese compounds, a hospital, and cultivated fields. The village of Pe is 3/4 hr further; here is where the Tsangpo narrows, at times only 100 m wide. (A ferry crosses to Timpe on the north—left—bank and then a trail goes northwest over the Nyima La to Tumbatse in the Rong Valley, see page 732.) Just after Pe is the Doshong La Valley (right), the main corridor to negotiate the Great Bend of the Tsangpo. (From the Doshong La, a trail leads precipitously down to Metok Xian at the southeast portion of the bend. From Pe [2923 m] to Metok Xian [760 m] involves a drop in altitude of over 2000 m.) (A truck goes from Pe to Miling Xian [west], on the Tsangpo's south bank every morning.)

Doshong La ('Rhododendron Fairyland')

In 1924, the English explorer-botanist, Frank Kingdon Ward, accompanied by Lord Cawdor, discovered an astonishing variety of rhododendrons on the Doshong La and described the pass as a 'Rhododendron Fairyland.' At a relatively low 4115 m, the pass is the main gateway between the northern and southern parts of the Tsangpo bend. (The much higher Nam La, 5287 m, is also used, but primarily by pilgrims.) It is noted for its abundant precipitation throughout the year. Warm, moist air from the southern slopes of the Assam Himalayas rushes up to shroud the region in rain and drizzle during the summer, from June to September. Snow storms and blizzards mixed with rain are frequent occurrences during the rest of the year. Heavy snow can fall in October and November and the pass is closed for the winter any time after mid-November. October can be frigid, with constant rain, snow and ferocious winds. Most of the heavy snow in the upper valleys melts in mid- or late June. Thus the best times to cross the Doshong La are the months of July, August, September, and October.

The route from Pe to Doshong La

From Pe, head east over a vehicular bridge at the entrance to the Doshong Valley. The army and civilian compound of Chutong is on the left. At this point, one branch of the jeep track forks to the right and heads to the pass, seen as a gap between two snow peaks. A forested ridge runs up between the two. The track bears east (left) of the Doshong Chu. Walk past houses and a small hydro-electric station and carry on up the ridge through dense pine forests, then a rhododendron belt. Beyond are grassy clearings and boggy meadows with grazing horses. Leave the jeep track from time to time to take short cuts up the forested slopes. The track deteriorates as it climbs, ending just below the alpine zone. Camp at this point, 4–5 hr after leaving Pe.

Near the campsite a small trail crosses a stream in the middle of an ice field. This stream joins the Doshong Chu, rushing from a steep valley to the left. Between this valley and the pass is a high rocky ridge. Flanking the valley leading to the pass is a high cliff. Cross the ice carefully. Further up, cross another gently sloping permanent ice field. Just before the pass is another, steeper ice field; kick steps in the ice to reach the top. The Doshong La is narrow and hemmed in by high cliffs; heavy mist and rain rushes up from the other side. There are no spectacular views. The descent is icy and sheer and the path indistinct. From campsite to pass is 2 hr.

Doshong La to Metok Xian (Pemakö)

The Doshong La sees many travelers from July to October. Mönpas from the Pemakö area cross to Kongpo, especially in September and October, when the Assam monsoon has died out. They are distinguished by puttee-like cotton strips bound very tightly around their calves to prevent leeches. The outposts of civilization on Namche Barwa's southern slopes generally cling to both banks of the Tsangpo, here called the Dihang. They are among the most isolated communities in Tibet, and Metok Xian is the only *xian*-level town in a huge tract of territory that has no road link to the rest of the country. The area is agriculturally self-sufficient but needs manufactured goods, now transported by helicopter from Ningchi. Other trails lead into Pemakö from the Pomi district by way of the Su La (the main pass), Chimdro La, Zik La, and Dochu La.

Metok Xian (Pemakö)

The entire Metok Xian district is designated a Nature Preservation Zone by Beijing and Lhasa. Stunningly beautiful, formidable, and virtually inaccessible, it is bounded on the north by Pomi and on the east by Zayul. South of Metok Xian is the disputed McMahon Line that demarcates Tibet from India. The highly contorted Tsangpo Valley within Pemakö proper is long and narrow, entrenched within the high mountains of the Namche Barwa range. Being on the south slopes of the Himalayas, Pemakö receives the bulk of the Assam monsoon. Its climate is hot and wet (over 300 cm of rainfall per year), due to the low altitude. The fascinating flora extends from rain forests (600 m) to high alpine (4500 m). One of the best times to travel in the region is April–May, before the heavy rains, and August–September, before snow closes the passes.

According to Tibetan tradition, Pemakö is one of 16 earthly paradises, a promised land free of worry, the ultimate hidden haven (*beyul*). When China invaded East Tibet at the beginning of the 20th C., many Khampas made the long, difficult trek to Pemakö for succor and refuge. Pemakö in turn encompasses 16 sacred regions. According to one Tibetan pilgrimage guide, it is consecrated to the female divinity, Dorje Phagmo, and its mythic geography is linked to the sleeping goddess. Her head, in the northeast, is Kangri Karpo, a prominent peak between Pemakö and Zayul. The neck is Mt Dorjeyang, situated between Metok Xian and Ningchi Xian. Rinchenpung Monastery, near Metok Xian, is the navel. Her left breast is sacred Mt Kondü Potrang and the right is the Pemasiri River of east Pemakö. Its water, milk of the goddess, rises south of the Nam La and drains into the Tsangpo. Pomi is the deity's left hand, Kongpo her right.

Tradition says Guru Rinpoche was the first master to set foot in Pemakö. His 25 disciples came here as well—their caves can still be identified. Gampopa, a chief disciple of Milarepa and founding father of the Kagyü sect, visited this area and revealed a number of holy places. A major pilgrimage site in Pemakö is Buddha Tsepung (Budi Tsepo), sited near the Pepung La. It is made up of wondrous Lake Bokun, considered perhaps the most scenic spot in the region, and two temples, all consecrated to Dorje Phagmo. Guru Rinpoche meditated in a cave here and broke a clay pot. Pilgrims possessing a high degree of merit are supposedly able to find shards. Secret water (sangchab) of the goddess issues from a rock in the vicinity. Near Buddha Tsepung is Dorje Drakden Monastery, dedicated to the protector of Nechung. Other noteworthy places in Pemakö are Rinchenpung Monastery and Rinchen Phuk (near Metok Xian), and Kondü Dosem Potrang (see below).

Poisoners of Pemakö The Pemakö region has a macabre cult of poison, as does Kongpo (see page 653). Practitioners use poison to gain merit, spirituality, and perhaps wealth. This unique practice consists of the following. An egg is first buried in the ground. When a mushroom sprouts from the spot, a female practitioner (*dugma*) of the cult paints half of her face black and braids one side of her hair. She emerges under the full moon and makes a vow to use the poison within eight days on (in order of preference) a lama, a monk, a minister, her husband, her children, or herself. The poison is usually mixed with food, especially curd, beer (*chang*), eggs, or fruit. It is not used with *tsampa*, hot liquids, or hot food. Even though the intended victim may ask the poisoner to test the food or drink first, the poison, concealed under a fingernail, can still be skillfully inserted later. Poison can also be transmitted when the *dugma* lightly scratches a victim. Death comes within 3–6 hr. First the stomach rebels, then the throat.

The original inhabitants of Pemakö were the Abor, a hill tribe known to the Tibetans as Lopa. Later migrations included the Mönpas—who came from East Bhutan in the 19th C., the Kongpopas, Pobas from the district of Pomi, and Khampas from East Tibet. Today, the great majority of the population is Mönpa, as most Abor tribesmen have been driven south or assimilated. Mönpas also live near Tsona Xian and Lhüntse Xian (see page 243 and page 240).

Pe–Metok Xian: a route summary
Start the trip before 0600 to avoid the worst weather and strong winds on the Doshong La.

Day 1 • Pe–Doshong La–Harmi

Day 2 • Harmi–Arni (from Arni to Buddha Tsepung takes three days).

Day 3 • Arni–Maniyung-Bipung Qu on the Tsangpo. Near Bipung is Tirkung, birthplace of the renowned Dudjom Rinpoche.

Day 4 • Bipung Qu–Metok Xian at the Shumo Chu–Tsangpo confluence. Rinchenpung Monastery, consecrated to Tamdrin and seat of Drodön Lingpa, is further up the valley on a hill called Zangdok Pelri. A three-day walk from the monastery, via Tapak and the Dozhung La, brings one to Kondü Dosem Potrang. This celebrated

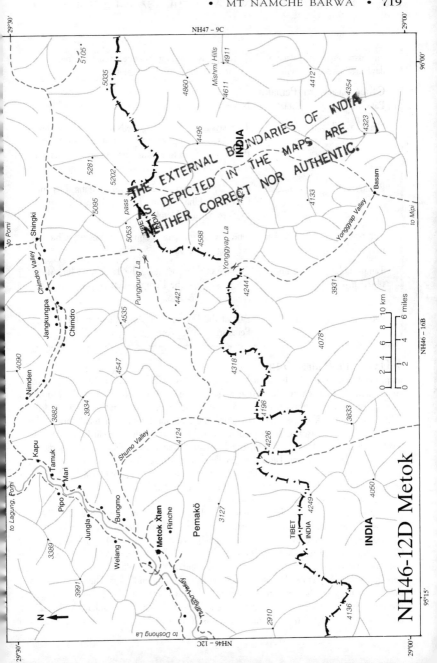

NH47 – 9C

NH46 – 12C

NH46-12D Metok

NH46 – 16B

THE EXTERNAL BOUNDARIES OF INDIA
AS DEPICTED IN THE MAPS ARE
NEITHER CORRECT NOR AUTHENTIC.

sanctuary, mythical palace of Dorje Sempa, is noted for its tame animals. Three more days are needed to perform the *khora* around this pilgrimage site.

Other passes to Pemakö

Pass	Start	Notes
Nam La (5225 m)	Kyikar	Two days to the pass along the Namlung Chu Valley; Nam Tso (glacial lake) at the foot of the pass. Follow the Nyalam Chu to Mandalting Monastery, then to Chiksha in Pemakö.
Pepung La	Pungkar	One day to the pass. Follow the Buddha Tsepung Chu to Buddha Tsepung (one day), then continue to Yortong and Metok.
Deyang La (3713 m)	Pungkar	One day to the pass. Follow the Nugong Chu to Sobrang in Pemakö.
Tamnyen La (4420 m)	Tamnyen	Two days to the pass along the Tamnyen Chu. After the pass follow the Dompu, then Nugong rivers to Sobrang in Pemakö.
Pero La	Pe	East of the Doshong La. After the pass, follow the Pemasiri Chu to Yortong.

❖ Day 3 Pe–Tripe 5 hr

Immediately east of the Doshong La Valley entrance is a Chinese-style compound (Chutong) on the left. A store is near the entrance. The presence of a Public Security Bureau officer means do not linger, although there is a guest house in the compound with four bedrooms. Follow the dirt track to continue east along the river for 1/2 hr to a small shrine with a painted footprint (*shabje*). Cross a small wooden bridge, then climb gradually to a rise with lovely views of the Tsangpo Valley, the Doshong La, and the Nyima La. Pass some ruins on the left. The village of Tatoka, overlooking a wide stretch of the river, is on a small ridge just ahead. 20 min further is Dzongluk (poorly stocked store), and soon Lingba appears on a terrace with good camping sites. The hills on the left bank are covered with firs, and lower down are prickly oaks (*partö*) and scrub.

Nyiting, 3/4 hr from Lingba, has a wood gate at the village entrance. The Tsangpo flows swiftly here. Further on (1 1/4 hr), a steep descent brings one to pretty Kyikar Village. The jeep track ends here and becomes a foot-trail. [A short distance from Kyikar is the Namlung Chu Valley, which leads south via the Nam La (5225 m) to Purarang and Metok Xian. The trail does not go along a valley but traverses a number of side valleys, and the pass is open only from July to September.] Cross a wooden bridge 20 min from Kyikar. Then, 5 min further, the trail splits; take the left fork for 5 min and cross another bridge (look up a valley to the right for a good view of awesome Namche Barwa). This is the Namlung Valley. Zigzag up the slopes to a level trail (20 min). Tripe is 20 min further on a small flat plateau. On the right side of the trail is a beautiful meadow with a stream that leads up the Tripe Valley to Namche Barwa. This is a memorable place to camp. Further up the narrow Tripe Valley are the tiny settlements of Tigiling and Rukar. A pasture called Tongshung, above Rukar is 1 1/2 hr from camp. From here it is possible to see across the Tsangpo to the Tong La, (see page 732) a pass that leads to Tumbatse in the Rong Valley. The Tong La, impassable for animals, is higher than the Nyima La (see page 729 for a trek crossing this pass). From Tongshung, drop down to the Tripe Chu, then climb 100 m up a ridge to find a spectacular receding glacier nearly 1 km wide. A spur of Namche Barwa drops to a point just beyond Tripe. This is a pilgrimage site consecrated by Guru Rinpoche and known as Atsom Neh. The *khora*, encircling the ridge, takes one day; there is an uninhabited temple on the circuit.

✤ DAY 4 TRIPE–BEACH CAMP 3HR

Carry sufficient water on this stretch to last for one day. After Tripe, pass through one wooden gate (5 min), then another in 1/2 hr. Longa is beyond on the left. Descend to a small river, the Palung, ford it, then walk up a slope until the trail levels. After 1/2 hr the level trail descends towards the Tsangpo. Walk through fern fields to Langpe, a derelict village of stone houses and corrals, tents and wide fields (1 1/2 hr from the last gate). Leave the village, pass through an oak forest, then descend to the river again at a sandy beach, a good place to camp (1 1/4 hr from Langpe). The isolation of this stretch is broken from time to time by helicopters bringing supplies to Metok from Ningchi. They fly in twos along the Tsangpo and cross the Assam Himalayas (Pachakshiris) via the Doshong La.

✤ DAY 5 BEACH CAMP–GYALA 4 1/2 HR

From this beach camp, the trail veers to the right, leaving the Tsangpo (1/2 hr). Pass flowery meadows, go around a bluff, then come down to the river again to cross a wooden bridge. The Tsalung Chu flows in from the right from a striking narrow cleft. (Beach to here is 1 1/2 hr.) In 1/2 hr, a cliff drops vertically to the Tsangpo. Start zigzagging up the side of its chiseled and dramatic rock face. Continue through a level oak forest, then reach a wide plain above the Tsangpo, site of Gyala, a pretty village with stone houses under walnut trees. Gyala is 3 hr from the Tsalung Chu.

   A secluded, pristine white sand beach is 1/4 hr down from the village. Forests and bluffs provide plenty of privacy and lovely grassy borders make for excellent camping. Occasionally fishermen arrive to fish. This is a magnificent spot; budget one or two extra days to rest here. The Tsangpo flows slowly by the beach, the rapids having ceased 2 km upstream, allowing for good swimming. The water attains its greatest height in September. Across the 100 m-wide river is the deserted Gyala monastery, Sinje Chögyal. Tradition states that the deity, Sinje Chögyal, is chained inside the stream that tumbles down a cliff next to the monastery. His image, in a small cave behind a waterfall, can be seen in the early spring when the water is low. Two dugouts lashed together ferry goods and men to the other shore when the Tsangpo is low and the current weak (spring and autumn). An indistinct trail from the monastery goes over the Tra (Pa) La to Lunang in the Rong Valley. Gyala is the starting point for climbing Gyala Pelri and a sulphur hot spring (submerged in summer) lies 1 1/2 hr downstream.

Return from Gyala

Gyala is a convenient place to turn back. One way retraces the route to Pe, where it is possible to find a truck to Miling Xian and the main road on the south bank of the Tsangpo. The

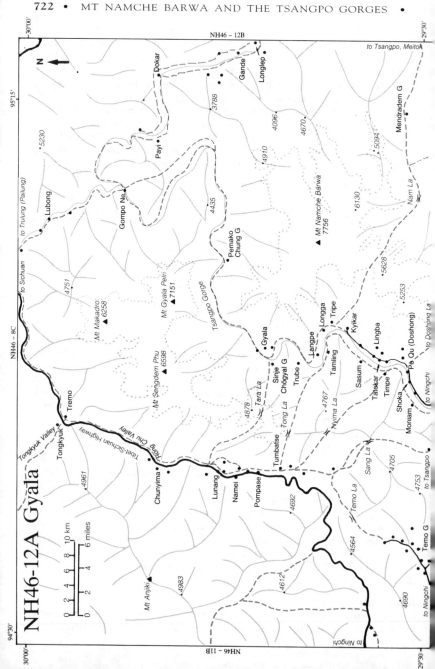

other route crosses the Tsangpo at Gyala and heads west, following the north bank of the river (see page 735).

THE TSANGPO GORGES: GYALA TO PEMAKÖ CHUNG MONASTERY (OPTIONAL PILGRIMAGE)

The trail to Pemakö Chung, a difficult 4–5-day walk beyond Gyala, is only passable from December to April (at other times the trail is likely to be submerged); daily progress rarely exceeds 12 km. This journey is for well-equipped, experienced trekkers only. It makes great sense to hire a guide from Gyala. The trail follows the Tsangpo beneath the magnificent Gyala Pelri (7151 m). Geographically, the region here is astonishing: the peaks of Gyala Pelri and Namche Barwa (7756 m), only 21 km apart from each other, tightly wedge between them the foaming Tsangpo. In penetrating these mighty ramparts, the river turns on itself before dropping 3000 m to the plains of India. No foreigner has ever succeeded in following the entire course of the indomitable Tsangpo gorges.

✧ Day 1 Gyala–Kumang   9 km
The trail east from Gyala goes through fields and then ascends to the top of a ridge. It becomes rough and narrow as it winds through a thick forest for 2.5 km before reaching the hot springs of Kenta Chu. After a steep climb, come to a sulphur mine, then ascend again for 1/2 hr to the top of a ridge. Continue up through a forest and then, after a slight descent, reach Kumang (3155 m), a deserted camp. The Tsangpo, far below, flows gently and the surrounding rugged mountains are sheer in places.

✧ Day 2 Kumang–Nyuk Sang   13 km
The trail first leads through bamboo forests. After 3 km reach the top of Musi La Ridge. From here, three peaks, the glaciers of Mt Sengdem and Sengdem Village, appear across the Tsangpo. A continuous snow ridge runs west from Gyala Pelri; the high mountain above Sengdem is Shegi Chörten. After some forests is Götshang Drubphuk, a cave below the trail on a ledge of rock, downstream from Sengdem. Below Sengdem, rapids in the river begin again (the river is mostly calm from Gyala to here). Descend 600 m through rhododendron and bamboo forests to reach a small river in a clearing opposite Gyala Pelri. Some 2.5 km further, after passing another clearing, come to a cave and campground under a high cliff called Nyuk Sang (2690 m). Lilies abound here. The Tsangpo, fast and furious, swirls 200 m below.

✧ Day 3 Nyuk Sang–Senge Dzong   12 km
Today's walk is difficult and dangerous, although the track improves near beautiful Mt Sanglung and Pemakö Chung. Climb from the cave to the Nyuk Sang La, a rise in altitude of about 200 m. In an hour cross another low spur, the Bong Sang La. Then, 8 km from the start, the trail appears to end in the river. A winter trail goes over rocks by the water, but when the river is high this trail disappears, making it necessary to scramble over steep slopes through dense forests. Ahead is the Gadza Oma River; ford it with difficulty. Continue along the increasingly difficult and overgrown trail to Senge Dzong (2605 m), an overhanging cliff. Beyond this, the trail goes over more partially submerged rocks. Travel this stretch between December and April. Marks on the sheer face of Senge Dzong were supposedly made by lions. Pilgrims make offerings of butter on the cliff.

✧ Day 4 Senge Dzong–Pemakö Chung Monastery 13 km

Walk through a forest, then emerge by the side of the river to begin a difficult section over boulders by the bank. During August and September the high water makes it impassable, forcing pilgrims to climb over a high ridge to the monastery (there is no trail). After leaving the river, walk through forests for nearly 10 km. The going is very rough and the trail overgrown. Staying generally high above the Tsangpo, eventually come to a trail junction. The path to Kinthup Falls drops steeply to the river, where the water rushes through a very narrow gap in the rocks. In the winter, pilgrims go from here along the edge of the falls to Pemakö Chung Monastery by way of a circuitous route. This way is not feasible in the summer.

Go back to the junction and continue to Pemakö Chung Monastery (a chapel and some houses). A nearby cave is reported to have 'lamps' that burn magically. This phenomenon is perhaps an emission of natural gas similar to Muktinath within the Kali Gandaki Valley of Nepal. [According to a local lama, a cave called Drakphuk Kawasum ('Cave of Three Pillars') exists two days downstream from Pemakö Chung. Concealed within is the key to the Hidden Valley of Pemakö (see page 703) as well as a secret text documenting its access. For Nyingma pilgrims, this cave is Pemakö's most important site.] Below, the Tsangpo makes a loop around Abu Dzong, a sacred rocky outcrop. Mt Namche Barwa rises to the southeast about 13 km away. Inhabitants leave this area in winter because of heavy snowfalls. The locals claim that no trail penetrates the Tsangpo gorges further downstream; they believe it impossible to follow the river's descent. Down river the view is blocked by a spur of Namche Barwa, but a rough herders' track continues for 2 1/2 km through forest to reach a glacial river. Beyond (1 km) is a hut called Seti. Pilgrims, mostly from Kongpo, come to Pemakö Chung on the 14th of the third lunar month. After paying homage to the monastery, they circle Kinthup Falls on the 15th, following a well-marked *khora*, and then they return home on the 16th.

EXPLORATORY TREK: PEMAKÖ CHUNG–GOMPO NE–TONGYUK (FIVE WEEKS)

This extremely difficult journey of five weeks traverses a section of the Tsangpo gorges. Do not attempt it without a competent guide and adequate gear. Excellent survival skills are a necessity. The first and most treacherous part of the route follows the Tsangpo. After negotiating some of the gorges, the river is left behind and a trail goes north to Gompo Ne, a small village and pilgrim site at the junction of the Tsangpo and Yigrong Chu. Kingdon Ward and Lord Cawdor did this trek in 1924. Since then, no foreigners have attempted it.

Stage 1

The trail east from Pemakö Chung passes through swamps and dense forest for a few km; the undergrowth is 2 m high. Cross the glacial Talung River (its source is Sanglung Glacier). The Tsangpo twists and turns along this stretch.

Stage 2

Below Kinthup Falls, the river makes a U-turn to the south around a sugarloaf peak, under the cliffs of Mt Sanglung (sulphur springs, submerged in the summer are here). Climb Sanglung's cliff (do not follow the U-bend of the river), then follow a narrow ledge around its face to another cliff. Ascend this via a narrow cleft. Continue along thick forests just above the

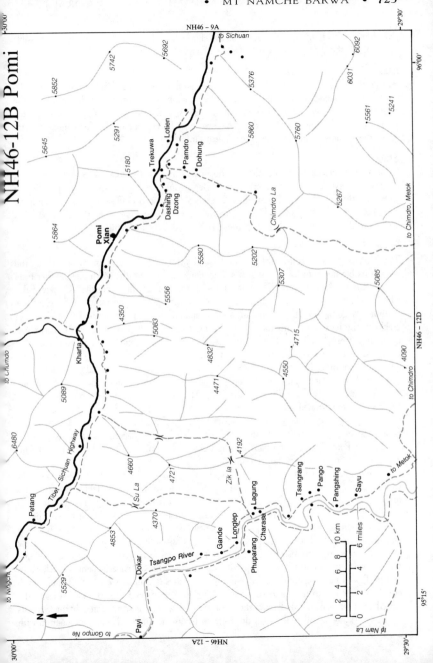

NH46-12B Pomi

river (during this tough stretch, expect to travel 6 km in 6 hr). Sheer cliffs make it impossible to go along the river banks. Come to a cliff and descend to a cave by the river.

Stage 3

Ahead, the large Churung Chu enters the Tsangpo from Sanglung. Hack a trail through the forest, then descend to the Churung; cross it, and follow a distinct path 300 m above the river. Descend a steep cliff (ropes may be necessary). Progress is very slow, averaging only 5 km per day for the next four days. A path must be cut out of the dense undergrowth. After the Churung, the Tsangpo veers northward.

Stage 4

Cross another glacial river, the Shegar Chu, which also comes from the Sanglung; in fact, its peak is very close and the foot of its glacier is only 3 km away to the south. Climb a steep cliff through thick undergrowth and reach a flat-topped cliff with pines and junipers. The Tsangpo is 300 m below. Descend to the river. Two streams enter the Tsangpo here, and soon after, the route along the gorge is blocked by a high cliff.

Stage 5

The Tsangpo smashes against the cliff's talus and swings sharply to the northwest (left), the start of its big northern loop. A spur from Sanglung juts in from the south and another from Gyala Pelri blocks the north. The river drops 12 m, creating the impressive Rainbow Falls. The Sanglung and Gyala Pelri spurs, now close together, tower over the rapids. Continue eastward by going over the steep east wall, scrambling up strips of scrub that grow out of cracks in the rock. After this tricky climb, come to a forest. Follow a hunter's trail through giant *tsuga* trees. Finally reach Sangchen La, the crest of the long Sanglung spur. Here the river and its gorges are on both sides! Continue northwest for 1 km through forests of huge *Abies* and tree rhododendrons, then start to descend the steep east face of the Sanglung spur.

Follow a clear trail due north along the face, then northeast along the crest of a smaller spur. The worst of this expedition is now over. The vegetation changes from conifer to oak, the steep descent arrested and the route now leads to cultivated fields (barley, maize, buckwheat, millet, apples), wood huts and the monastery of Payi (Payul) at river level. A rope bridge is just east of Payi. [A trail from here follows the left bank to Lagung and then ascends the Su La into Pomi. There is no path on the right bank; a high cliff blocks the route.] This whole area is populated by Lopas (Popas).

From Payi, leave the river to follow a path northwest up the Sorden La. Descend steeply to a single house and eventually reach the small village of Sengetong (three houses and a temple). Drop down to the Tsangpo and cross to the left bank by a rope bridge. The river is only 50 m wide here, at a point 6 km downstream (east) from the confluence of the Po Tsangpo (Yigrong) with the Tsangpo. The Tsangpo has fallen over 700 m since the Rainbow Falls and its rate of descent, 40 m per 1 1/2 km, is astonishing for a river of this size. The most violent section consists of a vertical drop of 40 m every 600 m. A long narrow spur comes down from the north. Traverse up to its crest and the little Kampa settlement of Tsachugang, one of Tibet's most superbly located villages. It perches 600 m above the river and affords breathtaking views to the south (the entire Sanglung massif) and west (Gyala Pelri and the jagged crest of Makandro). Follow the crest for 3 km, then descend through thick forests to the Po Tsangpo. Follow the river downstream (south) to Gompo Ne and its junction with

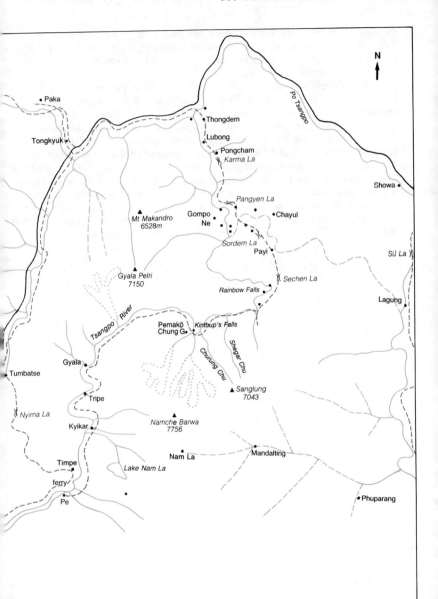

Heart of the Tsangpo Gorges

the Tsangpo. A *chörten* and deserted pilgrim hut stand 1 km from the confluence. To see Tsangpo's display of primordial force, cross the Po Tsangpo to its right bank by a rope bridge, climb a ridge to the west, cross a pass (again to the west), and continue southeast to the river. A 12-m waterfall is here too.

From Gompo Ne, return to Tsachugang and turn north up the gorge of the Po Tsangpo by climbing high above the village. Then cross a big spur at the Pangyen La, where the river bends sharply to the west. Carry on to the Karma La (2560 m) and descend steeply to Pongcham. Lubong, another Lopa village, is 6 km further to the north after crossing two rivers and two spurs. On the right bank is Pemaden; the two villages are linked by a rope bridge. The country north of the Karma La becomes progressively drier. From Lubong descend 300 m to the river, then immediately climb up over cliffs to Thongdem Village. Cross a broad river to reach the Rong Chu–Po Tsangpo junction. Further along (1 km) the Po Tsangpo is a rope bridge; cross it to Trulung on the right bank, then follow the Po Tsangpo back to the confluence downstream. Climb flights of steps over the shoulder of a high spur into the Rong Chu Valley. Finally, walk through pine forests to the Rong Chu–Tongkyuk junction and the town of Tongkyuk. Here a main road links Tibet with Sichuan.

NYIMA LA: FROM THE TSANGPO TO THE FLOWER GARDENS OF THE RONG VALLEY

Location	Kongpo, southeast Tibet
Map reference	NH46-12 A
Trekking days	5 (one-way)
Start–Finish	Pe–Tumbatse
Passes	Nyima La

OVERVIEW

This is an excellent, short trek for nature and flower lovers. It crosses part of Kongpo district, a pristine region that includes the delightful Nyima La and the lushly forested Rong Valley, a welcome change from the arid, barren landscape of most of Central Tibet. The route begins in Pe, a small village that is also the staging post of a trek to the great bend of the Tsangpo (see page 716). Here a ferry crosses to Timpe on the north (left) bank of the river, site of

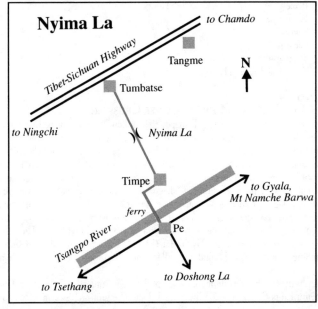

a revered Guru Rinpoche cave and monastery. A splendid footpath leads north to the Nyima La through some of the finest virgin forests and flower gardens in southeast Tibet. The idyllic walk passes a nomad camp, and encounters a wild profusion of poppies, primulas, and rhododendrons along the way. Many of the species abound on open moorland near the pass. Others grow by streams in the forests. Perhaps no other area in Tibet has so many varieties of poppy. A particularly spectacular plant, the giant sorel or rhubarb (*rheum nobile*), thrives on top of the Nyima La.

From the pass there are tremendous views of the Assam Himalayas, including nearby Gyala Pelri and Namche Barwa. The remote Salween Divide is also visible to the northeast. On the far side of the Nyima La is the Rong Valley, a beautiful, heavily forested valley that is luxuriantly carpeted with primulas and violet irises from May to July. Due to its relatively low altitude, this trek can be done virtually all year round—with the possible exception of February to April. The best time is from May to October. Rain can be expected from July to September.

Related sections
Great Bend of the Tsangpo, p 712

Access
Pe Village (see page 716), near the entrance of the Tsangpo gorge

Time Chart

Day	Place	Hours
1	Pe–Timpe	1 1/4 +
2	Sekundo	5 3/4
3	Clearing	5
4	Tumbatse	2 3/4
5	Tumbatse-*daoban* 111	1 3/4

Trail Notes
❖ DAY 1 PE–TIMPE 1 1/4 HR AND RIVER CROSSING
Walk from Pe directly down to the Tsangpo, then follow its south bank westward, passing prayer flags along the way. Reach a sandy beach in 20 min, the ferry docking point. The ferry has no fixed schedule but does run every day. Kongpo's distinctive ferryboats (*trus*), two 10 m-long dugouts lashed together, safely carry 3–4 horses and half a dozen people (Rmb 5 per person). Across the other side, walk 1 hr east on a flat track along the river to Timpe, a village with many Khampas. Old, gnarled trees topped with straw serve as rain shelters. The village entrance is a small square surrounded by buildings. Guru Drubphuk, a recently renovated monastery and cave consecrated to Guru Rinpoche, is located on the slopes overlooking Timpe. Locals say the master meditated here for three days. The monks can help hire horses to the top of the Nyima La (Rmb 15) or on to Tumbatse (Rmb 20–30). Good camping spots are just beyond the village, near a stone cottage and small river.

Guru Drubphuk This rebuilt monastery, on the slopes immediately west of Timpe, has a sacred Guru Rinpoche cave inside the second floor. The grotto, 10–12 m wide and equally deep, has *tsa-tsas* and clay images. Guru Rinpoche reputedly created the hole in the ceiling by shooting his arrow at a demon. Prayer flags line a short, ritual circuit (*nekhor*) of the monastery (1 hr).

✤ DAY 2 TIMPE–SEKUNDO 5 3/4 HR

The trail to the pass starts at Timpe's far end and leads north. In 1/4 hr, pass a house on the left and a cottage with a log roof on the right, then a flour mill, also on the right. Now enter a lovely forest trail lined with scrub oak and rhododendron; a river descending from the Nyima La is on the right. Reach a trail junction in 1/4 hr. Go left. The trail soon starts to climb. Cross a river coming in from the left by means of log planks (1/2 hr), then descend to a green meadow (good camping). Beyond is another junction (1/4 hr). Take the right lower trail. The route now narrows and steepens as it enters magnificent forests of larch, fir, maple, and birch. All along are fine campsites next to glorious flower gardens with lots of firewood. Cross a side river (1/2 hr), then cross to the left bank of the main Nyima La River by tree trunks (1/4 hr). One more side stream, coming from the left, must be crossed before recrossing the main river. Large clusters of poppies grow near the water. Again recross the main channel twice within 1/2 hr. After this, go up the narrow valley to a rise and then descend once more to the river. Cross to the left bank (1/2 hr). In 1/4 hr, cross and recross the river over logs. Ascend in a series of zigzags as the trail veers away from the river (1/4 hr), regain the banks of the river, then cross to the right bank on three long logs. Cross to the other bank in 1/4 hr. Climb to another constriction in the valley and cross a side stream, coming from the right, by stepping stones. The walk up is steady, the views good to the south (Tsangpo Valley and Doshong La). The trail is densely lined with flowers. Keep to the left bank until the settlement of Sekundo (1 hr), where friendly nomads offer superb yoghurt, buttermilk, bread, and cheese.

The blue poppy (Meconopsis betonicifolia) F M Bailey, a British officer attached to the Indian Civil Service, traveled widely in Tibet and discovered this legendary poppy in the Rong Valley in 1913. The bloom is a wonderful shade of turquoise with a golden eye, regarded as one of the most beautiful flowers anywhere. F Kingdon Ward, the renowned plant hunter, brought seeds of the flower to the West in 1924. The woodland blue poppy (M *Baileyii*) is a lovely poppy-wort that grows in clumps under bushes and along streams, attaining a height of over 1 m. The plant usually has six flowers, with four petals and deep yellow anthers, born on a single pedicel.

✤ DAY 3 SEKUNDO–CLEARING 5 HR

From Sekundo, follow an indistinct trail to the pass, bearing to the left up the slopes through dense carpets of flowers and scrub rhododendrons. Stone cairns mark the way near the pass. A short distance after Sekundo, cross the stream to the right bank, then recross to the left (1/2 hr). Pass a deserted hut on a crest to the right (1/4 hr), then walk along a narrow ridge flanked by two hills. Now reach the land of the giant rhubarbs. These amazing yellow-leaved vegetables (*rheum nobile*) grow to a height of 2 m. The path is indistinct, but generally keeps to the left. A stone cairn stands just before the Nyima La, 3/4 hr from the hut on the crest. At the pass, ascend a small hill on the right and look back for wonderful views of the strategic Doshong La, the Assam Himalayas, and Gyala Pelri.

The snow range in front to the right is the Po Yigrong range; its highest, most sacred peak is Namla Karpo.

Yellow pagoda, the giant rhubarb (Rheum nobile)

Perhaps the most spectacular plant in Tibet, this tall, yellow, eerily luminescent species grows only on a few passes in southeast Tibet. It springs up, one at a time, in splendid isolation among the dwarf rhododendrons. When fully grown, the plant is easily visible from over 1 km away. The pagoda-like trunk, covered with broad, overlapping yellow leaves, rises from a green, leathery leaf-bed and tapers at the top. Tibetans usually strip the yellow leaves and eat the narrow central stem. The taste, sharp and refreshing, helps quench thirst. The young leaves are edible and the root is a medicine. June and July are the best months to come across this remarkable vegetable.

On the descent, bear right and hug the right perimeter of the broad valley head. Do not go straight down through the scrub, even though this looks the easiest way. Be sure to follow a distinct trail down. Some distance further, the route, now along the right bank of the river, passes through *abies* (fir) and rhododendron forests and then evergreens. In 1 1/4 hr from the pass, cross a small river that drains into the right bank of the main course. Traverse an area of fallen trees (1/4 hr); afterwards, the path becomes more distinct. Cross another side stream in 1/4 hr. Walk along a narrow ridge through a constricted part of the main valley. The path is much drier here and there are good camping spots. Enter the forest belt (fewer flowers). In 1/2 hr, cross a tributary to a nice clearing with many purple irises (good campsites). Sheer short ravines mark the right side of the valley.

DAY 4 CLEARING–TUMBATSE 2 3/4 HR

The upper valley near the Nyima La is broad but the lower reaches near Tumbatse narrow considerably, with thick forests on either side. The river becomes a torrent and the trail stands out clearly. From the clearing, continue down the main valley. Cross a side river, then recross to the left bank on a long log that spans the river 5 m above the water (1/4 hr). Walk down the left bank, cross a side stream, and pass an enchanting iris and primula garden on the left. Cross back to the right bank (1/4 hr). Near Tumbatse the trail widens to a jeep track. Tumbatse (1/2 hr) is a logging village in the Rong Valley, with wooden houses and tin-roofed Chinese compounds. Good campgrounds lie outside the village among the primula gardens.

Passes of the Rong Valley The Nyima La and Temo (Tremo) La are the primary passes leading into the Rong Valley from the Tsangpo basin. Grain has to be brought in while butter is exported. The Nyima La is particularly blessed with numerous varieties of poppy, primula, and rhododendron. Tong La, immediately above Tumbatse, is easy to climb but the descent on the far side is steep and difficult. The Sang La lies just southeast of the Temo La. Perhaps the most difficult of all Rong Chu passes is the Tara La above Lunang. Both sides are equally daunting; only experienced yak herders use the Tara La and Tong La during the short summer season. Temo La,

⏵

the only pass in the area never closed by snow, has a motorable road. The Sang
La and Nyima La remain open all year, except February–April.

The alpine valleys leading up to the passes are usually semi-circular and broad,
even flat at the top, with moraines and scree. By contrast, the lower portions are
narrow and steep. Consequently, it is quite easy to go from one valley head to another,
or one range to another, by simply staying high, close to the passes. Yak herders
do this all the time. The few paths in the lower valleys are usually indistinct and
hard to find. In general, the best ones avoid the steep forests by staying near the
ridge crests. Villages and passes of the Rong Chu Valley are:

- Tumbatse–Tong La–Trube
- Tumbatse–Nyima La–Timpe
- Tumbatse–Sang La–Sang
- Lunang–Tara La–Sinje Chögye
- Tumbatse–Temo La–Temo

❖ Day 5 Tumbatse–Daoban 111   1 3/4 hr

From Tumbatse, follow the jeep road over the main bridge to an intersection. The dirt road
to the right goes to Lunang, Tongkyuk, Tangme, and Pomi. Take the left, which goes up
to the head of the Rong Valley. After 1/4 hr, reach another fork. Follow a truck path up
the slopes to the right to join the main Tibet–Sichuan highway. The walk from Tumbatse
to the main road takes 1 1/2 hr. On reaching the highway, walk left for 1/4 hr to the road
maintenance compound—*daoban* 111. Above it is a secluded primula garden marked by prayer
flags (good camping site).

Hitch from the *daoban* back to Ningchi and Lhasa or east to Chamdo and Sichuan.
There is plenty of traffic on this road. In summer, however, traffic might diminish if the
Tangme bridge is crushed by glacial eruptions and landslides. The return to Lhasa should
be relatively simple once you arrive in Ningchi.

Going east	Tumbatse–Lunang	10	km
	Lunang–Tongkyuk	29	km
	Tongkyuk–Trulung	30	km
	Trulung–Tangme	10	km
	Tangme–Pomi	89	km
	Pomi–Chamdo	481	km
Going west	Tumbatse–Ningchi	47 km, via Sekye La (4720 m)	
	Ningchi–Lhasa	420 km	

Along the Rong Valley

Below is a summary of an optional trek along the beautiful Rong Valley. A number of interesting
side trips also exist up secondary valleys. The route essentially follows the major Tibet–Sichuan
highway northeastward. From Tangme, at the trek's terminus, either hitch east to Chamdo
or west to Lhasa.

Place	Distance (km)	Notes
Tumbatse–Lunang	10	The track is flat and easy along the wide upper Rong Valley. Lunang is a logging community on a rise overlooking the valley.
Lunang–Tongkyuk	29	After Lunang, the valley narrows and steepens. Pass Chunyima, the first village in Pomi. Tongkyuk perches atop a hill.
Tongkyuk–Trulung	31	Descend 600 m to Trulung.
Trulung–Tangme	10	Tangme, at the Po Yigrong–Po Tsangpo junction, is noted for its Bhutan cypresses.

LEFT BANK OF THE TSANGPO: FROM MT NAMCHE BARWA TO GYATSA

Location	Southeast Tibet
Map reference	NH46-10 D, 46-11 C D, 46-12 A C
Trekking days	18 (one-way)
Start–Finish	Gyala–Gyatsa Xian
Passes	Kongpo Nga

OVERVIEW

This trek, going from east to west, takes in the seldom traveled stretch of the Tsangpo's north bank from Gyala at the base of Mt Namche Barwa to Gyatsa Xian near the Yarlung Valley. The 18-day itinerary can be regarded as a continuation of the Pemakö pilgrimage (see page 717) and can also be dovetailed with the Lhamo Latso route, a walk to Tibet's most important oracle-lake (see page 623). The Gyala–Gyatsa journey occasionally crosses the Tsangpo by means of dugout canoes and yak-skin coracles. One interesting section is between the Tsangpo-Giamda river junction and the village of Tu. A day or two from the river are the flower-rich passes of the Pachakshiri, the eastern extreme of the Himalayas. Most are but a stone's throw from the Arunachal Pradesh province of India. The Miling Xian Valley in the area still has settlements inhabited by Lopas, considered an ethnic minority in Tibet.

Further to the east, Trungkhang Monastery, birthplace of the 13th Dalai Lama, is visited. Other monasteries along the route include Temo Chemnak, Phurchu (one of Songtsen Gampo's celebrated demon-suppressing temples), Bangrim Chöde, Ganden Rabden,

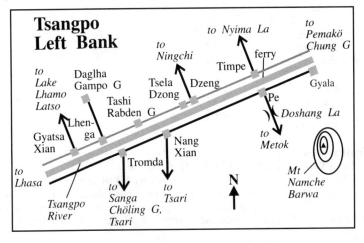

Tashi Rabden, and Dakpo Tratsang. Near Nang Xian is a major archeological site consisting of numerous ancient tombs (7th–9th C.), previously thought to exist only in the Yarlung area. From Nang Xian, one possible option is to hike north to access the sublime pilgrimage area of Tsari (see page 208). In the vicinity of Kyimdong Dzong (see page 238), a number of side valleys lead up to the watershed of the Pachakshiri range and to the headwaters of the mighty Subansiri river. This region of southeast Tibet is one of great physical beauty and diverse flora.

Related sections
Mt Namche Barwa, p 712
Bönri, p 741
Lhamo Latso, p 623
Tsari, p 208
The Yarlung Valley, p 515

Access
Begin from Gyala, within the Great Bend of the Tsangpo (see page 721).

Time Chart

Day	Place	Hours
1	Gyala–Tamling	4 1/2
2	Mönlam	4 3/4
3	Dzeng	6 1/4
4	Tsela Dzong	4 1/4
5	Dowoka	3
6	Lutö	5
7	Kangsar	5
8	Tu	2 3/4
9	Gacha	3 1/2
10	Opposite Tromé	4 1/4
11	Kamchung	4 1/2
12	Shu	3 1/2
13	Nye	2 3/4
14	Lu	7
15	Lhenga	3 1/2
16	Rapdang	2 3/4
17	Lenda	4 1/4
18	Dakpo Tratsang	2

Trail notes
✤ DAY 1 GYALA–TAMLING (21.7 KM) 4 1/2 HR
From the beach below Gyala, cross to the Tsangpo's north bank by dugout canoe. Gyala's Sinje Chögyal Monastery, with its sacred image of Yamantaka (Shinje), is in a cave behind a 10-m waterfall here (see page 721). To its right is another, smaller waterfall. The path west along the north bank is narrow and overgrown. Reach Lamo Chu in a deep ravine 5

km beyond the monastery. This was the boundary of the old Gyala district. Trubé, 13 km from Gyala, is next. Beyond it (2.5 km) is Tombolung Monastery and the Tong La River. (A trail follows the river up to the Tong La Pass and then descends to Tumbatse [see page 732] and Lunang in the Rong Valley. This journey takes 2–3 days.) Continue through bamboo and, after a steep climb, reach the Tamling Plateau (3000 m); the village is 1 km beyond.

✤ DAY 2 TAMLING–MÖNLAM (23.4 KM) 4 3/4 HR

Continue along the Tsangpo's north bank to Susum, on a terrace 9.5 km from Tamling. 5 km farther is Timpe, where a side valley leads to the Nyima La (see page 731). Mönlam (2955 m) is 8 km more along a trail called Trang. The Tsangpo in these parts is wide and calm, characterised by sandy beaches and islands. Downstream, the landscape is almost tropical with dense forests, but upstream from here the land is drier and flatter, with scrub and fewer forests.

✤ DAY 3 MÖNLAM–DZENG (30 KM) 6 1/4 HR

Sang is 13 km from Mönlam. The trail rises 150 m over a sanddune and then continues along the hillside above the water for the next 6.5 km before dropping to Kongmo and its small monastery . Some 9.5 km further is Dzeng (2895 m) at the entrance of the Temo Valley. Here is Temo Chemnak Monastery, formerly a large Gelugpa institution with 250 monks. A trail hugs the valley's west side and joins the ritual circuit around holy Mt Bönri (see page 741).

✤ DAY 4 DZENG–TSELA DZONG (20 KM) 4 1/4 HR

After Dzeng are the villages of Menri, Sekora, Mukdo, Gonjo, and Yungdrung Dzin. Near the last is a famous Yarlung-dynasty stone inscription (see page 761). Continue past the villages of Luding (6.5 km) and Chigu (2.5 km). 1.5 km further is the wide delta of the Giamda Chu, here divided into many channels. Go north up the Giamda to Chukor where a coracle crosses to the river's west bank at Phurchu Village and monastery (see page 746). This important institution is reputed to be one of King Songtsen Gampo's demon-suppressing temples. Walk south to the Giamda–Tsangpo junction and Tsela Dzong (2955 m).

✤ DAY 5 TSELA DZONG–DOWOKA (14 KM) 3 HR

Continue west along the north bank past Karma and Ama Yuma to Dowoka (2925 m). On the opposite bank is Paka, and Lamdo. A trail from there leads to Lopa settlements and the Lungma La.

✤ DAY 6 DOWOKA–LUTÖ (25 KM) 5 HR

Tse is 9 km from Dowoka. Upstream from Tse, on the other bank, lies Shoka at the entrance of a large valley. Lopas came here to trade as well. The valley called Nyaga (Nyung) Chu, a tributary of the Giamda, lies in the mountains north of the Tsangpo. Its villages have watchtowers like those near Bayi (see page 653). These were damaged during the Mongol invasion of the early 18th C. The village of Lungdo, opposite Lutö (2910 m), has a tower in good condition.

✤ DAY 7 LUTÖ–KANGSAR (25 KM) 5 HR

Past Lutö are the villages of Lungtaka and Shoteng (1.5 km). Beyond, off the trail, is Gyama on the river bank (1.5 km). Here, a ferry crosses the Tsangpo to Miling Xian, except in summer. Miling Xian, the district headquarters, is at the entrance of the Nayu Valley, a main avenue for Lopa traders. Settlements up this valley are still predominantly Lopa. Tashi Rabden Monastery is 13.5 km from Lutö and 1.5 km up the Sungkar Valley. It once supported 130 monks. After the monastery, cross the Sungkar River by bridge. Opposite, on the Tsangpo's south bank, the Yusum Kungbu Valley goes south to the Pachakshiri, the Assam Himalayas. Lopas once traveled this valley. Pass the villages of Chanda and Lunga (9 km from Tashi Rabden) to reach Kangsar (3000 m), 1.5 km west of Lunga.

✤ DAY 8 KANGSAR–TU (12.5 KM) 2 3/4 HR

Walk 3 km to Sengbo and its ferry crossing. Tranda is a further 2 km. Just before Tu, on the opposite bank, is Lilung at a large valley entrance. Nepa is a half-day walk up this valley. Mönpas also used to come down this valley to trade. Cross the Tsangpo at Tu (3030 m) on two dugouts tied together.

✤ DAY 9 TU–GACHA (17.5 KM) 3 1/2 HR

The trail on the south bank goes over sand and through forests. Gyapang is 7.5 km from the ferry. Chukor, on the bank of a large side river, is 14.5 km from Tu. Gacha (3100 m), a former *dzong*, is sited across another river, which has Orong Dzong on its right bank.

✤ DAY 10 GACHA–OPPOSITE TROMÉ (20 KM) 4 1/4 HR

Me is 5 km beyond Gacha. Cross the Trendopu Chu in a further 2.5 km (a trail up it leads to Lelung and Kyimdong Dzong). Sampé is 1 km more. Villages passed on the far north bank are Trumi and Kyami. Walk from Sampé for 11 km to reach a grassy campground across from Tromé. From Tromé (3050 m), a trail goes to Lhasa via the Pi La Pass.

✤ DAY 11 OPPOSITE TROMÉ–KAMCHUNG (21.5 KM) 4 1/2 HR

The trail goes through thorny forest for 6.5 km to a place opposite Changdrong (on the north bank), then continues for 5 km to Rishö. Carry on to Chake (3 km) and Kamchung (3090 m).

✤ DAY 12 KAMCHUNG–SHU (16.7 KM) 3 1/2 HR

Rip is 2.5 km from Kamchung and the She Chu River is a further 2.5 km. A short distance beyond is the small King Chung Rakar River, the border between Dakpo and Kongpo (the route now enters Dakpo). Villages are distinguished by their mature walnut and apricot trees. Pass through a barren, empty gorge for 10.5 km. Just before the She Chu, a cliff has a summer trail over it; the winter trail is at its base, close to the Tsangpo. Reach the junction of Kyimdong Chu and the Tsangpo; turn up the former and cross a bridge after 1 km. Shu (3170 m) lies 1 km farther upstream. Up the valley are the tiny villages of Melong and Shutsang. Kyimdong, a center for lead mines, lies beyond. Trails south from here access the sacred Tsari region (see page 208).

> **The Lishan tombs** East of Shu is the village of Li, on Kyimdong Chu's right bank. About 1.5 km from here is a ridge called Lishan. Scattered along its southern slopes are tombs that are among the largest, most important Yarlung-dynasty burial sites in Tibet (see page 373).

✤ DAY 13 SHU–NYE (18.5 KM) 2 3/4 HR

The trail climbs over and around a spur that descends to the Kyimdong Chu confluence. A difficult short cut can be used in winter to ford the Kyimdong Chu near the confluence to avoid the bridge. Cross a river 8 km from Shu. (Upstream are the villages of Udzu and Talam.) Walk past Trö, then Tungkar Monastery, to reach Nye (3230 m), a scattered village. Yaks appear for the first time since Gyala; below Tungkar Monastery is a ferry.

✤ DAY 14 NYE–LU (24 KM) 7 HR

The trail west leads over a ridge that descends from the south below the Drisam Chu–Tsangpo confluence. Follow the left bank of this side river over a bridge (3 km from Nye), then climb steeply for 2.5 km to Kyalo. Reach the Kongpo Nga La (4440 m) after a further 2.5 km. The reason this pass must be crossed is because the Tsangpo flows through a sheer gorge along this stretch and there are no paths along the river—rapids in the gorge cannot be negotiated by boats. It is possible to walk along the river within the gorge, but this is quite difficult. Descend westward to another village called Kyalo, then reach Chörten Shu on the bank of the Lapu Chu (2.5 km). (Upstream is Lador. A trail here goes from Nang Xian to Tsari in two days, see page 227.) The environs here are far wetter than those along the Tsangpo and there are thick forests of larch, birch, and rhododendron, with undergrowth of rose thickets. Walk down the river's bank for 1 km, then cross to the left and descend for 3 km to a cantilever bridge. The trail again follows the Tsangpo's south bank. Reach a ferry and cross the river by coracle 5 km from the bridge. Walk west to Lu (3260 m).

✤ DAY 15 LU–LHENGA (17 KM) 3 1/2 HR

Do lies 4 km west of Lu. Beyond it is Bangrim Chöde Monastery, once home to 200 monks (see page 354). West of this is the district of Gyatsa; east is Nang. Behind the monastery is the broad Rong Valley. Tsilung is 5 km from Do and Tashiling villages, at the Ku Valley entrance. 3 km further reach Trungkhang, a monastery and the birthplace of the 13th Dalai Lama (b 1876). He revisited his birthplace only once, in 1900. His residential quarters are sealed. Another monastery lies farther up. Continue for 2.5 km to Lhenga (3230 m).

✤ DAY 16 LHENGA–RAPDANG (12.5 KM) 2 3/4 HR

Walk 3 km up river past Trong-Nge to a ferry. Cross to the south bank of the Tsangpo by coracle to Tromda. From here, go 6.5 km up the Trulung Valley to Ganden Rabden Monastery, a dependent of Ganden Monastery near Lhasa. (About 5 km farther up this valley is Guru Namgye Dzong.) The rushing Trulung Chu has a bridge 3 km below the monastery. Cross it and walk down the left bank to the Tsangpo junction. Then follow the Tsangpo's south bank to Rapdang (3290 m). A nunnery lies 1 km farther. Across the river, opposite the Trulung Valley, is the famed Daglha Gampo Monastery (see page 352).

✤ DAY 17 RAPDANG–LENDA (20 KM) 4 1/4 HR

From Rapdang, the trail passes below cliffs most of the way to Panda. Ford the Pulung River 1 km before the village. (A trail upstream leads to Charap.) Walk 8 km on the slopes of cliffs to a ridge, then reach Lenda after 3 km more. A river flows through the scattered village.

✤ DAY 18 LENDA–DAKPO TRATSANG (10 KM) 2 HR

From Lenda, the trail follows the base of cliffs for 9.5 km to Dakpo Tratsang Monastery (see page 641) in the middle of Gyatsa Xian, a large district office with many houses. This is also a convenient point to begin the trek north to the oracle-lake of Lhamo Latso (see page 623).

To Tsethang To continue to Tsethang, see the Lhamo Latso pilgrimage, page 640.

THE HOLY PLACES
OF PRE-BUDDHIST BÖN

For the small number of Tibetans who still practice the ancient religion of Bön, Mt Bönri and Mt Kailash are the most important pilgrimage destinations. Located in Kongpo (southeast Tibet), Bönri has a magnificent ritual circuit that allows the complete circumambulation of the range in a few easy days. Far to the northwest, in the fastness of the eerily beautiful Changtang, are fabled Lake Dangra and Mt Targo. Both are major sites of worship for the Bönpos and the month-long trek to the region traverses hitherto unknown territories. Menri and Yungdrungling, near Shigatse, are the two most significant Bön monasteries in Tibet today.

BÖNRI: A CIRCUMAMBULATION OF BÖN'S MOST SACRED MOUNTAIN

Prehistoric sites—testaments to magical duels between the Bönpo patriarch and his demonic archrival

Location	Southeast Tibet, near Ningchi
Map reference	46-11 D, 46-12 C
Trekking days	7
Start–Finish	Bayi–Lusha
Passes	Bönri

OVERVIEW

Kongpo Bönri is regarded as the holiest mountain (*neri*) of the Bön religion. This ancient, pre-Buddhist pilgrimage site was explored and officially 'opened' to believers in the early part of the 14th C. by the hermit Kuchok Ripa Drukse (b 1290), who circumambulated Bönri and subsequently laid out precisely the path to be followed by pilgrims. A principal reason for the uncommon sanctity of Kongpo Bönri is its close

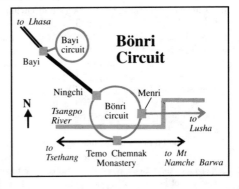

association with Tönpa Shenrab. This legendary figure, patriarch of the religion, is considered as the Bönpo equivalent of Sakyamuni Buddha. He first achieved prominence in Tibet by engaging in magical contests, and finally subduing his arch-rival, Kyapa Lagring, on the mountain. Most of the sacred sites along the Bönri circumambulatory path (khora) are associated with the struggles between the two.

Of the eight Bönpo monasteries in the area, four (Tagtse, Sigyal Gönchen, Tag Drosa, Gyeri) have been restored and are thriving. Each year Bön pilgrims from every part of Tibet, especially from Dzade and Khyungpo near Chamdo in East Tibet, travel long distances to circumambulate and pay homage to the mountain, which is also venerated by the local Kongpo population, no matter their sect. The tenth and 15th day of each Tibetan lunar month see flocks of Kongpopas rubbing shoulders with far-flung Bön pilgrims, all circling the mountain counter-clockwise in the classic Bön way. A number of them will prolong their stay by performing the arduous korgya—100 circumambulations! The old customs of offering free food and lodging to pilgrims and travellers are still alive and well in the Bönri and Kongpo area. Most villages along the pilgrimage route are Bönpos; this region is one of the last surviving enclaves of the indigenous religion. The most important Bön villages are Khar Semo, Tagtse, and Bangna.

Bönri (also Shenri) is one of three peaks of a range (the others are Muri and Lhari Gyangtö). According to tradition, the mythical first king of Tibet, Nyatri Tsenpo, descended from heaven to earth via this mountain (some sources say it was the Yala Shampo in Yarlung). [Seven of the early kings of Tibet descended onto sacred mountains: three at Bönri (Lhari Gyangtö), two at the Marpo Ri, site of the Potala in Lhasa, and two at the Yala Shampo (Shampo Lhatse).] This legendary associaton with the early kings gave rise to many myths and hypotheses concerning the origins of Tibetan civilization. Prof R A Stein of Paris theorized that Drena (Trena) Village on the khora was the place where the descendants of Chenresi, Bodhisattva of Compassion (in the form of a monkey), and of Drölma (in the form of an ogress) first settled. It is likely Drena also witnessed the funeral rites of King Drigum Tsanpo, one of Tibet's earliest rulers. The Tibetan scholar, Samten Karmay, believes an earth mound located at the cemetery of Miyul Kyithing (at the Tsangpo–Nyang Chu confluence) is in fact the tomb of Drigum Tsanpo. This tumulus might well be Tibet's first royal tomb, predating even the celebrated ones of the Yarlung Valley.

Kongpo Bönri's climate is much milder than most of Tibet. The base of the mountain stands at only 2995 m and the region's lush environment is famous for its rhododendrons and alpine flowers. A pilgrimage walk around Bönri is one of the most delightful experiences in Tibet. It can be done throughout the year, but expect rain during the summer monsoon season. Extreme cold is never a factor. It takes only a few days to completely walk around the mountain, stopping from time to time at its numerous mythical spots.

Adjacent to Bönri, only a few days' walk away, is Pemakö, perhaps the most fabled 'hidden valley' of Tibet (see page 717). On its periphery are the twin mountains of Namche Barwa and Gyala Pelri, both over 7000 m in height. The Tsangpo rushes as a series of cataracts through the gap created by these two peaks to form what is arguably the deepest chasm of Asia.

Kongpo Bönri is reached from either Bayi or Ningchi. The Ningchi start is more direct, and within a special enclosure near here grows Kushak, the sacred tree of Bön, a magnificent juniper more than 2,000 years old. However, the route from Bayi allows one to take in the monasteries of Phurchu, Zangdhok Pelri, Chemnak, and the holy site of Bönri Ama (Mother of Bönri). Also near Bayi is Bayi Pelri, a sacred hill consecrated to Guru Rinpoche, with a short half-day *khora* circuit. Along the route are a number of rock-formed iconographical marks, attributed to Guru Rinpoche.

For information on the journey from Lhasa to Bayi via Medro Gongkar and Kongpo Giamda, see page 708.

Related sections
Mt Namche Barwa and the Tsangpo Gorges, p 712
Kailash, p 273

Access: Bayi
The town of Bayi is located on the main Lhasa–Ningchi–Chengdu highway. Coming from Lhasa, Bayi's main street is on the right, perpendicular to the highway. Bayi's original old village, Drakchi, is now overrun by a town that boasts diversified industries, an army camp, and the Bayi Qu administrative compound. The population, about 20,000, is rising rapidly. Han Chinese are attracted to the temperate climate and the quick-paced development of commerce. The Tibet Agriculture and Husbandry College is located here, as is the Ningchi Textile Factory (woollen textiles and carpets), the biggest in Tibet, with nearly 1,000 workers. Sichuan and Moslem restaurants in Bayi are good and cheap; there is even a 'coffee house' on the main street. The thriving free market is mostly dominated by Chinese traders. Stores are full and transportation to Lhasa is frequent and relatively easy to procure.

BAYI PELRI
(A Tibetan pilgrim supplied the following information):
Bayi Pelri is also known as Zangdhok Pelri, Guru Rinpoche's Copper Mountain Paradise. According to legend, the entire Bayi area was once a vast lake with a small mountain island at its center. The Tantric master, out to explore the un-known and untamed Kongpo district, flew overhead and was intrigued by the area's geomantic profile. In order to pre-pare the place for future habitation, Guru Rinpoche went into a deep trance on top of the mountain. His meditation generated enormous forces that dried up the lake, but evil beings, unhappy at this upheaval, vowed to rid their land of the intruder. The showdown between the negative and positive forces was played

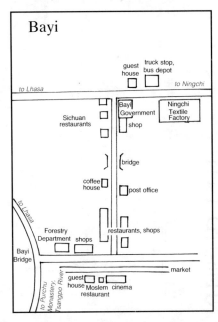

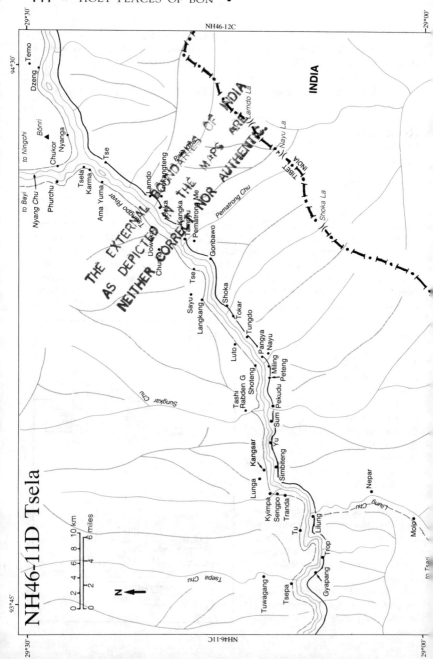

out on the holy mountain of Bayi Pelri, a hill a short distance east of present day Bayi. Good, naturally, triumphed. The hilltop circuit (*tsekhor*) has many natural landmarks that evoke the epic battle. All of them are testaments to Guru Rinpoche's passage through the area, when he played hide and seek with the multitude of demons.

Due east of Bayi's main street is Bayi Pelri. A trail leads east from near the highway junction, follows the left bank of a small river and then passes a brick factory on the left. Go through small villages and fields, then traverse some low foothills to approach the Pelri. A dirt logging track to the right leads also to the mountain. The *khora* circuit takes 2–3 hr.

Guru Chakje The Guru Chakje, handprint of Guru Rinpoche, is the first significant site on the *khora*. This flat area is marked by prayer flags strung on trees and the *chakje* is on the face of a large rock surrounded by mandalas and *mani* stones.

Phagmo Drupa Chörten Up the slopes from Guru Chakje is a small plateau marked by a white *chörten*. It was built in dedication of Phagmo Drupa, who reputedly died here after a long battle with leprosy (his tomb is said to be at Jang Tana Monastery, near Nangchen in Kham). The monument was erected in hopes that all debilitating diseases of mankind would one day be eradicated. Near the *chörten* is a cemetery (*durtrö*) consecrated by Guru Rinpoche.

Bayi Pelri's summit From the *chörten* walk to the right down the slope to the village of Ludrong (Pelri Drong). Cross a bridge near the beginning of the settlement, and walk up the other side of the valley. At this point, the trail joins with the dirt road. A short distance further is the top of Pelri, marked by a *lhatse* and prayer flags. Kongpo Bönri can be seen to the southeast. At its foot is the large town of Ningchi. To the south is Pab Ri, west of the Nyang Chu–Tsangpo confluence. Phurchu Monastery is below it. (See page 746.) Two trails lead down from the top of Bayi Pelri. The larger left one goes on to Ningchi. Follow the right trail to an open area; at its far end is a small rise with prayer flags, then a cemetery.

Khandro Bum Gyi Tshokzhong A short distance from the cemetery is a large rock. On top of its flat top is a smaller rock with a well-defined hollow; legend says this was the cauldron where 100,000 *dakinis* prepared their *tshok* (ritual *tsampa*) offerings. Along the rim of the hollow is a vague imprint of the 'Om Ah Hum' *mantra*.

Guru Kuje The trail circles down to the base of the rock. Two Guru Kuje (bodyprint) depressions in the rock face, representing Guru Rinpoche in meditation, are here.

Guru Zhengku Around the corner from the Guru Kuje is a cleft in the rock. Next to this is the Guru Zhengku (full bodyprint) of the master, a larger-than-life indentation in the rock.

Bardo Trang Above Guru Zhengku is a narrow passage formed by two rocks, the Bardo Trang ('Tunnel of Bardo'), a 'sin-gauge' that reveals a pilgrim's readiness to negotiate the 49-day passage after death prior to rebirth. Bardo Trang is a tight squeeze: the slight slope up and the polished surface of the rock make the test more difficult.

Sky Rock Walk back up to the main trail to a small oval-shaped rock embedded in the ground (right of the trail). On its top is a small dent, created when Guru Rinpoche dug his knee in here during his contests with the demons. They fired many arrows at him and one found its mark, penetrating his knee. Simultaneously, a piece of rock fell from heaven and the wound was made whole when Guru Rinpoche put his knee against it. Pilgrims make a point of coming here to press their own injuries or ailments to the 'kneeprint'. They also make a mud paste of water and earth in the hollow. The mixture, a highly prized relic from Pelri, is then distributed as a cure to family members or used as an important source of blessing.

Guru Kuje After the Sky Rock, go left down the short slopes to three more imprints of Guru Rinpoche's body. These were created when he sat in meditation against a rock while doing battle against the demons. The first took form when he came out of his retreat and became one of his eight manifestations. As Guru Nyima Wösel ('Seven Beams of Sunlight'), he directed powerful sun beams at his opponents, neutralising them completely.

Kyilkhor Rangjung Walk back up the slopes to the main path. A round rock represents a 'self-manifesting' mandala (Kyilkhor Rangjung). Guru Rinpoche proclaimed this an embodiment of the Zhitrö (peaceful and wrathful protectors) Kyilkhor. Next to this is a stone with a hollow top, the *tshokzhong* (cauldron for making *tshok*) of Guru Rinpoche. The trail descends to the dirt road, which leads back to Bayi.

KONGPO BÖNRI: THE BAYI START
Time Chart

Day	Place	Hours
1	Bayi–Chemnak	hitch
2	Menri	4 1/4
3	Sembön Dhungshing	3 1/4
4	*daoban* 114	5 1/2
5	Ningchi	3 3/4
6	Luding	5 1/2
7	Lusha	4

✤ DAY 1 BAYI–CHEMNAK (HITCH OR WALK)

Allow at least one day for this section, and more if visiting the Phurchu, Zangdhok Pelri monasteries, or taking a hike up Mt Pelri.

- Bayi to Gongga Bridge: 45 km
- Gongga Bridge to Chemnak: 23 km

From the free market area of Bayi, walk west to the Bayi Bridge that spans the Nyang Chu (also Nyangpo). The road to Lhasa goes northwest just before the bridge. Cross the bridge and follow the west (right) bank of the river southward. Hitchhiking is generally easy (trucks typically charge Rmb 2–5 per person for the 45 km journey to the Gongga Bridge).

Phurchu Monastery

Phurchu (now Gelugpa but once Nyingmapa) is 29 km from Bayi, easily recognised by its gold temple roofs and distinctive Chinese architecture. This was one of the original monasteries King Songtsen Gampo built to subdue Tibet's great demoness prior to the building of Lhasa's Jokhang (see page 43). Thus Phurchu's foundation may well date from the 7th century. In front of the main building is a courtyard and along its sides are the kitchen (left) and quarters for monks. An entrance foyer, with new paintings of the Four Guardian Kings, has been rebuilt. Within the ground floor, an old chapel at the back (center) houses statues of Songtsen Gampo, Guru Rinpoche, Chenresi, and a footprint of Guru Rinpoche. Phurchu's gilded pagoda roof is most unusual for this part of Tibet. Mt Pelri (4350 m), to the south, towers over the monastery. Climb through oak and rhododendron forests to the top for a pleasant side trip and good views of the Himalayas. Mt Namche Barwa can be seen to the southeast, and the Salween Divide to the northeast.

Zangdhok Pelri Monastery

The Nyingma monastery of Zangdhok Pelri perches on a hill 4 km south of Phurchu. It was the main monastery of Dudjom Rinpoche, the patriarch of the sect, with over 100 monks. Completely destroyed during the Cultural Revolution, only the chapel walls remain of the original. Resurrection of the religious community began in 1985. From Phurchu, walk south along the main road for 10 min and turn right onto a flat, straight trail. After 1 hr, cross a small river (to the left), then zigzag up to Lamaling, the name of a house (3/4 hr). Ten min beyond is Zangdhok Pelri, which is being rebuilt among the impressive ruins. A small path to the right leads from the monastery to a square chörten. Nearby is a rock with a red face. Dudjom Rinpoche's brother-in-law, Chuni Lama, painted it. He is presently one of the two highest ranking lamas in Tibet. (The other is Drigung Rinpoche, who lives in Lhasa behind the Jokhang.) Zangdhok Pelri is the name of Guru Rinpoche's mythical paradise. As such, this site is considered a highly sacred place.

From Phurchu to the Gongga Bridge is 26 km. A soldier guards the bridge and might ask for identification. Just show the Chinese visa in your passport. Walk or hitch east along the south bank of the Tsangpo for 23 km to reach Temo Chemnak Monastery (see below). Traffic is scarce on this stretch, but the walking is agreeable along a flat dirt road.

Nyang Chu–Tsangpo confluence (2900 m)

The Nyang Chu, draining from the Mangshung (Kongpo) La, flows southeast to join the Tsangpo below Ningchi. This river junction is a particularly sanctified area with many important monasteries. The major ones are:

• Phurchu	Right bank of Nyang Chu
• Temo Chemkar	Near Menri, on the Bönri khora circuit
• Temo Chemnak	South bank of Tsangpo, opposite Menri
• Tagtse Yungdrungling	Bön, on the khora
• Zangdhok Pelri	Near Phurchu
• Sigyal Gönchen	Bön, on the khora near Ningchi
• Chujo	Near Menri, on the khora
• Jakhyung	Garuda monastery near Menri, on the khora
• Gönjo	On the khora; has an 8th-C. doring

At the confluence, the Nyang Chu is about 3 km wide, with four main channels and islands of pasture and scrub in between. Most islands become submerged in the summer. The mountains of Pelri and Kongpo Bönri flank the junction, and the Assam Himalayas (Pachakshiri), immediately south of the Yarlung Tsangpo, are but a stone's throw away. The villages here, unlike most in Tibet, are graced by plentiful trees—apple, poplar, willow, elm, walnut, and others. The Tsangpo River immediately south of Kongpo Bönri is distinguished by a beautiful stretch of wide, pristine sand dunes and unspoiled white beaches. The scenery is superb, especially when the weather is clear and Mt Namche Barwa, highest peak of the Assam Himalayas, is visible downstream. Idyllic islands in the river provide excellent grazing grounds for yaks.

Flora

The Nyang Chu–Tsangpo confluence lies in a transition zone between the Tibetan plateau flora and the temperate forest flora of the upper gorge country of the Hengduan Mountains, the narrow range in southeastern Tibet that encompasses the great rivers of the Irrawaddy, Salween, Mekong, and Yangtse. The plateau flora has practically no woody plants, and only a few hundred species of sub-arctic flowering plants, whereas the temperate forest flora includes evergreen conifer forests at the higher elevations and deciduous forests lower down.

The alpine meadows around the Nyang–Tsangpo confluence are rich in flowers; many of Tibet's finest come from this region. In particular, the narrow wooded valleys leading south to the main Himalayan range are botanically outstanding. Small clearings within this alpine zone of flowers can be reached in 2–3 hr from the south bank of the Yarlung Tsangpo. During May and June, huge clumps of the beautiful, 1.2-m-tall sky-blue poppy (*Meconopsis betonicifolia*) abound. Each flower can be as big as 10 cm across. Many lovely primulas (*P baileyana*, *P calderiana* etc) grow beneath rhododendron forests (for example, *R wardii*, with its uncommon yellow flowers).

Rhododendrons common to the slopes of Kongpo Bönri and Pelri are:
• *R taliense* (7 m) pink flowers
• *R triflorum* (3 m) pale yellow flowers
• *R barbatum* (7 m) light pink or ivory white flowers
• *R lapponicum* bright purple flowers

Wheat, barley, turnips, potatoes, and peas are the principal crops in the river junction area. Apples and peaches are also plentiful. The weather here is influenced to a certain extent by the Assam Himalayas. Intermittent rain and foul weather can be expected even in May and June. Most of the rain however comes in July and August.

Temo Chemnak Monastery

This charming Gelugpa monastery, on a wooded ridge overlooking the highway, reflects a strong Kongpo influence in its architecture: huge winged roofs gently slope over the handsome main stone structure. The old monastery (Dechenling) was destroyed by an earthquake in 1950 and rebuilt in 1983. Quite a few monks now live outside the main monastery on a neighboring ridge. The chapel's main images are Maitreya and Tsong Khapa. A thousand 15-cm-tall Tsong Khapa statuettes surround the latter. In front of the monastery courtyard is a sacred site (*neh*) on a small rise, consecrated to Chana Dorje. Prayer flags surround it and the view overlooking the monastery with Kongpo Bönri just across the river is spectacular. On the west side of the Chemnak ridge is a village named Dungsar inhabited by the Lopas, a Tibetan ethnic minority. (Miling, 19 km west of the Gongga Bridge, also has surviving pockets of Lopas.)

Temo Chemnak forms half of an important twin-monastery configuration. Temo Chemkar is the other half. The two were built across from each other on opposite shores of the Tsangpo. (From Temo Chemkar, a road leads over the Temo La to the Rong Valley, then onto the heavily-forested area of Pome.) The color of the monasteries—Chemnak is black, Chemkar is white—symbolically links them to their landscape. The south bank of the Tsangpo is dark with forests, whereas the north is drier and lighter.

Thim Drakphuk

Near Temo Chemnak, this is a cave consecrated to Guru Rinpoche. The saint once saw an evil red spirit with horns at this spot. It turned into a small bird and disappeared. Guru Rinpoche threw his thunderbolt (dorje), which managed to seek out the spirit and destroyed it (thim means to disappear).

Bönri Ama

A short distance to the east of Temo Chemnak, on the south side of the road, is another neh. Two prominent concentric circles of prayer flags, about 20 m in diameter, enclose a circular corridor on a small knoll. Pilgrims circumambulate (counter-clockwise) this sacred site, which commemorates the mother of Bönri, mythical progenitor of the mountain.

Nyangpo, Dakpo, and Kongpo: Three provinces centering on Bönri

An ancient Bönpo text, Zermik, states that Kongpo Bönri stands at the junction of three valleys (lung sumdo) and three mountains (gongkar sumdo). The former are Nyangpo, Dakpo, and Kongpo. Dakpo is the region to the west of the Nyang Chu–Tsangpo confluence, Nyangpo the valley of the Nyang Chu, and Kongpo lies east of the Nyang. These three were also mentioned in the authoritative Dunhuang documents, which recorded that they were part of the 12 princely states before Central Tibet, an amalgamation of the 12, came under a single authority, namely that of Namri Lotsan in the 6th century. The people of Nyangpo, Dakpo, and Kongpo later rebelled against Songtsen Gampo briefly before being permanently subjugated under the Yarlung Dynasty. Kongpo was singled out for preferential treatment because its princes were related to the kings of Tibet. The Zermik describes the people of these regions as barbaric: the Dakpopas are depicted as frog- and snake-eaters and Nyangpo's inhabitants as carnivorous. It recounts that the Kongpopas commit incest between brothers and sisters, and that murder between uncles and nephews was common.

The three mountains are Tselha Gang in the west, Ri Luwang in the south, and Kongpo Bönri in the east. Together they constitute a triangle surrounding the confluence of the Nyang Chu and the Tsangpo. Bönri's topography is likened to a scorpion. The right horn is the Nyang, the left is the Yarlung Tsangpo and the head points towards Tselha Gang. Towards the east, the combined waters of the two rivers form the body, while the tail lies further downstream. The rivers' waters as they flow east do not mingle, thus keeping their own separate identity: the water of the Tsangpo is darker than the Nyang (also Giamda) and therefore the district along the right bank is Chemnak (Black Water) and that on the left is Chemkar (White Water).

✤ DAY 2 CHEMNAK–MENRI 4 1/4 HR

1 hr east of Chemnak, on the left side of the road, is the village of Lhumbak. Here a coracle service ferries people and goods to Menri, a small village on the Bönri Khora. The crossing takes 1/2 hr and costs Rmb 2 per person. There are no fixed schedules; just go to the village and ask for the ferrymen. As you cross the Tsangpo, the massive shape of Mt Lhari Gyangtö can be seen across the river; the mountain on the right bank is Luwang.

Lhari Gyangtö

Three peaks make up the Bönri range. Bönri, in the center, is flanked by Muri on the west, and Lhari Gyangtö to the southeast. The last is considerably lower than the first and one of its corners is at the Nyang Chu–Tsangpo confluence. According to a myth, Lhari Gyangtö was the site where the first king of Tibet, Nyatri Tsenpo, first landed on earth; ever since then it had close connections with the genesis of Tibetan civilization. In early times, the name Lhari Gyangtö probably referred to the high center peak, today's Kongpo Bönri. The Bönpos began to call it Bönri at the time when the epic stories of their patriarch, Shenrab, began to circulate. Apparently a transfer of names took place and one of the lesser peaks received the name of Lhari Gyangtö. One of the most important sites here is the cemetery of King Drigum Tsanpo. His interment and tomb building set the precedent for burials of later Yarlung-dynasty kings.

Along the north bank of the Tsangpo

The coracle docks at an isolated stretch along the sandy north bank of the river. Walk north via a tractor track to an army camp, then follow a dirt road east to Mukdo (3/4 hr). Continue east to the village of Sekora (1/2 hr). A bit further (1/4 hr) is the Chujo Monastery (Nyingmapa), a newly rebuilt monastery on a low rise overlooking the Tsangpo. An important statue, the Dho Jowo of Gonjo, was brought here from Gonjo (see page 761). The scenery along this stretch is memorable: untouched beaches and densely forested mountains of the Assam Himalayas drop down to the south bank of the river.

Chujo Monastery

This small, insignificant chapel contains one of the most sacred images of southeastern Tibet—the Dho Jowo (Stone Sakyamuni). At some distant time, a pilgrim from Kongpo suffered untold hardships to make the long pilgrimage to Lhasa. In those days the trails were not well developed and the journey through thick forests was full of hazards. He finally reached the Jokhang and the scruffy man carried his tattered shoes on his shoulders to enter the Jowo chapel in order to pay respects to Tibet's greatest image. There was an instant rapport between the two. After some time, he decided to visit Ramoche Temple, and asked the Jowo to look after his shoes. The statue agreed and he went. When the *könyer* (caretaker) came in and saw the shoes, he was aghast—these filthy objects defiled the chapel. At this, the Jowo spoke, reassuring him that everything was all right. The pilgrim eventually returned, thanked the Jowo and invited him to come to his home in Kongpo. The image replied that he could not go now but would try to visit later. The Kongpopa was instructed to keep an eye on the river. On his return, he told the story to his wife and they started a vigil. One day they were rewarded with the sight of the Jowo floating down the river towards them. After emerging, the image sat on a stone and feasted on a sumptuous spread of offerings prepared by the couple. Later, when it was time to depart, the Jowo regretted that he could not be in two places at once. As a consolation he offered the stone to the couple and to the people of Kongpo, telling them it would

➠

be equivalent to having the original. At that he dissolved into the stone, which gradually took on the form of the Jowo and was installed in the Dho Jowo (Stone Sakyamuni) Lhakhang. This stretch of the river has since been known as the Chujo. The chapel was destroyed in the Cultural Revolution, but due to the quick action of a monk, the statue was buried deep in the ground and saved.

Further along the flat dirt road from Chujo is Kongpo Menri (1/2 hr), on top of a small ridge and reached via a footpath to the left of the road. A big cluster of prayer flags marks the entrance to the village. Right of the main village street, halfway down, is a harvest yard with a long barn on one side. The barn is divided into eight or nine compartments, each with a rickety wood gate. A leaky shingled roof provides some shelter from summer rain. Firewood is plentiful. This is a good, quiet spot to spend the night before starting the Bönri *khora* proper.

The mythology of Bönri

Kongpo Bönri is an ancient, pre-Buddhist site associated with some of the most influential saints and sages responsible for the dissemination of the Bön doctrine. The most eminent was Tönpa Shenrab, who first expounded the precepts of this primeval religion in Ölmo Lungring, the mythical kingdom where Bön originated. Its inhabitants were believed to be well advanced on their way to enlightenment. The precise location of the territory is disputed. Some scholars believe it was in the region of Mt Kailash or perhaps northwest of Tibet. Ölmo Lungring supposedly took the form of a square. Within it, mountains and rivers partitioned small outlying kingdoms, each filled with enchanting cities and landscapes of great beauty. Eight square districts enclosed the central core, a nine-tiered sacred peak. On top was the king's throne. Each of the nine levels, dotted with the caves of meditating hermits, represented one of the Nine Ways of Bön, the system of teachings that has enlightenment as its ultimate aim. According to prophecy, a great teacher following in the footsteps of Tönpa Shenrab will again leave his abode at Ölmo Lungring. He will undertake the arduous journey to the outside world at a time when all semblance of religion has died out. His task will be to bring forth a new, relevant form of the old spiritual teachings.

The founder of Bön, Tönpa Shenrab, considered by some to have lived in the 2nd millennium BC, left Ölmo Lungring for Tibet primarily because a demon called Kyapa Lagring, who lived in Kongpo, stole his seven horses, and hid them inside the castle of Kongje Karpo. In addition to repossessing them, Shenrab also wanted to use this opportunity to teach the Tibetans the essence of his religion. He desisted when he found they were not ready to absorb the doctrines. (His disciples later spread the Bön precepts, first in Shangshung and later in other parts of Tibet.) En route, Shenrab traversed a burning desert. It was here that he encountered his arch-rival, Kyapa Lagring. The battles between the two opponents, magical contests of ferocious intensity, provide much of the drama and color of Bön folklore. In one story, the demon stood on top of a high black mountain on the south bank of the Yarlung Tsangpo to block Shenrab from entering the region. As a riposte, the Bön lama miraculously created Kongpo Bönri, a mountain even higher than the black one. The more Shenrab struggled to overcome Kyapa by transforming himself into wrathful divinities, the less success he had. In the end, he simply secluded himself in retreat. This proved to be the ultimate weapon and the demon, overwhelmed by Shenrab's wisdom and compassion, renounced his past and returned the seven horses to the sage at Drena. Eventually he became a disciple. Bönri's sacred sites commemorate the places where Shenrab and Kyapa Lagring tested their powers. The most important ones are:

• Semo Bönthang (Khar Semo, near Ningchi)	Conversion of 100 demon transformations
• Drakar Shabje	Shenrab shot arrow at demon
• Bemdrong (across river)	Kyapa's nine iron shields erected here
• Chumik Dadrang (Bela)	Arrow extracted by king's daughter
• Kunzang Thuka (near Bönri La)	Shenrab concealed two teeth, armour-shield, bow and arrows, conches
• Kushuk Demdrug	Shenrab offered turquoise juniper tree by Kongtsen Lhamo, a local demoness
• Drena (near Mijik Tri)	Shenrab got his horses back

Kongtsen Lhamo

Tönpa Shenrab also vanquished a local demon named Kongtsen Lhamo. She subsequently became his disciple and was entrusted with the protection of the Bön doctrine in Bönri. As a token of her gratitude, she offered a remarkable juniper tree to Shenrab. The tree, imbued with the unchanging color of turquoise and eternal life, was blessed and consecrated by Shenrab. Known as Kushuk Demdrug (Bönri Kushuk), it is considered to this day the most sacred object of Bönri (see page 759).

Kongyul Drena

Tönpa Shenrab stayed at a place called Kongyul Drena, on the khora, near the sacred cemetery of Mijik Tri. Here devotees offered him gold and turquoise measured in dre, a Tibetan measure that gives Drena its name. Chörtens, tombs, and graveyards were built to commemorate the site.

Monasteries of Bönri

Bönri's importance was not known until 1300 when a Bön lama, Kuchok Ripa Drukse, received divine guidance and traveled from Kham to Bönri. He first stayed at Nyitri Thö (present day Ningchi) and founded the monastery of Sigyal Gönchen. His meditation cave there is called Drukse Drubphuk. From that time on, the fame of the holy mountain spread far and wide.

Below are monasteries established on Bönri:

Monastery	Founder	Present status
Sigyal Gönchen	Kuchok Ripa Drukse	restored
Taktse Yungdrungling	Yungdrung Wangyal (Dhongom Tenpa Lhündrub)	restored
Yungdrung Gatsheling (at Tag Drosa)	Kudün Mönlam Tashi	restored
Dzong Khyung Teng	Trulzhik Yungdrung Tsultrim	destroyed

Gyelri Gön	Zeri Migyur Gyaltsen	restored
Gompa Teng	Khyung Trul Yungdrung	
	Phüntshok	unknown
Samtenling	Patshe Wang Wözer	unknown
(at Sinmo, Tha Tsa)		

Five sacred *rangjung* caves, known collectively as Sangphuk, are located at cardinal points on the mountain:

- Sangwa Yong Dzong (center)
- Taklung Drubphuk (east)
- Sinmo Drubphuk (north)
- Jati Drubphuk (west)
- Nyima Drubphuk (south)

THE BÖNRI KHORA PROPER: MENRI TO NINGCHI TO LUSHA

The pilgrimage route around the mountain does not actually circle the peak. Rather it winds along to the west, south, and east slopes and avoids the summit. The ninth, 10th, and 11th lunar months (October–December) see the most Bön pilgrims. This is when the harvests are finished and there is sufficient time to travel the great distances from eastern Tibet's Bön strongholds like Khyungpo Tengcheng (see page 586) and Dzade. From Menri, allow 9–10 hr to reach Bönri La. This is a leisurely pace that allows time to visit all the important sacred spots. The spiritual ambience and the natural environment along this stretch are outstanding. Take your time—two days or more are recommended.

✦ DAY 3 MENRI–SEMBÖN DHUNGSHING 3 1/4 HR

From the barn walk east out of Menri along a clear path. On the left, about 100 m from the path is Basha, a cemetery with one prayer flag and a phallic stone. The broad Temo Valley entrance is on the right, trending towards the northeast, and a Chinese-style village with brick houses is nearby. Temo Chemkar, a destroyed Gelugpa monastery, is further to the north near the valley's right side.

The path starts to ascend a wooded ridge left of the Temo Valley. In 1/2 hr, reach Drakar Shabje, a big flat rock, surrounded by prayer flags with a footprint of Tönpa Shenrab, the Bön patriarch. This marks the place from which Shenrab shot an arrow to subdue the local demon, Kyapa Lagring. The arrow went through his opponent's shields at Bemdrong on the opposite bank of the Tsangpo, and ultimately pierced the earth at Chumik Dhadrang (see below).

Droger Shabje is left of the main path. A small stone hermitage, Tsakhang (Thatched House) is 5 min from Drakar on the right. A friendly old monk from Khyungpo Tengcheng has been here for several years. A short distance away is Drakar Monastery (destroyed). Within its perimeter wall is a large cavity in the ground, where a stone in the center bears the footprints of Guru Rinpoche and Kuchok Ripa Drukse. Beyond Tsakhang (1/2 hr), on the left, is Lhamo Shika. A family lives here in a house marked by prayer flags. About 5 min further is a rock with the footprint (*shabje*) of Karmo Sigyal (White Sipe Gyalmo, Queen of Existence) chief goddess of the mountain and protector deity of Tönpa Shenrab. After 10 min, cross a sacred stream called Shangshung Chu. Pilgrims sprinkle its water on their heads three times to receive blessings and protection. The path then climbs steeply up a deeply eroded channel to some ruins. This is the site of an old Bön monastery, Dzong Khyung Teng. One source says it was destroyed in the 1950 earthquake, the same that laid waste to Temo Chemnak Monastery. 5 min further (1 hr from Drakar Shabje) is a *mani* pile. An unidentified saint's footprint marks a black rock. The entire path up to this point is well defined and clearly identified by masses of prayer flags.

Sacred earth On the sides of the path, deep pockmarks have been dug out of the earth banks by pilgrims. This earth, usually mixed with blessed relics and medicines, produces a sacred pill called *jinlab*. Only the earth of a few specific places on the *khora* has the requisite supernatural powers. Further up the steep ridge (1/2 hr), is a flat rock smothered with prayer flags. This is Shenrab Shugtri (Shenrab's throne); pilgrims touch the base of this rock with their heads and prostrate three times. The prayer flags are printed with images of various Bön deities. Another sacred stream Chu Lung is crossed after 1/4 hr. Water again is splashed on the head. This is the last water source on the *khora* until the main road on the other side of the mountain is reached. In another 1/4 hr, the path widens into a flat area between two rocks. This spot is known as Khandro Drora (*dakini* dancing place). A small *shabje* inspires pilgrims to touch their heads to the rock.

Sembön Dhungshing An amazing tree, Sembön Dhungshing, stands to the left of the path after 10 min. Its name roughly translates to 'Silver Fir of Shenrab's Awareness'. The huge trunk as well as many branches support up to 30 or more wooden crates. Blankets, hats, plastic bags, and talismans also dangle from the tree. Each crate, in fact a tiny coffin, contains a dead baby. The blankets and plastic bags contain the infants' few possessions. Along the lower portion of the tree trunk are numerous human teeth pressed into the bark. Decayed teeth are left behind, along with the sins that caused the toothache. Sembön Dhungshing, an arboreal cemetery for babies, is an unique phenomenon, unseen elsewhere in Tibet. This sacred tree, consecrated by Kuchok Ripa Drukse, the Bön patriarch who rediscovered Bönri in 1330, is believed to have everlasting life. Bönpos consider any change in its color, shape, or health is a harbinger of momentous events to come in Tibet. Sembön Dhungshing is a famous landmark throughout Kongpo; dead babies are brought here from far and wide in the belief that their sins, committed in this and past lives, will be cleansed by the tree. Pilgrims customarily make offerings by placing *khatas*, clothing, locks of hair, bangles, pins, and *sungdü* (consecrated thread) on the tree. (Another sacred tree across the valley, supposedly visible from this spot, is known to pilgrims as Tsenden Dhongpo [Sandalwood Tree]. Local tradition states it was brought by Guru Rinpoche from South India and planted by him here.) A small clearing 5 min from here is a good place to camp.

✤ DAY 4 SEMBÖN DHUNGSHING–DAOBAN 114   5 1/2 HR

Sembön Dhungshing to Taklung Drubphuk

Some 5 min from camp along the pilgrim trail is a small headprint of Kuchok Ripa Drukse, on a rock to the left. In another 5 min, reach a sacred rock dedicated to Sipe Gyalmo on the left. Touch heads to it. This spot commands a fine view of the Tsangpo Valley and most of the Bönri ridge, with the high mountains of Pachakshiri to the south.

Sonam Chechung Tasa Watch out for two deep holes within a rock. Pilgrims stick their arms inside, grabbing whatever comes to hand; bits of animal wool are auspicious, whereas dead insects signal calamity. Along this part of the path are many cut branches, about 1 m long, propped up against rocks. Notches are cut along the entire length, making the branch represent a miniature ladder.

Zhingkham Dzekke These scale ladders are called Zhingkham Dzekke, 'the Ladders to Paradise'. Pilgrims believe that their souls, by climbing to the end of a ladder, may then reach Pure Land or Paradise. Prayers accompany these notched branches when the are placed along the side of the path. Pilgrims also tell of the important protector, Abdze Nensa, who lives in the rocks of Bönri. The ladders allow their spirits to walk to a place under the protection of this deity. This helps them get through *bardo*, the rebirth cycle, more easily. The ladders also symbolize longevity.

Yak skulls Next to these miniature ladders are yak skulls, complete with horns, brought from far and wide. *Mantras* are carved or written on the bare bones as offerings to the gods for protection of the yak herds. The skulls of other slaughtered animals are brought here as well, a sign of uncommon respect for the source of one's meat. About 10 min after the rock of Sipe Gyalmo, a side trail goes to the right. Near the path junction, facing east across a wooded gorge, is a meditation cave called Taklung Drubphuk. The Bön saint, Taklung Mebar, meditated here. His image, carved in stone, is at the back. The cave is 1 hr from the small clearing above the tree of Sembön Dhungshing.

Taklung Drubphuk to Dhikpa Pabsa ('Sin Resting Place')

Return to the main trail. In 10 min, reach the meditation spot called Toura (4085 m). A self-manifesting (*rangjung*) Bön *mantra* is impressed on a rock to the right after 5 more min. Near here is a boulder (3 m by 5 m) above the path on the left, with a flat, disc-like surface. This is Tönpa Shenrab's drum; it supports many miniature ladders. Further on is Hum Chendrak, the rock that represents the eye of wisdom. Onto it is carved the syllable *hum*, one part of the famous 'Om Mani Padme Hum'. Nearby, on the left, is a *rangung* horseprint and an imprint of Tönpa Shenrab's saddle. Behind Hum Chendrak is Bardo Trang: a narrow cleft is formed of two rocks. Squeeze through, say a prayer, and you will be protected from losing your way. Another rock cleft, 1/2 m wide and formed of three rocks, tests how successful a pilgrim will be in his after-death (*bardo*) journey.

Netsab Nga Near Bardo Trang is a cluster of five rocks representing the five paramount pilgrimages (Kailash, Tsari, Kawa Karpo, Jago Phungro Ri of Bodh Gaya and Lapchi). The rock representing Kailash is lower than the others. This symbolizes the fact that the Bönpo master, Naro Bönchung, lost the mountain to Milarepa. By circumambulating these rocks, the pilgrim accumulates a measure of merit even though he is unable to actually visit the holy places.

Sadhak Tshok ('Assembly of Lords of the Earth') 5 min from Bardo Trang is a yellowish rock bearing Tibetan inscriptions. Legend has it that the *dakini*, Chersa Pomo, wrote these with her finger. A blue bag containing hair hangs from a branch. Pilgrims leave some hair behind in the belief that the act will promote longevity and help the dead in *bardo*. Tibetans generally consider hair to be sacred and inviolate. For example, they think blindness or deafness may result from someone inadvertently stepping on one's hair. As the Bönri *khora* is a representation of the route to paradise or enlightenment, leaving some hair along the way makes it possible to cast off one's sins. This act is also a symbol of renewal. With the holy mountain as witness, a pilgrim cuts a lock of hair and vows to start afresh, refraining from all crimes and immorality.

In 5 min, left of the path, is a small rock called Dhikpa Pabsa, 'place for setting down sins'. Pilgrims sit down on the rock and let it slowly extract their sins. Sometimes they recline and press their backs to the stone. During this process, they visualize a heavy burden on the back and shoulders. This weight is then abandoned, and with it sins and physical ailments, such as backaches.

Dhikpa Pabsa to Bönri Pass

About 10 m ahead is a grey rock, Drukta Ngonpo ('Blue Rock of the Dragon-Horse'), that resembles Tönpa Shenrab's steed (the teeth can just be made out). The Dragon-Horse is the mythical charger of Tibetan folklore, and the rock a well-known landmark on the Bönri *khora*. Bönpos mount the rock and imagine they are riding the Horse of Happiness (Kyi Kyi Taphoche). Just beyond, a 3 m by 3 m rock represents the throne of Karmo Sigyal. Many miniature ladders are here.

The ridge becomes steeper and much narrower, and nearly every tree is hung with prayer flags. This portion of the circuit is known as Langla Bola, 'forest path'. Bönri La can be seen in 20 min and the forest begins to thin out. In 1/2 hr, reach Kunzang Drak, a rock (2 m by 1 m) with inscriptions attributed to Kuchok Ripa Drukse. Pilgrims often sit here in meditation. According to legend, Kuntu Sangpo, a primordial Bön deity, sat here in contemplation and Tönpa Shenrab concealed *terma* in the rock which were later discovered by Kuchok Ripa Drukse. Higher up is a 5 m by 3 m rock inscribed with a handsome Bönpo *mantra*. It is known as Kunang Drakor Kunzang Thuka, 'the hiding place of Tönpa Shenrab's teeth'. In another 5 min, a large pile of stones and prayer flags appears just below the pass. This spot is Tsewang Rinzin Thuka (4480 m), 'the heart (*thuka*) of Tsewang Rinzin'. Nephew of Guru Rinpoche, Rinzin deposited his spirit here. It was from this point that Guru Rinpoche and Kuchok Ripa Drukse made an offering to the mountain. The Indian master, in a gesture of goodwill, set aside all claims to the sacred site and allowed the Bönpos to take over Bönri as a refuge for their ancient religion.

A flat trail from here leads left to the pass. Another goes right to a marginally higher pass, on the right. Pigeons gather here to poke among a large heap of abandoned effects left as offerings by pilgrims. The *thuka* marks the beginning of Wöser Jalam, 'the light ray rainbow path', and leads in 15 min to the two passes. Bönpo believe this spot is endowed with profound powers. It is not unusual for them to spend hours here, reciting prayers and offering incense (*sang*). The prolonged rites known as Serkyem Chöpa, liquid offerings, are conducted to invoke and appease various divinities and to dedicate the moment to universal peace. The right path leads to Shenri Dham Dham, Tönpa Shenrab's mountain consecrated to Demchok. This mountain represents the deity's Pure Land and Bönpo pilgrims hold it in the same reverence as Bönri. The right and left paths eventually rejoin below the far side of the passes.

Lake Sipe Gyalmo

From Shenri Dham Dham, a trail leads to Sipe Gyalmo Tso, the sacred Bönpo oracle-lake near Lunang. This is a two-day walk. Lunang, on the main Tibet–Sichuan highway, is 57 km northeast of Ningchi; cross the Dakmo Serkyem La if traveling from Ningchi to Lunang. After Lake Lhamo Latso (see page 623), the people of Kongpo and Poyul hold Sipe Gyalmo Tsho to be the most powerful oracle-lake in Central Tibet. Subsequent to obtaining a clear visualization at the lake shore, Bönpo pilgrims often head back to Bönri to seek out a Bönpo lama for interpretation. Tsewang Rinzin Thuka is reached in 2 1/4 hr from Dhikpa Pabsa. The Bönri Pass (4540 m), to the left (15 min from the *thuka*), offers a beautiful view of the Yarlung Tsangpo Valley.

The Bönri summit

To go to the Bönri summit, spend the night below the pass in the vicinity of Taklung Drubphuk and begin the ascent in the morning. The top of Bönri is 4 hr from the pass; walk up the ridge through an exquisite forest. The peak, known as Muri Mukpo, 'brown sky-mountain', is so called because it is manifested from a brown ray of light emanating from Shenrab's heart. One sees this peak prominently from Ningchi. Behind the top is a ridge that leads southward to some pastures. Here is a yak herders' hut, occupied from June to October during the prime pasturing season. In summer, cheese, curd, milk, and firewood are usually available. Snow can be expected after October. From the hut, reach Lhari Gyangtö, Bönri's highest peak, in 2 hr. Situated magnificently above the confluence of the Giamda (Nyang) Chu and the Yarlung Tsangpo, it has a footprint attributed to Nyatri Tsenpo, the legendary first king of Tibet. Going east from Lhari Gyangtö, following the ridge, the Bönri Pass can be regained in 4–5 hr.

Bönri Pass–Daoban 114

The path descending from the pass is gradual and hugs the left side of the valley. After 1/2 hr, make a sharp turn to the left and enter a rhododendron forest. In 10 min reach Shapchin Dong, where pilgrims look back towards Bönri and prostrate. The ridge narrows and the going becomes steeper. Unlike the ascent along the south side of the range, there are few prayer flags lining the path this side of the pass. In 10 min, some prayer flags mark two sacred rocks, 100 m apart, and the path passes through idyllic rhododendron and fir forests. In 1/2 hr, come to a tree with many small stones wrapped in red strings. Some are suspended from the branches, others are simply piled at the bottom. This is Dhikpa Dhotak, the 'sin-stone tying place'. Transgressions are left behind by tying red string around a stone and leaving it at the tree. The path now zigzags down the steep, narrow ridge. In 1/2 hr, come to a grove of rhododendrons. Nearby is a small rock with a *shabje* and prayer flags. This is Chemar Gang ('Creamed Tsampa Terrace'). Final prayers of thanksgiving for successfully completing the pilgrimage are offered here. Tradition calls for an elaborate picnic. Beyond, look for a pile of walking sticks, symbols of sacrifice offered to Bönri. Their abandonment expiates sins and marks the start of a newly purified life. New sticks are cut and the mountain divinities called upon to bless them, each one a treasured souvenir for friends and family. After 15 min, a left fork descends steeply to a road maintenance compound (*daoban* 114), next to the main Ningchi–Chamdo road. This stretch will take 20 min. The right fork, a more gradual path, also goes down to the main road; turn left to reach the *daoban*. Allow 2 hr from the pass to the compound (3720 m). Pitch a tent inside the compound or stay in a shack with the friendly caretaker's family.

✤ Day 5 Daoban 114–Ningchi 3 3/4 hr

Walk out of the compound and turn right along the unpaved road, the major artery between Lhasa, Ningchi, and Sichuan. After 10 min, the road makes a sweeping curve to the right. At this spot, prayer flags mark the beginning of a small trail that leads left down the slopes, away from the road. This is a shortcut much used by pilgrims to avoid the busy road. Three sacred trees to the right of the path stand as 'self-manifesting' representations of Tönpa Shenrab and two flanking goddesses (*Drölmas*). Bönpos usually stay here for some time making offerings of butter and coins. After 1/2 hr, rejoin the main road at road marker 1142 km. Prayer flags mark the junction. Also here is a small, water-driven prayer wheel within a wood frame.

Turn left at the main road to go downhill towards Ningchi. In 20 min, take a flat and narrow side trail to the left to reach Darbong ('Tiger Dancing Place'; 3/4 hr). Lovely purple irises line the trail. This Bön village of nearly 20 households has a new monastery set up by a Bönpo lama from Shigatse's Menri Monastery (see page 765). From Darbong, follow the trail to a large compound, the Ningchi School for Cadres (1/2 hr). Continue along a dirt path to Jibu (20 min). The village entrance has many prayer flags around a small shrine. 20 min later, cross a small rise to reach a roadside shrine that holds both Buddhist and Bön stone carvings. Beyond is the big village (100 houses) of Khar Semo, site of Shenrab's victory over the 100 devil-transformations. From here, follow a well-defined dirt track for 10 min to reach a bluff overlooking the sprawling town of Ningchi. The path forks at this point. Go right down the bluff to the main road. Turn right, cross the Ningchi Bridge over the Koro Chu to reach the town center. The Ningchi Guest House is on the left after the bridge (20 min). Just beyond are small Sichuanese restaurants that serve good food.

Ningchi

Ningchi (Linzhi Xian, Tib. Nyitri) stands on the east bank of the Giamda Chu, near its junction with the Koro Chu, 19 km southeast of Bayi. At the town, the Tibet–Sichuan highway leaves the flat bank of the Giamda Chu to climb up through narrow gorges and virgin forests of the lush Pome District. The guest house has comfortable rooms (4 beds) for Rmb 3 each on the second floor. Ningchi's population is an equal mix of Chinese and Tibetan. Stores are well stocked. The Ningchi prefecture controls Bayi and most of Kongpo. Recently, the remote Metok (Pemako) area, southeast of the Yarlung Tsangpo's big bend, came under the Ningchi's administration as well. The Ningchi Public Security Bureau cannot extend visas.

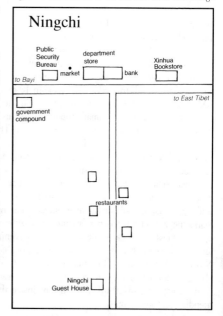

Kushuk Demdrug, the sacred tree of Bön

From the center of town walk west along the road to the Bayi–Lhasa road and turn left onto a dirt track that leads to Kushuk Drong, once part of old Ningchi. This enclave retains the characteristics of a traditional Kongpo settlement. Village houses surround a walled enclosure surmounted by prayer flags. Within is Kushuk Demdrug (Bönri Kushuk), the sacred tree of Bön, a magnificent specimen (considered a juniper by the Tibetans) perhaps 2,000–2,500 years old. Locals believe it to be the Original Tree, as old as the universe. Another tradition ascribes its genesis to Tönpa Shenrab, Bön's patriarch; the demon, Kongtsen Lhamo, offered him this tree of eternal life in tribute. According to some, 13 circumambulations around the enclosure, anti-clockwise (the Bön way), is equal in merit to a single Bönri *khora*. The locked compound is looked after by a nun from Khyungpo Tengcheng. In the past, pilgrims abused the tree by stripping its bark for relics. Now they can view it only during special days. The tree's cones (*shukdhok*) are greatly prized as protection against dangerous animals, weapons, and bad luck; pilgrims hunt for them outside the enclosure. Kushuk Drong is entirely Bönpo or Nyingmapa. The Ningchi Valley has strong ties to Bön and is one of its few surviving strongholds in the country. When Buddhist pilgrims come here they follow the Bönpo custom of circumambulating the holy sites anti-clockwise.

✤ Day 6 Ningchi–Luding 5 1/2 hr

Backtrack over the Ningchi Bridge and take the trail up the bluff on your left (20 min). Notice Muri Mukpo, a prominent peak of the Bönri range. Follow the dirt road to Khar Semo (Semo Bönthang; 35 min).

Sigyal Gönchen Monastery

After the village is a junction. The dirt trail to the right follows the Bönri *khora*. The left climbs a hill to the monastery of Sigyal Gönchen, dedicated to the Bön goddess, Sipe Gyalmo (Sigyal). Don't be misled by the many logging trails that lead to nowhere. Follow the clear ridge path through rhododendron and conifer forests until the prayer flags of the monastery appear (1 hr). Built in the 14th C. by Kuchok Ripa Drukse, it remains an important place of pilgrimage for the people of Khyungpo and Hor. It was destroyed in the Cultural Revolution; reconstruction began in 1983. The main assembly hall is in the middle of the complex. A small house with a huge prayer wheel stands to the left. Farther left is a small building containing four meditation cells. The kitchen and a provisional assembly room are housed in a building to the right of the main chapel. A nice grassy camp site lies beyond. Only a few Bönpos reside here permanently, although the number of monks and nuns fluctuates seasonally. Pilgrims on the Bönri *khora* regularly come here to contribute free labor, especially during idle winter months. In the old days, Sigyal Gönchen had over 100 monks.

Continue along the *khora*. Be sure to follow the well-defined trail. In general, stick close to the Giamda Chu and the motor road below, and head southward hugging the left side of the valley. Beyond Khar Semo, 20 min from the junction, is a 2 m by 2 m rock with Tibetan inscriptions and a footprint attributed to Tönpa Shenrab on the left. A blue flag marks the site. In another 10 min, the trail splits. Take the lower, well-traveled route. Later, take the upper, diminished trail immediately after crossing a small stream. Round the bend of the mountain in 1/4 hr. At this point, the trail forks again at two tall flagpoles. Take the upper, level trail. Reach a huge rock named Yeshe Armo, 1/4 hr later. It rests

30 m above the path and is dedicated to Sipe Gyalmo. Soon stone houses come into view, and 10 min later the trail goes up to the left to the ruins of the Bön monastery of Tagtse Yungdrungling.

Tagtse Yungdrungling Monastery

This monastery is used primarily by pilgrims from Amdo. Its reconstruction started in 1985. Near the entrance are dwellings for a few monks and nuns. The monk in charge, Nyankyab, came from Amdo in the mid-1980s. He had spent time in the great Bön monasteries of Yungdrungling and Menri (see page 763), near Shigatse, before settling here. Tagtse Yungdrungling was founded by Dongom Tenpa Lhündrub, an ascetic from Amdo. An earthquake damaged it badly in the 1930s and the Chinese demolished the rest in the 1960s. A footprint of Yumdrok Wangyal, the abbot, is here, and a tooth, attributed to Tönpa Shenrab, is the monastery's most important relic.

The motor road below the monastery can be reached in 3/4 hr. Follow it to the southeast along the east (left) bank of the Giamda (Nyang) Chu. After 1 hr, come to a spring next to prayer flags and *mantras* carved on rocks. These mark the most sacred of the 108 tributaries that flow down from Bönri. Beyond the spring is the village of Bangna.

Chumik Dhadrung

The spring is called Chumik Dhadrung, 'Arrow Originating Spring'. According to one legend, it was created by Tönpa Shenrab's arrow when it landed on this spot. Princess Kongza Tricham, daughter of Kongpo's king, extracted it, thus starting the flow. The water cures diseases and confers longevity on those who believe.

Reach an army compound in a further 20 min. A shop to the right sells beer, instant noodles, and biscuits. The village of Drena is on the right after 1/4 hr. Beyond is a destroyed monastery at Chigu. Lara, a site marked by prayer flags, is on the left (10 min).

Mijik Tri

Continue to the village of Miyul Kyithing, where Giamda Chu joins the Yarlung Tsangpo. Nearby is Mijik Tri Durtrö ('Indestructible Throne Cemetery'), the most sacred Bön burial ground. According to the historical text, *Deton Chöjung*, the first king of Tibet, Nyatri Tsenpo, stopped here first after his descent from heaven to Mt Lhari Gyangtö. Historical documents from Dunhuang state that King Drigum Tsanpo once lived in the castle of Chingwa Taktse (see page 528) at Yarlung. He went into battle against Lo-ngam, ruler of Yul Myangro Shampo (perhaps Nyangpo of the Nyang Valley). The king was killed and his body thrown into a river. His sons, banished to Kongpo, managed to retrieve their father's remains downsteam in Drena. They then buried them in a tomb at a place called Gyangtö Labub at the southwest foot of Mt Lhari Gyangtö. The spot can perhaps be identified with Miyul Kyithing. Among the ruins here is an earth mound that closely resembles one of the minor king's tombs in Yarlung. Samten Karmay, a Tibetan historian, believes this is the actual burial site referred to in the Dunhuang texts. Pilgrims believe the cemetery to be located originally much higher up in the mountains. Over the centuries, so the legend goes, it moved imperceptibly down towards the river. Supposedly, when it finally reaches the water, the universe as we know it will begin a slow but inexorable process of disintegration. There will be a hellish seven years of universal suffering when Mijik Tri is actually submerged. Finally, the world will cease to exist once it emerges from the other side.

Arrive at the pretty village of Luding, 'Home of the Nagas', on the right near the river, after 20 min. This was the site where Kyapa tried to poison Shenrab, and consequently pilgrims fear this village.

✤ DAY 7 LUDING–LUSHA 4 HR

Drena (Kongyul Drena) is 15 min beyond Luding on the left. This village is steeped in history and tradition. The funeral rites of King Drigum Tsanpo took place here, and nearby are two springs where Tönpa Shenrab washed his horses after he reclaimed them from Kyapa. After Drena the valley opens up to reveal Yang-o, a relaxed army base, and sandy beaches on a bend of the Tsangpo. Lhari Gyangtö rises impressively, close by on the left.

The Temo inscription

The village of Yungdrung Dzin, site of the Temo Inscription (just to the east), is reached in 3/4 hr. This important 9th-C. relic, carved on a stone *doring* and well protected inside an enclosure, states that Tibet's first king appeared on Mt Lhari Gyangtö. It also recounts how the two sons of King Drigum Tsanpo worshipped Kula Demo, the goddess of Lhari Gyangtö. The purpose of the proclamation was to confirm special powers and privileges bestowed on Kongpo's king, who ruled this area—one of 12 principalities of Tibet. The *doring* is 2.6 m high and 1.5 m wide. Most of the characters are still legible. The base has a carved Bön reverse swastika.

Thongmon-Gonjo, a charming area with good camping sites is 15 min from here. Continue for 10 mins to an army camp; then another in 10 min. Just beyond is Mukdo, the point reached earlier by coracle (see page 750). Follow the wide *khora* path to Sekora (1/2 hr). A side trail on the left (5 min after the village) ascends to Jakhyung Monastery (20 min), built atop a small ridge.

Jakhyung Monastery

This monastery was rebuilt in 1986 from private funds contributed by the surrounding villages. The interior of the Nyingma chapel has ten unusual, large chunks of rock in front of the altar. According to a local Bön legend, these rocks absorbed and concealed the mythical birds of Jakhyung (*garuda*). The footprint on stone of an unknown lama is next to a tablet carved with Chenresi's image; a huge prayer wheel revolves in a corner of the chapel. Menri, 1/4 hr down the road from Sekora, is where the Bönri *khora* begins.

Menri (Bönri) to Lusha and Namche Barwa

Mt Namche Barwa and the uncharted Tsangpo gorges are natural and easily accessible extensions to the Bönri pilgrimage. Secluded deep within these mountains of the Assam Himalayas is the mythic, hidden valley (*beyul*) of Pemakö (see page 717). From Menri, walk back down to the jeep track and continue east along the north bank of the Tsangpo. Go past Jimba (20 min) and Karmapa's stone image (10 min), marked by prayer flags. Gongmo Monastery (Karmapa) is near here. Cross a wooden bridge and walk to the lower village of Temo (Demo). This isolated stretch of road is built on a flat, narrow ledge between the mountain slopes on the left and the river. Reach the Lusha ferry in 3/4 hr. A long, thin boat, attached by a winch to an overhead cable, crosses the Tsangpo in only 5 min but it may take time to find the boatmen (Rmb 1 per person). Lusha, a big village with Chinese compounds and party cadres (avoid it if possible), is the staging post for the trek to Namche Barwa.

Side trip A trail southward from the settlement leads over the Lusha La into Assam, India. Twelve Lopa villages exist up the Lusha Valley, 1/2 hr–1 hr south of Lusha. An army outpost is located at the base of the Lusha La. The Lopa are tribal people living on Tibet's southern border.

YUNGDRUNGLING AND MENRI: THE MAJOR BÖN MONASTERIES

OVERVIEW

Within the Tsang valleys of Wuyuk and Tobgyal, which lie within the western portion of Central Tibet, are three of Tibet's most important Bönpo monasteries. Yungdrungling is situated at the entrance of the Wuyuk Valley; Menri and Kharna are at the upper reaches of the East Tobgyal (Shung) Valley. All are only a short distance east of Shigatse. Although other active Bönpo communities exist in Tibet (Khyungpo, Kham, Amdo, Lake Dangra, Bönri, Chumbi Valley), Menri and Yungdrungling are the religion's premier establishments and draw pilgrims and students from all over the country.

Related sections

The Lhasa–Shigatse north route, p 815
Shang Valley, p 869
Rinpung Dzong, p 841

Map Reference NH45-12 D

YUNGDRUNGLING MONASTERY

Yungdrungling is most easily reached from Shigatse (from Lhasa, see page 821). Go east from town and follow the Tsangpo's south bank along the Shigatse–Lhasa north route. The Tadruka ferry, at road marker 168 km (new marker 4821), is some 80 km east of Shigatse. Cross the river (5 min) on a metal barge and walk along the main road. Yungdrungling Monastery, on a shelf of land on the right, across from the Wuyuk Ma Chu (Longkung Chu) River, appears after a bend. 200 m beyond this point is a path that goes down to the Wuyuk Ma Chu. Follow it, walk across the sandy river bed, and wade across the shallowest part. After 200 m turn sharply to the right, away from the monastery, towards a grove of trees. Double back towards Yungdrungling through cultivated fields. On reaching the shelf of land, either scramble straight up or take the main path to the right, then left, up the slope to the monastery (3/4 hr from the ferry). Ralak Village is below. Sunset views overlooking the river to valleys and mountains beyond are superb. It is possible to stay in a clean, dry room at the monastery. Monks provide water, *tsampa*, and firewood.

The site

Yungdrungling was founded in the middle of the 19th C. by Nangtön Dawa Gyaltsen. After destruction by the Gelugpa villagers of Ralak in 1959 and 1967, the present structures were rebuilt on the original site. A feud still simmers between the monastic community and the villagers. They treated the present abbot badly during the Cultural Revolution by beating him regularly. Before 1950, up to 700 monks stayed here. Many were temporary visitors from other Bönpo centers. Today, there are about 30 monks and one incarnate lama.

The ruins cover a large area. Chief among them is the assembly hall, which used to have 108 pillars; it is now restored on a smaller scale. Behind it is the large Thongdröl Lhakhang. Within is a *chörten* that replaces an old one that once contained the remains of Yungdrungling's founder. The *chörten's* copper casing was made in Chengdu. (In the past, five such *chörtens* existed.) Along the back wall is a painting of the founder together with many woodblock prints of Shenrab, the Bön patriarch. The other three walls display 12 rather mediocre mandalas called Chöga Chunyi Ki Kyilkhor ('Mandalas of the 12 Rituals'). West and to the rear of the assembly hall are ruins of the *labrang*, the abbot's residence. Further away are other buildings, including the *drubkhang* (Ritual Temple) and the *lopön's* (headteacher's) residence. New images, murals, and relics of the founder and other lamas are inside the *drubkhang*. More buildings are being constructed in front of the assembly hall. Two monastic colleges (*tratsangs*), Yungdrungling and Namgyal Kungsaling, once stood here. The ridge behind the monastery is Wölha Gyal, one of Bön's 13 holy mountains. A path from Yungdrungling goes east along the Tsangpo River to Nub Chölung Monastery (1 1/2 hr). It is at the entrance of a small valley, under a 5383-m peak. Yulungling Monastery is 2 hr to the west (north bank) of the ferry.

TOBGYAL VALLEY

Tobgyal (Tobphu) Valley opens north from the Tsangpo, west of the Wuyuk Ma Chu. Within this valley are the Bön monasteries of Ensakha, Kharna, and Menri. The Gelugpa monastery of Drungshi is also here on the west branch of the Tobgyal.

Tadruka ferry to Menri Monastery

To reach the Tobgyal Valley, follow the dirt track leading west from the Tadruka ferry and Yungdrungling Monastery, along the north bank of the Tsangpo. The village of Tsobzang is 1 1/2 hr west of the ferry. In 3/4 hr, a track leaves the Tsangpo to head north up a small side valley. The valley divides in 1 hr at beautiful Lungbuk, a Bönpo village of about 25 houses whose inhabitants have close links to Menri Monastery. Take the left branch northwest and ascend for 3 hr to a pass (5050 m). Then walk north on the level along a contour to a second pass (3/4 hr). At this point Menri becomes visible. Descend 1/2 hr to the monastery. The villages of Dingphu (Dingchen) and Khulung (see below) can be seen much farther down the valley.

Menri back to the Tsangpo

From Menri, don't go straight down the valley towards Dingphu but walk back up to the second pass. Then follow a distinct path and small stream down to the village of Alé (Menri to Alé, 1 hr), a Bönpo settlement on the right side of the valley. In 1/4 hr, the stream joins the Shung Chu (eastern branch of the Tobgyal), which flows south to the Tsangpo. At the junction is Trashun. On the far (west) side, on a hilltop, are the remains of Kharna, another Bönpo monastery. Turn left down this larger valley. A short distance further is Kangba (Kanga) and beyond it the ruins of Bönpo Ensakha Monastery, Menri's precursor. Continue south down the Shung Chu to the main village of Tobgyal Qu, situated at the confluence of the eastern and western branches of the Tobgyal. Here is the restored Gelugpa monastery of Ganden Rabgye (Alé to here, 2 1/4 hr). The Tsangpo's north bank is a further 1 1/4 hr. Cross by coracle (Rmb 6) to Drakchik on the south bank. In the river is a rock crowned with a small shrine. Next to the main Lhasa–Shigatse north route is a teashop—a convenient spot (road marker 187 km; new marker 4840) to catch a ride west to Shigatse (road marker 250 km; new marker 4903).

MENRI MONASTERY

Until the founding of Yungdrungling and Kharna in the 19th C., Menri was Tibet's leading Bönpo center and the principal place of transmission for the sect's teachings. It was an unrivaled pilgrimage site, and monks from other Bön monasteries studied here to complete their religious training. Today, 50 monks live here; before the Cultural Revolution Menri housed 350, the majority from Kham and Gyarong. The acting abbot is from Tsarong in Kham. According to him, the monastery was destroyed in 1959, not 1967, by the villagers of Dingchen and Khalung further down the Tobgyal Valley. It was restored at the beginning of the 1980s.

The site

The monastery backs onto steep hillsides among the ruins of its former, clustered buildings. Its main assembly hall is centrally located and faces east, while the Phari Dukhang is at the edge of the complex. Next to the main temple is Drubkhang Marpo ('Red Ritual Temple of the Protective Deities'). This was the first structure built by Nyame Shenrab Gyaltsen, the founder. Further up the mountain are two shrines (*lhatsug*) consecrated to the Bönpo protective deities, Pomra and Sigyal. Between them is a stone throne marking the founder's place of death. A School of Dialectics (Tshanyi Khang) was established in the middle of this century. Menri, like Ensakha, had four colleges (*tratsangs*). A large rock just above the complex, painted to resemble a serpent's head, is a striking monument. It represents the water-serpent goddess, Chusin Phawang. Three sacred caves (Sangphuk, Wösel Phuk, and Waldhung Phuk) in the vicinity of Menri Luga Ri were once used by Dru Gyalwa Yungdrung.

The reconstruction of Menri was important for the religion's continuity. It provided a focus for Bön monks of different monasteries and also for disparate lay people. Menri fulfilled the role of a center for higher religious training in Bön doctrines.

Foundation of Menri

According to one Bönpo tradition, Menri's foundation was predicted by Tönpa Shenrab, Bönpo's equivalent of Sakyamuni. En route to Kongpo (see page 653), the master stopped here and told a little boy that this would be the site of a great monastery. He then left the imprint of his left foot. Menri was modeled on the monastery of Yeru Ensakha (further down the Shung Chu or East Tobgyal Valley), itself founded in 1072 by Druje Yungdrung Lama. This important institution was destroyed in 1386 by a flood. After this tragic event, Nyame Shenrab Gyaltsen, abbot of one of Yeru Ensakha's four colleges and a renowned master, spent the night within the ruins. In the morning he found that one of his shoes was missing. On the snow were fox tracks leading up the mountain. The lama followed them to a flat ledge, where he found both the fox and his shoe. Taking this as auspicious, he decided to build an alternative to Yeru Ensakha at the spot. Menri was eventually completed in 1405.

Another story tells that Nyame Shenrab Gyaltsen came to this area when he was 50 years old. He gave a bundle of marbles wrapped in a monk's shawl to his disciple, Rinchen Gyaltsen, who was told to close his eyes and deposit one marble on the ground for every nine paces walked. After this was done the disciple heard a loud noise. Upon opening his eyes, he saw that each marble had spontaneously become a monk's room. Altogether 60 rooms made up 12 khangtsens (a *khangtsen* is a unit of a *tratsang*; some *tratsangs* have 30–40 *khangtsens*). Since that time, Menri's fame spread and many Bönpo disciples came to learn from Nyame Shenrab Gyaltsen.

Kharna Monastery

This Bönpo monastery, located a short distance down the Tobgyal Valley from Menri, was founded after Yungdrungling by Shenrab Yungdrung (b 1838). The caves of Kharna Ri, however, have been used by Bön meditators for centuries. Nyame Shenrab Gyaltsen meditated and composed treatises in one of them. The Bönpo saint, Drempa Namkha, also came for retreat. At the foot of the Kharna ridge is the Khamlung River and in its vicinity is a large, black stone with the footprint of Dru Gyalwa Yungdrung, a Bön patriarch of the Dru clan. Kharna, smallest of the region's three Bönpo monasteries, has only 30 monks.

Khulung is the birthplace of Khulung Yönten Gyatso. This master supposedly taught Milarepa the art of sorcery.

LAKE DANGRA AND MT TARGO: A ONE-MONTH EXPEDITION TO THE SACRED LAKE AND MOUNTAIN OF BÖN

From the pilgrim valley of Mu to the steppes of the Northern Plateau

Location	Northwest of Shigatse
Map reference	NH45-7 C, 45-11 A C D, 45-6 B D, 45-2 D
Trekking days	30 (circuit)
Start–Finish	Lhatse–Sommai Qu
Passes	Chang-La-Pö, Ting, Tarbung

OVERVIEW

This pilgrimage is one of a few in this book that truly explores the wild, north-plateau country of the Changtang. More than half the walking time of this journey is spent north of the great Nyenchen Tanglha range—the watershed of the Tsangpo that effectively divides the inhabited valleys of Tibet's main river from the Changtang. Here is the sacred Bönpo territory of Mt Targo and Lake Dangra, which lies within the seldom-visited Tibetan district of Naktsang. This unparalleled combination of one of the largest lakes of Tibet with the haunting magnificence of the high snow-capped range

Dangra and Targo

makes this area one of the most superb in the country. Here is a world unknown to outsiders. Much wildlife still abounds and, during the latter half of the trek, there will be plenty of opportunity to come into close contact with it. The climate, however, is notoriously severe and changeable; ideally, this itinerary should only be attempted within a couple of narrow windows during the summer months.

About ten days will be spent in the circumambulation (over 300 km) of Lake Dangra—one of the most remote of all major Bönpo strongholds in the country. Due to its uncommon isolation and despite the inevitable ravages of the Cultural Revolution, the customs and way of life of this pre-Buddhist sect have survived until the present time. A number of Bönpo monasteries are in the vicinity of the lake, under the shadow of Mt Targo. Associated with these are some cave hermitages still used by ascetics. One of the biggest and most important Bönpo monasteries, the Sezhik Gompa, is at the southern tip of Lake Dangra. Over 50 monks are still attached to this very secluded retreat. Along the eastern shore of the lake there is a Guru Rinpoche cave and chapel called Orgyan. Nearby is the celebrated Khyung Dzong, the former castle of the king of Shangshung—the land (including Lake Dangra and certain parts of Changtang) where the Bön religion originated. Near the northeastern tip of the lake is the large settlement of Ombu which has another monastery consecrated to Guru Rinpoche. Near it is the Bönpo cave hermitage of Yungdrung Lhatse. It is interesting that these two earliest of Tibet's religions (Bön and Nyingma) are represented in this region side by side.

The first half of the route to Lake Dangra lies along the Mu Chu Valley—a major trade and pilgrimage artery. Its sanctity is attested to by numerous prayer flags, rock-paintings, and impressively long *mani* walls. It is one of the few in the region that succeeded in forging its way through the formidable ramparts of the Nyenchen Tanglha. The valley, one of the most fascinating in Tsang, serves as a conduit between the high plateaus of the Changtang and the low-lying valleys of the Tsangpo. On the trek, it is likely that a number of yak caravans carrying goods from the north to the big settlements of the south will be encountered from time to time. The trail along the middle and upper stretches of the Mu Valley goes through some stupendous gorge country; within the latter is a sacred cave called Phukchung Ramo, located on the Taphu Shelkar ridge. At the head of the Mu Chu is the high Chang-La-Pö-La pass that straddles the Tsangpo–Changtang Divide.

Before starting north up the Mu Chu Valley, the pilgrimage goes past Pindsoling and Jonang monasteries, both sited at the confluence of the Tsangpo and the Raga Tsangpo. The Jonang Kumbum, a renowned multi-chapel *chörten* of the country, has just been renovated. The surroundings of these seldom-visited monuments are memorable. The trail head is at Lhatse, a major stop on the Friendship Highway that links Nepal with Tibet. It is very convenient to just get off the bus and start trekking. The return journey from the lake is via Sommai Qu. Trucks from this small district office near the the southern tip of the lake go regularly to Sangsang on the Lhasa–Kailash highway.

This is a long trek. Because of the inhospitable nature of the region, it is important that it be undertaken at the most ideal time possible. This becomes less of a factor if you only want to explore the Mu Chu Valley, foregoing the crossing of the Chang-La-Pö-La and the trek around the lake (this in itself is a great itinerary). Otherwise, it is essential that you know what you are doing, have adequate experience in trekking in isolated areas, and are well equipped. The Changtang is one area in Tibet that demands the utmost respect from the traveler. It is wise to hire a Tibetan guide who knows the area of Lake Dangra well before venturing beyond the pass.

Related sections
Trans-Nyenchen Tanglha Valleys, p 847

Access

Lhatse (road marker 400 km; new marker 5051) on the Friendship Highway (see pages 868, 990).

Time Chart

Day	Place	Hours
1	Lhatse–Chaptrang	6
2	Pindsoling Monastery	6
3	Tangna	5
4	Lingo	6
5	Tong	8 1/2
6	Dhira	8 1/2
7	Kathing	4 1/2
8	Sapsee	4 1/2
9	Tagma Linka	4 1/2
10	Low	5
11	Camp A	-
12	Tserok	10 1/2
13	Chang-La-Pö-La	8
14	Pass crossing	9
15	Nomad tent	8 1/2
16	Sommai Qu	3
17–18	Targo Tsangpo	-
19–28	Lake Dangra	-
29–30	Sommai Qu	-

(Mark Salmon contributed to the trail notes.)

LHATSE TO LINKA MONASTERY

✦ DAY 1 LHATSE–CHAPTRANG 6 HR

From Lhatse walk east along the Friendship Highway to road marker 399 km (new marker 5050). Turn left (north) along a dirt track that goes through the fields of a very wide valley. On your right, near the entrance of the valley, is a ridge (4930 m) with some interesting-looking ruins on the top. Lhatse Chöde, the monastery sited within the large village of Lhatse Dzong, is reached in 1 1/2 hr (see also Shigatse to Lhatse Trek for more details of this region; page 847). At Lhatse Chöde (or Lhatse Dzong) two dirt roads go downstream on either side of the Tsangpo. (To follow the left bank, take the road that goes west over a bridge, go north and then northeast along the river.) Opt for the right (east) bank. Walk due north from Lhatse Chöde; then curve west around a 4710-m peak before heading northeast towards Pindsoling. Lhatse Chöde to Tremo is 2 1/2 hr on a flat dirt road. Chaptrang is a further 2 hr.

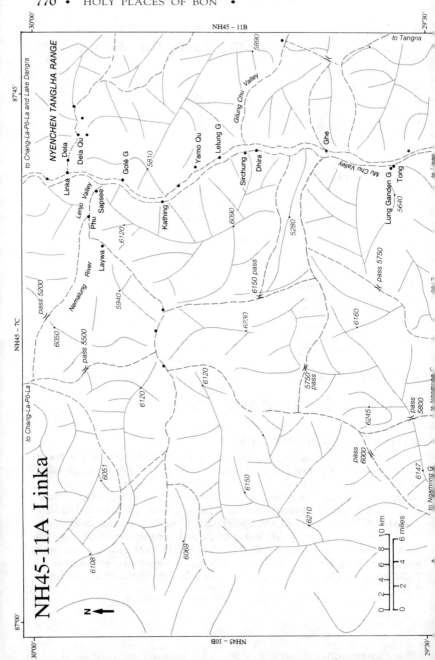

Optional treks

Yundre to Mu Chu Valley

Before Tremo, notice a side valley on the other side of the river with the village of Yundre at its entrance. A trail goes northwest along the valley to eventually reach the south bank of the Raga Tsangpo after crossing a 5400-m pass. At this point you can then turn right (east) and follow the south bank to the entrance of the Mu Chu. This provides an alternative route to the main pilgrimage, which goes via the Pindsoling Monastery.

Chaptrang to Thongmön

A big wide valley is on the right before the village of Chaptrang; a trail leads east to Momo Dzong on the Friendship Highway, via a 4800-m pass. From Momo, a dirt road goes north to Thongmön (see Shigatse to Lhatse Trek, page 852).

✤ DAY 2 CHAPTRANG–PINDSOLING MONASTERY 6 HR

Continue northeast and then east along the right bank of the Tsangpo. Quite a few villages are passed. They are sited at the entrances of small valleys that lead north to south up a 5000-m high range of mountains. One of these is Laisa (1 1/2 hr). 1 hr beyond is Pindsoling Qu, a dilapidated compound, on the right (1 hr); the main body of the settlement is left of the road. The junction of the Raga Tsangpo (the northerly river) and the Tsangpo is reached in a further 2 1/2 hr. Turn right (east) at this point along a very sandy track to the Pindsoling Village and monastery (1 hr; see page 863 for a description of the important monasteries of Pindsoling and Jonang). This segment of the walk, from Lhatse to the monastery, can be done in a four-wheel drive. The last part, from the junction on, is pretty difficult for motorized vehicles because of the large amount of sand on the road.

✤ DAY 3 PINDSOLING MONASTERY–TANGNA 5 HR

From Pindsoling Village, cross the new bridge to the north shore (next to the ancient *chaksam* [iron-chain] bridge which, since the turn of the century, had not been used). At this point, coracles can make the trip down to Shigatse in four or five days during spring. In the summer, the trip is faster, taking only two or three days. The latter is the preferred time to travel as there is less danger—the banks and rocks in the river bed are avoided. A village, Chaga (4012m), is here on the north shore of the Tsangpo. It is home to the official of Pindsoling. Across the river, the striking ruins of Pindsoling sit on the crest of a ridge that culminates in a peak called Mt Nagya. West of the ridge is the very large and prominent sand-dune, one of the most unforgettable landmarks in the area, known to the locals as Chiri. Upstream from Chaga, the Tsangpo goes through a very narrow passage called Chibuk and the track has to cross the small pass of Chikchung Chang via a gorge in the northwest. West of the pass, descend steeply to the valley floor, which at this point is over 1 km wide, and to the junction of the Raga and the Tsangpo rivers.

The trail leads west along the left (north) bank of the Raga, which in this area— from here west to its junction with the Mu Chu—is known as the Dok Chu. Walk past three short and insignificant valleys: Changra, Yangyang, and Dsho, all opening to the north. In summer, rain makes the path indistinct. There is no real difficulty though; just follow the river. The small village of Tangna, the fourth from Chaga, is 6 hr from Pindsoling. Quite a few ruins are seen on hilltops. A couple of short valleys open from here to the northeast. The trail to the west weaves along alluvial terraces cut by dry ravines.

> **Chulung Monastery** This is a picturesque 16th-C. monastery located 3 hr north of Tangna. There are supposed to be two Guru Rinpoche caves and some hot springs nearby. Just before it is a triple peak representing three sacred mountains, one of which looks like Mt Kailash.

❖ DAY 4 TANGNA–LINGO 6 HR

The path crosses ridges at Beruchang and Sibri above the wet valley bottom. Along this portion of the route the landscape is pretty dramatic. Large sand dunes are interspersed with granite slopes, and in between are grassy slopes and cultivated fields next to settlements. The Dok Chu as a rule keeps to the south side of its river valley, only occasionally touching the north. It is bounded by two ranges, one on either side of the river. The crests of the southern one are considerably closer than that of the north and thus its valleys are steeper.

About 3 hr from Tangna is the village of Machang, beautifully located at the base of steep cliffs on the northern side of the valley. There are some great granite blocks in the bottom of the valley. One in particular has its eastern side polished smooth by wind and sand, and the villagers have painted a tricolor design on it. From time to time, *mani* walls divide the track and rock paintings are seen. On the tops of flanking ridges are ruins of walls and towers, an indication that more people populated the area in the past. Lingo (4070 m), a village of ten houses at the entrance of the Mu Chu, is 3 hr from Machang. Here, the Dok Chu is divided into three or four branches, while the north–south Mu Chu is more placid. Lingo is a short distance below the confluence. The soil here is poor and the harvest is unreliable. In the summer, some of the villagers have to migrate north for 5–6 days with their herds in order to find better pastures.

❖ DAY 5 LINGO–TONG 8 1/2 HR

The route now turns north to enter the sacred Mu Chu Valley, and prayer flags, *mani* piles, and Buddhist rock-paintings are met with frequently. The environs, characterized by wonderful rock formations, are dotted with many caves. The rock carvings and paintings along the path are impressive—some images of divinities being as high as 5 m. The sacred Six Syllables ('Om Mani Padme Hum') are ubiquitous. Several of the mani walls are well over 100 m long. The valley is obviously an important pilgrimage route as well as one used frequently for trade; yak and mule caravans can occasionally be seen. However, it becomes more difficult for pack animals after Lingo; the stony path makes for tricky footing.

It is possible to go north up the Mu Chu Valley on both sides of the river (there used to be quite a few bridges). Near the entrance of the valley, the ruins of the nunnery of Gunda Tammo can be seen high up on a rocky terrace. Around Lingo, a colossal cone of round blocks of granite makes it difficult for animal traffic to pass. Villages to the north are Oktsangma, Chisu, Do, and Tagmura. At Tagmura, 5 hr from Lingo, the Mu Chu has spectacular terraces supporting villages high up on both sides. Tong (100 houses) and its neighboring Gelugpa monastery, the totally destroyed Lung Ganden, are both situated at quite a height above the floor of the Mu Chu Valley. There are numerous fields in the apparently fertile area and they support a multitude of smaller villages. A high peak called Takpoche, due west from here, has an altitude of 5640 m. Lung Ganden is sited at the southern foot of Mt Yayura, whereas the village is built on a terrace at the entrance of the side valley called Tongpuchen.

✤ DAY 6 TONG–DHIRA 8 1/2 HR

North of Tong, on the left (east) bank, are the villages of Sar, Lelung, and Ghe. (About 1 1/2 hr outside Tong is a totally destroyed nunnery.) Along the way are well-developed, striking fluvial terraces, some 30–40 m high, especially on the valley's western side. The comparatively large valley of Ghepu comes in from the east and at its mouth is the village of Ghe or Tsalada. At the head of the valley is the 5750-m pass known as Tsa La. (A well-defined path leads beyond the pass, down south to the Tsangpo at the village of Tangna, between Pindsoling and Lingo.) West of the Mu Chu at Ghe is another longish valley called Lingbopu (the village of Lingbo is at the entrance) and there is a 6000-m ridge in its background. A recently built road links this section of the Mu Chu (up to Yamo Qu, the district office of the valley) to the Raga Tsangpo. From the river it continues southwest to the main town of Ngamring, next to the Ngamring Lake. A 5800-m pass is crossed. From Yamo (see below) to Ngamring is 80 km.

The Mu Chu in these parts is at its fullest in August and becomes impossible to ford. North of Ghe, the river is noticeably more turbulent, although there are the occasional quiet stretches. Its water takes on a deep blue glacial look and the surroundings, hemmed in by 6000-m peaks, are spectacular. Villages at side valley entrances usually have barley and pea fields. From time to time, black nomad tents are seen—some of these come from or are on their way to West Tibet. Mani walls and mounds are common. The side valleys north of Ghe and coming in from the east are: Tangma, Rogam, Chepu, Shavo, Ship, and Gilung. The last is opposite the village of Sirchung. Tributaries opening along the west bank are: Tsasa, Sanakpu, Dhira, Tongbuk, and Tinga.

After Ghe, the gradient of the Mu Chu becomes steeper and there are more and more rapids. Dhira (Dera) is on the right bank of the Mu Chu and is a good spot for a rest, since it has some wonderfully warm hot springs which, however, are only operative in the summer (they dry up in the winter). South of Dhira, at the side valley of Shavo, cross by bridge over to the right bank and then continue north to Dhira.

✤ DAY 7 DHIRA–KATHING 4 1/2 HR

About 1 hr north of Dhira on the right bank is Tinga, where the Mu is crossed by a bridge. In order to visit the Lelung Monastery and then continue to the Linka Monastery, cross the river to its left at Tinga. However, the left bank path requires the crossing of a steep ridge that is unsuitable for pack animals and generally more strenuous. The other alternative is to cross at Tinga, go to Lelung, and then return to the right bank via the same bridge, then continue north to Kathing.

• Dhira–Tinga 1 hr
• Tinga–Sirchung 1/2 hr

- Sirchung–Lelung 2 3/4 hr
- Sirchung–Yamo Qu 1 1/2 hr
- Yamo Qu–Kathing 1 1/2 hr

Sirchung is a fairly large village where several routes and side valleys converge. The sizeable tributary called the Gilung Chu comes in from the east and a trail goes up to its head, crosses a 5750-m pass and then turns down south to the Raga Tsangpo at Tangna. An extension of this trail continues further to the east and then abruptly turns south down to the Thongmön Valley (see Lhatse Trek, page 852). The Lelung Monastery is a short way north of the village of Nesar.

> ### Lelung Monastery
> This Nyingmapa temple is completely destroyed except for a small chapel. A few monks have returned in recent years. It was a famous shrine in the area mainly because of the duel between the Bön magicians, Shen Nyima Gyaltsen and Mupa Agon, which took place here. A long line of *chörtens* extends down the gully from Lelung to the Mu River. The ruins, sited on a point of rock far up a side valley that descends from the left to the Mu Chu, are impressive. From here there is a tremendous view of the valley. The monastery was founded in the 15th C. by Muchen Kunchog Gyaltsen, a pupil of Kunga Zangpo, the founder of the famous Ngor Monastery (Sakyapa; see page 834) near Shigatse.

Around this stretch the vegetation becomes more alpine in character and the valley has a desolate wilder feel. From this point on it is necessary to use yaks as pack animals as the terrain is becoming too difficult for horses or mules. It is possible to hire yaks from Kathing, which at 4229 m is only 400 m higher than Shigatse.

✤ DAY 8 KATHING–SAPSEE 4 1/2 HR

The route now goes along a spectacular gorge seemingly hollowed out of the solid rock of fine-grained granite. This section probably has one of the finest landscapes anywhere in Tibet. The well-defined road, following the west bank and fairly high up above the river, skirts along the base of high rocky cliffs overlooking the aquamarine water rushing over large polished boulders scattered in the river. Two 6000-m peaks on either side towers over the river. Side valleys to the west reveal several snow-capped mountains.

Go past the Golé Nunnery situated on the east side of the gorge; 3 km beyond this is a major river junction, where the large tributary of Lenjo (also called Laywa) comes in to join the Mu Chu from the west. At least one third of the volume of the Mu is derived from the Lenjo. A trail follows the Lenjo to the west, then south to the Raga Tsangpo at Dekyiling, before continuing on to Lake Ngamring. A high 6000-m pass has to be crossed on this route. Sapsee is 1 hr walk up the side valley of Lenjo (the other villages further up are Phu and Laywa, also known as Mashung). From Kathing to the confluence of the Lenjo and Mu is 3 1/2 hr. There was a very solid bridge, consisting of three arches resting on four stone piers, crossing the Lenjo at the junction (marked by a prominent and very steep pinnacle) but this has been down since the early 1960s. As a result it is necessary to cross the tributary by a bridge past Sapsee, then walk back down the left bank of the Lenjo to the river junction. The path can be dangerous if the river is high. Continue north along the Mu Chu to the Linka Monastery. Because of the detour it is generally not possible to go from Kathing to Linka in one day. Kathing to Linka (excluding the diversion to Sapsee) is 16 km.

Short-cut to the Chang-La-Pö-La

Another trail goes from the upper reaches of the Lenjo or Laywa to the Chang-La-Pö-La. It goes up to the higher section of the valley to reach a river junction (the Nemalung comes in from the north). Follow it to the Chang-La-Pö-La. This route supposedly takes four days rather than six.

✤ DAY 9 SAPSEE–TAGMA LINKA 4 1/2 HR

From Sapsee, continue up the right bank of the Laywa to a bridge that spans the river (1 hr). Cross this to the other bank and then walk back down the river until a river junction is reached. This is the Nemalung confluence. Cross the tributary by another bridge and then descend the Lenjo along its left bank.

• Sapsee–bridge over the Lenjo–1 hr
• Bridge–the Mu-Lenjo junction–2 hr
• Junction–Linka–1 1/2 hr

Before Linka is a difficult stretch of track known as the Tigutang. Here, it ascends above solid rock at the right bank where the Mu Chu Valley has now contracted to a gorge. The schist cliffs fall 40 m to the river and, in parts, the track is made of slabs of schist lying on branches inserted into cracks along the face. Beyond this the gorge suddenly opens out into the very beautiful Linka or Tagma Linka Valley (4302 m). To the west, within a short valley, the spectacular Linka Monastery is sited on the uppermost ledge of a steep flight of terraces.

Linka Monastery

Despite wanton destruction, this monastery still gives the impression of an enchanting fairy castle. Marking the site is a line of six *chörtens* in various states of ruin; within these are thousands of *tsa-tsas*. The top sections of the *chörtens* are decorated with large terracotta tiles imprinted with various designs. Before the monastery are several long lines of *mani* walls. A small new chapel has now been rebuilt and several monks are in residence. The view from here is superb. It looks down across the Linka Valley and then up the Chang Valley to its confluence with the Mu in the north. At the juncture are the mountains around Donglung, the place where the Mu Chu turns to the west.

Linka Monastery was founded in the 15th C. by Muchen Kunchog Gyaltsen, the same lama who built Lelung further down. Above the monastery was the chapel

➠

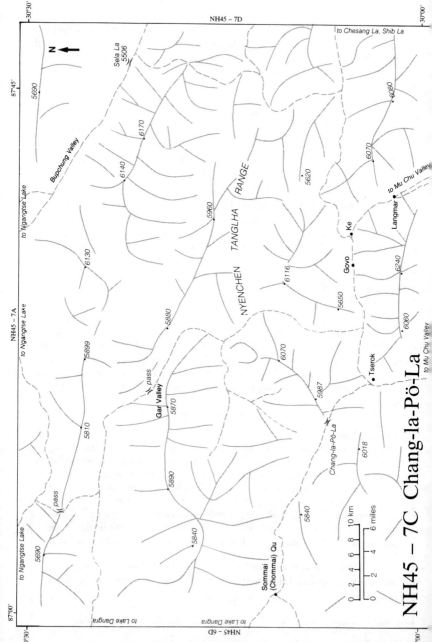

NH45 – 7C Chang-la-Pö-La

of Chori Gönkhang. In front of this was the Pesu Chapel, now completely destroyed, surrounded on three sides by a gallery. The hermitage of Linka, called Samde Phuk, is beyond Pesu. Situated on a small ridge between two side valleys it consisted of a *dukhang* and a couple of small chapels. Nearby was the windowless *drubkhang*, the meditation cell, made of very thick stone walls. In the past, when a monk went in here for extended retreats, the door was locked and walled over by stones. Food was delivered through a tiny tunnel. Within the small cell, a spring bubbled up in the center to provide drinking water.

North of the monastery is the village of Linka. There is another settlement across from the bridge that spans the Mu Chu, which in this point is about 20 m wide. An important river comes in from the east to join it at the Linka Valley. This is the Sha Chu, which in its higher reaches is called the Bup Chu—the greatest tributary of the Mu, with the possible exception of the Raga Tsangpo (also called the Dorzhung Tsangpo). Both the Mu Chu and the Sha Chu originate in the Pabla range. There is a good view of the Bup Chu from the Linka Monastery. In the background, due east, is the peak called Luchen, and along the river the villages of Tagmocha, Dela, and Linka Gyu can be seen. Between the two rivers is Linka.

An alternative trek to the Tsangpo East of the Mu Chu, near its confluence with the Sha, are the villages of Tagmocha and Dela. Dela Qu (formerly Chongda) is further upstream. From here, a trail goes along the Bup Chu to Chala Qu (here a trail goes southeast via the Chesang La to Thongmön Xian) and then to Chingdo (formerly Lajang). At this point, another trail leaves the Bup and turns south to Chabu, Namchi Qu, and Thongmön Xian, near the north shores of the Tsangpo (see page 852).

LINKA TO CHANG-LA-PÖ-LA

✦ DAY 10 LINKA–LOW 5 HR

From Linka, follow the right bank of the narrow Mu Chu Valley; it widens only at Takartang north of Linka. There is considerably less foot traffic here than in the lower parts. In 3 hr reach Langmar, at the entrance of the small side valley of Langma Phu. The Mu then makes an abrupt change in course. Instead of running north to south, it now flows from west to east, paralleling and quite near to the Nyenchen Tanglha watershed immediately to the north. Along the left bank of its upper reaches, the Mu receives its secondary sources of water directly from the great range itself. At the precise point where the Mu turns to the west, the Ke Tsangpo, the most important of all tributaries above the Bup Chu, comes in from the north. Ke is the name of the village at the junction. From here, an important trade route goes north to Thok Jalung, a famed gold depot of old. The mountains flanking the eastern side of the lower Ke Tsangpo are called Amirirung, while those of the west are the Namnam. According to the locals, the stretch of the Mu between Langmar and Govo, a village up the valley from Langmar, is known as the Langmar Tsangpo, formed by the Ke Tsangpo from the north and the Govo Tsangpo (the upper Mu) from the west. 1 1/2 hr from Langmar is Low, a village with barley fields up a side valley.

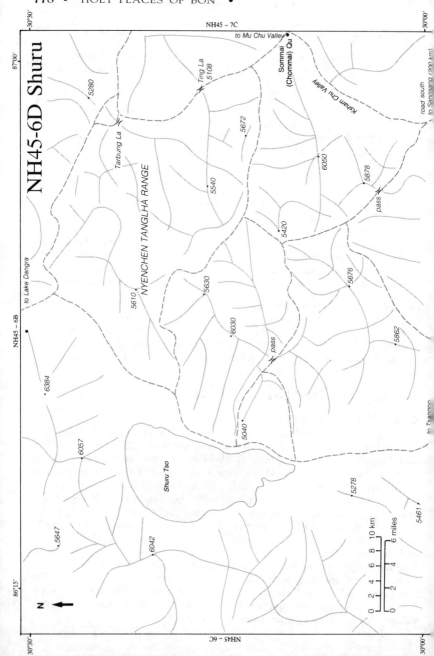

❖ Day 11 Low–Camp A

Low to Govo is 3 1/2 hr. Walk 2 1/2 hr from Low to the river junction of Mu and Gha. This is the point where you have to leave the Mu Chu behind by following the Gha. At the confluence, a bridge spans the latter. There are trails along both banks but the left, the wider and the better one, is blocked by a landslide—making it impassable for pack animals. The trail along the right bank is very stony but serviceable. From the bridge to Govo is 1 hr. The last villages of the upper reaches of the valley are progressively rougher. Govo consists of a few shambles of stone houses about 30 m above the bottom of the valley. Some barley is grown. The villagers, however, do not depend on the rather meager crop, since they own a substantial amount of sheep, goats and yaks, and in the summer they migrate northwards with them in search of pasture. Govo (4524 m), the last village on the way to the Chang-La-Pö-La, is also the last with cultivation. Black nomad tents replace the stone houses of further down, and there are quite a few herds of yaks and sheep grazing. Beyond Govo, the Mu, which has its source at the Chang-La-Pö-La, is known in the region as the Pashu Tsangpo. This main valley remains narrow and has terraces in several stories up to 50 m high. The rise is now steeper and the river forms rapids all the way. Several yak caravans are passed. Camp A is next to a large side river called Changlungi.

❖ Day 12 Camp A–Tserok 10 1/2 hrs

About 1 1/2 hr up the valley from camp A, reach the first large-sized valley coming in from the right (left bank). Ford the main river at a point just past where the side valley joins up. Walk up this side valley and then wade across to the other bank as well. This ford is impossible for a donkey as the water is at least 1 m deep. Yaks are necessary for this tricky crossing. The trail up the main valley is along the left bank. Follow this stony trail, with occasional tricky parts, for 3 hr. More wildlife—*kiang*, small deer and wild sheep—are visible around this region. The scenery is a combination of gorge country and snowy peaks. One of the challenges during the next 3-hr stretch is having to traverse an enormous landslide. At the end of this stretch the valley opens up and the river flows in a slow S-shaped bend. This is where it is necessary to ford over to the other side; the trail now follows the right bank. Tserok is a nomad camp with seven black tents that controls over 1,000 yaks and twice that many sheep and goats.

❖ Day 13 Tserok–Base of Chang-La-Pö-La 8 hr

Continue up the valley, passing hot springs and mineral formations that resemble steaming ant-hills. Follow the river closely, passing increasingly smaller tributary valleys. Eventually reach a large valley that looks like the head of the river. At the base of the mountains are some nomad tents just up on the left bank. The approach to the pass begins here.

Taphu Shelkar Drak This sacred mountain, near the base of the Chang-La-Pö-La, has a large grotto called Phukchung Ramo, which is entered by way of a small cave. The famous meditator, Sekar Tönpa, lived here.

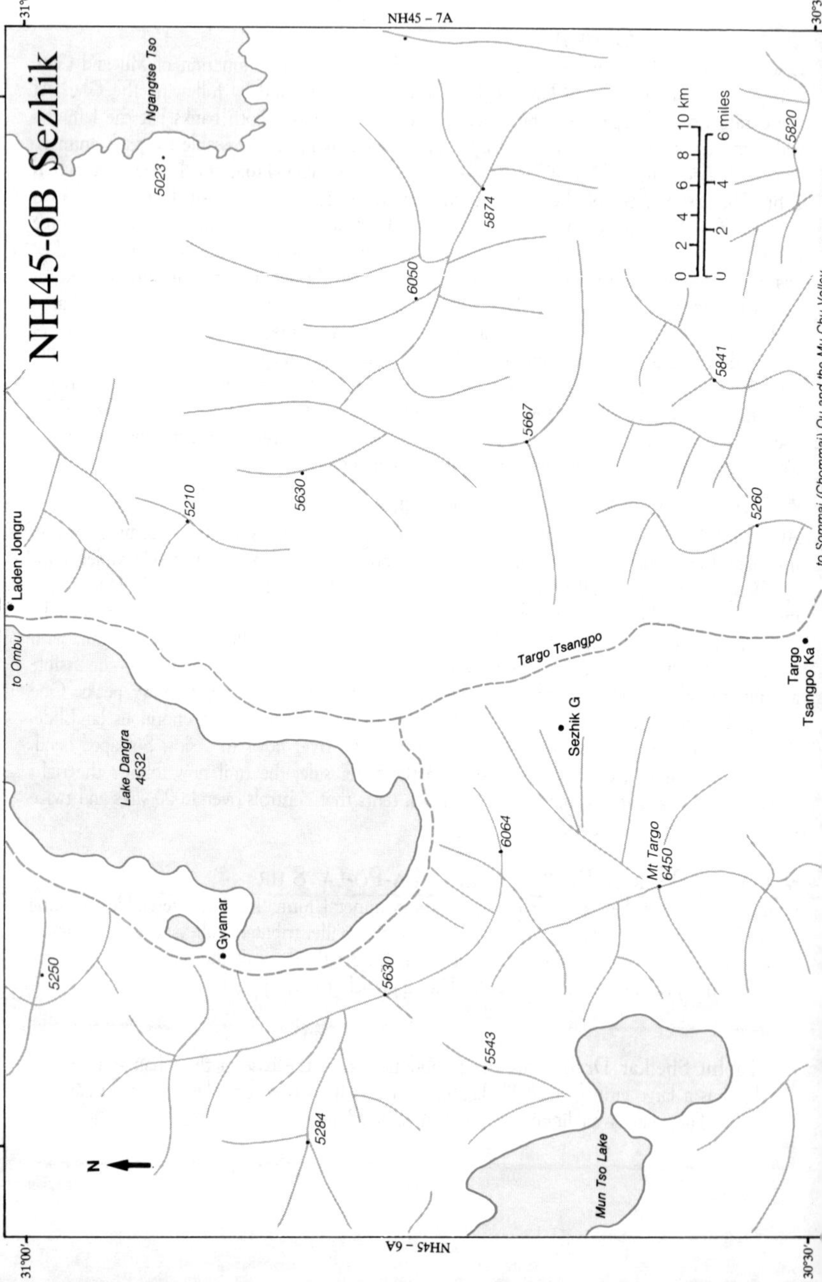

NH45 - 7A

NH45-6B Sezhik

NH45 - 2D

NH45 - 6A

31°00'

30°30'

87°00'

86°15'

Ngangtse Tso

5023

5874

6050

5667

5841

5260

5210

5630

Laden Jongru

to Ombu

Targo Tsangpo

Sezhik G

Lake Dangra
4532

Gyamar

6064

Mt Targo
6450

Targo
Tsangpo Ka

5250

5630

5543

5284

Mun Tso Lake

To Sormai (Chormai) Qu and the Mu Chu Valley

N

0   2   4   6   8   10 km

0   2   4   6 miles

5820

❖ DAY 14 CROSSING OF CHANG-LA-PÖ-LA 9 HRS

This is a long and tiring day. Follow the river for about 3 1/2 hr to where the valley divides. Take the left branch, which has no water. It is another 1 1/2 hr to the top of the pass. The ascent is steep and the snow and the strong wind make for difficult going. There is no distinct pass as such; the Chang-La-Pö-La (5572 m) is a flattish saddle (the watersheds in this high plateau area are all quite rounded rather than peaked). You have to continue up and across, all the time looking for a large pile of prayer flags. Directly northwest of the flags, descend comparatively steeply (much steeper than in the lower Mu Chu Valley) into a valley that eventually merges into the large Targo basin. The valley opens into a valley, the Shak Chu, which gradually becomes much broader to form a vast basin. The country is very open and the view stretches a long way. From the *lhatse* called Lapsen Tari the first view of the Mt Targo in the distance is seen. It is a dazzling snow peak, dominating the entire plateau. Flanking it are flat rounded mountains.

CHANG-LA-PÖ-LA TO THE TARGO TSANGPO

❖ DAY 15 NOMAD TENT 8 1/2 HR

Follow the valley and river to the Targo Tsangpo. Pass a valley mouth and continue into a new valley. The trail goes through a cross-mixture of topography: mountain gorges, caves and open plains. After 1 1/2 hr there is a settlement of permanent black tents at a large bend in the Targo Tsangpo.

❖ DAY 16 NOMAD TENT–SOMMAI QU 3 HRS

The river gets bigger and the trail improves. It is an easy walk to Sommai (or Chomai) Qu, the principal village of the region. A road from here heads back south to the main Lhasa–Kailash highway (see page 945). Fresh yaks to carry can also be procured here. It is necessary to negotiate an itinerary based on the complete circumambulation of the holy Lake Dangra, since any change of pack animals is difficult once there.

❖ DAYS 17–18 SOMMAI QU–CAMPSITE BELOW PASS–RIGHT BANK OF THE TARGO TSANGPO

From the Qu, follow the road and the river heading northwest towards Mt Targo. In order to cross the Ting La, before reaching the lake, leave the road and head up a well-trodden path below two ridges and look out for yak trains. The route to the pass lies within the right branch valley. It is advisable to camp just below the pass. It takes 1 1/2 hr to reach the top of the pass. There are spectacular views of Mt Targo and its many satellites. Head down towards a nomad encampment—two tents and a *mani* wall—on the valley bottom. Directly across the valley from the nomads, 2 km in the same direction as from the top of the pass, is a small side valley. It is discernible by the mixture of greenery and yellow sand-dunes. Head up this small valley to the top of the second pass, the Tarbung La. From here, another side valley runs down into the extensive Targo Valley and the Targo Tsangpo. Camp next to the river. The Targo Range, in all its majesty, rises up out of the valley bottom on the opposite bank.

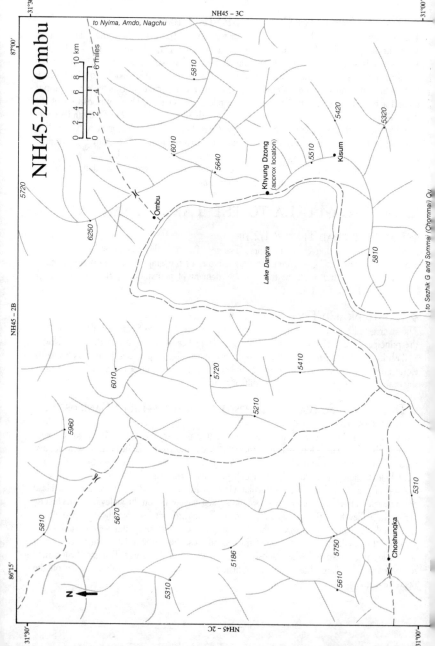

NH45 – 3C

NH45-2D Ombu

to Nyima, Amdo, Nagchu

10 km

6 miles

• 5810

• 5420

• 5320

• 6010

• 5640

• 5510

Kisum

Khyung Dzong
(approx location)

• Ombu

• 5720

• 6250

Lake Dangra

• 5810

to Sezhik G and Sommai (Chommai) Qu

NH45 – 2B

• 6010

• 5720

• 5410

• 5960

• 5210

• 5810

• 5670

• 5310

• 5186

• 5750

• 5610

Choshunqka

NH45 – 2C

N

31°30'

87°00'

31°15'

86°15'

31°30'

31°00'

31°00'

Targo and Dangra

The Mt Targo and Lake Dangra area is outstandingly beautiful. Sixteen peaks make up the Targo massif. To its south is the large lake of Shuru Tso and on the eastern flank of the range are five glaciers. The flat open valley of the Targo Tsangpo is to the east. Nyima Lung is the name of the area centered on Mt Targo; in the vicinity is the sacred Bönpo shrine of Sezhik Monastery (see page 785). The following are some principal places of pilgrimage with pre-Buddhist associations.

There is a sacred cave within the slopes of Targo called Zutrul Phuk, where the *mahasiddha*, Namkha Lodhen, spent time. Also in Targo is a pass called the Sakpa La. South of this was the famous hermitage of Targo Ganglung Ritrö. The *khora* around Mt Targo (6450 m) involves the crossing of one pass, the Barong (or Parung) La. Other sacred places in the region include Kyisum Labrang, which was the seat of the Shangshung Kyisum lineage; Dangra Yubun cave; Dangra Khyung Dzong (see below) with the ruins of the royal Shangshung palace, which was also a site where *terma* were hidden. Close to a small lake called Dangchung (the result of a mythical union between Targo and Dangra), further to the north, are a number of caves used by Bönpo recluses in early times. Later, these were taken over by the Nyingmapa. Buddhists also identify the Targo Dangra area as sacred. This is principally because of the exploits of Guru Rinpoche in the area.

THE CIRCUMAMBULATION OF LAKE DANGRA

✤ DAY 19 TARGO TSANGPO–CAMP A 8 HR

At the Targo Tsangpo there is a choice of routes. One is to cross the river if possible (not in late July and August) and go around the lake clockwise. The other is to circle the lake anti-clockwise, which is the Bönpo manner, and then cross the river after the circumambulation is completed. The latter course is preferable. Cut across to the right, away from the river towards the mountainous valley side. Dangra is very distantly visible but only once in a while. Camp near any of the scattered nomad sites where water and firewood are available.

✤ DAY 20 CAMP A–CAMP B 7 HR

Follow the eastern shores of the lake, crossing more arid steppes. There are plenty of *kiang* and other wildlife. After 4 hr reach the top of a ridge with wonderful views of the lake. The water (slightly salty, drinkable if necessary) is aquamarine blue and the shoreline sandy. Camp at a compound that is being rebuilt. In the late 1980s, an earthquake devastated the southern section of Dangra.

✤ DAY 21 CAMP B–CAMP C 8 HR

The terrain becomes more steep and the path keeps to the higher grounds above the lake. Pass a stone *chörten* and many prayer flags. Come down from the ridge to a small village where a Bönpo monastery is being rebuilt. This is the first cultivation seen since the upper reaches of the Mu Chu. Within the grounds of the monastery are 360 beautiful miniature Bönpo paintings on leather, probably of the 16th century. Four monks are here. Many vast gullies dissect the landscape from here until the main village of Ombu is reached.

❖ DAY 22 CAMP C–CAMP D 9 HR

This section, following the west to east part of the lake, is a tough one. A lot of steep ups and downs. It is nonetheless an exhilarating day with spectacular landscapes. The walk goes past the bottle-neck of the lake and there is a full view of the northern section. Camp D is at the village with cultivated fields in a side valley. There is a huge prayer flag in the middle of the field. The Tibetans here, long accustomed to isolation, are not the most friendly.

❖ DAY 23 CAMP D–CAMP E (KHYUNG DZONG) 7 1/2 HR

The route from the village follows the shores of the lake to the north. The topography of the region is still heavily dissected and there are plenty of strenuous ups and downs. After 3 1/2 hr come around the large corner of the lake to reach the beautiful, new Orgyan Monastery. There are about 20 monks in residence. The chapel is built around a huge cave, which is some 25 m deep and about 15 m high. Much of the interior—seats, drums, altar—is carved from the living rock. Shafts of sunlight came through the sacred grotto and the effect is biblical. The hand-print of Tönpa Shenrab, the Bön patriarch, is in the cave.

> **Orgyan Monastery**
> This Bönpo shrine was contemporaneous with Yungdrungling monastery (see page 763), and was founded by Mönlam Tenpa, one of the great *mahasiddhas*. In the area is another temple called the Kyisum Labrang; its founder was Lama Yungdrung Lhatse, a famous preceptor of Shangshung Nyen Gyü—a well-known tantric school of the Bönpos.

Further on, Khyung Dzong is located on top of a stunning outcrop of rock with a few nomad tents at the base. There are a couple of caves here and one Bönpo monk and a nun work to restore the shrine. Again, there is an amazing sense of spirituality in the area. Big cats are known and hunted in the area.

> **Khyung Dzong**
> This was the residence and castle of Limur Gyalpo, king of Shangshung, who supposedly ruled this part of Tibet from a very early time until the mid-7th C. Shangshung was an independent kingdom in West Tibet where the Bön religion had its pre-Buddhist roots. The Khyung Dzong ridge is where written treasures (*terma*) were hidden by two masters called Gyar Mi Nyiwo and Ma Tön Sizin. Also on this ridge are many *rangjung* prints, and *mantras*. A number of meditation caves are here. Included among these is a large cave with the hand-print of the Bönpo patriarch, Naro Bönchung. Khyung Dzong is one of the most important places of worship for Bönpo pilgrims in Tibet.

❖ DAY 24 CAMP E–OMBU–CAMP F 8 1/2 HR

Ombu (or Wompho), the main settlement of the lake, is reached by a good road that comes in from the east to the lake and then follows the shores anti-clockwise to the village. There is quite a bit of cultivation and a small monastery, consecrated to Guru Rinpoche, with three monks is here.

The Ombu Monastery

This small temple follows the tradition of Menri, the principal Bönpo institution of Tibet (page 765). In the vicinity is a cave hermitage called Yungdrung Lhatse, where many famous Bönpo masters stayed. Some distance north of Ombu is Ommo (or Wommo). To its north is a large sandy mountain with much pasture in the area. This place is known as Kakha Sermothang. One day away from here is Lake Dangchung, with a settlement and cave retreat called Mönlam Draktsa. Guru Rinpoche supposedly stayed here for some time.

Leave the road and the village behind to walk down to the lake. Continue for 2–3 hr to camp next to a small river that drains into the lake. Some *kiang* are about and there are wonderful sandy beaches.

✤ DAY 25 CAMP F–CAMP G 7 HR

Head west along the lake shore, generally following the road. The scenery is less spectacular than earlier. Camp next to some nomads at the mouth of a gully with fresh water. The northern tip of the lake is rounded and the route now heads in a southerly direction.

✤ DAY 26 CAMP G–CAMP H 9 HR

Walk up a 1000-m ridge in order to negotiate the bottle-neck of the lake. Keep to the road and pass a small freshwater lake halfway into the hike. Reach an area with quite a few nomad tents next to a river. There is also a village nearby. The road in these parts veers off to the west and leaves the lake; do not follow it.

✤ DAY 27 CAMP H–CAMP I 9 1/2 HR

This long walk is compensated by dramatic scenery and wildlife. There are herds of *kiang* galloping close by. Pass through a dried lake bottom with weird lunar-like land formations. Continue along the southwest shoulder of the lake. This region turns mountainous again and the route cuts through hilly, lateral valleys debouching into the lake from the west.

✤ DAY 28 CAMP I–SEZHIK MONASTERY 8 1/2 HR

The trail, after heading to the west up a ridge, now leaves the lake 1-hr's walk out of camp I. There is very little water in this stretch until Sezhik Monastery is reached. Locate a stream after crossing the fourth ridge. Mt Targo is seen again and so is the Sezhik monastery situated at the far side of the fluvial fan at the base of the mountain.

Sezhik Monastery

The 40 monks in residence here assert that this Bönpo monastery is the fifth most important in Tibet and contemporaneous with Menri (page 765), the premier Bön institution. Sezhik, constructed of stones and timber that came all the way from the ➡

Shang Valley (northeast of Shigatse), was traditionally supported by the nomads of the area. Most of the complex was destroyed and then restored in recent years. There are many retreat caves but no murals have survived. The ruins are impressive. It is said that there is another sacred lake with caves consecrated by Milarepa about 4 1/2 hr from Sezhik. To go, continue south to the base of the mountain and then turn north to below the fifth satellite of Targo. It is not easy to find; best take a guide along.

✤ Day 29–30 Sezhik Monastery–Sommai Qu

From Sezhik head back towards the Targo River, about a 2-hr walk across a flat plain. At the river, ask the local nomads for the best place to cross, since it varies according to the time of the year. Once back on the other side, retrace your route of Days 17–18. At the end of these two days, the district headquarters of Sommai Qu is regained.

Sommai Qu to Sangsang

Here there are trucks leaving roughly twice a week for Sangsang and Nebrang on the main Lhasa–Kailash highway. It is a 12-hr ride to Nebrang and it costs Rmb 20 per person. Sommai Qu to Sangsang is 200 km.

THE TIBET–SIKKIM HIMALAYAS

The remote Tibet–Sikkim divide has at its heart Chörten Nyima. This celebrated site is consecrated to Guru Rinpoche, that most powerful of Buddhist masters. The hermitage, which is virtually unknown to modern travelers, is claimed to be the gateway to Dremojong Beyul, a first-ranked 'hidden valley'. Today, pilgrims from all over the country make the long, arduous journey to pay homage to this potent site. Further to the west, the charming Chumbi Valley forms part of the traditional trade route between Tibet and Sikkim. Heading south from Gyantse to Yatung, several noteworthy Buddhist and Bönpo monasteries are encountered. Among them is Yemar, where fabulous statues created in the rare Central Asian style have survived.

CHUMBI VALLEY: THE TIBET–SIKKIM CARAVAN ROUTE

OVERVIEW

This chapter describes the old caravan route that goes from Gyantse south to Yatung on the Tibet–Sikkim border via the beautiful Chumbi Valley. Today, a good dirt road links the two towns. The first section of the route traverses a typical Tibetan plateau landscape. After strategic Phari Dzong, the scenery changes abruptly as the road descends into a lush Himalayan valley. Because of its low altitude, parts of the Chumbi Valley bring to mind the lower reaches of the Kyirong (see page 924) and Lapchi valleys (see page 248), both of which border Nepal. The itinerary ends at Yatung (2865 m), one of the country's lowest towns.

South of Gyantse, the Tibet–Sikkim road follows the Ralung and Tumbayung river valleys, where a number of side valleys open to the east and west. One leads to the Changpo Plain, a large open valley

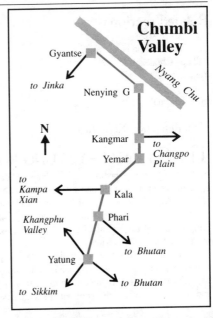

Chumbi Valley

Gyantse

to Jinka

Nenying G

Nyang Chu

N

Kangmar

to Changpo Plain

Yemar

to Kampa Xian

Kala

Khangphu Valley

Phari

Yatung

to Bhutan

to Bhutan

to Sikkim

within which drains the Gyantse River. A trail from here gives access to the seldom-visited Lake Phurma (see page 606). At road marker 315 km is the deserted monastery of Yemar (Iwang) (see page 390) with rare Central Asian-Pala statues. This small chapel is among the most important sites in Central Tibet for the study of early Tibetan art.

After the Gala checkpost, the road passes lakes Gala and Dochen to begin its imperceptible ascent to the main Himalayan watershed at the Tang La. This pass has good views of Mt Chomolhari (7314 m), straddling the Tibet–Bhutan border. Phari Dzong, one of Tibet's highest towns (4350 m), is next. It controls access to neighbouring Bhutan and has a number of sacred sites and holy mountains. This part of the valley is also known for its Bönpo settlements, some of the last in Central Tibet.

West of Chumbi is the delightful Khangphu Valley, known for its medicinal hot springs near Khangphu Monastery. Side valleys lead west to the Dongkya range, the watershed separating Sikkim from Tibet. Khangphu is an exciting place to explore; few outsiders have been here since the Younghusband Expedition of 1904. Its many side valleys provide fascinating trekking possibilities. Lower Chumbi is home to memorable villages such as Galinka and Dongkar. The latter, main seat of the Dongkar Oracle, hosted the Dalai Lama during his flight to India in 1950. Yatung Xian, the main town of lower Chumbi, stands near the border crossings to Bhutan and Sikkim.

Note As a result of India's more liberalized policies (as of 1992), there is much talk in Sikkim about reviving the ancient trade route that connects it to Tibet. One plan envisions tourists travelling from Gangtok (capital of Sikkim) north to Gyantse and Lhasa via the easy Jelep La (4386 m).

Related sections
Gyantse, p 412
The Gyantse Kumbum, p 447
Palkhor Chöde, p 419
Yemar, p 390
Jinka, p 327
Lake Phurma, p 606

Map Reference NH45-16 B D, NG45-4

THE GYANTSE–YATUNG ROAD

In 1904, a British expedition led by Francis Younghusband entered Tibet from Sikkim to open the country to trade and establish a British presence. This small army fought a series of battles with the Tibetans in the Chumbi Valley and in Gyantse before advancing in triumph to Lhasa. The Gyantse–Yatung road generally follows the expedition route. Logging trucks bring lumber up to Central Tibet and daily necessities from depots around Lhasa are in turn moved to the border regions.

Because of the Chumbi Valley's strategic position close to India, the Chinese have a checkpost at the village of Gala, 94 km south of Gyantse. Only vehicles and passengers with frontier permits can proceed. In the past, a handful of travelers bluffed their way through, and others—not wishing to confront the authorities—simply made easy detours around Gala.

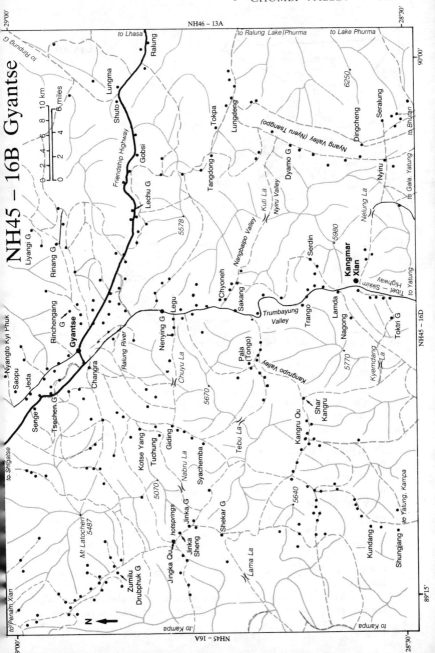

NH45 – 16B Gyantse

NH46 – 13A

to Lhasa
to Ralung Lake/Phurma
to Lake Phurma
to Rinpung G
to Bhutan
to Gala. Yatung
to Yatung
to Shigatse
to Yatung, Kampa
to Kampa
to Kampa
to Penam Xian

Ralung
Lungma
Shuto
Gobsi
Lechu G
Liyangi G
Rinang G
Nyangto Kyi Phuk
Rinchengang G
Gyantse
Saopu
Jeda
Senge
Tsechen G
Changra
Ralung River
Nenying G
Legu
Chuyu La
Chyoneh
Sakang
Trumbayung Valley
Trango
Pala (Tongo)
Nangbaipo Valley
Kuti La
Nyiru Valley
Tangdong
Tokpa
Lungdeng
Dyamo G
Nyang Valley (Nyeru Tsangpo)
Dingcheng
Seralung
Nyiru
Nelung La
Serdin
Kangmar Xian
Tibet – Sikkim Highway
Lamda
Nagong
Toktri G
Kyemdang La
Kangrupo Valley
Shar Kangru
Kangru Qu
Tebu La
Nabru La
Giding
Syachemba
Jinka G
Shekar G
Kotse Yang
Tuchung
Jingka Qu hotsprings
Jinka Sheng
Zumilu
Drubphuk G
Mt Latocheri
Lama La
Kundang
Shungjiang

Friendship Highway

5578
6250
5980
5770
5670
5070
5640
5487
5070

N

NH45 – 16A
NH45 – 16D

29°00'
28°30'
89°00'
89°15'

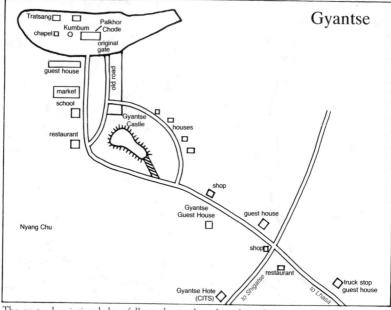

Gyantse

Tratsang
Kumbum
chapel
Palkhor Chode
original gate
old road
guest house
market
school
restaurant
Gyantse Castle
houses
shop
Gyantse Guest House
guest house
Nyang Chu
shop
restaurant
to Shigatse
to Lhasa
truck stop guest house
Gyantse Hotel (CITS)

The route description below follows the road markers from Gyantse to Yatung.

255   From the center of Gyantse (3927 m), walk 1 km west past the tourist hotel to the main highway junction (road marker 255 km). The right branch goes to Shigatse, the left south to the Chumbi Valley and Yatung along the west bank of the Ralung Chu, a tributary of the Gyantse (Nyang) River.

265   Nenying Monastery

Nenying Monastery

Founded by the Samye monk Jampal Sangba in the 11th or 12th C., Nenying was one of the oldest and most respected monasteries of Tsang, an important center for the Nyingmapas. It was taken over by the Gelugpa in the 17th C. and headed by Dorje Phagmo, the female incarnate residing at Samding Monastery (see page 590) on the shores of Yamdrok Tso. Even then, both monastic traditions were followed. A rarity among Tibetan institutions, Nenying remained open to many different schools of teaching. For this reason it became known as the Bodh Gaya of Tibet and given the epithet 'Dorjedan' (Tibetan for Bodh Gaya). Nenying is in good shape and quite active today. One of its chapels has early paintings executed in the rare Pala style (see page 51).

    The complex of several chapels and residences is surrounded by massive walls that were partly destroyed during the British Expedition of 1904. Nenying saw heavy fighting then and was nearly destroyed—the main chapel was rebuilt subsequently. The hermitage of Lungtang Kung is nearby and meditation cells can be found at another site called Kyigo, 1 hr from Nenying.

The site
From the main Gyantse–Yatung highway (at road marker 265), a dirt track on the right leads through Nenying Village to the old walls. The complex's entrance is to the side. Pass a courtyard to enter the rebuilt monastery, which contains a statue of Tsong Khapa. North of the main building is a dilapidated chapel, perhaps the sole remaining structure left over from the 11th–12th centuries. Within are ancient bare columns and walls with faded 14th–15th-C. paintings that exhibit a distinct Pala influence. These rare paintings are similar to those discovered at the Gyantse castle (see page 418). West of the monastery complex is Nenying's meditation retreat (1/2-hr walk). On the plain southwest of Nenying are the red walls of a ruined monastery.

269   A side valley on the right leads over the Chuyu La to Giding. The main road now enters the so-called Red Idol Gorge, named for rock carvings further south.

282   The Nangbaipo Chu flows from east to west to join the main Ralung Chu at this point. A trail on the right bank of the latter, starting from Choneh, goes east over the Kuti La and descends into the Nyang Chu Valley. From here a trail continues east to Pomo (Phurma) Tso Lake and then to the fascinating Lhodrak district (see page 681). Another goes south along the Changpo Plain while a third follows the Nyang Chu north and northwest to Gyantse.

284   Sakang Qu, a small village on the left. On the left before Sakang are colored rock carvings under a cliff, across from the river.

285   Bridge. The road now follows the east bank of the river, known in these part as the Tumbayung Chu. Instead of crossing the bridge, it is possible to follow a major side valley southwestward along the left bank of the Kangrupo Chu to Tongo, Kangru Qu, and Kundang. This route bypasses the checkpost at Gala by skirting the Gala and Dochen (Bam) lakes. It then rejoins the Kalimpong–Yatung–Gyantse road at Dochen.

301   Lamda is on the west bank of the Tumbayung. A trail follows a side valley to the southwest and then north to join the Kangrupo Chu Valley at Shar Kangru.

303   Kangmar Xian, a small town with an administrative compound, has jurisdiction over the district to the south, up to the northern limits of the Chumbi Valley proper. Situated near the entrance of a side valley, it is not visible from the main road. The government offices of the *xian* and a Public Security Bureau are located here. A jeep track goes east up the side valley and crosses the Nelung La

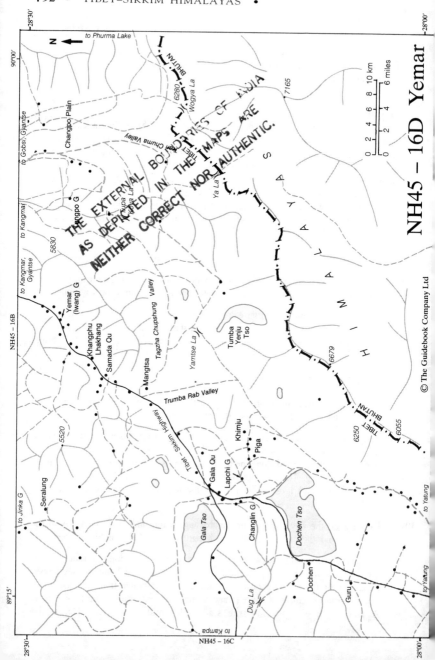

NH45 – 16D Yemar

© The Guidebook Company Ltd

to Phurma Lake

N

BHUTAN

6280

Wogya La

Changpo Plain

to Gobsi, Gyantse

Tibet Chuma Valley

Kari Chuma Valley

7165

THE EXTERNAL BOUNDARIES OF INDIA AS DEPICTED IN THESE MAPS ARE NEITHER CORRECT NOR AUTHENTIC.

to Kangmar

Chupa La

Thangpa La

Thangpo G

Ya La

HIMALAYAS

5830

to Kangmar, Gyantse

Yemar (Iwang) G

Khangphu Lhakhang

Samada Qu

Tagzha Chupshung Valley

Yamtse La

Tumba Yenju Tso

6679

NH45 – 16B

Mangtsa

Trumba Rab Valley

TIBET

BHUTAN

6250

6055

5520

Tibet–Sikkim Highway

Gala Qu

Lapchi G

Khimju

Piga

to Jinka G

Seralung

Gala Tso

Changlin G

Dochen Tso

to Yatung

Dug La

Dochen

Guru

to Yatung

to Kampa

28°30'

28°00'

90°00'

89°15'

NH45 – 16C

0 2 4 6 8 10 km
0 2 4 6 miles

(4755 m) to Nyiru on the Changpo Plain. It then continues east to the Pomo (Phurma) Tso. From Kangmar to Jida near the lake is 59 km.

312   Bridge. The road crosses to the west bank of the Tumbayung.

315   Yemar (Iwang), an important though deserted monastery, stands about 200 m on the right up a gentle incline. It is easy to miss from the road, being only a dilapidated, reddish building. Yemar's monumental statues, unique art treasures of Tibet, should not be missed (see page 390).

323   Samada Qu contains the ruins of Kyangphu Monastery. Riku Monastery lies about 2 km inside the Samada Valley, which trends to the west.

330   From here, a motorable track heads east for 19 km to Sermar along the Tagzha Chupshung Valley. At the valley entrance is the village of Mangtsa. The main road now begins to enter the large Gala Plain, leaving the Tumbayung Valley. At this point, the Tumbayung Chu receives two tributaries, Tagzha Chupshung from the east, and Trumba Rab Chu from the southeast. The road follows the main river.

347   Gala checkpost and village. West of the village is the brackish Gala Tso. The Kalimpong–Yatung–Lhasa highway squeezes into a bottleneck that is the checkpost. All traffic must stop and special frontier passes shown. One way to avoid the checkpost is simply to head towards the lake before the checkpost, then circle back to the main road at a point further south. At Gala a branch road splits from the main road to go southwest to Jangmu, Tratsang Monastery (via the 4942 m Lingdrub La), and Kampa Xian (see page 840). Gala to Kampa Xian is 110 km.

351   Chalu Village. A trail goes east via Lapchi Monastery (a branch of sacred Lapchi Monastery near Mt Everest, see page 265) to the Changpo Plain. The southern portion of the Changpo Plain forms the Tibet–Bhutan border. The road now skirts the north and west portions of the large, dry Dochen (Bam) Tso to reach Dochen, Guru (battleground during the 1904 Younghusband Expedition), and Tuna.

366   Dochen. A trail from this lakeside village goes northwest to Jangmu via the Dug La.

373   Turnoff to Guru, 1 km west of the main road.

387   Tuna Qu (4488 m), a site along Younghusband's route to Lhasa. A trail leads west to Maling. After Tuna is the flat Tang Pun Sum Plain.

395   Drakang. A motorable track goes west to Chi *daoban* (road maintenance compound No.7, 13 km), Chago La (24 km), Tratsang Monastery (25 km), and Kampa Xian (32 km). Another goes northeast along the Bhutan border to the Changpo Plain and Pomo Tso.

402   Tang La (4639 m), a gentle and scarcely perceptible pass, marks a main Himalayan watershed. The glacial peaks of Chomolhari (7314 m) rise to the east, only 8 km away. To the west are the snow peaks of Pawhunri (7065m) in Sikkim's northeastern

Phari

Phari, or Pig Hill, takes its name from nearby Phari Chökhor Lung, a mountain resembling a pig. The town, located at 4360 m, is one of the highest in the world. Winter is severe with temperatures reaching –30° C. Mt Chomolhari towers over the settlement, which is always cold and windy; crops have a difficult time here. Phari, strategically placed, commands the trails to Bhutan and Sikkim. The Bhutan border, at Tremo La, is only 7 km away to the southeast. (A trail leads from Phari into the Dukye Dzong and Paro areas of Bhutan via the Tremo La.) To the west is the Pawhunri range. Kanchenjunga and the lesser peaks of Siniolchum, Kabru, and Jonsong are further south. The important sacred places around Phari are:

Holy mountains
- Chomolhari (east of Phari)
- Kyoklung (northwest of Phari)
- Jowo Kyungdu
- Jowo Monbo (south of Phari)

Monasteries
- Korleb
- Samdrup Chöling
- Drathok Gang
- Richung Pathok
- Ngachen
- Ngachung
- Chatse Monastery, now restored with 30 monks, is 3 km north of Phari. The 13th Dalai Lama stayed here during his flight from the Chinese in 1910.

Guru Rinpoche's retreat
Taktsang Pephung (south of Phari near the Bhutan–Tibet border)

corner. A short distance west of the Tang La is the Kyaring La. A trail from here leads northwest to Tratsang Monastery and Kampa Dzong. The descent from the Tang La along the beginning of the Chumbi (Tromo) Valley to Phari Dzong is easy.

417   Phari Dzong (Phari Qu, 4360 m) is a small market town with Tibetan houses on one side of the road and Chinese mud compounds on the other. Beyond the market is the truckstop where a bed costs Rmb 1.5.

(For a continuation of the Gyantse–Yatung road, see page 798)

Khangphu Valley

Two routes go from Phari to Yatung. One is via the Chumbi Valley along the Gyantse–Yatung road. The other follows the Khangphu Valley, west of and parallel to Chumbi. A number of roads and trails lead from Phari to the Khangphu. The two most important are:

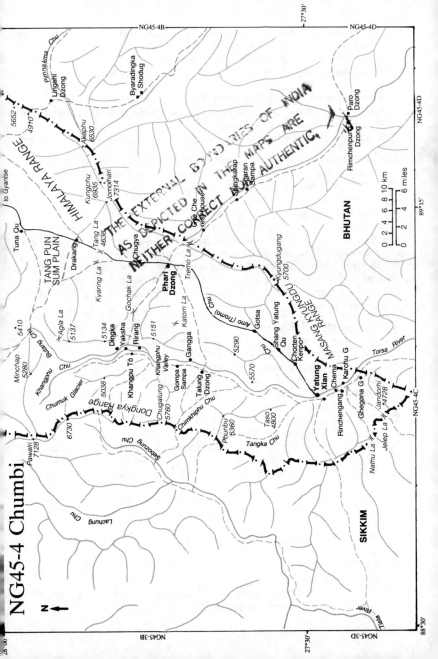

NG45-4 Chumbi

THE EXTERNAL BOUNDARIES OF INDIA AS DEPICTED IN THE MAPS ARE NEITHER CORRECT NOR AUTHENTIC.

1. Phari–Dingka (26 km) via the Gochak La on a motorable road. Close to Dingka are the villages of Yaksha and Larang, Khangphu Monastery and its hot springs. A few km south is Khangphu Tö Village (formerly Tawa Dzong).
2. Phari–Talung Dzong via a foot trail. Talung Dzong is 16 km south of Dingka.

Two optional, motorable routes begin from Dingka.
1. North to Kampa Dzong (see page 840) via Qi Daoban (26 km), Chago La (24 km), Tratsang (25 km), and Kampa Dzong (32 km).
2. South along the Khangphu Valley to Yatung (44 km). This is a lovely, two-day walk.

Khangphu is a beautiful valley hemmed in to the west by lush forests and the Dongkya Mountains of the Tibet–Sikkim border. Many tributaries flow east from the Dongkya into the Khangphu Chu, which drains into the Torsa of Bhutan (together with the Amo and Tangka rivers). These tributaries and the foot trails along them serve as lines of access to Sikkim. One such trail leads west from Talung Dzong via the Gaba La (4700 m). After crossing the pass, it follows the upper effluent of the Chimkhiphu Chu into Sikkim. Another, further south, starts from the junction of the Tangka and Khangphu rivers. It heads northwest along the Tangka into the Dongkya Mountains. Settlements and monasteries (eg Sampa and Khangphu) dot the Khangphu Valley. The Upper Khangphu is especially pleasant, with glacial springs and abundant medicinal plants. Hot springs near Khangphu Monastery and Dingka are said to be formed of five kinds of medicinal waters flowing from the rocks. There are 12 pools used to cure 440 diseases!

The hot springs of Khangphu

According to an old lama, the 12 springs of Khangphu each have specific curative powers.
1) The Lhamo Spring (Spring of the Goddess) can purge all sins.
2) The Chagu Spring (Spring of the Vulture) is good for women's diseases, sores, gout and fractures. Particularly effective for diseases below the waist.
3,4) The Pön Spring (Spring of the Official) is said to benefit hemorrhoids, kidney diseases and rheumatism.
5) The Dragye Spring (Spring Born of the Rock) helps the arteries and solves nerve problems. It is a tonic for blood and bile.
6) The Serka Spring (Spring of the Crevice) cures bile, nervous problems, and acidity. This is the place to go for chapped hands and feet, and diseases of the kidney and bladder. Do not soak here if you suffer from headache (arising from nervous catarrh) or if you have impurities of the blood.
7) The Thang Spring (Spring of the Plain) cures hemorrhoids, kidney diseases, rheumatism and venereal disease. Warning: too much use of this spring might cause the waist to bend like a bow.
8) The Dragyab Spring (Spring Behind the Rock) is beneficial to diseases of the arteries and helps anaemia.
9) The Tongbu Spring (Spring of the Hole) is good for white phlegm, brown phlegm and other phlegmatic diseases.
10) The Nub Spring (Western Spring) is good for liver diseases, blood impurities, kidney troubles, dyspepsia, brown phlegm, tumors, gout, rheumatism, gleet, flatulence and flatfoot.

11) The Dzepo Spring (Leper's Spring), counterpart of the Nub, can help cure hemorrhoids, gout, rheumatism and diseases of the feet. It is especially good for leprosy, sores and wounds.

12) The Lama Spring is a tonic for lung diseases, tumors, dyspepsia (both chronic and recent), poverty of the blood and venereal disease.

Chumbi Valley

This thumb-like protrusion of south Tibet inserts into the small gap between Sikkim and Bhutan. The British expedition of 1904 entered Tibet here, fought its way to Lhasa, and forced an agreement on the Tibetans whereby the British opened a trade center at Gyantse and received a financial indemnity from the Lhasa government. The Chumbi Valley remained in British hands until receipt of the payment and Charles Bell administered the district for the first 14 months of occupation.

Chumbi's vegetation is subtropical and lush; most of the valley lies below 3000 m. Yatung, the main town, has jurisdiction over the valley and controls trade between Tibet, Sikkim, and Bhutan. A juncture at Yatung divides the Chumbi Valley into two parts: Upper (including Phari) and Lower Tromo (Tromé). The Amo (Tromo) Chu drains the valley, then continues southeast through Bhutan to eventually join the Brahmaputra on the Bengal plains. Wondrously prosperous, the region's fertile land yields substantial quantities of barley, wheat, buckwheat, and potatoes. The wife of David MacDonald, British Trade Agent in Yatung, introduced the latter in the early 1900s. Upper Chumbi is much drier than Lower Tromo and the inhabitants depend on yak husbandry as a living. Most houses in the lower reaches are two storys of wood and stones with sloping roofs. They resemble Tirolese houses except for the elaborate, brightly painted wood carvings over the doors and windows. The houses are surprisingly big compared with those in other parts of Tibet. Lower Chumbi is rich in conifer forests and flowers, especially large bushes of wild roses that give the valley its lovely scent. Wild strawberries also abound.

North of Galinka and Lingma is the flat, open Lingmathang Plain, a terrace where the Amo Chu meanders slowly through several km of lovely meadows. Here is beautiful Dongkar Monastery, built on a spur overlooking the entrance to the plain. The Chumbi Valley narrows again to the north and dense conifer forests and birch line the valley. Near Phari the vegetation decreases dramatically. Gorges leading south from Phari to the Chumbi are home to varied game—monal, blood and tragopan pheasants, snipe, rock pigeon, and snowcock. Bears roam above Lingmathang and Yatung. Lower Chumbi's climate is quite temperate and rather similar to that of England, except that there is less rain and the winter is colder.

Bönpo communities of Chumbi

The Chumbi Valley has one of the last strongholds of Bön in Tibet. Four Bönpo monasteries are in Upper Tromo (Trotö), one of the sect's most significant enclaves. They are Sharmang, Nubmang, Dra Lhakhang, and Yungdrung Gönsar (now a Gelugpa institution called Tashi Chöling; the conversion occurred early this century). The first two are situated in Pungmo Ga, one of Trotö's four districts. A strong link existed between these monasteries and the main Bön centers of Yungdrungling, Menri, and Kharna, all near Shigatse (see page 763). Bönpos and Buddhists lived amicably in the valley until 1918, when a Gelugpa lama came to the area to convert the Bönpos. Within a short space of time, over 100 households went over to the Gelugpa.

In Upper Tromo, near Phari Dzong, is an area called Zhulung. The Tibetan government granted this land to a Bönpo lama named Zhu Namgyal Dragpa in recognition of his service during the building of the *dzong*. Before his appearance, each day's construction was mysteriously torn down at night. High lamas from all Buddhist sects performed rituals to prevent these bizarre, nightly incidents—all to no avail. Finally, the Buddhists asked Zhu to help. He determined that a demoness was the cause of the problem and subsequently converted her into a benevolent spirit, named Chomolhari. Her residence is the high mountain of the same name. As a reward, the lama received the land of Zhulung. Every three years a Bönpo monk performed propitiatory rites in Phari to the protectress. Three small Bönpo monasteries once stood in the area: Zhulung, Lhari Nyiphuk, and Khyungpa Gön.

451 Lingma (Shang Yatung). The first 14 km out of Phari are flat. Then the road descends into the gorge-like Chumbi Valley where, in dramatic contrast to the Phari

Yatung

Locals call this place Shasima and road signs in the area often use this name. The *xian*-level government offices are located in the north end of town and the Public Security Bureau is in a separate building towards the southern end, near the bridge. Yatung, center for all of Chumbi, is responsible for trade and security with Sikkim and Bhutan. It has a large, benign military presence. Travel across the Tibet–Sikkim border passes is strictly controlled. Determined traders, however, will find most of the border regions between Tibet, Bhutan, and Sikkim quite porous; it is easy enough to slip through by avoiding the main checkposts. Yatung has several truckstops with accommodation. Logging trucks from time to time travel the road

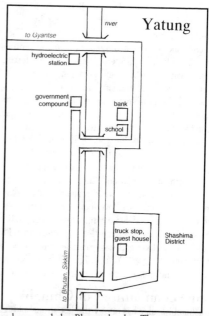

from Yatung to Rinchengang, Shingshang, and the Bhutan border. The main guest house in Yatung (Rmb 2 per bed in a 5-bed room on the second floor) is in a truckstop near the crossroad in the town's center. A tea house and kitchen here serve good fare: mutton, momos, vegetable dishes, and plenty of sweet milk tea. There is even the possibility of a shower, in a building across the street. The atmosphere is friendly. In fact, most of Yatung's people are very pleasant. Shops line the street near the post office and sell the usual assortment of tinned goods, sweets, and utensils.

area, a profusion of flowers and plants appear. The road follows the Amo (Tromo) Chu through conifers. Lingma Village has a few shops, including a small department store. The small, beautiful village of Galinka lies just beyond. Galinka Monastery (destroyed) is here as well as Dongkar Monastery, perched dramatically on a spur, home of the Chumbi Oracle. The present Dalai Lama stayed at Dongkar in 1950 during his flight from the Chinese. Two small hydro-electric stations are after Lingma and Galinka.

463   Yatung (2865 m), the main town of the Chumbi Valley, is at the junction of three rivers: the Tangka (from the northwest), Khangphu (from the north), and Amo (from the northeast).

SOUTH OF YATUNG

SIKKIM: THE JELEP AND NATHU PASSES

The main road continues south from Yatung. After 6 km, a sign-post marks a junction. The left branch goes to Bhutan (see below). The west (right) to Dorin (18 km), then to the Sikkimese towns of Gangtok and Kalimpong via the Nathu and Jelep passes. The Tibet–Sikkim border is about 15 km beyond Yatung and consists of the Dongkya range, which runs north to south. The Jelep Pass (4386 m), a few km south of the Nathu, is on the main trade route between Sikkim and Tibet. Near the top, the path is steep and stony; there is a gain of 1500 m in altitude from the Chumbi Valley. The route goes through forests of silver fir and pink rhododendrons.

THE BHUTAN ROAD

Chumbi is a small village along the left branch of the road after the junction. A shortcut up the mountain from here leads to Karchu Monastery on top of a ridge. The exterior of one remaining building is in good condition. Its interior was sacked but new murals have been painted recently. Monks live in a couple of tin-roofed rooms behind the monastery.

A dirt track goes up the hill to the right at Chumbi. This leads first to Karchu, then to the Bhutan border, 2 hr away by foot. Picturesque settlements (Rinchengang, Shingshang) with large stone houses are along the way after Chumbi. Army outposts are also here. A few trucks ply the road and Bhutanese traders from Thimpu and Paro pass through on their way to Yatung. Ghegona Monastery is near the border. From Chumbi to the Bhutan border is about 9 km. After the border a path follows the Torsa River southeast to Phüntsoling, on Bhutan's southern border. The Torsa is simply the lower reaches of the Amo, Khangphu, and Tangka rivers. It drains eventually into the Brahmaputra. No high passes separate Bhutan and Tibet at this border crossing point.

Routes to Bhutan

Do not attempt the following border crossings without official approval.
A number of trails along the Gyantse–Yatung highway lead into western and northwestern Bhutan. These originate near the Changpo Plain, the Gala Tso area, and the Chumbi Valley.   ➡

- Wagya La. From the southern end of the Changpo Plain, a trail following the headwaters of the Trari Chuma Chu goes over the Wagya La into north Bhutan.
- Ya La. The Yu Tso is a small lake 30 km east of the Gala checkpost. From here, a path skirts the small Tumba Yenju Tso and Tumba Monastery to reach the Ya La. This eventually joins the path from the Wayga La in north Bhutan.
- Phyen La. From Bamtö Village, south of Bam Tso, a trail goes over the Phyen La into Bhutan at Lingshi Dzong, then on to Punaka.
- Tremo La. This pass, less than 10 km southeast of Phari, leads into Dukye Dzong of Bhutan.
- South of Yatung. After Karchu and Ghegona monasteries, a trail follows the Torsa River into Bhutan.

CHÖRTEN NYIMA: A GURU RINPOCHE 'HIDDEN VALLEY'

Twin Nyingma sanctuaries centered between Tibet, Nepal and Sikkim

Location   Tibet–Sikkim–Nepal border
Map reference NH45-16 C D, 45-11 D, 45-12 C, 45-15 A C
Start–Finish   Sakya Bridge–Shekar Xian

OVERVIEW

Chörten Nyima is at the same time a mountain range, a monastery, and a mythological 'hidden valley' (*beyul*). It lies within a remote region of the Tibet–Sikkim Himalayas at the junction of three countries, Tibet, Sikkim, and Nepal. Pristine and untouched, this pilgrimage site is virtually unknown to outsiders and its scenic beauty rivalled only by Karchu (see page 693), Lapchi (p 248), and Tsari (p 208). From the complex, snow fields and glaciers are only an hour's walk away. Today, this ancient retreat in south Tibet again draws a constant flow of pilgrims; for some Nyingmapa followers, Chörten Nyima is perhaps a greater spiritual prize than Mt Kailash, mainly because of the sustained spiritual activities of Guru Rinpoche in the area. It is regarded as the North Gate of the magically powerful Dremojong Beyul, a 'hidden valley' situated deep within the Tibet–Sikkim Divide. This *beyul*, together with Pemakö (see page 717) and others, functions as a paradisaical refuge for all Tibetans in times of great national stress.

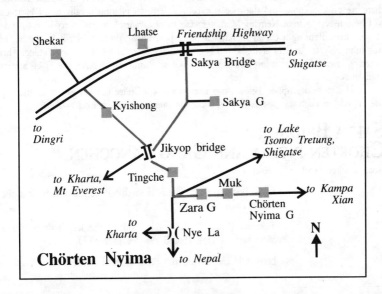

The hermitage's most important religious objects are three *chörtens* sited on a ridge overlooking the monastic complex. Within the Tamdrin Lhakhang are a number of treasured stone relics, each with a sacred imprint. West of Chörten Nyima is Gang Langchen, another renowned pilgrimage site. It sits on a distinctive ridge that resembles the head and trunk of an elephant. Consisting of a labyrinth of retreat caves, it is closely affiliated with the picturesque monastery of Zara. Nearby, the Nye La Pass leads to the Kharta Valley (see page 895) and the Kangshung Face of Mt Everest. It is also a key route into Nepal. After paying homage to Chörten Nyima and Gang Lanchen, return to civilization by means of a seldom traveled route along the isolated left bank of the great Phung Chu River. At the terminus is Shekar, near the Friendship Highway.

Related sections
Chumbi Valley, p 787
The Kangshung Face of Mt Everest, p 895
The Rhe and Ku valleys, p 831
North Bank of the Tsangpo from Shigatse to Lhatse, p 847
Lhatse to Sakya, p 890

Access: Sakya Bridge on the Friendship Highway
The Chörten Nyima area can be reached via the border towns of Kampa Xian and Tingche Xian. To reach Kampa Xian, take the Gyantse–Yatung highway south to Gala. Bypass a checkpost here and leave the main road. Take a secondary road westward to Tratsang and Kampa Xian (Gyantse–Kampa Xian, 204 km). A track continues west to Chörten Nyima (2-day walk). The route to Tingche Xian via Sakya Monastery (see below) is a better alternative because there are no checkposts and the road is excellent. Tibetan pilgrims usually travel by truck to Chörten Nyima from Nenying Monastery (south of Gyantse) or Sakya; try to get a ride at the latter. Renting a car in Lhasa is another possibility. Alternatively, it is possible to trek from Shigatse to Zara and Chörten Nyima via the sacred lake of Tsomo Tretung. This itinerary, briefly sketched below (see page 809), is a wonderful way to reach the Tibet–Sikkim Himalayas.

The route description below starts from the Sakya Bridge (24 km east of Lhatse) on the Friendship Highway (see page 989), and the numbers refer to road markers.

SAKYA BRIDGE TO CHÖRTEN NYIMA AND GANG LANGCHEN

Road marker (km)	Notes
0	Sakya Bridge turnoff. The road south follows the west bank of the Sakya Trom Chu.
21	Takchuk (Sakya Qu). A side road on the left leads to Sakya Monastery (4 km). (For Sakya, see page 880.)
24	Loba. Old *chörtens* on the right; an area worth investigating.

27	Lijun. Village next to hill.
37	Dango (Jungo) La. An easy pass. Beyond lie the headwaters of the Phung Chu, here called the Puchung Chu.
46	Chushö. Ruined *chörten* and stone tower. A side valley to the right leads to Puchung and Mt Hlako Kangri (6457 m).
52	Ladong. Ruined hermitage and caves within rocks on the right.
53	Village.
57	Mapcha Qu. On the right, the Puma Chu Valley trends off to the northwest to Hlako Kangri.
60	Village.
63	Pelag.
77	Jikyop Bridge. This wood bridge spans the Yeru Tsangpo; the Yeru flows into the Phung Chu, which becomes the Arun in Nepal. A side road on the right (0.5 km before the bridge) leads west along the Phung Chu Valley to the Friendship Highway near Shekar (see below, page 812).
80	Low pass; Mt Nyonno Ri (6724 m) rises to the southwest. The river below forms dangerous sections of quicksand.
87	The road makes a U-turn to go east along the Ko Chu Valley. The river flows north to join the Yeru Tsangpo.
88	Village of cave dwellings.
98	Wood bridge at Rongme. Rong Kong lies beyond. The road follows the Tingche Valley's left side. (A trail east follows the Chiblung [Jinlung] Chu to Kampa Xian or Sakya Monastery, see below.)
105	Tingche Xian. This strategic town on the edge of a plain is dominated by a big army compound and a cinema. A gas station at the far end of town is the only place to get gas for miles around.

The Tingche Plain The sluggish Yeru Tsangpo flows through the Tingche Valley; originating in the Chörten Nyima range, it heads west, and is then forced abruptly north by the granite peaks of Sangkar Ri and Nyonno Ri. It passes here before turning southwest to flow into the Phung Chu. The mountain on the Tingche Valley's west flank is Sangkar Ri (6226 m). Formerly, the Tingche Plain and village were known as Gyangkar Nangpa. During the summer rainy season, and even in winter, parts of the valley become shallow lakes; the road detours around them at the plain's west end.

106   Village.

111   Jena. Above is a ruined fort.

115   Swamp on the left.

121   *Daoban* (road maintenance compound).

126   *Daoban* with snow peak straight ahead. On the far east side of the
                valley is Chushar (Chushar Nango) with a ruined stone tower with
                machicolated galleries. A trail heads east, across the Tinki La (5210
                m) to Tinki Dzong, 30 km from Chushar. About 1 km from the
                Tinki Dzong are ruins of a large Gelugpa monastery.

From Chushar to Lake Tsomo Tretung A trail goes northeast from Tinki Dzong
for 20 km to Tashi Chirang on the west shore of Lake Tsomo Tretung (Tsomo Treling),
one of Tibet's four most sacred lakes. Dobtra, the main village on the north shore,
is a further 15 km. Allow two days to reach the lake from Chushar.

128   Stone shelters.

131   *Daoban.*

137   Kucha (Kochang).

140   Large rock painted red on the right.

142   Puguay, with military compounds, a rebuilt Kagyü monastery, and
                ruins with red monastic structures on a ridge above the village.

147   Zara (Sar). Overlooking the photogenic village is a craggy ridge covered
                by the ruins of a fort and monastery. Two chapels of the large Gelugpa
                monastery have been rebuilt and distinctive Gang Langchen
                ('Elephant Mountain') is in the background; it clearly resembles the
                head and trunk of an elephant. Within it is one of southern Tibet's
                most important pilgrimage sites (see below, page 810). Due west
                is Nyonno Ri (6724 m), part of the sacred north–south Ama Drimé
                range.

149   The road splits; the right branch goes south to Gompa Jang and
                the Nye La (13 km).

Nye La to Kharta
About 1.5 km before the Nye La, a trail leads due west over a pass in the Ama
Drime Range, then descends to Tashigang and Kharta, the jumping off point for the
Mt Everest–Kangshung Face trek (see page 895). This takes two days.

Nye La to Nepal

South of the Nye La Pass are the villages of Songchö, Dekyi, Riwo and Tashirak. 27 km farther south, is the Tipta La (5312 m) on the Tibet–Nepal border. After the border, a trail leads south to Wallungchung Gola and the small airport of Taplejung. Another trail from Tashirak goes southwest over the Rakha La (4957 m), also on the Tibet–Nepal border, then south to Num, Dingla and Tumlingtar along the Arun River.

To continue to Chörten Nyima, take the left branch eastward along the Yeru Chu Valley. (Road markers stop here; distances are given based on a Toyota Landcruiser odometer.)

152	Tashigang.
155	Dara, with a square stone tower.

Dara to Tashirak and Nepal A trail from here heads due south over the Langphu La to the Phu Chu and Tashirak, then to the Tibet–Nepal border at the Tipta La (see above).

The road continues along the desolate valley's right side.

163	Cave shelter. Another motor road, 2–3 km north across the east–west trending valley, heads east beneath the Sikkim Himalayas, on the right. The valley becomes dry.
168	Langma.
172	Changmu. A trail in a side valley on the right leads south (Lashar Glacier and the Chörten Nyima Range in the east) to Je and Gerwu Monasteries. Southwest of these is the Yangma Kangla La on the Tibet–Nepal border; beyond the pass is Wallungchung Gola and Taplejung.
173	Cross a bridge. Beautiful snow peaks on the right and the wide Yeru Tsangpo Valley on the left.
176	Village.
178	Village.
179	Village.
188	Muk (Muksi). Take the left (north) branch around a knoll, on top of which is the village.
189	The road splits; take the left branch.

197	The road splits again. Take the faint right branch straight ahead towards the mountains. The left continues to Kampa Xian via Tebung, Changlung (Neh), and Kampa Qu (Menda). Low hills are on the left; head towards a prominent snow peak through uninhabited land.
209	The road follows a stony river bed.
210	The road becomes better. Follow a canyon towards the snow peak. The Chörten Nyima Chu is on the left.
212	Cross the river (no bridge). The *chörten* and prayer flags of Chörten Nyima now appear.
214	Chörten Nyima Monastery at the base of low cliffs. In the background is the Chörten Nyima range. From Zara to here is 67 km, 2 1/4 hr by Landcruiser or 2 days by foot.

CHÖRTEN NYIMA (DORJE NYIMA)

Chörten Nyima was badly damaged during the Cultural Revolution but is now a thriving religious center with 12 nuns and some monks. Pilgrims come from all over Central Tibet, mostly by truck from Nenying Monastery or Sakya, and often number over 100 a day at peak season.

The farming villages of Muk and Changmu are the largest in the Yeru Tsangpo Valley; Muk lies one day's walk west of the monastery. Locals attribute the region's high crop yield to the supernatural potency of Chörten Nyima. The cave retreats and monastery of Gang Langchen are two to three days west, via the large Gelugpa monastery of Zara.

CHÖRTEN NYIMA RANGE

The Chörten Nyima range has 14 peaks (average height: 6700 m) dominated by Mt Chörten Nyima (6927 m), 5 km east of Sikkim's northwestern corner. Its eastern limit is the Kongra La and the Tista River, which flows south through Sikkim to Mangan and Kalimpong before joining the Brahmaputra River. The southwestern corner is defined by the Lhonak Chu, Goma Chu, and the South Lhonak glacier. Chörten Lapsang, a nomad camp 5 km south of the Tibet–Sikkim border and one day from the Chörten Nyima hermitage, is the Goma Chu's point of origin. Goma Chu joins Khora Chu to form the Lhonak Chu, which eventually flows into the large Tista. To the west, the range is bounded by the Lashar glacier, and to the east is Sikkim's Dongkya range.

THE HERMITAGE

At the entrance of the monastic complex is a row of *chörten*-like reliquaries (*tsakhangs*) for *tsa-tsas*. On top of the low ridge that flanks the canyon's west side is one of Chörten Nyima's three famous *chörtens*. The monastery has two courtyards separated by a row of one-story residences. On the left (east) is the newly built Tamdrin Drakpo Lhakhang. (Walk through some rooms and an open-air terrace into the chapel.) To the south are more one-story buildings.

The right courtyard is flanked on its west by the *dukhang* (rebuilt). Downstairs is the assembly room. Only paper *thangkas* decorate the walls. Upstairs are the Lhakhang Shar (East) and Lhakhang Nub (West) chapels. The former, smaller and cosier, has a 15-cm *rangjung* dagger (*phurpa*) engraved with the image of Tamdrin. It is kept within a cabinet on the altar. Another old *phurpa*, longer and wrapped in cloth, is next to it. Fine statues of Tamdrin, Jampelyang, and others, and a small bronze Kadampa Chörten are here as well. The Lhakhang Nub, left of the stairs, is bare.

South of the courtyard are the two chapels of Phüntsok Potrang and Tamdrin Zhiwa Lhakhang. Paper *thangkas* also hang in the former (also called Potrang Marpo) a building dedicated to Guru Rinpoche. Due west is the Tamdrin Lhakhang, Chörten Nyima's most important chapel. It stands along the rear wall of the front room. Within it is the low meditation cave used by Guru Rinpoche, which has an altar with offering implements and four highly treasured, sacred stones (*nedho*). One is called Marmo Dropa, Stomach of a Demon; another has Guru Rinpoche's clear footprint, supposedly impressed when he was eight years old. Next to the entrance is a 0.6-m-high bronze statue of Jowo (16th C.) the monastery's best art relic.

Guru Drubphuk, another cave of Guru Rinpoche, is 30 m west of the monastery at the base of the low cliff; it is now a nun's retreat. On top of the cliff are the three celebrated *chörtens* of Chörten Nyima.

MYTHOLOGY OF CHÖRTEN NYIMA

According to a small minority of Tibetan pilgrims, the monastery and pilgrimage sites of Chörten Nyima and Gang Langchen are the supreme sacred places of the Universe, more important even than Mt Kailash, Lapchi, and Tsari. A few Nyingmapa go as far as to regard them superior to Bodh Gaya, Buddhism's holiest shrine. (The region north of Sikkim, centered on Chörten Nyima and Gang Langchen, is a stronghold of the Nyingmapa.)

Namkhai Nyingpo, one of Tibet's first monks (8th C.), was the first great figure to practice here. He meditated in an earth cave (*saphuk*), near the present monastery. According to myths, Guru Rinpoche transformed himself into an old man and joined Namkhai Nyingpo at the cave. He was treated kindly and given food and shelter. One day, Namkhai Nyingpo perceived in a dream that the old man was, in fact, the Indian master. Namkhai Nyingpo showed his appreciation by building, with the help of Yeshe Tsogyal, Guru Rinpoche's consort, Chörten Nyima's three renowned *chörtens*.

The most important one is called Rangjung Shelgyi ('Self-originated Crystal') which contained within it a crystal *chörten* that supposedly fell from the sky. This event was predicted by Namkhai Nyingpo in a dream, and he subsequently saw the crystal *chörten* carried to earth at sunrise by a group of divinities; hence the name of the monastery (*nyima* means sun). A second group of powerful objects are the three sacred cemeteries (*durtrö*) founded by Guru Rinpoche and Namkhai Nyingpo, known collectively as the Chinang Sangsum (External, Internal, and Innermost) Durtrö. The Guru declared them to be enormously beneficial to mankind. He also stuck his trident into the ground at an auspicious site in the mountains behind Chörten Nyima. This gave rise to the sacred spring known as Guru Menchu—the third holy attribute of Chörten Nyima. A fourth is the 108 springs that spontaneously originated from Guru Rinpoche's 108 rosary beads, known as Chaktrang (rosary) Gya Dang Gye. Each possesses the Eight Qualities (sweet, cool, smooth, light, clear, clean, good for the throat, good for the stomach) important for the well-being of the practitioner. Further up the mountains are two oracular glacial lakes that supposedly divine the future. They are the fifth form of sacred phenonema in the area.

KORCHEN: THE LONG KHORA AROUND CHÖRTEN NYIMA

(A Tibetan pilgrim provided the following information.)

The pilgrimage around Chörten Nyima takes a day, although with sufficient time, it is worthwhile spending two days and camping by the glacial lake of Guru Latso. From the monastery walk east up a ridge to the three sacred cemeteries on top. The first one is enclosed by a low wall and within is a litter of old clothes, prayer flags, and offerings. A stone near the center is a *rangjung phurpa*. The middle *durtrö* consists of a large rock on top of which is Mipak Yangzhi, an imprint that resembles the full, flayed skin of a human. Over the centuries, the fame of these hallowed burial grounds has impelled pilgrims to travel for weeks or months to reach them. Typically, they roll around on the ground to absorb the site's potent vibrations, leaving behind pieces of clothing, fingernails and hair, even cutting their gums to spit blood on the stones.

Walk back down the ridge (west) along a trail and cross two rivers on the valley floor. Go up another ridge that flanks the valley's west side. On the top is a large rock, undercut by a tunnel, carved with the sacred Six Syllables. This is the 'sin-testing' stone of Dikpa Karnak. Crawl through the narrow opening; the ease or difficulty of the passage indicates your *karmic* debt. A short distance south is Guru Menchu, the Medicinal Spring of Guru Rinpoche. At this spot, marked by prayer flags, he stuck his trident into the ground to create the spring. Pilgrims also leave old clothes here as a symbolic depositing of past sins, therefore beginning life anew.

Continue south along the trail (stone *mandals* mark the way) and descend left (east) to the valley floor. Follow the river's left bank to the head of the valley and reach a small pass marked by a *lhatse*; beyond is another pass. A small lake lies between the two. Just after the second pass is Lake Guru Latso. Pilgrims come up here to divine the future by reading patterns on the lake's surface. Return to Dikpa Karnak. A side trail goes west across the ridge's top, and then drops down to a north–south trending valley. Wade westward across a river and hike up the right bank of a stream towards some stone buildings. Here is the source of Yanlak Gyeden Dutsi Chumik ('Spring of the Elixir of Eight Qualities'). It was believed created when Guru Rinpoche scattered his rosary beads on the ground. (A trail in the vicinity heads south for several hours to Khandro Latso, the 'soul-lake' of Yeshe Tsogyal.)

Return to the valley, cross the river again, and head north towards Chörten Nyima. Further down the valley, arrive at the three celebrated *chörtens*, all on top of a ridge flanking the monastic complex immediately to the west. The southernmost one is Dziwo (Shepherd) Chörten. The other two, aligned south to north, are Drokmo (Shepherdess) Chörten and Rangjung Shelgyi Chörten. The spectacular Chörten Nyima Range towers over the flat ridge and *chörtens* to create a superb and unforgettable setting. These *chörtens* have been renovated in recent years (the bases are perhaps original). The two southerly ones are 4–5 m tall, while the northernmost one, most sacred of the three, is nearly 7 m tall. This sealed monument is surrounded by prayer flags and *mani* stones; a trail descends sharply to the monastery. At the ridge's eastern base, across from the chapels, is the Saphuk Cave (Guru Drubphuk) of Guru Rinpoche. Namkhai Nyingpo stayed here as well; handprints of the two masters supposedly exist on the earthen wall.

DREMOJONG BEYUL

One day's walk south of Chörten Nyima, beyond the Chörten La, is the secret valley (*beyul*) of Dremojong (Drejong). In the heart of a mountain called Gangchen Dzö Nga, it is consecrated to Guru Rinpoche. Nomads, as well as Chinese and Indian soldiers, are in the area.

ALTERNATIVE ITINERARIES

1. KAMPA XIAN TO CHÖRTEN NYIMA: 2 DAYS

A dirt road goes west from Kampa Xian to Zara and Tingche Xian. Follow it from Kampa Xian to Kampa Qu (Mende, 10 km). Continue for 9 km to a road junction. The right, main branch goes to Zara. Take the left branch to Tranglung (4 km) or Neh. A dirt trail now goes south, then west, to the Chörten Nyima River (15 km), passing Sham along the way. Follow the river south to Chörten Nyima Monastery (17 km farther). Alternatively, from Kampa Qu, follow the road west past the road junction and continue west to Tebong (10 km from the junction) on the Chörten Nyima River. Follow the river south to the monastery (30 km).

The best route, however, bypasses Kampa Xian and Kampa Qu altogether. It starts from Serkhang (see page 840), a village 7 km northeast of Kampa Xian. Head west along a foot trail to the Kotsi hot springs by following the Yeru Tsangpo (3/4 hr). At Kotsi, leave the river by turning to the southwest, to reach a dirt road (1/2 hr). Follow this for 2 3/4 hr to Chungshu. From here, the route is Chungshu–Shobrang (2 hr)–Tranglung–Sham–Chörten Nyima.

2. SHIGATSE TO ZARA VIA LAKE TSOMO TRETUNG

This itinerary allows you to reach the pilgrimage sites of Gang Langchen (at Zara) and Chörten Nyima without resorting to hitchhiking or renting a vehicle. Allow eight to ten days to Dobtra on the north bank of sacred Lake Tsomo Tretung and three to four more days to Zara. From Shigatse, walk south along the Friendship Highway towards Gyantse for 6 km to a bridge that spans the Sha Chu. A dirt road on the right leaves the highway at this point. Follow it to the south.

Day	Village	Notes
1	Shigatse–Gerdu	Gerdu is on the Sha Chu's right bank.
2	Pass	Camp before the pass.
3	Bhadu	Cross the pass, then walk southwest past. Bending to Bhadu. Another trail just after the pass leads east to Duchung (see page 329).
4	Karu	Cross to the Shabu Chu's south bank. Walk west pass Sai Qu (Bongpa) and Chorju.
5	Gangde	Follow the Shabu Chu southwest to Wing. Turn south, leaving the river, to Gangde.
6	Longpu La	Camp before the pass. Before the pass is a route junction; the right trail goes to Jinlung (Chiblung) Qu along the Jinlung Chu. Do not take this, as it leads to Tingche.

7	Dungla	Descend from the pass due south. Near Dungla is the Chajong hot spring.
8	Dobtra	Walk southwest past Jiling (also called Dobtra) to Dobtra near Tsomo Tretung's north shore.
9	Tashichirang	Pass Bala en route to this village on the west shores.
10	Dönkang	Continue southwest past Gangnang.
11	Makra	Cross the Tinki La, then pass Nangkang.
12	Zara	Pass Nikek, and Lamadong and cross the Yeru Tsangpo. Zara is also known as Rongxar.

THE GANG LANGCHEN ('BIG ELEPHANT MOUNTAIN') PILGRIMAGE

This important pilgrimage site is intimately linked with Chörten Nyima. Gang Langchen, a Guru Rinpoche hermitage, is honeycombed with cave retreats.

ZARA MONASTERY

This Gelugpa monastery sits at the base of Mt Gang Langchen, west of Chörten Nyima. The flat motor road at Chörten Nyima goes west to Tingche Xian and Sakya. Follow it to Zara (67 km); try to get a ride on a pilgrim truck.

Zara Monastery is at the junction of the main road and a secondary one that leads south to the Nye La Pass. The monastic buildings are scattered along the spine of a craggy ridge crowned by an impressive fort (destroyed). Extensive ruins surround the site and only two major buildings remain: one up the slope and another, the three-storey dukhang, near the bottom. Both were renovated in recent years and house 20 monks. A large cave is at the ridge's southeast base. Zara Qu and Zara Village are near the monastery's dukhang. Behind the ridge (west) is Mt Gang Langchen, which when viewed from the east looks remarkably like the head and trunk of an elephant (Langchen means 'big elephant'). A distinct track leads left of the mountain up towards the snow peak of Nyonno Ri (6724 m), part of the north–south trending Ame Drime range. West of the range is the Phung Chu (Arun) Valley, an easy conduit into Nepal. In this valley is Kharta, the staging post for treks into the famed Kharta and Kama valleys and to the Kangshang Face of Mt Everest.

ZARA KHORA

A short khora surrounds the monastery. From the dukhang, circle the ridge clockwise. Towards the south-eastern perimeter, a short trail goes up the slope to the large cave. Continue the circuit around the hill to a cave nunnery near the village's south end. Follow the trail up to the fort—beyond this is a khandro drora (dakini dancing place). Go back down to the main path, a branch of which follows the motor road up towards the Nye La. Take this to the Lubuk Jowo, a house that once contained a Jowo (Sakyamuni) image. According to locals, it was smuggled to Dharamsala. From here to the pass, along a trail rather than the motor road, takes 2–3 hr. The Tibet–Nepal border is one day further. Some trade between the two countries is conducted at this crossing. Return from Lubuk Jowo to Zara.

ZARA MONASTERY TO GANG LANGCHEN

(A Tibetan pilgrim contributed the following information.)

A foot trail to the Gang Langchen Hermitage starts from behind the Zara ridge and goes up the Gang Langchen Valley, parallel to the northwestern section of the Zara Chu Valley. The walk along the well-defined path takes half a day and is frequented by pilgrims from all over Tibet. From Zara, walk up a rise, then continue up the valley to a level area (a pond is to the right of the path). A short distance after the pond, look out for a spot marked by stone *mandals* and a large rock. Within the latter is a Guru Rinpoche cave with a handprint of the saint above the entrance. The trail divides here; both branches lead up to Gang Langchen. Pilgrims generally take the left branch. Climb gradually to four white *chörtens*. The monastery of Gang Langchen is up the slopes on the right. Much of the complex has been destroyed. A renovated white *chörten* stands in front of the main entrance and beyond this is a large courtyard. Pilgrims have rebuilt some sections and it is possible to spend the night staying in a room or in the kitchen. A rock outside the monastery walls has on its surface the large *rangjung* syllables 'Om Mani Padme Hum'. To the rear a special walled area is considered particularly hallowed and pilgrims congregate here to eat and drink.

Walk down the slopes to an animal shelter and a site of two rocks. Guru Rinpoche supposedly split this once large rock; the taller section has a narrow tunnel underneath, the Bardo Trang ('Tunnel of Bardo'). Wriggle through the narrow opening to gauge your accumulated sin. A short distance beyond is another large rock, the Laekyi Melong ('Mirror of Karma'), marked by *mandals*. Pilgrims prostrate and offer prayers here; people with sufficient merit are sometimes rewarded with a vision of Chenresi or other divinities. The rock also has the power to expedite wishes. Follow the slopes on the valley's right side across a small river to a pass at the head of the valley. Beyond the pass are the sites of two *khandro drora*, each marked with stone cairns. *Dakinis* danced here to commemorate Guru Rinpoche's miraculous creation of 108 caves in Gang Langchen. This he achieved after spending three years, three months, and three days in retreat. Beyond is a narrow, striking ridge that descends gradually from the Gang Langchen peak. Its top and lateral surfaces contain numerous meditation caves. A cluster to the left has a prominent Guru Drubphuk, which has within it a painted image of Sakyamuni on a rock slab and some natural rock altars. Behind this cave, under a large rock, is an opening that leads down into an underground cave. Along the slope are many other caves, some with enclosures at the entrances. Some distance above the Guru Drubphuk is Tsogyal Latso, the soul-lake of Yeshe Tsogyal, a pond where pilgrims come to read their futures.

Walk to the flat top of the cave-dotted ridge. The largest cave here is the retreat's *dukhang* (*tshokhang*); enter via a rock tunnel. Within is an altar with many *mani* stones and Guru Rinpoche's handprint is at the back wall. North of the *dukhang* is Siwatsal, a cemetery enclosed by a wall—one of eight *durtrös* (four major, four minor) at Gang Langchen. A short distance west of the ridge is the site, marked by prayer flags, of a sacred spring, the Menchu, created when Guru Rinpoche struck his trident into the ground. Nearby is a walled-in cave that serves as a kitchen and two unusual underground houses (*sawok khangpa*), chambers dug into the ground and covered by stone and earth roofs. South of these is a large fissure in the rock face that bears a *rangjung* image of Chenresi. North of the prayer flags is Menlha Drubphuk (Medicine Buddha Cave) where Guru Rinpoche and Yönten Gönpo (Tibet's famed physician) reputedly stayed. Water from the ceiling is considered as long-life water (*tsechu*) by pilgrims. The narrow ridge is flanked on the east by mountains that make up the Gang Langchen Valley's east wall. A trail leads up the slope to Guru Latso, the soul-lake of Guru Rinpoche. Along the slopes are images of 1,000 Buddhas, and above them rainbow-shaped lines that lead the worthy to heaven.

BEYOND GANG LANGCHEN

The motor road from Zara Qu (road marker 147 km) goes north to Tingche Xian, 42 km away. West of Zara at Pugyay (road marker 142 km) are the extensive ruins of a Kagyü monastery at the base of a ridge. Renovation has started. Next to this is a Chinese army compound that has taken over parts of the original complex. From Tingche, follow the motor road north to Sakya (89 km) or northwest to Shekar and the Friendship Highway (134 km).

TINGCHE XIAN TO THE FRIENDSHIP HIGHWAY VIA THE PHUNG CHU LEFT BANK

Rather than retracing the route from Tingche Xian north to Sakya and Lhatse, consider taking a secondary road to the Friendship Highway near Shekar. This seldom-traveled route starts 31 km north of Tingche. It saves 77 km on the way to Nepal by avoiding a long section of the busy Tibet–Nepal highway. In general, it follows the flat, wide Phung Chu Valley, an arid, isolated area with few villages. Below is the route measured in km; road markers end after the Jikyop Bridge, 31km from Tingche Xian.

Jinlung Valley to Sakya Monastery via the Sogu La The road on the right goes up a hill along the Jinlung Chu Valley (the dirt road is replaced by a track after about 15 km). At the valley's head is the Sogu La (5904 m). A trail on the other side follows the Sakya Trom Chu northwest to Sakya. Villages passed are Mekar, Chösa, Thenga, Salagang, Nawoche, Kapu, Jinlung Qu, Luru, Phu, Jinlung Phu, Dungkung, Dangdor, and Sakya. The walk from the turnoff takes two to three days to the pass and one day more to Sakya.

Distance from Tingche Xian (km)	Notes
28 (road marker 80 km)	Road junction; keep straight.
31	Jikyop Bridge *daoban*.
31.4	Road junction (not obvious). Take the left fork, a secondary track up the ridge (the main road continues north to Sakya). It doubles back on itself above the bridge and then heads west.

NH45-15A Shekar

LADAKH RANGE

Pula Ri 6401

to Lhatse

Maphu La 5252

Mangkar Phu

Tubken Gephel

to Lhatse

Mabbo (nomad camp)

to Sakya C

N

to Sakya G

Jikyop
r.m. 77 km 4100

hot spring

Nyishar Shar

Nyishar Nub

Phar Chu

Lhako Kangri 6457

Mangkar Valley

Trangsö Qu

So Nga • 4488

Trangsö 5208

Trangsö Chumbab

to Tingche Xian

Tsonga

Kyiphu

Rigor

Pejorgang

Chulho

Muto (Ani G)

Phu G

Trupshi Ramchen

Trita

Kyishong

Chala

Balba

Friendship Highway

Lolo Chu

Phung Chu

Shekar Dzong

Dorje

4455

Lhumchen

Shekar

Pangla

Gyanor

Phu G

Gyaphu

Gyal Chu

Tse

Pang La 5250
to Everest East Face

Tsogo Shika

Tse La • 5600

r.m. 494 km

to Dingri

NH45 – 15C

NH45 – 14B

NH45 – 14B

0 2 4 6 8 10 km
0 2 4 6 miles

29°00'

28°30'

87°45'

87°00'

28°30'

35   Stone cairn.

36   Compound. The sandy road traverses a grassy field crosses streams; hot springs are near here.

40   Compound.

42   *Daoban.* The road heads south instead of northwest. Cross the Pangchö Phu Chu (Phar Chu). A trail follows this river northwest to Lhatse (see page 891) via the sacred Mangkar Valley (a branch goes to 44 *daoban* half way between Lhatse and Shekar). Hlako Kangri (6457 m) is east of the Mangkar Valley.

55   The road turns to the right (northwest) at the entrance of the Phung Chu Valley (5 km south of here is the Phung Chu–Yeru Tsangpo junction). The Phung Chu and the road hug the right (north) side of the valley. The Yeru Tsangpo is left behind.

78   Shar Trangso. Villages on the right, a long lake farther on.

80   T-junction. Take the left, wide road (the right branch leads to the many villages of Trangso Tse).

90   Cherna Village with new monastery.

94   A bridge to a village and Phu Monastery up the hillside to the left. Do not cross the bridge.

94.5   Pejorgang (Kyishong).

102   Kyishong ruins on top of a hill. Site of five *chörtens*, built to imprison an evil demon. South of Kyishong is a 5905-m peak.

117   Friendship Highway junction at a point between road markers 484 and 485 km. Turn right to go to the Shekar turnoff and the Tibet Guest House. A check-post now stands at road marker 489 km just before a bridge. Dingri and the route to Mt Everest are 60 km west along the Friendship Highway.

Go west to Dingri and Nepal or east to Shigatse and Lhasa.

SHIGATSE: CAPITAL OF TSANG

Shigatse, second largest city in Tibet, is the seat of the Panchen Lamas. A number of little-known pilgrimages start from here. The trek south along the Rhe and Ku valleys allows pilgrims to visit remote monasteries such as Ngor and Rhe. After traversing an isolated nomadic region, the itinerary reaches the foothills of the Tibet–Sikkim Himalayas and the important garrison town of Kampa Dzong. Another walk follows the easy Rong Valley southeast to the turquoise lake of Yamdrok Tso; the historic fortress of Rinpung Dzong is passed en route. Near Shigatse are the Wuyuk and Tobgyal valleys, home to highly respected Buddhist and Bönpo institutions. This region, north of the Tsangpo, is criss-crossed by a complex system of tributary valleys highly conducive to protracted treks.

LHASA TO SHIGATSE: THE FRIENDSHIP HIGHWAY NORTH ROUTE

OVERVIEW

In the 1950s the Chinese built this little-traveled portion (247 km) of the Friendship Highway. For trekkers, an advantage of the north route over the more popular south route (Lhasa–Gyantse–Shigatse) is its isolation and access to remote areas. A good staging point is Yangpachen Monastery (see page 679), center of the Shamarpa sect. One route follows the Lhorong Chu Valley to Dorjeling Nunnery and on to Tsurphu Monastery, main seat of the Karmapa (via the Lhasar La). Another option is to head south from the nunnery to Nyemo Xian near the north bank of the Tsangpo. Further along the north route, the Shogar La Pass offers a close-up panorama of Jomo Gangger, one of Central Tibet's most memorable mountains.

The next important start for treks and pilgrimages is at Majiang. One itinerary goes from Sanshang north to Puchiding via the high Jangyung La (5769 m). Puchiding is at the base of the Kalamba La pass, which provides access—via an isolated stretch of nomad territory—to Namtso, the sacred Sky Lake (see page 657). After crossing the Dongu La Pass, the north route descends into the Longkung Chu Valley. At its upper reaches, an old salt-trade route leads north to the Zambu Hermitage (see page 869), perhaps the most sacred retreat in all of Tsang (West-Central Tibet). The Zambu Valley and the upper part of the Jomo Chu are known for spectacular geothermal activities. From Zambu, the Shang Valley, the Zogpo pilgrimage, and Shigatse are natural extensions.

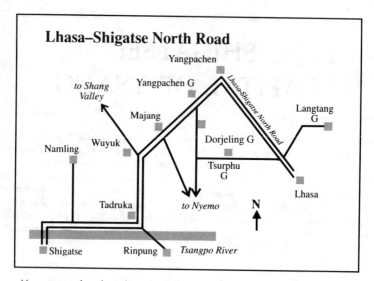

Lhasa–Shigatse North Road

Yangpachen

Yangpachen G

to Shang Valley

Majang

Langtang G

Dorjeling G

Namling   Wuyuk

Tsurphu G

Tadruka   to Nyemo   N   Lhasa

Shigatse   Rinpung   Tsangpo River

Numerous trails radiate from the small town of Wuyuk Qu, also next to the north route. Access from here the Tobgyal Valley, home of Bönpo villages and Bön monasteries. Other footpaths trend north to the wild Kadong and Zambu valleys, whose rivers contribute to the large Shang Chu. Another trail, via Lingkar Dzong, heads southeast to the Tsangpo and the historic Rinpung Dzong Valley (see page 841). Back at Wuyuk, Gho Ngön Monastery is reputed to be one of King Songtsen Gampo's monasteries, founded fully 1,200 years ago. The north route eventually meets the Tsangpo at the Tadruka ferry. (To the west is Shigatse, 2 hr away by truck.) Near the ferry is Yungdrungling Monastery (page 763), the most important Bön institution in Tibet. Other premier Bön temples, Menri and Khana, are close by.

Map Reference   NH46-9 A B, 46-5 C, 45-12 B D

Related sections
Namtso, p 657
Tsurphu, p 671
Shang Valley, p 869
Yungdrungling and Menri, p 763
Rinpung Dzong, p 841

The route
Most Lhasa–Shigatse buses go via the south route, so to travel the north route charter a vehicle or hitchhike. One way to start is to take a bus towards Damxung and Nagchu and get off at Yangpachen (Yangbajing) at road marker 1848 (new marker 3804). The bus starts every morning at 8 am from the bus station one block east of the Post Office (see Namtso, page 660). From Lhasa's center go west to the gas station past Drepung Monastery. Here, turn

right (do not turn left towards the airport and Gyantse) at road marker 1941 (new marker 3879). For this first section, follow the paved Tibet–Qinghai highway north to Yangpachen (town and geothermal power station). At this point, the north route leaves the Tibet–Qinghai highway and makes a sharp turn to the southwest (left) to reach the 5454-m Shogar La. After the pass the road descends along the Wuyuk Valley to the north bank of the Tsangpo at Tadruka. Here a ferry crosses the Tsangpo and a good road goes west to Shigatse along the south bank.

LHASA–YANGPACHEN

For this section, see Namtso (page 660); Tsurphu (page 671).

YANGPACHEN–TADRUKA

After Yangpachen, the paved road to Golmud divides. The left branch, now a dirt road, goes southwest to the Tsangpo and Shigatse; the right one continues to Damxung, Nagchu, and Golmud. A highway sign at this junction initiates the road markers (starting at zero) for the north route. Shigatse, the terminus, is at road marker 247 km (new marker 4904). The numbers below correspond to the markers.

1 A dirt track branches to the southwest (left) along the foothills of a mountain range. The route leads to Dorjeling Nunnery and the Lhasar La (see page 678). This is an alternative way to reach the nunnery, rather than approaching it from Yangpachen Monastery (see page 679).

15 Yangpachen geothermal power station.

16 Galu Nunnery. A trail goes up the slopes behind the power station to a Karma Kagyü nunnery (70 nuns). It takes 1 hr to reach the settlement: a line of white buildings with a red chapel in the centre. Galu was rebuilt in 1985 with donations from nomads.

18 Yangpachen (Yangchen) Monastery. On the right side of the road is Shungtse, a village with a *chörten* and the Lhorong Chu flowing next to it. See Tsurphu, page 678 for information on the monastery and a trek from here to Tsurphu.

20 A mountain range, the Jomo Gangger, is straight ahead. The river forks here and the road follows the right branch. The left goes southeast to Nakar and Nenang Monastery in the Tsurphu (Drowolung) Valley.

Excursions from Yangpachen Monastery
- Yangpachen–Dorjeling Nunnery–Tsurphu Monastery: four days (see Tsurphu, page 67)
- Yangpachen–Nenang Monastery: three days
  Walk south (towards Shigatse) from Yangpachen Monastery along the main road. In 20 min reach a river junction. Take the left branch to the southeast and walk up the wide valley to Yangre (3 hr). Continue to a 5850-m pass in 7 hr, then descend to Nakar in the Tsurphu Valley (5 1/4 hr). Above the village is Nenang Monastery, 1/2 hr up the north slopes. See also Tsurphu, page 675.

26 Bridge at the broad Lhorong Chu Valley.

28 Dirt track, on the left, to Dorjeling Nunnery.

31 Dirt track, on the left, also to Dorjeling Nunnery (4 hr). It hugs the eastern foothills of a north–south trending mountain range on the west bank of the Lhorong Chu. This is the most direct of all the routes to the nunnery. After Dorjeling it continues south along the Lhorong Chu to Gedar and Nyemo Xian near the north bank of the Tsangpo. Several hermitages and monasteries exist along this route.

33 The highway enters a narrow valley and starts to climb.

38 Nomad camps.

40 The mountain straight ahead is Jomo Gangger (7048 m). Another high snow peak (6175 m), one of the Jomo Gangger range, is only 10 km away to the north (right).

49 *Daoban*. A road maintenance compound is on the left and the road starts to zigzag up to the pass.

56 Shogar La (5259 m); beautiful views of the 7048 m-high snow dome of Jomo Gangger.

86 Majiang Village on left.

89 Nyemo Ma Chu, a wide valley on the left. A major dirt track goes south along it to Nyemo Xian near the north bank of the Tsangpo (50 km).

Nyemo Xian via the Nyemo Ma Valley: two days Follow a dirt track southward along the Nyemo Ma Chu Valley. In 1 hr cross to the west (left) bank of the river. In 4 1/2 hr reach a valley junction at Paku Qu. Take the right fork southeast to Shola (4 hr). Beyond is Nyemo (1 1/2 hr) and Nyemo Xian (a further 1 1/2 hr). The north shore of the Tsangpo is another 3 hrs.

---

93 Sanshang Village and valley junction. A trail up a north-trending side valley goes to the Jangyung La (5769 m), then descends north to Puchiding, where another trail leads north to the Kalamba La and Lake Namtso (see page 657). This short-cut to Namtso avoids Shigatse and the Shang Valley.

Sanshang to Puchiding: two days Walk north up the side valley. After 2 hr the valley divides. Take the right fork. The trail divides after 1 3/4 hr; this time take the left fork to the Jangyung La (5 1/2 hr). Descend to the northwest, then north, to Puchiding (3 1/4 hr) on the north (right) bank of the Jomo Chu.

---

100 The road climbs.

104 Dongu La Pass (4846 m).

114 Bridge across the Longkung Chu.

131 Domthang Village at the entrance of the Mong Valley, which opens to the north (right).

Dingma Monastery On a hill near Domthang is the 12th-C. Kadampa Dingma Monastery, seat of Ram Dingma Desé Jungne, a disciple of Potowa (1031–1105). A spring flows from the hallowed meditation cave of Nyong Dröl Jigje, and the monastery is noted for its Nyungne Khang chapel, a special room used by penitents to experience the suffering of others. A *chörten* above the monastery contained the relics of Ram Dingma.

Domthang to Zambu Monastery A trail goes north up the valley to Rin Dzong and Thangshe. It then joins the Zabso pilgrimage (see page 877) at Zambu (Shang Zambulung) Monastery after crossing the Mong La. Zambu and its counterpart, Zogpo Hermitage, in the neighboring Dzeshö Valley, represent the most important pilgrimage destinations in Tsang. The Zambu area is a center of geothermal activities.

---

138 Wuyuk Qu, on the right bank of the Longkung Chu, is an administrative center with a guest house. This is the starting point for a number of interesting treks.

Wuyuk Qu and Gho Ngön Lhakhang

This town's full name is Wuyuk Gho Ngöna and its monastery is the Wuyuk Gho Ngön Lhakhang. According to some literary sources, this is one of the Thadul temples built by King Songtsen Gampo in the 7th C. to subdue Tibet's great demon. Guru Rinpoche, Namkhai Nyingpo (one of Tibet's first ordained monks), and Terdak Lingpa (founder of Mindroling), all visited here. Gho Ngön Lhakhang once held a collection of weapons used personally by King Trisong Detsen. A meditation cave of Guru Rinpoche exists at Ludong, between Wuyuk and Domthang.

Excursions from Wuyuk Qu

- Wuyuk Qu–Kadong: two days
  Go northwest to Kadong at the junction of the Shang and Kadong valleys, on the Zabso pilgrimage route (see page 877). This trail, 31 km long, crosses the 4650-m Par (Yar La) (6 hr to the pass, 4 hr more to Kadong).
- Wuyuk Qu–Yanwu: three days
  A trail leads east into the side valley of Lungkar Dzong (Lungkar Zhidho Dzong). Reach the fortress town in 2 hr. Continue up the valley (southeast) to the ➡

5500-m Penpo La (7 1/2 hr). Descend to the southeast for 6 hr to Yanwu, 1/2 hr from the north bank of the Tsangpo. Follow the Tsangpo west to Rinpung Qu (or Shangba) to join the Rinpung Trek (see page 841), or walk east to Nyemo Xian.

• Wuyuk Qu–West Tobgyal: three days
  Another trail goes northwest from Wuyuk Qu to Sogchen (Baisa, 3 hr), turns abruptly southwest to ascend a 5000-m pass (4 1/2 hr), then descends southward along the western branch of the Tobgyal Valley to Chulung (3 hr) and Tobgyal Qu, also called Magada (3 hr). The north bank of the Tsangpo is a further 1 1/2 hr.

• Wuyuk Qu–East Tobgyal: two days
  Walk west to the wide entrance of the Wuyuk Valley (1/2 hr) and follow a trail southwest up a side valley to a 5350-m pass (5 1/2 hr). Descend to Dingphu and the Bön monasteries of Menri and Khanak (see pages 765, 766).

• Wuyuk Qu–Zambu Monastery: three days
  From Wuyuk Qu walk north up the Wuyuk Valley for 3 3/4 hr to Mongre (Wongpudor). Here the valley divides. Take the left branch north to a 5100-m pass (7 hr). Descend to the north. After 3 hr, enter the Zambu Valley. Turn west (left) to Zambu Monastery (1 hr), the most sacred hermitage in Tsang.

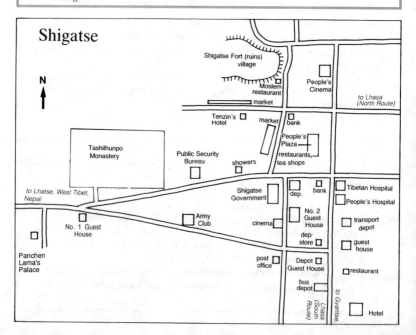

156   Numagang, the Longkung Chu Valley's largest village, is on the left. Numerous small, steep terraces, unusual for Tibet, are reminiscent of Himalayan cultivation.

168   (New marker 4821) Tadruka Ferry, on the Tsangpo's north bank. The crossing takes only 5 min and is free for vehicles and pedestrians. Tadruka Village, on the south bank, has a guest house. East of the ferry (3/4 hr) is the Bön monastery of Yungdrungling. Wade across the wide estuary of the Longkung Chu to reach it (see page 763). The high-water crossing from August–September might be tricky.

Yungdrungling and other Bönpö monasteries

Before the Cultural Revolution, the Menri Monastery (see page 765) was the largest and most important Bön center in Tibet. Now, however, it is much reduced in size and Yungdrungling has taken over. There are 30 monks and one lama, Kurzon Lhodrö Rinpoche, residing here. Many of the monks came from Amdo and Kham. A track from the ferry goes west along the north bank to Tobgyal Qu and the Tobgyal Valley. Within this valley are the Bön monasteries of Menri and Khana.

---

187   (New marker 4840) Drakchik Ferry. Coracles cross the Tsangpo to the entrance of the Tobgyal Valley. The crossing costs Rmb 0.6. Drakchik means 'single rock' and indeed there is a huge rock with a shrine in the river.

202   (New marker 4853) Jangdong Qu, site of Shigatse's airport, is on the right.

217   Samdrubling, a historic center of Tsang.

226   (New marker 4879) Tama Ferry. A wooden boat crosses the Tsangpo at the entrance of the north-trending Shang Valley. Within the prosperous valley are Namling Xian and many villages. Trails lead from the head of the valley to the Zabso pilgrimages (see page 877).

247   (New marker 4900) Shigatse. The road enters the town over an ornate bridge.

TASHILHUNPO: MONASTIC CITY OF THE PANCHEN LAMAS

Tashilhunpo, principal monastery of Tsang Province, is one of the Great Six centers of the Gelugpa sect. The others are Sera, Drepung, and Ganden, all in or near Lhasa, and Labrang and Kumbum in Amdo (southern Gansu/Qinghai provinces). Tashilhunpo is the largest, most vibrant monastery in Tibet, the only one that does justice to the term 'monastic city'. Founded in 1447 by Tsong Khapa's nephew and disciple, Gedundrub, the First Dalai Lama, it was substantially enlarged under the Fourth Panchen Lama, Lobsang Chökyi Gyaltsen (1570–1662). The latter completed many works on liturgy, tantrism, and Kadampa doctrines, becoming Tashilhunpo's abbot in 1600 and Drepung's abbot in 1617. The emphasis on Drepung, the *de facto* center of Gelugpa power, meant that Tashilhunpo drifted directionless for some decades. This changed after 1642. The Fifth Dalai Lama conferred on Chökyi Gyaltsen the title of Panchen Rinpoche, Great Precious Teacher, and created the Panchen Lama lineage. Each incumbent was known as an incarnation of the Buddha Amitabha (Wöpame: Buddha of Infinite Light). Kedrub Je, one of Tsong Khapa's two foremost disciples, was retroactively designated as the First Panchen. Subsequent abbots of Tashilhunpo, whether appointed or elected, became—together with the Dalai Lamas—the most important religious figures in Tibet. Wöpame is the spiritual source of Chenresi, who is incarnated in the Dalai Lamas, and thus the Panchen Lamas are considered by some religiously superior. The last Panchen, the Tenth, died in 1989.

The site

This large Gelugpa institution is sited at the base of a low ridge called Drölma Ri. At the western perimeter of Shigatse, its entrance gate is beside the main Lhasa–Shigatse–Nepal road, about 20 min walk from the Tibetan market. Tashilhunpo had four colleges (*tratsangs*): Kyikhang, Thösamling, Shartse, and Ngagpa. This last still functions but the other three have been incorporated into the Tsenyi Tratsang—the site of the debating garden near the monastery's main entrance. The main buildings of the complex are the Jamkhang Chenmo, the palace of the Panchen Lamas, the Kudhung, with its magnificent *chörten*-tomb of the Fourth Panchen Lama, and the Kesang Lhakhang, which, with its large courtyard, constitutes the center of the monastery. A 3-km (1-hr) *Lingkhor* (pilgrims' walk) surrounds the monastery, hugging closely Tashilhunpo's northern perimeter walls and ascending the ridge behind the complex. This is a most rewarding feature of the monastery and should not be missed.

JAMKHANG CHENMO

The tall red building with a gold roof at the complex's northwestern corner is the Jamkhang Chenmo, the first building reached by the short *khora* (ritual walk) behind the monastery. It was built in 1914 by the Ninth Panchen Lama and contains a 26 m-high statue of Jampa (Maitreya), the Future Buddha. The entire building is hollowed out to make room for the giant. Its exterior is made of gilded bronze and the interior, for support, has a large juniper trunk from the famous juniper grove at Reting Monastery. Jampa's ornaments, embellishing ears, hands, and neck, are studded with precious stones. The ears are fully 2.6 m long and each finger 1.2 m. Nearly 300 kg of gold and 150 metric tons of copper and brass were used for the construction. In its left hand is a vase symbolizing hidden treasures. The right has an emblematic wheel (*khorlo*) that denotes the Sakyamuni Buddha. Inside the statue are copious relics, texts, and gold. The surrounding walls of the cavernous interior space have gold line paintings of 1,000 Jampas on a red background; murals of the Kadampa triad of Atisha, Dromtönpa, and Ngok Legpai Sherab; and the Gelugpa protective deities, Sangdü, Demchok, and Dorje Jigje. It took four years and 900 laborers to build the Jampa Lhakhang. According to documents, the Ninth Panchen Lama and his teacher officiated during the first day of construction. Gold, copper, and paint were imported from India and the stones used to build the walls came from a quarry behind Shigatse's fort. To compensate the laborers, the government supplied 1.5 million kilos of grain. Artists, carpenters, sculptors, and specialists were given land, houses, and tax exemption. The building has 15 chapels on two floors. Described below are the most important ones:

Pedhek ('Made Sublime by Lotus Flowers') Lhakhang
The murals on the east side of the room are of the three tantric divinities, Yamantaka (Dorje Jigje), Guhyasamaja (Sangdü), and Chakrasamvara (Demchok). To the west is Neserwa surrounded by Tsong Khapa and other female divinities (west).

Kuké ('Hip') Lhakhang
The west wall has paintings of various religious implements used by ordained monks. Other

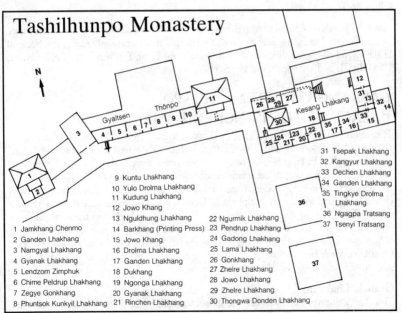

Tashilhunpo Monastery

1 Jamkhang Chenmo
2 Ganden Lhakhang
3 Namgyal Lhakhang
4 Gyanak Lhakhang
5 Lendzom Zimphuk
6 Chime Peldrup Lhakhang
7 Zegye Gonkhang
8 Phuntsok Kunkyil Lhakhang

9 Kuntu Lhakhang
10 Yulo Drolma Lhakhang
11 Kudung Lhakhang
12 Jowo Khang
13 Nguldhung Lhakhang
14 Barkhang (Printing Press)
15 Jowo Khang
16 Drolma Lhakhang
17 Ganden Lhakhang
18 Dukhang
19 Ngonga Lhakhang
20 Gyanak Lhakhang
21 Rinchen Lhakhang

22 Ngurmik Lhakhang
23 Pendrup Lhakhang
24 Gadong Lhakhang
25 Lama Lhakhang
26 Gonkhang
27 Zhelre Lhakhang
28 Jowo Lhakhang
29 Zhelre Lhakhang
30 Thongwa Donden Lhakhang

31 Tsepak Lhakhang
32 Kangyur Lhakhang
33 Dechen Lhakhang
34 Ganden Lhakhang
35 Tingkye Drolma Lhakhang
36 Ngagpa Tratsang
37 Tsenyi Tratsang

panels have a *chakra* (used by astrologers to calculate the movements of planets), *sipa khorlo* (wheel of life) etc. The wall west of the Jampa Buddha has paintings of Atisha, Dromtönpa, and other disciples. To the west are portraits of Tsong Khapa and his chief disciples.

Zhelre ('Face') Lhakhang

This room allows pilgrims to pay homage directly to the face of the Jampa. On the exterior wall of this chapel are paintings of mystical continents, like Tashi Tsekpa; the Five Dhyani Buddha; Mount Meru; Ngonga Zhingko ('Paradise of Joy'); the Six Classes of Existence (Ridruk Ne); and episodes showing the Buddha vanquishing demons while seated in meditation. On the south wall is the complete pictorial history of the Jampa Buddha, describing his 12 Deeds. Along the west wall, Jampa is surrounded by the lineage holders of the Kriya *Tantra* (Gyachen Chögye). Jampelyang, flanked by Nagarjuna, Chandrakirti, and other lamas of a tantric school known as Zabmo Tagyü, are on the east wall. Other paintings are of the 16 Arhats.

Ütrok ('Crown-facing') Lhakhang

Above the Zhelre Lhakhang, this chapel opens onto the huge Jampa's crown. The east wall has paintings of Jampelyang, Tsong Khapa, and his retinue, and the White Amitayus. To the west are images of Jampa, the 13th Dalai Lama, the Ninth Panchen Lama, and his teacher. In the four directions surrounding the crown are paintings of the Four Guardian Kings.

Ganden ('Tushita Heaven') Lhakhang

This chapel, directly in front of the main entrance of the Jamkhang Chenmo has 1,000 small statues of Tsong Khapa.

Leave the Jamkhang Chenmo and continue east along a principal east–west lane to the palace of the Panchen Lamas, the Labrang Gyaltsen Thönpo. It is immediately east of the Namgyal Lhakhang, a building constructed during the time of the Ninth Panchen Lama, Chökyi Nyima (1883–1937), and used for the study of philosophy.

LABRANG GYALTSEN THÖNPO, PALACE OF THE PANCHEN LAMAS

The important Gyaltsen Thönpo ('Highly Glorified Victory Banners') Palace was built by the Sixth Panchen, Pelden Yeshe (1738–80). Its tall white walls extend from east to west behind a long red-walled building housing seven interconnected chapels, all filled with innumerable small bronzes. These chapels are briefly noted below from west to east. The palace was the residence of the first abbot, Gedundrub, and all subsequent Panchen Lamas; it is generally closed. Its original foundation, completed by Gendundrub, consists of three floors of 15 main rooms. The residential quarters, known as the Phüntsok Kunzik, contain the principal image of Sendeng Nakdröl, made of medicinal clay. It stands next to a painting of the Paradise of Sendeng Nakdröl, the first painting of Tashilhunpo. The name of the palace was conceived when Gedundrub had a vision of 11 victory banners (*gyaltsen*) on the roof, a sign that the monastery would be under 11 successive Panchens.

Gyanak Lhakhang

This chapel, distinguished by its Chinese shrine, was built by the Sixth Panchen in dedication to his pupil Qianlong, the Chinese emperor. Dorje Chang, the tantric form of Sakyamuni, is the dominant figure. Other statues include Tsong Khapa and his two disciples, the Medicine Buddha, and Drölma.

Lendzom Zimphuk

Here the Panchen Lamas received visiting dignitaries. Hanging in the chapel are 17 woven *thangkas* from Hangzhou, commissioned by the Ninth Dalai Lama.

Chime Peldrup Lhakhang

This chapel is consecrated to Tsepame, one of the long-life divinities. Other statues in the room are Sakyamuni and Jampelyang. A complete set of the *Kangyur* and *Tengyur* is also kept here.

Zegye Gönkhang

This protector chapel is dedicated to Chamzing, the red female protective deity, special guardian of Tashilhunpo.

Phüntsok Kunkyil Lhakhang

The principal statues are Tsong Khapa and his two disciples. Next to them is an image of Kedrub Sangye Yeshe, tutor of the Fourth Panchen.

Kuntü Lhakhang

No single image dominates this chamber. Instead there is a collection of statues taken from various traditions.

Yulo Drölma Lhakhang

This celestial paradise of Drölma has 21 statues representing all the manifestations of the goddess.

East of the palace is the Kudhung Lhakhang. It can be reached by stairs from the Yulo Drölma Lhakhang or directly through its front entrance.

KUDHUNG LHAKHANG

This large, red building containing the *chörten*-tomb of the Fourth Panchen Lama, Chökyi Gyaltsen, is crowned by a gilded roof similar to the Jamkhang Chenmo. The consecration of the tomb in 1662 coincided with the first anniversary of the second Manchu Emperor's coronation. Kudhung Lhakhang's main entrance is through a door on the building's east side. Within, a courtyard leads into the mausoleum. The ornate, silver *chörten*, containing the Fourth Panchen's relics, is in the middle; statues of the long-life divinities Tsepame, Drölma, and Namgyalma are in front of it. This silver-and-gold burial *chörten* is 11 m high. According to the diary of the artist who constructed the tomb (Lhabab Chörten model), the Panchen's entire body was placed standing within the structure. Burial relics included a thousand-year-old manuscript and two sets of embroidered *thangkas* from the Manchu emperor. The chapel is elaborately decorated with expensive brocade and silk and the walls depict the 1,000 Buddhas. On the gold roof is a spacious balcony decorated with two golden victory banners, symbols of Buddhism's flourishing. Round, brass emblems (*pengyan*) engraved with mythical animals protect against disasters caused by the planets and elements.

After leaving the Kudhung Lhakhang, turn left and continue along the principal east–west lane to the east. Follow the high red walls to a passsageway on the left; turn into this to the flagstoned courtyard of the Kesang Lhakhang.

KESANG LHAKHANG

Centering on the monastery's courtyard, the Kesang Lhakhang is Tashilhunpo's largest complex. It is made up of two major parts, the assembly hall and the surrounding buildings. The courtyard walls, called Kelsang Khyrama and built in 1472, consist of rock slabs carried from Khalung Phuk, a retreat west of Tashilhunpo founded by Gedundrub. Carved on their surfaces are images of many Buddhas whose iconography is derived from the text of Dhodhe Kesang. Below the deities are descriptive inscriptions and short expressions of praise. An elevated stage is at the courtyard's northwest corner. North of this are engraved images of Gedundrub, Sakyamuni and his two disciples, and the Six-Ornament Scholars. At the center of the stage are seats of the abbots.

This courtyard is the venue of all important religious festivals and ceremonies as well as cultural events (eg Cham dancing) and many daily rituals. Monks debate and teachers teach here. South of the stage are paintings of the Regent Dharma Rinchen and many *chakras* (wheels). The center of the open yard has a special flagpole (*dhukar khorlo darchen*) decorated with a white umbrella symbolizing spiritual victory. Kesang Lhakhang is a complicated structure with myriad small chapels around the courtyard.

DUKHANG

The assembly hall on the western side of the courtyard was begun in 1447 by Gedundrub and finished 12 years later. Inside is a large throne for the Panchen Lamas. Statues attached to columns represent the benign and wrathful forms of Chenresi and the long-life divinities of Drölma, Namgyalma, and Tsepame. The hall's main image is Mipham Gön (Jampa), flanked by clay images of Chenresi and Jampelyang. Supposedly constructed by Je Sherab Senge, it came about in the following way. The lama was dreaming of Jampa when the First Panchen Lama came into the *dukhang* and told him that the creation of the Jampa would further the cause of Buddhism and benefit all beings. Je Sherab Senge thus began immediately to raise funds for its construction and sent for well-known Newari artists staying at Chung Riwoche Monastery. They could not come because of other commitments, but eventually artists of Nenying and six Newari artists living in Chudhu arrived to craft the statues.

They first completed a 1- m-high model of the Jampa. It was well made and many important relics, including special *mantras* transmitted by Tsong Khapa, were placed inside. Auspiciously, an image of Tsong Khapa appeared at the statue's right ear. At that time, the First Dalai Lama's disciple, Drachom Charka, had a vision of two suns, one large and one small. Their light filled the hall; the lesser sun symbolized the small Jampa and the larger indicated that a still bigger one would be built. During the reign of the Ninth Panchen, the huge Jampa in the Jamkhang Chenmo was crafted. An illustrious assembly of the religious community consecrated the Jampa proper. During the ceremony, a flower suddenly bloomed on the statue's forehead and a fine rain ('flower rain') accompanied by a rainbow shrouded the site. The same night, Je Sherab Senge saw in a dream the Jampa in the yellow robes of a monk. The Buddha looked pleased and subsequently dissolved into his body. At dawn came another dream. This time an ordained monk announced that Je Sherab Senge should be exultant for contributing so much to the well-being of Buddhism and all mankind.

Notice the embroidered *thangkas* with colored tassels hanging from the ceiling. These are paintings of the 17 incarnations of the Panchen Lama, and were made in Hangzhou, China in the 1920s.

Interior chapels

The *dukhang* has two interior chapels: a left one is consecrated to Sakyamuni, the other to Drölma.

Drölma Lhakhang This old chapel was built by Gedundrub in 1466. The principal image is the White Tara (Drölkar) with seven eyes. This statue, crafted by Newari artists from Nepal, contained many important religious relics. Two Green Taras flank it and around them are Tsepame and Je Sherab Senge. Behind the White Tara is a painting of a Green Tara, believed drawn personally by Gedundrub.

Jowo Lhakhang Next to the Drölma Lhakhang. The central image of this large chapel is Sakyamuni, flanked by his chief disciples Sariputra and Maudgalyayana. Around them are the Eight Great Bodhisattvas and two images of Jampelyang. On two columns are statues of Gedundrub and Lobsang Chökyi Gyaltsen, the Fourth Panchen Lama.

SOUTH CHAPELS

Along the south wing of the Kesang complex (southwest of the courtyard) is a row of two-story chapels built at the beginning of the 17th C. by the Fourth Panchen Lama. These rooms all contain numerous small, fine bronzes. The first three chapels are on the lower floor, the last four on the upper.

Ngonga ('Great Joy') Lhakhang This is located at the southeast corner of the complex, the easternmost room attached to the *dukhang*'s south side. The main object here is a sandalwood Kadampa *chörten* with many small statues and *chörtens* around it.

Gyanak ('Chinese') Lhakhang This chapel, west of Ngonga, has as its central image a large Sakyamuni made of Indian silver. Surrounding it are the 16 Arhats and the Ninth Panchen Lama.

Rinchen ('Precious') Lhakhang This is the last chapel on the *dukhang*'s south side. The principal image is a *rangjung* Maitreya made of bell metal (*li*). Other images are Dorje Chang (Vajradhara), Drölma, and Chenresi. Beyond this room, a flight of stairs leads to an upper level. The Ngurmik Lhakhang is directly above the Ngonga.

Ngurmik ('Orange') Lhakhang The main image is Drölma, a famous statue commissioned in the mid-12th C. by Darma Nyingbo, an expert on Abhidharma teachings. He wore orange robes during lectures and thousands attended. One day, he asked four disciples to go to India to bring back a statue of the Orange Tara (Drölma Ngurmik). Unable to locate it, they therefore asked an artist to create one. The night before casting, the artist discovered his workshop suffused with light and the Tara statue spontaneously created. The king of India was notified of this miraculous happening and he gave permission for it to go to Tibet. On the way, the four disciples fell asleep and the statue disappeared. Shocked by this turn of events, they shouted in surprise and sorrow, 'Kure'; thus, this place became known as Kure Dong. Eventually, the statue reappeared and spoke out loud of its contrition for making them upset. The retinue continued on to Tibet, carrying the statue on their backs. At a high, difficult pass, the disciples wished to be unburdened. Reading their minds, the Tara statue proceeded to walk over the pass; since then, it has been known as the Mondrö La, 'the Pass where Prayers are Fullfilled'.

Pendrup Lhakhang (Chapel of Panditas and Sages) The main image is the Fourth Panchen Lama, made of Indian silver. To the left is a statue of Dugkarma, the multi-headed female manifestation of Chenresi, distinguished by its white parasol. On the right is a thousand-armed, eleven-headed Chenresi (Chaktong Chentong Chenresi). The murals consist of Drölma and Jampelyang encircled by concentric rings of *mantric* inscriptions.

Gadong Lhakhang Here is a life-size image of Jampa made of bell metal and consecrated personally by the Fourth Panchen.

Lama Lhakhang The main image is Tsong Khapa in gold and copper. Renowned teachers of various sects are here as well.

After this chapel, descend to the main floor, and then proceed to the back to the Kesang Lhakhang's north wing.

NORTH CHAPELS

Gönkhang (Protector Chapel) This chapel at the *dukhang*'s northwest corner has as its main image Dorje Jigje in clay. Others include the Six-armed Mahakala and the White Mahakala. All were sponsored by the *mahasiddha*, Zangpo Gyaltsen. The Second Dalai Lama, Gedan Gyatso, specially commissioned the statues of Chögyel (Dharmaraja), a wrathful, bull-headed protector much worshipped by the Gelugpa, and Palden Lhamo. He decorated the human skull held in the hands of the latter and entrusted the monastery to her protection. Subsequently, the Fourth Panchen embellished this statue with red and white pearls and a gold crown adorned with images of the Five Dhyani Buddhas, studded with turquoise. Here also are ritual implements used by the different protectors. On the walls are paintings of Chögyel and Palden Lhamo.

Zhelre Lhakhang This chapel on the *dukhang*'s northeast side allows pilgrims to view the head and shoulders of the Mipham Gön (Jampa) statue in the assembly hall below.

Another flight of stairs leads up to the *dukhang* (attached to the Phende Kunkyil and Zimjak bedrooms) of the Kunzik Palace, built in 1816 by the Seventh Panchen Lama.

Dukhang of the Kunzik Palace This unusual hall has statues of Sakyamuni and his two disciples (made of medicinal clay), the 16 Arhats, the Four Guardian Kings, and a set of wrathful Gelugpa protectors, including Palden Lhamo. All are installed in cabinet-shrines (*chösam*). The room's heavy atmosphere is reinforced by many funereal tantric hangings and two stuffed snakes. Here also is a large library.

Go downstairs to yet another Zhelre Lhakhang.

Zhelre Lhakhang This chapel looks onto the face of the Sakyamuni statue in the *dukhang*'s Jowo Sakyamuni Chapel. Here are *thangkas* of the Six-Ornament Scholars (early Indian Buddhist philosophers Nagarjuna, Aryadeva, Asanga, Vasubhandu, Dignaga, Dharmakirti) and the Two Supreme Philosophers (Indian masters, Shakyaprabha and Gunaprabha, authors of the *Vinaya*). On the altar is a black stone inscribed with the Six Syllables in white.

Go upstairs via another set of stairs to the Thongwa Dönden Lhakhang.

Thongwa Dönden Lhakhang Founded by the Second Panchen Lama, Zangpo Tashi, in 1478, it was originally called the Namthar Lhakhang. Within the chamber is the *chörten*-tomb of Gedundrub, Tashilunpo's founder, and a statue of Mitrukpa. Also here are the *chörten*-tombs of the Second and Third Panchen Lamas. The room was renovated by the Fourth Panchen, who added the large Namgyal Chörten. Since then the chapel has been known as Thongwa Dönden ('Meaningful to be Seen'); it holds eight *chörtens*, most with relics of former abbots.

CHAPELS FLANKING THE EAST AND SOUTH SIDES OF THE KESANG KHYAMRA COURTYARD

The chapels of the first floor, from the courtyard's northwest corner, are listed first, then those of the second floor, all in a clockwise progression.

First floor
These rooms are attributed to the Fourth Panchen Lama, Lobsang Chökyi Gyaltsen (1570–1662).

Jowo Khang The main statue is Sakyamuni, surrounded by the Thousand Buddhas.

Nguldhung Lhakhang (Chapel of the Silver Tomb) The central silver *chörten* was a gift to Tashilhunpo from Gushri Khan, leader of the Qosot Mongols, who helped install the Fifth Dalai Lama as the undisputed ruler of Tibet in the 17th century. Dorje Chang (Vajradhara) is the main statue.

Barkhang (printing press) A corridor leads into this room where Tibetan folios (*peychas*) are printed; the press stores woodblocks of the *Kangyur* and *Tengyur*.

Jowo Khang This chapel, consecrated to Sakyamuni, is similar to the one before the Nguldhung Lhakhang.

Drölma Lhakhang Drölma is the central image. *Thangkas* on the walls are replicas of the 17 Hangzhou scrolls that depict the incarnations of the Panchen Lamas, found in the Kesang Lhakhang.

Ganden Lhakhang (Chapel of the Tushita Heaven) The main image is Tsong Khapa, considered an incarnation of the Buddha. Stairs lead down to the Kesang Lhakhang assembly hall.

Second floor
These chapels are attributed to the Fifth Panchen Lama, Lobsang Yeshe (1663–1737).

Tsepak Lhakhang This chapel is consecrated to Amitayus (Tsepame), the Bodhisattva of Infinite Light.

Kangyur Lhakhang This contains the complete set of *Kangyur*; monks congregate here regularly to recite *sutras*. The images are of Sakyamuni and his two chief disciples. Silk Hangzhou *thangkas* decorate the walls.

Dechen Lhakhang The main image is Wöpame (Amitabha), one of the Five Dhyani Buddhas, flanked by Jampa and Jampelyang. This Buddha of Infinite Light reigns in the Paradise of Sukhavati (Dechen). On the walls are paintings of the fabulous continents of Dechen.

Ganden Lhakhang The main statue of Tsong Khapa is surrounded by the Sixth and Eighth Panchen Lamas, lineage holders of the Lamrin tradition (Stages on the Path to Enlightenment). An unusual statue here is of the Fifth Dalai Lama, perhaps the only one of a Dalai Lama in the entire monastery. On the walls are the life episodes of Sakyamuni.

Tingkye Drölma Lhakhang The main image is a famous standing Drölma called Tingkye 'later born' made by the Kache Pandita (Sakyasri, 1145–1243) to prevent fires. Outstanding 300-year-old murals depict the 12 major episodes in the Buddha's life, the paradises of the Medicine Buddhas, and the history of Jampa.

OTHER MAJOR BUILDINGS IN THE TASHILHUNPO COMPLEX

NGAGPA TRATSANG (TANTRIC COLLEGE)

This is next to the main path that leads north from Tashilhunpo's main entrance. It is the only one of four colleges (*tratsangs*) to survive the Cultural Revolution. The college's old, dark *dukhang* is on the first floor, reached via a flight of steps from the courtyard. Its main statues are Tsong Khapa and his two disciples and the Fourth Panchen Lama. Each morning, monks come here to perform tantric rituals accompanied by liturgical music.

TSENYI TRATSANG

South and below the Ngagpa Tratsang is the chapel of the Debate College. It has a statue of Sakyamuni and, in front of it, a small image of the Ninth Panchen Lama, Chökyi Nyima. By the inner chapel's door, behind the main hall, are six figures. On the left are Gedundrub, the founder, Tsong Khapa, and Chökyi Gyaltsen, the Fourth Panchen. On the right are renowned lamas. Within the chapel are large images of Sakyamuni and his two disciples. Surrounding these are the Eight Boddhisattvas, the 16 Arhats, and the Ninth Panchen Lama. Upstairs is a *gönkhang* consecrated to Chamzing, the red female divinity, the special protector of Tashilhunpo. The debate courtyard is a charming tree-lined place.

THANGKA WALL

A large, white, free-standing wall rises at the complex's northeast corner. During three days in July, a 40-m *thangka* (*gheku*) hangs from this wall for a festival.

THE RHE AND KU VALLEYS: NOMAD TERRITORY BETWEEN SHIGATSE AND THE TIBET–SIKKIM BORDER

Location	South of Shigatse
Map reference	NH45-12 C, 45-16 A C
Trekking days	7
Start–Finish	Shigatse–Kampa Qu (Mende)
Passes	Shago, Tonga, Kyogo

OVERVIEW

The exploration of this seldom–visited area south of Shigatse begins conveniently from the city; simply walk out of the town towards the large Tashilhunpo Monastery. Shigatse to Kampa Qu takes about a week, and none of the three passes along the way is difficult. The first stretch of the route, along Rhe Chu River, takes in several of Tsang Province's important monasteries: Narthang, Ngor, Rhe, and Chumik Ringmo. Narthang, a 12th-C. Kadampa institution, was the headquarters of the Narthangpa, a sub-sect of the Kadampa. Ngor Ewam Monastery, formerly renowned for its Newar-style paintings and mandalas (see below, page 834), is rarely visited. Rhe and its surrounding valley have been virtually forgotten by outsiders since the 1940s.

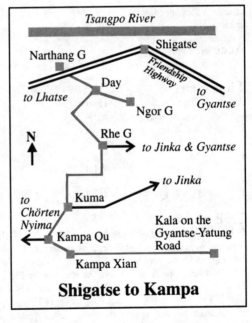

Shigatse to Kampa

After the Rhe Valley, the trek crosses the Nujin Sangra range via the Kyogo La Pass (4884 m) to follow the Ku Chu River through wild, isolated nomad country. The outpost of Lukri usually has many black tents in the warm months. Settlements are once again encountered in the southern portion of the valley, and Kotsi, a pleasant hot spring on the broad Yeru Tsangpo, is just north of Kampa Dzong, the principal town of the district. Kotsi, being near the main road (one branch of which goes east to Kala, then north along the Tibet–Sikkim road to Gyantse), is a good place to start hitching back to Gyantse (see page 412) or to explore the Chumbi Valley (see page 787). Kampa Qu, also on the road, is another plausible place to begin hitching. Avoid entering Kampa Dzong (Kampa Xian), now primarily an army camp and the administrative headquarters. Its old, impressive fort, quite ruined, is atop a spectacular ridge. No traditional Tibetan houses remain in the *xian*, only drab Chinese compounds. Kampa Qu (Mende), on the south bank of the Yeru Tsangpo, is a nice, compact village with excellent views of the Sikkimese mountains. Another option after completing the trek is to continue to Chörten Nyima, a renowned pilgrimage site (see page 801). Both Kampa Qu and Kampa Dzong are appropriate places to start.

Note Day 3 and day 5 of this trek are long. Consider adding a couple more days for the journey.

Related sections
Shigatse, p 815
Chörten Nyima, p 801
Chumbi Valley, p 787
Jinka, p 327

Access
Shigatse is a major stop on the Friendship Highway (see page 989).

Time chart

Day	Place	Hours
1	Shigatse–Ngor	6 1/4
2	Rapdeling	2 3/4
3	Bhadu	8 1/4
4	Yago	5
5	Kuma	9 1/4
6	Serkhang	5
7	Kampa Qu	4 1/2

Trail notes
✤ DAY 1 SHIGATSE–NGOR MONASTERY 6 1/4 HR
From the front gates of Tashilhunpo Monastery, turn right (southwest) on the main road, the Shigatse–Lhatse portion of the Friendship Highway. After 1 km the yellow palace of the Panchen Lama appears on the left. At road marker 262 km (new marker 4913, 2 hr from Tashilhunpo), turn left onto a dirt road that traverses a wide, open area. Head southwest towards a prominent, isolated hill. The village of Dzong (3/4 hr) stands at its base. The road goes between hill and village, then veers left, bypassing a side valley on the right in the distance. (This leads to Rapdeling and the Tonga La, see page 836). (The village of Day [1 hr to walk from Dzong] guards this valley's entrance on the right. Pack animals can be hired here. Close by is Chumik, site of the ancient Chumik Ringmo Monastery, destroyed in a 15th-C. flood.) Turn southeast into a valley to reach Berong (1 1/4 hr). Here the track stops; motor vehicles cannot continue. Ngor is a further 1/2 hr up the valley. Tashilhunpo

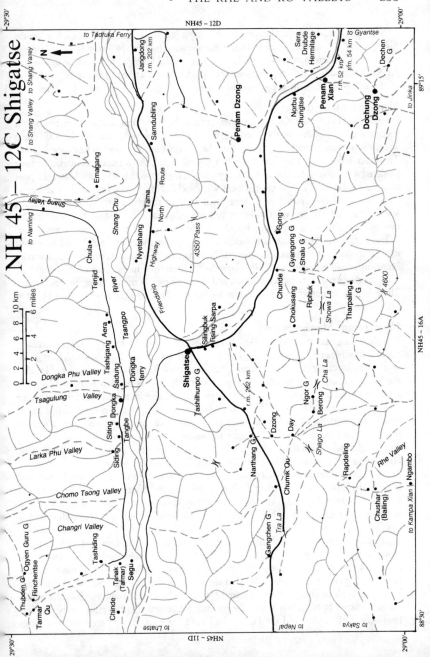

NH45 – 12D

NH 45 – 12C Shigatse

N

to Tádruka Ferry

to Shang Valley
to Shang Valley

to Naming

to Gyantse

to Jintsa

Jangdong
r.m. 202 km

Sera
Drubde Hermitage

r.m. 52 km
p/m. 54 km

Dechen
G

Penam
Xian

Dochung
Dzong

Samdubling

Norbu
Chungtse

Penam Dzong

Emagang

Shang Valley

Shang Chu

Tama

North Route

Chula

Nyetshang

Highway

4350 Pass

Gong

Gyangong G
Shalu G

NH45 – 16A

Tenjid

Friendship

River

Chunde

Riphuk

Showa La

r. 4600

Tsangpo

Silingbuk
Tsing Sarpa

Chokusang

Tharpaling
G

Aera

Tashigang

Sadung

Dongka

Dongka ferry

Shigatse

Tashilhunpo G

Cha La

Siting Dongka

Tangbe

Dongka Phu Valley

Ngor G
Berong

Tsagulung   Valley

Narthang G

Dzong

Day

Shago La

Rapdeling

Rhe Valley

Larka Phu Valley

Siding

r.m. 262 km

Chumik Qu

Chomo Tsong Valley

Chushar
(Baiing)

Ngambo

to Kampa Xian

Changri Valley

Tra La

Gangchen G

Thuden G
Ogyen Guru G

Tashiding

Rinchentse

Tarmar
Qu

Tanak
(Tarmar)

Segu

Chinde

to Lhatse

to Nepal

to Sakya

NH45 – 11D

0   2   4   6   8   10 km
0   2   4   6 miles

88°30'   88°45'   89°00'   89°15'

29°30'   29°00'

to Ngor is a 5 1/2-hr walk. Alternatively, start from Narthang village and monastery, on the right (north) side of the Shigatse–Lhatse main road. They are 14 km west of Shigatse at road marker 266 km (new marker, 4917). The walk is 2 1/2 hr; try to find a ride from Shigatse. At Narthang, walk due south, across an open plain and a river bed to Dzong, at the bottom of the distinctive hill; then continue to Berong and Ngor. This will take 1 1/2 hr.

Narthang Monastery

Founded in 1153 by the Kadampa teacher Tumton Lodrö Drakpa, a disciple of Sharapa, it became the headquarters of the Narthangpa, a Kadampa sub-sect. From the 13th C. on, it was the seat of the Chimtön Namkhar Rinpoche and considered the font of Kadampa doctrine. The main image here was Chumik Drölma (Spring Tara). As a printing center, Narthang produced a valuable collection of the *Tengyur* and *Kangyur* wood blocks, which took 12 years to complete (1730–42). Also created were woodblocks of the *Jakata Tales of the Buddha* and eight famous blocks, created by Polhane, used to print *thangkas* of the 16 Arhats. Only a few *Kangyur* and *Tengyur* woodblocks survive, and only one of the *Arhats*. The latter depicts two *arhats* in the upper corners, Sakyamuni in the center, and two Kadampa lamas below. A huge, intricate, 14th-C. *chörten*, similar in age and design to Gyantse's, stood here until its destruction in the Cultural Revolution. Narthang today is an impressive, extensive ruin. Monks in a small, rebuilt chapel (1987) keep the tradition alive. In the range north of Narthang is the meditation cave of Jangchen Ritrö, and the hermitage of the Narthang Sangye Gompa. These formed an important retreat center for the Kadampa, and are now occupied by a few practitioners.

Ngor Ewam Monastery

Ngorchen Kunga Zangpo (1382–1444), a Sakyapa master, founded Ngor in 1429. The monastery subsequently became the seat of the Ngorpa, a Sakyapa sub-sect, and was widely regarded as the most important Sakyapa monastery after Sakya itself. Known as a great center of Lamdre, the Sakyapa discipline of meditation, it had a rich collection of Sanskrit texts, and Nepalese artists decorated its chapels. Ngor's murals (destroyed) and illuminated manuscripts were among Tibet's greatest artistic treasures. Within the complex were once 18 colleges under five different monasteries. Ngor's two meditation caves of Ngorchen Kunga Zangpo were highly revered; they contained the images of the Lamdre lineage of teachers.To reach them, take the path on the right and cross a stone bridge just before reaching Berong. Go around a hill and climb (1/4 hr) to the grottoes. A footprint (*shabje*) of Ngorchen lies within.

Below and before the rebuilt monastery is a row of recently renovated *chörtens*. Constructed in the mid-15th C., these *chörtens* of the Tathagatas numbered 60 and in the old days contained mandala paintings (rescued). The monastery's main structure was renovated in 1985. Ngor now has about 25 monks, half of them young (400 monks lived here before the Chinese came). The primary buildings of the complex are the Lamdre Lhakhang and Tartse Labrang. Ngor's chapels once contained invaluable murals and Indian and Pala-style (9th–11th C.) bronzes. Some were hidden and are now slowly being brought back to the monastery. Ngor's principal deity is Kye Dorje (Hevajra) and its protector is Mahakala. The rebuilt Lamdre Lhakhang displays several sacred relics. On the left are a 'dragon's egg', old statues (including Birupa), a tooth of Phagpa (Sakya patriarch), and a voluble Tara (*sung gyur*). In the middle are new statues of Ngorchen Kunga Zangpo and Sakyamuni. On the right are new statues (including Tarik Tulku) and the Fifth Dalai Lama's felt boot. Beyond these are two statues of Mahakala (two- and four-armed), covered with white scarves (*khatas*). Ngor's four main lamas are Kangsa Rinpoche, the incarnate, who lives in India (he has come back to visit), Tartse Rinpoche in the United States, Tende Rinpoche in France, and Lobdin Rinpoche also in India.

An optional trek from Ngor to Shalu Monastery

Instead of heading southwest from Ngor to the Rhe Monastery (main trek), consider a short but interesting walk east to the celebrated Shalu Monastery. This itinerary, which involves the crossing of two ridges, can best be performed in two days.

◇ **Day 1** Walk down from Ngor Monastery to the row of rebuilt *chörtens*. Look for a narrow side valley that trends east towards the top of a ridge. Follow a trail within it to the Cha La (1 1/4 hr), which is marked with a large stone cairn. Descend steeply to a small stream (1/2 hr), then zigzag down the slopes of a valley. Go past a small pond and then to a small village sited above another pond. From the pass to here is 2 hr. This is a good place to camp before tackling the second pass.

◇ **Day 2** Descend from the village along the north side of the valley to reach some more villages in 3/4 hr. These are sited along the upper parts of a wide alluvial fan. Walk down to a dirt road (3/4 hr) and valley floor that trends south along the east bank of a river (this road in the north joins the main Shigatse–Gyantse road). (Turn left at the junction to reach Shigatse in a few km; if you follow the road south, you can reach the sacred pilgrimage of Chörten Nyima in about two weeks [see page 801].)

The area here is surprisingly arid and cultivation non-existent. Turn right at the road and head south for 10 min. Then walk due east up the slopes on your left to connect with a trail leading up to the Showa La. Reach the top in 2 3/4 hr. Like the Cha La, it is also marked by stone cairns. Descend along a dry and gravelly valley in 1 hr to a village consisting of two small groups of houses and some barley fields. From here, follow a dirt track that goes north along the Shalu Valley to Shalu (1 3/4 hr). Along the way, walk past several more villages and more cultivation. For more information on Shalu, one of the most memorable monasteries in Central Tibet, see page 400.

Chumik Ringmo Monastery

Chumik Ringmo, formerly a vital pilgrimage site of Tibet, is a short distance south of Day at the junction of the Rhe Chu and a river that flows east from the Pö La into the Nyang Chu at Shigatse. Founded by Chögyal Phagpa in the 11th C., it belonged first to the Kadampa before its Sakyapa conversion. The Chumik Council took place here in the late 13th C., after Phagpa's return from the Mongol court. The monastery was destroyed by a pre-15th-C. flood and nothing remains. Ngor grew in importance after the flood.

✦ DAY 2 NGOR–RAPDELING 2 3/4 HR

From Ngor walk back down to Day (1 1/4 hr). Pass the village and take a path on the left southwestward. Reach the Shago La after a 1/2 hr gradual ascent from Day. About 3/4 hr from the pass is a village, then prosperous Rapdeling (1/4 hr further), a green oasis amidst a dry, sandy plain at the junction of a number of side valleys.

✤ DAY 3 RAPDELING-BHADU 8 1/4 HR

Head southwest along a flat path. Cross a river after 1/4 hr, then take the left, ascending path around a hill to reach the entrance of a sandy, stony valley. Here is the village of Chushar (Bailing). Go south, then southeast along the stony valley, crossing several rivers, towards the Tonga La (4550m). Reach the Ngambo 3 hr from the valley entrance. If you have donkeys, replace them with yaks here to traverse the pass. (Spend the night in Ngambo if you want to break the walk to Bhadu.)

Go east for 1/4 hr past a deserted village on the right. The valley now forks; take the right branch. Shortly it splits again; this time go left. After 1/4 hr, the path starts to ascend the Tonga La, 1 1/4 hr away. The first half of the climb is steep and narrow as it follows a ridge; the scenery from the top is beautiful. Tonga La's far side is flat; yak herds graze in a wide meadow. Head southeast past the villages of Lulung and Sheka (the latter is 1 3/4 hr from the pass). Sheka, poor and exposed on a dry plateau, has peculiar, conical houses. The tapering, 4-m-high walls are stone with openings for a door and a hole at the tip of the cone for ventilation. Walled enclosures help cut the wind. These houses were perhaps granaries originally.

From Sheka, two villages are visible to the south. Two different paths lead to them (a swamp lies between); the right one goes to Rhetö, the left to Bhadu. Take the left, distinct trail along the west bank of the Rhe Chu. After 3/4 hr, wade to the east bank, head southeast for 1/2 hr, skirting a swampy area to the west, to reach Bhadu. Rhetö and Bhadu are both on the right (north) bank of the Rhe Chu. Rhe Monastery is a 10-min walk northeast, above Bhadu, which is a big village with a shop and open-air cinema. No Chinese appear to be present. Rhe is hidden from the village. To find it, skirt south around a hill, then reach another hill with a shrine (lhatse) on top. (To the south [3/4 hr] is Tramo Monastery; locals assert that its statue is a 'cousin' to the Jowo of Lhasa.)

Rhe Monastery

This Gelugpa monastery's full name is Rhe Rinchentse. Its impressive, fortress architecture dominates a razor-sharp ridge. Walls lead down to the river; in the old days these served to protect the water supply. Rhe's location was strategic; trails from here led to Sakya Monastery, Shigatse, Gyantse, and Kampa Dzong. Remdapa (Shonnu Lödro), Tsong Khapa's teacher, was born nearby. Palden Rhe Gyur Tratsang, a tantric college, was the focus of the monastery. The site is mostly in ruins, the result of natural decay over the centuries. A square and white building (new) stands near the top of the complex, solitary home of Kay Gyur Rinpoche. In the middle of the ruined dukhang, inside a walled compound next to the new building, is a tall banner mast (darchen) and a wooden box above a sacred well. The spring, purportedly created by Guru Rinpoche, conceals his meditation cave beneath the well. Pilgrims sometimes carry this miraculous water all the way to Nepal. In front of the ruins, on a hill, is a tiny shrine (lhatse) that contains the image of Penjay, the local protector (yulha). Rhe and Bhadu (3 hr to the east) monasteries have been incorporated at this one site.

Ngor–Bhadu via the Sisung La Take this direct route to Bhadu over a narrow, sometimes treacherous, trail. If you have pack animals, it is necessary to go back to Day (1 1/4 hr, northwest), and cross the Tonga La.

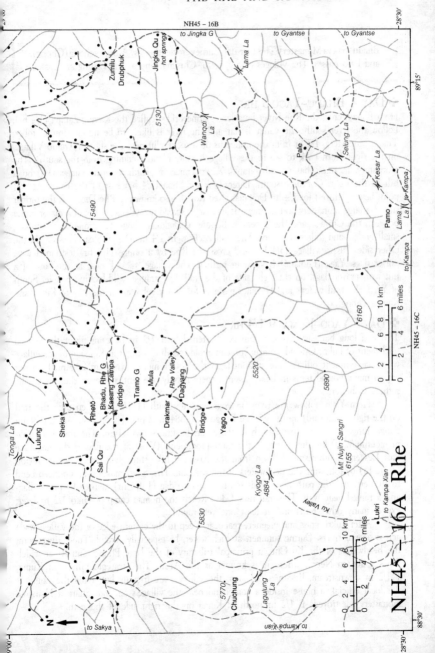

NH45 – 16B

to Jingka G

Lama La

to Gyantse   to Gyantse

Zumilu

Drubphuk

Jingka Qu
hot springs

5130

Wanqoi La

Pale

Selung La

Kesar La

to-Kampa

Lama La

Pamo

to Kampa

5490

6160

10 km
6 miles
8
6   4
6
4   2
2
0   0

NH45 – 16C

5520

Bhadu, Rhe G
Kasang Zabpa
(bridge)

Tramo G

Mula

Rhe Valley

Dagyang

5890

Drakmar

Bridge

Yago

Mt Nujin Sangri
6155

Rheto

Sheka

Tonga La

Lulung

Sai Qu

Kyogo La
4884

Ku Valley

Lukri

to Kampa Xian

NH45 – 16A Rhe

5830

10 km
6 miles
8
6   4
6
4   2
2
0   0

5770

Chuchung

Lagulung La

to Kampa xian

to Sakya

N

28°30'

89°15'

28°30'

29°00'

88°30'

88°30'

Bhadu–Sakya Monastery This four-day journey crosses the easy Adro, Lachong (Chong), and Latö passes. The villages of Sai, Karu, Chisung, Shaga, and Lasung are passed.

✤ DAY 4 BHADU–YAGO 5 HR

From Bhadu, cross the Rhe River by a large, stone bridge called the Kasang Zampa (1/4 hr). Follow the river south; the valley is flat and the river is likely to be frozen after October. Tramo Monastery, 1/2 hr from the bridge, is up a rocky cliff near the start of Tramo Village, on the right (turn back to see it; the village is more obvious coming from the south). The monastery, in ruins, has no inhabitants. After Tramo, a guardian shrine (*sungma*) is on a hill to the right. Continue south. Later, look for Mula (3/4 hr) east of the river. At this point bear southwest for 1/4 hr. Drakmar (Red Rock), also known as Rhe Dzong, is the former site of a large monastery and nunnery. It is a large, spread out village, scene of a major battle between the Chinese and the Tibetans. Beware of Drakmar's dogs. Continue south, cross a small bridge, and follow the river. The trail is clear. In 1/4 hr, Dagyang can be seen on the other side. Pass a village (3/4 hr) and cross the Rhe by a bridge (1/4 hr) festooned with prayer flags. Yago (Pholané) is an hour further. The village, tucked away at the base of a hill with prayer flags, on the right side of the trail, has strange, wild-looking people. South of Yago, the trail widens and becomes passable for motor vehicles all the way to Kuma and Kampa Dzong.

✤ DAY 5 YAGO–KUMA 9 1/4 HR

This is a long but easy day that can be shortened by 1 1/2 hr by camping at the nomad settlement of Lukri. One advantage: you can avoid spending a night at Kuma, a major village where government officials are stationed. In the colder months (November–April) do not expect many nomad tents in Lukri. Even if there is only one tent, however, there is usually sufficient shelter.

From Yago, follow the river on your left due south (1 1/2 hr), then take the trail on the right (westward) up the gradual Kyogo La (4884 m, 2 hr). This pass crosses the Nujin Sangri range from east to west where there can be fine snowy vistas. The rounded 6155-m mountain, 10 km due south, is the most prominent. (West of the pass is the Lagulung La.) Descend southwestward down from the pass and hike through a barren, windy region (2 1/2 hr) by following the headwaters of the Ku Chu. The valley makes a pronounced bend to the left, and the path now heads south. Cross a ridge (1 1/4 hr) marked by prayer flags and a ruined *mani* wall. The trail now fades. Reach the nomad camp of Lukri 1/2 hr later; expect many other tents and at least one year-round.

After Lukri, grass and greenery reappear. Keep to the eastern edge of the valley; wade across several rivers. During summer, at high water, be especially careful. These rivers form the headwaters of the Ku Chu, a principal tributary of the large Phung Chu River which flows south to Nepal, where it is known as the Arun. The strategic village of Kuma, 1 1/2 hr downstream, lies in a flat area; the villagers are friendly but avoid the home of the local official, a house inside a compound near the village's far end. Shari, a Nyingma monastery (destroyed) is 1/2 hr north of Kuma on the right side of the path.

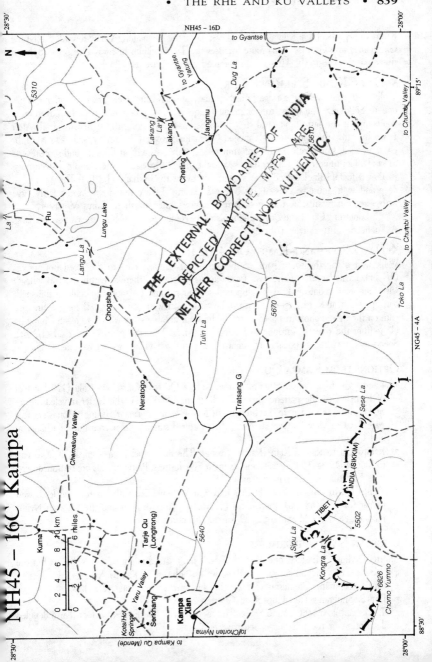

NH45 – 16C Kampa

THE EXTERNAL BOUNDARIES OF INDIA AS DEPICTED IN THE MAPS ARE NEITHER CORRECT NOR AUTHENTIC.

Kuma to Gyantse From Kuma, trails lead east along the Chemalung Valley towards the Nyang Chu Valley and Gyantse. This route bypasses the Tibet–Sikkim highway (see page 787) and the Kala checkpost. (It skirts the motor road along its western flank.)

✤ DAY 6 KUMA–SERKHANG 5 HR

Walk south-southwest up a ridge to a flat, sandy area (1/2 hr). Here are two optional trails; one to Serkhang, the other to Longtrong (Tarje Qu). It is best to avoid the government compound at the latter and head straight to Serkhang by taking the right-hand trail. After 1 3/4 hr, cross the wide, multi-branched Chemalung River (15 min to wade across). 1 hr later, a paved, stone path begins; unfortunately, it only lasts a short distance and soon reverts to sandy. Continue for 1 1/2 hr, then bear right in a southwesterly direction up a steep ridge (4900 m) for 3/4 hr. Descend steeply south-southwest to Serkhang (1/2 hr). The Yeru Chu, deep and swift, must be crossed just before Serkhang. Take care. The village is fairly large with wary inhabitants. A trail from here goes west, then north to Sakya Monastery.

Longtrong Qu (Tarje Qu), an administrative compound, is 1/2 hr to the east of Serkhang. A Public Security Bureau is here.

✤ DAY 7 SERKHANG–KAMPA QU 4 1/2 HR

Walk west along the south bank of the Yeru Chu (a short cut) to the Kotsi hot springs (3/4 hr), located north of the river (wade across). Here is a thermal bathhouse (no village) with four small rooms and several dispersed sulphur streams. (A motor road along the south bank passes near Kotsi.) After a bath, follow the road west (on flat sand) for 1/2 hr, to a path on the right. Follow this path. After 3/4 hr, wade across a shallow river to reach Chungshu (1 hr from the river). Continue to Kampa Qu (Mende) on the main motor road (1/2 hr). Spend as little time as possible in Kampa Qu, a *qu*-level village with government officials.

OPTIONS FROM KAMPA QU

- Kampa Qu to Gyantse. Hitchhike from Kampa Qu to Gyantse via Kala (120 km east of Kampa Qu). Be patient; there is little traffic. At Kala is the better-traveled Tibet–Sikkim road (see page 787). Hitch north to the amazing Yemar (Iwang) Monastery (see page 390) to view its Central Asian, Pala-inspired statues. Then continue to Khangmar and Gyantse.
- Kampa Qu to Kampa Xian (Kampa Dzong). The main road from Kampa Qu leads east to Kampa Dzong, 10 km away, and its impressive fortress. Party officials are stationed here. It is best not to linger in the area.
- Kampa Qu to Tingche Xian. From Kampa Qu or Kampa Xian, the motor road leads west to Sar (or Zara; 68 km), then north (42 km) to Tingche Xian and the Chörten Nyima pilgrimage. Sakya Monastery is 89 km to the north.

CHÖRTEN NYIMA PILGRIMAGE

Chörten Nyima Monastery, one of south Tibet's most sacred pilgrimage sites, lies within the spectacular Tibet–Sikkim range, two days' walk southwest of Kampa Xian.
- Day 1. Serkhang–Chungshu (3 1/2 hr), Chungshu to Shobrang (2 hr).
- Day 2. Shobrang–Tranglung–Sham–Chörten Nyima.
  Trucks can go all the way to Sham. The monastery is 1 hr further on foot. For a detailed description of the pilgrimage, see page 801.

RINPUNG DZONG: FROM SHIGATSE TO LAKE YAMDROK VIA THE RONG CHU VALLEY

Location	East of Shigatse, north of Gyantse
Map reference	NH45-12 C D, 46-9 C
Trekking days	5 (one-way)
Start–Finish	Shigatse–Yasik (on Friendship Highway)
Passes	None

OVERVIEW

This easy trek heads east from Shigatse along the south (right) bank of the Tsangpo. After the Tadruka ferry, it leaves the Tsangpo Valley for the Rong Chu Valley and its old fortress town of Rinpung Dzong. Finally, the Rong Chu is followed to its source at the Scorpion Lake of Yamdrok Tso. Wonderfully varied scenery distinguishes this route. Fertile river valleys with fields of brilliant green barley and golden mustard contrast with barren moonscapes. The flora is made up of colorful forget-me-nots, gentians, daisies, dandelions, sweet peas, and pungent herbs. Monasteries and villages, some perched on dramatic promontories, add human and historical interest to the trek. Near Tadruka is Yungdrungling Monastery,

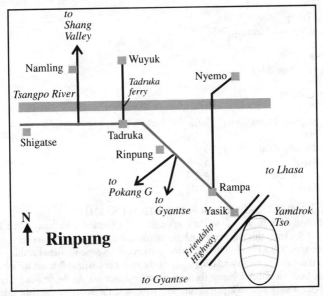

probably the most important pre-Buddhist Bön institution in Tibet. Rinpung was once a major principality; during the 15th and 16th centuries its princes controlled all of Tsang (West-Central Tibet). Rinpung Dzong, a picturesque fortress town, is on the itinerary. Next to the town of Rinpung Xian is Rong Chuchen, a monastery that once had a mighty Jampa statue.

Interesting side valleys open to the north and south. From Dewapaling, walk to Pökang Monastery, once a vital Gelugpa shrine. A good dirt road leads from Dekyiling via the Yung La to Gyantse. Near Rampa, two trails go north to the Tsangpo and Nyemo. Another runs south to Ralung Monastery via the spectacular Nyadong La. An alternative trek involves hiking downstream along the Tsangpo from the Tadruka ferry to the town of Nyemo. From there, either continue along the Tsangpo to Chusul and Lhasa or turn north up the Nyemo Valley to Tsurphu Monastery.

The Rinpung trek is ideal for new arrivals who are still acclimatizing to Tibet's altitude. Its route is well defined along dirt roads and flat river valleys. There are no passes to cross. Hitchhiking is relatively easy along the one unremarkable and rather dusty section of the Shigatse–Tadruka road. (Two or three vehicles pass from Tadruka to Rampa each day.) The final stretch after Rampa is more isolated. Hiring donkeys to carry packs should not be difficult; numerous villages are passed en route. May, June, October, and November are the best months to go. During the summer rainy season hot, cloudless days (sometimes too hot for walking until late afternoon) alternate with stretches of heavy rain.

Related sections

Shigatse, p 815
Shang Valley, p 869
Ralung Monastery, p 611
Yamdrok Tso, p 587
Yungdrungling and Menri, p 763

Access

Shigatse (see page 821).

Time Chart

Day	Place	Hours
1	Shigatse–Tadruka ferry	hitch (80 km)
2	Shangba	5 1/2
3	Rinpung Xian	3
4	Kyemi	5
5	Rampa Qu	4 1/4
6	Yasik	6 1/2

✤ DAY 1 SHIGATSE–TADRUKA FERRY: HITCH (80 KM)

This portion of the itinerary follows the north route of the Friendship Highway to the Tadruka ferry. (After the ferry, this important road goes north to Yangpachen and Lhasa via the Wuyuk Valley, see page 819.) Plan to hitch from the outskirts of Shigatse to Tadruka; this relatively busy road is not conducive to a relaxing walk. At the center of town, walk towards Tashilhunpo Monastery from the Tibetan bazaar (beneath the ruined fortress). At the first major crossroad turn left (northeast) and walk past department stores and the bank on the right side of the

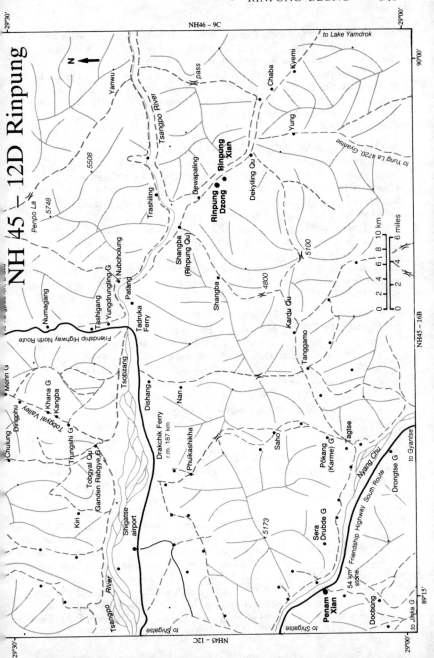

NH45 – 12D Rinpung

street. Continue northeastwards, then east onto the Friendship Highway, which follows the south bank of the Tsangpo. Try to hitch a ride from any point after the bank. Shigatse East (the airport) lies 42 km from Shigatse and is at road marker 4853. The small village of Tadruka, 38 km further (road marker 4821), has a guesthouse and military camp. (The free ferry to the north bank of the Tsangpo takes both people and motor vehicles and runs frequently until 2100.) Nearby, the Bön monastery of Yungdrungling (see page 763) on the north bank is a 3/4 hr-walk from the ferry. This is the most important Bön institution in Tibet and should not be missed.

✤ DAY 2 TADRUKA FERRY–SHANGBA 5 1/2 HR

From Yungdrungling, take the ferry back to the south bank. Walk east along the Tsangpo, first to the northeast around a ridge, then to the southeast. Pass the villages of Chigpa, Dorpan (ruined), and Kulung. After Kulung, a sandy beach 20 m below the road on the left, is suitable for camping. The beach is idyllic, away from habitation and completely private. There is driftwood for a fire, but the river water tastes foul and must be boiled. (A footpath across the river runs to Rinpung and Thompa.) Shangba (Rinpung Qu), 5 hr from Tadruka, is located where the valley broadens. (Along the way pass Chedeling, a monastery and village 3/4 km from the banks of the Tsangpo.) The road goes right through the village beneath a little shrine on the right. This attractive area is a good place to hire a donkey. At Shangba, the Tsangpo receives the waters of the Rong Chu and alters course from southeast to east. Leave the Tsangpo here to follow the left bank of the Rong. After Shangba, camping sites become more scarce.

Shangba to Pökang Monastery: Two days

Shangba is at the entrance of a side valley that opens to the southwest. Follow this valley and in 3 1/2 hr reach another Shangba at its upper reaches. Cross a 4800-m pass in 3 3/4 hr, then descend westward to Kardu Qu (1 3/4 hr). A dirt track leads along a wide valley to Pökang Monastery (see page 329) in the village of Karme (3 1/2 hr). The Nyang Chu (Gyantse River) flows just 7 km away next to the Gyantse–Shigatse road. Drongtse Monastery is across this river. Tagtse, 4 km south of Pökang, was once site of the Tara Monastery (8th century).

✤ DAY 3 SHANGBA–RINPUNG XIAN 3 HR

Continue southeast along the Rong Valley, passing Dewapaling on the right. This village is situated at the entrance of a side valley that opens to the southwest and leads also to Kardu and Pökang Monastery. Rinpung Dzong is 1/2 hr from Dewapaling. The main track skirts the bottom of the ridge capped by the ruined fortress. To reach the town, follow the trail leading to the right from the road, then cross a small bridge and head up the slope through houses. The fortress, at the end of town, appears as one structure, a high wall on the right, and crumbling walls to the left; the surrounding scenery is stark and imposing. One option is to stay here for the night and spend time in the town—this location is one of the centerpieces of the trek. Rinpung Dzong has about 100 houses and a store is in the center of town. It is good place to hire donkeys. Attractive camping spots with flat, mossy ground, and firewood can be found 10 min before and after Rinpung. The ruler of Rinpung principality, Rinpung Depa Norbu Sangpo, took control of Tsang (West-Central Tibet) in 1435. From that time on, the princes of Rinpung ruled this part of Tibet until 1565.

Continue along the flat left bank of the Rong Chu towards Rinpung Xian. Cross a bridge and follow the main road. The next landmark is a hydro-electric station on the right below a garish carving of Jampa. Take the path to the right immediately after the station; Rinpung Xian lies ahead. Rong Chuchen Monastery is in front (100–150 m) and to the right. The Xian is a graceless Chinese town with about 100 houses and a large military presence. A well stocked store (beer, kerosene, canned food, noodles) is on the right on the way out of town. Rong Chuchen (Rong Chamchen), a large Gelugpa monastery, has as its main building a U-shaped chapel that has an expansive front with three floors and numerous windows. This institution, active and in good condition, was built approximately 80 years ago below the ruins of the old, original monastery. The main *dukhang* is cluttered with statues, *thangkas*, butter lamps, and carved butter statues. A hermitage, Rilung Phuk, is across the Rong Chu.

Rong Chuchen Monastery

The Rong Valley's principal monastery was built by a Rinpung prince in 1367. Its spiritual founder was Zhonnu Gyalchok, and the complex contained one Gelugpa and four Sakyapa colleges. At the beginning of the 17th C., the princes of Tsang took control. The Rinpung chief, Norbu Sangpo, donated a huge (10 m) Jampa statue to the monastery, one of the largest in Tibet. The early 20th C. saw 1,500 monks in residence and villages studding the surrounding plains.

✦ DAY 4 RINPUNG XIAN–KYEMI 5 HR

Follow the road southeast into a wide, beautiful valley surrounded by mountains. Dekyiling Qu, at the entrance of a side valley to the right, is 1 1/4 hr away.

Dekyiling to Gyantse: Two–three days
A jeep road 1/2 hr after Dekyiling branches south to Gyantse (68 km) and crosses the 4720-m Yung La in the process.

Monasteries near Dekyiling
• Kyatsal. This monastery at Kishong, near Dekyiling, was founded in 1449. Norbu Sangpo, the Rinpung prince, established an ecclesiastical school here.
• Kambulung, located 10 km up the Kishong River, on the right bank.
• Drölma Lhakhang, surrounded by the ruins of a monastic college.
• Gangra Nesang Dorjeling, 7 km south of Drölma Lhakhang.

The attractive village of Kyemi is reached 3 3/4 hr after Dekyiling (passing Chaba on the right bank along the way). Camp at Kyemi or walk out of town for 3/4 hr for a quiet campsite. The road dips down to a small bridge, then rises again to cross a stream issuing from a side valley. Here are grassy areas and firewood. The water is good for drinking and washing— the first time since Shigatse! This is an excellent place to spend a rest day. Make sure you have sufficient supplies.

✤ Day 5 Kyemi–Rampa Qu 4 1/4 hr

Continue up the road to the southeast along a superb stretch of the Rong Valley. After 1/2 hr pass a bridge leading to the right bank of the river. (The valley widens and to the left is a ruined fort. Above it, on a promontory, are the neglected ruins of Kotto Monastery.) Keep to the left bank of the river, and 1/2 hr from the bridge is Chutsen Village. Its dirty, dribbly hot spring can be bypassed, and soon the river narrows to create a steep, dramatic gorge. The valley divides 3/4 hr from Chutsen. Take the left branch and walk along a straight, exposed road to the Rampa Qu and Rampa Monastery (destroyed).

Rampa to the Tsangpo

Rampa is above the road. Just before its entrance, the road splits. The left branch goes north up a side valley to Yarde Qu, then on to the Tsangpo's south bank. Nyemo is across the river to the east. The right branch continues east along the Rong Chu.

✤ Day 6 Rampa Qu–Yasik 6 1/2 hr

The Rong Valley soon narrows again into a gorge that makes a sharp turn south before reverting east. There are a few places to camp in the gorge, but they are not all that attractive. About 1 hr from Rampa is a side valley with Chungda Village at the entrance; it opens to the north. A trail follows this side valley to the south bank of the Tsangpo via the villages of Phu, Padong Qu, and Sarda.

Ralung Monastery 1 1/2 hr after Rampa, a side valley opens to the south (right); this leads to the Nyadong La (5050 m). The Friendship Highway and Ralung Monastery are on the other side.

Continuing due east along the Rong Chu, go through Tsasum (left bank), Tsathang (right bank), and Gyathang (right bank). Mountains on both sides diminish as the valley widens into a lush, open plain. Reach Tsandung by fording the river on a rough, stone road. Yasik lies 1 1/2 hr further along, at the tip of a small finger of Yamdrok Tso. At this point the dirt track meets up with the Friendship Highway. There are good campsites before the road junction. For drinking water walk to the lake, then bear left for 5 mins to a spring.

From Yasik, hitch east to Lhasa, west to Gyantse and Shigatse, or trek around Yamdrok Tso (see page 587).

TRANS-NYENCHEN TANGLHA VALLEYS: LONGITUDINAL CORRIDORS OF THE TSANGPO–CHANGTANG DIVIDE

It is possible to walk directly from the banks of the Tsangpo northward all the way to the hauntingly beautiful Changtang Plateau, via the great natural corridors of the Nyenchen Tanglha Range. They cut through the mighty mountains and provide essential communication between the settled population of Central Tibet and the nomadic regions of the north. Many of these valleys are religiously significant. Throughout most of the year, when the passes remain open, pilgrims on their way to distant hermitages rub shoulders with traders and herders. In the entire region of Tsang (West Central Tibet) there are no more powerful sites of worship than Zabso, two renowned retreats sited within the Shang drainage system. The east–west route from Shigatse to Lhatse, along the Tsangpo's north bank and via the monasteries of Pindsoling and Jonang, is also described.

NORTH BANK OF THE TSANGPO FROM SHIGATSE TO LHATSE

Location	The Tsangpo Valley west of Shigatse
Map reference	NH45-12 A C, 45-11 B C D, 45-7 A D
Trekking days	5 (one-way)
Start–Finish	Shigatse–Lhatse
Passes	None on main trek

OVERVIEW

The north bank of the Tsangpo, roughly from Shigatse west to Lhatse, is distinguished by four major valleys that open to the north. Piercing the great Nyenchen Tanglha range, these longitudinal corridors ultimately lead to the seldom-visited Changtang and its sublimely beautiful lakes. For experienced trekkers who want to explore the nomadic culture of the high plateau, this chapter includes two major routes, through north-trending valleys, that lead over the

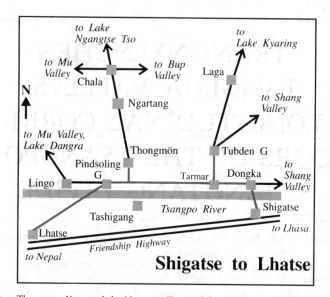

Shigatse to Lhatse

mountains: Thongmön Xian to Lake Ngangtse Tso, and from Tarmar to Lake Kyaring Tso. (Two other itineraries, the Mu Chu–Lake Dangra pilgrimage and the Shang Valley–Lake Namtso trek are detailed in separate chapters; see pages 767 and 869.) The Nyenchen Tanglha range is the watershed between the Tsangpo basin and the isolated, inhospitable Changtang Plateau. It separates the settled population of south Tibet from the nomadic north, a desolate, magnificent world rich in wildlife. These valleys to the north are veritable highways for Tibetans who travel back and forth to trade and to find suitable pastures for their herds.

The main trek from Shigatse to Lhatse along the Tsangpo's north bank is level and easy. The week-long route first goes north from Shigatse to the river, then heads west to avoid the busy Friendship Highway. Begin from either Shigatse or Lhatse simply by walking out of town. Starting from Lhatse is a good option for travellers coming to Tibet via Nepal.

Along the way, pass the important Yeshung and Tanakpo valleys. The latter was once a major artistic center. Pindsoling, Jonang, Tubden, Lhatse Chöde, Gyang Bumoche, and the Bönpo monastery of Tarting are important religious monuments visited. Both Pindsoling and Jonang, sited in striking locales, were noted for their Indian-inspired wall paintings. Drampa, the ancient district centered around Lhatse Chöde, has a number of small chapels associated with early historical personages. Drampa Gyang Lhakhang was supposedly built in the 7th C. by Songtsen Gampo. Guru Rinpoche stayed in a cave near the chapel of Gyang Yönpolung; and Gayadhara, the famed 11th Kashmiri *pandita*, consecrated the Gayadhara Lhakhang, a cave temple in the center of Lhatse Dzong. The monastic center of Lhatse Chöde still retains 17th-C. murals which document a transition stage when Tibetan painting finally moved away from the influences of India and Nepal to develop its own unique style.

During most months it is also possible to hire a coracle—an age-old mode of transport—to travel down the Tsangpo. Changtang portions of the routes are rated Exploratory Treks and can be extremely arduous at certain times of the year. However, the lake districts of

Ngangtse and Kyaring are well-worth the effort; this region has some of Tibet's most stunning scenery.

Related sections
Lake Dangra and Mt Targo, p 767
Shigatse, p 815
The Shang Valley, p 869
Lhatse to Sakya, p 890
The Jonang, Gyang, and Jampaling *kumbums*, p 463

When to go
Avoid the rainy season of July and August; June and September can also be wet. From December to June, the Tsangpo Valley between Shigatse and Pindsoling is characterized by a strong westerly wind that blows from noon until late in the evening. This sand-laden wind rushes east along the river and contributes to the valley's barrenness. It also makes heading west difficult. With the first rains of early July the wind stops. During the summer, the Tsangpo rises dramatically and makes travel by coracle difficult; at times, high water forces the trail to go over ridges rather than along the banks.

Access: Shigatse
From Shigatse, walk past the Tibetan market and the destroyed fort on the hill, then follow the main dirt road away from Tashilhunpo Monastery. This initial, busy stretch passes through areas of construction (about 5 km) on the way to the Dongka ferry. Turn left (west) along the Tsangpo River after crossing the river (2 hr from Shigatse).

Note: Lhatse to Shigatse
The reverse of this trek, from Lhatse to Shigatse, begins at road marker 399 km (just east of Lhatse) by the side of the Friendship Highway. Near here is the turnoff for a dirt track to Lhatse Chöde Monastery and the village of Lhatse Qu; follow it north up the Lhatse Valley.

Time Chart
Day	Place	Hours
1	Dongka ferry–Tanak	6 1/2
2	Thongmön Xian	8
3	Pindsoling Monastery	8
4	Lhatse Chöde	9
5	Lhatse Xian	1 1/2

Trail Notes
✤ DAY 1 DONGKA FERRY–TANAK 6 1/2 HR
Cross to the Tsangpo's north bank on the Dongka ferry, an iron platform pulled by steel cables (5 min, free). The ferry does not operate during lunch, between 1300 and 1500. Nearby are pylons that carry power to Shigatse from the Tanakpo Valley. Follow a dirt track due north from the ferry to the main road along the river's north shore (1/2 hr). At the junction are the villages of Dongka and Sadung situated near the entrance to the north–south Dongka Phu Valley. The Tsangpo in this region is about 5 km wide.

Dongka Phu Valley A trail from Sadung goes north up the valley to its upper pastures, passing the side valleys of Nyangra, Mudik, and Charo. These regions are mostly inhabited by nomads. Reach the 5500-m Dongka La after two days, then descend eastward to the prosperous Shang Valley at Chom, 10 km south of Namling Dzong (see page 872). From the pass to Chom takes one day.

Walk west from the junction along the Tsangpo's north bank. Traffic is rare on this dirt road. The first side valley on the right is called Tsagulung (1 hr); the village of the same name lies up the valley. Pass Siting, Chöni, Tugay, and Tangbe, sometimes crossing ravines adjacent to fields of corn and wheat. Tangbe is 3 hr from the junction. The next valley to the north is the Larka Phu. Beyong are the villages of Pani, Sepuk, Gede, and Segu (a picturesque village at the eastern entrance of the large Tanakpo Chu Valley.) Finally reach Tanak (known locally as Tarmar) at the beginning of the wide Tanakpo Valley, 3 hr from Tangbe. A ferry is near here.

The Tanakpo Valley

This is the largest of the north-trending valleys between Shigatse and Thongmön Xian. At its mouth the river divides into several branches and nearby are Rangjön and the monasteries of Tragun and Tashiding. Farther up are Yangyu, Drölma Phuk, Rigu, Nasa, and Hlagu. Tanak is a good place to hire coracles for the trip downstream to Shigatse. At the village's center is Tanak Monastery (rebuilt); no trace remains of its original foundation. There is also a store here. A trail within the valley leads north to Tubden and Ogyen Guru monasteries and the hot springs of Bur Chutsen.

Tubden Monastery

Follow the Tanakpo Valley north, with the river on the left, to Tashiding and Dingyi (1 hr). [In the hills east of the path is Drölma Phuk meditation cave, which will take about 1 hr to reach.] Continue to the Tong Chu hydro-electric station set close to a village (1 1/2 hr). It supplies much of Shigatse's electricity. A number of tributaries flow east and west to this river junction. Cross a wooden bridge and continue along the valley's west side; soon the jeep road veers to the left (ruins appear across the river on the right). A side road leads to a small wooden bridge with a stone foundation. Do not cross it but continue to the monastic complex of Tubden in the Tanak (Tarmar) Qu (1 hr from the power station), after crossing a different bridge. A lama lives near the foot of a hill in a stone house; several fine *thangkas* hang in a small chapel. Rebuilt Tubden Monastery, halfway up the hill, was founded in 1478 as a major Sakyapa center. Surrounding buildings, once owned by Tubden, are now occupied by villagers. The head lama is also the village doctor. Be sure to visit his house beyond the monastery where one room on the roof has sculptures, *thangkas*, ritual objects, and a plethora of medicinal herbs. There are more than 20 monasteries farther up the Tanakpo and its tributary valleys. One of these is Ogyen Guru Monastery (1 1/2 hr from Tubden).

➡

Ogyen Guru Monastery

Walk back down the road from Tubden, cross the small bridge again and turn right down the Tanakpo Valley. A side valley is to the left (east) and some ruins (seen earlier) are at the valley's entrance on the right side. Cross the small wood bridge with stone foundations to Niu, one of several villages in the area well known for terracotta pottery. Follow the side valley up, along its right slopes, to a dry canyon on the right. A path goes up its steep sides to Ogyen Guru at the top. Several nuns live in a restored building. The original walls are intact and the charming monastery has the appearance of a fortress (dzong).

Tarting Monastery (see also below, p 854)

From Tubden, an alternative route leads to the next (west) valley and the Bönpo Monastery of Tarting. Instead of returning to Tanak, continue along the Tubden Monastery side valley (west) to Chökong (1 3/4 hr) and the Jeh La (5500 m, 2 3/4 hr). Descend for 2 1/2 hr to Keshong; Tarting Monastery is 1/2 hr away on a hill.

Upper reaches of the Tanakpo Valley

The eastern branch of Upper Tanakpo leads to the Shang Valley (see page 869). The western branch has two important tributaries, one of which leads to the large Thongmön–Yeshung Valley (see page 854) and another which crosses the Nyenchen Tanglha range to Lake Kyaring Tso.

1. To the Shang Valley

From Tubden at a valley junction, follow a branch of the Tanakpo Valley to the northeast. Trails follow both sides of the river. Reach Namgyagang in 2 1/2 hr. Continue northeast to Lekyepa (3 hr) on the left bank. Beyond is a river confluence and Laga (1 3/4 hr). Take the right branch (the left goes west to the Thongmön Valley, then northwest to the Changtang via Lungsang Qu). Follow the right bank past the village of Tanakpo to reach the Bur Chutsen hot spring (2 hr). This renowned site is where lamas and monks come for cures. Chaga is 3/4 hr farther. Continue northeast to cross a 5000-m pass (5 hr), then descend due east along a river valley that eventually joins the Shang Valley in 7 hr. From here, either head north to Lake Namtso (see page 657) or south to Namling Dzong (1 1/2 days) and Shigatse (see page 815).

2. To Lake Kyaring Tso by crossing the Nyenchen Tanglha range: Two weeks

In Tsang, four main routes penetrate the Nyenchen Tanglha range, north of the Tsangpo, to reach the large lakes lying on the Changtang. From west to east, they are:
• Mu Chu Valley to Lake Dangra via the Chang-la-Pö-La Pass (see page 767).
• Thongmön Xian to Lake Ngangtse Tso via the Sela La Pass (see page 855).
• Tanak (Tarmar) to Lake Kyaring Tso via the Tanakpo Chu (see below).
• Shang Valley to Lake Namtso via the Kalamba La (see page 869). ➡

Tanak (Tarmar) to Lake Kyaring Tso via the Tanakpo Chu: A Brief Sketch
From Tubden Monastery, go to Laga, at a river junction (see Shang Valley, above), take the left (northwest) branch (the right goes to the Bur Chutsen hot springs). Walk up the valley for 3 1/2 hr to another junction. Follow the right branch north to Lungsang Qu (4 1/2 hr) and an important trail junction. The right branch (east) leads to the Shang Valley, while the left (north) crosses a high 6050-m pass after 6 hr. The valley beyond heads northeast to Nibo Nima (2 1/2 hr). Continue for 1 1/2 hr more to Kungchu, situated at a valley junction. Take the north valley to the large Chinma (Shencha) Chu Valley (3 1/2 hr), then the left (west) branch to the shores of a twin lake in 2 hr (not on map). The trail now curves north to the wide plain of the Shencha Tsangpo (2 1/2 hr), a basin that runs from the Nyenchen Tanglha's northern edge to Lake Kyaring Tso.

Allow six more days from here for the trek north to Shencha (Shentsa) Xian, a district headquarters for this part of the Changtang. From here to the lake (northwest) is a 2-hr walk. At Shencha a dirt road with regular traffic leads to the dirt highway that links Nagchu to Ali (Shiquanhe) in West Tibet. Shencha to Amdo is 391 km; Amdo to Nagchu is 138 km. Buses ply between Nagchu and Lhasa.

✤ DAY 2 TANAK–THONGMÖN XIAN 8 HR

Follow the sandy road along the Tsangpo, traversing sand dunes along flood plains. The entrance of the north-trending Lagong Valley is near Chinde. Pass the Siglung, Lungpa Shar, and Pooshan valleys. Dewa Lungcha, Dzong Chöde, Ogyen Dzong, and Tsukung are villages along this stretch of the Tsangpo, here divided into two main branches. The trail widens as it veers southwest to Rungma. To the right (north) the Sabget La Mountains rise immediately above the river. Rungma, a village of 30 houses, is built on a terrace of gravel and shingle (4 hr from Tanak). Wheat, corn, peas, and radishes grow here. [On the

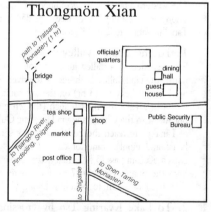

Tsangpo's south bank is the mouth of the Shab (Shablung) Valley. At its entrance, west of the river, is an isolated rock with Chöni Kera Monastery on top.] Continue west to Chom Lamchang. On a hill above it are the ruins of the Chöding Nunnery. Follow the road to Karu at the eastern entrance of the Thongmön Valley. Above it is Karuphu Valley. Continue to Thongmön Xian (locally pronounced Thomay), a strategic settlement at the center of the Yeshung Plain. The village's original name was Ye (or Zhe), now known as Zhe Thongmön (officially Thongmön Xian). The original Thongmön lies some distance to the southwest.

(For the continuation of Trail notes, see page 862).

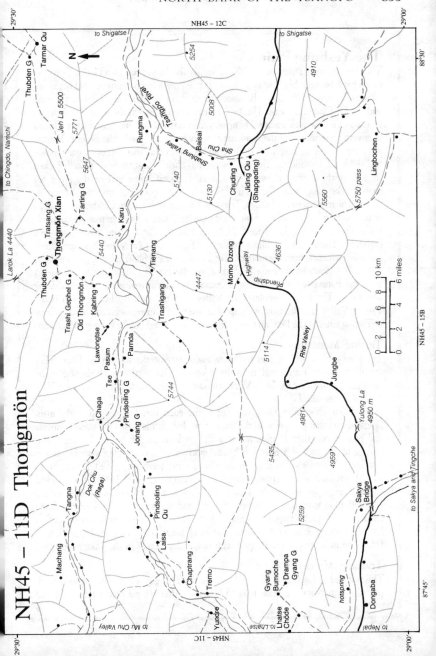

NH45 – 11D Thongmön

NH45 – 12C

N

to Shigatse
to Shigatse

29°30'
29°30'

88°30'

Thubden G
Tarmar Qu

Jeh La 5500
5771

Tsangpo River
5254

4910

5008

to Chingdo, Namchi

Shablung Valley
Sha Chu

5647
Rungma
Baisai

5130
Chuding
Jiding Qu (Shapgeding)

Tarting G
5'40
Karu
5440

Larok La 4440

Tratsang G
Thubden G
Thongmön Xian

Momo Dzong
4636
5560
5750 pass

Lingbochen

Trashi Gephel G
Old Thongmön
Kabring
Tienang
4447

Friendship Highway

Lawongtse
Parnda
Tse Pasum

Trashigang

5114

10 km
8
6
4
2
0

6 miles
4
2
0

Chaga
Pindsoling G
5744
Jonang G

Rhe Valley
Jungbe

Machang
Tangna
Dok Chu (Raga)
Pindsoling Qu

Laisa
4981

Yulong La 4950 m

Sakya Bridge
to Sakya and Tingche

Chaptrang
Tremo
5435
4959

5259

29°00'
29°00'

Yundre
to Mu Chu Valley

Gyang Bumoche
Drampa Gyang G

Llatse Chode
to Lhatse

hotspring
Dongaba

to Nepal

87°45'

NH45 – 11C

NH45 – 15B

The Yeshung Plain

The vast Yeshung Plain, nearly 100 sq km, is the largest flat area of the Tsangpo's north bank between Shigatse and Lhatse. It has quite a few monasteries and numerous villages. Several rivers drain the area; among them are the Rung Chu in the west and the De Chu in the east. The Yere Tsangpo flows through the plain; the Tsangpo delimits its southern perimeter. Thongmön Xian is the center of a large district. Organs of government, including the Communist Party office and the Public Security Bureau, are here as well as hospitals, schools, and a compound that serves as guest house and residence for officials. The guest house has cheap, plentiful food. A well-stocked store is at the centre of town 5 min from the guest house and nearby are a tea shop, market, and post office. The PSB is in a compound around the corner.

The monasteries of Tubden, Tratsang, Tangna, and Ganden Chöding are grouped at the north perimeter of the plain. Tashi Gephel, once a large, impressive complex, lies to the west (see below, page 862). Several small valleys radiate from the western perimeter. These include Didung (leading to Sumno Monastery and Ngompo Ritse), Kuratse originating from the mountains of Tanak Sila, and Sharchuk Nang. An isolated spur called Ngunchu runs north–south along the plain's eastern sector and within it are the transverse valleys of Yunggung and Chetö La as well as Ngunchu Chödzong Monastery. The wide Ngunchu Tang Valley is to the east. Farther east still is the Tarting Valley and the famous Bönpo monastery of Tarting, sited above the village of Tarting Chöro. The De Chu flows within this valley and nearby is Tanga Monastery.

Tarting Monastery

The pre-Buddhist sect of Bön has three major monasteries in Central Tibet. They are all in Tsang: Yungdrungling in the Wuyuk Valley northwest of Shigatse is the most important (see page 763); Menri Monastery (near Yundrungling, see page 765); Tarting is the third.

From Thongmön Xian, walk out of the guest house compound to the main Shigatse road that starts next to the town store. Turn left and pass the market, cinema and post office. After 15 min, follow a dirt track to the left to the Tarting Chöro Village at the foot of a hill (1 hr). The monastery ruins are clearly visible above; a steep path zigzags up to them in 20 min. Tarting (originally called Tarting Sergo Tamo) was built a few centuries before Tashilhunpo (founded 1447). It was sacked by the Dzungar Mongols in the 17th C. and then by the Chinese during the Cultural Revolution. A main temple has been restored and nearby is a small, charming shrine festooned with prayer flags and Bönpo tridents. Faint murals remain in a large, roofless hall that once contained 42 pillars. The head lama has a house in Tarting Chöro below the monastery; a tall flagpole with prayer flags stands in the village courtyard.

Tratsang Monastery

This restored Gelugpa monastery is 1 hr from the Thongmön Xian Guest house. Walk past the turnoff for the main road to Shigatse. After several blocks turn right and

➡

cross a bridge outside the village. A path goes through cultivated fields and up a hill to a small valley. Tratsang lies just beyond a village. Careful restoration has preserved many old walls with original murals. The central chapel is surrounded by monks' quarters now used by the villagers (70 monks lived here before 1966). An old monk buried sculptures and ritual objects during the upheavals, thus saving for the monastery a surprisingly good collection of artefacts.

Thubden Monastery

This destroyed center west of Tratsang has not been rebuilt. Immediately to its southeast is the nunnery of Ganden Chöding (destroyed).

Ngunchu Chödzong Monastery is southwest on a ridge that divides the Yeshung Plain along its eastern sector.

Exploratory Trek: From Thongmön Xian to Lake Ngangtse Tso on the Changtang

This strenuous 17-day, 250-km trek from Thongmön Xian up the Zhe Valley to Lake Ngangtse Tso traverses the Nyenchen Tanglha range and crosses eight passes. This route is classified Exploratory and should only be attempted by experienced, well-equipped trekkers. Those that do would be amply rewarded by breathtaking scenery, timeless nomadic culture, and plentiful wildlife. (Getting a guide for the Changtang portion is critical.) The Swedish explorer, Sven Hedin, in the first decade of this century, was the first Westerner to travel this route; no outsiders have set foot on the shores of Lake Ngangtse Tso or crossed any of the eight passes since. It is possible to undertake this trek even in winter with the proper gear. The passes are almost never closed, as those of the Himalayas are. Very cold temperatures and strong winds can be expected north of the Sela La, but little snow. The route from the Yeshung Plain to Lake Ngangtse Tso is well used for most of the year, especially in summer when nomads and traders are on the move. However, people with inadequate equipment should turn back south of the Sela La and not attempt to cross the Changtang to the lake. The following is a route summary.

✧ Day 1 Thongmön Xian–Shepa Kawa (Dokang)   15.6 km

From Thongmön Xian, walk northwest on a well-used trail through eroded granite terrain and cross several ravines that run southwest to the Rung Chu and the Yeshung Plain. Continue to the Larok La, a steep, 4440-m pass situated on a secondary range of the Nyenchen Tanglha. From here the Himalayas are visible; the Rung Chu can be seen to the west and the huge Yeshung Plain is dotted with small villages. After the pass, descend northwest along the left bank of the Do Chu (Pema Nagpo Chu). On the left is Chaga Monastery on a hill at the foot of Mt Hasha. The river from the pass, flowing south, joins the Rung Chu at Tsolung; the region below it is called Amnak Rung. (South of this is the Yeshung Plain.) Mountains west of the trail are the Dongra and the Gasa ranges. After passing the Yulung Tanka Plain, reach Shepa Kawa by the banks of the river. A ruined *dzong* here is called Dokangpe and the area is sometimes known as Dokang.

✧ Day 2 Shepa Kawa–Kabalo   7.2 km

Walk north along the Do Chu Valley; the river is a tributary of the Rung Chu. The valley is bounded on the west by a sizeable range of mountains with many transverse valleys. (About 3 km after Shepa Kawa a side trail leads west over a 5000-m range to the Rung Chu, only 7 km from this turnoff.) In the middle of the valley is the ruined fort and village of Arung Kampa. Tiny Kabalo (4344 m) stands at a river junction with at least three possible routes. The way left leads to the Gula Valley and the Rung Chu. One branch of the Do Chu continues northeast for three days to Chingdo, a major nomad encampment with many tents.

✧ Day 3 Kabalo–Ngartang   21.8 km

From Kabalo, take the center Tokja Valley (north-northeast), another branch of the Do Chu, to the Ta La (5436 m, 11.8 km from Kabalo). The pass, situated between two rocky crags, is steep but the view of the snowy Himalayas is one of the best in Tibet. Descend steeply to the west-northwest on a trail marked by stone cairns. After about 5 km the valley becomes the Gelung Plain. Continue in the same direction along the Talung Valley to the triangular Ngartang Plain (10 km from the pass). Nomad tents are here year-round. Look back due south to locate the entrance to the deep, narrow Rung Gorge that leads to the Yeshung Plain. This difficult, summer-only route avoids the Ta La and Larok La passes. The Rung, flanked on the east by massive Mt Chumbulung (5620 m), is a series of rapids and waterfalls. To the north-northeast is the Sanglung River, a branch of the Rung Chu; a trail follows it to Chingdo.

✧ Day 4 Ngartang–Tamring   24.4 km

Follow a branch of the Rung Chu north-northwest. It receives smaller tributaries from both sides. About 13 km from Ngartang is the Dangbe La (5250 m), the watershed between the Bup Chu and Rung Chu rivers. Descend along the Dangbe Valley to the north-northwest. From the pass to Tamring is 11.4 km; high mountains rise on both sides of the settlement. Two small valleys, Nalung and Dalung, merge at the villages of Lhündrub and Tamring.

✧ Day 5 Tamring–Tak Rera   13.7 km

From Tamring, follow the Dangbe Chu, an easy descent, to the major valley junction at Chala Qu (7.7 km), an administrative center in the narrow Bup Chu Valley. Bup Chu, the most significant river in these parts, runs east to west to join the Mu Chu Valley to the west at Linga Monastery (see page 775). In the summer, the swollen river requires a ferry to cross. Sechen lies east of the junction and beyond is the great mountain mass of Shakchen (6150 m). The Sham Valley opens due north and a trail within it leads to the Chesang La (5474 m). Sham, a warm valley, never sees snow in the summer when it turns into a wet, marshy area where many streams converge. From the Sham Chu–Bup Chu junction, continue along the Sham Valley for 6 km to the Tak Rera campground (4635 m). Large herds of sheep and yak graze on the mountain sides and a 50-m *mani* wall here is constructed from thousands of sculpted *mani* stones.

✧ Day 6 Tak Rera–Ogma Tagar   20.7 km

The 10-km ascent from Tak Rera to the Chesang La (5474 m) follows the Yangser Valley (called Terungpa in its upper reaches). After the pass, descend northward along a graded path within the Chesang Valley to the small nomad encampment of Chialung. The side valleys

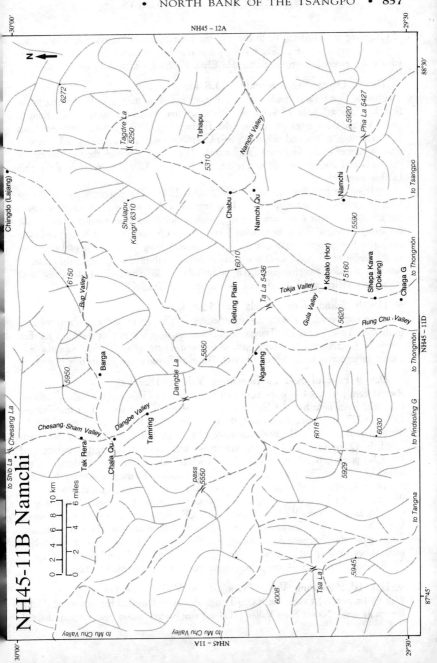

NH45 – 12A

NH45-11B Namchi

of Chagelung and Lungsang lie to the east; the latter leads to Chingdo, a large and noted nomad encampment. Ogma Tagar, a valley junction at the east–west valley of Muwa Chechen (this valley proceeds westward to the Mu Chu), is 10.6 km from the pass.

✧ Day 7 Ogma Tagar–Selindo   23.8 km

The trail at Ogma Tagar climbs immediately northeast along the Ogma Tagar River to the Shib La (5349 m), only 3.8 km away. This valley has two tributaries; the Tagar Kungma on the left and the Kaling Ogma on the right. The crest of the Shib La affords a wide panorama in all directions. It is second only to the Sela La in importance in this itinerary and represents a true watershed of the Nyenchen Tanglha range. Two stone cairns mark the top. The eastern one has a trail leading eastward to a region called Lanang. All the rivers south of the Shib La flow westward.

From the pass down to Selindo (4832 m) is 20 km. The descent along the Porung Valley is generally to the northwest and the trail, marked by mani walls, is forced to follow the left slopes. About 6 km from the top, a side valley enters from the left (west) at the hot springs of Mensé Tsaka. In a further 3 km is Tsaka Chutsen (Salt Hot Water) and more sulphurous hot springs. To the east is the wide Terkung Rung Valley with a trail that leads to the region of Chingdo. Continue straight ahead (north-northwest) along the valley of Selenang. Selindo, a camping ground, is distinguished by eroded terraces. To the left (southwest) is the Sela Valley, which trends west to join the Mu Chu.

✧ Day 8 Selindo–foot of Sela La   15.8 km

Continue north-northwest along the wide Selenang Valley; its river is a northern tributary to the Sela Valley's river (Ke Tsangpo in its lower reaches), a branch of the Mu Chu. The valleys of Tingring and Shinglung open to the west; Horyu is to the east. Near the Sela La, the valley curves to the left (northwest). There are nomad encampments here in summer.

✧ Day 9 Foot of Sela La–Bupchung Valley   18.9 km

Ascend steeply for 2.9 km to the northwest to the Sela La (5506 m), the highest point on this trek. From here to Lake Ngangtse Tso (4694 m) is 92.3 km and to the Tsangpo (3930 m) 127 km. As one travels west, the height differential between the Tsangpo and the northern plateau lessens; the rivers' corrosive effect is greatest in the east. The Sela La is called the Chang La or Pö La as are other passes that demarcate Chang (Changtang) and Pö (Tibet proper). North of the pass, the Nyenchen Tanglha's many rivers drain into the inland lakes of the Changtang, none of which have outlets. To the south, rivers drain into the Tsangpo basin and, ultimately, the Indian Ocean. North of the Sela La, the route follows the large Naong Tsangpo and Tagrak Tsangpo to the northwest. Tributaries originating in the Pabla range, between the Sela La and the Mu Chu to the west, flow north to the Naong Valley. Names of side valleys often are derived from the Pabla peaks from which they originate. For example, the Bupchung River comes from Bupchung Ri. These valleys on the Pabla's north slopes are deep and narrow. Descend gradually to the north-northwest for 16 km to the Bupchung Valley (5344 m), a high frigid area generally not used by nomads.

✧ Day 10 Bupchung Valley–Naong Sung Valley   14 km

Walk 14 km northwest along the Naong Tsangpo Valley, well marked between rounded hills. Eventually reach Naong Sung Valley (5134 m) that merges into a plain. Again, descend

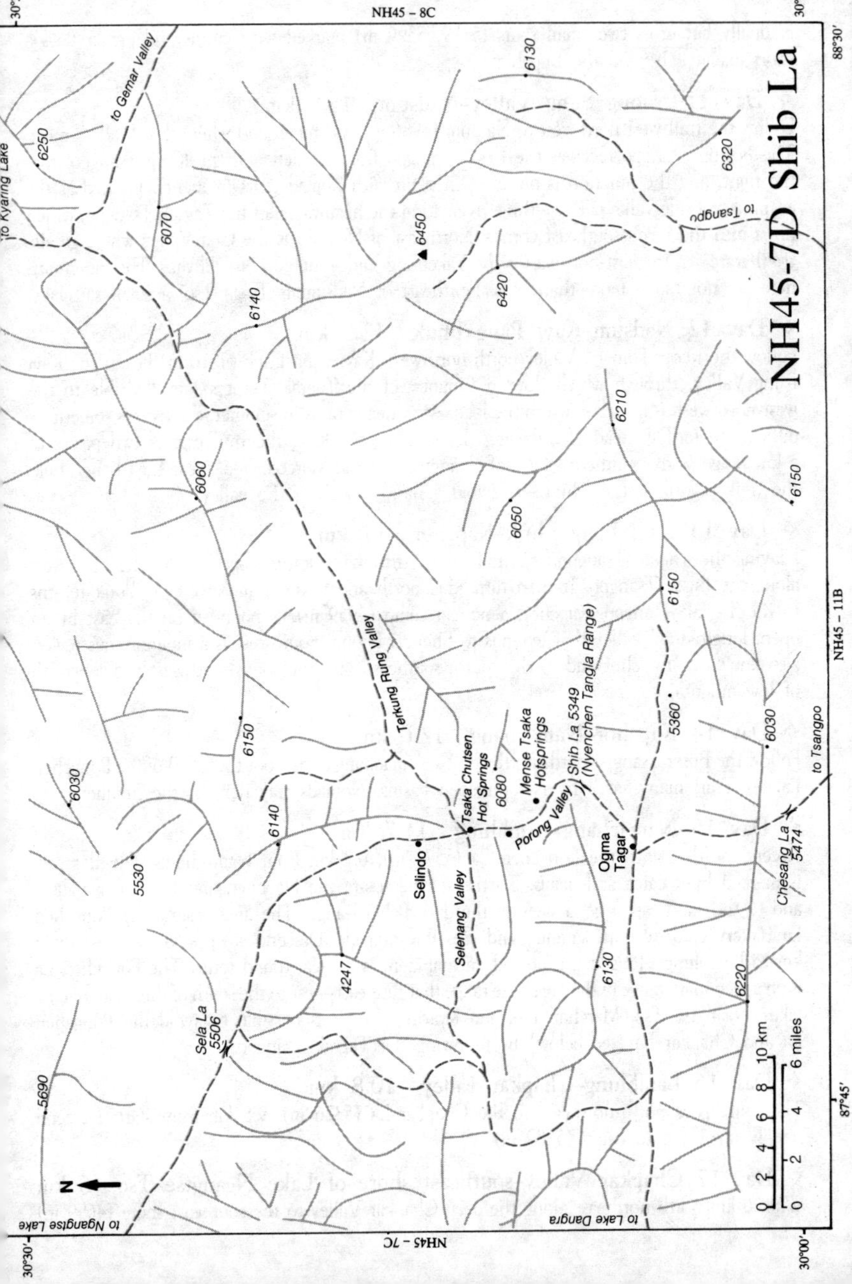

NH45 – 8C

NH45-7D Shib La

30°30'

30°00'

88°30'

to Gemar Valley

to Kyaring Lake

6250

6070

6140

6060

6150

6030

5530

6150

6140

4247

Terkung Rung Valley

Selenang Valley

Selindo

Sela La 5506

5690

to Ngangtse Lake

to Lake Dangra

6130

5349

Tsaka Chutsen Hot Springs

Mense Tsaka Hotsprings

Shib La 5349 (Nyenchen Tangla Range)

Porong Valley

Ogma Tagar

Chesang La 5474

6130

6220

6030

5360

6150

6150

6210

6050

6420

6450

6130

6320

to Tsangpo

to Tsangpo

NH45 – 11B

NH45 – 7C

87°45'

N

0   2   4   6   8   10 km

0   2   4   6 miles

gradually but cross two small spurs (5199, 5399 m) marked with cairns and prayer flags a short distance beyond the Bupchung.

✧ Day 11 Naong Sung Valley–Nadsum   15.8 km

Follow the trail west-northwest to Nadsum (4986 m), a campground where three valleys meet. The Naong Tsangpo receives the Kesar Tsangpo from the left and the Kung Tsangpo from the right, and the junction is on an open plain with nomad tents frequently pitched at the entrances of side valleys. These three rivers form the headwaters of the Tagrak Tsangpo, which flows into the lake's southeast corner. Northeast of Nadsum is the Goa Valley where gazelle (*goa*) graze. To the east-northeast is the Yakchung Valley, habitat of wild yaks. The mountains here are not much more than hills. Northeast of Nadsum is Tsaga Tso, a small salt lake.

✧ Day 12 Nadsum–Kayi Pang Phuk   12.2 km

Follow the Kesar Tsangpo Valley north-northwest. Kayi Pang Phuk (4910 m) lies in the Kayi Rung Valley, through which flows a tributary of the Tagrak Tsangpo, itself visible to the west-northwest as it runs down to the lake. After heavy rains in summer, the river is sometimes difficult to ford. Instead of following the river to the lake, the trail crosses two passes of a low range at the southern shores of Ngangtse Tso and Marchar Tso. Near Kayi Pang Phuk, the trail negotiates the Chi La to avoid a narrow neck of the valley.

✧ Day 13 Kayi Pang Phuk–Kapchor   17 km

Leaving the Tagrak Tsangpo, the trail for the first half of this stage goes to the northwest along the Buser Tsangpo. It then turns due north and 9 km from Kayi Pang Phuk returns to the Tagrak Tsangpo. Kapchor, a nomad camp (4959 m), is bounded on the east by an open, longitudinal valley that extends to Shentsa Dzong. Southwest is a mountainous region also known as Kapchor and to the south, southeast, and the south-southwest is a labyrinth of low mountains.

✧ Day 14 Kapchor–Namachang   12.6 km

Follow the Buser Tsangpo north-northwest to Namachang at the foot (5055 m) of the Pongchen La. At Tsari many small rivers form open basins. Nomads stay here in the summer.

✧ Day 15 Namachang–Lamblung   11.7 km

Ascend northwest to the Pongchen La (5371 m), 6.7 km from Namachang. The flat pass is marked by a cairn and *manis*. To the northeast are the Ngochen and Ngochung valleys and to the southeast a good view of the dark Pabla Range. The area around the Pongchen La is very cold even in summer and sees few nomads. Descend steeply to the west for 5 km to Lamblung (4895 m), a nomad encampment with year-round tents. The Pongchen La is on a secondary range of the Ngangtse range that runs east–west to the south of three Changtang lakes: Ngangtse Tso, Marchar Tso, and Kyaring Tso. It is possible to avoid the Pongchen La and Chapkar La (see below) by following the Tagrak Tsangpo.

✧ Day 16 Lamblung–Chapkar valley   10.8 km

The route goes north-northeast to the Chapkar La (5326 m), 9.8 km from start. Descend steeply for 1 km to camp (5189 m).

✧ Day 17 Chapkar Valley–southeast shore of Lake Ngangtse Tso   6 km

Walk 6 km north-northeast along the deep Chapkar Valley to the southeast shore (4699 m)

NH45-7A Ngangtse Tso

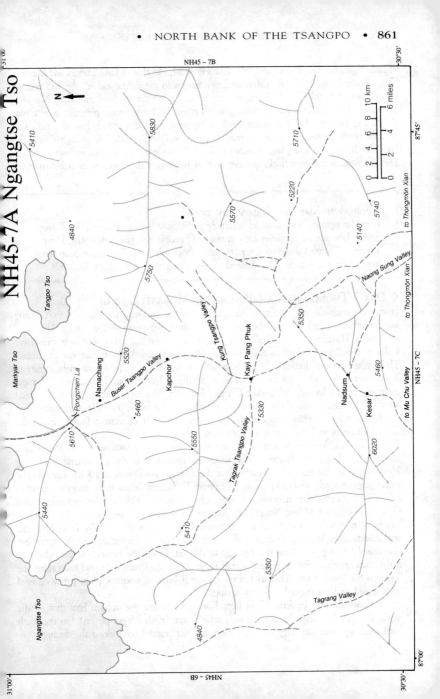

NH45 – 7B

5410 •

5830 •

5710

5220

5570 •

5740 •

4840 •

Tangpo Tso

5750 •

5140 •

Naong Sung Valley

to Thongmön Xian

to Thongmön Xian

5520 •

Kung Tsangpo Valley

Kayi Pang Phuk

5350

Markyar Tso

Pongchen La

5610

Namachang

Buser Tsangpo Valley

5460

Kapchor

Tagrak Tsangpo Valley

5330

Nadsum

Kesar

6020

5460

to Mu Chu Valley

NH45 – 7C

5550 •

5440 •

5410 •

5350 •

Ngangtse Tso

Tagrang Valley

4840 •

NH45 – 6B

0 2 4 6 8 10 km
0 2 4 6 miles

31°00'

30°30'

87°45'

87°00'

30°30'

of Lake Ngangtse Tso. The water of the lake (4694 m), like that of Lake Dangra and Marchar Tso, is undrinkable due to salt. (Marchar Tso is narrow in the middle and one day will become two lakes.) Only the Tagrak Tsangpo, with its many tributaries, flows into Lake Ngangtse Tso from the southeast. Waters flowing north from the Pabla Range generally empty into the Naong Tsangpo. The mountains north of Ngangtse Tso are relatively low; it is necessary to walk north for nearly 100 km to reach a pass, the Piké La, only 500 m higher than the lake. To the west, a wide plain stretches to low hills bordering the eastern perimeter of Lake Dangra. Nomads and great flocks of sheep and yak reside near that lake's western and southern shores.

Thongmön Xian to Shigatse by coracle

From Thongmön Xian, consider returning to Shigatse by coracle down the Tsangpo River; Tibetans for centuries have transported people and goods this way. There is a ferry at Tsorgu Village on the river bank, about 4 hr from Thongmön Xian. From here, charter a coracle for a leisurely cruise down the river (about Rmb 80).

❖ DAY 3 THONGMÖN XIAN–PINDSOLING MONASTERY 8 HR

From the guesthouse of Thongmön Xian, return to the crossroad (on the way to Tratsang Monastery) and turn left. Soon the road makes a sharp right through the town's old section and leaves Thongmön Xian. Walk up a canyon and down the other side to a wide river valley with villages on both banks. Come to Thongmön (2 hr), the former district capital. Thongmön Labrang Monastery is in the middle of the village. A path leads right (west) to Tashi Gembe Monastery (destroyed), also in a village, 1/2 hr from Thongmön. Down the plain are Dewe Chasang and Gompa Chang Monastery. The mountains on the right (west) are the last ramifications of the Nyenchen Tanglha. To the left is the ridge of Ngunchu that divides the great Ye Plain into eastern and western parts. At its western foot is small Ribu Tinsi Monastery and the village of Sharchen.

Continue from Thongmön along the wide valley to the southwest. Pass the villages of Kabring, Chögo, and Shatsa, at the southern promontory of the isolated ridge. Ünsang Monastery is on the right of the path. Near the Tsangpo are Dewuk and Kabu Kangsa. The path zigzags up a steep cliff to a plateau, 1/2 hr from Thongmön; below are meandering branches of the Tsangpo (the river narrows as it approaches Shigatse). Walk over an easy ridge called Gyang La (4130 m). Milung Nangbe, a village to the right at the opening of a double valley, can be seen. Reach Lawongtse (1 hr), surrounded on all sides by low hills. From here, the trail descends steeply to the Tsangpo Valley floor. Along here is a tributary from the northwest, also called Lawong, that joins the Tsangpo to the left. Ignore the canyon on the right with a flat track inside it. Follow instead a trail to the river, then turn right and hike along the Tsangpo for about 1 km. This stretch of the north bank is a narrow plain partly covered with gravel and interrupted by dry ravines.

Cross the river by ferry 1/2 hr from Lawongtse. Locate the wooden boat that usually works the shores all day; the crossing only takes 5 min (Rmb 0.5 per person). On the south bank walk up from the ferry to a dirt road and turn right (west) along the Tsangpo.

Lawongtse to Shigatse via the Friendship Highway (four days)

From Lawongtse, walk to the Tsangpo River, cross by the ferry, then turn left (east) along the road to Tashigang. Continue to Silung on the Friendship Highway. This flat 100-km walk has no passes.

Pass the village of Parnda (1/2 hr from the ferry) and continue along the narrowing Tsangpo Valley to Pindsoling (2 hr) on the slope of a hill left of the road. A new bridge spans the river on the right and close by is the original *chaksam* bridge, built by the great Tangton Gyalpo (1385–1464). It has large stone foundations on both shores and is made of iron chains and ropes like the bridge near Reting Monastery (see page 561). Nearby are Pindsoling and Jonang monasteries. The area is superb: the Tsangpo emerges around a bend through a narrow valley and a huge sand dune, like a shimmering white mountain, rises just beyond the village. A small compound in Pindsoling has very basic rooms, with straw on the floor for mattresses. Across the river is Chaga Village with a walled compound where the district head lives. To its left are ruins on a hill.

From Lawongtse to Pindsoling along the north bank of the Tsangpo

An alternate way from Thongmön Xian to Pindsoling simply follows the Tsangpo's north bank from Lawongtse. It is impossible for vehicles to traverse this stretch completely. Beyond the ferry (3/4 hr) is Pasum, a village about 60 m above the water on the gravelly fan of the Ngolung Valley. Below Pasum, the track follows the river and soon Pindsoling Monastery can be seen on the crest of a ridge. Tse, another village at the mouth of a tributary, is 1/2 hr from Pasum. The Tsangpo valley here is about 400 m wide. Beyond, granite cliffs descend nearly to the river. Tangnak is 3/4 hr from Tse and Chaga, opposite Pindsoling, is 1 1/4 hr further. This is a stony section and the path sometimes disappears.

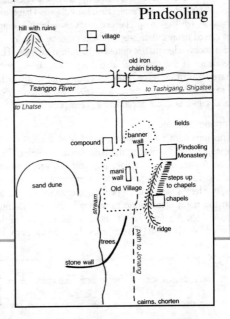

Pindsoling

hill with ruins — village — old iron chain bridge — Tsangpo River — to Tashigang, Shigatse — to Lhatse — fields — banner wall — compound — Pindsoling Monastery — mani wall — sand dune — Old Village — steps up to chapels — chapels — stream — path to Jonang — ridge — trees — stone wall — cairns, chorten

Pindsoling Monastery

The large red building enclosed by a courtyard in the middle of the village is the monastery. Pindsoling and neighboring Jonang were restored early in the 17th C. by the scholar Taranatha (Kung Nyingpo) as a means of countering the growing influence of the Gelugpa; in this he had the support of the princes of Tsang and Ngamring. Taranatha (b 1575) belonged to the Jonangpa, a Kagyü sub-sect, and wrote many tantric and historical treatises. After his death, the Fifth Dalai Lama converted the monastery to the Gelugpa tradition. A printing house here printed vast numbers of historical and religious texts on wooden blocks. Close to the monastery is a shrine dedicated to the protector Begtse, founded by the Bodongpa Rinchen Tsemo in the 12th century.

Enter the monastery by means of a wooden gate in the courtyard wall nearest the hillside. The main, well-preserved, four-story temple is usually locked. Within the inner *tsangkhang* chapel, dedicated to Jowo Choklé Namgyal, are statues of Mitrukpa and the Eight Bodhisattvas. Its celebrated murals and those of the Jonang Kumbum up a side valley, were influenced heavily by Indian traditions and share little with most Central Tibetan monasteries. Their uniqueness lies in the Indian styles applied to the depiction of Tibetan tantric mythology. This probably resulted from Taranatha's frequent contacts with India and his support of Indian masters and artists. (On the walls of ruined chapels up the hill are faint remnants of paintings. One sees this influence in smooth flowing lines, sensuous rendering of svelte women, and active, energetic images.) In the 1940s, Tucci, the renowned Tibetologist, saw large collections of sacred texts printed in gold on pages tinted with indigo. They lined the walls of the chapels. In one room, filled with masks for ritual dances, he saw beautiful Indian-style paintings of the type mentioned. Another room had Chinese-inspired murals and the atrium works were a blend of Indian and Chinese styles. Pindsoling and nearby Jonang thus seem to be the center of an exciting artistic school virtually unknown elsewhere in Tibet.

Outside the monastery near the village is a large, free-standing wall used to hang enormous *thangkas* (*gheku*) on special occasions. Nearby is a long *mani* wall with many stone plaques of carved figures. A zigzagging flight of stone steps leads from near the courtyard up the spine of a rocky ridge that is dotted with ruined chapels. The Taranatha Potrang (destroyed), the residence of the master, is at the top. Here, traces of the murals remain; an atrium used to have large frescoes analogous to central and southern Indian styles. Also at the top was the Trogyal Gönkhang (protector chapel). Magnificent views extend over the valley, the huge sand dune, and the meandering Tsangpo.

Jonang Kumbum

This important multi-chapel *chörten* is in a small side valley near Pindsoling. Spend a day reaching it and exploring the large Jonang complex. The easy walk from the monastery takes 2 hr. A path from the village goes past the long *mani* wall on the right and skirts the bottom of the Taranatha Potrang ridge. A grove of trees enclosed by a stone wall is farther on the right. Here a side valley opens to the south. A trail follows its left slope with the stream on the right; many stone cairns mark the way. Eventually reach a better path lined with stone walls. A round *chörten* stands at the entrance of the heavily damaged religious complex. Sacred Jomo Nakgyal (5744 m) rises above the valley to the south and Guru Rinpoche meditated in a cave below the peak.

For a description of the Jonang Kumbum, see page 463.

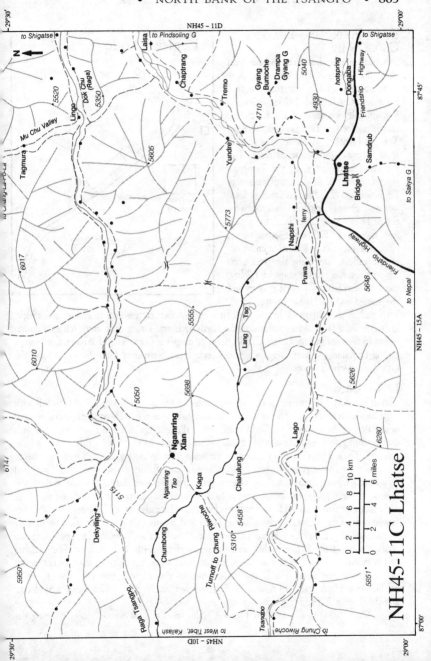

NH45 – 11D

to Shigatse

to Pindsoling G

to Shigatse

Laisa

Chaptrang

Tremo

Gyang Bunoche

Drampa Gyang G

5040

hotspring

Dongaba

Friendship Highway

DoK Chu (Raga)

5520

5350

Lingo

Mu Chu Valley

5605

Yundre

4710

4930

Lhatse

Samdrub

Tagmura

to Chang-La-PO-La

Bridge

to Sakya G

6017

5773

Napshi

ferry

Friendship Highway

Puwa

5648

to Nepal

NH45 – 15A

6010

5555

Lang Tso

5626

Ngamring Xian

5050

5698

Lago

6280

Ngamring Tso

Kaga

Chakulung

614?

5115

Chumbong

Turnoff to Chung Riwoche

5458

5310

Dekyiling

5950

Raga Tsangpo

to West Tibet, Kailash

Tsandpo

to Chung Riwoche

5851

0 2 4 6 8 10 km

0 2 4 6 miles

NH45-11C Lhatse

NH45 – 10D

DAY 4 PINDSOLING–LHATSE CHÖDE 9 HR

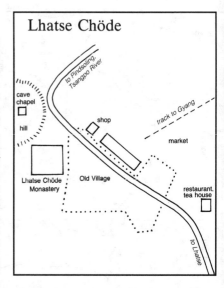

Lhatse Chöde

Descend from Pindsoling to the dirt road along the Tsangpo. The huge sand dune is ahead and on the left; this beautiful but sandy stretch, about 1–2 km in length, is a difficult one for vehicles. Reach the confluence of the Tsangpo and the Raga Tsangpo (2 hr), a wonderful area of sand spits, islands, and scattered trees. The path now turns left along the Tsangpo's right (east) bank to the small village of Pindsoling Qu (2 1/2 hr) on a rise. A desolate government compound with rooms for the night is on the other side of the path from the village. Follow the serene valley, passing idyllic villages located at entrances of side valleys. Eventually the river turns left and enters a narrow gorge (3 1/2 hr). Continue to Lhatse Chöde Monastery and the ruined fort of Lhatse Dzong (1 hr), both within the village of Lhatse Qu. This ancient district was and is known as Drampa. It centers on a large plain anchored in the north by Lhatse Dzong. Important religious monuments in the area include Lhatse Chöde, the cave chapel of Gayadhara Lhakhang, the Drampa Gyang Lhakhang, Gyang Yönpolung Monastery, a cave retreat of Guru Rinpoche, and the Gyang Bumoche *chörten*.

Lhatse Chöde

This three-story Gelugpa monastery in the center of Lhatse Qu is sited next to a hill with some fortress ruins on top. The monastery, anomalously, is in relatively good shape and escaped destruction at the hands of the Red Guards. Since the mid-1980s, artists have proceeded with their painting and restoration work. Some original murals in the ground floor *dukhang* have survived. These 17th-C. works represent a transition from an early to modern stage in Tibetan art. The panels were painted when Indic influences were finally dying, to be finally replaced by a homogeneous, quintessentially Tibetan genre that prevailed during the rule of the Dalai Lamas. In these paintings, archaic traditions as seen in the superb murals of Shalu (see page 400) and Gyantse (page 412) can still be detected. The rather stocky, massive Buddhas are reminiscent of the 15th-C. Gyantse works. Traits of this earlier art phase also show up strongly in the colors. The yellow, blood red and dark blue in these few *dukhang* paintings are characteristic of the bolder, richer tones of works of the 14th–15th century. The Buddhas and *bodhisattvas* are not merely dry iconographic exercises, a trademark of more recent works, but expressive and alive. The Lhatse Chöde painters paid close attention to each figure to produce individual, animated results. Faces are refined, although some details, such as clouds, already show a later Gelugpa influence.

Once 1,000 monks lived at Lhatse Chöde, an important religious center during the

Sakyapa period (13th C.). Today, there are about 30 monks. The inner chapel on the ground floor, the *tsangkhang*, has a finely sculpted *torana* (halo) that shows a strong Indian influence.

Gayadhara Lhakhang

This cave temple built into the living rock on the north side of a hill immediately adjacent to Lhatse Chöde was named after the 11th-C. Kashmiri *pandita*, Gayadhara, who died in Tibet. The site was originally the retreat of Drokmi Lotsawa, a lineage holder of a tradition initiated by the Indian *mahasiddha*, Birwapa. This discipline was later absorbed into the Sakyapa teachings by the founder of the sect, Kong Chögyal Po. Drokmi was a renowned translator, a master of the Lamdre teachings, and a teacher of Marpa Lotsawa. Student and *guru* met at this cave.

The main grotto is preceded by an atrium and an ancient figure of Vairocana carved in the rock decorated the chamber's central wall. Wooden panels, and especially the lintels with sculpted figures, confirm the cave-temple's antiquity. Some sources claim that Indian artists were responsible for the decoration. The temple entrance is festooned with prayer flags and painted with red. It is not possible to see the cave chapel and its opening from the monastery below. Farther up the ridge are the ruins of Lhatse Dzong (destroyed), former residence of the district governor.

Drampa Gyang Lhakhang

The Drampa Gyang Lhakhang (ruined) sited at the eastern perimeter of the Lhatse Plain, is considered one of 12 temples built by King Songtsen Gampo in the 7th C. to suppress the demoness of Tibet (see page 43). The chapel was designed to pin down the monster's left hip and the king himself supposedly built a statue of Vairocana here. This chapel, together with Chocho Mashing (not located) and the Gayadhara Lhakhang, were the three major shrines in the Lhatse area favored by the Panchen Lamas. As a result, all received generous gifts of money, statues, and ornaments. In the vicinity of the Drampa Gyang Lhakhang were five other chapels called collectively Namnang Rigna Lhakhang (not located), supposedly built by King Trisong Detsen and Bodhisatta.

Gyang Bumoche Chörten

Northwest of Drampa Gyang is the large, destroyed *chörten* of Gyang Bumoche Monastery. At the edge of Lhatse Chöde, a dirt track hugs the hills on the left while a dirt road on the right leads along telegraph poles to Lhatse Xian on the Friendship Highway. Follow the track; it passes through cultivated fields traversing from the valley's left side to the right. The earthen *chörten* on a hill can already be seen just outside the village on a hill. Weather has eroded whatever traces once existed of the valuable murals; Tucci was the first and last scholar to study this monument. A pyramidal *chörten* stands at the entrance of a side valley.

For more information on this *chörten*, see page 465.

Gyang Yönpolung

East of Gyang Bumoche, within a lush ravine, are the ruins of a small Nyingmapa monastery called Gyang Yönpolung. Lopön Drubphuk, a meditation cave of Guru Rinpoche, is located at nearby Terlung Khangdho. It is also the celebrated place where the *Leudunma*, a major 'hidden text' of the Nyingmapa, was discovered by the *terton*, Sangpo Drakpa. Outside the cave was a shrine called Chirol Lhakhang and nearby was Namkhai Nyingpo's meditation cave, expanded by Kunzang Rikdrol. Next to Gyang Yönpolung is Yeshe Tsogyal's retreat, the Tsogyal Drubphuk.

✣ DAY 5 LHATSE CHÖDE–LHATSE 1 1/2 HR

This easy, idyllic walk follows the telegraph poles outside Lhatse Chöde on the far side of the monastery. A track bears left to Gyang Bumoche, and a trail right to Lhatse. Follow the latter (south) through the center of the valley, along the jeep track through fields. Ruins stand on a hill to the left. Reach the Friendship Highway after 1 1/4 hr. Turn right to Lhatse (1/4 hr) at road marker 399.

Lhatse

Considerable traffic stops here, mostly en route between Lhasa and Nepal. A guest house in a compound across the street from the gas station serves poor meals at set times. It is preferable to eat at small Moslem and Sichuanese restaurants near the western part of town next to the highway. A cinema and post office are around the corner from the guest house on a large street perpendicular to the main road. Beyond is a store with a reasonable selection of tinned goods.

Lhatse to Lhasa or Nepal

Hitchhike or catch a bus east or west on the Friendship Highway.

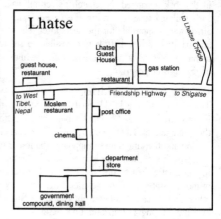

Lhatse

to Lhatse Chöde

Lhatse Guest House

guest house, restaurant

gas station

restaurant

to West Tibet, Nepal

Moslem restaurant

Friendship Highway   to Shigatse

post office

cinema

department store

government compound, dining hall

SHANG VALLEY: TREKS TO THE ZABSO PILGRIMAGE

Location	North of Shigatse
Map reference	NH45-12 A B C, 45-8 A C
Trekking days	20 (round-trip)
Start–Finish	Shigatse–Zambu Monastery–Shigatse
Passes	None

OVERVIEW

The Shang Valley is one of four principal routes in Tsang (West-Central Tibet) that traverses completely the great Mt Nyenchen Tanglha. This range, lying east to west north of the Tsangpo basin, forms the watershed between the vital Tsangpo Valley and the isolated Changtang Plateau. The mountain represents a dividing line between the settled population of south Tibet and the nomadic people of the north. From west to east, the four routes that penetrate the range are:

Shang Valley

- The Mu Chu Valley.
Sacred Lake Dangra on the
Changtang can be reached via the Chang-la-Pö-La Pass (see page 767).
- Thongmön Xian to Lake Ngangtse via the Sela La (see page 855).
- Tanak (Tarmar) to Lake Kyaring via the Tanakpo Chu (see page 852).
- The Shang Valley to Lake Namtso via the Kalamba La.

The route along the Shang Valley goes from Shigatse north to Zambu Monastery and the Kalamba La (5242 m) which straddles the Nyenchen Tanglha. The Lake Namtso section (see page 657) sketches an itinerary from Lhasa to Namtso and the upper reaches of the Shang Valley. It forms a logical extension of this chapter.

The twin hermitages of Zambu and Sogpo, sited within side valleys of the Shang, constitute the fabled Zabso pilgrimage. These ancient places, consecrated to Guru Rinpoche, are widely regarded as the most holy in Tsang. Sogpo has a network of cave retreats and passages within limestone cliffs. At Zambu are hot springs, spouting geysers, and a thriving monastic community. Zabso is not to be missed.

Near the main town of Namling are the monasteries of Ganden Chökorling and Zhong Zhong. The latter is an 11th C. center founded by Khyungpo Naljor, patriarch of the Shangpa sect. Monasteries within the Shang Valley included Bachen, Dechen Rabgya, Tagna, Peting, and others. Shang's upper reaches are made up of two main tributaries. To the east is the Jomo (Labu) River, which leads to Zambu and the Kalamba La. The western branch is formed from the waters of four rivers: Drung, Dzeshö (Sogpo is here), Nyangra, and Rindu. Trails along these rivers access a network of valleys of the Shigatse area. From Zambu, it is possible to walk away from the Shang drainage system and enter that of the Wuyuk to the east. A trail from Sogpo goes over the Sha Rindzin La to join the Tanakpo (Tanak) Valley (see page 850). From Tagna Monastery, one day's walk from Namling, another path leads up a side valley and eventually turns south to the Tsangpo basin. The Drung heads west and then south also joining the large Tanakpo Valley, which has its entrance on the north bank of the Tsangpo. The Shang area allows for a large number of excursions beyond the main valley. To thoroughly explore this region would take months.

The isolated upper stretches of Shang are characterized by vigorous geothermal activity. At the head of the Jomo (Labu) Chu are a number of hot springs and geyser sites, and eruptions in the water are especially spectacular in the winter, when high, frozen towers of water are formed. The climate here is much less severe than the Changtang. Nevertheless, though not far from Shigatse, this area of upper Shang has notoriously unsettled weather, even in the height of summer. Snow and hail storms are frequent. Cultivation (peas, potatoes, radishes, barley) in the valley stops at Nako, a day's walk south of Zambu. North of here is the domain of the nomads and yakherds. The valley, noted for food production, has dirt roads and regular traffic in the lower reaches. Five or more vehicles per day go from Namling, the major town, to Shigatse. Hitching a ride from Shigatse to Namling is possible and saves three days of walking. However, plan to travel by foot to explore the cultural and religious sites north of Namling.

Related sections
Shigatse, p 815
Namtso, p 657

Access
From Shigatse (see page 821) to the beginning of the Shang Valley along the north bank of the Tsangpo is described below (Day 1). An alternative way to reach the valley is via the Shigatse–Lhasa north route (see page 815), which follows the Tsangpo's south bank. Hitch east from Shigatse to road marker 226 km (the new marker is 4879). Here, the Tama ferry crosses to the north bank of the Tsangpo at the entrance to the Shang Valley.

Time Chart
Day	Place	Hours
1	Shigatse–Chula	7 1/2
2	Dokjit Qu	5
3	Namling Xian	5 1/4
4	Nija	4
5	Tongie	4 1/2

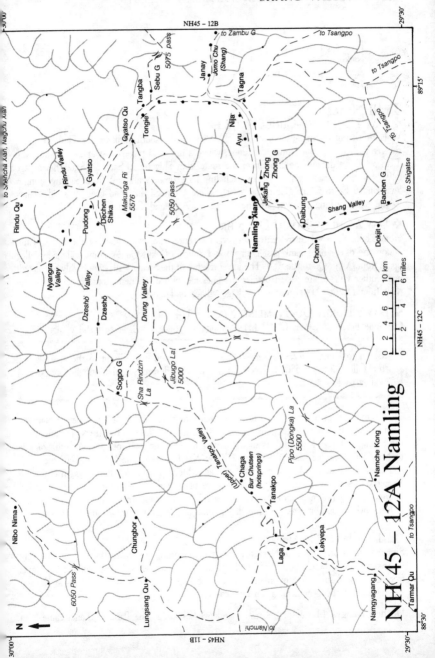

6	Janay	4 3/4
7	Paou Monastery	4 1/2
8	Naikor	4 1/2
9	Zambu Valley entrance	4 3/4
10	Zambu Monastery	1 1/2

Trail Notes

✦ DAY 1 SHIGATSE–CHULA 7 1/2 HR

Walk north out of Shigatse to the Dongka ferry on the south bank of the Tsangpo. Cross the river, then continue north to Sadung, where a dirt road travels east and west along the Tsangpo. For a detailed description of the route from Shigatse to Sadung (Shuda), see page 849. Shigatse to Sadung is 2 1/2 hr excluding ferry time. Walk east from Sadung along a level dirt track to Chula (Chuyada, 5 hr), where a branch dirt road goes up a side valley to the north. Along the way are the villages of Aera and Tenjid.

✦ DAY 2 CHULA–DOKJIT QU 5 HR

From Chula the road turns gently northward to enter the wide valley of the Shang Chu. Follow the river's right bank past Drongtö and Yang to Dokjit Qu. A short, wide side valley opens from Dokjit Qu to the west. The lower reaches of the Shang Valley are highly populated; many other villages are passed besides the ones mentioned. Bachen Monastery is across the river from Dokjit. At its foot is the large village of Hrangpa.

✦ DAY 3 DOKJIT QU–NAMLING XIAN 5 1/4 HR

Continue north to Chom (2 1/2 hr). A monastery once stood west of the village.

> **Chom to Dongka ferry** A major side valley veers off from Chom to the west. A trail follows it to the 5500-m Pipo (Dongka) La, then descends south along the Dongka Valley to Dongka ferry.

From Chom the main road heads northeast to Singa, the village just before Namling Xian (a grassy area next to the stream is good for camping). Perhaps five trucks per day travel the Shang Valley and hitchhikers should expect to pay Rmb 5–10 per person from Shigatse to Namling. A bridge spans the Shang Chu at Namling, the valley's largest settlement. (If you cross to the left bank, you can walk to Tagna Monastery via Jekang, the 11th-C. Zhong Zhong Monastery, and Pemadong. There may be places farther on to ford the swift river [10 m wide and over 1 m deep].) At Namling a side valley opens to the north; a trail within it leads over a 5050-m pass to drop down into the Drung Valley, a journey of 8 hr.

Ganden Chökorling Monastery

Situated on the steep cliffs of Namling, Ganden Chökorling used to be the largest monastery in Shang with 30 buildings and 150 Gelugpa and Sakyapa monks. It was founded by a lama from Chom and subsequently enlarged by one of Tsong Khapa's disciples. Ruins at the top are remains of the provincial governor's castle.

Dechen Rabgya Monastery is near Ganden Chökorling. The Panchen Lama came from this small monastery. In 1774, Bogle, the English explorer, stayed here as a guest of the Third Panchen Lama.

Zhong Zhong Monastery

Khyungpo Naljor, founder of the Shangpa sect, a sub-sect of the Kagyüpa, established this important monastery. Originally a Bönpo, this illustrious lama converted to the Dzokchen sect after receiving teachings from Naropa's wife, Niguma. He went to Kathmandu, Nepal, to learn Sanskrit, and he also spent many years in India studying Buddhism. Tradition says Khyungpo then traveled to Shang and founded 108 monasteries. Zhong Zhong, 5 km east of Namling on the south bank of the Shang Chu, is one of them. He died here. The monastery is also known as Dorjedan (the Tibetan name for Bodh Gaya), a name that developed when Khyungpo, nearing his death, predicted that if his body was spared cremation and put in a vessel of gold and silver, the shrine would become as great as Bodh Gaya. Zhong Zhong's present condition is unknown. It is located on the south bank of the Shang Chu.

✢ DAY 4 NAMLING XIAN–NIJA 4 HR

From Namling follow the north (right) bank of the Shang Chu along a good dirt road. Walk past the villages of Chu, Bitee, Shegong, and Pemadong in an easterly direction. Look for inscriptions on the hillside above the last village. After Pemadong a large waterfall appears on the left. Beyond is a power station, some barracks and the village of Ayu. Between the road and the river is an irrigation canal. Continue east past the villages of Dolom, Cholong, Lanchu, and Nija, where a dam controls the irrigation system. Across the Shang River from Nija is Tagna Monastery, situated on a hillside above Tagna Village at the entrance of a side valley that opens to the southeast. (A path up this valley leads over a 5250-m pass to the north bank of the Tsangpo, a journey of two to three days.) From Nija onwards the region becomes more isolated and trucks are seen only once or twice a day.

✢ DAY 5 NIJA–TONGIE 4 1/2 HR

After Nija, the road makes a sharp turn to the left and ascends the Shang Valley in a northerly direction. Walk north past the villages of Chara (Gyara), Laya, Lensing, Dong, and Naptra before reaching Tongie, a small village with a modern building that encloses a large courtyard. Here the road continues north and northwest. This route leads past the Drung Valley entrance to a junction of three valleys. One of these heads west to join the important Sogpo pilgrimage (see page 879). A bridge at Tongie, suitable for vehicles, spans this western branch of upper Shang Chu. (This river is made up of the Drung, Dzeshö, Nyangra, and Rindu tributaries. The last three come together at Gyatso.)

✢ DAY 6 TONGIE–JANAY 4 3/4 HR

Cross the bridge at Tongie, then turn right and head south, back down the left bank of this upper tributary of the Shang. The road degenerates and no more vehicles are seen. Shitso is the first village reached and just beyond are the village and monastery of Tangba at the entrance of a lush side valley. (A trail up this valley goes east to a 5075-m pass and then descends to Lhanag, a nomad settlement, and Pangtö, situated inside the eastern branch of upper Shang). The villages in these parts are neat and attractive; good places to spend a day of rest. (A short distance up the side valley is Sebu Monastery.) Continue south. The path, high above the river, disappears at times but there is no chance of getting lost with

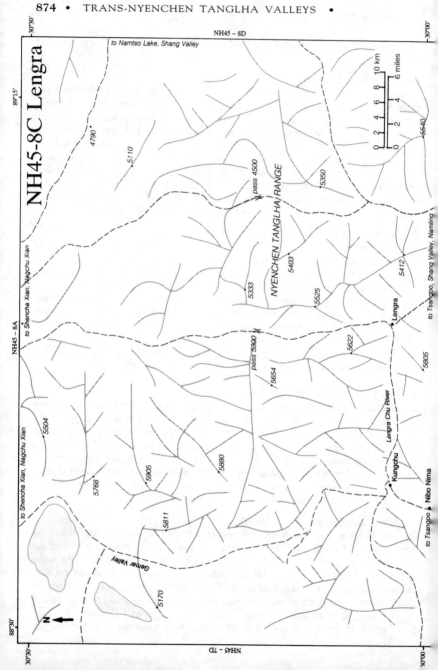

NH45 – 8D

NH45-8C Lengra

to Namtso Lake, Shang Valley

NYENCHEN TANGLHA RANGE

pass 4500

to Tsangpo, Shang Valley, Namling

to Shencha Xian, Nagchu Xian

NH45 – 8A

to Shencha Xian, Nagchu Xian

pass 5800

Lengra

Lengra Chu River

Kungchu

to Tsangpo ● Nibo Nima

Gemar Valley

NH45 – 7D

4790
5110
5350
5403
5412
5333
5525
5622
5805
5654
5504
5905
5880
5768
5811
5170
5640

Lengra

N

10 km
6 miles
0 2 4 6 8
0 2 4 6

30°30′
89°15′
88°30′
30°30′
30°00′
30°00′

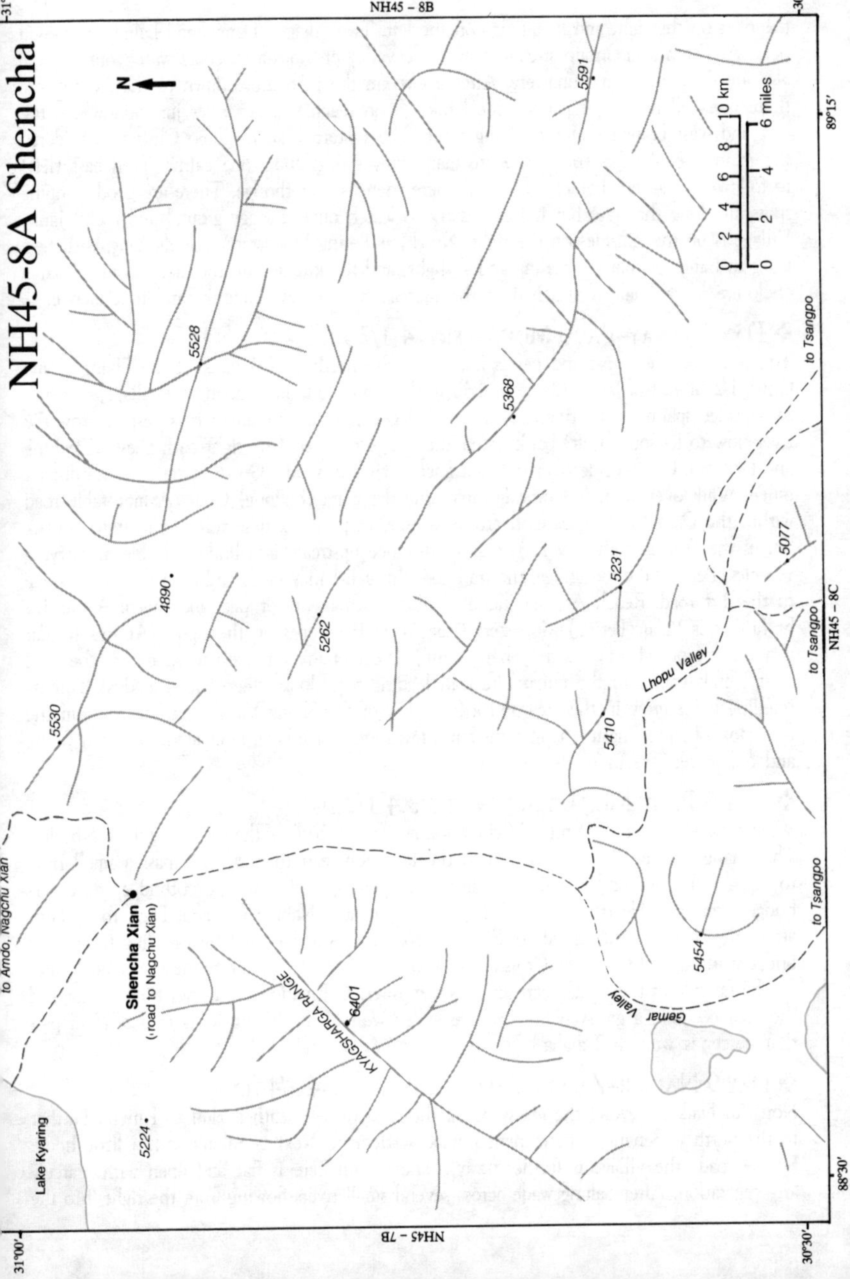

NH45-8A Shencha

NH45 – 8B

N

31°00'

30°30'

31°00'

30°30'

89°15'

88°30'

to Amdo, Nagchu Xian

to Tsangpo

to Tsangpo

to Tsangpo

Lake Kyaring

Shencha Xian
(road to Nagchu Xian)

KYAGSHARGA RANGE

Lhopu Valley

Gemar Valley

5591

5368

5528

4890

5262

5231

5530

5410

5077

5454

6401

5224

NH45 – 8C

NH45 – 7B

0 2 4 6 8 10 km
0   2   4   6 miles

the river on the right and mountains on the left. Two villages, Damya and Lalun, are passed next. At Lalun a mountain stream from a side valley provides a welcome water source. Here also are the ruins of a monastery. After a few km the path drops down to the river where there is excellent camping along the banks. Soon reach a major river junction where the east and west branches of the Shang meet. The eastern branch (Jomo Chu) is considered the main one. At this confluence are many prayer flags and stone cairns. Turn east (left) to follow this eastern branch to Janay, where there is a footbridge. There are good camping spots all along the river but it is necessary to watch out for soggy ground and rocks. Janay Village is up the hillsides on the right. Nearby is Peting Monastery. The *dukhang*, with new *thangkas* hanging from the ceiling and skylight, and the kitchen are the main rooms. A large enclosure for animals is attached to the monastery, and seven monks are in residence.

✤ Day 7 Janay–Paou Monastery 4 1/2 hr

The trail continues east and passes Larum on the north (right) bank of the Shang (Jomo Chu), 1/2 hr east of Janay. Gamet is 1 hr further and the trail, bisecting the village, descends to a bridge spanning the river. As the trail degenerates after Gamet, it is best to cross the river now to its south (left) bank. After the bridge turn left (the right path goes to Peching and Dodgay). Cross a side river to reach Lachi. Beyond is Labu Qu (Redong), a small district office. Walk over another footbridge spanning the Cara (Kadong) Chu. (A motorable road within the Cara Valley goes east, crosses a 4650-m pass and descends southeast to Wuyuk Qu in the Wuyuk Valley; 9 hr.) A short distance upstream is a bridge capable of carrying vehicles. Beyond the footbridge, the trail goes through barley fields and then up a steep slope to the dirt road. Reach Atso, a friendly village with plenty of yaks and sheep. About 1/2 hr further is Paou (Peting) Monastery situated up the slopes on the right. (At this turnoff is another footbridge across the Shang Chu.) The monastery is hard to spot from the road as it blends well into the cliffs. The trail leading to it looks steep but is gradual. Potent-smelling herbs grow in the area and a fine view of the Shang Valley can be had from the top. Most of the monastery is in ruins but a few rooms have been renovated. Over ten young and old monks are in residence.

✤ Day 8 Paou Monastery–Naikor 4 1/2 hr

Walk back down to the main road (which follows the left bank of the river) and the footbridge. The Shang Chu begins a sharp turn to the left, from east to north. Go past a small river to Zigpa (Sika), beyond which is a side valley opening to the east (a footbridge and a car-bridge span this side tributary). Walk past Stonejo and Nalung to Sabu. High rocky cliffs are to the right. At the far side of Sabu the road makes a sharp left turn leading to another bridge spanning the Kye River. Cross this and continue north to Naikor. Stone animal enclosures on the far side of the village can serve as campsites. Cultivation ceases north of Naikor and the area becomes a grassy plain. (A side valley west of the Shang leads to a 5075-m pass that descends west to Tangba.)

✤ Day 9 Naikor–Zambu Valley Entrance 4 3/4 hr

North of Naikor, beyond the grassy plain, the road runs beneath a bluff to Pangtö. Further to the north is Senang, a permanent nomad settlement. Next is Salung with a little house by the road (the village is further away). The terrain here is flat and open with scarcely any vegetation. After Salung wade across several small rivers flowing from the right into the eastern branch (Jomo Chu) of the Shang Chu. On the far side is the village of Dong Nyag at the entrance of a twin valley. (The southern valley leads to the 5400-m Enak La; the northern one leads to a peak called Jo Rongtse Ri.) The road, now actually a trail, curves around a steep slope to cross another stream. At a flat plain, the valley forks where the side valley of Zambu joins the main one of Jomo. (The left trail of the Jomo Valley is narrow and impassable by motor vehicles. It continues northeast, then east, to the Kalamba La.) To the east (right) follow an obscure trail steeply through a grassy, rock-strewn meadow. This is a nice place to camp with plenty of yak dung for fuel. Stone animal enclosures can provide shelter. Find fresh water farther up the hill, 1/4 hr from where the trail again becomes distinct. The Zambu Chu Valley, with its hot springs giving off steam, is 70 m below. It is a steep descent for a bath. Nomad tents are pitched on a flat area across the Zambu Chu ravine.

Jomo–Zambu valley junction to the Kalamba La

Take the left trail at the valley junction and walk up the narrow valley northeastward. In 2 hr reach the nomad settlement of Labuphu (Salung Sumdo). The trail now veers towards the east; Korlung (Phusum) is 2 hr further. (A side trail from here goes north up the Talung valley.) Continue east past sacred Naisum Chuja (3 1/2 hr), Dungchaka, and Puchiding (2 1/2 hr from Naisum Chuja). From Puchiding walk north up a side valley to the Kalamba La to connect with the route to Lake Namtso (see page 670).

Puchiding to the Wuyuk Valley

A trail from Puchiding goes south, crosses the high 5769-m Jangyung La (5 1/2 hr), then descends to Sanshang of Wuyuk on the north Lhasa–Shigatse Highway (5 hr).

✦ Day 10 Zambu Valley Entrance–Zambu Monastery 1 1/2 hr

Hike for 1 1/2 hr up the Zambu Valley to reach Zambu Monastery. The ascent along the river is gradual and easy. Zambu Village is marked by a rather unusual round building. A footbridge crosses the river 1/4 hr beyond this landmark. If you miss this bridge it is easy to wade across. The village and monastery are spread out; 40 monks and perhaps 10–20 lay people live in the area. The monastery, east of the village, consists of a chapel with a statue of the Jowo within a small cave at the back right corner. Next to the cave entrance is an altar with statues and offerings. Another cave, behind the round building, lies next to a chapel within a courtyard. A kitchen is behind this chapel.

The Zabso Pilgrimage

Zabso, the most important pilgrimage in the Tsang Province, takes in two premier religious sites, Sogpo and Zambu monasteries.

Zambu

Zambu Monastery, also called Shang Zambulung, is located in Zambulung, a broad, moraine-filled valley. It is consecrated to Sakyamuni (Jowo) and Guru Rinpoche, and legend has it that Guru Rinpoche once hid 108 sacred texts here. In myth, Zambulung is surrounded by 13 snow mountains and 13 lakes. According to the *Padma Thangyig*, an old Tibetan text attributed

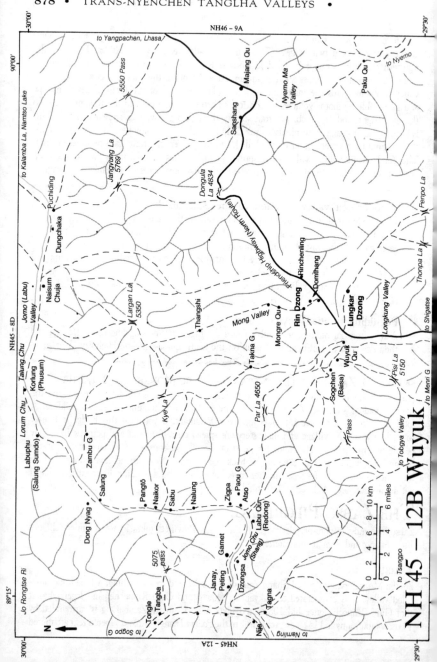

NH46 – 9A

NH 45 – 12B Wuyuk

to Guru Rinpoche, 'there are five valleys, one country, three districts, 20 glaciers, and in the middle of all is Zambulung'.

SOGPO

This seldom-visited hermitage is located within the Dzeshö Chu Valley; its river is one of three that make up the large western tributary of the Shang Chu. The other two side rivers are the Nyangra Chu and the Rindu (Lotsai) Chu.

Access From Tongie (see above, p 873), continue northwest up the western branch of the Shang. In 1 hr, a side valley called Drung opens to the west (left). (A trail within it crosses the 5000-m Jibugo La, descends to the southwest, then south to the Tanakpo Valley, see page 850.) At its entrance is the large village and district headquarters of Gyatso Qu. (This place is eulogized in Milarepa's songs.) Continue up the main valley. In 2 hr reach the villages of Gyatso and Pudong, both near the junction of the Dzeshö, Nyangra, and Rindu valleys. Take the one on the far left (Dzeshö) to due west. (The middle valley is Nyangra.) Within Dzeshö Valley is Dechen Shika (1 hr). South of this village is the peak of Makunga Ri (5576 m). Dzeshö village is a further 3 3/4 hr. The area is home to nomads and hundreds of yaks. In 2 3/4 hr, the valley splits. Follow the southern branch into limestone country with narrow gorges and steep cliffs. Sogpo Monastery, 1 3/4 hr further, is high up on sheer cliffs. The steep trail up is not easy to find—approach the monastery from the south.

Sogpo is a remarkable complex of interconnected cave hermitages. At the end of the chain of caves is the *sanctum sanctorum*: the Cave of Enlightenment. Here, a hole in the rock is reputed to be the penis-print of Guru Rinpoche. A larger hole supposedly leads to Emagang, a village at the eastern limit of the Shang Valley's entrance. A distinct break in the mountain chain to the south marks the Sha Rindzin La, a pass Guru Rinpoche supposedly crossed riding a deer.

ZAMBU TO THE WUYUK VALLEY: 2–3 DAYS

From Zambu Monastery, a salt trade route continues up the Zambulung Valley, heading first to the east and then southeast. Cross the Mong La (5250 m) 5 hr from Zambu. Descend the Mong Valley and walk due south to Mongre Qu. Carry on to Rin Dzong (1 1/4 hr), where tracks radiate to the Lhasa–Shigatse north route (3/4 hr) and to the Wuyuk Valley. (Nomad salt routes always lead precisely north to south, unhindered by east–west mountain chains.) From the Lhasa–Shigatse road walk south to Wuyuk Qu (1 1/2 hr) at road marker 138 km (see page 819). 30 km further south is the Tadruka ferry on the Tsangpo's north bank. (Nearby is Yungdrungling Monastery.) A highway follows the south bank west to Shigatse.

Zambu to Lake Namtso or the Tsangpo River

After Zambu, either go north to Lake Namtso via the Kalamba La (see page 670) or return south to the Tsangpo and Shigatse via the Shang Valley or one of its many side valleys.

THE SAKYA PRINCIPALITY

SAKYA MONASTERY: THE MASSIVE CITADEL OF THE SAKYAPAS

Sakya originally consisted of two large complexes, Sakya North and Sakya South, constructed on the north and south banks of the Trum River. There were over 40 chapels and monastic buildings; the earliest structures (Ütse Nyingpa, Ütse Sarma, Gorum Lhakhang, Zhitok Labrang, Lhakhang Shar) were all to the north. Before the Cultural Revolution, Sakya was one of the country's largest monasteries, surpassed only by Tashilhunpo, Ganden, Sera, and Drepung, the famed monastic cities of Central Tibet. Today pilgrims come primarily to pay homage to the fortress-like Lhakhang Chenmo, a centerpiece of the Tsang province. Although Sakya is almost entirely represented by this southern structure, the renovated chapels and entire hillside of ruins to the north are still impressive.

The Sakya region is drained by three major river valleys: the Trum, Shap, and Phu. Trum first originates near the monastery and then flows northwest to join the Tsangpo near Lhatse. The Shap, east of Sakya, flows from south to north to merge with the Tsangpo west of Shigatse. Phu, a headwater of the Arun, begins west of Sakya and flows south. The southernmost part of Sakya's domain ends at Kharta (see page 903) near Mt Everest. Within the territory are two other minor river valleys. The Mangkar (see page 892) is due south of Lhatse and north of Mt Lhako Kangri. It is a major retreat center and contains a number of ancient monasteries and hermitages. The other is the Mo, which parallels the Shap River on the west and runs from south to north into the Tsangpo. Chimlung River, another of the Arun's headwaters, defines the domain's southeast boundary.

Access
Follow the Friendship Highway west from Shigatse to road marker 377 km at the Sakya Bridge. Immediately after the bridge is a side road to the left (south). Take this to Sakya Qu (21 km) where the road branches. The left (east) goes to Sakya Monastery (4 km), the right to Tingche Xian and the superb Chörten Nyima pilgrimage (page 801).

History
Sakya North, on the north bank of the Trum, was founded in 1073 by Kong Chögyal Pho, whose family goes back to the times of King Trisong Detsen (755–97). He studied with Drokmi, a teacher of Marpa (founder of the Kagyüpa) and built a chapel on the south slopes of Ritrö Hill. During the sect's beginning, its doctrine was incomplete and the monasteries small and inconsequential. Kong Chögyal Pho's son, Kunga Nyingpo, was an unusually dynamic man

who traveled extensively to learn from other teachers. He finished what his father had begun—a full compilation of Sakyapa religious doctrine, the *Sakya Lamdre Chögyu*. Buddhist precepts, according to the Sakya interpretation, involved three stages: 1) the actual moment (the student's existential moment); 2) the path (meditation, yoga mystical insights); 3) the result (attainment of ultimate enlightenment). In later years, Kunga Nyingpo was given the title of Sachen and became popularly known as the first of the Five Sakya Patriarchs. He practiced at the Lhakhang Shar, a small chapel with meditation caves on the slopes of Ritrö Hill. A driving force in the expansion of the North Monastery, he and his sons, Sonam Tsemo and Trakpa Gyaltsen, founded the principal structure of Ütse Nyingma. During the 13th C., the Ütse Sarma was built further to the west. Still later, more buildings were added to the north complex, which was irrevocably destroyed during the Cultural Revolution (today, the small Namgyalma Lhakhang has been rebuilt and Kunga Nyingpo's reconstructed *chörten* overlooks the ruins).

Sakya South was built by the Sakya Panchen (regent), Sakya Zangpo, on the orders of the famous Sakya Patriarch, Phagpa (1235–80). Also known as Lödro Gyaltsen, he was the last of the Five Patriarchs. An unusually gifted child, he was able to recite complicated *sutras* at age eight, and by nine he was already teaching other monks. He accompanied his uncle, the scholar Sakya Kunga Gyaltsen (grandson of Kunga Nyingpo, also known as Sakya Pandita), to Liangzhou, seat of the Mongol Emperor Godan. After the death of Sakya Pandita in 1251, Phagpa became the head of the Sakya domain and was much favored by the Mongol Emperor Kublai Khan (1216–94). During this time he made large donations for the monastery's further expansion. This was the period of the special patron-priest relationship (*yonchö*) that existed between China and Tibet. Phagpa was the spiritual advisor of the emperor, who in turn was patron and protector of Buddhism. Phagpa returned to Sakya in 1265 and in 1268, Sakya Zangpo, his regent, started to draw up plans for the enormous South Monastery, which was completed in 1276. During this time there were over 70,000 monks in the area. To celebrate the monastery's completion, Phagpa convened the Council of Chumik Chökor (see page 832) and, according to tradition, feted 100,000 people. He was effectively the ruler of Tibet (Rinchen Chögyal) as well as the undisputed leader of Sakya's vast holdings (Sakya Tripa). This was the start of the practice to join religious and political bodies to govern the country.

In 1265, Phagpa organized the *labrang* system to look after his holdings and treasures. At the time of Kunga Lodrö Gyaltsen in the first half of the 14th C., the ruling Kong family split into four *labrangs*. Each rotated to accede to the Sakya Tripa, effective ruler of the Sakya domain. These four are Zhithok, Lhakhang, Rinchengang, and Duchö. Zhithok Labrang housed the Secretariat, Sakya's governing body. Lhakhang Labrang, site of Phagpa's death in 1280, was situated south of the Lhakhang Chenmo within a three-story fortress, topped by a pagoda roof nearly as tall as the main hall. Rinchengang and Duchö were built during Phagpa's time. By the 15th C., three of the *labrangs* were unable to produce heirs. Two brothers of the Duchö fought over the succession to the Sakya Tripa and each built separately the Phüntsok and the Drölma Potrang. Heads of these two institutions then became the Tripa by rotation. At Sakya, unlike other Tibetan Buddhist sects, the abbotship passed from father to son rather than through the system of incarnate lamas.

The Sakya sect controls 11 enclaves in Tibet. The most important is Sakya proper, site of the capital (Sakya Densa). Most of the other 10 areas are scattered in West-Central Tibet. Two are in Kham. Sakya's 11 enclaves are:

Name	Location
• Sakya	Sakya Monastery area
• Tsedong	North bank of the Tsangpo, east of Shigatse; strongly linked to the capital; a few monasteries remain.
• Mu	North bank of the Raga Tsangpo, 100 km from Sakya; Tamoling Monastery.
• Yulchen	South bank of the Tsangpo, 160 km due west of Sakya; Yulchen Monastery.
• Pukar	100 km southwest of Sakya
• Dingri Tesa	30 km due west of Pukar, near Dingri
• Rhe	70 km southeast of Sakya (see page 831)
• Apo	Halfway between Sakya and Yulchen
• Chökar	Between Yulchen and Mu
• Markham Gyachag	South of Markham, between the Mekong and Yangtse rivers; East Tibet
• Demkhog	Southwest bank of the Yangtse; East Tibet, near the Yunnan border; three monasteries in the area

The Sakyapa has a history of over 900 years. It was the undisputed ruler of Tibet for the second half of the 13th C. and in those years accumulated many important cultural relics. Its collection of Buddhist texts is especially impressive; they are kept in shelves or cabinets known as Kunga Rawa. Within the South Monastery, these can be found along the rear and left and right side walls of the *dukhang*. There are over 20,000 large and small volumes, some particularly valuable hand-written manuscripts. The largest (1.3 m by 1.1 m) is the Gyatong Pa, a summary of the *Kangyur* and *Tengyur*. This beautiful work, completed in Phagpa's time, was handwritten in silver and gold powder on indigo leaves. Within the collection are rare Sanskrit manuscripts consisting of folios of banana leaves. According to a survey, 18 such texts have a total of 3,193 pages. Sakya is also the depository of over 3,000 *thangkas*. Those of the Sung, Yuan, and Ming dynasties number over 360. Because of this large collection of irreplaceable Buddhist texts, Sakya is sometimes referred to as the Second Dunhuang. The monastery also has over 20,000 sculptures. Many are rare and predate the 14th century. There are over 2,200 porcelain pieces, most from the Yuan and Ming dynasties and some from the Sung.

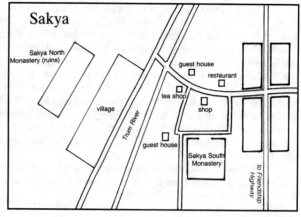

Devout Buddhists venerate four particularly sacred objects. The first is a statue of Gönpo Gur (Mahakala), one of the most significant statues to come from Bodh Gaya, India. It was brought here by the Indian *mahasiddha*, Birwapa, whose doctrines formed the basis of the Sakya school. The statue, made of the skin of an Indian king, supposedly secreted holy water periodically. The second is a statue of Jampelyang (Manjusri), called Siwo Barba, which is the *yidam* of Sakya Pandita. Pilgrims believe they can gain immeasurable wisdom if they recite the *Wisdom* Sutras in front of this Kashmiri image for seven days. The third is a statue of Drölma (the *yidam* of Phagpa), and the last is the Namgyalma Chörten, built by the translator Bari. Apparently sacred water also oozes from this *chörten*, which contained the Buddha's relics and robe.

NORTH MONASTERY

The North Monastery, founded in the 11th C., represented a minor watershed in Tibetan architecture. For the first time, construction of religious monuments utilized fully the design principles of indigenous civilian buildings. Prior to this, the monasteries of early Tibet, notably those of Tholing (see page 425), Samye (page 295), and the Jokhang (page 62), were copies of famous Indian temples. Unlike the rigorous geometry of the South, the North Monastery was a seemingly haphazard collection of lay and monastic buildings, with no apparent formal plan or symmetry. A dynamic congregation of buildings of varying sizes and placement gradually evolved over the ages.

The complex was multi-functional. It consisted of a conglomeration of chapels, aristocratic and common dwellings, administrative buildings, and defensive structures, all thrown together along the general slope of the ridge. Sakya North resembled a sizeable village. Main buildings were sited in commanding positions near the top of the ridge or near the monastery's epicenter and were among the tallest and most massive of the complex. Apart from size and position, their architecture closely resembled civilian dwellings.

Sakya began life as a modest cluster of buildings congregated around the meditation retreat of Kong Chögyal Pho. Later, during the 13th C., fortifications appeared and as the institution's prominence increased, more grandiose buildings were added. The 16th C. was a pivotal time for restorations and additions. Despite these later works, it is still easy to make out the early structures.

According to the Sakya tradition, there were 108 chapels in the complex. The 16th-C. *Guide to Sakya* by Kunga Rinchen listed four major temples (including the two Ütses), eight minor temples, four principal *labrangs*, and numerous other buildings. It is likely that in its heyday the monastery accommodated about 3,000 monks.

The Namgyalma Lhakhang (recently renovated) was founded by the translator Bari during Sakya's inception. Within it is the restored Namgyalma Chörten, originally erected by Bari and said to contain relics of the Buddha. A painting of the white-haired master can be seen on the altar. Overlooking the ruins of the North Monastery is a large, white chörten, rebuilt recently to replace the original 12th-C. one commemorating Kunga Nyingpo. An important pilgrimage site at the now-destroyed Lhakhang Shar is a cave (with a spring) where Sakya Pandita meditated under the guidance of Baripa. A distinguishing feature of Sakya is the vertical stripes of white, red, and blackish blue on the external walls of its buildings. These rare decorative elements probably had religious overtones that followed the precepts of the Vinaya; a white background interspersed with black and red was a sacred configuration of colors.

SOUTH MONASTERY (LHAKHANG CHENMO)

Sakya South was designed as an extraordinary fortress. Excluding the Potala, it is probably the most massive building in Tibet (14,760 sq m). Before the Chinese occupation, it was home to 300 monks (the North had about 200). Near both monasteries are more residential buildings that belonged to the Secretariat and to administrators.

Sakya South, founded in 1268 by Phagpa, underwent several major renovations. A great fire gutted the monument in the 16th C. and the Lhakhang Chenmo was partially rebuilt at that time. Another significant change occurred when the wood partitions in the assembly hall were upgraded to stone and mud walls. Many of the murals were repainted then. The last program of works was accomplished in 1948. Despite reconstruction, the main complex retains much of its original grandeur.

It was said that Phagpa used a temple near Lhasa as the model for Sakya South, which was eventually finished by Panchen Kunga Zangpo, who succeeded to the Sakya throne in 1275. The principal building, the Lhakhang Chenmo, was the first constructed, followed by

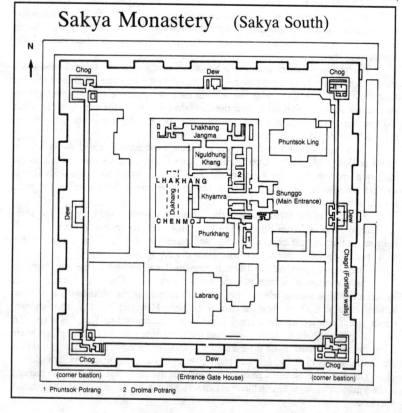

Sakya Monastery   (Sakya South)

N

Chog

Dew

Chog

Lhakhang Jangma

D

Phuntsok Ling

Nguldhung Khang

2

LHAKHANG

Dukhang

Khyamra

Shunggo (Main Entrance)

CHENMO

Phurkhang

Dew

Chagri (Fortified walls)

Dew

Labrang

Chog

Dew

Chog

(corner bastion)

(Entrance Gate House)

(corner bastion)

1 Phuntsok Potrang   2 Drolma Potrang

the external walls, other chapels, dwellings and administrative buildings. Each side of the complex's perimeter wall was 100 m in length. The square main building, with sides of 40 m, has two storys and stands on the complex's primary axis, in line with the main entrance. Because of its great height, this edifice served as the focus even though it was not situated at the monastery's center.

The Lhakhang Chenmo's main entrance is to the east and its walls are parallel to the perimeter walls of the complex. The ground floor is divided into two principal halls; attached to them are secondary structures. The first hall after the entrance is the Jowo Khang, separated from the second, the sumptuous *dukhang*, by a large courtyard. Side chapels contain the funerary *chörtens* and prized libraries of the monastery. The upper floor has other funerary *chörtens*, more books, and other sacred relics. An external staircase to the left of the *dukhang* entrance leads to the roof. Porticos cover all sections of these unusual, archaic stairs. Left of the Lhakhang Chenmo is the administrative building; it was totally demolished and then reconstructed in 1948. Surrounding the main chapel, somewhat asymmetrically, are the monks' residential quarters, *labrangs* of important abbots, and lesser chapels. Being lower and smaller, all are subordinate to the Lhakhang Chenmo.

Although the South Monastery differs drastically in appearance and architecture from the North, both their sacred areas are delineated by perimeter walls, and the main entrances open to the east. Direct, unimpeded access exists between the main buildings and the entrances. Sakya South was designed as a citadel: the walls are heavily fortified and the massive entrance gates are typical of Tibetan fortresses and castles. Watchtowers stand at the four corners and at the center of each of the four sides. A second perimeter wall (largely destroyed), enclosed by a moat, was beyond the present one. This type of monastic architecture is unique in Tibet, yet its prototype probably existed in both India and Central Asia. Some scholars even suggest a similarity to Yuan Chinese defense architecture; although a north–south axis, a traditional Chinese design element, is completely absent. Similarly, the typically courtyard-dominated plan, another hallmark of Chinese monuments, is lacking. Sakya's principal axis is off center and slightly displaced to the north. More conventional arrangements have the entrance, courtyard, and main building perfectly aligned. This peculiar trait of Sakya South is perhaps a reflection of the Tibetan architects' disdain towards formal, unvarying symmetry.

The construction material used at Sakya is mainly stone and unbaked brick. Its woodwork, especially in the oldest parts of the chapels, is typically Indian influenced (clouds and peony decorations, however, are derived from China). Interesting carpentry exists in the unusual four-story stairway (Kyaring Sebu), left of the *dukhang* entrance, which leads up the main building's external facade to the roof. At the top of the columns upholding the staircase porticos are cruciform consoles with wave-like profiles. The same Indian-inspired design can be seen in the atrium of the destroyed Kyangphu Monastery (see pages 793, 390), a complex founded in the 11th century. These stairs lead up to a terrace. Flanking the west and south sides of the terrace are two wide, spacious corridors with original murals. The south is painted with the leading figures of the Sakya lineage, while the west has large mandalas. These 16th-C. paintings are in good condition and the colors are as fresh as ever because traditional minerals were used.

Architectural elements first pioneered at Sakya were soon adopted by other Central Tibetan monasteries. One is the three-sectioned front facade of the central building. The center one, extending outward from the other two, is conspicuous for its large windows fronting the spacious, airy balconies (*rabsels*). Also used frequently in later monasteries is the raised platform, flanked by two massive lateral pillars, that provides dramatic access to the entrance. Chökorgye Monastery (badly damaged) near Lake Lhamo Latso (see page 638) was strongly influenced by Sakya. Its near-quadrangular perimeter walls, great square towers, and the unusual height of the central edifice are all trademarks of Sakya. Bhutan's numerous *dzongs* also retain architectural features that go back to Sakya.

In the center of the Lhakhang Chenmo complex is the main courtyard (Khyamra) with a tall flagpole (Darchen Ringpo). On its eastern (entrance) side, stone steps left of the main gate lead to the second floor and the Phüntsok Potrang Dhungten Khang. Right of the gate, another flight of steps leads to the Drölma Potrang Dhungten Khang. Directly in front of the main entrance is the main assembly hall while the Nguldhung Khang (Silver Chörten Hall) is to the right (north). The Phurkhang flanks the courtyard on the south.

Dukhang

The main assembly hall has an area of 5775 sq m and the enormous walls that enclose it are fully 16 m high and 3.5 m thick. 40 huge wooden columns support the roof. The four central ones, nearest the entrance, are especially famous. They are formed of four single tree trunks, each about 2 m in diameter. The one to the northeast, the Gyanag Sechen Kawa, was a gift from Kublai Khan, the monastery's most important donor. It was carried by hand from China, and the marks of the iron spikes that held the carrying frame remain visible. Each New Year, the Shapé (senior government official) hung a *khata* on the column. The ceremonial scarf was also offered whenever the monastery received a large donation. Another one to the southeast is the Tag Kawa or Tiger Column. According to legend it was carried here from India on the back of a tiger that expired on arrival because of its exertions. Its pelt, 6 m from nose to tail, was fastened to the column. The tree, probably a cedar, suffered over the years as pilgrims chipped away most of the bark of the lower section. A third, the Changpo Kawa column (southwest) was delivered on the horns of a black yak. Just south of Yalung is a pass called Yak's Tears Pass. The yak that carried the tree supposedly wept here and created a spring that has become a pilgrimage spot. The last of the four great columns is the Nagpo Chashak Kawa (northeast), the column that 'bleeds black blood'. Legend has it that a protector spirit (*naga*) lived inside the tree that was a destined to become the column. On being chopped down, the spirit's black blood spouted from the cut. This tree (barkless) came from India and, when propitiated, supposedly cures diseases. The lower portions of the pillars are wrapped in plastic to prevent further damage. All the upper sections of these columns have vivid green and red designs reminiscent of totem poles.

Along the assembly hall's front walls are paintings of the Buddha's former lives as told in the Paksam Trishing. The larger-than-life sculptures in the Lhakhang Chenmo are unusual for also serving as reliquaries for Sakyapa lamas. These bronze images, with ornate head-dresses, are interspersed among smaller ones, all clothed in original, richly decorated robes. Many of these date back to the 14th–15th centuries. Below are the main statues, presented in a clockwise progression.

Left (south) wall
- Sakyamuni (relics of Sakya Zangpo)
- Chenresi
- Guru Rinpoche

Back (west) wall • Sakyamuni (relics of Sakya Pandita)
  • *Chörten* (relics of Ngawang Tutob Wangchuk, the previous Tripa)
  • Statues of important Sakya lamas; to the right and below are the
    37 deities of the tantric Kunrig cycle, the longevity deities—Tsepame,
    Drölma, Namgyalma
  • Three thrones for Sakya abbots
  • Sakyamuni (relics of Sakya Pandita)
  • Three White-coated Patriarchs of Sakya: Kunga Nyingpo flanked by
    Sonam Tsemo and Drakpa Gyaltsan
  • Jampelyang
  • Jampa
  • Dorje Chang
  • *Chörten* (relics of Sakya lamas)
  • Sakyamuni (relics of Aklen, Phagpa's minister)
  • Jampelyang
  • *Chörten*
  • Sakyamuni

Right (north) wall • Sakyamuni (relics of Kungawa Rinchen Pel, Phagpa's minister)
  • Small statues of lamas and deities
  • Mural of the Five Patriarchs–Kunga Nyingpo (center), Sonam Tsemo,
    Drakpa Gyaltsan, Sakya Pandita, Phagpa

Like Lhasa's Jokhang, the ceiling beams of the hall are carved with many lion-faced figures.
Richly embroidered brocade banners hang from the rafters and columns. The best time to
visit the Lhakhang Chenmo is in the morning, when sunlight from the skylight suffuses the
entire assembly hall in a rich, magical glow.

Drölma Potrang Dhungten Khang
This second floor chapel, residence of one of the two chief Sakya lamas, has five burial *chörtens*
that entomb important abbots. On one wall are paintings dedicated to Guru Rinpoche and
on the other is the longevity triad of Tsepame, Namgyalma, and Drölma.

Nguldhung Lhakhang and Lhakhang Jangma
On the north side of the courtyard is the Nguldhung Lhakhang (Silver Chörten Chapel).
It has 11 silver *chörtens*, each containing the relics of past Sakya rulers. Behind them are
murals of the Five Dhyani Buddhas; portraits of the Five Sakya Patriarchs are painted above
each divinity. On the left side wall is a library, behind which are murals of the Rigsum Gönpo:
Chenresi, Jampelyang, and Chana Dorje. A door along the back wall opens to the rich, cosy
Lhakhang Jangma. Within it are five more ornate *chörtens* and behind them huge murals of
patriarchs and *bodhisattvas*. On other walls are paintings of mandalas.

Phurkhang
The Phurkhang is on the courtyard's south side. Inside are large, new bookcases and larger-
than-life sculpted figures, dominated by Sakyamuni and Jampelyang. Between them is the complete
Kangyur. The left wall has images of Sakya tantric deities including Hevajra, the favorite of
Drokmi, the lama and teacher of Kong Chögyal Pho who started the Sakya order. Drokmi

translated the Hevajra *tantra* from Sanskrit into Tibetan. Along the back wall are paintings of Tsepame, Namgyalma, Drölma, and the Medicine Buddha. Numerous bronzes range along the right-hand wall surrounding a central Drölma. Sakya's monks recite the Phurpa Drubchö *sutra* in this chamber.

Phüntsok Potrang Dhungten Khang

Like the Drölma Potrang, this chapel is located on the second floor at the courtyard's southeast corner. It served as the residence for one of the two chief Sakya lamas. The principal statue is Jampelyang, surrounded by sculpted images of Drölkar (White Tara), Namgyalma, Tsepame, Dorje Chang, Dorje Sempa, and Sakya Pandita.

LESSER MONASTERIES AND NUNNERIES WITHIN THE SAKYA PRINCIPALITY

Chökorlünpo This important monastery, 2 hr on foot due west of Sakya (south of the Trum River), was founded in the 14th or early 15th C. and had 200 monks. It had a special relationship with the Phüntsok Potrang branch of the ruling Kong family.

Donga Chöde This monastery, halfway between Sakya and Lhatse, also on the south bank of the Trum, is a 2-hr walk northeast along the river from Chökorlunpo. The abbot outranked all the others outside Sakya due to family connections with the Trichen (supreme ruler).

Tubken Gephel South of Lhatse, this monastery is at the entrance of the Mangkar Valley (see page 892) on the east bank of the Mangkar Chu. It is a 3/4-hr walk from the village of Mangkar Phu, itself 6 1/2 hr from Lhatse. Within the monastery is one of the Mangkar Valley's Great Caves. Tubken Gephel was rebuilt in 1985 amidst the ruins. Out of 200 monks that lived here in 1965, only one remains.

Chundu This site on the Phu Chu's west bank, 3 hr north of the Phu-Phung confluence, had 40 monks.

Kabale Location unknown (contained 40 monks).

Nishar The monastery, 2 1/2 hr southwest of Chundu, is on the north side of a road that leads west to the Friendship Highway and Shekar. It had 24 monks.

Dechen The monastery has 15 retired monks and five retired nuns. It is near the headwaters of the Phu Chu, on its right (west) bank. The road which follows the Phu Chu south (to Kharta from Sakya) is across the river.

Chagur A 1 1/2-hr walk due east of Sakya leads to the retreat of Khetsun Trapa, abbot of Sakya in the 12th century. It had 15 monks.

Kyilé Also known as Tsau Tra Dzong, its location is 4 1/4 hr west of Sakya on the north bank of the Semawre River; the villages of Nyambo and Lage stand across the water. Pretty Kyilé is a jumble of ancient ruins mixed with houses and sheds on a plateau. To its west, across sandy ravines, are *chörtens* and a circular stone wall that mark a sacred pilgrimage site. Kong Chögyal Pho, founder of the Sakyapa, was born near here in 1034.

Dradre Dradre, a monastery of eight retired monks, is on the west bank of the Shap River near its junction with the Tsangpo. The prosperous Shap Valley has many settlements.

Tragpoche On the east bank of the Phu, south of Dechen, it had eight monks.

Truma This was the birthplace of Sachen (Sakya Chenpo Kunga Nyingpo, 1092–1158), second abbot of Sakya and one of the sect's major teachers. Eight retired monks lived here. It is 1/2 hr south of Chagur, 1 1/2 hr east of Sakya.

Jashong A large, 11th-C. monastery previously housed 1,000 monks. It is north of Dradre, about 1 hr from the Shap–Tsangpo confluence.

Jikyop 1 1/2 hr east of Chagur.

Sazang A nunnery, 1 1/2 hr west of Sakya, on the Trum's north bank. It was previously a monastery and has about 60 nuns.

Rinchengang This former nunnery of 50 nuns is 1 hr east of Sakya North, north of the Trum.

Kagung Located in the area of Kochag, north of Kharta and immediately west of the Nyonno Ri massif (6749), this nunnery had about 50 nuns.

Tsedrung Also in Kochag, with 50 nuns.

Lashar In Kochag, north of Kagung, a nunnery with 30 nuns.

Gönpa Gya A nunnery north of Sakya and west of the Shap Chu. It had 20 nuns.

LHATSE TO SAKYA: FROM THE FRIENDSHIP HIGHWAY PAST THE VALLEY OF THE THIRTEEN CAVES

Location	Lhatse and Sakya area
Map reference	NH45-11 C, 45-15 A
Trekking days	5 (one-way)
Start–Finish	Lhatse–Sakya
Passes	One low pass

OVERVIEW

This relaxing, five-day pilgrimage goes from Lhatse to Sakya, a profoundly important monastery in the history of Tsang Province and all Tibet. It is easy to reach Lhatse; most vehicles plying the main road between Nepal and Lhasa make an obligatory stop here. Sakya, however, is more difficult to get to, being 25 km off the main road. Most people get there by chartering a vehicle or finding a ride on a pilgrim truck. Walking to Sakya from Lhatse thus provides a convenient, pleasurable alternative. (Returning to the Friendship Highway from Sakya is much easier than trying to find a way in; trucks regularly head that way.)

The walk passes through an area considered to be within Sakya's sphere of influence. Rebuilt monasteries (Samdrub, Tubken Gephel) are highlights along the way. The most important sanctuary, however, is the remarkable hidden valley of Mangkar, the Valley of the Thirteen Caves. In the past, these secret hermitages were frequented only by serious practitioners, including the illustrious Indian lama, Dampa Sangye (d 1117). Certain caves were established in the early days of Buddhism in Tibet. Dragur Lotsa Phuk, for example, was where the first Tibetan texts were translated from Sanskrit in the 8th century. Later, in the early 11th C., advanced ascetics made their homes here. Unfortunately, we have little contemporary information on Mangkar. The trek merely skirts its entrance.

Related sections

Sakya Monastery, p 880
North Bank of the Tsangpo, p 847
Chörten Nyima, p 801
West Tibet, p 943
Chung Riwoche, p 451

Access

Lhatse (Lhatse Xian) is 151 km west of Shigatse on the Friendship Highway at roadmarker 402 km (new marker 5052). Buses and trucks coming from either Lhasa or the Nepal–Tibet border usually stop here to refuel. Stay at the Lhatse Guest House, a compound with plenty of cheap rooms, diagonally across from the gas station. See page 868 for more information on Lhatse.

Time Chart

Day	Place	Hours
1	Lhatse–Samdrub	3
2	Mangkar Phu	4
3	Drum Chok	4 1/2
4	Tsau	4
5	Sakya	4 1/4

Trail Notes

✤ DAY 1 LHATSE–SAMDRUB 3 HR

Walk out of the Lhatse Guest House, go past the gas station, and then turn right on the main road. At the first major intersection turn left (south). There is a post office on the left, then the ornate town cinema in a large compound on the right. Further along is Lhatse's 'department store', on a corner on the left. Continue straight ahead past the grounds of the Lhatse Communist Party and the local school. Leave the town behind; the road soon joins another dirt road curving in from the right (west). Follow this to the east, making a left turn from the original direction.

The path goes along the valley floor towards the southeast with the river on the left and a steep ridge to the right. Notice a large rock on the left 3/4 hr after Lhatse. Cross the river just before this rock. Reach Mangkar in 3/4 hr from this point. Across from the village are *chörtens* near some houses at the base of the valley's south ridge. Continue southeast along the valley to Samdrub, a village of 100 families. (The villages along the way all have electricity.) A trail from Samdrub leads left (north) up a side valley to Samdrub Monastery (1/2 hr). This 14th-C. institution once had 100 monks, though that number had dwindled to 25 by 1950. In 1965, the place was badly damaged by the Chinese, but was rebuilt in the mid-1980s.

✤ DAY 2 SAMDRUB–MANGKAR PHU 4 HR

From Samdrub, the path veers south; the river is on the right. Walk past Mangkar Til, a village on the right. Further along, on the left, are buildings constructed over the site of a destroyed monastery. The next village is Cup, 1 1/2 hr from Samdrub. Continue along the river valley southward, past villages and ruins on the right. Across the valley from the ruins are Tibetan inscriptions on the hillsides. Beyond are more ruins, then the valley divides. At this junction, near the entrance of the left-hand valley, is the village of Mangkar Phu (Mang Phu), 2 1/2 hr from Cup. A trail leads up the right-hand Mangkar Valley to the monastery of Tubken Gephel (3/4 hr from Mangkar Phu).

Tubken Gephel Monastery

This was the monastery of Tsarchen Losel Gyatso (1502–67) of the Sakya Tsarpa lineage. Destroyed in 1965, it was rebuilt in the mid-1980s. Only a handful of the original 200 monks of the 1960s live here. One of the Mangkar Valley's 13 Great Caves is enclosed within the monastery. Near here are ruins of an unknown monastery, perhaps Ganden Dargyaling. Reputedly, hot springs lie one day's walk away. Tsachen Monastery is also up this west-trending valley.

The Mangkar Valley

Mangkar, the Valley of the Thirteen Caves, is the mystical corridor of access to the sacred Lhako Kangri range. The valley's retreats and hermitages are built around 13 historic meditation caves. Near the head of the valley, to the south, is the range's highest peak, Mt Lhako Kangri (6457 m) and an important trail junction. The trail heading right (northwest) leads to the Friendship Highway at *daoban* 44, by the banks of the Lolo Chu, halfway between Lhatse and Shekar. The other trail goes south. After crossing a high pass, it follows the Pangchö Phu (Phar) Valley southward to eventually meet the Tingche–Shekar road near the Jikyop bridge (see page 803).

THE MANGKAR CAVE RETREATS

Lower Mangkar

There are two main monasteries here.

- Se Karchung (Ngog Karchung). This 11th-C. monastery was founded in 1064 by Drubchen Sekarchungwa, a master of the Lamdre practice. Choklé Namgyal, a Bodong Monastery patriarch of the 14th-C. stayed here in retreat during the last years of his life.
- Dar Drongmoche. Tsarchen Lösel Gyatso (1502–67), head of the Sakya Tsarpa school, founded this monastery. He belonged to a lineage derived from the Sakyapa teacher, Dampa Sonam Gyaltsen (1312–75) of Rinchengang Monastery, a branch of Sakya. Tsarchen taught the young Tsong Khapa for a short time at Nethang Monastery (see page 472) near Lhasa. His tomb is at Dar Drongmoche.

Middle Mangkar

- The birthplace of Ma Rinchen Chok. The 8th-C. translator Ma Rinchen Chok was born in a village of the middle Mangkar Valley. An early translator in Tibet, he was one of Guru Rinpoche's 24 disciples, a contemporary of King Trisong Detsen. His great achievement was the translation of the *Cycle of Guhyagarbha*. Ma Rinchen Chok was murdered during the turmoils at the time of King Langdarma's assassination (842).
- Retreat of Sonam Chöpel. Sonam Chöpel was a Teacher of Mantras (*ngagcheng*), a title common among the Sakyapa. He was reputedly a magician and lived in an isolated spot in this area.

Upper Mangkar

- Sungnak Lamdre Phuk. The Indian sage, Dampa Sangye (see page 272), taught the secrets of Lamdre in this cave.
- Dragur Lötsa Phuk (Dragur Gyagar Phuk). Sanskrit texts were translated into Tibetan here in the 8th century. Translators came from both India and China; the Chinese worked on astronomical and medicinal texts as well as sacred Buddhist literature.
- Wösel Dawa Phuk. This was the meditation cave of Drokmi Pelgyi Yeshe (Sakya Yeshe, d 1074), a scholar-traveler, and one of Guru Rinpoche's 24 disciples. A

➡

pupil of Santibhadra, he was a contemporary of Rinchen Zangpo (see page 425), the West Tibet translator. Drokmi transmitted into Tibet the teachings of the Indian tantric master Birwapa (Virupa), and the Sakyapa derived their system of instruction from Birwapa's theories. Drokmi tutored Konchok Gyalpo, founder of mighty Sakya Monastery (1073), and also taught Marpa Lotsawa, Milarepa's guru. Other principal retreats of this translator include the cave at Lhatse Dzong (see page 807) and the cave of Nyugu Lung.

- Nyugu Lung. This retreat, founded by Drokmi in 1043, is near Wösel Dawa Phuk. He taught the illustrious Marpa here.
- Tsalung Dorjedrak Dzong. Jetsun Drakpa Gyaltsen, a 12th-C. lama and third son of Sachen Kunga Nyingpo (successor in 1172 to Sonam Tsemo as Sakya's abbot), came here for retreats. Tsarchen Lösel Gyatso also meditated here in the 16th century.

✤ DAY 3 MANGKAR PHU–DRUM CHOK 4 1/2 HR

Take the left valley from Mangkar Phu towards the southeast. (Directly south are the sacred snow peaks of Lhako Kangri; the highest is 6457 m. A side valley at the Mangkar Phu junction leads towards this lofty range and its remote meditation caves. The village of Gadong is also up this valley.) In 1/2 hr, cross to the right bank of the river; shortly thereafter recross it to the left. Steep hills border the valley.

Further along on the left, across the river, are caves at the foot of a ridge. They are used by herders for shelter. 1 1/2 hr after the first river crossing, come to a tiny *chörten* on the right. The valley veers to the right (east) and widens. Steep ridges on both sides give way to less dramatic, low hills. There is no habitation; the only sign of life is sheep. The last portion of the day's walk is along a stone wall on the left that peters off into a barbed wire fence. The trail is indistinct, but just follow the fence eastward, swinging somewhat to the valley's left side. Reach Drum Chok (Gung Chok), beyond the fence, in 1/2 hr after the tiny *chörten*. It is the most secluded village on the trek; a good place to rest and explore the surrounding hills.

✤ DAY 4 DRUM CHOK–TSAU 4 HR

This thoroughly isolated stretch has no distinct path or habitation along the way. Hire a guide for the day if possible, and yaks to carry packs. *Chörtens* beyond Drum Chok soon mark a point where the valley divides. Take the right branch, which is flanked by low hills and rises gently uphill. Reach a low pass 1 3/4 hr after Drum Chok. Descend eastwards into the next valley. Pass a couple of *chörtens* and a stone animal enclosure (1hr from the pass). Further to the east, two sandy ravines open to the left. Then cultivated fields start to appear; reach Tsau (Tsau Tra Dzong, Kyilé), on the river's left bank, 1 1/4 hr after the stone enclosure. This village, a jumble of ancient ruins juxtaposed with houses and animal sheds, is situated on a beautiful plateau overlooking the river. Steep cliffs flank Tsau to the south; it is a long drop to the valley floor. Donkeys are available here. Tsau, a pilgrimage site is the birthplace of Kong Chögyal Pho (b 1034), founder of the Sakyapa sect.

✤ DAY 5 TSAU–SAKYA 4 1/4 HR

A short distance beyond Tsau is Nyambo on the right bank of the Semare River. Further along is a pond. The path now crosses to the right (south) bank, passing the village of Lagé. Reach some ruins with prayer flags (1 hr from Tsau). Walk past Rimba. The valley soon becomes blocked by steep hills; the path curves to the left. The left (north) side of the valley is bordered by cliffs that taper into low and sloping hills with caves and ruins at the base. Pass several *chörtens*. Round the corner to reach an open sandy area, which is just before the main road leading from the Sakya bridge to Sakya Monastery. At the junction of the road and the trail is the village of Tsucheting (1 1/2 hr from the ruins with prayer flags). Follow the dirt road to Sakya (1 3/4 hr).

MT EVEREST: THE KANGSHUNG FACE AND RONGPHUK

The following sections describe an extensive network of treks in the region north of Mt Everest. Most major valleys (within Tibet) emanating from the world's highest mountain are surveyed. These include the fabled Karma, Kharta, and Arun which since the First British Everest Expedition (1921) are familiar to a small circle of explorers. The trek to the Kangshung Face is relatively unknown to most present-day visitors: the North Face is by far the more familiar. It goes through pristine, untouched areas such as the superb Valley of the Lakes and the luxuriant Damdong Valley. The return leg goes north to Sakya Monastery via the Yeru Tsangpo or to Shekar on the Friendship Highway. Also included is an ascent of the high Lakpa La, which allows an approach to the Kangshung Face directly from Rongphuk Monastery.

THE KANGSHUNG FACE: EXTENSIVE TREKS IN THE EASTERN REGIONS OF MT EVEREST

Explorations of the legendary valleys of Karma, Kharta, and the Valley of the Lakes

Location	East of Mt Everest
Map reference	NG45-3 A, NH45-14 B D, 45-15 A C
Trekking days	16 (circuit)
Start–Finish	Road marker 494 km–Kangshung–Shekar
Passes	Pang La, Langma La, Shao La

OVERVIEW

This section, when combined with 'Rongphuk: A trek to the North Face base camp' (see below, p 913), constitutes a very thorough exploration of the Everest region. Two points (Dingri and road marker 494 km) on the Friendship Highway allow access to the villages of Peruche and Kharta. The latter is the staging post for a reconnaisance of the fabulous Kharta and Karma valleys. The Kharta River originates in the Kharta Glacier which descends from west to east from the Everest massif. It joins the Phung (Arun) Chu and the combined waters

to Nepal
road marker (494 km)
Shekar
to Lhatse
Friendship Highway
Sakya G
Dingri
to Shekar
Nyomda
Lamar La
Peruche
Jikyop
Pasum
Karkhung
Doya La
Chukhor
to Tingchi, Chörten Nyima
Rongphuk G
Dra
Lhundrubling
Yueba
Kharta
to Chörten Nyima
Langma La
Yulok
Nye La
to Mt Everest
Shao La
Valley of the Lakes
Pethang Ringmo
Sakyetang
Lungto
Everest: Kangshung Face
to Nepal
N

flow southwards into Nepal through a greatly constricted gorge. Because of this tremendous narrowing, the monsoon precipitation rushing up from Nepal is effectively stopped at Kharta—with the result that within the space of a few km, the dry barren plateau climate of Tibet abruptly cedes to the moist one of Nepal. The lush vegetation of Kharta and Karma reflects this transition dramatically. Kharta is a well-populated valley with a good harvest of barley. At an elevation of 3750 m, it has an almost ideal climate; the air is always warm but never hot, the sun shines brightly, and the rain is not too heavy.

The Karma Valley, at 4300 m, is characterized by magnificent alpine scenery and rich flora and contains the highest known forests in the world. Three of the world's five highest peaks—Everest (8848 m), Lhotse (8501 m), and Makalu (8463 m)—overlook the valley. Views of the last are especially unforgettable. Four glacial rivers, including one from Everest's Kangshung Glacier, contribute to the Karma River which flows through a pristine, isolated area. There is no habitation except for the occasional yak herders. Beyond Kharta, after crossing the Samchung La to the south, is the amazing Valley of the Lakes. Within this alpine plateau is a string of 14 emerald green lakes. Just beyond it, on the far side of the Chog La, is sacred Lake Rudam Latso where Tibetans come annually to circumambulate. East of the Samchung La is the secluded valley of Damdong. The vegetation here is outstanding and there are plenty of lovely campsites. Only a few locals wander into this area occasionally. To the western extremity of the Karma Valley is the famed Kangshung Glacier which appends from the eastern face of Mt Everest. A route follows the glacier's northern perimeter to Pethang Ringmo, the magnificent alpine camp for assaults on Everest's Kangshung Face. It passes beneath the jagged peaks of Chomo Lonzo and Makalu and allows an intimate look at the eastern approach to Everest. Cross back to the Kharta Valley via the Langma or Shao La.

Kharta can also be reached from the Rongphuk base camp via a more direct route (see Everest base camp to Kharta via the Doya La, p 899). One of two return legs of the main trek (from Kharta) goes north back to the Friendship Highway. The other follows the Phung (Arun) Chu Valley northwards to Chukhor, where the route veers to the northeast to continue along the banks of the Yeru Tsangpo. It eventually connects with the main highway that links Tingche Xian with Sakya Monastery. This allows for the exploration of the Chörten Nyima pilgrimage (see page 801). Or, if you are short of time, it is only a short journey to Sakya and the Friendship Highway. For those with mountaineering experience, a 9-day crossing from the Rongphuk Valley into the Kharta Valley via the high Lakpa La (6849 m) is also described (Exploratory Trek).

Because of the considerable monsoon effect that penetrates the Kangshung area (via the Arun/Phung Chu corridor), the best time to trek is pre- and post-monsoon, ie May to mid-June and September to mid-October. However, the North Face of Everest (following chapter) is blessed with a longer season. The sheer wall of the mountain effectively stops most of the precipitation. It is possible to trek here for most of the year, May to October being the best bet (expect rain in July and August in the lower regions).

Related sections
Rongphuk, p 913
Chörten Nyima, p 801
Lapchi, p 248
Dingri, 918
Tzipri, p 921

Access: Near Shekar
At road marker 494 km on the Friendship Highway, 11 km west of the Shekar turnoff, is a dirt track that hugs the extreme right side of a tributary valley. It trends to the south and leads over the Pang La to the village of Kharta (3750 m), staging post for the trek to Mt Everest's Kangshung Face.

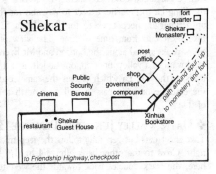

Shekar

fort
Tibetan quarter ☐
Shekar Monastery ☐

post office ◇

shop ◇
path around spur, up to monastery and fort

Public Security Bureau

government compound

cinema

Xinhua Bookstore

restaurant • Shekar Guest House

to Friendship Highway, checkpost

Time Chart

Day	Place	Hours
1	Rm 494 km–Valley junction	5 1/2
2	Valley junction–Peruche	3 1/4
3	Peruche–Khorta	5 3/4
4	Khorta–Tsa	6 1/4
5	Tsa–Dra	5 3/4
6	Dra–Kharta	4 1/2
7	Kharta–Yueba	2 1/4
8	Yueba–Base of Langma La	6
9	Base of Langma La–Cave	5 1/4

10	Cave–Pethang	4
11	Pethang–Pethang Ringmo	4 3/4
12	Pethang Ringmo–Pethang	4 1/4
13	Pethang–Sharlung	5 1/2
14	Sharlung–Sharo	4 3/4
15	Sharo–Yueba	6
16	Yueba–Kharta	2 1/4
17	Kharta–Shekar	hitch

FRIENDSHIP HIGHWAY TO KHARTA

Expect to walk to Kharta along a jeep track which sees very little traffic. If you have sufficient time, this is a most delightful way to go. It is also possible to get a ride (probably on a tractor), although you will be charged for the privilege.

Trail Notes

✤ DAY 1 ROAD MARKER 494 KM–VALLEY JUNCTION 5 1/2 HR

Walk south from the road junction (hugging the west slopes of the valley) to Tse (1 hr), a village in a valley junction. In recent years, a toll has been set up here. Foreign trekkers are typically charged 50 Rmb per person and motor vehicles 200 Rmb. These fees, however, can be bargained down considerably. Tse is a good place to hire donkeys for the trip over the Pang La to Peruche; expect to pay also for the handler's return to the village. Continue up a zigzagging jeep track to the Pang La, a 5250-m pass (3 1/4 hr). Leave the road and take short cuts from time to time. The view of the Himalayas at the top is magnificent. Snow peaks spread along the horizon and Mt Everest is a small triangle far to the left. Descend southward to a valley junction, on the left, in 1 1/4 hr. (The side valley to the left [northeast] leads to the Tse La which crosses the same secondary range as the Pang La but further to the east. Beyond the pass, a trail goes north to rejoin the jeep track some distance south of Tse.)

✤ DAY 2 VALLEY JUNCTION–PERUCHE 3 1/4 HR

Take short cuts but generally follow the jeep track south and southeast. The river is on your right. Cross to the other bank after 3/4 hr. 1/4 hr further is the village of Omalung. From here, the track doubles back towards the west to Nyomda at a valley junction (1 1/2 hr). A dirt track goes up the western valley via the Lamar La (5662 m) to Dingri. The southern valley leads to Peruche (Padrug), also situated at a confluence of valleys (3/4 hr). (The valley on the right trends southwest to the Rongphuk Monastery and Everest Base Camp [North Face]. To the left, the jeep track continues east, then south to Kharta.)

Peruche is an extensive village with a dilapidated guest house called the Chomolungma Hotel. It has a restaurant and shop with expensive goods. Donkeys and horses can be hired here; prices tend to be stiffer than normal so bargain hard. Strong winds buffet the area after midday. Thösamling Monastery, about 2 km east of Peruche, has been restored; it is noted for the collection of masks for Cham dances. For the continuation of this route, see page 902.

Dingri to Peruche via the Lamar La

A variety of routes lead to Peruche: the jeep road from road marker 494 km (above), the route from Dingri or the Everest Base Camp, and an obscure way from Dingri via the Lamar La that takes three days.

✧ Day 1   4 hr

From Dingri, walk east along the Friendship Highway to the eastern perimeter (1/2 hr) of the large Dingri Valley that trends southward towards the Himalayas. Cross a bridge over the Ra Chu and turn right (south) along a rough track which runs at the base of a line of hills on the left. Reach Razam (Raju) at the entrance of a tiny side valley on the left (3/4 hr). In 15 min the ruins of Chölung Monastery appear, and in 15 min more the track splits into three. The left branch goes up the slopes to Shelung, the right goes to due south towards the Himalayas along the Ra Chu's left (west) bank, and the center one veers southeast. Take this last way to Nelung (1 1/2 hr) on the far side of a branch valley. Follow the river along its right bank. In 3/4 hr, after crossing a low ridge, come to a major trail junction. The right trail goes southeast over a 5180-m pass and then follows the left (north) bank of the Ding Chu to its junction with the Dzakar Chu. Take the left trail.

✧ Day 2   5 3/4 hr

The left trail heads east to the Lamar La (5662 m). In 1 hr, cross the river to its left bank. The pass is reached in a further 1 3/4 hr. Descend to the east along the right (south) bank of the Nyo Chu and ford numerous streams. In 3 hr, reach Gara, a large village.

✧ Day 3   3 hr

Gara is sited on the banks of the Nyo Chu. Reach Trongpa, a village next to Karé Monastery (1/2 hr), then Nyomda (1 1/4 hr) at a junction of valleys. Here, the jeep track from the Pang La and road marker 494 km joins the trail from the Lamar La. Turn right (south) and follow the jeep road to Peruche (3/4 hr). The left (north) trail leads back to the Friendship Highway via the Pang La.

Everest Base Camp to Kharta via the Doya La and the Chongphu Chu Valley

This itinerary to Kharta starts from the Everest Base Camp and Rongphuk Monastery. It crosses the Doya La and avoids the Friendship Highway–Peruche–Kharta jeep road almost entirely. An alternative route to Kharta from Rongphuk bypasses the Doya La by simply following the Dzakar Chu Valley to Chö Dzong and then to Peruche. From here, continue to Kharta along the jeep road (see main trek).

✧ Day 1   Rongphuk Monastery–Zambu Valley   6 hr

Walk south along the right (east) bank of the Rongphuk River, following the jeep

➠

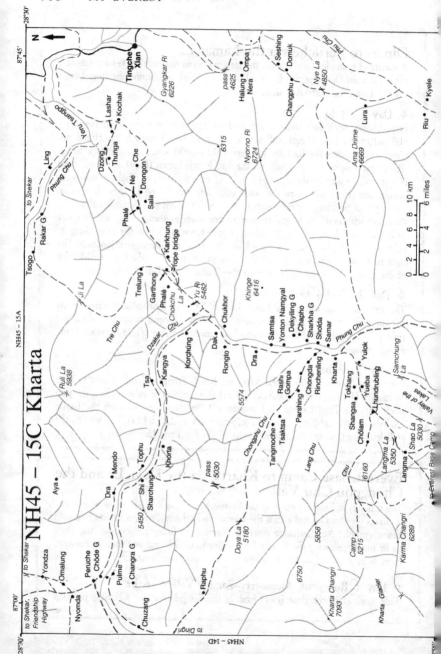

NH45 – 15C Kharta

NH45 – 15A

28°30'

87°45'

87°00'

28°30'

road. Use footpaths from time to time as short cuts. In 3 1/2 hr, reach a cantilever bridge at the confluence of the Rongphuk and Gyachung rivers. (The latter flows south from the Gyachung Glacier [west of the Rongphuk Glacier].) These two form the Dzakar Chu. Just before the bridge, a dirt road turns to the right to follow the Dzakar's south bank. Walk along it to the north, then northeast with the river on the left. In 2 hr, Chöbu appears next to some ruins on the left across the river. Beyond (1/2 hr), is a side valley across the river that leads to Zambu.

✧ Day 2 Zambu Valley–Lelung 5 hr

Continue along the right bank of the Dzakar Chu; the dirt track trends to the east to Chö Dzong (1 3/4 hr). After the village, cross a steep pass 400 m above the valley, then descend steeply to Lelung (3 1/4 hr), a prosperous village within the Thömar Chu Valley.

Note: Chö Dzong to Peruche 1 day (6 3/4 hr) From Chö Dzong, the Dzakar Chu flows east to Peruche (see Friendship Highway to Kharta, page 898). Follow its south (right) bank to a new cement bridge (1 1/4 hr). (A short distance beyond the village, look for a side valley on your right across the Dzakar. This leads southeast to the Doya La.) In 1 1/4 hr, cross a bridge over a river draining from the Ding La (the Ding Chu flows into the Dzakar from the west), then continue along the left bank of the Dzakar to Pasum (3/4 hr), a major settlement of the valley that has a small guest house for trekkers. The river now trends to the northeast. Walk along its left bank, passing the ruins of Chetang Monastery (3/4 hr) on top of a ridge, and the villages of Palding and Lashing. Peruche is 3/4 hr from Pasum. Budget two to three days from Rongphuk Monastery to Peruche.

✧ Day 3 Lelung–base of Doya La 6 3/4 hr

Walk north down the Thömar Chu Valley to a valley junction (1 1/4 hr). The side valley that enters from the right leads southeast to the Doya La. Ascend this valley to Tontra (1/4 hr), then cross over to the river's right bank and continue to Ratsal (3/4 hr). Cross again to the other bank and go upstream to Raphu (Rebu, 1 3/4 hr) after crossing a spur. This picturesque village straddles the river. The valley divides after Raphu. Take the left trail with the river on the right to the foot of the Doya La (2 3/4 hr).

✧ Day 4 Base of Doya La–valley junction 4 3/4 hr

Continue east for 2 1/2 hr to the Doya La (5180 m), then descend to the east to the Chongphu Chu Valley. In 2 1/4 hr, reach a valley junction. The side valley on the left has a trail that leads north to the Dzakar Chu Valley. For the remaining trip down the Chongphu Chu Valley to its junction with the Phung Chu and then to Kharta, see box, page 902.

✤ Day 3 Peruche–Khorta 5 3/4 hr

From Peruche, follow the flat jeep track eastward along the Dzakar Chu's left (north) bank. The walk to Kharta passes many ruined villages, an indication that this area south of the Friendship Highway was once more densely populated. The population declined during the 18th-C. wars with the Nepalese Gurkhas. In 1/2 hr, walk past the ruins of Chöde Monastery. Continuing due east to Dra (Dila) Dzong, a village of two-story houses. Here the track makes a right turn to Nazon and a bridge (Peruche to bridge is 2 1/2 hr). Nearby is Tashigang. Cross the bridge and follow the right (south) bank of the Dzakar Chu River, which along this stretch is lined by sheer cliffs. (Across the river, a gorge with a village at its entrance trends to the northeast. After passing Mendo and Kenga, a trail crosses the high Ruli La (5938 m) to the small town of Tsogo and its monastery of Rakar, sited on the main road between Tingche Xian and Shekar, see page 812). After the gorge, the Dzakar Chu bends to the southeast. Go past the villages of Langdong, Shi, Sharchung (2 hr from bridge), and Kalirong to Khorta (3 1/4 hr from bridge). Beyond Khorta the valley narrows significantly and enters a forest of tall trees, the first encountered in the region.

Sharchung: To Kharta via the Chongphu Chu Valley

A side valley opens to the right at Sharchung. A path along this side valley goes due south over a pass and then follows the Chongphu Chu River southeast to Kharta. This alternative route takes 12 hr to walk and avoids altogether the Peruche–Kharta jeep road; locals use it as a short cut.

✧ Day 1 6 1/4 hr

Walk southward along the right (east) bank of the river in the side valley. In 2 1/2 hr, reach a valley junction. Take the right branch up and over a 5030-m pass in 2 3/4 hr. Descend south into the Chongphu Chu Valley (1 hr). Camp here. To the west, a trail leads to a lake at the head of the valley and then to the Doya La (see page 901).

✧ Day 2 5 3/4 hr

Follow the Chongphu Chu downstream (southeast) along its left (north) bank. A strong head wind typically comes up the valley. In 2 3/4 hr, reach the Lalung Monastery situated across the river from the villages of Tangmoche and Tsaktsa. Continue to Trusar (1hr), Rashi Gompa (1/4 hr), Kharnga (1/4 hr), Pula (1/2 hr), Chongda (1/4 hr), and Tashigang (1/4 hr) sited just before a bridge over the Chongphu Chu. Here is its confluence with the large Phung Chu, which becomes the Arun in Nepal. Cross the Tashigang bridge to Rinchenling. Kharta is 1/2 hr further to the south. Houses in the Chongphu Valley are built of brown stone and are quite heavily fortified. They have virtually no windows, only small loopholes.

✤ Day 4 Khorta–Tsa 6 1/4 hr

Walk east along the Dzakar Chu; no villages exist between Khorta and Tsa. Go past a stream that flows into the main river from the right. Cave dwellings appear on the other side. Farther along, by the left side of the track, are corral shelters with firewood; spend the night here if necessary. Reach a second side valley flanked by snowridges (3 1/4 hr) with many steep footpaths going up the hills to the south. These lead over 5000-m saddles to the Chongphu Chu Valley. Across the Dzakar, on both sides of a side valley, are more cave dwellings. Walk past another side valley with ruins a short distance up it. There are good camping spots here. Beyond, the river valley widens into a plateau. At the far end is Kangya with a sacred spring marked by two large trees festooned with prayer flags. Just after the village is a path that leads to a bridge spanning the Dzakar River. On its north bank is Tsa (3 hr) and a corral in the midst of barley fields. Donkeys can be hired here.

✤ Day 5 Tsa–Dra 5 3/4 hr

After Tsa, the Dzakar Chu Valley bends from east to southeast. Cross back to the right (south) bank and continue along a dirt track. An intense head wind makes the going slow. Walk past a *chörten* and the village of Lajung. Reach Korchung (Horchung) on the left side of the road (2 3/4 hr). Farther downstream, across the river, is Tungme (Lungme) which has a handsome house near tall poplar trees that used to belong to the Shekar Dzong government. At a forest the river makes a pronounced turn to the right; some distance beyond is a bridge. Do not cross it. Later, come to the confluence (3 3/4 hr from Tsa) of the Dzakar Chu and the Phung Chu, which flows through the Himalayas to Nepal. Dramatic peaks rise to the east. On the Phung Chu's left bank are Patso and Samtsa; the large village of Chukhor is farther downstream. A footpath goes south along this side as well. (East of the bridge, the Phung Chu forces a passage through a deep gorge. The peak flanking the gorge to the north is Yu Ri, 5482 m.) Follow the right (west) bank of the river's combined waters (now known as the Phung), and in 2 hr reach a wide plain with the twin villages of Combu and Dra, separated by a path. The latter is on the right perimeter near the entrance of a side valley. A bridge spans the wide and quite unfordable Phung Chu near here.

✤ Day 6 Dra–Kharta 4 1/2 hr

Walk past a side valley on the right; two of its streams flow into the Phung. The track now hugs the base of the valley's west walls; most habitation and traffic are on the far side. The villages on the left bank, from north to south, are Samtsa, Yönton Namgyal, Dekyiling Monastery, Chapho, Sharkha Monastery, Sholda, and Samar. Farther downstream a bridge crosses the Phung. Do not cross it. Continue to its junction with the Chongphu Chu (a trail within this valley leads west to the Doya La; see above). The track crosses the former by a bridge to continue south down the latter. Across the bridge is Rinchenling (4 hr). Kharta is 1/2 hr further. The district headquarters consists of several Chinese compounds. One contains a guest house (Rmb 1.5 per bed) and a shop with bare necessities. Beyond the compounds, farther downstream, is the old Tibetan village of Kharta. Potatoes, turnips, and meat can be bought here. Kharta is sited on the left (north) bank of the Lang Chu, which at this point flows into the Phung Chu. Just south of the village the dirt track crosses a bridge over the Lang Chu and turns west to travel up the left (north) bank of the Kharta Chu to Yulok and Yueba. The latter is the staging post for treks into the Kangshung Valley.

KHARTA TO THE KANGSHUNG FACE BASE CAMP OF EVEREST VIA THE LANGMA LA

❖ DAY 7 KHARTA–YUEBA 2 1/4 HR

From Kharta, cross the bridge over the Lang Chu, then follow the left (north) bank of the crystal-clear Kharta Chu westward. This beautiful, inhabited valley has many villages and good camp sites. Walk past Yulok on the south bank (1 1/4 hr) and Yulong, then reach Yueba (2 1/4 hr from Kharta) on the south bank by a bridge. (A trail from Yulok goes south over the Samchung La to the Valley of the Lakes; see page 907.)

Yueba sits on a small rise above the river; hire yaks here for the trek to the Kangshung Face base camp (Rmb 5–10 per day per yak; the services of the handler are also the same rate per day; be prepared to stay overnight so the animals can be rounded up). Villages on the north bank of the Kharta include Tokhang, Namgo, Shangsa, Ganden Monastery, and Tangtö.

❖ DAY 8 YUEBA–BASE OF LANGMA LA 6 HR

Continue west along the Kharta Valley on a tractor track past Yarbu, a village near the entrance of a side valley that trends south (1 1/4 hr). A footpath in this side valley leads over the Shao La into the Karma Valley and then to the Kangshung Face. (This trek returns via the Shao La.) 3/4 hr beyond the Shao La turnoff is the large village of Lhündrubling. (A trail continues westward up the Kharta Valley past the villages of Lhading, Chölam, Lhamdo and Riphu. From Lhündrubling to a campsite on the river's right bank, near the base of the Kharta Glacier, is 7 1/2 hr.) Go through the village to walk up to the top of a ridge (1 1/4 hr) that constitutes the east wall of the valley leading up to the Langma La. Descend a short distance to the river, cross it and then walk up the other side. Follow this uninhabited side valley southwestward for 2 hr to the top of another ridge. Walk through a short gorge to a small grassy area with large boulders. Under a couple of these are makeshift cave shelters (3/4 hr). Mountains with snow and ice are all around. The Langma La is a rocky cliff with sheer sides.

❖ DAY 9 BASE OF LANGMA LA–CAVE 5 1/4 HR

This difficult day crosses the steep, three-tiered Langma La Pass. Cross the first tier in 1 1/4 hr (gain 300 m in altitude), then walk along a broad, level, rocky shelf with a 1 km-long glacial lake. Climb 150 m to another giant shelf then a final 150 m to the top of the Langma La (2hr, 5350 m) for a truly magnificent view of the Himalayas. To the left (southwest) rises massive Makalu (8463 m) with its four sharp jagged peaks. Mt Chomo Lonzo, Makalu's northern peak, is in front. Mt Everest, to the right (west) is less impressive than Makalu from this viewpoint. To the west is a wonderful amphitheater of jagged snow peaks and glaciers. Three great glaciers converge in the deep, green valley of the Karma Chu: the Kangshung Glacier from Everest in the west; the Kangdoshung Glacier from the cliffs of Chomo Lonzo in the southwest; and the third from Karma Changri (6289 m), a beautiful peak north of the Karma Valley. To the east, beyond the Phung Chu Valley, are high snow peaks of the Ama Drime range (6669 m). From the pass, descend southward through grassy uplands and a couple of small lakes. Follow stone route markers. In 2 hr, reach a substantial cave beneath a huge boulder. En route, pass Shurim Tso, a deep blue glacial lake. This is a flat area dotted with large rocks and patches of grass. Closed in by craggy peaks, it is often shrouded by fog. When the weather clears, there are wonderful views of Mt Makalu.

✦ DAY 10 CAVE–PETHANG 4 HR

Head down the valley from the cave to a long, narrow terrace 300m from the bottom of the Karma Valley. Here is a cave called Tangshum (2 hr), situated near the edge of a bluff overlooking three valleys: the Langma La, the Karma, and the Chog La to the east. Across the Karma Valley are the astounding cliffs of Chomo Lonzo, which rear to nearly 8000 m. Near the valley confluence, a path leaves the terrace to descend to the Langma Chu and crosses to its right bank, a pretty area with grassy meadows and meandering streams (3/4 hr). [A short distance to the east is a wood bridge spanning the Karma Chu; from here a trail also leads up the Shao La.] Turn right (west) here up the Karma Chu Valley to Pethang, a grassy plain with stone huts for herders. Walk through rhododendron scrubs along the way and wade across one stream (1 1/4 hr).

✦ DAY 11 PETHANG–PETHANG RINGMO (KANGSHUNG BASE CAMP) 4 3/4 HR

Go west up the Karma Valley by following the river's left (north) bank. Moraines and landslides make the going difficult. In 1 3/4 hr, round a bend called Orga to view Mt Everest properly for the first time. It looms large at the head of the valley beyond the Kangshung Glacier. On the left, a few km away, is Chomo Lonzo (7815 m) and behind it, the multi-peaked Makalu. The Karma River issues from beneath iceblocks farther up. Scramble from rock to rock along the river. After the Orga bend, traverse to the right and ascend a 150 m ridge that parallels the right bank along a clear path. On top of the ridge, follow a path westward. Below are the river and the glacier. Reach the Kangshung Face base camp (5000 m) in 3 hr. This large, grassy area with stunning views of Mt Everest (8848 m) and Lhotse (8516 m) to the left (south) is known as Pethang Ringmo. Stone huts constructed like igloos are used by the yak herders in the summer. Try to budget at least one day for this superb camp site.

It is possible to walk farther along the glacier to the west by climbing up a 5950-m ridge (2 1/2 hr to ascend 1000 m). From here, Mt Everest is only 5 km away, and to the southeast is a striking amphitheater of peaks dominated by Lhotse. Makalu rises dramatically farther to the southeast. Between Lhotse and Makalu, on the left along the Nepal–Tibet border, is the conical peak of Pethangtse (6724 m).

KANGSHUNG FACE TO KHARTA VIA THE SHAO LA

✦ DAY 12 PETHANG RINGMO–PETHANG 4 1/4 HR

Return to Pethang.

✦ DAY 13 PETHANG–SHARLUNG 5 1/2 HR

Walk back up to a point just below the cave called Tangshum (2 1/2 hr). Turn right along a ridge that overlooks the river valley, on the right, which extends to the northeast and the Chok La. Continue to the end of the ridge to its end and descend for a short distance to another cave, the Sharlung, situated next to an emerald lake within a cwm. During the summer, the astounding giant rhubarb (*Rheum nobile*) grows here on the hillsides (see page 732).

✤ DAY 14 SHARLUNG–SHARO 4 3/4 HR

From Sharlung turn north and cross two ridges to reach a wooded valley. The path then follows a beautiful crest that descends to a side valley (4000 m) with dense forests of juniper, silver fir, mountain ash, willow, birch, and tall rhododendron. Primulas, meconopsis, gentians, and ferns are everywhere. The abundant moisture of the Karma Valley derives from Makalu; the mountain attracts storms and foul weather that transform into rain and mist. Turn left at the valley (do not take the trail heading right) and begin the ascent towards the Shao La. Makalu's eastern glacier appears and all around the path are sheer, black cliffs. At the foot of the pass, on the left, is a cave called Sharo; the peaks of Makalu are directly opposite.

✤ DAY 15 SHARO–YUEBA 6 HR

From the cave to the Shao La Pass (5030 m) is an easy 2-hr ascent. Descend northward to an open area next to a lake. The trail continues north to the Kharta Valley at Yarbu. Turn right (east) along the right bank of the Kharta River to head back to Yueba.

✤ DAY 16-17 YUEBA–KHARTA–SHEKAR

Walk east to Kharta (2 1/4 hr), then hitch a ride by tractor to Shekar (Dingri Xian), 7km north of the Friendship Highway. Expect to pay around Rmb 30–40 for the dusty, 120-km trip.

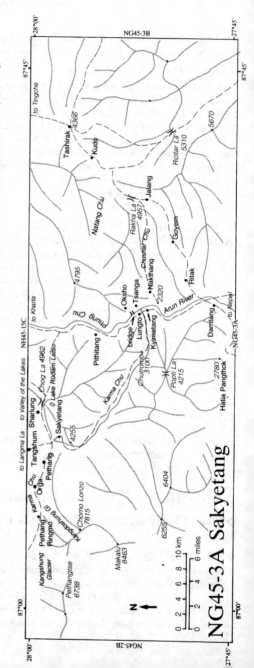

KHARTA TO THE VALLEY OF THE LAKES AND THE KARMA CHU–PHUNG CHU JUNCTION

At Kharta, consider exploring the superb Valley of the Lakes and the lush Phung Chu Valley near Nepal's border instead of returning to Shekar and the Friendship Highway.

✧ Day 1 Kharta–Samchung La-camp   7 1/2 hr

Walk from Kharta to Yulok in 1 1/4 hr (see Day 7, page 904). A stony foot trail zigzags steeply up the mountains from behind the village. Reach a wide valley with a river; further upstream are a few glacial lakes. Wade across the river and ascend a ridge that forms the valley's far side (another path follows the valley's north slopes; it also leads to the Samchung La, 4600 m, but this is a more difficult option as the route is sometimes covered in snow). The steep, 1000-m ascent along a rough trail passes through dense vegetation of rhododendron, mountain ash, and juniper near the pass. Sandwiched between two peaks, the trail switchbacks up for its final approach to the Samchung La (4 hr from Yulok). Expect snow, even in late spring and early autumn. Directly below is the Valley of the Lakes.

The Valley of the Lakes

The entire valley floor, flanked by ridges and peaks, is dotted with 14 large and many small lakes created by a receding glacier. Their color varies from turquoise to blue to green to near black, and two or three are nearly 1 km in length. Corrals give shelter to herders who occasionally come here with their yaks.

From the Samchung La Pass, the main trail to the Chog La (4962 m), which leads to the sacred Rudam Latso Lake, veers far to the left and stays high along the top of a ridge that flanks the valley. This wide, direct route is often covered waist-deep in snow. To the right, another path plunges steeply to the Valley of the Lakes. Tibetan herders going to Sakyetang via the Chog La favor this more difficult route. (The lush Damdong side valley, east of the pass, leads to a confluence with the Phung Chu [see below]. Across the Phung are fine views of the mighty Ama Drime Range.) A path between these two trails follows a gentler gradient by traversing the valley's steep western slopes to the floor of the Valley of the Lakes (2 hr from the pass). Camp next to a lake and hillock. (An alternative to this long day is to camp some distance beyond Yulok; then start the walk to the Valley of the Lakes the next day.)

The Damdong Valley

Descend steeply from the Samchung La to the south, then turn left (east) into the Damdong Valley. A logging trail on the valley's north slopes follows the left (north) bank of the river; prominent peaks are to the right. Beyond the peaks, the trail zigzags down to an open plain with good campsites. To the south, rhododendrons cover the hillside. The trail traverses the slopes north of the valley; steep sections must be negotiated by sharp switchbacks. Reach some logging huts on a small plain. (A trail branches from here to the south, leading to the Yindong La and the Phung Chu's west bank.)　　➡

Further on, look back to see some waterfalls. The path leads to another logging camp sited near a large rock (from the Samchung La to here is 4 hr). Beyond the camp, the trail turns a corner to the left (north) to follow the Phung Chu's right bank northward. The way becomes steep and poor after the bend. Eventually, the trail ends at sheer cliffs near a side valley (from logging camp to end and back is 3 1/4 hr). En route to here are rock caves and ledges used as make-shift shelters by loggers. Firewood and water are readily available. From the logging camp at the large rock to the base of the Samchung La takes 5 1/4 hr; the pass to Yarbu in the Kharta Valley is a further 3 hr.

✧ Day 2 Valley of the Lakes–Chog La–Lake Rudam Latso

Walk south along the valley past numerous lakes and streams that run east to the main river. The valley is generally covered with snow by late October. [Due to heavy snow, the Chog La was blocked in the autumn when this trek was undertaken; the route description beyond the pass to the Karma Chu–Phung Chu confluence is thus necessarily sketchy.] If free of snow, the approach to the Chog La (4900 m) takes 5 1/2 hr. A wall across the pass formed a defense against the invading Gurkhas in the 18th century. Immediately to the north is a glacier. South of the pass is a deep, sacred lake called Rudam Latso. The water is wonderfully clear to a depth of 10 m. Pilgrims come here annually to circumambulate it. There are good campsites nearby.

✧ Day 3 Lake Rudam Latso–Sakyetang–Chutromo

Descend steeply for 6.5 km to Sakyetang (3690 m) along a foaming cataract, through zones of varied, luxuriant vegetation. Idyllic uninhabited Sakyetang (Pleasant Terrace), is situated on a terrace 300 m above the confluence of the Karma Chu and Chog La Chu. Once a sizeable village, it suffered an outbreak of disease that wiped out the population. Belief in a demon active in the area has prevented people from returning. Follow the left (north) bank of the Karma Chu south, then southeast. The trail descends steeply through a forest of junipers. In an earlier time, this was one of the most magnificent in Tibet. Old, enormous silver firs merge with the junipers; ancient trees, fully 30 m in height and many with their trunks approaching 6 m in circumference, existed in this primordial region. Reach a herders' camp called Takpa Kyisa. Beyond, at Chutromo (3100 m), is a 20-m-long wooden bridge that spans the Karma Chu. Cross the bridge and camp in an open space. Expect leeches here in summer.

✧ Day 4 Chutromo to Karma Chu–Phung Chu confluence

The next 10-km stretch (southeast, then east) follows the Karma Chu's final stages to its confluence with the south-flowing Phung Chu. This beautiful, difficult walk entails abrupt ups and downs that total 1500 m of altitude gain and loss. Pass a shelter (overhang) called Korabak and descend to the cascading river, now fed by four glacial rivers (Karma, Tangma, Shao, Chog). The flora at the Karma–Phung confluence (2300 m) is subtropical and the undergrowth consists of wild roses, berberis, wild currant, and raspberry. Just before the junction is a bridge. Lungtö is on the left bank, 350 m above. (The Phung Chu, from here upstream to Kharta, flows through an impenetrable gorge. Below here it opens wide to several hundred meters for a few km, with villages on both banks. Then it narrows into a gorge again.) Cross the bridge to the right bank and reach Kimonanga, a pretty village on a terrace 200 m above the river. The village across the Phung at the junction is Tsanga.

KHARTA TO SAKYA VIA THE YERU TSANGPO: FIVE DAYS

This optional itinerary goes directly from Kharta to Sakya Monastery. It basically follows the Phung Chu north and then northeast to its confluence with the Yeru Tsangpo. From here it continues to Sakya via the Jikyop Bridge. If you do not want to retrace your steps to Peruche, the Pang La and the Friendship Highway, this is a recommended alternative.

✧ Day 1 Kharta–Chukhor 5 hr

Retrace the route north along a dirt road on the Phung Chu's right bank. Pass Rinchenling and a bridge spanning the Chongphu (Sambön) Chu. In 3/4 hr, cross a bridge to the Phung Chu's left (east) bank. Effectively bypassing the jeep road, walk north along a track, passing the villages of Sharkha (former monastery), Chaphö, Dekyiling (former monastery), Yönton Namgyal, and Samtsa. Wade across tributaries flowing from the east. Chukhor is a cluster of villages sited at the point where the Phung bends to the right (east). Here is the last bridge to the river's right bank before it enters a gorge.

✧ Day 2 Chukhor–Karkhung 6 hr

Cross the Chukhor bridge to the right (west) bank where the track makes a U-turn southward up the slopes before heading north along a jeep road. Pass the Dzakar–Phung confluence; here the road zigzags up to a rise and then levels off. After skirting a hill to the left, cross a bridge over the Dzakar River to its left bank (3/4 hr from Chukhor). Cross a gentle plain and walk along sand and short grass to the northeast. Find a distinct trail at the base of a ridge and follow it up to the Chokchu La (2 hr). On the way, pass a ruined fort and other military ruins. To the east, Yu Ri (5482 m) appears as an elongated, rocky peak, first of a series that runs to the south.

From the pass are remarkable views of Makalu, the valleys of Dzakar, Kharta, and Karma, and even the Samchung La. To the right, the Phung Chu enters a deep gorge. Descend northeast to reach a river that flows from the left to join the Phung Chu. Near here is Phalé. Continue down to Garthong on the Phung's right bank, where a rope bridge with a single strand and leather harness spans the river (2 hr). Cross it to follow a trail on the east bank that leads steeply up a spur next to the river. At the flat top, the way leads north to Karkhung (Kongyuk, 1 1/4 hr), on the right, a short distance from another bridge. The Dok Chu flows into the Phung just before the village.

✧ Day 3 Karkhung–camp 8 hr

Continue up the left (east) bank of the Phung Chu. The trail ascends the valley wall on the river's left bank. Descend to a side valley, cross it, and ascend to the top of the valley wall. Pass a corral, descend again to the Phung Chu Valley, cross a stream (good camping and corrals), then climb steeply up the side valley wall again, passing some ruins on the top. Descend once more to the river. A steep gorge is on the opposite bank (2 1/4 hr). The Phung Chu Valley has many shepherds tending their herds.

The trail now enters a region of villages sited at the entrances of tributary streams: Phalé, Sala, Drongon, Ne (2 1/4 hr). It zigzags below them through barley fields and climbs in and out of many tedious tributary ravines. Perhaps an easier route exists to the left (west), closer to the Phung Chu. The river in this region meanders through loops and channels next to a large plain on the right. Pass a flat area on the left where the river bends left. After some ruins on the right, ascend past the villages of Dzong, Thunga, Lashar, and Kochak. An unsual settlement, left of the path, has developed out of a ruin amidst strange cliff formations. Cross a spur and then descend westward towards the river. Camp at a wonderful spot next to a trout-filled spring (3 1/2 hr). Good water to this point has been scarce and the Phung Chu's water must be treated before drinking. The Yeru Tsangpo joins the Phung Chu here. From this junction, the trail improves and follows the left (east) bank of the Yeru rather than the Phung. Tingche Xian (see page 803) lies across the Nyonno Ri range (6724 m) to the east.

✧ Day 4 Camp–Jikyop Bridge   4 hr

Follow the jeep track across barren landscape, passing more ruins on the left. In 1 1/2 hr, the track turns right (east) into the Ko Chu Valley. (The main road in this valley follows the river's right bank to Tingche Xian and joins the Chörten Nyima pilgrimage, see page 801.) Cross a bridge after a short distance, then walk west to leave the Ko Chu Valley. Near its entrance is road marker 86 km. (Tingche Xian stands at road marker 105 km. The Sakya turnoff is road marker 21 km.) From camp to here is 2 hr. Continue along the road and then zigzag up to a small pass. The snow peak to the south is Nyonno Ri. Descend to a valley junction at road marker 80 km. Here the road splits; the right branch goes up the Chiblung (Jinlung) Valley to the southeast and east (see page 809). A good path within it leads to Sakya Monastery in three to four days. Take the left branch along the main road to the Jikyop Bridge at road marker 77 km (2 hr). A road maintenance compound (*daoban*) provides shelter for the night.

✧ Day 5 Jikyop Bridge–Sakya Monastery

From the bridge to the Sakya Monastery turnoff (road marker 21 km) is 56 km. (The monastery lies 4 km right [east] of the turnoff.) The walk along this excellent road takes 12 hr. (Try to hitchhike to Sakya if you don't feel like walking.) For more details about the road portion to Sakya, see page 802.

EXPLORATORY TREK: RONGPHUK TO KHARTA VIA THE LAKPA LA (6849 M)

This difficult, nine-day trek requires crampons, ice axe and fixed rope, and demands previous mountaineering experience. Starting from the Rongphuk Monastery (see page 918), it negotiates the Rongphuk East and Kharta glaciers before crossing the high Lakpa La (Windy Pass). Go with competent guides and hire yaks for transport. The pass marks the transition from the dry, barren Rongphuk Valley to the lush, green Kharta Valley, and it takes in tremendous views of Mt Everest and Mt Changtse.

Acclimatization

Before starting, acclimatize properly by spending several days around Everest Base Camp

(5200 m). Walk from Base Camp to Camp 1 at 5500 m and spend the night there, then ascend to the top of a hill (6000 m) above the camp. Return to Base Camp the same day and rest one more day.

Rongphuk Monastery to Base Camp 2 1/2 hr

A jeepable track connects the Everest Base Camp to the Rongphuk Monastery. From the monastery (5030 m), follow it south along the right (east) bank of the Rongphuk River. After 2 km, reach the ruins of Samdrupo Monastery and some stone meditation huts sited on a ridge to the left. Stay near the middle of the valley with the river still on the right. Pass glacial lakes on the left. Just beyond these, to the right, are the caves of Tündrupling. To the left, up the ridge are the ruins of the Jangchub Tarling Nunnery (one chapel is now rebuilt). Below them is a rock slide whose base is marked by a *chörten* and two stone structures. The base camp (5178 m) lies at the junction of the Rongphuk River and a glacial stream called Xarlungnama, which issues from the Qianjing Glacier. To the left is the entrance to the Qianjing Valley. Ahead, 3/4 km away, is the Rongphuk Glacier's terminal moraine.

✧ Day 1

From base camp, ford the Xarlungnama, then follow the eastern edge of the Rongphuk Glacier southward along the glacial moraine and scree slopes. Small glacial lakes and ice formations are on the right. On the left are the rocky ramparts of the Lixin Massif (7113 m). To its north is the Qianjing Glacier. 1 1/2 hr south of the base camp, between the glacier and the ridge on the left, is a tiny camp site. The trail divides here. Take the left, which zigzags steeply up the ridge. Reach Camp 1, identified by numerous tent sites amidst large boulders, in 1 1/4 hr.

✧ Day 2

Rest and acclimatize. Yaks can carry supplies to Camp 2.

✧ Day 3

Beyond camp 1, the route leads left up the East Rongphuk Glacier. Follow a moraine route up the central spine of the glacier. Look out for stone path markers. The faint path weaves in and out of rock slides, ice patches and large boulders—a difficult section for yaks. This is a dramatic area of huge 10–20-m ice seracs and treacherous crevasses. This is the Highway of Miracles of early British expeditions. Camp 2 is sited at the base of towering cliffs. Expedition debris litters the area which is at a glacial division. The right (west) arm is the Changtse Glacier (Day 4 goes along the left arm), which has at its head Changtse (7583 m), Mt Everest's north peak. Camp 1 to Camp 2 (6088 m) is 5 1/2 hr.

✧ Day 4

Follow the narrow moraine ledge on the western perimeter of the East Rongphuk Glacier's east branch. After 2 hr, cross ice fields to the glacier's east side to reach Camp 3 (6368 m), next to a tiny glacial lake at the base of the Lakpa La. Mt Everest rears beautifully close by. The peak on the right beyond the glacier is 6855 m high. To the south-southeast, the Rabu La (6548 m) leads to the Kangshung Glacier. Immediately behind it are the jagged peaks of Makalu (8463 m). An indentation on the rim of a bowl to the east is the Lakpa La (6849 m). Rest here for the remainder of the day.

✧ Day 5

Start at 0500 and walk 4–5 hr northeast to Lakpa La. The steep, icy, 400-m ascent is manageable with crampons, ski poles, or ice axes. Once at the pass, consider climbing an easy 6883-m peak a short distance to the south. Use a 40-m fixed rope to descend the pass's precipitous eastern side. (This tricky, 250 m-long section is very difficult if attempted from the Kharta Valley side.) After the descent, the route bears to the left of an amphitheater at the head of the Kharta Glacier and follows an easier gradient. Be careful of crevasses 1 1/2 km from the pass. Descend 6–7 hr from west to east through an icefall that blocks the Kharta Glacier's upper reaches. Above and to the left are superb, fluted, snow ridges. The day's camp (6065 m) is located at the eastern base of an east–west ridge at the center of the glacier's upper amphitheater (to the left).

✧ Day 6

From the tip of the ridge, cross the upper Kharta Glacier to its northern perimeter (6025 m) of moraines and scree slopes. Travel east-northeast across snow fields and pass Khartse (6350 m), a white, conical peak on the glacier's right (south) flank. Stay high along a 6000-m contour, above the glacier's left side. Below, at the end of the glacier, skirt a lake (5643 m) to its left (west) by following a river that issues from a small lake (5801 m). The peak to the left is Ritung Lhabu (6171 m). Camp near the lake at an altitude of 5600 m (6 hr).

✧ Day 7

Go up and around a cliff (gain 200m of altitude). Beyond the lake, walk down the upper Kharta Valley by following its river along grassy meadows. Locate a prominent *chörten* just in front of a 6000-m peak. Camp by the river (5200 m) (5 hr).

✧ Day 8

Leave the Kharta River and walk along the valley's left (north) side. Soon, pass prayer flags opposite a distinctive pyramidal peak. The steep descent reaches a terrace with a wonderful view above a lake sited at the entrance of a side valley that divides the Kharta and the Karma valleys. Here is a grassy area with alpine flowers and huts. Stay above the river, then reach a nomad camp by the river (4450 m). Find a place to ford; the swift current may require ropes. Continue down the valley along the right (south) bank to reach Kharta's first village, Riphu, after 7 hr. Beyond the settlement a bridge spans the river.

✧ Day 9

Continue down the right bank of the Kharta River past the villages of Lamdo, Chölam, Lhading, Lhündrubling, Yueba, Yulok, to Kharta (3750 m, 5 hr).

RONGPHUK:
A TREK TO THE EVEREST NORTH FACE BASE CAMP

Location	South of Dingri; near the Tibet–Nepal border
Map Reference	NH45-14 B D, Mt Everest (Detail)
Trekking days	5 (one-way)
Start–Finish	Dingri–Mt Everest Base Camp
Passes	Lamna

The Mt Everest North Face Base Camp trek is among the most popular for trekkers in Tibet. Being near Dingri on the Friendship Highway, it is relatively easy to access. And the walk is not particularly strenuous—only one low pass must be crossed. Near the Base Camp is the reconstructed monastery of Rongphuk, once one of the largest monastic complexes in the region. The views from here of the Everest North Face, perhaps the most dramatic of all its sides, are unforgettable. Well-acclimatized trekkers without mountaineering expertise have a number of interesting options, including going up to more advanced camps.

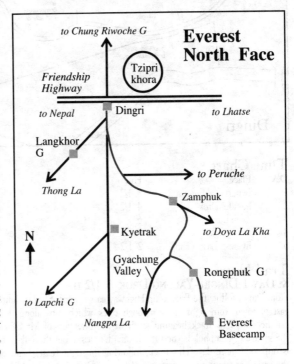

This is made possible by the relatively gentle gradient and the lack of dangerous glaciers and crevasses in the initial stages. For extensive hikes in the east Everest region, see Mt Everest: The Kangshung Face (p 895).

Related sections
Kangshung Face, p 895
Lapchi, p 248
Dingri Monasteries, p 918
Tzipri, p 921

Access
Dingri on the Friendship Highway (see pages 250, 990).

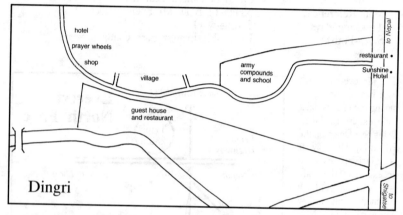

Time Chart

Day	Place	Hours
1	Dingri–Yalung	5 1/2
2	Lamdu Drok	4 1/2
3	Zamphuk	6
4	Rongphuk	6
5	Everest Base Camp	2 1/2

Trail Notes
✤ DAY 1 DINGRI–YALUNG DROK 5 1/2 HR
From Dingri follow the Friendship Highway east towards Shekar. Immediately after the bridge east of town, turn right along a rough track which runs along the base of a line of hills on the left. This track heading south in the direction of Mt Everest, goes all the way to the village of Zamphuk beyond the Lamna La pass. From the village to the Everest base camp is only one more day. This track, following the right (east) bank of the Ra Chu, provides the easiest access to the mountain. 3/4 hr after Dingri, pass the village of Razam (also Rizong) some distance on your left. It is possible to hire yaks here. Turn right out of the village and follow a rather obscure part of the track. Langpe can be seen on the west side of the Ra Chu valley at the base of a sandy hill. A branch of the Ra Chu is on the right. In 1 hr reach the entrance of a very wide valley on your left. Along its southernmost wall is

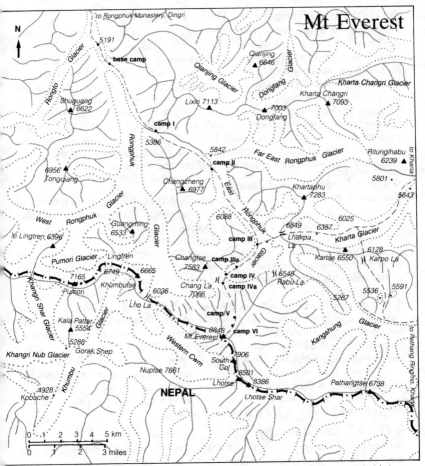

a trail that leads east up the Lamar La via the village of Nelung which is 3 1/2 hr from Dingri. Continue along the track. After passing the wide valley (1 3/4 hr) notice the thin wedge of a ridge on the right. This is a prominent landmark of the Dingri Plain which runs north to south. At its northernmost tip is the village and monastery of Chölung. 1 1/4 hr beyond it is Lunja (Langja), a friendly place with yaks for hire. (A short distance beyond the village is the turnoff, on the right, to Ding La and Ding valley which eventually also leads to the Everest base camp via Pasum and Chödzong). One option is to stay in a village house. Another is to continue below a ruin on the left and climb over a low ridge; about 2 km down the track at the base of a plateau is a grassy campsite beside the river. This is Yalung Drok (3/4 hr). Above the camp, about 1 hr away, climb up the slopes for good views of the Dingri valley and Dingri itself. No large peaks are visible and Cho Oyu is hidden from view.

✤ Day 2 Yalung Drok–Lamdu Drok 4 1/2 hr

Lunja is the last village on the Dingri Plain. Until Zamphuk (Zangbo) is reached (beyond the Lamna La) there is no habitation except for the occasional nomad camp. Follow the track above camp, contouring slightly around the base of the hills on the east side of the Ra Chu. Continue along the base of the hills on the north side of the river by means of a footpath; this will avoid unnecessary river crossings. After 1/2 hr the valley broadens into an open plain. The track has already crossed the river to the south side of this plain (if you follow the track without shortcuts, ford the river 3 hr from the day's start). An indistinct footpath veers into a side valley to the northeast, across marshy ground. Take this longer route which skirts a low ridge and which has access to water and grazing. 1 hr from this marshy area is the Lamdu Drok campsite near a stone corrall and stream. Another possible campsite is 1 hr away, across a slaty ridge and into the next valley.

✤ Day 3 Lamdu Drok–Zamphuk 6 hr

Head up the valley towards the obvious col in the distance. Follow a poorly-defined trail that contours along the base of some low hills on the right. Climb towards the col and after 3/4 hr reach the top of a black, slaty ridge. Descend into a river valley. Follow it along its east side, below screes slopes. 2 1/2 hr from Lamdu reach a stone corrall on the right. Here the trail ascends to the Lamna La Pass after only 1/2 hr of climbing. The track can be seen to the south. There is no trail but head generally down from the summit cairn. The valley is wide and bends towards towards the east. After 2 hrs cross the stream to the left side of the valley and hike to a rocky promontory (a gentle climb through rocks on a clear track). Beyond the promontory is the village of Zamphuk (or Zangbo) sited high above the Zamphuk valley. If you are feeling energetic, climb over the ridge of hills to the south for a magnificent view up the Rongphuk valley. In its upper reaches are the Everest base camp and the Rongphuk Monastery. At its head is the north face of Mt Everest. There is an obscure yak trail over these hills, crossing a pass, that also leads to the valley; use this only in good weather. Due to the altitude there is no cultivation in Zamphuk; the villagers rely on animal husbandry for a living. Many of the yaks used for Everest expeditons come from here. There are possible camping sites before the village near a stone corrall or further east, down the valley after Zamphuk. The Rongphuk valley is a further 3 hr away.

✤ Day 4 Zamphuk–Rongphuk Monastery 6 hr

Descend from the village to rejoin the track from Dingri. Follow this to the southeast along the Zamphuk river to its confluence with the large Dzakar Chu (1 1/2 hr) which in its upper stretches is known as the Rongphuk Chu. Before the confluence ford to the right (south) bank of the Zamphuk. Then follow the left (north) bank of the Dzakar upstream (to the southwest). In 1/2 hr, the ruins of the cave monastery of Chöphuk, sited within high cliffs, can be seen. Follow the base of the cliffs, ascend a small gorge then descend to a wooden bridge (1 hr) which spans the Rongphuk River. Cross it to its right (east) bank to join the dirt road linking Peruche (see Kangshung Face of Everest, page 898) with Rongphuk Monastery. Walk up the road (due south) to the large Peyul (Nepal) Chörten (1 1/2 hr). The Rongphuk Monastery is 1 1/2 hr more from here. For a description of the monastery see Dingri Monasteries, page 918.

✤ Day 5 Rongphuk Monastery–Everest Base Camp 2 1/2 HR

Follow the dirt road south; the Dzakar Chu, now much reduced in volume, is on your right. Soon the valley broadens and the road leaves the river to continue its ascent on the other side, swerving to avoid a rock slide. At the base of the slide is a *chörten*; at its top are the ruins of the Samdrupo Nunnery (a small chapel has been rebuilt). The Everest Base Camp is just beyond some moraine hills.

If you are sufficiently acclimatized, it is possible to take a couple of short excursions beyond the Base Camp. One is to climb the moraines of the Central Rongphuk Glacier, immediately south of the camp, to some small glacial pools. The other is a trek to the Qianjing glacier. Head up a small canyon east of the Base Camp to a rough track that crosses a vast lateral moraine 200 m above camp. Follow this south on a relatively level platform high above the Central Rongphuk Glacier. At the end of the moraine is the Qianjing Glacier, about 4 hr from the Base Camp. To the south are fine views of the Everest North Face.

Further Excursions
Base Camp–Camp 1

From Base Camp, a trail runs along the east side of the Central Rongphuk Glacier, below the lateral moraines to the left. After 1 hr the trail divides. Ahead, 3 km away, lie the ice seracs of the Central Rongphuk Glacier. Take the trail up the steep hill to the east. From this trail the peaks of Lingtren and Pumouri are clearly visible. Camp 1 as defined by expeditions in the twenties and thirties, is located after the trail stops climbing steeply, 3 hr from base camp. From here an hour's climb rewards the trekker with close-up views of gigantic ice seracs. The trail upward to Camp 2 is ill-defined. It is possible to camp at Camp 1 as nearby water is available. Take extreme care on this walk because altitude sickness is a real danger. Budget eight hours.

This chapter was contributed by Bob Gibbons and Sian Pritchard-Jones.

For more information on a trek from Base Camp to Camp 1 and beyond, see Rongphuk to the Kharta Valley via the high Lakpa La, page 910.

DINGRI: MONASTERIES OF THE DINGRI–EVEREST REGION

The Dingri area is a large tract of over 1,000 sq km centering around the headwaters of the Phung (Arun) River. Most of its 10–15,000 inhabitants live on the Dingri Plain with Dingri Ganggar, commonly called Dingri (Old Dingri), the *de facto* center. Shekar Xian (New Dingri), 67 km to the west, is the prefecture's headquarters; the Shekar Monastery, perched on a ridge, overlooks the small town. Pastoralists live in the hundred or so villages in the surrounding valleys.

Two monastic systems co-exist here. One is the *serkyim*, an informal organization of village chapels with no presiding lamas, whose members have jobs and are not celibate. There are nearly 30 of these religious communities scattered throughout the area. The other is the formal, traditional system of monasteries with celibate monks and lamas totally devoted to religious service. Before the Cultural Revolution, Dingri had over 30 large and small monasteries. Some of these are in the process of being revived.

SERKYIM MONASTERIES

It is difficult to distinguish *serkyim* ('yellow household') monks from those in established monasteries—both shave their heads and wear robes. Each *serkyim* community has a chapel (usually locked) similar to regular houses of the village. The monks perform services for the villagers in their own homes and also work in the fields. Most are associated with the Nyingmapa Rongphuk (Dzarong) Monastery at the base of Mt Everest and often go there to study with the lama.

In Dingri, the *serkyim* monasteries predate the lama monasteries. The oldest (11th–13th-C.) chapels are:

- Langkor   Home of Padampa (or Dampa) Sangye
- Lhadong   Home of Yangönpa
- Chag Chumo   Small shrine
- Gönda Phuk   The largest; Tsari Lama presided over the monastery at the turn of the century

Other *serkyim* chapels: Drak Karpo, Gönsar, Nganyan, Tongtröling, Mugpa, Dargyaling, Raphuk, Chagpu, Gyedring, Nalum, Chuwar, Gönsam, Mugchung, Gön Lhadong, Chölung, Tsari Phuk, Sharlung, Gönpa Jang, Lhading, Riwoche, Lungjang, Yöldong, and Dzakya. On the 10th and 25th days of every lunar month, members of the *serkyim* community gather at their chapels to make offerings to Guru Rinpoche, their patron saint.

Before the destruction of the 1960s, most of these monasteries were headed by a lama. A few have made modest comebacks and religious services are held in simple renovated chapels. Some of the most significant are:

RONGPHUK (DZARONG) MONASTERY

Founded in 1902, this largest monastery of the region once had over 500 monks and nuns.

It is located at the foot of the Rongphuk Glacier, near Mt Everest's North Face Base Camp. A couple of centuries before the complex was built, a small group of nuns in meditation huts braved the severe conditions regularly experienced at this sobering altitude of 4980 m. This religious community of nuns was the precursor of the Dzarong Monastery. In the early years of the 20th C., Ngawang Tenzin Norbu catalysed the flowering of Rongphuk. He also went to the Khumbu area of Nepal to start the monasteries of Thamé, Tengboche, Takshingdu, and Chiwong. These became Rongphuk's satellite monasteries.

By 1940 (the year of his death), he had established seven chapels at the Rongphuk complex, four Sherpa monasteries in Nepal, and five nunneries near Dingri. Chung Riwoche Monastery (see page 451) and its multi-chapel *chörten*, a particularly sacred Nyingmapa pilgrimage site near Sangsang (north of Dingri and the Tsangpo), was a dependency of Rongphuk until 1957, when Tashilhunpo Monastery took over. Chapels and hermitages of the Rongphuk complex are:

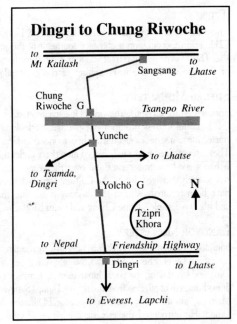

Dingri to Chung Riwoche

to Mt Kailash

Sangsang

to Lhatse

Chung Riwoche G

Tsangpo River

Yunche

to Lhatse

to Tsamda, Dingri

Yolchö G

N

Tzipri Khora

to Nepal

Friendship Highway

Dingri

to Lhatse

to Everest, Lapchi

• Dzarong
• Dongak Chöling (main monastery; the site of present renovations)
• Samten Chöphuk (4 hr down the Rongphuk Valley)
• Tashi Thongmön
• Chölingkor
• Jangchub Tarling (nunnery)
• Rongchung (nunnery)
• Rongphuk Toshe Rabling (near the complex)

The complex now has about ten monks and ten nuns. An important image in the assembly hall of Dzarong is Ngawang Tenzin Norbu, next to that of the Mindroling Lama (see page 496). A *shabje* of Rongphuk Namgyal Zangpo is to the lower right of the image. Next to the rebuilt chapel is a monastic guest house, which provides adequate accommodation for trekkers. Rongphuk's branches in the Dingri area are:

• Chökorgang
• Langkor
• Labtran
• Jangding
• Tramar

TZIPRI

These monasteries are noted under Tzipri: The Holy Mountain of Dingri (see below, page 921). Tzipri Götsang, on a cliff face southeast of the massif, is the most important pilgrimage site. This Drukpa Kagyü retreat was founded by Götshangpa Gompo Pel (1189–1258), a disciple of Tsangpa Gyaré, the first explorer of the great pilgrimage site of Tsari (see page 208).

SHEKAR MONASTERY

Shekar (White Crystal), the only Gelugpa monastery in the area, once had 300 monks at this beautiful fortress site on a craggy ridge overlooking Shekar Xian. Like Rongphuk, Shekar started life as a series of meditation huts founded in 1266 by the Sakyapa lama, Sindeu Rinchen. They later evolved into a full-fledged monastery under the Fifth Dalai Lama in the 17th century. It had a good printing center and over the years assembled a fine woodblock library. Shekar was severely damaged during the Cultural Revolution. Since 1984, some buildings and chapels have been repaired. Within the *dukhang* is an altar that holds new images of Tsong Khapa and his two disciples, Dorje Chang and Guru Riñpoche. It is now a thriving center of worship.

LANGKOR MONASTERY

Founded by Padampa (also Dampa) Sangye in the late 11th C., this monastery's architecture resembles Tengboche of Khumbu, Nepal. A full set of *Tengyur* and *Kangyur* are held here. On the 14th day of the sixth lunar month, Langkor is the site of a celebrated festival that draws hundreds of pilgrims from the region. Dampa Sangye was a disciple of the Bengali *mahasiddha*, Maitripa, and was a key figure in the Second Diffusion of Buddhism in Tibet, especially around Dingri. He introduced the esoteric disciplines of Chö and Zhije. The former involved purification and offering rituals at cemeteries, whereby the mind and body of the practitioner are symbolically given up to the negative forces that inhabit these places of sky-burial. The second is a path to enlightenment by means of a specialized method of meditation. For more details of this monastery, see Lapchi, page 271.

GÖNDA PHUK MONASTERY

This Nyingmapa monastery on a hill has 30 monks and one chapel has been restored. A village is below.

LAMA RALÖ PHUK

This cave is a 3/4-hr walk from the village of Ngoru near the southeast face of Mt Shishapangma. Lama Ralö (Ra Lötsawa), an 11th-C. translator, was born in Nyalam and studied in Nepal with Mahakaruna, a member of Naropa's lineage. He used this cave as a hermitage, which today contains a statue of the founder. Under the altar is his *shabje*.

TSA MAMBO MONASTERY

Located in the village of Tsa Mambo, this is the only habitation on the west side of Pekhu Tso. The monastery is active today.

TZIPRI:
THE HOLY MOUNTAIN OF DINGRI

Tzipri and Langkor are the two principal mountains of pilgrimage in the Dingri area. In the 11th C., the Dingri sage, Dampa Sangye, lived here for nearly 20 years and brought fame to both. A five-day circuit around the Tzipri Range starts a few km north of Dingri—the staging post for the Mt Everest Base Camp trek (see above). To thoroughly explore the various scattered hermitages of the range takes a few days more. At least 17 retreat centers and small monasteries punctuate the route; three are nunneries. Some remote shrines entail steep hikes. The best seasons to undertake this pilgrimage are spring (May, June) and autumn (Sept, Oct, Nov). Summer is more of a problem because rivers and streams tend to become swollen and difficult to ford. In winter there are no special difficulties except for the cold.

BACKGROUND

Dampa Sangye made Dingri famous as a place of pilgrimage. He came from South India and was a pupil of Maitripa, one of the 84 *mahasiddhas*. Local tradition claims Dampa Sangye founded the strategic settlement of Dingri, which commands access to Rongphuk Monastery (Dzarong Phuk), the Lapchi Range, and the Kharta and Karma valleys. The legend tells how Sakyamuni personally instructed Dampa to go to Tibet to teach the *dharma*. The Buddha threw a stone that landed with a resounding 'ding' on top of a hill far to the north. Dampa was ordered to search for the stone, find it, and stay in that area to spread Buddhism. Sakyamuni named the area Dingri. After a long fruitless search he came to the mountain of Tzipri, where he met a protectress (*dakini*) who led him to the stone that had landed in Langkor, a village south of Dingri. The master then spent his life in the vicinity teaching and meditating.

Since that time, Tzipri and Langkor have became the focus of pilgrims, who every year hold religious events and festivals. The poet-saint, Milarepa, also added to the folklore and mystique. He and Dampa met on top of the Thong La (see Lapchi, page 271) while travelling and teaching in the early part of the 12th century. The First Dalai Lama (1391–1474), Gedundrub, was an important pilgrim to this area. Dampa and his chief disciple, Machik, the yogini, founded the religious practices of Chö and Zhije. These are characterized by meditation in cemeteries and emphasize the immediate attainment of *prajna*, or wisdom. After Dampa and Machik came the teacher, Götsangpa, and his local student, Yangönpa, who was born in Lhadong, a village at the northwest corner of Tzipri. During Yangönpa's life, many monasteries grew up around his birthplace. Tzipri became an important center for the Drukpa-Kagyü sect and many followers came to study with him.

In 1934, Tzipri Tripön Lama (Tripön Pema Chögyal), a nationally recognized teacher from central Tibet, came here to meditate. He took long, solitary retreats without students and admirers. Apart from Tzipri, he visited Zapulung, Lapchi, Chuwar, and Kyirong, all mystical haunts of Milarepa and Dampa. The *tripa* (abbot) eventually established a center in Tzipri. Vast, glorious monastic monuments were not what he was after. Instead he created a carefully thought-out network of retreats in the mountains and asked his students to lead simple, ascetic lives. He set up 11 hermitages, eight for monks and three for nuns. None of these could have more than 13 students and only the most dedicated were admitted. Tzipri Tripön Lama also founded a very fine library, the Nerang Barkhang southwest of Tzipri. This held over 10,000 woodblocks, representing a rare anthology of Buddhist works. He died in 1958 at his own retreat of Kiutsang Tzipri (south Tzipri). Another important teacher at Tzipri was Tzipri Singtra Lama. He founded Samling (Singtra Gompa) in the mountains in 1870, and spent a good part of his life in the Kyirong Valley.

THE TZIPRI RETREATS

The 11 retreats of Tzipri Tripön Lama are:
• Kyaphuk • Tashi Thongmön • Dingpoche • Samdrub Chöling • Nyanang Dechenteng (near Nyalam) • Kiutsang • Samling • Nerang • Yuloko • Tashi Chöteng • Langtso

All are located in the Tzipri mountains except for Nyanang Dechenteng, which is near Nyalam on the Friendship Highway. The last three listed are nunneries. Regarded as the most important are the retreats of Kiutsang (Tripön's center) and Samling (Singtra's center). Nerang once held the Nerang Barkhang library. Other monasteries in the vicinity of the mountain are: Chözang, Namding, Surphu, Natra, Ngonga, and Götsang. Chözang is located in the north. It was built as the private residence of Tzipri Chözang, a head lama of Shekar. He lived in this modest retreat with his students and servants. It looks onto Shekar Monastery, built on a ridge overlooking Dingri Xian (New Dingri), from across a wide river valley. Namding is located at the southwest corner of the range; Surphu and Natra are at the eastern end. Ngonga is in the north. Götsang is a famous retreat built into a sheer cliff on the southeast side of the mountain. It was an important place of meditation for the Kagyüpa, built by Götsangpa Gönpopal (1189–1258) of Lhodrak. He was a disciple of Tsangpa Gyaré, the renowned ascetic, and studied at the monasteries of Ralung and Druk.

THE TZIPRI KHORA

The circumambulation of the sacred Tzipri (map reference NH45-14 B, 45-15 A) starts at Dingri, a strategic village on the Friendship Highway, and goes north along the Lobo Chu. The Lobo, which originates at Mang La to the north, flanks the western limit of the Tzipri range. The dirt track of the khora follows along its west (right) bank. For more information on the Dingri area, see above, and for Lapchi, see page 248.

Time Chart

Day	Place	Hours
1	Dingri–Kongtsa	4 1/2
2	Kongtsa–Nagoling	5
3	Nagoling–Pangla	5 3/4
4	Pangla–Friendship Highway	7 1/4
5	Friendship Highway–Dingri	

✤ DAY 1 DINGRI–KONGTSA 4 1/2 HR

From Dingri, walk east along the Friendship Highway, cross a bridge, and come to the start of a dirt track, going south, which hugs the hills bordering the eastern perimeter of the Dingri Valley (1/2 hr). This spot is just east of road marker 539 km. Across the highway, on the north side, is another dirt track heading to the north. This is the start of the khora; follow it, with the Lobo Chu on your right, and skirt a low hill also on the right. The terrain is quite flat. After leaving the hill, wade across several small streams to reach a broad river, which is shallow and can easily be forded. Continue north through a valley entrance straight ahead. A cold spring and clear pool are landmarks on the west (left) side. Ruins of a fortress appear on top of a hill to the east; three smaller ruins stand at the foot of the hill. Shimde (Shirida) is 1 1/4 hr from road marker 539 km. 3/4 hr further is Lingshar. Immediately to its east, 1/4 hr away, is Kemar. (From Kemar, a trail leads due east to the hermitage of Surphu, [3/4 hr]. Due north of Surphu is Natra [1 hr].)

Continue north from Lingshar (past the village is a water reservoir) to Temi (1/4 hr). Go through a compound; beyond is the village of Manju (Mankhyung) where the trail splits (1/2 hr). Jagged rocky hills are off to the east. The north trail goes on to Yöldong and Yölcho Monastery, then to the Mön La (see Riwoche trek, page 459). Do not take this. Take the right fork, which trends to the northeast, to Kongtsa (1 1/4 hr). Ford the Lobo River along the way. Dzakya hermitage, a short distance to the southeast of Kongtsa, is up the slopes of Tzipri. Dongphuk, another retreat, is further to the east, near the upper parts of the mountain.

✤ DAY 2 KONGTSA–NAGOLING 5 HR

Kongtsa lies at the northwest corner of the Tzipri range. From here the pilgrimage track heads east by following the Shi Chu to Shekar Dzong (Dingri Xian). The river flows from northwest to southeast and forms the northern perimeter of the Tzipri range. From Kongtsa, walk east up a spur, one of the foothills of Tzipri. The top is reached in 2 hr. Then descend to the east to follow the north (left) bank of the Shi Chu. In 1 1/2 hr, come to the entrance of a small side valley on the left. Enter the valley and follow a trail north to Ngöndam (1/2 hr) and Pangbo (1 3/4 hr). Continue east along the main track. Another side valley to the left appears in 1 1/2 hr. The hermitage of Nagoling is 1/2 hr up it.

✤ DAY 3 NAGOLING–PANGLA 5 3/4 HR

Walk back to the main valley to follow the Shi Chu down to Ganden (3 hr). (Halfway to Ganden, a trail on the right leads to Ngonga Monastery.) Farther on (1/2 hr) is Newa, at the mouth of a large tributary which flows from the north. Continue to Phalé (3/4 hr), Newo, and Pangla (1 1/2 hr).

✤ DAY 4 PANGLA–FRIENDSHIP HIGHWAY 7 1/4 HR

About 2 hr downstream from Pangla is a junction of two tracks. The village across the Shi Chu is Lhumchen. The track on the left goes northeast over a spur to Shekar (1 1/2 hr); the right one crosses the Shi, heads west and returns to Dingri. Take the latter. In 3/4 hr, a trail junction is again reached. The left goes south to join the Friendship Highway at road marker 494 km. On the south side of the highway, this trail continues southward to Kharta (staging post of the Mt Everest Kangshung trek, page 903). Take the right trail, staying close to the foothills. It eventually veers south to join the highway (4 1/2 hr). Along the way, wade across a number of tributaries descending from the Tzipri mountains to the north. The numerous streams to the west prevent a straight route along the foothills of Tzipri, and thus the track has to turn south to the highway.

✤ DAY 5 FRIENDSHIP HIGHWAY–DINGRI

About 1 hr to the west of this point is Tsakor. Memo, a village on the south side of the highway, is 1 1/2 hr further along the heavily trafficked road. Try to hitch a ride back to Dingri.

KYIRONG: MILAREPA COUNTRY IN THE TIBET–NEPAL HIMALAYAS

VALLEY OF HAPPINESS: A SONGTSEN GAMPO DEMON-SUBJUGATING TEMPLE, GURU RINPOCHE CAVES AND THE BIRTHPLACE OF MILAREPA

Location	West of Dingri and Nyalam Valley
Map reference	NH45-13 B D, 45-14 A
Trekking days	8 (one-way)
Start–Finish	Friendship Highway (road marker 615 km)– Nepal border
Passes	Jakhyung La

OVERVIEW

Gungthang and Mangyul are two ancient districts west of the Nyanang (modern-day Nyalam) Valley. Mangyul, with Kyirong as its capital, is the northern extension of the Trisuli Valley of Nepal and one of the lowest areas of Tibet (Kyirong's elevation is only 2774 m). The lush, green landscape resembles Nepal's alpine zone rather than the high, dry plateau of most of Tibet. Gungthang is immediately north of Mangyul. On the Tibet Plateau proper, this tract of land is arid and barren. It was once part of the Ngari Khorsum (West Tibet) Kingdom, and Dzongka, the main town, was the seat of the Gungthang kings.

In his later years, Milarepa, Tibet's greatest poet-saint, spent a great deal of time in the Mangyul-Gungthang region. Together with Lapchi (see page 248), Chuwar (page 256), and Lhodrak (page 681), these are important pilgrimage sites associated with the Kagyü ascetic. His birthplace, Tsalung (Kya Ngatsa), is near Dzongka. Drakar Taso, Milarepa's most important hermitage during the latter part of his life, is at the Gungthang–Mangyul border. Other sacred sites, mostly meditation caves and small shrines, are found throughout these two districts. Milarepa, one of the most beloved religious figures in Tibet, rejected the world of comfort: houses, clothes, family life, and social standing. For him, blue skies, flowers, birds, animals, and inner freedom were the things to be celebrated, and he imbued in others this love of nature.

The early part of this pilgrimage crosses the wide plain of Digur Thang to reach the beautiful, seldom-seen Pelku Lake, a prime grazing area for nomads at 4600 m. A moonlike setting of subtly colored, barren mountains is on one side of the lake; high snow peaks towering over enormous sand dunes on the other. After the Jakhyung La Pass, the path follows the Sarong Chu and the Kyirong River Valley to the towns of Dzongka and Kyirong and finally to the Nepalese border post of Rashuwa.

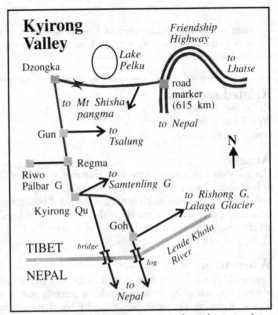

The countryside along the route is exceptionally varied; the transition from plateau to alpine zone is one of the highlights of this itinerary. Another is the close approach to Shishapangma and its stupendous glaciers. At 8012 m, it is the highest mountain located entirely within Tibet. The rare vantage point from the north later also takes in the Nepalese giants of Ganesh (7406 m) and Langtang (7232 m). Dzongka, located on a plateau between two rivers, is a thriving old Tibetan fortress town with an impressive monastery.

In the area of Günda to the south are Milarepa's birthplace and his renowned Drakar Taso ('eagle's nest' hermitage), where the master meditated in absolute solitude high up on a sheer cliff. The Regma Valley has a Guru Rinpoche cave and the monastery of Riwo Palbar, one of the most superbly located in Tibet. Near Kyirong is the ancient monastery of Jamtrin, built long ago in the 7th C. by King Songtsen Gampo to suppress demons of the border. Its distinctive architecture is influenced strongly by the Nepalese style.

Kyirong is the 'Village of Happiness' of Heinrich Harrer, author of *Seven Years in Tibet*. He wrote in this book, 'If I can choose where to pass the evening of my life, it will be in Kyirong.' It is indeed a lovely village set in an enchanting valley. Surrounding Tibetan villages are charming, out-of-the-way places, virtually untouched by the Chinese. There is even a Bönpo monastery near the town.

A two-day walk to the Lende Khola region is a fitting option at the end of this pilgrimage. This is a superb area of serene valleys and rich pastures for grazing yaks and cattle. Snow mountains of the Tibet–Nepal Divide underscore the magnificence of the whole setting. A day hike goes up to destroyed Samtenling Monastery. The extensive ruins overlooking the Kyirong Valley, immediately below a hanging glacier, are impressive.

> **Note** If the Nepal border south of Kyirong is closed (see page 935), retrace your steps to the Friendship Highway and head south to Zhangmu and Nepal or east to Shigatse and Lhasa.

Related sections
Mt Everest, p 895
West Tibet, p 943
Lapchi, p 248

Access
The trek starts from a point on the Friendship Highway, west of Dingri, where the road begins to head south down a gorge to Nepal. At this spot is a wooden road sign in Chinese with two arrows, one pointing to Nyalam near the Nepal border, the other to Kyirong. Coming from Dingri, take the right branch to the broad plain of Digur Thang. From Nepal, turn left after descending the Lalung La Pass. The road marker 615 km is very near the junction, 75 km west of Dingri.

When to go
Kyirong (2774 m), has a climate similar to the well-known Langtang Valley of Nepal and is strongly influenced by the monsoon. Rains generally start in the middle of May and last through September. December, January, and February are cold but pleasant. The best times are March–mid-May and October–November.

Food and shelter
The long stretch between the Friendship Highway and Dzongka has few villages. Nomads along the way will usually supply *tsampa* and sometimes mutton. Water can be scarce; be sure to bring a large water bottle and purification tablets. Freeze-dried food is ideal for this route, though impossible to get in China. Stock up in Lhasa on food that requires no cooking. Once in Dzongka and the Kyirong Valley, food and shelter are plentiful.

Time Chart

Day	Place	Hours
1	Friendship Highway–Selung	8 1/2
2	Pelku Lake nomad camp	7
3	Base of Jakhyung La	6 1/2
4	Dzongka (Kyirong Xian)	8 1/2
5	Gün	5 1/4
6	Drothang	4 3/4
7	Kyirong Qu	4
8	Rashuwa (Nepal)	6 1/2

Trail Notes
✤ **DAY 1 FRIENDSHIP HIGHWAY–SELUNG 8 1/2 HR**
Follow the jeep track from the junction near road marker 615 km, down to the wide beautiful

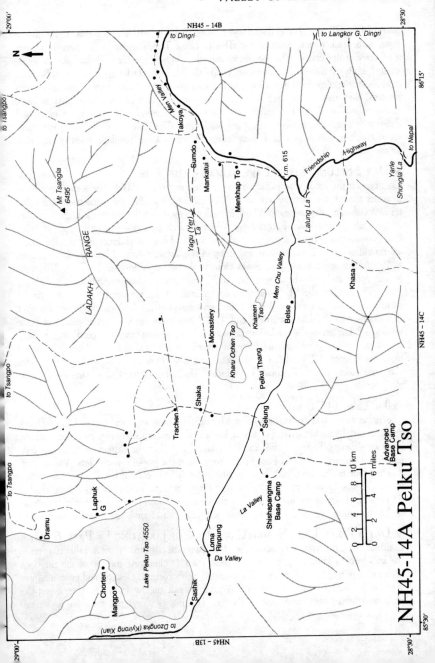

NH45-14A Pelku Tso

plain of Digur Thang. Travel directly west. After 2 1/2 hr, arrive at a ruined tower on the right, with black nomad tents nearby. This is Tanga Tempa. Next to the ruins is a river, a tributary of the Pungro Chu that drains into the southeast corner of Pelku Lake. A strong wind typically starts in the late afternoon. Follow the flat, stony track west. The scenery becomes more dramatic; huge sand dunes loom in the foreground and stunning snow mountains with glaciated sides rear up from behind them. Continue past Khamen and Kharu Orchen lakes, to the right (north) and not visible from the road. At the end of the day, reach more sand dunes with ruins at their foot, and a few black tents. The Tibetan couple living here have seven children, four horses, and many sheep. Selung is a small village 1 km off the road to the left.

✤ Day 2 Selung–Pelku Lake Nomad Camp 7 hr

Continue on the sandy road (which has an average one truck a day). The scenery continues to amaze towards the southeast corner of Pelku Lake, but the afternoon wind makes the going uncomfortable. Shishapangma (8012 m), immediately south (on the left) is the highest member of the multi-peaked Pelku Kangri range, which extends to a point directly south of Pelku Lake's southwestern tip. Glaciers approach the road and huge sand dunes abut the ice. There are no villages, only herds of goats and sheep in the distance. After 2 hr, the southern shore of Pelku Lake appears; the road passes close to the water in another 2 1/2 hr. The sense of vast space and overwhelming silence make this an eerie, haunting place.

The road at the lake's southwest corner makes a distinct bend to the right (north) to follow the western shores. Reach a mud enclosure (on the left) on the bank of a river that drains into the lake's southern end. (1 1/2 hr). From here, an encampment of black tents is 1/2 km left of the road. An enclosure full of goat droppings is a good place to keep out of the wind. Nearby, farther from the river, is a herder's mud hut. After 1 hr, reach more black tents, 1/2 km left of the road. Sandstorms blow up occasionally and the soft, clay sand makes the road difficult for vehicles. The ferocious wind now starts early in the afternoon.

Pelku Lake (4550 m)

The name Pelku is a corruption of Pal Khyung. The common local name, Lhatso Zhitso, describes the lake's kidney shape, which has a neck-like constriction at its center. (In the songs of Milarepa, Pelku is called the Pal Thang Tso.) Near the eastern shore, at the constriction, a Milarepa cave—La Phuk Pema Dzong—is at the foot of vertical cliffs. A monastery, La Phuk Gompa, has been built here. Nearby is the 'hidden' cave of Bae Phuk Mamo Dzong, where the sage Ludzi Repa stayed. Across the neck of water to the west is a large *chörten*. At Betse, a village at the foot of a hill, is the cave of Dhoyön Dzong; a monastery overlooks it. To the east of the lake is Porong District, a vast tract of land, home mainly to nomads.

✤ Day 3 Pelku Lake Nomad Camp–Base of Jakhyung La Pass 6 1/2hr

Continue along the western lakeshore for 3 hr. Pass on the right the brown hill that compresses the lake into its kidney shape. The road now starts to climb. At the top of the rise, look back for an unforgettable view of Pelku Lake and Shishapangma. Descend and enter a narrow gorge with spectacular rock formations. After 2 hr, exit the gorge onto a wide, desert-like plain bounded by high mountains on the left. This is a very dry area; there are no streams or rivers. Walk to the foot of the pass, on the left, in 1 1/2 hr. There is a road junction here. The right fork follows telegraph poles to Saga, 69 km away, north of the Tsangpo. This easy walk has only one hill. From Saga, hitch either east to Lhatse and Shigatse or west to Zhongba (Tradum) and Mt Kailash, a distance of 532 km. The left fork ascends to the pass. Spend the night here at its base to have the whole of the following day to cross it.

✤ DAY 4 BASE OF JAKHYUNG LA–DZONGKA (KYIRONG XIAN) 8 1/2 HR

It takes 4 hr to climb the steep road to the Jakhyung La (Ma La) Pass (5180 m). The wind at the top is biting and cold. (Milarepa crossed this pass enroute to Pelku Lake and Dzongka). Jakhyung La to Dzongka is 34 km. The descent is westerly along a ravine, then up a small spur, then along the side of a ridge. Soon the road zigzags down the mountain. Chungkar Monastery (present condition unknown) can be seen in the distance on a hill to the right.

Chungkar Monastery

Chungkar is short for Khyunglung Karpo, a castle built by Bönkar Khyung at this superb site. The castle-palace, consecrated to Chenresi, was well known for its *chörtens*, built by expert Nepalese artists; and the multi-doored Tashi Gomang *chörten* was of a type, similar to the one at Sakya (destroyed), known as Rinchengang. Other holy sites in this myth-filled area include Kyirong Kang Sengkar, Longkar Lhakhang Marpo, and Kalsang Lhakhang. The celebrated Gungthang La, where Guru Rinpoche first entered Tibet from India, is nearby to the northeast.

A river is on the left during the descent. Take in views of Langtang Himal (7232m) in Nepal (left) and the town of Dzongka at the bottom of the valley. Ganesh Himal (7406 m) is to the right, behind Dzongka. The descent takes 4 hr. Pass a village, then come to Dzongka after a further 3/4 hr.

Dzongka (Kyirong Xian, 4039 m)

These days few people use the name Dzongka, a word meaning 'high mud walls' (they once encircled the town). The Chinese have renamed it Kyirong Xian (*xian* means county town and here denotes the headquarters for the entire Gungthang-Mangyul district. Kyirong proper, further south, is called Kyirong Qu to signify that it is a smaller center under the control of the *xian*). Dzongka was the residence of the Gungthang-Mangyul kings. This branch of the West Tibet kingdom produced the celebrated Jangchub Ö, who invited Atisha, the Indian Buddhist master, to Tibet in the 11th century. Rechungpa, Milarepa's biographer, was born here as well. The town stands dramatically on an elevated section of the plateau, sandwiched between two river canyons. Chinese compounds with tin roofs spread around the outskirts; the old Tibetan sector is at the town's southern end. Cultivated fields in the valley floor are ringed by low hills, each imbued with a different, marvelous hue of yellow or brown. High mountain ranges rise to the north, east, and west.

Dzongka's two rivers are the Sarong, flowing from the northwest, and the Gyang, whose origin is the Jakhyung La Pass. The combined waters flow south to Kyirong, where they become the Trisuli of Nepal. In the old days, Dzongka was enclosed by huge, 8-m-tall,

2-m-thick mud and stone walls, about 400 m long on each side. Some sections have survived, particularly at the southwest corner (much was destroyed in the Gurkha wars of the 19th C). The old town is a fascinating jumble of alleyways and houses amidst crumbling ruins. Dzongka's environs are archeologically interesting. North of the town are several prominent ruins situated on hilltops. Next to Lhamog Monastery is an ancient cave settlement (similar to those in Mustang, Nepal; for example, Luri). The caves, dug out of rock, are decorated with murals and have remnants of wood sculptures. Many clay *tsa-tsas* litter the floor. Near the town are the caves of Za Og Phuk of Rala Village and Wösel Phuk of Ronphu Village. Dzongka was an important trade center with many goods coming up from Nepal destined for Lhasa and other parts of Tibet. The small town enjoys a much milder winter than most other Tibetan towns. Even in January, it is very rare for it to have snow.

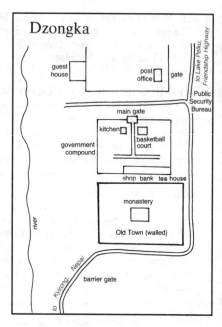

Trade routes out of Dzongka

- Takgya La (5400 m). This route follows the Sarong Chu out of town to Shomang Simna, then goes up to its headwaters near the Takgya La Pass, north-northwest of Dzongka. After the pass, the trail descends to the south bank of the Tsangpo via Abchen Menna, then travels west to Tradum (Zhongba) or north to Saga.
- Yurwo La. This route runs due north from Dzongka. Beyond the Yurwo Pass is Kegye, a ferry on the Tsangpo.
- Shangye La. This route goes east of the Yurwo La and crosses the Ladakh range.
- Gungthang La. Religiously and historically the most important. Guru Rinpoche crossed this to reach Tibet from India. From Dzongka, the route goes northeast to Gönser and then to Chungkar, a tiny village. Nearby are the ruins of Chungkar Monastery (see page 929).
- Jakhyung La (Ma La). Due east of Dzongka, this route leads to the Pelku Lake and Dingri.

Stay clear of the Public Security Bureau of Gungthang-Mangyul district, which is within the government compound. A small tea shop, the main store, and a bank (no money changed) are clustered nearby. The guest house is outside, adjacent to the large compound. It has ten rooms; some are usually occupied by Khampa traders from eastern Tibet.

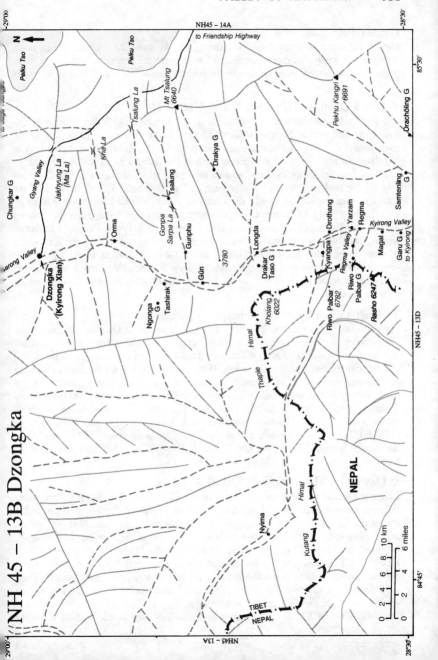

NH 45 – 13B Dzongka

Ganden Pelgyaling

Ganden Pelgyaling Monastery is in the center of the old town. The structure, though much damaged, still stands, and recent restorations have brought the institution back to life. Some original murals and good wood carvings on the columns remain, and over 20 original sculptures have been salvaged.

✤ DAY 5 DZONGKA (KYIRONG XIAN)–GÜN 5 1/4 HR

The route now goes due south for 68 km along the Kyirong River Valley to Kyirong Qu. Follow the road outside the town walls to the fort's southwest corner, then descend to the river, passing a lumber inspection station. Follow the Kyirong River (Trisuli, Bhote Kosi in Nepal) into a narrow canyon immediately south of the Dzongka plains. Go through this to reach the beautiful village of Orma, situated on a small, elevated plateau (2 hr). Enormous yaks till the land, and caves here were once used as dwellings. (A small track from here leads east over the Kha La Pass to the southwest corner of Pelku Lake, where it joins up with the main road.) 3/4 hr from Orma is a distinctive earth *chörten* that marks the entrance into the long Kyirong Gorge, which extends all the way south to Regma Village, 15 km before Kyirong Qu. The scenery around here is spectacular. Follow the road into the gorge; the Kyirong River is on the right. Reach Gün (Günda) after 2 1/2 hr. A desolate, forsaken place, this consists of a mud compound with a roadside tea shop. It is possible to stay in a room next to the family room, which doubles as the kitchen. Nepalese traders come through here en route to Dzongka.

Tsalung: the birthplace of Milarepa

Just north of Gün is a side valley with a trail that leads east to Günphu and then to the Gönpa Sarpa La. Tower-like houses line this portion of the route. Unfortunately, most are in ruins. South of the pass a large structure (perhaps a destroyed monastery), with three large *chörtens*, can be seen. Then reach Tsalung (Kya Ngatsa, 4300 m), the celebrated birthplace of Milarepa, consisting of two groups of houses at the valley's end near a moraine. To the north, beyond an east–west trending ridge, are the villages of Rungpu and Sharkhang. Above Tsalung, the valley forms a wide, flat basin; snow peaks with descending glaciers are visible to the south and east. The most prominent peak, to the south, is also named Tsalung (6700 m). Below the village is a *chörten*, the only religious monument of Milarepa left in the vicinity. Beyond Tsalung is the high Tsalung La Pass (5800m), which leads down to Pelku Lake.

✤ DAY 6 GÜN–DROTHANG (3320 M) 4 3/4 HR

Continue south along the gorge and ford a stream 1/2 hr from Gün. Reach a point where the river valley widens; prayer flags on the left form an unusual gateway (1 1/4 hr). (Just east of the flags is the village of Longda and the cave of Lingwa Drak. North of Longda, a side valley trends to the east. Near its head, at the base of the snow-capped Tsalung Ri [southwest face] is the Drakya Monastery, built next to the Milarepa cave of Drakya Dorje Dzong.) The hillside next to the road has emblazoned Tibetan characters and orange, white, and grey vertical stripes. Across the river are prayer flags and more colored stripes. These mark the approach to Drakar Taso, Milarepa's hallowed hermitage for 12 years. It is precipitously situated on top of the cliffs on the western bank.

Continue for 3 hr down the narrow gorge (the road hugs its side 10–20 m above the

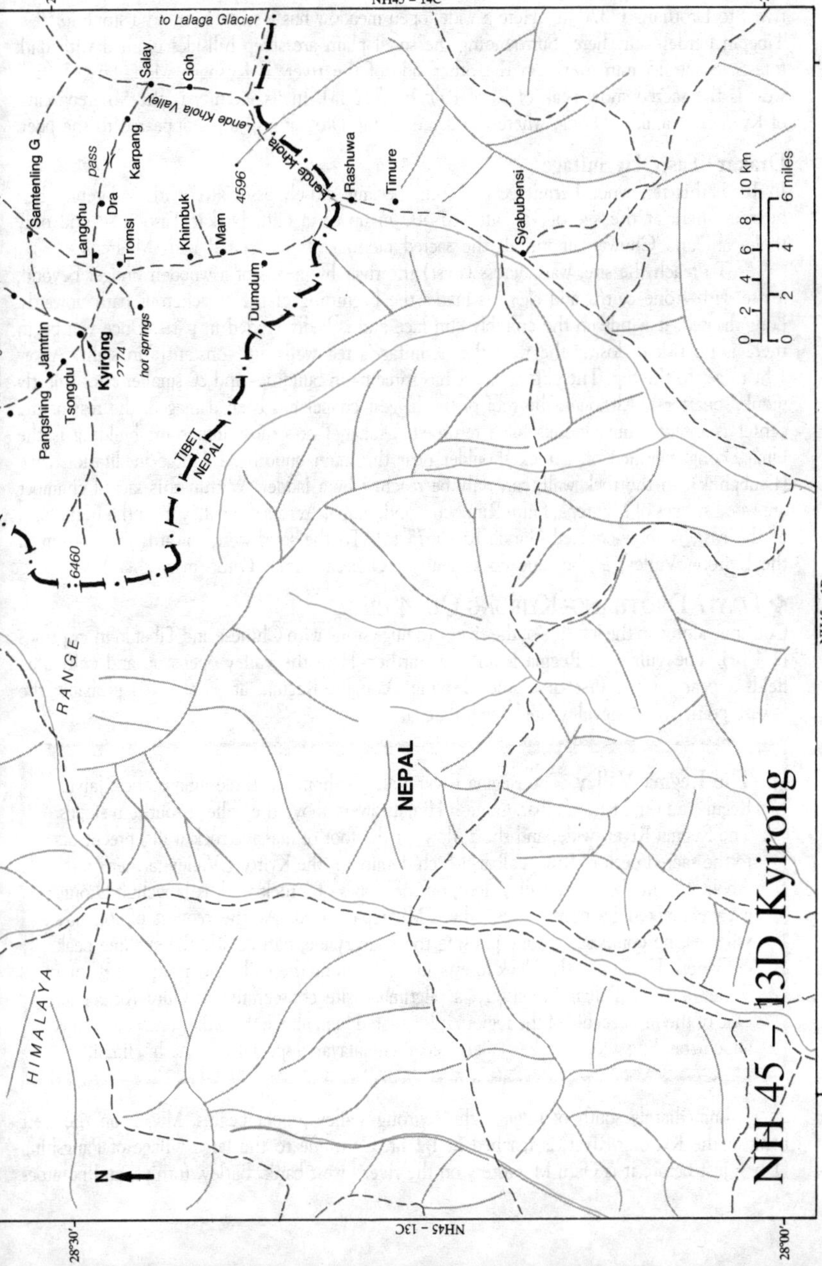

NH45 – 14C

85°30'

28°30'

28°00'

to Lalaga Glacier

Salay   Goh

Samtenling G

pass

Karpang

Langchu   Dra

Khimbuk

Tromsi

Mam

4596

Rashuwa

Timure

Syabubensi

Jamtrin

Pangshing   Tsongdu   Kyirong
                            2774

hot springs

Dumdum

TIBET
NEPAL

6460

RANGE

NEPAL

HIMALAYA

N

NH45 – 1B

NH45 – 13C

84°45'

NH 45 – 13D Kyirong

Lende Khola Valley

Lende Khola

0 2 4 6 8 10 km

0   2   4   6 miles

river) to Drothang (3320 m). Here a wide, open meadow has a stone hut and a stone fortress. Tibetan herders stay here. Surrounding the small plain are steep hillsides clothed with dark forests. Some 15 min away, on the other side of the river, is Kyangpa Monastery. To the west is the sacred snow peak of Riwo Palbar (6797 m). In its vicinity is the Milarepa cave of Kyangpa Namkha Dzong, where the demon king, Drothang Gyalpo, appeared to the poet.

Drakar Taso Hermitage

In 1083, this renowned hermitage (3600 m) became closely associated with Milarepa when he came here at the age of 43. Situated 300 m up on a cliff, Drakar Taso is second only to Lapchi and Chuwar among all the sacred monuments associated with Milarepa.

To reach the site, walk across (west) the river by means of a wooden bridge. Beyond, a rise with stone cairns and *chörtens* marks the beginning of the treacherous path upwards. Long disused, it winds up the crumbly cliff face and is badly eroded in parts. Once you begin there is no risk of losing the way; the hermitage's red walls are constantly in sight. Allow 1 hr to get to the top. The cliff complex has three main buildings and 20 smaller ones (mostly monks' quarters). Although the roof of the biggest chapel has been damaged, the rest of the center is intact. Some monks have returned. Drakar Taso's most important building is the Uma Dzong, perched on a rock shoulder near the main building. Its large meditation cave (Drubphuk), in the rock wall, can only be reached by a ladder. Within this sacred chamber are wood statues of Milarepa, Guru Rinpoche, and Jampa. Across the valley from the hermitage, to the east, is snow-covered Günda Ri (6675 m). To the southwest, towards the bottom of the Kyirong Valley, is the blue cockscomb of Ganesh Himal (7406 m).

✤ Day 7 Drothang–Kyirong Qu 4 hr

Continue along on the left side of the river to a huge stone with Chinese and Tibetan inscriptions (1/4 hr). The village of Regma is an hour further. Here the valley opens up and cultivated fields appear for the first time since leaving Dzongka. Regma, at 3000 m, is probably the lowest point in Mangyul visited by Milarepa.

The Regma Valley The Regma River Valley is home to three monasteries: Jaiyul, Regma, and the Riwo Palbar. Ganesh Himal towers above the valley's southern slopes. The Regma River, wide, and short, flows at the foot of massive rock walls, precursors to the sacred peak of Riwo Palbar, which dominates the Kyirong Valley farther south. About 150 m above the valley floor, on the slopes of a rock wall, is Jangchub Dzong, a cave marked by prayer flags, where Milarepa stayed. At the request of Regma's villagers, he composed a song praising the countryside, particularly the sublime peak of Ganesh Himal and the black forests and lakes along the valley floor. Up the Regma Valley is Riwo Palbar Monastery, a pilgrimage site consecrated to Guru Rinpoche. One of the most scenic of the region, it is situated high above the valley and commands an outstanding view of the Tibet–Nepal Himalayas, especially Ganesh Himal.

Immediately south of Regma, the Kyirong Valley proper begins. Magal, on the west bank of the Kyirong River, is reached in 1/2 hr. Continue to the large village of Pangshing (1 hr); just before it is Garu Monastery on the river's west bank. Barley, turnips, and potatoes grow here. Chamding (Jamtrin) Village is beyond Pangshing, left of the road, as is the small, renovated Jamtrin Monastery. In 1/2 hr arrive at Tsongdü. The road now descends, curving to the right. On the right is a beautiful grassy glen with peculiar stone formations. Beyond, on a hill to the left overlooking Kyirong, are Chinese army barracks. From here to Kyirong is 3/4 hr. All along the Kyirong Gorge, from Orma to Kyirong, are good camping and picnic spots near the river.

Jamtrin (Chamding)

One of the fabled Yangdul monuments (see page 43) of King Songtsen Gampo, this monastery was founded in the 7th C. in order to hold down the right foot of Tibet's great demoness. Jamtrin, small and insignificant, is typical of monasteries in the Kyirong area. It is configurated as a four-story pagoda—quite unlike the usual stone fort design—and the delicate lines are a radical departure from the squat, massive architecture of Tibet. Some original murals remain on the second floor.

✤ DAY 8 KYIRONG QU–RASHUWA (NEPAL) 6 1/2 HR

From Kyirong to Rashuwa on the Nepal border is 29 km. Villagers on both sides of the border move freely between the two countries within a buffer zone that stretches from Dzongka and Kyirong in Tibet to Syabrubensi and Dunche (trailhead for the Langtang trek) in Nepal. If you have a Nepalese visa and want to cross at Rashuwa, check first at the Nepalese embassy in Lhasa. (A one-month visa can be obtained there [FEC 30], available one day after application.) At the time of writing, this border crossing is not opened to tourists.

Follow the dirt road east out of Kyirong (see above). The road forks after a small rise. Take the right along the Kyirong River. Reach Tromsi after 1 1/2 hr. Descend gradually to Khimbuk (1 1/2 hr) and then continue to Mam and Paimenesa (2 hr). From here the border bridge over the Lende Khola, which separates Nepal from Tibet, is 1 1/2 hr. Rashuwa Fort is just across the bridge. If allowed to enter Nepal, you can reach Syabubensi Village in one day, passing along the way the Timuri military check point. In Syabubensi, stores, restaurants and lodges, and a local hot spring, cater to trekkers. Another day's walk brings you to the big Nepalese town of Dunche. Catch a jeep to Trisuli the following morning. Buses leave from Trisuli to Kathmandu around noon, arriving the same day.

KYIRONG

Kyirong (2774 m) is a mixture of Tibetan houses, drab Chinese compounds, and a pagoda-style monastery, all at the bottom of an alpine valley. The snow mountain of Serkham Gang, east of Ganesh Himal,

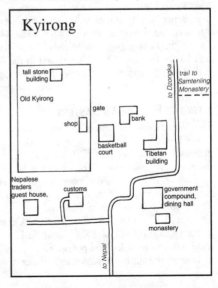

Kyirong

tall stone building

Old Kyirong

shop

gate

bank

basketball court

Tibetan building

to Dzongka

trail to Samtenling Monastery

Nepalese traders guest house.

customs

government compound, dining hall

monastery

to Nepal

rises west of the valley; Nepal is a one-day walk south. Most of the village is on the right (west) side of the road. On the left is a Tibetan-style compound and the four-story pagoda monastery of Kyirong Pomba (Phagpa Gompa), a rather ramshackle structure with firewood and machinery piled all around it. The Kyirong Qu administrative compound is next to the monastery. Go to the traders' compound farther south for lodging. In the old village, the 160-odd houses are constructed mostly of dark stones with sloping shingled rooves held down by rocks.

Near the river is a huge boulder with stone houses perched on top; a distinctive landmark. Nearby are large houses that belonged to the former chief of the village. An old flat-topped building, the Dzong Shar (East Fort), still stands; in earlier times it was the district office. A customs house processing goods from Nepal is in a compound further south. Depending on current regulations, the Public Security Bureau here has the authority to stamp you into the country if you arrive from Nepal with a valid Chinese visa (one day away is the frontier at Rashuwa, where you can be stamped in or out as well). Beyond is a compound where traders from Tibet and Nepal congregate. A small very basic room with horrendously dirty mattresses is available. This is the only regular lodging in Kyirong (the alternative is to stay with a family). Nepalese and Tibetans sleep outside in the big hall and build makeshift fires on the earth floor to make tea and cook. Stacks of Tibetan wool are everywhere, waiting to be taken to Nepal. A store in the village stocks milk powder, dried apples, tins of chicken, pork, and mandarin oranges.

Kyirong's low altitude (2774 m) allows three crops annually. Wheat and barley are sown in October and harvested in June. Another variety of barley, *neh*, is sown in July and harvested in October. Two other grains, *parpa* and *saso*, are grown. Rice is imported from Nepal. In general, the climate in Kyirong is pleasant year round. Even in winter, the temperature seldom falls below 10° C. The monsoon rains fall between May and September. Vegetation here is rich and varied, including large varieties of rhododendrons and primroses. About 2 hr southeast of Kyirong are sulphur hot springs (40° C) in a bamboo forest near the Kyirong River. Other hotsprings lie near the end of the Dobli Gorge (where the Kyirong River disappears), near Chang (northwest of Rashuwa), and in the Lende region. Once 26 monasteries thrived in the Kyirong–Lende area. Only three of these belonged to the Gelugpa sect: Phagpa, Samtenling, and Jamtrin. From Kyirong north to the Tsangpo River is a walk of eight days.

KYIRONG PHAGPA MONASTERY

This Nepalese-style monastery still retains murals on the outside walls that depict the holy city of Lhasa, the great monasteries of Ganden, Samye, and Tashilhunpo, and the renowned pilgrimage of Tsari (see page 208). It is dedicated to Phagpa Changra and once held a famous statue of Jowo (Sakyamuni). The statue was 'banished' to Kyirong Phagpa from Central Tibet by ministers of King Trisong Detsen (r 755–97) who were hostile to Buddhism. It was then moved to Drepung in 1656, and again to the Potala when rumors grew of war with Nepal. This Jowo was spirited out of Tibet and into India at the time of the Chinese invasion in 1959, and is now supposedly in Dharamsala. Other important Jowo statues in the Tibet are in the Jokhang (Lhasa), and Korja, near Taklakot (Purang) in West Tibet. Kyirong Phagpa and Jamtrin monasteries (and perhaps Ushang, see page 491) are two of the few institutions in Tibet to be built in the pagoda style of Nepal. Above the entrance to the Kyirong Phagpa

Monastery was an inscription: 'Whoever goes through this door will be freed of all sins accumulated over a thousand eons.' At the top of the building is a golden ornament (*sertok*) with a jewel ornament (*norbu*). A second *norbu* is on the third floor. The top two floors are beautifully crafted, with many fine decorations and details.

JADUR MONASTERY

Yangchu Thangkar is a large village near Kyirong with 500 households; 10 per cent of these belong to the Bönpo sect and support Jadur Monastery, an affiliate of Menri (see page 765), Bön's premier establishment near Shigatse. The Matri festival, lasting for 12 days during the fourth lunar month, was held here annually. Bönpo monks from Menri, Yungdrungling, and other Bön centers, who were on their way to Mt Kailash, took part and thus assured themselves of a sufficient supply of *tsampa* to last until the seventh month, when they returned to Jadur for the festival of Namgyal Tong Tshok (12 days). They then gathered enough supplies to return to Central Tibet.

EXCURSIONS FROM KYIRONG

KYIRONG TO SAMTENLING MONASTERY

This very pleasant excursion from Kyirong requires the minimum of a full day (4 hr to go up and 3 hr to come down). Allow time for rest and a picnic. It makes sense, however, to spend the night at Samtenling and explore its wonderful surroundings the next day. The monastery, high up the Kyirong Valley, is enclosed by dramatic snow peaks and glaciers. Milarepa's disciple, Repa Zhiwa, meditated here, as did the guru Yeshe Gyaltsen Pandita. In its later years, the monastery was converted from the Kagyüpa to the Gelugpa by a lama of Shekar Monastery (see page 920). Samtenling was once a huge complex of chapels and monks' dwellings but was virtually leveled during the Cultural Revolution. Remains of the main hall and chapel stand on the lower portion of a slope; 50 stone houses of varying sizes are further up the hillside.

Follow a side valley (on your right, if you are walking north up the road from lower down the valley) northeast from Kyirong Phagpa Monastery and the Tibetan-style building and compound. The trail follows the contours of the right-hand slope (army barracks are visible across the valley). After traversing some cultivated fields, the path climbs to a beautiful plateau (2 hr). Two pretty villages, Nanu and Nanshö, are spaced a few km apart in a lovely, green field. High snow peaks of the Langtang and Ganesh Himals provide an exquisite backdrop. Nearby are the ruins of a monastery, its reddish earthen walls contrasting superbly with the emerald fields.

Continue for 15 min along a level path left of the first village. The path then forks. Take the left lower, level fork (the right hand path climbs up the mountain). After 3/4 hr in a forest, arrive at a clearing called Sema, site of a few shepherds' huts and a herd of yaks. Fresh yoghurt (*shö*) and Tibetan bread (*kora*) are available from the herders. An ill-defined path now goes up from the clearing through more forests to a ruined chapel built below a huge rock (1 hr). Some murals and the remains of the broken statues can still be seen. Outside, there are paintings on a stone outcrop above the building. To the left, a path leads to the top of this outcrop; from there climb to Samtenling in 20 min. The return trip goes back down to Sema, where a more direct, though obscure path, takes you straight down to Kyirong. It crosses a dense forest to follow a small river to the ridge of the Chinese army barracks. The cultivated valley floor is on the left. Go through fields to emerge on to the motor road at a point across from the Tibetan-style building.

KYIRONG–GOH (NEPAL BORDER)

This lovely walk of two or three days through the pristine Lende region, with its numerous unspoiled Tibetan villages, is one of the highlights of Kyirong. Across the river is a very isolated part of Nepal, virtually unknown to trekkers.

Follow the jeep track (a continuation of the track from Dzongka) that leaves Kyirong heading southeast. After 3/4 hr go over a rise that overlooks Kyirong. Here, the road forks. Take the left track (the right leads to Rashuwa and Nepal), following a wide cultivated, side valley for 1 3/4 hr. The village of Langchu, on the left, is 1 km from the main road. Electricity poles go along the track, now impassable for vehicles. Reach Dra after 1 1/2 hr of climbing. An empty building in the village center can be used for lodgings; it has no beds, only an empty room and an earthen fireplace for cooking. A ruined monastery with beige walls sits on top of a hill overlooking the village. Cross a low 4005-m pass after 3 hr. *Chörtens* dot the area. Descend for 1/2 hr to reach a plateau with many more *chörtens* and stone cairns. Unusual designs, occupying an area of 4 m by 2 m, are cut into the earth—a unique phenomenon, (perhaps similar to that below Yamalung Monastery, page 627).

Continue the gentle descent to Karpang (2 1/2 hr) above a small river that drains into a tributary of the Lende Khola. There is one monk in a makeshift monastery in the center of the village. Up the hill is a building that once housed the Muluk Monastery. Prolabrang Monastery is also in the area. Cross the small river and continue downward towards the Lende Khola tributary. Pass Pangboche and Salay to reach a wooden bridge over the river (fine scenery here). The path now ascends a short distance up the eastern hillside flanking the tributary to the grassy plateau of Lende. Here is the handsome village of Goh (2 hr from Karpang). Beyond it, a cliff face towers over the entire plateau where horses and cattle graze. Goh is an elongated settlement on the plateau above the river, with architecture similar to that of Kyirong: stone houses with wood plank roofs held down by stones.

From Goh an easy, level trail leads along the edge of the plateau southward, passing a village in a clearing (1 hr). In another hour descend from the plateau to the Lende Khola River, the boundary of Tibet and Nepal. A giant log makes it possible to cross into Nepal at this isolated spot. A trail leads through idyllic and deserted countryside to the Nepalese village of Sadang Kadu (3 hr). From there, carry on for a day to Syabubensi, a frequent stop for trekkers going to Langtang National Park.

WILDLIFE OF LENDE

Locals in Kyirong believe two types of bear exist in the region, a carnivore (*lhadom*) and a vegetarian (*shingdom*). In actual fact, there is only the omnivorous Himalayan bear, small and black with a white collar. It is fiercer than the placid Tibetan bears. Other animals sighted in the area are leopards, *thar* (large wild goat), and *muntjak* (*Muntiacus*), the barking deer.

Lalaga Glacier

A trip to the Lalaga Glacier passes through the beautiful Rishong Valley and includes Rishong Monastery, the glacier, and the peak of Kakaga Ri (6666 m).

Continue east along the Lende Khola (from the giant log), with the river on the right. Reach the Rishong Monastery (3 hr), then walk east along the north bank of the Rishong. After 2 km the river bends to the north; follow it to Dzedzö. (Just before this village, a bridge crosses the river. Pethang is on the opposite bank.) Continue along the right (west) bank to Timpu (3 km), Kongmen (4 km), and Lalaga (1 km). 2 km north beyond Lalaga, on the western tip of the Lalaga Glacier, is Sumgyong (the villages of Tashithang and Shingtro are on the river's opposite bank). Lalaga is located directly west of the main Shishapangma peak.

THE SHISHAPANGMA MASSIF: TREKS NEAR TIBET'S HIGHEST MOUNTAIN

NORTH ROUTE

A road to Shishapangma's North Base Camp is between road markers 613 and 614 km on the main highway (see page 990) between Nyalam and Dingri. The road heads west around low hills, then enters a broad valley. After 1/4 hr it drops to a river, 10 km from the turnoff. In another 12 km is a village at the base of cliffs, then the village of Siling after 8 more km. Nearby to the north is a picturesque lake and camp site. Consider hiring yaks at Siling.

From Siling, just off the main track, the route continues to large Pelku Lake. A few trucks use this route in summer to supply Kyirong. No proper road reaches the North Base Camp from Siling, but it is easy to drive across country. A vague track follows the base of southern hills to an open valley with low hills to the east. Two cairns mark the first part of the track. About 15 km from Siling is a river crossing and nearby campsite. Strong, icy winds blow here. From this base camp, the peaks of Shishapangma (8012 m) and Phola Gangchen (7661 m) appear close to the south. A continuous ridge runs west from Shishapangma to Lalaga Ri. To the northwest, Pelku Lake is visible, a 1-hr drive from Siling.

Day hike from the North Base Camp

Continue along the valley to the south, keeping to the west side or if no wind, trek along the top of low hills adjacent to the camp. After 1 1/2 hr, reach a large boulder with a corral in the middle of the valley. After this point, the valley narrows and turns southward. Continue for 1 1/2 hr before entering a narrower gorge. Make camp in this area before continuing to the advance base camp below the great mountain. A further day is required to reach the moraines.

The high altitude of this region makes it particularly important to acclimatize lower down, perhaps at Shekar or Dingri. The Base Camp region lies at approximately 4900 m.

EAST ROUTE

A side road at road marker 667 km on the main route between Nyalam and the Lalung La Pass appears to lead to the eastern regions of Phola Gangchen and Shishapangma. Camp at the junction of the main road and this track if necessary.

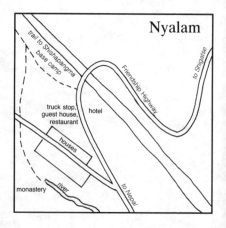

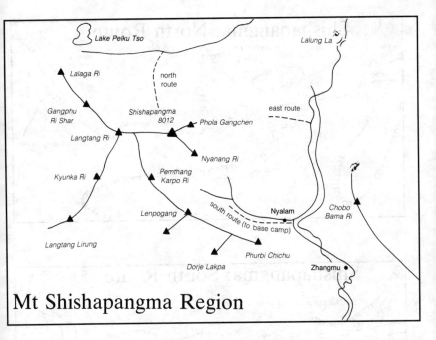

Mt Shishapangma Region

SOUTH ROUTE

The route from Nyalam gives stunning views of the north side of Nepal's Jugal Himal, the upper peaks of the Langtang Valley, and Shishapangma's south face. During the summer monsoon season, this region is subject to heavy rains, snow, and unsettled weather. The ideal seasons appear to be April–June and October–December.

The route to Shishapangma's South Base Camp follows the Nyanang Chu Valley. From Nyalam, a trail heads west from the monastery at the end of the Tibetan part of town. Cross fields to a well-defined trail and follow it for 1 hr to an isolated settlement of stone buildings below the hillside to the west. Yak herders and dogs inhabit this area. From here the trail splits into tracks, but the narrowing valley can be followed around a bend into a wide valley with parallel sides. On the south side of this valley is a steep, level plateau, about 800 m above the valley floor. The distances here are deceptive and a further day's hike is necessary to reach even the near peaks. Climb the plateau ridge to the south to view Shishapangma's South Face and also to descend slightly to a glacial lake. Immediately south is the peak of Phurpu Chichu; a grassy ridge leads to its great glaciers. It is possible to camp by this lake, but the region (4300 m) is extremely cold.

This chapter was contributed by Bob Gibbons and Sian Pritchard-Jones.

(see over page for maps of the north and south routes.)

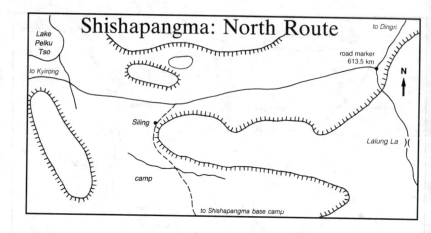

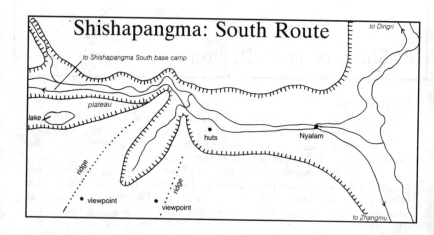

WEST TIBET: THE ANCIENT KINGDOMS OF GUGE, PURANG, AND RUTOK

West Tibet, home to the premier pilgrimage site of Mt Kailash (see page 273) and Lake Manasarovar, also has some of Tibet's most significant art and architecture. Within the royal chapels of Tsaparang, capital of the ancient Guge kingdom, are sumptuous Kashmiri-inspired paintings and statues. The ruins themselves are stunning; the castles and troglodytic communities provide an archeological chronicle of the region since the 10th century.

The West Tibet Routes section (below) gives detailed descriptions on how to get there and it includes a section on Purang, a petty kingdom that made up the West Tibetan territory of Ngari Khorsum. A walk along the upper Satlej River allows access to the incomparable canyon country of West Tibet. En route are the sacred hot springs of Tirthapuri and the famed Bönpo shrine of Khyunglung, where the pre-Buddhist religion supposedly originated. The Rutok petroglyphs, farther to the north along the Tibet–Xinjiang highway, uniquely document Tibet's prehistory.

WEST TIBET ROUTES: FROM CENTRAL TIBET, NEPAL, AND XINJIANG TO GUGE AND MT KAILASH

OVERVIEW

Most travelers make the strenuous, sometimes very expensive trip to West Tibet (Ngari) in order to pay homage to Kailash (see page 273), the holiest mountain for both Buddhists and Hindus. Two other important West Tibet sites for pilgrims are Lake Manasarovar and Tirthapuri (pages 614, 961). A major destination of monumental cultural and artistic interest is the Kingdom of Guge (see page 430), founded in the mid-10th C. and sited northwest of Kailash. Its twin centers of Tsaparang and Tholing preserved Buddhism in Tibet during the turbulent downfall of the Yarlung Dynasty. Most importantly, they still retain exquisite 15th-C. works of art. The Satlej River Valley (see page 964) was the focus of Guge and is a thoroughly fascinating, albeit difficult, region to explore on foot. Khyunglung, a cave monastery within the valley, is reputed to be the Bönpo religion's place of origin. Within the vast territory of West Tibet are the sources of some of Asia's most important rivers—the Tsangpo, the Indus, the Karnali and the Satlej. The strategic frontier town of Purang (Taklakot) is about 100 km southwest of Mt Kailash; it links West Tibet with India and Nepal. This chapter outlines the routes from the urban centers of Central Tibet to Shiquanhe (Ali), West Tibet's capital. Alternative routes from Nepal and Xinjiang are also described. From Shiquanhe, there are itineraries to Mt Kailash, Guge, and Purang.

Related sections
Kailash, p 273
Lake Manasarovar, p 614
Tsaparang, p 430
Tholing, p 425

Access to West Tibet
The large territory of West Tibet (Ngari) is bounded in the east by Nagchu district and in the southeast by Shigatse district. To the south are India and Nepal; Kashmir forms the border in the west. North of Ngari is Xinjiang, the huge Uighur Autonomous Region of China, the so-called Chinese Turkestan. Ngari extends 750 km from north to south, over 300 km from east to west, and comprises approximately a quarter of the Tibet Autonomous Region. Its population, almost entirely Tibetan, is about 50,000. Shiquanhe, the capital of West Tibet, is difficult to reach. Some people hire vehicles or go with expensive tourist agencies, but for hitchhikers the route from Lhasa is one of the most problematic in the country. Traffic is sparse and seats in any vehicle are at a premium.

A number of different routes lead to Mt Kailash, but the most straightforward is the North Route, which runs through Shiquanhe. From here, continue southeast to Tholing and Tsaparang or south to Mt Kailash. The South Route, through Lhatse and Saga to Kailash, although more direct, is much harder to hitch and even with the help of expensive Landcruisers, the chances of reaching the holy mountain are by no means certain. The options are:

1 Lhasa to Shiquanhe (north route), 1756 km
2 Lhasa to Amdo to Shiquanhe, 1793 km
3 Lhasa to Lhatse to Mt Kailash (south route), 1188 km
4 Kathmandu to Shiquanhe via Lhatse, 1586 km (from Zhangmu near the Nepal–Tibet border)
5 Kathmandu to Mt Kailash direct, 817 km (from Zhangmu)
6 Kashgar and Yecheng to Shiquanhe, 1100 km

From Shiquanhe to Tsaparang via Gar and Nabru is 271 km and takes 10 hr in a jeep or truck. The old route from Tsaparang to the main road and then south to Mensi and Mt Kailash is a further 330 km. A good, new road, also from Tsaparang, to Mensi via Ba'er military camp is 160 km and takes 6 hr. Mensi to Barga at the foot of Mt Kailash is 71 km further.

Traffic is scarce and uncertain from Shiquanhe to either Tsaparang or Mt Kailash. For the latter, try to find a pilgrim truck, the cheapest though not the most comfortable way to the mountain. Tsaparang is not on the pilgrimage itinerary and pilgrim trucks bypass this ancient capital. To visit both Kailash and Guge, try to rent a vehicle from the Shiquanhe tourist authorities (expensive). There might be a cheaper Beijing jeep available (bargain hard).

1. Lhasa to Shiquanhe (North Route) 1756 km
The north route to Mt Kailash is the easiest and the most widely used (the south route is

the shortest and most direct). It goes from Lhasa to Lhatse along the Friendship Highway, then branches north at Raga, and crosses the Changtang to Shiquanhe (Lhasa–Lhatse is described in Friendship Highway, page 987; Lhatse–Shiquanhe is described below, page 947). To get a direct ride from Lhasa, try the Ngari Office that coordinates all traffic to and from Shiquanhe. It is located on the main road (Chingdrol Lam) to Sera Monastery (see Lhasa map for directions), tel 22729. A guest house here called Baizhou accommodates foreigners for about Rmb 15 per night; plan to stay a few days to increase the chances of a ride. Expect to pay at least Rmb 200 for the eight-day ride by truck and perhaps Rmb 400 for a seat in a Beijing jeep. A Toyota Landcruiser seat will be far more expensive. Be patient and bargain. If you are able to secure a ride all the way from Lhasa to Kailash via Shiquanhe, expect a minimum travel time of six to seven days.

From Lhatse on the busy Tibet–Nepal road, the best chance for a ride to West Tibet is to walk 6 km west out of town (at road marker 5057) to where the Friendship Highway forks. The left branch turns south to Nepal, the right goes to Kaga, Sangsang, and Raga. Take the right and walk 2 km more to the Tsangpo ferry. Here all traffic must stop and wait for the barge. Try your luck here. At Raga, a truck route turns north to Shiquanhe.

2. LHASA TO SHIQUANHE VIA AMDO, 1793 KM

This long, circuitous route is perhaps the most fascinating and least attempted, but the best to experience the strange, euphoric feeling of the Changtang and its still-abundant wildlife. The route goes north from Lhasa towards Golmud along the Tibet–Qinghai highway and crosses the Nyenchen Tanglha range. Just before the Tangula range that separates Tibet from Qinghai, a secondary road branches to the west at Amdo, 138 km north of Nagchu. It then traverses practically the entire southern portion of the Changtang Plateau to reach Shiquanhe. Traffic is extremely scarce on this road and hitching is very difficult. Villages are few; nomads, yak herds, and black tents are more common. Winter temperatures on the Changtang often plummet to –40°C and the average temperature is –5°. Attempt this route between May and September only.

From Lhasa to Amdo is relatively easy because many trucks and buses go each day from Lhasa to Golmud. (Lhasa to Nagchu is 317 km, Nagchu to Amdo is a further 138 km.) The rough 'road' to Shiquanhe heads due west and passes through Dongchio (94 km), then Dogyaling on the north shore of the huge Lake Siling after another 222 km. From Dogyaling it is 104 km to Nima (still within sight of Siling) and a further 421 km to Gerze, where the road joins the north route. A direct ride from Amdo to Gerze takes four to five days. The 497-km section from Gerze to Shiquanhe portion is far easier to hitch.

3. LHASA TO MT KAILASH VIA LHATSE (SOUTH ROUTE) 1188 KM

The spectacular south route from Lhasa to Kailash is 568 km shorter than the north route. This way guarantees superb vistas and close encounters with *kiang* and antelopes, especially west of the Maryum La. The route is normally open for only two limited periods, from May to early July (after the snows and before the monsoon) and from October to November (after the monsoon). Few drivers will consider this road at other times because of the dangers of flooding and high rivers. Landcruisers and trucks have been known to founder for days in one spot. Another disadvantage of the south route is that after reaching Mt Kailash, if you want to go on to Guge (Tsaparang and Tholing), rides are very difficult to come by. To follow the south route, take a bus or hitchhike to Lhatse, then walk 6 km out of town to where the road forks. Take the right fork to Raga, then continue west to Mt Kailash via Saga, Zhongba, and Paryang. From Raga to Mt Kailash is 590 km. Take plentiful supplies. A Landcruiser from Lhasa to Kailash on the south route requires four to five days, assuming that the road conditions are not particularly onerous.

4. KATHMANDU TO SHIQUANHE VIA LHATSE (NORTH ROUTE) 1586 KM (FROM ZHANGMU)

The standard route goes north from the Friendship Bridge on the Tibet–Nepal border via Zhangmu, Nyalam, and Dingri to Lhatse, a distance of 335 km. From Lhatse, continue to Shiquanhe via the north route, or to Mt Kailash via the south route.

5. KATHMANDU TO MT KAILASH DIRECT, 817 KM (FROM ZHANGMU)

This is a more interesting and scenic route than the previous one. After reaching the Tibetan plateau from the Nyalam Valley, take the left (west) fork at a road junction marked by a wooden Chinese signpost near road marker 615 km (instead of going east to Dingri and Lhatse). Cross the Digur Thang (Porang) Plain to beautiful Pelku Lake (see Kyirong, page 928). The impressive Shishapangma massif is close by on the left. From the lake's western shore turn north to Saga on the north bank of the Tsangpo, then west to Zhongba and Mt Kailash. This route is effectively closed from mid-July through mid-September because of heavy rain. Expect very little traffic between the signpost and Saga. From the Friendship Bridge to Saga is 285 km. Barga (near Kailash) is a further 532 km. A lucky direct ride to Mt Kailash takes about five days.

6. KASHGAR AND YECHENG TO SHIQUANHE, 1100 KM

This route is for those who have traveled to Kashgar from Lanzhou, Turfan, or Urümqi. Or from Pakistan via the Khunjerab pass.

Yecheng (Karghalik) is a one-day bus ride southeast of Kashgar (Kashi). Catch the bus from the bus station near Chairman Mao's statue in the centre of Kashgar. At Yecheng, head for the truck stop and guest house 8 km south of town, next to the main road to Shiquanhe and Tibet. Most traffic coming from Tibet stops here. Spend the night and try to arrange a ride south. (The main government guest house at the centre of Yecheng has troublesome officials; the Public Security Bureau might send you back to Kashgar. Do not stay here.) The usual rate for a seat in the cab of the truck going to Shiquanhe is about Rmb 50–100, but expect to pay more. Old Russian trucks, usually driven by Uighurs, ply between Yecheng and Shiquanhe. The trucks have deep blue cabs and a bed behind the driver. Look for them in the center of Yecheng. The journey takes about three days and is possible throughout the year except from December to February, when snow closes the high pass between Xinjiang and Tibet.

LHATSE TO SHIQUANHE: THE NORTH ROUTE (1263 KM)

Lhatse is situated at road marker 400 km (new road marker 5051) on the Nepal–Tibet highway. Walk out of the Lhatse Guest house, opposite the gas station, and turn right. Turn right again after the gas station and follow the main road west out of town. Pass a large bridge and in 1 hr the road forks (road marker 5057). Take the right branch (the left goes to Nepal) and walk 2 km further to the Tsangpo ferry. This is the best place to get a ride. From now on, all times specified are based on a pilgrim truck averaging 25 km per hour. The road after the ferry enters a river valley with dry hills on both sides. Pass Lake Lang Tso on the left and the town of Kaga (on a small lake) is reached 51 km from the ferry.

Routes from Kaga

- To Ngamring Monastery. A side road heading east goes around the eastern side of Lake Ngamring to the village of Ngamring (1 1/4 hr walk). Here is Ngamring Monastery, founded in the 13th C. by a Sakyapa teacher. The Gelugpa under Tsong Khapa converted the monastery only partially, and by the end of the 17th C. it was in the unusual position of having 15 Sakyapa and ten Gelugpa colleges.
- To Chung Riwoche. The dirt road turnoff (to the left) to the great Riwoche Chörten (see page 451) is 0.5 km before Kaga; it is indistinct and easy to miss.

Across the road is a compound for the road maintenance crew; a kitchen here sells steamed dumplings and vegetables, and accommodation is available. This is a good place to stay as all traffic west passes directly in front. The next town is Sangsang, 60 km away (2 1/2 hrs). The 13th-C. Sangsang Nerang Monastery once stood here.

Sangsang to Chung Riwoche A well-used trail leads southwest and then south, over a pass to the *chörten* of Chung Riwoche (see page 460).

From Sangsang to Raga is 122 km. Raga is a settlement of mud compounds on the right hand side of the road that exists to service and fuel trucks. The landscape of the area is gorgeous. The guest house has cheap and basic rooms but food is not readily available. Trucks going to Shiquanhe and West Tibet usually stop here, as the turnoff to the north is only a few km ahead. Those going west to Saga (60 km away) and Zhongba (145 km further) do not usually stop. The road branches soon after Raga. Follow the dirt track that turns off the road to head north to the small town of Tsochen, 242 km away. This is the start of the north route proper. The main road continues west from Raga to Saga and Zhongba. (Another track leaves the main road 8 km from this Raga junction. It heads south to the Tsangpo and then goes on to the eastern and western shores of Pelku Lake.) The north route is generally good and flat. Pass steaming geysers and hot spring pools about 1 hr from the turnoff, then beautiful lakes before crossing the Semo La. Wildlife is abundant on the plains. Wild antelope (*kiang*), horses, herds of sheep and goats are common; stretches before and after Tsochen are superb. The north route follows a long valley and, exiting a gorge, reaches the settlements of Tsochen Qu and Tsochen Xian.

Tsochen Qu and Tsochen Xian

Tsochen Qu is a small settlement of mud houses and tents in a side valley 35 km before Tsochen Xian. The Tibetans here all wear huge, tattered, yak-skin coats and make their living by hunting and selling animal skins. 12 hr from Raga, arrive at the small town of Tsochen Xian, an important center for trucks and nomads; the next place of any consequence is Gerze Xian, 278 km to the north.

Tsochen Xian near the left (west) bank of the Tsochen Tsangpo, is on a wide plain bordered to the east by huge Lake Zhari Namtso, 15–20 km away. The guest house (populated mostly by Khampas) is in a compound at the town's south end. A square in the center of Tsochen has a store on the east side. The post office is farther to the north, after the school. The town secretary lives in a compound just west of the guest house and can help arrange rides. From time to time official vehicles (mail trucks) go from here to Shiquanhe and back. Mendong Monastery (destroyed) is 20 min beyond the north end of town. Instead of a *mani* wall the area is strewn with *mani* stones. A new chapel is looked after by a few monks.

After Tsochen Xian, the road traverses a long grassy plain, 10–15 km wide, bounded by low hills. Black tents appear from time to time. The people here eat much more meat than their Tsangpo valley counterparts, and herds of more than 1,000 sheep and goats are not uncommon. Sheepskins are plentiful. The sheep originally migrated from eastern Tibet (Kham) during the mid-19th century.

Reach Daxung in 2 1/2 hr (64 km), then Tung Tso, south of Tung Tso salt lake, in another 4 hr (115 km). The salt on the lake shores forms a hard, white crust that is collected, cleaned, and then dried in the sun. Black tents stand right (north) of the road. About 4 hr (99 km) from here is Gerze Xian (Gertse), 30 km north of Lake Lagkor. Gerze Xian, smaller than Tsochen Xian, is sited in a vast, desolate area. Compounds line both sides of a main street. The guest house is on the north side and meals are served at precise hours. A store on the south side of the street sells cheap, heavy, wool-lined coats. The town secretary, in a big government complex next to the store, can be helpful. One of his staff coordinates vehicles to and from Shiquanhe. (Most government officials in charge of towns and villages in Tibet are Tibetan and are known as *shuji*, secretary.)

Large herds of sheep transport grain in this region. Each animal carries a pair of woolen panniers capable of hauling 12 kilos. West and south of the road out of town is a wide, 50-km stretch of salt deposit and beyond it are more black tents. Reach Wuma (Öma) in 3–4 hr (90 km) from Gerze. It is distinguished by its fortress walls and guard houses with rifle slits. After this is the large salt lake of Qagcaka (Yan Hu), in another 4 hr (94 km). The salt deposit here stretches for nearly 40 km. For the next 6 hr (170 km) the road continues westward. At the small village of Pongba the road enters the Shiquanhe (Indus River) Gorge (the river source is further south near Mt Kailash). The scenery is quite magnificent. Reach Gegye in 1 hr (30 km). Its two halves are separated by 2 km; the town hosts a large trade fair each July and August. Cross the Chiyi Bridge after 2 1/2 hr (70 km) and continue for

1 1/2 hr (42 km) to Shiquanhe (Ali), the capital of West Tibet.

SHIQUANHE

Sited at the junction of the Indus (Shiquanhe) and Gar rivers, this new town, built by the Chinese, administers the vast region of western Tibet. Dusty Shiquanhe (commonly called Ali) is the only shopping center for hundreds of kilometers. It is a surprisingly good place for stocking up on food supplies, eating, and relaxing in reasonable comfort before heading south to Mt Kailash or north to Kashgar.

Food and lodging The Ali Hotel is nice enough, with a bed in a four-bed room for Rmb 10 per night. The staff might insist on FEC. The toilets are outside, left of the main building. Cold showers exist but are normally locked. Reportedly, hot showers can be had at the government compound in front of the Tibetan hotel. Electricity comes on around dusk and stops at midnight. The only Public Security Bureau to deal with foreigners is in the Ali Hotel; its officers are usually friendly. Ali's PSB has in the past arranged rides with trucks to the Kailash region for reasonable rates (Rmb 30–50). The Tourist Corporation, next to the PSB office in the hotel, rents an expensive Landcruiser (Rmb 3 per km). Enquire about a much cheaper Beijing jeep.

The government guest house has 20–30 rooms in a large compound. Each room is heated with a coal stove. A restaurant next to the main building of the Ali Hotel serves excellent Sichuanese food. Between May and October, an outdoor market sells delicious Uighur bread cooked in a stone oven. A Uighur bakery is down the street towards the bridge and

Shiquanhe (Ali)

to Xinjiang

cinema · playing field · government office · Public Security Bureau · truck stop · Ali Hotel

to Lhasa

post office · Xinhua Bookstore · department store (top floor tea room) · tourist office

Moslem bakery · Ali Guest House

shops · mail truck depot

school

to Purang, Zanda Xian

Indus River

truck stop

in the area are tasty, cheap shish kebabs. Just before the Uighur food stalls on the left is a dumpling and noodle restaurant with thick bread. Fresh fruit (especially the renowned Hami melons) and vegetables are available in the outdoor market near the stalls. A well-stocked store is nearby on the main road (smaller ones are scattered about town).

For rides to Xinjiang or the Kailash region, simply ask truck drivers. Trucks in front of the Ali Hotel generally go to Xinjiang and those on the river bank next to the market generally go to Lhasa or the Kailash region. Expect to pay about Rmb 50–200 to get to Kashgar and Rmb 20–80 for the trip south to Darchen (Mt Kailash) or Purang.

Longjiu Geothermal plant Most of the electrical power for Shiquanhe and neighboring villages comes from this plant, 30 km from town. Small holes drilled 80 m deep tap the energy source; powerful jets of steam shoot 40 m in the air. There are hot springs and a nearby river spawns large fish.

ROUTES OUT OF SHIQUANHE

Three main routes leave Shiquanhe. The first goes north to Yecheng and Kashgar, in Xinjiang province; the second returns to Lhasa; and the third goes south to the former Kingdom of Guge, Mt Kailash, and Purang.

1. Yecheng and Kashgar

Considerable traffic goes between Shiquanhe and Yecheng during most of the year. Expect to wait some days to make all the arrangements or for a vacant seat. The blue, vintage Russian trucks driven by Uighurs are usually a good bet. License plates of trucks going to Yecheng and Xinjiang begin with the numbers 87-50 and 27-66. Local trucks (West Tibet) have plates that start at 23-60.

The route

(All timings based on a Chinese truck) The dirt road to Yecheng and Kashgar goes north from near the market (two windmill generators are on the left). The first stretch is a desolate area devoid of habitation. After 3 1/2 hr (147 km) reach a road junction. The left fork goes to Rutok Xian, the right to Yecheng.

Rutok Xian and its pre-historic rock carvings

Rutok Xian, 10 km from the junction, is worth exploring. The Jesuit priest Andrade established a mission here in the beginning of the 17th C., the second one in West Tibet after Tsaparang. In the vicinity are ancient petroglyphs (see page 980) that resemble those of Gilgit and Ladakh. Rutok's fort once stood on a low hill above the village and four monasteries were sited in the area: Sharje, Lhakhang, Marpo, and Nubradan. 15 km away is the great Pangong Tso, a slender lake that measures 170 km from east to west. In most places it is only 5 km wide. Half the lake is in Ladakh, India, and half in Tibet. Another small lake 4 km north of Rutok teems with wildlife and is a place of pilgrimage. On its northeast shore is Kalpi Mai, a site so hot that the ground smokes and wood ignites if placed on it.

From the junction the road goes north (along Pangong Tso's eastern shore) to reach the village and military camp of Dorma after 4 hr (149 km). Dorma, in a long narrow valley, has two guest houses; one provides food and lodging specifically to the Xinjiang–Tibet traffic. After Dorma the landscape becomes more striking, with velvety colors dominated by subtle sheens of green, pale browns, and purple. In 4 hr (136 km), reach the Tibet–Xinjiang border at a pass marked with a plaque. Below is a beautiful blue lake with snow mountains in the background. The road now descends from Tibet's high plateau to the Aksai Chin, a disputed territory between India and China. Lake Aksai Chin is west of the road. Reach Dahongliutan in 5 hr (203 km), then Mazar (Chinese compounds and barracks), in another 253 km, by following the Yecheng (Yarkand) River Gorge. A small compound next to the militia on the right side of the road has a guest house and serves noodles. A side road just before the village turns sharply right to Yecheng.

K2 base camp

The main road from Mazar leads for 35 km to a junction with a side track turning sharply left. (Another side road turns to the right 26 km from Mazar; ignore it.) This dirt track goes to Pakistan and India. About 55 km after the turnoff, reach a point only 25 km northeast of K2 (8611 m), the world's second highest mountain. Glaciers and spectacularly high mountains surround the area, the heart of Chinese Karakoram. Eric Shipton in 1936 wrote of K2's north face in *Blank on the Map*:

... nothing interrupted my view of the great amphitheater about me. The cliffs and ridges of K2 rose out of the glacier in one stupendous sweep to the summit of the mountain, 12,000 feet above. The sight was beyond my comprehension, and I sat gazing at it, with a kind of timid fascination, watching wreaths of mist creep in and out of corries utterly remote.

Mazar Daria, a small village along the track, is a place to hire camels to carry equipment. Pay about Rmb 10 per day per camel. The camel driver costs Rmb 5 or less per day. Reach K2 Base Camp in four–five days of walking along the Surukwat River from the Mazer Daria River. The route: pass Ilik to reach the Surukwat Gorge. From here, ascend to the Aghil Pass (4875 m), then descend to the Shaksgam River canyon, 300 m below. Cross the river and continue on its far bank to the Shaksgam–Sarpo Laggo confluence. The K2 Base Camp of Suget Jangel (3800 m) is nearby, with gorgeous views of the peak. The advance base camp is a further two-day hike (camels cannot go from the base camp to the advance base camp).

This road now climbs a steep, narrow gorge to one of China's highest road passes, the unforgettable Chiragsaldi (4970 m). Descend to a long, narrow river valley. Finally, small desert towns with extensive irrigation channels and stately poplars appear. It is 6 hr (249 km) from Mazar to Yecheng.

Yecheng

The guest house for trucks originating from Tibet is 8 km before the town, next to the main road. (Travelers heading south to West Tibet should stay here and look for transportation.)

A gracious solid place, it is a welcome change from the hovels along the way. Beds cost about Rmb 5. A paved road leads to the center of Yecheng, the first since leaving the streets of Lhasa. The guest house manager will help arrange a lift to Yecheng. The government guest house at the centre of town is around the corner from the bustling bazar. Tourists are likely to be put in the expensive wing, with its fixtures, cupboards, and dressers straight out of the 1940s. The bazaar in Yecheng is wonderful, a small paradise after the austerity of Tibet. This Uighur town of about 200,000 people has a minority Chinese population.

Kashgar

There is a daily early morning bus from Yecheng to Kashgar. Buy the ticket the day before to assure a seat. The 249-km route on a paved road in the middle of the desert passes surprisingly large areas of irrigated fields. Go through the large towns of Shache (Yarkand, 24 km from Yecheng) and Yingjisha (Yangi Hissar, 124 km from Shache) before Kashgar. The bus arrives at Kashgar around 1600.

Lodging At the station, donkey or horse carts go to various hotels. The Xin Binguan, with extensive grounds and hot showers, is 1/2 hr out of town. Another guest house, closer to the center, is behind the main square. It was formerly the British Mission in Kashgar, known as Chini Bagh (Chinese Garden). Eric Shipton, the mountaineer and author, was the consul here from 1940–42. Rooms for budget travellers are on the left side of the compound.

2. Lhasa

The 6–10 day trip from Shiquanhe to Lhasa costs at least Rmb 200 per person on a truck and might take days to organize. Walk around town and talk to drivers of trucks or jeeps. (See page 945)

3. Tsaparang, Tholing, Mt Kailash, and Purang

The Kingdom of Guge, with its ruined capital of Tsaparang and its principal monastery of Tholing, is not on the direct route from Shiquanhe to Mt Kailash. Due to its spectacular archeological relics (see pages 425, 430), it is well worth a detour. Hitching out of Shiquanhe to Guge and Kailash is difficult. Arrange a ride in town with truck drivers.

Hitchhiking Exit the town on the main road, cross the bridge over the Indus, and start hitching. Tell any driver you want to go to Zanda (Tholing), a distance of 253 km. Some 40 km west of Shiquanhe, cross the Luma Bridge and continue for 71 km to Gar (Gargunsa). In another 25 km, reach Nabru and follow the turnoff, away from the Gar River Valley that is flanked in the east by the Kang Tise range. Head southwest to Zanda, a district seat, where it is easier to catch a ride back to Shiquanhe or to the main road and on to Mensi and Barga (Kailash).

A. To Tholing (Zanda Xian) and Tsaparang 8 1/2 hr

(Timings based on a Beijing jeep)
The first part of the journey requires leaving the Shiquanhe (Indus) Valley and turning south to an immense corridor that trends from northwest to southeast. Sandwiched between the Kang Tise range and the mountains of Ladakh and Zanskar, it extends over 300 km from near Shiquanhe to Mt Kailash and Lake Manasarovar. There are few settlements after Shiquanhe.

Gar and Gartok

Pass the small village of Gar (Gargunsa) on the right 111 km from Shiquanhe. It was once the winter capital of West Tibet. The summer capital was Gartok (Garyersa), 60 km further south. These two settlements administered a gigantic region and were loosely controlled by Lhasa by the stationing of two officers. There were four provinces in West Tibet: Rutok, Purang (Taklakot), Dawa, and Tsaparang. Before the Chinese takeover, Gartok was the most important center in West Tibet and every year it held a huge fair in late September. Merchants from all over Tibet and from India (mainly Almora, Garhwal, and Ladakh) came here to sell their goods. The *pashmina* goat in this region is world-famous. Its soft undercoat provides *pashma* wool for shawls and the clothing industry in Kashmir. A small Gelugpa monastery here was under the jurisdiction of Tholing. The village 25 km south of Gar is Nabru, where the road to Zanda forks right and crosses tributaries of the Gar River to reach the valley's western side.

Alternative routes

An alternative road to Zanda begins farther south from Gartok. It crosses the high Bogo La (5900 m) to Dongbo and Zanda. Another, a new road built in the mid-eighties, branches from the Shiquanhe–Kailash–Purang road at a point 14 km south of Gartok (70 km north of Mensi) to go to Zanda. The turnoff is at the large army camp of Song Sha (Sung Sarga). From here it is 200 km west to Tholing via a low pass over the Ladakh range. Most drivers choose this route to reach the Kingdom of Guge.

Cross the Ayi La (5610 m), then the Laoche La (5250 m), to descend to the great Satlej River Valley. Two hours before Zanda (Tholing), enter an amazing canyon system. Lama Govinda, in *The Way of the White Clouds* wrote of this area:

> The mountain scenery is more than merely a landscape. It is architecture in the highest sense. It is of awe-inspiring monumentality, for which the word 'beautiful' would be far too weak. . . Whole mountain ranges have been transformed into rows of gigantic temples with minutely sculpted cornices, recesses, pillared galleries, bundles of bulging cones, intersected by delicate ledges, crowned with spires, domes, pinnacles, and many other architectural forms... How the wonders of this Tibetan canyon country, covering hundreds of square miles, could have remained unknown to the world is almost as surprising as seeing them with one's own eyes.

Near Tholing, on top of a ridge on the right, are the ruins of a castle that blend so well into this fantasy landscape it is nearly impossible to tell the structure is man made. Cross the Satlej on a modern bridge and soon reach Zanda.

Zanda Xian (Tholing) 3660 m

Zanda Xian is on the left (south) bank of the Satlej River Valley. An old *chörten* and caves dug out of the soft clay are right of the road. Reach the new part of town first; a side road

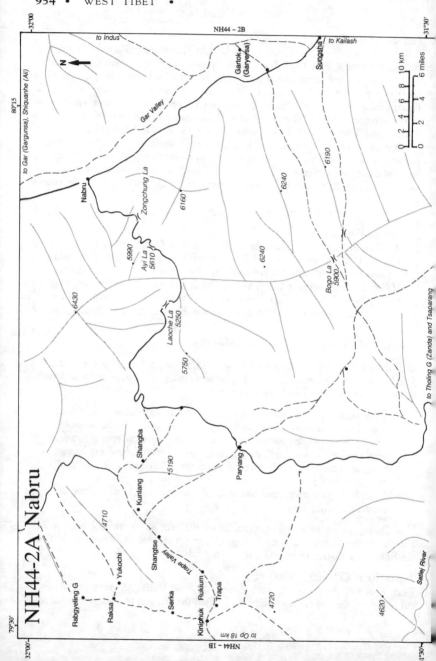

to the right leads to the guest house and local government compounds. The guest house has a few rooms, each with a wood stove (Rmb 3 per bed). A restaurant is down the road past a military compound. At an intersection, further down the side road, is a one-story store. Across the street, along another side road, is a clinic with Chinese doctors. At the intersection, turn left to reach Tholing Monastery which is within the town.

Zanda Xian (Tholing)

school Tholing Monastery — shop — government office — communal kitchen — Public Security Bureau — shop — post office — bank — guest house — truck stop — to Tsaparang — to Shiquanhe — Indus Bridge

Tholing Monastery

Tholing was West Tibet's most important monastery. It was built c.1020 by Rinchen Zangpo who, together with Atisa from India, led the revival of Buddhism in the country. For a discussion of Tholing, see page 425.

Tholing to Tsaparang For the route to Tsaparang and a description of the Guge capital, see page 430.

B. From Zanda Xian to Mt Kailash

Zanda to Mensi 8 hr (Timings based on a slow Beijing jeep)

From Zanda, drive back across the Satlej Bridge. After 1 1/2 hr, leave the amazing canyon country and reach a fork with a signpost. Three names are given: Ba'er, Zanda, and Shiquanhe. The new road to Ba'er goes to the southeast; follow it. This is a short cut to Mensi. Pass a military camp, then another junction and signpost 5 hr (120 km) from the first Ba'er signpost. Three options are here: Ba'er, Shiquanhe, and Purang. Take the road towards Purang, a major town near the borders of Nepal and India, 104 km south of Mt Kailash. Reach Mensi after 1 1/2 hr (60 km) on a bad, bumpy road. This desolate place administers the Mensi coal mines, 20 km to the northeast, and is an appropriate place to break the journey to Kailash. A compound has a comfortable guest house with large rooms, sofas, and coal stoves. Food is available at another compound.

Options from Mensi

• **Mensi to Tholing Monastery along the Satlej River** This 125-km footpath along the Satlej contains some of Tibet's most fascinating villages and monasteries and is of significant archeological and cultural interest (see page 970, day 7).

• **Mensi to Tirthapuri** For a description of this important pilgrimage site, see page 961.

• **Mensi to Mandi** A road from Mensi leads due south over two passes to Mandi (Gyanima Mandi), 45 km away. This was the biggest market in western Tibet. Wool, sheep, yaks, and hides were traded with Bhotia merchants of the Indian borderlands (Almora, Garhwal)

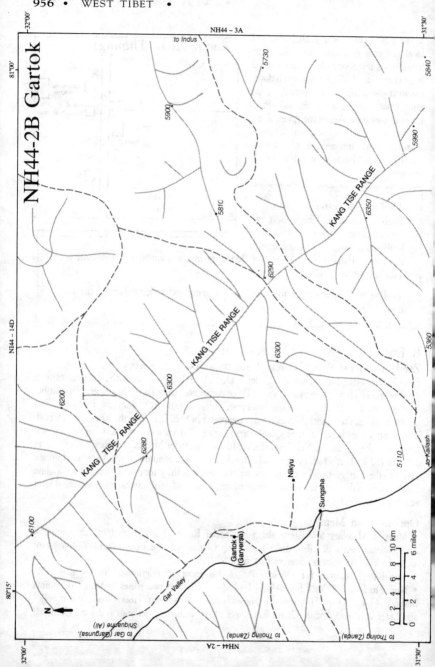

for cloth, utensils, and other Indian commodities. The trading took place between May and October. Purang (Taklakot) was the second biggest market; a brisk trade between Nepalese and Tibetans still goes on today.

• **Mensi to Darchen (base of Mt Kailash) 2 1/2 hr**

From Mensi, the road continues southeast along the flat Gar River Valley with the Kang Tise range on the left. After 1 hr the dramatic snow cone of Mt Kailash rises from the brown mountains that ring its base. On the right (southwest) is the massive mountain, Gurla Mandhata (7728 m). Tibetans call it Memo Nani. This magnificent peak rises sheer from the plains and the entire massif is unobstructed from the road. In the foreground is Lake Raksas Tal and beyond are the Nepalese mountains of Api (7130 m), Nampa 6746 m), and Saipal (7034 m). Reach the village of Barga in another hour (71 km from Mensi). It is a sheep center and an important stop on the Xinjiang–Lhasa Highway (south route). From Barga to Darchen along a dirt track is 10 km. Another dirt track about 10 km before Barga leads left towards Mt Kailash. Take this (easy for a jeep) for 1/2 hr to the small village of Darchen (4600 m) at the southern base of Mt Kailash. This is the beginning and end of the Mt Kailash *khora*. For a detailed description of the pilgrimage route, see page 273.

C. Mt Kailash to Purang (Taklakot) 2 3/4 hr

From Barga, a road goes south between lakes Manasarovar (Mapham) and Raksas Tal (Lhanak) to Purang Xian (2 3/4 hr, 104 km). This substantial administrative center is only 19 km from the Indian border at the Lipu Lekh Pass. Interesting places in the Purang area include Tanga (a great Nepalese market), Korja Monastery, Simbiling Monastery (ruined), cave dwellings, the cave village of Gukung. Some sites along the route:

Gurla La Pass (5120 m)

Reach the pass 1 1/4 hr from Barga. The ascent from the lakes is gradual and the pass is marked with cairns and prayer flags. The Gurla Mandhata (Memo Nani) Massif is on the left (southeast) and to the south is a stretch of high mountains. In the north are sacred lakes with Kailash in the background.

Toyo

This village, 5 km before Purang, is known for its ruins of Zorawar Singh's tomb. In the first half of the 19th C., this Dogra general from Jammu conquered Ladakh. In 1841 he went from Leh into West Tibet, pillaging and destroying villages and monasteries all the way to Purang. Tibetans, with the help of the Chinese, ambushed and killed Zorawar Singh at Toyo. Despite the invasion, the general is well respected for his courage, and locals have erected a *chörten* in his honor.

Purang

Taklakot is the old Nepalese name for this town on the banks of the Karnali River. The town's two main parts are separated by a ravine and aqueduct. The first part is older and consists mostly of walled compounds on the right side of the main road. A guest house is in one of these and a couple of stores are inside a compound across the street. From the guest house, a path leads down to a suspension bridge. Here, a small tent market sells beer, utensils, clothing, and goods from China and Nepal. It is very active in the summer. Purang's

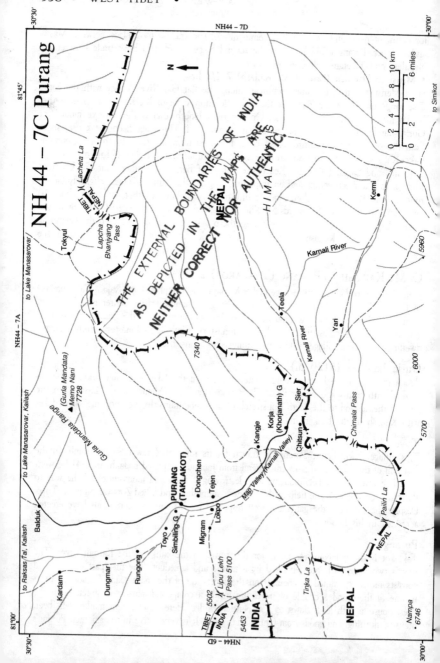

second section is a 20-min walk along the main road, past the ravine and aqueduct. The main government compound is on the right; across the street from it is a military camp. A government guest house in the compound is nicer and more expensive than the guest house at the other end of town. The road continues south for 15 km to Korja (Khojarnath) Monastery (see below).

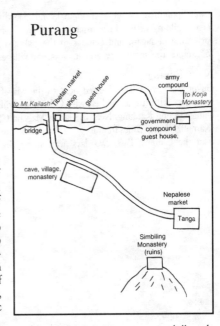

Tanga (Pilitanga)

Begin the 1/2-hr walk to this bustling Nepalese market from the first part of Purang. Cross the suspension bridge and immediately ahead is a village made up of caves and small houses. Farther along the path are old, whitewashed houses built into a cliff. More cave dwellings are higher up and within a complex is Tsegu, a cave temple marked by prayer flags and a wooden bal-cony, nine storys above the base of the cliff. This was the home of Sudhana, the protagonist of the Buddhist epic *Gandhavyuha Sutra*.

The path rounds a bluff to reveal the ruins of Simbiling Monastery on a hill to the right. It was the largest monastic institution in the region. Below the ruins is a small plateau with some 50 roofless stone houses, built closely in a maze-like manner; some have canvas coverings. This is Tanga, a market where traders from Nepal and India have come for centuries, though now only Nepalese merchants are allowed access. This amazing, active place has wonderful scenes of bargaining and interaction between Nepalese (mostly from Darchula) and Tibetans. Yaks, donkeys, and goats abound. The traders come here by crossing the Tinka, Langa and Yangri passes during the summer. The Tinka, main point of access from Nepal, is less than a day's walk away and nearly every day in the summer, mule caravans bring cloth, incense, cane sugar, rice, household utensils, and many other items. (The adjacent Lipu Lekh Pass is the traditional route to Mt Kailash for Indian pilgrims.) Tibetans in turn trade wool, rock salt, tea, borax, and Chinese manufactured goods. The busiest months are July and August and these are wonderful times to be here. Some of the Nepalese speak good English as well as Tibetan. The houses of Tanga have no roofs because the Younghusband treaty of 1904 between British India and Tibet specifically prohibited them. Across the river are several interesting-looking villages.

Korja Monastery

This monastery is at the centre of Korja, a pretty village 15 km southeast of Purang by the banks of the Map Chu (Karnali) River. Between Purang and here are several delightful villages of handsome, well-crafted Tibetan houses. About ten monks hold regular services in a well-appointed chapel with original, undamaged murals. Across a square is the monastery's larger building with a huge assembly hall and high ceilings. Korja was founded by Khor, an early king of Ngari, and belongs to the Sakyapa. This is a beautiful place; set aside time to explore the monastery and its adjacent village.

Near Purang

Gukung, a cave village located next to the Map Chu, 1 km from Tanga, has a three-story monastery within one of the caves. Other cave villages in the area are Garu, Doh, Ringung, Dungmar, and Kardung. Near the last is Mapcha Chungo, traditional source of the Map Chu (Karnali). Water issues from a spring that flows into the river below. The actual glacial source is at the Lampiya Pass, two days' walk from here.

TIRTHAPURI:
THE THIRD MAJOR PILGRIMAGE
SITE IN WEST TIBET

Tirthapuri is considered the third most holy pilgrimage site in West Tibet, after Mt Kailash and Lake Manasarovar. Sanctified by Guru Rinpoche and his consort, Yeshe Tsogyal, it is known for medicinal hot springs and a geyser. Both Hindus and Buddhists make obligatory stops here and the pilgrimage to Mt Kailash is considered unfinished if this site is not visited. From May to October, pilgrims congregate to complete a ritual circumambulation around the ridge and to dig for sacred relics (*jinlab*) within the earth. The temple of Tirthapuri, consecrated to the goddess Dorje Phagmo, is on the *khora* path.

Access: Mensi on the Ali–Purang road
Tirthapuri is situated on the right bank of the Satlej River approximately 10 km from Mensi (see page 955), itself 71 km northwest of Barga (near Darchen and Mt Kailash) on the Ali (Shiquanhe)–Purang road. At Mensi, next to the main road, is a dirt road heading south. Follow it to a T-intersection (7 km from Mensi). Head left at the T and proceed for another 3 km to the pilgrimage site of Tirthapuri. (Map reference NH44-2 D)

Topo Mopo On arrival at Tirthapuri, on the right, is an open area where pilgrim trucks parked. Here is Topo Mopo, consisting of a series of white and red limestone terraces. A geyser at the top spouts hot water which cascades down the terraces; it is believed to have powerful healing properties. Pools at the bottom have varying temperatures and pilgrims immerse themselves for ritual ablution. White mineral deposits are prized as sacred relics (see below).

The pilgrimage route around Tirthapuri
The circumambulation of Tirthapuri takes about 1 hr but spend more time to linger at sacred caves and a monastery. From Topo Mopo, turn left up a small ridge called Sindura. Halfway up is a terrace and the cemetery (*durtrö*) of Tsogyal Durtrö, consecrated to Yeshe Tsogyal. Clothing and belongings of the dead are left here. Beyond is a trail junction; the right branch is a short-cut down to Tirthapuri Monastery, the left continues to the top of the ridge.

> **Jinlab Sa Ngarmo Sa Kyurmo** Along the short cut is Jinlab Sa Ngarmo Sa Kyurmo ('Blessed Sweet and Sour Earth') where large holes have been dug out along the slopes. These have been created over the centuries by pilgrims, who take the earth home as a relic and as medication.

Continue up the ridge. The top has good views of the Satlej River. A *lhatse* and prayer flags mark the spot. Pock holes on the ground some distance away were also the handiwork of pilgrims who dug out this orange earth (*sindura*) to bring home as blessed substance. Descend to Tirthapuri Monastery by following the pilgrim path and pass another cemetery on the way.

Netsab Nga   Near the cemetery, overlooking the chapel, are five *rangjung* (self-manifesting) earth *chörtens* that represent the Five Sacred Mountains (Kailash, Kawa Karpo, Tsari, Jago Phungpo Ri of Bodh Gaya, and Bönri). They are known collectively as the Netshab Nga (the Five Representation of Pilgrimage Sites).

TIRTHAPURI MONASTERY

Before the Kazakh invasion of 1941, this important monastery was attached to Hemis in Ladakh. It has been completely rebuilt since the Cultural Revolution. The chapel, constructed on the slopes of the ridge, is reached through a courtyard. Within the assembly hall on the ground floor is the main image of Sakyamuni flanked by Guru Rinpoche and his two consorts. These statues are new. The most sacred relics in the hall are two footprints (*shabje*) that belonged to Guru Rinpoche and Yeshe Tsogyal. A small Guru Rinpoche image is carved in rock at the back of the chapel. Behind the monastery is a meditation cell (*tsamkhang*), consecrated to the goddess Dorje Phagmo and used by Guru Rinpoche.

Dhikpa Karnak   Near the *tsamkhang* is a rock with a cavity that contains black and white pebbles. Known as Dhikpa Karnak ('Black and White Sin-testing Place'), pilgrims close their eyes and select a handful of stones. The proportion of the colors indicates their *karmic* state.

Farther along the *khora* path, a short distance from the chapel, is a big red rock said to resemble Shiva's *lingam*. At this point, either descend towards some ruined *chörtens*, then take a steep short cut to retreat caves near the base of the ridge; or detour left to some *mani* walls and drop down to the river to reach the caves. Near the *chörtens* are *chörten*-like rocks considered to originate spontaneously from deep within the earth. These are among Tirthapuri's most significant objects of power.

Before the caves is a life-size color painting on a rock. After passing the first three caves (above the path) look out for two sets of twin caves (not easily seen). The first two were occupied by Guru Rinpoche when he meditated on Shinje (Lord of Death) and then by Milarepa. Later, his consorts, Mandarawa and Yeshe Tsogyal, also stayed here. Since that time no women have been allowed to meditate in these caves. In one, along the back wall, is a hollow where pilgrims have deposited offerings. The walls are thickly covered with black soot. The next set of twin caves is called the Sindura Drubphuk. Innumerable pilgrims have gouged out pockets of earth with crude implements (animal horns) to obtain a powdery, yellowish substance (*sindura*). It supposedly facilitates one's after-death journey (*bardo*) towards a higher state of rebirth. It is also mixed with medicinal herbs to make magical pills. These are deposited within statues or ingested as medicine.

Farther along the low ridge is a cave with a walled entrance. A gully separates this ridge from the next, which has more caves. Another set of twin caves, on a cliff face, have walled enclosures outside their entrances. These were used by the lamas, Khyirepa and Rechungpa, important disciples of Milarepa. Two nuns from Gerze occupy Rechungpa's cave, the larger of the two. Then come to another walled cave once used by Guru Rinpoche. It is usually locked. A rock next to the path has the *rangjung* image of Jambala, God of Wealth. Beyond a cave with a wide, walled opening is a rock with a shaft through the middle, said to be created by Guru Rinpoche's arrow when he subdued a demon. Another tradition ascribes its creation to Yeshe Tsogyal during the consecration of the hot spring. Pilgrims make offerings of butter and coins here and believe the rock can expedite the granting of wishes.

> **Jangsem Karma**
> Reach the walls of a ruined retreat center. Behind them is a cave with rocks tinged in red and white. These colors represent the discharge (mucus) from the nostrils of an enlightened person and are considered a sure indication of *bodhisattva*-hood. The discharge is called Jangsem Karma; according to local tradition, the colored rocks here are manifestations of the Jangsem Karma of Mandarawa and Yeshe Tsogyal.

Continue along the river to return to the open area and the Topo Mopo hot spring.

PELDHUNG CHUTSEN ('RELICS FROM THE HOT SPRING')

Pilgrims come to Tirthapuri in droves to look for *ringsels*, pearl-like mineral deposits. Tibetans hold that these rare objects are best found near hot springs and they search diligently for them in both the water and the nearby earth, particularly on auspicious dates like the full moon. Once found, the authenticity of a *ringsel* is tested by its attraction to a statue made up of the *li* metal. If deemed genuine, it is swallowed and remains in the body until the person is traumatized by disease or injury. It then extrudes through the wound to cleanse the passage and cure the malady. The *ringsel* is re-swallowed, but to insure the relic's perpetual purity, it must never come into contact with dead bodies or menstrual blood. It is believed that *ringsels* can replicate spontaneously. The white salt-like deposit found around the hot spring is called Kangri Chu Kyugang. Considered an essence distilled from water, it becomes a potent antidote to harm when mixed with herbs and minerals. Diverse magical substances with unusual powers are found at Tirthapuri and every visiting pilgrim wishes to take home some. They believe luck and karma will determine the richness of their find. Nowadays, local Tibetans collect sacred rocks, earth, and plants and sell them to devotees.

UPPER SATLEJ RIVER: CANYON COUNTRY FROM LAKE MANASAROVAR TO THOLING MONASTERY

Visits to the forgotten cave-cities of the Guge kingdom

Location	West Tibet
Map reference	NH44-7 A, 44-2 C D, 44-1 B D
Trekking days	17 (one-way)
Start–Finish	Chiu Monastery (Lake Manasarovar)–Tholing Monastery (Zanda Xian)
Passes	Ninchung, Tsaldot, Münto Mangbo, Shangtso

OVERVIEW

Virtually unvisited monasteries still exist along the Satlej, the great river that flows from Mt Kailash in West Tibet to India. Some were built by the translator, Rinchen Zangpo, leader of Buddhism's revival in the 11th C., and founder of celebrated Tholing Monastery. Others have substantial cave dwellings once occupied by monks and laymen. At Mangnang and upper Tholing, subterranean passages link chapels and residences elaborately carved from cliffs that border the canyons. Today, most of these religious sites are in ruins, destroyed over time by erosion and neglect. Surprisingly, these have generally escaped the wanton ravages that occurred in the Cultural Revolution.

Although in decline, centers like Mangnang, Dawa Dzong, and Khyunglung are fascinating places to explore. Khyunglung, in particular, is one of the most sacred pilgrimage sites for Bönpo adherents, the place of genesis for the pre-Buddhist sect. With its amazing cave temples and castled ruins, it is a powerful, striking place, widely believed to be the capital of Shangshung, an ancient, independent kingdom. The region was conquered by Tibet in 645 and has since become one of three provinces of Western Tibet (Ngari Khorsum). Remnants of megalithic construction and unusual circular structures, perhaps hermitages of ancient Bönpos, still stand. Nearby is the cave colony of Pangtha.

Ruined Mangnang Monastery, sited near the end of this trek, is, according to Tucci the Tibetologist, 'a monument of outstanding importance in the history of art'. Here, some decades earlier, he saw beautiful murals painted in the 11th C. by Kashmiri artists. Tholing Monastery, principal shrine of the Guge kingdom, was the most magnificent temple in West Tibet. Early murals executed in the rare and wondrous Kashmiri style still survive (see page 425).

The strenuous 17-day trek along the Satlej River begins at Chiu Monastery, on the shores of sacred Lake Manasarovar, and ends at Tholing Monastery. It goes through an isolated region with few inhabited settlements. Even nomads are rare. During the first days the path

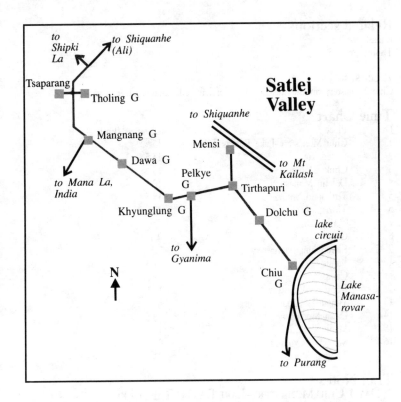

to Shipki La

to Shiquanhe (Ali)

Tsaparang

Tholing G

Satlej Valley

Mangnang G

to Shiquanhe

Mensi

Dawa G

to Mana La, India

Pelkye G

to Mt Kailash

Tirthapuri

Khyunglung G

to Gyanima

Dolchu G

lake circuit

N

Chiu G

Lake Manasarovar

to Purang

follows a flat section of the river valley, but later it periodically leaves the celebrated water course. For long stretches, the river flows through deep gorges with steep sides. It is thus necessary to follow a very irregular trail that snakes in and out between hills and cliffs, and numerous low passes near the banks of the river have to be negotiated. The route after Guru Gem and Khyunglung monasteries enters a maze of confusing canyons that twist and turn amidst blocks of table land, a gigantic, natural labyrinth. This area is absolutely without peers in Tibet. The natural environment is simply stupendous, and the closest thing to it is perhaps the Mustang Khola gorge between Kagbeni and Tsarong in Nepal. To reach Tholing, it is best to try and find a guide who knows the area well. Water can be scarce. Travel beyond Guru Gem in the summer is particularly onerous because of the monsoon rains that obliterate the trails. The swelling Satlej makes it virtually impossible to follow the banks of the river through its narrow gorges. Summer, however, is the ideal time to explore the canyons and monasteries of West Tibet; the temperature drops drastically during late autumn and winter. The best time to go is May and June or September and October (less rain). Avoid if possible July and August, the worst months for rains.

Related sections
Kailash, p 273
Tholing, p 425

Access:
Chiu Monastery on the western shore of Lake Manasarovar (see page 617)

Time Chart

Day	Place	Distance (km)
1	Chiu Monastery–Lake Raksas Tal	15
2	Serlep Yung	13.5
3	Chukta Lungpa	13
4	Dölchu Monastery	10
5	Tirthapuri Shung	15.5
6	Tirthapuri	12
7	Gerik Yung	7.9
8	Camp	9.5
9	Khyunglung Monastery	7.5
10	Kande	21.3
11	Camp	19.8
12	Dongpo Monastery	11.5
13	Yungu Tsangpo	8
14	Dawa Monastery	18.5
15	Manlung Karla	13
16	Mangnang Monastery	9
17	Tholing Monastery	21

Trail Notes

✤ DAY 1 CHIU MONASTERY–LAKE RAKSAS TAL 15 KM
From Chiu Monastery, sited on the western shore of Lake Manasarovar, follow the north bank of the Nganga channel, which flows between lakes Manasarovar and Raksas Tal. The flat trail goes northwest to the northeastern corner of the latter; the area north of the lake is used in winter by the villagers of Barga for its excellent pastures.

✤ DAY 2 LAKE RAKSAS TAL–SERLEP YUNG 13.5 KM
Continue northwest across the Dama Chu, which is derived from the rivers draining the small subsidiary range south of the Topchen La (see page 985). Shortly thereafter, cross the Lha Chu, which forms the lower reaches of the Khaleb Chu (formed of two Kailash rivers: Lhachu from the west valley; and Topchen from the east). Then, 2 km before the campground of Serlep Yung (4585 m), cross a small, swampy depression; southeast of here are stagnant pools, the former bed of the Satlej. Serlep Yung is on the left side of this bed, a site with pools and a spring.

✤ DAY 3 SERLEP YUNG–CHUKTA LUNGPA 13 KM
For the first 5.3 km, go northwest along the left bank of the Satlej's old bed. The channel becomes increasingly distinct. Opening to the southwest are several ravines—all quite dry except

NH44 – 7A

to Barga to Barga to Purang

Satlej Valley

Chumersara

Chuiatol 5555

Chaldu camp

Amlang camp

Shinglabtsa La

Shinglabtsa camp

Ringtachu camp

Gyanima Chakra camp

Gyanima

THE EXTERNAL BOUNDARIES OF INDIA AS DEPICTED IN THE MAPS ARE NEITHER CORRECT NOR AUTHENTIC.

Langchen Tsangpo

to Gartok

Mandi camp

Tage camp

Lama Chujia camp

Chorten camp

Mingchin Chu

Chugar camp

Bhawiti camp

Silangtar camp

Khagia Sumna camp

Lampia Dhura La 5530

Mangsha Dhura La

TIBET

INDIA

Jinakhar camp

Liktsephu camp

Gunj Yankti

to Khyunglung G

Gomyachin camp

NH44 – 6D

Chilamkurkur 5145

Thazang camp

Tsom Buga camp

natural stone bridge

Talla Chaldu camp

Mingchin Chu

Shib Chu

Shib camp

Chilam camp

Lochambelki Chak camp

Chitchun ford

to Indus Valley

Shokhong camp

Dakar camp

Kanchego camp

Jankung camp

5700 Ghatamemin

Chitchun camp

TIBET

INDIA

Manum camp

INDIA

to Dongpo Gompa

Khumar camp

Bancha Dhura 5748

Bancha Dhura La

N

0 2 4 6 8 10 km
0 2 4 6 miles

INDIA

NH44-6B Gyanima

NH44 – 6A

31°00'

30°30'

30°30'

81°00'

80°15'

during the rainy season. To avoid these ravines, the trail goes northwest and leaves the Satlej on the left; the river begins to enter the Rongchung, first of many constricted gorges. The mountains south of the river are the Amar. (At this point, a side trail originating from Barga crosses the Satlej, goes up a ridge on the river's left bank and continues west to the campground of Ringtachu, then to Gyanyima Dzong, the junction of many trails.) Cross a flat ridge with a cairn, the Ninchung La (4645 m). Chukta Lungpa is on a tributary to the right of the river. Its small gorge burrows through the cliffs on the left to join the main river.

✤ DAY 4 CHUKTA LUNGPA–DÖLCHU MONASTERY 10 KM

The trail trends west-northwest to Dölchu Monastery on the right bank of the Satlej. Along the way it crosses a ridge and descends to the well-defined Chukta Kongma Valley, 1 hr from Chukta Lungpa. West of this, cross another small ridge to a plain to the south (low hills are to the north). The terrain falls southwards towards the Satlej, which cannot be seen here. The small Gelugpa monastery of Dölchu, a dependent of Tholing, sits on the flat slope of a hill near the Satlej, here a series of braided streams.

✤ DAY 5 DÖLCHU MONASTERY–TIRTHAPURI SHUNG 15.5 KM

The next stage of two days to the important monastery and pilgrimage site of Tirthapuri is considerably more difficult: the crossing of two tributaries of the Satlej, the Trokpo Shar and Trokpo Nub, can be treacherous. From Dölchu, the trail follows the south base of the hill to the river. (On its left bank are the tributary valleys of Sheri Namking and Charike Tangma.) It then crosses to the left bank and the river valley widens. Recross to the right to reach the mouth of a 50-m-wide tributary coming from the Kang Tise range. For the rest of the day follow the Satlej's right bank. From this point on, the river is much fuller and the trail confined to the floor of the valley. Cross another tributary coming from the right. Springs well up from the valley floor to drain into the Satlej, here divided into several channels. For a few km the river flows west-northwest. Its bed is 100–200 m wide between terraces (good pastures). Some 5 km from Tirthapuri Shung reach Mapcha Tibu, a red hill on the left. Near here the trail goes up along an eroded terrace and then descends back to the river. Opposite Tirthapuri Shung, the Tara Kungyok tributary enters the Satlej from the left.

✤ DAY 6 TIRTHAPURI SHUNG–TIRTHAPURI 12 KM

Beyond Tirthapuri Shung (1/2 km), the Satlej enters (to the northwest) a very narrow gorge with precipitous sides. The trail is forced to ascend the 50-m-high right terrace. At this point, the large Trokpo Shar River comes in from the north. It is divided into three channels (maximum depth 1 m). After this tributary, go up another 50-m terrace and cross two or three dry ravines. Beyond these is another tributary with two channels called Trokpo Nub, the western companion of the Trokpo Shar. From this river, the trail ascends another terrace and follows along it for some time. Pass stone cairns, *mani* piles, and small ravines. To the right are low hills and beyond them the snow mountains of the Kang Tise range. To the left, the Satlej, now a torrent, makes its way through a deep gorge tunneled out of solid rock.

Tirthapuri

The third most important pilgrim site in West Tibet (see page 961 for more details). Just before Tirthapuri (4345 m), the trail winds among low hills and slopes. The Drukpa Kagyü monastery of Tirthapuri is built on a terrace of white and reddish-yellow rocks; their distinctive

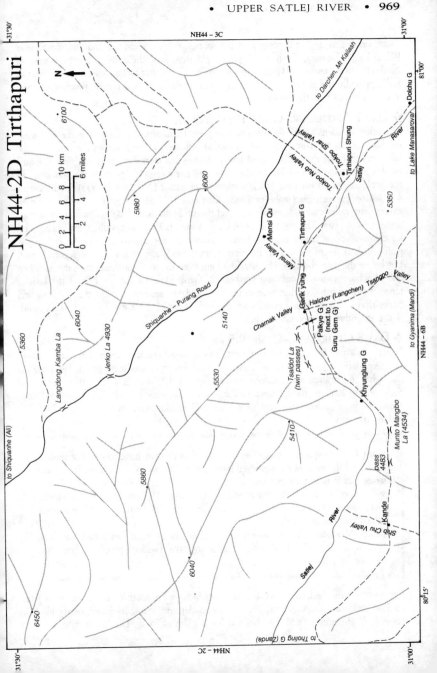

NH44 – 3C

NH44-2D Tirthapuri

N

to Darchen, Mt Kailash

to Shiquanhe (Ali)

to Thöling G (Zanda)

Langdong Kamba La

Jerko La 4930

Shiquanhe – Purang Road

Mensi Qu

Mensi Valley

Chamak Valley

Tsaldot La (twin passes)

Genk'yüng

Halchor (Langchen) Tsangpo Valley

Palkye G (next to Guru Gem G)

Tirthapuri G

Trakpo Nub Valley

Trakpo Shar Valley

Tirthapuri Shung

Satlej River

to Lake Manasarovar

Dolchu G

Khyunglung G

Munto Mangbo La (4534)

pass 4483

Kande

Shib Chu Valley

Satlej River

NH44 – 6B

to Gyanima (Mandi)

6100

6060

5980

5360

6040

5140

5530

5410

5860

6040

6450

5350

NH44 – 2C

31°30'

31°00'

31°30'

31°00'

81°00'

80°15'

10 km
0 2 4 6 8
6 miles
0 2 4 6

coloration due to sulphur deposits from hot springs. Below are *chörtens* and a *mani* wall over 100 m long. The name Tirthapuri is probably derived from the Sanskrit *pretapuri*, 'town of the dead'. It is the most sacred pilgrimage area in West Tibet after Kailash and Lake Manasarovar, and supposedly the place where spirits of the dead dwell. During certain times of the year it is possible to ford the Satlej here.

✤ Day 7 Tirthapuri–Gerik Yung 7.9 km

The valley broadens significantly downstream from Tirthapuri. Continue down the trail west-northwest along the base of the lowest eroded terraces, on the Satlej's right bank. To the left, parallel to the river, is a strip of lush pasture. 4 km from Tirthapuri, the river is joined by the 20-m wide Mensi Chu, coming from the northwest. (7 km from this junction, on the banks of the Mensi Chu, is the settlement of Mensi Qu (see page 955), an important way station between Shiquanhe or Zanda Xian and Mt Kailash.) At this point the Satlej, close to the valley's left side, heads west and the trail follows it along the base of the terrace across a large plain. The small village of Gerik Yung (4295 m) is a well-known campground for caravans. Some barley is grown here. Continue on the dirt road to the far end of the plain. A short distance below it, the river again enters a narrow gorge through a rock gate. Just before the gate, the large Halchor Chu joins from the south; it comes from the Minchen and Minchung valleys. North and northeast of Gerik Yung are the low hills of the Ladakh range. To the northwest, they become the main Ladakh range that divides the Garthang and Satlej rivers. Behind these low hills are the high peaks of the Kang Tise and to the south is the extensive Halchor Chu Valley.

✤ Day 8 Gerik Yung–Camp 9.5 km

Today's walk trends to the west-southwest. The up-and-down trail north of the river crosses two secondary ridges. From Gerik Yung, the trail first goes southwest past a low ridge on the right, and swamps and meadows with springs on the left. On a projecting spur of the Satlej are the Kardong ruins, former dwellings of the Guge royal family. Below them is Pelkye Monastery on a promontory. Next to it is Guru Gem Monastery, in a cliff facing the Satlej and its tributary.

Guru Gem Monastery Guru Gem, on the Satlej's right bank, consists of shallow caves and the ruins of the destroyed monastery built into an escarpment. Its red and white facade is easy to spot. A trail snakes up to the lone, roofless chapel. On the valley floor are impressive ruins testifying to a more vigorous monastic settlement. Guru Gem, a Bönpo haunt, had chapels that date back to the 11th C. and many ruined *chörtens* are in the vicinity.

Pelkye Monastery Pelkye (destroyed) is on the plain downstream from Guru Gem. Within the low ridge behind the chapels are cave dwellings populated from time to time by pilgrims.

Just west of here, the large Charnak Chu comes in from the north from the important Jerko La Pass straddling the watershed between the Satlej and Indus. Its water, nearly black in color, is divided into several branches and has a width of 75 m. The largest tributary so far is the Halchor, some distance back. At the Charnak–Satlej junction, the valley is broad and flat and the main river divided into several channels. The terrain begins to change: the trail now enters the fabled canyon country of West Tibet. Instead of mountain ranges, this landscape is distinguished by the vertical chasms that cut deep into the earth. Wade across the Charnak to its right bank to a large rock with ruins of *chörtens* (erected by the Bönpos) and chapels at its base. From this point on, the Satlej becomes much more difficult to follow as it enters the labyrinthine canyons. The trail by necessity climbs up and down the myriad gorges and at times is indistinct and difficult to follow. It is best to have a guide if you can find one.

Just beyond the broad valley, the Satlej again enters a narrow gorge and it becomes impossible to follow its banks during the summer. The trail therefore crosses two ridges on the right. About 2 km west of the Charnak–Satlej junction is the narrow Tsaldot Valley entrance. After this, the trail zigzags steeply among gravelly ravines to the Tsaldot La (4495 m). The sight of ridges and canyons as far as the eye can see is magnificent. Beyond the pass, the rocky trail keeps 200 m above the river and sometimes passes dangerous abysses. Go up to the second pass, also called Tsaldot La (4535 m). Descend for 300 m to a grassy campground through a labyrinth of ravines, ridges and valleys. Here the 60-m-wide Satlej emerges from its gorge. Ford here in the dry season to proceed along the left bank instead of the more difficult right.

✤ Day 9 Camp–Khyunglung Monastery   7.5 km

The trail heads to the southwest and follows the river's right bank fairly closely. At a small gorge, it descends to a narrow cornice in the solid rock, then goes up and down, in and out, along projecting spurs and into gorges. Progress along it is painfully slow. After this difficult section, descend to the river and go along the base of the right terrace. The Satlej becomes greatly constricted and the water is a rushing torrent with white-water rapids. A bridge at Khyunglung Monastery spans the 10-m-wide river. Soon the river again flows in a broad channel.

Khyunglung Monastery

Khyunglung Monastery (4259 m), located in a spectacular canyon of the Satlej, is built above the river's right bank on a terrace with fantastic, eroded sides. In the area are astonishing multi-hued cliffs of yellow, green, red, and white. Across the river are grassy flatlands and a village. The monastery (ruined) consists of two levels of castled structures, the upper about 200 m above the lower. Surrounding them are numerous cave dwellings. Below are several long rows of *manis* and red *chörtens*. Perched on the cliff tops are strange ruins of circular buildings that were perhaps ancient hermitages of Bönpos. Old *tsa-tsas* with Sanskrit inscriptions have been found here. Unlike their Buddhist counterparts, these ancient Bön temples are called *serkhangs*, not *lhakhangs*. Other chapels are Buddhist and perhaps date to the 16th century. Tall wooden columns crowned with carved capitals still stand among the rubble. About 2 km east of Khyunglung are more castle-like ruins built with large, white rocks instead of common clay bricks. These megalithic structures are unique in Tibet. After crossing the bridge to the left bank, come to some hot springs in lovely surroundings. Khyunglung

➠

was once a volcanic area; a huge mound of calcium deposits is the site of numerous cave dwellings. Downstream from the bridge are more chapel ruins. The village is some distance upstream.

This impressive area is considered the site of Shangshung, an ancient kingdom where the Bönpo sect originated. Once many villages filled this region. Historians tend to equate Shangshung with Guge, a post-7th-C. appellation. Shangshung in fact was a territory separate and distinct from Tibet and its language seems to belong to the Indo-European group. Khyunglung is still a major pilgrimage site of Bön. Although many Shangshung sages and saints are believed to have blessed the site, few Bönpos have lived here this century. Only after Khyungtrul Jigme Namkha Dorje (1897–1956) built Guru Gem did Bönpos return. This lama originally came from a rich family in Hor. After studying in the Bönpo monastery of Kharna (see page 766), he went on pilgrimage in 1917 to Bhutan, Nepal, Kinnaur, and other places, before establishing Guru Gem in this remote area. It became an important institution for Bönpos and Buddhists and he taught both Nyingmapa, and Bönpo doctrines. About 60 nuns and monks lived here when he died.

Pangtha About 20 km southwest of Khyunglung is the deserted cave colony of Pangtha, at the junction of the Sibchu and Tsumchu rivers, 8 km downstream from Sibchilim. Two terraces of a few hundred caves rise 100m above the river. A Sakyapa monastery with murals in the upper terrace once flourished in the 13th or 14th century Today, shepherds stay here in winter and early spring.

✤ DAY 10 KHYUNGLUNG MONASTERY–KANDE 21.3 KM
Follow the Satlej's left bank for 1 hr, passing a nomad camp. The gorge here is a tremendous sight with the powerful river forging its way between sheer cliffs. Several transverse valleys enter the main valley from both sides and freshwater springs make the valley swampy in places. Come to a point where the river again enters a narrow gorge with perpendicular cliffs. Ascend the ridges of the left bank to reach the flat saddle of Münto Mangbo La (4534 m). Here are cairns and a view of the Satlej Gorge but not the river itself. Descend gradually and pass a series of stone cairns. After the last one, drop down steeply to a deep valley, a left tributary of the Satlej. Follow this to its head and a second pass (4483 m), also marked by cairns. Beyond is another canyon and the trail leads down to its floor (4369 m) before climbing up to its top (marked by a cairn) along the left slopes. At this point the trail turns from west-southwest to southwest and follows a ridge between the canyons. The top of this ridge forms a level plain that falls imperceptibly to the Satlej. After walking along it for 2 km, reach another canyon with a substantial river, the Shib Chu (20 m wide), flowing from the south. Its lower reaches are joined by the Lunak, coming from the southwest. The combined waters then drain into the Satlej, now running northwestward through a narrow gorge. A campground on the Shib Chu's right bank is called Kande (4270 m).

✤ DAY 11 KANDE–CAMP 19.8 KM
The route today first goes west, then northwest, and finally north. Cross a terrace between the Shib Chu and its left tributary; a few ruined houses are on top. After descending from

the terrace, ford the clear tributary. The trail goes steeply up the canyon sides immediately after the crossing, and the Shib Chu Gorge with its near-vertical terraces is seen to the right. Continue to cross three more terraces and a tributary bed, then ascend a valley. Turn northwest to enter the large Sang Serpo Valley. On the left are more ridges and hills and from them emerges a broad tributary. Finally the trail veers to the north and the valley widens (it again narrows in the north).

✤ Day 12 Camp–Dongpo Monastery 11.5 km

Follow the Sang Serpo Valley (now narrow). Cross several small streams to where the valley turns right and broadens. The trail then leaves the floor to ascend some hills to the left. At the top, cross an eroded ravine to arrive at the edge of a deep valley. Descend its steep slopes to the northeast and north. A side valley from the right joins it and the combined valley turns west. Stone cairns, *manis*, and ruins of houses are encountered from time to time. From the left (south) one more side valley joins the main one; the route now veers to the north and north-northeast. The Satlej is some distance away to the north and cannot be seen. Descend steeply to the Gelugpa Dongpo Monastery (4081 m), above the Dongpo River. This is the largest monastery since those of the Kailash area. It once had a rich collection of *thangkas* painted in the Guge style (see page 55).

✤ Day 13 Dongpo Monastery–Yungu Tsangpo 8 km

From the monastery, the trail ascends steeply through a series of ravines and eroded channels between ridges to flat, open country. The general appearance of the flatland is deceptive, as it is crisscrossed by deep canyons that are southern tributaries of the Satlej. All have near-vertical sides and, to follow the great river, the route becomes a never-ending series of abrupt ascents and descents. Follow the trail northwest across three deep, dry channels. The last and the largest trends to the north-northwest. After them, reach the edge of the substantial Yungu Tsangpo Gorge, which is very similar to the Dongpo. Descend for 350 m to its floor (4068 m).

✤ Day 14 Yungu Tsangpo–Dawa Monastery 18.5 km

The first half of today's route goes west, the second turns to the northwest. From the canyon bottom, ascend two 25-m terraces to barley fields on the uppermost one. Beyond these, the grueling process of zigzagging up to the Tanga tableland begins. The top edge of the canyon is marked by a stone cairn. Pass a short, flat stretch then cross four or five eroded channels. After this tedious trek, the trail turns northwest and crosses four more channels. To the left is a deep valley, a branch of the large Dawa River, and to the right, a tributary to it. Beyond is Dawa Monastery (Gelugpa) on top of a terrace 100 m above the valley floor. Another group of ruined chapels is next to the old house of the Dzongpön (leader of the fort). This area is in the heart of the Guge kingdom.

Dawa Monastery

Large *chörtens* encircle the ruined monastery's three main buildings: the *dukhang*, the Jampa Khang, and the Lama Khang. The complex's oldest chapel is probably the ➠

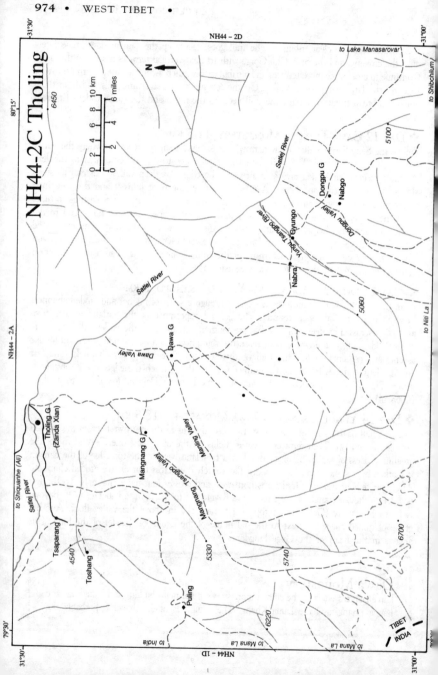

small one on a rock above the Dzongpön's house. Superb Guge-style murals representing the Eight Medicine Buddhas once adorned this place, as well as invaluable Indian statues, perhaps brought by pilgrims in the 10th century.

By the entrance of a side valley is the village of Dawa, surrounded by a stunning landscape of natural stone pyramids and cones, each separated from the next by a very narrow vertical cleft excised from the terraces. It is a phantasmagoric place of make-believe castles, towers, and crenellated walls, all chiselled into amazing shapes by rain and other elements. The *chörtens*, of typical West Tibet design and similar to those of Tholing, are outstanding. Lama Govinda wrote of the area in *The Way of the White Clouds*:

> . . . enchanted world of rock formations which had crystallized into huge towers, shooting up thousands of feet into the deep blue sky, like a magnetic fence around an oasis, kept green by the waters of springs and mountain brooks. A great number of these nature-created towers had been transformed into dwellings—nay into veritable sky-scrapers—by the people who had lived here many hundreds of years ago. They had ingeniously hollowed out these rock towers from within, honeycombing them with caves, one above the other, connected by inner staircases and passages, and lit up by small window-like openings. The center of a crest was crowned with temples, stupas, monasteries, and the ruins of ancient castles, whence one could get a beautiful view into the valley, bordered by phalanxes of towers rising up, row after row, like organ pipes and perforated by hundreds and hundreds of cave-dwellings and their windows.
>
> In ancient times, this strategic site of the Guge kingdom was the premier trading center on the Tibet–India route. Traders from Garhwar came regularly to barter for goods and attend a grand, annual fair.

To see a slightly lesser version of this, make the expedition to Luri monastery of Mustang, a Tibetan enclave in Nepal.

The trail steeply descends the right side of the tributary and crosses several channels. Ford the tributary and go up a ridge marked by a cairn. Descend steeply to the floor of the Dawa Valley and to the monastery. Here the river that eventually drains north into the Satlej is divided into several branches. The mountains to the south are the Hundes, those to the north the Chumurti.

✦ DAY 15 DAWA MONASTERY–MANLUNG KARLA 13 KM

The entire day consists of a series of strenuous ups and downs, across transverse canyons and eroded channels. From the monastery, the trail enters a side valley that leads to the southwest, west, and north-northwest. The last section begins in a gorge so narrow (2–3 m wide) that the slopes appear as tight, perpendicular walls. At the gorge's head is the Shangtso La, about 200 m above the Dawa Valley. The trail then enters an easier valley that drops north-northwestward. It is joined by another valley trending to the north-northeast. The trail follows the floor of the latter, then ascends to open, flat country. Cross two more tributaries

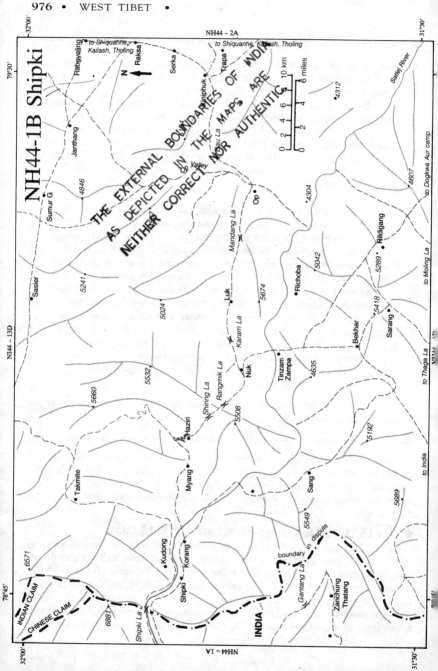

NH44 – 2A

NH44-1B Shipki

THE EXTERNAL BOUNDARIES OF INDIA AS DEPICTED IN THE MAPS ARE NEITHER CORRECT NOR AUTHENTIC

NH44-1D Mana La

of the Satlej. Within the valley of the second are ruins of houses and *chörtens* and barley fields. The next stretch goes through a maze of hills, each separated by steep ravines and eroded gullies. Cross another valley; it opens to the northeast but gradually veers to the left (north). Ascend on its far side to the top of a platform, then carry on to the next substantial valley of Manlung Karla. Within it is the Manlung Tsangpo, a river impossible to ford after heavy rains.

✤ DAY 16 MANLUNG KARLA–MANGNANG MONASTERY 9 KM

The first part of the walk goes west-northwest. From the Manlung Karla Valley, the trail climbs very steeply to the next platform. After 2 km, it again descends to the narrow Anggong Valley, which eventually joins the Mangnang Valley. The trail turns around a corner to proceed west-southwest. At this point, Mangnang Monastery, surrounded by a grove of poplars in a serene oasis can be seen. Beyond is the final push through the convoluted canyon country that lies between Mangnang and Tholing.

Mangnang Monastery

Mangnang, formerly a huge complex, has its largest group of chapels on a ridge overlooking the Mangnang River. The setting is unusual: the damaged site is on the level valley floor, not on the cliffs above. Reach them by crossing the valley to its far side and following the trail up. Castle ruins and red chapel walls dominate the valley. There is no sign of life. A labyrinthine network of passages links a multitude of subterranean chapels within the cliff face. Inside are remnants of paintings, stucco statues, and piles of discarded manuscripts. In the area are numerous cave dwellings.

Mangnang Village, near the bridge on the left bank, is surrounded by many fields. Inside the settlement are three ruined chapels that also belonged to the monastery. The two smaller ones are earlier. Tucci, the acclaimed Tibetologist, wrote that one had extremely rare paintings that belonged to the Kashmiri-Ajanta genre. A third chapel, built much later, is better preserved and retains late, poor quality paintings.

✤ DAY 17 MANGNANG MONASTERY–THOLING MONASTERY 21 KM

The route goes from north-northeast to northwest and drops 300 m from the Mangnang Valley to the banks of the Satlej at Tholing Monastery. Just below Mangnang, ascend three terraces, then cross several channels and flat hills. Finally reach a large, impressive, 300-m-deep canyon. The trail follows its edge for 2 km to a point where the slope becomes more gradual; descend the precipice here along a tortuous route through some of the most wonderful canyon country in West Tibet. Finally, the great Satlej appears once again. Tholing Monastery is on the left bank on a terrace 20 m above the river.

Tholing Monastery For details on this preeminent monastery, see page 425.

Tholing to Shiquanhe to Lhasa For a description of the trip from Tholing (Zanda Xian) to Shiquanhe, capital of West Tibet, and then back to Lhasa, see pages 952, 945.

RUTOK:
RECENTLY DISCOVERED
PREHISTORIC ROCK CARVINGS

The prehistoric petroglyphs (rock carvings) of Rimo Thang, Luri Langkar, and Karke Sangri, discovered in 1985 by Lhasa's Cultural Relics Institute, are all situated within Rutok Xian county. This is the first time such archeological finds have been reported in Tibet. These unique, substantial carvings cover a wide range of subjects and are important for the study of early nomadic culture. Rutok Xian is a small town 127 km north of Shiquanhe (Ali), the capital of West Tibet.

The sites
RIMO THANG CARVINGS, RISHUNG QU
Rishung Qu is 40 km south of Rutok Xian on the main Tibet–Xinjiang road (see page 950), and the rock carvings of Rimo Thang are 1.5 km southeast of Rishung Qu. West of these two places is a wide, marshy valley drained by streams that flow northwest to Maga Tsangpo River. The north–south trending valley, an ideal pasture, was perhaps a main traffic corridor in ancient times. Dorma Qu (see page 951), a short distance west of Rimo Thang and Rishung Qu, is also served by the Tibet–Xinjiang road. The name Rimo Thang comes from these carvings; *rimo* means 'picture' in Tibetan. Numerous carvings are scattered along the lower surfaces of 100-m cliffs. They vary in size from 0.3 to 12 sq m and each panel has from one to several dozen images. A piece of hard rock was first used to delineate the outline; subsequent careful chiselling make them stand out more boldly. In some cases, the enclosed surface area is similarly worked on. Rimo Thang has four main groups of carvings, each along one of the cliff faces. The first has 14 panels, the second 4, the third 12, and the last 5.

LURI LANGKAR CARVINGS, RUTOK QU
Rutok Qu is 20 km west of Rutok Xian and the Luri Langkar carvings are 12 km west of Rutok Qu. To their north is a secondary road that connects Rutok Qu with Chulung and Reju (65 km west of Rutok Xian). Flowing next to the road is the Chulung River; its north bank forms a wide pasture. The carvings run along six cliff faces on the north side of Luri Langkar, each no more than 4 m above the ground. They resemble those of Rimo Thang, but each panel has fewer individual images.

KARKE SANG CARVINGS, DORMA QU
Dorma Qu, on the Tibet–Xinjiang road, is 159 km northeast of Rutok Xian. The petroglyphs of Karke Sang are about 25 km south of Dorma Qu. In the neighborhood, trending north–south, are the wide, open Tapo pastures within which flow rivers that drain west into the Dorma Chu.

Three main groups of carvings are scattered along the west side of the Karke Sang ridge and within a cave halfway up the cliffs. Inside the large cave (25 m deep, 22m wide, and 12 m high) are several panels of rock paintings colored by mineral-based paints and depicting Buddhist subjects. These are of later vintage than the rock carvings, although earlier images can be seen beneath them.

The petroglyphs

North of Rutok Xian are the Kunlun Mountains and Xinjiang, to the west is Kashmir. The counties of Gar Xian and Gegye Xian are to the east. Most of this vast, mountainous territory, with many rivers and lakes, is over 4600 m. All three cliff sites containing rock carvings are situated on valley floors. Their grassy surroundings are flat and open, ideal for animal grazing. Many of the carvings are within 3 m of the ground; only some panels at Rimo Thang are carved on a slope and very few are 7 or 8 m above the ground.

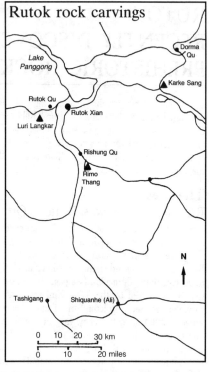

Rutok rock carvings

The Rutok petroglyphs depict people, sheep, yak, deer, wolf, dog, camel, fish, don-key, sun and moon, swastika, and reverse swastika. Subjects include nature, pre-Buddhist offering and sacrificial scenes, pre-Buddhist nature worship, herding, hunting, dance, travel etc. The animals at Rimo Thang and Luri Langkar generally have realistic proportions and their main features are portrayed clearly. Yaks, for example, have large horns, thick necks, and short, fat legs; the simple outlines convey well their essence. Most animals depicted are still numerous in the region. Human figures wear long robes, similar to those worn by today's Changtang nomads. Some figures wear masks, a tradition still seen at festivities. The carvings were created in four ways:

Spot chiseling. Hard, sharp rocks were used to make small indentations to form the basic outlines.

Continuous outlines were created by rubbing a sharp piece of rock back and forth on the rock surface.

An initial outline was first delineated by making a thin, shallow depression and then the enclosed surface deepened by one of the above methods.

Painted outlines, only seen at Karke Sang. Red, mineral-based colors were used to paint thick outlines.

Other images include Six Syllable *mantras* created by metal implements, the work of more recent pilgrims. Rimo Thang is the richest site and its carvings can be divided into three periods, early, middle, and late. Some co-exist on the same rock surface and some cluster according to period.

The early phase has the most images; humans and animals are rendered realistically with simple, lively strokes. Two methods were used. In one, small spots were chiseled over the entire body rather than just confined to the outlines. This technique is rarely seen in the middle period and not at all in the late. The second method, where only the outline was delineated, was used in all three periods. Early images can be distinguished by their archaic, simple rendering, but their arrangement on the rock faces is haphazard. Age and erosion have made many of them indistinct.

The middle period has fewer works. In addition to subjects of the early phase, it also has images of birds, wild pigs, and pottery. The limbs of figures are now formed by double outlines, but animals still lack eyes. Many have horizontal S-patterns on their bodies. Very few have chiseling over the entire surface; only along the outlines. More attention was given to the organization of the entire panel and the placement of individual images has its own logic. Thus there are complex scenes of offering ceremonies and dancing. The late period has few carvings which mostly portray deer, leopards, wolves, and birds. Detailing of the animals are considerably more refined. In some cases, images from different periods are carved on top of each other.

Most carvings at Luri Langkar are from the early period, although some animal figures—notably those with horizontal S-patterns—are derived from the middle period. None from the late phase are found here. Some Karke Sang images are painted. However, their use of pre-Buddhist symbols (moon, sun, trees) categorizes them in the middle period. Rutok's three sites generally have similar techniques, subjects, and style. All exhibit strong local flavor and can readily be differentiated according to age. The early carvings, for example, are distinguished by their use of discontinuous outlines to depict the dual horns, ears, and limbs of animals. In the middle period, the horizontal S-shaped pattern is a common motif; whereas in the late period, animal figures are more elaborately rendered and scroll patterns appear on the bodies. These designs are seldom encountered in rock carvings in other parts of China and Central Asia.

The Rutok works were probably accomplished before the 7th century This hypothesis is supported by two pieces of evidence. First, the carvings were created by blunt stone implements. There is no indication that metal tools were used. According to literary sources, metal utensils were common only after the 7th century Second, there are no Buddhist images or motifs and Tibetan inscriptions are also absent. Since the start of the Yarlung era (7th–9th C.), many instances of cliff carvings depicting Buddhist subjects as well as textual inscriptions were found. From that time on, simplistic subjects such as animals, human figures, and Bön symbols were dropped in favor of Buddhist ones.

Early Chinese literary sources mentioned the territories of Taiping and Dayang Tong, both of which can be ascribed to West Tibet. Dayang Tong is now commonly known as Shangshung, an ancient kingdom conquered by the early Yarlung kings. It is likely that the authors of the Rutok carvings were nomads of Taiping and Dayang Tong. Some Rutok carvings exhibit characteristics that belong to the pre-Buddhist religion. The Bön sect had strong elements of nature worship and certain mountains and lakes were endowed with supernatural properties. Rituals required that deer and goats be beheaded and their blood and meat offered to mountain gods as sacrifice. Many of the carvings depict yaks, goats, and deers and these may reflect the desire of early Bön proponents to present these animals as offerings to deities residing in rocks and mountains. A dramatic Rimo Thang panel has images of over 100 goat heads;

it appears to commemorate the ritual sacrifice of a large herd. In the same panel is an unusual image of a long fish bent to form a circle. Within its stomach are ten small fish and next to it are four masked figures dancing. Three small fish swim nearby. This scene perhaps denotes the worship of some subterranean deity (*lu*) and the wish of the artist for its protection. Ten carved vases may well symbolize *chang* offerings. At Rutok, the swastika symbol can be seen in a few places. Two panels show a reverse swastika; these are found once each in panels of the middle and late periods. The others are found in the early and middle periods. This may suggest that the standard swastika is an earlier symbol than the reverse.

Most of China's known petroglyphs are in the north: Inner Mongolia (Lang Shan), Xinjiang, Gansu (Hei Shan), Qinghai (Gyancha Xian, Halung Valley, Dulan Xian, Baha Muli Valley), and Ningxia. Most of these territories are populated by nomadic tribes and the art works reflect their pastoral and hunting concerns. The Rutok works have much in common with them. Below are characteristics particular to the petroglyphs of Rutok and these regions:

• Petroglyph sites are usually near pastures.

• The most common subjects are animals; infrequent scenes show herding activities, dance, war etc.

• Implements were mainly shaped from stone; there are few instances of color.

• Two basic techniques: spot chiseling and continuous lines rendering the outline; within the outlines, chiseling or rubbing creates an indented surface.

• Animals are all in profile while humans are frontal and mostly wear long robes.

Rutok is the first instance of such petroglyphs being discovered in Tibet. Subsequently, others have been found at Gegye Xian (112 km east of Shiquanhe on the banks of the Indus, see page 948), and Shuang Hu Qu in Nagchu Xian county. The latter site, with about 100 panels, is located at Jialing Shan near Yibo Chaka Lake (1400 km from Lhasa; 1000 km from Nagchu; 380 km from Shuang Hu District Office). From Rongma Qu, drive 15 min to the petroglyph site in the Derdung Valley.

SOURCE OF THE INDUS: MT KAILASH TO THE LION-MOUTHED RIVER

Location	West Tibet, Mt Kailash area
Map reference	NH44-3 C
Trekking days	4 (one-way)
Start–Finish	Drira Phuk Monastery–Jekung La
Passes	Tseti, Tseti Lachen

OVERVIEW

The trek to the source of the Indus starts from Drira Phuk Monastery on the sacred Mt Kailash circuit. Pilgrims and herders routinely travel this stretch and cross the Kang Tise Range, of which Kailash is the most prominent peak. The headwaters of the Indus, unlike the Kailash area, are surprisingly green and lush, especially during the summer. The source of the river, well-marked by prayer flags and *mani* stones, can be reached from the monastery in three days. To some scholars, a number of tributaries, notably the Lungdep and Munjam, actually carry higher volumes of water and have good claim to be the Indus's empirical source. These are superb valleys, touched only by nomad encampments. One day beyond the source is the Jekung La, which leads to large tracts of pasture frequented by the Changtang nomads. From Mt Kailash, a good way to pay homage to the holy site is to follow a circuit. First cross the Tseti La to reach the source, then traverse the Topchen La at the head of the Lungdep Valley. This route twice penetrates the Indus–Satlej Divide to form a loop that ends by returning to the monastery and village of Darchen at the start of the Mt Kailash *khora*.

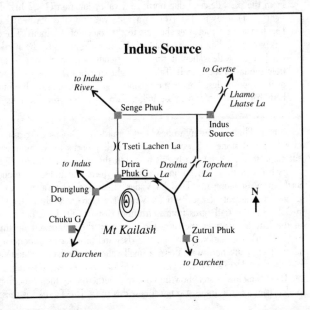

Indus Source

to Indus River

to Gertse

Lhamo Lhatse La

Senge Phuk

Indus Source

Tseti Lachen La

to Indus

Drira Phuk G

Drolma La

Topchen La

Drunglung Do

Chuku G

Mt Kailash

Zutrul Phuk G

N

to Darchen

to Darchen

Related sections
Kailash, p 273
Lake Manasarovar, p 614

Access
Drira Phuk Monastery on the Mt Kailash *khora* (see page 284).

Time Chart

Day	Place	Hours
1	Drira Phuk Monastery–Tseti Lachen La	6 3/4
2	Senge Buk	6 3/4
3	Indus River source	3 1/4
4	Jekung La	5 1/2

Trail Notes
✤ DAY 1 DRIRA PHUK MONASTERY–TSETI LACHEN LA 6 3/4 HR
Start at Drira Phuk Monastery (5081 m) on the Mt Kailash *khora* in the La Chu Valley.
(Further downstream [west] the valley is joined by the rivers of Drunglung and Chamo Lungchen
[Belung] at the important Drunglung Do junction.)

Drunglung Valley to the pastures of the Singtö nomads
A trail leads up the Drunglung Valley in one day to the Drunglung La (5550 m).
From the pass, descend due north to a valley junction (1 1/2 hr). The fork on the
right (east) leads in 1 1/4 hr to a wide valley at the northern base of the Tseti
La, then joins a trail over the pass to the source of the Indus. The left (northwest)
fork goes to a long, narrow lake (1 1/2 hr). Continue to the north end of the 7-
km lake. A wide valley at this point trends north-northwest to a junction (4 hr
from the lake's south end). Take the right (northeast) branch to reach the left bank
of the upper Indus. This is the expansive grazing grounds of the Singtö nomads, on
both banks of the uppermost Indus. Two days from the Tseti La Pass.

Leave Drira Phuk Monastery to head east towards the Drölma La, crossing the Tseti La River
on a bridge of stone and wood. The river valley opens to the northeast on the left. The
stiff climb to the Drölma La begins here. On the right (south), the pilgrim trail to the pass
zigzags between the Tseti La and Drölma La rivers. An indistinct though easier trail leads
north-northeast along the Tseti La Valley. Take this. The valley floor is quite swampy in
summer; the ascent of the Tseti La Valley gives progressively better views of Mt Kailash.
In 2 1/2 hr, the trail turns from north-northeast to east. Look out for the first side valley
on the left, 1/2 hr after the turn. Go northeast, then northwest up this valley. The Tseti
La (5628 m) is a platform between two rises and provides no panorama (2 3/4 hr from the
side valley). Walk northward down a small valley to the Sande Phuk Valley junction (1 hr
from the pass). Here a river flows left (west) to join another river descending from the Drunglung
La. Their combined waters flow into a lake's southern end, then issue from its north to enter
the left bank of the Indus. Do not follow this river. The Tseti La is thus not the true divide

between the Satlej and Indus. The real watershed is the Tseti Lachen La (5466 m) on the crest of the Kang Tise range. Stone cairns and prayer flags mark a glacial pond that gives rise to a stream which goes northeast and then north. It forms the north-flowing Tseti Chu, a left tributary of the Indus.

✤ DAY 2 TSETI LACHEN LA–SENGE BUK 6 3/4 HR

Follow the Tseti Chu; in 1 1/4 hr it veers to the north. Along this almost level valley are nomad camps, flocks of sheep (beware of dogs), and four azure lakes. After 5 1/2 hr from Sande Phuk, the north-trending Tseti La Valley joins the Indus at Senge Buk (5079 m). To the east, the valley is broad and open but the Indus is only a small stream. (Below the junction, the Shinglung Öta, a tributary of the Indus, opens to the right [north]. It leads to the Ngoma Chande La. Beyond, a trail goes north for two–three days to Tashi Toche, an uninhabited region. From the Indus-Tseti Chu junction, another trail goes downstream [northwest, then northeast] to the settlement of Gechu Rap on the banks of the Indus.)

✤ DAY 3 SENGE BUK–INDUS RIVER SOURCE 3 1/4 HR

Turn right (east) at Senge Buk to follow the Indus to its source. Nomad encampments are generally far apart. The river is joined by the Lungdep Chu on the right after 1 1/4 hr.

The Lungdep Valley and the return loop to Darchen

The Lungdep Chu carries a greater volume of water than the Indus but is regarded by Tibetans as its tributary. Empirically, the Lungdep has better claim to be the source if the sole determining factor is flowage. Its source is at the Topchen La (5650 m), two-and-a-half days due south from the Indus–Lungdep Chu junction. The pass also straddles the Kang Tise range. From here, a trail goes south, then southwest for a day to Darchen at the south base of Mt Kailash. The Lungdep Valley provides an alternative route for the return to Darchen.

◇ **Day 1** From the Indus–Lungdep Chu junction, follow the flat Lungdep Valley south-southeast. The gradient does not become significant until the top end of the valley. After 3 hr reach two glacial lakes, each 2 km long. At their southwestern end is an isolated, 5125-m peak. Reach a third lake in 2 hr. Camp here.

◇ **Day 2** The valley forks 1 hr from the lake. Take the right fork to the south-southwest. In 1 hr this valley also branches. Follow the left, main branch. Reach another fork in 2 1/2 hr and take the right. This divides again in 1 hr. Camp here.

◇ **Day 3** The left valley from camp goes due south to the Topchen La (3 hr). Descend due south along a long, narrow valley that slowly curves to the south-southeast. It bends to the west at its lower reaches. In 4 1/2 hr from the pass, the valley is joined on the left (north) by a similarly narrow valley. Zuthulphuk Monastery is located within it. The valleys' combined rivers flow southwest to Darchen (2 hr).

After 1 1/2 hr, the Munjam Chu joins the Indus from the right (southeast). It originates at the Jamé La in a region called Jamé Membar. A short distance northeast of the Munjam-Indus junction is a rugged cliff with a hole known as Senge Yura. Above the junction, the Indus carries little water; some of the volume comes from the Bokar Tsangpo that joins it from the southeast.

Tibetans call the source of the Indus Senge Kebab 'Lion Mouth'. It is 1/2 hr east of the junction, just north of the trail. It trickles from a conical slope covered with detritus. At its foot is a horizontal slab of white rock topped by *mani* piles. The source, issuing from a few springs below this, drains into the Bokar Tsangpo, one of the headwaters of the Indus. Many *mani* stones and prayer flags mark this sacred place. Tibetans for centuries have acknowledged this spot as the true origin of the Indus. Pilgrims drink the water and sprinkle their faces and heads.

✤ Day 4 Indus River Source–Jekung La 5 1/2 hr

From Senge Kebab, continue northeastwards along the right bank of the Bokar Tsangpo Valley, which broadens immediately. The dark, rounded mountains and ridges to the south-east are called Jungson and the prominent peak is Yama Koto. In 1 1/2 hr, reach the entrance of the large Shinglung Ngota Valley, which opens to the northwest; here is the Jekungra campground and the Jekung Tso, a tiny salt lake left of the trail. Continue northeast along the Bokar Tsangpo Valley for 4 hr to the Jekung La (5294 m). At the southeast base of the pass, the Bokar is joined by the Lamo Tsangpo. Several large valleys exist beyond the Jekung La; to explore them, find a nomad herder as guide. Alternatively, return to the Lungdep Chu Valley and cross the Topchen La to regain Darchen.

Beyond the Jekung La

On the pass's far side, a trail goes up the wide Lamo Tsangpo Valley to the Lamo Lhatse La (5426 m), watershed between the Indian Ocean and the Changtang Plateau. Beyond the pass is the Lamo Lhatse Lungpe Do Valley, which merges into a large plain after three days of walking. This is part of a pilgrim route that Tibetans use to reach Mt Kailash from the settlement of Gerze, Senkor, and Yumba Matsen. From Lungpe Do, it is a 15-day walk to Gerze, the important staging post on the north Lhatse–Kailash route (see page 948). The district of Yumba Matsen, three days from Lungpe Do, is known for its summer pastures and nomads. In winter, they migrate to the shores of Lake Mugu.

Much of this chapter's trekking information was supplied by John Bellazza.

THE FRIENDSHIP HIGHWAY

LHASA TO THE TIBET–NEPAL BORDER VIA GYANTSE

The Friendship Highway (also known as the Arniko Highway) goes from Lhasa west to Gyantse, Shigatse, Lhatse, and the Nepal border. An important artery of commerce, it is also Tibet's most popular tourist route. An alternative road for the Lhasa–Shigatse section goes via Yangpachen, the Wuyuk Valley, and the south bank of the Tsangpo (see page 815). This, however, bypasses the important town of Gyantse with its magnificent Kumbum Chörten, and the Turquoise Lake of Yamdrok Tso. Most of the Friendship Highway is marked by kilometer stones. The numbers at the beginning of each location below correspond to road markers in kilometers. Note that the sequence changes from sector to sector and that some markers have been removed or destroyed by road works. To complicate matters further, as of 1989 a new system, identified by red numerals, has been put into place. Where applicable, both new (in parenthesis) and old markers are given. For more information on Notes, look under appropriate entries in the Place-Names Index.

LHASA TO THE CHUSUL BRIDGE

Road marker (km)	Notes
2	Dongkar Bridge, dirt road on right to Kyormolung Monastery and the sacred pond of Zhongpa Lhachung; before this, at the petrol station, a paved road turns right to Golmud and Qinghai
9	Coracle crossing to Shugseb Nunnery on the Kyi Chu's left bank
11	Rock carving of Buddha
17 (4662)	Nethang Drölma Lhakhang
18	Valley on right; follow red pipeline to Ratö Monastery
27	Coracle crossing
29	Nam Village at the entrance of the Nam Valley; a trail leads northwest to Tsurphu Monastery
33	Coracle crossing
40	Sakyaling Monastery
41	Valley on right; small monastery 1 km up the valley

47   Village 1/2 km up side valley

51   Chusul near the Kyi Chu–Tsangpo confluence; a trail in the Chusul Valley leads north to Tsurphu Monastery

60   Chusul Bridge spans the Tsangpo; turnoff to Tsethang and the Yarlung Valley
(4705)

Chusul Bridge to Gyantse

65   Jangtang; new road on right follows the Tsangpo's south bank westward to Shigatse

97   Kamba La (4794 m); descend to Yamdrok Tso

103   Tamalung; ferry across Yamdrok Tso

123   Pede Dzong; trail north over the Nyapso La to the Tsangpo

134   Yarsik (Pede), road forks on the shores of Yamdrok Tso; right branch goes to Rinpung Dzong, left continues to Gyantse

150   Nakartse Dzong; start of Yamdrok Tso circuit

160   Road forks; left branch goes to Taklung Monastery (17 km) and Lhodrak

182   Karo La (5045 m); Mt Nojin Kangtsang (7191 m), on the right, Mt Jetung Chusang (6242 m) on the left (northeast)

188   Namru Chu Valley on right; a trail leads north over the Nyadong La to the Rong Valley and Rinpung Dzong

199   Ralung; a trail from the village leads east to Ralung Monastery and Lake Phurma

207   *Daoban*

212   Lungma; large valley to right leads north to the Rong Valley and Rinpung Dzong

220   Kangwang; Nyeru Tsangpo Valley on left leads south to the Changpo Plain and Bhutan

224   Simi La

244   Road forks; right branch goes east to the Yung La and on to Rinpung Dzong in the Rong Valley

252   Gyantse

255   T-junction; right branch goes to Shigatse, the left south to the Chumbi Valley and Yatung along the Ralung Chu's west bank

256   Side road on left leads to Changra and the Jinka Cave Hermitage

Gyantse to Shigatse

Another set of road markers begins after Gyantse.

87   Ruins of Tsechen Monastery (seat of Rendawa, principal teacher of Tsong Khapa)

on top of a steep hill on the left

71	Drongtse Monastery
65	Nesar Monastery, one of the oldest in the area
56	Sera Drubde Hermitage on the Nyang Chu's right bank
54	Turnoff to Jinka Cave Hermitage
52	Concrete bridge
50	Penam Xian; small town with monastery and dirt road leading south to Duchung, Wongdan Qu (28 km from the Friendship Highway), and Jinka
46	Norbu Chungtse
24	Valley on left; track south leads to Duchung and Jinka
18	Turnoff on left to Shalu Monastery
3	Shigatse

SHIGATSE TO LHATSE

The road markers change sequence again after Shigatse.

(4904)	Tashilhunpo Monastery
262 (4917)	Dirt road on left leads to Ngor Monastery
266 (5014)	Narthang Monastery
275	Valley on left leads north to the Tsangpo's south bank
291	Tra (Tso) La (4050 m)
296	Gangchen Monastery
310	Jiding Qu; (bridge, ruins of a fort, and Jiding on the left); side road on left leads south to Zesum Qu (Shungma) and Sai Qu (55 km) within the Rhe Valley; valley on right leads north to Chuding and the Tsangpo
326	Turnoff on right leads north to Tashigang Qu, the Tsangpo's south bank, and Pindsoling Monastery
349	Shrine on hill next to village
363	Gyatso La (4950 m)
377 (5028)	Sakya Bridge; turnoff on left to Sakya Monastery (25 km). This road leads to Tingche Xian and Chörten Nyima pilgrimage
389	Hot springs within a compound on right side of road (1/2 km from highway);

sign in Tibetan and Chinese.

400   Incense burner; dirt road on right to Lhatse Dzong

401   Lhatse Xian
(5052)

LHATSE TO ZHANGMU (TIBET–NEPAL BORDER)

407   Major road junction; right branch (road marker 0 km, 5058) goes west to Mt Kailash, West Tibet; left branch continues to Nepal border along Lola Chu Valley

432   Jachor La (5252 m) or Lagpa La
(5082)

470   Hot springs by roadside

482   Baiba; bridge and right turnoff to Shekar Dzong (7 km)

484   Turnoff on left to Tingche Xian and Chörten Nyima pilgrimage

489   Checkpost; show passports

494   Dirt road on left goes up side valley to the Pang La and Mt Everest

512   Hermitage halfway up hill; village below

542   Bridge; Rachu Village turnoff

543   Dingri; routes south to Rongphuk Monastery, Mt Everest Base Camp and Lapchi pilgrimage; routes north to Chung Riwoche Chörten and the Tsangpo

555   Tsamda hot springs ; dirt track on right leads to Langkor Monastery; springs are 0.5 km west of the village.

581   Gutsuo army camp with guest house

587   Menkhab Me (Menpu Qu) on north bank of Men Chu; trails lead east then north to a major north–south valley. Within it Satso Qu, 17 km from Menpu Qu, which leads to Tagtse on the Tsangpo

601   Two large caves 100 m from the road on the right; meditation chambers built around them

604   Sumo, pretty village on the right across the river on a cliff; impressive ruins; a trail within the valley (north bank of the Men Chu) leads west via the Yer La to Shaka, Pelku Tso, and Kyirong; another trail goes north to the Tsangpo

606   Tibetan sign and prayer flags mark valley entrance on left

612   View of Mt Shishapangma (8012 m)

614   Turnoff to Kyirong Valley; wood road sign (arrows point to Nyalam and Kyirong); follow right branch to Kyirong and Mt Shishapangma base camp

625   Lalung La (5124 m), first of a double pass across the Himalayas

630   Descend to valley junction at bridge and house; wide valley leads east to Langkor Monastery and Dingri via 5150-m pass

638   Yarle Shung La (second of double pass, 5200 m); on right is massive flank of Mt Shishapangma; descend along the Majang Tsangpo

652   Dulung; bridge and trail along wide valley on left leads east to the Thong La, Langkor Monastery and Dingri; stone cairns mark valley entrance

656   Lasi; three villages on left; ruins at entrance of east-trending valley

659   Yarle; government compound and village

662   Ngoru Tsangpo Valley on right; trail leads up to Ngoru on Mt Shishapangma's southeast face, and Lama Ralo Phuk, consecrated to Ra Lotsawa (3/4 hr from village)

664   Bridge and ruins on cliffs; village on left

667   Ngoru Village turnoff; dirt track on right leads east to Mt Phola Gangchen area

675   Cross bridge; narrow valley to the left with a village

678   Tsangdrung (Nesar) Qu

680   Trail up valley on left leads to Tashigang and the Lapchi pilgrimage; impressive views

682   Phegyeling Monastery and Milarepa's cave; cross from here to opposite bank of Majang Tsangpo

693   Nyalam Xian (3750 m); just before the bridge, on the right, is track to Mt Shishapangma base camp

705   Chushang Hotel; new hotel for tourists

724   Zhangmu (2300 m); Tibet–Nepal border town; Chinese customs and immigration

116   (new system begins) Friendship Bridge on Tibet–Nepal border

0   Kathmandu, Nepal

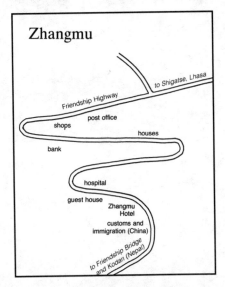

Zhangmu

to Shigatse, Lhasa

Friendship Highway

shops

post office

houses

bank

hospital

guest house

Zhangmu Hotel

customs and immigration (China)

to Friendship Bridge and Kodari (Nepal)

PRACTICAL
INFORMATION

TRAVELING IN TIBET

TRAVEL ADVISORY

Regulations concerning travel in Tibet are in a state of constant flux. From 1984 to 1987 no special restrictions were placed on individual travel to Lhasa but sporadic demonstrations, which led to a period of martial law, caused the authorities to limit access to Tibet to organized groups only. Tourism in 1989 declined to ten per cent of its 1987 volume, but gradual relaxation of regulations and increased confidence amongst travel agents has caused an upsurge during the 1990s.

The 'open cities' have been defined as Lhasa, Shigatse, Gyantse, Nagchu, Tsethang and Zhangmu—thus opening the routes from Golmud (Qinghai) to Lhasa and the road to Nepal. Travel permits, obtained from the Public Security Bureau (*Gong An Ju*) in any major Chinese city are, at present, no longer required for these cities, but travel to Tibet for individuals is still somewhat restricted due to control over access routes imposed by the authorities. Plane tickets from Chengdu or Kathmandu, or bus tickets from Golmud, require a certain amount of finagling (see below). Most travelers are therefore forced into *ad hoc* budget groups in Chengdu or Kathmandu, paying local travel agents for the privilege. It is expected that these restrictions will be relaxed during the 1990s. The overland route from Golmud to Lhasa (two days on a bus) is the best bet for individual travelers.

VISAS

A standard Chinese visa is required to enter Tibet. These are obtained from most Chinese embassies and consulates, although rules of issuance vary from country to country. The best and easiest place to get one is Hong Kong, where visas for single/double entry are issued for 30, 60, or 90 days. Cost ranges from HK$90 to 250 (US$12 to 32), and one day 'express' service is available. The cheapest visas are from the Chinese Visa Office, 5th floor, East Wing, China Resources Building, Gloucester Road, Wanchai. However, it is generally more convenient to use a travel agent. China Travel Service has several offices in Hong Kong and Kowloon. Time Travel, 16th floor, Block A, Chungking Mansions, 40 Nathan Road is the budget travelers' favorite. Try also Phoenix Services (722 7378), Room B, 6th Floor, Milton Mansions, 96 Nathan Road, Kowloon, or Traveller Services (367 4127), Room 704, Metropole Building, 57 Peking Road, Kowloon.

Visas are not generally issued to individuals at the Chinese embassy in Kathmandu, so it is necessary to use a local travel agent who will telex your details and itinerary to a Lhasa travel agent. They in turn will telex the embassy who then issue a visa. The process is costly and effectively creates a 'one man group'. It is generally cheaper to join one of the budget groups organized by the Kathmandu travel agents. (Arniko Travel is a good one.) Chinese visas sometimes start from day of issue, so apply for the visa shortly before commencing your journey. Individual travelers willing to try the Tibet–Nepal border crossing on their own should secure a Chinese visa before entering Nepal.

Visas for Nepal

Visas for Nepal are available at the Nepalese embassy in Lhasa, situated between the Holiday Inn and Norbu Linka. Two-week visas can be obtained at the Nepalese border (Kodari) or Kathmandu airport and can be extended at Central Immigration in Kathmandu.

Getting There

By Air

Tibet's only commercial airport is at Gongkar, 96 kilometers from Lhasa, and is accessible only from Chengdu or Kathmandu. Two flights leave Chengdu daily at 06:50 and 07:00, while flights from Kathmandu are limited to Tuesdays and Saturdays. A direct flight from Hong Kong to Lhasa is expected to be available shortly and the Xian–Golmud–Lhasa route may also be reinstated. Shigatse airport is due to open in the mid-1990s and there are constant rumours that airports in east and west Tibet are scheduled to open later in the decade.

The Chengdu (US$190) and Kathmandu (US$200) flights are both spectacular—the former giving views over the river gorges and the high snow-capped peaks of east Tibet, the latter of the Himalayan range, including Everest.

From Kathmandu, twice-weekly flights to Lhasa begin in the third week of April and continue until the end of November. In principal, tickets are only sold to groups. If you are not with one try the following. First procure a Chinese visa from Hong Kong or your home country, which is generally very easy. It is not possible, at the time of writing, to obtain a visa in Nepal without joining a group. Either purchase a Kathmandu–Lhasa–Chengdu ticket through one of the following travel agents in Kathmandu or go directly to China Southwest Airlines (411302), show them your Chinese visa, and buy the ticket yourself. This should allow you to fly into Lhasa. Once there, regularize your status by getting an Aliens Travel Permit from the Public Security Bureau in Tsethang, Shigatse or Lhasa. (The best places to do so are perhaps Tsethang and Shigatse.) However, if you don't want to go on to China, you may lose the Lhasa–Chengdu portion (about US$190) of your ticket. The China Southwest Airline office in Kathmandu will possibly give a refund.

Nepal travel agents specializing in budget Tibet tours:

Marco Polo (tel 414192; fax 9771 220143)
Arniko Travel (tel 414594; fax 9771 411878, 226912; tlx 2703 ARNIKO NP) The specialist in Kathmandu.
Tibet Travel and Tours (tel 410303; fax 9771 220143)
Nepal Travel Agency (tel 413188, 412899; fax 9771 227782, 419021)
Mountain Travel (tel 414508; fax 9771 419126)

From Chengdu, the best plan is to procure both a Chinese visa and a Chengdu–Lhasa ticket from China Airlines (CAAC, tel 8610322) in Hong Kong. Mera Travels (tel 3916892), the best adventure travel company in Hong Kong, has a lot of connections with Lhasa and can perhaps tailor something for you. China Tibet Qomolongma Travels (tel 5418896) is the agent for CITS in Lhasa. They have a brochure outlining some thirty tours to Tibet, most costing about US$150 per day. Once you are in Chengdu it is considerably more difficult to purchase a ticket. You might have to resort to one of several travel agents specializing in Tibet tours—

for example Golden Bridge Travels, a commercial arm of the People's Liberation Army—who can probably get you a ticket at a premium. The other possiblility is to join one of their budget tours. CITS, the state travel company, has a four-day tour (accommodation and transport) to Lhasa which costs about 1400 FEC per person. If you manage to form a group of ten, the price drops to 900 FEC. This is one of the cheapest options available.

By Road

Kathmandu–Lhasa The route from Nepal to Lhasa (900 km) takes at least three days, with overnight stops in Zhangmu and Shigatse. The road crosses several passes at around 5,000 m and the journey is cold, dusty and exhausting. Frequent landslides disrupt traffic for 30 km on either side of the border and it is generally necessary to walk the 8 km between Kodari and Zhangmu, the two border posts, although porters are readily available. Nevertheless the journey is rewarding, with many of Tibet's important religious sites en route and scenic views of Lake Yamdrok (on the Gyantse route from Lhasa), Mount Everest at Dingri and the Himalayas at Lalung La pass.

To enter Tibet via the Kathmandu–Kodari–Zhangmu land route as an individual traveler is possible though not officially sanctioned. A valid Chinese visa is essential, yet the chance always remains that you will be turned back at the Zhangmu. This raises the problem of re-entering Nepal at Kodari; make clear to the Nepalese immigration officer on departure that you might be back in a few hours. Rules and regulations concerning Tibet have a habit of changing overnight so this might be worth a try. In the event that you are allowed entry, getting a seat on a Landcruiser, minibus, or bus to Lhasa is not a problem. Most drivers have unloaded their passengers at the border and will be glad to take paying tourists back to Lhasa. Expect to pay from US$30–80. Hiring an entire vehicle (*bao che*) costs US$150 (Beijing Jeep) or more.

Going from Lhasa to Kathmandu the logistics are considerably easier. The authorities have no quibbles with individuals who want to go to Nepal by road provided you have a valid Chinese visa. The main problem is that there are very few buses going from Lhasa to the border, although things may change, especially in the busy summer months. The best option for budget travelers at present is to take buses to Shigatse (daily) or Sakya and hitch to the border (see the section on hitchhiking). Another possibility is to get a group together in Lhasa (see Car Hire p 1000) or Shigatse and hire a Landcruiser (from Tenzin Hotel or Shigatse Hotel) for the remainder of the trip to Nepal. If you rent a Landcruiser or minibus directly from Lhasa, the charge is around 4 FEC per km (this includes the driver's return). Four passengers are standard for a Landcruiser but sometimes you can squeeze in five.

Golmud–Lhasa These days most individual travelers enter Tibet by way of Golmud, a large sprawling town in the desert heartland of Qinghai at the end of the railway line from Xining. CITS (Chinese International Travel Service) and other travel companies may have cheap budget tours to Lhasa which charge only transport costs. Most travelers succeed in getting a bus ticket. If problems arise, another possibility is to get a permit to go to Tuotuohe from the Public Security Bureau. This small settlement, halfway between Lhasa and Golmud, is the staging post for the source of the Yangtse. With this permit you can get a seat on the Golmud–Lhasa bus (about 70 Yuan). Alight before the turnoff to Tuotuohe and hitch the rest of the way to Lhasa. In the off-season months (before and after summer), you might be refused this permit. One option is then to hire a taxi for a day trip out of town. Once you get past two checkposts (one is in the suburbs, the other is about 20 km out on the

Golmud–Lhasa road), start hitching south to Lhasa. This 1115-km journey along the Qinghai–Tibet highway takes between 30 and 50 hr by bus, and only a little less by Landcruiser. The road is bleak and cold, particularly on the high Tangu La pass, and facilities en route are very poor. Most vehicles travel throughout the night with only brief stops at Nagchu and Damxung for refreshments. If you are in one of the decrepit Chinese buses, make sure you have heavy woollens and a sleeping bag.

If you are hitching to Golmud from Lhasa along the Qinghai–Tibet highway, start some distance beyond the large gas station in the western suburbs of the city (past Drepung Monastery). Once out of sight of soldiers and officials, truck drivers are more likely to stop for you.

Chengdu–Lhasa This is a logistically difficult journey of over 2,400 km. Buses and trucks take anywhere from one to three weeks, with delays frequent in all seasons. Facilities are generally limited to dirty concrete truck stops and poorly provisioned roadside restaurants. Tour groups are only permitted to use this route if operating through an approved travel agent with an agreed itinerary.

Kashgar–Lhasa Kashgar, a major town in western Xinjiang, can be reached from Pakistan via the Karakoram Highway. For the journey from Kashgar to Lhasa, see the West Tibet section.

Hitching It is hard to get a realistic view of how difficult it is to hitchhike in Tibet. During the golden days of Tibet travel, between 1984 and 1987, many travelers hitched to all kinds of exotic destinations on a whim and a song. Then, because of a series of road accidents involving foreigners, and because of the severe clashes between Tibetans and the Chinese, the authorities imposed substantial penalties on drivers who gave hitchhikers rides. This mode of transport became extremely difficult. However, since the early 1990s, most people who have tried to hitchhike have reported that things are improving. Although you might have to wait a while to get a ride, truck and jeep drivers, anxious to make some money on the side, are again willing to take on hitchhikers. Individuals are more likely to succeed. The unwritten tariff charged per head is Rmb 10 per hundred km. Surprisingly, in quite a few recent cases, drivers have declined accepting money. Contrary to conventional belief, army vehicles, expensive Landcruisers and Beijing jeeps are not averse to picking up travelers. Tractors driven by Tibetans are good bets but the drawback is that they are slow, painfully uncomfortable and often ply only short distances.

An alternative to hitching by the road is to try the truck depots which exist in every city. Lhasa, for example, has several along the Lingkhor Road leading to the sky-burial site of Sera. Should a ride be agreed upon, the manager will generally charge you a reasonable price and then write out a proper ticket.

BUDGET AND TIME

Tours arranged in Chengdu or Kathmandu cost US$65–120 per day, including hotel, guide/interpreter and transport (not airfares). Minimum group size is officially three, but one-man groups are available at a premium. Discounts can be obtained with groups of 15 or over. Those arranging their own food and accommodation in Lhasa can survive on US$5 a day, although hired transport can be expensive.

CLIMATE—WHEN TO GO

The best time to visit Tibet is between early spring and late autumn. Spring is generally short, cool and dusty but clear skies are good for sightseeing. The rainy season, June–September, has 70–95 per cent of annual precipitation, causing snow on the hills and night rain in the valleys. The weather is, however, still predominantly dry with low humidity, the hills are at their greenest and temperatures are mild. Large diurnal temperature variations exist in all seasons, so carry extra layers of clothing even on short daytrips. Lhasa can be surprisingly pleasant even at the end of December, although nights are frigid. During the cold winter months, many nomads converge on Lhasa and, with few tourists, this is a most interesting time to visit.

CLOTHING AND EQUIPMENT

(see also Trekking equipment checklist, page 1005) The changes in temperature make it advisable to bring many layers of clothing into Tibet. Polypropylene long underwear is especially good in the colder seasons. For protection against dust, bring a silk scarf to cover mouth and nose and get gauze masks in Lhasa. Consider leaving contact lenses at home. Good dark glasses—preferably with side protectors to help against dust and glare—are necessary and a hat is useful, though one can be bought in Lhasa. Sunblock cream and lip guard are essential.

Bring strong, comfortable walking shoes and a windproof jacket; a down jacket is good against cold and as padding on uncomfortable journeys. Pile jackets take up more space but they dry quickly. A sleeping bag is useful but not strictly necessary (unless trekking), as nearly all hotels provide adequate bedding, although outside the larger towns this bedding is often filthy.

Other essentials: Take a metal water bottle, a tin cup to make use of thermoses of hot boiled water (widely available), a flashlight for visiting monasteries, batteries (local ones are not good), film (see photography), a can opener, water purifying tablets such as Micropur or iodine, toilet paper and soap. Take some food for emergencies. Kit for a long trek needs careful planning.

PUBLIC SECURITY BUREAU

China's Public Security Bureau is an internal police force that covers everything from traffic problems to political dissent. Foreigners deal with the Foreign Affairs branch of the PSB; it extends visas. Officers have a reputation of friendliness to foreigners and a few speak English. The PSB has two offices in Lhasa, one in Shigatse and branches in other major towns.

CUSTOMS

Register watches, radios, cameras, calculators, and other devices on entering Tibet and China and account for them on leaving. Do not lose the declaration form or you may be required to pay a hefty fine on departure. Do not take in printed matter, cassettes, or anything considered seditious by the Chinese, which includes Tibetan flags or literature pertaining to the Tibetan independence movement.

You can take in four bottles of liquor, two cartons of cigarettes, up to 72 rolls of still film, and 1,000 meters of 8mm moving film. There are no obvious restrictions on video equipment. Artifacts made before 1959 are officially considered antiques and cannot be exported. Rugs and small religious objects can be taken out but tourists considered to be carrying 'too much' may have goods confiscated. Body searches are unlikely.

MONEY

China has two different systems of currency, Renminbi (Rmb) for locals and Foreign Exchange Certificates (FEC, Waihuijuan) for foreign travelers. There is a double pricing system which means that foreigners are usually charged double for buses, lodging and services and are generally required to pay in FEC. Rmb are widely used on the street by tourists and it is sometimes possible to pay for transportation (renting landcruisers, bus tickets) in this local money. Airplane tickets require FEC. Outside the main centers (on a trek for example), bring lots of Rmb because it is difficult to change foreign money. The unit of money is the *yuan*, divided into 10 *jiao* (*mao*) or 100 *fen*.

In Tibet, travelers' cheques and foreign currency can be changed formally at the Lhasa Hotel, the Bank of China in Lhasa, Shigatse, Zhangmu and Shiquanhe (travelers' cheques only). Bank hours are 0830–1200 and 1530–1830. Keep the exchange receipts to convert FEC back into foreign currencies. At the Nepalese border you can change Rmb into Nepalese rupees informally, but the rate is unattractive.

COMMUNICATIONS

Sending letters by airmail or packages by air or surface from Tibet is surprisingly reliable. To receive mail in Lhasa, have it addressed to Post Restante, Main Post Office, Lhasa, Tibet, China. Telegrams are commonly used. It is very easy to dial or fax direct to Europe or the States. International calls can be made at large hotels or at the Telecommunications Office. Telexes and faxes are available to guests at the Holiday Inn, and at the Telecommunications Office, which has cheaper rates.

ELECTRICITY AND BATTERIES

An adequate electrical supply (220 volts, 50 cycles AC) exists in nearly all towns and major villages. The hours of operation are, however, unpredictable. Rely on battery-operated equipment. Tibet has no facilities for reprocessing of batteries—they are merely dumped. Take used batteries out of the country when you leave.

PHOTOGRAPHY

Photography is controlled in monasteries. In some cases you must pay per photograph, in others you may be refused permission to shoot at all. Respect these rules but get around them sometimes by being nice to the monks. Do not photograph Chinese military installations, bridges or airports.

Take plenty of film; sometimes print film runs out of stock even in Lhasa. Kodachrome and Fujichrome are generally not available. Be prepared for the strong light and appalling dust of Tibet. A lenshood and a polarizer can help the exposure problem. It is best to photograph in the early mornings and late afternoons to avoid the harsh light and it is worth underexposing by half a stop to one stop at other times. Kodachrome 25 film is useful and Fujichrome 100 is considerably better than Ektachrome 100 which is ill-suited to cope with the harsh light. Nothing will completely keep out the dust but plastic helps. A strong flash is needed for many temple interiors. Take flash photographs of wall murals at an angle to avoid reflection.

Do not give money in exchange for taking photos; it is a quick way to create beggars. On the whole, most Tibetans are happy to let you photograph them.

GETTING AROUND

Car Hire All car hire includes vehicle and driver—foreigners are not permitted to drive in Lhasa. Rates depend on vehicle and mileage, with a daily charge applied if mileage is low. Rates start at 3 FEC per km for Landcruisers and 4.5 FEC for minibuses. (The price is for a one-way trip and includes the driver's return to Lhasa.) Daily charge is around 150 FEC. Numerous agents in Lhasa will hire out these vehicles but the rates vary significantly. It is important to shop around and to bargain.

Rental companies are generally willing to take you to remote, little known areas— provided you know precisely where to go and have a good map. Most drivers are only familiar with standard tourist routes. Before you set off, have the itinerary carefully defined. Include the names of all villages and monasteries you want to visit, the approximate time you want to spend at each place and the number of days for the trip. Write this information down and have the document signed by both the company manager and the driver.

CITS (across from the Lhasa Holiday Inn)
Lhasa Holiday Inn
Taxi Company (next to the Yak Hotel)
Lhasa City Tourist Company (offices in Sunlight Hotel)
Xuelian (Snow Lotus Hotel, inside the military compound on the Kyi Chu River)
Lhasa City Reception Office (behind the Potala on the same side of the main road as the Public Security Bureau, but closer to the Lukhang)
Himalaya Hotel (near the Kyi Chu River, south of the Sunlight Hotel; its vehicles are geared for trekking and mountaineering groups)

Buses Public buses, well-used by individual travelers, are infrequent except for those plying the main routes to Shigatse, Golmud, Tsethang and Ningchi. Most are slow, decrepit and uncomfortable—particularly in the back seats. Several private bus companies now operate— notably pilgrim buses to Ganden, Drepung and Sera monasteries—although some go as far as Golmud. Check that your luggage is securely tied on the roof and protected against the elements. Keep a daypack and carry dry food and water. If possible, try to get on a Japanese vehicle which is usually more reliable and comfortable.

Lhasa has three bus stations: the central station is near the Lhasa Hotel and the Norbu Linka, another is one block east of the post office, and a third is across from Tibet University. Each services different routes. Buses cost double for tourists and tickets must be paid in FEC. (Try bargaining and paying in Rmb or get a Chinese or Tibetan friend to buy a ticket for you.) Get your ticket 1–2 days in advance.

Trucks Almost everything enters Tibet by truck. Roads are usually unpaved, dusty, and bumpy and the condition of vehicles varies greatly. Japanese and recent Chinese trucks are good but the dark green, pre-1950 models should be avoided. You can sometimes negotiate a ride on the back of a truck (squeezed in with Tibetans) or, occassionally, in the cab. The police strongly discourage drivers from taking foreigners.

Truck travel is greatly enhanced by speaking a bit of Tibetan or Chinese, or providing cigarettes and sharing food. Expect to negotiate a price with the driver. If you travel in an open truck, be sure to have plenty of warm clothes, a hat and protective sun cream. Have your sleeping bag near you on long journeys, especially between Lhasa and Golmud. Try to arrange rides at truck depots, petrol stations and hotels frequented by drivers. Otherwise, simply wave down vehicles on the road.

Pack animals In small villages or nomad camps you can often hire a guide and pack animals, but remember that farmers need their animals during the harvest. A yak can carry 50–80 kg (3–4 backpacks) and travel up to 25 km each day. Horses and donkeys (they carry half the load of a yak) are also possible, depending on the terrain. Bargain for the price, but expect to pay over Rmb 20–30 per day per beast (this includes the handler).

Lhasa rickshaws Cycle rickshaws ply the main roads in Lhasa and are a pleasant way to see the city. The rate for the journey from the Holiday Inn to the Jokhang is 7 FEC, but be prepared to haggle.

Lhasa mini-buses/taxis These follow set routes, going from the front of the Jokhang to the Holiday Inn, and to the main monasteries of Sera and Drepung. When you see one going past simply flag it down and squeeze in. Prices are reasonable.

FORMING YOUR OWN BUDGET TIBET TOUR

One way for individual travelers to enter Tibet is to join a so-called budget tour operating from Kathmandu, Nepal. They typically cost close to US$1,000 for seven or eight days. This includes the flight to Lhasa, overland transport to Kathmandu, all hotels, meals and visa. Some travelers have joined one of these and simply jumped tour in Lhasa pleading sick; this however requires going to the Public Security to get a stamp in the passport. A cheaper way is to form your own group, effectively bypassing the intermediaries. This has become a more viable option as telecommunication between Lhasa and the rest of the world took a quantum leap in the early 1990s. Using faxes, it is now very easy to work out itineraries (including trekking to remote areas), agendas and prices with several reliable travel companies in Lhasa. The basic procedure is to fax sufficiently detailed information (number of persons in the group, length of stay, first or second class accommodation, meals required and the itinerary) and request a quote. It is a good idea to shop around as prices vary significantly. You are responsible for all airfares; the agent handles all ground matters including visas.

FORMING YOUR OWN TREKKING GROUPS

The basic procedure applies as above. However, there is additional information that the Lhasa travel company needs before it can give you a firm price. You must draw up two itineraries in considerable detail: getting from Lhasa to the trailhead, and the trek itself. To do this use the Tibet Handbook to give you the basic framework. For the trek to the Everest Kangshung Base Camp, for example, first define the number of days you budget for your Landcruiser trip from Lhasa to Kharta, the trailhead. You might want to spend a night each at the major pilgrimage centers of Gyantse, Shigatse, Sakya and Dingri, or you may simply want to go as fast as possible and overnight only at Shigatse and Shekar. As for preparing for the trek, the agent will want to know if he is to supply all trekking equipment (including tents, stove, kitchen gear, etc), food on the trek, pack animals and guides. Read the trail description in the book to get an approximate idea of the length of the trek from Kharta to the Kangshung Base Camp and back, and add the desired sidetrips and rest days.

LHASA TRAVEL AGENTS

[For telephone and fax, the international code is 86 and the Lhasa code is 891]

Holiday Inn Lhasa Tour Dept
Holiday Inn Lhasa
Tel 32221
Fax 35796
Tlx 68010 HILSA CN / 68011 HILSA CN

Tibet Tourist Corporation / Chinese International Travel Service Lhasa Branch (TTC/CITS Lhasa)
Holiday Inn Lhasa, Room 1112
Tel 35277 / 36626
Fax 35277 / 36315
Tlx 68009 ZMLAS CN / 68018 TTC CN

Chinese Workers Travel Service Tibet Branch (CWTS)
Holiday Inn Lhasa, Room 1104
Tel 34472
Fax 34472
Telex 69025 WTBC CN

Lhasa Travel Agency
Sunlight Hotel
Tel 23196
Fax 35675
Tlx 68016 TRCLS CN

Tibet Mountaineering Association (TMA)
8 East Lingkor Road (next to Himalaya Hotel)
Tel 22981
Fax 36366
Telex 68029 TMA CN

Chinese Youth Travel Service Tibet Branch (CYTS)
Holiday Inn Lhasa, Room 1106
Tel 24173
Telex 68017 CYTS CN

Tibet International Sports Travel (TIST)
Himalaya Hotel
Tel 23775 / 22293
Fax 34855
Telex 68019 TIST CN

Golden Bridge Travel Lhasa Branch (GBT)
13 Minzu Lu (near Holiday Inn Lhasa)
Tel 23828 / 24063
Fax 25832
Tlx 68002 GBTCL CN

ACCOMMODATION

Lhasa The Holiday Inn in Lhasa (Lhasa Fandian) is the only top-ranked western style hotel in Tibet. In recent years this has been heavily booked by tour groups and individual travelers have not been accepted. Its only real competition is the nearby Tibet Guest House, owned by CITS, which also possesses good facilities but caters mainly to Chinese guests.

The Himalaya Hotel near the university and river, and the Sunlight Hotel both provide reasonable facilities at a moderate price (US$20) and are used by the budget tour groups. Individuals generally use the Yak Hotel, centrally located north of the Barkhor, although the Banak Shöl and Snowlands are also popular. Prices are under US$3 per bed.

Outside Lhasa Gyantse, Shigatse, Tsethang, Shekar, Nyalam and Zhangmu all contain tourist class hotels but most are run down and dirty. Cigarette burns on the carpet, squalid bathrooms and an infrequent supply of hot water annoy many visitors. Tour groups use these hotels but individuals are discouraged by the high prices and poor facilities.

Small guesthouses, offering little more than a bed and washbasin, operate in most towns. Truckstops, consisting of a bare concrete cell with beds and dirty bedding, are the best that can be expected in others. Costs range from US$2–5 per bed per night.

Below is a list of hotels and guest houses in Tibet's main centers.

Hotels
(1) good facilities, expensive (US$60)
(2) reasonable facilities, medium price (less than US$30)
(3) basic accommodation, cheap (less than US$3 per bed)

Lhasa

- Holiday Inn (Lhasa Fandian) (1) The Holiday Inn management has upgraded the service considerably. Western style rooms with private bathrooms; the food (Western and Chinese) is good by Lhasa's standards; telex and fax available. Bad location in the west part of town.
- Himalaya (Tibet Sports Association) Hotel (2) Near the university and river.
- Tibet Guest House (1) In the western suburbs, a short distance west of the Lhasa Hotel.
- Sunlight Hotel (2) Across from the university; Tibetan style architecture; close to the Barkhor.
- No. 1 Municipal Guest House (1, 3) Near the Friendship Store and bookshop; Chinese-style compound with good location; plain Chinese set meals.
- Kirey Hotel (3) West of the Banak Shöl Hotel. Good location, good two- or three-bed rooms; shower; reasonable latrines. Tibetan management.
- Plateau Hotel (3) Across from the telecommunications office; showers; good rooms; Tibetan management.
- Hotel Banak Shöl (3) Tibetan-run hotel; small rooms with thin walls; showers; latrines. Still very popular with travelers; also caters to many Chinese and Tibetan visitors.
- Snowlands Hotel (3) Excellent location near the Jokhang; friendly Tibetan management; no showers; poor latrines; small rooms with thin walls; Sichuan food in restaurant.
- Yak Hotel (3) Central location, next to the Taxi Company; good atmosphere (large sofas, pleasant courtyard). Friendly Tibetan management (speak English). Best of the budget hotels.

Shigatse

- Tenzin Hotel (3) Near the Tibetan bazaar; Tibetan-run. Popular with travelers.
- Shigatse Hotel (2) New hotel; reasonable service; caters mainly to tours.
- No. 1 Guest House (3) Tibetan hotel across from Tashilhunpo Monastery; friendly and basic; cheap Tibetan food.
- No. 2 Guest House (2, 3) Across from the cinema; nice suites or dormitory-style rooms; best value in town.
- Truck stop hotel (3) Two of these are near the big department store west of the Shigatse Hotel on the main road into town; good Chinese restaurants nearby.

Gyantse

- No. 2 Guest House (3) Truck stop; dormitory accommodation; near bus station.
- No. 1 Guest House (3) Three-bed rooms; cold water tap; near bus station.
- Gyantse Hotel (2) Caters to tour groups; near center of town.

Tsethang

- Tsethang Hotel (2) Double rooms with

bathrooms and periodic solar-heated showers; caters mainly to groups; adequate Cantonese food.

- Tsethang Guest House (3) The top floor's last wing has comfortable rooms reserved for foreigners; shared cold water washrooms; two restaurants, one simple and cheap, the other with Chinese set meals; best value in town.

Sakya

- Transport Depot Guest House (3) At the northwest corner of Sakya Monastery.
- Sakya Xian Guest House (3) Around a courtyard near the monastery's northeast corner, beyond the market street.
- Sakya government compound (3) The guest house here is outside the east wall of the monastery.

Shekar

- Mt Everest Hotel(Dingri Xian Guest House) (3) Three-bed rooms; reasonable restaurant; rates vary.
- Shekar Hotel (2) Recently built; used mainly by tour groups and expeditions.

Dingri

There are two hotels here. The first (3) is the only structure of Dingri Village located north of the main road. Small kitchen; dormitory; arrangements for yaks, horse carts etc. The Dingri Hotel (3) is located directly across from the center of the town's old section; 17 double room, one 10-bed dormitory.

Rongphuk Monastery

Ten rooms with wood stoves and 2–5 beds in each. Prices depend on whether quilts are required. Food occasionally available (3).

Nyalam

- Nyalam Hotel (2) The largest in town, mainly for groups. Dirty bathrooms; no locks on doors.
- Tsongdü Hotel (3) One dormitory, seven rooms.
- Truck stop hotel (3) Located in the main square by the road where trucks usually stop.

Zhangmu

- Zhangmu Hotel (2) Private double rooms (balcony with great views) with attached bathrooms (unpredictable plumbing); mainly for tour groups. Uninspired service despite direct control by CITS. Food in restaurant can be quite good.
- Reception Office Guest House (3) Simple accommodation in the middle of town.
- Friendship Lodge (3) In center of Zhangmu, run by Nepalis. Many small, inexpensive lodges are for budget travelers.

Mt Kailash

- Pilgrim Guesthouse (3) at the foot of Mt Kailash (Darchen Village).

Shiquanhe (Ali)

- Shiquanhe Hotel (2) Near the center of town.
- Shiquanhe Guest House (3) Rooms arranged around a compound; coal stoves in each room; good, reasonably priced meals.

FOOD AND DRINK

Tibetan Food Tibet's staple food is roasted barley flour (*tsampa*) which is mixed with butter tea into doughy mouthfuls. Generally this is not served in restaurants but is offered on most visits to Tibetan homes. Dumplings filled with meat or vegetables (*momo*) and soup noodles with meat or vegetables (*thukpa*) are widely available in cheap restaurants. Tibetan banquets are arranged occasionally by the Holiday Inn and are also available in some local restaurants—ask your tour agent or a Tibetan friend.

Local Restaurants Sichuanese food is widely available in Lhasa—particularly in the small restaurants outside the Holiday Inn and those near the Yak Hotel. The wider range of vegetables now available has increased choice but few meals rate better than adequate. Several Moslem restaurants can be found in central Lhasa serving a limited menu of noodles and lamb dishes. These are some of the best bets in town. For road trips it is advisable to carry food—bring instant drinks and food that can be reconstituted with hot water. The main vegetable market is behind the post office to the east of the Potala. Tinned goods are available in many department stores near the Barkhor.

TREKKING EQUIPMENT CHECKLIST

The following is an essential checklist which is compiled with high-altitude trekking in Tibet in mind. Personal items like shirts and underwear are excluded.

- Thermal underwear. Long johns made of polypropylene; a good item to bring if passes are to be crossed. Shirt is optional.
- Down or fiberfilled jacket. A highly compressible down jacket (about 1 kg) eliminates the need for a bulky sweater which occupies much the same space. Useful for those chilly couple of hours in early morning and before crawling into the sleeping bag. Fiberfilled jackets occupy more room.
- Trekking boots. Medium to lightweight. Preferable to running shoes. This is the better choice if you are carrying a substantial pack; they give greater protection in marginal situations (snow, icy patches, crossing of passes). Go for Goretex if you can afford it. Be sure to break the boots in. A pair of optional lightweight sneakers is good for camp and for river crossings (avoid wading barefoot if possible). Moleskins for blisters.
- Sleeping bag. Three-season down bag that weighs about 2 kg. Try to get one with zippers that open both ways: if it is too warm in lower altitudes you can stick your feet out. A cotton or silk liner is a good idea.
- Foam pad. A standard closed-cell type, preferably 2 cm thick. I personally prefer Therm-a-Rest, a self-inflating mattress that allows for a good night's sleep on virtually any surface. A 3/4-length one rolls into a surprisingly compact bundle.
- Groundsheet. Best to have a plastic groundsheet under both the pad and the sleeping bag if you plan on staying overnight in Tibetan villages and nomad tents.
- Backpack. Do not skimp on this one. With your trekking boots, this is the most vital piece of equipment on the trek (unless you have porters or pack animals). Make sure the shoulder and waist straps are well-constructed and cushioned; the latter takes most of the weight of the pack. A good sweat-evaporating back panel is important.
- Tent. Well-designed 2-man tents weighing about 2 kg (with a waterproof flysheet) are widely available. Most have advanced features that will allow you to pitch tent within five minutes, an important consideration when you arrive in camp exhausted. Having a tent in Tibet means you do not always have to stay in smoke-filled and noisy Tibetan village houses (or nomad tents). Privacy is an important issue on the trek. Inquisitive villagers or nomads can at times be overwhelming, and being able to camp in splendid isolation at the top of a secluded ridge is one of the greatest pleasures in life.
- Stove. Kerosene stoves are high priority items. Like the tent, it gives you sufficient flexibility and independence from village houses so that you can concentrate on appreciating the environment. I have always taken an MSR Whisperlite which is both light and reliable.

It can use gasoline as well as kerosene, an important consideration in Tibet.
- Rain gear. A roomy, hooded poncho that also covers the backpack is best.

Miscellaneous

- Iodine. An essential item. Comes in tablet, solution or crystal forms to purify water. Tablets are the most convenient: dissolve one in a liter of water and wait 20 minutes. Iodine solution is cheaper: put eight drops in a liter and wait 20 minutes. Its drawback is its taste.
- Medical kit. See Health and Medicine. Be sure to have a small but complete one. It is difficult to find the medicine you need, even in Lhasa.
- Cup. A large one is useful for the enormous amount of butter tea you will be treated to on trek and in monasteries. Good for eating tsampa and meals out of.
- Flashlight. Do not leave home without it. Splurge and get a good one. Do not be tempted by cheap Indian or Chinese flashlights.
- Water bottle. Essential. Again, get a good one like Sigg (Swiss-made).
- Plastic bags. Take five or six good-sized ones for carrying food, fuel, garbage, etc..
- Suntan lotion. Essential in Tibet where exposure to strong ultraviolet light is constant.
- Glacial goggles. Invaluable for crossing passes with snow. At the very least, bring a pair of good dark glasses.
- Toilet paper. Bring plenty. It is available in most big centers. Burn after use.
- Swiss-Army knife.

HEALTH AND MEDICINE

by Robin Houston M. D.

Travel in Tibet, whether limited to a few larger towns or farther afield, poses specific health hazards, primarily altitude and isolation. All visitors are exposed to high altitude. While this may cause only minor symptoms in some, it can rapidly develop into a more dangerous situation in others. Recognizing early symptoms is of paramount importance in preventing major problems. Nearly all travelers will also be at risk of isolation from medical help. This chapter is divided into four sections: 1) Preparation; 2) First Aid and Emergency; 3) General Illness; 4) Problems Specific to Tibet.

PREPARATION

Travelers to Tibet should review their immunization status, put together a small medical kit on advice from their physician (include any chronic medications used), and give careful thought to cold-weather gear.

IMMUNIZATIONS

There are no immunization requirements for Tibet. There are, however, recommended immunizations similar to those for other Asian countries. Diseases such as polio and tetanus are rare in the West, but endemic in Asia. Being up to date in these basic immunizations is important. The following shots are discussed:

1. Rabies

   Dog bites are common in Tibet, and dogs can be the most common source of rabies. The current immunization (HDCV) is extremely effective, but expensive, and requires a specific series to be effective. These shots are painless, but carry some risk of allergic reaction. The prophylactic series consists of three shots, given over a 21-day period. 5 shots plus a shot of concentrated immune globulin (RIG) is the full series. These should be given within ten days. Only two shots are required for an exposure in someone who has had the prophylactic series. In addition, the prophylactic series may give some protection in the interim before the last two shots.

   Treat any dog bites by washing the wound immediately and carefully with a disinfectant, preferably iodine.

2. Hepatitis

   There are two immunizations for hepatitis, a three-shot series for hepatitis B, and immune globulin (gamma globulin) for hepatitis A. There is no current shot for Non-A, Non-B hepatitis. The hepatitis B series is effective, but expensive, and recommended primarily for medical personnel at risk through contact with blood products. Gamma globulin is recommended for travelers to Tibet.

3. Meningitis

Travelers to Asia may be at some risk from meningococcal meningitis. The immunization against meningitis is effective, but often difficult to find (Kathmandu is a good place to get it). Note that it is not effective until two weeks after injection.

4. Typhoid

Typhoid fever is common in Asia, and can be a serious disease. Although there are new immunizations against typhoid being tested, the current shot is not 100 per cent effective, and often causes a painful arm and low grade fever upon injection. The exact risk in Tibet is unknown.

5. Others

Yellow fever immunization is not necessary for Asia, unless there has been previous travel to a yellow fever area, in which case there are country-specific recommendations. The cholera immunization is only good for six weeks, is not that effective, and not recommended by many authorities. Since respiratory disease is common in Tibet, some travelers, such as those susceptible to respiratory illness, and older travelers, may wish to consult their physician on the importance of pneumococcal and flu immunizations.

MEDICAL SUPPLIES

In many parts of Asia medical supplies, including prescription drugs, are readily available, and in the larger cities in Tibet drugs may also be available. However, it is wise to carry a kit that has some basic supplies. The following list represents a very basic kit, and could be supplemented with other medications on an individual basis. Any medications taken regularly should be included. All drugs and their dosage should be reviewed with a physician, allergic history and drug interaction discussed, and self-treatment only attempted with full understanding of the risks and side effects of the medications. The first figure indicates the number of pills to take with you, the second describes the strength of each pill.

- **Antihistamine**
  diphenhydramine: for allergic symptoms, hives, itching: 5 (50 mg)
- **Antibiotics**
  tetracycline: for sinusitis, bronchitis, some skin: 30 (250 mg) infections, dysentery

  trimethoprim sulfa: for dysentery, some skin infections, urinary tract infection: 30 (100mg)

  metronidazole: for amoebic dysentery, giardiasis: 30 (200 mg)
- **Analgesics**
  aspirin: for pain, joint inflammation, fever: 20 (250 mg)
  codeine: for more severe pain, cough: 20 (15 mg)
- **High altitude**
  acetazolamide: for prevention of altitude symptoms: 10 (250 mg)
- **Disinfectants**
  iodine: for water purification

- **Others**

tape:	for first aid, bandaging etc.
dressings:	including bandaids, gauze pads
sunscreen:	particularly for nose, ears etc.

In the dry air of Tibet, throat lozenges can give symptomatic relief and cold preparations ameliorate symptoms of nasal congestion. Topical antibiotic ointment may be useful for minor cuts and abrasions to help prevent infection. An ankle wrap or knee brace can give support for weak joints. Other medications are discussed under specific illnesses, with some comments on their pros and cons.

FIRST AID AND EMERGENCY

CUTS, SCRAPES, AND BURNS

Most minor cuts, scrapes, and burns are readily amenable to treatment with materials at hand. First, the injury must be carefully examined to determine the extent of injury, and whether any deeper structure has been injured. Bleeding can invariably be controlled by direct pressure over the wound, though it may begin again with washing. Scrapes (abrasions) can be left open if they can be kept clean. Burns should be evaluated to determine severity and size. A small burn that blisters but maintains its sensation can be treated like other wounds, with careful observation for infection. However, burns that appear greyish, with loss of sensation should be taken seriously, since the entire thickness of skin may no longer be viable, and grafting could be necessary. As a first measure, burns should be covered with an antibiotic ointment and a sterile dressing. Any wound, no matter how small, can become infected. The classic signs of early infection are increased redness, tenderness, and swelling.

SPRAINS AND FRACTURES

Perhaps the most common trail injury is the sprained ankle, and the majority of these are minor. Any joint can be sprained from trauma, and the treatment of minor symptoms is similar. First determine the extent of injury, in order to rule out a fracture. Then apply cold compress and raise the limb initially to decrease swelling. Finally, avoid stressing the injured joint later. While ankles are the most likely to be sprained, knees can cause pain just from excessive use. Treatment is rest and the use of an anti-inflammatory medication such as aspirin or ibuprofen. Unfortunately, the problem may reoccur.

EYE PROBLEMS

Perhaps the two most common problems relating to the eye are infection (pink-eye) and a foreign body in the eye. Conjunctivitis, or pink-eye, is a viral or bacterial infection of the superficial tissue. Since this tissue is very vascular, early treatment with hot soaks (using a washcloth and a dish of hot water) will often curtail the infection. Sometimes ophthalmic antibiotic drops or ointment are required. Conjunctivitis can be contagious, and care should be taken with hand-washing.

Getting something in the eye is very painful. Most foreign bodies rinse themselves clear, but some may adhere to the cornea (clear part of the eye) causing severe discomfort. It is important to remove these, as they can be the focus for infection.

One other precaution is worth mentioning. The eye is affected by ultra-violet radiation, and the intensity of this radiation is greater at altitude and when there is a reflective surface such as snow. Should a trekker find himself on snow on a bright day, snowblindness is the rule, even after only a few hours, if adequate dark glasses are not worn. This condition can be extremely uncomfortable, requiring that the eyes be patched, and may take two days to resolve. It is completely preventable with the use of dark glacial glasses, which have hoods on the stems.

ABDOMINAL EMERGENCIES

Diarrheal disease with its associated cramps is common in Asian travel. The more serious intestinal illnesses include appendicitis, intestinal obstruction or torsion, and perforation. The abdomen usually will respond to irritation within the gut, i.e. from diarrheal disease, with increased activity—thus the gut becomes noisy or hyperactive. Crampy pain is experienced in a variety of locations. When the abdomen is palpated, it may be tender, but remains soft. More serious illnesses tend to quiet the abdomen, have pain restricted to an area, such as the right lower quadrant in appendicitis, and when palpated, the abdomen may feel hard to the touch. Nausea, vomiting and fever may sometimes accompany both serious and less serious illness. They can also be indicators of a worsening situation.

The urinary tract is commonly affected by infection either in the bladder or kidneys, and by stones. Symptoms include painful urination, frequent urination, and a sense of having to urinate frequently. More serious infections may cause fever, backache, and abdominal pain, often to the side or in the back just below the ribcage. Most infections respond well to antibiotic therapy.

Pain caused by the liver or gallbladder can be difficult to diagnose. Hepatitis, which is endemic in Asia, causes pain in the right upper quadrant of the abdomen,. This is often a less significant finding than the other symptoms of hepatitis, namely fatigue, anorexia, dark urine, and jaundice.

As a general rule, abdominal pain is more likely to be serious, regardless of cause, if it is persistent and constant (rather than crampy), causes the abdomen to become quiet and hard to the touch (muscular guarding) or is associated with vomiting or fever. Whenever there is a question as to the seriousness of abdominal pain, medical help should be sought immediately.

GENERAL ILLNESS

I. RESPIRATORY PROBLEMS

Given the geography and climate, Tibet is a set-up for respiratory infections. The altitude tends to dry the air, which can cause irritation in the nasal passages, facilitating entry of viruses or bacteria. Dust in the air and smoke from cooking fires also aggravate the respiratory tract, casuing respiratory infections. The most common problem is the common cold; antibiotic treatment is not required, and other medications (aspirin for the fever, antihistamines for drying up secretions) are basically for symptomatic relief only. However, the common cold may pave the way for a more serious infection, and knowing just when this has happened is not always easy.

When discussing respiratory illness in the context of high altitude it is critical to remember that one of the serious elements in altitude illness is pulmonary edema, a respiratory disease. Therefore, it is very important to be absolutely clear that the respiratory symptoms are not signs of altitude illness, since the treatment is quite different. Individuals enthusiastic about their trip to Tibet commonly deny this possibility, blaming symptoms on a minor 'cold'. They are at significant risk if altitude illness has not been ruled out. Altitude problems are discussed later.

Sinusitis The sinuses are air spaces in the skull that can become infected. Sinusitis may follow a common cold, or may develop on its own. The most common sinuses affected are located just above the eyebrows and just below the eyes. When drainage is obstructed, pain may develop in the area of the infected sinus. In addition there may be fever and a purulent discharge from the nose, or draining down the back of the throat. All of these symptoms can be present with the common cold, and the points of differentiation are subtle. Headache and pain located 'behind the eyes' or in the upper teeth, associated with fever (and particularly if it follows a cold), is likely to be sinusitis.

This condition frequently requires antibiotic therapy, using penicillin or tetracycline. In addition, it is helpful to thin the secretions and open the nasal passages. Increasing fluids, doing steam inhalations (perhaps with a bit of Tiger Balm in the water), and using a nasal spray decongestant can all be helpful.

Bronchitis As an extension of the naso-pharynx, the upper airway is also susceptible to irritation and infection, and when the bronchus is infected it is termed bronchitis. Smokers are at significantly increased risk for developing bronchitis, and some will have a chronic bronchitis that can worsen in the face of a new infection.

Like sinusitis, bronchitis can be subtle, developing from a cold. Though a low grade fever may be present, the hallmark symptom is a productive cough. Classically, bronchitis appears as a cough accompanied by significant green or yellow, thick sputum. Fatigue, malaise, and sometimes pain in the lower throat with coughing, may be present. Like sinusitis, the symptoms tend to be low-key, lingering but persistent.

Treatment of bronchitis is similar to sinusitis—attempting to thin secretions with steam inhalations, increasing fluids, stopping smoking etc. Antibiotics are often necessary, with tetracycline being a good choice. It is not uncommon for a slightly longer course to be required—up to 14 days, for more severe cases.

Pneumonia Pneumonia is an infection in the smaller air sacs of the lungs, and represents one of the more serious respiratory infections. Before antibiotic therapy, pneumonia carried a very high mortality rate, and even today is responsible for many deaths in older people and children in the developing world. It is a disease not to be taken lightly.

Pneumonia begins as a cough, usually productive, often with 'rusty' or blood-tinged sputum. This is accompanied by fever, often quite high (39.5°C, 103°F) and chills. There may be chest pain in the area of the infection, or referred pain that goes to the back or shoulder. It may come on rapidly, but more commonly it develops gradually, with all symptoms worsening over one to two days.

Many other illnesses can cause chest pain, including heart disease, pneumothorax (lung collapse), pulmonary embolus (blood clot in the lung), and pulmonary edema. It is therefore important to carefully review the history of the illness, look for any other risk factors, including age, other medications, and be sure of the diagnosis before considering self-treatment. In general, it is best to seek medical attention for pneumonia to avoid misdiagnosis, and to have back-up in case of treatment failure. As mentioned before, it is critical to rule out altitude-related pulmonary disease in Tibet, since it can mimic pneumonia.

Treatment is antibiotic therapy and rest. Symptomatic treatment such as cough suppressants should be used with caution, and patients monitored closely to be sure they are improving. The choice of antibiotics depends on the organism, and this is not easy on a trek. For most adult pneumonia, injectable penicillin is the treatment of choice. Oral penicillin is not as effective; a cephalosporin may be a better choice. Hydration is very important, and aspirin or tylenol can be used for fever control. Severe pneumonia may require oxygen, particularly at the higher altitudes of Tibet.

Others   Shortness of breath is a non-specific symptom that is common at altitude. Most people in Tibet will experience shortness of breath with exercise, but this should disappear when resting. In association with illnesses such as pneumonia, this condition may occur. However, it may also be an early sign of altitude sickness for someone poorly acclimatized. Since altitude sickness symptoms can be so subtle, shortness of breath in that context should be carefully evaluated.

Nosebleeds are common at altitude because of the dryness of the air. Most are from the anterior septum of the nose, and thus easy to stop by direct pressure. A common problem is failing to pinch the nose for long enough—it may take up to five minutes. Keeping the nose and the septum lubricated may be a good preventive measure, and this can be done with vaseline to prevent chapping.

Sorethroat may again be just from the cold, dry air, or can be from the start of a cold, or other infection. Climbers at higher altitudes often use throat lozenges to help keep the throat moist to prevent irritation.

II. INTESTINAL PROBLEMS

Of all the things that plague travelers to Asia, intestinal problems are the most common. For many parts of Asia, including Tibet, a complete variety of intestinal pathogens is endemic, and travelers with limited prior exposure (and thus little immunity) are particularly susceptible. Luckily, most of the illnesses, though quite unpleasant, are self-limited and not life-threatening. Frequently, they run their course without treatment. However, it is not uncommon to contract something for which treatment may be important.

The pathogens causing diarrhea are either parasites (amoeba, giardia), bacteria (salmonella, shigella), viruses, or occasionally helminths (worms). Symptoms overlap almost completely, running the spectrum from little or no sickness to severe diarrhea with dehydration. Treatment is determined by the organism, and differs for each group. In addition to eradicating the germ, there are medications to give symptomatic relief, to slow down the diarrhea or prevent the cramping. Drugs to stop diarrhea are controversial; some authorities feel they may prolong the course of the illness. These should perhaps be reserved for long, necessary bus rides, or severe cramps, and should absolutely not be used for children.

Nearly all intestinal illness described here is transmitted through contaminated food and water. Thus proper attention to correct water purification and the food you eat are important preventive measures. In addition, wash your hands frequently.

Amoebiasis

Entamoeba histolytica is a parasite that can cause diarrhea, and it also has the ability to invade the gut wall and thus migrate elsewhere, usually the liver. Although not common, this facility for invasion makes amoebiasis a potentially serious illness, and one that should be treated carefully. In addition, amoeba can cause sudden onset of severe, bloody diarrhea. At its worst, expect fever, very frequent bloody diarrheal stools, headache, and extreme fatigue. In a milder form, it can cause occasional cramping, on and off diarrhea, separated by a day or so of constipation, then the return of diarrhea. Treatment is with the metronidazole group of drugs, followed by diodoquin to rid the system of the more resistant cyst form of the parasite. After taking the pills, a rapid decrease in symptoms usually results.

Giardiasis

Giardiasis is a common illness in the Western world, and occurs frequently in Asia. The parasite, like amoeba, has a cyst form that is quite happy in cold water at high altitudes. In addition, the organism survives in wild animal hosts, and thus is present in wilderness areas. Unlike amoeba, giardia do not invade, and are therefore less dangerous.

The classic symptom of giardiasis is gas—both flatulence, and the infamous 'sulfur burp'. Perhaps more than diarrhea, bloating and explosive flatulence are the most unpleasant side effects. In more chronic cases, low-grade diarrhea may continue for many weeks, and be associated with fatigue. Some individuals may have minimal symptoms, and carry the organism with them for years.

Treatment for giardiasis is with quinacrine or drugs of the metronidazole group. Usually this results in cure, though an occasional case is refractory.

Bacterial Diarrhea

Many bacteria can cause diarrhea. The most common include the E. Coli group, Salmonella (also responsible for typhoid), and Shigella. Like the parasitic illnesses, the bacterial diarrheas have a wide spectrum of symptoms, and are not simple to diagnose. Most bacterial diarrheas will cure themselves over time, although some have the potential for serious illness. In all cases, the severity of the diarrhea (and vomiting, if present) determines the extent of associated dehydration, which can be dangerous. Fever, malaise, abdominal cramps, diarrhea, and sometimes bloody diarrhea are the common symptoms, with little to distinguish one organism from another. Sometimes extreme fatigue may be the major symptom.

Treatment is either with antibiotics, or with letting the illness run its course, and there is controversy about this. In severe cases, taking the appropriate drug is necessary, and should be started 'in the field'. In mild cases, it may be alright to take a 'wait and see' approach, since symptoms may stop on their own. When possible, confirming a diagnosis with a stool specimen is best. Once the decision to start antibiotics is made, it is difficult to determine which is best, since the intestinal pathogens are notorious for their resistance to drugs. Naladixic acid (and related drugs), tetracycline, trimethoprim sulfa, chloramphenicol, and ampicillin are all good intestinal drugs. Antibiotics should be continued for a minimum of five days.

Bacterial intestinal illness can be more serious, and it is important to judge the level of improvement on a day-to-day basis. Since intestinal perforation can occur, abdominal pain that becomes constant (rather than crampy), fever that persists, and an abdomen that is hard and tender on palpation are all worrisome signs.

Hepatitis

Though not strictly a diarrheal disease, hepatitis is included here because the common type (hepatitis A) is transmitted by the same route as most of the diarrheal diseases. Hepatitis is an infection of the liver caused by a particular set of viruses. The inflammation of the liver produces many symptoms, including anorexia, which can be severe, fatigue, mild diarrhea, fever, and itching. In addition, in most cases there is associated jaundice, or yellowing of the sclera (white) of the eye, and of the skin. Most instances of hepatitis A cause significant illness, which except for mild cases would terminate a trip. However, the disease usually resolves itself without causing permanent damage to the liver. There is no treatment. The gamma-globulin shot recommended for travelers can be a good preventive measure, and even if hepatitis is contracted, may decrease its severity.

Hepatitis B is the more serious form, and is most commonly contracted through contact with blood or blood products. It is much less likely to be a cause of concern in travelers.

PROBLEMS SPECIFIC TO TIBET

ALTITUDE ILLNESS AND COLD INJURY

For travelers exploring towns and cities in Tibet, without trekking, this section will have little relevance. For those who plan on walking, the issue of cold injury, which includes frostbite, is important. Except in rare cases, proper equipment and planning will prevent frostbite and related problems.

Although most areas of Tibet visited by foreigners are not far to the north, Tibet is of uniform high altitude, and thus can be cold at any time of the year. In addition, it is relatively simple to walk to even higher altitudes, where cold temperature, wind, and altitude combine to make cold injuries much more likely. Understanding the early symptoms, and being adequately equipped for the trek, are critical and may save lives.

Frostbite

Frostbite occurs when there is tissue damage due to freezing. The most common areas affected are the hands and feet, although spots of frostbite also occur on the nose, ears, or cheeks. With freezing, there is impaired circulation, and in the process of healing, maintenance of circulation is very important.

The early signs of frostbite are pain and discoloration, progressing to numbness. On the face, 'white' patches may signify early frostbite, while on the hands or feet, a digit may become greyish. In time, the tissue may ultimately turn black. During the early phases the exact extent of injury is difficult to estimate—blistering or persistent discoloration are poor prognostic signs. As a preventive measure, extremities that lose their sensation should be warmed up immediately, even if this involves the common field treatment of placing icy feet on another's warm abdomen. Attention to these early signs of pain or numbness can easily prevent serious frostbite in most instances.

Once frozen, tissue is damaged, and further trauma will significantly worsen the prognosis. Perhaps the worst case situation is to allow the area to be refrozen, and this should be avoided at all costs. Some authorities say it is better to walk on a frozen foot than thaw it if there is a chance of refreezing.

The ideal treatment for a frostbitten extremity is to rewarm in a water bath kept just above body temperature. In addition, the victim should be warm and adequately fed. Water temperature should be monitored, and great care exercised that it not be too hot (above 42°C or 108°F) since all sensation may be lost. After thawing, the affected area must be kept clean; infection can occur. Digits can be separated by clean cotton to prevent rubbing. Avoid further traumatization; a victim with thawed feet should be carried.

During a trek, it is often difficult to make judgements about frostbite. Early detection is important. Should an extremity be numb, remember that warming by a stove or fire is dangerous, since the tissue can be burned easily in the absence of normal sensation. Caught early, a nipped extremity may not in fact have significant frostbite. It is thus possible to continue walking in an emergency.

Perhaps the commonest frostbite in trekkers occurs while crossing passes: where there is snow to walk through, when the weather deteriorates, or when a party is caught by weather or darkness and is forced to bivouac. Wet feet in dropping temperatures are at risk, and the judgement should be not how to treat the frostbite, but whether to cross the pass.

Hypothermia

The most insidious illness common in mountainous areas is hypothermia, a condition where the body's core temperature is too low. Due to its gradual onset and debilitating powers, hypothermia is a dangerous condition. When unrecognized, it can be fatal.

The body's internal temperature is protected at the expense of the periphery. As the temperature drops, there are protective mechanisms that attempt to preserve the 'core' temperature. First, there is peripheral vasoconstriction: decreasing blood flow to the arms and legs and thus increasing it to the heart and lungs. At a certain point, the body responds to cold by shivering, basically a muscular contraction, which produces heat (and also requires calories). If the core temperature drops below a certain point, the body's normal shivering response fails, and the core temperature is free to continue to drop. Unless this is reversed, someone in this condition may lapse into a coma and die.

Various factors contribute to heat loss and subsequent hypothermia: temperature, wind, moisture. A wet person loses heat through evaporative loss, and with wind, it is possible to lose a great deal of heat quickly. There are reports of fatalities from hypothermia in these conditions even at temperatures well above freezing. Finally, the availability of calories to enable the body to produce heat is important.

Hypothermia is commonly seen in situations where an individual is working hard (trekking, climbing, skiing) and is wet from sweat or rain on a windy day at relatively low temperatures. Altitude contributes to the process, making trekkers in Tibet particularly vulnerable. Understanding this is important, since the early signs of hypothermia are difficult but vital to recognize.

The most common symptoms of hypothermia are the loss of muscular coordination and impairment of judgement. The trekker who complains of being cold, and later says he will just stop and rest a bit, may be suffering from this condition. There are reports of bizarre behavior, such as eating ski wax, and of poor judgement in the extreme, such as removing a parka in the face of worsening weather and dropping temperatures. Sometimes the victim has failed to keep up with caloric needs, say by skipping lunch, and although cold to the point of shivering, may simply stop walking. At the point of mental impairment, if the victim continues to cool down, he may become lethargic, and then comatose. It is not uncommon to have frostbite as a concurrent problem.

Severe hypothermia can be difficult to treat, since the heart is very susceptible to dangerous rhythm disturbances when cold. In most field situations, mild hypothermia can be alleviated by warming the victim and meeting caloric needs. At the earliest signs, stopping is mandatory, and the victim must be rewarmed by the most efficient methods. These include using hot (but not hot enough to burn) water bottles placed on the abdomen or at major arteries (groin, armpit), using a warm person in the same sleeping bag, and having the victim drink warm sugary drinks. If caught early, these techniques should be safe and effective.

Altitude illness

Everyone going to Tibet will be affected by altitude. Many will have unpleasant symptoms. A few may even develop life-threatening symptoms. The bulk of the Tibetan Plateau lies above 3300 m and many passes are over 5000 m. Furthermore, descent, which is the mainstay of treatment for altitude problems, can be difficult: the lowest points are distant and difficult to reach quickly. Most visitors to Tibet will arrive at high altitudes quickly, i.e. by flying from Chengdu or driving from Nepal. All these factors combine to make altitude problems significant.

The mildest form of altitude illness has been called 'acute mountain sickness', or AMS. Headache, nausea, lassitude are all common symptoms. However, other signs may also be a result of mild AMS. These include diarrhea, sleepiness, shortness of breath, 'flu' symptoms, and general malaise. The rate of ascent and altitude reached determine the severity of these symptoms, which may represent precursors to more serious problems.

A second form of altitude sickness is pulmonary edema, or HAPE ('high altitude pulmonary edema'). When the body's acclimatization mechanisms fail, fluid begins to accumulate in the lungs, causing difficulty with oxygen absorption. Pulmonary edema can be severe, even fatal, and is difficult to treat. The classic symptoms are shortness of breath, particularly at rest, a cough, and later, the production of pink frothy sputum. This dangerous condition can be rapidly progressive, requiring emergency treatment.

The third form of altitude sickness is 'high altitude cerebral edema' (HACE). As with the lungs, altitude can cause swelling in the brain, which can develop to such an extent that neurologic symptoms such as headache and ataxia or loss of balance are present. Headache is difficult to evaluate, since it is a common symptom of the more benign AMS. However, headaches that are severe, that are associated with vomiting, or that persist in spite of rest at the same altitude are worrisome. Cerebral edema is a real possibility. Ataxia can be easily tested by having the individual walk a straight line with one foot in front of the other. If off balance for this test, in the presence of headache, the victim may well have early cerebral edema, and should descend immediately.

The classic signs of pulmonary or cerebral edema are obvious, but usually their manifestation is more subtle. It is safest to assume that any symptoms at altitude may be warning signals, and that further ascent is unwise. If more severe problems show up, the only choice is to descend. Since the body does acclimatize, the rate of ascent is important. Most people, if given long enough time to ascend, will have minimal symptoms even up to 5000 m or more. The general rule is not to go more than 300m per day above 3000 m, and to go less per day above 4500 m.

Additionally avoid potential problems by building reasonable rest days into the itinerary. If flying into Lhasa, there should be at least two rest days before moving to higher altitudes, and then the general rules should be followed as closely as possible. However, even more important is to listen to what the body is saying. If there are symptoms that could be attributed to altitude, do not ascend.

There are medications that can ameliorate the symptoms of mild altitude illness. The most commonly used is acetazolamide (Diamox), which helps prevent headache and malaise. In addition, Diamox helps prevent the unpleasant sleeping disturbances many encounter at altitude, particularly the breathing pattern called Cheyne-Stokes—breathing characterized by a deep breath followed by an abnormally long pause. The drug can be taken once or twice per day, and may cause increased urination (it is a diuretic). Steroids have been used to prevent altitude illness, with promising results, but they have the potential for serious side effects and their safety for use at altitude has not been established. Other medications should be used with caution, since little is known about their effects at altitude. In particular, drugs that depress respiration, such as strong pain medications or tranquilizers (codeine, diazepam) should be avoided, since these may contribute to the development of more serious altitude illness.

There is no better treatment for significant altitude illness than descent; to consider medical treatment as a substitute is completely irrational. If there are signs of significant altitude illness the victim must descend as quickly and to as low a level as possible.

The treatment of AMS is also descent, although in the case of mild symptoms, simply avoiding ascent and allowing the body's normal acclimatization mechanisms to catch up may be appropriate. Acetazolamide is usually not curative, but rather should be used as a preventive measure. If rest and time do not alleviate symptoms, then descent should be considered. Under no circumstances should a symptomatic individual be left to their own devices while the rest of the party moves on, under the misguided notion that the affected individual can catch up later. Too often the victim worsens, with his support group merrily walking on ahead.

Two other points are worth mentioning. First, fluid intake is important at altitude. Although the severe expressions of altitude illness involve excess fluid, it is misplaced fluid, not true excess. High altitude air is dry, and fluid loss is significant even in the absence of sweating. Most authorities feel that maintaining a fluid intake that keeps urine output high, with nearly colorless urine, is an important preventive measure. Second, the notion that being fit keeps altitude illness away is not supported by experience. Some would say that being out of shape is desirable, since upon reaching a higher altitude, an unfit individual is less apt to be active, and may rest and acclimatize. A fit person probably wants to exercise after a long flight, and this is most foolhardy for the first day above 3000 m. In addition, the fit individual tends to be ahead of the group, moving beyond his capacity to acclimatize.

SPOKEN TIBETAN

by Sylvie Grand-Clement

CONTENTS

Introduction
How to use Spoken Tibetan
Abbreviations
Punctuation

The Basics
KEY TO PHONETICS
    vowels, consonants, nasals,
    retroflex, aspirations

ELEMENTARY GRAMMAR
    word order, to be, personal
    pronouns, to have, possessive
    pronouns, verbs, tenses,
    questions, negation, adjectives:
    comparative and superlative,
    must/need

NUMBERS
    how to count, ordinal numbers

TIME AND DATES
    time, terms relating to time,
    adverbs, age, duration

IDIOMATIC EXPRESSIONS

A Phrasebook for Trekkers and Pilgrims
GREETINGS
    ordinary and honorific forms,
    tashee-delay, common phrases

TREKKING
    weather, equipment, preparat-
    ion, guide and pack-animals, the
    countryside, trail, direction,
    rivers, pass, shelter

MONASTERIES
    in the courtyard, preliminaries,
    general queries, statues, frescoes,
    history, foundation, destruction,
    reconstruction, special events, in
    the neighborhood, life in the
    monastery, rituals, meeting the
    lama, blessings, staying in the
    monastery, festivals

PILGRIMAGE
    pilgrims, places, practises, retreat

INTRODUCTION

The purpose of this manual is to allow the reader to communicate orally with Tibetans while trekking and/or on pilgrimage. There are two sections. The core of the first, The Basics, is an elementary grammar. This is indispensible for those who intend to spend a significant amount of time in Tibet. The second part is highly specific. It focuses exclusively on the needs of a traveler while he or she is in a monastic or pilgrimage situation. Having some rudimentary concepts of grammar is useful.

To avoid the problem of dialects, the system of pronunciation of Lhasa has been adopted here. It is the most common throughout the country. In the Phrasebook, however, the honorific form is not stressed as much as in classical Lhasa dialect. Instead, it is offered as an option according to need. The system of phonetics used here is simple and fairly close to reality, and the syllabic rhythm is presented as in normal conversation.

How to use Spoken Tibetan
First familiarize yourself with the Key to Phonetics. Skip Elementary Grammar and go straight to the Phrasebook, experimenting with key phrases in Greetings and Monasteries. After you have picked up some knowledge of sentence structure, immerse yourself gradually into the main components of Grammar: pronouns and possessive pronouns, verbs and tenses, and questions. After a week or two, depending on inclination and progress, start work on the rest of Basics and the Phrasebook.

List of abbreviations
A few Chinese and Hindi terms, commonly used these days in Tibet and in India by the Tibetans, are indicated in this manual by (c) and (hi). Tibetan terms are in italics, so are the Sanskrit ones preceded by (skt). (H) means the form is honorific.

Punctuation
Punctuation in Spoken Tibetan has the following function:

, a comma separates two synonyms.

; a semi-colon separates the ordinary from the honorific forms.

/ a slash indicates a pause in a Tibetan sentence. It puts the stress in the right place.
eg: now, let's go
        da/dro gee-yin

... triple dots indicate the place where to put the changing term which is chosen from the list below it.
eg: this hat is/   **shamo dee/... ray**
black   **nakpo**
new   **sarpa**
This hat is new   **shaamo dee/sarpa
                    ray**

- a hyphen unifies the particles with the auxiliary:
eg: He will not come. **korang yong gee-
                       ma-ray**

or can be used also to avoid confusion in the phonetics:
ex : cinema   **lo-nyen**

The punctuation in English follows the rules given below:

a hyphen separates the word order in a Tibetan sentence:
eg: can you speak English ?
        kirang/injikay shen-gee-yö-pay?
        you-English-speak-int.

THE BASICS
Key to Phonetics
Tibetan belongs to the Sino–Tibetan family and more specifically to the Tibeto–Burmese group. Primarily mono-syllabic, it was probably an oral language up to the eighth century AD. At that time, a Sanskrit script called lentsa was introduced from India. The alphabet is composed

of thirty consonants and five vowels. Each consonant contains the basic sound a. Other vowels are denoted by accents. There is a standardised system of transliteration into Roman characters. This system is not phonetic because all consonants are not pronounced, and the association of several letters may produce a new one.

The phonetics presented in this manual have been designed in a simple way specifically for English-speaking readers. The purpose is to allow anyone to converse in Tibetan without knowing the Tibetan script. In this system, all letters are pronounced.

VOWELS

Most of the vowels are pronounced as in English, except for ö and ü.

a*	as a	in lack	eg: **nga** (I)
aï	y	shy	eg: **kwaï** (money) (c)
ay	ay	ray	eg: **ray** (to be)
e	e	lens	eg: **meling** (America)
i	i	quick	eg: **chini** (sugar)
ö	eu	French jeu or German schön	eg: **pö** (Tibet)
ee	ee	seem	eg: **dee** (this)
o	o	go	eg: **sho** (come here)
oo	oo	boot	eg: **namdroo** (plane)
u			only used for Sanskrit terms and names eg: **stupa** (skt)
ü**	u	French rue or German über	eg: **yül** (country)
ye	ye	yell	eg: **trongyer** (town)

Note
* aa gives the same sound as a at the end of a word.
  ex : **daawa** (moon)

** To pronounce **ü**, pronounce several times **ou** as in you, (eg: ou,ou,ou,ou...), then pronounce **ee** as in see. Keep the mouth in the **ee** pronunciation position, and try pronouncing **ou** of you, without moving the mouth or the lips.

y never alters the preceding sound.
  eg: **koyö** is pronounced **ko-yö**
      saaya   **sa-ya**

NASALS

Nasal sounds are quite important in Tibetan. The main ones are **an** and **on**. They are made by nasalizing the vowels **a** and **o**.
  eg: **tanda** (now)
      gonda (sorry)

CONSONANTS

All consonants are pronounced and most of them are similar to English.
At the end of a syllable, **k** is hardly pronounced—it shortens the preceding sound
  eg: **drook** (six)

ng is softened like **ing** in coming.
  eg: **ngö** is similar to **ng-a** in sing-again

ang as ung in sung eg: ch'ang (beer)

eng (times)	ang	gang	eg: **teng**
ing (today)	ing	ring	eg: **tering**

ong   ong   gong   eg: **song**
(auxiliary)

There are several ways to combine the consonant n with vowels.

ön as   un   in run   eg: **lopön** (master)

en   en   men   eg: **len** (answer)

in   in   sin   eg: **yin** (auxiliary)

ann   in   man   eg: **sanntsam**
                                     (border)

onn   on   son   eg: **dronn-do** (want
                                    to go)

kyoo   cu   cute   eg: **kyooma**
                                    (ordinary)

gyoo   gu   regular   eg: **gyoo** (run)

ün is the combination of ü and n
(like une in French)   eg: **dün** (seven)

RETROFLEX CONSONANTS

A retroflex sound is made by moving the tip
of your tongue along the palate.
The **r** is slightly rolled.

tr as tr in train   eg: **tri** (knife)
dr as dr in drill   eg: **dro** (go)

ASPIRATIONS

Aspirations, denoted by an apostrophe, are similar
to an aspirated **h**.
They are applied to the consonants **k**, **p**, **dr**,
tr, **dz**, **ts**, **j**, **l**, **ky** and **ch**.
They are important for they change the meaning
of the word.
Thus: **tsangma** means clean, and **ts'angma** all.

Elementary Grammar

WORD ORDER

The word order in a Tibetan sentence is as
follows:
Subject–Complement–Verb

The subject always comes first and the verb
is found at the end, whatever the tense.

eg: I am going to Tibet
        I-to Tibet-am going
        nga/pöla dro-gee-yin

ARTICLES AND PRONOUNS

In Tibetan, there is no definite article (the),
nor plural articles. The indefinite article **one**
is translated by the cardinal number (**chik**).

All the adjectives, except for the possessive
ones, follow the noun they qualify.

Noun–Adjective

eg: A good friend
        friend-good-a
        drokpo yakpo chik

Definite articles are often replaced by the
demonstrative adjectives:

         this   **dee**
         that   **day**

eg: this coat   eg: that car
      dooklo dee   **motra day**

Demonstrative pronouns are similar to demonstrative adjectives. They usually come first in
a sentence and can refer to a thing as well
as to a being.

         this one   **dee**
         that one   **day**

eg: This is mine. eg: That one is the
                          chief.
   dee/ngay ray day/gootree ray

Plural

Pronouns and adjectives become plural by adding
the particle **ts'o** to them.
Noun–Adjectives–Article–Plural
Demonstrative pronouns and adjectives become
nasalized as below :

     dee —> **din-ts'o**   these, these ones
     day —> **den-ts'o**   those, those ones

eg: these thick black clouds
       cloud-black-thick-this-plural
       trinpa nakpo t'ookpo din-ts'o

Prepositions

Prepositions follow the noun instead of preceding it.

Noun-preposition

Some prepositions:

after	**jela**	since	**nay**
before	**nyela**	to	**la**
in	**nangla**	under	**wola**
near	**chila**	within	**yamdoo**
on	**gangla**		

eg: in the house
       house-in
       k'angpa nangla

Conjunctions

For the most part, the conjunctions follow the subordinate proposition that they introduce.

Subordinate Proposition–Conjuction–Main Proposition

Some conjunctions:

after	**nay, jay**
before	**ma + (verb) + gongla**
because	**tsang**
if	**na**
while	**kabla**

eg: If he does not come, I will go
       he-neg-come-if-I-go-future.
       kong ma p'ay-na/nga dro gee-yin

TO BE

In Tibetan, there are different ways to express the notion of **to be**. According to the situation, it can be **ray**, **doo** or **yoray**.

Ray

It can express a state or a quality.

(I) am	**(nga) yin**

(you) are	**(kirang) ray**
(he/she/it) is	**(korang/morang/kong) ray**
(we) are	**(ngaats'o) yin**
(you) are	**(kirangts'o) ray**
(they) are	**(korangts'o/ morangts'o/kongts'o) ray**

eg: He is a teacher.
       he-teacher-is
       kong/gegenla ray (H)

eg: That hat is yellow.
       hat-this-yellow-is
       shaamo dee/serpo ray

Doo

It can express:
– a location or
– the result of a personal experience or
– the possession of something or
– the impersonal mode (used to express feelings)

(I) am	**(nga) yö**
(you) are	**(kirang)doo**
(he/she) is	**(korang; morang; kong (H)) doo**
(we) are	**(ngaats'o) yö**
(you) are	**(kirangts'o) doo**
(they) are	**(korangts'o; morangts'o; kongts' o (H)) doo**

eg: The post-office is close to here.
       post office-from here-distance-close-is. **dak'ang dee-nay/t'a-nyepo doo**

eg: Today it is very hot
       today-very-hot-is
       tering/pay-ts'apo doo

eg: He has a house.
       to him-house-a-has
       korangla/kangpa chik doo

eg: I am tired
       I-tired-am
       nga/t'ang chay-gee-doo

Yoray

This auxiliary is the same for all persons in the singular and plural.
Yoray is used for a general affirmation, for something everybody knows. It is often translated as there is or there are. It can also be used to express possession.

eg: There are many yaks in Tibet.
       in Tibet-yak-many-there are
       pö-la/ya mangpo yoray

PERSONAL PRONOUNS

Personal pronouns are the same whether they are subject or object.

person	singular	plural
1st	nga (I)	ngaats'o (we)
2nd	kirang (you)	kirangts'o (you)
3rd (M)	korang (he)	korangts'o (they)
(F)	morang (she)	morangts'o (they)
(H)*		kong (he/she)
		kongts'o (they)

* (H) means the form is honorific

TO HAVE

The verb **to have** does not exist in Tibetan. To express possession, the verb **to be** (**doo** or **yoray**) is used in the possessor's person. The subject is followed by the particle of attribution **la** (meaning to).

I have	**nga-la yö**
you have	**kirang-la doo**
he/she has	**korang-la; morang-la; kong-la (H) doo**
we have	**ngaats'o-la yö**
you have	**kirangts'o-la doo**
they have	**korangts'o-la; morangts'o-la; kongts'o-la (H) doo**

Possessor–particle la–Complement–Auxilliary

eg: I have two children.
       to me-children-two-have
       (1st person)
       nga-la/poogoo nee yö

eg: They have a lot of property.
       to them-property-a lot-have
       korangts'o-la/gyoo mangpo doo *
       (personal experience) **yoray***
       (in general)

* The use of the auxiliary **doo** or **yoray** at the end of the sentence depends on whether it refers to personal or general knowledge.

POSSESSIVE PRONOUNS

Possessive adjectives and pronouns are similar.

person	singular	plural
1st	**ngay** (my, mine)	**ngaatso,** (our, ours)
2nd	**kirangee** (your, yours)	**kirangtso,** (your, yours)
3rd (M)	**korangee** (his)	**korangtso,** (their, theirs)
(F)	**morangee** (hers)	**morangtso'** (their, theirs)
(H)	**kongee** (his, hers)	**kongtso,** (their, theirs)

Order

Possessive adjectives always precede the noun they qualify.
Possessive Adjective-Noun-Adjective

eg: his long hands
       his/hand/long/plural
       kongee ch'akpa ringpo-dints'o (H).

VERBS

A Tibetan verb is composed of a root and an ending to indicate the tense. The verbal root is formed by taking the verb as the infinitive and suppressing the ending **pa** or **wa**.

meaning	infinitive	root	ending
To think	sampa	sam	pa
To eat	saawa	sa	wa

Note!

Though this verbal root is used only for the present/future tenses, in spoken language one can often use it for the past tense. The ending then determines the tense. The main exceptions are:

verb	present root	past root
To go	dro	ch'in
To eat	sa	say

TENSES

To conjugate a verb, one needs:
– to know the verbal root (see above),
– to add to it the proper particle (gee or pa)
– followed by the correct auxiliary (ray, doo or yoray for present tense, song or joong for past tense).

Note!

The second and third persons are always the same. There is no difference between singular and plural.

(1) Present

particle	auxiliary	person
root +	gee yö	1st
root +	gee doo	2nd & 3rd

eg: We seek
we/seek/pres.
ngaats'o ts'el gee-yö

eg: She eats
she/meal/eat/pres.
morang/k'aala sa gee-doo

In the future tense gee-yin-pay becomes kay.

(2) Past tense

(a) Simple past
This is the most common form of the past tense. It indicates the action is completely over. Because there is no need for a helping particle, it is very easy to use.
The auxiliary is then in the past tense (song or joong).

All verbs of perception (to see, to hear, to feel..) use this past form.
verbal root + song

eg: He understood
korang/haago-song

The auxiliary joong is chosen when the speaker is refering to himself.

eg: I won.   eg: He saw me
ngay/t'ob-joong   **korang/nga
t'ong-joong**

(b) Present perfect
This is a narrative past form used to recall past events.

	particle	auxiliary	person
verbal root +	pa	yin	1st
		ray	2nd & 3rd

eg: I have been dancing all night
night-all-we-dance-past
ts'en-gang/nga/shaabro-gyab pa-yin

eg: They have eaten bad food in this restaurant.
restaurant-this-in-they-food-bad-eat-past
korangtso'/k'aala dookcha say pay-ray

(c) Past with consequences in the present

	auxiliary	person
verbal root +	sha	1st
	song	2nd & 3rd

The pronoun subject I need not be mentioned.
eg: I forgot
jay-sha or **nga/jay-sha**

eg: He fell down
korang/ree-song

(3) Future

	particle	auxiliary	person
verbal root +	gee	yin	1st
	gee	ray	2nd & 3rd

eg: I shall talk to him
      I-him-to-talk-future
      **nga/korang-la/kecha
      shö gee-yin** (H)

eg: you will come
      you-come-future
      kirang/lay gee-ray

(4) Imperative tenses

There are several levels of imperative (or injunctive) from the most polite to a very direct command. The polite form, or honorific form denoted (H) is made by adding **ro-nang** to the verbal root.

eg: Please sit down.
      sit down/imp
      shoo ro-nang (H).

A common way is to add **nang-da** or more easily **da** to the verbal root:

eg: Could you repeat please?
      say/again/imp.
      soong-gyo nang-da

The ordinary form needs only to add **ah** to the verbal root:

eg: Work well !
      work-well-imp.
      leka yakpo jay-ah !

A very familiar expression uses the verb alone:

eg: Go !
      dro !

To express a demand, one uses **gay** :

eg: Take us !
      us/take/imp.
      ngaats'o/tri-nang-gay

QUESTIONS

Anticipation of the answer

The auxiliary used in the question is the same as the auxiliary expected in the answer. In that way, the answer is anticipated.

A literal translation would be: 'Am you a Tibetan? Yes I am '.

In a question the pronoun always precedes the auxiliary.

		Ray	Doo
am-(I)?	(nga)	ray-pay?	doo-gay?
are-(you)?	(kirang)	yin-pay?	yö-pay?
is-(he)?	(korang)	ray-pay?	doo-gay?
is-(she)?	(morang)	ray-pay?	doo-gay?
are-(we)?	(ngaats'o)	ray-pay?	doo-gay?
are-(you)?	(kirangts'o)	yin-pay?	yö-pay?
are (they)?	(korangts'o)	ray-pay?	doo-gay?
	(morangts'o)	ray-pay?	doo-gay?

eg: Are you a Tibetan? Yes, I am
      you-Tibetan-are-int.-am
      kirang/pöpa yin-pay? la*-yin

eg: Am I learning Tibetan?
      Yes, you are
      I-Tibetan-learn-are-int.-are
      **nga/pökay lobjong-jay-gee-doo-gay?
      la*-doo**

* In this usage **la** is only a signifier of politeness without any meaning in itself.

Questions with the answer yes or no

This type of question is expressed by adding an interrogative particle to the verb, at the very end of the sentence. This particle can be **pay, gay** or **ngay** according to the auxiliary (see below).

Auxiliary	Particle
yin; ray; yoray;	pay
doo	gay
song; joong	ngay

eg: Do you eat meat?
      you-meat-eat-int.
      kirangee/dee nyay song-ngay?

eg: Did you find it?
      you-it-find-past-int.
      kirang/sha sa gee-yöpay?

eg: Will he come back?
he-back-come-future-int.
korang/lo-yong gee-ray-pay?

Note!

There are two condensed forms in the second person. In the past tense **pa-yin-pa** becomes **pay**:

eg: Have you been to Lhasa?
L'aasa-la p'ay-pay? (H)

In the future tense **gee-yin-pay** becomes **kay**:

eg: Would you like some tea?
söcha shay-kay (H)

Other questions

The main interrogative terms are:

what	**kaaray**	who	**soo**
where	**kaaba**	whose	**sü**
when	**kaadü**	to whom	**soola**
how	**kanday**	why	**kaaray-jenay**
how much)	**kaatsay**	which	**kaagee**
how many)			

When the question has an interrogative term, the interrogative particle is not necessary. The interrogative term comes immediately before the verb to which it applies.

eg: When did you meet him?
you-him-when-meet-past
kirang/kong/kaadü t'ook-song?

eg: Whom is he speaking to?
he-who-to-speak-present
korang/soo-la kecha shö gee-doo?

eg: What are you doing?
you-what-do-present
kirang/kaaray jay gee-yö?

Note!

The condensed forms in the second person are the following. In the past tense **pa-yin** becomes **pa**:

eg: Where are you coming from?
kaanay yong-pa ?

In the future tense **gee-yin** becomes **ka**:

eg: Where are you going?
kaaba dro-ka ?

NEGATION

In the negative form, the auxiliary is preceded by the particles **ma** (past) or **mi** (present/future) .

There is a nasalization between **mi** and **doo**. —> **min-doo**. **Ma-yin** and **ma-yö** are both condensed in the single form **may**.

	Ray	Doo
(I) am not	may	may
(you) are not	ma-ray	min-doo
(he) is not	ma-ray	min-doo
(we) are not	may	may
(you) are not	ma-ray	min-doo
(they) are not	ma-ray	min-doo

eg: I don't understand.
understand-neg.-past
nga/haago ma-song

eg: He does not know
know-neg.-present
korang/shen gee-min doo

eg: We will not forget.
we-forget-neg.-future
ngaats'o/jay gee-may.

ADJECTIVES: COMPARATIVE AND SUPERLATIVE

The adjective does not vary with the gender. It comes right after the noun it qualifies. It can take the plural mark **ts'o**.

The root of an adjective is formed by suppressing the last syllable.

eg: **ringpo** (long) —> **ring**

A comparison between two things is made by

presenting the second object of comparison first, followed by the particle **lay** (meaning than). This is followed by the main object, the adjective and the verb.

B–particle (**lay**)–A–adjective–Verb

The adjective in the comparative form is often made of the root followed by the endings **a** or **wa** .

> eg: **tsangma** (clean) —> **root:tsang —>tsanga** (cleaner)

> eg: This room (A) is cleaner than that one (B)
> B (that one)–**lay** (than)–A (this room)–adjective (cleaner)–verb (is)
> that one-than-room-this-cleaner-is
> **day-lay/nyekang dee tsanga ray**

The superlative of an adjective is built by simply adding the particle **shö** to the root of the adjective.

> eg: **ringpo** (long) —>**ring** (root) —>**ringshö** (the longest)

MUST/NEED

The verb **go** can express a duty or a need depending on the structure of the sentence.

(1) Must

Subject–Complement–   1st person
Verbal root–**go-yö**

Subject–Complement–   2nd, 3rd person
–**go-ray**

> eg: I must buy this
> I-this-buy-must
> **nga/dee/nyo go-yö**

> eg: You must go
> you-go-must
> **kirang/dro go-ray**

(2)To need

The auxiliary is the same in all persons.
Subject–Particle **la**–Complement–Root–**go gee-doo**

> eg: I need this
> to me-this-need
> **nga-la/dee go gee-doo**

Not to want

The verb is the same in all persons
Noun + **mo-go**

> eg: I do not want this hat
> I-hat-this-do not want
> **nga/shaamo dee mo-go**

Numbers (angdrang)

HOW TO COUNT

0	lekor	10	choo		
1	chik	11	choo-chik		
2	nee	12	choo-nee	20	nee-shoo (tsa)
3	soom	13	chok-soom	30	soom-choo (so)
4	shee	14	choop-shee	40	ship-choo (shay)
5	nga	15	chon-nga	50	ngap-choo (nga)
6	drook	16	choo-drook	60	drook-choo (ray)
7	dün	17	chop-dün	70	dün-choo (dün)
8	gyay	18	chop-gyay	80	gyay-choo (gya)
9	goo	19	choor-goo	90	goop-choo (go)

100	gya-t'ampa	200	nee gya-t'ampa
1000	tong-dra	2000	nee-tong
10000	tr'i	20000	nee-tr'i
100000	boom	200000	nee-boom

It is easy to learn how to count in Tibetan:

the tens are built by combining two numbers:
    ex : 30 = 3-10 = **soom-choo**

the same rule is applied to hundreds:
    ex : 500 = 5-100 = **nga-gya-t'ampa**

to each ten corresponds a helping particle (see above) to insert between the tens and the units. For instance **so** is the particle associated to the thirties.

eg: 32 = 3-10-particle-2 = **soom-choo-so-nee**

Note!
The numbers from 11 to 19 do not have any helping particle: they are made by direct combination like above.

eg: 12 = 10-2 = **choo-nee**

However most of them are pronounced irregularly (see above).

From 100 on, **dang**, meaning **and**, comes between the hundreds, and the tens and the units.

eg: 154 = 100-and -
54 = **gya-dang-ngap-choo-nga-shee**

ORDINAL NUMBERS
The ordinal numbers are made by adding **pa** to the cardinal ones.

eg: sixth = **drook-pa**

The only exception is **dangpo**, which means first.

Time and Dates
TIME (CH'OOTSÖ)

What time is it? **ch'ootsö kaatsay ray?**
At what time. . . ? **ch'ootsö kaatsay-la. . .?**

The term **ch'ootsö** means hour or o'clock and can also designate a clock or a watch.

To tell the exact time, one uses ordinal numbers (see preceding chapter). **Ray** is usually the auxiliary.

It is one o'clock	**ch'ootsö dangpo ray**
It is ten o'clock	**ch'ootsö choo-pa ray**

minute	**karma**
five minutes	**karma nga**
half-hour (30 mn)	**cheka**
quarter-hour(15mn)	**karma chon-nga**

eg: It is quarter past three
o'clock-three-being-quarter hour-is
Ch'ootsö soom/ynay karma chon-nga ray

eg: It is half past two
o'clock-two-and-half hour-is
ch'ootsö nee/dang cheka ray

Note!
The auxiliary **doo** is used only when it is before the hour.

eg: It is ten to five
o'clock-five-minus-minutes-ten-is
ch'ootsö nga/simpa-la karma choo doo

TERMS RELATING TO TIME

morning	shokay
midday	nigoong
afternoon	ningoong-gyab
evening	gonda
night	ts'enmo

yesterday morning	kesa-shokay
this morning	t'arang
tomorrow morning	sangsho
day before yesterday	kanoob
yesterday	k'asang
today	tering
tomorrow	sangnee
yesterday night	dan-gong
tomorrow night	san-gong

two years ago	shay-ninglo
last year	da-ninglo
this year	d'alo
next year	d'sang

ADVERBS
The adverb usually precedes the verb it qualifies.

He will ... come here

	korang/day/... yong gee-ray
always	kaad-yinay
continuously	mootnay
immediately	lamsang

never	kad +neg, gynay +neg
often	yangsay
sometimes	tsamtsam-la, kabkab-la
soon	gyokpo
usually	chirtang

AGE

How old are you?	kirang/lo kaatsay ray?
I am. . .	nga/. . .yin
old	gengo
young	shnoo
30 years old	lo soom-choo

DURATION

How long does it take?	dee/kaatsay gor gee-ray?
It takes a/an	chik/gor gee-ray

instant	kechik	second	karcha
minute	karma	hour	ch'oots
day	neema	24 hours	shakpo
week	düntra	month	daawa
year	lo	century	lo-gya

since when (+verb)?
(verb)-nay/kaatsay ch'in-song?

how long ...?   gyün ringlö ...?

how many years (+verb)?
(verb)-nay/lo kaatsay ch'in-song?

Idiomatic Expressions

Here are some typical Tibetan idiomatic expressions. They seem difficult at first glance but once you get used to them, you will find that they are liberally sprinkled in all conversations.

Lö

is a prefix of quantity that, when connected to the root of an adjective, expresses the question 'how . . ?'

eg: ringpo (long)–ring-lö (how long)

This form is used to express a question dealing with quantity or quality such as 'how long is

the distance?' or 'how good is this restaurant ?'. The interrogative particle is not necessary at the end of the sentence.

eg: How long does it take?
      duration-how long-take?
      gyün-ringlö gor gee-ray?

eg: How far is it?
      distance-how long-is?
      t'a-ringlö ray?

Nyen

Nyen (also pronounced ken) deals with the one who performs the action. It means literally 'the one who ...' and comes right after the verb it qualifies.

eg: the one who talks: **shay-nyen**

It can refer to a person or to a thing or it can be used to express a relative proposition:

eg: The bus that goes to Samye
      to Samye-the one who goes-bus
      Samyay-la dro-nyen motra

eg: For my father who has died
      my-the one who has died-father-
      ngay tr'ong-nyen paalagee chedoo

It can also perform a function that defines:

eg: The driver (the one who drives)
      motra tang-nyen

... nay/... ch'in-song

This refers to a duration of time belonging to the past. It means literally 'since ... / ... .have past.' It is commonly used to express 'for how many ....?' when it deals with hours, days, years etc.

If the duration is vague one should use 'gyün-ringlö..?' (see above)

eg: For how many years have you been living here?
      you-here-stay since-year-how many-have past ?
      kirang/day shoo nay/lo kaatsay ch'in-song ?

eg: I have been waiting for two hours
     I-wait-since-hour-two-have past
     nga/goo-day nay/ch'ootsö nee ch'in-song

Nyong

Nyong is a verb meaning literally 'to have the experience of ....' It is always preceded by an other verb, usually of perception. In interrogative and negative forms it gives a notion of 'ever' or 'never.' Used affirmatively, it means 'already' and is often followed by **yoray**. (See grammar p 00.)

subject-verbal root- **nyong-yoray** (aff)
nyong-ngay?   (int)
ma-nyong   (neg)

eg: He has already seen the ocean
     (affirmation)
     the-ocean-see-to have the experience
     korang/gyamts'o t'ong nyong-yoray

eg: Did you ever ride a horse?
     (interrogation)
     you-horse-ride-to have the experience?
     kirang/ta shön nyong-ngay?

eg: I have never been so cold in my life (negation)
     I-like this-human life-in-at all-cold-to have the experience
     nga/dindess/mi-ts'ay nanla/ky'nay ky'a ma-nyong

... long-may

'.. **long-may**' means 'not to have the time to ...' It qualifies the preceding verb.

eg: I do not have the time to go
     I-to go-have no time
     nga/dro long-may

Tsee

'**tsee gee-doo**' or' . . . **tsee gee-yö**' means 'to intend to. . .'

As above, it follows the verb to which it applies.

eg: I intend to buy this
     I-this-to buy-intend
     nga/dee/nyo tsee-yö

eg: He intends to come too
     he-too-to-come-intend
     kong/yang p'ay tsee-doo

... na/dree gee-ray-pay ?

The verb **dree** means to agree. It is used in the expressions:

it's alright   **dree gee-ray**
is it alright?   **dree gee-ray-pay ?**
it's enough   **dree-song**

A very common way of asking permission: '(verb)-na/**dree gee-ray-pay** ?' meaning literally 'if/... will it be alright?'

eg: Could I come with you?
     nga/kirang nyamdoo yong-na/dree gee-ray-pay ?
     I-you-together-to come-if-will it be alright

A PHRASEBOOK FOR TREKKERS AND PILGRIMS

Greetings

ORDINARY AND HONORIFIC FORMS

In Tibetan, there are two forms in the spoken language: one is ordinary and the other one is polite or honorific, denoted as (H). The former (**kyüma**) is used to speak of oneself or to someone equal or inferior. The honorific form (**shesa**) shows respect towards the person one talks to. Outside of Lhasa, this form is mostly spoken by educated people.When addressing a lama this form is imperative. Each form has its own vocabulary and verbal structure. Therefore it is important not to mix both in the same phrase. The particle **la** can also show politeness and respect.

When addressing someone by name or title, one usually adds **la** :

eg: **Tashee-la**
or **aani-la** for a nun.

In the expression yes/no, **la** precedes the auxiliary when it is monosyllabic.

eg: '**la-may t'oo-jay-chay**' meaning 'no, thank you.'

La also appears in the expression **laso**, often pronounced **loss**, with the meaning of alright.

TASHEE-DELAY

This is probably the first word that you will learn for it is extensively used as a greeting, a good-bye or to say thank you. Literally, it means good merit or good luck.

COMMON PHRASES

Welcome	ch'a p-nang
Please take a seat	shoo den-ja, shoo-ro-nang (H)
How are you ?	koosoo depo yin-pay?
I am well	depo yin
Thank you	t'oo-jay-chay; t'oo-jay-nang (H)*
Please	koochee, (verb)+ ro-nang
Alright	loss, laso (see above)
You are welcome	la-ong
Sorry	gonda*

* thank you and sorry are not used as much in Tibetan as in English.

The way to express goodbye varies with the situation.
If you are going, you should say to others stay slowly.
If you are staying, say go slowly to someone leaving.

good-bye	kaalay shoo-ah (if you go)
	kaalay p'ay-ah (if you stay)
What is your name ?	kirangee mingla kaaray ray?
or	kirangee ts'enla/ kaaray shoo gee-yö' (H)
My name is Tashee	ngay mingla Tashee ray
See you soon	gyokpo jay-yong
See you tomorrow	sang-nee jay yong

Trekking

WEATHER (NAMSHI)

moon	daawa	mist	mookpa
rainbow	jaatsön	sky	nam
star	karma	storm	traachar
sun	neema		

How is the weather today?
tering/namshee kanday doo ?
Today it is ...
tering/namshee ... doo

cold	dr'angmo
fine	yakpo
hot	ts'aapo

The sun is shining
neema shar gee-doo

A strong wind is blowing
l'akpa ch'enpo gyab gee-doo

It is going ...... gee-ray

to hail	sera tang
to rain	ch'arpa p'ap
to snow	kang tang

to thunder (lit:dragon voice)
drookay gyab

The storm is raging
loong-tsoob tor-shik

a dust storm	t'eloong
a hail storm	sera loong-tsoob
a snow storm	poo-yook

Four seasons (dü-shee)

spring	chika	summer	yarka
autumn	tönka	winter	goonka

EQUIPMENT

axe	taari	mattress	den
backpack	gyabkoor	needle	kab
candle	yangla	pot	aayang
cigarette	t'aama	rope	t'akpa
flashlight	bejilin (hi)	scissors	chemdzay
kerosene	saanoom	stick	gyookpa
kettle	hoo	stove	t'ab
knife	tri	string	kpa
ladder	gyo	tent	g'oor
lamp	shooma	water bottle	ch'oodam
matches	mooksi	map	saptra

PREPARATION

We are walking to ... monastery
ngaats'o/g'ompa gyab-nay/...la dro gee-yö

Could you show me the way to ... on the map?
saptray nanla/ ... gee lam ten ro-nang?

Difficulties (ka-nyel)

Is it difficult to get there?
p'agay/k'aalay-k'aapo yoray-pay ?

What is the diffficulty?
ka-nyel kaaray doo ?

It is raining a lot
charpa mangpo p'ap gee-doo

It is easy to get lost
lam nor-ya/lel'aapo ray

There are wild animals
saacha dee-la/chensen yoray

The rivers are high at this time
t'anda/ch'oo ch'enpo yoray

There are bandits on the way
lamka-la/ch'akpa yoray

GUIDES AND PACK-ANIMALS
(LAM-TRINYEN DANG KEL-SEMCHEN)
Is it possible to find the way alone?
ngaats'o/lamka lamsang nyay gee-ray-pay?

I have lost my way
nga/lam nor-song

Have you ever been to ...?
kirang/...-la/p'ay nyong-ngay ?

We need a good guide to come with us
ngaat' o/lam-trinyen yakpo gö doo

Our bags are heavy
ngaatso chaala/jiboo sheta doo

We need a . . . to carry the luggage
ngaatso chaala ky'ay-nyen/. . go gee-doo

porter	dopo ky'ay-nyen
pack-animal	kel-semchen
donkey	p'oongoo
horse	ta
yak	ya

How much does it cost ... ?
... kaatsay ray?

per day	neema chikla
altogether	dom-nay

Is the food included?
k'aalakee rinpa/tü yoray-pay?

It is too expensive	gong ch'enpo ray
It is alright	dree gee-ray

Do we need to take food with us?
  ngaats'o/sabchay ky'ay go-ray-pay?

For how many days?
  neema kaatsay chedoo ?

Are there villages on the way?
  lamka-la/tr'ongsay yoray-pay?

Can we ride the horses?
  ta/shön ch'o gee-ray-pay

Is this area forbidden?
  loongpa dee-la/dro ch'o gee ray-pay?

Could we be arrested?
  simyay/nyenka yoray-pay?

THE COUNTRYSIDE

cave	traapook
flower	meto
dried (yak) dung	joowa
forest	shingnak
field	shinga
glacier	ky'akpa
firewood	meshing
hill	ri
grass	tsa
hot spring	sch'ootsen
juniper	shookpa
lake	ts'o
leech	espepa
nettle	saptsö
path	lam
river	dyook-ch'oo, tsangpo
snowy mountain	gangri
trees	hindong
snow	gang

Trail (lamka)

How is the trail?	lam kanday doo ?
The trail is ...	lam/... yoray
bad	dookcha
broad	gya-ch'enpo
dangerous	nyenka-ch'enpo
downward	gy'en
dry	kampo
hard to find	nyay-kakpo
long	ringpo
muddy	dam-nyok
narrow	dokpo
steep	sarbo
upward	t'oor
wet	lönpa

What is the easiest way?
  lamka deshö/kagee ray?
Is it a hard walk?
  lamka/kaalay-k'aapo yoray-pay ?

DIRECTION (CH'O)

trail-marker	lamtak
prayer flag	darcho
cairn	laatsay
wool in the trees (trail-marker)	p'es

Which path is the way to...?...
  drosa/kagee ray ?

I am looking for a place called ...
  ngay/...ming chepay/sacha ts'ay gee-yö

How long does it take?
  kaatsay gor gee-ray ?

a compass	shar-noob

Cardinal directions

east	shar*
south	l'o
west	noob*
north	jang

* East is the main direction of reference for Tibetans because this is where the sun rises. Therefore, most of the monasteries have their main gate towards the east. **Shar** and **noob** are also verbs describing the rising and setting of the sun.

Take the trail to the right
  lamka yay-ch'ola/gyoo

After the crossing ...
    lamka shitsam-nay /...

turn to the left   yön-la gyoo
go straight ahead   kartoo gyoo

Have you seen my companion?
    ngay rokpa/t'ong-song-ngay ?

I lost my companion
    ngay rokpa/la-song

I have not seen anybody
    soochik/t'ong ma-song

RIVERS (CH'OO)

bridge   sampa
coracle   kowa
ferryman   drü-dakpo
ferry   droodzin
flag   dar
stream   ch'oo

Should we cross the river?
    tsangpo gyay go-ray-pay ?

Is the bridge strong enough?
    sampa dee/tempo yoray-pay ?

If there is no bridge
    sampa may-na

how can we cross the river?
    ch'oo kandess gyay go-ray ?

Where does the ferryman live?
    drü-dakpo desa/kaaba doo ?

Could you take us across the river?
    kirang-nga tsangpo dee/gyay ro-nang

PASS (LA)

What is the name of this pass?
    la dee/mingla kaaray ray ?

Is the pass blocked by the snow?
    lam gangee/ka doo-gay ?

How high is the pass?   la t'ol yoray?

The pass is ...   la dee/...doo
difficult   t'ampo
easy   lel'aapo
high   t'opo
low   maapo

SHELTER (NEDZANG)

in the open air   ch'ilola
tent   goor

Is there a shelter in the area?
    dep'ar/nedzang ra gee-ray-pay ?

Where can I sleep?
    nga/kaaba nyel go-ray ?

Can I sleep in your house tonight?
    d'ogong/nga/kirangee nanla nyay-na/dree
    gee-ray-pay?

Where can I put the tent?
    ngay goor/kaaba pi go-ray ?

Can I camp near your house?
    nga/kirangee kangpay tr'ila g'oor pi-na/dree
    gee-ray-pay ?

Could we get into trouble here?
    ngaats'o/dep'ar nyoktra yong gee-ray-pay?

Monasteries (gompa)

This section provides the phrases you will need when visiting a monastery, and the terms necessary to understand the cultural activities connected with Tibetan Buddhism. Some useful phrases are included for those who wish to meet a lama or to stay in a monastery.

IN THE COURTYARD

courtyard   ky'amra
prayer banner (lit:wind-horse)   loong-ta
prayer flag   darch'o
prayer mast   darch'en
prayer wheel   maani-laakor
juniper stove   sang-kang
stupa   ch'öten

PRELIMINARIES

In certain instances, it is necessary to buy tickets to enter main monasteries. This should be considered in lieu of the offering that pilgrims give. Most of the monasteries are back to normal.

Do we have to buy tickets?
paasay nyo go-ray-pay?

How much is it per person?
mi ray-ray-la/ngö kaatsay ray?

Can I keep my ticket?
paasay nyar-na/dree gee-ray-pay?

Should I take off my shoes?
ngay hangö/pi go-ray-pay?

Could we visit upstairs?
ngaats'o/t'okar ch'in-na/dree gee-ray-pay?

What is the name of this chapel?
l'aakang dee mingla/kaaray ray ?

Where is the ...?	... kaaba doo ?
chanting room	dook'ang
garden of debate	chödra
library	pendzö-k'ang
monastic college	dratsang
printing room	park'ang
reliquary room	koodoong-k'ang
protector room	gönk'ang
retreat center	droop-k'ang

Each temple has its caretaker (könyer) who is in charge of the shrine and of the welfare of the chapel. He is the only one who has the key and who can tell you the history of the religious objects.

The doors are locked	go/gyab doo
Who has the key?	demik/soo-la yoray?

Who is in charge of this room?
l'aakang dee könyer soo ray?

Can you open it for us?
ngaats'o/go ch'ay ro-nang

Do you have a . . . ?	kirangla/...yö-pay
butter	marmay
flashlight	bejilin (hi)

Can we take pictures ...?...
/par gyab/ch'o gee-ray-pay?

inside	nanlola
outside	ch'ilola

Can we pay only 10Y for this room?
ngaats'o/gormo choo tray-na/dree gee-ray-pay?

Can I take only one picture?
nga par chik mato/ gyab na/dree gee-ray-pay?

On the shrine   ch'öshom-gang

What do you offer?
kirang/kaaray pü gee-yö?

offering	chöpa
the seven offering bowl	ting-düntsa
butter lamp	chömay
incense	pö
kapala	töpa
ritual dagger (skt:kilaya)	p'oorba
ritual cake	torma
mandala	lakeel-kor
grain mandala	latsomboo keel-kor
sand mandala	dültsön keel-kor
vase	boompa

GENERAL QUERIES

Is there any monk who knows more about this place?
sacha dee korla/chip-tsaako jay-nay/haago-nyen kooshola yoray-pay ?

What is there inside this stupa?
chöten dee nanla/kaaray shoo yoray?

relics	ringsel
clay mould	tsaatsa
text	pecha

Which one is a reliquary?
    koodoong/kaagee ray?

What is the meaning of this?
    dee/dönda kaaray ray?

Those are offerings
    dents'o/chöpa ray

Where does this come from?
    dee/kaanay joong-pa-ray?

Which objects belonged to . . ?
    gee ngöchay/kaaray yoray-pay?

Could you please show me one of these sacred texts?
    nga-la/pecha ningpa dee-nay/chik ten-ro-nang

STATUES (KOONDRA)

What are the statues made of?
    koondra dintso' gyoo/kaaray ray?

Are they old?
    dints'o/ningpa ray-pay?

Which ones are old?
    kaagee/ningpa ray-pay?

How old are they?
    lo kaatsay ray?

What is the story of this statue?
    koondra dee/logyü kaaray ray?

Does this statue contain anything?
    koondra dee nanla/kaaray yoray?

Who does it represent?
    dee/sü/draakoo ray?

Where did they hide the statues?
    koondra dee/ kaaba bay-song?

In the ground
    sa-wola

This statue has talked
    koondra dee/soon-jönma ray

What did it say?
    dee/kaaray soong-song?

To whom did it talk?
    soola soong-song?

How did it happen?
    dee/kandess joong-song?

Did that occur several times?
    dee/t'eng mangpo joong-song-ngay?

This statue appeared spontaneously
    koondra dee/ranjoong ray

FRESCOES (TEBRI) AND PAINTINGS (TANKA)

to paint   l'a-dree(pa)
painter   l'a-dripa
drawing   rimo

What style of painting is this?
    rimo-dritang/kanday ray?

Kashmiri   kachay
Chinese   gyana
Newari   pepo

What is the name of the school?
    l'adri dee look/kaaray ray?

Where did it originate?
    dee/t'okma kaanay joong-pa-ray?

Where is it possible to see old ones?
    koong-dak dents'o/kaaba jelgyoo yoray?

Are these original frescoes?
    tebtri dee/ning-rik ray-pay?

From which period?
    dütsö/kaanay ray?

Are the colors vegetable dye?
    dints' o/shingts'ön ray-pay?

Has it been repainted recently?
    dee-la nyejar ts'ön/tang pa-ray-pay?

This fresco has been damaged
  tebtri dee/nyamcha sheta song-doo

Are you going to restore it?
  tebtri dee/nyamso shoo gee-ray-pay?

HISTORY (GYERAB)

cabinet	kaasha
general	mapön
minister	lönpö
prince	say
princess	semo
regent	gyeltsab
queen	tsünmo, gyelmo
king	gyelpo
soldier	makmi
fortress	kar, dzong
palace	podrang
stone-pillar	doring
demonstration	ngamtön-tr'omkor
freedom	rangwang
independence	rangtsen
riot	ngogöl
trouble	strookpa
war	mak
to build	gyab(pa)
to destroy	tor(wa)
to escape	tö'(pa)
to establish	ch'ak-tab(pa)
to fight	ma-gyab(pa)
to lose	shor(wa)
to rebuild	kyerdoo-gyab(pa)
to restore	namso-jay(pa)
to win	t'ob(pa)

FOUNDATION (MANGSHI)

Who established the monastery?
  densa dee/ch'ak-t'ab nyen soo ray?

When was it founded?
  kaadü/ch'ak-t'ab pa-ray?

To which lineage does it belong?
  kongee gypa/kaaray ray?

How long did it take to build?
  gompa dee/ch'ak-tab paala/dütsö'kaatsay
  gor-song?

How many monks used to live here?
  day/nyela/trapa kaatsay shoo-song?

DESTRUCTION (TORSHIK)

Which part of the building is old?
  k'angpa ch'o/kaagee ningpa ray?

Has the place been completely destroyed?
  gompa dee/tsaanay/torpa ray-pay?

It has been partially destroyed
  haalam ts'angma/torpa-ray

Did all the monks leave at that time?
  day-dü/traapa ts'angma/t'ön song-ngay?

Who destroyed it?	sü/tor-song?
the Mongols	sokpö
the Gurkhas	pep
the Chinese	gyami
the Manchus	dzoongar-gee

Has it been bombed?
  nam-tor-nay/pardzay yook song-ngay?

Has there been any fight here?
  day/mak-drook joong-ngay?

Why was it not completely destroyed?
  kaaray jay-nay/ts'angma tor-ma-song?

When did it happen?
  dee/kaadü joong-song?

Who was the head lama then?
  day-dü/lama tsowo soo ray?

RECONSTRUCTION (KYERDOO-GYABPA)

When did you start to rebuild?
  kirangtsö'/dee nyamso kaadü go-tsoo-pa-
  yin?

Since when can you perform rituals again?
  kaadü-nay/gompa tsok chöra/roo-t'ook-
  song?

SPECIAL EVENTS

What does this commemorate?
dee/kaaray tsö'n gee-yoray?

Who wrote it down?   **dee/sü tri-song?**

What is it about?   **dee/kaaray kor ray?**

What makes this monastery famous?
gompa dee/kaaray jay-nay kedra ch'a-pa-ray?

Did any special event/day take place here?
day/miksel-gee logyü/kaaray joong pa-ray?

IN THE NEIGHBOURHOOD

Which are the other monasteries?
poogön shen/kaagee ray?

Are they far from here?
dee-nay/t'a ringpo yoray-pay?

Is there a hermitage nearby?
dee tsa-la/ritrö'yoray-pay?

Who stayed in this cave?
droopook dee nanla/soo shoo-song?
For how long?
gyü-ringlö shoo song?

Is there anybody staying here now?
paagay/t'anda/soo-nyen doo-gay?

LIFE IN THE MONASTERY

monk	traapa
nun	aani
monk keeping discipline	dob-dob
cook	maajen
benefactor	jindak
layman	mikya

(to) take vows	dompa-len(pa)
(to) receive ordination	rabjoong-dompa t'ob(pa)

How many monks are living here ?
day/traapa kaatsay shoo gee-ray?

Are you staying here permanently?
kirang/da/takpar shoo gee-yö-pay?

We have a three years assignment
ngaats'o/dee-roo/lo soom-ray/rem day-gee yin

What is the name of your chief?
kirangee magön/kaagee ray?

Is there a lama in this monastery?
gompa dee nanla/laama yoray-pay?

Is he here currently?
t'anda/laama shoo yoray-pay?

What is the name of the lama?
laamay ts'enla/kaaray shoo gee-doo?

Is the lama allowed to teach?
ch'soong tch'o-gee-ray-pay?

Does he give teachings sometimes?
tsamtsam-la/soong-ch'nan-gee-ray-pay (H)?

RITUALS (CHOGA, SKT:POOJA)

chant master	oomdzay
ritual assistant	chö'pön
gesture(skt:mudra)	ch'aagya
offering ritual (skt:ganachakra)	tsok

(to) perform a fire ritual
sang tang(wa) ; koosang pü(wa) (H)

(to) pray (in a loud voice)	dön (pa)
(to) recite	tr'ang(wa)
mantras	maani*, nga
praise	töpa
wishing-prayer	mönlam

Do you perform rituals everyday?
neema ray-ray-la/choga tan-gee-ray-pay?

At what time does it start?
ch'ootsö kaatsay-la/go-tsoo gee-ray?

Where does the ritual take place?
choga/kaaba tsoo gee-ray?

Is it possible to attend the rituals?
  nga/kirangee choga tang-sar jel-na/
  dree gee-ray-pay?

in the morning   shokay-la
in the evening   gonda-la
What ritual is it?   choga dee/kaaray ray?

Could I borrow a text?
  ngay/pecha yar-na/dree gee-ray-pay?

Can the lama give initiations?
  laamay/wang nang gee-ray-pay?

Which initiation is this?
  t'anda kaaray wang nang gee-doo?

Who is the main ...of the monastery?
  .../ tsowo kaagee ray?

divinity   yidam
historical figure   logyü-nang tr'akpay-mi
protector   soongma

We need information about ...
  ngaats'o/ ... kor/netsö go

Do you know anybody who could help me?
  nga-la rok jenyen/kyen gee yö-pay?

MEETING THE LAMA (LAMA-DZAYWA)

Is it possible to see the lama now?
  nga/t'anda/laamay koondön char-na/dree
  gee-ray-pay?

At what time?   ch'ootsö kaatsay-la?

When should I come back to see the lama?
  laama jekar/yangkyer kaadü yong go-ray?

Can I come in?
  nga/nanlola yong-na/dree gee-ray-pay?

Am I disturbing you?
  ngay/kirangla t'ook-tro ma-song-ngay?

Should I take off my shoes?
  ngay hango/pi go-ray-pay?

If you are busy
  kirangla ch'aalay yö-na

I could come back later
  nga/jela/char gee-yin

I have a letter for you from ...
  nga/... nay/yigay chik kyer-yö

Do you have a translator?
  kirang la/kay-gyoor yö-pay?

Could I record what you say?
  ngay/kirangee soong chook-na/ dree gee-
  ray-pay ?

I am a disciple of ...
  nga/... loma yin

I have been studying Dharma for three years
  nga/ch'öjang-nay/lo soom ch'in-song

I need an introduction letter to . . .
  gee chedoo/nga-la ngotrö-kee yigay gö-doo

Thankyou for your help
  kirangee rokpa nang-pa la/t'oo-jay-chay

BLESSINGS (JINLAB)

protection string   soongdü
blessed water   dütsi
blessed pill   jinden
reliquary   gao
rosary   (sk: malla) tr'engwa
white scarf   k'aata

Could you please grant me your blessing?
  nga-la/ch'awang nan-ro-nang

Could you bless my rosary?
  ngay tr'engwa-la/jinlab nan-ro-nang

Do you have some relics to put in my reliquary?
  kirangla/ngay gao nanla/soong-shook jinlab
  nangya yö-pay?

Could you dispel the obstacles to my journey?
  kirangee/ngay drimdrül parch'ay/ sel t'oob
  gee-ray-pay ?

Could you perform a ritual so that our pilgrimage goes smoothly?

> ngaats'o nekor-la/nyobtra ma yong-na saawa-la/kirangee koorim nan-ro-nang

Could you perform a long life ritual?

> kirang tsedroob tang-ro-nang

We have paid a visit to the lama

> ngaats'o/lamay koondünla char pa-yin

STAYING IN THE MONASTERY

Can I sleep in the monastery?

> gompay nanla nyay-na/dree gee-ray-pay?

Are women allowed to stay here?

> day/pümay/day ch'o gee-ray-pay?

Can I share your meals?

> nga kirang nyamdoo k'aala sa/ch'ogee-ray-pay?

Tell me if there is any problem

> day/ngay t'oknay nyobtra joong-na/soo-ro-nang

FESTIVALS (DÜCH'EN)

What is the festival today?

> tering/kaaray düch'en ray?

How long is the festival?

> düch'en dee/neema kaatsay yoray?

What does it celebrate?

> kaaray t'emdray/jay gee-ray?

Where do the dances take place?

> ch'am/kaaba ts'oo gee-ray?

What is there to see over there?

> paagay temo/kaaray yoray?

How long does it last?

> dee/gyü-ringlö gor gee-ray?

What is the subject?

> kaaray kor ray?

Could you please give me some explanations about this performance?

> temo dee-kor/telshay nan-ro-nang?

There is a break now

> t'anda/ts'am chay-song

What is going to happen?

> kaaray jay gee-ray?

We are going	gee-ray
to dance	shabro-gyab
to play cards	taasi tsemo-tsay
to play dice	sho-gyab
to play music	baaja tang
to get together	rooroo-jay
to sing	loo-tang

Pilgrimage (nekor)

Pilgrimages are very popular among Tibetans. Their purpose is to purify sins and to accumulate merit in order to overcome obstacles in practice or in daily life.

PILGRIMS (NEKORPA)

sacred place	nay
to visit (a sacred place)	jel(wa) (lit:to meet)

Are you on pilgrimage?

> kirang/nekorla t'ay-pay? (H)

I am on pilgrimage

> nga/nekorla dro gee-yö

Which area are you from?

> kirangee pa-yö/kaanay ray?

How did you come here?

> kirang/day/kandess p'ay-pa? (H)

on foot	g'om gyab-nay
by truck	motra nanla

How many days have you been traveling?

> ch'ola tö'-nay/neema kaatsay ch'in-song?

Have you been on pilgrimage to Lhasa?

> kirang/L'aasay nekorla/p'ay-pa? (H)

Have you visited other places?
nay shemba/jay nyong-ngay?

Where are you going now?
t'anda/kirang kaaba p'ay-ka? (H)

Is it an important place for pilgrimage?
nay dee/tsa-ch'enpo ray-pay?

Who has been staying there?
day-la/soo shoo-song?

What happened there?
day /kaaray jay-song?

May I come with you?
nga/kirang nyamdoo dro-na/dree gee-ray-pay?

How long will it take to reach there?
par jorpa/kaatsay dro go ray?

When you meet someone in a place of pilgrimage you should greet him with:
May you be blessed!   **jinlab jay-ah!**

PLACES (NAY)

Could you please come with me to ..?
kirang/nga-nyamdoo .. -la p'ay ro-nang (H)

Can someone who knows the way...
lamka kyay-nyen/mi chik rokpa...

...take me to...?   **.. tang-na/dree gee-ray-pay..?**

the cemetery	**doortrö**
the hermitage (in the mountain)	**ritr'ö**
the life tree	**laashing**
the meditation cave	**droopook; simpook** (H)
the place for retreat	**tsamk'ang; simk'ang** (H)
the sacred lake	**laats'o**
the sacred mountain	**laari**
the sacred spring	**droopch'oo**
the medicine river	**mench'oo**
the long life river	**ts'ay-choo**

PRACTICES (NYAMLEN)

The main practises on pilgrimage are:

The offering of ritual scarfs (**k'aata**) to statues and thrones, which represent the presence of the lama; offering of light in the form of butter to fuel the butter-lamps (**chömay**) and of food in the form of barley grains (**tsampa**) inside monasteries; the offering of butter (**mar**) to be put on statues and rocks.

sacred water	**dütsi**
relic pill	**ringsel**
sacred pill	**jinden**

As they go around the monasteries, pilgrims undertake different practises in order to to pay respects to and ask blessings from past spiritual masters.

whose ... -print is this?	**... -jay dee/sü ray?**
hand	**ch'ak** (H)
foot	**shab** (H)
head	**ü**(H)

To keep healthy there is a custom to touch different parts of the body to the stone where a great master sat. Holy places are touched with the forehead as a sign of respect. Pilgrims put sometimes their head into a hole under the statue to receive its blessing.

What am I supposed to do here?
day/kaaray jay go-ray?

Can you show me how to do it?
nga kaaray jay-go-ray/lab ro-nang

Put your head in the hole.
kirangee oo/ik'oong nanla shoo ro-nang

Put your ... against the stone.
kirangee .../do-la dar-ro-nang

back	**gyab**
forehead	**chiwo**
knee	**pemo**

Is it possible to go round the mountain?
ri dee/kora gyab t'oob gee-ray-pay?

Could you please show me all the holy places on the way?
korlam-la/nay tsa ch'enpo ganga/ ten-ro-nang?

Do you know the meaning of this practise?
nyamlen dee dönda/shen gee-yö-pay?

RETREAT (TS'AM)

In Tibet, great masters would retire to caves for three years and three moon-phases (one month and a half).

hermit	**gomch'en**
person staying in retreat	**ts'amla-denyen**
yogi	**neljorpa**
hermitage	**ritrö**
meditation cave	**droopook**

retreat center   **droopk'ang**

Is it possible to reach these caves?
tr'apook dints'o nanla/drossa yoray-pay?

Are there hermits in these caves?
tr'apook dints'o nanla/gomch'en yoray-pay?

Are you in retreat?
kirang/ts'amla shoo-yö pay? (H)

I am in retreat.
nga/ts'amla day gee-yö

Could I stay in retreat here?
day/nga/ts'am-la day-na dree gee-ray-pay?

I will stay here for a few days
nga/neema nee/day gee-yin

Is there an empty room?
kangmik tongpa doo-gay?

APPENDICES

TIBETAN GLOSSARY

(S = Sanskrit; C = Chinese)

A

Abhidharma (S) (Tib. Nyongpa) Seven collected works of systematic teachings that analyze elements of experience and search for the nature of existence; an extensive philosophical and psychological tradition that speculates and comments on Buddha's teachings

Ajanta (S) Buddhist cave temples and monasteries in Maharashtra State (western India); founded between 1st century BC and AD 7th century.

amban Chinese representative to oversee the Dalai Lama's government; the office was created in 1727 and abolished in 1913 by the 13th Dalai Lama

Amdo Tibet's northeastern region bordering on China

ani nun

apsara (S) angel

Arhats (S) The first monks to attain the state of Buddhahood; usually 16 Arhats

asura (S) demon

B

bardo state of consciousness between death and rebirth

barkhang middle or second floor

barkhor an intermediate circumambulatory passage or corridor

bodhi (S) enlightenment

bodhicitta (S) enlightened mind

bodhisattva (S) a being devoted to the salvation and enlightenment of all sentient beings

Bön native religion of Tibet that preceded Buddhism but now has many attributes of a Buddhist sect

Brahma (S) chief god of the Hindus, the personification of divine reality in its creative aspect

Buddha (S) the Enlightened One; generally refers to Sakyamuni, the historical Buddha who lived in India in the 6th century BC

bumpa the bell-shaped part of a *chörten*

Butön 14th-century scholar who organized the Tibetan Buddhist canon; abbot of Shalu Monastery

C

caitya (S) small *chörten*

Chana Dorje (S. Vajrapani) *bodhisattva* who personifies the energy and power of the Buddha

chagri fortified walls

chakje handprint

chaksam suspension bridge of iron chains

chaktsal prostration

chaktsal gang site of prostration

cham religious masked dance

chang barley beer

Charya Tantra (S) the second of the four divisions of the Buddhist tantras

Chenresi (S. Avalokiteshvara) Bodhisattva of Compassion

chigye foreigner

chikhor outer circumambulation passage

chö (S. Dharma) teachings of the Buddha

Chöd tantric system based on the Perfection of Wisdom (Prajnaparamita) texts, introduced to Tibet by Dampa Sangye

chödhung conch

chog corner bastion

Chögyel (S. Dharmaraja) wrathful bull-headed protector important in the Gelugpa pantheon

chökhang offering hall

Choknyi Two Supreme Ones: Shakyaprabha and Gunaprabha, two Indian masters who wrote on the Buddhist monastic rule (Vinaya)

Chökyi Gyaltsen 16th–17th-century teacher of the Fifth Dalai Lama; the Fourth Panchen Lama

Chökyong (S. Dharmapala) protector of the Dharma; a type of deity whose function is to protect the practitioner from deception and waywardness

chömay butter lamp

chöpa offerings

chöra debating courtyard

chörten multi-tiered monument often containing sacred relics

chösam cabinet-shrine

chu river, stream

chuba long robe worn by men and women

chumik spring

chura cheese

chutsen hot spring

D

da arrow; the lower, flat part of a valley

dagshing Pure Land or paradise

Dalai Lama the incarnate lama recognized as a manifestation of Chenresi; they ruled Tibet from the 17th century; the first was Gedundrub, nephew and disciple of Tsong Khapa, founder of the Gelugpa; the present Dalai Lama is the 14th

damaru small ritual drum used in tantric ceremonies

daoban (C) road maintenance depot

darchen flagpole for prayer flags

Demchok (S. Chakrasamvara, Samvara) deity of the supreme yoga *tantra* of Tibetan Buddhism. He usually has two or 12 arms and is in *yabyum* with Dorje Phagmo; their union symbolizes the union of emptiness and bliss

Deno (S. Pitaka) the Buddhist canon is divided into three 'baskets', or *pitakas*, and is known as Tripitaka

depa regent or ruler

deva (S) god

devi female deity

Dewachen (S. Sukhavati) Pure Land of the West, or Western Paradise, where the Buddha Wöpame resides

deyang large courtyard

dhensa main monastery of a high lama

Dhyani Buddha (S) the original Adi Buddha created five Dhyani Buddhas, who in turn created the universe of each human era; Amitabha is the Dhyani Buddha of our era

Dipankara (S) Past Buddha

Döndrub (S. Amoghasiddhi) one of the Five Dhyani Buddhas

doring stone pillar, often with inscriptions

dorje (S. Vajra) 'diamond scepter', the active symbol of the means for attaining wisdom; frequently, a hand-held ritual object

Dorje Chang (S. Vajradhara) 'the Bearer of the Vajra', all-embracing Buddha nature; the tantric form of Sakyamuni Buddha

Dorje Drakden protector divinity who speaks through the Nechung oracle

Dorje Neljorma (S. Vajrayogini) the highest *dakini*, who embodies all Buddha wisdom

Dorje Sempa (S. Vajrasattva) the Body of Bliss aspect of Akshobhya, the *bodhisattva* who personifies the purity of enlightenment

Dorje Thegpa (S. Vajrayana) the Diamond Vehicle, or Tantricism; this Buddhist path based on the *sutras* and *tantras*, offers a rapid means to spiritual liberation

Drakpa Gyaltsen one of the Five Patriarchs of the Sakyapas

drakphuk an enclosed overhang forming a meditation retreat

dre demon

drilbu a hand bell used with a *dorje* in tantric rites; symbol of the feminine principle

Driza (S. Gandharva) a class of deities that live off odors; celestial musicians

drokpa nomads of the high plateaus

Drölkar White Tara

Dröljang Green Tara

Drölma (S. Tara) goddess redemptress, venerated as the *bodhisattva* of compassion; feminine aspect of enlightenment

Dromtönpa 11th-century disciple of Atisha, founder of the Kadampa and Reting Monastery

drubdra meditation school

drubkhang hermitage

drubphuk meditation cave

duchen large assembly hall

dud demons

Dugkarma Lady with the Umbrella, a multi-headed deity

dukhang assembly hall

Dükhor (S. Kalachakra) Wheel of Time, a complex yogic *tantra*, associated with the mystical land of Shambhala; also a deity

Dülwa (S. Vinaya) teachings and rules of moral conduct for monks and nuns

dungkar conch

durtrö cemetery

Dzogchen Great Perfection, a practice of the Nyingma and Kagyü sects to obtain supreme realization in one lifetime

dzong fort

E

Eight Great Bodhisattvas (S) Avalokiteshvara, Manjusri, Vajrapani, Maitreya, Samantabhadra, Akashagarbha, Kshitigarbha, Sarvanivaranaviskambini

F

Four Guardian Kings four kings of the four cardinal directions, found at temple entrances; Dhritarahta (east), Virupaksha (west), Virudhaka (south), Vaishravana (north)

G

Gampopa chief disciple of Milarepa, founder of the Kagyüpa

Ganden (S. Tushita) Pure Land where the Future Buddha Jampa presently resides

gang snow field

gangri snow mountain

garuda (S) the man-bird vehicle of Vishnu

gau reliquary worn around the neck

Gedan Gyatso (1476–1542) Second Dalai Lama

Gedundrub (1391–1474) the nephew and disciple of Tsong Khapa; founder of Tashilhunpo Monastery; First Dalai Lama

gelong (S. Bhiksu) ordained monk

Gelugpa (Virtuous Ones) Tibetan Buddhist sect founded by Tsong Khapa (15th century); his *Lamrin Chenmo*, based on Atisha's *lamrin* texts, became the sect's central focus and thus assimilated much of the Kadampa teachings

geshe title of one who successfully completes the Gelugpa highest order of examination

gomdrak meditation cave monastery

gompa monastery

gongpo enchanter

gönkhang chapel where protective deities are kept and worshipped

Gönpo Guru special protector of the Sakyapa

götshang 'eagles' nest' mountain hermitage

Guru Rinpoche (S. Padmasambhava) 8th-century tantric master who established Buddhism in Tibet; known to Tibetans as the Second Buddha

Gushri Khan Mongolian emperor; patron of the Fifth Dalai Lama in the 17th century

gyalpo ruler

Gyaltsab Je disciple of Tsong Khapa

gyaltsen 'victory banner' that surmounts monastery roofs

Gyalwa Rigna (S. Dhyani Buddhas) five Buddha 'families' associated with aspects of existence: Vairochana, Ratnasambhava, Amitabha, Amoghasiddhi, Akshobhya

gyaphip ornate gilt-copper roof

Gyendruk Six Ornaments; six important Buddhist philosophers of ancient India: Nagarjuna, Aryadeva, Asanga, Vasubhandu, Dignaga, and Dharmakirti

gyü (S. tantra) teachings that employ magic and other skilful means to obtain liberation rapidly; a class of Buddhist scriptures that teach through symbolic language

H

Heruka wrathful male tutelary deity; manifestation of *tantric* energy

J

jalu (rainbow body) transformation of the body into multi-hued light

Jamchen Chöje Sakya Yeshe founder of Sera Monastery and student of Tsong Khapa

Jampa (S. Maitreya) Future Buddha

Jampelyang (S. Manjusri) Bodhisattva of Wisdom

Jamyang Chöje founder of Drepung Monastery and student of Tsong Khapa

Jamyang Zhepa founder of Labrang Monastery in Amdo

Jangchub Gyaltsen 14th-century abbot of the Phagmo Drupa sect

Jonangpa Tibetan Buddhist sect that emphasizes the practices and doctrines of the Kalachakra Tantra

Jowo Precious One, title of highly venerated statues of Sakyamuni; Buddha as a prince aged eight

K

Kadampa Tibetan Buddhist sect based on the teachings of Atisha (982–1054), noted for the rigor of its Vinaya practice; its teachings later assimilated by the Kagyüpa and Gelugpa schools

Kagyüpa Tibetan Buddhist sect founded by Marpa (1012–96), great yogi and translator

kalon officer of the Tibetan cabinet

kalpa (S) an eon, sometimes reckoned at 4,320 million years

Kamalashila Indian student of Santarakshita, winner of the Samye debate (c 792)

Kangyur Translation of the Word, part of the Tibetan Buddhist canon that contains discourses attributed to the Buddha

karma (S) Buddhist and Hindu law of cause and effect, which continues from one life to another

Karmapa lineage of incarnate lamas of the Kagyüpa whose main seat is Tsurphu Monastery; the first Karmapa, Düsum Khyenpa (1110–93) was a disciple of Gampopa; the Karmapas are the head of the Karma Kagyü sect

karuna (S) compassion

Kashag cabinet of the Dalai Lama

kawa column

Kedrub Je disciple of Tsong Khapa; the First Panchen Lama

Kham eastern province of Tibet; parts of it are now in the Chinese provinces of Sichuan and Yunnan

khandroma (S. dakini) class of celestial beings, usually female tantric deities who protect and serve Tantrism; they personify the wisdom of enlightenment

khang house

khangchung small house

khangtsen 'house' of a monastery college (*tratsang*); residential quarters for monks

khanpo abbot

khata offering scarf

khora ritual circuit clockwise for Buddhists, counter-clockwise for Bönpos

khorlo Dharma wheel

khyamkhor corridor surrounding a courtyard

khyamra courtyard

khyamtö terrace

khyung (S. garuda) bird of Indian mythology said to hatch fully grown, hence a symbol for the awakened mind

Kong Chögyal Pho 11th-century founder of Sakya Monastery, father of Kunga Nyingpo

könyer caretaker

ku (S. kaya) modes of existence; the Buddha is conceived as having three such modes: body, speech and mind

kudung khang reliquary room

kumbum large multi-chapel *chörten*

Kunga Nyingpo (Sachen) one of the Five Patriarchs of Sakya

Kuntu Zangpo (S. Samantabhadra) the Adi Buddha, who through ceaseless meditation, gives rise to the Five Dhyani Buddhas; often shown seated on an elephant

kuten a Buddha image

Kye Dorje (S. Hevajra) a major tantric deity, depicted in two-, four-, six-, 12-, or 16-armed forms, dancing in union with his consort, usually Nairatmya; especially worshiped by the Sakyapa

Kyerab (S. Jataka) stories of Buddha Sakyamuni's previous lives

kyilkhor (S. mandala) a symbolic, graphic representation of a tantric deity's realm of existence; a psycho-cosmogram

L

la pass

labrang residence of abbots; palace

lam path

lama (S. guru) spiritual teacher; enlightened master

Lamdre the Way and its Fruit; tantric Sakya meditation introduced by the 9th-century Indian adept Virupa, which integrates the teachings of *sutra* and *tantra* into a course designed to induce enlightenment within a single lifetime

Lamrin 'Stages on the path to Enlightenment' tradition expounded by Tsong Khapa; the discipline represents the series of steps the meditator must go through in order to achieve the final goal of enlightenment

lamtak stone trail markers

Langdarma 9th-century king, last of the Yarlung Dynasty; he persecuted Buddhism

le (S. karma) the sum and consequences of a person's actions during the successive phases of his existence

lha god, life-spirit

lhakhang chapel

lhari life-spirit mountain

lhashing life-spirit tree

Lhatotori mythical 28th king of the Yarlung Dynasty; received the first Buddhist texts from the sky

lhatse cairn or *chörten*, usually on a pass

lhera corral-like stone shelter

lingkhor external circumambulatory circuit

linka garden or park

Lobsang Gyatso Fifth Dalai Lama (1617–82)

Longchenpa 14th-century teacher of the Nyingmapa; text-finder (*terton*)

Losar Tibetan lunar New Year, usually in February or March

lötsawa Tibetan translators of Buddhist texts from India

lu (S. naga) long-life serpent deities that inhabit bodies of water

Ludrup (S. Nagarjuna) 2nd-century Indian Buddhist philosopher

lukhang chapel of the serpent-protector

lungi (S) long piece of printed cotton wrapped around the waist and worn as a skirt

lungta prayer flag

M

Mahakala (S) (Tib. Nagpo Chenpo) wrathful deity; wrathful aspect of Chenresi

mahasiddha (S) (Tib. Drubchen) an enlightened being; yogic magician; Tilopa, Naropa, and Maitripa are among the famed 84 Mahasiddhas

mahavihara (S) large monastery

Mahayana (S) Great Vehicle; major development of Buddhism with emphasis on compassion and *bodhisattva* ideal

Maitreya (S) (Tib. Jampa) Future Buddha

makara (S) mythical water monster, often appears as a water spout on buildings

mandal stone pile offering

mandala (S) see Kyilkhor

Mandarava consort of Guru Rinpoche

Manjusri (S) (Tib. Jampelyang) Bodhisattva of Wisdom

mantra (S) sacred formula; syllables and words that communicate the nature of tantric deities, grant powers, or lead to realization

Marmaze (S. Dipankara) Past Buddha

Marpa (1012–96) founder of the Kagyüpa; teacher of Milarepa

Maudgalyayana one of two chief disciples of the Buddha

Mikyö (S. Akshobhya) one of Five Dhyani Buddhas; sometimes used to represent Sakyamuni

Milarepa (1040–1123) poet-saint; teacher of Gampopa and founding patriarch of the Kagyüpa

Miyöwa (S. Acala) the Immovable; a wrathful protector

momo steamed dumpling

Mönlam prayer festival started by Tsong Khapa in 1409; takes place at the Jokhang in Lhasa after the lunar New Year celebrations of Losar

Mt Meru (S) (also Sumeru) axis mundi; sacred mountain at the center of the universe

N

Naga (S) serpent deity

Namgyalma (S. Vijaya) female deity associated with longevity

Nampa Nangse (S. Vairochana) one of the Five Dhyani Buddhas

Namtose (S. Vaishravana) Buddhist god of wealth; Guardian King of the North

Namse god of wealth

nangkhor inner circumambulatory passage

nangpa Buddhist

Nangwa Thaye (S. Amitabha) one of the five Dhyani Buddhas; Buddha of Infinite Light

Naropa 11th-century Indian *mahasiddha* who was the teacher of Marpa

nay barley

ne place of pilgrimage

nechen important pilgrimage site

nekhor pilgrimage circuit around a holy site

nekorpa pilgrim

neljorma *yogini*

neljorpa *yogi*

Neten Chudruk 16 Arhats, immediate disciples of Sakyamuni in the Theravada tradition

neyig pilgrimage guidebook

ngakpa wandering tantric practitioner, usually Nyingmapa or Kagyüpa

Ngok Lötsawa famed translator; principal disciple of Atisha

nguldung silver burial *chörten*

nirvana state of Buddhahood; an unconditioned state free from birth, suffering, and death

nojin nagpo black demons

norbu wish-fulfilling gem; the Buddha is often called *norbu*

Nyatri Tsenpo mythical first king of Tibet who descended from heaven onto a mountain in the Yarlung Valley

Nyingmapa Tibetan Buddhist sect that maintains the lineages carried to Tibet during the 7th–9th century; lineages established by Guru Rinpoche (Padmasambhava), Vimalamitra, Santarakshita, and Vairochana

P

Paksam Trishing (S. Avadanakalpata) a work by the Buddhist poet, Ksemendra, which recounts previous lives of the Buddha

Palden Lhamo wrathful protectress of Tibet

Panchen Lama lineage of incarnate lamas, recognized as manifestations of Amitabha Buddha; abbots of Tashilhunpo Monastery

pandita great Buddhist scholar; usually refers to scholars from Kashmir and India

pecha religious text in folio form

Phagmo Drupa 12th-century founder of Densatil Monastery and disciple of Gampopa; dynasty founded by Jangchub Gyaltsen, successor to the Sakyapa

Phagpa 13th-century patriarch of the Sakyapa; appointed by Kublai Khan as spiritual and temporal ruler of Tibet

phu the upper part of a valley

phuk, phukpa cave

phurpa ritual dagger

pöba wooden drinking cup

pöda farmer

Prajnaparamita (S) Perfection of Wisdom; group of Mahayana texts; female deity who personifies wisdom

prasad (S) relic infused with sacred power; a blessing

puja (S) religious offering or prayer

Q

Qianlong (C) 18th-century Chinese Manchu emperor who defeated the Nepal Gurkhas in 1792

qu (C, pronounced chu) administrative district; district center

R

rabsel balcony

Ralpachen (806–38) last of the Three Religious Kings of the Yarlung Dynasty (others: Songtsen Gampo, Trisong Detsen)

rangjung 'self-manifesting'; refers to sacred objects such as handprints, statues, stones etc. that originated miraculously

Ratnasambhava one of the Five Dhyani Buddhas

Rechungpa disciple of Milarepa

ri mountain

Rigsum Gönpo Three Protectors of Tibet: Chenresi, Chana Dorje, Jampelyang

rilbu medicinal capsule, often contains sacred substances blessed by a lama

rima sheep and goat dung

Rinchen Zangpo (958–1055) West Tibetan translator who, with King Yeshe Ö, invited Atisha to the Kingdom of Guge

ringsel small, hard, glittering objects found in the ashes of certain great lamas

rinpoche honorific term for a Tibetan guru

rishi (S) great sage of old; distinguished poet, philosopher or spiritual personality

ritrö mountain retreat

rongpa farmer; valley dweller

S

sadhanas (S) special tantric practices for gaining certain spiritual attainment

sadhu (S) Hindu ascetic who has renounced family and caste to wander, beg and pray

Sakya Pandita (1182–1251) one of the Five Patriarchs of the Sakyapa

Sakyapa Tibetan Buddhist sect that traces its lineage to Drogmi Sakya Yeshe (b 1147); the tradition emphasizes both study and practice

Sakyamuni (S) Sage of the Sakyas; the historical Buddha who lived in India around 500 BC

Sakyathupa Historical Buddha

samadhi state of meditative absorption

sampa bridge

samsara (S) the cycle of birth, death, and rebirth

sang offering of scented wood; juniper

sangchö incense ritual

Sangdü (S. Guhyasamaja) deity of the supreme yoga *tantras*, represented with three faces and six arms

sannyasi (S) religious ascetic who has cut all ties with normal society

sangha (S) community of monks and nuns; practitioners of Buddhism

Sangye Gyatso (1652–1705) the regent of the Fifth Dalai Lama

Santarakshita S. (Tib. Khenchen Bodhisatta) Indian Buddhist philosopher invited by King Trisong Detsen to Tibet in the 8th century; one of the founders of the Samye Monastery

shabje footprint

Shambhala mythic land associated with Kalachakra

Shangpa Tibetan Buddhist sect based on the lineage brought to Tibet by Khyungpo Naljor (11th century); later absorbed by the Kagyüpa, and Gelugpa

Shariputra disciple of the Buddha

Shenrab founder of the Bön religion

sherab (S. prajna) knowledge, discrimination

shika manor, estate

shikara (S) a style of temple consisting of a tapered cigar-shaped tower set over a square shrine

Shinje (S. Yamantaka) bull-headed wrathful form of Jampelyang; represents wisdom that subdues death

shiwa peaceful deities

shukpa juniper

shunggo central gate

siddha (S) one who has accomplished the *siddhis*, complete attainment

sinmo ogress

Six Ornaments six early Indian Buddhist philosophers: Nagarjuna, Aryadeva, Asanga, Vasubhandu, Dignaga, Dharmakirti

Sonam Tsemo one of the Five Sakya Patriarchs, son of Kunga Nyingpo

Songtsen Gampo (7th century) first of the Three Religious Kings of the Yarlung Dynasty

sungjönma sculpted or painted deity that miraculously talks

sungkhang chapel of a guardian-protector

sungkhor (S. Yantra) amulet worn around the neck; contains *mantras* or pictures of deities

sungma wrathful guardian of the doctrine; oracle-medium

sunyata (S) emptiness; Nirvana

sutra (S) scriptures

T

Tamdrin (S. Hayagriva) tantric deity and wrathful protector with a horse's head emerging from his flaming hair

Tangton Gyalpo (1385–1464) bridge builder; founder of Chung Riwoche Chörten; creator of Tibetan opera

tantra (S) a mystic philosophy developed in ancient India that profoundly influenced both Hinduism and Buddhism

Taranatha founder of the Jonangpa, master of the Kalachakra tantra

Tathagata title of the Buddha

Tegmen (S. Hinayana) Lesser Vehicle; earliest form of Buddhism in which one is concerned with one's salvation alone

tengwa rosary

Tengyur Translation of the Commentaries, part of the Tibetan Buddhist canon that contains the Indian commentarial literature to accompany *sutras*

Tenzin Gyatso (b 1935) 14th Dalai Lama who currently lives in Dharamsala, India

terma concealed treasures: texts, ritual objects, relics; *terma* convey essential teachings suited for the time and place in which they are discovered

terne pilgrimage sites where *terma* has been found

terton discoverer of *terma*

thang plain

thangka religious painted or embroidered scroll

Thirty-five (35) Buddhas of Compassion class of archetypal Buddhas; believers confess unwholesome deeds before them

Thönmi Sambhota (7th century) minister of King Songtsen Gampo; inventor of the Tibetan alphabet

Three Jewels Buddha, Dharma, Sangha

thumo practice to develop mystic inner heat; type of tantric yoga

tirtha (S) Hindu pilgrimage site

tokdhen professional cremator

torana gateway; arch over a sculpted image

torma cake made of *tsampa*, butter, and sugar; offering in religious ceremonies

trapa monk

tratsang monastic college

tribhanga (S) exaggerated S-shaped body posture found in early Indian works

Trichen (Tripa) supreme ruler of Sakya Monastery

Tripitaka (S) Three Baskets; earliest most complete collection of Buddhist sacred literature, comprised of monastic rules (Vinaya), the discourses of the Buddha (Sutra), and scholasticism (Abhidharma)

Trisong Detsen (r 755–97) Yarlung-dynasty king who proclaimed Buddhism as the state religion

Tritsun Nepalese wife of King Songtsen Gampo

trowa wrathful deities

tsamkhang hermitage; meditation room

tsampa roasted barley flour, Tibet's staple food

Tsang West-Central Tibet centering on Shigatse

tsa-tsa small clay icon of a deity or other religious symbol

Tsechigma (S. Ekajati) protector; wrathful *dakini* with one topknot, one eye, one fang, and one breast; personifies mental concentration; important protector of the Nyingmapa

tsechu long-life water

Tsepame (S. Amitayus) Buddha associated with the long-life initiation
tshokchen great assembly hall
tshok ritual offering made of *tsampa*
tshokhang assembly hall
tso lake
tsomchen reception hall
Tsong Khapa (1357–1419) founder of the Gelugpa
Tsuglag Khang grand temple
tulku incarnate lama
Two Supreme Philosophers Indian masters, Shakyaprabha and Gunaprabha, authors of Vinaya treatises

U

Ü Central Tibet centering around Lhasa
ütse topmost part of a monastic complex
ushnisha (S) protuberance or hair-bun on skull of a Buddha

V

Vairocana (Tib. Nampa Nangse) one of the Five Dhyani Buddhas
Vajrayana Diamond Vehicle; Tantrism, a division of Mahayana Buddhism
vihara (S) a monastery, temple
vinaya (S) monastic codes of conduct

W

Wencheng Chinese wife of King Songtsen Gampo
Wheel of Dharma cycle of teachings given by the Buddha
Wöpame (S. Amitabha) Buddha of Infinite Light
Wösung (S. Kashyapa) Buddha of the Past

X

xian (C; pronounced shian) county; administrative center

Yabse Sum Tsong Khapa and his two principal disciples

Y

yabyum tantric symbol or representation of male and female energies; mystic sexual union
yaksa (S) demon
Yangchenma (S. Sarasvati) Melodious Lady; Indian goddess of music
yatra (S) pilgrimage
Yeshe Tsogyal consort of Guru Rinpoche; former wife of King Trisong Detsen
yidam tutelary deity; personal protector and guide
yu turquoise
yuan (C) Chinese dollar
Yutok Yönten Gönpo (b 729) physician; founder of Tibetan medicine

Z

Zangbala (also Jambala) God of Wealth
zhidak protective spirit of a place
zhitro peaceful and wrathful deities
Zhije Buddhist teachings brought to Tibet by Dampa Sangye, 12th-century Indian master
zimkhang hermitage
zimphuk 'sleeping cave'; cave retreat

TIBETAN FESTIVALS

Lunar Month	Date	
First	1st–7th	New Year Festival (Losar). Week-long drama and carnivals, horse races, archery. Time for family and friends. Lots of beer (*chang*). Pilgrims make incense offerings on hills around Lhasa.
First	4th–25th	Mönlam or Great Prayer Festival, begun by Tsong Khapa. Hordes of pilgrims at Lhasa's Jokhang. The Future Buddha (Jampa) is paraded around the Barkhor.
First	15th	Lantern Festival to commemorate Buddha's miracle at Sravasti. Fires on roofs, lamps in windows. Gigantic butter sculptures erected around the Barkhor.
Second/ Third	28th–19th	Festival to drive out evil and expel the scapegoat. Lamas and monks encircle Lhasa with trumpets.
Fourth	7th	Important month for pilgrims. Birth of Buddha Sakyamuni.
Fourth	15th	Sakyamuni's enlightenment and entry to Nirvana. Outdoor opera. Captured animals set free. Thousands of pilgrims in the Jokhang.
Fifth	14th–16th	Hanging of giant *thangka* at Tashilhunpo, Shigatse.
Fifth	15th–24th	Worship of the Buddha. Bonfires and picnics under trees, at Norbu Lingka and parks.
Sixth	4th	Feast of Buddha's first sermon. Pilgrims climb holy mountains around Lhasa, especially the Gephel Ri behind Drepung Monastery.
Sixth	30th	Hanging of giant *thangka* at Drepung Monastery. Cham dances in the main courtyard.
Seventh	1st–7th	Shötun (Yoghurt) Festival. Drepung and Norbu Linka are venues for Tibetan operas, Cham dances, and much merry-making.
Seventh (end) and Eighth		Golden Star Festival to wash away greed, hate, and delusion. Ritual bathing in rivers. Picnics.

Eighth	1st–10th	Dajyur Festival at Gyantse and Damxung. Horse racing, games.
Eighth	1st–7th	Harvest Festival. Prayers, dancing, singing, drinking.
Ninth	22nd	Lhabab Düchen. Buddha's descent from heaven after preaching to his mother. All monasteries open. Lots of pilgrims gather in Lhasa for this important festival.
Tenth	15th	Palden Lhamo Festival. Procession around the Barkhor of Palden Lhamo (protectress) statue.
Tenth	25th	Memorial festival of Tsong Khapa's death. Fires on monastery roofs, many lamps. Image of Tsong Khapa carried in procession.
Twelfth	1st–7th	New Year Festival at Shigatse.
Twelfth	5th–6th	Meeting of the Eight Guardians and demons. People stay indoors to avoid evil outside.
Twelfth	29th	Festival to drive out evil and the Old Year. Houses are meticulously cleaned and Cham dances performed.

The Tibetan lunar calendar lags approximately four to six weeks behind the solar calendar. For example, Tibetan First Month usually falls in February, the Fifth Month in June or early July, and the Eighth Month in September.

ICONOGRAPHY

Sakyamuni (Sakyathubpa)

Atisha

Milarepa

Marpa

Gampopa

Padampa

Buton

Sakya Pandita

Tsongkhapa

Khedrub Je

Fifth Dalai Lama

Vajrabairava (Dorje Jigje)

Guhyasamaja (Pal Sangwa Dupa)

Chakrasamvara (Khorlo Dompa)

Kalachakra (Dykyi Khorlo)

Hevajra (Kye Dorje)

Manjughosa (Jampayang)

Vajrapani (Chana Dorje)

Avalokiteshvara (Chenresi)

Kshitigarbha (Sayi Nyingpo)

Maitreya (Jampa)

Samantabhadra (Kuntu Zangpo)

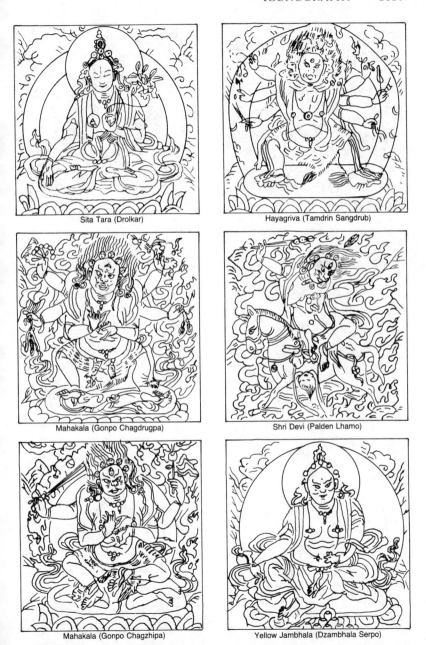

Sita Tara (Drolkar)

Hayagriva (Tamdrin Sangdrub)

Mahakala (Gonpo Chagdrugpa)

Shri Devi (Palden Lhamo)

Mahakala (Gonpo Chagzhipa)

Yellow Jambhala (Dzambhala Serpo)

Mangala (Tashi Tseringma)

Vaishravana (Namtose)

Amitayus (Tsepame)

Vairocana (Namnang)

Alsobhya (Miyowa)

Ratnasambhava

Amitabha (Wopame)

Amoghasiddhi (Dondrub)

SELECT BIBLIOGRAPHY

Allen, C, A Mountain in Tibet: The Search for Mount Kailas and the Sources of the Great Rivers of India (London, 1982)

Aris, M & Kyi, A S S, Tibetan Studies in Honour of Hugh Richardson (Warminster, England, 1980)

Aris, M, Bhutan, the early history of a Himalayan kingdom (Warminster, England, 1980)

Aschof, J, Tsaparang-Königsstadt in Westtibet (Munich, 1989)

Aschof, J & Meyer, H, Tsaparang (Freiburg, 1987)

Aufschnaiter, P, 'Prehistoric sites discovered in inhabited regions of Tibet', East and West, vol VIII (1956-57), pp 74-88
        —'Lands and places of Milarepa', East and West, vol 26 (new series: 1976) nos 1-2, pp 175-190
        —Sein Leben in Tibet (Innsbruck, 1983)

Avedon, J F, In Exile from the Land of Snows (London, 1984)

Aziz, B N, Tibetan Frontier Families (New Delhi, 1978)

Aziz, B & Kapstein, M, ed, 'Soundings in Tibetan Civilization', Proceedings of the 1982 Seminar of the International Association for Tibetan Studies held at Columbia University (New Delhi, 1985)

Bailey, F M, China–Tibet–Assam, A Journey (London, 1945)
        —No passport to Tibet (London, 1957)

Batchelor, S, The Tibet Guide (London, 1988)

Bernbaum, E, The Way to Shambhala (New York, 1980)

Bezruchka, S, The Pocket Doctor (Seattle, 1988)

Blondeau, A M, 'Les Pèlerinages tibétains, Les Pèlerinages', Sources Orientales, 3 (Paris, 1960)

Booz, E, A Guide to Tibet (London, 1986)

Bowman, G, Anthropology of Pilgrimage, Dimensions of Pilgrimage: An Anthropological Appraisal (New Delhi, 1985)

Brauen, M & Kvaerne, P, Tibetan Studies (Zurich, 1978)

Cassinelli, C & Ekvall, R B, A Tibetan Principality: the Political System of Sa-skya (Ithaca, New York, 1969)

Chang, G C C, The Hundred Thousand Songs of Milarepa, 2 vols (Boulder, Colorado, 1977)

Chayet, A & Meyer, F, 'La chapelle de Srong-btsan sgampo au Potala', Arts Asiatiques, XXXVIII (Paris, 1983), pp 82-85

Csoma de Koros, A, Tibetan Studies. A Collection of his Contributions to the Journal of the Asiatic Society of Bengal, ed E Denison Ross (Calcutta, 1912)

Dalai Lama, My Land and My People (New York, 1983)

Dargay, E M, The Rise of Esoteric Buddhism in Tibet, (New Delhi, 1977)

Das, S C, Journey to Lhasa and Central Tibet, ed W W Rockhill (London, 1902)

David-Neel, A, My Journey to Lhasa, (London, 1983)

De Schaunesee, R M, The Birds of China, (Washington DC, 1984)

Denwood, P, 'Forts and Castles—An aspect of Tibetan Architecture', Shambhala occaisional papers of the Institute of Tibetan Studies, no 1 (London, 1971), pp 7-17

—'The Tibetan temple-art in its architectural setting' in *Mahayanist Art after AD 900*, ed W Watson (London, 1971)

—'Introduction to Tibetan Architecture', *Tibet News Review*, vol 1, no 2 (London, 1980) pp 3–12

Dowman, K, *The Power Places of Central Tibet: The Pilgrim's Guide* (London, 1988)

Ferrari, A, *mk'yen brtse's guide to the holy places of Central Tibet* (Rome, 1958)

Filibeck, E de Rossi, 'Two Tibetan Guide Books to Tise and Laphyi'. *Monumenta Tibetica Historica*, Abteilung 1, Bund 4 (Bonn, 1988)

Fleming, P, *Bayonets to Lhasa, The British Invasion of 1904* (Oxford, 1984)

Fletcher, H, *A Quest for Flowers* (Edinburgh, 1976)

Francke, A H, *A History of Western Tibet* (London, 1905)

Gensser, A, *Geology of the Himalayas* (London, 1964)

Gerner, M, *Architekturen im Himalaya* (Stuttgart, 1987)

Gold, P, *Altar and the Earth*, (Ithaca, 1987)

Goldstein, M C, *A History of Modern Tibet, 1913–1951* (Berkeley, 1962)

Gordon, A K, *The Iconography of Tibetan Lamaism* (Rutland and Tokyo, 1985)

Govinda, A, *The Way of the White Clouds* (Berkeley, 1962)

Gyatsho, T, *Gateway to the Temple: Manual of Tibetan monastic customs, art, building and celebrations* (Kathmandu, 1979)

Haarh, E, *The Yar-lung dynasty* (Copenhagen, 1969)

Hackett, P H, *Mountain Sickness—Prevention, Recognition and Treatment* (New York, 1980)

Harrer, H, *Seven Years in Tibet* (London, 1955)

Hedin, S, *Transhimalayas*, 3 vols (London, 1910)

—*Southern Tibet*, 9 vols (Stockholm, 1917)

Henss, M, *Tibet* (Zurich, 1981)

Hopkirk, P, *Trespassers on the Roof of the World* (Oxford, 1982)

Howard-Bury, C K, *Mount Everest, The Reconnaisance, 1921* (London, 1922)

Jisl, L, Sis, V & Vanis, J, *L'Art Tibetain* (Paris, 1958)

Karmay, H, *Early Sino-Tibetan Art* (Warminster, 1975)

Karmay, S G, 'The Treasury of Good Sayings: A Tibetan History of Bön', *London Oriental Series*, vol 26 (London, 1972)

Klimburg-Salter, D, *The Silk Route and the Diamond Path* (Los Angeles, 1982)

Kling, K, *Tibet* (London, 1985)

Kwang, C Y et al, *The architecture of the buildings of the Guge kingdom* (Beijing, 1988)

Ling Rinpoche, K, 'The history of Ganden, Drepung and Sera', Dreloma no 1, *Drepung Loseling Library Society* (Mundgod, India, 1978), pp 7 ff

MacDonald, A W & Imaeda, Y ed, *Essais sur l'art du Tibet* (Paris, 1977)

Maraini, F, *Secret Tibet* (Paris, 1952)

McGregor, J, *A Chronicle of Exploration* (London, 1970)

Moran, K & Johnson, R, *Kailash: On Pilgrimage to the Sacred Mountain of Tibet* (London, 1989)

Müller, K & Raunig, W, *Der Wegzum Dach der Welt* (Innsbruck, 1982)

Nebesky-Wojkowitz, R de, *Oracles and Demons of Tibet* (Den Haag, 1956)

Norbu, T J & Turnbull, C, *Tibet: Its History, Religion and People* (London, 1968)

Pal, P, *Art of Tibet* (Los Angeles, 1983)

Pal, P *Tibetan Paintings* (Basel, 1984)

Pranavananda, S, *Pilgrim's Companion to the Holy Kailash and Manasarovar* (Allahabad, 1938)

Richardson, H, *Tibet and its History* (London, 1962)

    —*A Corpus of Early Tibetan Inscriptions* (London, 1985

Shakabpa, W D, *Tibet: A Political History* (New Haven and London, 1967)

Sherring, C A, *Western Tibet and the British Borderland* (London, 1958)

Snellgrove, D, *Indo-Tibetan Buddhism* (Boston and London, 1987)

Snelling, J, *The Sacred Mountain* (London, 1983)

Stein, R A, *Tibetan Civilization* (Standford, 1972)

Swift, Hugh, *Trekking in Nepal, West Tibet and Bhutan* (San Francisco, 1989)

Taring, A, *Map of Lhasa*, ed Chie Nakane (Tokyo, 1984)

    —*Lhasa Tsug-Lag Khang Gi Sata and Karchlag [The index and plan of Lhasa Cathedral in Tibet]* (Rajpur, 1979)

Teichman, E, *Travels of a Consular Officer in Eastern Tibet. Together with a History of the Relations between China, Tibet and India* (Cambridge, 1922)

Tucci, G, *Indo-Tibetica*, 4 vols (Rome, 1932–41)

    —*Santi e briganti nel Tibet ignoto* (Milan, 1937)

    —*Tibetan Painted Scrolls*, 2 vols (Rome, 1949)

    —'The tombs of the Tibetan kings', *Serie Orientale, Roma*, 1 (Rome, 1950)

    —*A Lhasa e oltre* (Rome, 1950)

    —*Transhimalaya* (Geneva, 1973)

Tulku, T, *Ancient Tibet* (Berkeley, 1986)

Uebach, H and Panglung, J L, eds, *Tibetan Studies: Proceedings of the 4th Seminar of the International Association for Tibetan Studies* (Munich, 1985)

Ugyen Gyatso, *Records of the Survey of India*, vol VIII (Dehra Dun, India, 1915–22)

Vaurie, C, *Tibet and its birds* (London, 1989)

Vitali, R, *Early Temples of Central Tibet* (London, 1990)

Waddell, L A, *The Buddhism of Tibet, or Lamaism* (London, 1895)

Wylie, T V, *The Geography of Tibet according to the 'Dzam-gling-rgyas bshad'* (Rome, 1962)

Zwalf, W, *Heritage of Tibet* (London, 1981)

MAP INDEX
Topographical (Trekking) Maps

Ref no.	Name	Page
NG45-3A	Sakyetang	906
45-4	Chumbi	795
NH44-1B	Shipki	976
44-1D	Mana	977
44-2A	Nabru	954
44-2B	Gartok	956
44-2C	Tholing	974
44-2D	Tirthapuri	969
44-3C	Kailash	276
44-6B	Gyanima	967
44-7A	Mapham	616
44-7C	Purang	958
NH45-2D	Ombu	782
45-6B	Sezhik	780
45-6D	Shuru	778
45-7A	Ngangtse Tso	861
45-7C	Chang-la Pö La	776
45-7D	Shib La	859
45-8A	Shencha	875
45-8C	Lengra	874
45-8D	Kalamba	668
45-10C	Raga	461
45-10D	Riwoche	457
45-11A	Lingka	770
45-11B	Namchi	857
45-11C	Lhatse	865
45-11D	Thongmön	853
45-12A	Namling	871
45-12B	Wuyuk	878
45-12C	Shigatse	833
45-12D	Rinpung	843
45-13B	Dzongka	931
45-13D	Kyirong	933
45-14A	Pelku Tso	927
45-14B	Dingri	252
45-14C	Nyalam	269
45-14D	Rongphuk	255
45-15A	Shekar	813
45-15C	Kharta	900
45-16A	Rhe	837
45-16B	Gyantse	789
45-16C	Kampa	839
45-16D	Yemar	792

Ref no.	Name	Page
NH46-4D	Tengcheng	585
46-5A	Namtso	666
46-5B	Namtso Qu	662
46-5C	Yangpachen	659
46-5D	Reting	565
46-6A	Langlung La	562
46-6B	Chakpatang	558
46-6C	Drigungtil	554
46-6D	Jinda	559
46-7A	Lharigo	576
46-7B	Alado	577
46-7C	Giamda	573
46-7D	Draksum	650
46-8A	Pemba	579
46-8B	Shopado	583
46-8C	Tangme	581
46-8D	Chumdo	586
46-9A	Tsurphu	676
46-9B	Lhasa	626
46-9C	Chusul	593
46-9D	Dranang	473
46-10A	Medro Gongkar	547
46-10B	Jashing	645
46-10C	Tsethang	517
46-10D	Gyatsa	220
46-11C	Nang	228
46-12A	Gyala	722
46-12B	Pomi	725
46-12C	Lusha	714
46-12D	Metok	719
46-13A	Phurma Tso	591
46-13B	Yamdrok Tso	605
46-13C	Manda	703
46-13D	Lhodrak	684
46-14A	Drigu Tso	213
46-14B	Sanga Choling	216
46-14C	Tsona	244
46-14D	Lhuntse	241
46-15A	Chikchar	224
46-15B	Tsari Sarpa	236

Map Location Index	20
Topographical Map Legend	18

PLANS

King Songsten Gampo's Demon Suppressing Temples	44
Jokhang (Ground Floor)	76
Jokhang (2nd Floor)	86
Jokhang (2nd Floor, East Wing)	88
Jokhang (2nd Floor East Wing)	89
Jokhang (3rd Floor)	93
Jokhang (Roof)	95
Potala	101
Potrang Marpo (The Red Palace)	105
Ramoche Monastery	118
Meru Nying Monastery	120
Ganden Monastery	141
Drepung Monastery	146
Tsomchen (Ground Floor)	147
Sera Monastery	158
Tsokchen	162
Lukhang	176
Gesar Lhakhang	178
Norbu Lingka: The Summer Palace	182
Lapchi: The Holy Places	264
The Samye Complex	302
Samye Ütse	303
Khamsum Sangkhang Ling	309
Tsogyal Latso Lhakhang	321
The Chongye Tombs	356
A Serkhung Tomb (section)	369
The Lishan Tombs	373
Khachu Lhakhang	382
Yemar (Iwang) Monastery	391
Dranang Monastery	395
Shalu Serkhang (Ground Floor)	403
Shalu Monastery (Top Floor)	408
Gyantse Palkhor Chöde	420
Palkhor Chöde (Tsuglug Khang)	422
Tholing Monastery	427
The Guge Kingdom	431
The Winter Palace	433
The Palace Precinct	435
Lhakhang Karpo	437
Lhakhang Marpo	441
Gyantse Kumbum	449
Chung Riwoche Chörten	453
Mindroling Monastery (Ground Floor)	497
Mindroling Monastery (2nd Floor)	499
Gyaling Tsokpa Monastery	504
Dingboche Monastery	506
Yarchen Monastery	508
Trandruk Monastery (Tsuglug Khang)	535
Yumbu Lagang	541

Tashilhunpo Monastery	823
Sakya Monastery	884
Rutok Rock Carvings	980

TOWN PLANS

Lhasa	64–5
Lhasa: The inner City	67
Lhasa: The Barkhor	69
Tsethang	519
Chongye	527
Nakartse	589
Yangpachen	660
Bayi	743
Ningchi	758
Gyantse	790
Yatung	798
Shigatse	820
Thongmön Xian	852
Pindsoling	863
Lhatse Chöde	866
Lhatse	868
Sakya	882
Shekar	897
Dingri	914
Dzongka	930
Kyirong	935
Nyalam	940
Shiquanhe (Ali)	949
Zanda Xian (Tholing)	955
Purang (Taklakot)	959
Zhangmu	991

ROUTE MAPS (NOT TO SCALE)

Tsari	209
Lapchi	248
Mt Kailash	273
Ganden to Samye	314
Drakyul	317
Jinka Cave	327
Lhasa to Tsethang	471
Shugseb Nunnery	487
Drachi Valley	495
Dranang Valley	501
Yön Valley	510
Yarlung Valley	515
Lhasa to Reting	544
Gyalam	571
Yamdrok Circuit	588
Lhasa to Chongye	595
Yamdrok to Phurma	606
Ralung	611
Lake Manasarovar	615
Lhasa to Lhamo Latso	623

Rutok Dzinchi   642
Lake Draksum   647
Lake Namtso   657
Tsurphu   672
Lhodrak   682
Lhasa–Ningchi Road   708
Mt Namche Barwa and Vicinity   712
Nyima La   729
Tsangpo Left Bank   735
Bönri Circuit   741
Lake Dangra and Mt Targo   767
Chumbi Valley   787
Chörten Nyima   801
Lhasa–Shigatse North Road   816
Shigatse to Kampa   831
Rinpung   841
Shigatse to Lhasa   848
Shang Valley   869
Everest: Kangshung Face   896
Everest: North Face   913
Dingri to Chung Riwoche   919
Kyirong Valley   925
Satlej Valley   965
Indus Source   983

ROAD MAPS

West Tibet   21
Central Tibet   22–23

OTHER MAPS

Mt Kailash Circuit   278
Mt Namche Barwa (section)   715
Heart of the Tsangpo Gorges   727
Mt Everest   915
Mt Shishapangma Region   941
Mt Shishapangma: North Route   942
Mt Shishapangma: South Route   942

General Index

Key to abbreviations:
Dran = Dranang
D = Drepung
Jok = Jokhang
Ks = Kailash
K = Karchu
LL = Lhamo Latso
NL = Norbu Linka
P = Potala
RG = Rigsum Gönpo
Rp = Rongphuk
S = Sera
Tlp = Tashilhunpo
Ts = Tsaparang

Bold type denotes principal entry

A

Abdze Nensa   755
Abhidharma   394
Abor   718
Abu Dzong   724
Ache Dzong   595, 602
Ajanta [India]   54, 68, 80, 121, 126, 429
Aksai Chin   951
Akshobhya Vajra   117
Alado   570, 574, 575
Alchi   28, 50, 436
Altan Khan   29
Ama Chömo Taktse   648, 651
Ama Drimé Range   804, 810, 904, 907
Ambu Phuk   620
Amdo   27, 639, 760, 944, 945
Amdo Khangtsen   143
Amo (Tromo) Qu   797, 799
Amolongkha   75
Amshuvarma   94
ancient columns   80
ancient door frames   78
Anshuvarman   26, 63
Antonio de Andrade   427, 430, 950
Arig   575
Arniko   83, 400, 402, **406**, 407, 408, 411, 455, 464
Arun River [Nepal]   271, 458, 805, 838
Arunachal Pradesh [India]   209, 735
Arya Lokeshvara   97, 99, 108
Ashang Kang La   710

Assam   221, 425
Assam Himalayas (see Pachakshiri)
Atisha   **28**, 29, 32, 34, 50, 303, 338, 341, 381, 385, 390, 401, 405, 408, 411, 425, 429, 430, 470, **472**, 475, 490, 497, 527, 545, 564, 638, 929
Atsa   570, 574, 656
Atsom Neh   721

B

Ba Salnang   297
Ba'er   955
Bacheng   584
Bailey, F M   731
Bairo Phuk   516, 525, **526**, 628
Balo   380, 710
Balpo   43
Balti Rinpoche   674
Bamian   121
Banda La   574, 656
Bangna   742
Bangrim Chöde   226, 353, 354, 735, 739
Bangso Marpo   357, 528
Bardo   334
Bardo Trangchen Chobgye   334
Baré La   214
Barga   292, 293, 617, 952, 957, 966
Bari   883
Barjung   578
Barkhang   100, 204
Barkhor   43, 62, 84
Batsak   560
Bayi   571, 643, 648, 653, 655, 708, 711, 737, 741, 742, **743**, 746
Bayi Bridge   746
Bayi Pelri, Mt   743
Bell, Charles   797
Bemdrong   752, 753
Bengal [India]   51, 68, 393, 399, 429
Benpa   681, 689
Benpa Chakdhor Monastery   690
Benpa Drukral Monastery   690
Benpa Qu   245
Benpa Valley   686
Bentsa Serki   706
Bepa Gong   267
Bepa Og   267
beyuls   **39**
Bhadu Monastery   329, 331, 335, 336, 809, 836

Bhama Ri 169, 178
Bhata Hor Monastery 165, 308
Bhutan 46, 243, 245, 412, 429, 606,
    612, 692, 787, 797, 799, 988
Bihar [India] 47, 68, 393, 398
Bimathang Monastery 649
Bimbi La 210, 235, 237
Birupa 33
Birwapa 867, 883, 893
blue poppy 731
Bodh Gaya [India] 36, 38, 40, 78,
    79, 114, 281, 286, 807, 883, 962
bodhicitta 39
Bodhisatta 867
Bodong 892
Bödong Chokle Namgyal 590
Bödongpa 590
Bokgong Mönpa Lodro Gyaltsen 99
Bomchen 363
Bomtö 569
Bonington, Chris 257
Bönkar Khyung 929
Bönpos 66, 82, 189, 273, 276, 297,
    319, 335, 344, 359, 388, 539,
    570, 584, 617, 622, 636, 639,
    664, 713, 741–9, 750, 754–9,
    763–8, 783–6, 787–8, 797–8,
    815–6, 848, 854, 873, 937, 943,
    964, 970–2
Bönri Ama 742, 749
Bönri, Mt 707, 713, 737, 741–62,
    962
Botö Gön 690
Brahmaputra 46, 712, 797
Buddha 36, 37
Buddha Tsepung 713, 717, 718
Bul Tso 667
Bumda Sebum 218, 226
Bup Chu 777
Bupchung Valley 858
Bur Chutsen Hot Springs 850, 851
Butön 298, 300, 400, 408, 409, 411,
    414, 415

C

Capuchin chapel 75
Central Asia 27, 47, 48, 49, 53, 66,
    111, 121, 378, 389, 390, 392,
    398, 399, 428, 429, 885
Ceylon 32, 49
Ch'an 300, 692
Cha 600
Cha La 218, 222, 234, 240, 245, 835
Chagar Monastery 641

Chago La 796
Chak La 194, 560, 561, 564, 567
Chakpatang 577
Chakpo Ri, Mt 48, 85, 97, 122,
    138–139, 178, 624
Chakpur Chen, Mt 682, 692, 693,
    694
Chakra 578
chaktshal 40
Chala Qu 777
Cham, Mt 700
Chamdo 570, 572, 580, 582, 584,
    656, 733, 742
Chanda La 607, 610
chang 41
Chang'an 27, 63
Chang-La-Pö-La 768, 775, 779, 781,
    852
Changju 627
Changkhang Shar Phuk 199
Changpo Plain 91, 793, 799, 988
Changra 365, 414, 416, 495, 988
Changra Tombs 365
Changtang 587, 767, 768, 847, 848,
    855, 869, 945
Chapel of the Prefect 56, 432, 435,
    444
Chaptrang 769, 771
Char Chu 209
Charmé 212, 219
Chartö Valley 212
Chasi Nunnery 321
Chatse 794
Chayul 217, 219, 242, 247
Chayul Qu 209
Che La 488, 493, 599
Chedeling Monastery 844
Chega Monastery 855
Chegona 799
Chemnak 742
Chenga 545, 564
Chengdu 994, 995, 997
Chengye Monastery 528
Chenresi 35, 40–1, 304, 401, 402
Chenresi Senge Dra Lhakhang 83
Chenresi, Mt 702
Chensel Lingka (NL) 190–2
Chensel Potrang (NL) 190–1
Cherkip 619
Chermen 372, 379
Chesang La 777
Chesang La 856
Chetang Monastery 901
Chetsün Sherab Jungne 401, 402, 404,
    407

chezing 41
Chiali Xian 574
Chickchar 227, 230, 231, 235
Chilay 240
Chim Tso 211
Chimdro La 717
Chime Tsokyil Potrang (NL) 192
Chimlung Tsemo 510
Chimlung Tsemo Tombs 371
Chimpu 386, 489, 624, 630, 631,
    632, 686, 702
Chimpu Range 371
China 26, 30, 43, 47, 49, 52, 53, 55,
    62, 63, 70, 179, 378, 386, 392, 393,
    406, 418, 440, 451, 465, 518, 648
Chinese Turkestan 52
Chingdo nomad camp 856, 858
Chingwa Taktse 60, 360, 516, 526,
    528, 540, 760
Chiragsaldi 951
Chiri 771
Chitishio 471, 481, 599
Chiu Monastery 617, **618**, 622, 966
Cho Oyu, Mt 251, 915
Chö 636, 920, 921, 521
Chöde Gang Monastery 516, 531, **532**
Chöde Wo Monastery 516, **531**
Chöding Khang (S) 164
Chöding Monastery 512
Chog La 896, 905, 907, 908
Chögar 578
Chögle Namgyal 454, 464
Chogola 667
Chögong 60, **375**
Chögro Lugyaltsen Chörten 629
Chögyal Phagpa 835
Chögyal Drubphuk (P) 43, 48, 97,
    110, 378, 536
Chögyal Gyaphip 94
Chögyal Songtsen Lhakhang 91
Chögyal Thönmi Lhakang 85
Chögyal Trungben 91
Chökhor Valley [Bhutan] 44
Chökorgye Monastery 624, **638**, 644,
    886
Chökyi Gyalpo 482, 822
Chökyi Gyaltsen 822
Chökyi Wangchuk 45
Chölung Monastery (LL) 624, **637**
Chölung Monastery (Rp) 899, 915
Chölung Tsokpa 521
Chom Lhakkang 561
Chomdo 572
Chomolhari, Mt [Sikkim] 788, 793,
    798

Chongmoche 500
Chongphu Chu Valley 901, 902
Chongye **355–61**, 365, 368, 373, 500,
    501, 526–9, 595, 683, 702
Chongye Xian 526, **527**
chöpa 41
Chörten Kangnyi (Ks) 280
Chörten Karchung 256
Chörten Karra 246
Chörten La 808
Chörten Lapsang 806
Chörten Namu 218, 222, 227
Chörten Nyima 787, **801–14**, 832,
    835, 840, 897, 910, 989, 990
Chörten Nyima Range 806
Chösam 209, 217, 222, 226, 227,
    229, 230, 231, 232, 234, 239,
    880
Chou En Lai 472
Chöyul 492
Chözang 922
Chujo Monastery 747, **750**
Chukenda Monastery 452
Chukhor 897, 903, 909
Chuku Monastery (Ks) 281
Chuku Rinpoche 281
Chulung 772
Chumbi Valley 337, 390, **787–800**,
    832, 988
Chumdo 580
Chumdo Kyang 212
Chumdo Kyang Qu 209
Chumelung 171
Chumik Dhadrang 752, 753, 760
Chumik Ringmo Monastery 831, 832,
    835
Chung Riwoche 54, 379, 447, **451–62**,
    463, 464, 541, 826, 919, 947
Chungboche 250, 256
Chungkar Monastery **929**, 930
Chuni Lama 747
Chupsang Nunnery 134
Churli 683
Chusang 268, 637
Chushar 804
Chusul 99, 470, 477, 607, 672, 674
    842, 988
Chusul Bridge 379, 516, 631, 988
Chusul Xian 674, 675
Chusum 212, 225
Chutsen 310, 312, 315, 620
Chuwar Drejik Drubphuk 256
Chuwar Monastery 249, **256**, 260,
    265, 921, 924, 934
Chuwo Ri, Mt 27, 470, **478**, 629, 685

Chuyu La 791
Council of Chumik Chökör 881
Cultural Revolution 15, **31**, 37, 52, 157, 385, 432, 452, 453

D

Da Drongmoche 892
Daglha Gampo 28, 226, **352–4**, 624, 640, 641, 739
Dagpo Gompa Tsultrim Nyingpo 88
Dagri Nyalse 360
Dakmema 700
Dakpo 352, 738, 739, 749
Dakpo Rinpoche 353, 354
Dakpo Tratsang 480, 624, **641**, 736, 739
Dalai Lama, 1st 822, 921
Dalai Lama, 2nd 145, 438, 638
Dalai Lama, 3rd 115
Dalai Lama, 5th **30**, 35, 48, 56, 98, 113, 145, 168, 175, 453, 464, 516, 527, 539, 587, 671, 678, 704, 920
Dalai Lama, 5th, tomb of 114
Dalai Lama, 6th 30, 107, 113, **114**, 175
Dalai Lama, 7th 30, 103, 106, 180, 183, 296
Dalai Lama, 7th, tomb of 109
Dalai Lama, 8th 107, 175, 180
Dalai Lama, 8th, tomb of 109
Dalai Lama, 9th, tomb of 109
Dalai Lama, 10th 114
Dalai Lama, 11th 114, 644
Dalai Lama, 12th 114
Dalai Lama, 13th 30, 100, 175, 180, 181, 184, 188, 189, 190, 639, 735, 739
Dalai Lama, 13th, tomb of 107
Dalai Lama, 14th 31, 103, 180, 185, 186, 188
Dalai Lamas **29–30**, 35, **56–57**
Damchen Gara Nakpo 701
Damdong Valley 895, 896, **907**
Dampa Sangye 271, 393, 482, 492, 521, 568, 636, 890, 892, 918, 920, 921
Dampa Sonam Gyaltsen 892
Damxung 563, 657, 660, 664, 665, 673, 816, 997
Damxung La 642, 643
Damxung Xian 661
Damzung 561
Dandanuiliq 387

Dangra Khung Dzong 783
Dangra Yubun 783
Dantig 27
Dar Drongmoche Monastery 892
Dara 805
Dara Tza Monastery 331
Darbong 758
Darchapa 160
Darchen 274, 275, 277, 293, 617, 950, 957, 983
Darchen Monastery 275
Darchula 621
Dargye Chöding 502
Darma Dhodhe 699
Darma Dzong 689
Dawa Drakpa 341
Dawa Dzong 444, 964
Dawa Gyaltsen 549
Dawa Monastery 973
Dawa Phuk 339
Dechen 171, 316, 321, 380, 546, 549, 623, 624, **625**, 626
Dechen Chökor 479, 480
Dechen Dzong 318
Dechen Rabgya Monastery 872
Dechen Xian 140, 569
Dedra Lhartse, Mt 578
Dege metalwork 75, 103
Dekyiling 845
Dela Qu 777
Demchok 46, 52, 274
Demchok Lhakhang 90
Demchok Tso 640
Demo Chemkar 735, 737
Demo La 748
Demo Labrang 168, 202
Demo Qutuqtu 168
Deng Xiaoping 31
Densatil Monastery 28, 29, 34, 197, 518, 567, 612, **635**
Depa Norbu Sangpo 844
Derge 204, 678
Derong 501, 505, 508
Desheg Gye Lhakhang (Jok) 73
Devikota [India] 36, 130, 210, 523, 682, 692, 694
Dewachen 46
Dewapling 842, 844
Dewe Chasang Monastery 862
Deyang La 720
Deyang Nub (P) 102, 115
Deyang Shar (P) 100, 103, 433
Deyang Tratsang (D) 154
Dhaggo Kani 122
Dhaggo Rungkhang 73

Dharamsala [India]   42, 79, 127, 811,
   936
Dhedruk Labrang   202
Dhelekling   370, 503, 506
Dhemik Gön   690
Dhikpa Pabsa   756
Dho Ngakling Monastery   312
Dhochok Phuk   463
Dhok Ri   130
Dhoko Ri   495
Dhoku Ri Tomb   366
Dihang   717
Ding La   915
Ding Tso   619
Dingboche Monastery   370, 502,
   505–8, 618
Dingka   796
Dingma   819
Dingna Qu   380
Dingri   249, 250, 271, 451, 456, 458,
   814, 895, 899, 906, 913, 914,
   918–20, 921, 922, 940, 990, 991,
   996, 1004
Do Chu Valley   856
Do La   336
Dochen   787
Dochu La   717
Dode Valley   193–4
Dodhu   582
Dok Chu   771
Dokham Longtang Drönma   44
Dokjit   872
Dokong La   715
Dölchu Monastery   968
Dolpopa   454
Dolpopa Sherab Gyaltsen   463
Domoko   387
Dongka ferry   849, 872
Dongka Phu Valley   850
Dongkar   210, 242, 243, 787
Dongkar Bridge   673, 987
Dongkar Me Tomb   363
Dongkar Monastery   797
Dongkar Valley   356, 360, 689
Dongkya   590, 787
Dongkya Mts   796
Dongkya Range   806
Dongom Tenpa Lhundrub   760
Dongpo Monastery   973
Dongu La   815, 818
Dorbai Qu   452
Dorchen   651, 652
Doring Chima   196
Doring Nangma   99, 196
Dorje Drak La   234

Dorje Drak Monastery   33, 317, 318,
   322, 324, 385, 470, 482, 488, 493,
   494, 496, 497, 509, 595, **598**,
Dorje Drakden   165, 718
Dorje Dudjom   323
Dorje Gyalpo   28, 492
Dorje Jigje Lhakhang (Ts)   432, 434,
   443
Dorje Lingpa   45, 344, 485
Dorje Phagmo   52, 590, 790
Dorje Phagmo Latso   233
Dorje Phurpa   46
Dorje Shugden   166
Dorjeling Nunnery   658, 660, 672,
   678, 815, 817, 818
Dorjeyang, Mt   717
Dorkya Lugudong   665, 668
Dorma Qu   979
Dorpita   75
Doshong La   713, **716**, 718, 720, 721,
   731
Dowman, Keith   639
Doya La   897, 899, 901
Dra La   479, 481
Dra Lhakhang   797
Dra Yugang Drak   502, 508
Drachi   **365–6**, 367, 470, **495**
Drachi Qu   365, 366
Drachi Valley   484
Drachom Ngagye Durtrö (Ks)   279
Dragla Lugug   43, 48, 60, **121–7**, 492
Dragur Lotsa Phuk   892
Drak   471, 483
Drak Sinmo Barje   681, 689
Drak Yerpa   28, 60, **338–43**, 685
Drak Yong Dzong   37, 45, 317, 318,
   321, 483, 522, 595, 598
Drakar   753
Drakar Shabje   752, 753
Drakar Taso   924, 925, 932, **934**
Drakchik ferry   821
Drakda   319
Drakear   130
Drakmar   249, 251, 386, 389
Drakmar Drinzang   295, 624, **628**
Drakmar Keutsang   633
Drakmar Khyunglung   261–3
Drakmar Yamalung   45
Drakpa Gyaltsen   400, 401, 404, 406,
   464, 893
Drakphuk Kawasum   724
Draksum Dorje Drak   648
Draksum Kye La   648, 655, 656
Draksum Latso (see Lake Draksum)
Drakya Monastery   932

Drakyul 317
Drama Gyang Lhakhang 867
Dramai Xian 603
Drampa (district) 866
Drampa 848
Drampa Gyang 43
Dranang Monastery 28, 49, 50, 51,
    52, 319, 329, 367–70, 378, 390,
    392, 393–9, 470, 475, 484, 497,
    501, 509, 548
Dranang Valley 463, 465, 483
Dranang Xian 370, 483, 484, 502
Drang Monastery 346
Drapa Ngönshe 393, 394, 482, 501
Drathok Gang 794
Dremojong beyul 39, 787, 801, 808
Drempa Namkha 765
Drena 742, 752, 760
Drepung Lingkhor 155
Drepung Monastery 29, 30, 43, 56,
    61, 71, 98, 145–56, 157, 165,
    166, 167, 416, 595, 631, 822,
    880, 936, 1000
Drib 170, 470, 488, 595
Drib La 471, 595, 600
Drib Tsemchok Ling 170
Drib Valley 481, 482, 595, 600
Drigu Qu 683
Drigum Tsanpo 637, 742, 750, 760
Drigung 544
Drigung Durtrö 545, 556
Drigung Dzong 552, 560,
Drigung Kyapgön 28, 34
Drigung Qu 545, 552, 553
Drigung Rinpoche 747
Drigung Tsa 561
Drigungpa 52
Drigungtil Monastery 28, 34, 53, 344,
    346, 544, 552, 553, 557, 561,
    571, 620, 709
Drime Lingpa 634
Drin 249
Drintang 249, 258, 260, 263
Drinzang 386
Drira Phuk Monastery 274, 283, 284,
    290, 618, 983, 984
Driza Zurphu Ngapa 70
Dro Trimalod 386
Dro Trisumje 388
Drodön Lingpa 718
Drögon Phagmo Drupa 34, 197, 612,
    635, 688 (see also Phagmo
    Dorje Gyalpo)
Drokmi 887
Drokmi Lötsawa 33, 409, 867, 880

Drokmi Peleyi Yeshe 892
Drölma 52
Drölma La (Ks) 274, 285, 286, 287,
    984
Drölma La (Tsari) 231, 233
Drölma Lhakhang (Jok) 72
Drölma Ri 822
Dromtönpa 28, 34, 43, 50, 303, 385,
    429, 472, 475, 545, 567
Drongtse Monastery 328, 844, 989
Drönyang Deru 356, 361
Dröshul 690
Drothang Gyalpo 934
Drowa Gön 690
Drowolung Monastery 682, 697, 698
Drowolung Valley 673, 675
Dru Gyalwa Yungdrung 766
Drubchen Sekarchungwa 892
Drubden 249, 257
Drubthob Chenpo Kuchora 136
Drubthob Lhakhang 127, 136
Drubtra Samtenling 677
Druje Yungdrung Lama 765
Drukla 649, 653
Drukluk 480
Drukpa Kagyu 612
Drukpa Kunlek 290, 688
Drukpa Rinpoche
Drukse Drubphuk 752
Drum La 682, 698, 702
Drunglung La 984
Drunglung Valley 984
Drungshi 764
Dücho 881
Dudjom Lingpa 33
Dudjom Rinpoche 33, 651, 718, 746
Dudul Phuk 266
Dugu La 589
Dükhor Lhakhang 109
Dulung 991
Dumburi 546, 548, 549
Dumo Tso 587, 589
Dungkar 429
Dungpu Chökor Monastery 470, 481,
    482, 599
Dungsar 748
Dunhuang 27, 47, 48, 51, 52, 111,
    121, 125, 126, 387, 389, 399,
    429, 463
Dusong Mangpoje 357
Düsum Khyenpa 28, 34, 678, 699,
    704
dutsi 38
Dzade 742, 753
Dzakar Chu 899, 901, 902, 909

Dzakhol 580
Dzeng Dharmabodhi 344
Dzeshö Valley 819
Dzinchi 624, 637, 642, **644**, 710
Dzogchen 45
Dzokchen **33**
Dzokchen Nyingtik 492, 508, 509
Dzong Khyung Teng 752, 754
Dzong Kumbum 317, 318, 321, **325**, 483, 595, 598
Dzongka (Kyirong Xian) 924, 925, 926, **929**, 935
Dzongka Chöde Monastery 214, **215**
Dzongyap Lukhang dorings 195

E

Ensakha 764, 765
Everest Base Camp 898, 910, 911, 917
Everest, Mt 251, 814, **895–917**, 923, 990, 996
Eyul 641; see also Lhagyari

F

Fa Xian 49
Farhad-Beg-Yailaki 387
First Diffusion of Buddhism 386
First Karmapa 478
Five Discoverer Kings 686, 701
Five Patriarchs 34, 881
Foreign Exchange Certificates (FEC) 999
Four Friendly Brothers 58, 104
Four Royal Monasteries **168–70**, 596
Four Tsokpas 504
Friendship Highway (Tibet–Nepal) 270, 271, 272, 328, 458, 462, 594, 601, 607, 608, 610, 679, 702, 768, 769, 802, 803, 809, 812, **815–21**, 868, 880, 890, 895, 897, 898, 914, 923, 926, 945, **987–91**, 996

G

Gaba La 796
Gachung 673
Gadhe Zangpo 80
Gadong Monastery 200, 660, 672, 673, **674**
Gaktsa 483
Galingka 797
Galu 817

Gampopa 28, 34, 260, 352, 354, 197, 512, 635, 637, 641, 644, 678, 699, 700, 717
Ganden Chöding 854, 857
Ganden Chökorling Monastery 870, **872**
Ganden Chungkhor Monastery 564, 567
Ganden Lingkhor 143
Ganden Monastery 29, 30, 35, 43, 61, 71, **140–4**, 157, 171, 380, 416, 527, 546, 549, 569, 624, 627, 630, 638, 739, 880, 1000
Ganden Pelgyaling Monastery 932
Ganden Potrang (D) 98, 145, 146,
Ganden Rabden Monastery 214, 217, 226, 735, 739, 764
Gandenpa 29
Gandhara 52
Gandharan 428
Ganesh Himal, Mt [Nepal] 925, 929, 934, 937
Gang Langchen 802, 804, 806, 807, 809, 810, 811
Ganga Chu 614, 617, 618
Gangchen Monastery 989
Gangri Tökar, Mt 470, 488, 491, **492**
Gangtok [Sikkim] 788, 799
Ganze 44
Gar (Gargunsa) 952, 953
Gar, Lompo 392, 542
Garhwal [India] 443, 953, 955
Garmiton Yönten Yungdrung 644
Garphuk 637, 644
Gartok (Garyersa) 953
Gatshal Phuk 502, 505
Gauhati [India] 36, 694
Gawa, Mt 702
Gayadhara 848, 867
Gayadhara Lhakhang 867
Gazhi 328, 330, 331
Gedrub Je 416
Gedun Gyatso 338
Gedundrub 35, 511, 822, 824, 826, 829
Gegye Xian 948, 980, 982
Gelek Zibar Serdhung 109
Gelugpa 'Great Six' 43
Gelugpa **29**, 35, 412, 416, 450, 465
Genghis Khan 28, 52
Gephel Ri, Mt 156, 672, 674
Gephel Ritrö 156
Gephel Ütse 145, 156
Germany 36
Gerwu 805
Gerze 945, 948, 986
Gesar Lhakhang 178–9
Geshe 200

Geshe Jayul 552
Geshe Tsakpuwa 259
geshe 35
Gevo La 280
Ghari Ani Gompa 134
Gheden Yeshe Chengye 531
Gho Ngön 816
Gho Ngön Lhaklung 819
Giamda 571, 656, 711, 743
giant rhubarb (rheum nobile) 655,
    731, 732, 905
Giga La 715
Gilgit [Pakistan] 436, 950
Go La 233
Go Lotsawa Shonnu Pal 496
Gochak La 796
Godan 881
Godan Khan 28, 53, 462, 705
Godavari [India] 265
Godemchen 599
Gökar 293, 627
Gökar La 314, 380, 625, 627
Gokpo Ri 140
Golé 774
Golmud 557, 660, 673, 817, 945,
    987, 994, 996, 1000
Gomang Tratsang (D) 153, 168, 312
Gompa 197
Gompa Chang Monastery 862
Gompo Ne 713, 724, 727
Gönda Phuk Monastery 918, 920
Gongdeling 644
Gongga Bridge 746
Gongkar 470
Gongkar airport 480, 995
Gongkar Chöde 466, 470, 479, 493
Gongkar Chöde branch chapel 119
Gongkar Dzong 98, 478, 600
Gongkar Xian 481
Gongmo 761
Gongpo Rabsal 27, 50, 401, 485,
    497, 644
Gönjo 747
Gönpo Drashe Marpo 131
Gönpo Khang 104
Gönpo Ri, Mt 26, 364, 515, 519,
    533, 629
Göntang 516
Göntang Bumpa Chörten 525
Gonzo La 653
Göring La 668
Gorsum Chörten 246
Gossul Monastery 614, 621, 622
Gosung Nangma 697
Götsang 922

Götshangpa 279, 281, 284, 285, 288,
    290, 291, 347, 566, 692, 920,
    921, 922
Govinda 441
Gowa 66
Great Six 141
Guge 27, 28, 52, 53, 55, 378, 425,
    429, 430, 434, 435, 436, 437,
    441, 442, 943, 944, 946, 950,
    952, 972, 973
Guge art style 425, 440, 444
Guge school 55-6
Gukung 957, 960
Gulung 251
Gün 932
Günda Ri, Mt 934
Gungru Gungtsen 111
Gungsong Gungtsen 360
Gungthang 347, 429, 924, 929
Gungthang La 108, 929, 930
Gungyal Lodrö Rinchen 160
Gupta 47, 49, 51, 52, 62, 66, 77,
    111, 383, 387, 398
Gurkhas 179, 196, 930, 680
Gurla La 957
Gurla Mandhata Range 277, 293, 614,
    957
Guru Chuwang 681, 683, 685, 686,
    692, 696, 705
Guru Drubphuk 730
Guru Gem Monastery 965, 970
Guru Latso 808, 812
Guru Lhakhang 90, 606, 683, 692,
    702
Guru Namgye Dzong 218, 226, 232,
    234, 739
Guru Namgye Qu 209
Guru Nangse Silnyon 120
Guru Rinpoche 27, 33, 37, 45, 121,
    130, 165, 245, 272, 279, 282, 292,
    295-8, 303, 304, 310, 312, 317,
    320, 328, 332, 338, 339, 344, 354,
    380, 413, 478, 485, 508, 511, 513,
    522, 526, 530, 575, 578, 587, 592,
    598, 606, 608, 609, 618, 620, 630,
    631, 632, 637, 644, 647, 651, 672,
    674, 681, 683, 685, 691, 692, 694,
    695, 696, 698, 701, 706, 717, 730,
    743, 745, 754, 787, 794, 801, 807,
    809, 811, 819, 836, 848, 866, 867,
    869, 892, 893, 918, 925, 929, 930,
    934, 961, 962
Guru Tsengye 114
Gurubum Lhakang 73
Gushri and Desi Mural 70

Gushri Khan **30**, 33, 56, 61, 71, 142, 671, 829
Gyachen Chögyue 113
Gyal La 691, 713
Gyal Lhakhang 50, 201, 705
Gyal Metoktang 624, 633, 640
Gyala Pelri 712, 721, 726, 727, 730, 731, 735, 742
Gyalam 545, 553, 557, 561, **570–86**, 648, 656, 710
Gyalchen Zhi Lhakhang 70
Gyaling Gatsal Phuk Monastery 505
Gyaling Tsokpa Monastery 470, 495, 502, 503, **504**
Gyalmashing Valley 140, 545, 546, 549, 630
Gyalmo Mizen 691
Gyalmo Tsün 311
Gyalpo Chok 99
Gyalpo Kongkar Monastery 545, 546, **548**
Gyalrab Salwai Melong 125
Gyaltsab Je 141, 157, 642, 646
Gyaltsab Rinpoche 646, 677
Gyalzang Tombs 371, 372, 510
Gyama 131
Gyama Trikhang 546, 548, 549
Gyama Valley 315, 380, 511, 514
Gyamo Dumburi Monastery 549
Gyamo Trikhang Monastery 548
Gyang 54, 447, 465
Gyang Bumoche Chörten 451, 453, 454, 455, 463, 4,64, **465,** 867
Gyang Yönpolung 867
Gyangdrak Monastery (Ks) 279, 280, **293**, 620
Gyangkar Nangpa 803
Gyangong 50, 400, 401
Gyangro 412
Gyangtö 742
Gyantse 56, 328, 330, 336, 337, 349, 390, **412–24**, 439, 443, 455, 541, 611, 797, 832, 834, 836, 840, 845, 994, 988, 987, 1003
Gyantse Castle (Fort) 55, 417–8, 423, 450, 536
Gyantse *gönkhang* art style 424
Gyantse Kumbum 54, 55, 56, 57, 410, 412, 416, 421, 436, 444, **447–50**, 451, 452, 453, 454, 455, 463, 464
Gyantse main art style 424, 448, 450
Gyantse princes 413
Gyantse school **55**, 455, 465
Gyantse transitional art style 424
Gyanyima Dzong 968

Gyargom Tsultrim Senge 492
Gyarong 765
Gyasa Drubphuk 127
Gyasa Gönchu Potrang (P) 132, 133
Gyatsa Gye 529, 530
Gyatsa Qu 352, 353, 640
Gyatsa Xian 225, 480, 520, 641, 740
Gyatso La 989
Gyatso Qu 879
Gyeling Tsokpa 521
Gyelri Gön 753
Gyeri 742
Gyürme Monastery 197
Gyürme Tratsang 171
Gyurtö 339
Gyürtö Tratsang 116

H

Hamdong Khangtsen (S) 162
Hatha Yoga 34
Hebu Valley 315, 316, 631
Hedin, Sven 614, 855
Heinrich Harrer 103, 925
Hemis [India] 619, 962
Hengduan Mountains 748
Hepo Ri 295, 298, 624, **629**, 631
Hepo Ri Lhakhang 630
Heruka Sangye Gyaltsen 72
Hlako Kangri, Mt 803, 814
Hong Kong 994
Hor 43, 356
Hor Qu 617
Hoshang 300
Huntington 446

I

India 26, 27, 31, 32, 36, 40, 47, 49, 51, 53, 56, 66, 68, 79, 121, 166, 180, 271, 386, 392, 393, 425, 429, 436, 885, 943, 944, 959
Indus 42, 274, 284, 289, 430, 943, 948, 983, 985, 986
Islam 50, 51, 201
Iwang (*see* Yemar)

J

Jachor La 990
Jador 658, 665, 667
Jadur Monastery 937
Jago Phungro Ri .755, 962
Jaiyul Monastery 934
Jakhyung La 925, 929, 930

Jakhyung Monastery 747, **761**
Jamgang 268
Jamgang La 265, 268, 270
Jamgön Kongtrul Rinpoche 677
Jamkhang 106
Jamkhang Chenmo (Tlp) 822
Jampa Chezhi Lhakhang 84
Jampa Gönpo Lhakhang 83
Jampa Gyaphip 94
Jampa Ri 672, 678
Jampa Sangba 790
Jampa Truze Lhakhang 79
Jampaling 54, 367, 447, 454, 463,
    464, **465**, 481, 501, 502
Jampaling Chörten 38
Jampaling Nunnery 411
Jampalinga 480
Jamtrin Monastery 45, 925, **935**, 936
Jamyang Chöje (D) 145, 155
Jamyang Zhepa 145
Jang 412, 544, 561
Jang Chöling 475, 674
Jang Gyi Dhoke 102
Jang Rigsum Lhakhang (RG) 128
Jang Tana 745
Jang Tsangpa Lungnön 44, 45
Jang Tsha Lhe Bön 359
Jangchen Ritrö 834
Jangchen Tharlam 102
Jangchub Gyaltsen 29, 98, 320, 413,
    518
Jangchub O 929
Jangchub Tarling Nunnery 911
Jangra 328, 661
Jangsang Lhamo 612
Jangse Kunga Sangpo 312
Jangter 497, 599
Jangto 475
Jangyung La 815, 818, 877
Janzik Lhakhang 84
Jasa Lhakhang 485
Jasa Ri Tombs 372
Je 575, 805
Je Rinpoche Lhakhang 77
Je Sherab Senge 171, 826
Jeba 651, 652, 654
Jebum Gang 200
Jeh La 851
Jekung La 983, 986
Jelep La 788, 799
Jetung Chusang, Mt 612
Jibugo La 879
Jigme Lingpa 33, 305, 528, 532, 634
Jikyop Bridge 909, 910
Jincheng 47, 82, 85, 116, 358, 383,

386, 388, 629
Jing 485
Jinka 317, **327–37**, 988
jinlab 42
Jinlung Valley 812
jinpa 41
Jisnugupta 63
Jokhang 26, 27, 31, 37, 40, 42, 43, 47,
    51, 60, 61, **62–96**, 116, 121, 179,
    295, 342, 355, 393, 533, 534, 541,
    746, 936
        (Outer) 68–74
        (1st Floor/Ground Floor) 75–85
        (2nd Floor) 85–91
        (3rd Floor) 92–4
        (Roof) 94–6
Jokhang dorings 195
Jomo Chu 668, 815, 818, 870
Jomo Nakgyal, Mt 864
Jomo Sisi, Mt 193
Jonang Kumbum 55, 83, 447, 451,
    453, 454, 455, **463**, 768, 771
    847, 864
Jonang-Kagyu 463
Jonangpa 83, 551, 864
Jooker La 140, 315, 316
Jowo Gyaphip 94
Jowo Lhakhang (Jok) 62, 82
Jowo Lhakhang (K) 381
Jowo Mikyo Dorje 63
Jowo Rinpoche 82
Jowo Sakyamuni 37, 63, 304
Jowo Utra 70
Jungden Monastery 467
Jyekundo 582

K

K2, Mt 951
Kachu 385
Kachu Lhakhang 27, 47, 49, 50, 85,
    119, 121, 358, **378–89**, 393, 470,
    510, 511, 540
Kadam 34
Kadampa art style 57
Kadang 214
Kaga 451, 462, 945, 947
Kagyü 34
Kagyüpa 415, 700
Kailash, Mt 38, 40, 46, 208, 248,
    273–94, 386, 429, 461, 462, 531,
    545, 587, 613, 681, 751, 755, 807,
    943, 944, 945, 946, 949, 950, 952,
    957, 959, 961, 962, 983, 984, 990,
    1004
Kakaga Ri, Mt 939

Kala   328, 337
Kala Tso   793, 799
Kalamba La   658, 668, 815, 818, 851, 869, 877
Kalimpong   799, 806
Kalung Dzong   460
Kama Valley   810
Kamba La (Tsari)   217
Kamba La (Yamdrok)   587, 607, 988
Kambulung Monastery   845
Kampa Dzong   336, 337, 796, 815, 831, 836, 838
Kampa La   315, 514, 550, 706
Kampa Qu (Mende)   806, 809
Kampa Xian   328, 793, 802, 803, 806, 809, 840
Kanchenjunga, Mt [Sikkim]   794
Kandro Thang Tso   233
Kang Pema, Mt   223, 230, 237
Kang Tise Range   459, 615, 952, 957, 968, 970, 983
Kangchen La   249, 263
Kangchung La   263
Kangjam Chu   284
Kangjam Glacier   285
Kangmar   609, 791
Kangpam   799
Kangri Karpo   717
Kangri Tsosum   273
Kangshung Face (Everest)   802, 804, 810, **895**
Kangso Khang   91
Kangwa   661
Kangxi   30, 100, 107, 113, 178, 195
Kangyur   33, 163
Kapilavastu   82
Kar Nga Dong   201
Karakhoto   51, 52, 399
Karakoram Highway [Pakistan/China]   997
Karchen   320
Karchu *khorchen*   693–6
Karchu La   691
Karchu Monastery (Lhodrak Karchu)   45, 681, 690, 691, 692, **693**, 799, 800, 801
Karchu Tadhong Karmo   692
Kardo   194
Kardong   970
Karé Monastery   899
Karkyü La   234
Karma Changri, Mt   904
Karma Chu Valley   895, 896, 905, 906, 908
Karma Gardri art style   75

Karma La   728
Karma Lhadeng   678
Karma Lingpa   45
Karma Pakshi   677, 678
Karmalasila   300
Karmapa   52, 291, 678
Karmapa Dusum Khyenpa   490
Karmapa Rangjung Dorje   592
Karmashar   200
Karmashar Oracle   206
Karmo Gong La   689
Karmo Sigyal   753, 757
Karnali River [Nepal]   274
Karo La   587, 594, 611, 613, 988
Karpo Chu Valley   **217**
Karro Pumri Range   263
Karshung Phuk   122
Karu   60, 375
Karu Lhakhang   526
Kashag   100
Kashgar   944, 946, 949, 950, **952**, 997
Kashmir [India]   28, 47, 49, 50, 52, 53, 56, 112, 201, 378, 392, 425, 429, 436, 441, 443, 944, 953, 980
Kashmiri art   49, **52–3**, 49, 56, 430, 437, 438, 441
Kashmiri paintings   426, 436
Kashmiri art style   50, 54, 56, 429, 430–2, 436, 439, 440, 442, 445
Kathang Denga   46
Kathmandu Valley [Nepal]   48, 400, 405, 407
Kathmandu [Nepal]   196, 935, 621, 944, 991, 994, 995, 996
Katsal Monastery   28, 43, 540, 545, **550**
Kawa Karpo   755
Kawa Paltsek Chörten   629
Kazhima Lhakhang   320
Kedrub Je   141, 157, 529, 624, 822
Kelsang Dekyil Potrang (NL)   191–2
Kelsang Potrang (NL)   183–5
Keru (*see* Karchu)
Kesang Lhakhang (Tlp)   822, **826**
Keser La   336
Keutsang   164
Khachar Monastery   425
Khache Lingka   201
Khache Panchen Sakyasri   329, 495
Khalip   230
Khalung Phuk   826
Kham   27, 386, 572, 653, 765
Kham Taktsang   513
Khamsum Sangkhang Ling   309
Khanak   820
Khandro Jewa Bum Drubphuk   697

Khandro Kiri Yongdzong 345
Khandro Latso 808
Khandro Nyingtrik 633
Khandro Sanglam (Ks) 285
Khangphu Monastery 794
Khangphu Valley 794, 796
Khar Semo 742, 752, 758
Khardrak, Mt 92
Kharna 763, 764, 766, 797, 816
Kharta 221, 242, 802, 804, 810, 880,
    895, 897, 898, 899, 901, 903,
    906, 909, 912
Kharta Chu Valley 895, 896, 904,
    910, 912
Kharta Glacier 895
khata 41
Khembalung [Nepal] 39
Khentse Chemo 466, 478
Khetsun Zhönnu Drub 590
Khongcha Tombs 365, 495
Khor 329
Khotan 27, 47, 48, 49, 301, 386,
    392, 535
Khothing 44, 682, 686, 692
Khulung 766
Khulung Yönten Gyatso 766
Khunjerab Pass [Pakistan/China] 946
Khuwön 549
Khyamra Chenmo 62, 71
Khyamra Gochor 68
Khyangphu 793
Khyenrab Norbu 127, 204
Khyense Chenmo 463
Khyense school 463
Khyirepa 962
Khyung Dzong 768, 784
Khyung Gong Phuk 256, 257
Khyunglung 429, 943, 964, 971
Khyungpa Gön 798
Khyungpo 742
Khyungpo Naljor 870, 872
Khyungpo Neljorpa 496
Khyungpo Tengcheng 504, 557, 570,
    578, 582, 584
Khyungtrul Jigme Namkha Dorje 972
Kiang La 669
King Gesar 178, 287, 292, 413, 575,
    628, 647, 652
King of Tsang 145
Kingdon Ward, Frank 713, 716, 724,
    731
Kinthup Falls 713, 724
Kiri Yongdzong 545
Kiutsang 193
Kizil oasis 463

Ko 656
Kodari 996
Koko Nor 27, 657
Kon Chögyal Pho 28, 33, 867, 880,
    883, 888, 894
Kond Potrang, Mt
Kondü Dosem Potrang 713, 718
Kong La 663, 664, 665
Kongchok Gyalpo 699, 893
Kongmo 737, 742
Kongpo 575, 647, 653, 717, 718, 729,
    738, 741, 743, 749, 765
Kongpo Aki Gyalpo 715
Kongpo Bönri 746, 749
Kongpo Giamda 571, 648, 655, 708,
    711
Kongpo Kings 653
Kongpo La 217, 222, 226, 234, 239
Kongpo Menri 751
Kongpo Nga La 226, 739
Kongtsa 923
Kongtsen Lhamo 752, 759
Korja Monastery 936, 957, 959
Korleb 794
Koro Chu 758
Kosi Hot Springs 809
Kotsi 831, 840
Ksemendra 74
Ku Nga Gönkhang 91
Ku Valley 831
Kublai Khan 28, 53, 197, 400, 406,
    678, 881, 886
Kuchok Ripa Drukse 741, 752, 754,
    757, 759
Kudhung Lhakhang (Tlp) 825
Kula Cham, Mt 702
Kula Demo 761
Kula Kangri, Mt 607, 682, 700, 701,
    702, 706
Kuma 337
Kumbum late art style 449
Kumbum Monastery 157, 822
Kumbum narrative style 448
Kumbum variation 449
Kunde Ling 169, 597
Kunga Döndrub 402, 408, 411
Kunga Döndrup 116
Kunga Gyaltsan 881
Kunga Namgyal 480
Kunga Ngonshe 513
Kunga Nyingpo 880, 883, 888, 893
Kunga Phagpa 414, 417
Kunga Rinchen 883
Kunga Zangpo 774, 884
Kunlun Range 980

Kunrik Lhakhang 73
Kunzang Jedro Khang 112
Kunzang Thuka 752
Kur La 324
Kure La 459
Kushak 742
Kushan 49, 91, 111
Kushuk Demdrug 752, 759
Kusinagara [India] 36, 129, 130, 523
kuten 37
Kuti La 791
Kuyi Gyalpo Monbuputra 200
Kyangbu Monastery 390, 392
Kyangpa Monastery 934
Kyapa Lagring 742, 751, 753
Kyaring La 794
Kyaring Tso 848, 849, 851, 869
Kyatsal Monastery 845
Kyekye 212
Kyenri murals 479
Kyenri art style 466
Kyerong Ngawang Trakpa 519
Kyetrak 251
Kyi Chu (Lhasa River) 84, 97, 99, 165, 193, 487–94, 555–69, 683, 705
Kyichu Lhakhang Monastery 43, 705
Kyigo 791
Kyilé 893
Kyilkhor 231, 232
Kyilkhor Thil 75
Kyilkhor Trangdruk 332
Kyimdong 373
Kyimdong Dzong 210, 235, 239, 736, 738
Kyimdong Qu 209, 373
Kyimphu 219
Kyiphuk Ritro 463
Kyipo Shing Tshal Chen 500
Kyirong 37, 45, 256, 265, 787, 921 924–42, 990
Kyirong (Phagpa) Monastery 936, 937
Kyirong Qu 935
Kyiru Lhakhang 503
Kyishong 814
Kyisum Labrang 783, 784
Kyogo La 831, 838
Kyormolung Monastery 660, 671, 673, 674, 987

L

La Phuk Monastery 928
La Tsho Ogma 257
Labrang Gyaltsen Thönpo (Tlp) 824

Labrang Monastery 145, 157, 822
Labrangteng 68
Labu Valley 668
Lachato 622
Lachen La 656
Ladakh Range 459
Ladakh [India] 28, 52, 201, 425, 429, 430, 437, 950, 952, 953, 957
Lagpa La 990
lagpön 43
Lagulung La 838
Laiya La 251
Lajang Khan 145
Lake Atsa 557, 574, 656
Lake Bokun 717
Lake Dangchung 783, 785
Lake Dangra 741, 767, 781, **783**, 848, 851, 862, 869
Lake Draksum 557, 575, **647–56**
Lake Drigu 603, **683**
Lake Kurkyal Chungo 619
Lake Manasarovar 273, 277, 284, 292, 293, 587, 481, 526, 589, 600, 601, 602, 607, **614–22**, 640, 687, 701, 702, 706, 815, 943, 966
Lake Namtso 561, 587, **657–70**, 701, 815, 816, 818, 869, 879
Lake Ngamring 773, 774, 947
Lake Ngangtse 848, 849, 851, 855, 860, 862, 869
Lake Pelku 925, **928**, 930, 932, 940, 946, 990
Lake Pemaling 613, 681, 682, 697, **701**, 706
Lake Phurma 587, 606, **609**, 683, 706, 788, 791
Lake Raksas Tal 277, 293, 614, **622**, 957, 966
Lake Siling 945
Lake Sipe Gyalmo 756
Lake Tsogar 230, **235**
Lake Tsomo Tretung 804, 809
Lake Wothang 63, 75, 84
Lake Yamdrok 471, 479, 481, 482, 494, 526, **587–94**, 600, 601, 602, 606, 607, 640, 687, 701, 702, 706, 815, 841, 846, 987, 988, 996
Lake Zhari Namtso 948
lakhug 37
Lakpa La 895, 897, 911, 912
Lalaga Glacier 939
Lalung La 926, 940, 991, 996
Lama Dewachen 530
Lama Govinda 430, 953, 975

Lama La   336
Lama Ralo Phuk   920, 991
Lama Shang   165, 197, 490, 511, 512
Lama Ugyen Gyatso   327
Lamar La   899, 915
Lamdre   33, 834, 867, 892
Lamna La   914, 916
Lamo Monastery   28, 497, 546, **548**
Lamo Lhatse La   986
Lamo Valley   140
Lamrim Chenmo   **35**
Lamrin Lhakhang   113
landscape tradition   57
Lang La   238
Langak Tso   614, 622
Langdarma   27, 60, 70, 323, 340, 359,
       386, 390, 399, 413, 430, 485,
       533, 569, 652, 704, 892
Langkhor   492
Langkor Dzong   225, 641
Langkor Monastery   249, 271, 393,
       636, 918, **920**, 921, 990, 991
Langma La   896, 904
Langong   239
Langphu La   805
Langpöna   618, 619
Langri Songtsen   360
Langri Tangpa Dorje Senge   568
Langtang Himal, Mt [Nepal]   925,
       929, 937
Langtang Monastery   28, 34, 193, 546,
       564, 566, **568**, 672, 673, 674
Langu La   337
Langu Tso   337
Lanji La   562
Lanzhou   28, 946
Lapchi   37, 39, 42, 46, 208, **248–72**,
       531, 545, 681, 755, 793, 801,
       807, 921, 924, 934, 990, 991
Lapchi Kang Chu   264
Lapchi Kang Range   46, 249, 268
Lapso Dzong   641
Lapu   739
Larchen La   661
lari   37
Larok La   855
lashing   37
Latö   55
Latö art style   **455**
Latö school   **54**, 450, 451, 464, 465
latso   37
Lawapa
Lawongtse   863
Layak Guru Lhakhang   705
layü   37

Le La   511, 514, 710
Lekpe Sherab   79
Lelung Monastery   773, **774**
Len   649, 653
Lende Khola   925, 935, 936, 938
Lenjo   774
Lha Chu Valley   277, 280
Lha Totori   360, 539
Lhabab Ri   37, 516, 524
Lhabum Lubum (P)   96
Lhabzang Khan   30
Lhachag Shokhang (P)   96
Lhachu   672, 673
Lhadro Namgyal Khangzang   697
Lhagyari   225, 470, 573, 641
Lhajang Khan   114
Lhakhang   681, 685, 686, 691, 692, 696
Lhakhang Chenmo (Sakya)   880, **884**
Lhakhang Karpo (Ts)   425, 430, 432,
       434, **437–41**
Lhakhang Marpo (Ts)   425, 430, 432,
       434, 437, 438, 440, **441–3**, 444
Lhako Kangri Range   893
Lhalung   513, 607, 609, 613, 681, 682,
       701, 702, 704
Lhalung Paldhor   70, 130, 338, 340,
       343, 569, 701, 704
Lham Chukir Valley   290
Lhamo Kharchen   682, 692, 693
Lhamo Latso (Oracle Lake)   37, 42,
       352, 548, 587, **623–41**, 642, 644,
       710, 735, 740, 757
Lhamo Nying, Mt   639
Lhamo Yangchen   615
Lharchen La   663, 665
Lhari Gyangt, Mt   749, 760
Lhari Gyantö   757
Lhari Nyiphuk   798
Lharigo   557, 570, 574, 656
Lharing Longchen Drak   491
Lharje Chojang
Lharje Gewabum   84
Lharu Mengye Monastery   521, **529**
Lhasa   30, 42, 56, **60–139**, 165, 168,
       349, 375, 379, 412, 415, 429,
       430, 437, 494, 516, 577, 561,
       596, 611, 630, 631, 708, 733,
       738, 743, 944, 945, 952, 987,
       994–1003, 1005
Lhasa Khardrak   386
Lhasar La   672, 678, 815, 817
Lhatag   683
Lhatak Monastery   705
Lhatotori   26
Lhatse   450, 451, 455, 456, 458, 462,

768, 769, 802, 814, 847, **868**, 890, 891, 944, 945, 947, 987, 990
Lhatse Chöde 769, 848, **866**
Lhatse Dzong 43, 848
Lhatse Monastery 580, 849
Lhatse Nyipa, Mt 580
Lhatsün Labrang 133
Lho Rigsum Lhakhang (RG) 128
Lhodrak 46, 210, 245, 526, 587, 597, 607, 610, 613, 653, **681–706**, 924, 988
Lhodrak Karchu 45, 522
Lhodrak Lungpa 704
Lhodrak Nub Chu 692, 696
Lhodrak Shar Chu 685, 692, 696
Lhodrak Xian 607, 608, 609, 686, 687, 692, 698, 702, 705, 706
Lhogo Melongchen 84
Lhorong 557, 570
Lhorong Chu 672, 679
Lhorong Xian 582
Lhoter 497, 599
Lhotse, Mt 896, 905
Lhündrub Dzong 194, 567
Lhündrub Lhakhang 588
Lhündrub Xian 545, **561**, 660
Lhündrubling 904, 912
Lhuntse 214, 247
Lhuntse Dzong 231
Lhuntse Xian 209, 215, 240, 243, 685, 718
Li Gotama 430, 438
Licchavi 48, 78
Lilung 218, 738
Limur Gyalpo 784
Ling Gesar 664
Ling Rinpoche 552
Linga Monastery 856
Lingdrub La 793
Lingkar Dzong 816, 819
Lingkhor 43
Lingma 797
Lingrepa 599, 612
Lingrepa Pema Dorje 635
Lingshi 305
Lingshi Lhakhangs 299
Lingtö Dhokpa 490
Lingtren Lhakhangs 299
Lingtrens 307
Lingtsang Labrang 202
Linka Monastery 769, 773, **775**
Lipu Lekh La 957, 959
Lishan Tombs 363, 365, 367, 372, **373–4**, 738
Little Potala 531

Lo-ngam 760
Lochen La 575
Lodro Pelsang 527
Lokmo 655
Longchen Rabjampa 303, 508
Longchenpa 33, 305, 488, 490, 492, 501, 552, 632, 634, 685, 686
Longdhöl Lama 476
Longdhöl Monastery 348, 547, 705
Longdo 706
Longjiu Geothermal Plant 950
Longmen 125, 126
Longpu La 809
Lonjok 592
Lopa 718, 735, 737, 762
Lord Cawdor 713, 716, 724
Lorepa 693
Loro Chu 209
Loro Dol 253
Lorong 580
Loseling Tratsang (D) 152
Lotang Lhakhang (Ts) 432, **446**
Löton Dorje Wangchuk 50, 401
Lotsawa Shonnu Pal 504
Loyul 637
Luding 737
Lugong Sanggo 70
Lukhang 75, 175–7
Luma Dzog Dzog 254
Lumbini [Nepal] 36
Lume 50, 340, 343, 386, 390, 394, 485, 496, 548, 551
Lumé Tsultrim 27
Lunang 733, 757
Lung 222, 352, 353, 642
Lung Ganden 773
Lung La 637, 638, 644, 710
Lungden Phuk 267
Lungdep Valley 985
Lungdo 737
Lungma La 737
Lungsang La 475, 674
Lungshö 545, 522, 560
Lungtang Kung 791
Lusha 713, 741, 753, 761, 762
Lusha Gyala
Luyi Gyalpo 175
Lwang
Lyungdrung Gönsar 797

M

Ma Rinchen Chok 633, 892
MacDonald, David 797
Machik 921
Machik Labdrönma 271, 492, 521, 636

Madra La 644, 710
Madra Latso 642, 644, 710
Magadha [India] 47, 51
Magön La 642, 644, 710
Magsorma 94, 639
Maha Ketongwa 349
Mahabodhi 297
Mahakarma 930
mahamudra 34
Mahayana **32**
Mahayoga 114
Maitripa 720, 921
Majiang 815, 818
Makalu, Mt 896, 904, 905, 906, 909, 911
Makandro 727
Manasarovar (*see* Lake Manasarovar)
Manda 607, 609, 610
Manda La 609, 692, 698
Manda Qu 702, 705
Mandala Lhakhang (Ts) 433, 437, **445**
Mandarawa 328, 333, 962
Mandi 955
Mang La 922
Mangkar Valley 814, 890, **892**
Mangnang Monastery 52, 964, **978**
Mangra 545, 552
Mangra Chu 560
Mangra Valley 545, 551
Mangshung (Kongpo) La 747
Mangshung La 798, 710
Mangsong Mangtsen 356, 357
Mangyul 924, 929
Mangyul Jamtrin 44, 45, 935
mantras **40**
Mao Tsetung 30
Mapham Tso (*see* Lake Manasarovar)
Mar Sakyamuni 27
Marchar Tso 862
marme 41
Marpa **28**, 34, 481, 681, 698, 699, **700**
Marpo Ri, Mt 48, 98, 99, 179, 742
Martön Chökyi Jungne 341
Masa Gongi Lhakhang 386
Maurya 49
Mawochok Monastery 681, **685**
Mazar 951
Mazar Tag 540
McMahon Line 235, 717
Me La 243, 246, 608, 609
Medro Gongkar 171, 380, 545, 546, 550, 560, 571, 624, 643, 708, 709, 743
Medro Gongkar Valley 511
Meiji Shan 126

Melong Dorje 325, 696
Melung Tse 251
Memo Nani 614
Mende 831, 840
Mendong 609, 687
Mendrub Kongsar 529
Mendrub Kongsar Chörtens 530
Menla Desheg Gye Lhakhang (Jok) 78
Menlung Tse, Mt 257, 261
Menlung Valley 249, **257, 687**
Menpa Qu 346, 553
Menpa Tratsang 138
Menpu Qu 990
Menri Monastery 741, 749, 753, 760, 763, 764, **765**, 785, 816, 820, 937
Mensang La 687
Mensi 952, 955, 957, 961, 970
Mentsi Khang 203
Meru Nyingba 60, 68, 73, **119–20**, 169, 509
Meru Sarpa Tratsang 120, **173**
Meru, Mt 42
Meshul 690, 691
Metok 653, 713
Metok Xian 713, 716, **717**, 720
Michungri 193
Migyitun 227, 231, 235, 237
Migyur Paldrön 499
Mijik Tri 752, 760
Mikyö Dorje 677
Mila Drubphuk (Ks) 290
Mila Tse 347, 525, 539
Mila Tse Tower 525
Milarepa 28, 34, 37, 248, 259, 262, 270, 273, 280, 282, 283, 286, 289, 291, 338, 481, 511, 513, 555, 612, 617, 641, 644, 671, 679, 681, 682, 698, 699, **700**, 893, 921, 924, 932, 937, 962
Miling 748
Miling Xian 716, 721, 735, 737
Mindroling Monastery 33, 470, 478, 484, 495, **496–500**, 501, 503, 504, 599, 628, 688, 819
Ming Dynasty 29, 55, 43, 414, 415, 424, 450, 455, 882
Minling Terchen 33, 497, 511, 522, 671, 678
Minyag 27, 43
Minyag Gomring 553
Mipa 233
Mitrukpa 66
Miwang Polha 77
Miyul Kyithing 742, 760

Mo La   217, 242
Moga Lengye Valley   247
Momo Dzong   771
Mön Bumthang   44
Mön La   456, 459, 923
Mong La   879
Mongols   26, 29, 30, 33, 34, 35, 45,
      53, 61, 195, 402
Mongza Tricham   60, 111, 338
Monka Senge Dzong [Bhutan]   45, 46,
      522, 690
Monka Sridzong   45
Monkey Cave   516, 520
Monla Karchung La   706
Monlam   61, 70
Mönlam Dorje   80
Mönlam Draktsa   785
Mönlam Festival   70, 98
Mönlam Tenpa   784
Mönpas   718
Mor   599
Moragyel   50
Moslem (see Islam)
mosques   201
Mu Chu Valley   768, 772, 856, 869
Mu Gön Kar   696
Mughal   49
Muk   805
Muktinath [Nepal]   724
Mune Tsenpo   357
Münto Mangbo La   972
Mura, Mt   356, 358
Muran Jampa Thukje Pal   679
Murchen Kunchog   755
Muri   750
Muri Mukpo   757, 759
Mustang [Nepal]   930, 965, 975
Mutik Tsenpo   360
Myarma Monastery   425

N

Nab   690
Nabru La   328, 330, 331, 336
Nagchu   574, 584, 660, 710, 816, 945,
      994, 997
Nagchu Xian   667, 673, 852
Nagchuka   550
Nagoling   923
Nagpo Chenpo   52
Nagya, Mt   771
Naisum Chuja   668
Nakartse   587, 588, 589, 590, 594,
      602, 607, 608, 609, 611, 688,
      698, 702, 706, 988

Nako   669
Nakpo Dzumme   685
Naktsang   767
Nalanda Monastery [India]   28, 51, 193,
      297, 481, 495, 546, 564, 566,
      567, 568, 673
Nam La   716, 717, 720
Nam Valley   470, 475, 672, 987
Nambu   654
Nambu La   654
Namche Barwa, Mt   274, 615, 707,
      712–28, 730, 735, 742, 747, 748,
      761
Namche Bazaar   253
Namdröl Yangtse   528, 683
Namgyal Gön   575
Namgyal Tratsang   98, 102, 115, 146,
      503, 551
Namkading   470, 478
Namkha Lodhen   783
Namkha Pelzangpo   141
Namkhai Nyingpo   341, 485, 682, 694,
      695, 696, 807, 819, 868
Namla Karpo, Mt   648, 651, 652, 654,
      732
Namling   870, 872
Namling Xian   821
Namo Zampa   521
Nampa La   478, 675
Namrab   470
Namrab Valley   478, 480
Namri Lotsan   749
Namri Songtsen   26
Namring Drubphuk   485
Namse   655
Namse Monastery   711
Namseling   483
Namther Gosum Lhakhang   71
Namtso (see Lake Namtso)
Namtso Qu   658, 661, 663, 667
Nanam Dorje Wangchuk   50
Nang Xian   209, 222, 225, 226, 227,
      240, 353, 354, 373, 736, 739
Nang Xian Tombs (see Lishan Tombs)
Nangchen   745
Nangkhor (Jok)   43, 72, 116
Nangkhor paintings   74
Nangpa La   251, 253
Nangtön Dawa Gyaltsen   763
Nangtseshag Prison   119, 203
Narendradeva   63
Naro Bönchung   274, 286, 289, 291,
      617, 755
Naropa   28, 34, 474, 699, 700, 872,
      920

Narthang Monastery 54, 204, 400, 453, 455, 831, **834**, 989
Narthang Sangye Gompa 834
Narthangpa 831
Nasen Bumpa 194
Nathu La 799
Natra 242
Natshok Rangdrol 509
Nawokyok 688
Nayu Valley 737
Nebrang 786
Nechu Lhakhang 73, 96
Nechung Monastery 120, 145, **165–7**, 200, 308
Nechung Oracle 493
Nedong 367, 635
Nedong Xian 363, **521**
Nego Che Cave 599
nekhor **40**
Nelung La 791
Nenang Monastery 671, **675**, 817
Nenying Monastery 390, 450, 455, **790**, 802, 803, 805, 826
Nepal 26, 47, **48**, 49, 53, 54, 56, 62, 63, 66, 121, 126, 249, 253, 258, 267, 271, 378, 389, 412, 418, 436, 438, 451, 455, 458, 465, 617, 787, 802, 805, 810, 812, 836, 926, 935, 936, 938, 943, 965, 959, 944, 994, 995
Nepalese paintings 444
Nepalese art style 436, 463
Nepu Chölung 599
Nerang Monastery 462, 922
Nering Senge Dzong 45
Nesar Qu 991
Netang 564
Neten Lhakang 549
Neten Lhakhang 28, **126**, 497
Neten Rongyelwa 141
Nethang Drölma Lhakhang 28, 51, 349, 470, **472–5**, 485, 698, 705, 987
Netsab Nga 755
Neudzong Palace 489
Neuzurpa 549, 568
Newari 26, 53, 54, 62, 63, 78, 88, 389, 404–7, 411, 417, 450, 452, 454
Newari art style 48, 423
Newari-style murals 400, 436
Newari-style paintings 417
Nezhi 686, 688
Nezhi Zhiitrö Monastery 688
Nezur 194

Nezurpa 194
Nga La 609, 610
Ngachen 794
Ngachö Tratsang 518
Ngachung 794
Ngadrak Monastery 319, 320
Ngagkhang 203
Ngagpa Tratsang (D) **152**
Ngagpa Tratsang (S) **159**
Ngagrim Chenmo 35
ngakpa 33
Ngam Chö Khang 141
Ngamring Monastery 458, 460, 462, 773, 947
Ngamring Xian 451
Nganga Channel 966
Ngangtse Tso (see Lake Ngangtse)
Ngangtsul Jangchub 522
Ngar Phuk 325
Ngari Drubthob Chenpo 136
Ngari Tratsang 380, 510, 634, 635, 636
Ngaripa Tsondru Nyingpo 79
Ngödru 582
Ngok Chöku Dorje 697
Ngok Jangchub Jungne 343
Ngok Legpai Sherab 303, 385, 490
Ngok Loden Sherab 476
Ngokton Chokyi Dorje 481
Ngor 34
Ngor Monastery 400, 774, 815, 831, 832, **834**, 959
Ngorchen Kunga Zangpo 834
Ngorpa 834
Ngunchu Chödzong Monastery 855
Ninchung La 968
Nine Ways of Bön 751
Ninga Dzong 626
Ningchi 60, 375, 520, 571, 643, 648, 708, 711, 741, 742, 745, 753, **758**, 1000
Ningchi Road 707, 733
Ninggong 316, 627, 631
Nojin Kangtsang 611
Nojin Kangtsang, Mt 608, 613
Nojin Khang 75
Nomun Qan Qutuqtu 169
Non 60
Norbu Chungtse 989
Norbu Khungshak 74
Norbu La 345
Norbu Lingka **180–92**, 698
Nub Cholung 764

Nub Gong (Nub Ghang) La   570,
    572, 574
Nub Gyi Dhoke   102
Nub Nyima Nyingpo
Nub Rigsum Lhakhang (RG)   128
Nubmang   797
Nyadong La   611, 613, 842, 846, 988
Nyaga (Nyung) Chu   737
Nyaknyön Sewa Rinchen   72
Nyakwön Sonam Zangpo   483
Nyalam   249, 926, 940, 946, 990, 991,
    1003, 1004
Nyalam Valley   270, 271, 787, 924, 940
Nyalme Geridrak   685
Nyame Shenrab Gyaltsen   765, 766
Nyamjang Chu Valley   210, 242
Nyan   60
Nyang clan   60
Nyang   653
Nyang Chu   349, 355, 653, 746, 747,
    791
Nyang Tingedzin   45, 121
Nyang Tingzin Zangpö   632
Nyango   379
Nyango Druka Chaksam   379
Nyango ferry   379
Nyangpa Tenzin Zangpo   127
Nyangpo   749
Nyangral Nyima Wösel   46
Nyangtö   413
Nyangtö Kyi Phuk   349–51
Nyapso La   594, 988
Nyatri Tsenpo   26, 516, 524, 539,
    742, 750, 757, 760
Nye   226
Nye Chu   209, 217, 240, 640
Nye La   802, 804, 810
Nyemo   450, 611, 613, 842
Nyemo Valley   672
Nyemo Xian   815, 818, 820
Nyen Gomphuk   569
Nyenchen   557
Nyenchen Tanglha Range   557, 560,
    570, 574, 627, 637, 658, 663,
    667, 670, 767, 847, 848, 851,
    855, 858, 869, 945
Nyenkar   60
nyensong   41
Nyergawo   66
Nyeru   609, 793
Nyewo Valley   575
Nyima La   707, 716, 720, 721,
    729–34, 737
Nyima Wösel   45, 681, 685, 686
Nyingdho Monastery   370, 502, 504

Nyingma   33
Nyingsaka   639
Nyingtö Yönton Gönpo   136
Nyiseb Gön   582
Nyitri Thö   752
Nyiwö Nub Sonam Lekhyil   104
Nyiwö Shar Gadhen Nangsel   104
Nyiwö Sonam Lekhyil   112
Nynen Lung   893
Nyomba Chutsen   620
Nyonno Ri   803, 804, 810

O

Odantapuri   299, 427
Ogyen Guru Monastery   850, 851
Oljadu   401, 406
Ölmo Lungring   751
Om Mani Padme Hum   41, 441, 445
Ombu   768, 783, 784
Ombu Monastery   785
Onchangdo (see Ushang)
Onpa Dzong   656
Oodungpu La   263
Orgyan Dorje Lingpa   45, 522, 524
Orgyan Lingpa   33, 45, 46, 50, 509
Orgyan Monastery   768, 784
Orgyan Padma Lingpa   45
Orma   932, 935
Orong Dzong   738

P

Pab La   478
Pab Ri   745
Pabonka Durtrö   129, 134
Pabonka Labrang   202
Pabonka Monastery   36, 43, 60, 63,
    121, 129–35, 157, 164, 694
Pabonka Rinpoche   135
Pabonka Rock   132
Pachakshiri Range   209, 210, 232, 238,
    735, 738, 747
Pachung Rinpoche   556
Padampa Sangye   338, 344
Padma Lingpa   45
Pagor   526
Paka   575, 655
Pakistan   946, 997
Pal Gi Phuk Ring   682
Pala   62, 68, 88, 90, 112, 301, 378,
    384, 390, 392, 393, 396, 398,
    429, 436, 399, 404, 405, 454,
    464
Pala manuscript covers   442

Pala art style   50, 484, 590
Pala-Sena art style   429
Pala-style murals   501
Pala-style paintings   484
Palden Lhamo   37, 62, 130, 587
Palden Lhamo Lhakhang   92
Palkhor Chöde   55, 412, 416, **419–24**,
    448, 449, 450, 465
Palkhortsan   413, 417
Palung   238
Palung Ri   641
Panchen Lama   35, 465, 867, 872
Panchen Rinchen Lingpa   504
Pang La   897, 898, 990
Panger   578
Pangtha   964, 972
Pangtö   560
Pangyen La   728
Par (Yar La)   819
Pardu   560
Paro Kyerchu [Bhutan]   44, 45
Paro Taktsang Phuk [Bhutan]   45
Paro Taktsang [Bhutan]   513
Pato Kyerchu [Bhutan]   44, 45
Pawhunri, Mt [Sikkim]   793
Pawo Rinpoches   320, 671
Pawo Tsuklak Trengwa   121, 125, 675,
    704
Payi   727
Pe   716, 730
Pehar   **165**, 200, 304, 308
Pejorling (Tön)   217
Pel Kortsen   485
Pelde Dzong   **594**, 988
Pelgyi Phuk Ring   690, 696
Pelha Bedhongma Lhakhang   92
Pelha Gönkhang Zimgo   92
Pelha Yum Drakmo Lhakhang   94
Pelhachok Dukhang   92
Pelku Tso (see Lake Pelku)
Pelkye Monastery   970
Pelri   528, 747
Pelri Gön   696
Pema Chuling   501, 503
Pema Dzong   321
Pema Karpo   506, 612, 693
Pema Khyng Dzong   677
Pema Tso   42
Pema Wöber   176
Pemakö   39, 259, 324, 653, 707, 712,
    717–8, 721, 735, 742, 761, 802
Pemakö Chung   713, 723, 724
Pemaling Tso   613, 682, 697, 700,
    706
Pemalingpa   681, **701**, 704, 705

Pemasel   633
Pemasiri   720
Pemasiri River   717
Pemba Monastery   557, 570, **578**
Pemba Xian   580
Pembo Valley   560
Pempogo La   193, 568
Penam Xian   328, 989
Penpo   60, 820
People's Museum   100
Pepung La   717, 720
Pero La   720
Persia   49, 111, 112
Peruche   895, 898, 899, 901, 916
Pethang Ringmo   896, 905
Pethangtse, Mt   905
Peto   601
Phagmo Drupa sect   **29**, 197, 413,
    415, 465, 484, 521, 635, 678
Phagmo Drupa Dorje Gyalpo   29, 197,
    334, 348, 531, 533, 567, 635,
    688, 694, 745 (see also Drögon
    Phagmo Drupa)
Phagmo Drupa Dynasty   515
Phagmo Lhakhang   231
Phagmodru   98
Phagpa   **28**, 34, 53, 406, 413, 881,
    884
Phagpa Changra   936
Phagpa Lhakhang
Phagpa Pal Sangpo   413, 414, 417
Phagpa Rinchen   414
Phagri   414
Phakpa Lhakhang   43, 48, 97, 107,
    108, 542
Phanyul   194, **544**, 568, 672
Phanyul Valley   34, 481, 567
Phari   **794**, 797, 798
Phari Chökhor Lung   794
Phari Dzong   787, 788, **794**
Phegyeling   249, 270, 271, 991
Phola Gangchen, Mt   940, 991
Phongdo Dzong   566
Phu Nublung Tombs   363
Phugyang Phuk cave   578
Phukchung   768
Phung (Arun) Chu Valley   895, 903,
    904, 918
Phung Chu   458, 802, 803, 810, 812,
    838, 895, 897, 908
Phuntsok Dulam   102
Phuntsok Köpa   106
Phurchok Labrang   202
Phurchu Monastery   44, 735, 737, 742,
    745, **746**, 747

Phurdruk 347
Phurma 613
Phurma Tso 683, 706, 791, 988
Phurma Yutso 609, 610
Phurpa Chok 160, 164, 193
Phurpa Chok Ri 157
Phyen La 800
Pi La 738
Pibang Monastery 648, 649, **652**
Pindsoling Monastery 83, 463, 768, 769, 771, 847, 863, 989
Pindu 594
Po Tsangpo 728
Po Yigrong 570, 575, 654, 656, 732
Po Yigrong Range 648, 651, 655
Po Yigrong Valley 711
Pökang Monastery 329, 842, 844
Polhane 561
Pomé 231, 717, 727, 733
Pomi 570, 580, 654
Pongchen La 860
Pongong La 331
Pönri Monastery 618
Pönri Ngaden 273
Porong 928
Potala 30, 48, 60, 61, 85, **97–115**, 503, 742, 936
Potho Namkha Dzong 261
Potö 194
Potöpa 194
Potowa 34, 130, 545, 564, 567, 568, 819
Potrang 211, 529
Potrang Karpo (see White Palace)
Potrang La 225, 641
Potrang Marpo (see Red Palace)
Pozé La 253
Pozo Sumdo 227, 235
Pradün Tse 44
Prajnaparamita 34
Princess Kongza Tricham 760
Puchiding 818
Puchung 194
Puchungpa 194
Puchungwa 34, 545, 564
Pugyay 812
pungjal 81
Purang (Taklakot) 28, 292, 435, 444, 617, 621, 936, 943, 950, 955, **957**
Purmoche 130
Pusha 598
Puti Gön 580, 582

Q

Qagcaka 948
Qiang 26, 689
Qianjing Glacier 911, 917
Qianlong 55, 107, 113, 178, 196, 201, 824
Qing Dynasty 30
Qinghai 26, 201, 982, 987
Qosot Mongols 56
Queen Döndrubma 441
Queen Jincheng
Queen of Goats 84

R

Ra Chu 914, 915, 916
Ra Lotsawa 296, 532, 569, 920, 991
rabne 38
Rabsel 27
Rabtan Kunsang Phag 415, 416, 419, 420, 421, 448
Raga 945, 946, 947
Raga Chok 164
Raga Tsangpo 462, 771
Ragya 130
Rainbow Falls 713, 726
Raksas Tal (see Lake Raksas Tal)
Ralpachen 27, 47, 70, 112, 119, 173, 195, 338, 360, 378, 384, 388, 491
Ralung Monastery 28, 34, 347, 348, 587, 606, 610, **611**, 612, 683, 706, 842, 846, 988
Ram Dingma Dese Jungne 819
Rama Shika 194
Ramagang 195
Ramding Nan Phuk 267
Rame Monastery 470, 481
Ramo 768
Ramoche Monastery 43, 60, **116–8**, 121, 295
Rampa 842
Rampa Qu 846
Rangjung Dorje 677, 679
rangjung 38
Rapdang 226
Rasa Trulnang 63
Rashuwa [Nepal] 925, 935, 938
Ratna Lingpa 45, 681, 690, 696
Ratö Monastery **476**, 987
Rawa Laepa 481
Rechen 266
Rechung 700
Rechung Phuk Monastery **347–8**, 525
Rechungpa 34, 253, 260, 262, 270, 347, 678, 705, 929, 962

Red Guards 37, 97, 441, 451
Red Palace (Potrang Marpo) 99, 100, 105
Regma 932, 934
Regma Valley 925, **934**
Rekhu La 805
Rendawa 328, 988
Renminbi (Rmb) 999
Repa Zhiwa 937
Repna 557
Reting Labrang 173, 202
Reting Monastery 28, 34, 50, 53, 164, 173, 341, 545, 552, **563-4**, 660, 705, 709, 876
Reting Regent 394
Reting Rinpoche 639
Reting Tulku 173
Rhe Monastery 331, 335, 336, 337, **836**
Rhe Valley 815, 831, 835, 836, 838, 989
Ri Luwang 749
Ri Mar tombs 364
Richardson, Hugh 358, 540, 551, 682
Richung Pathok 794
Rigdzin Chenpo Gye 114
Rigdzin Godem Truchen 45
Rigdzin Lhakhang 114
Rigdzin Pema Trinle 394, 599
Rigong Kha 575
Rigsum Gönpo **128**
Rigsum Gönpo Lhakhang 133
Riku 793
Rilung Phuk 845
Rimon 683
Rin Dzong 819
Rinchen Gyatso 328
Rinchen Pel 545, 553, 556, 561, 635
Rinchen Pelzang 506
Rinchen Zangpo **28**, 32, 50, 56, 425, 427, 428, 430, 437, 446, 497, 964
Rinchengang (Rinjigon) Monastery 546, 548, 549, 881, 892
Rinchenling 710
Rinchenpung 713, 717, 718
Rinpung 635, 678, 706
Rinpung Dzong **841-6**, 988
Rinpung princes 29
Rinpung Valley 611, 613
Rinpung Xian 844
Rinpungpa 415
Rip La 222, 232, 234
Riphuk 400, **411**
Rishong Monastery 939

Rishung Qu 979
Ritang 243
Riwo Chöling 529, 539
Riwo Dechen Monastery 526, **527**
Riwo Namgyal 502, 503
Riwo Palbar Monastery 925, 934
Riwo Palbar, Mt 934
Riwo Tratsang, Mt 462
Riwo Tsenga, Mt 488, **491**
Riwoche 567, 678
Rong 225
Rong Chuchen Monastery 845
Rong Valley **245**, 707, 716, 721, 728-34, 748, 841, 844-6, 988
Rongkhor 46, 231
Rongpa Pass 701, 706
Rongphuk Glacier 911, 917
Rongphuk Monastery 249, 895, 898, 899, 910, 913, 916, **918**, 921, 990, 1004
Rongphuk Valley 897, 910, 916
Rongsha Mongsul 689
Rongshar Valley 39, 46, 249, **253**
Rontönpa 481, 490, 568
Route of Religion 412
Route of Wood 412
Route of Wool 412
ru 43
Ruatung 582
Rudam Latso 896, 907, 908
Ruli La 902
Rumtek 675
Runo 43
Rutok 28, 430, 444, 710, 943, 950, **979-82**
Rutok Monastery (LL) 642, 644
Ruyong Gyalmo Tsün 121, 125

S

Saga 44, 930, 944, 946, 947
Saga Dawa 277, 279
Sai Qu 809
Sakya **33**, 989, 1004
Sakya art style 454
Sakya Bridge 802, 803, 880, 989
Sakya Monastery 28, 50, 53, 100, 168, 406, 408, 412, 414, 545, 555, 802, 803, 806, 810, 812, 880-9, 895, 897, 909, 910, 989, 1004
Sakya Ngape 120, 174
Sakya Pandita **28**, 34, 53, 303, 409, 881, 883
Sakya Tsarpa 891

Sakya Yeshe 157
Sakya Zangpo 881
Sakyaling 477, 987
Sakyamuni 36, 304, 305
Sakyapa 28, 412, 413, 414, 415, 417, 450, 465
Sakyapa art style 53, 436, 452
Sakyasri 504, 521, 548, 685
Sakyetang 907, 908
Salween 557, 578, 582, 651
Salween Divide 570, 648, 655, 656, 730, 747
Samada 397, 398, 885
Samada Qu 793
Samantabhadra 112
Samchung La 896, 904, 907, 908
Samding Monastery 587, 590, 592, 789, 790
Samdrub 690
Samdrub Ling 564
Samdrub Potrang 636
Samdrubling 821
Samdrup Chöling 794
Samdrupo Nunnery 911, 917
Sami Dün 299
Samling Monastery 637, 922
Sampa 796
Samten Karmay 742
Samtenling 925, 936, 937
Samye Chimpu 45, 114, 295, 338, 339, 631–3, 522
Samye Monastery 27, 45, 48, 57, 81, 112, 121, 140, 165, 168, 169, 195, 295–313, 314, 316, 317, 318, 320, 325, 339, 349, 378, 380, 385, 393, 394, 425, 427, 428, 483, 494, 510, 513, 533, 541, 545, 548, 549, 553, 623, 624, 629, 630, 634, 710, 788, 790
Samye Ütse 57, 509
Sang Ngag Zimche 519
sang 41
Sanga Chöling Monastery 212, 215, 218, 219, 232, 233, 234, 240, 242, 247
Sanga Chöling Qu 209
Sangda 356, 361
Sangda Karchung Monastery 489
Sangda Kumbum 490
Sangka Ri, Mt 803
Sanglung 246, 727
Sanglung Glacier 724
Sanglung, Mt 723, 724

Sangphu Monastery 28, 34, 481, 487, 489, 490, 568, 678
Sangphu Valley 489
Sangpo Drakpa 867
Sangsang 452, 456, 460, 462, 768, 786, 919, 945
Sangwa Ne 592
Sangye Gyatso 30, 71, 99, 106, 175
Sangye Lingpa 45, 524, 575, 647, 648, 652
Sangye Lingpa Monastery 649
Sangye Rabdün Lhakhang 85
Sangye Sangwa 386
Sangye Wantön 549
Sangye Yeshe 323
sannyasi 39
Sanshang 818
Santara Chörten 629
Santarakshita 27, 45, 130, 295, 297, 298, 303, 312, 630
Santibhadra 893
Sarnath [India] 36
Sassanid 392
Sasum Namgyal 106
Sasum Ngonga Serdhung 109
Sati 36
Satlej River 274, 426, 430, 943, 953, 955, 961, 964–78, 985
Satso Qu 990
Scythian 91
Se 171
Se Karchung 892
Se Karchung Monastery 892
Se La 314, 627, 656, 710
Sebu Monastery 873
Second Diffusion of Buddhism 27, 32, 50, 340, 390, 391, 393, 399, 401, 413, 429, 472, 485, 487, 497, 527, 548, 698
Sekye La 733
Sela La 855, 858
Selung La 336
Selung Monastery (Ks) 280, 294
Sembön Dhungshing 753
Semo Bönthang 752, 759
Semo La 947
Senge Gön 610
Senge Qu 696
Senguti 223
Sephuk 131, 380
Ser Tri Khang 142
Sera Dhaggo 73, 119
Sera Drubde 329, 989
Sera Je Tratsang 160, 173

Sera Me Tratsang 158
Sera Monastery 29, 30, 43, 61, 71,
        129, **157–64**, 171, 375, 416, 637,
        822, 880, 1000
Sera Ütse 157, **164**, 193
Seralung Monastery 617, 618, 619,
        620
Serdhung Dzamling Gyenchik 114
Serdhung Gelek Dhojo 107
Serdhung Lhakhang 142
Serdung Chuksum 280
Serkhang (Shalu) 400, 401, 402,
        403–11, 809
Serkhar Guthok 607, 609, 613, 681,
        682, 689, 696, 697, **698**, 706
Serkhar Qu 698, 699
Serkhung 503
Serkhung Tombs **367–70**, 467
Serkyem La 757
Serkyim 918
Serlingpa 474
Sershung (Ks) 280
Setrabchen 548
Setsun 637
Sezhik Monastery 768, 783, **785**
Sha Rindzui La 879
Shagam La 233
Shago La 835
Shajiang 225
Shakhapa 55
Shalu Monastery 40, 50, 53, 54, 57,
        349, 351, 378, 393, **400–11**, 414,
        455, 464, 465, 835, 989
Shalupa 410, 411, 412, 415, 450
Sham Tso 619
Sham Valley 856
Shama Ri, Mt (Ks) 285
Shamarpa 671, 679, 815
Shambala 39, 40, 109
Shanda La 595, 603
Shang La 689
Shang Lama 28
Shang Shong 496
Shang Valley 657, 658, 669, 786,
        815, 821, 851, **869–79**
Shangba (Rinpung Qu) 844
Shangpa 570
Shangshung 26, 273, 401, 767, 783,
        784, 964, 972, 981
Shangtse 240, **444**
Shangtso La 975
Shangü La 234
Shangye La 930
Shao La 896, 905, 906
Shapje La 280

Shar Gong La 570, 572, 578
Shar Gyi Dhoke 102
Shar Khalep Pass 623
Shar Rigsum Lhakhang (RG) 128
Shara Bumpa 41, 194, 564, 566, 567,
        1003
Sharapa Yönten Drak 34, 568
Sharchen Chok 99, 102
Sharchung 902
Shariputra 340
Sharkhapa 414, 415, 450
Sharmang 797
Sharmapa 641, 675
Shekar Monastery 336, 802, 812, 918,
        920, 922, 937, 990, 1003, 1004
Shekar Xian (New Dingri) 918
Sheldrak Drubphuk 37, 45, 130, 338,
        339, 362, 485, 516, **522**, 537
Shenpe Dhiklak Chu (Ks) 287
Shenrab Yungdrung 766
Shenri Dham Dham 756
Shepa Kawa 855
Shera La 687
Shersha 212, 215
Shersha Qu 214
Sherteng 560
Shi Dzong 655
Shib La 858
Shide Tratsang 173, 174
Shigatse 29, 56, 328, 349, 390, 400,
        429, 518, 658, 668, 763, 809,
        815, 877, 821, 831, 836, 842,
        847–849, 862, 987, 988, 994,
        995, 996, 998, 1000, 1003
Shingjang 626
Shingtri Tsanpo 652
Shinje Chögye 713, 721, 736
Shinje Rolpa Potrang 321
Shipton, Eric 951, 952
Shiquanhe (Ali) 617, 667, 944, 945,
        946, 947, 948, **949**, 952, 978,
        1004
Shirap 204
Shishapangma, Mt 615, 920, 925,
        928, 939, **940–2**, 946, 991
Shiva 274
Shivadeva 26, 63
Shivaists 464
Shobo Qu 209, 211, 215, 240, 531
Shobo Tu La 214
Shobosang 215
Shoga 655
Shoga Dzong 649, 653
Shogar La 660, 815, 817, 818
Shopado 557, 570, 580

Shopado Monastery 580
Shoralung Valley 687
Shoto Tö 251
Showa La 835
Shuang Hu Qu 982
Shugseb Jetsunma 482
Shugseb Nunnery 127, 318, 319, 470, 487, **492**, 636, 987
Shugtri 200
Shugtri Chenmo 71
Shuntse 488, 491
Shurim Tso 904
Shuru Tso 783
Sigyal Gönchen Monastery 742, 747, 752, **759**
Sikkim 390, 787, 788, 797, 799, 806
Sili Götshang 566
Siling Tso 657
Silk Road **48**, 49, 121, 390, 392, 429, 463
Simbiling Monastery 621, 957, 959
Simi La 988
Sinden Rinchen 920
Sinje Chögye 733
Sinmo Drak, Mt 697
Sino-Newar school 464
Sinpo Ri, Mt 478
Sinpori 493
Sipe Gyalmo 759
Sipe Gyalmo Tso 756
Sisung La 836
Situ's pilgrimage guide 592, 689
Siwatshal (Ks) 286
Six Long-living Beings 104
Six Yogas of Naropa 34
Siyom 237
Sizhi 546, 548
Smallpox Edict 70
Sobhe La 654
Sobje La 250, 261, 263, 655
Söduk Drangsa 259
Sogpo 869, 873, 877, **879**
sogshing 38
Sogu La 812
Soldeb Lewu Dünma 46
Solnag Tangboche 50. 394
Solo-Khumbhu 253
Somapura 301
Sommai Qu 768, 781, 786
Sonak Tangboche 28, 497
Sonam Chöpel 892
Sonam Gyaltsen 296, 304, 472, 480, 519
Sonam Gyatso 29, 409
Sonam Rabten 105

Sonam Rinchen 127
Sonam Tsemo 881, 893
Song Sha 953
Songtsen Gampo **26**, 37, 42, 47, 48, 60, 63, 108, 111, 116, 121, 127, 128, 129, 136, 138, 303, 318, 338, 339, 353, 355, 356, 378, 388, 399, 466, 511, 516, 527, 533, 539, 542, 545, 548, 551, 641, 682, 692, 705, 708, 735, 737, 746, 749, 816, 819, 848, 867, 925, 935
Songtsen Monastery 711
Sorden La 727
Sordruk Rinpoche 556
Southeast Asia 49
Spiti [India] 28, 425
Stein, Prof R A 742
Su La 717, 727
Subansiri 46, 209
Sudhana 959
Sumbatse 237
Sumeru, Mt 274, 299, 301
Sumke Go 103
Sumke Gochor Wok 103
Sumo 990
Sumpa 50
Sung Chöra 73, 200
Sung Dynasty 882
sungdud 42
Sungjönma **38**
Sungnak Lamdre Phuk 892
Sungrabling (Suruling) Monastery 483, 599
sungten 37
Sur La 222, 227, 229, 240
Surkhar 297, 325, 513, 624, 627
Surkhar Chörtens 295, 312, 319
Surkhar Do 630
Surkhar Ferry 630
Swat 297
Swat Valley 45

T

Ta La 856
Tab 589, 590, 592, 608
Tadruka ferry 763, 764, 816, 817, 821, 841, 842
Tag Drosa 742
Taglung Monastery 193, 607, 687, 706
Tagna Monastery 870, 872, 873
Tagpa Chörten 77
Tagri Nyanzig 60
Tagtse 742, 990

Tagtse Yungdrungling Monastery 747, 760
Tagtshang Gormo 102
Tai Situ Jangchub Gyaltsen 635
Tai Situ Rinpoche 677
Taizong 26, 63
Taizu 415
Takar La 222, 233, 234, 380, 513, 710
Takchen 516
Takchen Bumoche 530
Takchen Bumpa 529, 530
Takgya La 930
Takialing Chu 264, 268
Taklung Drubphuk 754
Taklung Mebar 755
Taklung Monastery 28, 34, 194, 545, 546, 561, 564, 566, 988
Taklung Tangpa 28, 34, 566, 635
Taklung-Kagyu 564
Taklungpa 551
Taknya Lungten Phuk 682, 699
Takpa 760
Takpa Shelri, Mt 46, 209, 230, 231
Takpo Tratsang 226
Taksang Pephung 794
Takshang 476
Takten Migyür Potrang (NL) 185–8
Taktsangpa 476, 511, 513
Taktse Monastery 215
Taktse Yungdrungling 752
Takyawo 60
Talung Dzong 796
Tama Ferry 872
Tama La 233
Tamalung 594, 601, 607, 988
Tamdrin Drönkhang (Ks) 282, 292
Tamdrin Sangdrub chapel 73
Tamdrin Sangdrub Lhakhang 73
Tamnyen Darchen 96
Tamnyen La 720
Tamshul 685
Tanak 850–2
Tanakpo Valley 848, 850–1, 869, 870
Tandul 43
Tandul monasteries 551, 682, 692, 705
Tang Annals 26, 48
Tang Dynasty 26, 47, 48, 52, 382, 386, 387, 392
Tang La 732, 787, 793
Tanga 957, 959
Tangba Monastery 872, 873
Tangboche Monastery 516, 526, 527, 548

Tangda 600, 601
Tangkor 527
Tangkya 43
Tangma La 222, 227, 240
Tangme 733, 734
Tangton Gyalpo 127, 379, 451, 452, 454, 455, 460, 465, 478, 561, 863
Tangton Gyalpo Nunnery 127, 492
Tangu La 997
Tankya Monastery 551
Tantrism 32
Tantric pilgrimage 42
Tapgyü La 234
Tapho 28, 50, 56, 404, 436
Taphu Shelkar Drak, Mt 768, 779
Taplejung 805
Taranatha 464, 864
Tarboche (Ks) 277
Tarbung La 781
Targo Ganglung Ritrö 783
Targo Tsangpo 781
Targo, Mt 741, 767, 781, 783, 785
Tarim Basin 49
Tarmar 848, 850, 869
Tarting Monastery 851, 854
Tasak Qutuqtu 170
Tashang 249, 251, 254
Tashi 657
Tashi Chöde 529
Tashi Chöling 134, 157, 683
Tashi Dhenga, Mt 700
Tashi Doka Monastery 380, 385, 510, 511
Tashi Dor Chungchung 663
Tashi Dor Thuje 663
Tashi Dorje 657, 663, 665
Tashi Gembe Monastery 854, 862
Tashi Gomang 447, 466
Tashi Gön 582
Tashi Namgyal 481
Tashi Rabden 735, 738
Tashi Tobgye 599
Tashi Tongme 242, 247
Tashi Wöbar Serdhung 109
tashi gomang 464
Tashiding Monastery 850
Tashigang Monastery 270, 472, 991
Tashilhunpo Monastery 29, 35, 56, 157, 416, 512, 822–30, 831, 880, 919, 989
Tashiling 696
Tashirak 805
Tatipu Range 157
Taxila 306

Tebura 240
Techen Phagtö 171
Temo Chemnak Monastery 747, 748
Temo inscription 761
Temo La 732
Temo Valley 753
Tengboche Monastery [Nepal] 919, 920
Tengcheng 584
Tengye Ling 168, 597
Tengyur 33
Tenma Chok 99
Terdak Lingpa 485, 497, 501, 509, 628, 819
Terdrom 344–6, 485, 545, 552, 553, 557, 561
terma 29, 33, 45, 66
tertons 33, 45, 66
Tew Mul 94
Thadul Temples 819
Thalchok Ling 349, 351
Thekchenling Chapel 73
Theravada 32
Thim Drakphuk 749
Thimpu 799
Thinley Sangpo 561
Thirteen Buddha-lamas 393
Thökhar 43
Tholing Monastery 28, 50, 52, 56, 378, 425–9, 435, 441, 555, 698, 943, 944, 946, 964, 955, 952, 965, 975, 978
Thomni Sambhota 26, 466
Thong La 249, 270, 271, 921, 991
Thongdröl Nunnery 520
thongdröl 38
Thongmön Valley 774, 851
Thongmön Xian 771, 777, 848, 852, 854, 855, 862, 863
Thonmi Lhundrub 466
Thönmi Sambhota 26, 49, 119, 129
Thönpa 203
Thösamling Monastery 898
Thubden Monastery 855
Thugo Sumna 667
thugten 37
Thuje Chenpo Lhakhang 73, 78
Thuje Chenpo Rangjung Ngaden 79
Thuje Gyaphip 94
Thukje Dzingbu 41
Thumpa Punzhi 104
Thupa Ridruk Lhakhang 91
Thuwang Tsokhor 90
Thüwang Khang 110
Tibetan Book of the Dead 177

Tibet–Nepal road (see Friendship Highway)
Tibet–Qinghai highway 563, 658, 660, 817, 944, 945, 996
Tibet–Sichuan highway 197, 380, 571, 636, 642, 648, 654, 655, 656, 707–11, 733, 757, 758, 997
Tibet–Sikkim highway 832, 840
Tilopa 34, 281, 700
Ting La 781
Tingche 809
Tingche Xian 802, 803, 809, 810, 811, 840, 880, 897, 910, 989, 990
Tingedzin 552
Tinki Dzong 804
Tinki La 804, 810
Tinkye Monastery 345
Tipta La 805
Tirkung 718
Tirthapuri 277, 281, 943, 955, 961–3, 968
Tobgyal Valley 43, 763, 764, 815, 816, 820, 821
Togon Temur 414, 417
Tokden Drakpa Senge 675
Tokdhen Drubphuk (P) 135, 164
Tokdhen Gyaluk 135
Tölung 470, 475, 564, 660
Tölung Dechen Xian 673, 674
Tölung Valley 671–80
Tombolung 737
Tomo Mopo 620
Tönang Sangwa Ri, Mt 587, 592
Tong La 721, 737
Tonga La 832, 836
Tongie 873
Tongkyuk 648, 654, 724, 728, 733, 734
Tongshoi 483
Tongten 136
Tongzhi 105, 108
Tönpa Shenrab 273, 742, 751, 753, 755, 756, 758, 759, 761, 765, 784
Topchen La 966, 983, 985
Topo Mopo 961
Topserma 622
torma 42
Toro 572
Torsa 796
Toyo 957
Tra La 580, 721, 989
Tragtse 673
Tragun Monastery 850
Trakor 240
Trakpa Gyaltsen 881

Tramo Monastery 331, 337, 836, 838
Trandruk Monastery 43, 66, 121, 211, 295, 364, 516, 519, 521, 522, 525, **533–8**, 541, 548
Trango La 314
Trangser Trangmar cliffs 292, 293
Trasum Kye La 557
Trathang 483, 502
Tratsang Monastery 793, 794, **854**
Trebuling Monastery 518
Tremo La 794, 800
Tri Tsangkhang Chapel (Dran) 393, 395
tribhanga 126
Trichen Tenpa Rabgyal 132
Tride Songtsen 359, 381, 489
Tride Tsugtsen 47, 48, 116, 304, 335, 358, 378, 381, 382, 383, 385, 386, 387, 388, 489, 629
Trijang Labrang 202
Trijung Rinpoche 202
Trinen Songtsen 360
Tripang Sum 60
Tripe Valley 721
Trisong Detsen **26**, 45, 47, 112, 130, 178, 196, 295, 297, 303, 304, 311, 312, 320, 323, 335, 338, 344, 356, 358, 478, 378, 385, 388, 509, 522, 526, 819, 867, 880, 936
Tritsun 26, 47, 48, 63, 91, 112, 116, 339
Trö La 557, 572, 656
Tromda 217, 226, 239, 710, 739
Tromo Tretung Lake 400
Trön 221
Tröphu Monastery 54, 410, 453
Trorang La 222
Trotö 797
Trowo Ritrö 697
Trugo Monastery 621
Trulung Chu 218, 739
Trum Chu Valley 880
Trungkang 226
Trungkhang 735, 739
Trungrab Lhakhang 115
Tsa 560
Tsa La 609, 773
Tsa Mambo Monastery 920
Tsachen 891
Tsachungang 727, 990
Tsakpuwa Drubphuk 259
Tsaldor La 971
Tsalung 932
Tsalung Dorjedrak Dzong 893

Tsalung La 932
Tsamda 271
Tsamkhung 121, **136–7**
Tsang 33, 50, 55, 413, 415, 436, 442, 443, 455, 869, 880
Tsang Dram 43
Tsangnyön Heruka 347
Tsangpa Gyare 28, 34, 208, 348, 472, 501, 502, 504, 566, 612, 705, 920, 922
Tsangpa Karpo 548
Tsangpo Gorges 707, 713, **723–8**, 761
Tsangpo River 15, 33, 54, 274, 362, 379, 447, 451, 452, 453, 456, 458, 460, 462, 463, 577, 651, 712–30, 747, 847–68, 943
Tsangpo-Changtang Divide 768
Tsantang tombs 362
Tsantang Yuyi Lhakhang 362, 522
Tsaparang 28, 50, 53, 56, 378, 425, 426, 429, **430–46**, 555, 943, 944, 946, 952
Tsar 34
Tsarchen Losel Gyatso 891, 892, 893
Tsari 46, **208–47**, 248, 281, 342, 347, 348, 354, 373, 500, 501, 502, 531, 545, 566, 612, 681, 705, 738, 739, 755, 801, 807, 962
Tsari Kyilkhor 210
Tsari Lama 918
Tsari Rongkhor 210
Tsari Sarpa 210, 237, 239
Tsarong Vinaya 673, 674
Tsau 893
Tse 898
Tse Lobdra 97, 102, 103
Tse Tsokpa Monastery 521, 536
Tse-o-na 600
Tseb 545
Tseb La 314, 514, 549
Tsechen Monastery 328, 414, 988
Tsechok Ling 488
Tsecholing 318
Tsechu 516
Tsechu Bumpa 522, 523
Tsechu Kopa 478
Tsegye 614
Tsela Dzong 737
Tselam Pel Ri 696
Tselha Gang 749
Tselha Namsun Lhakhang 85
Tsemalung 687
Tsemchok Ling 170, 595, **596**
Tsemo La 289

Tsenden Dhongpo 754
Tsenyi Tratsang 822, 830
Tsepa Drungchen Kunga Dorje 156
Tsepak Lhagu Lhakhang 85
Tsepak Lhakhang 110
Tsepame Lhakhang 51
Tsering Jong Nunnery 528
Tsering Tsenga Lhakhang 96
Tseringma, Mt 249, 256, **260**
Tsethang 209, 211, 225, 240, 379,
     470, 486, 494, 515, 516 **518**,
     519, 543, 641, 740, 994, 995,
     988, 1000, 1003–4
Tseti Guest House 617, 618, 623
Tseti La 284, 289, 983
Tseti Lachen La 984, 985
Tseu Marpo 308
Tseumar 168, 304
Tsewang Rinzin 756
Tshal Gungthang Monastery 28, 80,
     84, 96, 140, 165, 171, **198**, 318,
     453
Tshalpa Kagyu 512
Tshalpa Monastery 52, **197**
Tshamkhung 60, 121
Tshangpa 45
Tshanipa 476, 477
Tshena 490
Tshepong 60
Tshering Drukhor 104
Tshezik chörtens 510, **512**
Tsho Ngön Serkhok 114
Tshokchen (S) 162
Tshokchen Chapel 71
Tshokchö 70
Tshomchen (D) 147
Tshomchen Nub 97, 100, **113**
Tshomchen Shar 97, 101, 105
Tshur Lhalung 678
Tsi Nesar 43, 50, 329, 390, 392, 398,
     989
Tsila Monastery 218
Tso Bunang 210, 227
Tso Kapala 280, 293
Tsochen Qu 948
Tsochen Xian 948
Tsogar Lake 210, 235
Tsogyal Drubphuk 485
Tsogyal Latso 318, 319, 811
Tsokyil Potrang (NL) 188–91
Tsomi 356, 681, 683, 686, 688
Tsomi Xian 526, 683, **685**
Tsomo Dretung 701
Tsomo Tretung 802, 803
Tsomön Ling 164, **169**, 597

Tsomsikhang 116, 140
Tsona 214, 242, 243, 246, 247, 641
Tsona Dzong 686
Tsona Xian 209
Tsondu Drak 92
Tsong Kapa 989
Tsong Khapa 29, **35**, 61, 79, 141,
     145, 157, 197, 303, 328, 416,
     476, 485, 503, 510, 511, 521,
     527, 564, 590, 637, 644, 674,
     872, 892
Tsongdü Tsokpa Monastery 28, 365,
     471, **495**, 497, 505, 521, 548
Tsongo 575, 651, 652, 654
Tsongtsun Sherab Senge 390
Tsophu La 575
Tsosum Monastery 647, 648, **651**, 652
Tsuglag Khang 63
Tsultrim Jungne 50
Tsungda 400
Tsünmo Dingi Ri 141
Tsurphu Durtrö 678
Tsurphu Monastery 28, 29, 34, 96,
     352, 470, 475, 613, 658, 660,
     671, **675–8**, 815, 817, 842,
     987, 988
Tsurung 552
Tubden Monastery 850
Tubken Gephel Monastery 891
Tucci 304, 306, 342, 367, 393, 428,
     438, 439, 441, 442, 446, 482,
     487, 489, 540, 864, 867, 964,
     978
Tugdam Tsuglag Khang 550
Tugsum La 280, 294
tulkus 678
Tumba 800
Tumbatse 716, 730, 732
Tumbe Monastery 336
Tumlingtar 805
Tumton Lodrö Drakpa 834
Tungkar 739
Tungo La 318, 595, 597
Tungshak Lhakhang 122
Tuotuohe 996
Tzipri 249, 456, 458, 920, **921–3**
Tzipri *khora* 922
Tzipri Singtron Lama 922
Tzipri Tripon Lama 921

U

Uddiyana 40, 45, 699
Ueyon Kung Sangpo 72
Ü Gyi Dhoke 102

Urgyen Tmadha   570, 578
Üri   56
Ushang   27, 491, 932
Ushangdo   112, 195
U-Tsang   415
Utse Teng Monastery   511, **512**

V

Vairocana   303, 307, 338, 485, 525,
   526, 627, 628, 632, 633
Vajrayana   32
Valley of the Kings (see Chongye)
Valley of the Lakes   895, 896, 904
   907
Valley of the Thirteen Caves (see
   Mangkar Valley)
Vikramasila [India]   28, 45, 51, 63,
   297, 301
Vimalamitra   552
Vinaya   34, 314, 883
Vinaya school   528
Virupa   33, 409
visas   994
Visvakarman   82
Vitali, Roberto   350, 385, 398, 403,
   412, 417, 419, 447, 452, 464,
   536

W

Wa   60
Wagya La   799
Wallungchang Gola   805
Wangku Ri   140, 315
Wencheng   26, 43, 63, 70, 82, 84,
   112, 116, 127, 138, 339, 522,
   533, 538
White Palace (Potrang Karpo)   97, 99,
   100, **103**
Wöde Gungyal   636
Wöka   636, 637, 642, 646
Wöka Dzong   642, 644, 710
Wökar Drak   485
Wölha Gyal   764
Wongde La   336
Wöpame Lhakhang   77, 81
Wösel Dawa Phuk   892
Wösung   28, 359, 430
Wutai Shan   40, 491
Wuyuk Qu   819, 820
Wuyuk Valley   763, 815, 816, 817,
   842, 876, 877, 879, 987

X

Xinjiang   26, 944, 946, 950, 980, 982
Xixia   51, **52**, 390, 392
Xixia Kingdom   390, 393, 396, 398,
   399
Xixia style   50
Xixia-Pala   470, 475
Xuan Zang   45, 49
Xuande   55, 415
Xuanzong   386

Y

Yala Shampo   26, 37, 362–4, 516, 742
Yala Shampo, Mt   17, 531, 627
Yamalung Monastery   316, 318, 380,
   511, 513, 550, 624, **627**, 627,
   631, 710, 938
Yamdrok Tso (see Lake Yamdrok)
Yamo Qu   773
Yamure   553
Yangchenma   320
Yangdul   43
Yangkar   319
Yangma Kanghi La   805
Yangönpa   918, 921
Yangpachen   660, 816, 817, 842, 987
Yangpachen Monastery   171, 658, 660,
   669, 671, 672, 675, 678, **679**,
   805, 817
Yangri Gön   553
Yarap   231
Yarchen   501, 508
Yarchen Lhakhang   503
Yarle Shungla   991
Yarlung Dynasty   16, 26–7, 32, 43,
   47–50, 295, 355, 358, 378, 382,
   384, 386, 399, 404, 417, 421,
   425, 427, 429, 430, 487, 534,
   943
Yarlung Tombs   **355–61**, 371–2, 526
Yarlung Valley   **26**, 43, 45, 46, 50,
   347, 362, 379, 386, 393, 394,
   395, 429, 465, 470, 494, 500,
   515–43, 539, 603, 611, 681,
   683, 742, 988
Yarsik (Pele)   988
Yartö   211, 531
Yartö Drak   140, 199, 317, 488, 599, 622
Yartö Tra La   211, 531
Yartse   94, 356
Yarzang   516, 531
Yasang Pass   683
Yasik   594, 846

Yatung   390, 787, 797, **798**, 988
Yecheng   944, 946, 950, **951**
Yeh La   610, 706
Yemar (Iwang) Monastery   49, 50, 52, 329, **390–2**, 397, 398, 399, 475, 485, 698, 787, 793, 840
Yer La   990
Yerngo   620
Yerpa   522, 704
Yerpa Da   339
Yerpa Drubde   28, 338
Yerpa Lhari   341
Yeru Tsangpo   803, 805, 809, 814, 897, 909
Yeshe Gyaltsen   27
Yeshe Ö   **28**, 32, 50, 56, 425, 427, 430, 436, 472
Yeshe Tsogyal (Princess Karchen)   319, 320, 328, 332, 344, 354, 511, 513, 522, 633, 652, 696, 807, 808, 868, 961, 962
Yeshu Gong Chenpo   75
Yeshung Plain   854
Yeshung Valley   848, 851
Yigrong Valley   711
Yo Gejung   27
Yokmo Tso   289
Yol Rigong   478
Yölcho Monastery   458, 923
Yön Qu   371, 379, 380
Yön Valley   **371–2**, 386, 470, **510–4**, 520, 710
yöncho   406, 415
Yong Yashede Chörten   629
Yong Zhungza   629
Yongdzin Jampal Pawo   480
Yongle   55, 115, 415
Yönpodo Monastery   587, 592, 606, 607, **608**, 704, 706
Yönpu Taktsang   380, 511, **513**
Yöntan Gyatso   83
Yönten Gönpo   812
Younghusband, Francis   30, 788, 793
Younghusband Treaty   959
Yuan Dynasty   29, 53, 400, 402, 404, 406, 407, 408, 411, 413, 414, 415, 418, 455, 463, 464, 671, 678, 737, 749, 882
Yuan-influenced Newari art   404, 407
Yueba   903, 904, 906, 912
Yuena   552
Yugyal Chok   99
Yul Myangro Shampo   760
Yuldruk Barkhor   349
Yulok   903, 907, 912

Yulung   638
Yulung Chu Valley   624
Yulungling   764
Yumbu Lagang   211, 360, 362, 429, 516, 521, 529, **539–43**, 681, 698
Yumé   221, 232, 234
Yundre   771
Yung La   842, 845, 988
Yungdrung Dzin   737, 761
Yungdrung Gatsheling   752
Yungdrung Lhatse   767, 785
Yungdrung Lhatse   784
Yungdrung Menri   797
Yungdrung Phuk   84
Yungdrungling Monastery   741, 760, **763**, 784, 816, 820, 821, 841, 844, 937
Yungtön Dorje Pal   349
Yuro Dzong   706
Yurwo La   930
Yüthok Zampa   203
Yutö   222, 233, 234
Yutok Yönten Gönpo   127, 472, 315, 328, 335

Z

Zabmo Tagyue   114
Zabso   658, 849, 877
Zabso pilgrimage   668, 819, 821
Zahor [India]   165
Zambu   819, 820, 901
Zambu Hermitage   815
Zambu Monastery   819, 869, 877
Zamphuk (Zongbo)   914, 916
Zanda Xian (Tholing)   425, 432, 952, **953**, 955
Zangbala Lhakhang   119
Zangdhok Pelri   632, 742, 747
Zangdhok Pelri Monastery   747
Zangkar Lotsawa   83, **87**, 90
Zanglingma   46
Zangmu   991, 994, 996, 1003, 1004
Zangpo Drakpa   46
Zangri   636, 710
Zangri Karmar   635, 636
Zangri Qu   636
Zangyak Namkha Drak   491
Zanskar [India]   952
Zapulung   921
Zara   802, 803, 804, 806, 809, 810, 840
Zayul   717
Zhang   227, 229

Zhangmu 250, 270, 926, 944, 946, 991, 996
Zhari Namtso 657
Zhayi 545
Zhayi Lhakhang 551, **552**
Zhe 653, 699
Zhe Chu 706
Zhe Chu Valley 697, 698, 855
Zhelre Lhakhang 62, **87**
Zhelye (Tshokhang) Lhakhang 122
Zhije 920, 921
Zhithok Labrang 881
Zhöl 99, **100**, 101, 102
Zhong Zhong Monastery 870, 872, 873
Zhongba 947
Zhongpa Lhachung 674
Zhonnu Gyalchok 845
Zhu Namgyal Dragpa 798
Zhulung 798
Zhungo 75
Zik La 717
Zikpa Lhakhang 132
Zimchung Chime Namgyal 104
Zimchung Ganden Yangtse 104
Zimchung Kadam Khyil 107
Zimchung Phuntsok Dhokhyil 104
Zimchung Tri Thok Khang 142
Zingpo Sherapa 674
Zitho 570, 580, 582
Zogpo Pilgrimage 815
Zok Xian 584
Zorawar Singh 957
Zorong 545, 557
Zorong Chu 560
Zorong Gorge 552
Zorong Valley 346
Zorthang 520, 542
Zoto Valley 345, 557
Zumilu Drubphuk 330
Zung 480
Zung Trezhing 480, 481
Zur Ug Pa Lung 690
Zurchung Rabsel 104
Zutrul Phuk (Zuthulphuk) Monastery 274, 280, **290**, 619, 985